THE ENCYCLOPEDIA
OF
JUDAISM

THE ENCYCLOPEDIA
OF
JUDAISM

VOLUME II

J – O

Edited by

JACOB NEUSNER

ALAN J. AVERY-PECK

WILLIAM SCOTT GREEN

PUBLISHED IN COLLABORATION WITH THE
MUSEUM OF JEWISH HERITAGE
NEW YORK

CONTINUUM • NEW YORK

1999

The Continuum Publishing Company
370 Lexington Avenue
New York, NY 10017

Copyright © 1999 by Koninklijke Brill NV, Leiden, The Netherlands

Distribution in the United States and Canada by The Continuum Publishing
Company, 370 Lexington Avenue, New York, NY 10017-6503, USA

Distribution in the rest of the world by Brill, Plantijnstraat 2, P.O.Box 9000,
2300 PA, Leiden, The Netherlands

This book is printed on acid-free paper.

Printed in The Netherlands

Library of Congress Cataloging-in-Publication Data

The encyclopedia of Judaism / editors, Jacob Neusner, Alan J. Avery
    -Peck, William Scott Green.
        p.   cm.
    Includes bibliographical references and index.
    Contents: v. 1. A–I.
    ISBN 0–8264–1178–9 (set : alk. paper)
    1. Judaism—Encyclopedias.   I. Neusner, Jacob, 1932–   .
II. Avery Peck, Alan J. (Alan Jeffery), 1953–   III. Green, William
Scott.
BM50.E63   1999
296'.03—dc21   99–34729
                                                  CIP

Volume 2   ISBN 0-8264-1176-2

TABLE OF CONTENTS

VOLUMES I-III

J

JERUSALEM IN JUDAISM: The Rabbinic Judaism that emerged after the destruction of the Second Temple in 70 C.E. took for granted that the city Deuteronomy spoke of as "the place God would choose," God's capital city, is Jerusalem. The rabbis thus canonized the view expressed explicitly in the Bible only in Solomon's dedicatory prayer (1 Kgs. 8; 2 Chr. 6), that Jerusalem and the Temple Mount are a conduit for prayers to the one God of all the universe. The later history of Judaism revolves, at least in part, around the unfolding of this idea, with Talmudic rabbis explaining the source of Jerusalem's special sanctity and medieval Judaism's encouraging perpetuation of beliefs contrary to fact, such as Jerusalem's being the center of the universe and its being higher in altitude than any other city.

Jews from 135 C.E. onward perceived their loss of Jerusalem as a punishment for their failure to observe God's laws, set forth in the Hebrew Scripture and by the rabbis. They were acutely aware that their Christian neighbors, by contrast, believed that the city's destruction was a just punishment of the Jews' failure to adopt Christianity. Consequently, in 1967, many Jews saw the Israeli army's seemingly miraculous capture of East Jerusalem, including the city's medieval walls and the Temple Mount, as a vindication of their religion and a harbinger of the messianic era. But, concomitantly, as the second millennium C.E. draws to a close, some Jews firmly believe that Israel's failure to establish a Jewish presence on the Temple Mount itself may irrevocably turn back the clock and prevent the arrival of the messiah. Jerusalem and the Temple Mount thus retain the mythic place they have held within Judaism for more than two thousand years.

Located on two hills twenty miles west of the Dead Sea and thirty miles east of the Mediterranean Sea, Jerusalem stands in the center of the land of Israel, atop a limestone plateau some 2500 feet above sea level.[1] Inhabited as early as 3200 B.C.E., the city is referred to as Rushalimum in the Egyptian Execration Texts of the twentieth and nineteenth centuries B.C.E.[2] These bowl fragments from Thebes, now found in the Berlin Museum, mention two rulers of Rushalimum, Yaqar-ʿAmmu and Setj-ʿAnu. From a later period, six of the fourteenth century B.C.E. Amarna Letters emanated from scribes writing on behalf of Abdi-Hepa king of *Urusalim*; Assyrian and Babylonian scribes of the Iron Age refer to Jerusalem as *Urusilimmu*.

According to Josh. 10, while Jerusalem was not initially conquered by the Israelites, Joshua executed the city's Amorite king, Adoni-Zedek. Judg. 1:1-8 relates that only at some undesignated time after Joshua's death did an army of the tribe of Judah capture and burn the city. Even so, Josh. 15:63 states that the Israelites failed to evict the aboriginal Jebusites, so that they shared Jerusalem with them "until now." Judg. 1:21 states that it was the tribe of Benjamin that failed to evict the Jebusites but concurs that, as a result, Israelites continued to share the city with this indigenous people. Apparently confirming this image, Judg. 19 describes a xenophobic Levite's tragic decision not to spend the night in Jerusalem, because it was "a gentile city."

According to 2 Sam. 5:4-10 (cf., 1 Chr. 11:1-9), after David had reigned over Judah at Hebron for seven and one half years, he conquered Jebusite Jerusalem and made the city the capital of the united kingdom of Judah and Israel. Most scholars concur that

David deliberately chose for this purpose a previously non-Israelite city outside the territories of both the southern (Judah and Benjamin) and the northern (Israel) tribes. This guaranteed the city's acceptance by Judahites and Israelites alike. The famous modern analog is the establishment by the founders of the United States of America of the nation's capital in Washington, D.C., outside the boundaries of any state and, like Jerusalem, at the border between North and South.

The biblical roots of Jerusalem's holiness: Throughout human experience, holiness has been believed to be embodied in places (lands, mountains, rivers, cities), times (festivals and sabbaths), and movable objects.[3] In the biblical books of Genesis, Joshua, and Judges, cities and altars derive their holiness—and so become proper places for future generations to worship—because of a meeting between God and an Israelite hero. Examples include Shechem (Gen. 12:7; 33:18-20), Beth-El (Gen. 12:8, 28:10-22, 35:7, 14-15), Hebron (Gen. 13:18), Beersheba (Gen. 21:33), Gilgal (Josh. 4:20; 5:9), and Ophrah (Judg. 6:24). 1 Chr. 22:1 makes explicit that the altar set up by David at the threshing floor of Ornan is in fact the site of the future Temple. Contrast 2 Sam. 24 and especially 1 Chr. 21:29-30, which apologize for David's having sacrificed on that site rather than at the Mosaic Tabernacle and altar, which were at Gibeon!

In Deut. 12, 14, 15, 16, 17, and 23, God repeatedly promises that at some undesignated time in the future, when the people of Israel will be able to live in tranquillity after the peoples of Canaan have been subdued, God will choose a particular, as yet undesignated, location as the one legitimate place for sacrificial worship and the consumption of sacrificial meals. Many passages in the so-called Books of the Former Prophets, including 2 Sam. 7:1 and 2 Kgs. 17:7-23, identify this place with Jerusalem. This identification is taken for granted by the prophets Jeremiah (627-586 B.C.E.; see Jer. 2:20, 3:1-13, 7, 17:1-2, 26, and passim) and Ezekiel (593-573 B.C.E.; see Ezek. 6:13, 18:6, 11, 15, and passim) as well as Is. 40-66, Ezra-Neh., and 1-2 Chr.

Altogether independently of Deuteronomy, the eighth century B.C.E. prophets Amos and Isaiah both conceive of Jerusalem as not only the capital of the state of Judah and the Davidic dynasty but also as God's capital. For example, Amos, who sees nothing intrinsically wrong in sacral pilgrimages to the holy cities and sanctuaries of Beth-El, Gilgal, and Beersheba (Amos 4:4, 5:5, etc.), declares, "The Lord roars from Zion, and from Jerusalem he thunders" (Amos 1:2). Isaiah's vision of a future era in which all peoples will recognize the sovereignty of the one God includes both altars dedicated to God in diverse places (Is. 19:19) and pilgrimages by members of all nationalities to Jerusalem to submit to God's judgment (Is. 2:2-4).

The Psalms contain numerous hymns, many of them likely from the First Temple period, such as Pss. 20; 48; 50; 65; 76, that refer explicitly to Jerusalem/Zion as God's home city. Additionally, numerous psalms take for granted that all people know which place is called "*the* mountain of the Lord/his holy place" (Pss. Ps. 15:1; 24:4).

Umberto Cassuto argues that the author of Gen. 22:14 deliberately refered to the place Abraham bound Isaac on the altar (Gen. 22) as "the mountain of the Lord" in order to indicate that this was the Temple Mount at Jerusalem, which is explicitly called "the mountain of the Lord" at Is. 2:3, 30:29, Mic. 4:1, and Ps. 24:3.[4] Post-Exilic 2 Chr. 3:1 identifies the site of the Temple with Mt. Moriah and thus alludes to the narrative of the binding of Isaac. Notably, this identification is imperfect, since Gen. 22:2 in fact refers rather vaguely not to Mt. Moriah but to "the land of Moriah." In all events, by not giving that place the name of Jerusalem, Gen. 22, like Deuteronomy as a whole, appears to treat the ultimate identification of Deuteronomy's "place he will choose to establish his name there" as a mystery yet to be revealed.

While other sacred cities referred to in Genesis and the Prophets derived their sanctity from a meeting between heaven and earth negotiated by a patriarch or prophet who gave the place its name, Deuteronomy suggests—and the prophetic books confirm—that "the place he will choose" was not singled out because of any specific event but as a matter of God's inscrutable will, comparable to God's choice of Israel, who was to be given the Promised Land, according to Deut. 9:5, "not because of your virtues and your rectitude . . . but to fulfill the oath that the Lord made to your ancestors. . . ."

As we shall see below, precisely because Scripture left open the question of what precisely qualified Jerusalem to be chosen by God as God's holy city, the Mishnah is free to derive from Scripture its own most fascinating rationale. The Mishnah's reasoning, in turn, has far-reaching implications for the comprehension of holiness in Judaism from the Mishnah's day to our own.

The legacy of late Second Temple Judaism: The second century B.C.E.[5] Book of Enoch 26:1 locates Jerusalem at the middle of the earth, while Jubilees 8:19, from the same period, declares Mt. Zion to be the center of the navel of the earth. Both of these ideas recur in Rabbinic literature and together with the contents of the Hebrew Scripture belong to the common legacy that Judaism and Christianity inherited from the Judaisms of the second century B.C.E.

Deut. 23:10-15 prescribes that when the people of Israel will be organized as a military camp in the course of the conquest of Canaan, persons who are impure from semen must reside outside the camp so as not to defile it. Similarly, facilities for defecation must be located outside the camp. Application of these rules of purity to Jerusalem indicates the special holiness applied to the city by the Temple Scroll, recovered from Qumran Cave 1 and dated by Yadin to the reign of John Hyrcanus I (135/4-104 B.C.E.). The Scroll designates the entire city of Jerusalem as "The Temple City" and "My [i.e., God's] Temple City" and applies to it in its entirety the rules of purity Deut. 23:10-15 demands in the military camp. Thus col. 45, lines 11-12, states: "When a man has intercourse with his wife [and ejaculates] semen, for three days he may not enter any of the Temple City wherein I cause my name to dwell." Col. 46, lines 13-14, states: "You shall provide for them a marked place outside the city where they may defecate on the northwest side of the city: roofed buildings containing pits into which the excrement may descend."

Jewish apocalyptic literature of the first centuries C.E. (Apocalypse of Baruch 4:3, 4 Ezra 7:26, 8:52-53, 10:44-50) speaks of a heavenly Jerusalem that, in the time to come, will descend to earth. This view reappears in Jewish apocalyptic literature of the Geonic period. To the limited extent that such an idea is reflected in pre-Islamic Rabbinic literature, it holds that the Jerusalem to be built by the Jews on earth will reach up to heaven, while the Temple, now located in heaven, will, at God's appointed time, descend to earth. The same idea is reflected in the Zohar.[6] This notion, that the Jew may not rebuild the Temple, but must wait until God sends one down from heaven, should put to ease any who fear that believing Jews today might actually attempt to take matters into their own hands and, at the expense of the peace of Jerusalem and the world, try to build a Temple in Jerusalem.

In some phases of Christianity, the idea of a heavenly Jerusalem replaced the earthly one. But this notion is virtually unheard of in Judaism, which, at least in this respect, remained bound by and faithful to the literal meaning of the Prophets and the Hagiographa: Deuteronomy's "place that he will choose" is the Jerusalem located here on earth. Considering Christianity's spiritualizing of the concept of Jerusalem, it is perhaps ironic that, for almost five centuries, up until the Arab conquest of the city in 638 C.E., the Christian Byzantine Empire denied Jews and Judaism access to the earthly Jerusalem.

From the Mishnah to modernity: The Judaism of the Mishnah inherited and took for granted the view reflected over and over again in Samuel, Kings, Jeremiah, Ezekiel, and Chronicles, that Deuteronomy's "place that he will choose to establish his name there" is Jerusalem. The Mishnah, however, is acutely aware that, in its time, another numerically significant religious community, the Samaritans, shared Judaism's deity, festivals, and, for the most part, Pentateuch, but disagreed regarding interpretation of that crucial recurring phrase in Deuteronomy. The

Samaritans held that God's chosen place was not Jerusalem but their own cultic center, Mt. Gerizim. Consequently, in its discussion of idiomatic expressions employed in vows, M. Ned. 3:10 explains that the phrase "those who ascend on pilgrimage to Jerusalem" refers exclusively to Jews, whose single place of religious pilgrimage is the Holy City of Jerusalem. This excludes from the vow that other Israelite community, the Samaritans, whose single place of religious pilgrimage is Mt. Gerizim.[7]

The idea reflected in the second century B.C.E. Temple Scroll from Qumran Cave 1, that the entire city of Jerusalem is "God's Temple," is also reflected in several passages in the Mishnah. M. R.H. 4:1 declares, "When the holy day of the New Year fell on a Sabbath, they used to sound the ram's horn in the Temple [i.e., Jerusalem] but not in the rest of the country [*medinah*]." Moreover, T. Suk. 2:10 proves[8] that when M. Suk. 3:12 and M. R.H. 4:3 tell us, "Formerly [i.e., before 70 C.E.] the *lulav* [the bouquet prescribed in Lev. 23:40 for use on Tabernacles] was taken [in hand] in the Temple [i.e., Jerusalem] seven days but in the rest of the country [*medinah*] only one day," also there the word "Temple" denotes the entire city of Jerusalem. The idea that all of Jerusalem and not only the Temple is holy again is reflected in the anonymous M. Ned. 1:3: "As for a person who declared [concerning any comestible], 'it is like the altar,' 'like the sanctuary,' 'like Jerusalem' . . . such a person thereby has vowed [to present] a sacrifice." Jerusalem thus appears to be holy and dedicated to sacrificial use in the sense that animals or produce might be designated for use on the Temple altar.

The continuation of this passage quotes Judah b. Ilai to the effect that whoever declares that an object is "like Jerusalem" has not thereby uttered a vow. Behind this controversy between the anonymous Mishnaic passage and the typically dissident Judah b. Ilai, who himself indicates that minority opinions are not to be followed (M. Ed. 1:6), is the Mishnah's equivocal stance concerning Jerusalem as Temple. We have seen that, for the Temple Scroll, all of Jerusalem has

the status of the camp of Israel, as alluded to in Deut. 23:10-15. A similar idea is set forth in Jer. 3:16-18, according to which, in the future, the status of God's throne will be transferred from the Ark of the Covenant to the entire city of Jerusalem. In contrast to the view presented in the Temple Scroll, T. Kel. B. Q. 1:12 states:

> Now just as in the wilderness there were three camps—the camp of the Divine Presence [*Shekinah*], the camp of the Levites, [and] the camp of Israel—so there were [also] in Jerusalem: From the entrance of Jerusalem to the entrance to the Temple Mount is the Israelite camp. From the entrance to the Temple Mount to the Gates of Nicanor is the camp of the Levites. From the Gates of Nicanor inward is the camp of the Divine Presence.

The implicit purpose of this passage is not historical reminiscence but prescription for the time to come, when God will see fit to restore to Jewry Jerusalem and the Temple Mount (see T. Men. 13:23). Maimonides (1135-1204) in his monumental codification of Rabbinic law and theology, the Mishneh Torah, Laws of the Temple 7:11, rewrites T. Kel. B.Q. 1:12 and makes the Rabbinic document's implicit purpose explicit:

> There were three camps in the wilderness: the camp of Israel, which consisted of four camps [i.e., Judah, Reuben, Ephraim, and Dan; see Num. 2:1-31]; the camp of the Levites, concerning which it is stated in Scripture, "They shall encamp around about the Tabernacle" (Num. 1:53); and the camp of the Divine Presence [*Shekinah*], which is located from the entrance to the front courtyard of the Tent of Meeting inward. Corresponding to these [three camps of the wilderness period] there are for all time [*ledorot*]: from the entrance to Jerusalem to the Temple Mount corresponding to the camp of Israel [in the wilderness]; from the entrance to the Temple Mount to the entrance to the Temple Court, i.e., the Gate of Nicanor, corresponding to the Levite camp; and from the entrance to the Temple Court and inward *is* the camp of the Divine Presence [*Shekinah*].

In comparing the first of the two divisions of Jerusalem to the corresponding camps in the wilderness, Maimonides employs the preposition *ke*, 'corresponding to, like.'

However, Maimonides does not employ a prepositional phrase to *compare* the innermost of the three "camps" at Jerusalem to the camp of the Divine Presence but a nominal sentence, which *equates* them. For Maimonides as for Mishnah-Tosefta and for all of Rabbinic Judaism down to the close of the twentieth century C.E., Jerusalem thus is not a witness to the past or a future potentiality but an eternal embodiment of varying degrees of hierarchical holiness. It is this sincerely and firmly held belief, which Second Temple Judaism inherited from Scripture and which Maimonides inherited from the Rabbinic corpus and passed on to Judaism in modern times, that keeps most Jews even today from setting foot on the Temple Mount until God in his own good time will provide in accord with Num. 19 and M. Par. the means of purification from corpse uncleanness. In the interim this respect for God's holy place keeps Jewry from treading on the Temple Mount and thereby offending the religious sensitivities of Muslims, who see the Temple Mountain as *their* holy place.

At M. Kel. 1:6 the Mishnah supplies an answer to the question never raised in Scripture, of why God promised the Land of Canaan to the people of Israel:

> There are ten degrees of [hierarchical] holiness: the Land of Israel is more holy than all lands. Now what constitutes its holiness? [Its greater holiness consists of the fact] that from her [the Land of Israel, which, like the Hebrew word for land and like all lands and cities, is feminine] people are commanded to offer up to God the first sheaf from the barley harvest [on the second day of Passover; Lev. 23:10], and the two loaves of bread [presented on Pentecost; Lev. 23:17], the first fruits (Deut. 26:2), which people are not commanded to offer up from any other lands.

Building upon an idea taken for granted in Scripture, that the entire Land of Israel is sacred space and that all other lands are the opposite, namely, unclean (see Hos. 9:3-4, Amos 7:17, Ezek. 4:13), the Mishnah declares once and for all time that the greater number of opportunities to fulfill the positive precepts that connect humankind with God (see also M. Qid. 1:9) sets the Land of Israel apart from all other lands. In keeping with this idea, Rashi (1040-1105), in his biblical commentary at Num. 34:11, which in medieval manuscripts is written inside of a schematic map of Canaan, explains that the need to know precisely where to obey the commandments incumbent only in the Land of Israel obliged God, at Num. 34, to designate precise boundaries of Canaan.[9]

M. Kel. states that cities within the Land of Israel surrounded by walls have a greater sanctity than the rest of the Land because in them two additional commandments apply, namely the expulsion of lepers (Lev. 13:46) and the circumambulation of the dead.[10] M. Ar. 9:6 provides a list of such cities, ending with Jerusalem. The legal category of walled city is found already in Lev. 25:9 and is alluded to also in Deuteronomy's frequent reference to "your gates" (e.g., Deut. 6:9, 16:18, 17:2) meaning, "your cities surrounded by walls furnished with gates."

Strangely, M. Kel. 1:7 is followed immediately by the enigmatic M. Kel. 1:8, which begins: "What is inside the wall is more sacred than are they [i.e., the walled cities such as Sepphoris, Gischala, Gamla, etc., listed in M. Ar. 9:6]." Without warning, M. Kel. thus moves on from the holiness of walled cities in general to the eight degrees of hierarchical holiness beginning with the area within the city walls of Jerusalem and ending with the inner sanctum of the Temple, commonly called the Holy of Holies. Jerusalem, however, is not mentioned by name in this passage. It is simply stated, "Inside the wall [of Jerusalem] it is more sacred than they [other walled cities] for there [in Jerusalem alone] they eat sacrifices of lesser holiness (Deut. 12:7, 12) and second tithe (Deut. 14:22-26)."

Perhaps it was the trauma of the Jews' being forbidden by Roman edict to enter Jerusalem after the defeat of Bar Kokhba (135 C.E.) that made the Mishnah's authors, as it were, choke on the word Jerusalem and create, momentarily, the impression both here in M. Kel. 1:8 and in M. Ar. 9:6 that Jerusalem is just another walled city. Silently getting on with one's routine and establishing a new routine are proven strategies for dealing with trauma. Thus M. Ta. 4:6 treats the destruction of the Second Temple, the capture by the Romans of Bar Kokhba's last stronghold, Beitar, and the plowing over of the city of Jerusalem by Hadrian as just three more in a series of events going back to the Mosaic era that fell on the ninth of the month of Av. The very same strategy is reflected also in M. R.H. 4:1-3, which explains, first, that Yohanan b. Zakkai was able to create a new routine by transferring from Jerusalem to his self-appointed government in exile at Yavneh the practice of blowing the ram's horn on a New Year festival that coincided with the Sabbath and the use of the *lulav* all seven days of the Festival of Tabernacles. M. R.H. 4:2 then has the colossal nerve to state, "In this [matter of the conditions under which the shofar was sounded] also Jerusalem surpassed Yavneh." While on the surface this passage notes Jerusalem's unique superiority, it is in fact remarkable that the Mishnah's authors could even imagine comparing Yohanan b. Zakkai's seat of government to the eternal city of Jerusalem, chosen by God Almighty!

Time, they say, is a healer of sorts. And so Maimonides' Mishneh Torah, Laws of Temple 7:14, in an amazingly successful attempt to imitate and outdo the Mishnah, adds the words on which the Mishnah's authors choked with tears at M. Kel. 1:8: "Jerusalem is more holy than the other walled cities for there they eat sacrifices of lesser holiness and second tithe within her walls." Here we have fully revealed the secret implicit in Deut. 12 and almost spelled out with a gasp in M. Kel. 1:8. Jerusalem's sanctity derives from a divine decree that sacral meals in which, as it were, God joins together in God's capital city with all Israel—men and women, boys and girls—may only take place in Jerusalem.

Throughout the almost two millennia during which neither second tithe nor sacrifices of lesser holiness have been consumed in the Holy City of Jerusalem, Rabbinic Judaism has made the holiness embodied in Jerusalem a part of everyday life for Jews around the world. First, the so-called Eighteen Benedictions, recited three times every week-day, include a petition asking God to rebuild Jerusalem as well as a concluding affirmation in which the believer expresses trust that

the rebuilding of the city's walls is already in progress. A similar benediction is included in the Grace After Meals, recited as many times in the day or night as one has eaten a meal including bread. Inspired by Is. 60:4, the Rabbinic liturgy prescribes that the Scripture reading from the prophets (*haftarah*) on Sabbaths, festivals, and fasts be followed by a series of benedictions that include, "Blessed are You, O Lord who makes [personified] Zion rejoice with her children." These children are the Jews returning from exile referred to in Is. 60:4. Similarly, the benedictions recited under a wedding ceremony and for six days thereafter are inspired by Is. 54:1:

> May the barren woman [i.e., personified Jerusalem] truly rejoice at the joyful ingathering of her children [i.e., Israel returned from exile] within her [Jerusalem the Holy City]. Blessed are You, O Lord, who makes [personified] Zion rejoice with her children.

Moreover, possibly inspired by an unbroken tradition reflected already in Dan. 6:11 and encouraged by the two versions of the prayer attributed to Solomon at the dedication of the First Temple (1 Kgs. 8, 2 Chr. 6), T. Ber. 3:15 prescribes that, when they pray, persons living outside the Land of Israel face the Land and that persons living in the land face Jerusalem. Accepted in every code of *halakah* to this day and concretized in the floor plans of synagogues throughout the world from antiquity to the present from Kaifeng in the East to Kalamazoo in the West, from Cophehagen in the North to Capetown in the South, and practiced by individual Jews in lands of freedom, in Soviet prison camps, and in Nazi death camps, this simple regulation of the Tosefta embodies the biblical belief that the Holy City and the Temple are a conduit for prayers of men and women of every nationality to the universal God whom even the heavens cannot contain (1 Kgs. 8:28-53).

Constantly reminded by the liturgy of Jerusalem and its special spiritual energy but barred by Roman edict from physically entering the city, the imagination of Jews and Judaism lavished praise and admiration upon Jerusalem very much in the way that lovers lavish praise upon each other or that parents bestow praise upon their children. Thus B. Qid. 49b records: "Ten measures of beauty descended to the world, and Jerusalem received nine of them." Midrash Tehillim at Ps. 48:3 states: "The common saying is: 'One is not what one's mother says, but what one's neighbors say.' This is not true of Zion; all people acknowledge her beauty: Even when she lay in ruins it was said, 'Is this not the city which people call the crown of beauty?' (Lam. 2:15)."

Reminded by the precepts of their religion of Jerusalem's centrality but barred by imperial decree from visiting the city, the sages who grew up in the post-Bar Kokhba era should not be blamed too harshly for letting their imagination get away from them so that they deduced from the redundancy in Deut. 17:8—"You shall *get up*, and you shall *ascend* to the place that he will chose"—that the Land of Israel is higher in elevation than all other lands and that the Temple is higher in elevation than all the Land of Israel (Sifre Deut. 152).

Lasting testimony to Judaism's commitment, from the Tannaitic era onward, to the restoration of the Jews, the Temple, and Judaism's sacred rites to Jerusalem is found not only in the Mishnah, Tosefta, Talmuds, and Midrashim but also in the innumerable elegies (*qinot*) over Jerusalem composed for the anniversary of the destruction of the Temple on the ninth of Av.[11] Similar in force are the elaborate poetical compositions for the Additional Service (*musaf*) of the Day of Atonement, which describe the words and symbolic acts of the high priest in the Temple on that day and which lament the irreparable loss of that sacred service and beg God to restore it speedily. In this category too are the *selihot* or penitential prayers for fast days and the period leading up to New Year and the Day of Atonement, when the heartfelt loss to the Jewish people of Jerusalem was expressed time and again.[12]

A Christian pilgrim from Bordeau who visited Jerusalem in 333 C.E. testified that on the ninth of Av the Jews were allowed to visit Jerusalem and to mourn its loss. It is this slight mitigation of the long-standing ban upon any Jewish presence in Jerusalem that seems to be reflected also in Lam. Rabbah 1:17: "In the past I used to go up to Jerusalem in a noisy celebration, but now I go up [to Jerusalem] in silence, and I descend [from Jerusalem] in silence."

Upon the Arab conquest in 638 C.E., Jews were once again allowed to live in Jerusalem, which they did. Four hundred and sixty one years later, the Crusader capture of the city, July 15, 1099, led to the massacre of Jerusalem's Jews. They were invited back about a century later, when the Muslim Saladin retook the city in 1187. It is of no little significance that, given the chance to fulfill the dream inculcated by Scripture, the liturgy, and by Rabbinic law and homily of returning to the Holy City of Jerusalem, not a few Jewish spiritual leaders did make the trip. In fact, as time went on, more and more Jews came to live there, so that, by the end of the nineteenth century, they constituted a majority of the population of the Holy City, as they do at the end of the twentieth century.

Indeed, as art historians were among the first to point out, the medieval maps of Jerusalem and the Holy Land, the diagrams of the Temple, the pictorial illustrations of the candelabrum, the table of the shewbread, and other Temple vessels in both Rabbanite and Karaite Bibles from as early as the tenth century C.E. reflect the renewed interest in this period in the re-establishment of the earthly Jerusalem and its Temple as a prelude to the end of days. The biblical commentary of Rashi and Maimonides' Commentary on the Mishnah and Mishneh Torah suggest this same interest.

Among the most famous medieval Jewish thinkers and poets to set out for Jerusalem was Judah Halevi (1075-1141). Tragically, he died before achieving his goal. In 1121, three hundred rabbis from England and France settled in Jerusalem, while in 1247 Moses Nahmanides settled and even founded a *yeshivah* there. Despite serious economic problems and frequent setbacks, many Jews, inspired primarily by the belief that Jerusalem is God's eternal capital, continued to settle in Jerusalem in increasing numbers from the Muslim Conquest of the seventh century C.E. until the Crusades and again from the time of Saladin until the close of the twentieth century C.E.

The nineteenth and twentieth centuries: The Rabbinic corpora (e.g., Lev. Rabbah 22:8, B. Ber. 32b) and Maimonides' Guide to the Perplexed (3:8) include a few statements to the effect that sacrificial worship in the Temple on Mt. Moriah might not be the best that humankind can do in the way of communicating with God; and that God might actually have done the Jews a favor by scattering them all over the world (B. Pes. 87b). These statements, however, do not constitute a consistent ideology or program for the authors or redactors of any of the works in which they are found. Yet, in the same sense that the Mishnah was innovative in creating a comprehensive program that incorporated numerous ideas found in Second Temple Judaism, so Reform Judaism of the nineteenth century C.E. was innovative in creating a new vision of Judaism as a religious denomination in which Jerusalem and the Temple were matters of the past and of interest only as facts of history.

For example, Gustavus Poznanski, the spiritual leader of Charleston, South Carolina's prestigious and pretentious (hence the long name) Kahal Kadosh Beth Elohim declared in his address at the dedication of the congregation's new edifice March 19, 1841: "This synagogue is our *temple*, this city our *Jerusalem*, this happy land our *Palestine*, and as our fathers defended with their lives *that* temple, *that* city and *that* land, so will their sons defend *this* temple, *this* city, and *this* land."[13]

Another example of nineteenth century Reform Judaism's view of Jerusalem is the long prayer of thanks prescribed for recitation on the anniversary of the destruction of the Temple, the ninth of Av, in the prayerbook, *Olat Tamid*, written by David Einhorn. The same idea is reflected in the recasting of the Service of the High Priest on the Day of Atonement in that same volume and in subsequent prayer books of the Reform movement in America throughout the twentieth century. Typical is *The Union Prayer Book* (Cincinnati, 1922), *part 2*, p. 255: "And though we cherish and revere the place where stood the cradle of our people, the land where

Israel grew up like a tender plant, and the knowledge of Thee rose like the morning-dawn, our longings and aspirations reach outward a higher goal." Accordingly, when Reform Judaism officially accepted Zionism as part of its program, it never was able to explain to itself or to anyone else the *religious* significance of Jewish sovereignty in Jerusalem and over the Temple Mount as opposed to the *political and cultural* efficacy of a Jewish state in part of the Land of Israel.

It is continually pointed out in the triumphalist historical literature of modern Zionism that by the end of the nineteenth century the Jews constituted a majority of the inhabitants of Jerusalem.[14] The reason for making this point is very simple. The Zionist historians who collect and publish these statistics attempt to show that, according to the standards of fair play accepted in the western world, a permanent electoral majority going back one hundred years should guarantee the Jews their right to declare Jerusalem part and parcel of the Jewish state reestablished in the Land of Israel with the support of the United Nations in 1948. Of course, the very same western world cannot and does not recognize the Jewish claim to Jerusalem for a very simple reason: Most Christians of the post-135 C.E. era interpreted the barring of the Jews from Jerusalem in theological terms. In the Byzantine era and later in the Crusader period, Christians saw in their own occupation of Jerusalem and their filling it up with churches and monasteries visible symbols of their having become the new and authentic Israel. Now come the Jews, and they call their state Israel, and in defiance of the United Nations, they set up their parliament and their government ministries in Jerusalem. They also want the world to recognize Jerusalem as their eternal capital, established by King David. What is more, in a defensive war of six days duration in 1967, just nineteen years after the establishment of the state, this Jewish state brings under its control the entire city of Jerusalem including the Temple Mount.

The majority of Israeli Jews and many of their fellow Jewish and gentile sympathizers throughout the world see in these events, both momentous and seemingly miraculous, the harbinger of the messianic era, the veritable reversal of the insult and injury heaped upon God's Holy City by the Romans in the year 70 C.E. and in the year 135 C.E. In much the same way that some of the sages who were products of earliest Rabbinic Judaism became supporters of the would-be Messiah Bar Kokhba, so in the years after 1967 it is the world of modern Orthodox Judaism, also called National Religious (Religious here means Orthodox) Judaism, that nourishes the hope that the establishment of a Jewish State in the Land of Israel with its capital at Jerusalem will lead shortly to the governing of that state by the law of the Torah and the reestablishment of the sacrificial cult on Mt. Moriah. Indeed, an extremist branch of this persuasion has established in the Old City of Jerusalem a *yeshivah* called *'Atteret Kohanim*, i.e., 'Diadem of the Priests,' in which the rules of Temple service are studied in preparation for the imminent restoration thereof. The Old City of Jerusalem also is home to a unique museum, which concerns itself not with understanding the past but with the future: the Temple vessels and the priestly vestments to be employed when the Temple cult will have been reestablished.

As easy to define as are the National Religious—they are generally recognized as those whose males wear knitted skullcaps—so easily demarcated are the Haredi or Pre-Modern Orthodox, whose official position is that the establishment of the State of Israel with its capital at Jerusalem has no theological significance at all. This is the case even though the present circumstances, in which the nations of the world let the Jews run their own affairs in the Land of Israel, so that the civil holidays include the Jewish festivals, makes it a very convenient place for the nurturing of their brand of Judaism. Still, the majority of Israelis, generally defined by themselves and others as non-religious or secular, share with the National Religious the belief that the events of 1948 and 1967 portray God's love for Israel. They fully believe that Jewish sovereignty in Jerusalem is the fulfillment of biblical prophecy and Jewish religious belief, even if they are divided as

to whether sharing sovereignty in Jerusalem with a Palestinian Arab State is a betrayal of biblical prophecy and the providence believed to have been revealed in the seemingly miraculous creation and defense of the State.

Given the possibility that a Temple might tomorrow be sent down from heaven to rest on Mt. Moriah, the only people who have an idea what to do with it are the Orthodox. This, however, can be explained if we remember that all of Rabbanite Judaism begins with the Mishnah, which fully explains how you build a Temple for sacrificial service. No Jewish movement in the last two millennia or the last two centuries has produced an alternative comprehensive program of life and belief based on Is. 56:7, which envisions the restored Jerusalem as the location of "a Temple of prayer for all peoples." In the meantime, the people of Israel, who have indeed seen so much of Is. 40-66 reenacted before their eyes—the return to Jerusalem, the ingathering of exiles, the rebuilding and rehabitation of the waste places of the land of Israel—grope in darkness as did the Jews whom Is. 40-66 addressed in the sixth cent. B.C.E. and whom the sages of Yavneh and Usha, who created Mishnah, addressed in the first and second centuries C.E. Meanwhile, the only Jewish movement, religious or secular, that has a fully published vision of the future of Jerusalem and Israel and humankind is Orthodoxy, in the eyes of which the vision set forth in the Rabbinic corpus has been fully vindicated by the events of the twentieth century. What the future may bring is anyone's guess.

Conclusion: One of the many city-states that dotted Syria-Palestine as early as the Chalcolithic period (3200 B.C.E.), Jerusalem became the capital of King David's empire at the beginning of the Iron Age (c. 1000 B.C.E.) and soon afterwards the site of King Solomon's Temple. By the middle of the eighth century B.C.E., Jerusalem was perceived by many religious and political leaders in Israel and Judah as God's capital city. In 622 B.C.E., this belief was reinforced by King Josiah of Judah's destruction of all temples of the Lord other than King Solomon's at Jerusalem.

The belief that Jerusalem is God's capital city was cultivated by Rabbinic Judaism, which emerged after Roman armies had twice conquered and destroyed the city. By the time the Mishnah was published, Jews were forbidden by Roman edict from setting foot in Jerusalem. In response, inspired in part by Ps. 137, traditional Judaism required that, twice in each of the three daily worship services and again at the end of each meal and at the solemnization of marriages, Jews mention and pray for the restoration of Jerusalem as God's capital. This idealization of Jerusalem and of its possession as a signifier of the messianic age meant that, by the time Jews were again allowed in significant numbers to set foot in the city, after the Arab conquest of the seventh century C.E., they had been fully convinced of the truth of what their religious leaders so vividly imagined, that the city was the most beautiful in the world, located at the umbilicus of the universe, and situated atop the world's highest mountain.

From late antiquity until the end of the twentieth century C.E., it was widely agreed by Jews and Christians alike that the banishment of the Jews from Jerusalem demonstrated God's displeasure with the original covenant people. Accordingly, at the end of the second millennium C.E., a reunited Jerusalem's standing as the capital of a Jewish state called Israel has significant theological and religious implications, understood by some to vindicate the Jews' claim to remain the true covenant people, and, by others, as a serious insult to competing claims to be the only true monotheistic faith.

Bibliography

Abiram, Yosef, ed., *Jerusalem Through the Ages* (Jerusalem, 1968).

Oesterreicher, John M., and Sinai, Anne, *Jerusalem* (New York, 1974).

Poorthuis, Marcel, and Safrai, Chana, *The Centrality of Jerusalem: Historical Perspectives* (Kampen, 1996).

Prawer, Joshua, and Ben-Shammai, Haggai, *The History of Jerusalem: The Early Muslim Period: 638-1099* (New York and Jerusalem, 1996).

Notes

[1] The specifics of this location, as we shall see below, assume a great importance both in Jewish religious literature of the Second Temple and in post-70 C.E. Rabbinic Judaism.

[2] See James B. Pritchard, ed., *Ancient Near Eastern Texts Relating to the Old Testament* (3d ed., Princeton, 1969), pp. 328-29.

[3] See Mircea Eliade, *The Sacred and the Profane* (New York, 1951).

[4] Umberto Cassuto, "Jerusalem in the Pentateuch," in Umberto Cassuto, *Biblical and Oriental Studies* (Jerusalem, 1973), vol. 1, pp. 71-78.

[5] The date now given for the Aramaic original of this book, which belongs since the fourth century C.E. to the Old Testament of Ethiopian Christianity, rests upon the date assigned to the Aramaic fragments recovered from Qumran; see Michael A. Knibb, *The Ethiopic Book of Enoch* (Oxford, 1978), pp. 8-9.

[6] See E.E. Urbach, "Heavenly and Earthly Jerusalem," in Yosef Abiram, ed., *Jerusalem Through the Ages* (Jerusalem, 1968), pp. 156-71.

[7] It is of course typical of the Mishnah, which often portrays what its authors wished to to be as though it already were, to speak in the third century C.E., when Roman law forbade Jews to enter Jerusalem, of "those who ascend on pilgrimage to Jerusalem"!

[8] See S. Safrai, "Jerusalem in the Halacha," in Marcel Poorthuis and Chana Safrai, eds., *The Centrality of Jerusalem: Historical Perspectives* (Kampen, 1996), p. 112.

[9] Catherine Delano Smith and Mayer I. Gruber, "Rashi's Legacy: Maps of the Holy Land," in *The Map Collector*, no. 59 (Summer 1992), pp. 30-35.

[10] On this rite, see Mayer I. Gruber, *The Motherhood of God and Other Studies* (Atlanta, 1992), pp. 157-59.

[11] See Abraham Rosenfeld, *Authorised Kinot for the Ninth of Av* (London, 1965).

[12] See Abraham Rosenfeld, *The Authorised Selichot for the Whole Year* (London, 1969), pp. 65, 127, 171, 195, and passim.

[13] Charles Reznikoff, with the collaboration of Uriah Z. Engelman, *The Jews of Charleston* (Philadelphia, 1950), pp. 140 and 296-97.

[14] See Michael Avi-Yonah, "Jerusalem in Archaeology and History," in John M. Oesterreicher and Anne Sinai, *Jerusalem* (New York, 1974), p. 18.

MAYER GRUBER

JESUS AND JUDAISM: Recent study of Jesus has emphasized the Hellenistic setting of his activity and of his movement as a whole. Sometimes—for example in the work of John Dominic Crossan, discussed below—the result has been an evidently programmatic extraction of Jesus from the Judaic environment of his day. Our purpose here is not simply to redress that imbalance, but (while redressing it) to show how pivotal issues within the critical study of Jesus may only be resolved by attending to his Judaic milieu. That Jesus was called "rabbi," that he commissioned twelve followers to take up his activity for the kingdom of God, that he occupied the precincts of the Temple, and that his execution involved high-priestly intervention with the Romans—these are well accepted points of reference within contemporary research. None of them may be assessed apart from an appreciation of early Judaism, and—so appreciated—they constitute in aggregate a fundamental orientation in the assessment of Jesus.

In an influential book, E.P. Sanders has complained that scholars have focused on the sayings of Jesus to the exclusion of a study of what he did. Sander' own suggestion is that we concentrate on certain of the deeds of Jesus that may be regarded as "almost indisputable facts."[1] However much the perspectives of scholars might diverge, the data they seek to understand and interpret include Jesus' baptism at the hands of John, his ministry of preaching and healing within Israel, his calling and sending of disciples, and his confrontation with cultic authorities in the Temple.

The corrective Sanders suggests is pertinent, because there has been a tendency to interpret Jesus' teaching as a set of abstract assertions, without precise context. Considered in the abstract, Jesus' sayings can be reduced to a few banalities, the supposed religious truth that remains the same through the ages. Obvious problems emerge when sayings are removed from the culture in which they were produced and are transplanted into the environment of what we think of as truth in the present.

By keeping Jesus' practices in mind, as well as his teaching, we keep the issue of cultural context clearly in view. "Deeds" have no meaning apart from the culture in which they are accomplished; they cannot be understood in the abstract (any more than sayings can be). At the same time, it is important to bear in mind that what a person says is often the best commentary there is on what that person does. We will only understand Jesus historically, in his impact on his followers and

the movement that continued in his name, to the degree that we appreciate both his teaching and his characteristic activities in their original contexts and in relation to one another.

Jesus developed a well articulated and distinctive understanding of the kingdom of God. The challenge Sanders has rightly issued involves relating Jesus' teaching of the kingdom to what he did, to his public activity. If Jesus focused his attention as keenly on the kingdom as his sayings make it seem, then his public activity must have been, not merely characteristic, but programmatic: a conscious response to the claim which God made as truly king.

Jesus as rabbi: Many of the "almost indisputable facts" Sanders lists might have pertained to any rabbi within Jesus' period. Teaching, healing, and calling disciples were typical activities among the rabbis. Not every rabbi was noted for all three, but in aggregate they were known to be active in those ways. In addition, rabbis were especially reputed for their expertise in adjudicating matters of purity. "Purity" is not on Sander' list, but there is practically no question that Jesus engaged in discussion and controversy concerning purity. In all these aspects, then, Jesus presents a typically Rabbinic profile.

The reference to Jesus as a rabbi can easily cause confusion, because the dominant movement we know of as Rabbinic Judaism did not emerge until after 70 C.E. The destruction of the Temple and the resulting displacement of high priestly authority created a vacuum of power. Local sages and teachers, who had previously been engaged in issues of purity and conduct, stepped into the breach and organized themselves in centers of learning in cities such as Sepphoris and Tiberias. The rabbis who had been local and rural sages before 70 C.E. increasingly became formally trained Rabbis after 70 C.E.: hierarchical and metropolitan authorities who attempted to formulate what it meant to be Israel. Rabbinic literature only emerged, beginning with the publication of the Mishnah in 200 C.E., as a result of mature development of Rabbinic Judaism.

Note that the term "rabbi" *was* used in

relation to teachers before 70 C.E. Joshua
ben Peradija, c. 104-78 B.C.E., is known in
that way according to M. Ab. 1:6 (see also
M. Ab. 1:16). An ossuary from Jesus' period
also attests the usage.[2] In a culture that respects learning, it is only to be expected that
a student might address a respected teacher
as "great," which is what the term *rab* means.
When I call a teacher "great," I indicate that
I defer to him; he is greater than I am in the
expertise that is involved. That relational
understanding becomes emphatic in the form
rabbi, "my great one." In the book of Daniel,
Daniel himself is named by King Nebuchadnezzar "*rab* of the prefects of the wise" (Dan.
2:48; see also 4:6; 5:11). Within the Aramaic
usage involved, the natural way for one of
those beneath Daniel to address him would
have been as "rabbi."

Jesus is addressed in the Gospels as rabbi
more than under any other designation; it is
obviously what his followers called him (see
Mat. 26:25, 49; Mark 9:5; 10:51; 11:21;
14:45; John 1:38, 49; 3:2; 4:31; 6:25; 9:2;
11:8). The designation comports well with
his characteristic activities, especially with his
adjudications regarding purity and his public dispute with the authorities in the Temple.
When, during the course of the twentieth century, scholars have expressed reservations
about referring to Jesus as a rabbi, they have
had in mind the danger of identifying Jesus
with the Rabbinic movement after 70 C.E.,
which was more systematized than before
that time, and which amounted to the established power within Judaism.

Unfortunately, anxiety in respect of that
anachronism can result in the far greater
error of bracketing Jesus within "sectarian"
Judaism. The Judaism of Jesus time was so
pluralistic that depicting a dichotomy between "orthodox" and "sectarian" forms of
the religion is not helpful. Worse still, denying Jesus the address of *rabbi*, which his first
followers used, can be part of an attempt
to place him apart from Judaism. The most
famous attempt recently is John Dominic
Crossan's: he would make Jesus into one
of the "Cynic" philosophers whom Crossan
styles as "hippies in a world of Augustan
yuppies." The argument can only be main-

tained by ignoring the cultural context of the
Gospels and by an extremely elastic understanding of what a "Cynic" might have been.[3]
That Jesus was a teacher from Galilee, a
rabbi from peasantry, is a finding in which
most critical scholars concur.

Once Jesus is understood as a local sage,
some of his behavior is easily explained.
Teaching, calling disciples to learn from his
example, discussing issues of purity, even
healing, all belong to the general category of
what such a teacher might be expected to do.
We might compare Jesus to two of his most
famous near contemporaries, Hanina ben
Dosa and Hillel.

In a story that is very similar to Mat. 8:5-
13, Luke 7:1-10, and John 4:46-53, Hanina
is reputed (B. Ber. 34b) to have successfully
prayed for healing at a distance.[4] Both Hanina
and Jesus are said to receive a request from
a person concerning that person's child or
servant. (In the case of Luke and Berakhoth,
emissaries make the request; the father or
master appears in person in Matthew and
John.) Both Hanina and Jesus have the pray-
erful insight to know that healing has been
achieved, and the child or servant indeed is
healed from the time that each rabbi said so.
Fascinating divergences among the stories
cannot be treated here; neither can we here
settle the question of the tales' historical reliability. Only the cultural similarity between
the memory of Hanina and the memory of
Jesus is our present concern. In each case, a
rabbi is attested in a similar way to have been
involved in healing.

Hanina lived during the first century, but
after the death of Jesus. Hillel, on the other
hand, was a slightly older contemporary of
Jesus. The Talmud relates that Hillel once
was approached by a man who wanted to be
taught the Torah so as to convert to Judaism
quickly, while he stood on one foot. Hillel
told him: "That which you hate, do not do
to your neighbor. That is the whole Torah,
while everything else is commentary: go and
learn!" (see B. Shab. 31a). Jesus' teaching
concerning the principal of love in the Torah
is an obvious analogy (see Mat. 22:34-40;
Mark 12:28-34; Luke 10:25-26).

Whether viewed from the perspective of

prayer and healing (as in the case of Hanina) or from the perspective of teaching and thought (as in the case of Hillel), Jesus appears to have been comparable to his Rabbinic colleagues. Such a comparison may be pursued along other lines of similarity. But comparison is never fruitful if it becomes a form of simplistic reduction. To say simply that Jesus was a rabbi is no more informative than saying that Hillel or Hanina was a rabbi, that Caiaphas was a priest, or that Pilate was a Roman prefect. All such statements represent no more than points of departure in historical description. They do not constitute categories that are adequate to convey just who these people were, although they do provide an indication of the social fields in which they were active.

Once we appreciate the field within which a person's memory was preserved, we are in a position to analyze what makes that memory distinctive. Hillel's skill in the oral tradition, Hanina's repute as a thaumaturge, Caiaphas' acquiescence to Roman administration in Jerusalem, Pilate's tendency to bait the Jews, all become apparent when they are studied and compared to those with whom they are generally similar and yet from whom they are strikingly different. The same principle applies in the study of Jesus' memory within the Gospels.

Much of what Jesus is remembered to have done and said comports well with Rabbinic activity: the concern regarding purity and ablutions (a concern that included the practice of baptism), the programmatic emphasis on teaching and healing, the development of characteristic themes within his teaching (such as "the kingdom of God"), the gathering of disciples for whom that teaching was presented in a repeatable form, like the Rabbinic Mishnah (a noun that derives from the verb *shanah*, "to repeat"). Most of the passages that present Jesus in dispute with his Pharisaic, scribal, and priestly contemporaries are also in line with some of the vigorous arguments one encounters in the Rabbinic literature. In all of those aspects, Jesus' activity seems broadly similar to what might have been expected of a rabbi.

Within that broad similarly, however, two strong aspects of distinctiveness appear. First, Jesus is remembered not only to have gathered disciples but to have sent out twelve of them in order to teach and to act in his name. The correspondence between the number of disciples and the Scriptural number of the tribes of Israel reinforces the impression that Jesus sent the twelve as a consciously distinctive act.[5] Second, although Rabbinic controversies in the Temple could result in disorder, violence, and even bloodshed,[6] Jesus' controversy in the Temple, involving both his occupation of the great, outer court and ultimately his execution at the order of Pilate, stands out as an unusual confrontation between a rabbi's authority and the priestly authority in the Temple, which had been underwritten by Rome. No historical description of Jesus can claim to be adequate that fails to explain the causes of that fateful confrontation, because that is just where he becomes a figure whom history has not forgotten. However memorable Jesus' teaching may have been on its own merits, it was his crucifixion as a result of his occupation of the Temple that became the centerpiece of the Gospels and of the movement that bore his name.

Jesus' Sending of the Twelve: Catchpole[7] and Vaage[8] are both competent guides in the attempt to understand Luke 10:1-12, the commission of the seventy or seventy-two disciples (the number varying with the manuscripts that are followed). The former adduces much Rabbinic material to elucidate the text, while the latter cites a range of Cynic sources. Both sorts of analogy are helpful in understanding the literary shape of the commission, but the focus here is different. Our purpose is to understand the commission of the disciples in terms of the kingdom, and the kingdom in terms of the commission. If, as seems to be the case, Q in its earliest, oral phase represents Jesus' charge to his disciples as he sent them out to be his representatives, it should reflect his own programmatic activity more lucidly than any inference we might draw regarding his intentions. Jesus' commission is the closest thing there is to his own commentary on his actions.

What the disciples are told to do seems

strange, unless the image of the harvest at the beginning of the charge (Luke 10:2) is taken seriously. (The metaphor of harvesting is also applied to discipleship by Tarfon in M. Ab. 2:15.) Because they are going out as to rich fields, they do not require what would normally be required on a journey: purse, bag, and sandals are dispensed with (Luke 10:4). Their charge is to treat Israel as a field in which one works, not as an itinerary of travel; even greeting people along the way (which would only lead to diversions from the task) is proscribed in Luke 10:4.

In addition, staffs are also prohibited, although they were normally used on journeys for support and protection. That is a detail that we actually know from Luke 9:3, the commission of the twelve (rather than the seventy). Luke 9:3 also prohibits carrying a bag, a provision of bread, money, or a change of clothing. Mat. 10:9-10 agrees in regard to money, a bag, clothing, sandals, and staff, but nothing prohibits bread. Mark 6:8-9 prohibits bread, bag, and money, but both a staff and sandals are positively prescribed!

All those additional privations comport with the command to go without sandals and were a part of the original charge. Each Gospel softens the stringent requirements somewhat. Matthew omits the prohibition of bread; Luke divides the prohibitions between the twelve (9:1-6) and the seventy (10:1-12). In a more radical way, Mark 6:9 turns the prohibition of sandals into a command to wear them. By the same transformation, Mark 6:8 specifies that a staff "alone" should be carried, so that the imagery of discipleship shifts from treating all Israel as one's household to passing through territory that might prove hostile. Such variations reflect differences in primitive Christian practice and in conceptions of discipleship. Similarly, the number of disciples in Luke 10:1, seventy or seventy-two, accommodates to the traditional number of the nations of the world, while the earlier figure of 12 in Mat. 10:5 and Mark 6:7 represents both the intention of Jesus to address all Israel and the earliest stage of Q. The image of Israel as a field ripe for harvest dominates the details of the charge to the disciples in the earliest form of the commission.

Another powerful analogy is at work with the commission. The Mishnah reflects the common practice in Jerusalem of prohibiting pilgrims to enter the Temple with the bags and staffs and sandals they had traveled with (M. Ber. 9:5). All such items were to be deposited prior to worship, so that one was present simply as a representative of Israel. Part of worship was that one was to appear in one's simple purity. The issue of purity also features prominently in the charge to the disciples (although it is overlooked far too often).

The very next injunction (Luke 10:5-8) instructs the disciples to enter into any house of a village they enter and to offer their peace. They are to accept hospitality in that house, eating what is set before them. The emphasis upon eating what is provided is repeated (Luke 10:7, 8), so that it does not appear to be a later, marginal elaboration. Within Pharisaic constructions of purity, such as are reflected in the Mishnah, the foods one ate and the hospitality one offered and accepted were carefully regulated. In the M. Dem. 2:2, which concerns tithing, one who undertakes to be faithful must tithe what he eats, what he sells, and what he buys, and may not accept hospitality from any "person of the land" (am ha-aretz), a phrase used since the time of Zech. 7:5 to refer to people whose practices could not be trusted. M. Dem. 2:3 further specifies that a faithful person must not sell to a person of the land wet or dry produce and must not buy from him wet produce—understood to be susceptible to uncleanness. The passage goes on to make the rule against hospitality more reciprocal, insofar as he cannot have a person of land as a guest when that person is wearing his own (probably impure) garments: he must first change his clothing. These strictures clearly reflect a construction of purity among the "faithful" (haverim) that sets them apart from other Jews by limiting the foods they might eat and by restricting the trade, commerce, and fellowship they might enjoy.

Jesus' insistence that his disciples accept hospitality in whatever house would accept them is fully consonant with his reputation as a "glutton and a drunkard" (see Mat. 11:19

and Luke 7:34). There is a deliberate care-lessness involved, in the precise sense that the disciples are not to have a care in regard to the practices of purity of those who offer them hospitality. Their hosts are to be considered true Israelites. When they join in the meals of the kingdom that Jesus' disciples have arrived to celebrate, when they accept and grant forgiveness to one another in the manner of the Lord's Prayer, what they set upon the table of fellowship from their own effort is by definition pure and should be gratefully consumed. The twelve disciples define and create the true Israel to which they are sent, and they tread that territory as on holy ground, shoeless, without staff or purse.

The activities of the disciples in the fellowship of Israel are essentially to be the activities of Jesus. As Luke presents Q, they are to heal the sick and preach that the kingdom has drawn near (Luke 10:9); as Matthew presents Q, they are to preach that the kingdom has drawn near, to heal, raise the dead, cleanse lepers, and caste out demons, all the while taking and giving freely (Mat. 10:7-8). As Catchpole observes, the wording of Matthew correlates the disciples' activities with Jesus' activities, and he thinks the correlation was introduced when the Gospel was composed (p. 167). But the correlation involves material in Q: Jesus' statement of what John the Baptist should be told he is doing (Mat. 11:5 and Luke 7:22). For that reason, Matthew at this point may be held to represent the more primitive wording. In any case, the coordination of the disciples' activity with Jesus' is manifestly an organic aspect of the charge in Q.

The extent of the identity between what Jesus does and what the disciples do is clearly represented at the close of the charge, when the disciples are instructed to shake off their feet the dust from any place that does not receive them (Luke 10:11). That gesture is, of course, vivid on any reading. But on the understanding of the charge we have developed here, the symbolism is particularly acute. Towns that do not receive the disciples have cut themselves off from the kingdom of God and can expect worse than what is in store for Sodom (Luke 10:11-12).

The fact that the kingdom has drawn near is the foundation of everything that is commanded, and the disciples are to address the people they gather in towns and villages in order to announce that dawning reality. Their preaching in itself is a witness to the nature of Jesus' eschatology. Likewise, their engagement in a ministry of healing attests to the immanence of the kingdom. The strong man of ailment is bound in order that the stronger man of the kingdom might prevail (see Mat. 12:28-29; Mark 3:27; Luke 11:20-22). That triumphant immanence of the kingdom, whether marked by healing or the wider range of victories indicated in Mat. 10:8 (cf., Luke 10:9), appears in the context of purity. The purity of the kingdom is such as to accept that each forgiven and forgiving Israelite is clean in himself and clean in what he produces. Much of the charge to the disciples is arranged to emphasize the understanding of purity that enables the triumphant immanence of the kingdom. To reject that kingdom, in the shape of its emissaries, alone can render the very dust of the town unclean. Accepting or rejecting the kingdom is the sole ground on which judgment ultimately is conducted.

Sending the disciples to announce the kingdom as promise (Luke 10:9) and as judgment (Luke 10:11) establishes that Jesus' eschatology is of an ultimate future that impinges upon the present. Their ministry of healing warrants the dynamic, transforming immanence of that divine power that finally must be all in all (Luke 10:9). What they teach, in its finality, amounts to a standard according to which hearers will be judged (Luke 10:10-12). And they enact the generic purity of Israel, which is the presupposition of the kingdom's revelation (Luke 10:5-8).

In the Gospel according to John, Jesus' brothers taunt him for not going to Jerusalem for the feast of Tabernacles. They say to him, "No one acts in secret and seeks himself to be in the open. If you do these things, show yourself to the world" (John 7:4). The idiom of the Gospel at this point is thoroughly christological, in that the concern is with Jesus' identity. But the question may well be asked in the idiom of the kingdom (and the question may originally have been asked in that way): if the kingdom is upon us and immanent, the standard of final judgment and the index of purity, then what is its public point of manifestation? How can all that Jesus says in parable and in action be true, how can the extension of his ministry by his disciples be valid, unless somewhere the kingdom is in the open, a matter of how public Israel radiates its truth to the world?

That urgent issue, as we will see in the next section, is what brought Jesus to Jerusalem and to the cross.

Jesus' occupation of the Temple: Critical discussion of Jesus during the modern period has been daunted by one crucial historical question. Anyone who has read the Gospels knows that Jesus was a skilled teacher, a rabbi in the sense already described. He skillfully wove a portrait of God as a divine ruler ("the kingdom of God," in his words) together with an appeal to people to behave as God's children (by loving both their divine father and their neighbor). At the same time, it is plain that Jesus appeared to be a threat both to the Jewish and to the Roman authorities in Jerusalem. He would not have been crucified otherwise. The question that has nagged critical discussion concerns the relationship between Jesus the rabbi and Jesus the criminal: how does a teacher of God's ways and God's love find himself on a cross?

The critical pictures of Jesus developed during the past two hundred years portray him as either an appealing, gifted teacher or as a vehement, political revolutionary. Both kinds of portrait are wanting. If Jesus' teaching was purely abstract, a matter of defining God's nature and the appropriate human response to God, it is hard to see why he would have invested himself in argument in Jerusalem and why the local aristocracy there turned against him. On the other hand, if Jesus' purpose was to encourage some sort of rebellion against Rome, why should he have devoted so much of his ministry to telling memorable parables in Galilee? It is easy enough to imagine Jesus the rabbi or Jesus the revolutionary. But how can we do jus-

tice to both aspects and discover Jesus, the radical rabbi of the first century?

The Gospels all relate an incident that sheds light in this dark corner of modern study (see Mat. 21:12-16; Mark 11:15-18; John 2:14-22, and Luke 19:45-48). In the passage traditionally called "The Cleansing of the Temple," Jesus boldly enters the holy place where sacrifice was conducted and throws out the people converting the currency of Rome into money acceptable to the priestly authorities. Such an action would arouse opposition from both the Roman authorities and the priests. The priests would be threatened because an important source of revenue was jeopardized. The Romans would be concerned because they wished to protect the operation of the Temple, which they saw as a symbol of their tolerant acceptance of Jews as loyal subjects.

The conventional picture of Jesus as preventing commercial activity in God's house is appealing in homiletic terms. It enables us to conceive of Jesus as transcending the worship of Judaism, and that is the intention of the Gospels. They are all written with hindsight, in the period after the Temple was destroyed (in 70 C.E.), when Christianity was emerging as a largely non-Jewish movement. From the early fathers of Christianity to the most modern commentaries, the alluring simplicity of the righteous, philosophical Jesus casting out the "money-changers" has proven itself again and again.

As is often the case, the conventional picture of Jesus may only be sustained by ignoring the social realities of early Judaism. There were indeed "money-changers" associated with the Temple; their activities are set down in the Mishnah. Every year, the changing of money—in order to collect the tax of a half shekel for every adult male—went on publicly throughout Israel. The process commenced a full month before Passover, with a proclamation concerning the tax (see M. Sheq. 1:1), and exchanges were set up outside Jerusalem ten days before they were set up in the Temple (M. Sheq. 1:3). According to Josephus, the tax was not even limited to those resident in the land of Israel (*War* VII, 218; *Antiquities* XVIII, 312), but was collected from Jews far and wide. An awareness of those simple facts brings us to an equally simple conclusion: the Gospels' picture of Jesus is distorted. It is clear that he could not have stopped the collection of the half shekel by overturning some tables in the Temple.

A generation after Jesus' death, by the time the Gospels were written, the Temple in Jerusalem had been destroyed, and the most influential centers of Christianity were cites of the Mediterranean world such as Alexandria, Antioch, Corinth, Damascus, Ephesus, and Rome. There were still large numbers of Jews who were also followers of Jesus, but non-Jews came to predominate in the primitive Church. They had control over how the Gospels were written after 70 C.E. and how the texts were interpreted. The Synoptic Gospels were composed by one group of teachers after another during the period between Jesus' death and 95 C.E. There is a reasonable degree of consensus that Mark was the first of the Gospels to be written, around 71 C.E. in the environs of Rome. As convention has it, Matthew was subsequently composed, near 80 C.E., perhaps in Damascus (or elsewhere in Syria), while Luke came later, say in 90 C.E., perhaps in Antioch. Some of the earliest teachers who shaped the Gospels shared the cultural milieu of Jesus, but others had never seen him; they lived far from his land at a later period and were not practicing Jews. John's Gospel was composed in Ephesus around 100 C.E. and is a reflection upon the significance of Jesus for Christians who had the benefit of the sort of teaching the Synoptic Gospels represent.

The growth of Christianity involved a rapid transition from culture to culture and, within each culture, from sub-culture to subculture. A basic prerequisite for understanding any text of the Gospels, therefore, is to define the cultural context of a given statement. The cultural context of the picture of Jesus' throwing money-changers out of the Temple is that of the predominantly non-Jewish audience of the Gospels, who regarded Judaism as a thing of the past and its worship as corrupt. The attempt seriously to imagine Jesus' behaving in that fashion only

distorts our understanding of his purposes and encourages Christian anti-Semitism. Insensitivity to the cultural milieu of the Gospels goes hand in hand with a prejudicial treatment of cultures other than our own.

Jesus probably did object to the tax of a half shekel, as Mat. 17:24-27 indicates. For him, being a child of God (a "son," as he put it) implied that one was free of any imposed payment for the worship of the Temple.[9] But a single onslaught of the sort described in the Gospels would not have amounted to an effective protest against the payment. To stop the collection would have required an assault involving the central treasuries of the Temple as well as the local treasuries in the land of Israel and beyond. There is no indication that Jesus and his followers did anything of the kind, and an action approaching such dimensions would have invited immediate and forceful repression by both Jewish and Roman authorities. There is no evidence that they reacted in that manner to Jesus and his followers.

But Jesus' action in the Temple as attested in the Gospels is not simply a matter of preventing the collection of the half shekel. In fact, Luke 19:45-46 says nothing whatever about "money-changers." Since Luke's Gospel is in some ways the most sensitive to historical concerns in the New Testament, the omission seems significant. Luke joins the other Gospels in portraying Jesus' act in the Temple as an occupation designed to prevent the sacrifice of animals that were acquired on the site. The trading involved commerce within the Temple, and the Jesus of the canonical Gospels, like the Jesus of the Gospel according to Thomas, held that, "Traders and merchants shall not enter the places of my father" (Thomas, saying 64).

Jesus' action in the Temple, understood as a means of asserting the sanctity of the Temple, is comparable to the actions of other Jewish teachers of his period. Josephus reports that the Pharisees made known their displeasure at a high priest (Alexander Jannaeus) by inciting a crowd to pelt him with lemons (at hand for a festal procession) at the time he should have been offering sacrifice (*Antiquities* XIII, 372, 373). Josephus also recounts the execution of the rabbis who were implicated in a plot to dismantle the eagle Herod had erected over a gate of the Temple (*Jewish War* I, 648-655; *Antiquities* XVII, 149-167). By comparison, Jesus' action seems almost tame; after all, what he did was expel some vendors, an act less directly threatening to priestly and secular authorities than what some earlier Pharisees had done.

Once it is appreciated that Jesus' maneuver in the Temple was in the nature of a claim upon territory in order to eject those performing an activity he obviously opposed, it seems more straightforward to characterize it as an "occupation" rather than a "demonstration;" the traditional term "cleansing" is obviously an apologetic designation. The purpose of Jesus' activity makes good sense within the context of what we know of the activities of other early Rabbinic teachers. Hillel was an older contemporary of Jesus' who taught (according to the B. Shab. 31a) a form of what is known in Christian circles as the Golden Rule taught by Jesus, that we should do to others as we would have them do to us. Hillel also reportedly taught that offerings brought to the Temple should have hands laid on them by their owners and then be given over to priests for slaughter (see the citations below). Recent studies of the anthropology of sacrifice show why such stipulations were held to be important. Hillel was insisting that, when the people of Israel came to worship, they should offer of their own property. Putting one's hands on the animal about to be sacrificed was a statement of ownership.

The followers of a rabbi named Shammai are typically depicted in Rabbinic literature as resisting the teachings of Hillel. Here, too, they take the part of the opposition. They insist that animals for sacrifice might be given directly to priests for slaughter; Hillel's requirement of laying hands on the sacrifice is held to be dispensable. But one of Shammai's followers was so struck by the rectitude of Hillel's position, he had some 3,000 animals brought into the Temple and gave them to those who were willing to lay hands on them in advance of sacrifice (see the B. Bes.

20a-b; T. Hag. 2:11; Y. Hag. 2:3; and M. Bes. 2:4).

In one sense, the tradition concerning Hillel envisages the opposite movement from what is represented in the tradition concerning Jesus: animals are driven into the Temple rather than their traders expelled. Yet the purpose of the action by Hillel's partisan is to enforce a certain understanding of correct offering, one that accords with a standard feature of sacrifice in the anthropological literature. Hillel's ruling, in effect, insists upon the participation of the offerer by virtue of his ownership of what is offered, while most of the followers of Shammai are portrayed as sanctioning sacrifice more as a self-contained, priestly action.

Jesus' occupation of the Temple is best seen—along lines similar to those involved in the provision of animals to support Hillel's position—as an attempt to insist that the offerer's actual ownership of what is offered is a vital aspect of sacrifice. Neither Hillel nor Jesus needs to be understood as acting upon any symbolic agenda other than his conception of acceptable sacrifice, nor as appearing to his contemporaries to be anything other than a typical Pharisee, impassioned with purity in the Temple to the point of forceful intervention. Neither of their positions may be understood as a concern with the physical acceptability of the animals at issue: in each cases, the question of purity is, What is to be done with what is taken to be clean?

Jesus' occupation of the Temple took place within the context of a particular dispute in which the Pharisees took part, a controversy over where the action of acquiring animals for sacrifice was to occur. Insofar as the dispute was intimately involved with the issue of how animals were to be procured, it manifests a focus upon purity akin to that attributed to Hillel and Jesus. The Gospels describe the southern side of the outer court as the place from which Jesus expelled the traders, and that is what brings us to the question of a dispute involving Pharisees. The exterior court was unquestionably well suited for trade, since it was surrounded by porticos on the inside, in conformity to Herod's architectural preferences. But the assumption of

Rabbinic literature and Josephus is that the market for the sale of sacrificial beasts was not located in the Temple at all but in a place called Hanuth ("market" in Aramaic) on the Mount of Olives, across the Kidron Valley. According to the B. A.Z. 8b, B. Shab. 15a, and B. San. 41a, some forty years before the destruction of the Temple, the principal council of Jerusalem was removed to Hanuth from the place in the Temple called the Chamber of Hewn Stone. Around 30 C.E., then, Caiaphas both expelled the Sanhedrin and introduced the traders into the Temple, in both ways centralizing power in his own hands.

From the point of view of Pharisaism generally, trade in the southern side of outer court was anathema. Purses were not permitted in the Temple according to the Pharisees' teaching, and the introduction of trade into the Temple rendered the ideal of not bringing into the Temple more than would be consumed there impracticable. Incidentally, the installation of traders in the porticos would also involve the removal of those teachers, Pharisaic and otherwise, who taught and observed in the Temple itself (see M. San. 11:2; B. Pes. 26a).

From the point of view of the smooth conduct of sacrifice, of course, Caiaphas' innovation was sensible. One could know at the moment of purchase that one's sacrifice was acceptable and not run the risk of harm's befalling the animal on its way to be slaughtered. But when we look at the installation of the traders from the point of view of Hillel's teaching, Jesus' objection becomes understandable. Hillel had taught that one's sacrifice had to be shown to be one's own, by the imposition of hands; part of the necessary preparation was not just of people to the south and beasts to the north, but the connection between the two by appropriation. Caiaphas' innovation was sensible on the understanding that sacrifice was simply a matter of offering pure, unblemished animals. But it failed in Pharisaic terms, not only in its introduction of the necessity for commerce into the Temple, but in its breach of the link between worshiper and offering in the sacrificial action. The animals were correct in

Caiaphas' system, and the priests appropriate, but the understanding of the offering by the people appeared—to some at least—profoundly defective. The essential component of Jesus' occupation of the Temple is perfectly explicable within the context of contemporary Pharisaism, in which purity was more than a question of animals for sacrifice being intact.

For Jesus, the issue of sacrifice also—and crucially—concerned the action of Israel, as in the teaching of Hillel. His action, of course, upset financial arrangements for the sale of such animals, and it is interesting that John 2:15 speaks of his sweeping away the "coins" (in Greek, *kermata*) involved in the trade. But such incidental disturbance is to be distinguished from a deliberate attempt to prevent the collection of the half shekel, which would have required coordinated activity throughout Israel (and beyond), and which typically involved larger units of currency than the term "coins" would suggest.

Jesus shared Hillel's concern that what was offered by Israel in the Temple should truly belong to Israel. His vehemence in opposition to Caiaphas' reform was a function of his deep commitment to the notion that Israel was pure and should offer of its own, even if others thought one unclean (see Mat. 8:2-4; Mark 1:40-44; Luke 5:12-14), on the grounds that it is not what goes into a person that defiles but what comes out (see Mat. 15:11; Mark 7:15). Israelites are properly understood as pure, and therefore what extends from a person, what one is and does and has, manifests that purity. That focused, generative vision was the force behind Jesus' occupation of Temple; only those after 70 C.E. who no longer treasured the Temple in Jerusalem as God's house could (mis)take Jesus' position to be an unqualified prophecy of doom or a global objection to sacrifice. When Jesus cited Jer. 7:11 in equating Caiaphas' arrangement in the Temple with theft, he implicitly invoked Jeremiah's prophecy of the Temple's destruction (see Mat. 21:13; Mark 11:17; Luke 19:46). But the implication was only that, and it was exaggerated by Caiaphas for one purpose and (later) by non-Judaic Christians for another purpose. The force of Jesus' message concerned what the Temple should be, not its demolition.

Jesus' crucifixion and the Kingdom of God: Jesus' interference in the ordinary worship of the Temple might have been sufficient by itself to bring about his execution. After all, for as long as it stood the Temple was the center of Judaism. Roman officials were so interested in its smooth functioning at the hands of the priests they appointed that they were known to sanction the penalty of death for gross sacrilege (Josephus, *Antiquities* XV, 417). Yet there is no indication that Jesus was arrested immediately. Instead, he remained at liberty for some time and was finally taken into custody just after one of his meals, the last supper (Mat. 26:47-56; Mark 14:43-52; Luke 22:47-53; John 18:3-11). The decision of the authorities of the Temple to move against Jesus when they did is what made it the final supper.

Why did the authorities wait, and why did they act when they did? The Gospels portray them as fearful of the popular backing Jesus enjoyed (Mat. 26:5; Mark 14:2; Luke 22:2; John 11:47-48), and his inclusive teaching of purity probably did bring enthusiastic followers into the Temple with him. But in addition, there was another factor: Jesus could not simply be dispatched as a cultic criminal. He was not attempting an onslaught upon the Temple as such; his dispute with the authorities concerned purity within the Temple. Other rabbis of his period also engaged in physical demonstrations of the purity they required in the conduct of worship, as we have seen. Jesus' action was extreme, but not totally without precedent, even in the use of force. Most crucially, Jesus could claim the support of tradition in objecting to siting vendors within the Temple, and Caiaphas' innovation in fact did not stand. That is why Rabbinic sources assume that Hanuth was the site of the vendors.

The delay of the authorities, then, was understandable. We could even say it was commendable, reflecting continued controversy over the merits of Jesus' teaching and whether his occupation of the great court should be condemned out of hand. But why

did they finally arrest Jesus? The last supper provides the key; something about Jesus' meals after his occupation of the Temple caused Judas to inform on Jesus. Of course, "Judas" is the only name the traditions of the New Testament have left us. We cannot say who or how many of the disciples became disaffected by Jesus' behavior after his occupation of the Temple.

However they learned of Jesus' new interpretation of his meals of fellowship, the authorities arrested him just after the supper we call last. Jesus continued to celebrate fellowship at table as a foretaste of the kingdom, just as he had before. As before, the promise of drinking wine in the kingdom of God united his followers in an anticipatory celebration of the kingdom (see Mat. 26:29; Mark 14:25; Luke 22:18). But Jesus also added a new and scandalous dimension of meaning. His occupation of the Temple having failed, Jesus said over the wine, "This is my blood," and over the bread, "This is my flesh" (Mat. 26:26, 28; Mark 14:22, 24; Luke 22:19-20; 1 Cor. 11:24-25; Justin, *Apology* I.66.3).

In Jesus' context, the context of his confrontation with the authorities of the Temple, his words can have had only one meaning. He cannot have meant, "Here are my personal body and blood;" that interpretation only makes sense at a later stage in the development of Christianity. Jesus' point was rather that, in the absence of a Temple that permitted his view of purity to be practiced, wine was his blood of sacrifice, and bread was his flesh of sacrifice. In Aramaic, "blood" (*dema*) and "flesh" (*bisra*, which may also be rendered as "body") can carry such a sacrificial meaning, and in Jesus' context, that is the most natural connotation.

The meaning of "the last supper," then, actually evolved over a series of meals after Jesus' occupation of the Temple. During that period, Jesus claimed that wine and bread were a better sacrifice than what was offered in the Temple, a foretaste of new wine in the kingdom of God. At least wine and bread were Israel's own, not tokens of priestly dominance. No wonder the opposition to him, even among the twelve (in the shape of

Judas, according to the Gospels) became deadly. In essence, Jesus made his meals into a rival altar.

That final gesture of protest gave Caiaphas what he needed. Jesus could be charged with blasphemy before those with an interest in the Temple. The issue now was not simply Jesus' opposition to the siting of vendors of animals, but his creation of an alternative cultus. He blasphemed the law of Moses; Josephus deems blasphemous attacks on Jews (*Against Apion* I, 59, 223), on Moses (*Antiquities* III, 307; *Apion* I, 279), or on patriarchal law (*Apion* II, 143). The accusation regarding Jesus concerned the Temple, in which Rome also had a vested interested. Pilate had no regard for issues of purity; Acts 18:14-16 reflects the attitude of an official in a similar position, and Josephus shows that Pilate was without sympathy for Judaism. But the Temple in Jerusalem had come to symbolize Roman power as well as the devotion of Israel. Rome guarded jealously the sacrifices that the Emperor financed in Jerusalem; when they were spurned in the year 66 C.E., the act was a declaration of war (see Josephus, *Jewish War* II, 409). Jesus stood accused of creating a disturbance in that Temple (during his occupation) and of fomenting disloyalty to it and (therefore) to Caesar. Pilate did what he had to do. Jesus' persistent reference to a "kingdom" that Caesar did not rule, and his repute among some as messiah or prophet only made Pilate's order more likely. It all was probably done without a hearing; Jesus was not a Roman citizen. He was a nuisance, dispensed with under a military jurisdiction.

At last, then, at the end of his life, Jesus discovered the public center of the kingdom: the point from which the light of God's rule would radiate and triumph. His initial intention was that the Temple would conform to his vision of the purity of the kingdom, that all Israel would be invited there, forgiven and forgiving, to offer of their own in divine fellowship in the confidence that what they produced was pure (see Mat. 15:11; Mark 7:15). The innovation of Caiaphas prevented that, by erecting what Jesus (as well as other rabbis) saw as an unacceptable barrier between Israel and what Israel offered.

The last public act of Jesus before his crucifixion was to declare that his meals were the center of the kingdom. The kingdom that was near and immanent and final and pure was now understood to radiate from a public place, an open manifestation of God's rule. The authorities in the Temple had rejected what some people in Galilee already had. Just as those in the north could be condemned as a new Sodom (see Luke 10:12), so Jesus could deny that offerings coopted by priests were acceptable sacrifices. It is no coincidence that the typical setting of appearances of the risen Jesus is while disciples were taking meals together (see Luke 24:13-35, 36-43; Mark 16:14-18 [not originally part of the Gospel, but an early witness of the resurrection nonetheless]; John 21:1-14). The conviction that the light of the kingdom radiated from that practice went hand in hand with the conviction that the true master of the table, the rabbi who began it all, remained within their fellowship.

Bibliography

Chilton, Bruce, *Pure Kingdom. Jesus' Vision of God: Studying the Historical Jesus* (Grand Rapids: Eerdmans, 1996).

Chilton, Bruce, *The Temple of Jesus. His Sacrificial Program Within a Cultural History of Sacrifice* (University Park: The Pennsylvania State University Press, 1992).

Crossan, John Dominic, *The Historical Jesus. The Life of a Mediterranean Jewish Peasant* (San Francisco: Harper and Edinburgh: Clark, 1991).

Neusner, Jacob, *Judaism in the Beginning of Christianity* (Philadelphia: Fortress, 1988).

Sanders, E.P., *Jesus and Judaism* (Philadelphia: Fortress, 1985).

Vaage, Leif E., *Galilean Upstarts. Jesus' First Followers According to Q* (Valley Forge: Trinity Press International, 1994).

Notes

[1] Sanders, E.P., *Jesus and Judaism* (Philadelphia, 1985), pp. 3-13.

[2] J.P. Kane, "Ossuary Inscriptions of Jerusalem," in *Journal of Semitic Studies 23* (1978), pp. 268-282.

[3] John Dominic Crossan, *The Historical Jesus. The Life of a Mediterranean Jewish Peasant* (San Francisco and Edinburgh, 1991), pp. 421-422.

[4] George Foot Moore, *Judaism in the First Centuries of the Christian Era. The Age of the Tannaim 1* (Cambridge, 1927), pp. 377-378.

[5] Ben F. Meyer, *The Aims of Jesus* (London, 1979), 153-154.

[6] Bruce Chilton, *The Temple of Jesus. His Sacrificial Program Within a Cultural History of Sacrifice* (University Park, 1992), pp. 101-103, 183.

[7] David Catchpole, *The Quest for Q* (Edinburgh, 1993).

[8] Leif E. Vaage, *Galilean Upstarts. Jesus' First Followers According to Q* (Valley Forge, 1994).

[9] Bruce Chilton, "A Coin of Three Realms (Matthew 17.24-27)," in D.J.A. Clines, et al., eds., *The Bible in Three Dimensions. Essays in Celebration of Forty Years of Biblical Studies in the University of Sheffield: Journal for the Study of the Old Testament, Supplement Series* 87, 1990, pp. 269-282.

BRUCE CHILTON

JOSEPHUS AND JUDAISM: For any number of reasons, the Judaism of Flavius Josephus has not been a subject of burning inquiry these past two thousand years. He began his literary career saddled with the reputation of a heinous traitor to the Judean people; his works were first preserved by those who had destroyed the Second Temple and then by Christian leaders such as Eusebius, who were in the process of building a state that would limit Jewish civil rights. None of these early users of Josephus had any motive to reckon seriously with his perspectives on Judaism.

Nor, by and large, have his more recent users. Critical scholarship on Josephus, as on classical and biblical literature in general, received its major impetus from a kind of source criticism that was impatient with any supposition of authorial integrity. From about 1870 to 1920, Josephan scholarship was quite preoccupied with the quest for Josephus's sources, which the historian was thought largely to have cobbled together ineptly.[1] Since 1920, scholarship has tended to look *through* Josephus to the events behind his narrative rather than examining the compositions themselves for a coherent statement. This trend has been abetted by the (otherwise welcome) flourishing of Judean archaeology since 1967, for archaeologists lead all historians in poking about in Josephus without worrying much about his literary aims or religious values.

So, paradoxically, although Josephus with his thirty volumes would appear to offer us a rare opportunity to examine the outlook of a first-century Judean, very few books or even articles have probed the issue of his Judaism.[2] Those that have done so have tended to begin with the assumption that he was or wanted to be seen as a Pharisee. But this is an insupportable assumption and, as we shall see, one that skews the rest of the evidence. Because of the fragmented state of the scholarship and the relative lack of interest in the question of Josephus's Judaism, we cannot simply summarize the state of the question here; we must make a new attempt to sketch the contours of Josephus's Judaism.

Definitions, red herrings, and false premises: In order to approach this topic fruitfully, we must first clarify what is obvious in principle but requires constant reiteration in practice: in the ancient world, religion in general and Judaism in particular could not be isolated from other aspects of life. In societies that had no understanding of a "separation between Church and state," where political leaders were often priests and priests were politicians, and where every aspect of public life from education and military service to public holidays was replete with symbols of piety toward the god(s), there were no words for "religion" as a distinct experience. One's external obligations might be differentiated in the slogans "piety towards the god(s) and justice towards one fellows," but these two virtues were inextricably tied together.[3]

In talking about Josephus's Judaism, therefore, we are not talking about some isolable component of his writings or world view: we cannot simply look up a section on "religion." He was a *Ioudaios* (Greek for Judean, Jew), and this meant to his contemporaries that he represented the whole culture of the Judean people, who lived throughout the eastern Mediterranean. Just as every other city had its sanctuaries in which animals were slaughtered by priestly experts in order to appease a deity, Jerusalem had its famous Temple, sacrificial system, and priesthood. Just as every nation had its laws and customs passed down from time immemorial—often from heroes who were gods or had encountered gods—so the Judeans had their famous constitution from Moses, who had conversed with God. Just as each nation had its regimen of special holidays and (in some cases) diet, so too the Judeans had theirs. Although

Josephus cannot devote a book to "religion," his writings about Judean origins, philosophy, wars, and other history are suffused with issues of piety and faithfulness toward the deity. The best that we can do is focus our exploration on these aspects of Josephus's writings, while bearing in mind that they cannot be excised from the tapestry to which they belong.

Before we explore Josephus's writings, we also need to disabuse ourselves of two false but common presuppositions. The first is that Josephus's personal character renders his writings—no matter how sublime they might be in places—insincere or at least suspect. This widespread belief rests on a methodological oversight, for Josephus's character can only be reconstructed from what he says about his actions in his writings. Although countless readers have brought a rigid morality to those texts and found Josephus wanting—among other things, he is accused of having abandoned his people while he was their "general," having invented stories of a divine mission as a cover-up, having avoided death for ignoble reasons, and having sold his soul as propagandist for the Romans— we must remember that ancient writers generally relate only what they think will persuade readers of their intelligence, character, and trustworthiness. Since Josephus evidently meant to impress his readers with his wily resourcefulness in the service of an ultimately noble cause, rather like Homer's hero Odysseus (or for that matter, the biblical Jacob), it makes no sense for us to use his cheerful testimony about his lies and tricks as evidence against his character. We must simply admit that we know nothing in advance about his character: that remains to be reconstructed hypothetically from the literary evidence *after* we have a firm grasp of the texts.

Second, we may not begin with the standard assumption that Josephus either was or claimed to be a Pharisee. His major works make no such claim and, indeed, the *War* and *Antiquities* give the strong impression that he disliked the Pharisees. In *Life* 12, after he has described his education among the Judean philosophical schools and his prolonged period of study with Bannus in the wilderness,

he acknowledges in somewhat puzzling language that his entry into public life upon his return to the *polis* of Jerusalem entailed a certain "following" of the Pharisees. But this seems best understood as a sequel to his earlier remark that even Sadducees must defer to the Pharisees *when they assume public office* (*Ant.* 18.17).[4] Since Josephus does not make any claim to personal Pharisaic allegiance, we ought not to be strait-jacketed by the conventional reading of *Life* 12, but should rather cultivate a view of his religion inductively, from what he says as a whole.

The *Judean War*: Josephus's first known work, the *Judean War*, is critical for our assessment of his Judaism. This work has borne the brunt of scholarly and popular distaste for Josephus because it is typically understood as a service to Roman propaganda. That understanding is grounded in Josephus's situation while writing—allegedly as a Roman favorite, well compensated in Rome for his betrayal; in the work's obvious flattery of Vespasian and Titus; and especially in Josephus's claim that the Greek *War* more or less translates an earlier Aramaic version he had sent to Jews and others living in the Parthian kingdom (1.3, 6). Richard Laqueur and Henry St. John Thackeray argued that this earlier *War* must have been written in order to prevent disturbances from Rome's longtime enemy, Parthia, by showing what had happened to the Judeans.[5] In support of this view, they pointed to Josephus's comment in *War* 3.108: after a detailed account of Roman military training, Josephus allows that he included it "to deter others who may be tempted to revolt." Plainly, if the *War* was a work of Roman propaganda, we ought not to examine it too closely for genuine religious thinking.

In fact, however, this entire scholarly edifice is groundless. To begin with, Josephus was not well compensated in Rome: his benefits reached only to the Roman citizenship that was common to most of his compatriots in Rome, relief from taxation (common to teachers of his time), some sort of stipend and accommodation, and some land in Judea (*Life* 417-29). He did not receive anything like what the truly favored received: equestrian (or even senatorial) rank, property in Italy, and social prominence.[6] He remained an utterly marginal figure, known to others as a captured Judean who made a prediction, not as a significant figure in Rome. Second, the surviving *War* is not a translation of the Aramaic account, but a new Greek work, as the language and literary forms (e.g., prologue, speeches, philosophical discussions) make clear.[7] And what is there in the Greek *War* does not answer well to the needs of propaganda. Flattery of Vespasian and Titus is undeniable, but such adulation was widely understood to be unavoidable for historians of contemporary events.[8] Josephus's comment about deterring revolt plainly does not refer to the aim of his whole work; it is part, and only part, of his excuse for a digression on the Roman army. He also says there that he included the digression to console those conquered by the Romans—a motive that would not suit the Parthian addressees at all—and to inform those who do not know about such matters (*War* 3.108-109). These appear to be "throw-away" editorial lines explaining a brief digression much more than the author's programmatic statements about the *War* as a whole.

War's programmatic statements, which come in the prologue, in the major speeches (crafted by an ancient author as vehicles of his perspective), and in editorial asides, are all but ignored by the conventional view.[9] These passages present a consistent agenda, however, which cannot fairly be described as Roman propaganda. Josephus claims to write because other accounts of the recent war in Judea have either praised the Romans or vilified the Judeans. A Jerusalemite priest who fought on the Judean side and later observed from the Roman side, he wishes to set the record straight (1.1-3, 6-9). Was he sincere in this elaborate statement of his purpose?

Although the particular anti-Judean works to which he refers have not survived, it appears from what has survived of contemporary literature that the view of the war challenged by Josephus was indeed quickly entrenched among his Roman contemporaries. Namely: the Judeans revolted in keeping with their national character, which was

seen as anti-social and troublesome for the rest of humanity; the Roman victory represented the decisive defeat of the Judean God by the Roman gods.[10] Thus the revolt brought to a head the old accusations that Judeans were misanthropic (because of their refusal to mix with others) and atheistic. The triumphal procession of Titus, the issue of *Iudaea Capta* coins, and the diversion of the Temple tax to Jupiter Capitolina must all have contributed to a jingoistic atmosphere in Rome, which would have been difficult for Roman Judeans and their friends to endure. Josephus's *War* develops arguments to counter precisely these attitudes. Whether he was personally sincere or not, the *War* appears to be a coherent response to a hostile postwar situation for Judeans in the 70s.

Josephus's argument is two-fold. First, he defends the national character. Already in the prologue he announces his thesis that the revolt and consequent destruction of the Temple resulted from the activities of a very few "tyrants" who initiated a civil war among the Judeans (1.10); he picks up the venerable Greek theme of civil insurrection (*stasis oikeia*) as an explanatory model (see, e.g., *Thucydides* 1.2). In the unfolding narrative, the reader is reminded constantly that the Judeans are excellent world citizens: although courageous warriors against evil when necessary—this is illustrated by their stunning defeat of the monstrous Seleucids (1.34-35)—their most famous king, Herod, whose descendants were still prominent in Roman society, embodied all the traits of the faithful ally. No misanthrope, he.

On Herod's death, a revolt was sparked by a handful of rebels, who almost led the nation to ruin before they were put down by Varus. This revolt lays much of the groundwork for the more recent conflict. Josephus has Nicolaus voice the obvious charge against the Judean character: "impatient of all authority and insubordinate towards the sovereigns" (2.92). But in spite of the self-serving royal pretenders and militants who arise from time to time, Josephus insists that the Judeans as a whole and their legitimate leaders favor peace (2.73, 302, 324, 333; 6.344). This becomes increasingly clear as Josephus describes the "philosophical school" of Judas the Galilean, with its belief that the Judeans must tolerate no master but God, for he insists that proper Judean philosophy, in its three forms, has nothing to do with this kind of thinking (2.117-19). The subsequent narrative and especially the major speeches created by Josephus for his characters drive home repeatedly the point that the Judeans (represented most brilliantly by the Essenes) respect legitimate authority (2.91, 140).

To be sure, the present sketch simplifies Josephus's narrative greatly. In a sophisticated way, he works in important nuances. For example, he makes it clear that the later Roman governors were thoroughly corrupt and wicked, so that the reader cannot be entirely unsympathetic toward the rebels (2.272, 277). He allows that the Judeans' initial victories gave them courage, and he may even suggest that *he* was persuaded to join the revolt at this point—or perhaps he was "forced" (2.562). He remarks astutely on the various pragmatic motives that came into play—not only an insatiable thirst for power but also hopes for economic and spiritual deliverance (2.426-27) or, on the part of the aristocrats, the view that no matter how bad the Romans were, victory against them was simply impossible and acquiescence the only prudent course (2.339, 397-99). Otherwise, horrifying reprisals would—and did—follow (2.457-93). He describes many scenes of extreme Roman cruelty (2.308, 352; 3.329, 336). So this is not a simple story told in black and white terms. Nevertheless, his thesis that the Judeans are, in spite of all provocations, peaceful and faithful subjects undercuts the charge that the revolt was symptomatic of a bellicose national character.

Josephus develops an equally nuanced argument to the effect that the Roman victory did not represent the defeat of the Judean God. On a superficial reading, his many remarks about Roman fortune might be understood as part and parcel of a Roman world view. But that would be a superficial reading indeed. Such remarks are deeply grounded in another view of things, which holds that the Judean God is ultimately in control of human affairs, having caused various nations to rise and fall and, in fact, having brought the Romans to their current hegemony (2.365-87; esp. 3.368; 5.2, 367). Without God, they could not have achieved this power.

What about the destruction of this God's Temple? Was it not a defeat? On the contrary, Josephus argues that, because of the sacrilege committed by the rebel leaders in the sacred precincts, the Judean God withdrew from his sanctuary (6.127, 300) and used the Romans to purge his city (2.393-4; 5.19; 6.110, 249; 7.328-32). If the Judeans had simply served God and waited for him to right any wrongs perpetrated against them, he would have come to their aid. But by taking matters into their own hands, they violated the national tradition and caused irreparable damage. The Temple and city had to be destroyed (5.19). But it was the Judean God, as even Titus appears to acknowledge (6.409-13), who engineered the entire remedy; the Romans were merely his pawns.

Josephus does not here address what lies in the future for the Judeans. There are hints, perhaps—in Titus's acknowledgment that all human affairs are in flux (3.396) and in the claim that the city has been purged and the malefactors punished (5.19)—that things will improve for the Judeans. But this is nowhere made explicit in the *War*. Josephus instead focuses steadfastly on the causes of the revolt and the resulting image of the Judeans. Against charges of impiety and injustice, he takes every opportunity to insist that Judeans are normally the most virtuous of all people, upholding piety towards the deity and justice towards their fellows (e.g., 2.139). Given his circumstances, in a hostile post-war Rome, it is difficult not to see this as a courageous essay in defense of Judean character, even an effort to prevent further reprisals against his compatriots.

But what of *War*'s underlying "religious" assumptions? Were there, for instance, views current in Judean circles that matched Josephus's outlook? Was this an *ad hoc* ploy or does it fit plausibly with broader currents of Jewish thought?

Within the Bible itself, the texts that provide fertile soil for Josephus's outlook are those attributed to Jeremiah and Daniel. The priest Jeremiah, who lived when the first Temple was destroyed, had counseled submission to the Babylonian super-power, on the argument that God was using the Babylonians to punish the Judeans for wickedness (including Temple sacrilege). In response, he was maligned as a traitor to the national cause. It is quite clear that Josephus has Jeremiah in mind throughout his works. He compares the recent destruction to the ancient one (5.391, 411; 6.104, 268, 437, 439); he borrows Jeremiah's "lamentation" as a key semantic field (1.9, 12; 2.400, 455; 3.263; 3.501; 4.128, 412; 5.20, 418, 515; 6.7, 96-111, 267, 271-74);[11] he explicitly compares himself with the famous prophet as he faces possible death at the hands of his fellow Judeans (5.391-93); and, as one of the mysterious omens preceding the fall of Jerusalem, he has a man named Jesus walking around for seven years citing Jeremianic verse (6.301; cf., Jer 7.34). The horrible famine and cannibalism story of *War* 6.193-213 vividly recalls Lam 2.20: "Should women eat their offspring, the children they have borne?" And the whole story of the rebels' assassination of aristocrats recalls the completion of that verse: "Should priest and prophet be killed in the sanctuary of the Lord?" It is probably no coincidence, in this context, that Jeremiah's famous remark about the Temple's having become a den of robbers (Jer 7.11) corresponds to Josephus's most typical description of the rebel leaders as robbers: he uses the same Greek word (*lēstēs*) as the Septuagint translation of Jeremiah, and accuses his robbers of the same crimes (Jer 7.9; *War* 5.402).

Although Daniel is not mentioned in the *War*, we have good reason to suppose that Josephus also had this work in mind. *A priori* considerations include the extreme popularity of Daniel in that period and the fact that Daniel was thought to be another prophet of the Exile, following the destruction on the first Temple. Details in the *War* bear out the supposition that Josephus knew and treasured Daniel. The book of Daniel, both in the six chapters of narrative and the six chapters of dream visions, has a clear message: nations rise and fall under the sovereignty of God

(2.21; 4.14, 22, 29); whatever happens, God will protect his own people as long as they are faithful and, under God's protection, it is even possible for them to prosper in the courts of foreign power (1.20; 2.48; 3.30; 6.29); it is entirely wrong to assert oneself to end foreign domination (8.14), for only God can bring an end to foreign oppression, which he will do through a kingdom *not* made with human hands (2.34, 45; 8.25); the "wise," who understand God's ways (1.17, 20; 2.30, 47; 5.11-12; 11.33-35), are to be distinguished from the "many," who are open to persuasion for good or ill (8.25; 11.33). All of these themes, as we have seen, are prominent in the *War*. Josephus writes as a new Daniel, protected by his piety from his accusers in the courts of foreign power.

Literary reminiscences of Daniel also appear in various places. In some tension with his earlier praise of the Hasmoneans as courageous opponents of evil, his speech favoring pacifism laments that when the Judeans opposed Antiochus IV, the Temple lay desolate for three years and six months (5.394), a period specified only in Daniel (Dan 7.25; 9.27; 12.11); 1 Maccabees (1.54; 4.52) changes the timing in hindsight. Again, when Josephus speaks of Archelaus's deposition, he strangely places soothsayers alongside *Chaldeans* among the ethnarch's entourage that tries to interpret his ominous dream (*War* 2.111-13). The only parallel to this construction in all of Josephus is his description of Nebuchadnezzar's entourage in *Ant.* 10.195. So it seems likely that Josephus is anticipating his own story of Daniel, which will come in the *Antiquities*. Third, the passage from Jeremiah about the "den of robbers," noted above, is interesting because the Hebrew word used of the robbers there (*peritz*) also appears in Dan 11.14, to describe the "violent ones" who wrongly assert themselves to fight foreign oppression. Although we cannot prove it, it would make sense if Josephus had both Jeremiah and Daniel in mind when he used this charged language.

Most telling, however, are the various allusions in *War* to mysterious oracles and dreams about future events. In one place, Josephus claims that an ambiguous oracle in the sacred writings foretold the rise of a world ruler from among the Judeans, which many of the "the wise" misunderstood as referring to a Judean, when in fact it pointed to Vespasian, who was acclaimed in Judea (6.312). And about half-way through what may have been the earliest version of the Greek *War*—volumes 1 to 6—Josephus tells the story of his surrender as a result of his divine call to predict the rise of Vespasian and Titus (3.350-408).

If we ask in which of the sacred books Josephus found these mysterious oracles, we shall have to answer with most scholars who have worked on the question: Daniel, for Daniel alone lays out detailed timetables, and Josephus's reference to "the wise" betrays his source. Since the pivotal surrender episode has to do with dream interpretation, we cannot escape noticing that in all of his writings, Josephus credits only three parties besides himself with this gift: his biblical namesake Joseph(us), his beloved Essenes, and Daniel. These are all mentioned in *Antiquities*, but the only reference to "interpretation of dreams" in the *War* comes in Josephus's self-description in 3.352, which again suggests an affinity with Daniel and the others. Exactly which portions of Daniel Josephus may have had in mind is debatable. I simply note here that any Judean who read Daniel after 70 C.E. would be sorely tempted to understand Vespasian as the tenth horn of the fourth beast of Dan 7.7-25 (counting from Julius Caesar—cf., Suetonius, *Lives; Sib. Or.* 5.12-15; Rev 13.1), and Titus or Domitian as the arrogant eleventh horn, before whom three small horns (Galba, Otho, and Vitellius) had fallen. Although the parallels are not precise, the general picture might have been compelling.[12]

It seems undeniable, then, that Josephus had come to own important aspects of the theology represented by Jeremiah and Daniel. There is little occasion in this work about the recent revolt for him to discuss the ancient texts per se, but their themes provide an appropriate substructure for his view of the world.

Another essential feature of Josephus's Judaism in *War* is his commitment to the priestly aristocracy. The priests play a major role in *War* as the legitimate guardians of the national traditions. What goes wrong in the story is that the priests lose their control over the people, who, sheep-like, are vulnerable to the enticements of illegitimate pretenders. Such a theme was perfectly familiar to Josephus's Roman readers. For example, Sallust had long before pointed out that when the nobility failed (*Catilinarian Conflict* 37.3):

> In every community those who have no means envy the good, exalt the base, hate what is old and established, long for something new, and from disgust with their own lot desire a general upheaval.

Josephus repeatedly points out that the masses were duped into hoping for economic, political, and religious salvation by popular leaders whose only claim to leadership was a lust for power.

Josephus immediately identifies himself, by contrast, as a proud priest (1.3). It is not long before he has shown that the priests, with the high priest at their head, are the legitimate aristocrats of Judea. It was a family of priests who fought off the evil Antiochus (1.36) and, when they assumed the high priesthood, created the most recent golden era of Judean history—the glorious Hasmonean dynasty (1.53, 68). Affairs deteriorate rapidly once Aristobulus converts the nation to a monarchy (1.70). Early on, Josephus establishes the priestly theme of Temple piety: Antiochus IV was punished for desecrating the Temple and interrupting the course of sacrifice (1.32); Pompey was a good general because, although he saw the sacred Holy of Holies, he did not touch the Temple vessels (1.152-53). When Gabinius arrived, he reconstituted the nation as an aristocracy, which was welcomed by the Judeans (1.170).

After his portrayal of Herod, who appears somewhat inconsistently as a good king—at least, his usefulness to Josephus here as exemplary Judean world citizen outweighs his assumption of royalty—Josephus begins to feature the high priests increasingly as his narrative builds toward the revolt. During the governorship of Cumanus, the chief priests interpose themselves between the people—who are clamoring for revenge against the

Samaritans (who killed a Galilean pilgrim to Jerusalem)—and the Syrian governor Quadratus, asking the former to restrain their anger and the latter to discipline the Judean governor (2.237-44). With the rise of guerrilla assassins (*sicarii*) and false prophets under Felix, however, the priests begin to lose control of the populace, and the *sicarii* actually kill the high priest Jonathan (2.256). Under Gessius Florus, the chief priests again try to calm tensions by pleading with the governor to spare the peaceful majority of Judeans rather than punish them for the rash actions of a few. But the Roman utterly undermines the priests' standing by sacking the city and massacring the inhabitants, thus making popular revolt inevitable (2.301-8). In a moving scene, the chief priests gather the people and arrange to make peace with the Romans, but again their intentions are undercut by Florus, who is bent on massacre (2.315-29). When the chief priests undertake to maintain perfect order as the governor withdraws from the city, the reader has a strong sense of pathos (2.332): it is already clear that the rebellion is out of their hands.

In the sequel, the chief priests enlist the offices of King Agrippa II to stem the tide (2.336), but the effect of his eloquent and reasoned speech is short-lived; he is expelled from the city, realizing that "the passions of the revolutionaries were now beyond control" (2.407). Although the young son of a high priest takes a leading role in the revolt by stopping the daily sacrifice for the emperor, Josephus makes it clear that the chief priests as a group were appalled by this radical departure from the national tradition; they fully anticipated the charge of impiety that would result (2.414). Josephus remarks, however, that "not one of the revolutionary party would listen to them" (2.417). Indeed, from this point onward the chief priests become thoroughly odious to the various rebel factions and thus targets for assassination. The rebels set fire to the house of the former high priest Ananias (2.426-29) and then kill him and his brother (2.441). But their impiety reaches its height when they arrogate to themselves the right to appoint high priests (4.147-50), appoint a simple villager to the

post (4.155), and, finally, after the chief priests make a valiant attempt to rally the people against the Zealots, the Idumean allies of the latter kill the high priest Ananus as well as Jesus (4.236-325). Josephus presents this despicable crime against those who tried to maintain peace as a singular cause (among many other singular causes!) of the divine punishment that ensued (4.318-25). The ultimate crime of the Idumean rebel faction was that they destroyed what remained of "our political system" (7.267).

In spite of the failure of the chief priests to maintain control, Josephus does not waver in his commitment to the legitimate authority of his class. His authentic priestly training enabled him to interpret divine utterances at the fateful hour when he surrendered to the Romans (3.352). Indeed, his whole explanation of the Temple's fate—that pollution requires purging—stems from a priestly perspective, and he even uses the count of sacrificial animals as his basis for estimating the size of the Passover crowd caught in Jerusalem's destruction (6.423-25). He looks pathetically at the masses who have been led astray by the false hopes of salvation proffered by would-be saviors (6.285-87). If the priests had only been able to maintain their rightful role as aristocrats, the debacle would have been avoided.

It remains to point out some contours of Josephus's personal piety in the *War*. Most obviously, he champions the views and practices of the Essenes, who "irresistibly attract all who have once tasted of their philosophy" (2.158). He consistently presents Judaism as a *philosophy*, a comprehensive way of seeing and living in the world. He is much absorbed with questions of Fate (or God) and free will (6.310), and he preserves the biblical, especially Danielic, tension between a fatalistic view of the world and one in which human repentance (*metanoia*, a change of thinking) will issue in a change of circumstance. He is also concerned with the soul and afterlife, showing off his ability to construct philosophical speeches either in favor of or opposing suicide, depending upon the speaker and situation (3.361-78; 7.341-57). His view of the afterlife remains vague, but it sounds very much like a one-time, morally conditioned reincarnation, when the soul will experience either reward or punishment; he claims to endorse the "Greek" view (2.155-56; cf., 3.371-74). For the rest, he assumes the exquisite character of the Judean code as practiced by the Essenes, with their simplicity of lifestyle, training in the occult practices of healing and prediction, extreme discipline, and even sun-worship. His jarring footnote on the "marrying kind" of Essenes (2.160-61) may well be his own creation, to justify his implied connection with the group. Josephus presents himself and his kind of Judean as philosophers.

In sum: the content of the *Judean War* cannot support the customary treatment of the work as Roman propaganda. It is a thoroughly Judean story, representing the piety of a priest from Jerusalem. The kind of Judaism revealed is one that has roots in priestly and prophetic strands of the Bible and equally in the heritage of Greece. By Josephus's time, however, one could not distinguish Greek ideas from those of any other Mediterranean region; Josephus had absorbed the broadly shared assumptions of his age and social class. His was an outward-looking Judaism that had found ways of getting along in the larger world while also claiming a unique, proudly maintained constitution. From this vantage point he could assume the rhetorical posture of criticizing Greek values while also owning them unconsciously at a profound level.

Judean Antiquities/Life: In his magnum opus, the twenty-volume *Judean Antiquities* and its appendix, the *Life*, Josephus shows that his fundamental place in Judaism has not changed even though his literary aims are significantly different. Once again, we need to begin by offering some adjustments to the conventional scholarly wisdom on this collection.

Analysis of the *Antiquities/Life*, taken as a whole composition, has been as haphazard as that of the *War*. We have partial explanations of the text but nothing comprehensive and therefore satisfying. Paradoxically, the tiny *Life* has received the most concentrated study, no doubt because of its manageable size and unusual significance for understanding Josephus. But part of the problem is just that: the *Life* has been read in isolation from the work that it completes.

The single most common explanation of the *Antiquities* holds that is an apologetic for gentiles, that Josephus writes to defend his nation against the widespread slanders about Judean origins and early history.[13] To the extent that the *War* is viewed as Roman propaganda, the *Antiquities* must then be read as a work of either sincere repentance or opportunistic rehabilitation—perhaps meant to catch the eyes of the rabbis of Jamnia (Yavneh), who are allegedly gaining political power in the 80s and 90s.[14] A slightly different view is that Josephus writes for Roman authorities, to present the Yavnean rabbis (implicitly, since they are nowhere mentioned) as the local leadership group to be sponsored in post-war Judea.[15] The *Life* is most commonly understood as a quite separate response to Justus of Tiberias's history maligning Josephus. A minority of scholars has argued, however, that the *Life* addresses other special concerns, including a bid to present Josephus as a Pharisee (to make intelligible his alleged backing of the rabbis in *Antiquities*), and that the response to Justus is incidental, confined to particular sections of the book.[16]

Detailed discussion of these proposals, most of which I have accepted at some point, is precluded by available space. Fatal objections are that the apologetic concerning Judean origins explains *at best* the first half of the *Antiquities*, which deals with the older history; that even then, however, the work is not defensive in tone but rather quite positive; that it is implausible to imagine the Judeans' detractors sitting patiently through this meandering story, and the writings of such people as Tacitus (*Hist.* 5.1-13) accordingly reveal no awareness of Josephus's claims; that scholarship on Yavneh has minimized the significance of that movement before at least the late second century;[17] that the Pharisaic precursors of the rabbis receive generally harsh treatment in the *Antiquities/Life*; and that the *Life* asks to be read as part of the *Antiquities*. In a nutshell, scholarship has not yet explained the question that the *Antiquities* as a whole answers, the need that it satisfies. It has not posed the legal question: who stands to benefit (*cui bono*)? Which gentiles could have been expected to read this work, and why?

As in the case of the *War*, we had best begin with the prologue and major themes of the *Antiquities/Life*. In doing so, we notice first that Josephus celebrates the *War*, describing it as a work of precise eye-witness accuracy; he would already have treated ancient history in that book if he could have done so with literary proportion (*Ant.* 1.1-6). This opening reprise, taken together with Josephus's repeated references back to the *War* in the body of *Antiquities/Life* (e.g., *Ant.* 13.173, 298) and his boast about the two works together in *Against Apion* (1.47-56), precludes the theory discussed above that Josephus felt a need to improve his image after the *War*. It is impossible to detect the faintest blush in these works: he is proud of the *War* and seems to imagine that he is writing from a broadly consistent place in Judaism. The *War* as propaganda is a figment of modern imagination.

The main part of the prologue to *Antiquities/Life* introduces two large themes, or constellations of themes, that persevere through the entire work. It also forces the question of Josephus's audience. First, Josephus announces that the book will be about the Judean constitution (*diataxis politeumamatos*, 1.5; *politeia*, 1.10), its origin and development. As the prologue continues, he asserts that this constitution is the noblest and most effective in existence, vastly superior to the codes of all other nations. In fact, this constitution operates universally, for the Judean God acts through it to punish *all* who violate its demands and to reward all those who observe it (1.14, 20). Moses grounded this constitution in the laws of nature and, especially, piety (1.21), which is why it is superior to all other constitutions, which are built upon fables and grotesque stories of the gods (1.15, 22). Unlike all other systems, the Judean code is invariably effective in providing for a virtuous society. Josephus will demonstrate this thesis not only by means of the

kings of Israel and Judah and sundry other biblical characters, but, also, in the second half of the book, with figures more familiar to his readers: King Herod, his descendants, and Gaius Caligula.

It is too easy for scholars to read all of this as a tame rehash of the Bible's Deuteronomic covenant (e.g., Deut. 28): the righteous prosper and the wicked perish. But in Josephus's day, the question of the proper constitution was a burning issue. Theories of government had been debated vigorously since Plato (*Republic*) and Aristotle (*Politics*), and Rome itself had become a violent proving ground. The world capital had long since found itself unable to maintain a traditional senatorial oligarchy based on the rule of a few patrician families; the Catilinarian conspiracy and then a long civil war had issued in the Augustan settlement by which a *princeps* became first citizen among his peers. By the time that Josephus wrote the *Antiquities* (completed, 93/94), however, this fiction had more or less evaporated before a ruler who was a monarch in all but name. Domitian (81-96 C.E.) ruled on the basis of a small court of advisors, only infrequently stayed in Rome, and intimidated the senate; he was very much the king.[18] Even when Josephus arrived in Rome in 71, immediately after the bloody "year of the four emperors" (69 C.E.), questions of government were on everyone's mind. This political uncertainty was matched by widespread disillusion about the social conditions of city life, where theft and violence appeared to reign. Hopes for a stable society, in which crime could be effectively checked, were common.

In this context, Josephus presents his ideal Judean constitution, which he describes as an *aristocracy*. As in the *War*, only now in greater detail, he argues that the Judeans were properly governed by a priestly elite: the high priest presided over a senate (*gerousia*) comprising his fellow priests. Already the prologue identifies the high priest Eleazar as the leader of the nation at the time of Ptolemy II (1.11). Josephus pointedly notes that Moses consigned the laws received from God to the high priest and his colleagues for safe-keeping (4.304). Moses tells the people that "aristocracy, and the life associated with it, is the noblest" (4.223). Josephus's interpretation of the Bible has a marked priestly bias; he alters Joshua and Judges to introduce a senatorial aristocracy (5.15, 43, 55, 135), and Samuel's objection to monarchy is made to rest on the fact that he is "strongly committed to aristocracy" (6.36).

The following experiment with monarchy turns disastrous and, so, after the Exile, the Judeans return to priestly aristocracy (11.111). Further flirtations with monarchy are predictably catastrophic (13.300-1), especially the famous rule of the "half-Judean" Herod (14.403). Herod's lineage is one of a number of factors in Josephus's new portrayal of him in *Antiquities*—as an incorrigible offender against the Judean constitution who accordingly suffered horrors of divine punishment. This change of perspective does not seem to bother Josephus: it was considered a virtuoso rhetorical performance to make very different cases from the same evidence. Josephus's radical revision of his portrait of Herod in *Antiquities* fits with his determination to show that the Judean priestly aristocracy supervises the best known constitution. He routinely pauses to let the reader know who the serving high priest was at various times, provides a partial summary at the half-way point (10.149-153), and then furnishes a comprehensive list of high priests at the book's end (20.224-51).[19] The Judean priestly aristocracy, a singularly ancient nobility with divine sanction, was unique in the Greek-speaking East. Josephus presents this as the best constitution.

Alongside and tightly interwoven with the constitutional *Leitmotiv* of *Antiquities* is the theme of philosophy, which emerges from the claim that the Judean constitution is thoroughly philosophical. For his Roman audience, too, philosophy was closely connected with constitutional issues. Greek philosophers had first debated constitutions in general, and Stoic philosophers had led the charge against the Roman departure from senatorial aristocracy. Recently, the names of Seneca, Lucan, Rubellius Plautus, Thrasea Paetus, Helvidius Priscus, Musonius Rufus, Barea Soranus, and Epictetus headed the list of those who had

suffered exile or death for their philosophical commitments in the face of tyranny. The committed philosophical life, which required a kind of "conversion," was still considered fanatical and inappropriate among the Roman upper class, a potential threat to those in power, though the mood would change somewhat by the time of the philosopher-*princeps* Marcus Aurelius in the mid-second century.

In this social context, it is most significant that Josephus links the Judean aristocratic constitution so closely with philosophy. It accords perfectly with the laws of nature—Moses considers the construction of the world before giving his laws (1.21)—and so it can uniquely promise well-being (*eudaimonia*), the recognized goal of philosophy,[20] to those who follow it (1.14, 20). Although the Egyptians were widely credited with having made fundamental discoveries about the universe, Josephus eagerly asserts that Abraham discovered monotheism and virtue (1.154-55) and taught the Egyptians astronomy and arithmetic (1.166-67). He presents Solomon as the ideal king, because he was the wisest philosopher who ever lived (8.42), and Josephus directly challenges the Epicureans by means of the demonstrable fulfillment of Daniel's predictions (10.277). As in *War*, he again portrays the Pharisees, Sadducees, and Essenes as the mainstream Judean philosophical schools (*Ant.* 13.171-73; 18.12-21; *Life* 10), now explicitly comparing the Essenes to Pythagoreans (15.371) and the Pharisees to Stoics (*Life* 12).

In this context it is particularly interesting that Josephus not only presents Judaism as the supreme philosophical system but also holds open the possibility of conversion. Just like the character who discovers the joy of philosophy in Lucian's *Wisdom of Nigrinus* (e.g., 6), Josephus promises not to make a secret of or be stingy with the good things the Judeans have (1.11-12). Abraham was the first to convert to belief in one God and was willing to convert to the Egyptian way if he found it superior, or to convert them to his way (1.161). Early in the book, the Midianite Balaam proclaims the Judeans uniquely happy (*eudaimon*) and announces that they will one day dominate the earth by numerical growth and fame (4.115-16). This promise is partially realized near the end of the book, where Josephus celebrates the conversion of the royal house of Adiabene to Judaism (20.17-96).

After this brief survey of its two major themes, we may return to our question of *Antiquities'* purpose and audience. What purpose does the book satisfy, and for whom? I would argue that *Antiquities* is best understood as a comprehensive manual or primer in Judean history, law, and culture. In the former half, Josephus renders the somewhat difficult collection of law and duplicated history in the Bible as a single, continuous, and appealing narrative for Greek speakers; the latter half interprets the famous events of more recent Judean and world history in light of the ancient constitution. All of this presumes a gentile audience highly sympathetic to Judaism. This is exactly the audience Josephus envisions when he refers to Epaphroditus (1.8-9) and to other Greek "lovers of learning" (1.12). A wide variety of evidence outside Josephus—literary evidence, funerary inscriptions, and legal rulings—confirms that attraction and even conversion to Judaism were easily observable phenomena in Josephus's Rome.[21] It may be more than a coincidence that, within two years of the appearance of Josephus's *Antiquities*, Domitian had his cousin Flavius Clemens executed and banished Clemens's wife Domitilla on charges of drifting into Judean ways.[22] It was perhaps for sympathizers such as these that Josephus wrote his magnum opus. Indeed, the Epaphroditus who was executed by Domitian in about 95 may have been the man to whom Josephus dedicated his later works.[23] Laying such speculation aside, we may conclude at least that the *Antiquities* answered the need for a manual of the Judean constitution and its effects.

As we have seen, the *Life* is usually understood as an independent work responding to Justus of Tiberias. The main problem with this view is that Josephus introduces the work as an appendix to the *Antiquities*, and the manuscript tradition supports this link. Josephus decides to cite his own credentials while reflecting on his success—remarkable by any standard—in completing the mammoth book (20.267). Those credentials must include, according to ancient canons, one's genealogy, early training, and public activities.[24] And that is just what Josephus provides. After an account of his noble blood line and education, he flags his return to the city and embarkation upon public life with appropriate language (*polis* and *politeuesthai* in *Life* 12). From there, he begins the story of his public life from about age 26. At the end of all this, Josephus allows that he has presented a case for his "character" (*Life* 430), a critical feature of persuasion in ancient rhetoric, always made with reference to public activities.[25] Thus Josephus describes in detail his virtuous treatment of friends and enemies while he held a position of leadership. Scholars have often assumed that the five-month focus of the *Life* is so peculiar that Josephus must have been forced by Justus's work to write about this period. But the fact is that only this period really illustrated Josephus's public Judean career, which was the necessary proving ground for his character. So the *Life* is best understood as a direct continuation of the *Antiquities*, showing the character of the author through his public life.

In keeping with this continuity of theme, the *Life* begins by introducing Josephus as a shining example of the priestly aristocracy that he has been speaking of at such length (*Life* 1-6). It then moves quickly to describe his philosophical training, which culminates in just the rigorous, Essene-like lifestyle, under the tutelage of Bannus, that we might have expected from the *War* (Life 10-12). Throughout the *Life*, Josephus maintains an emphasis on his priestly authority, on the mischief caused by pretenders (189-98), and on his philosophical views. Especially noteworthy is his statement about refusing to compel refugees to convert to Judaism, so that each person might choose how to worship God (113).

Josephus's direct response to Justus, as several scholars have pointed out, is restricted to a passage late in the work (*Life* 336-67). The best explanation of the positioning and tone of this passage seems to be that Josephus uses Justus in a sporting way, not because he was seriously threatened by the challenge but because Justus provided him easy fodder with which to fill out his resounding portrayal of his own character. Refutation (*refutatio*) was the standard co-efficient of proof (*probatio*) in ancient rhetoric.

Josephus's religious outlook in the *Antiquities/Life* remains consistent with that reflected in the *War*, even though his literary aims have shifted somewhat. As in the *War*, he continues to assume and propagate a priestly-aristocratic viewpoint. Throughout Judean history, he indicates, major challenges to propriety have come from those who arrogated royal status to themselves, but also from the Pharisees, who assume a consistent role as historic trouble-makers in the *Antiquities/Life*: their nefarious activities extend all the way to Josephus's own career (*Ant.* 13.288, 401, 431-32; 17.41-45; *Life* 189-98).

Josephus also makes conspicuous the affinities with Jeremiah and Daniel that we uncovered beneath the surface of the *War*. Indeed, he arranges his work such that the first ten volumes end with the destruction of the First Temple and Babylonian Exile, to parallel the second ten volumes on the Second Temple. This means that he can devote much of volume 10 to Jeremiah and Daniel; the latter he considers "one of the greatest prophets" (10.266). It is peculiar that scholars have preoccupied themselves with the dissonance between this claim and the later Rabbinic tradition that excludes Daniel from the prophets altogether. The really interesting thing, surely, is the implication for our understanding of Josephus. He considers Daniel one of the greatest because that prophet alone gave a detailed schedule of future events, to the time of Antiochus Epiphanes, which has been fulfilled with stunning and easily verifiable accuracy. Whereas modern scholarship has adopted the insight of the fourth-century philosopher Porphyry, that Daniel must actually have been written at the time of Antiochus, Josephus was apparently innocent of this viewpoint. In that case, he must have been as deeply impressed as he appears to have been with the notion that the Judean God controls all of history. No wonder he

uses Daniel's fulfilled predictions as irrefutable evidence of his main thesis, against the Epicureans (10.277-81). Jeremiah, too, wrote a book (presumably, he means Lamentations) about the recent capture of Jerusalem by the Romans (10.79).

His detailed consideration of Jeremiah and Daniel in the *Antiquities* allows Josephus to suggest numerous parallels with his own life. Jeremiah he introduces as a priest-prophet from Jerusalem (10.79-80) who warned the people incessantly that they should abandon hope of alliances (compare the hopes of the Judeans for possible alliances with Parthia; *War* 2.398-99!), because they were destined to be overthrown by the Babylonians (10.89). Refusing to listen to Jeremiah, however, the people and their leaders accused him of treason and even desertion (10.90, 114, esp. 119). Surrender to the Babylonians, God had shown him, was the only way to avoid having the city and Temple burned to the ground (10.126). Josephus even notes that Jeremiah and King Zedekiah colluded in a barefaced lie to cover the real nature of their discussion (10.129-30)—just as Josephus freely admits in the *War* to having lied to others about his intentions (e.g., *War* 2.595-607; 3.136-37, 193-202, 389). God was clearly "on the Babylonian side" (10.139), just as he is now on the Roman side (*War* 5.2). Parallels with Daniel are equally compelling: this precocious young Judean nobleman finds himself in the court of the foreign king, where he lives with extreme piety on a carefully selected diet (10.186, 189-90, 194; cf., *Life* 8-10, 20); as a result of his piety he is given the ability to interpret dreams (10.194), and he consequently prospers in the foreign courts.

The size and different aim of *Antiquities/Life* allow Josephus to drop much broader hints than he had in *War* about the future success of the Judean people, which is in any case a natural consequence of his thesis about their vastly superior constitution. We have noted Balaam's predictions of singular prosperity and growth. In his discussion of Daniel, moreover, Josephus develops rather boldly the image of the final kingdom of Daniel, the stone that will smash to pieces the last worldly kingdom, which must be

Rome (10.207). He says quite enough here to disturb any sensitive Roman reader, even though he prescinds from further elaboration upon the stone (10.210). Evidently, he expects a sympathetic audience.

As for personal theology and practice, Josephus continues to exhibit the traits he had revealed in the *War*: a marked preference for Essene-like views (10.250; 15.371-79; esp. 18.20) and a rigorously ascetic, philosophical lifestyle, which unfortunately but understandably he had to relax upon his entry into political life (*Life* 11-12a).

In sum, the *Antiquities* as a whole addresses itself to sympathetic gentiles who have asked a question much like the following: "Please tell us about the Judean constitution and philosophy!" Josephus obliges with a wide-ranging manual, which argues through countless examples that the inflexible but humane constitution of the Judeans, which operates in harmony with nature, is the most effective in the world. Though inexorable in punishing the wicked, it alone promises its followers prosperity. One day, it will be supreme. Those who wish to adopt it as their own are welcome to do so, with the assurance that God will protect them from the social consequences described so vividly by Tacitus (*Hist.* 5.5).

Against Apion: Thus far we have seen Josephus writing, first, a refutation of postwar slander (*War*) and then a celebratory manual of Judean history, law, and culture with an appendix on the author's character (*Antiquities*/*Life*). In spite of the different aims of these works, they both presuppose a well-disposed gentile audience: Romans who are *a priori* sympathetic to things Judean. These friendly gentiles, Josephus hoped, would broker the truth about the Judean revolt and also find encouragement in his account of Judean culture. When we turn to Josephus's final known composition, the so-called *Against Apion*, we must ask how this work fits in with his previous audience and literary aims.

Josephus did not call the work "Against Apion" (he confronts Apion only in the first half of the second volume) but perhaps something like "On the Antiquity of the Judeans."

Indeed, refutation of slander does not explain the whole content of the work. In his unusually brief prologue, Josephus says that he will consider the antiquity of the Judeans for three reasons: to refute slanderers (who should have realized their errors after the *Antiquities*), to inform the ignorant, and to instruct those who desire to know the truth (1.3). The final group in this list corresponds well with the "lovers of learning" mentioned in *Ant.* 1.12. That correspondence, taken with Josephus's dedication of this work to the same Epaphroditus who appeared in *Antiquities* (*Apion* 1.2) and, through him, to all who wish to know the truth about the Judeans (*Apion* 2.296), along with the assumption of this work that readers know of his earlier writings (*Apion* 1.47-56), suggests that Josephus is continuing his appeal to roughly the same group of Judeophiles in Rome. To this friendly audience, he first makes a summary case for the antiquity of the Judeans (1.6-56), then moves to the body of the work, which contains both proof of Judean antiquity (1.60-218) and refutation of false claims about the Judeans (1.219-2.144), then finally returns to a positive statement of the Judean constitution (2.145-295).

To understand Josephus's aims in this work, we cannot treat it as if it appeared in a vacuum. Determining his likely audience is critical for imagining the extra-textual resources shared by him and his readers, and thus his purpose; for the same words have different meanings in different contexts. For example, it would be easy to suppose that because Josephus rhetorically targets the Judeans' detractors, he really meant to confront them directly—to dissuade them from their views—and perhaps also some neutral gentiles who wondered naively about the truth. In that case, the work would be an example of "forensic" rhetoric, the kind that set out to persuade the hearer about what had really happened in the past, as in a criminal case. The problem is that in the ancient world, one could not normally produce a book by simply leaving the text in the hands of a publisher to disseminate to a targeted audience. Authors needed first of all a real circle of readers/hearers: people who would willingly gather in homes and lecture halls to listen to the author recite. The *War*, though it is fundamentally a refutation, assumes such a patient group, as does the *Antiquities/Life*. Neither work could plausibly have been aimed directly at the Judeans' enemies, and indeed the accounts of Tacitus and Suetonius (also Dio) in later generations show no knowledge of Josephus's literary claims.[26] Similarly, although *Against Apion* unquestionably devotes a great deal of space to refutation of slander, we must ask who the intended readers were and what they should have expected to glean from it. What if any larger goal does the refutation of slander serve?

Two features of the text deserve special consideration. First, it has been observed that Josephus's arguments, though clever, would not have answered the hard objections of a determined critic.[27] He demonstrates a great deal of wit, but wit is appreciated more by a kindred spirit than by a genuine antagonist or even someone who is coldly neutral. He tips his hand with his plan to expose the "utterly absurd slanders of the slanderers of our nation" (1.59) and "to deprive our jealous enemies" of a pretext for controversy (1.72). He is preaching to the converted, so to speak. For example, when he traces current slander to expatriate Egyptians, who were allegedly jealous of the Judeans, he remarks: "These frivolous and utterly senseless specimens of humanity, accustomed from the first to erroneous ideas about the gods, were incapable of imitating the solemnity of our theology, and the sight of our numerous admirers filled them with envy" (1.225). Would the Egyptian expatriates themselves have been impressed by this? Or, again, he sarcastically describes Apion's suffering from ulceration of the genitals and submission to circumcision, after Apion had mercilessly ridiculed circumcision (2.144). These barbs could only be appreciated by a sympathetic audience (cf., 2.115, 318). His attempts at humor recall his refutation of Justus in the *Life*: in both cases, we should probably conclude that Josephus is not, and does not expect his readers to be, seriously shaken by the challengers. He asks readers, in effect, to join him in a somewhat triumphalist demolition of opponents' claims.

Second, Josephus encloses this refutation of slander between a positive introduction that assumes a familiar audience (1.6-218) and the most sublime exaltation of Judaism in his entire corpus (2.145-296). That concluding passage once again presents the Judean constitution as the noblest imaginable, as uniquely effective in creating a stable and crime-free society, and as welcoming everyone who wishes to come and live under it. As we have seen, refutation of opposing views was an expected rhetorical function of proving a positive case. Even the lecture inviting hearers to begin a life of philosophy (called a *logos protreptikos*) typically included substantial elements of dissuasion from other life choices and refutation of other claims.[28] So the prominence of refutation in *Against Apion* does not automatically imply that Josephus's chief or sole motive was direct confrontation with the opponents of the Judeans.

Reading *Against Apion* as a sequel to *War* and *Antiquities/Life*, prepared for a group of friendly gentiles in Rome, it is difficult to avoid understanding its purpose somewhat as follows. Inhabitants of Rome keenly interested in Judean culture encountered widespread antipathy toward the Judeans following the failed revolt. We know from Tacitus (*Hist.* 5.1-13) that characterization of the Judeans as misanthropic and bellicose went hand in hand with depictions of their origins as base and derivative of greater cultures. Josephus appears to target all of his works at a group of interested hearers who are aware of the slanders, but still enough "on side" to be heartened by his spirited attacks and defenses. He intends both to consolidate their support and to use them as brokers of a better image of Judeans to the society at large. In the *War*, he forthrightly challenges the negative image of the Judeans the war had catalyzed. In the *Antiquities/Life*, he offers his readers a comprehensive positive statement about Judean culture that also invites further exploration. Although the *Life* is essentially a positive statement of his character, it too includes refutation of an opposing view (Justus's). Finally, here in *Against Apion*, Josephus returns to refutation, this time in a systematic rebuttal concerning Judean origins. As in both of the earlier works, his ultimate goal is positive and forward-looking: he at once encourages his readers and defuses the slander with clever assaults, leaving them to ponder the exquisite Judean constitution. As before, any forensic rhetoric here serves the larger aims of deliberative and epideictic rhetoric, that is, sympathetic exhortation and preparation for future decisions.

A marked continuity of religious perspective underlies this consolidating function of *Against Apion*. Nowhere does Josephus make it clearer that the Judean laws have produced a peerless constitution, administered by the most ancient and authentic aristocracy. Oriental nations as a group are superior to the Greeks in preserving old records (1.28), he argues, and the Judeans lead the Orientals in the precautions they take for preserving a pure priestly aristocracy (1.29). As in the closing section of *Antiquities/Life*, he celebrates the high-priestly succession that has come down from remotest antiquity (1.36). The Judean constitution was written by prophets and preserved by priests; as he showed in the *Antiquities*, it is internally harmonious (1.37-41), known and observed by all Judeans (1.42-43). Josephus's own priestly ancestry, as he implied or stated throughout *War* and *Antiquities*, makes him a rare expert in the "philosophy" of the national traditions (1.54-55).

After his systematic refutation of slanders, Josephus turns to a final presentation of the Judean constitution (2.145) that marks the climax of his literary legacy. He will show that this constitution promotes piety (*eusebeia*), friendly relations with one another (*koinonia*), and humanity (*philanthropia*) towards the world—responding forthrightly once again to charges of impiety and misanthropy (2.146-47). The ancient priestly aristocracy that guarantees the preservation of this constitution, under divine mandate, is so special that Josephus ventures to coin the term "theocracy" for it (2.165):

> Could there even be a more excellent or just [constitution] than that which, having established God as ruler of all things, having assigned to the priests as a body the admin-istration of the greatest issues, has entrusted the rule of the other priests to the high priest? (2.185)

According to Josephus, this constitution produces a social harmony that is unmatched elsewhere (2.179-81). Though humane, it absolutely controls vice (2.211-17, 276-78). It promotes such a high level of virtue that it instills contempt for death, the sure sign of an effective philosophy (2.232-33, 271-75). For these reasons and more, it is the envy of the entire world, and the major Greek philosophers borrowed extensively from it (2.168; cf., 1.162, 166-67, 175, 182, 190), though they could not actually implement their ideals on a large scale (2.220-31). A big difference between Moses and these other philosophers—and here Josephus articulates fully what he has often implied—is that Moses welcomed all those from other nations who wished to come and live under this constitution (2.209-10, 257-61).

Although it is not a major theme of *Against Apion*, one can easily detect the continuing substructure of Jeremiah and Daniel in Josephus's outlook, particularly in his critique of Apion. There he confronts the claim that the Judeans have typically found themselves in servitude to others: "It has been the lot of a few, by waiting on opportunity, to gain an empire, and even they have, through the vicissitudes of fortune, been reduced once more to servitude beneath a foreign yoke" (2.127). His mention of Athenians and Spartans as examples recalls the words *War* put in the mouth of Agrippa II (*War* 2.358-59). Josephus continues to hold that nations rise and fall under God's sovereignty. Significantly, whereas *War* had left only the vaguest hint of future Judean supremacy, and *Antiquities* had been more forthright, Josephus now seems to believe that he is witnessing the rise of Judean influence. At the end of *Against Apion*, he dwells on the vitality and spread of Judean customs throughout the entire world (2.279-86). None of this, least of all the closing address to his friend Epaphroditus, inclines us to classify *Against Apion* as a work targeted directly at the Judeans' opponents. It seems rather to be his last effort for friendly gentiles.

Conclusion: A responsible picture of Josephus's particular kind of Judaism emerges from a survey of his works, which combine history, law, narrative, philosophy, entertainment, and much else. Thus we side-stepped the scholarly tradition that fragments Josephus's literary corpus, deeming the *War* Roman propaganda; the *Antiquities*, a vaguely conceived apologetic for unspecified gentiles; the *Life*, a response to Justus of Tiberias's hostile account of Josephus's Galilean career; and *Against Apion*, a statement to hostile or neutral outsiders (if Josephus did not steal it bodily from some other writer).

Indeed, this survey has turned up many differences among Josephus's works, but not those that are usually proposed. He wrote the *War* to defend his people and their tradition against post-war accusations of impiety and misanthropy. He maintains there that the Judean God controls history and has used the Romans to punish the few leaders of insurrection in Judea, especially because of their Temple pollutions. Acceptance of God's sovereignty permits the Judeans to be the exemplary world citizens they normally are, as long as the people follow their duly constituted leaders. Josephus wrote the *Antiquities/Life*, a single work, to present the breadth and depth of Judean culture to an interested audience, presumably much the same group that brokered his *War*. It depicts a universal, philosophically respectable, and uniquely effective constitution, administered by an ancient high priesthood and senate. This new literary agenda causes Josephus to change much of his evaluation vis à vis *War* 1-2, especially concerning the Hasmoneans and Herods, but the rhetorical changes do not seem to have bothered him. He also appends a portrait of his own character, as priest, philosopher, and man of affairs, which also is rather different in its details from his self-portrait in *War*. The *Antiquities/Life* obviated, more than rebutted, common slanders about Judean antiquity. But Josephus finally decided to arm his friendly gentile audience with a presentation of Judean antiquity and refutation of common slanders on this issue, while also reasserting his claims about the Judean constitution, in the systematic essay we know as *Against Apion*. His writings exhibit many differences in detail and even genre.

Nevertheless, amid the many great and small changes from work to work, we find a broad consistency of outlook:

1. Josephus is a proud member of the ancient priestly aristocracy that has divine sanction to administer the Judeans' matchless constitution.
2. When the Judeans follow their constitution and their proper leaders, they prosper. Otherwise, disaster invariably follows; the war is only the most recent example. In a world apparently falling into social chaos, the Judean constitution alone promises stability and punishment of vice.
3. Inauthentic Judean leaders who have led the people away from their constitution have included ancient usurper kings, the demagogue Pharisees, and the assorted pretenders and false prophets of recent times. (Josephus's picture of Herod changes from *War* to *Antiquities/Life*.)
4. The Judean constitution has deep roots in natural philosophy, and the Judeans as a nation are philosophically inclined. They live simply, faithfully, and with discipline; they hold no fear of death.
5. Josephus claims to favor the kind of rigor in lifestyle that he attributes to his best examples of Judean philosophers, the Essenes and Bannus.
6. Because it is the finest in existence, the Judean constitution has attracted widespread interest, ever since the philosophers of old borrowed heavily from it. Josephus encourages full conversion and promises divine protection from the social consequences.
7. Josephus's priestly piety shows particular affinity with the writings of Jeremiah and Daniel. From an interpretive tradition of these texts, he has learned a lesson with practical benefits: to recognize the rise and fall of nations under the sovereignty of God and to allow God to bring about changes in world-rule. Josephus expects that the Judeans, with their superior constitution, will one day take their turn on center stage. By the time of his last known composition, he imagines that he sees this dream being realized.

All of this is of course a literary construction, a summary of the "implied author's" outlook. It says nothing directly about Josephus's personal piety. To be sure, we have no shortage of passages in which he appears, by modern standards of spirituality or even religiosity, extremely arrogant and self-absorbed and above all inconsistent in his judgments. Although it would be easy to join in the customary dismissal of his piety as false and opportunistic, we must remember that he lived long before the Western tradition of introspection had developed. He lived in a very public world, where religion was political and character was determined by public roles. He also lived at a time in which rhetorical conventions that seem strange to us so thoroughly colored all discourse that we can hardly penetrate to an author's real views. In these circumstances, it seems hazardous to claim much certain knowledge of Josephus's real perspectives.

But even the question, "What sort of person could have devoted this kind of energy to such a literary occupation?" might give us pause to rethink the traditional assessments of Josephus and Judaism.

Notes

[1] The end product of this approach was G. Hölscher's article for the Pauly-Wissowa *Realenzyklopädie des classischen Altertumswissenschaft* (1916), vol. 18, pp. 1934-2000.

[2] Partial coverage of the question may be found, for example, in H. Paret, "Über den Pharisäismus des Josephus," in *Theologische Studien und Kritiken* 29 (1856), pp. 809-844; J.A. Montgomery, "The Religion of Flavius Josephus," in *Jewish Quarterly Review* 11 (1921), pp. 277-305; H. Rasp, "Flavius Josephus und die Religionsparteien," in *ZNW* 23 (1924), pp. 27-47; F.J. Foakes Jackson, *Josephus and the Jews* (London, 1930); A. Schlatter, *Die Theologie des Judentums nach dem Bericht des Josephus* (Gütersloh, 1932).

[3] E.g., Plato, *Gorgias* 507b; Polybius, *Universal History* 22.10.8; Xenophon, *Memorabilia* 4.8.7.

[4] See S. Mason, "Was Josephus a Pharisee? A Re-Examination of *Life* 10-12," in *Journal of Jewish Studies* 40 (1989), pp. 31-45.

[5] R. Laqueur, *Der jüdische Historiker Flavius Josephus* (Darmstadt, 1970 [1920]), p. 126; H. St. John Thackeray, *Josephus: The Man and the Historian* (New York, 1967 [1929]), pp. 27-28.

[6] See Peter White, "*Amicitia* and the Profession of Poetry in Early Imperial Rome," in *Journal of Religious Studies* 68 (1978), pp. 74-92, esp. pp. 90-92. Suetonius, *Vespasian* 5.6.4; Cassius Dio, *Roman History* 65.4. The fourth-century Eusebius mentions a statue of Josephus in Rome (*Church History* 3.9.2), but he is our only witness for it; we do not know when it was erected, if it ever existed.

[7] See T. Rajak, *Josephus: The Historian and His Society* (London, 1983), pp. 86, 176; G. Hata, "Is the Greek Version of Josephus' 'Jewish War' a Translation or a Rewriting of the First Version?" in *Jewish Quarterly Review* 66 (1975), pp. 89-109.

[8] E.g., Lucian, *How History Should be Written* 7, 11-13.

[9] An important exception is H. Lindner, *Die Geschichtsauffassung des Flavius Josephus im Bellum Iudaicum* (Leiden, 1972), which undertakes a careful study of the speeches.

[10] Tacitus, *Histories* 5.1-13; Philostratus, *Apollonius of Tyana* 5.33; Celsus, *The True Word*, cited in Origen, *Against Celsus* 5.41; Minucius Felix, *Octavius* 10, 33.

[11] Cf., Lindner, op. cit., pp. 133-140.

[12] See S. Mason, "Josephus, Daniel, and the Flavian House," in F. Parente and J. Sievers, eds., *Josephus and the History of the Greco-Roman Period* (Leiden, 1994), pp. 161-191.

[13] Thackeray, *Josephus* 52.

[14] Laqueur, op. cit., pp. 258-261; Hans Rasp, "Flavius Josephus und die jüdischen Religionsparteien," in *ZNW* 23 (1924), pp. 27-47, esp. p. 46; S.J.D. Cohen, *Josephus in Galilee an Rome: His Vita and His Development as a Historian* (Leiden, 1979), p. 145; Seth Schwartz, *Josephus and Judaean Politics* (Leiden, 1990), pp. 199-201.

[15] M. Smith, "Palestinian Judaism in the First Century," in M. Davis, ed., *Israel: Its Role in Civilization* (New York, 1956).

[16] Cohen, op. cit., p. 144; T. Rajak, "Justus of Tiberias," in *Classical Quarterly* 23 (1973), pp. 345-368.

[17] E.g., L.L. Grabbe, *Judaism from Cyrus to Hadrian* (Minneapolis, 1992), vol. 2, pp. 592-595.

[18] See B.W. Jones, *The Emperor Domitian* (London, 1992), pp. 23-30.

[19] That the incidental notices do not correspond perfectly to the summaries is a famous literary-historical problem, but it does not affect our observations about the impression that Josephus wished to leave with his readers.

[20] Aristotle, *Nicomachean Ethics* 10.6.1.

[21] See S. Mason, "The Contra Apionem in Social and Literary Context," in L. Feldman and J.R. Levison, eds., *Josephus' Contra Apionem: Studies in its Character and Context with a Latin Concordance . . .*, (Leiden, 1996), esp. pp. 188-195.

[22] Cassius Dio, *Roman History* 67.2-3.

[23] Dio 67.14.4; Suetonius, *Domitian* 14-15.

[24] G.A. Kennedy, *A New History of Classical Rhetoric* (Princeton, 1994), p. 5.

[25] Aristotle, *Rhetoric* 1.2.

[26] Tacitus, *Hist.* 5.13, does show a knowledge of three omens mentioned by Josephus in *War* 6.294-300. But these might understandably have gone into wide circulation as omens of the Flavians' rise, wrenched from their context in Josephus.

[27] S.J.D. Cohen, "History and Historiography in the *Contra Apionem* of Josephus," in *History*

and Theory 27: *Essays in Jewish Historiography* (1988), pp. 1-11.

[28] Philo of Larissa in Stobaeus, *Anthology* 2.7.2.

STEVE MASON

JUDAISM, CONTEMPORARY EXPRESSIONS OF; NEW AGE JUDAISMS: New Age Judaism refers to a style of Jewish thought and practice within American non-Orthodox Judaism. It emerged in the late twentieth century as a result of Judaism's encounter with the American counter-culture and as a reaction to an American Judaism that had become, in the view of many, stultified and in need of renewal. In the period following World War II, the movement of Jewish veterans into suburbia caused synagogues and Jewish community centers to flourish. But the Judaism these institutions housed fit too comfortably into the classic American pattern. To be American, President Dwight D. Eisenhower declared, was to be religious. But this was without regard for *which* religion or *what* spiritual content. As a result, to be "religious" in the 1950s was often a function of sociology, a way of belonging and conforming rather than a result of theological conviction or a search for spirituality that touched the inner life. Jewish institutions had grown, but Judaism had shrunk into a pediatric instrument, into life cycle and holiday observances primarily aimed at children and which did not touch the core of life.

By the late 1960s, as the result of a number of factors, American Judaism was poised for a spiritual revival. The first important factor was the growth of ethnicity, which ended White Anglo Saxon Protestant hegemony in American culture. Ethnic pride had grown among various hyphenated Americans. In particular, American blacks created new kinds of art, music, social service agencies, dress, and hair styles. In this atmosphere of cultural pluralism, some American Jews started to feel comfortable expressing their distinctiveness. The growth of black studies in academia similarly contributed to the growth of Jewish studies, and, in the late 1960s, the Black Panther Party offered a model of militancy for those who created the Jewish Defense League. In this same period, the growth

of the counter-culture and a youth culture created an atmosphere of rebellion. Alternative music, cinema, art, literature, and journalism flourished, and these soon had their analogues in an emerging Jewish counter-culture In addition, Jews increasingly became involved in various secular and alternative therapies—meditation, ashrams, EST—that created new models of community and opened the door to spirituality.

These developments were encouraged by the Israeli-Arab Six Day War of 1967, which brought in its wake an explosion of American Jewish pride. The Jewish theologian Abraham Joshua Heschel wrote: "In those days many of us felt that our own lives were in the balance, and not only the lives of those who dwelt in the land; that indeed all of the Bible, all of Jewish history was at stake. . . . I had not known how deeply Jewish I was." The Six Day War's victorious conclusion transformed the image of the beleaguered Jew into the powerful Jew, and Israeli military power soon became trans-valued into American Jewish spiritual power. A new Jewish activism emerged, affecting not only American Jewish support for Israel but for Soviet Jews—refused the right to leave Soviet tyranny—as well.

So, too, there was a growing hunger for community. While ostensibly critiquing Reform Judaism, Leonard Fein spoke for many observers of the synagogue world:

> The Reform temple appears an unlikely site for the effort to create community. Our survey data show that most people are not disappointed in their temple; the demands and expectations they have of the temple are too minimal for them to experience disappointment, even when they experience alienation. The temple is assigned certain limited functions, notably with respect to the young, and it is judged in terms of its performance of these functions. The large majority of our respondents report very few close friends among their fellow temple members . . . the temple is a joyless place; the house of worship is not a home, except to a tiny few.

Or, to quote Abraham Joshua Heschel's observation from the 1950s:[1] "The modern temple suffers from a severe cold. The services are prim, the voice is dry, the temple is clean and tidy. . . . No one will cry, the words are still-born."

The havurah movement: The longing for community and intensity gave birth to the havurah (pl.: havurot), literally, a fellowship group, typically consisting of ten to fifty Jews who meet regularly for Torah study, worship, and doing mitzvot. The havurah movement's impact on American Jewry far exceeds its numbers, for many veterans of this movement have found places within synagogues as rabbis, cantors, educators, Jewish scholars, communal professionals, and lay leaders. In addition, the movement has had a massive programmatic and spiritual impact on Conservative, Reconstructionist, and Reform Judaism and on the college campus. Beginning in the 1960s, it comprised along with the New Left the ideal place to find a political or religious identity. In Paul Cowan's words, both movements, "developed almost identical styles, which encouraged intimacy and virtually outlawed authority.[2]

The concept of the havurah—a holy community taking on religious obligations—originated in the land of Israel in the first century B.C.E., and there also were early adumbrations of the havurah model in the traditional synagogues of Eastern Europe. Certain synagogues were devoted to people with distinct trades, e.g., synagogues for tailors. This created a sense of camaraderie and shared purpose. So, too, there were fellowship groups (*hevreh*) that were centered around certain sacred activities, e.g., a group to study Mishnah or to dower brides, to visit the sick, or to tend the dead for burial.

In the U.S.A., early experiments in havurot included *Breet K'tanah* (sic), a short-lived group led by Rabbi Roland B. Gittelsohn in the late 1950s at Temple Israel in Boston, Massachusetts. Participants agreed to perform various basic religious duties, such as attending services, devotions at the Sabbath table, study, various Jewish practices, and undergoing ethical inventories. There were also Reconstructionist havurot/fellowships in Denver in the 1960s.[3] The most enduring seeds for the havurah, however, were planted in the Conservative movement's Camp Ramah, which taught a 24 hour a day Judaism

that became increasingly attractive to a cadre of young Conservative Jewish activists.

The first independent havurah in America was *Havurat Shalom*, founded in 1968, in Somerville, Massachusetts. It started as an alternative seminary with a faculty that included Rabbi Zalman Schachter (now Schachter-Shalomi). *Havurat Shalom* was a place for serious and intense prayer and study. The curriculum included Buber's *I and Thou*; an introduction to Talmud, and techniques in *davening* (intense prayer). Teachers and students were equals. They spent the Sabbath together and shared communal meals. A typical service would be in the round. It could include the singing of one prayer for fifteen minutes and then bypass a third of the service to the *Shema*, the affirmation of God's unity. As Rabbi Michael Paley recalls, "The order of the service was completely obliterated for the sake of this unbelievable *kavannah* (inner spiritual meaning)."[4] There was a great deal of Hasidic chanting and meditation, especially the wordless chants called *niggunim*.

The second classic example of the havurah was the New York Havurah of the 1970s, located in a large, rambling apartment on the Upper West Side of Manhattan, in which some participants lived (fig. 63). Whereas *Havurat Shalom* attempted to create a seminary, the New York Havurah established a religious school in which parental participation was required. It thus foreshadowed Jewish family education programs that would subsequently emerge. Other examples are the *Aquarian Minyan*, founded by Zalman Schachter in Berkeley, and the Havurah of South Florida, a network of independent havurot found in 1980 by a Reform rabbi, Mitchell Chefitz. An umbrella organization, the National Havurah Committee, has sponsored various gatherings, including week-long summer institutes devoted to intensive study and prayer.

The havurah phenomenon was both a conscious *rejection* and *re-invention* of the synagogue. Rather than "a limited liability community, which we belong to for clearly-defined goals,"[5] the havurah was to be a community of unlimited liability, an alternative

Figure 64. The New York Havurah, a Jewish counterculture group, celebrates Sabbath outdoors in New York City, 1979. Photograph by Bill Aron.

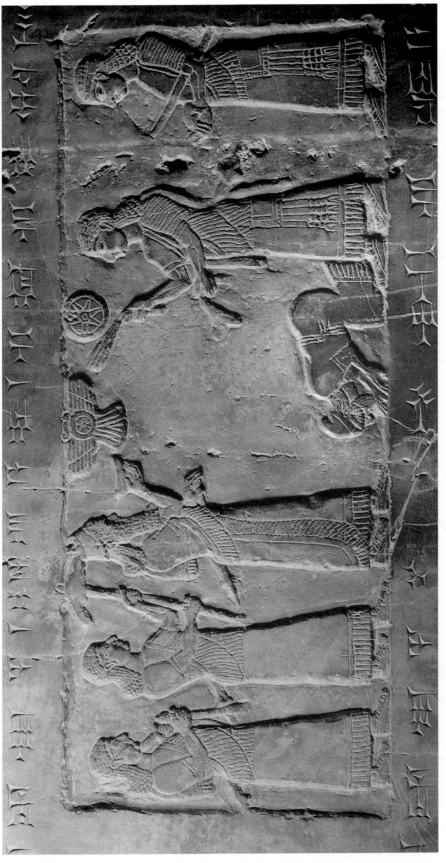

Figure 65. Black Obelisk of Shalmaneser III, Assyrian, seventh century B.C.E. Detail of King Jehu, king of Israel, bowing before Shalmaneser III, after the Assyrian king conquered the Northern Kingdom of Israel.

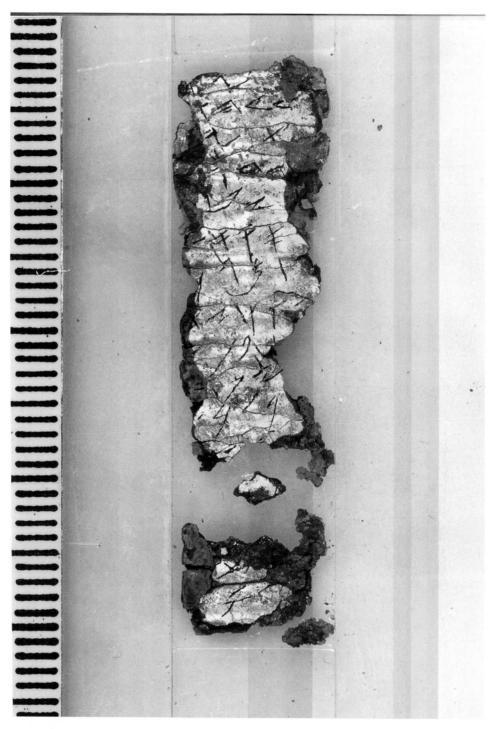

Figure 66. Inscribed silver amulet, Hinnon Valley, Jerusalem, c. First Temple Period. This amulet is one of two discovered in burial caves of the Hinnon Valley. It is inscribed with the earliest known version of the Priestly Benediction.

Figure 67. Greek inscription from the balustrade (*soreg* in Hebrew) of the Jerusalem Temple, c. first century C.E. Many such inscriptions placed on the balustrades leading from the Court of the Gentiles into the Court of the Jews forbade gentiles from entering the inner precincts of the Herodian Temple under penalty of death.

Figure 68. Silver shekel coin commemorating the first or third year of Jewish freedom in the war against Rome. Minted in Jerusalem, c. 66-69 C.E.

Figure 69. Coin commemorating the Bar Kokhba revolt against the Roman army. Simeon bar Kokhba was the charismatic-messianic leader whose government gave rise to hope of rebuilding the Jerusalem Temple after its destruction by the emperor Titus in 70 C.E.

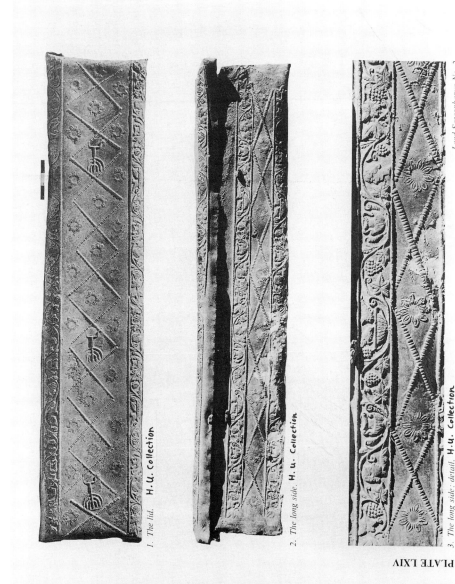

1. The lid. H. U. Collection

2. The long side. H. U. Collection

3. The long side: detail. H. U. Collection

Lead Sarcophagus No. 2

PLATE LXIV

Figure 70. Sarcophagus from Beth Shearim catacomb, Lower Galilee, Israel, c. second-fourth centuries C.E.

to large, impersonal synagogues with professional clergy in robes who preached *to*, prayed *to*, and sung *to* a passive audience, often accompanied by choirs and organs. Moreover, the havurah responded to the spiritual compartmentalization of American Judaism by becoming holistic, seamless, and radically counter-cultural—a conscious rejection of American secular and corporate values.

To accomplish their goals, the first havurot had several distinctive characteristics. First was an emphasis on intimacy, the notion that smaller is better, a conscious rejection of the large synagogues of suburban Judaism. Within such a setting, learning and leadership were de-centralized, meaning, by extension, that, unlike in large synagogues, people could not join a havurah in name only; active, passionate participation was required.

Another aspect of the rejection of the suburban aesthetic of American Judaism was the (romanticized) embrace of the Eastern European *shtetl* as a communal model. In the havurah, the *shtetl* survived in the form of liturgy and worship, through Hasidic music and meditations. It also survived in a sociological sense, through the emphasis on small groups, mutual support, and informality. Yet, clearly, the havurah did not recreate the actuality of *shtetl* life at all, based as it was (and is) on principles of egalitarianism between men and women and the notion that individual Jews can and should create their own Judaism. On the first point, nowhere has the lowering of barriers for full female participation in Jewish life been as radically realized as in the havurah world, where egalitarianism became a basic cardinal of faith and practice. On the second point, regarding "Do it yourself" Judaism, the havurot reacted to American Judaism's pattern of "surrogacy," in which primary Jewish tasks were farmed out to rabbis, cantors, and professional teachers. Havurot, by contrast, placed all religious responsibilities upon the individual, from the crafting of personal ritual objects to the development of a spontaneous, disorderly, and informal mode of worship.

Within this setting, and clearly unlike in the *shtetl*, Jewish rituals were re-interpreted to express counter-cultural values. In prayer, a Paul Simon or Bob Dylan song could suddenly become a Psalm, an Allen Ginsberg or Lawrence Ferlinghetti poem, a responsive reading. *The Jewish Catalog* (see below), for instance, suggested that people create a *ner tamid* ("eternal light," reminding worshipers in a synagogue of God's eternal presence) for the home: "Attach to each section one of a string of variously colored lights on a random-flashing sequence chain," so as to create, that is, a sixties light show. Similarly, the *mikveh* (ritual bath) is, in traditional Judaism, a place where women purify themselves after separation during the menstrual period, for men to purify themselves after seminal emissions, and for the performance of conversions to Judaism. Now, as Rachel Adler interpreted it in *The Jewish Catalog*, *mikveh* was to represent "the original living water, the primal sea from which all life comes, the womb of the world, forcing participants to confront life and death and resurrection." Thus members of the original havurot rethought Jewish ritual in light of, as Marshall Sklare put it, the "regnant pieties of American youth culture."

Overall, the havurot expressed a post-denominational liberal Judaism, a thick stew of contributions from every Jewish movement. Conservative Judaism contributed its scholarship; Reform, its social activism and its liberalization of Jewish theology; Reconstructionism, its perspective on Jews as a historical and cultural force; Hasidism, its joy; Orthodoxy, its sense of text, tradition, and authenticity. The historical parallels with Hasidism are the strongest. Both Hasidism and the havurot were revolutions that responded to a growing sense of spiritual anomie. Even their practices seem similar, with Hasidism's institutionalized meditation and use of wordless chants paralleling the havurah's emphasis on singing and experimenting with a personal high.[6]

The havurah movement also looked for inspiration to the writings and life examples of several modern Jewish theologians. Mordecai Kaplan's theology contributed a sense of the power of the community within Jewish life, in which *belonging* takes precedence even over *believing*. Martin Buber's theology contributed a sense of true relationship, in which the I-Thou mirrors the human relationship with God. Abraham Joshua Heschel's theology contributed religious awe mixed with social action. And Franz Rosenzweig, the German Jewish theologian, may have been the master teacher of this movement that emerged forty years after his death. Rosenzweig re-entered Judaism from the very portals of the Church, just as the "new Jews" of the havurot had re-entered Judaism from the portals of secularism. In reclaiming Judaism for himself, Rosenzweig re-entered a relationship with God, sensing that commandment flows from that relationship, but that human autonomy remains implicit and necessary. In doing whatever we can, we participate in the act of *mitzvah*, and thus we are personally commanded. Such would be the attitude towards *mitzvah* among young Jews re-entering the Jewish community.

The major texts of the movement: The organizing principles behind the nascent havurah movement appear in the three volume work *The Jewish Catalog*, edited by Michael and Sharon Strassfeld and Richard Siegel (who departed after the first volume). By the early 1980s, *The Jewish Catalog* (New York, 1973, 1976, and 1980) had sold more than 200,000 copies—more than any other Jewish Publication Society book other than the Hebrew Bible. It rapidly became the unofficial handbook of the havurah movement.

The Jewish Catalog combined the detailed approach of the *Shulhan Aruch* (the classic, definitive, sixteenth century code of Jewish law) with the "do-it-yourself" aesthetic of the *Whole Earth Catalogue*, describing thereby a Jewish life that easily could be reconciled with the regnant counterculture. A chapter in volume I, "Using the Jewish Establishment— A Reluctant Guide," demonstrates a marked 1960s sensibility towards the institutions of the Jewish world. "Teachers" offers names of directors of college Hillel centers (from which many of the leaders of the havurah movement emerged), Hasidic *rebbes*, some professors of Jewish studies, and some pulpit rabbis. Subsequent volumes of the Cata-

log expanded the purview from ritual to the rest of Jewish life—e.g., Israel, charity, living Jewishly in small communities. Michael Strassfeld subsequently expanded the *Catalog* approach in a book on the Jewish holidays, which treats each holiday as a sacred text, going into layers of interpretation and discourse and including comments in the margins by havurah luminaries.

The havurah movement also produced a number of magazines and journals. Of primary importance was *Response*, a Jewish student journal that continues to function as a regular chronicle of the intellectual developments of the movement and a constant call to activism. There was also the short-lived journal *New Traditions* (1984-1985, published by the National Havurah Committee) and the infrequently published *Kerem: Creative Explorations in Judaism*.

Synagogue Havurot: The havurah as a self-contained spiritual community that functioned in lieu of the synagogue eventually had an impact on the synagogues themselves, in the process, transforming synagogue Judaism. This happened as the same hungers that gave birth to the independent havurot affected the synagogue, which many believed had become too large, losing spirituality and intimacy. In response, some synagogues, like the Germantown Jewish Centre in Philadelphia, opened themselves up to havurot that existed within the community, thus infusing the synagogue with new life and allowing it to stand firm against changing demographics.

The major pioneer in the area of synagogue-based havurot has been Rabbi Harold Schulweis, of Temple Valley Beth Shalom, a large Conservative synagogue in Encino, California. After arriving at Valley Beth Shalom in 1970, Schulweis sensed that he was dealing with a new kind of Jews: "psychological Jews," who regarded community with as much suspicion as they regarded religion. This led to the existence of barriers —Schulweis calls them *mehisot*, using the term for the partition that divides men from women in the traditional synagogue—between "the pulpit and the nether-world of a pew; then the *mehitza* between "Sanctuary

Judaism" and Jewish life *in profanum*; finally the *mehitza* that divides one congregant from another."[7] Schulweis' answer was the creation of a network of havurot. Each was comprised of ten families and contained social, cultural, and celebratory ingredients. By autumn, 1984, there were more than sixty such havurot, involving about one third of the congregation's families. In this model, the rabbi became less a figurehead and more a teacher, a leader of activists rather than of passive followers. Lamenting the need for rabbinical ubiquity, Schulweis further pioneered the use of para-rabbis, training congregants to render help and aid, thus to become their own spiritual leaders.

By the early 1980s, Charles Silberman estimated the number of synagogue havurot at about three thousand. Another estimate suggested that fully one quarter of all congregations in the United States had havurot. Such synagogues tended to be large, suburban, non-Orthodox, and founded after World War II. Havurot were so successful that many synagogues came to view them as programmatic panaceas, and rabbis needed to warn that simply re-naming an ongoing class or a committee a havurah did not make it so. In fact, many synagogues found such programs unwieldy to administer, and some protested that the havurot were elitist, contributing to a further splintering of the synagogue. Often, participants complained that while they participated in havurot, they were not, in fact, *haverim*—friends—with the people in the group.

To address such problems, synagogues fostered various styles of havurah organization. Sometimes these became neighborhood groups or affinity groups revolving around a particular religious task. Groups met to study Torah, to worship, or to attend synagogue functions together. Some havurot became involved in family retreat weekends, social action concerns, *tzedakah* (charity) collectives, or writing a prayer book. As with the independent havurot, the styles of liturgy and study were largely informal, with many synagogues debating the role of their professional leaders within these groups. Still, many of the groups simply became extensions of the

rabbi's personality and barely functioned independently of professional leadership. Others fostered true lay leadership, leading to the growth of a genuine American Jewish spirituality.

New kinds of synagogues: The havurah movement helped create a transformed American synagogue, which flourished in the 1960s through 1990s. One of the first, Congregation Solel, in Highland Park, Illinois, was founded as a northern branch of KAM-Isaiah Israel and was led by Rabbi Arnold Jacob Wolf. The new community was, in Wolf's words, "intellectual, political, and exceedingly innovative and radical in its expectations." This synagogue pioneered egalitarianism and focused on study, prayer, and action.

Wolf would ultimately list Solel's major successes: lay participation in congregational services; no fund raising (synagogue dues paid for everything) and no plaques for donors; democracy without an entrenched board of trustees; a de-emphasis on sermons, with no sermon titles published in the bulletin and discussions or debates taking the place of sermons. Solel developed a serious adult study program with a minimum of guest lecturers. The synagogue was involved in innovative social action projects, notably, running a day camp for black youngsters. Most radically, they abolished the *bar mitzvah* celebration, seeing it as problematic and perhaps irrelevant. At Solel, the rabbi was seen as teacher, not as administrator or politician.

Rabbi Wolf's assistant at Solel was a young rabbi named Lawrence Kushner. In 1971, following his apprenticeship at Solel, Kushner moved to Congregation Beth El of the Sudbury River Valley, in Sudbury, Massachusetts. There he carried the Solel model into the next generation. Indeed, few congregations have adapted the havurah model as effectively as Beth El. For instance, soon after arriving at Beth El, Kushner helped the congregation write its own prayer book for the High Holy Days. This was followed by the congregation's creating of its own Sabbath prayer book, *Vetaher Libenu*, as well as a prayer book for the mourning period.

Following the havurah's pattern of using

the shtetl as the "usable past," Kushner created a style of "Neo-Hasidic" Reform Judaism. He introduced *niggunim* (wordless Hasidic melodies and chants). In the words of member Anita Diamant, "Through its simple repetition, it forces the analytic, critical side of yourself to shut down and opens you to other ways of knowing and being present." The worship style consists of chairs gathered around a table that holds candles, *hallah*, and wine. Kushner rejects the "priestified" Rabbinic role and therefore leads services from the same level as the congregation. Martin Buber's I-Thou relationship finds its echoes at Beth El as well. As Diamant remarked, "We greet the Sabbath by looking not at the backs of heads, but by meeting each other's eyes across a table." There is a certain lightness and informality. As Kushner notes, "Not much is taken too seriously except for one's personal search for how to be in the presence of God and what God wants. The primary reason we have a synagogue is to encourage the primary Jewish acts of prayer, study, and good deeds."

Kushner hopes the congregation will grow into a confederation of semi-independent religious family groups—havurot—with the synagogue serving as a central Jewish clearing house, providing Jewish resources. Towards this end, Kushner organizes family retreats and insists that parents of bar and bat mitzvah candidates participate in his weekly Torah class. Evoking the havurah principle that "smaller is better," the congregation experimented with limiting the size of its membership. Beth El also became one of the few Reform synagogues with a *hevra kaddisha*—"holy society"—a group that prepares the dead for burial.

Solel and Beth El were created with the havurah model at least partially in mind. (Solel's founding principles in fact pre-dated and were even prescient of the havurot.) Other synagogues similarly were founded on havurah notions, such as, for instance, that of *intentional community*, which holds that members cannot just join but must be involved. Thus Congregation Mishkan Shalom, a Reconstructionist synagogue in Haverford, Pennsylvania, holds that Judaism is inextri-

cable from social and political action. Members therefore must make a covenant with the synagogue to participate in programs that fulfill the congregation's vision.

Alongside synagogues *founded* on the havurah model are many formerly moribund congregations that gained new life by being *re-created* in this pattern. The two best examples are found on the Upper West Side of Manhattan in New York City. Long a Jewish neighborhood, this area underwent a Jewish renaissance at least partially because of the presence of both the Jewish Theological Seminary and the *New York Havurah*. The havurah had a particular impact on the restoration of Congregation Anshe Hesed. This old, established synagogue was entirely re-created by havurah veterans (especially the co-authors of *The Jewish Catalog*; Michael Strassfeld serves as the congregation's rabbi), so as to become a major communal and worship center.

So, too, Congregation B'nai Jeshurun, the oldest Ashkenazic Conservative synagogue in New York. In 1985, the congregation called Rabbi Marshall Meyer to be its spiritual leader. Meyer had distinguished himself through selfless duty during the *junta* in Argentina, where his activism and left-wing politics earned him the nickname *El Royo Rabbino*, "the Red rabbi." At B'nai Jeshurun, he found a once-proud synagogue with severe structural problems and even worse spiritual problems, a congregation that could not even muster the quorum of ten Jews needed for communal worship. Meyer reached out to the homeless, AIDS patients, and the spiritually hungry, creating a worshipping community that sometimes numbered close to a thousand on a Friday night. After Meyer's untimely death in 1993, his assistant, Rolando Matalon, became the congregation's senior rabbi. Friday night services remain jubilant, with music, chanting, and dance—so popular that one must line up as early as five o'clock to get a seat.

Finally, we can credit the havurah movement for critiquing conventional synagogues and for producing Jewish professionals willing to change them. Most ambitious is the "Synagogue 2000" project, funded by the

Cummings Foundation and directed by Lawrence Hoffman and Conservative educator Ron Wolfson. They clearly recognize that the synagogue must be re-invented for the next century, for, as their promotional material states: "Beyond the coldness of the corporate-consumer culture lies the spiritual ambiance of the synagogue as community and home, a place where people feel welcome, connected, and intellectually alive—partners on a sacred odyssey of a sacred people, completing creation and thereby themselves."

New kinds of Jewish education: Inevitably, the transformation of the American synagogue affected the methods and content of Jewish education. This transformation began with a mass protest by student activists at the Council of Jewish Federations General Assembly in Boston in 1969. Arguing that Jewish education was woefully underfunded and inadequate, the activists, many of whom became founders of the havurah movement, initiated the organized Jewish community's confronting of its funding policies and asking of hard questions about the proportion of money sent to Israel and the amount retained for domestic needs, especially for education.

Soon the transformation of Jewish education began. Creative Jewish educators began experimenting with new techniques, curricula, and technologies. A major, and hitherto unheralded, contribution to this process was the Rocky Mountain Curriculum Planning Workshops, founded in 1971 by educator Audrey Friedman (Marcus). Friedman pioneered the concept of taking groups of Jewish college students, rabbinical students, and teachers on retreats, where they would invent new curricula and techniques. Over three summers, the Rocky Mountain workshops innovated approaches such as sociodrama, values clarification, and creative engagement with the arts. Friedman's efforts led her to found Alternatives in Religious Education, Inc., an independent publishing house for Jewish educational materials. Her efforts were paralleled, years later, by other such companies, including Torah Aura Productions in Los Angeles, California, founded by Joel Grishaver.

The full maturation of Jewish education resulted from the dynamic leadership of CAJE—the Coalition for Advancement of Jewish Education—founded in 1976 as the Coalition for *Alternatives* in Jewish Education. CAJE has become the major activist Jewish educational organization, raising consciousness about the need for creativity, better curricula, and more communal funding. To echo an often-stated theme, CAJE is both trans-denominational and post-denominational, bringing together Jewish educators, rabbis, cantors, youth workers, academics, social workers, writers, and artists from all sectors of Jewish life. It sponsors an annual national conference as well as local conferences and is actively involved in the creation of curriculum banks and resources. Like many of the recent institutions of American Jewry, CAJE emerged from a radical critique of American Jewish apathy, in this case, towards Jewish education and the career needs and goals of Jewish educators, but has quickly been accepted within the mainstream.

New kinds of charities: The havurah movement continually critiqued the style and substance of American Jewish fund-raising, viewed by many as more concerned with honoring donors with plaques and lavish dinners than with serious world transformation. So, too, there developed an ongoing critique of decisions regarding where funding should go. These critiques, combined with the new aesthetic, more redolent of the *shtetl* than the ballroom, led to alternate *tzedakah* collectives, which collected money and decided locally what it should support. On this model, new decentralized, non-corporate charities have emerged. Among the most successful is the Ziv Tzedakah Fund, administered by the poet and educator Danny Siegel, which distributes money to small projects in the United States and Israel. The SHEFA Fund, supporting socially responsible projects, and the New Israel Fund, which funds programs in Israel concerned with Jewish/Arab relations, religious pluralism, civil rights and liberties, women's rights, and community action, are similar. MAZON, The Jewish Hunger Fund, has been remarkably successful. Founded by activist and author Leonard Fein, MAZON exploits American Jew's penchant for celebration, asking people to donate three percent of the cost of a celebration to help feed the hungry. MAZON allocates the funds to various domestic and foreign organizations.

In addition, Caring Community programs have emerged in many synagogues, training congregants to visit the sick, comfort the bereaved, bury the dead, take care of the hungry, and perform other mitzvot. Like havurot, such programs signal at least a partial reclamation of a pre-modern Jewish sociology— a sociology of the *shtetl*, of mutual interdependence and the insistence that the holy acts of a Jewish community cannot be the sole responsibility of professionals.

New Jewish music: An earlier generation of Reform Jews preferred synagogue music performed by organ and choir, while Conservative Jews favored traditional *hazzanut* (cantorial chant). Now, as a result of the Reform and Conservative camping movements, the counter-culture, and the havurah, a new Jewish aesthetic has emerged. It focuses on the guitar and other informal instruments, and it promotes new melodies, combining contemporary pop and folk idioms with Hasidic and Eastern European traditions, as well as Israeli folk music, to engage the soul and create community.

This new tradition began with Rabbi Shlomo Carlebach (1926-1995), a popular singer and story-teller. His neo-Hasidic style blended traditional *niggunim*, Israel song, and American folk style, and his concerts in the United States and Israel were popular both in religious and nonreligious circles. At the same time, the greatest center of musical activity was the Reform camping and youth movements, giving birth, for instance, to *Kol B'Seder* (Rabbi Daniel Freelander and Cantor Jeffrey Klepper), which adopted classical and modern Jewish texts for guitar and voice. In this mode, Debbie Friedman is regarded as the master Jewish songstress of her generation, inheriting the mantle of Shlomo Carlebach and producing a body of spiritually moving works that have galvanized audiences.

Like the havurah movement, this music is informal, "do-it-yourself," often written on Thursday and sung the next evening on the Sabbath. It is much more concerned with creating group transcendence than with formal artistry. And yet, like the havurah movement, much of this music has survived its critics, transcended camps and youth, and become standard synagogue fare.

The new spirituality: Contemporary Jews increasingly have sensed that much of what has been central to Jewish life in recent decades is *necessary*, but not *sufficient*. Social activism has increasingly been recognized as unable to keep Jews Jewish; ethics have been revealed as generalized goodness without a nuanced examination of virtue; even the post-1967 craze of Jewish ethnicity, Israel, and Holocaust consciousness has begun to lose steam, with many Jewish leaders and educators concerned about the *detrimental* effects of Holocaust consciousness, especially upon the young. Ethnicity and folk Judaism too have lost their appeal for a generation without immigrant ties.

At the same time, ever since the 1960s, the self has become increasingly important in American culture, leading to an often radical individualism. As the need for individual nurturance became dominant, spirituality rushed in to fill the void, for Jews in particular emerging from both the turn to the self and the desire to re-discover the inner substance of Jewish living. Jewish spirituality, like the havurot, began in a critique of a dry and lifeless institutional Judaism. But there was a larger cultural context as well, since this spiritual thirst coincided with a general American interest in mysticism: Eastern religion and meditation; Indian music; the writings of Hermann Hesse, Gurdjieff, Carlos Castenada, and Alan Watts; and various occult practices, such as astrology, I Ching, and tarot cards. Psychedelic drugs similarly pointed towards new levels of reality, and an easy syncretism emerged between psychedelics, various New Age religions, self-help movements, and kabbalah—Jewish mysticism.

Jewish mysticism became popular for a number of reasons. First was the massive intellectual achievement of Gershom Scholem, who almost single-handedly redeemed Jewish mysticism from its prior disparagement by Jewish rationalists. Scholem demonstrated that Jewish mysticism had been a constant and ubiquitous theme within historical Judaism and that it was commingled with rational forces not only within Judaism but even within the lives of individual sages. To this was added the massive outreach success of Lubovitcher Hasidism, which saw kabbalah as the salt that flavors the basic meat of Judaism. Thus there was a renewed interest in Hasidic stories, with Martin Buber's retelling and re-shaping of them winning new popularity and Elie Wiesel's presentation in *Souls on Fire* gaining a wide readership. Finally came popular books on Jewish meditation, especially the work of Aryeh Kaplan, a physicist and Orthodox rabbi whose *Jewish Meditation* (New York, 1985) was the first modern effort to compose a simple and contemporary do-it-yourself guide to mystical meditation.

Kabbalah's increased popularity is an interesting foundation for what many Jews perceive as a return to a more *authentic* Judaism. Traditionally, Rabbinic authorities inveighed against the study of mysticism until one was forty, married, a parent, and learned in Torah. Yet kabbalah today has become a cottage industry, represented in an avalanche of popular books—many of uneven intellectual depth—and media celebrities who flock to Rabbi Philip Berg's Kabbalah Learning Center. But, for better or worse, the Jewish mystical trend has allowed Jews to sense the intuitive and the non-rational in Judaism, opening the soul in the process. Reviving spirituality among American Jews, its roots are similar to those of Hasidism, which began as a revolt against an institutional Judaism divorced from the emotions and needs of common people. Also similar to Hasidism, the new Jewish spirituality relies on charismatic teachers who move the "masses" to a higher level of inwardness. Chief among these are Arthur Green (1941-), the founder of *Havurat Shalom* and an academic who has clearly articulated the principles of Jewish spirituality,[8] and Lawrence Kushner (1943-), referred to above, a prolific author and teacher, perhaps the American congrega-

tional rabbi most responsible for recapturing Jewish spirituality. His work is best known for its elegant use of personal narrative as a platform for restating in a contemporary idiom the truths of mysticism and Hasidism.[9]

One outgrowth of the new Jewish spirituality is a revolution in Jewish ritual expression. For instance, in the past twenty-five years, the *havdalah* ("separation") ceremony that traditionally marks the conclusion of the Sabbath has returned to non-orthodox Judaism. This has largely been a result of Jewish summer camps, where the sensuousness of the ceremony's candles and spices entranced a generation. Other reclaimed ceremonies include *tashlich*, in which, on Rosh Hashanah, sins are symbolically thrown into a body of water, and the mystical *Tu B'shevat seder*, held on the Jewish New Year of Trees to celebrate the various kinds of fruits in the world. As already noted, the *mikveh* has also been reclaimed as a ritual of welcome for converts and for ritual immersion before marriage. It thus has a new symbolic meaning, far removed from its traditional use in matters of family purity and sexual separation during menstruation.

The new Jewish spirituality in general demonstrates an openness to individuals' search for personal meaning. Even its spatial metaphors reveal this emphasis. Rather than focusing on *ascent* (i.e., Jacob's ladder or Mount Sinai), now viewed as too hierarchical, the contemporary master metaphor is the *journey*, implying that the destination is by no means determined. Here the biographical model of Franz Rosenzweig is revealed in all its potential power, as the dominant theme for this generation has become *teshuvah*— return to Judaism—and thousands of young Jews have become *baalei teshuvah*—newly Orthodox. But even among many who have not become Orthodox, Jewish practice has increased. Indeed, a new confessional autobiographical form has emerged, in which previously estranged Jews speak of their spiritual journeys back to Judaism. The most prominent of these books are Paul Cowan's *An Orphan in History* (Garden City, 1982) and Anne Roiphe's *Generation Without Memory: A Jewish Journey in Christian America*

(New York, 1981). In both books, prominent Jews speak of their return from either being Jewish "WASPs" or from an apathy that bordered on self-hatred. Finally, presaging New Age Judaism's flirtation with other religious traditions, in *The Search for God at Harvard* (New York, 1991), Ari Goldman, former *New York Times* religion editor, chronicles his experiences as a visiting student in the theologically multi-cultural Harvard Divinity School.

Finally, the new Jewish spirituality has become much more open to conversion to Judaism, represented in the silent semantic revolution through which the word "convert" is increasingly shunned and "Jew-by-choice" is preferred. The Reform movement has taken massive leadership in this area, especially since Rabbi Alexander Schindler's 1978 call for a new, assertive receptivity to those who would enter the Jewish people. Such calls for understanding and acceptance have been renewed perennially. In most cases, candidates for conversion are entering Jewish families through marriage. And yet, increasingly, non-Jews unconnected to Jewish families are converting as well, sometimes after re-claiming a long-buried Jewish family legacy. A model of this is the life story of the black activist and academic Julius Lester, found in his autobiography *Lovesong: Becoming a Jew* (1988).

Gender issues and prayer: The feminist influence on prayer and worship has been profound and pervasive, with even mainstream Jews becoming increasingly uncomfortable referring to God as "he," "father," "king," and "Lord." As a result, gender-conscious liturgies have become standard in all liberal Jewish movements. Sometimes the language is truly neutral, with God referred to as "loving parent," "ruler," etc. But God also has been re-imagined and renamed as feminists have experimented with authentic Jewish female terms for divinity, e.g., *Shekhina*, the traditional term for the feminine presence of God. Perhaps most radical, Marcia Falk, *The Book of Blessings* (San Francisco, 1996), replaces the traditional opening of blessings, "Blessed are You, Lord our God . . .," with the first new blessing formula

in more than fifteen hundred years: *Nevarekh et eyn hahayim*, "Let us bless the wellspring of life." Such renaming and re-addressing of God has had a far-reaching impact on Jewish theology, with feminist influences contributing to a new sense of the divine. Feminism, for instance, has prompted the mining of mystical texts for non-human conceptions of God: God as fountain, source, well-spring, locked garden, and sea of wisdom.[10] This loss of the patriarchal God has made the divine-human relationship seem less hierarchical and more horizontal, bringing new metaphors in its wake: God as friend, partner, lover.

A major figure in the feminist revival of ritual for more than two decades, Rabbi Lynn Gottlieb has been creating a feminist Judaism. Her poetry and ritual feature the *Shekhina*, the mystical sense of God's feminine presence, and her search for the female face of divinity has led her even into a celebration of the ancient Near Eastern creation goddess, Tehom. Inspired by Elie Wiesel's storytelling from the Bible (a narrative that largely ignored the presence of women), Gottlieb has pioneered the passionate reclamation of women's stories. Lilith, Adam's first wife; Eve; the matriarchs; Hagar; Shifra and Puah, the Egyptian midwives; Yocheved, the mother of Moses; Miriam, the sister of Moses—all find their renewed places in her poetry and ritual inventions. She has been particularly successful in bringing a feminist consciousness into the deliberate creation of community, stressing openness and hospitality.

Life cycle celebrations: The new spirituality has increased Jews' emphasis on the personal, even sometimes at the expense of the communal. This emphasis is expressed in particular in the creation of new life cycle celebrations, many of which have been created for women in order to redress historical gaps. Thus there has been a growth of baby-naming ceremonies for girls, often with new rituals intended to parallel circumcision, the mark of the male child's entry into the covenant. Such rituals include feet-washing (evoking an ancient Middle Eastern form of greeting) and even, though rarely done, a ceremony invented by Mary Gendler in which the hymen is broken, a conscious imitation of the power and pain of ritual circumcision. The last two decades also have seen a growth of celebration of *Rosh Hodesh*—the first day of the Jewish month—as a woman's festival, and many synagogues now mark this day with women's observances and study. So, too, there has been a growth in women's Passover seders, focusing on the role of women in the Exodus story.

At the same time, ritual has increasingly been seen as a path to healing in moments of vulnerability. Jewish feminists thus have created rituals of mourning for infertility, of healing after abortion or miscarriage, and of recovery after rape. Other ceremonies apply equally to men: rituals have been invented for divorce, getting a new job, losing a job, and retirement. While traditional life cycle rituals primarily marked the individual's bonding to Torah and community, these newer ones witness many phases of the individual's life, seeking to bring Judaism's wisdom to bear on all personal times of passage.

Healing: Through the pioneering work of the National Center for Jewish Healing and its branches (now more than twenty), healing has been a new focus in synagogue programming and worship, signifying a return to faith and its traditional language. Here, the new Jewish spirituality is as indebted to modern science and medicine as Maimonides was to the medicine of his day. For research indicates that faith and prayer are far more efficacious than rational minds once thought, with prayer, in conjunction with modern medical treatments, sometimes bridging the gap between illness and recovery.[11]

Accordingly, many Reform, Conservative, and Reconstructionist synagogues now offer healing services, which include psalms, singing, meditations, and recitation of the names of those who need healing. As one leader in the healing movement has noted, the purpose of such services is not *cure* but *care*, to bring Buber's I-Thou relationship to its logical conclusion by demonstrating that the community—and, by implication, God—is with those who suffer. These services have become a rich resource for those who seek to integrate more emotional elements into liturgy. Most significant, the healing phenomenon is not limited to synagogues but has become popular within the secular world of the Jewish Federation as well.

Another aspect of the concern for healing is the recent sea change in American Jewish attitudes towards Jews and addictions. The recognition that addiction is a medical *and* spiritual problem, not just a disease, combined with the fact that Jews, like non-Jews, have found spirituality in Twelve Steps groups, led to the creation of an American Jewish addiction literature. Much of this material seeks to establish theological linkages between Twelve Steps therapy and Jewish wisdom: for instance, the "Higher Power" of Twelve Steps becomes the God of Judaism. The pioneer in this field is Orthodox rabbi-therapist Abraham Twerski. Additionally, Kerry Olitsky, Hebrew Union College-Jewish Institute of Religion, has created a literature of recovery, much of it based on daily meditations, affirmations, and texts linked to the weekly Torah portions. He has been particularly adept at utilizing the lectionary and festival cycle to help those in recovery.

Gay and lesbian inclusiveness: Starting in the mid-1970s, gay and lesbian Jews began to create a movement of liberation, which has taken several different forms. One of these is gay synagogues, the first of which was *Beth Chayim Chadashim* in Los Angeles, founded in 1972 and affiliated with the Reform movement in 1973. Other gay and lesbian outreach synagogues have been established in such cities as New York (Congregation Beth Simchat Torah, the largest gay outreach synagogue, with some 1100 members), San Francisco (Sha'ar Zahav, which has pioneered creative gay/lesbian inclusive liturgy), Philadelphia, Atlanta, Washington, D.C., Chicago, and Miami. Second, while gays and lesbians have always been quietly active in Jewish education and communal work, recent years have seen a massive increase in the numbers of openly gay and lesbian rabbis. Both the Reform and Reconstructionist movements ordain openly gay and lesbian rabbis and have taken official steps to counter overt discrimination in hiring practices.

Finally, a gay and lesbian liturgical and ritual movement has emerged, so that, for instance, Jewish commitment ceremonies have been developed and "coming out" celebrations are now a common feature of the gay and lesbian Jewish world.

Yet even as a significant number of Reform and Reconstructionist rabbis consent to honor such relationships publicly, liberal Jewish movements continue to struggle with the official place of gay and lesbian weddings and commitment ceremonies. There has been a growth of consciousness in this area within the Conservative movement as well, with such prominent rabbis as Harold Schulweis, Stuart Kelman, and Bradley Shavit-Artson pioneering new theological and ethical assessments of such unions, albeit alongside many dissenting views.

The Jewish Renewal movement: The end of the counter-culture made the original havurah passé. The havurot had too little infrastructure to sustain themselves and, as a result, became largely a one generation phenomenon: the children of havurah members did not replicate the structures created by their parents. The havurah movement does, however, have a successor in the Jewish Renewal movement, a true movement with a clear infrastructure and singular identity. Its retreat center—Elat Chayyim, near Woodstock, New York—hosts week-long conferences every summer, and its renowned rabbinical leaders and authorities produce various publications and have a dedicated following of several thousand Jews.

Despite its corporate trappings, Jewish Renewal follows the havurah ideal of nurturing communities that are intimate, participatory, and egalitarian and of assisting the spiritual growth and healing of individuals, communities, and society as a whole. As post-denominational as the earlier havurot, the movement has been described by William Novak as "a new Judaic impulse fed by the best qualities in each of the recognized branches of Judaism: the authenticity of Orthodoxy; the liberalism of Reform; the scholarship of Conservative Judaism; the social awareness of Reconstructionism; the excitement of Hasidism." Indeed, Jewish Renewal

shares with the havurah a deep attachment to the wisdom of Jewish mysticism and Hasidism as well as of the prophets and Talmudic rabbis, all of which it infuses with the insights of contemporary ecology, feminism, and participatory democracy. This New Age Judaism blends the styles of human potential movements, therapeutic psychology, and inclusive interpretation of ancient texts.

Even while developing the previously-discussed trends in Jewish spirituality, Jewish Renewal adds its own unique signature to Judaism. It fosters a new intensity regarding prayer, seeking to deepen the intentionality, spiritual meaning, and direction of worshipers through the use of chant and meditation, including guided imagery, new music, dance, and even yoga. The movement also has developed new ways of creating and learning Torah, with the process of *midrash* (Scriptural interpretation) continuing well into postmodernity. Poets, especially David Curzon and Joel Rosenberg, and scholar/translators, such as Everett Fox, have "re-written" Torah for this generation.[12] There has also been increased interest in synthesizing textual criticism with psychological techniques. Psychotherapist Peter Pitzele pioneered "bibliodrama" and role playing techniques as ways of entering the inner life of sacred texts.[13] Closely related are scholars and authors who integrate family dynamics issues with their reading of the texts.[14]

Jewish Renewal is marked by its comfort with a more intimate—rather than transcendent—sense of God as suffusing the world with divinity. Here, theology works closely with the New Age design of Jewish sacred space. Instead of the rabbi acting as God's surrogate up on the *bimah*—the raised platform in the synagogue—Jewish Renewal participants prefer to pray in a circle, with the leader one among many in its circumference. "God," says Rabbi Leonard Gordon of the Germantown Jewish Center in Philadelphia, "emerges out of the circle and is not something beyond you."[15] The movement also has reclaimed previously ignored theological options, for instance a re-birth of interest in angels in Jewish lore, made easier by the prevailing culture's interest in New Age phenomena. More significant, there has been a serious new interest in issues of life after death, leading to Jewish Renewal's recapturing of traditional Jewish views of the immortality of the soul, reincarnation, and even a flirtation with the idea of the messianic resurrection of the dead.[16]

Jewish Renewal rejects the earlier American Jewish bifurcation of the world into categories of "relevant to Judaism" and "irrelevant to Judaism." Rather than restricting Judaism's pertinence to prayer or Torah study, for instance, it returns to an earlier model, applying Jewish teachings to all aspects of life—food, money, sex, health, politics—and thereby working to raise to a higher level everything that a Jew does. In this setting, the personal becomes religious, for instance, with sexuality, even at its most intimate, being sanctified.[17] Along these lines, recent years have seen the cautious beginnings of a Jewish men's movement, which asks how Judaism views masculinity and men's life issues. Another aspect of the incorporation of all aspects of life is the search for new ways of supporting and celebrating cultural pluralism, in particular, by inviting into the community gays and lesbians, alternate families, and the intermarried. And feminism—even in its most radical manifestations—also has been made a matter of faith, represented in the great interest in the redemption of Biblical women and in a mild flirtation, in some quarters, with goddess worship, even, though rarely and most radically, Wicca (witchcraft).

Creating radically de-centralized authority structures and new leadership models, Jewish Renewal follows the *havurah* movement's post-denominational disinterest in traditional models of authority. Important in this regard is private rabbinical ordination, which takes place outside the aegis of recognized seminaries. The result is a distinctive style of Jewish Renewal rabbi, many of whom teach and work in New Mexico, "the national cutting edge of Jewish spiritual renewal."[18] Even as private ordination makes a concerted statement that the established models for training and leadership no longer work for many people, we find in this a reclamation of the older Eastern European model, in which rabbis often studied for private ordination and in which a plethora of quasi-professional roles for religious leadership existed.

Zalman Schachter-Shalomi has been particularly active in this regard, advocating new kinds of religious leadership with new titles:[19]

> There have been people in our community who have demonstrated their skills, often immense, in leading services and I have named them *ba'alei tefilah* ("masters of prayer"). Others have become discerning and inspiring *mashpi'im*, spiritual directors. Still others have honed their God-given gifts of teaching *mussar* (ethics) by parable . . . and earned the title *maggidim* (those who teach through stories) . . . [or] preparing to serve as eco-kosher *mashgichim* (supervisors).

The encounter with other religions: Jewish Renewal's respect for other spiritual paths often goes deeper than mere posturing, including active learning from those traditions. In the words of Rabbi Jeff Roth of Elat Chayyim, such engagement represents "the mining of other traditions for vitamins and minerals that we need in our own community." This has led to a certain syncretism between kabbalah and Eastern faiths, seen already in the work of Schachter-Shalomi. Sheila Peltz Weinberg, a Reconstructionist rabbi, similarly remarks, "Over the years, I have sampled a lot of teachers and forms of Eastern practice and New Age offerings including karate, yoga, tai ch'i, Sufi dancing, the Gurdjieff work, vision-questing and the twelve steps."

Such spiritual interaction is found especially in the Jewish Renewal encounter with Buddhism, particularly Tibetan Buddhism, depicted in Rodger Kamenetz's theological travelogue, *The Jew in the Lotus*, which describes a journey of American Jewish intellectuals and teachers to India to meet with the Dalai Lama. The Dalai Lama requested this remarkable meeting because he sensed that Jewish wisdom and history could counsel him on how to maintain a nation in exile from its homeland. While mostly an account of the dialogue between the Dalai Lama and the Jews, the book also brings to light the existence of numerous "Jubus"—Jews who integrate Buddhism into their life styles and philosophy—in India and elsewhere. Kamenetz's work is followed by Sylvia Boorstein's *Funny, You Don't Look Buddhist*, a memoir of a Jewish life enriched and even defined by Buddhist insights.

Buddhism's power in part is that it offers spirituality without the problems modern secular Jews have with God. Since Buddhism presents no personal god, it creates no conflict with science or reason and eliminates the problem of theodicy. Buddhist thought, rather, encourages practitioners to see suffering in one's life as a microcosm of suffering in the world and provides tools to understand and alleviate suffering. New Age Jews also find Buddhism's body-based activities attractive, for they do not require learning a new language, vocabulary, or even ideas. Finally, many are attracted simply because these traditions are *not Judaism.*

Jewish Renewal similarly has begun a process of intellectual cross-pollination with Hinduism, Sufism, and the Society of Friends. In her book *Miraculous Living: A Guided Journey in Kabbalah through the Ten Gates of the Tree of Life* (New York, 1997), Rabbi Shoni Labowitz explores and creates new linkages between Jewish spirituality, Buddhism, and the teachings of Lao Tzu. Jewish Renewal implicit teaches that all spiritual paths are similar and that all spiritual wisdom is interchangeable, even to the point of flirting with syncretism. Speaking of his experiences praying with Trappists, Native Americans, and Sufi mystics, Zalman Schachter-Shalomi has said, "I see myself as a Jewish practitioner of generic religion."[20]

Principal Teachers—Zalman Schachter-Shalomi: Three principle teachers of Jewish Renewal bear noting. Foremost is Zalman Schachter-Shalomi, born in Poland in 1924 and affectionately known as "Reb Zalman." Schachter-Shalomi grew up in Vienna and then fled to Antwerp, where he attended both a Zionist gymnasium and a Lubovitcher yeshiva. He became a passionate missionary for *Habad*, and was ordained a rabbi in 1947. Blessed with a fertile imagination and a creative intellect, Schachter-Shalomi's intellectual interests soon took him into psychology

and to a doctoral dissertation on Hasidic modes of counseling. Ultimately he was drawn into the use of psychedelics to enhance the religious experience. Of all the leaders of New Age Judaism, he has been the most assertive in creating linkages with other spiritual traditions, such as Sufism, Zen, Native American religions, and Tibetan Buddhism. In the words of Eugene B. Borowitz, "Zalman is unique in that he was willing to learn from the mystics of all religions, not only to learn from their texts but to experience the ecstasy of their saints."[21]

Schachter-Shalomi was active in the inception of the *havurah* movement. He created P'nai Or Religious Fellowship, now ALEPH: The Alliance for Jewish Renewal. His publications include *The First Step*, which translates Jewish mysticism into a popular, practical idiom, and *Paradigm Shift*, a collection of his Jewish Renewal writings. While he has written relatively few books, in the style of a true hasidic *rebbe*, his impact has come from his charismatic leadership.

Arthur Waskow: A second leader of the Renewal movement is Arthur Waskow, a veteran of 1960s activism who returned to Judaism in the aftermath of the assassination in 1968 of Rev. Martin Luther King. Witnessing the riots in Washington, D.C., Waskow saw King as the Moses of his people and the armed policemen as Pharaoh's soldiers. This insight led to the creation of an interreligious Freedom Seder, published in 1970, incorporating universal themes of freedom—for blacks, Vietnamese, and all oppressed peoples. He was a founder of Farbrengen in Washington, D.C., *Breira*, which actively criticized Israeli policies, and the Shalom Center, the Jewish address for the antinuclear movement. In 1978, he began editing "Menorah: Sparks of Jewish Renewal," now titled "New Menorah" and published by ALEPH.

Waskow's major books emphasize the integration of Jewish truths with social justice and transformation. *God Wrestling* (1978; updated in 1996) begins a process of "wrestling" with Judaism's sacred texts in order to hear how Torah speaks to us today. *These Holy Sparks: The Rebirth of the Jewish*

People goes further, re-imagining Jewish sociology, education, charity, and Zionism. *Seasons of Our Joy*, Waskow's Jewish Renewal interpretation of the festival cycle, presents new methods of celebration, and *Down to Earth Judaism* rejects the compartmentalization of Jewish life, offering new ways of imagining and addressing God and of acting Jewishly in our everyday lives. Waskow offers a new/old Jewish ethic for dealing with money and charity, champions a sexual ethic that sanctions gay, lesbian, and non-marital sex, and advocates the expansion of kashrut into "eco-kashrut," which goes beyond food to other consumables: coal, oil, paper, wood, and plastics. Waskow asks: "Is it eco-kosher to eat vegetables and fruit that have been grown by drenching the soil with insecticides? Is it eco-kosher to drink Shabbat Kiddush wine from non bio-degradeable plastic cups? Is it eco-kosher to use 100 per cent unrecycled office paper and newsprint in our homes, our synagogues, our community newspapers? To destroy great forests, to ignore insulating our homes, to become addicted to automobiles?"[22]

Michael Lerner: The Jewish life of Michael Lerner, editor of *Tikkun* magazine, a left-wing Jewish intellectual journal, was saved by the Conservative Camp Ramah and by a relationship with the great theologian-activist Abraham Joshua Heschel. Lerner has become famous through his brief intellectual friendship with First Lady Hillary Rodham Clinton, an outgrowth of his philosophy called "the politics of meaning," which holds that politics and public life should speak to the inner anguish of the contemporary individual. Lerner believes that the secular Left has failed because it only addresses economic issues, not spiritual issues, which the Right, by contrast, willingly engages. Lerner's "politics of meaning" is centrally concerned with human values anchored in spirituality. His message is that we can re-discover and enliven authentic Jewish teachings in our lives and institutions.

Lerner's major work is *Jewish Renewal: A Path to Healing and Transformation*. True to his training as a psychologist, he brings to his analysis a psychoanalytical critique of Judaism, noting that Judaism began with a trauma. According to ancient legend, Abraham shattered his father's idols. In response, his father, Terach, took him to King Nimrod, who put him on trial for heresy against the gods. Nimrod cast the boy into a fiery furnace, but he was redeemed by an angel. Abraham is the first proto-martyr of the Jewish people, and he is the first *survivor* as well. As a survivor of child abuse, he abuses others, for instance, selling his wife to Pharaoh (Gen. 12:11-20; Gen. 20) and allowing her to abuse their handmaiden, Hagar (Gen. 16:6) after she has conceived a child with Abraham (Gen. 21:14-21). Finally, in the classic Jewish text known as the *Aqedah* (the binding of Isaac, Gen. 22), the angel stops Abraham from sacrificing his son. Only then can Abraham stop the great chain of pain.

Lerner suggests that the angel was, in reality, Abraham's redemptive voice speaking within him, and this inner struggle of Abraham repeats itself over the generations. Abraham's dueling inner voices—the voice of pain vs. the voice of healing—create two competing voices in Torah. The bad voice of Torah manifests itself in many ways: the Israelites killed Sihon, the king of Heshbon, because he would not let them pass through his territory (Num. 21:23-24); Deuteronomy's various fantasies about the Israelite annihilation of the Canaanite nations; the book of Joshua, which records the conquest of Canaan; King Saul's refusal to kill the cruel Amalekite King Agag, and the prophet Samuel's overt willingness to finish the task (1 Sam. 15:32).

Lerner believes that far too much of contemporary Israeli policy is the bad voice of Torah. "This is not the voice of God. It is the voice of pain and cruelty masquerading as the voice of God." The good voice expresses compassion, justice, freedom, and fights racism, sexism, homophobia, classism, and so on. Whatever Jews do to strengthen the good voice of the tradition, on a private, communal, institutional, international, and cosmic level, helps redeem Judaism, redeem the Jewish people, and heal the world.

Conclusion: New Age Judaism continues

to struggle with the massive issues that face it. How can one construct a Jewish identity that is rooted in the past and yet is creative and individualistic? How can a movement be authentically Jewish and yet be nourished by so many non-Jewish intellectual and theological streams? And will this movement prove to be fertile, replicating itself into the next generation? Overall, it remains to be seen whether New Age Judaism will become a fifth movement within American Jewry. But even absent such an official designation, there is no doubt that it has successfully brought many people back from the peripheries of Jewish connection to a deepened sense of Jewish belonging. Jewish renewal is deeply American, intuitively Jewish, and a classic late twentieth century illustration of an ongoing principle in Jewish history, that all historical Judaisms have borrowed from the majority culture and have wrestled with that culture. In the words of Ecclesiastes, they have known that there is "a time to embrace, and a time to refrain from embracing." New Age Judaism needs to discern exactly what to embrace and what to refrain from embracing. Therein will lie its unique blessing.

Bibliography

Green, Arthur, *Seek My Face, Speak My Name: A Contemporary Jewish Theology* (Northvale, 1992).

Salkin, Jeffrey K., *Putting God on the Guest List: How to Re-Claim the Spiritual Meaning of Your Child's Bar or Bat Mitzvah* (Woodstock, 1996).

Salkin, Jeffrey K., *Being God's Partner: How to Find the Hidden Link between Spirituality and Your Work* (Woodstock, 1994).

Waskow, Arthur, *God Wrestling—Round 2: Ancient Wisdom, Future Paths* (Woodstock, 1996).

Notes

[1] *Quest for God* (New York, 1954), p. 49.
[2] *An Orphan in History: Retrieving a Lost Jewish Legacy* (Garden City, 1982), p. 214.
[3] Note that the Reconstructionist synagogue body is titled "The Federation of Reconstructionist Congregations and *Havurot*."
[4] In Judy Petsonk, *Taking Judaism Personally: Creating a Meaningful Spiritual Live* (New York, 1996), p. 192.
[5] Lawrence A. Hoffman, "The Synagogue, the Havurah, and Liable Communities," in *Response* 38 (1979-1980), p. 37.
[6] Ibid.

[7] Harold Schulweis, "Changing Models of Synagogue and Rabbi's Role," in *CCAR Yearbook* LXXXV (1975), p. 136.
[8] Green's major books are *Tormented Master: The Life and Spiritual Quest of Rabbi Nahman of Bratslav* (Woodstock, 1992); *Jewish Spirituality: From the Bible Through the Middle Ages* (New York, 1988); *Seek My Face, Speak My Name: A Contemporary Jewish Theology* (Northvale, 1992); and, with Barry Holtz, *Your Word is Fire: Hasidic Masters on Contemplative Prayer* (Woodstock, 1993).
[9] Kushner's major books are *The Book of Letters* (Woodstock, 1990); *The Book of Miracles: Jewish Spirituality for Children to Read to Their Parents and Parents to Read to Their Children* (New York, 1987); *God Was In This Place and I, I Did Not Know: Finding Self, Spirituality, and Ultimate Meaning* (Woodstock, 1991); *Honey From The Rock.* (Woodstock, 1990); *The River of Light: Spirituality, Judaism, Consciousness* (Woodstock, 1990); *The Book of Words* (Woodstock, 1993); *Invisible Lines of Connection: Sacred Stories of the Ordinary* (Woodstock, 1996).
[10] See Judith Plaskow, *Standing Again at Sinai: Judaism from a Feminist Perspective* (New York, 1990), p. 165.
[11] See Larry Dossey, *Healing Words: The Power of Prayer and the Practice of Medicine* (San Francisco, 1993).
[12] It is significant to note that, although it was published in 1996 by Schocken, Fox's translation of the Five Books of Moses began in the pages of *Response* almost a quarter century ago—a clear example of how the *havurah* movement has contributed to modern scholarship.
[13] Peter Pitzele, *Our Fathers' Wells: A Personal Encounter with the Myths of Genesis* (San Francisco, 1995).
[14] See, e.g., Norman J. Cohen, *Self, Struggle and Change: Family Conflict Stories in Genesis and Their Healing Insights for Our Lives* (Woodstock, 1995).
[15] Quoted in Rodger Kamenetz, *The Jew in the Lotus* (San Francisco, 1997), p. 49.
[16] Note in this regard a course title from the 1997 Elat Chayyim Catalog: "Judaism and the Mysteries of Death, Grief, and the World Beyond." So, too, Neil Gillman's recent *The Death of Death: Resurrection in Jewish Thought* (Woodstock, 1997).
[17] Note a course title from the 1997 Elat Chayyim brochure: "Menstruation, Birth and Sexuality as Individual States of Sacredness."
[18] Judith Fein, "Beyond the Fringe," in *Hadassah Magazine* 78:3 (November, 1996), p. 19.
[19] Zalman Schachter-Shalomi, "Reverends Needed," in *Sh'ma* 27/158 (February, 1997), p. 5.
[20] Zalman Schachter-Shalomi, *Paradigm Shift* (Northvale, 1993), p. 257.
[21] Eugene B. Borowitz, *Choices in Modern Jewish Thought: A Partisan Guide* (West Orange, 1995), p. 253.

22 Arthur Waskow, "Eco- Kosher!," in *Jerusalem Report*, April 3, 1997, p. 37.

JEFFREY K. SALKIN

JUDAISM, DEFINITION OF: A Judaism is a religion that [1] for its way of life privileges the Pentateuch and finds in the Five Books of Moses the main rules defining the holy way of life, [2] for its social entity identifies the group that embodies faith as the Israel of which the Hebrew Scriptures speak, and [3] for its world view recapitulates the experience of exile and return that the Pentateuch sets forth.

Deriving from God's revelation to Moses at Sinai, Judaism is a monotheistic religion, as are Islam and Christianity, which affirm that same revelation (to Christians, it is the Old Testament; to Moslems, the Tawrat). Distinguished from polytheist and non-monotheistic religions, all three maintain that God is one and unique, transcendent, not subject to the rules of nature but wholly other. Judaism differs from Christianity in recognizing as God's revelation the Hebrew Scriptures but not the New Testament. It differs from Islam in holding Moses to be unique among prophets and in recognizing no prophecy beyond the scriptural record.

The diversity of Judaisms: Differentiating Judaism from Christianity and Islam is easier than defining Judaism, because, the word "Judaism" applies to a variety of closely related religions, past and present. These share a number of traits. For example, all of them revere the Torah (literally: the teaching, that is, "revelation," often mistranslated, "the Law") revealed by God to Moses at Sinai—even if they do so to different degrees. But they also differ among themselves in important ways. So to define Judaism as a unitary and uniform religion, unfolding in a single continuous history from beginning to present, is simply not possible. The world today knows a number of Judaisms, and times past witnessed diversity as well.

We cannot treat as single, unitary, and harmonious the quite diverse versions or systems of Judaism that have flourished in time. The conception people commonly hold is that there is such a thing as a religious tradition that is continuous, has a history, and unfolds in a linear continuity. Those who believe that Judaism is played out over time believe that there is only one Judaism at a time—one Judaism for all time. They do not recognize other Judaisms or a Judaic system. They claim that Judaism develops in incremental steps, yielding at its zenith Judaism as "we" know "it."

But who is that "we"? The answer must always be theological: the "we" of course is that group of Jews that identifies "it"—its particular system—not as a choice but as "Judaism pure and simple." We assume that the Judaism we participate in is both the epitome and the norm. Thus, the Reform rabbi near at hand, the Orthodox *rebbe* of a Hasidic sect in Bnai Braq in the State of Israel, the Chief Rabbi of this town in the State of Israel, the Chief Rabbi of the Judaism(s) of European origin in the State of Israel—each considers his Judaism the true religion.

Indeed, some followers of the Lebovitcher rebbe, a Hasidic group in Brooklyn, believe that their leader is the messiah. No other Judaism concurs. But as their separate assumptions indicate, there is not now and there never has been a single Judaism that (speaking descriptively) dominated to the exclusion of all others. In modern times, we all recognize, there are a variety of Judaisms. Indeed, each Judaism, that is, each system, begins on its own and then—only then—goes back to the received documents in search of texts and proof-texts that can validate its role as "the Judaism."

All Judaisms claim to be Judaism: So all Judaisms see themselves as incremental developments, the final and logical outcome of *The* History of Judaism. And every Judaism traces its origins retrospectively in a canon of relevant historical facts or holy books that it selects to support its reality and that believers imagine constitute an *a priori* justification for their Judaism. All Judaisms therefore testify to humanity's power of creative genius, its ability to make something out of nothing more than hope—or God's intervention. Each creates and defines itself. Every Judaism in modern times alleges that it is the natural, or historical, Judaism, but that allegation always denies the obvious fact. Each Judaism begins in its own time and place and then goes in search of a useful past. Every system serves to suit a purpose, to solve a problem, in our context, to answer through a self-evidently right doctrine a question that none can escape or ignore. Orthodoxy, no less than Reform, takes up fresh positions and presents stunningly original and relevant innovations. It is in the nature of theology to follow this pattern, and from the perspective of the theologian, one can imagine no other.

Dealing with the diversity of Judaisms within Judaism proves somewhat easier if we simplify our terms and speak not of "the religion, Judaism" but of a "Judaic religious system." A religious system comprises three components:

[1] A world-view. This world-view explains who the people it encounters are, where they come from, what they must do. In general, what a Judaism defines as "the Torah" will contain that world-view.
[2] A way of life. This way of life expresses in concrete deeds the religious system's world view. It thereby links the life of the individual to the community. Each Judaism's way of life comprises what it sets forth as the things someone must do. (Thus the Judaism of the dual Torah foregrounds *halakhah*, the law.)
[3] A particular social group. This is the group to whom the world-view and way of life refer. For a Judaic system, obviously, that group is "Israel" or, more specifically, the group it considers to constitute Israel—beginning with itself.

So a Judaic system or (in shorthand) a Judaism, comprises a world-view, a way of life, and a group of Jews who hold the one and live by the other. How do we tell when all three are present and thus define a social group, a Judaism? We look for the emergence of a striking and also distinctive symbol, something that expresses the whole all together and at once, a symbol—whether visual or verbal, gestured, sung, danced, or precipitated in the cultural formation (like a redefinition of the role of woman)—that captures the whole and proclaims its special message: its way of life, its world-view, its conception of Israel. For a Judaism, such a generative symbol may be "Torah," God's

revelation to Moses at Sinai. Or it may be "Israel," God's holy people. Or, of course, the generative symbol may come to concrete expression in the conception of God.

Through the history of the Jewish people, diverse Judaisms have won the allegiance of groups of Jews here and there, each system specifying the things it regards as urgent both in belief and in behavior. Yet all systems in common allege that they represent the true and authentic Judaism, or Torah, or will of God for Israel, and that their devotees *are* Israel. And each Judaism ordinarily situates itself in a single historical line—hence, a linear history—from the entirety of the past. Commonly a Judaism sees itself as the natural outgrowth, the increment of time and change. These traits of historical or even supernatural origin characterize nearly all Judaisms. How then do we distinguish one Judaism from another? We can do so when we identify the principal symbol to which a given system on its own appeals, when we uncover its urgent question, define the answer it considers natural.

The formation of Judaism—Urgent questions, self-evident answers: All Judaisms, wherever formed, whatever type of question they have deemed urgent, must face up to the same persistent social facts that all Jews for all time have confronted. Jews are few in number, divided among themselves on many important questions, participants in different cultural and political systems, yet convinced that they form an ethnic group and that what happens to all of them matters to each one. Now when we identify these facts, we can explain the urgent questions that all Judaisms address. But, however diverse the answers that to different groups of Jews appear to be self-evident, the questions form variations on a single question, the answers upon one uniform pattern. That is why we may see Judaism as one family of closely related religious systems, different from all other families of religious systems.

The Pentateuch and Judaism(s): If we ask what all Judaisms identify in common, we home in on the Pentateuch, or the Five Books of Moses ("the Torah"). The Torah comes "in the beginning," and so explains "where it all began" (or, "where *they* all started"). It is important because, as a matter of fact, it forms a critical component of the holy writings of every Judaism ever known. The key issue is what problem does the Pentateuchal authorship—the people who put it all together as we now have it—find urgent? And can we translate that problem into terms that are socially relevant wherever Jews have lived, from then to now? If we can, then we can account for *any* Judaism and *every* Judaism.

The generative event: Judaism finds its origins in two sequential happenings that together form a single event.

[1] In 586 B.C.E. the Temple of Jerusalem was destroyed. In addition, the political classes of the Jewish state and the persons of economic worth, the craftsmen and artisans—anybody who counted—were taken away to the homeland of the conquering empire. They were settled in Babylonia, where the Tigris and Euphrates rivers come close to one another (a province of antiquity now encompassed by the nation Iraq). And, similarly to mix the populations of the polyglot empire, the Babylonians brought other populations to the land of Israel. These mixed with the Israelites who had not been taken away into exile. It was simply good public policy to form heterogeneous populations. The Babylonians divided and conquered.

[2] Around "three generations later," toward the end of the sixth century B.C.E., the Babylonian empire fell to the Iranian one led by the Persians. The Persian emperor Cyrus, as a matter of public policy, sought to win the loyalty of his diverse empire by restoring to their points of origin populations removed from their homelands by the Babylonians. Consequently, the Jews of Babylonia were given the right to return to the land of Israel. At this time, only very small numbers of them took the opportunity. These Jews made a start at rebuilding the Jerusalem Temple. And some time later, in the middle of the fifth century (ca. 450 B.C.E.), a successor of Cyrus allowed a Jewish high court official, Nehemiah, together with a top bureaucrat and civil servant, Ezra, to go back to Jerusalem and with the support of the state to rebuild the Temple and establish a Jewish government in the surrounding region.

These two events come together as "exile and return" and are framed in terms as mythic and transcendent in their context, as rich and intense in their human messages, as "the Holocaust and Redemption" of contemporary Judaism. But, as a matter of fact, in making that comparison, we turn matters on their head. For the historical events of 586 and 450 are transformed in the Pentateuch's picture of the history and destiny of Israel into that generative myth of exile and return that characterizes every Judaism, then to now.

Event and paradigm—The secret of persistence: In order to grasp its main point, the vital concern that its compilers dealt with, we have first to understand how the Pentateuch took shape. The Five Books of Moses (Genesis, Exodus, Leviticus, Numbers, and Deuteronomy) speak of the creation of the world and God's identification of the children of Abraham, Isaac, and Jacob (who also was called "Israel") as God's people. That people is portrayed as taking shape in Canaan, which was promised to Abraham and his seed and would be called the land of Israel. It is portrayed as then going down to Egypt, being freed of the bondage of Egypt by Moses, who led the people to Sinai, where they were given the Torah by God. The Torah is described as comprising rules that were to govern Israel's holy community and Israelites' service to God in the cult and in the temple that would be built in time to come. It also comprised the message that when Israel kept the covenant, the contract made with God by the patriarchs and given substance at Sinai, God would favor Israel, but when Israel did not comply, then God would punish it.

This thumbnail sketch of the Torah suggests that the narrative is uniform and comes from the time of the events themselves. But as a matter of fact, the Pentateuch is made up of a variety of discrete writings, each marked by its own style and viewpoint. The writings that speak of the caste system—priests, Levites, Israelites—and of the Temple cult, the special tasks and duties and rights of the priests, for instance, are ascribed to a priestly authorship; these writers produced Leviticus and most of Numbers, as well as passages in Exodus that deal with the tabernacle. The entire book of Deuteronomy, attributed to Moses as he looked back and narrated the story of the formation of Israel, represents an altogether different authorship, with its own points of interest. One difference, for instance, is that the priestly writers in Leviticus take for granted that sacrifice to the Lord may take place in any appropriate holy place, while the authorship of Deuteronomy insists that sacrifice may take place only in the place that God will designate, by which it means Jerusalem's Temple. These striking differences alert us to the question, where and when did the whole get put together as we now have it?

The answer to that question is important, because if you read the Torah as one sustained narrative you are receiving the message as a whole, in the composition, proportion, order, and sense that *final* group of authors, editors, and compilers imparted. The Pentateuch as we now have it is the work of an authorship of a particular period. So the message of the Pentateuch, encompassing diverse prior viewpoints and messages to be sure, addresses the social world of the ultimate authorship, which has put everything together to say that one thing. To understand the Pentateuch, therefore, we require one further set of facts: what had happened before the age of formation and conclusion of the Torah, and what problems pressed upon the authorship of the Torah?

The facts are simple. The ancient Israelites settled the land before 1000 B.C.E. and lived there for five centuries. The details of their history, culture, and religion need not detain us, because they do not define the history of Judaism. Only as these details were *reshaped* after a world-shaking event and formed into the Torah (and certain other writings) does the life of Israel from the conquest of the land to that utter break—a caesura in time—matter to Judaism.

Now we may return to the issue addressed by Judaic systems from the Pentateuch onward. Each Judaism responded to events within the pattern laid out by Scripture in the original encounter with the destruction of the Temple in 586 and the return to Jerusalem in the beginning of the fifth century. That event was, to begin with, interpreted as a paradigm of death and resurrection. The destruction of the Temple and the subsequent exile symbolized death, while the return from exile with the rebuilding of Jerusalem and reinstitution of the temple cult constituted resurrection. It answered the question, who is Israel?, by defining the rules that govern what it means to be Israel:

[1] the formation of Israel and its covenant with God, time and again insisting on the holiness of Israel and its separateness from the other peoples;
[2] the conditional possession of the land as the mark of the covenant.

The people has the land not as a given but as a gift. So long as the people accord with the covenant, the land will be theirs, and they will prosper in it. If the people violate the Torah, the conditions of the covenant, they will lose the land. The key chapters are Lev. 26 and Deut. 32. But if you review the narrative of Genesis, with its account of how the people took shape and got the land, you see that the relationship of Israel to the land is the theme throughout. Everything else depends upon it. When you get to the land, you build the temple. When you get to the land, you obey these laws. When you get to the land, you form a godly society and carry out the Torah. So the condition of the people dictates their right to the land, and in losing the land, the people is warned to keep the Torah and the conditions that it sets forth. What that means, of course, is that in recovering the land, the people enjoys a redemption that is conditional: not a given but a gift.

Difference and destiny—resentment provoked and appeased: The Torah stresses the distinctive rules that govern Israel, the unique character of Israel among the nations. If we may translate those points of stress into secular and neutral language, we may see a chronic concern for defining Israel—for discovering (if we may here slip into contemporary political language) "who is a Jew?" In one way or another Israel, the Jewish people, wherever they lived sought means of declaring themselves a group distinct from its neighbors. One reason that the concern with difference persists is that the Jews, wherever located, are simply a very small group surrounded by others that are larger, more powerful and more important. If a small group under diverse circumstances wishes to sustain itself, it does so by underlining the points of difference between itself and everyone else. It will furthermore place a high value on these points of difference, going against the more common impulse of a minority to denigrate points of difference and so identify with the majority.

Throughout the Torah's narrative—in Genesis, where the patriarchs go "home" to Babylonia to obtain their wives; in Leviticus, with its exclusion of the Canaanites, whom "the land vomited out" because of their wickedness; in Deuteronomy, with its command to wipe out some groups and to proscribe marriage with others—the stress is the same: form high walls between Israel and its nearest neighbors. The stress on exclusion of the neighbors from the group, and of the group from the neighbors, in fact runs contrary to the situation of ancient Israel, which, with its unmarked frontiers of culture, participated in the constant giving and receiving among diverse groups characteristic of ancient times.

The persistent stress on differentiation, yielding a preoccupation with self-definition, also contradicts the facts of the matter. In the time of the formation of the Pentateuch, the people Israel was deeply affected by the shifts and changes in social, cultural, and political life and institutions. When, a century and a half after the formation of the Pentateuch under Ezra and Nehemiah, the Greeks under Alexander the Great conquered the entire Middle East (ca. 320 B.C.E.) and incorporated the land of Israel into the international Hellenistic culture, the problem of self-definition came up again. And when the war of independence fought by the Jews under the leadership of the Maccabees (ca. 160 B.C.E.) produced an independent state for a brief period, that state found itself under the government of a court that accommodated itself to the international style of politics and culture. So what was different, what made Israel separate and secure on its land and in its national identity? In that protracted mo-

ment of confusion and change, the heritage of the Five Books of Moses came to closure. And that same situation persisted that had marked the age in which the Pentateuch had delivered its message, answering with self-evident responses the urgent question of the nation's existence. That, briefly stated, constitutes the formative chapter in the history of all Judaisms: exile and return as the history of Judaism.

In the formation of a Judaism, do events define systems, or do systems select events? Now we may address a question important in the study of any religion: where does it all start? Do things happen that people then interpret? Or do people start with a system and then select events to form the structure of the social world that, to begin with, they comprise? The case of Judaism strongly suggests that events come after the fact and that the social requirements of a system dictate the criteria by which people identify the events to which, later on, they attribute the origin of their system.

The principal givens of the Pentateuchal Torah's model, namely, Israel's heightened sense of its own social reality, its status as an elected people standing in a contractual or covenantal relationship with God, inhere in the system. They express *its* logic, not a logic intrinsic in events, even in events selected and reworked; they apply *its* premises, not the data of Israel's common life in either Babylonia or the land of Israel. This is particularly evident in that the system not only selected the events it would deem consequential, but from the perspective of a vast population of Israel—of Jews who remained in the land all along; of exiled Jews who never returned to the land from Babylonia—it spoke of events that simply had never happened.

Consider the Jews who remained in the land after 586, or those who remained in Babylonia after Cyrus's decree permitting the return to Zion. To these people who never left, or who left and never came back, since they each belonged to a distinct generation that knew only one mode of living—in exile or out of it—*there was no alienation, and also, consequently, no reconciliation.* That is, the normative—the "right" and "true"—was not complicated by change. It corresponded to the way things were—and things were only one way. In effect, to be Israel meant to live like any other people, wherever it happened to locate itself.

By contrast, for the exile who returned, exile and return were normative. Further, this doubled normalcy imparted to the exile the critical and definitive position. It marked Israel as special, elect, subject to the rules of the covenant and its stipulations.

But for much of Israel—those who never left, and those who never returned—some system other than the system of the normative alienation constructed by the Judaism of the Torah necessarily appeared self-evident. Obviously, for example, to those who stayed put, the urgent question of exile and return, with its self-evident response of election and covenant, bore slight relevance. Exile did not constitute a problem, so return was not a question worth asking, and such a question could provide no answers worth believing.

Still, there are few more powerful examples of a religious system's creating a society than we find in the operations of the Pentateuch's conception of Israel as it tells people not only the meaning of what had happened but details what had happened, creating for Israelite society a picture of what it must be—and what therefore had been. (We should credit here not only the Pentateuch but also associated post-586 B.C.E. writings.)

Exile and return as the structure of (all) Judaism(s): What happened in 586 and after and the pattern fabricated out of what happened do not correspond. Scripture said, in both the Torah and the prophetic-historical books, that Israel suffered through exile, atoned, attained reconciliation, and renewed the covenant with God (as signified by the return to Zion and the rebuilding of the Temple). The Judaic system of the Torah made normative that experience of alienation and reconciliation. But only a minority of "Israel" in fact had undergone those experiences. Thus the Judaic system expressed by the Five Books of Moses, as well as by some of the prophetic books, did two things. First, it precipitated resentment, a sense of insecurity and unease, by selecting as meaningful events

only a narrow sample of what has happened (exile). Second, it appeased the same resentment by its formula of how to resolve the tensions of events of dislocation and alienation (return). That is, Judaism in its initial model guaranteed its own persistence by creating resentment at how things now are but also providing a remedy for that anger. It is this power both to create a problem and to solve it that made this early Judaism into Judaism's initial, originating model, a paradigm, or pattern, for time to come. Consider:

[1] The paradigm (pattern) began as a paradigm, not as a set of actual events transformed into a normative pattern.
[2] The conclusions generated by the paradigm, it must follow, derived not from reflection on things that happened but from the logic of the paradigm—there alone.
[3] That same paradigm would create expectations that could not be met, and so would renew the resentment encapsulated in the myth of exile. But at the same time it would set the conditions for remission of resentment, so resolving the crisis of exile with the promise of return.
[4] This self-generating, self-renewing paradigm formed that self-fulfilling prophecy that all Judaisms have offered as the generative tension and critical symbolic structure of their systems.

Clearly, the paradigm that has imprinted itself on the history of this period did not emerge from, was not generated by, the events of the age. First came the system, its world-view and way of life—formed whole we know not where or by whom. Then came the selection, by the system, of consequential events, and their patterning into systemic propositions. And finally, at a third stage (of indeterminate length) came the formation and composition of the holy writings that would express the logic of the system and state those "events" that the system would select or invent for its own expression. Since chief among the propositions of the system as the Torah of Moses defined it is the notion of the election of Israel effected in the covenant, we may say that, systemically speaking, Israel—the Israel of the Torah and historical-prophetic books of the sixth and fifth centuries—selected itself.

At the very foundations of the original and generative Judaic paradigm, the account of the events from 586 (when the Israelites were exiled to Babylonia) to ca. 450 (when they had returned to Zion and rebuilt the Temple), we find history systemically selected. That is, by definition it is invented, not described. This would make slight difference—everyone understands the mythopoeic (myth-creating) power of belief—except for one thing. We err if we think that a particular experience, going into exile and returning home again, was subjected to interpretation, that is, was transformed by a religious system into a paradigm of the life of the social group. What really happened is that the particular experience—exile, return—itself happened, to begin with, in the minds and imaginations of the *authors* of Scripture. No one who left Jerusalem in 586 came home in 450, so as a totality, the Pentateuch's narrative was not an experience interpreted, but invented; and once people imagined things in that way rather than in some other, they also found in real, everyday experiences examples of the same experience of exile and return that, to begin with, they were predisposed to find by the lessons of the faith.

But as to its restoration and reconstruction, people clearly differed—the incessant complaints of the post-exilic prophets about the neglected condition of the altar attest to this fact. No one denied that some of Israel had stayed home, some had gone into exile. But as to the exclusion of those who had stayed home and not undergone the normative experience of alienation and return, opinion surely differed, since it was only by force that the dissolution of families was effected.

The same is so for a long list of systemic givens, none of them, as a matter of fact, "given" and self-evident except to those to whom they were self-evident. It follows that it is Scripture—and Scripture alone—that says that what happened was that Israel died and was reborn, was punished through exile and then forgiven, and that therefore—and this is critical—to be *Israel* is in a genealogical sense (since no individual can have lived that long) to have gone into exile and returned to Zion. But the very normative stand-

ing of that experience forms what was at issue in the time of Ezra and Nehemiah, who imposed upon the Judean society of the fifth century the norm of exile and return, that is to say, of death and resurrection.

What emerges therefore is a striking paradox. What happened to people does not correspond to what people were told had happened. The paradigm imparted to events that meaning that was expressed in narrative and law alike; the paradigm, not events, generated meaning. Most people after 586 stayed in Babylonia, but called it exile. A few migrated to Jerusalem, where they found themselves a tiny minority among a larger group of Israelites whose ways they found improper—but told themselves they had come "home," had "returned to Zion." Call it what you will, by their own word they did not find much familiar about this "home" of theirs, since most of the people who lived there followed rules they declared alien. So on both sides, the "exiles" and those who had come "home," the systemic paradigm transformed what was happening into something else.

The persistence of the paradigm— Why all Judaisms rehearse pentateuchal Judaism: But why did the system persist as paradigmatic? Why did its structure prove definitive long after the political facts had shifted dramatically, indeed, had ceased to pertain at all? As long as the Torah continued to be authoritative for Israel, the experience to which it originally constituted a profound and systematic response was recapitulated, age after age. Reading and authoritative exegesis of the original Scripture that preserved and portrayed the system perpetuated it as paradigmatic. Jews repeated: "Your descendants will be aliens living in a land that is not theirs ... but I will punish that nation whose slaves they are, and after that they shall come out with great possessions" (Gen. 15:13-14).

The long-term reason for the persistence of the priests' Judaism as the self-evident explanation of Israel's life derives from two facts. First, the Scriptures themselves retained their authority. But that begs the question. Why should the Scriptures remain authoritative? One answer is that, second, the priests' system in its basic structure addressed, *but also created*, a continuing and chronic social fact of Israel's life.

Of course, so long as the people perceived the world in such a way as to make urgent the question that Scripture framed and answered, Scripture appeared authoritative beyond all need for argument. It enjoyed (self-evidently) the status of God's will revealed to Israel. And the people perceived the world in this way for a very long time. Yet Scripture gained its own authority, too, independent of the circumstance of society. The priests' paradigm therefore imposed itself even in situations in which its fundamental premises hardly pertained. Thus, although when the world imposed upon Jewry questions of a different order, Jews would go in search of more answers and even different answers, a great many Jews continued to envision the world through that original perspective created in the aftermath of destruction and restoration, that is, to see the world as a gift instead of a given, themselves as chosen for a life of special suffering but also of special reward. And the modern Judaism of Holocaust and Redemption—which sees the destruction of the Jews of Europe as a cause for the formation of the Jewish state, the State of Israel—fits quite neatly into the Pentateuchal paradigm. Indeed, it fits more comfortably than other Judaisms of a more classical character, for here we have exile in its most brutal form, mass murder, followed by restoration in its most concrete and real form in all of the history of the Jews, an actual return to the land of Israel and rebuilding of the State of Israel. Ironically, then, although in any age but this one the power of the paradigm might be subject to dispute, in the twentieth century it enjoys the status of self-evident truth. It seems an indisputable fact.

Two reasons account for the perennial power of the priests' system and perspective. One is that the generative tension precipitated by the interpretation of the Jews' life as exile and return, which formed the critical center of the Torah of Moses, persisted. Therefore the urgent question answered by the Torah retained its original character and definition—and the self-evident answer, read in the synagogue every Sabbath morning as well as on Monday and on Thursday—retained its relevance. With the persistent problem renewing, generation after generation, that same resentment, the product of a memory of loss and restoration joined to the recognition, in the here and now, of the danger of a further loss, the priests' authoritative answer would not lose its power to persist and to persuade. But the other reason is that people saw what was not always there, because through the Torah of Moses they were taught to.

The second of the two reasons—the one explaining the long-term power of the Judaic system of the priests to shape the world-view and way of life of the Israel addressed by that Judaism—is the more important: the question answered by the Five Books of Moses persisted at the center of the national life and remained, if chronic, also urgent. The answer provided by the Pentateuch therefore retained its self-evident importance. The question persisted, to be sure, because Scripture kept reminding people to ask that question, to see the world as the world was described, in Scripture's mythic terms, out of the perception of the experience of exile and return. To those troubled by the question of exile and return, that is, the chronic allegation that Israel's group-life did not constitute a given but formed a gift given with conditions and stipulations, the answer enjoyed the status of (mere) fact.

The human condition takes on heightened intensity when God cares what you eat for lunch and will reward you for having a boiled egg. For a small, uncertain people, captured by a vision of distant horizons, behind and ahead, a mere speck on the crowded plain of humanity, such a message bore its powerful and immediate message as a map of meaning. Israel's death and resurrection—as the Torah portrayed matters—therefore left nothing as it had been and changed everything for all time. But the matter—central to the history of Judaism—demands yet another angle of analysis. We have to ask what was at stake and try to penetrate into the deepest layers of the structure to state the issues at their most abstract and general. For the sacred persistence in the end rested on judgments found self-evident in circumstances remote from the original world subject to those judgments.

Why then does the paradigm of exile and return characterize all later Judaisms? Because the problems addressed and solved by the Judaism of the Five Books of Moses remained chronic long after the period of its formation, from the seventh century onward down to its final editing in the time of Ezra and Nehemiah. Since that question would remain a perplexity continuing to trouble Israelites for a long time, it is not surprising that the categorical structure of the Torah's answer to it, so profound and fundamental in its character, should for its part have continued to define systems that would attract and impress people.

The Torah encapsulated, as normative and recurrent, the experience of the loss and recovery of the land and of political sovereignty. Israel because of its (in its mind) amazing experience had attained a self-consciousness that continuous existence in a single place under a long-term government denied others (and had denied Israel before 586). There was nothing given, nothing to be merely celebrated or at least taken for granted in the life of a nation that had ceased to be a nation on its own land and then once more had regained that (once-normal, now abnormal) condition. Judaism took shape as the system that accounted for the death and resurrection of Israel, the Jewish people, and pointed for the source of renewed life toward sanctification now, and salvation at the end of time.

But Judaism as it flourished from antiquity to our own day appeals not only to the Pentateuch or even to the entire Hebrew Scriptures. Its canon encompasses a range of holy books that speak of the Pentateuch as "the written Torah" and call into being a Torah that is not written but formulated and preserved in memory, a part of the one whole Torah revealed by God to Moses at Sinai that is called "the oral Torah." Hence, we know the formative history of Judaism does not close with the Pentateuch. But on that basis we also anticipate that a principal event will be selected by a nascent system to account for its origin, and to that event we shall now turn.

The power of Judaism and its success: The power of all Judaisms to precipitate and then assuage resentment offers a useful point at which to conclude, because it suggests a theory of the nature of religion that can be tested in the study of other religions. Judaism must be classified as a living and highly vital religion, because its adherents frame the world in its terms and form a social entity in its definition.

Why is that the case? The reason is that the generative paradigm, formed in the Torah of Moses or the Pentateuch, asks a question and answers it, creates a problem and solves it, and that question and problem correspond to the social world people perceive or are taught to perceive. That is to say, Jews see their life together not as a given but as a gift, stipulated and subject to conditions. That creates a measure of anxiety or resentment, and these translate that discomfort with being different, which any minority group feels, into spiritual terms. But then, the Torah teaches, the Jews' difference is destiny: holiness is in the here and now, salvation comes at the end of time. So the anxiety or discomfort on account of difference is turned into a good and hopeful feeling: things have deep meaning now, and will matter even more in time to come.

In psychological terms, what "religion recapitulates resentment" means is that a generation that reaches the decision to change (or to accept or to recognize the legitimacy of change) expresses resentment of its immediate setting and therefore its past, its parents, as much as it proposes to commit itself to something better, the future it proposes to manufacture. In political terms, the meaning of "religion recapitulates resentment" is that each Judaism addresses a political problem not taken up by any other and proposes to solve that problem. Accordingly, resentment—whether at home or in the public polity—produces resolution. The two, when joined, form a religious system, in this context, a Judaism.

At issue when we study religion, as in the case of the Judaism, therefore, is how religious ideas relate to the political circumstances of the people who hold those ideas. Religion as a fact of the practical life of politics constitutes a principal force in the shaping of society and imagination alike, while politics for its part profoundly affects the conditions of religious belief and behavior. So one thing we should want to know when we study a religion, as we have seen in this study of Judaism(s), is how stunning shifts in the political circumstance of a religion affect that religion's thought about perennial questions. When we understand the interplay between this world and our aspirations to transcend this world, we know what, within the limits of human knowledge, we can find out about religion.

The power of Judaism forms a striking contrast with the pathos of the Jewish condition. The Jews from the formation of the Pentateuch in 450 B.C.E. to the present day have been scattered, few in number, lacking a clear definition for themselves. They are not joined by a common language, though Hebrew serves in synagogues everywhere. They do not share a common set of ethnic or social or economic or political traits, though Scripture imputes to them a common identity. They assuredly do not derive from a single, unitary history, though through Scripture they contemplate in common a single past and future. So Judaism describes what reality does not present, which is one people, with one land, one language, one faith, one destiny. In the contrast between Judaism's perspective and the Jews' everyday circumstances, we grasp what Judaism accomplishes for the Jews. It is to make them see not what is but what ought to be, to shape their vision so that the facts of the everyday, whatever they are, conform to the structure of the faith, everywhere. Judaism makes Jews see things that no one else sees, and to see them in a way that only they find self-evident.

The Jews, diverse and scattered, called themselves "Israel" and saw themselves as the people to whom God speaks in the Torah. Weak and subordinated, disliked because they were unlike, and some times abused and even murdered because of the difference, they rejoiced in who and what they were and

wanted to continue to be different and to form a distinct and important people in the world. And they always had the choice, except in the Holocaust, to be or not be a Jew, and they always chose to be Israel. Had they not made that decision in every generation, "Israel" the holy people—counterpart to the Church, the mystical body of Christ—as well as the Jews, the this-worldly ethnic group, would have disappeared from humanity.

But the Jews remain a visible presence in many parts of the world, and holy Israel and its Torah—that is, Judaism—endures as a vital religion as well. That simple fact shows the amazing power of what we call Judaism and what Judaism calls "the Torah" to exalt the humble, to strengthen the weak, to give joy to the disappointed and hope to the disheartened, to make ordinary life holy and sacred and significant for people who, in the end, are not much different from everybody else, except that believing has made them so. To take the full measure of the success of Judaism, one has to realize that, when it comes to religion, Jews really do like being Jewish and do not want to be anything else.

JACOB NEUSNER

JUDAISM, HISTORY OF. PART I. ANCIENT ISRAEL. TO 586 B.C.E.: How does the Hebrew Bible as a redacted whole describe the historical emergence and subsequent history of the Israelite people? This is not the picture that scholars have developed of what actually happened in each of the formative ages of Israelite religion, from the patriarchal period and on. It is, rather, the history of the world and of Israel as it was perceived in the period of the composition of the Hebrew Scriptures, sometime after the Babylonian exile, and as it was accepted by believing Jews and non-Jews in the centuries since then.

Historians and textual critics know that this story, beginning with creation and ending with the Babylonian exile, is a composite. It proposes a linear development in which each historical event over thousands of years demarcates a divine plan conceived at the time of creation and revealed already to the earliest Israelite patriarch, Abraham. Similarly, this view anachronistically proposes that what later Israelites did and believed invariably represented the practices transmitted by God to earlier generations as well. Thus Scripture equates later beliefs, practices, and institutions of worship and rule with the history of the people, making no reference to changes and developments that occurred over time. For the Bible understands Israelite religion, like Israelite history, to be static and unalterable, the direct revelation of God, made known through a series of historical events that define what Israelites are to believe and do.

This normative perspective views the Torah as the divine work and word of God. While this God is called by varied names—Lord, Lord God, El Shaddai, for example—the text admits no perception of the existence of different beliefs and attitudes that reflect distinct religious ideologies or characterize different periods. Rather, all beliefs and attitudes, particularly those represented in "The Law," that is, the Pentateuch, are presented as the word of God, transmitted to Moses at Sinai. If humans perceive contradictions, the flaw is not in Scripture—which is perfect, unalterable, and unchanging—but in their misunderstanding of what the text says and means. Thus Scripture depicts the inherent unity of the Torah: all of God's ways set forth for humankind are uniform, just as God, who is the only deity, is one (Deut. 4:35; 6:4). Thus, the history of the Israelite nation attests to God's activity in the world, to the unfolding of a divine plan that begins with the choice of a single man and the determination to create of his family a great and mighty nation worshipping only the one true God.

From creation to the expulsion from Eden: Israelite religion begins before any of the theophanies experienced by the patriarch Jacob/Israel, from whom the Israelites' national name and identity is derived. It begins when God created Adam in his own likeness and image, giving him dominion over the fish, birds, cattle, wild things, and all creeping things (Gen. 1:26-29), thereby making him second only to God himself. God placed Adam in his own garden to till and care for it (Gen. 2:15). But Adam had no helper, the cattle, birds, and wild animals created to be his partners in the Garden turning out not to be suitable for the task (Gen. 2:18-20). Only for this reason does God create Eve as Adam's helpmate (Gen. 2:15-23).

Humankind's original utopian existence in Eden was lost because Adam and Eve disobeyed God. Eve was lured by the serpent, and Adam followed her lead in disobeying God's injunction against eating the fruit of the Tree of Knowledge of Good and Evil (Gen. 3:1-6, 11). This is the basis of their guilt, which is not mitigated by the fact that neither initiated the violation. There is no justification for any violation of God's command. The serpent's guilt is in having enticed Eve to eat and to give the fruit to Adam to eat. The very act of being cursed by God is punishment. The separation from God this punishment represents is emblematized by expulsion from Eden.

While God curses all three participants in the event in the Garden of Eden, the allocation of guilt is not as we would expect. The two active parties, the serpent and Eve, suffer curses limited to their own kind. Serpents must henceforth crawl, eat dust, and be hated by women (Gen. 3:14-15), and women are to bear children in pain and suffering and to desire their husband, who is to be their master (Gen. 3:16). But Adam, who seems to have taken the least active part in the sin, suffers the broadest curse. He is to be the cause of the earth's curse, because of which he must labor for food and win bread by the sweat of his brow. In contrast to the patriarchs, who would be blessed and a cause of blessing, Adam is to be a curse as well as cursed. Moreover, Adam and, after him, all people are to become mortal, subject to death (Gen. 3:17-19).

To both of these ends, God expels *Adam* from the Garden (Gen. 3:22-24). Because Eve is part of (Gen. 1:27) and derived from (2:21-23) her husband, to whom she is to be subject, she too is expelled, thereby also becoming subject to death. So, the hierarchy of male over female is affirmed; the nature of productivity is defined—males bring forth food and bread, females bring forth children—and death becomes the lot of all humankind. Henceforth, humans cannot obtain the immortality offered by eating of the fruit of the Tree of Life or even that offered by remaining in the Garden and doing God's service. The only immortality they now can experience is the continuation of their line through procreation. Oddly, this is exactly what God already had ordained when he commanded them to be fruitful and multiply (Gen. 1:28, renewed for Noah and his sons, Gen. 8:17; 9:1, 7). According to God's mandate, after leaving the Garden, Adam and Eve experience sexuality and bear children who will be the ancestors of all the earth's inhabitants (Gen. 4). By their obedience in fulfilling the injunction to be fruitful and multiply, Adam and Eve obtain immortality, even if it is only via the line descending from Adam's third born son, Seth (Gen. 4:25-5:32).

The Eden narrative establishes perhaps the most basic paradigm of Israelite religion: while punishment consequent on sin is inflicted on human and beast alike and whoever disobeys or even causes others to disobey God's commands will be punished, a return to the path set by God repairs the human-divine relationship. This illustrates and epitomizes God's concern for his creations, a point later illustrated over and over in the example of the Israelites: in almost all circumstances, God redeems those who repent of their sin.

From the expulsion to the flood: The primordial, deathless period ended because of the sin of Adam, Eve, and the serpent. Not only Adam and Eve die, but also, with the exception of Enoch, all of the pre-flood forefathers descended from Adam via Seth, from the expulsion to the period of Noah (Gen. 5). Only Enoch, who walked with and is taken away by God (Gen. 5:24), does not die.

The first murder—a "non-natural" death representing a crime against a person—occurs when Cain, the eldest son of Adam and Eve, kills his brother Abel (Gen. 4:1-8). Because this opposed as well as hindered fulfillment of God's commandment for humankind to be fruitful and multiply, it was a sin of disobedience. More important, because Adam was created in God's likeness and image (Gen. 1:26-27), the murder of a human destroys a likeness and image of God

(Gen. 9:6). This is a disrespectful, insolent, haughty, and presumptuous act of faithlessness toward God. Because God is forgiving, however, he does not retaliate in kind, extracting an eye for an eye. Rather than putting Cain to death, he curses him to "living-death" as a wanderer and a fugitive (Gen. 4:9-12). God responds to Cain's fear that this renders him vulnerable to those who would put him to death, promising vengeance against anyone who does so (Gen. 4:13-15).

Despite this period's acts of disobedience and faithlessness, sin was not ubiquitous prior to the age of Noah (Gen. 5). But as the aggregate of humankind fulfilled God's commandment to be fruitful and multiply, sin increased. Then the sons of the gods' fornicating with the daughters of man (Gen. 6:12, 4) defied God's original mold, whereby each kind was designed after its own kind (Gen. 1:21, 24-25), save for man, designed in God's image and likeness (Gen. 1:26-27). To punish this hubris, God limited the human life span (Gen. 6:3). After this, for the great wickedness, corruptness, and violence that filled the world, and in particular for the evil of humankind, God nearly eliminated people, animals, creeping things, and birds altogether by bringing about a flood (Gen. 6:5-7, 11-13).

The flood and Noah, the righteous hero: God looked with favor on Noah because he remained obedient and faithful (Gen. 6:8-9; 7:1). God's reaction to humankind's commingling of species is an expansion of the parameters that define disobedience and faithlessness, that is, sin or crime. By implication, Noah has not commingled with those of other species, thereby violating the divine ordinance. As had Enoch before him (Gen. 5:24), the righteous Noah "walked with God," that is, was obedient and faithful to him. In Scripture, only a few besides Noah are deemed righteous: David, Abner son of Ner, Amasa son of Jether (relatively so), and Job (who even questions whether mortals can be righteous before God at all; Job 4:17; see also Job 15:14; 25:4). Likewise, only a few besides Noah are called "blameless:" Abraham, David, Job, Daniel. Noah therefore is in a select company, even if, particularly in Psalms,

Proverbs, and the canonical prophets, there are numerous references to "the righteous" in general.

God wishes to save Noah, his family, and a pair of every living creature (Gen. 6:17-20) precisely because the righteous, blameless Noah had won his favor (Gen. 6:8-9; 7:1). Commanding Noah to build an ark into which he will bring his family and the various beasts, creeping things, and birds, God establishes the circumstances whereby his mandate that all living creatures can be fruitful and multiply will be brought to fruition (Gen. 8:17; 9:1, 7). Thus, unlike Adam, who separated himself from God by his actions in the Garden, Noah has joined himself to God by his actions in the world. As he is blameless, he is not held liable for the sin of others. Most importantly, because Noah preserved the integrity of the species, he is more than passively guiltless for not having sinned: he is actively righteous. Consequently, God rewards Noah as if he were a second Adam. God thus makes an unconditional covenant with him, his descendants, and all living creatures (Gen. 9:8) never again to destroy all living things on the earth or the earth itself by means of a flood (Gen. 9:8-11). God establishes his weapon (Hab. 3:9), the rainbow, as a sign to remind him of this covenant (Gen. 6:18, 9:9-17).

Noah is commanded to be fruitful and multiply, as were those in Eden at the time of creation (Gen. 1:28). Noah, who has not sinned, populates the earth (Gen. 9:18-19), just as Adam and Eve, who had sinned, had done after they were sent into the world. Just as God at first gave Adam dominion over all that he created in the Garden (Gen. 1:26, 28), so he blesses Noah, giving him and his descendants dominion over the earth (Gen. 9:2). The only limitations he places on Noah and his descendants are interdictions against eating flesh with lifeblood and shedding human blood (Gen. 9:36). In the latter case, God really interdicts Noah from desecrating man, created in the likeness and image of God (Gen. 1:26-27; 9:6), an act of hubris and a sin. Noah, a second Adam, and his descendants are bounded by religious constraints not imposed on Adam. These retain an un-

changing religious valuation throughout the rest of Israelite history.

Noah's sons, Shem, Ham, and Japheth, bear sons whose families develop into the nations of the earth (Gen. 10), all of whom still speak one language (Gen. 11:1, 6). Some, traveling east, build a city and a tower with its top in the heavens so as to make a name for themselves, fearing they will be scattered all over the earth (Gen. 11:24). God finds this an act of hubris. So he confuses their language and scatters them all over the earth (Gen. 11:6-9).

The historical era—patriarchal religion: A new age, dated by historians to around 2000 B.C.E., begins with the patriarchs Abram/Abraham, his son Isaac, and Isaac's son Jacob/Israel. It is a period of wandering bounded by Abram/Abraham's ascent from Mesopotamia and Jacob/Israel's decent into Egypt. This tradition commences when Terah, father of Abram, Nahor, and Haran (Gen. 11:26), takes Abram, Sarai, and Lot from Ur of the Chaldees. Although their destination is Canaan, they settle in Haran (Gen. 11:31-32). Although Abram/Abraham, Isaac, and Jacob/Israel are characterized as wanderers, promises of the land (stable location) and progeny characterize and underlie the religion they practiced. But the Israelites must never forget that they are descended from a wandering Aramaean (Deut. 26:5) and that their forefathers enjoyed a different relationship with God than for the most part they do.

Although God's name, the Lord, by which people began to call on him at the time of Enosh (Gen. 4:26), was known prior to the flood, God kept it from those who lived after the flood until he revealed it to Moses (Exod. 3:13-15; 6:3; Ezek. 5-7). Still, the patriarchs, like those whom they followed, interacted directly with God, both in person and in dreams and visions. They needed no intercessor, whether prophet, priest, seer, or other mediator. They built their own altars and offered sacrifices on whatever "high place" and at whatever time they deemed appropriate. Alongside this direct interaction with God, the patriarchs' religion is characterized by the unilateral, though not necessarily unconditional, covenants God made with each of them, in which God blessed them and made them a blessing to others, promising them innumerable progeny as well as possession of the land, a perhaps not unexpected feature of the religion of wanderers.

Abram/Abraham: God has a personal relationship with Abram/Abraham, interacting directly with him when granting covenants. He speaks directly to Abram (Gen. 12:13; 13:14-16), and he appears to Abram in a vision (Gen. 15, 17). Although God makes covenants with Abram/Abraham at several different times, he promises the same things in each: Abram/Abraham is to have innumerable progeny and develop into a great nation (Gen. 12:2; 15:5; 17:4-6, 16; 22:16-18). His name shall be a blessing (Gen. 12:2-3). He and his descendants shall possess all the land (Gen. 13:14-18; 15:17-21; 17:8). Notably, after completing the second covenant, God orders Abram to "walk" the length and breadth of the land, thereby establishing ownership of it.

Of all these materials, the covenant of Gen. 15 is the most momentous. Not only does God promise to be Abram's protection, but he also informs him of his progeny's future. Conjoined with this is the covenant of Gen. 17, which offers a different perspective. Offering more than a set of promises, Gen. 17 sets forth what Abram/Abraham and his descendants must do for the covenant of Gen. 15 to be enabled. Under its tenets, they must obediently and faithfully circumcise all males throughout their history. In addition to the prior conditions of faithfulness and obedience to God, circumcision now becomes the *sine qua non* of Israelite religion.

Isaac: Scripture does not give many details about Isaac's relationship to God; only the covenant in which God promises him many descendants is described (Gen. 26:24). Isaac's importance as a patriarch is shown from two different vantage points: his father's action and his reaction. At God's request, Abraham—who does not know that God is only testing him—is willing to sacrifice Isaac on Mt. Moriah (Gen. 22:1-3). And, although Isaac does question his father about the allegedly missing sacrificial victim, he neither protests nor shows distrust or disobedience

to God or his father when his father places him on the pyre and prepares to sacrifice him.

The relationship between Abraham and Isaac is analogous to that between God and Abraham. Just as Isaac does not protest when he (must have) realized that he was the sacrifice, likewise Abraham did not protest when God commanded him to sacrifice his son. Without hesitation or question, Abraham remained faithful and obedient to God (Gen. 22:1-19). Therefore, God makes an unconditional covenant with him, promising him innumerable progeny. He also promises him that his descendants will possess their enemy's cities (Gen. 22:15-18). Interestingly, God's test of Abraham comes to emblematize the precept that the first born belongs to God (see Exod. 13:1-2, 12-13; 34:19-20), though it may be redeemed if a substitute sacrifice is offered. This redemption of the first born becomes a part of Israelite religion together with the establishment of the Passover, to which, as we shall see, it is also related (Exod. 34:20).

Jacob/Israel: Far greater attention is given God's relationship with Jacob than his interactions with Abram/Abraham and Isaac. The focus on the relationship between God and Jacob is ongoing, occurring both before and after the theophany at the river Jabbok that results in Jacob's renaming as Israel. Nevertheless, God's covenants with Jacob are much the same as those he concluded with Abram/Abraham and Isaac. The first is at Bethel, where God commands Jacob to be fruitful and multiply and promises him innumerable descendants. He also promises to be with Jacob, to protect him, and to bring him back to the land he gave to him and his descendants (Gen. 28:13-15; 35:10-12; 48:3-4).

After crossing the river Jabbok, Jacob wrestles with a "man" until daybreak. The victorious Jacob demands a blessing, which is forthwith given. Jacob's adversary declares Jacob's name now to be Israel, for Jacob had successfully vied with God and men (Gen. 32:24-29). But Jacob, now Israel, is not unscathed. Wounded in the hip socket, he and his descendants cease eating the corresponding portion of a butchered animal (Gen. 32:31-32). For Jacob/Israel, the confrontation by the Jabbok is awesome in every sense of the word. It alters both him and the place, leaving each of them renamed (Gen. 32:30). When the patriarch returns to Bethel from Paddan-aram (Gen. 35:9-10), his new name, Israel, is acknowledged by God. Notably, Jacob/Israel's relationship with God is different from Isaac's or even Abram/Abraham's. God and Abram/Abraham had a host/guest relationship and friendship, and the two engaged in social discourse. Jacob's relationship, which lacked social discourse and included neither a host/guest connection nor friendship with God, is characterized by Jacob's courage and physical prowess.

Jacob is faithful to God's command to be fruitful and multiply (Gen. 28:3; 35:11). Leah, whom he was tricked into wedding, and Rachel, whom he wed for love, contend for his love by bearing children. Additionally, each has a concubine who bears Jacob/Israel children on her mistress's behalf. At Paddan-aram, all of Jacob's children except for Benjamin are born (Gen. 29:32-30:24). Leah, the elder but unloved wife, bears the patriarch one daughter, Dinah, and six sons, Reuben, Simeon, Levi, Judah, Issachar, Zebulun. Her concubine, Zilpah, bears him Gad and Asher. Rachel, the younger but beloved wife, bears him Joseph, and her concubine, Bilhah, bears him Dan and Naphtali. The birth to Rachel of one last son is special. He is born in what will be the land of Israel, between Bethel and Ephrathah (Gen. 35:16-19; but see Gen. 35:22-26). Moreover, as soon as Rachel names him Benoni, she died. His father called him Benjamin (Gen. 35:18). Jacob/Israel, his remaining wife, concubines, and sons then settle in Canaan (Gen. 37:1).

The sons of Israel—Joseph and his brothers: The sons of Leah and those of both concubines hate Joseph, because Jacob loves him more than all of them and gives him a special coat. They also hate him because he is has dreams that elevate him above the entire family, which shocks even Jacob/Israel (Gen. 37:3, 45, 8, 11). So the brothers act opportunistically in attempting to kill Joseph. However, Reuben and Judah persuade them instead to sell him to a band of Midianites,

who then sell Joseph to Ishmaelites making their way to Egypt (Gen. 37:18-22, 25-28). The Ishmaelites, in turn, sell Joseph into slavery in Egypt, where he becomes a servant in Potiphar's house (Gen. 39:1).

Joseph rises quickly in Potiphar's service, and God blesses the household because of him (Gen. 39:2-6). But Potiphar's wife, who had become enamored of Joseph, accuses him of attempted rape after he spurns her advances; consequently, Potiphar casts Joseph into prison (Gen. 39:6-20). There Joseph the dreamer—one of the very things that had caused his brothers to hate him and had shocked even his father—becomes renowned as an interpreter of dreams. When Pharaoh has troubling dreams (Gen. 40), which neither his magicians nor wise men can interpret (Gen. 41:8), he sends for Joseph, who is recommended to him (Gen. 41:1-36). Pharaoh positions Joseph to carry out what he had interpreted and God had planned, establishing Joseph as lord over all Egypt, second only to Pharaoh himself (41:39-45).

Since Pharaoh received divine knowledge (Gen. 41:25-32), it is not surprising that he accepts Joseph's interpretation of the dreams. Indeed, when Pharaoh's actions indicate that he understands that his dreams have been correctly interpreted, Joseph properly attributes to God rather than to himself this as well as the situation foretold in the dream (Gen. 41:16, 32). When Pharaoh now puts Joseph in charge of saving Egypt from the forthcoming famine, Joseph does what is necessary. He gathers the food produced in Egypt during the coming seven good years, storing huge quantities of grain (Gen. 41:46-49) in accordance with God's plan for Israel.

The subsequent seven years of famine bring people from everywhere to Egypt to buy grain (Gen. 41:57). To this end, Jacob sends the ten sons of Leah and the concubines to Egypt and, in particular, to the lord of Egypt, whom neither he nor his sons know to be Joseph (Gen. 42:1-5). When Joseph sells grain to his brothers, who do not recognize him, he alone knows how long the famine will last. He demands that the brothers bring Benjamin with them if they return to Egypt for yet more grain, and he secretly returns their silver to them, thereby setting conditions in which Jacob/Israel, Benjamin, and in fact the entire family of Israel will descend to Egypt to survive (Gen. 42:6-28). The brothers recognize what has happened as of God's devising (Gen. 42:2-8), but they do not yet realize that it is part of God's larger plan for Israel's salvation.

After using up the grain, Jacob/Israel must again send his sons to Egypt, this time with Benjamin (Gen. 43:1-15). In Egypt, Joseph again tests his brothers (Gen. 44) before revealing himself to them (Gen. 45:1-5). The brothers, properly repentant of their sin, are dispatched to bring Jacob and his entire household to Egypt (Gen. 45:16-28), thereby completing God's plan. Now, at the very end of the saga, the brothers see that God caused everything that happened. Now they recognize Joseph as a visionary and seer whom God chose as an instrument for Israel's ultimate salvation and see even their own actions as part of God's plan.

The salvation paradigm: In converse order, just as Terah, the father, began his son Abram's ascent into the land that ultimately is to be the land of salvation, Joseph, the son, began the descent of his father, Israel, into Egypt, which is to become the land of oppression. As the patriarchs are characterized by their relationship to the land and to the oppression of the Israelites, all Israel shall later be characterized by its relationship to the land and to its bearing on God's salvation of them. As Abram/Abraham enters and takes possession of the land, Isaac dwells in it, and Jacob/Israel departs from it, the Israelites shall enter and take possession of the land, they shall dwell in it, and they too shall depart from it. But, even in exile, Israel shall have the expectation of being again saved by God and restored to the promised land. So, because of the pledges made to the patriarchs as well as the paradigms regarding their relationship to the land, it too becomes one of the foci of Israelite religion.

The descent of Jacob/Israel and all that is his into Egypt, in around 1600 B.C.E., is necessary because God determined to make Israel a great nation in Egypt (Gen. 46:2-3). However, it is also in Egypt that Israel's compliance with God's command to be fruitful and multiply, to become a great nation, places the people in danger (Gen. 47:27; Exod. 1:7). So, the very descent into Egypt sets the circumstances whereby God will rescue the Israelites and lead them to the land promised to Abraham, Isaac, and Jacob. This rescue becomes paradigmatic for all salvation experiences henceforth. It is epitomized by God's granting Israel the Great Covenant (Exod. 19:2b-Num. 10:11), whereby he is their sole God and they his people. Because Israel's status is now limited and demoted to that of God's vassal, the expectation of direct interaction with God is restricted. Moses, Joshua, and yet others such as Samuel must henceforth act as intermediaries between God and Israel. Moreover, when God has not chosen some individual as an intermediary, the priests are to serve in that capacity.

The Mosaic period: This salvation paradigm requires the Israelites to fall into bondage so that God can save them. When an Egyptian Pharaoh who did not know Joseph, that is, one who was unaware of Joseph's role in saving Egypt, takes power, he instigates harsh measures to prevent the Israelites from growing greater, oddly advancing the divine plan exactly by preventing that which God ultimately desires. One of the measures specifies that male Israelites be put to death (Exod. 1). Therefore, when the Israelite child who Pharaoh's daughter will call Moses is born, his mother hides him until he is three months old and then sets him adrift in a basket on the Nile. Pharaoh's daughter rescues him, names him, and rears him as an Egyptian noble, saving him from death (Exod. 2:1-10).

When Moses grows up, he experiences a personal salvation, which allows him to be the covenant mediator in Israel's great salvation experience. After killing an Egyptian soldier, he ascends from Egypt to Midian (Exod. 2:11-15) and thence to Sinai/Horeb, where he experiences God (Exod. 3:1-4:17, 19). At God's command, Moses goes back to Egypt to save the Israelites (Exod. 4:18-31). Ultimately, in about 1280 B.C.E. according to historians, he leads them out of Egypt, across the Sea of Reeds, and, by a circuitous route, to Sinai/Horeb, where God grants them the Great Covenant. After wandering for many years in the desert, Moses leads the people up to, but not into, the land.

In sending Moses back to Egypt, God shows himself faithful to his covenants with Abraham, Isaac, and Jacob, in which he promised them descendants and the land (Exod. 6:2-8). Nevertheless, God determines that salvation shall not be easy. He hardens Pharaoh's heart, on the one side, and makes Moses' signs and wonders that much the more effective, on the other. Thus God makes the Israelites understand that he himself, using Moses, forced Pharaoh to release them from bondage and allow them to leave Egypt (Exod. 7-11; 12:28-36).

Just before the last of ten plagues brought by God against Egypt, the Israelites celebrate the first Passover (Exod. 12:1-28; 13:3-10; 23:14-15; 34:18, 23; Num. 9:1-14; Deut. 16:1-8). This feast henceforth is kept by all generations of Israelites, who also are to see themselves as personally redeemed from Egyptian bondage. After the midnight slaying of the firstborn of all living things in Egypt save those of the Israelites (Exod. 12:29-30), who are saved by blood placed on the doorposts and lintels of the houses in which the Passover is celebrated (Exod. 12:7, 13), God institutes the Israelite practice of "dedication" of the firstborn (Exod. 13:1-2, 11-13), already emblematized in the binding of Isaac. Because each firstborn properly belongs to God (see also Num. 3:13; 8:17), the dedication of the firstborn is relevant to the redemption from slavery in Egypt for all generations (Exod. 13:14-16). The Passover, thereafter, is a reminder that the firstborn are God's to give or to take.

The Exodus and wandering: Freed from bondage, Moses and the people follow a messenger of God who leads them into the desert, traveling in a pillar of cloud. After they cross the Reed Sea, enter the Wilderness of Shur, and reach Marah, God grants them a conditional covenant (Exod. 15:22-26). God will protect them if they adhere to him, do what is right in his eyes, and obey his commands and statutes (Exod. 15:26), some of which are later expounded in the Great

Covenant, by which Israel is henceforth to be governed (Exod. 19:2b-Num. 10:11).

At various stations in their journey, the Israelites complain to Moses about their circumstances (Exod. 16:2-3; 17:1-4). This discontent, expressing faithlessness and lack of trust in God, is manifest even in the midst of the miracle of redemption. This failure of faith before the conclusion of the Great Covenant (Exod. 19:2b-Num. 10:11; Deut. 1:19-33; 4:10-20; 5:2-32) may be somewhat comprehensible, since the Israelites have not yet formally accepted God. But the continuation of this discontent during the covenant ceremony itself (Exod. 32; Deut. 9:6-29) and afterwards (Num. 11; 13; 14:1-45; Deut. 1:34-40; 9:22-24) is hardly likely to elicit understanding from Moses or God. Even while Moses is learning the terms of the Great Covenant, the Israelites are making and worshipping a golden bull-calf (Exod. 32:1-6; see also Exod. 32:19-24; Deut. 9:12-16). Moses placates God by reminding him how the Egyptians would view the destruction of the nation, and, more important, by reminding him of the covenants with Abraham, Isaac, and Israel (Exod. 32:11-13).

Given the sanctity of the land and its relationship to God, it is eminently appropriate that there should be a covenant renewal or even a new covenant struck just before the Israelites are to cross the Jordan (Deut. 4-29). This occurs at Pisgah in Moab, a mount from which Moses, whose sin prevents him from entering the land, can view it. The Israelites must truly be God's people before they can come into the land (Deut. 5:31-6:9), and they must remain God's people thereafter, continuing to show faith by observing his statutes, commandments, ordinances, etc. If they should henceforth fail in faith and obedience, they will be punished. But, even in setting forth these circumstances, God continues to offer hope of salvation (Lev. 26:40-45; Deut. 4:29-31; 30:1-10).

The Great Covenant: The most meaningful covenant in Israelite religion is given by God at Sinai/Horeb and either renewed or supplemented by a new covenant at Pisgah (Exod. 34:27; Deut. 29:14). This covenant, which God as suzerain gives to his people as vassals, is conditional, with its terms and conditions set by God. The Israelites accept it (see esp. Exod. 20:18-21) in the third month after the Exodus (Exod. 19:1-2), first acknowledging the covenant as thus far expressed (Exod. 19:8) and then accepting it totally (Exod. 24:3, 7). They thus become God's special possession, his holy nation, and a priestly kingdom (Exod. 19:5-6).

The Great Covenant's mandatory tenets are announced (Deut. 4:12-13). If the Israelites fulfill their obligations, God will protect them from the inhabitants of the land, and he will make them fruitful so that they may take possession of the land (Exod. 23, esp. 23:20-33; Lev. 26:9). But the covenant is clear that fulfillment of its promises, indeed, its reaffirmation in the land, depends on the Israelites' faithfulness and adherence to its stipulations (Lev. 26). Consequently, when they are in the valley opposite Bethpeor, Moses reiterates tenets of the Sinai/Horeb covenant and, additionally, lays down the statutes and laws that the Israelites must observe in the land itself (Lev. 26; Deut. 48; 12:1-26:15). These statutes and laws are preconditions for entering and dwelling in the land. The Israelites are to start observing them right away (Deut. 8:1; 11:8-9).

The tenets of this covenant, some of which are imparted to the Israelites at different times during the covenant conclusion, include the entire basic format of Israelite religious law and practice. They are specifically set forth in the Decalogue (Exod. 20:2-17; Deut. 4:13; 5:6-21) and in the collection of laws now called the Book of the Covenant (Exod. 20:22-23:33), as well as in the description of the Tabernacle (a portable sanctuary; Exod. 25:8-31:17), the institution of the Aaronide priesthood and all pertaining to it (Exod. 27:21-29:46; 40:12-15), and the various matters and appurtenances necessary for the cult (Exod. 30; Deut. 12:10-18, 26-27).

Speaking from the Tent of Meeting, God gives Moses additional rules concerning the offerings and sacrifices the Israelites are henceforth to make (Lev. 1-7:38). Now the nature of sacrifice is changed: individuals no longer may prepare and offer their own sacrifices on high places as they had done dur-

ing the patriarchal era. God specifies Sabbath observance as an eternal covenant (Exod. 31:12-17), the stipulation of which is included in the Great Covenant. He also specifies the pilgrimage festivals that all Israel is to observe (Deut. 16:1-17). The covenant laws are repeated in Deuteronomy, where they appear in a more compressed format than in the Tetrateuch.

Priestly matters: Henceforth, there will be officials (priests) in charge of sacrifice and other cultic matters (Num. 18) related to the newly delineated movable sanctuary (the Tabernacle and/or Tent of Meeting) and the Ark of the Covenant/Ark of Testimony (Num. 4:1-4, Deut. 10:8), among other things. The first priests, Aaron and his sons, were ordained by Moses (Lev. 8) according to God's command. Next, God himself delineates the various priestly matters, telling Moses and Aaron to inform the Israelites of the dietary laws—including which animals may and may not be eaten (Lev. 11)—and other rules of ritual purity and purification (Lev. 12-16)—such as the "Holiness Code" (Lev. 17:1-26:46)—and the rules regarding vows (Lev. 27).

Neither the priesthood nor the laws, statutes, commandments, and ordinances were necessary before the Great Covenant. All of this emerges as part of the Great Covenant, when it becomes basic to Israel's faithfulness and obedience to God. Moreover, God now commands Moses to appoint the Levites to serve and minister to Aaron (Num. 3:5-10), as a substitute for the consecrated firstborn in Israel (Num. 3:11-13, 44). This appointment recognizes the Levites' response to Moses' rallying call and their consequent execution of Israelites for the sin of the golden calf (Exod. 32:26-29; Deut. 10:8-9). They accordingly are given charge of carrying the Ark of the Covenant that leads the Israelites in the desert and in battle (Num. 10:33-36; Josh. 6) and are assigned as assistants to Aaron and his sons (Num. 3:9), to attend on and minister to God (1 Chr. 23:28, 32).

Also at Sinai, God gives the Israelites commandments that are not included in the other codes, regarding crimes against persons (Num. 5:5-31), the requirements for self-

Map 2. The Tribes of Israel in Canaan.

Map 3. The United Kingdom of Israel Under David and Solomon.

dedication as a Nazarite (Num. 6:1-21), and the blessing Aaron and his sons are to use in blessing the Israelites (Num. 6:22-27), although after Aaron's death, the Levites are to bless in God's name. The duties of the priestly orders do not stop with the establishment of God's permanent sanctuaries. The priestly orders will later function in Israelite temples: at Shiloh (1 Sam. 2:15; 2:27-36) and especially at Solomon's Temple at Jerusalem (1 Kgs. 6:14-7:51; 1 Chr. 16:39-42; 2 Chr. 26:17-19).

The priests are to take care of everything cultic, including the cultic aspects of punishing those who disobey the covenant's tenets. This becomes apparent when, after leaving Sinai, the people complain and rebel against God (Num. 11:1-34). Only after Israel has become a holy nation by ratifying the covenant do purification rights and the priests who are to administer them become necessary. So God establishes Aaronide and Levitical rights (Num. 18). Moreover, he establishes the statute regarding the red heifer and its role in purification (Num. 19).

The rights and role of the priesthood are further clarified and amplified precisely because, at Shittim, the Israelites violate the covenant's tenets by having intercourse with Moabite women—perhaps the human equivalent of commingling species—sacrificing to their gods, and worshipping the Baal of Peor (Num. 25:1-6). This blemishes the purity implicit in the acceptance of the covenant. Because Eleazar's son and his descendants responded appropriately to this great act of disobedience, God grants them the priesthood for all time (Num. 25:7-15).

The death of Moses: Unlike Abram/ Abraham, Isaac, and Jacob/Israel, Moses and Aaron sin: they are not totally obedient to God at the waters of Meribah (Num. 20; 27:14; Deut. 32:48-52). Additionally, Moses is blamed for the Israelites' sins (Deut. 4:21). Their punishment is that neither enters the land. Aaron dies on Mt. Hor (Num. 22:28). And, after fulfilling his charge of commissioning Joshua to lead the people in his place (Num. 27:15-23) and after seeing the land (Num. 27:12-15), Moses dies in Moabite country. He is buried in some unknown place

in a valley opposite Bethpeor (Deut. 34:5-6). Although Moses' burial site is unknown, he himself will be remembered for all time, since the Israelites must always remember the salvation event God worked through him (Deut. 34:10-12).

The covenant with Joshua: After Moses ordains his successor Joshua by laying his hands on him and Joshua becomes filled with wisdom (Deut. 31:7-8, 14-15, 23; 34:9), God directs Joshua to prepare to cross the Jordan to enter the land he is giving to the Israelites in accordance with his promise to Moses (Josh. 1:1-6). Joshua operates with greater restrictions than were imposed on his predecessors. Since the law now is established in its entirety, Joshua must be faithful and obedient in observing it, reflecting on it day and night, if he is to fulfill his charge (Josh. 1:7-9). God's own actions illustrate Israel's new status. In entering the land, God no longer precedes the Israelites in a pillar of smoke. Rather, the Lord of the Israelites, enthroned on the Ark of the Covenant, leads the people into the promised land (Josh. 3:3-5). So, under the new covenanted circumstances, just as they did at Sinai/Horeb, the Israelites must consecrate themselves for the miracle that is to follow (Josh. 3:5).

The crossing of the Jordan is a covenant and salvation event, analogous to the Exodus from Egypt and crossing of the Reed Sea. It is in tandem with, and consequent on, the salvation event of the Great Covenant, by which the Israelites are transformed from slaves who had not yet accepted God into free individuals who are God's chosen people. Only now, Israel is transformed from a nation to whom the land has been promised into a nation actually taking possession of the land. The crossing of the Jordan, with the setting up of the twelve stones at Gilgal, is of the greatest importance (Josh. 3-4). As an act of faithfulness, the people are commanded to tell their descendants, and their descendants to tell their descendants, the significance of the stones (Josh. 4:19-24). This ritual enactment is completed with circumcision and the celebration of the Passover (Josh. 5:1-12), the same Passover that is to be celebrated throughout the generations of

Israelites because of the miracle of salvation God worked on their behalf.

The religious basis of the conquest: The conquest, dated to the period 1250-1200 B.C.E., represents the fulfillment of the covenants given to Abraham, Isaac, and Jacob, that their descendants would inherit the land. However, this is itself conditional and predicated on the acceptance of the terms of the Great Covenant. Only after they have accepted God as their Lord and God has accepted Israel as his people can the Israelites come into possession of the land promised the patriarchs. The conquest, then, is neither of human design nor executable solely by Israelite power. Rather, it is effected by God's hand through his chosen leader, Joshua.

Because the Israelites are under covenantal warrant and bound by law, they must act according to God's wishes; so, the conquest of the land progresses in tandem with Israel's obedience. Where Israel disobeys, it suffers defeat, and the people must be punished and reconsecrated (Josh. 7). However, after victory, the Israelites show their faithfulness and obedience by worshipping God as prescribed by Mosaic law. Accordingly, Joshua does what is necessary and appropriate: he builds an altar on Mt. Ebal without using iron tools; he makes the prescribed offerings; and he engraves the law of Moses on stone blocks (Josh. 8:30-33). Victory has religious benefits and rewards as well as obligations. Hence, the Great Covenant is renewed, reaffirmed, and reconcluded with the ritual arrangement of the people on one side and the Levites on the other side of the Ark of the Covenant and the ritual pronouncement of the blessings and curses (Josh. 8:30-35). Because of their compliance with the covenant, the Israelites, under Joshua's leadership, take the whole land that God promised to the patriarchs as well as to the Israelites themselves. Then, the land has peace (Josh. 11:23).

After the land is subdued, a great assembly is held at Shiloh. The Tent of Meeting is established there and the distribution of the land completed (Josh. 18-22). The Israelites must remember that God acted for their sake and fought for them. Because everything they had accomplished must be attributed to him

(Josh. 23:1-5), they must observe and do everything in Moses' law. In particular, they must be faithful to God, neither disobeying him (Josh. 23:6-8) nor violating his covenant. Failure to comply will be punished by loss of the land (Josh. 23:11-13, 16). So, the Great Covenant is reaffirmed at Shechem (Josh. 24:1-28), and Joseph's bones are buried (Josh. 24:32). Joshua dies and is buried in the hill country of Ephraim (Josh. 24:29-30), as is Eleazar, Aaron's son (Josh. 24:33). Unlike Moses and Aaron, Joshua and Eleazar are buried in the land. The fidelity of the Israelites to God during Joshua's leadership and that of the elders who survive him is noted in conjunction with these burials (Josh. 24:31).

From the kingship of God to the kingship of Saul and David: Once in the land, the Israelites' relationship to God deteriorates. During the time of the Judges, believed to cover the period 1200-1020 B.C.E., each man acts as he thinks best. Israelite actions are epitomized by the paradigm that henceforth characterizes Israelite history: the people sin, God punishes them by sending an oppressor, the people cry out to God in repentance, God sends a redeemer, and once again the people sin. This is particularly relevant to the Israelites' virtually treasonous actions toward God during the time of Samuel, the last of the Judges.

Samuel: The birth of Samuel heralds a new facet of Israelite religion. Dedicated as a Nazarite by his pious mother, Hannah (1 Sam. 1:11, 28), he is to serve God as a faithful priest (1 Sam. 2:11, 18, 21, 26, 35) and be in God's presence all his life (1 Sam. 1:22, 28, 2:21). Samuel is a visionary with whom God speaks in dreams (1 Sam. 3), and, after receiving his call, he becomes the preeminent priest, seer, and judge in Israel, going on a regular circuit to Bethel, Gilgal, and Mizpah (1 Sam. 7). In the aftermath of the sins of Eli's sons (1 Sam. 2:11-17, 22-34), Samuel supplants the house of Eli the priest (1 Sam. 2:35-36) at the temple at Shiloh.

Saul: When the aged Samuel's sons do not follow in his ways (1 Sam. 8:1-3), the Israelite elders ask him to appoint a king to rule over them (1 Sam. 8:4-5). Samuel holds that the most important religious precept is faith and obedience to God (1 Sam. 12:6-15), so that, in demanding a king, the Israelites sin (1 Sam. 12:16-17). Still, he follows God's injunction and complies with the people's wishes (1 Sam. 8:6-9, 22). Oddly, God now deems the desire for a king to be a slight, a form of hubris analogous to the Israelites' lack of faith when God brought them out of Egypt (1 Sam. 8:4-9, 10:17-19). By demanding a king such as rules other nations, the people reject the kingship of God, clearly at least a partial abrogation of the Great Covenant, which depicts God as the people's only sovereign.

In an act God may have intended to fail, Samuel chooses Saul (1 Sam. 9:15-17) to be king over Israel, following God's instructions and, in a secret ceremony, pouring anointing oil over his head (1 Sam. 10:1). Later, by a ruse, God and Samuel together bring Saul to the attention of the Israelites, declaring him king without the people's knowing that he had already been anointed (1 Sam. 10:20-24). Samuel induces the people to renew the kingship again, at Gilgal, and, in 1020 B.C.E., Saul is made king by and in the presence of the Israelites (1 Sam. 11:14-15). But, for two reasons, Saul's kingship is doomed: it represents the people's denial of God's kingship, and Saul himself cannot keep God's commandments (1 Sam. 13:8-15; 15:10-31).

David: Well before the death of Saul, whom God found unsatisfactory, God commands Samuel to anoint David king (1 Sam. 16). In about 1000 B.C.E., Saul thus is supplanted by David (2 Sam. 3:9), who is first anointed king of Judah by the Judahites in Hebron (2 Sam. 2:1-4), ruling Judah for seven years and six months (2 Sam. 5:5). Then he is made king of all Judah and Israel by the Israelite elders who come to Hebron for that purpose (2 Sam. 5:1-5). David's subsequent taking of Jerusalem, from whence he ruled Israel and Judah for thirty-three years (2 Sam. 5:5), alters the focus of Israelite religion, insofar as the city becomes a permanent locale for the Ark of the Covenant.

Because of his great love for David (2 Sam. 22:51; Ps. 18:50), God promises that a descendent of his (and of his son Solomon) will always sit on the throne (2 Sam. 7:12-16;

1 Kgs. 2:45; 1 Chr. 17:10-15; 22:10; Is. 16:5; Jer. 33:17; Ps. 89:4), provided his line remains faithful to God (1 Kgs. 2:3-4; 8:25-26; 9:3-9; 1 Chr. 28:5-7; 2 Chr. 6:16-17; 7:18; Jer. 17:24-25; 22:3-6; 33:19-22). He also promises God's peace for him and his descendants (1 Kgs. 2:33) and that, because of David's line, which will continue forever, he will not to destroy Judah (2 Kgs. 8:19; 2 Chr. 21:7). These promises, comprising a David and Zion (Jerusalem) theology, are a cornerstone of Israelite faith but do not supersede the basic theological precepts based on the patriarchal practices, the Great Covenant, and the entire desert experience. Rather, the promises of possession of the throne in return for faithfulness are analogous to the earlier covenantal promises of possession of the land, which were not fulfilled until the Israelites ratified the Great Covenant.

Still, David sins, responding to his desire for Bathsheba, the wife of Uriah the Hittite, by conspiring to bring about Uriah's death (2 Sam. 11). Consequently, their firstborn child dies, and David's family is never to have peace (2 Sam. 11:26-12:19). They have another child, Solomon, who inherits the throne even though he is not first in succession (1 Kgs. 1:28-48). Those who had a prior claim, Amnon and Absalom, die because of their own sins (2 Sam. 13-19:4); Adonijah, for his part, who thought to take the throne without David's consent (1 Kgs. 1:3-26), dies because he attempts to take it treacherously from Solomon (1 Kgs. 2:13-25). David thus makes Solomon king (1 Kgs. 1:8) in accordance with God's wishes and Bathsheba's plotting.

Solomon: Reigning from 961-922 B.C.E., Solomon was a just and righteous king who honored God and enriched and extended the kingdom. Because of his righteousness and because of God's promise to David (2 Sam. 7:13; 1 Chr. 17:11-13), he was granted the privilege of building God's Temple in Jerusalem. The court of Solomon was a place of splendor, and God's Temple was built with the best and most costly materials from inside and outside of the kingdom. The Temple became a permanent home for the Ark of the Covenant, the Throne of God.

Israel and Judah: When Solomon died in 922 B.C.E., the people of the northern kingdom, Israel, were not willing to accept rule by the Davidic line and separated themselves from Judah and Jerusalem (1 Kgs. 12:1-24). From this time onward, two kingdoms of Israelites stood: Israel, in the north, and Judah, in the south. But the rulers and aristocracy of Israel, which no longer had a Davidic king, repeatedly sinned. They worshipped Baal and other gods of the nations, built temples in which they publicly followed their sinful faith, dishonored God's prophets and the men of God, and oppressed the poor. Such sinfulness and apostasy increased until, in 722 B.C.E., the nation fell (2 Kgs. 17), the result of God's punishment of the people, accomplished at the hand of Assyria (fig. 65). Most of the people were taken into Assyrian captivity, and their Israelite identity was lost; only some few escaped to Judah.

Even though Davidic kings remained on the throne of Judah, only a few truly worshipped God. For the most part, the rulers and aristocracy of Judah sinned just as had the leaders in the north. But even as their sinfulness and apostasy increased, three good kings arose: Joash (2 Kgs. 12:1-3), who, however, failed to remove the foreign shrines; Hezekiah (2 Kgs. 18-20); and Josiah (2 Kgs. 22:1-23:30). The latter, on finding a lost book of Moses' law in 622 B.C.E., attempted to restore the proper form of God's worship. Unfortunately, the people had already fallen into such a state of sinfulness that it was not possible for Judah to be saved. The Babylonians conquered Judah and Jerusalem in 597 B.C.E., taking into exile the Temple's treasures and all but the very poor (2 Kgs. 24; 2 Chr. 36:6-10). In 586 B.C.E., they burned the Temple, taking the rest of the leaders and aristocracy into exile in Babylonia (2 Kgs. 25; 2 Chr. 36:17-21; Jer. 21:3-7; 44:2-6; Lam. 2), an act whereby God too allowed himself to be brought into captivity so as to punish his sinful people.

Conclusion: God created Adam to till the Garden of Eden, but, because of Adam's and Eve's sin, expelled them from it. But even after expelling them from the garden, God did not reject Adam and Eve, but watched over them and their posterity as they procreated in accordance with God's command to be fruitful and multiply.

God made covenants with specific descendents of Adam and Eve: God never again would destroy the earth by means of a flood (Noah); they would have progeny too numerous to count (Noah, Abraham, Isaac, and Jacob); they and/or their progeny would inherit the land (Noah, Abraham, Isaac, and Jacob). After bringing about the Exodus of the Israelites from Egypt, God made a covenant with the Israelites at Sinai/Horeb. He became their God, and they became his people, now possessing a divinely given law by which the nation would henceforth be governed. At this time, God also established the Aaronic priesthood (fig. 66).

According to the biblical narrative, everything that happened to the Israelites throughout the generations occurred because God willed it to happen. Israelite history thus is comprised of a chain of events devised by God's will and determination of what is to be. Just as fulfillment of God's commandments is part of this chain of events, so is Israel's failure to fulfill them: that is, Israel's sin and consequent punishment are as much of God's devising as is the goodness and righteousness toward him practiced by some Israelites. Sin, an ever-present problem, thus is an undesirable, but expected, aspect of the relationship between the people and God. It is a human failing, the consequences of which can be corrected through acts of atonement: Israel is punished because of sin, viewed inevitably as some type of apostasy; but God always offers the possibility of redemption, granted when the people renounce their apostasy and call to God for help.

One of the gravest acts of apostasy is Israel's desire for a king, which God construes as a rejection of himself as king. Nevertheless, God agrees to the anointing of a human king over Israel and uses Samuel as king maker. Despite this divine sanction, appointment of a king hastens Israel's fall into apostasy, manifest in the division of the United Monarchy after Solomon's death and then in the fall of the Northern Kingdom, Israel, in 722 B.C.E. Despite Josiah's reform,

Judah too is doomed by apostasy, falling to the Babylonians in 597 B.C.E, with the Temple being destroyed in 586 B.C.E. God could not be defeated by Babylonian idols but actually caused the Temple's destruction and Judahites' exile, punishments for the people's sins against him. God thus controls all nations, using them to advance the divine purpose, and assuring that he has the power, ultimately, to hear the people's cry and send a redeemer to free them from the captivity God himself had devised.

SARA MANDELL

JUDAISM, HISTORY OF, PART II: SECOND TEMPLE TIMES (586 B.C.E.-70 C.E.): A complex entity, the religion of the Jews in the Second Temple period encompassed strands that, with the passage of time, evolved and developed in their own separate ways. Not only were these individual elements important but also the way they interacted with and influenced one another. As metaphors for this phenomenon, we might think of the trajectories of bodies in motion or currents of flowing water. But whatever analogy we use, it must express the important aspect of motion. This religion was not a static phenomenon that can be described and systematized as such; on the contrary, any description must either grasp the whole in its historical development or be limited to a slice representing a single, short time.

In one regard, Second Temple religion forms a part of the continuum that stretches from ancient Israel to the present. Many of the religious practices known from the Hebrew Bible continued in this period (though we must keep in mind that some biblical texts present an idealized picture and may not always reflect the actual society and cult). In the same way, the developments after 70 C.E. and during the Talmudic period, which form the basis of modern Judaism, involved many innovations and alterations based upon the practices and beliefs of the preceding period. Yet even as we recognize such connections, we must also see the period of the Second Temple in its own terms, for it has its own character and complexities that cannot be explained from either the Bible or the Talmud.

One of the main, distinctive characteristics of Second Temple Judaism that separates it from both earlier and later forms of the religion is its center in the Jerusalem Temple. The importance of the sacrificial cult, so alien in many ways to modern sensibilities, must at all times be understood and kept in mind. Another factor that especially developed during this period was a world-wide diaspora, so that now the majority of Jews lived outside of Judah. Their distance from the Temple and their life as a minority religion and population among the dominant Persians, Greeks, or Romans produced modifications that affected not only post-70 Judaism but also in many cases had consequences for Palestinian Judaism in the pre-70 period.

Jewish Identity: Religion in the ancient Near East was mainly ethnic. Although certain gods were worshipped across national boundaries, each people tended to have its favorite deities. Even those cults preferred by the ruler, which would receive special attention under the royal patronage, usually were traditional to the people. Only very occasionally would a ruler break with the past by emphasizing another deity (e.g., Akhenaton; Nabonidus). But this was unusual and, in any case, did not normally involve a rejection or suppression of other cults.

Judaism in the Second Temple period was similarly inseparable from the Jewish people. To be Jewish was to be a part of the Jewish *ethnos*, and this ethnic identity was a major feature of Judaism as a religion. The idea of religion as merely a freely chosen system of beliefs did not generally apply at that time. With very few exceptions, you were born into the religion; you were a Jew because you were born a Jew.

Apart from this strong ethnic element, however, a great deal of variation existed in religious practice, and finding a common set of characteristics by which to define Second Temple Judaism is not easy. For almost every characteristic suggested, a counter example can also be thought of. For example, even our statement regarding the centrality of the Jerusalem Temple can be questioned. For although traditional Judaism indeed laid a great deal of emphasis on that temple's role as the sole place for the cult, other temples stood, not only at Gerizim (the Samaritan community) and at Elephantine (in Egypt) through part of the Persian period but, more important, at Leontopolis, where a temple was founded by Onias IV, of the line of Jerusalem high priests.[1]

General characteristics of Judaism: Certain characteristic beliefs and practices defined and were associated with various forms of Judaism. The focus on a temple seems to have been distinctive of all types of Judaism, though, as just noted, the particular choice of temple varied. Still, the Jerusalem Temple was by far the dominant center, even of forms of Judaism whose adherents thought it was polluted in its current state (e.g., the Qumran community). A second characteristic of all Jewish groups was belief in the one God, the God of Israel. For, by the late Second Temple period, if not quite a bit earlier, Judaism had become monotheistic. In addition, almost all groups claiming to be Judaism used the Pentateuch in some form and often other books that became part of the normative canon.

There were other common traits. For example, it is difficult to find any group that rejected physical circumcision, even if an occasional voice may have questioned its absolute necessity (Josephus, Ant. 20.2.3-4, 41-43; Philo, *Migration of Abraham* 89-93). The Jews were not the only ones of the ancient Near East who required circumcision, but both from within and without the community, it was seen as a Jewish characteristic. Other elements of practice frequently mentioned both by Jewish writers and gentiles are adherence to certain food laws (especially the rejection of pork), the maintenance of other purity laws, and the observance of the Sabbath and certain annual holy days. While these characteristics do not necessarily define Judaism, their presence generally suggests that we are dealing with a Judaic system.

Beyond this, tremendous diversity existed, so that to speak of "orthodoxy," or even "orthopraxy," is problematic. And this diversity was the norm not only in the land of Israel but also in the diaspora communities, which developed their own peculiarities.

Diaspora: A diaspora existed as early as the deportation of people from the Northern Kingdom by the Assyrians in 722 B.C.E. (the fictional background of the book of Tobit). An additional series of deportations seems to have taken place as the kingdom of Judah came to an end: in 597 B.C.E., 587 B.C.E. (when Jerusalem fell), and apparently even later (cf., Jer. 52:30). There may have been others (cf., Ezra 4:2, 10). These deportations resulted in an extensive Jewish population in the Mesopotamian area, about which we hear little for a number of centuries. With the coming of the Greeks, Jewish communities sprang up in various cities around the Hellenistic Near East, until the inhabitants of Judah were a minority population of Jews. Perhaps one of the best documented is the Jewish community in Alexandria and others in Egypt. We also know the names of some Jewish leaders there, such as Philo (ca. 20 B.C.E. to 50 C.E.), who wrote a series of biblical commentaries (mostly on Genesis), works on biblical figures (e.g., Moses), and other treatises (e.g., on his mission to emperor Gaius Caligula). In addition to Egypt, we also know of Jewish populations in various cities in Syria and Asia Minor and even as far away as Rome, as well as around the Palestinian area but outside Judah proper.

This development of a major diaspora eventually had a significant effect on Judaism as a religion. Many of the particular features of Judaism that became characteristic after the fall of the Second Temple were those that we find already developing in diaspora religious practices. YHWH, the God of Israel, became the God of a people rather than just of a nation. The Jerusalem Temple was still the focus of religious worship, but in many ways it became a distant ideal, especially the further from it one lived. Many diaspora Jews desired to visit the Temple, and certainly in late Second Temple times pilgrimage to worship in Jerusalem expanded greatly.

Nevertheless, the reality was that visits to the Temple were very infrequent and, for most of the diaspora population, probably non-existent. This meant that the traditional worship centering on the cult was simply not possible. The home and family replaced the Temple and community as the focus of worship. Prayer, acts of piety, and faithful observance of some aspects of the law (Sabbath, circumcision, food laws) replaced the sacrificial cult. None of these were incompatible with the Temple cult; indeed, they were part of the traditional practice of religion. The difference in the diaspora was that they were given greater emphasis, because that was all that could be done.

Many scholars have speculated that the synagogue had already developed in the exilic period, but the evidence for this is very precarious. On the contrary, from the available sources, it appears that worship among diaspora Jews originally took place privately in the home. This was the case until the third century B.C.E., when we have the first evidence of synagogues for communal worship.

Proselytization, conversion, God-fearers: As noted above, like most religions at this time, Judaism was primarily an ethnic religion; even so, from early on, it was envisaged that outsiders could become part of the community and take on its religious identity (cf., Exod. 12:43-49; Deut. 23:4-9; Ruth 1:16-17). Sojourners among the people were expected to conform to Jewish religious practices even while remaining outsiders (Num. 15:15). We have no evidence of wholesale conversion to Judaism nor of any Jewish "mission" to make converts,[2] yet we know of a number of specific examples in antiquity in which gentiles were converted to Judaism as well as of a general attitude that allowed conversion. The whole royal house of Adiabene was apparently converted around the turn of the era, and queen Helena was instrumental in helping to avert a famine in Judea (Josephus, *Ant.* 20.2.3-5, 41-53). The New Testament mentions examples of conversion (Acts 6:5), as does Rabbinic literature.

The main obstacle to conversion was the requirement of circumcision, which is why more women than men converted. This is also why there developed a group of adherents to the community, often men, who took on Jewish observances without making the full step of circumcision and complete conversion. These were frequently designated by the term "God-fearer" (*theosebes* in Greek).

The existence of these individuals has been disputed, partly because many of the references to "God-fearers" in the early sources are simply to pious Jews. Acts mentions gentile adherents to the synagogue who were called by similar terms (*seboumenoi, phoboumenoi*), but the main source in the recent debate is the Aphrodisias inscription from the city in Asia Minor. This is now generally interpreted as demonstrating the existence of a special class of gentiles who undertook most Jewish religious practices apart from circumcision.

The process of conversion is nowhere described in pre-70 sources. For men, circumcision is clearly the main formal step. In an anecdote told by Josephus (*Ant.* 20.2.3-4, 41-43), the king of Adiabene was told by one Jewish merchant that he could convert without circumcision because of his special status as king, but another Jew convinced him that circumcision was necessary. He followed the latter advice. This is the only example to even suggest that circumcision was not a *sine qua non* for full entry into the Jewish community. Rabbinic sources suggest that women had to undergo a ritual baptism, a requirement also for men in addition to circumcision, but no pre-70 sources indicate this.[3] It may well be that the baptism ritual developed under the influence of Christianity.

Temple and Torah—Centrality of the Temple cult: The principal difference between worship before and after 70 C.E. was the centrality of the Temple cult. Apart from a few decades during the neo-Babylonian period (612-539 B.C.E.) when the Temple lay in ruins, from ancient Israel until 70, the sacrificial cult lay at the heart of religion. The performance of the *tamid* (daily) offering was essential. Even during the brief period of three years when this sacrifice ceased during the Maccabean revolt, it was as if the cosmos was shaken to its foundations and the endtime was near (Dan. 7-8). Similarly, after the destruction of the Temple in 70 C.E., the authors of 4 Ezra and 2 Baruch expected the imminent intervention of God to destroy the Roman empire.

The Temple personnel held an important position in society. During the periods in which there was no king, the priesthood in general and the high priest in particular were in positions of political as well as religious power. There is evidence that the Levites were especially drawn on for the scribal skills necessary to run the nation as well as the Temple.[4] The Temple personnel had the education and leisure for intellectual pursuits and thus constituted the bulk of those who read, wrote, and commented on religious literature. They were also the primary teachers in religious matters. Thus, not only the cult but also a large portion of the religious activity of other sorts, including teaching and development of the tradition, took place in the Temple context.

Place of Scripture, tradition, and interpretation: Little is known for certain about the development of the Bible, and the subject is currently being intensely debated. An older consensus of traditio-historical critics concerning how the tradition grew has now come under strong challenge from both conservative and radical perspectives. It is difficult to predict which way the debate will move. Some see an extensive development of what became the Bible already in the time of the Israelite monarchy, with some traditions even likely to be pre-monarchic. Others argue that since the text is first attested in manuscripts of the late Second Temple, that is the context in which we should interpret them. Having been rewritten and incorporated into a late document, any earlier traditions in all events only represent the views and thinking of the latest editors.

The question of when the written text became important and what place it had in the development of the religion thus is difficult. But some matters are indisputable. We have evidence that some of the later biblical writers were aware of and drew on earlier traditions,[5] even if the extent of that reuse and reinterpretation is a moot point. The first positive evidence for writings being treated in some way as scripture and canon appears in Ben Sira, probably written soon after 200 B.C.E. In a section known as the "Praise of the Fathers" (Sir. 44-50), the author recites a long list of figures in Israel's history. Although these do not always correspond to

specific biblical passages, and even if it cannot always be demonstrated that the information comes from our current biblical text at all, a close coordination exists between his list and the general contents of the biblical text we now have. For example, Sir. 49:10 talks of the "the twelve" prophets, clearly suggesting that the prophets in our Minor Prophets already formed a unit.

The Greek version of Ben Sira's book is even more informative. Produced about 132 B.C.E. by the author's grandson, its prologue talks several times about "the law, the prophets, and the other writings" (the Prologue has no verse numbers). This suggests that, for the grandson already, a somewhat authoritative list of books (canon?) consisted of our Pentateuch, a collection of "prophets," which probably did not differ significantly from our present Former and Latter Prophets (since it included the Minor Prophets as a unit), and a number of others writings, some of which are probably part of our present-day canon, though not necessarily all.

This impression is confirmed, but also complicated, by information from other sources. The corpus of Dead Sea Scrolls contains every book of the Hebrew canon but Esther; but many other books are also in the collection and cited as authoritative, suggesting that canonical boundaries were either much wider (embracing a much larger number of books) or possibly much narrower (a small core with special status, such as the Pentateuch, with a much wider collection of non-canonical but nevertheless significant books). The last view fits well some other communities, such as the Samaritan in which only the Pentateuch and a version of Joshua are canonical but other books are known and used in a semi-authoritative way. Similarly, Philo cites a number of the books of the canon at one time or another, but he focuses his main activity on the Pentateuch, and his text is the Septuagint (he apparently knew little if any Hebrew).

Developments in the Persian period: The Persian period was seminal for the development of Judaism. It was here that the transition was made from a monarchic system, with the king as the chief religious and cultic figure, to one in which the high priest was the main religious leader. This change from a monarchy, as well as other changes in the status of Judah, unavoidably led to changes in the religion. It is thought by many that the crystallization of the biblical literature came about primarily in the Persian period, as the Jews began to feel the loss of their monarchic past and the need to interpret it and explain the new situation.

High Priest and Sanhedrin: Although the high priest had important authority in the Temple and cult during the First Temple period, as envisaged by a number of biblical passages, the king was still the chief cultic official.[6] This situation changed considerably in the Second Temple period because of the loss of the monarchy. The priesthood, especially in the person of the high priest, was in a position to fill that vacuum, at least in part. We must accept that the power of the high priest is likely to have varied from time to time, and a lot may have depended on the personality and strength of character of the individual holding the office. Nevertheless, the high priest was the leading political as well as religious figure through much of the Second Temple period.

One of the first concerns with the coming of Persian rule was to rebuild the Temple, which had been destroyed by the neo-Babylonians. This is credited to a diarchy of Zerubbabel, appointed by the Persians as governor of Judah, and the high priest Joshua (Hag. 1:1; 2:2, 21; Ezra 1; 3). As the official Persian appointee, Zerubbabel would have had the preeminence. But Joshua is clearly seen as a partner and active player in the restoration of the cult (Zech. 3; 4; 6:9-15), since, in the absence of a king, he was now the chief cultic official. We have evidence of other Persian governors of Judah, including Sheshbazzar (Ezra 1:8-11; 5:14), Nehemiah (Neh. 5:15-18), and Bagohi.[7] It is possible that they were mostly or all Jewish, though we cannot be certain. It seems likely that the Persians would have continued to appoint an official governor of the province throughout their period of rule, but the last part of the Persian period is largely a blank. However, we have some hints that the high priest may

have been appointed as governor, thus combining the two offices. This is based on coins that mention "Hezekiah the governor" and an individual by the same name (Greek: Ezechias), mentioned by Josephus as high priest at the coming of the Greeks (*Ag. Apion* 1.22, 187-89), suggesting that they may refer to the same man.

In most of the references we have from the period of Greek rule, the high priest acted as spokesman for the Jewish community. His power no doubt waxed and waned, depending on the political circumstances. For example, because of the high priest Onias II's refusal to pay a tribute to the Ptolemaic court, some of his authority seems to have been taken by Joseph Tobiad, a member of a prominent Jewish family across the Jordan (*Ant.* 12.4.2, 160-66). The skimpy amount of information we have also suggests that, throughout much or all this period, the high priest had an advisory council.[8] It has recently been argued that no such official decision-making council existed as a continuous body,[9] though an ad hoc council might be called into existence when the need was felt for it. The problem is how you define such a body. It is likely that any ruler would have had his advisers, whether they were "official" or not, and the existence of an advisory council is attested by various sources (*Ant.* 12.3.3, 142; 2 Macc. 4:43; Acts 5:21-41). The power of this council (*gerousia*: "council of elders," *boule*: "advisory council," or Sanhedrin: from Greek *sunedrion*: "assembly") is likely to have varied, being completely subservient to strong high priests but perhaps dominating the decision-making process under weaker leaders.

There is nothing to argue against the existence of such a regular body throughout much of the Second Temple period, though its status—both *de jure* and *de facto*—may have varied considerably from period to period. This seems a simpler explanation than the claim that all the references are merely to ad hoc assemblies. However, it is difficult to know how early such a body developed, since the earliest references are to the Greek period. Although an advisory Sanhedrin can easily be postulated for the Persian period, we have too little information to be certain.

Move to Exclusive Monotheism: The question of when monotheism developed in Israel has been much debated in the past decades, though the recent trend is to put it later rather than earlier. It may be that YHWH was always the most important God for the Israelites, and certain groups may have worshipped "YHWH-alone" even at an early period.[10] Yet the evidence is that other gods were worshipped alongside YHWH through much of the period of the monarchy.[11] Theophoric names with Baal are found in the biblical text (1 Chr. 8:33, 34; 9:39, 40), and various Israelite inscriptions (e.g., the Samaria ostraca) show names compounded with Baal or other pagan elements.[12] The Jewish community at Elephantine in Egypt not only had their own temple but also worshipped what were apparently consorts of YHWH: Anat-Yahu and Anat-Bethel.

The Ten Commandments begin with a henotheistic declaration that mandates the worship of YHWH for the Israelites but recognizes the existence of other gods (Exod. 20:2-6; Deut. 5:6-10). Deuteronomy has statements that might be taken as monotheistic, but perhaps the first clear declaration of the non-existence of other gods is found in Deutero-Isaiah (Is. 40-55). This is normally dated to the exilic period, though some have recently put it later.[13] We cannot assume, however, that all Jews accepted the viewpoint of Second Isaiah, and the spread of exclusive monotheism may have continued well into the Second Temple period. Zoroastrianism, which became the official religion of the Persian rulers, may have helped in this, though there is no evidence that the Persians imposed particular religious practices on anyone.[14]

Other heavenly beings—angels and demons—were acknowledged, but they were distinct from and inferior to God (some have suggested they were simply the old gods demoted to an inferior status). Indeed, the development of a complex angelology and demonology is a characteristic of Second Temple Judaism, well illustrated from 1 Enoch 6-9, 20. The divine name YHWH was still given special honor by not being pronounced and, often, by being written in paleo-Hebrew script in some Qumran manuscripts. In non-Hebrew manuscripts it was often translated as "Lord" (*kurios* in Greek) and in Hebrew manuscripts (e.g., the Qumran scrolls) God was usually called *El* or *Elohim*.

Crystallization of Tradition: In the past century something of a consensus emerged about how the various biblical books grew up and were edited. The last couple of decades have seen that consensus crumbling. The documentary hypothesis on the sources of the Pentateuch is no longer so widely accepted,[15] and many would put the final editing and perhaps even the major composition of many or all the biblical books as postexilic. In such a condition of flux in scholarly debate itself, it would be unwise to make confident statements. What one can say is that many would put in the Persian period the main editorial work of collecting and crystallizing the traditions into the present biblical books, though some would place it even later. I think that scholarship as a whole is unlikely to accept the Roman period for much of this activity, since the Qumran scrolls show many of the biblical books to have been in essentially their present form before the coming of Pompey (the Roman general who brought Judah under Roman rule) in 63 B.C.E. As for the Ptolemaic period as the main period of editorial activity, the book of Ben Sira suggests that many books were regarded as authoritative by his own time in the late Ptolemaic period. The question is whether this suggests a certain passage of time since they were written.

The situation is complicated whatever position one takes. We have more than one version of some biblical books, suggesting that they continued to grow and develop over a considerable period of time. Dan. 7-12 is almost universally accepted as being written at a late date, at the time of the Maccabean revolt about 165 B.C.E. (though many would be happy to accept a third-century date for Dan. 1-6). The question is not only when the different biblical books were written or edited but to what extent they continued to grow and develop before finally reaching a stable form.

Textual Developments: Something of the development of the biblical text is known from the variety of text-types attested from antiquity.[16] A good portion of the books are known in at least two distinct textual forms, and some in three or more. Most of the biblical books were found among the Dead Sea Scrolls, which has generally complicated the picture. For the Pentateuch, we know at least three textual forms: the Masoretic text or traditional Hebrew text, the Septuagint , and the Samaritan Pentateuch. When we add the Dead Sea Scrolls, we only increase the variety of readings. Two versions of Samuel, the Masoretic and the Septuagint, were once known. Now, some of the scrolls of Samuel found at Qumran (4QSam[a,b,c]) show at least a third version. The Septuagint of Jeremiah and Job are quite a bit shorter than the Masoretic version, and many scholars think the Septuagint to Jeremiah is more original. Both forms of Jeremiah (but not of Job) are attested at Qumran. Other books (e.g., Isaiah) show essentially the same text in both the Masoretic version and the Septuagint, a position confirmed by the Isaiah manuscripts found at Qumran. However, there are many variant readings of individual verses even if the overall text belongs only to one type.

The Dead Sea Scrolls show that all the various textual types are early. It was once speculated that the Masoretic text was a late development, since our earliest knowledge of it was in medieval manuscripts. But many of the Qumran manuscripts of the Masoretic type go back to the first century B.C.E. or earlier. Similarly, because the Septuagint is a translation into Greek, one could argue that its differences from the Masoretic text were due to translation technique or to corruption by Greek scribes. Now, however, in many cases we have Hebrew manuscripts that show that a variant Septuagint reading at a particular point was due to a different Hebrew reading in front of the translator, who translated faithfully. When the Samaritan Pentateuch was discovered by Western scholars in the eighteenth century, some thought it was simply a corrupt form of the Masoretic text, especially since many of the manuscripts are very recent. Although the text itself tends to be closer to the Masoretic one in its primary readings (though often closer to the Septuagint in its secondary expansions), the Qumran finds show that it is an ancient text, going back well before the Common Era.

What this variety shows is that the text was not finalized until quite late and that the Jewish communities seem to have tolerated a variety of different textual forms. The exclusive use of the Masoretic text-type by the entire community seems to have come about only after the fall of the Temple in 70.

Other Greek versions (the so-called Minor Versions of Aquila, Theodotion, and Symmachus) are a further complication. At one time it was widely believed that the last two were late translations by Christian scholars. We now have evidence that Theodotion has an early Jewish revision of the Septuagint (called the *kaige*) at its base (no later than the first century C.E.), though a historical Christian Theodotion may have made some stylistic revisions. It has become common to think of Aquila as a second century C.E. Jewish revision of the Septuagint, designed to replace the Septuagint for Jewish readers who did not know Hebrew and to use the exegetical techniques of Aqiba. However, both these assumptions have been challenged, with the argument that Aquila was an independent translator and that there is no clear connection with Aqiba.[17]

Assimilation versus exclusivism: The extent to which Jews were allowed to conform to the lifestyle and ways of the peoples around them was already debated at an earlier time. Some argued that worship of YHWH did not allow the worship of other gods (Exod. 20:3), that Israel was a holy nation that should be different from other nations (Exod. 19:6), and that association with gentiles would only corrupt and lead Israelites astray from the true religion (Deut. 7:1-5). How much this debate was really carried on while Israel was a nation can only be speculated on; it became a reality, however, as the community sought religious reconstruction in the early Persian period.

We know from the books of Ezra and Nehemiah that the question of relations with the other peoples living in the Palestinian region became acute. Apparently many of the returnees by the second or third generation had married wives from the surrounding peoples. This was opposed by Nehemiah when he came as governor in 445 B.C.E. (Neh. 9-10; Ezra 9-10 gives a similar picture, though its relationship to the Nehemiah episode is debated), and many Jews were compelled to send away their wives and the children of the marriages. The odd thing is that these "peoples of the land" were probably in many cases the descendants of those from the Northern and Southern Kingdoms who had not been taken captive and were thus as much Israelite as those who returned from Babylon.

The relationship of the Jewish community to the broader world continued to be debated, and the "inclusivists" seem to have won the initial battle when, in the Greek period, the community opened itself up more and more to outside influences. The greatest example of this was perhaps the "Hellenistic reform" under Jason, when Jerusalem became a *polis*, or Greek city. This incident has often been misinterpreted as an embracing of paganism, but the issue was not initially that of religion but of culture.[18] However, the suppression of Judaism soon brought the religious question up in a very sharp way. The Jews of Judea fought off this threat and restored the desecrated Temple; nevertheless, the Hasmonean state that arose out of the Maccabean revolt continued to be very much open to influences from and relations with other nations.

Modern scholars have frequently phrased the question as whether or not one could be a faithful Jew and still embrace Hellenism. The answer naturally depends on the extent to which the process of Hellenization was purely a cultural one and to what extent it also affected religion. We know of many Jews who were thoroughly Hellenized but were completely faithful to their ancestral religion (e.g., Philo of Alexandria). See further in the next section.

Impact of Hellenization on Judaism: Hellenization (or Hellenism) has been a bad word to many writers on early Judaism. This is often due to a misunderstanding or to a disproportionate focus on Judaism in isolation

from other subject peoples of the Greek empires. Some aspects of Greek culture were new in the ancient Near East, but not all were, and the Greek conquerors were in many ways as influenced by the peoples among whom they settled as they influenced them. What is very clear from recent studies is that Greek culture did not displace the native; it only added another element to the complex mixture already in place.

Hellenization in the diaspora: The process of Hellenization occurred everywhere that came under Greek rule and even reached areas over which Alexander's spear had not extended. No sharp distinction can therefore be made between Jews in Palestine and those elsewhere under Greek rule; most of the Jews in the world found themselves in one of the Greek empires that followed the forty years' fighting of the Diadochi ("successors") after Alexander's death. In Babylonia a large Aramaic-speaking population lived from an early time, and the Hellenistic influence was probably smaller than elsewhere, since this area was taken over by the Parthians after less than a century of Greek rule. But many Jews also lived in Egypt, Syria, or Asia Minor, usually in Greek-speaking cities. Many lost their knowledge of Hebrew and Aramaic as, for example, Philo, who clearly knows little or no Hebrew, certainly not enough to use the Bible in the original.[19] This is why the Septuagint was originally created: to provide a Bible the Greek-speaking Jews could understand (the explanation in the *Letter of Aristeas*, that it was translated for the library of Ptolemy II [282-246 B.C.E.], is generally rejected by scholars). Even those who retained a knowledge of Hebrew and Aramaic would not have escaped the strong influence of their Greek-speaking environment.

We know of Jews in the diaspora from several sorts of sources. First comes some literature from the diaspora Jews, though it is often fragmentary. Second, we know of the presence of Jewish communities at various ancient sites because of inscriptions, e.g., from synagogues. Only in Egypt have some documents written on papyri survived. A third source is the references to Jewish communities in literary sources, such as Josephus (a Jewish historian of the first century C.E.) and the Greco-Roman writers.

The writings of Jews in the diaspora cannot always easily be separated from those of Palestinian Jews who chose to write in Greek. However, it is generally accepted that 2 Maccabees was an epitome of a larger work written by a diaspora Jew, Jason of Cyrene (1 Maccabees seems to be a translation from a Hebrew original). Philo of Alexandria has left us extremely valuable material, not only about Jewish interpretation of the Bible, but also many passing references to the Alexandrian community. Other writings written by Greek speakers include the Wisdom of Solomon, Sibylline Oracles 3-5, Pseudo-Phocylides, Testament of Abraham, and 4 Maccabees. Some of the Fragmentary Jewish Writers in Greek[20] were written in the diaspora, though a number of them were probably written in Palestine itself. Translation of literature from Semitic originals also seems to have become a major endeavor, probably mostly in the diaspora, producing Greek translations of Ben Sira, 1 and 2 Enoch, Tobit, Testaments of the Twelve Patriarchs, Psalms of Solomon, not to mention the Bible itself.

What we find in all this literature, most of it religious, is the adoption of Greek literary devices and modes of communication. This does not mean that the religion itself was compromised, but the way of expressing that religion was adapted to the rhetorical and literary characteristics of the vehicle in which it was conveyed, namely, Greek literature.

Hellenization in Palestine: Like any other peoples of the Syria-Palestinian region, the Jews were influenced by Hellenization, the more so as time went on. It thus can be said that, from some time fairly early in the Greek period, "all Judaism must really be designated 'Hellenistic Judaism' in the strict sense."[21] Greek administration reached to the lowest levels of society, and the Greek language was widely (though not exclusively) the language of administration. Greek "culture" in the narrow sense was longer in making itself felt, because the Greeks had little interest in spreading it; on the contrary, they saw it as a part of the privileges that they kept to themselves. But many of the natives, especially of the upper-classes, found it attractive for various reasons. A knowledge of Greek was a way of rising in the world, and some evidently found other aspects of the Greek way of life attractive. Thus, as time went on, Greek identity shifted from emphasis on ethnic descent to one of language and education. One with a good knowledge of the Greek language and a Greek education could go far, even if not born Greek.

Yet most Jews drew the line at matters of religion. Indeed, in all of extant Jewish literature we know of very few who are alleged to have abandoned their faith (e.g., Dositheos son of Drimylus in 3 Macc. 1:3; Julius Tiberius Alexander in *Ant.* 20.5.2, 100). Even Jason the high priest who is so reviled in the books of Maccabees does not appear to have compromised Temple worship when he established the Greek constitution in Jerusalem.[22]

We find, then, a complicated situation. All Jews in Palestine came into contact with the Greek administration, while many learned some Greek, and a few learned it well. The extent to which a Greek lifestyle was adopted varied greatly, with the peasants probably the least affected and the aristocracy the most. But apart from the way of life for those who were citizens of a Greek city (an extremely small number), Greek influence was most evident in the areas of literature and architecture. Influence on literature could be very subtle, though, as already noted, many Jewish writings of this period were written in or translated into Greek.

Perhaps one of the most interesting features of this influence is the presence of Greek forms in religious practice. For example, it has been argued with good reason that the Passover celebration took on the form of a Greek symposium or drinking party, which we know of from philosophical and other literature. Some aspects of the Festival of Tabernacles (and Hanukkah) are reminiscent of Dionysus worship (Greek god of wine). It is difficult to say whether these characteristics arose in Palestine or outside, but regardless they show definite Greek influence.

Religious toleration: Religious tolerance

has two aspects: tolerance by the surrounding gentile peoples of Judaism, and tolerance by the Jews of other religions. The Jews were generally allowed to practice their religion without hindrance in their polytheistic environment. Polytheism is necessarily tolerant, since it accepts the existence of many gods; the Jewish god was only one among many. As long as the religion did not cause sedition and revolt, there was no reason the ruling powers should interfere with it. This is easily forgotten after a two-thousand-year history of the persecution of Jews. But through most of the Second Temple period, Jews did not suffer anti-Semitism as we know it. Only two major threats to Judaism are known from antiquity. The first of these was the forcible suppression of Judaism by Antiochus IV (168-165 B.C.E.). The cause(s) of this will no doubt continue to be debated for a long time to come without a clear solution, but there is no question that the Seleucid government attempted to outlaw Jewish religious practices in Palestine (it is not clear that Jews outside Judea were affected). Only the Maccabean revolt brought a revocation of the decree.

The other incident was a threat that was never carried out: the plan by the Roman emperor Gaius Caligula to place his statue in the Jerusalem Temple. The precise reasons are still not clear, though it may have been a punishment for an act of Jewish religious intolerance (see below). The Jews resisted by everything short of a revolt, and even this might have taken place if Caligula had carried out his plan. But he was persuaded to abandon it, and his assassination not long afterward meant that if he was still contemplating such an act, it had no chance of being realized.

This does not mean the Jews always had an easy time or that they were not discriminated against. In towns and cities outside Palestine, they were a minority population, and Josephus preserves a number of alleged decrees in their favor, mainly issued by the Romans and relating to communities in Asia Minor (*Ant.* 14.10.1-26, 185-267). Although the genuineness of these has been disputed, many of them are probably based on actual decrees,

even if they have been collected and edited by Jewish scribes. In all events, what stands out is the very need for such decrees, which suggests that in some cases Jewish civic rights indeed were being severely abridged.[23] The practice of Judaism was not strictly being forbidden, but the surrounding gentile community was making it difficult for Jews to follow their own customs as freely as the Greek citizens of the cities.

The reverse side of the coin was Jewish intolerance of other religions (fig. 67). Some biblical passages envisage the extermination of the Canaanites (e.g., Deut. 7:1-4). As noted, in the period of Ezra, Jewish men were forced to separate from wives and families thought unsuitable, even though there is a good chance that many of these wives were descended from Jews or Israelites (Ezra 9-10; Nehemiah 9-10). The Hasmonean rulers removed non-Jewish worship from their borders as they conquered new areas and converted the Idumeans and Itureans to Judaism.

Under Roman rule Judaism was a permitted religion, and in Judea proper other religions were apparently excluded, including pagan altars and the emperor cult. However, Roman policy also expected the Jews to tolerate other religions in most areas. A careful examination of the sources shows that an act of intolerance is likely to have precipitated the plan of Caligula to place his statue in the Jerusalem Temple. Philo notes that some rash Jewish youths tore down a pagan altar to the emperor in the area of Yavneh (*Legation to Gaius* 199-202). This was outside Judea proper, so Roman altars were to be allowed to function without hindrance.

Personal piety and popular religion: As noted above, the focus of Judaism before 70 was on the Temple cult. For Jews in Palestine or otherwise near the Temple, a regular pilgrimage to the Temple would have been customary and expected; however, the further one lived form the Temple, the more difficult to make the journey and the less frequently it took place, especially for those who were not wealthy. This naturally led to a change in the actual practice of religion, even where the theory of the Temple as center was fully maintained. This also meant that alongside the official cult, a large body of local, family, and individual forms of piety and worship developed. Some of these go back for centuries and were officially frowned on (magic, cult of the dead). Yet even where we do not have a great deal of data, we have strong hints that such things flourished, not confined to the masses but, in some cases, cultivated also by an educated elite.

Prayer and worship: Prayer, one of the most basic forms of worship, is exemplified in many biblical and early Jewish examples of actual or literary prayers and of cases in which people exercised their religion by praying. Prayer in its widest sense of praise, petition, and talking to God suffused Jewish piety from an early period, and the existence of the sacrificial cult in no way constrained this natural expression of devotion. The sacrificial cult embodied a theory of formal atonement and removal of sins in which the actual carrying out of the cultic act was efficacious. It was not necessary to have this accompanied by prayer, singing, or other liturgical forms, but these were probably the norm most of the time while the Temple stood.

Unfortunately, the amount of information on the actual day-to-day conduct of the Temple service is brief, and despite helpful attempts to reconstruct it, much is guesswork. Nevertheless, there are indications that prayer and singing were important elements of the daily worship. The Temple as a place of prayer is taken for granted (1 Kgs. 8:29-34; 2 Chr. 7:15; Is. 56:7; Ps. 122; Luke 18:10; Acts 3:1). Among the duties borne by Temple personnel were singing, with individuals specifically allocated the task of producing songs, and perhaps other forms of music (Ez. 2:65, 70; Neh. 7:67, 73; *Ant.* 20.9.6, 216-18). The songs preserved in the Psalms and elsewhere are types of prayer; conversely, it is normally prayers that are set to music.

Prayer could be conducted anywhere and not just at the Temple. We find many examples of people praying individually, and most of these examples involve private prayer. Daniel prays three times a day in his room (Dan. 6:11); Judith prays on top of her house

(Jdt. 8:5; 9:1; 10:1-2). Tobit prays and also celebrates the Jewish festivals in his home (Tob. 2:1-5; 3:1-6, 10-17). The indication is that this was the norm for a long time. Yet we have examples of group public prayer early as well, especially in times of crisis (1 Chr. 5:20; Neh. 9; 1 Macc. 5:33; 2 Macc. 10:26-27). The books of Maccabees give other examples as well in which the people prayed, apparently as a group (1 Macc. 3:44-54).

Although viewed as the quintessential place of Jewish worship, the synagogue seems to have developed late, in the diaspora, where it was a community center and place of worship for those unable to go to Jerusalem.[24] The idea that synagogues immediately sprang up where the Jews were removed from the Temple (e.g., during the Exile) is unsupported. No early Jewish writing mentions gatherings for communal worship, suggesting that the synagogue was a late development even in the diaspora. Judaism could be practiced in the home and among one's family, whether in prayer and devotion or celebration of the festivals, as the book of Tobit well illustrates.

The first attestations of synagogues are from the third century B.C.E. and are in Egypt, though we find evidence for them elsewhere in the Mediterranean not much later. These were called *proseuchai*, which means "places of prayer," suggesting this was their main function even if they had other uses. The Alexandrian Greek writer Agatharchides of Cnidus (ca. 215 to 140 B.C.E.) mentions that, each Sabbath, Jews came together in their "temples" to pray. What other activity went on there is mainly a matter of speculation. Whether they also served as community centers, for example, is not known in most cases, though it makes sense that this was sometimes a fact (cf., *Life* 54, 277-80).

Synagogues seem to have come to Palestine only very late, well after the Maccabean revolt.[25] Whether there were any synagogues in Judea proper before 70 is still a debated point, though we have literary evidence for them in Tiberias (*Life* 54, 277-80), Dora, and Caesarea (*War* 2.4.4-5, 285-89; *Ant.* 19.6.3, 300-5), and possible archeological evidence for Gamla. Whether Masada and Herodium show evidence of being synagogues is disputed. The Theodotus inscription, which seems to have come from a synagogue in Jerusalem, describes the synagogue as a place of study and also hospitality to travelers. It is commonly dated before 70 C.E., though some argue it is post-70.

This evidence shows the need people felt for public and communal worship. Private prayer and devotion were not felt to be sufficient to meet the religious needs of the people. The requirements of the diaspora people, removed form the Temple, produced innovations (such as the synagogue) that were in turn imported into Judea itself. These then served as a convenient vehicle for worship when the Temple was destroyed, with the greatest evidence of growth in the third and fourth centuries C.E.

Pilgrimage: From the indication of all our sources, worship at the Temple was the expected norm for Jews living in the region of Judah (cf., Luke 2:41). But many thousands of Jews lived too far away to even contemplate making a pilgrimage more than very infrequently. Philo seems to have attended the Temple at least once (*On Providence* 2.64), but he was better placed than many to meet the expenses. Still, the picture we have is that by the first century C.E., a large traffic of Jewish pilgrims came each year to the annual festivals. Even if male Jews came only a few times in their lifetime, the diaspora population was sufficiently large to yield a large influx of visitors each major festival period. All indications are that the number of people employed in catering for these visitors was substantial, and the tourist industry became quite important for the regional economy. Unfortunately, the Temple did not long survive the most developed aspect of this type of devotion, for one suspects that, with time, pilgrimage for all diaspora male Jews once in a lifetime would have become an expected part of the religion, as it later became in Islam.

Esoteric arts: An important feature of religion is those darker elements that are often overlooked in standard treatments: divination, magic, and the "esoteric arts. The condemnation of these in the biblical and other sources (e.g., Deut. 18:9-14; Is. 65:3-4) has

often been taken at face value, to indicate that these things had no place in Judaism. The evidence indicates otherwise, though the matter is complicated. Divination was officially practiced by the priests at an early time through use of the Urim and Thummim, and it was certainly present among the people even when some frowned on it. This evidently included cults for the dead, even though the evidence for these has been largely suppressed.[26] While evidence for cults of the dead is lacking in the later Second Temple period in particular, other forms of contact with the spirit world are well-documented.

Although astrology was associated with the Babylonians, its main development was actually during the Hellenistic period, and Jewish interest in astrology is indicated in a variety of ways.[27] Several texts among the Qumran scrolls refer to astrological signs (4QBrontologion; 4Q186). During the first few centuries C.E., synagogue mosaics and decorations often have astrological motifs. Judging from 1 Enoch 72-82, the astronomical knowledge among the Jews was not particularly sophisticated in comparison to that known in some parts of the Greco-Roman world, but the heavenly bodies were thought to be extremely important. Part of the reason was the importance of the calendar for Jewish worship.

Jews had a reputation for magic going back to an early time. In Second Temple sources, Solomon was credited with controlling and exorcising demons (*Ant.* 8.2.5, 45-49; cf., *Testament of Solomon*). The Jews accepted the common view that demons were the cause of many of the physical and mental illnesses in society, and exorcism was an accepted if not always honored profession (cf., Mat. 12:27 and the many other examples in the Gospels). Some Qumran texts have the aim of controlling various demonic figures (4Q510-511; 4Q560; 11QPsAp[a]).

Celibacy, virginity, abstinence: Judaism is not normally associated with asceticism. Despite the lack of emphasis on such things, contrary to Christianity, we nevertheless find some streams of asceticism, with celibacy and virginity given a positive religious value. The best-known group is the Essenes, who are said by most of our sources to live in celibate communities (even though Josephus says one group married for purposes of procreation alone). The Therapeutae of Egypt were claimed to be celibate communities of both men and women (Philo, *De vita contemplativa*). When Tobit and Sarah pray before their wedding night, they note that what they do is not done in lust (8:7). This reminds one of Philo's view (taken from his Platonic philosophy) that the passions of the lower body must be severely resisted and controlled (*Special Laws* 1.195-203). Judith not only lived in an unmarried state after her husband died after only a few years of marriage, but she fasted all the days except the eves of the Sabbaths and the Sabbaths themselves (Jdt. 8:6). In the Second Temple period, fasting, which in the Bible is a sign of mourning, thus became a religious act and means of invoking the deity (4 Ezra 5:20; Mat. 6:16-17; 9:14-15; Luke 18:12).

Prophecy, apocalypticism, eschatology: It was widespread belief that prophecy had in some way come to an end with the biblical prophets (1 Macc. 4:46; cf., *Ag. Apion* 1.41). Yet Josephus, who is one of those telling us this, also implies that he himself was a prophet (*War* 3.8.9, 403-7). One of the problems is how to define the prophet. Many want to disassociate the "classical" prophets of the Bible from the apocalypticists, charismatic figures, foretellers, and prophets of later times. But whether such a neat division is possible has to be questioned.[28] In any case, there continued to be figures throughout the Second Temple period whom the sources call "prophet." Their exact characteristics are not always easy to determine, but the ability to discern the future is often a central attribute (*War* 2.8.12, 159; Acts 11:27-28; 15:32; 21:10-11).

Apocalypticism has characteristics known from biblical prophecy and prophets but also from mantic wisdom (which includes divination and other modes of communication with the spirit world). We have evidence of it already in the third century B.C.E., but it may have developed as early as the Persian period. Although eschatology is an important part of the apocalyptic world view, it is by no means the only component. The revela-

tion of heavenly mysteries of all sorts is a major feature of apocalypticism, including the secrets of nature and the universe. Knowledge of the heavens, heavenly beings, and the divine plan were all part of a body of learned and revealed knowledge. The model sage was not only the one who had mastered "proverbial" (that is, traditional) wisdom by study but also the revealed knowledge that came from living piously and devoting life to the search for divine wisdom.

In the literature of the Second Temple period, we find a variety of beliefs in the afterlife.[29] Some such as Ben Sira followed what was probably the older Israelite view, that there is no afterlife, only the shadowy existence of the life essence in the underworld. Dan. 12:2-3 envisaged that some (not all) would be resurrected to stand judgment; these seem to be the extremely righteous, perhaps the martyrs (who would become like the stars of heaven), or the extremely wicked, who had not been properly punished in this life. The *Psalms of Solomon* also seems to be thinking of resurrection for the righteous alone (2:31; 3:12). Resurrection and judgment were often associated with an apocalyptic end of the world, in which the cosmos would be shaken and God would personally intervene to bring in a new age. Yet the apocalyptic vision was only one Jewish perspective on the subject. In writers such as Philo, the Wisdom of Solomon, and the *Testament of Abraham*, it was thought that the soul was immortal (or potentially so) and that each person would face individual judgment immediately at death. The question of a general resurrection or an apocalyptic end to history is not discussed by them and may have been absent from their thinking. All this shows that views of the development of history, the future, and the afterlife varied widely among Jews in this period.

One subject that exercises many, especially Christians, is the Jewish belief in a messiah. Again, we find enormous variety.[30] The concept of the messiah arose from the biblical data in which the king and the high priest were anointed with oil (*meshiah* in Hebrew; *christos* in Greek). The idea that an ideal king, modeled on David, would be raised up to rule over Israel already occurs in many biblical passages (e.g., Jer. 23:5-6; 30:8-9; Ezek. 34:23-24). These two figures—the kingly and the priestly—became the basis of most later messianic speculation. The *Psalms of Solomon* (17-18) think of a larger-than-life Davidic figure. A number of texts from Qumran seem to think of two or three messianic figures: a priestly messiah, a messiah from Judah, and perhaps a prophet (*Cairo Damascus Document* 12:23-13:1; 19:10-11; 1QS 9:11; 1QSa 2:11). A few texts have a heavenly figure that seems to serve in the messianic role (4 Ezra 13; 11QMelchizedek 2:4-18). Thus we may not speak of *the* messianic expectation or *the* Jewish messiah; different messiahs and eschatological figures were imagined, depending on which Judaism one followed.

Sects, preachers, teachers, revolutionaries: Discussions of Second Temple Judaism often focus on the various groups and sects of this period. But this can lead to a distortion, since these sects comprised only one aspect of the religion. While their place and influence should not be ignored, we must accept that our knowledge of them is imperfect. According to Josephus, the Pharisees, Sadducees, and Essenes were the three main groups or "philosophies" (*Ant.* 18.1.2, 11). None was evidently very large, though, since the figure of six thousand is given for the Pharisees (*Ant.* 17.2.4-3.1, 41-47) and only four thousand for the Essenes (*Ant.* 18.1.5, 20; Philo, *Probus* 75). The Sadducees were presumably even fewer. This suggests that whatever influence these groups had, they were minority movements to which the bulk of the Jewish people did not belong. Josephus actually tells us little about them, and their description in the New Testament is unavoidably a caricature (e.g., Mark 7 and parallels). A major debate remains regarding the relationship of the community in the Qumran scrolls and the Essenes.

We first meet the Pharisees and Sadducees in the second century B.C.E. as two opposing parties who seem to have the political aim of influencing the Hasmonean ruler. The Pharisees are alleged to have dominated the rule of Alexandra Salome (76-67 B.C.E.), but

then they drop out and we hear nothing of them until the time of Herod. They tried to influence members of his household, and he had some executed as a result. Greek sources say Gamaliel I and his son Simeon, in the first century C.E., are Pharisees, but they are the only ones who appear to have held public office. The Pharisees give the impression of being a closed table fellowship sect[31] whose main influence was in the period of Yavneh after the fall of the Temple. The Sadducees were supposed to have a number of prominent members of society among their numbers, including at least one or two high priests, but we hear little about their beliefs (other than that they accepted only the written law) or of individuals who belonged to their group.

Revolutionary and messianic groups: Perhaps more straightforward than the "religious groups" were the revolutionary and messianic groups that wanted to change society by direct action. Apart from several uprisings by the last of the Hasmoneans and their descendants, several revolutionary groups arose at various times of political instability, such as at the time of the Herod's death. Shortly after this time, the "Fourth Philosophy" originated as a resistance movement to the census at the time Judea became a Roman province in 6 C.E. In the middle of the first century C.E. the Sicarii ("assassins") came up as heirs of the Fourth Philosophy. The Zealots were formed once the war with Rome began in 66 C.E., and, until the Romans set siege to the city, they fought against other revolutionary factions, including the Sicarii. Messianic and eschatological beliefs seem to have characterized some of these groups, though we have no evidence that such ideologies motivated all of them. Some groups may have been no more than revolutionary movements. In most cases, we have little information, and trying to extract goals and ideals is difficult.

Other groups: In addition to the major sects and groups, we have knowledge or hints of many other groups.[32] Some of these seem to have had only a brief existence. Others are known mainly because of their later history. Figures such as John the Baptist and the *Fourth Sibylline Oracle* indicate that baptismal sects existed already in the first century

C.E. Some of the later Gnostic and related groups (Mandeans, Manicheans) show knowledge of Jewish traditions, which suggests they may have arisen from within Judaism, even if they eventually manifested anti-Jewish attitudes. If nothing else, these groups indicate the complex nature of Judaism of the time, but they also show why trying to identify a common set of characteristics integral to all forms of Judaism is so difficult.

Charismatic individuals and leaders: The sources also sporadically name individual religious figures or leaders.[33] These are not necessarily identified with a particular movement, though in some cases (e.g., Jesus) we know that they founded movements that became very important. We have little more than anecdotes about certain individuals. For example, we hear of Onias (Honi) the Circle-drawer who was able to cause rain. Another figure is Hanina ben Dosa who, though "rabbinized" in the later tradition, does not appear as a typical Rabbinic sage but is better known for his miraculous powers. The historical Jesus is also often thought to fit in with such individuals as a charismatic miracle worker. In his case, we have an extensive tradition, though it has been heavily interpreted by the later church. These all show that the Rabbinic sage, known from the later Rabbinic literature, was only one possible model of leadership; the Second Temple period was characterized by its lack of adherence to a single or dominant paradigm.

Conclusion: The religion of the Jews during the Second Temple period is intimately tied up with their history, though one is not necessarily the mirror image of the other. The Judaism that emerges in the Persian period carries forward many elements known from pre-exilic times. The Temple was rebuilt and continued to be the formal focus of worship throughout this period. The Temple also served as the center of much other activity associated with the religion, such as teaching, discussion, and much theological speculation that fed into the developing tradition. The Temple personnel, who had already been important under the monarchy, now increased in power and influence, at least partially filling the vacuum created by the loss

of the king. The zenith of priestly power was under the Hasmoneans, when the high priest was also king.

Already during the Persian period there is evidence that the tradition was beginning to be crystallized into books and collections, which later became a part of the canon (though the fixing of text and canon may not have taken place before the Yavnean period). The written Torah became an important focus in its own right and, naturally, did not require the Temple to be studied. The growth of a large diaspora population, geographically separated from the Temple but with access to some religious books, led to innovations and developments, some of which eventually had their influence on the religion of the homeland (e.g., synagogues).

Beyond a few basic beliefs and practices (e.g., circumcision, the Sabbath and festivals, some purity laws, loyalty to the God of Israel) it is difficult to find general characteristics that all Jews and Jewish groups had in common. Within certain broad parameters, it seems that no hierachy attempted to—or at least was successful in attempts to—impress a uniformity of belief and practice on all Jews. There was no agreed set of holy books or even uniform text. The freedom of biblical interpretation and the diverse form it takes is especially notable to an outsider.

Without a central authority, not surprisingly there were many different groups, movements, sects, leaders, and teachers, each with distinct beliefs or at least different emphases. Alongside the central sacrificial cult were not only private prayer and devotion but also ascetic practices, magic, divination, and even secret cults. Most characteristic of Second Temple Judaism is its enormous variety. Still, a major aspect of Jewish identity was membership in the Jewish people. Religion and ethnicity went closely together, whatever the degree of religious pluralism.

If one stands back and views the Second Temple period as a whole, what immediately strikes the observer is the extent to which *Urzeit wird Endzeit*—the end recapitulates the beginning. We find at the start of the Persian period a people, conquered and under foreign rule, but allowed to reconstitute some sort of national existence and to rebuild their ruined Temple. There were expressions of hope for the future, sometimes couched in more idealized terms but sometimes concentrating more on practical possibilities. The Second Temple period ended in destruction of the nation and the Temple, but despite this we find expressions of hope in the future—in the soon-to-be-ushered-in Kingdom of God (4 Ezra; 2 Baruch; Revelation)—and, most importantly, we find the beginnings of a reconstitution of Judaism that no longer needed the physical Temple but had the power to survive and continue its existence to the present day.

Bibliography

Goodman, Martin, *Mission and Conversion: Proselytizing in the Religious History of the Roman Empire* (Oxford, 1994).

Grabbe, Lester L., *Judaism from Cyrus to Hadrian: Vol. 1: Persian and Greek Periods; Vol. 2: Roman Period* (Minneapolis, 1992).

Grabbe, Lester L., *Priest, Prophets, Diviners, Sages: A Socio-historical Study of Religious Specialists in Ancient Israel* (Valley Forge, 1995).

Grabbe, Lester L., *An Introduction to First Century Judaism: Jewish Religion and History in the Second Temple Period* (Edinburgh, 1996).

Saldarini, Anthony J., *Pharisees, Scribes and Sadducees in Palestinian Society: A Sociological Approach* (Wilmington, 1988).

Notes

[1] Gideon Bohak, *Joseph and Aseneth and the Jewish Temple in Heliopolis* (Atlanta, 1996).

[2] See Martin Goodman, *Mission and Conversion: Proselytizing in the Religious History of the Roman Empire* (Oxford, 1994).

[3] Shaye J.D. Cohen, "Conversion to Judaism in Historical Perspective: From Biblical Israel to Postbiblical Judaism," in *Conservative Judaism* 36 (1983), pp. 31-45.

[4] Lester Grabbe, *Priest, Prophets, Diviners, Sages: A Socio-historical Study of Religious Specialists in Ancient Israel* (Valley Forge, 1995), pp. 160-61.

[5] Cf., Michael Fishbane, *Biblical Interpretation in Ancient Israel* (Oxford, 1989).

[6] Grabbe, op. cit., pp. 38-39, 60-62.

[7] A. Cowley, *Aramaic Papyri of the Fifth Century B.C.* (reprint: Osnabruck, 1967), pp. 30-31.

[8] Lester Grabbe, *Judaism from Cyrus to Hadrian: Vol. 1: Persian and Greek Periods; Vol. 2: Roman Period* (Minneapolis, 1992; reprinted: London, 1994), pp. 389-95.

[9] David Goodblatt, *The Monarchic Principle: Studies in Jewish Self-Government in Antiquity* (Tübingen, 1994).

[10] Morton Smith, *Palestinian Parties and Politics that Shaped the Old Testament* (New York, 1971).

[11] Diana V. Edelman, ed., *The Triumph of Elohim: From Yahwisms to Judaisms* (Grand Rapids, 1995); Mark Smith, *The Early History of God: Yahweh and the Other Deities in Ancient Israel* (San Francisco, 1990).

[12] Jeffrey H. Tigay, *You Shall Have No Other Gods: Israelite Religion in the Light of Hebrew Inscriptions* (Atlanta, 1986), pp. 65-70.

[13] E.g., Philip R. Davies, "God of Cyrus, God of Israel: Some Religio-Historical Reflections on Isaiah 40-55," in Jon Davies, Graham Harvey, and Wilfred G.E. Watson, eds., *Words Remembered, Texts Renewed: Essays in Honour of John F.A. Sawyer* (Journal for the Study of the Old Testament Supplement 195, 1995), pp. 207-25.

[14] This is contra Bolin in Edelman, op. cit., p. 139; cf. Grabbe, *Judaism from Cyrus to Hadrian*, p. 130.

[15] R.N. Whybray, *The Making of the Pentateuch: A Methodological Study* (Journal for the Study of the Old Testament Supplement 53, 1987).

[16] Emmanuel Tov, *Textual Criticism of the Hebrew Bible* (Minneapolis, 1992).

[17] Grabbe, "Aquila's Translation and Rabbinic Exegesis," in G. Vermes and J. Neusner, eds., *Essays in Honour of 'Yigael Yadin (Journal of Jewish Studies*, 33, 1982), pp. 527-536; "The Translation Technique of the Greek Minor Versions: Translations or Revisions?" in *Septuagint, Scrolls and Cognate Writings: Papers Presented to the International Symposium on the Septuagint and Its Relations to the Dead Sea Scrolls and Other Writings* (Manchester, 1990; Atlanta, 1992), pp. 505-556.

[18] Grabbe, *Judaism from Cyrus to Hadrian*, pp. 276-281.

[19] Cf., Lester Grabbe, *Etymology in Early Jewish Interpretation: The Hebrew Names in Philo* (Atlanta, 1988), pp. 63, 233-35.

[20] Carl R. Holladay, *Fragments from Hellenistic Jewish Authors*, 3 vols. (Atlanta, 1983-1995).

[21] Martin Hengel, *Judaism and Hellenism* (Philadelphia, 1974), vol. 1, pp. 103-106.

[22] Grabbe, *Judaism from Cyrus to Hadrian*, pp. 278-80.

[23] John M.G. Barclay, *Jews in the Mediterranean Diaspora from Alexander to Trajan (323 B.C.E.-117 C.E.)* (Edinburgh, 1996), pp. 262-281.

[24] J. Gwyn Griffiths, "Egypt and the Rise of the Synagogue," in *JTS* 38 (1987), pp. 1-15; Martin Hengel, "Proseuche und Synagoge: Jüdische Gemeinde, Gotteshaus und Gottesdienst in der Diaspora und in Palästina," in J. Gutmann, ed., *The Synagogue: Studies in Origins, Archaeology, and Architecture* (New York, 1975), pp. 27-54.

[25] Paul V.M. Flesher, "Palestinian Synagogues before 70 C.E.: A Review of the Evidence," in Dan Urman and Paul V.M. Flesher, eds., *Ancient Synagogues: Historical Analysis and Archaeological Discovery* (Studia Post-Biblica 47; Leiden, 1995), vol. 1, pp. 27-39; M.J.S. Chiat, *Handbook*

Map 4. The Hasmonean Kingdom.

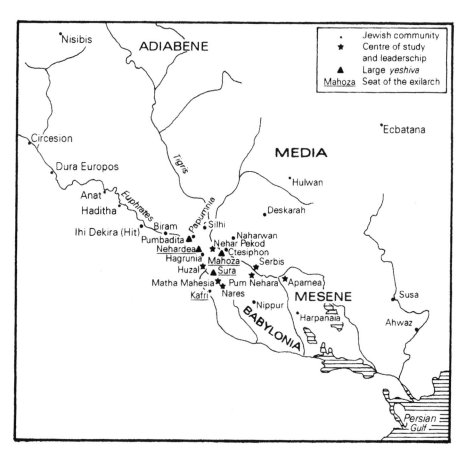

Map 5. The Jews in Babylonia in the Time of the Mishnah and Talmud.

of Synagogue Architecture (Atlanta, 1982), pp. 116-118, 204-207, 248-251, 282-284.

[26] Frederick H. Cryer, *Divination in Ancient Israel and its Near Eastern Environment: A Socio-Historical Investigation* (Journal for the Study of the Old Testament Supplement 142, 1994); Brian B. Schmidt, *Israel's Beneficent Dead: Ancestor Cult and Necromancy in Ancient Israelite Religion and Tradition* (Tübingen, 1994).

[27] B.L. van der Waerden, "History of the Zodiac," in *Archiv für Orientforschung* 16 (1952), pp. 216-30; James H. Charlesworth, "Jewish Interest in Astrology during the Hellenistic and Roman Period," in *ANRW II: Principate* (1987), vol. 20.2, pp. 926-50.

[28] Lester Grabbe, *Priest, Prophets, Diviners, Sages*: pp. 98-107, 176-78.

[29] G.W.E. Nickelsburg, *Resurrection, Immortality, and Eternal Life in Intertestamental Judaism* (Harvard Theological Studies 26, Cambridge, 1972); Lester Grabbe, *An Introduction to First Century Judaism: Jewish Religion and History in the Second Temple Period* (Edinburgh, 1996), pp. 73-93.

[30] Grabbe, op. cit., pp. 66-69.

[31] Jacob Neusner, *From Politics to Piety* (Englewood Cliffs, 1973).

[32] Grabbe, *Judaism from Cyrus to Hadrian*, pp. 507-19; *An Introduction to First Century Judaism*, pp. 94-110.

[33] Cf., Grabbe, *Judaism from Cyrus to Hadrian*, pp. 519-23.

LESTER L. GRABBE

JUDAISM, HISTORY OF, PART III: LATE ANTIQUITY: In late antiquity, the Judaism of the dual Torah ("Rabbinic Judaism") took shape. That Judaism in time became normative, the foundations for every system of Judaism, the religion, that flourished from then to now. We have evidence that, at that time, other Judaisms, besides that represented by the Rabbinic documents, also took shape, for archaeology of synagogues has produced decorations that hardly conform to the Rabbinic rules governing representational art. But only Rabbinic Judaism is fully represented in written evidence that permits us to formulate its history.

Judaism represented by archaeological remains: The two bodies of evidence that inform us about the condition of the religion, Judaism, in late antiquity, archaeological and literary, do not correspond. The Judaism portrayed in the material culture uncovered by archaeology takes over the images of Graeco-Roman paganism and integrate it into a Judaism represented by the remains of synagogue decoration, burial rites, and the like. This evidence proves homogeneous for all parts of the Roman Empire, and it suggests that beyond the pages of the Talmud, a Judaism flourished of which the Talmudic rabbis never could have approved. Even where some of the same symbols are mentioned in the Bible or Talmud and inscribed on graves or synagogues, it is not always obvious that the biblical antecedents or Talmudic references engage the mind of the artist. The artists follow the conventions of Hellenistic art, and not only Hellenistic art, but the conventions of the artists who decorated non-Judaic cultic objects and places in the same locale in which, in the Jewish settings, the symbols have turned up. A principal interpreter of the art of ancient Judaism, Erwin R. Goodenough, asks:

> Admitting that the Jews would not have remained Jews if they had used these images in pagan ways and with pagan explanations, do the remains indicate a symbolic adaptation of pagan figures to Judaism or merely an urge to decoration?[1]

He concludes:

> Indeed when the religious symbols borrowed by Jews in those years are put together, it becomes clear that the ensemble is not merely a "picture book without text," but reflect a lingua franca that had been taken into most of the religions of the day, for the same symbols were used in association with Dionysius, Mithra, Osiris, the Etruscan gods, Sabazius, Attis, and a host of others, as well as by Christianity later. It was a symbolic language, a direct language of values, however, not a language of denotation.[2]

Goodenough is far from suggesting the presence of a pervasive syncretism. Rather, he points to what he regards as pervasive religious values applied quite parochially by various groups, including some Jews to the worship of their particular "Most High God." These values, while connotative and not denotative, may, nonetheless, be recovered and articulated in some measure by the historian who makes use of the insights of recent students of psychology and symbolism:

> In taking over the symbols, while discarding the myths and explanations of the pagans, Jews and Christians admitted, indeed

confirmed, a continuity of religious experience which it is most important to be able to identify . . . for an understanding of man, the phenomenon of a continuity of religious experience or values would have much more significance than that of discontinuous explanations.[3]

These symbols, he holds, were of use "only in religions that engendered deep emotion, ecstasy, religions directly and consciously centered in the renewing of life and the granting of immortality, in the giving to the devotee of a portion of the divine spirit of life substance."

> At the end these symbols appear to indicate a type of Judaism in which, as in Philonic Judaism, the basic elements of "mystery" were superimposed upon Jewish legalism. The Judaism of the rabbis has always offered essentially a path through this present life the father's code of instructions as to how we may please him while we are alive. To this, the symbols seem to say, was now added from the mystery religions, or from Gnosticism, the burning desire to leave this life altogether, to renounce the flesh and go into the richness of divine existence, to appropriate God's life to oneself.
>
> These ideas have as little place in normative, Rabbinic Judaism as do the pictures and symbols and gods that Jews borrowed to suggest them . . . That such ideas were borrowed by Jews was no surprise to me after years of studying Philo.

What is perplexing is the problem of how Jews fitted such conceptions into, or harmonized them with, the teachings of the Bible.

While much debated, Goodenough's approach takes account of the realities of the Jews' situation in a cosmopolitan and diverse world, in which many different groups lived side by side. Under such circumstances, Jews learned from their neighbors and commented, in a way they found appropriate, on their neighbors' religions. Jews did not live quite separate from the diverse world around them. They assuredly spoke the same language as others, and they knew what was going on. There was no single Judaism, there was never an Orthodoxy, any more than today there is a single Judaism, Orthodox or otherwise. Indeed, both in the Land of Israel and throughout Babylonia (present day Iraq) Jews lived in the same many-splendored world, in which

diverse languages and groups worshipped different gods. The evidence is that the Jews in Babylonian, where the Talmud of Babylonia took shape, lived in relatively close contact, both physical and cultural, with their neighbors. Their main center, Nehardea, was not far from the great Hellenistic city, Seleucia on the Tigris. Greeks, Babylonians, pagan Semites, Jews, and Parthians inhabited the narrow strip of fertile land around the Royal Canal, which later historians so generously assigned to the Jews alone. It should be emphasized, therefore, that the Jews were only one minority in the region, and they were not the most numerous. And the same applies even to the regions of the eastern part of the Roman Empire that possessed sizable Jewish populations, Galilee, for instance.

Extensive Jewish participation in political, commercial, and possibly military affairs could not have been carried on by people "wholly isolated" from the culture of the government. One should expect to find among them substantial marks of knowledge of surrounding culture. Not the least of the contacts of the Jewish masses with that culture would have been through the coinage, which certainly yielded some information on the pagan religion of the Roman and Iranian Empires, and on the local Semitic and Hellenistic cults as well. It is too much to conclude that political, commercial, and military contacts had led to the utter assimilation of Babylonian Jewry into Parthian culture or the Jews of Graeco-Roman times in the Land of Israel into pagan culture in their setting. But we should not be surprised to find some kind of syncretistic, mystical tradition in the synagogues, such as the utilization of pagan symbols there suggests. That the synagogue's Judaism is not portrayed in the Rabbinic writings—which on every page denounce what sages rejected in the life of the Jews round-about—hardly presents a surprise. Goodenough's approach to the Judaism represented by synagogue symbolism is as follows:

> Symbolism is itself a language, and affected the original faith much as does adopting a new language in which to express its tenets. Both Christians and Jews in these years read

their Scriptures, and prayed in words that had been consecrated to pagan deities. The very idea of a God, discussion of the values of the Christian or Jewish God, could be conveyed only by using the old pagan theos; salvation by the word soteria; immortality by athanasia. The eagle, the crown, the zodiac, and the like spoke just as direct, just as complicated a language. The Christian or Jew had by no means the same conception of heaven or immortality as the pagan, but all had enough in common to make the same symbols, as well as the same words, expressive and meaningful. Yet the words and the symbols borrowed did bring in something new. . . .[4]

Describing that other Judaism out of the archaeological remains remains a difficult problem, and Goodenough's proposed solution—a mystical Judaic cult, celebrating immortality—meets formidable competition. We cannot describe the Judaism adumbrated in the silent stones, nor does that Judaism yield a history in any narrative framework. The competing Judaic system, by contrast, comes to richly detailed articulation and one kind of history—literary, not social, to be sure—emerges as well.

Judaism represented by surviving writings. Rabbinic Judaism: The literary evidence, in the form of well-crafted, systematic and coherent documents, presents us with a Judaism called "Rabbinic," by reason of the title of honor accorded many of its principal authorities, or "classical" or "normative," by reason of its later standing, or "Talmudic," because of its final and definitive statement, in the Talmud of Babylonia. Its governing myth, the story of how at Sinai God revealed the Torah to Moses in two media, written and oral, with the oral part finally given written articulation in the Mishnah and associated writings of rabbis themselves, contributes the title, "Judaism of the dual Torah."

The history of that particular Judaism as it took over and defined the life of the Jews in the first six centuries of the Common Era cannot be recovered. We have no evidence about the state of affairs for the Jews in general, such as would tell us how that Judaic system came to dictate the character of the Jews' social world and culture. One may argue that the evidence driving from synagogues, not that reaching us from the limited circles of learned sages, tells us about the common practices of the time. But, as we have noted, what sort of religious system emerges out of the material evidence remains to be determined.

How the Judaic system set forth in the Rabbinic writings related to the religious life of Jews beyond the circles of sages, the ways in which the particular way of life and world view set forth by that system came to define the actual character of the "Israel" to which that Judaism spoke—these are historical questions we cannot answer. The books tell us what their writers and compilers thought, but not about the world beyond their circle and its view of matters. And what we learn about "Judaism" from other than Judaic sources, for instance, pagan and Christian and Zoroastrian writers about Judaism, tells us no more than we know about Judaism from the written Torah. Christian writers about Judaism, for example, utilize the Hebrew Scriptures for their picture of the Judaism that they criticize.

But a different sort of history of Judaism in late antiquity emerges from the Rabbinic documents. It is the documentary history of the ideas that inform the religious system of Rabbinic Judaism. For if we follow the unfolding of the documents of that Judaism, stated in documentary terms, the formative history of Judaism tells a story in these sentences.

It shows how the Judaic system first emerged in the Mishnah, ca. 200 C.E., and its associated Midrash-compilations, ca. 200-300 C.E., as a philosophical structure comprising a politics, philosophy, economics. These categories were defined as philosophers in general understood them: a theory of legitimate violence, an account of knowledge gained through the methods of natural history, and a theory of the rational disposition (and increase) of scarce resources.

This philosophical system then was turned by the Talmud of the Land of Israel and related Midrash-compilations, ca. 400-500 C.E., into a religious system. The system was effected through the formation of counterpart categories: an anti-politics of weakness, an anti-economics of the rational utilization of an infinitely renewable resource, a philosophy of truth revealed rather than rules discovered.

The first stage in the documentary history takes up the urgent questions precipitated by the political calamities of the first and second centuries, the destruction of the Temple, the paganization of Jerusalem, and the chaos following the Bar Kokhba disaster (figs. 68-69). The second stage responds to the issues made urgent by the political triumph of Christianity and the consequent challenge to the situation of Israel as Jews read Scripture's account of their particular Israel. To the extent that the documentary history corresponds to the major turnings in political history, we may reconstruct not only the unfolding of ideas, but the relationship between ideas and the social world of the people that held those ideas, that the history of a religion proposes to narrate.

The crisis of 70 and the Mishnaic stage in the formation of Rabbinic Judaism: The Temple in Jerusalem, where sacrifices were offered to God, constituted the focus of Pentateuchal Judaism. Indeed, the cycle of holy time was marked by sacrifice. Thus the lives of the patriarchs repeatedly drew them into relationship with the sacrificial cult in various holy places, but especially in Jerusalem, and the laws of the Torah dealt in detail with the sacrifices, the priests, the maintenance of the priestly caste, and other cultic matters. So the power of the Torah composed in this time lay in its focus on the Temple. This central Temple cult, with its total exclusion of the non-Israelite, raised high walls of separation between Jew and "other." They underlined such distinctiveness as already existed. What made Israel Israel was the center, the altar; the life of Israel flowed from the altar. But in 70 C.E., in the course of a war fought by Jews against Roman rule in the Land of Israel, Jerusalem fell, and the Temple, except for the Western wall of the platform on which it stood, was destroyed.

How then, are we to define the urgent question and self-evident answer of the Judaic system of the Dual Torah, Oral and Written, that emerged in the Mishnah? The principal question formulated by the sages who pro-

duced writings beyond 70—writings that ultimately were portrayed as the oral part of the one whole Torah of Moses, "our lord," our *rabbi*—centered upon the sanctification of Israel now that the Temple, the locus of holiness, lay in ruins and the cult was no more. The Judaism of the dual Torah set forth a twin-ideal: 1) sanctification of the everyday life in the here and now would, when fully realized, lead to 2) salvation of all Israel in the age to come. But what remained to be sanctified, as the Temple had been sanctified through its cult, now that the Temple was gone? One locus of sanctification endured beyond 70: the holy people itself. That people's life would be made holy—in the holy land at first, but later, as this Judaism spread across the world through exile in the diaspora, everywhere the people lived. Holy of course meant separate and distinct from the ordinary, and the chronic question of who is a Jew and what is Israel would find its self-evident response in the same categories as the Pentateuchal system had defined for itself.

The stress of the Judaism of the dual Torah, of the post-Temple sages or rabbis who constructed it, on the sanctification of the home and the paradigmatic power of the Temple for the home points to a more extreme position within the priestly paradigm than that of the priests who wrote parts of Exodus, Leviticus, and Numbers. What the priests wanted for the Temple, the dual Torah's sages wanted for the community, Israel, at large. The premise of the written Torah rested on a simple allegation: if Israel observes the terms of the covenant, leading a sanctified life, Israel will enjoy prosperity in a serene land, a national life outside of history. The traumatic event of annihilation and rebirth, of death and resurrection of the nation (as manifested in the reworking of ancient Israelite writings into the Pentateuch) brought about yearning for one thing above all, no more. The picture of what had happened presented solace—that is why people wanted to accept the portrait of their world. The restoration gave Israel a second chance at life, but Israel also could rely on its knowledge of the rules that governed its national life, those of the Torah and its repeated allegations of an agreement, or covenant, between Israel and God, to make certain there would be no more experiences of exile and alienation (whether or not followed by reconciliation and restoration). This same paradigm governed in the framing of the Judaism of the dual Torah. What shifted was the redefinition of salvation from the here and now to the end of time. And that change, of course, was not only plausible, it also was necessary in light of the destruction of the Temple in 70.

The reason for the transfer of the hope for salvation from now to the end of time derives from a political event in some ways bearing greater weight than the destruction of the Temple in 70. This event is the failure to recover the city and rebuild the Temple through war three generations later. Had the war been successful, it could have replicated the events that began in 586 and ended in 450. That is, it could have restored the people to the land and the government and Temple to Jerusalem. Indeed, when the war broke out in 132, the Jews evidently expected that after three generations, God would call an end to the punishment as God had done by restoring the Temple some "seventy years" after its first destruction (586). But that did not happen. Under Bar Kokhba Israel again suffered defeat—a defeat worse than before. The Temple now lay in permanent ruins; Jerusalem became a forbidden city for Jews. So Israel, the Jewish people, necessarily set out to assimilate enduring defeat.

The Mishnah's Judaism of sanctification without the Temple: The Mishnah manifests the Judaism that took shape in the aftermath of the Jews' defeat in this Second War against Rome, fought from 132 through 135. Although later considered the written manifestation of the oral tradition that formed part of the Torah received by Moses at Sinai, and accorded proportionate status, the Mishnah was in fact a philosophical system in the form of a law code that responded to problems arising from the destruction of the Temple and Bar Kokhba's subsequent defeat. When in the aftermath of the destruction in C.E. 70 and the still more disheartening defeat of 135 the Mishnah's sages worked out a Judaism without a Temple and a cult, they produced in the Mishnah a system of sanctification focused on the holiness of the priesthood, the cultic festivals, the Temple and its sacrifices, and on the rules for protecting that holiness from Levitical uncleanness. Four of the six divisions of the Mishnah expound on this single theme.

In an act of supererogatory imagination, defying the facts of the circumstance of a defeated nation, the Mishnah's system-builders composed a world at rest, perfect and complete, made holy because it is complete and perfect. In mythic terms, the Mishnah reaches back to creation to interpret the world of destruction round about. The system of the Mishnah confronts the fall from Eden with Eden, the world in time beyond the closure of Jerusalem to Israel with the timeless world on the eve of the Sabbath of Creation: "Thus the heavens and the earth were finished and all the host of them. And on the seventh day God finished his work which he had done, and he rested on the seventh day from all his work which he had done. So God blessed the seventh day and hallowed it, because on it God rested from all his work which he had done in creation" (Gen. 2:1-3).

The Mishnah's framers posited an economy embedded in a social system awaiting the seventh day, and that day's divine act of sanctification which, as at the creation of the world, would set the seal of holy rest upon an again-complete creation. That would be a creation that was well ordered, with all things called by their rightful names, in their proper classification, from the least to the greatest, and from the many to the One. There is no place for action and actors when what is besought is no action whatsoever, but only unchanging perfection. There is room only for a description of how things are, for the present tense, for a sequence of completed statements and static problems. All the action lies within, in how these statements are made. Once they stand fully expressed, when nothing remains to be said, nothing remains to be done. There is no need for actors, whether political entities such as king, scribes, priests, or economic entities, householders.

That is why the Mishnah's framers invented a utopia, one that exists nowhere in particular, a fantasy related to whom it may concern. The politics of Judaism began in the imagination of a generation of intellectuals who, in the aftermath of the Jerusalem government's and Temple's destruction (70) and the military defeat Jews suffered three generations later (132-135), had witnessed the end of the political system and structure that the Jews had known for the preceding millennium. The political theory of Judaism laid out political institutions and described how they should work. In that way these intellectuals, who enjoyed no documented access to power of any kind and who certainly were unable to coerce many people to do very much, sorted out issues of power. They took account, in mind at least, of the issues of legitimate coercion within Israel, the holy people, which they considered more than a voluntary association, more than a community formed around a cult.

The Mishnah's principal message, which makes the Judaism of this document and of its social components distinctive and cogent, is that man is at the center of creation, the head of all creatures upon earth, corresponding to God in heaven, in whose image man is made. The way in which the Mishnah makes this simple and fundamental statement is to impute power to man to inaugurate and initiate those corresponding processes, sanctification and uncleanness, which play so critical a role in the Mishnah's account of reality. The will of man, expressed through the deed of man, is the active power in the world. Will and deed constitute those actors of creation which work upon neutral realms, subject to either sanctification or uncleanness: the Temple and table, the field and family, the altar and hearth, woman, time, space, transactions in the material world and in the world above as well. An object, a substance, a transaction, even a phrase or a sentence is inert but may be made holy when the interplay of the will and deed of man arouses or generates its potential to be sanctified. Each may be treated as ordinary or (where relevant) made unclean by the neglect of the will and inattentive act of man. Just as the entire system of uncleanness and holiness awaits the intervention of man, which imparts the capacity to become

unclean upon what was formerly inert, or which removes the capacity to impart cleanness from what was formerly in its natural and puissant condition, so in the other ranges of reality, man is at the center on earth, just as is God in heaven. Man is counterpart and partner and creation, in that, like God he has power over the status and condition of creation, through his intentionality putting everything in its proper place, through the exercise of his will calling everything by its rightful name. The goal then was the restoration of creation to its original perfection. Then it was that God ceased from labor, blessed creation, and sanctified it.

The Talmuds' Judaism of sanctification and salvation: The Mishnah enjoyed two centuries of study and amplification. Indeed, a massive system deriving from and connecting with the Mishnah's but essentially distinct from it emerged in the Talmud of the Land of Israel (closed ca. 400). The urgent question that predominates in that enormous document, and that takes the form of an extended elaboration of the Mishnah, is salvation: when and why will it come, and, above all, how long must it be postponed? The urgency of the issue derived from two events that we have already touched upon. First of all, in 312 Constantine legalized Christianity, and in the course of the next three generations, the state became officially Christian. In the course of suppressing paganism, the Christian state adopted rules that for the first time since the Maccabees, in the second century B.C., denied the licit practice of Judaism. That trauma was intensified by a brief moment of relief, when one of the heirs of Constantine, Julian, left Christianity, reaffirmed paganism and, in 361 proposed to discredit Christianity by permitting the Jews to rebuild the Temple in Jerusalem. Unfortunately, he died soon afterward and nothing came of the project.

The urgency with which the Jews pursued the question of salvation is hardly a surprising. The Christians' political triumph and the Jews' deep disappointment at Julian's failed scheme, allowed the Christians to claim that the political shifts in the standing of Christianity and Judaism confirmed the truth of

Christianity and underlined the falsity of Judaism. In particular, Christianity stressed the falsity of the Jews' hope for a coming messiah. It argued that the Jews had been saved in the time of the return to Zion (450 B.C.E.). That return, Christians claimed, fulfilled the Old Testament prophecies of Israel's salvation. But from that moment, by rejecting the messiahship of Jesus, Jews had lost all further standing in the divine scheme for saving humanity. So the question of salvation turned from a chronic concern to an acute crisis for the Jews—in positive and negative ways. And predictably, it was addressed by the sages who revised the Mishnah by setting forth the Talmud of the Land of Israel.

Two hundred years after that Talmud took shape, a second one, the Talmud of Babylonia, recast matters in a permanent and authoritative form (ca. 600). From then to the present, "the Talmud," meaning the Talmud of Babylonia, together with its commentaries, codes of laws deriving from it, and institutions of autonomous administration resting on it, has defined the life of most Jews and the Judaic system that prevailed as normative. Its successful definition of the essentials of Judaism for Jews living in Christian and the Muslim worlds depends on the compelling power of its account of who is a Jew, what it means to be Israel, and how the holy people must work out its life in the here and now so as to attain salvation at the end of time. This was, then, a Judaism intersecting with the Mishnah's but essentially asymmetrical with. It was a system for salvation focused on the salvific power of the sanctification of the holy people.

The Judaism of the dual Torah as portrayed in the two Talmuds shifted the focus from the Temple and its supernatural history to the people Israel and its natural, this-worldly history. Once Israel, holy Israel, had come to form the counterpart to the Temple and its supernatural life, that other history—Israel's—would stand at the center of things. Accordingly, a new sort of memorable event came to the fore in the Talmud of the Land of Israel. It was the story of Israel's suffering—remembrance of that suffering on the one side, and an effort to explain events of such tragedy on the other. And that story enjoyed the standing of self-evident, indeed self-validating truth because Jews found that it corresponded to and satisfactorily explained the powerless political situation they found themselves in.

The Mishnah: Judaism as a philosophy in the first and second centuries: From this brief account of the unfolding, in response to historical crises, of the Judaism of the dual Torah, let us turn to the intellectual characterization of each of its stages, with stress on the shift from philosophy to religion. The Mishnah presents a philosophical theory of the social order, a system of thought that, in the context of the same time and place, people generally deemed philosophers will have recognized as philosophical. The Mishnah's method of hierarchical classification in important ways is like that of the natural history of Aristotle, and the central component of its message proves congruent to that of neo-Platonism.

Specifically, the Mishnah's Judaic system sets forth in stupefying detail a version of one critical proposition of neo-Platonism, demonstrated through a standard Aristotelian method. The repeated proof through the Aristotelian method of hierarchical classification demonstrates in detail that many things really form a single thing, many species, a single genus, many genera, an encompassing and well-crafted, cogent whole. Every time we speciate—and the Mishnah is a mass of speciated lists—we affirm that position; each successful labor of forming relationships among species, e.g., making them into a genus, or identifying the hierarchy of the species, proves it again. Not only so, but when we can show that many things are really one, or that one thing yields many (the reverse and confirmation of the former), we say in a fresh way a single immutable truth, the core of this philosophy concerning the unity of all being in an orderly composition of all things within a single taxon. Accordingly, this Judaism's initial system, the Mishnah's, finds its natural place within philosophy because it appeals to the Aristotelian methods and medium of natural philosophy—classification, comparison and contrast, expressed in the forms of

Listenwissenschaft—to register its position, which is an important one in Middle Platonism and later (close to a century after the closure of the Mishnah) would come to profound expression in Plotinus.

The philosophical Judaism moreover utilized economics—the rational disposition of scarce resources—in order to set forth a systemic statement of fundamental importance. Entirely congruent with the philosophical economics of Aristotle, the Mishnah's economics answered the same questions concerning the definition of wealth, property, production and the means of production, ownership and control of the means of production, the determination of price and value and the like. And that fact signifies that the Judaic system to which the Mishnah attests is philosophical not only in method and message but in its very systemic composition. The principal components of its theory of the social order, its account of the way of life of its Israel and its picture of the conduct of the public policy of its social entity—all of these in detail correspond in their basic definitions and indicative traits with the economics and the politics of Greco-Roman philosophy in the Aristotelian tradition. Specifically, the Mishnah's economics, in general in the theory of the rational disposition of scarce resources and of the management and increase thereof, and specifically in its definitions of wealth and ownership, production and consumption, point by point, corresponds to that of Aristotle.

The power of economics as framed by Aristotle was to develop the relationship between the economy to society as a whole. And the framers of the Mishnah did the same when they incorporated issues of economics at a profound theoretical level into the system of society as a whole that they proposed to construct. That is why the authorship of the Mishnah will be seen as attacking the problem of man's livelihood within a system of sanctification of a holy people with a radicalism of which no later religious thinkers about utopias were capable. None has ever penetrated deeper into the material organization of man's life under the aspect of God's rule. They posed, in all its breadth, the ques-

tion of the critical, indeed definitive place occupied by the economy in society under God's rule. The points in common between Aristotle's and the Mishnah's economics prove no less indicative. Both Aristotle and the Mishnah presented an anachronistic system of economics. The theory of both falls into the same classification of economic theory, that of distributive economics, familiar in the Near and Middle East from Sumerian times down to, but not including, the age of Aristotle (let alone that of the Mishnah five centuries later). But market-economics had been well-established prior to Aristotle's time. Aristotle's economics is distributive for systemic reasons, the Mishnah's replicates the received principles of the economics planned by the Temple priests and set forth in the Priestly Code of the Pentateuch, Leviticus in particular. The result—fabricated or replicated principles—was the same. Both systems—the Mishnah's and Aristotle's—in vast detail expressed the ancient distributive economics, in their theories of fixed value and conception of the distribution of scarce resources by appeal to other than the rationality of the market. The theory of money characteristic of Aristotle (but not of Plato) and of the Mishnah for instance conforms to that required by distributive economics; exchange takes place through barter, not through the abstract price-setting mechanism represented by money. Consequently, the representation of the Mishnah as a philosophical Judaism derives from not only general characteristics but very specific and indicative traits held in common with the principal figure of the Greco-Roman philosophical tradition in economics.

There was a common social foundation for the economic theory of both systems. Both Aristotle and the Mishnah's framers deemed the fundamental unit of production to be the household, and the larger social unit, the village, composed of households, marked the limits of the social entity. The Mishnah's economic tractates, such as the tractates on civil law, invariably refer to the householder, making him the subject of most predicates; where issues other than economics are in play, e.g., in the political tractates such as Sanhedrin, the householder scarcely appears as a social actor. Not only so, but both Aristotle and the authorship of the Mishnah formed the conception of "true value," which maintained that something—an object, a piece of land—possessed a value extrinsic to the market and intrinsic to itself, such that, if a transaction varied from that imputed true value by (in the case of the Mishnah) 18%, the exchange was null. Not only so, but the sole definition of wealth for both Aristotle's and the Mishnah's economics was real estate, only land however small. Since land does not contract or expand, of course, the conception of an increase in value through other than a steady-state exchange of real value, "true value," between parties to a transaction lay outside of the theory of economics. Therefore all profit, classified as usury, was illegitimate and must be prevented.

The Mishnah's politics—its theory of the legitimate use of violence and the disposition of power in society—describes matters in a manner that is fundamentally philosophical in the Aristotelian context. Israel forms a political entity, fully empowered in an entirely secular sense, just as Scripture had described matters. To political institutions of the social order, king, priest, and court or civil administration, each in its jurisdiction, is assigned the right legitimately to exercise violence here on earth, corresponding to, and shared with, the same empowerment accorded to institutions of Heaven. These institutions moreover are conceived permanently to ration and rationalize the uses of that power. The picture, of course, is this-worldly, but, not distinguishing crime from sin, it is not secular, since the same system that legitimates king, high priest, and court posits in Heaven a corresponding politics, with God and the court on high exercising jurisdiction for some crimes or sins, the king, priesthood, or court down below for others. Three specific traits, direct our attention toward the philosophical classification for the Mishnah's politics in framing a systemic composition, even though, to be sure, the parallels prove structural and general, rather than detailed and doctrinal as was the case with economics.

First, like the politics of Plato and Aristotle, the Mishnah's politics describes only a utopian politics, a structure and system of a fictive and a fabricated kind: intellectuals' conception of a politics. Serving the larger purpose of system-construction, politics of necessity emerges as invention, e.g., by Heaven or in the model of Heaven, not as a secular revision and reform of an existing system. While in the middle second-century Rome incorporated their country, which they called the Land of Israel and the Romans called Palestine, into its imperial system, denying Jews access to their capital, Jerusalem, permanently closing their cult-center, its Temple, the authorship of the Mishnah described a government of a king and a high priest and an administration fully empowered to carry out the law through legitimate violence. So the two politics—the Mishnah's, the Greco-Roman tradition represented by Plato's and Aristotle's—share in common their origins in intellectuals' theoretical and imaginative life and form an instance, within that life, of the concrete realization of a larger theory of matters. In strange and odd forms, the Mishnah's politics falls into the class of the *Staatsroman*, the classification that encompasses also Plato's *Republic* and Aristotle's *Politics*. But, admittedly, the same may be said for the strange politics of the Pentateuch.

Second and more to the point, the Mishnah's sages stand well within the philosophical mode of political thought that begins with Aristotle, who sees politics as a fundamental component of his system when he says, "political science . . . legislates as to what we are to do and what we are to abstain from;" and, as to the institutionalization of power, one cannot imagine a more ample definition of the Mishnah's system's utilization of politics than that. While that statement also applies to the Pentateuchal politics, the systemic message borne by politics within the Pentateuchal system and that carried by politics in the Mishnah's system do not correspond in any important ways. Aristotle and the philosophers of the Mishnah utilize politics to make systemic statements that correspond to one another, in that both comparison and contrast prove apt and pointed. Both spoke of an empowered social entity; both took for granted that on-going institutions legitimately exercise governance in accord with a rationality discerned by distinguishing among those empowered to inflict sanctions. Both see politics as a medium for accomplishing systemic goals, and the goals derive from the larger purpose of the social order, to which politics is subordinated and merely instrumental.

But, third, the comparison also yields a contrast of importance. Specifically, since political analysis comes only after economic analysis and depends upon the results of that prior inquiry into a social system's disposition of scarce resources and theory of control of means of production, we have no choice but to follow up the results of the preceding chapter and compare the politics of Aristotle and the politics of the Mishnah, just as we did the economics of each system. For when we know who commands the means of production, we turn to inquire about who tells whom what to do and why: who legitimately coerces others even through violence. And here the Mishnah's system decisively parts company with that of the Pentateuch and also with that of Aristotle. As to the former, the distributive economics of the Pentateuch, in the Priestly stratum at the foundations, assigns both economic and political privilege to the same class of persons, the priesthood, effecting distributive economics and distributive politics. But that is not the way things are in the Mishnah's politics, which distinguishes the one in control of the means of production from the one control of the right legitimately to commit violence. The former, the householder, is not a political entity at all, and, dominant as the subject of most sentences in the economic tractates, he never appears in the political ones at all.

The point of difference from Aristotle is to be seen only within the context of the similarity that permits comparison and contrast. While the economics of Aristotle and the economics of Judaism commence with the consideration of the place and power of the person ("class," "caste," economic interest) in control of the means of production, the social metaphors that animate the politics of the two systems part company. Aristotle in his *Politics* is consistent in starting with that

very same person ("class") when he considers issues of power, producing a distributive politics to match his distributive economics. But the Mishnah's philosophers build their politics with an altogether different set of building blocks. The simple fact is that the householder, fundamental to their economics, does not form a subject of political discourse at all and in no way constitutes a political class or caste. When the Mishnah's writers speak of economics, the subject of most active verbs is the householder; when they speak of politics, the householder never takes an active role or even appears as a differentiated political class. In this sense, the economics of the Mishnah is disembedded from its politics, and the politics from its economics. By contrast the economics and politics of Aristotle's system are deeply embedded within a larger and nurturing, wholly cogent theory of political economy.

The Yerushalmi's transformation of philosophy into religion: The successor-system, represented by the Talmud of the Land of Israel and related writings, ca. 400-450, presented a theory of the social order lacking any theory of politics, philosophy, and economics of a conventional order. Now that we have seen the philosophical character of the initial system's world-view, way of life, and theory of the social entity, that is, its philosophy, economics, and politics, we ask how these same categories fared in the successor-system's documentary evidence. As a matter of simple fact, while sharing the goal of presenting a theory of the social order, as to their categorical formations and structures, the initial, philosophical Judaic system and the successor system differ in a fundamental way. What happened is that the successor-system held up a mirror to the received categories and so redefined matters that everything was reversed. Left became right, down, up, and, as we shall see, in a very explicit transvaluation of values, power is turned into weakness, things of real value are transformed into intangibles. This transvaluation, yielding the transformation of the prior system altogether, is articulated and not left implicit; it is a specific judgment made concrete through mythic and symbolic revision by the later authorships themselves. A free-standing document, received with reverence, served to precipitate the transvaluation of all of the values of that document's initial statement.

What the philosophical Judaism kept apart, the religious Judaism portrayed by the Talmud of the Land of Israel and related writings now joined together, and it is just there, at that critical joining, that we identify the key to the system: its reversal of a received point of differentiation, its introduction of new points of differentiation altogether. The source of generative problems for the Mishnah's politics is simply not the same as the source that served the successor-system's politics, and, systemic analysis being what it is, it is the union of what was formerly asunder that identifies for us in quite objective terms the critical point of tension, the sources of problems, the centerpiece of systemic concern throughout. Let me show how this process of reintegration was worked out in the categorical reformation underway in the Yerushalmi and related writings.

We begin with the shift from philosophy to Torah-study, that is from abstract reflection to concrete text-exegesis and digression out of sacred scripture; philosophy yields accurate and rational understanding of things; knowledge of the Torah, by contrast, yields power over this world and the next, capacity to coerce to the sage's will the natural and supernatural worlds alike, on that account. The Torah is thus transformed from a philosophical enterprise of the sifting and classification of the facts of this world into a gnostic process of changing persons through knowledge. It is on that basis that in the Yerushalmi and related writings we find in the Torah the counterpart-category to philosophy in the Mishnah. Now we deal with a new intellectual category: Torah, meaning, religious learning *in place of* philosophical learning. What is the difference between the one and the other? First comes appeal to revealed truth as against perceived facts of nature and their regularities, second, the conception of an other-worldly source of explanation and the development of a propositional program focused upon not nature but Scripture, not the

nations in general but Israel in particular, and third, the gnosticization of knowledge in the conception that knowing works salvation.

What was to change, therefore, was not the mode of thought. What was new, rather, was the propositions to be demonstrated philosophically, and what made these propositions new was the focus of interest, on the one side, and data assembled by way of demonstrating them, on the other. From a philosophical proposition within the framework of free-standing philosophy of religion and metaphysics that the Mishnah's system aimed to establish, we move to religious and even theological propositions within the setting of contingent exegesis of Scripture. Then how do we know that what was changing was not merely topical and propositional but *categorical* in character? The answer lies in the symbolic vocabulary that would be commonly used in the late fourth and fifth century writings but not at all, or not in the same way, in the late second century ones. When people select data not formerly taken into account and represent the data by appeal to symbols not formerly found evocative or expressive, or not utilized in the way in which they later on were used, then we are justified in raising questions about category-formation and the development of new categories alongside, or instead, of the received ones. In the case at hand, the character of the transformation we witness is shown by the formation of a symbol serving to represent a category.

To signal what is to come, we shall find the quite bald statement that, in the weighing of the comparative value of capital—which in this time and place meant land or real property, and Torah—Torah was worthwhile, and land was not. This symbolic syllogism is explicit, concrete, repeated, and utterly fresh for the documents we consider. On the basis of that quite explicit symbolic comparison we speak of transformation—symbolic and therefore *categorical* transformation, not merely thematic shifts in emphasis or even propositional change. Here we witness in the successor-writings the formation of a system connected with, but asymmetrical to, the initial, philosophical one. Then for the world-view of the transformed Judaism, the counterpart-category to philosophy is formulated by appeal to the symbolic medium for the theological message, and it is the category, the Torah, expressed, as a matter of fact, by the symbol of *Torah.*

Philosophy sought the generalizations that cases might yield. So too did religion (and, in due course, theology would too). But the range of generalization vastly differed. Philosophy spoke of the nature of things, while theology represented the special nature of Israel in particular. Philosophy then appealed to the traits of things, while theology to the special indicative qualities of Israel. What of the propositional program that the document sets forth? The philosophical proposition of the Mishnah demonstrated from the facts and traits of things the hierarchical order of all being, with the obvious if merely implicit proposition that God stands at the head of the social order. The religious propositions of the successor-documents speak in other words of other things, having simply nothing in common with the propositional program of the Mishnah's philosophy.

The shift in economics is no less striking. Consideration of the transvaluation of value brings us to the successor-system's counterpart category, that is, the one that in context forms the counterpart to the Mishnah's concrete, this-worldly, material and tangible definition of value in conformity with the familiar, philosophical economics. We have now to ask, what, in place of the received definition of value and the economics thereof, did the new system set forth? The transformation of economics involved the redefinition of scarce and valued resources in so radical a manner that the concept of value, while remaining material in consequence and character, nonetheless took on a quite different sense altogether. The counterpart category of the successor-system concerned itself with the same questions as did the conventional economics, presenting an economics in function and structure, but one that concerned things of value other than those identified by the initial system. So indeed we deal with an economics, an economics of something other than real estate.

But it was an economics just as profoundly embedded in the social order, just as deeply a political economics, just as pervasively a systemic economics, as the economics of the Mishnah and of Aristotle. Why so? Because issues such as the definition of wealth, the means of production and the meaning of control thereof, the disposition of wealth through distributive or other media, theory of money, reward for labor, and the like— all these issues found their answers in the counterpart-category of economics, as much as in the received and conventional philosophical economics. The new "scarce resource" accomplished what the old did, but it was a different resource, a new currency. At stake in the category meant to address the issues of the way of life of the social entity, therefore, were precisely the same considerations as confront economics in its (to us) conventional and commonplace, philosophical sense. But since the definition of wealth changes, as we have already seen, from land to Torah, much else would be transformed on that account.

Land produced a living; so did Torah. Land formed the foundation of the social entity, so did Torah. The transvaluation of value was such that an economics concerning the rational management and increase of scarce resources worked itself out in such a way as to answer, for quite different things of value from real property or from capital such as we know as value, precisely the same questions that the received economics addressed in connection with wealth of a real character: land and its produce. Systemic transformation comes to the surface in articulated symbolic change. The utter transvaluation of value finds expression in a jarring juxtaposition, an utter shift of rationality, specifically, the substitution of Torah for real estate. In the fifth century (but not in earlier compilations) Tarfon is said to have thought wealth took the form of land, while Aqiba explained to him that wealth takes the form of Torah-learning. That the sense is material and concrete is explicit: land for Torah, Torah for land. To show how Torah serves as an explicit symbol to convey the systemic world-view, let us note the main point of Leviticus Rabbah XXXIV:XVI:

1.B. R. Tarfon gave to R. Aqiba six silver centenarii, saying to him, "Go, buy us a piece of land, so we can get a living from it and labor in the study of Torah together."

C. He took the money and handed it over to scribes, Mishnah-teachers, and those who study Torah.

D. After some time R. Tarfon met him and said to him, "Did you buy the land that I mentioned to you?"

E. He said to him, "Yes."

F. He said to him, "Is it any good?"

G. He said to him, "Yes."

H. He said to him, "And do you not want to show it to me?"

I. He took him and showed him the scribes, Mishnah teachers, and people who were studying Torah, and the Torah that they had acquired.

J. He said to him, "Is there anyone who works for nothing? Where is the deed covering the field?"

K. He said to him, "It is with King David, concerning whom it is written, 'He has scattered, he has given to the poor, his righteousness endures forever' (Ps. 112:9)."

The successor-system has its own definitions not only for learning, symbolized by the word Torah but also for wealth, expressed in the same symbol. Accordingly, the category-formation for world-view, Torah in place of philosophy, dictates, as a matter of fact, a still more striking category-reformation, in which the entire matter of scarce resources is reconsidered, and a counterpart-category set forth.

Philosophical politics tells who may legitimately do what to whom. When a politics wants to know who ought *not* to be doing what to whom, we find in hand the counterpart-category to the received politics—anti-politics, a theory of the illegitimacy of power, the legitimacy of being victim. The received category set forth politics as the theory of legitimate violence, the counterpart-category, politics as the theory of *illegitimate* violence. The received politics had been one of isolation and interiority, portraying Israel as sui generis and autocephalic in all ways. The portrait in the successor-documents is a politics of integration among the nations; a perspective of exteriority replaces the inner-facing one of the Mishnah, which recognized no government of Israel but God's—and then

essentially ab initio. The issues of power had found definition in questions concerning who legitimately inflicts sanctions upon whom within Israel. They now shift to give an account of who illegitimately inflicts sanctions upon ("persecutes") Israel. So the points of systemic differentiation are radically revised, and the politics of the successor-system becomes not a revision of the received category but a formation that in many ways mirrors the received one: once more a counterpart-category. Just as, in the definition of scarce resources, Torah-study has replaced land, so now weakness forms the focus in place of strength, illegitimacy in place of legitimacy. Once more the mirror-image of the received category presents the perspective of the counterpart-category.

Now we find the answers to these questions: to whom is violence illegitimately done, and also, who may not legitimately inflict violence? With the move from the politics of legitimate power to that of illegitimate power, the systemic interest now lies in defining not who legitimately does what, but rather, to whom, against whom, is power illegitimately exercised. And this movement represents not the revision of the received category, but its inversion. For thought on legitimate violence is turned on its head. A new category of empowerment is worked out alongside the old. The entity that is victim of power is at the center, rather than the entity that legitimately exercises power. That entity is now Israel *en masse* rather than the institutions and agencies of Israel on earth, Heaven above—a very considerable shift in thought on the systemic social entity. Israel as disempowered, rather than king, high priest, and sage as Israel's media of empowerment, defines the new system's politics. The upshot is that the successor-system has reconsidered not merely the contents of the received structure, but the composition of the structure itself. In place of its philosophy, we have now a new medium for the formulation of a world-view; in place of a way of life formulated as an economics, a new valuation of value, in place of an account of the social entity framed as a politics, a new conception of legitimate violence. So much for the formation of counterpart categories.

From philosophy to religion. Systemic integration: What holds the system together identifies the critical question that the system as a whole means to answer, its aspect of self-evidence. Seeing the whole all at once, we may then undertake that work of comparison and contrast that produces connections from system to system. How then may we characterize the shift from a philosophical to a religious system? The answer derives from our choice of the systemic center, e.g., a symbol that captures the whole, that holds the whole together. Certainly, the integration of the philosophical system is readily stated in a phrase: the philosophical Judaism set forth a system of hierarchical classification. Having emphasized the succession—philosophy out, Torah in—one may ask whether for the religious system of Judaism, the systemic center is captured by the symbol of the Torah—focused on the holy man sanctified through mastery of revelation. The answer is negative, because, as a matter of fact, knowledge of the Torah forms a way-station on a path to a more distant, more central goal, it is a dependent variable, contingent and stipulative. Then wherein lies the systemic center? It is the quest for *zekhut*, properly translated as "the heritage of virtue and its consequent entitlements." It is the simple fact that Torah-study is one means of attaining access to that heritage, of gaining *zekhut*— and there are other equally suitable means. The *zekhut* gained by Torah-study is no different from the merit gained by acts of supererogatory grace. So we must take seriously the contingent status, the standing of a dependent variable, accorded to Torah-study in such stories as Y. Ta. 3:11.IV:

> C. There was a house that was about to collapse over there [in Babylonia], and Rab set one of his disciples in the house, until they had cleared out everything from the house. When the disciple left the house, the house collapsed.
>
> D. And there are those who say that it was R. Adda bar Ahwah.
>
> E. Sages sent and said to him, "What sort of good deeds are to your credit [that you have that much merit]?"
>
> F. He said to them, "In my whole life no man ever got to the synagogue in the morning before I did. I never left anybody there when I went out. I never walked four cubits without speaking words of Torah. Nor did I ever mention teachings of Torah in an inappropriate setting. I never laid out a bed and slept for a regular period of time. I never took great strides among the associates. I never called my fellow by a nickname. I never rejoiced in the embarrassment of my fellow. I never cursed my fellow when I was lying by myself in bed. I never walked over in the marketplace to someone who owed me money.
>
> G. "In my entire life I never lost my temper in my household."
>
> H. This was meant to carry out that which is stated as follows: "I will give heed to the way that is blameless. Oh when wilt thou come to me? I will walk with integrity of heart within my house" (Ps. 101:2).

What is striking in this story is that mastery of the Torah is only one means of attaining the *zekhut* that had enabled the sage to keep the house from collapsing. And Torah-study is not the primary means of attaining *zekhut*. The question at E provides the key, together with its answer at F. For what the sage did to gain such remarkable *zekhut* is not to master such-and-so many tractates of the Mishnah. It was rather acts of courtesy, consideration, gentility, restraint. These produced *zekhut*, all of them acts of self-abnegation or the avoidance of power over others and the submission to the will and the requirement of self-esteem of others. Torah-study is simply an item on a list of actions or attitudes that generate *zekhut*.

Here, in a moral setting, we find the politics replicated: the form of power that the system promises derives from the rejection of power that the world recognizes—legitimate violence replaced by legitimation of the absence of the power to commit violence or of the failure to commit violence. And, when we ask, whence that sort of power?, the answer lies in the gaining of *zekhut* in a variety of ways, not in the acquisition of *zekhut* through the study of the Torah solely or even primarily. But, we note, the story at hand speaks of a sage in particular. He has gained *zekhut* by not acting the way sages are commonly assumed to behave but in a humble way.

Ordinary folk, not disciples of sages, have access to *zekhut* entirely outside of study of the Torah. In stories not told about rabbis, a single remarkable deed, exemplary for its deep humanity, sufficed to win for an ordinary person the *zekhut*—"the heritage of virtue and its consequent entitlements"—that elicits the same marks of supernatural favor enjoyed by some rabbis on account of their Torah-study. Accordingly, the systemic centrality of *zekhut* in the structure, the critical importance of the heritage of virtue together with its supernatural entitlements—these emerge in a striking claim. It is framed in extreme form—another mark of the unique place of *zekhut* within the system. Even though a man was degraded, one action sufficed to win for him that heavenly glory to which rabbis in lives of Torah-study aspired.

The mark of the system's integration around *zekhut* lies in its insistence that all Israelites, not only sages, could gain *zekhut* for themselves (and their descendants). A single remarkable deed, exemplary for its deep humanity, sufficed to win for an ordinary person the *zekhut* that elicits supernatural favor enjoyed by some rabbis on account of their Torah-study. The centrality of *zekhut* in the systemic structure, the critical importance of the heritage of virtue together with its supernatural entitlements therefore emerge in a striking claim. Even though a man was degraded, one action sufficed to win for him that heavenly glory to which rabbis in general aspired. The rabbinical storyteller assuredly identifies with this lesson, since it is the point of his story and its climax.

Zekhut serves, in particular, that counterpart category that speaks of not legitimate but illegitimate violence, not power but weakness. In context, time and again, we observe that *zekhut* is the power of the weak. People who through their own merit and capacity can accomplish nothing, can accomplish miracles through what others do for them in leaving a heritage of *zekhut*. And, not to miss the stunning message of the stories cited above, *zekhut* also is what the weak and excluded and despised can do that outweighs in power what the great masters of the Torah have accomplished. In the context of a sys-

tem that represents Torah as supernatural, that claim of priority for *zekhut* represents a considerable transvaluation of power, as much as of value. And, by the way, *zekhut* also forms the inheritance of the disinherited: what you receive as a heritage when you have nothing in the present and have gotten nothing in the past, that scarce resource that is free and unearned but much valued. So let us dwell upon the definitive character of the transferability of *zekhut* in its formulation, *zekhut abot*, the *zekhut* handed on by the ancestors, the transitive character of the concept and its standing as a heritage of entitlements.

So *zekhut* forms the political economy of the religious system of the social order put forward by the Talmud of the Land of Israel and related writings. Here we find the power that brought about the transvaluation of value, the reversal of the meaning of power and its legitimacy. *Zekhut* expresses and accounts for the economic valuation of the scarce resource of what we should call moral authority. *Zekhut* stands for the political valorization of weakness, that which endows the weak with a power that is not only their own but their ancestors'. It enables the weak to accomplish goals through not their own power, but their very incapacity to accomplish acts of violence—a transvaluation as radical as that effected in economics. And *zekhut* holds together both the economics and the politics of this Judaism: it makes the same statement twice. *Zekhut* as the power of the powerless, the riches of the disinherited, the valuation and valorization of the will of those who have no right to will. In that conception the politics, social order, and theology of Rabbinic Judaism came together. For the millennium and a half that would follow, this is the Judaism that governed.

Notes

[1] *Jewish Symbols in the Graeco-Roman Period* (Princeton, 1962), vol. IV, p. 27.

[2] Ibid., p. 36.

[3] Ibid., p. 42.

[4] Ibid., vol. VIII, p. 220.

JACOB NEUSNER

JUDAISM, HISTORY OF, PART. IV:A. MEDIEVAL CHRISTENDOM: The term medieval does not apply smoothly to the course of the

Jewish past, for the notion of a medieval—or middle—period in history developed entirely outside of the Jewish world. Still, the idea of such a "middle age," preceded and succeeded by periods of greater creativity, has significant meaning in western Christendom, in which it developed. It is consequently reasonable to evaluate Jewish experience against the backdrop of that particular majority society, with its distinctive tensions, pressures, and challenges.

Medieval western Christendom is generally defined as stretching in time from the Christianization of the Roman Empire in the fourth century down through the breakup of a unified Christian society across Europe during the sixteenth century and as extending in space all across the sectors of Europe that were Roman Catholic during that millennium. Jewish experience varied markedly over that long stretch of time and that broad expanse of space, and the depth of our knowledge of Jewish experience over the course of the Western "middle ages" varies widely as well. For some areas and time periods we are relatively well informed; for others we have only the most fragmentary data. Even when and where we are relatively well informed, the evidence derives overwhelmingly from a limited segment of the Jewish population, from the literate and learned leadership class. Generally conspicuous by its absence is the sort of broadly based material provided in the medieval Cairo Genizah, emanating from a substantial cross-section of Jews.

Among the important substantive variations among the Jewries of medieval western Christendom, perhaps most significant is the distinction between the older and larger Jewries of the Mediterranean areas and the newer and smaller Jewish communities of northern Europe. While the earliest sites of Jewish history lay in the Levant—along the eastern shores of the Mediterranean and in Mesopotamia—by late antiquity Jews had moved westward and founded communities all across the Mediterranean basin. Although our information on Jewish life in the west during late antiquity is minimal, it does seem clear that stable Jewish settlement around the

Mediterranean Sea was never uprooted. To be sure, some of these western Jewries—particularly the important Jewish communities of the Iberian peninsula—did pass out of the Christian orbit and into Muslim control for a period of time. Nonetheless, Jewish circumstances in the southern sectors of western Christendom, those areas bordering the Mediterranean Sea, rested on a firm foundation of longevity, uninterrupted settlement, and substantial numbers.

For approximately the first half of the period under consideration, until the tenth century, the Jewish presence in the northern areas of western Christendom was negligible. Jews traded across this northern expanse, and occasionally small Jewish enclaves were created. But extensive Jewish life did not take root. Only sometime during the tenth century, as northern Europe began its remarkable efflorescence, were Jews attracted for the first time in considerable numbers. Jews found new opportunities available to them in the rapidly developing economy and were enticed northward by some of the most far-sighted rulers in the area. From the beginning of this migration, however, Jews encountered considerable resistance and a limited set of economic options, and, as a result, Jewish numbers remained fairly restricted. In important ways, the new Jewish settlements of the north contrasted markedly with the older communities of the south: in longevity of Jewish presence, in the sense of belonging, in size, and in economic diversification. These socio-economic contrasts had far-reaching implications for Jewish culture, including religious activity and thinking.

In the older and larger Jewish communities of the south, there was a higher level of social interaction with the surrounding majority and, as a result, greater receptivity to the cultural patterns and ideals developed within that majority. In the newer and smaller communities of the north, tensions between Jewish newcomers and their settled neighbors were more intense, leading to a tendency toward greater exclusivity on both sides. This is not to suggest anything like isolation from the Christian majority in northern Europe; it does mean that there was less readiness to accept from the majority and fewer channels for informal cultural and religious contact. At the same time, the size and economic diversification of the Mediterranean Jewries meant significant stratification within the Jewish world and the development of internal cleavages and tensions. In the smaller and economically more homogeneous northern settlements, there was less possibility for the development of such divisions and a stronger propensity toward uniformity of behavior and thought.

Both the older and larger Jewish communities of southern Europe and the newer and smaller ones of the north fell heir to the same legacy of Jewish cultural and religious norms. For both sets of Jewish communities, the Judaism adumbrated in the Rabbinic academies of Mesopotamia and Palestine set the basic parameters for Jewish religious activity and belief. The core of Jewish experience lay for all the Jewries of medieval western Christendom in the divine revelation vouchsafed to the Jewish people directly at Sinai and vicariously through a series of divinely elected prophets. Of the truth of this revelation, canonized in the Hebrew Bible, there could be no reasonable doubt. At the same time, God had—as it were—conferred a further revelation, an Oral Torah that accompanied the Written Torah. The specifics of this Oral Torah were worked out in complex ways through community consensus and, even more strikingly, through Rabbinic ratiocination, reflected in the larger and more sprawling corpus comprised of the Mishnah and the equally authoritative glosses of the two Talmuds, with the Babylonian Talmud by far the more influential. All this gave the Jewries of medieval western Christendom a sense of secure anchoring for individual and communal religious behavior and thought, while at the same time affording considerable latitude for change.

The Christian environment in which the Jews of southern and northern Europe found themselves proved itself both congenial and hostile to Jewish religious life. In a positive vein, the assumptions shared by Christians and Jews were numerous and weighty. These included the fundamental notion of a Creator God, who had set in motion the workings of the universe and the unfolding of human history and who remained concerned with his creation, guiding the course of cosmic and terrestrial affairs, rewarding the righteous, and punishing the wicked. More concretely, Christian tradition concurred with and reinforced veneration for the Hebrew Bible and for the biblical Israel whose history it chronicles. Abraham, Moses, Isaiah, and Jeremiah were all major hero figures to both communities, although these giants were perceived differently in the Christian majority and the Jewish minority. It is of no small significance that core beliefs reinforced each other so regularly. In many instances, as we shall see, even perceptions of laudable religious action and thinking were shared between the two groups. Still, the eyes of Christians and Jews were more regularly fastened on those issues that divided than those that united majority and minority. Despite the reinforcement afforded by the Christian ambiance, the more common sense was of the challenges posed by that environment.

The first major challenge involved physical safety. Given the tensions occasioned by conflicting Christian-Jewish claims to the same record of divine revelation and the deleterious impact of New Testament portrayal of Jews, especially the central role imputed to them in the death of Jesus, the potential for majority hatred of the Jewish minority was high. In the areas of older Jewish settlement, this potential was dampened somewhat by the historical record of long-time Jewish settlement and by Jewish economic diversification. In the northern areas of western Christendom, by contrast, the legacy of Christian anti-Jewish imagery was exacerbated by the resentment that is the normal lot of immigrants and by the complications of limited Jewish economic activity. When, during the twelfth century, the Jews of northern Europe turned increasingly in the direction of money lending and banking, the potential for hostility was sharply augmented. Jews were targets of fear and animosity out of both the historic Christian legacy and the immediate realities of relative newness, religious dissidence, and limited economic outlets that were often perceived as harmful.

Fear of and hostility toward Jews led to occasional outbreaks of physical violence. Again, the record of such violence is far more prominent in the north than in the south, although even in the north it was not sufficient to depress Jewish population growth until well into the thirteenth century. Still, this occasional physical violence posed a double challenge to the Jewish minority. On the most immediate level, it had to be combated; Jews had to find modalities for ensuring and preserving their safety. In more complex ways, the difficulties of Jewish existence, highlighted by but not confined to physical violence, played into a recurrent Christian claim and an underlying Jewish anxiety. For Christians, the record of Jewish limitation and suffering subsequent to the lifetime of Jesus served as compelling evidence to the truth of the Christian vision. Jesus's Jewish contemporaries had rejected him and had ultimately occasioned his death. Punishment was, in the Christian view, swift in coming. The classical Christian view of post-Passion Jewish history was a tale of exile, degradation, and suffering, as in fact God had ordained it to be. The record of Jewish tribulations had to be acknowledged by any ostensibly objective observer as substantiating Christian claims. But the Jews too needed to engage the omnipresent signs of Christian ascendancy and Jewish decline. It was surely not easy for the Jews of western Christendom to encounter everywhere the symbols of Christian power and success from the vantage point of a more-or-less restricted minority. A major challenge to the Jews of medieval western Christendom was to configure for themselves the historical record in a way that would reinforce, rather than jeopardize, Jewish existence.

The reality of a majority Christian ambiance posed an ongoing intellectual threat as well. Precisely because so much was shared between the Christian majority and the Jewish minority, contesting of the common legacy was ongoing and intense. While agreeing to the truth of revelation as realized in the biblical canon, Christians and Jews interpreted that revelation in profoundly different ways. Each community could hardly believe that the other might misconstrue so badly the record of revelation. Reading Christian and Jewish biblical interpretations side by side, one imagines partners to a dialogue regularly talking past one another, a common phenomenon in human history. Yet it is not inappropriate to ask whether on occasion the confident assertions of each side do not mask deeper concern and anxiety. Given the medieval propensity to avoid doubt and eschew uncertainty, we are rarely privy to such a deeper level of openness. In a profound way Christianity threatened Jews, just as Judaism threatened Christians.

The Christian environment that fostered Jewish existence while limiting it and pressuring it was diverse and rich. Although often excoriated as an age of darkness, in fact the "middle ages" of western Christendom set in motion much of what has come to characterize the modernity of the west. The Jewish minorities of medieval western Christendom contributed to the richness of majority experience and derived benefit therefrom. Jews were reinforced and challenged simultaneously, resulting in an enriched contribution to the flow of Jewish historical experience.

Communal structure and leadership: A number of circumstances in medieval western Christendom conspired to encapsulate the Jews in a segregated, protective, and coercive self-governing community. For their part, the secular authorities of the medieval west very much encouraged Jewish separatism, both out of support for the Church's traditional insistence on segregation of the Jews and for their own fiscal and administrative advantage. At the same time, the internal political and social needs of a small and often endangered minority dictated communal cohesion, useful for negotiating with the outside world and maintaining stability within the Jewish fold. In addition, the Rabbinic legacy to which the Jews of medieval western Christendom fell heir stressed emphatically the importance of communal self-rule, while leaving considerable latitude for the forms that it might take. The net result of this confluence of circumstances was a powerful communal authority, vested with a wide range of functions, both secular and religious. The internal leadership negotiated Jewish concerns with the non-Jewish powers, raised taxes within the Jewish community, maintained law and order among the Jews, created and sustained the institutions of Jewish education and social welfare, and set the parameters for Jewish religious and intellectual activity.

Parallel to the majority distinction between religious and secular leadership, the Jewish communities of medieval western Christendom recognized twin elites, the elite of Rabbinic learning and the elite of financial and political power. Members of the former won their position through mastery of the classics of Rabbinic thought, gained in institutions more or less well ordered. In theory utterly democratic, Rabbinic leadership—not surprisingly—tended to maintain itself in certain families. The elite of wealth and political clout was less formally constructed, somewhat more fluid, again theoretically democratic, but in practice highly oligarchic. The two elites by and large worked well with one another, although on occasion conflict could and did develop. Generally, the spheres of authority of the two elites were fairly well delimited, which certainly helped to minimize friction. In matters of intervention with the non-Jewish powers and in communal financial dealings, the Rabbinic leadership had little say; in matters of education and religious life, the elite of wealth and power was normally deferential. The area that provided the highest potential for strife was the court system, which impinged heavily on the "secular" lives of Jews, but which had to be run according to the norms of talmudic jurisprudence. Even in this potentially problematic sphere, conflict was normally held in check.

Since our concern is with Judaism, the religion, we shall focus on the roles of the Rabbinic elite. In the most general way, these authority figures were charged with responsibility for absorbing, transmitting, and clarifying the norms of Jewish law; for expanding these norms as ambiguous and evolving realities required; and for insisting on the implementation of the norms they studied and adapted. At the same time, they bore responsibility—although less exclusively—for identifying the core beliefs, ideals, and symbols of Judaism, for interpreting and reinterpreting those beliefs and values in terms that would be meaningful to wide numbers of their followers, for conveying to their constituencies the requisite ideals and symbols, and for combating views deemed harmful and inappropriate. In the domain of Jewish law, the elite of Rabbinic learning exercised sole dominion; in the domain of beliefs and symbols, the Rabbinic authorities played a key but hardly exclusive role.

The absorption and clarification of the legacy of Rabbinic law took place within the advanced Jewish schooling system of the medieval west. The most rudimentary type of advanced schooling involved, as it did in the majority milieu, discipleship of student to teacher. More sophisticated were the schools that eventually emerged in major population centers, again paralleling developments in the Christian majority. The core of the advanced curriculum focused on transmitting knowledge of the vast corpus of Rabbinic law. Out of the Jewish schools of western Christendom, especially its northern tier, there emerged—from the late eleventh century on—a rich literature of talmudic exegesis. The earliest layer of this literature, the influential commentary of Rabbi Solomon of Troyes (Rashi), was aimed at straightforward clarification of the often difficult talmudic text. Subsequently, the descendants and students of Rashi took the exegetical enterprise in striking new directions. The key to this innovative effort at clarification of Jewish law lay in the assumption that the sprawling talmudic corpus was internally consistent and that seeming contradictions were merely grist for the intellectual mill, problems to be solved through careful consideration of seemingly conflicting sources. This method of exegesis, ascribed to a group of northern-European Rabbinic authorities called the Tosafists, eventually came to dominate talmudic study throughout the medieval Jewish diaspora.

Beyond clarification of the law crystallized in the talmudic corpus, there were inevitably cases in which the prior legal legacy seemed inadequate, where the specific details of a situation required extrapolation from the previously known to the ambiguous or innovative. The tool for confronting and solving such difficulties was the Rabbinic responsum. This involved a query sent to an admired master of the legal tradition soliciting guidance in circumstances in which the precise dictates of the law seemed uncertain. The responses of venerated authorities to these queries came to constitute new elements in an expanding legal system. The authoritative pronouncements of distinguished experts like Rashi would be carefully preserved and widely quoted as noteworthy precedents. The Jews in the medieval Muslim world were heirs to a set of centralized institutions that became the acknowledged address to which such queries and answers concerning Jewish law were regularly forwarded. The Jews in medieval western Christendom, by contrast, enjoyed no such legacy. Their system was far less institutional and far more personal. Inquiries would be sent to scholars acknowledged for their expertise; the preservation and absorption of responses on difficult points of law reflected the slow and steady evaluation of the stature of the respondents over an extended period of time.

While the commentary literature focused heavily on the text, its direct meaning, and the complications engendered by seeming contradictions encountered elsewhere in the vast talmudic corpus, engagement with difficult contemporary issues was not totally absent. The Tosafist commentaries often addressed immediate issues of communal and individual behavior, identifying perplexing problems and providing solutions. Thus, in a variety of ways, the received tradition of Jewish law developed dynamically, addressing shifting and changing realities. Indeed, with Jewish law constantly invigorated by new understandings of the classical Rabbinic texts and by reflections on individual and communal experience, there was regularly a perceived need to organize in a rational manner the ever-expanding corpus of legal directives and to make them readily accessible to all Rabbinic leaders. To this end, from the twelfth century on, important codes of Jewish law appeared throughout western Christendom,

reflecting the ongoing vitality of Jewish life and Rabbinic learning.

In addition to its concern with clarification of Jewish law, the elite of Rabbinic learning was committed to pressing for the implementation of the legal norms, both personal and communal, that it sought so zealously to identify. This objective was achieved in a number of ways. The simplest avenue was exercise of the authority that expertise in the law conferred. Rabbinic leaders were generally venerated figures and utilized the respect accorded them to press for observance of the legal norms as they defined them. In addition, the efficacious alliance with the elite of wealth and political power was regularly exploited for reinforcing the demands of Jewish law. On occasion, there is evidence of links between the Rabbinic leaders and the non-Jewish authorities, and these links as well could be utilized for buttressing the demands of Rabbinic tradition.

Both the Jewries of the south and the north concurred in their recognition of the central place of Jewish law and, consequently, of the role of the elite of Rabbinic learning. Only the medieval Karaite movement, first developed in the sphere of Islam, overtly challenged the authority of Rabbinic law and hence of this Rabbinic elite. This movement, still obscure in many of its details, did make its way westward. Precisely how strong a foothold it achieved in medieval western Christendom has not yet been accurately determined. For the moment, the consensus is that the Karaite tendency made little real headway in the west, thus leaving us with a sense of the relatively unchallenged dominance of the Rabbinic elite in the sphere of Jewish religious behavior.

The effort to identify and reinterpret the core beliefs and ideals of Jewish tradition was somewhat more fluid. The Rabbinic leadership, enjoying respect for its role as transmitters and protectors of Jewish law, was necessarily central to this effort. While the talmudic corpus had much to say with respect to Jewish beliefs and ideals, its vast and sprawling nature made it somewhat difficult to use in a regular way for clarifying and transmitting key values and symbols. The biblical text, rich and varied in its own right, provided a much more manageable vehicle for clarifying and transmitting key Jewish beliefs and images. The centrality of the Hebrew Bible to Jewish liturgy provided a ready-made vehicle for regular communal engagement with the biblical text and the ideals it incorporated. Oral explication of the biblical text and its implications was a regular feature of synagogue life and provided a ready avenue through which the elite of Rabbinic learning might educate the Jewish masses to the core values of Jewish tradition. This oral teaching eventually led to the emergence of a literature of biblical exegesis. Once again, the late-eleventh-century northern-European figure, Solomon ben Isaac of Troyes (Rashi), played a central role. Rashi's commentary on the Bible proved as influential and enduring a work as his commentary on the Talmud. The remarkable popularity of Rashi's Bible commentary seems to flow from his success in transmitting key Jewish beliefs and values through the medium of biblical exegesis.

The exclusive role of the elite of Rabbinic learning in defining the norms of Jewish law was not paralleled in the sphere of Jewish beliefs and ideals. In this more fluid arena, other groupings exercised considerable leadership. Pietistic, mystical, messianic, and philosophic tendencies in the Jewish communities of western Christendom sometimes brought to the fore alternative leadership figures and groups. While these alternative leadership groupings did not overtly challenge the centrality of Jewish law and the role of the rabbis, they did take their own stances in the adumbration of the ideals of Jewish living. For example, in the martyrological enthusiasm of the First-Crusade period, the Rabbinic elite played a prominent role but shared that role with others in the Jewish community, on occasion even women, who were conspicuous in the strength of their spiritual enthusiasm and commitment. Major outbursts of pietism, mysticism, messianism, and philosophic speculation often brought new spokesmen to the fore in the effort to identify key Jewish values and to promote such values among the Jewish masses.

Thus, the elite of Rabbinic learning played a dominant role in the cultural and religious life of the Jews in medieval western Christendom. On occasion, these leaders had to share their authority with the elite of wealth and political power or the alternative leadership groupings just reviewed. Again, homogeneity was more prominent in the smaller and socio-economically less diversified Jewries of the north as contrasted with the larger and more stratified Jewries of the south. Throughout medieval western Christendom, however, was found a high level of uniformity, even if punctuated by recurrent outbreaks of innovative behavior and thinking.

Behavioral patterns—reinforcement and challenge: The talmudic tradition followed by the Jews of medieval western Christendom emphasized the application of Jewish law to both the individual and community, and, as we have seen, key factors in Jewish circumstances reinforced the grip of this law. This created a system of legal norms that encompassed every facet of Jewish existence. Indeed, even the occasional flashes of innovation that swept the community generally were in the direction of more, and not less, punctilious observance.

At the heart of the legal system as it affected the individual was a set of ritual observances that governed daily life. Purity regulations were extensive, addressing the major facets of biological existence, especially eating and sexual activity. Taboos regarding foods, sex, and death were omnipresent. Prayer was regularized into an extensive set of daily obligations. The weekly cycle was of great significance to every member of the community, with Sabbath observance central to the individual, the family, and the group. The yearly cycle was filled with special days celebrating central transitions in the solar calendar and highlighting major points of importance in the Jewish past. Critical points of passage in the individual lifetime were regulated and consecrated by Jewish ritual. Birth, coming of age, marriage, divorce, and death all fell under the sway of Jewish legal norms and were enriched by a plethora of observances.

As noted already, the Christian milieu both buttressed and challenged these individual religious behaviors. On the one hand, the Christian environment reinforced powerfully the centrality of taboos, prayer, weekly and annual cycles, and rites of passage. On the other, the differences in detail between Christian and Jewish observance raised difficulties of both a socio-economic and spiritual nature. Jews had to deal, for example, with the reality of the different Jewish and Christian days of rest and of alternate sets of religious festivals and celebrations. Occasionally, these differences were seized upon by the majority as problematic. The recurrent juxtaposition of the Christian Holy Week and Jewish Passover, for instance, led to frequent ecclesiastical complaints about public Jewish displays of ostentatious celebration on days of the Christian calendar reserved for commemorating the tragic event of the Passion. While the Jews simply desired properly to observe their own distinct festival celebration, Christian religious authorities perceived their actions as deliberately provocative.

More broadly, the alternative Christian observances had to raise some element of spiritual questioning in the minds of medieval Jews living as a restricted and secondary minority. One can only wonder at the psychological response of Jews residing in a segregated area of a medieval town to an elaborate procession wending its way up the town hill to the local cathedral. Once again, the overt response of the Jews of medieval western Christendom was to denigrate Christian spirituality and to exalt Jewish behaviors, to mock the lavishness of the Church and to laud the modesty of Jewish religious practice. We are of course not privy to the alternative feelings that might have occasionally roiled Jewish souls.

Far more difficult to assess is the influence of Christian ritual behaviors on the Jews. Given the richness of Jewish tradition, every new trend could find some element of justification in the Jewish past, and given the conservative bent of medieval Jewish (and Christian) thinking, for every innovation roots in the past indeed were zealously searched out and elaborated. To argue the impact of medieval Christian practice thus is extremely difficult. Nonetheless, an inescapable sense

of the influence of the Christian milieu on medieval Jewish practice remains. For example, a number of recent observers suggest that the extreme asceticism of the German Pietists (*Hasidei Ashkenaz*) of the twelfth and thirteenth centuries shows the influence of practices in Christian society, particularly its monastic sectors.

More striking yet was the unusual pattern of Jewish martyrdom that exploded with the assaults on Rhineland Jewry in 1096. While earlier Jewish tradition had enjoined passive resistance to demands for breach of certain central tenets of Jewish law, the Rhineland Jews who found themselves unexpectedly the object of crusader wrath did far more than is required by Jewish law, avoiding death at crusader hands by taking their own lives and—even more shockingly—by taking the lives of spouses and children. Interestingly, subsequent attempts by the Rabbinic authorities of the twelfth and thirteenth centuries to find justification for this innovative behavior foundered, although these authorities did not in any serious way question the propriety of the extreme martyrological behaviors. A number of recent observers have again suggested that these innovative Jewish behaviors must be understood against the backdrop of a Christian society caught up in religious frenzy and suffused with a sense of the heroic as a major dimension of religious experience.

The dictates of Jewish law extended well beyond the realm of the "religious." Jewish law as crystallized in the vast talmudic corpus included the normal interactions of family life, social relations within the Jewish neighborhood, business dealings among Jews, and business and personal interactions between Jews and their non-Jewish neighbors. Some facets of these activities were closely regulated in talmudic law; others were rather more vaguely articulated. Even in those areas closely regulated, for example the laws governing business practices among Jews and business dealings between Jews and non-Jews, the exigencies of changing circumstance often required significant modification of prior guidelines.

For example, talmudic law specified a

rigorous set of limitations on Jewish-non-Jewish business contact on or near non-Jewish festive occasions. The social and business implications of such limitations would have made life in western Christendom untenable for Jews whose economic activities were increasingly centered in the marketplace, and so ameliorations were introduced. More remarkable was the need for adjustment of the stringent limitations on money lending, as first northern-European and then southern-European Jews came increasingly to specialize in this business activity. In other areas, such as family relations, the dictates of Rabbinic law were from the outset more nebulous and hence required less adjustment. Despite the limited regulation, the Jews of medieval western Christendom and their Rabbinic leaders certainly saw such domains as belonging to the broad realm of God-given Jewish law.

Indeed, the norms of Jewish law applied far beyond the sphere of individual behavior. The Jewish community, so well organized and potent, likewise was governed by the rules of Jewish law, although in this sphere the legal prescriptions were generally more fluid. The area of communal activity most closely regulated by talmudic law was the Jewish court system. Not all cases involving Jews in fact came before the local Jewish court. In many instances issues had to be brought before one of the relevant non-Jewish judiciaries. The notarial registers from southern-France indicate that, on occasion, Jews opted of their own free will to appear before non-Jewish tribunals. Nonetheless, most of the litigation involving Jews did take place in Jewish courts, with the rules under which issues were adjudicated those of talmudic tradition. As noted, the utilization of talmudic law empowered the elite of Rabbinic learning, while the issues under consideration often involved concerns of the elites of wealth and power. Despite the potential for friction, there is only minimal evidence of serious conflict.

Other aspects of Jewish communal activity likewise were viewed as regulated by the dictates of Jewish law, but the regulations were far less fully articulated in the talmudic corpus. Communal taxation was understood as a given of Jewish life, buttressed by divine injunction. The precise forms of taxation, however, were not well defined and actual practice varied widely across the diverse Jewish communities of medieval western Christendom. The same is true for electoral procedures within the Jewish community, which varied considerably from place to place and period to period.

The Jewish leadership of medieval western Christendom had at its disposal potent weapons for securing its way with the Jewish masses, weapons that reflect the religious underpinnings of the communal structure. The simplest technique was to emphasize acceptance of communal dictate as a feature of Jewish law and hence as every individual Jew's sacred obligation. Where this failed, the allegiance of the bulk of the community to its religious leadership was utilized. Decrees of excommunication against those resisting communal authority were ultimately grounded in the willingness of most Jews to abide by the demands of group leadership and thereby to shun contact with offenders. In rare instances, the communal leadership found itself with no alternative but to turn to the non-Jewish rulers who were the Jews' overlords. Such an extreme move was avoided to the extent possible.

Indeed, one of the recurrent difficulties faced by the Jewish communities of medieval western Christendom involved the relationship of the Jewish community to its overlords. On occasion, well placed individuals within the Jewish community were tempted to exploit their own personal connections to the authorities to avoid internal taxation or to circumvent the dictates of community leadership. Stringent safeguards were established to obviate such personal appeals to non-Jewish rulers. These safeguards were rooted in the fundamental sense of communal authority as divinely ordained; hence acceptance of the demands of the communal leadership became part and parcel of the religious obligation of a God-fearing Jew.

Wherever we turn, accordingly, we encounter the evidence of a wide ranging legal system governing all aspects of Jewish behavior, individual and communal. The demands of the Jewish legal system found their ultimate grounding in the medieval Jewish sense of divine law revealed to the people of Israel at Sinai, adumbrated further in the Oral Law, and brought into the life of the community and its individual members by the elite of Rabbinic learning. Unyielding commitment to this divinely ordained legal system was perceived as the marker that distinguished decisively between the Jewish community and its errant neighbors. Christian failure to observe the dictates of divine law—indeed overt Christian repudiation of the dictates of divine law, as medieval Jews understood them—was seen as the fundamental intellectual and moral failure of Christian society. For medieval Jews living in difficult minority circumstances, adherence to God's commandments afforded a profound sense of rectitude and an unshakable guarantee of eventual divine reward and redemption.

Beliefs, values, symbols—reinforcement and challenge: Traditionally, the Jewish belief system was considerably less well enunciated than the Jewish behavioral system. This has occasionally been understood to mean that medieval Judaism was altogether free of dogma, an unwarranted inference from the relatively flexible definition for required Jewish belief. Medieval Jews and their leaders agreed that proper Jewish living involved a set of requisite beliefs, despite the fact that there was a certain looseness in their precise delineation. The far-ranging code authored by the great halakhist-philosopher, Moses Maimonides, represented a remarkable effort to define requisite Jewish beliefs. Jewish leadership in medieval western Christendom was not unsympathetic to the Maimonidean effort, although it was uncomfortable with some of the precise details of what Maimonides proposed. In a general way, then, this Jewish religious leadership remained convinced that there were guidelines to belief, but chose to leave these guidelines less than fully formulated. On occasion, particularly with the spread of Maimonidean philosophic thinking into sectors of southern-European Jewry, Rabbinic leaders felt that a critical line had been crossed and that unac-

ceptable beliefs had been circulated. Anarchy was certainly not envisioned by the Rabbinic leadership. Nonetheless, the enterprise of rigorously defining the parameters of Jewish belief was by and large left in abeyance.

Beliefs, as loosely as they might have been defined, represented only one element in the complex that animated Jewish practice and Jewish souls. Even more ambiguous and ill-defined were the ideals toward which medieval Jews strove and the symbols that moved them. In the sphere of amorphous values and images, there was much room for change and for the impact of the reinforcing and challenging Christian environment. To be sure, medieval Jews rejected the notion of evolving ideals and symbols, insisting that the values they espoused and the images that moved them were age-old. In fact, tracking the evolution of ideals and symbols is extremely difficult. Nonetheless, the sense that medieval Jews responded to an ever-changing set of values and images is inescapable.

As noted already, the most readily available vehicle for conveying to the Jewish masses essential Jewish beliefs, values, and symbols lay in the ongoing engagement with the biblical record of divine revelation. The Rabbinic elite—and others as well—regularly preached in the synagogues of medieval western Christendom, with the biblical text as their base and with identification, clarification, and transmission of Jewish beliefs and values as their ultimate objective. Little direct record of this preaching has survived, although toward the end of the "middle ages" manuals for preachers began to appear, and some collections of sermons have been saved. Sermons were generally grounded in the biblical text, yet they at the same time absorbed a variety of influences from the dynamic environment in which the Jews found themselves.

Evolving Jewish beliefs, values, and symbols were expressed in a variety of literary modes. Given the centrality of the Bible to all Jewish thinking, biblical exegesis became a significant modality through which beliefs, ideals, and images were communicated. In medieval western Christendom, biblical exegesis became a wide ranging literary endeavor, absorbing the energies and talents of a variety of major thinkers, Rabbinic and otherwise. This exegetical endeavor oscillated between two poles, the freewheeling Rabbinic midrash inherited from the prior period of Jewish history and a more rigorously limited search for the straightforward contextual meaning of the biblical passage. Caught up in this creative tension, major exegetes, such as the aforementioned eleventh-century Solomon ben Isaac, the twelfth-century Abraham ibn Ezra, and the thirteenth-century Moses ben Nahman all managed to introduce into their commentaries a variety of alternative cultural emphases as well.

Poetry, both sacred and secular, constituted another major vehicle through which beliefs, values, and symbols were articulated and transmitted. There developed also a literature of homily and exempla, strongly directed toward the articulation of ideals and images. The meager historical records that have survived likewise embody key values and symbols, generally those operative during points of crisis. Indeed, successful embodiment of such ideals and images assured the survival of these historical reports, in contradistinction to the larger body of historical information that was lost with the passage of time.

As noted throughout, the Jews in medieval western Christendom were reinforced in striking ways by the larger environment with which they shared significant core values. Reference has already been made to pietistic and martyrological Jewish behaviors. In both cases, the behaviors reflected powerful ideals and symbols, often shared with the surrounding Christian milieu. Let us focus briefly on the martyrological behaviors so prominent in northern-European Jewry during the early crusades. Ensconced in an environment alive with the value of heroic self-sacrifice, embodied in the imagery of Jesus as the ultimate divine-human offering, the Jews of northern Europe responded with their own potent ideals of self sacrifice, expressed in traditional Jewish imagery. The embattled Jews countered the Christian images of Jesus and Christian Jerusalem with their own vision of a Jewish Jerusalem, a rebuilt Temple, and dedicated human beings offering themselves up as sacrifices to the divine. These Jews negated Christian appropriation of the biblical Abraham-Isaac image (Gen. 22) by making themselves the heirs to the patriarchs in their willingness to answer the divine call for slaughter of beloved children. Ideals shared by the two neighboring communities found eloquent expressions in imagery particular to each.

Medieval western Christendom was rife with both philosophic and mystical speculation. Recognizing the dangers inherent in both these tendencies, the ecclesiastical leadership of Christian society strove to coopt the philosophical and mystical impulses and did so with considerable success. In parallel fashion, the Jews of medieval western Christendom responded to the appeal of both the philosophic and mystical tendencies and attempted to domesticate these impulses into the Jewish fold. New philosophic texts and knowledge had first been introduced into the Islamic sphere during the tenth century and had been engaged by both Muslim and Jewish thinkers. Moses ben Maimon, already mentioned, had created a widely ranging synthesis of the newly encountered philosophic truths, particularly those of the Aristotelian tradition, with normative Jewish thinking. While the Jews of northern Europe remained relatively aloof from the philosophic challenge and the philosophic-Jewish rapprochement, those of the Mediterranean lands quickly became familiar with the Aristotelian legacy and with the efforts at synthesis epitomized in the Maimonidean enterprise.

All through the closing centuries of the Christian "middle ages," significant numbers of southern-European Jews remained committed to the study and mastery of philosophy and to the conviction that traditional Jewish thinking was fully consonant with the philosophic enterprise. Indeed, such thinkers were convinced that Judaism was far more rational than Christianity and, therefore, that philosophic truth could be enlisted in the battle against the majority milieu. As in the prior case of pietistic and martyrological fervor, some medieval Jews shared the philosophic impulse and indeed saw themselves and their faith justified by it.

In medieval western Christendom, mystical tendencies were even more prevalent than the philosophic, for at the core of both Christianity and Judaism were profoundly mystical insights and texts. To be sure, there is some evidence for mystical impulses imported into medieval western Christendom from the outside, but that evidence is extremely difficult to assess. The Christian majority produced a series of major mystical movements and insights, as did the Jewish minority. Both the Christian majority and the Jewish minority had to wrestle repeatedly with the danger that mystical speculation could—like philosophic speculation—cross the fine line that distinguished legitimate insights from heretical flights of fantasy. Innovative mystical movements were often highly suspect, sometimes absorbed successfully into the mainstream and sometimes rejected.

Engagement with mystical insight was widespread through both large sectors of European Jewry, the northern and the southern. In the north, the major group associated with innovative mystical speculation was the *Hasidei Ashkenaz*, the Jewish pietists of twelfth- and thirteenth-century Germany. While known more popularly for their pietistic practices and teachings, these Jews have been recognized increasingly as bearers of important mystical traditions and as innovative speculators concerning many of the major mysteries of the divine and the human. By the thirteenth century, many of the insights and texts of the *Hasidei Ashkenaz* began to make their way into the larger Jewish communities of the south, where independent mystical traditions and lines of thinking were already much in evidence.

By the twelfth century, in Provence and on the Iberian peninsula, both centers of medieval Christian mystical speculation, a variety of lines of Jewish mystical thinking had begun to develop. By the thirteenth century, these small and relatively independent streams had begun to fuse, although there remained a serious commitment to maintaining these mystical ruminations in small and elitist groupings. But by the middle decades of the thirteenth century, the mystical speculation had entered the mainstream, with the towering figure of Moses ben Nahman

lending considerable credibility to these tendencies. During the closing decades of the thirteenth century, the so-called theosophic Kabbalah, focused on comprehension of the complex structure of the divine realm, conceived as a set of ten interlocking sefirot or domains, took shape as a dominant school. With the compilation of the Zohar as this school's authoritative text, the Kabbalah's major symbols were crystallized, and its place as the dominant school of medieval Jewish mystical speculation was assured. Throughout the remainder of the "middle ages," the theosophic Kabbalah and the Zohar as its classic expression penetrated ever more fully into every sector of world Jewry and into every facet of Jewish thinking. Once more, Jews shared a central inclination of their milieu, and once more they absorbed this inclination into a sense that they in fact were the bearers of the true religious tradition. Jewish mystical speculation regularly advanced the sense that it reached profounder levels of truth than its Christian counterparts.

Thus, medieval western Christendom reinforced its Jews in many ways, with the Jews both absorbing the tendencies in the larger environment surrounding them and claiming to have superseded that environment in depth of religious commitment and insight. As noted, Jews were necessarily challenged by the simple reality of living a minority and somewhat secondary existence within a successful host society. This sense of unremitting challenge surely is reflected in the constant Jewish effort to assert superiority with respect to pietistic, martyrological, philosophical, and mystical creativity. At the same time, the Christian milieu posed a number of far more specific and more self-conscious challenges to its Jewish minorities, and to these specific and self-conscious challenges we must now turn.

Both Jewish and Christian sources tell us that the onset of anti-Jewish violence in the Rhineland during the early months of the First Crusade generated the view that Jewish losses in and of themselves could admit no interpretation other than divine abandonment of the Jewish people. In a supercharged environment in which the hand of God was regularly seen in Christian victory, the emergence of such simplistic thinking is readily understandable. To cite but one instance of this argument, after the Jewry of Worms had been destroyed in a set of crusader-burgher assaults, a Jew who had found refuge with friendly townsmen outside Worms was accosted by her erstwhile protectors and urged to convert with the following argument: "Know and see that God does not wish to save you, for they [the Jews of Worms] lie naked at the corner of every street, unburied."

Parallel sentiments were voiced by Archbishop Ruthard of Mainz to his Jewish friend Kalonymous, a major figure in that town's Jewish community: "I cannot save you. Your God has abandoned you; he does not wish to leave you a remnant or a residue." Now, in a general way, catastrophe always leaves doubts in the minds of sufferers. Especially in a monotheistic community committed to the notion of divine control of human affairs, the possibility of divine abandonment can never be fully foreclosed. The crusade-related losses had to arouse in and of themselves such questions, especially since they were linked, by 1099, with remarkable Christian victory. As we have just now seen, the suggestion of divine abandonment was overtly advanced by Christian observers.

Catastrophe was of course hardly a new experience for Jews, and lines of rationalization were fully developed. However, the central thrusts of traditional Jewish thinking were problematic. To emphasize Jewish sinfulness as the basis for persecution in a sense played into Christian hands. Given the Christian perception that Jews suffered because of their historic crime of deicide, to acknowledge Jewish sin as the causative factor in the crusade-related persecution would hardly have been useful. Moreover, in the militant environment of crusading, Jewish sinfulness and resultant suffering failed to match the Christian mood and imagery of heroism and self-sacrifice. As a result, the Jews of the Rhineland and their memorializers created a striking and innovative Jewish counter-crusade mythology.

The challenging Christian interpretation of Jewish suffering elicited an audacious Jewish counter-view, as bold, at least, as the Jewish counter-behaviors and counter-symbols noted above. Rather than punishment for Jewish sinfulness, the anti-Jewish violence was interpreted as a divinely ordained ordeal. Just as God had chosen to test the most steadfast of the Jewish ancestors, Abraham, had found him willing to make the requisite sacrifice, and had promised abundant reward in the aftermath of this willingness, so too the Jewish losses of 1096 were projected as a divine test imposed on the most steadfast of generations. The success in meeting the divine test could only result in unimaginable reward on both the individual and communal level.

As crusading waned, the aggressiveness of the Christian environment took a new and more ecclesiastically acceptable form. Conversion of the non-believer had always been a central obligation of Christian society, an obligation generally observed in the breach. By the middle of the thirteenth century, however, western Christendom was profoundly committed to winning over through reasonable discourse those outside the faith, preeminently the Muslims but secondarily the Jews. Both Muslims and Jews living within the perimeter of the Christian world made an especially inviting target for missionizing ardor, because an element of coercion could be introduced. Forcible conversion had regularly been denounced by the Roman Catholic Church; but demanding Muslim or Jewish presence at missionizing sermons was seen as legitimate, since the eventual decision on baptism was left to the free will of the individual involved. Thus, in Christian lands, preeminently those of southern Europe, where the Muslim population was considerable, a program of forced sermons and forced debates was instituted, with the Dominican Order playing an especially prominent role in adumbrating new argumentation and carrying the innovative message to Muslim and Jewish auditors.

Given the millennium-old dispute between Christians and Jews, venerable lines of argumentation were readily available and relatively innocuous. The most common thrust of Christian (and Jewish) argumentation involved correct understanding of the biblical record of revelation. Christians had developed long-standing claims based on their readings of biblical verses, readings convincing to Christian audiences and meaningless to Jews. So long as there was no genuine commitment to actual missionizing, Christian authors could comfortably rehearse these time-worm arguments, leaving their Christian auditors and readers befuddled at Jewish intransigence. Once a serious commitment to proselytizing had developed, however, new lines of argumentation had to be sought. Proofs from history—again highly meaningful to Christian audiences—likewise seem to have made little headway among Jews. A new possibility emerged from the intensification of philosophic thinking and its appropriation by the Church. Such philosophic speculation could, however, hardly form the basis for popular missionizing. The level of abstraction and expertise required was simply beyond the capacities of most auditors, whether Christian, Muslim, or Jewish.

What emerged during the middle decades of the thirteenth century as a striking new alternative was the rigorous exploitation of Rabbinic exegesis of biblical texts. Aware that Jews had a rich tradition of biblical commentary that was regularly used to defuse Christian claims, churchmen investigated the Rabbinic corpus to extract therefrom readings that seemed to offer support for the Christian case. Indeed, the use of Rabbinic materials was extended to freestanding Rabbinic dicta. The essential claim was: Examine your own Jewish tradition and see how even the rabbis acknowledged fundamental Christian truths. This line of argumentation was pioneered by converts from Judaism to Christianity, equipped from childhood with first-hand knowledge of Rabbinic teachings. Quickly, however, schools were established in which Christian missionizers were trained in the languages and literatures of both Muslims and Jews and prepared to turn Muslim and Jewish texts against their adherents.

A major testing of this new missionizing argumentation was engineered in Barcelona in 1263, with the backing of a powerful royal figure, King James I of Aragon. A pioneer in the exploitation of Rabbinic texts for mis-

sionizing purposes, a former Jew turned Dominican preacher, Friar Paul Christian, engaged the great Catalan-Jewish Rabbinic authority, Moses ben Nahman, known as Ramban. While we cannot be certain of what precisely occurred in the Barcelona missionizing encounter, the Ramban's remarkable narrative account of the event lays bare the central lines of Jewish response to the new argumentation. The rabbi argued that the entire thrust of this innovative Christian attack was invalidated by the reality that the rabbis whose teachings were cited remained loyal Jews all their lives; moreover, he examined each and every text adduced and attempted to prove that not one substantiated Christian views; finally, he (at least in his beguiling Hebrew narrative) pointed recurrently to underlying flaws in Christian thinking that would make the alternative of conversion unthinkable to any sensible Jew. While Moses ben Nahman surely defended his faith ably and provided a concise and appealing refutation of the new (and old) lines of Christian thinking, he was not able to derail the new missionizing argumentation. Throughout the remaining centuries of western Christendom's "middle ages," Jews continued to be faced with these innovative claims.

The third of the great challenges to Jewish thinking and commitment in this period flowed from an altogether different direction, the rediscovered legacy of Greco-Roman thinking, a legacy that threw into doubt many of the firm foundations of both Christian and Jewish theology. Whereas physical assaults on Jews and the serious missionizing that began in the thirteenth century derived from Christian aggressiveness toward the Jewish minority, the philosophic challenge posed problems for both the Christian majority and the Jewish minority. To be sure, the intellectual leadership of both communities attempted to coopt philosophy, as we have already seen, with both Christians and Jews claiming that philosophic considerations bolstered the validity of their particular faith. In fact, however, both groups faced serious problems of squaring their particularistic traditions with the claims of universalistic science and reason.

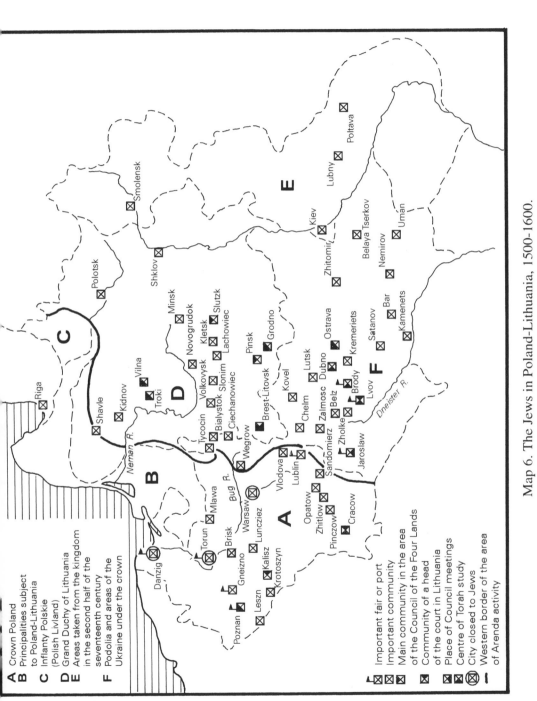

Map 6. The Jews in Poland-Lithuania, 1500-1600.

A Crown Poland
B Principalities subject
   to Poland-Lithuania
C Inflanty Polskie
   (Polish Livland)
D Grand Duchy of Lithuania
E Areas taken from the kingdom
   in the second half of the
   seventeenth century
F Podolia and areas of the
   Ukraine under the crown

⬛ Important fair or port
⊠ Important community
⊠ Main community in the area
   of the Council of the Four Lands
⊠ Community of a head
   of the court in Lithuania
⊠ Place of Council meetings
⊠ Centre of Torah study
⊗ City closed to Jews
▬ Western border of the area
   of Arenda activity

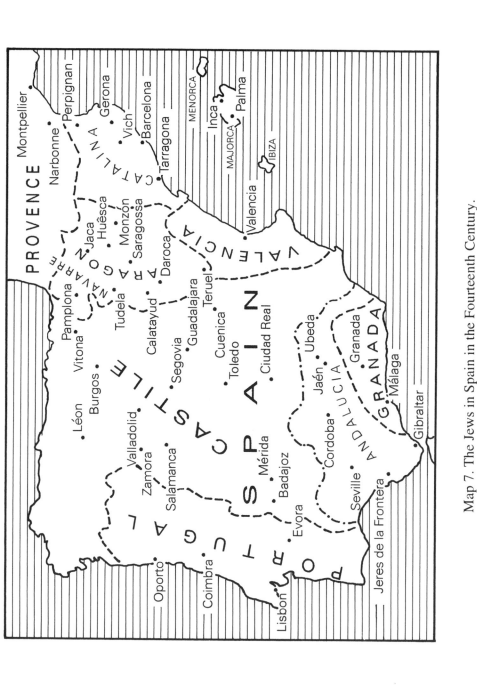

Map 7. The Jews in Spain in the Fourteenth Century.

Not surprisingly, the Jewish responses were strikingly parallel to those of their Christian neighbors. Some of the Jewish leadership negated philosophic insight, denying its truth claims and banning its study. Others felt profoundly that the challenge could not be avoided, that Judaism was in fact consistent with the best of philosophic truth, and that Jewish intellectuals had to be provided with the tools with which to understand and assimilate this truth. In this arena, the Jews of the Muslim world had first encountered the philosophic challenge and had adumbrated all these lines of response. Particularly striking and influential was the already-noted synthesis worked out by Moses Maimonides, from whose translated writings the Jews of the Christian sphere learned much.

The philosophic challenge remained a contentious issue throughout the latter centuries of the "middle ages," with no clear cut resolution ever achieved. When large segments of Iberian Jewry began to succumb to Christian conversionist pressures, many of the Jewish traditionalists claimed that the way to baptism was paved by the inappropriate Jewish espousal of philosophy. The philosophically inclined rejected this charge and continued to insist that philosophic inquiry was a solution to the Jewish quandary, not the cause of it. As was true for the other major challenges faced by the Jews of medieval western Christendom, this last too elicited lively and creative Jewish response.

Did these responses suffice to blunt both the Christian assaults and the philosophic challenge? No simplistic answer will do. On the one hand, Jews did defect from the Jewish communities of medieval western Christendom. But the defections in the direction of universalistic philosophic speculation were rather small in number, largely limited to a tiny group of intellectuals. The unremitting Christian pressures took a far greater toll. Jewish lives were lost through physical persecution, and the Christian argument that Jewish suffering proved divine abandonment registered with a significant number of Jews. One of the most important, influential, and well-documented medieval converts, the learned Jew Abner of Burgos who became

Alfonso of Valladolid, indicates the preponderant role the sense of divine abandonment played in his decision to leave the Jewish fold. The most extensive conversion of the period involved the Jews of the Iberian peninsula during the period from 1391 through 1492. The number of converts was massive, as Jews succumbed to the threat of violence, to the violence-grounded argument of divine abandonment, and to the steady pressure of intense Christian missionizing.

This evidence of conversion notwithstanding, it hardly seems fair to judge the Jewish responses to the challenges posed by the Christian environment as failures. The bulk of the Jewish population survived the physical and spiritual challenges, in the process adding creative new patterns of behavior and thought to the Jewish legacy. A difficult and challenging environment took a certain toll, while at the same time stimulating Jewish creativity in unforeseen directions.

ROBERT CHAZAN

JUDAISM, HISTORY OF, PART. IV:B. MEDIEVAL TIMES. ISLAM: It is virtually impossible to know what was normative Judaism and Jewish practice during the first two hundred years of the Muslim Caliphate, in the seventh through ninth centuries. The great Islamic Arab conquests of the seventh and early eighth centuries brought the majority of world Jewry living at that time from Spain to Persia and Central Asia under the rule of a single empire, the Dar al-Islam ("the Domain of Islam"). The two hundred years immediately preceding the Islamic conquests and following the redaction of the Babylonian Talmud were likewise a dark age in Jewish history, for which very little in the way of historical sources exist. One thing, however, is clear: This seeming dark age was one of tremendous social, political, and religious upheaval for all peoples living under the new Islamic world order, including the Jews. By the end of this period—around the middle of the ninth century—the Rabbinic form of Judaism had spread and consolidated itself into what became mainstream Judaism.

Under early Islam: Jews lived among Muslims in the *umma*, the earliest Islamic polity, established by the prophet Muhammad himself in Madina in 622 (the year 1 of the Islamic calendar). These Jews spoke Arabic, were organized into clans and tribes like their Arab neighbors, and seem, like other Jews of the Arabian Peninsula, to have assimilated many of the heroic values of desert society. The Arabic poetry attributed to Jewish bards such as Samuel ibn Adiya reflects the same rugged ethos of *muruwwa* (manly virtues) as expressed in the compositions of their pagan neighbors and have no identifiable Jewish content or character.[1] These Arabian Jews entered into alliances with other tribes, both Jewish and non-Jewish, and took part in intertribal feuds. At the same time, their distinctive religious practices and customs and their use of use of Aramaic and Hebrew loan words in their speech (some of which passed imperceptibly into general Arabic usage and were absorbed into the religious terminology and concepts of nascent Islam) caused them to be perceived as a separate group. The Jews of Madina soon ran afoul of the Allah's apostle, and between 624 and 627, two of the principal Jewish tribes, the Banu Qaynuqâ' and the Banu 'l-Naîr, were ousted from the community and the third, the Banu Quraya, were put to the sword. The few Jews who remained in Madina together with the Jews of the rest of the Arabian Peninsula (the oases of the northern Hijaz, Yemen, and Yamama on the Persian Gulf), most of whom came under Islamic hegemony by the time of Muhammad's death in 632, became tribute-bearing subjects.

The accounts of the early Muslim chroniclers (such as al-Wâqidî, Ibn Sa'd, and Ibn Isâq) of the life of the Prophet and occasional references to Jews and Jewish practices in Arabic poetry from this period just before and after the founding of Islam, provide a few details on Arabian Judaism at this early time.[2] Observance of the dietary laws and the Sabbath were the two outstanding hallmarks that distinguished Jews in the eyes of their Arab neighbors. Although "the books of the Jews" and "their writings" are referred to occasionally in the Arabic sources, the only Jewish texts specifically mentioned by the Arab poets, the Koran, and the earliest historians, are the Torah (Ar., *al-tawrât*) and the Psalms (Ar., *al-zubûr*). There is no mention of the Talmud at this time, but the typically Rabbinic practice of reciting a blessing over wine before its consumption is noted by several Arab poets. The Jewish scholars of Arabia are referred to in Arabic as *abâr*, apparently the Arabicised form of Hebrew, with *aberim* being the standard title designating members of the Tiberian academy of the Land of Israel.

The appearance in the Koran of midrashic forms of biblical stories indicates that, at the very least, oral versions of the aggada were current among Arabian Jews, although some of these midrashim could easily have come from Christian circles.[3] Furthermore, the Koranic verse (Sura 5:32) stating, "Thus, we ordained for the Children of Israel that whoever kills a person other than for taking a life or corruption on earth, it is as if he had killed all of humanity, and whoever saves a life, it is as if he had saved all of humanity," with its almost verbatim quotation from M. San. 4:5, would indicate that, among their otherwise unspecified "books" and "writings," the Jews of Arabia possessed the Mishnah.

A year after Muhammad's death, his followers poured out of Arabia and within less than a generation conquered most of the Middle East. The Jewish and Monophysite Christian population in the Byzantine Empire, which had been recently subject to persecution and were caught up in a wave of messianic expectation, viewed the Muslims as liberators. In some cities and towns in the Byzantine provinces, such as Emesa in Syria and Hebron and Caesarea in Palestine, Jews, Samaritans, and members of the non-Melkite Christian churches openly collaborated with the invaders. Among the few recorded Jewish sources for this period are the apocalyptic midrashim, written around the time of the conquest, such as the *Sefer Eliyahu* ("The Book of Elijah"), or, in the following century but incorporating earlier material, the *Nistarot shel Rabbi Shimon b. Yohai* ("The Secrets of R. Simeon b. Yohai"). In these midrashim, the Muslim conquest is viewed as a visitation from God upon the Byzantine persecutors. In the *Nistarot shel Rabbi*

Shimon b. Yohai, the angel Metatron tells Simeon, "Do not be afraid, Ben Yohai, the Holy One, blessed be he, has only brought the Kingdom of Ishmael in order to save you from this wicked one."[4]

During the invasion of Visigothic Spain in 711, the Jews, who had undergone intense persecution since the last decade of the seventh century, also collaborated with the Muslim conquerors, but on an even wider scale than in the Middle East. Even in the Persian territories, where they were considerably better off than in Christendom, the Jews, who were probably tired of the political and economic instability of the late Sassanian period, generally welcomed the invading Arabs. Sometime between 656 and 661, Isaac Gaon, head of the Pumbeditha Academy in Iraq, is reported to have greeted the Caliph Ali in Firuz-Shapur at the head of 90,000 Jews (Sherira Gaon, *Iggeret*, ed., B. Lewin, Haifa, 1921, p. 101).

Like the Christians and Zoroastrians, the Jews of the new Islamic Empire were considered to be People of the Book (Ar., *ahl al-kitâb*), that is, people who possessed a genuine divine revelation. If they accepted the overlordship of the Muslim community, they were, therefore, entitled to be its protégés (Ar., *ahl al-dhimma*). In return for the payment of special taxes—namely, the *jizya*, a poll tax, and the *kharaj*, a land tax—and acceptance of a legally defined, second-class social and political status, the *dhimmis* were granted the protection of their lives and property, the right to worship unmolested, and a great degree of autonomy in their internal affairs under their own communal religious leaders who were themselves recognized by the state authorities—no small concessions by medieval standards. This general tolerance and state recognition of religious leaders and institutions combined with several other factors in fostering greater centralization and standardization of Jewish religious life in the Caliphate. One of these factors was increased freedom of movement within the empire after the first century of Islamic rule. A second factor was the establishment of the Abbasid dynasty in 750 and the transferal of the political, cultural, and economic center of the Caliphate to the province of Iraq, which was Jewish Bavel (Babylonia), the foremost center of world Jewry.

The centralization of Jewish authority and spread of establishmentarian Judaism: Iraq/Babylonia was the seat of the talmudic academies (Heb., *yeshivot*; Aram., *metivata*) of Sura and Pumbeditha, each of which was under the leadership of a gaon (an abbreviation of the title *rosh yeshivat geon Yaaqob*—"the head of the academy of the pride of Jacob"). It was also the seat of the aristocratic official known as the exilarch (Aram., *resh galuta*), who was recognized as a descendant of the last king of Judah and had served as the governor of the Jews in the Sassanian Empire. The conquering Muslims confirmed the Jewish exilarch's authority over his coreligionists (as they did with the Nestorian catholicos). The process of consolidating and centralizing Jewish authority in the Caliphate was facilitated when the Sura and Pumbeditha academies relocated in the new capital of Baghdad shortly after its founding in 762, and the exilarch became a regular courtier at the Abbasid court. Though chosen within the Jewish community, both the exilarch and the geonim had to receive a caliphal proclamation and patent of office (Ar., *ijâza*), and such official patents became standard for Jewish communal officials in the Islamic world all the way down to the modern era. A number of these caliphal proclamations and writs of approval have survived. They clearly confirm the rights and privileges of the official, but also reiterate the restrictions of his own and his community's *dhimmî* status, as for example in the document given to Daniel b. Samuel Gaon in 1247, which is preserved by the Arab historian Ibn al-Fuwaî:

> I am appointing you leader of the adherents of your denomination of the people of your religion which has been abrogated by the Muhammadan religious law. You may lead them within the boundaries of their religion, command them in that which they are commanded by the religious law, forbid them that which they are forbidden by it. You are to judge between them in their conflicts and legal disputes in accordance with their religious law. Praised be to Allah for Islam.[5]

The geonim and in particular the exilarch enhanced their aura of authority with some of the pomp and circumstance of Abbasid court ceremonials. For example, the pageantry involved in the installation of the exilarch is described by the tenth-century chronicler Nathan ha-Babli and reported as well by the awe-stricken Benjamin of Tudela.[6] Gaonic and exilarchic authority had been great in Iraq even before the Muslim conquest. In Islamic times, it was extended far beyond the former Sassanian territories.

Under Islam, the exilarchs were essentially aristocratic figure heads,[7] whereas the geonim gradually became the ultimate diocesan leaders of the greater Jewish religious community. As religious authorities, the geonim based their claims to legitimacy and preeminent leadership on the contention that they were the sole possessors of the unbroken, living Rabbinic tradition that ultimately went back to Moses at Sinai. They were the expounders and propagators of the Babylonian Talmud, which they sought to make the constitutional framework for the entire Jewish community, first in Iraq and Iran and later in the entire Caliphate. For several centuries they had exerted a strong formative influence over the Jewish masses in Babylonia through the public educational sessions known as *kallot* that were held semi-annually during the months of Adar and Elul. They exerted even greater influence over the bourgeoisie, whose sons studied in the academies during the rest of the year. These alumni of the gaonic academies, many of whom belonged to the growing merchant class, helped further to disseminate the Judaism of the Babylonian Talmud. Additionally, as freedom of movement increased during the second half of the eighth century, they spread the prestige and influence of the geonim of Sura and Pumbeditha throughout the length and breadth of the Dar al-Islam. Some of these alumni, like the Ibn Shahins who settled in Qayrawan, Tunisia, or the Ibn Awkals who settled in Fustat, Egypt, acted as local representatives of the Babylonian academies in their diaspora communities.[8]

The Jewish communities of the diaspora sent queries (Heb., *sheelot*) on law, ritual, and textual exegesis to the academies, together with contributions for the support of the institutions and their scholars. Indeed, the geonim emphasized that these contributions were comparable in merit to the annual *shekel* paid to the Temple in antiquity. The contributions included both an annual fixed amount (Heb., *hoq*) and an occasional special collection (*pesiqa*). The communities received in return replies to their queries in the form of responsa (Heb., *teshuvot*). These were authoritative legal opinions that frequently bore the admonition, "This is the *halakha* and there is no moving from it."

The practice of issuing formal responsa and other halakhic developments at this time evolved within the shared cosmopolitan environment of Baghdad, where at the very same time, Muslim legal scholars were developing the *sharia* (Islamic law) and issuing responsa (Ar. *fatâwî*) of their own. One cannot say with any certainty who is influencing whom at what point and to what extent. There may have been at least with respect to the legal sources of the two systems what Gideon Libson has dubbed a "feedback model" at work, "according to which the Jewish system first influenced the Muslim, which at a later stage exerted influence on Jewish law."[9] But although the complexity of the interface between Jewish and Islamic jurisprudence may never be fully elucidated, the parallels of legal methodologies, concerns, and even the formulas used in the respective responsa of the geonim and the *ulama* (Muslim scholars) are striking.

Diaspora communities expressed their allegiance to the gaon and the scholars of the academy by reciting their name in the *reshut*—the formal introductory rhetorical request for permission to begin reciting the sanctification of wine, the grace after meals, or a public sermon—and in the *qaddish* doxology, which punctuates the component parts of congregational prayer services. More importantly from an administrative point of view, the local congregational functionaries, such as cantors, judges, scribes, and beadles, were appointed by the gaonic academy to which the community paid loyalty. However, these appointments involved in point of fact most often gaonic approval of local candidates recommended by the diaspora congregation.

There was a third academy outside of Iraq, the venerable Tiberian yeshivah in Palestine, which was a direct continuation of the Sanhedrin of Second Temple times. Sometime around the middle of the tenth century, the Tiberian academy relocated to Jerusalem. The constitutional basis of this Palestinian school was embodied in the so-called Jerusalem Talmud. Palestinian practice differed from the Babylonian on various points of law and ritual. For example, in the Palestinian rite, the Torah was read in the synagogue according to a triennial cycle, whereas in the Babylonian rite, the reading took only a year. Palestinians celebrated only the one biblically ordained day for each holiday, whereas the Babylonians celebrated two. Palestinians recited the *shema*-prayer standing, while Babylonians recited it while seated.[10]

Despite their differences of custom and legal interpretation, the several academies recognized each other's orthodoxy. At the time of the Muslim conquest, the Palestinian academy's authority extended throughout Italy and the territories of the Byzantine Empire, while the Babylonian academies held sway in the Sassanian lands. But following the shift of the political, economic, and cultural center of gravity in the Islamic world to Iraq and the steady flow of Jews from the east into the Mediterranean region, the Palestinian academy was increasingly overshadowed by Sura and Pumbeditha. Every major city and even many smaller towns (such as al-Mahalla, Tinnis, and Minyat Ghamr in Egypt, Baniyas in Palestine, and Palmyra in Syria) west of Iraq came to have two principal congregations—one following Palestinian practices (Ar., *kanîsat al-shâmiyyîn*) and one Babylonian (Ar., *kanîsat al-'Irâqiyyîn*). By the twelfth century, the Babylonian form of Rabbinic Judaism had become the dominant rite worldwide—with local variations, to be sure.

The ultimate triumph of the Babylonian rite among the Jews communities in the medieval world, and indeed eventually throughout the entire diaspora, was due in no small measure to the activism, creativity, and intellectual quality of its spiritual leadership during the ninth, tenth, and early eleventh centuries. The geonim of this period included such figures as Amram b. Sheshna, Saadiah b. Joseph, Sherira b. Hananiah, and Samuel b. Hofni.

Amram Gaon and Saadiah Gaon produced the earliest known prayerbooks, which contributed enormously toward the greater standardization of the liturgy. The first of these was the *Seder Rav Amram Gaon*,[11] which was sent to the Jews of Spain at their request around 860. This prayerbook included all of the regular prayers according to the annual cycle for weekdays, sabbaths and festivals, new moons, fasts, and the non-pentateuchal holidays of Hanukkah and Purim. Each section of prayers was prefaced with the pertinent laws. At the end of the *Seder Rav Amram* were the special prayers and benedictions for use in daily life (e.g., blessings to be recited before partaking of specific foods or at grace after meals) and for rites of passage in the life cycle (e.g., circumcision, marriage, and burial).

As a work of literature, Amram's prayerbook pales in comparison with Saadiah's liturgical masterpiece, composed sometime between 928 and 942, which bore the Arabic title *Kitâb Jâmi' al-alawât wa 'l-Tasâbî*.[12] Saadiah's prayerbook went far beyond Amram's and indeed most later prayerbooks in that it was not merely an arranged compilation of existing prayers. Rather, it offered the worshipper a complete and systematic introduction to the subject of liturgy, its historical evolution, its significance, and its rationale. It also provided helpful notes and comments to the service and to individual prayers—all in Arabic, rather than Hebrew, for easy understanding by the layman, since by the tenth century, Arabic had become the daily language of the Jews in the Dar al-Islam, both in speech and writing. In addition to the required prayers, Saadiah included liturgical poems (Heb., *piyyutim*) by great synagogue poets of the past, such as Yose b. Yose, as well as his own poetical creations, which were highly regarded by later generations (see, e.g., the Andalusian exegete Abraham b. Ezra's praise of Saadiah's liturgical poetry in his Commentary on Eccl. 5:1) and which served as thematic and linguistic models for liturgical poets of the Golden Age of Hebrew letters in Islamic Spain. Saadiah's prayerbook contained the oldest extant version of the Passover haggadah, and many later Oriental prayerbooks continued to follow the practice of including it, all the way down to modern times. Saadiah's prayerbook was widely used throughout the medieval Arabic-speaking world, although it eventually went out of circulation in the later Middle Ages with the widespread decline in literacy in Classical Arabic among Jews and with the appearance of regional prayerbooks.

The challenge of Jewish sectarianism: No less important than the standardization of the liturgy was the success of the Babylonian geonim in meeting the challenges posed to the Rabbinic form of Judaism both from within the Jewish fold by sectarian movements and from the society without by the philosophical rationalism of the Hellenistic renascence in the medieval Islamic world. Remnants of some of the sectarian movements of late Second Temple times may still have existed, including Gnostic and Judeo-Christian groups such as the Ebionites and the Elkasites, but the evidence is tenuous and contradictory.[13] One thing that is certain, however, is that the highly charged climate of the great Islamic conquests and the sanguinary early religio-political struggles of the first Islamic century sparked apocalyptic and sectarian outbursts among many peoples in the Dar al-Islam, including the Jews.

The earliest of these Jewish sectarian movements in the medieval Islamic world about which there is substantial historical information is the Isawiyya (also Isuniyya), the followers of the messianic pretender Abu Isa of Isfahan, who led an ill-fated rebellion against the caliphate. The sources, both Jewish and Islamic,[14] place him alternatively during the reign Abd al-Malik (685-705) and the reigns of Marwan II and al-Manur (744-750 and 754-775); both were periods of widespread millenarian political and religious ferment. Goitein has argued for the earlier of the periods, while more recently Wasserstrom has made a strong, but not entirely convincing, case for the later.[15]

Abu Isa preached that he was a prophet and apostolic harbinger of the messiah and that Jesus and Muhammad were genuine prophets, but only to their own communities. He instituted seven (or perhaps ten) daily prayers, which maintained the Rabbinic Eighteen Benedictions and the Shema. He prohibited divorce and the consumption of meat and wine, which he deemed permissible only when the Temple sacrificial cult would be restored. This last innovation resembles the ascetic practices of Jewish sects of late antiquity such as the Mourners for Zion, remnants of which may have survived into the early Islamic period or at least were reestablished at that time.

The Isawiyya did not end with the death of its founder on the battlefield, but continued to exist at least into the tenth century. A disciple of Abu Isa, Yudghan (Judah) of Hamadan, also claimed to be a prophet and was considered to be the messiah by his followers, who referred to him as the Shepherd. In addition to following the ascetic practices of the Isawiyya, the Yudghanites observed many fasts. They believed that observance of the Jewish holidays was not obligatory while Israel remained in exile, but were merely to be considered memorial days. They maintained that the Torah had a literal exoteric meaning and an allegorical inner meaning (Ar., *ta'wîl*), a notion common among Shiite sectarians vis-à-vis the Koran. Also like the Muslim Shiite sects of this period, these Jewish movements spun off splinter groups, such as the Mushkanites, about whom little is known for sure beyond their names. The followers of Yudghan further adopted the Shiite notion of occlusion (Ar., *satar*), which held that their leader had not died but had gone into hiding and would return.[16] Still, according to the tenth-century Karaite encyclopedist, al-Qirqisani, the Isawiyya—despite their idiosyncratic practices—continued to live alongside mainstream Rabbanite Jews, following the same calendar, observing the same holidays, and being able to intermarry with them without impediment, something the Karaites could not do.[17]

The Karaite Sect: It was thus the Karaite sect that, even as it served as a stimulus for a forceful and creative response, posed the most serious challenge from within the Jewish fold to the Babylonian Rabbinic tradition. The origins of Karaism go back to Anan b. David in mid-eighth-century Iraq. An ascetic member of the Davidic aristocracy, he may have become involved in sectarian circles such as the Isawiyya. According to Rabbanite tradition,[18] he was a disappointed candidate for the office of exilarch. Anan and his followers, who at this early time were known simply as the Ananiyya, rejected the authenticity of the Oral Torah, and hence of gaonic authority. Opposition to the notion of an Oral Torah and to those who claimed to be its authoritative transmitters and interpreters had a history extending back to late Second Temple times. However, it is by no means clear whether there is a direct link, as some scholars have tried to argue, between Anan and the Karaite movement and the ancient Sadducees or the Dead Sea sects.[19]

Anan insisted upon a fundamentalist acceptance of the biblical text (Heb., *miqra*, whence perhaps the later name of *Qara'im*, or "Bible readers") as the sole source of Jewish law. While, as noted, his scriptural literalism may have been inspired by presumed remnants of groups like the Sadducees, Muslim influences appear more likely.[20] Anan founded an independent legal school of Judaism (a *madhhab* in the Islamic sense and perhaps even influenced by the Islamic school of Abu Anifa, with its emphasis upon the use of *ray'*, or considered opinion), and created his own legal code, *Sefer ha-Mitzwot* ("The Book of Commandments"), which he composed in Aramaic and which his Rabbanite opponents disparagingly referred to as his "own Talmud."

Almost invariably, the laws he derived from the scriptural text are considerably harsher and more restrictive than in the Rabbinic tradition. For example, the Mosaic prohibition against kindling fires on the Sabbath (Exod. 35:3) is interpreted as constituting a total ban against all fire on the seventh day, even if the flame were kindled prior to sundown on Friday evening. Thus, it was customary for the followers of Anan to spend the Sabbath eve in total darkness; nor did they eat the traditional Sabbath day pot-au-feu. He also prohibited conjugal relations between husband and wife (one of the *ongey ha-shabbat*, or Sabbath joys, in Rabbinic Judaism) on the Sabbath. This was on the basis of an exceedingly forced interpretation of the ban on agricultural labor (Exod. 34:21) and perhaps under the influence of the koranic analogy of wives as fields and the sexual act as plowing (Sura 2:223).

Anan also went far beyond the Rabbinic tradition in his interpretation of the dietary and purity laws. The only fowl that he permitted for consumption were pigeons and turtle doves, since these were the only birds mentioned as sacrificial offerings (Lev. 1:14). He totally rejected the talmudic notion of the minimal quantities in which foods were ritually unfit. He extended the laws of incestuous relations to include all consanguineous marriages, with the result that his later followers often had considerable difficulties in finding permissible partners under the complicated system of marriage law that the Karaites designated as *rikkub* (union). Only fragments of the *Sefer Mitzwot* survived, and already by the tenth century it was only being used in an epitomized form known by the Arabic title *al-Falaka* ("The Summary").

The primary intellectual emphasis of the Ananiyya was upon studying and interpreting Anan's legal code. But during the ninth century a breakaway group was formed that devoted itself to Anan's scriptural fundamentalism, and it is this group that actually became the Karaite sect, eventually attracting away from the original movement some of Anan's own descendants, who bore the princely title of *nesiim*. In the ninth and tenth centuries, this new offshoot had outstanding intellectual leadership and became a force to be reckoned with within the Islamicate Jewish world.

The first significant figure of the new Karaite movement was Benjamin Nehawandi (second quarter of the ninth century), who in later Karaite tradition is second only to Anan. He established many of the principals and the methodology of Karaite scriptural exegesis and seems to have been influenced by the theological concerns of the Muslim Mutazilite rationalists, who were at that time the dominant theological school in the Caliphate. He vigorously fought against anthropomorphism in the Bible and in popular religious thinking. According to Benjamin, all of Scripture's references to creation, revelation, and theophany actually refer to an intermediary angel rather than God. This logos-like demiurge was rejected by later Karaites, who instead avoided the problem posed by scriptural anthropomorphism through allegorical exegesis. Benjamin composed two legal works, *Sefer Mitzwot* ("Book of Commandments") and *Sefer Dinim* ("Book of Laws"). Both books were written in Hebrew and may have been part of a comprehensive code.[21]

The second significant leader in the evolving Karaite movement was Daniel al-Qumisi in the late ninth and early tenth centuries. Like Benjamin and so many other Jewish sectarians in this period, he was from Persia. He was the first Karaite to settle in Palestine and to advocate passionately for *aliyah* to lament the destruction of the Temple and to supplicate God for its restoration, in the tradition of the Mourners for Zion:

> Therefore it is incumbent upon you who fear the Lord to come to Jerusalem and to dwell in it, in order to hold vigils before the Lord until the day when Jerusalem shall be restored, as it is written: "And do ye not give him rest" (Isa. 62:7). . . . Do not nations other than Israel come from the four corners of the earth to Jerusalem every month and every year in the awe of God? What, then, is the matter with you, our brethren in Israel, that you are not doing even as much as is the custom of the Gentiles . . .?[22]

Daniel was a strict rationalist and also seems to be influenced by the Mutazilites. He was a stringent legalist, far more so than Benjamin Nehawandi. His primary endeavors were in the realm of scriptural exegesis, and, like Benjamin, he wrote exclusively in Hebrew. But he was omitted from the later official Karaite memorial lists of the founding fathers because of his disrespectful remarks about Anan, whom he refers to as a "champion of fools" and one of "the failed wisemen." Still, it was Daniel al-Qumisi who was most responsible for giving later Karaism three of its most distinctive ideological characteris-

tics: the total rejection of all rabbinical teachings, the high priority given to *aliyah*, and the centrality of asceticism and mourning.

During the tenth and eleventh centuries Karaism produced a large number of scholars who wrote in both Arabic and Hebrew, men like Salmon b. Yeruham, Yefet b. Eli, and Jeshuah b. Judah. Because of the primacy they accorded the study of the biblical text, they were compelled out of necessity to develop the sciences of Hebrew grammar and lexicography as well as exegesis. They also seem to have been the first Jewish theologians to adopt the tools of Greek philosophy, which had come into vogue in Muslim circles only a short time before. The questions of anthropomorphism (with which Rabbinical literature abounded), rational knowledge of God, divine justice, and many other philosophical concerns were taken up by the Karaites at the very time that these issues were being raised by Muslim scholars and by freethinking intellectuals in the Jewish and non-Jewish communities. Furthermore the Karaites began at this time to send out missionaries far and wide, like the Shiite *dâ'îs* ("those who call") in the Muslim community, to disseminate their ideas among other Jews and to call them (another possible explanation of the name Karaites is "those who call") to their sectarian version of the faith.

For a while, the Karaites posed a serious threat to mainstream Judaism. In order to combat this threat effectively, the Rabbanite Jews took up the Karaites' same weapons and, of course, addressed some of the same burning intellectual issues. The challenge of Karaism thus proved to be an important stimulus to Rabbinic Judaism, especially in the areas of scriptural exegesis, Hebrew language studies, and philosophy.

Unlike the Isawiyya and other early sects of the Islamic era, the Karaites were perceived as having gone beyond the pale of normative Judaism and were considered heretical sectarians (Heb., *minim*). Because of their rejection of the Rabbinic mathematically calculated calendar and their reliance instead upon a visual sighting of the new moon (hence their Arabic nickname *al-mîlâdiyya*, mentioned by al-Biruni), Karaite holidays frequently did not coincide with the days celebrated by other Jews. Their prayer service consisted entirely of praises and other readings from the Pentateuch and Psalms and did not include the Eighteen Benedictions or any prayers of communal or personal supplication. Although, during the morning prayer service, Karaite men wore a fringed garment—like the Rabbinate *tzitzit*—they rejected the use of phylacteries, considering the biblical injunction at Deut. 6:8—"And you shall bind them as a sign upon your hand, and they shall be as frontlets between your eyes"—to have only a figurative and symbolic meaning. Similarly considering Deut. 6:9—"And you shall write them on the doorposts of your house and on your gates"—to be symbolic, they placed no *mezuzah* on their doorposts either.

Only in a few places at certain periods were there any sort of amicable relations between Rabbanites and Karaites. The most notable example was in Fatimid Egypt during the eleventh century, when the sense of Jewish community was strong enough and broad enough to embrace the Karaites as well. Among members of the Egyptian haute bourgeoisie, intermarriage between Rabbanites and Karaites was not uncommon. Marriage contracts between individuals of the two sects preserved in the Cairo Geniza show that special stipulations frequently had to be made in order to respect the religious sensibilities of each of the partners. Karaites in Egypt at this time also participated with the rest of the Jewish community in emergency philanthropic fundraising drives. During the Ayyubid and Mamluk periods (1171-1517), the highest official of the Jewish community in Egypt who was recognized by the Muslim authorities (called in Arabic *ra'îs al-Yahûd* ["chief of the Jews"] and in Hebrew *nagid*) was considered to represent the Karaites and even the more sectarian Samaritans. However, by this time, the easy and cordial relations between Rabbanites and Karaites no longer prevailed.

In the end, due to its emphasis upon individual interpretation, Karaism failed to create a well organized unified movement. The dictum attributed to Anan, "Search thoroughly in the Torah, and do not rely upon my opinion" left the movement open to continual divisions from within.

The medieval Islamic renaissance: During the ninth through mid-thirteenth centuries, the Muslim world experienced a revival of Hellenic science and philosophy in Arabic translation, which the Swiss historian Adam Mez has aptly dubbed "the Renaissance of Islam."[23] This medieval Islamic form of Hellenism exerted a profound cultural influence upon both Muslims and Jews that was felt in religious and secular thought.

The intellectual and spiritual ferment in the Caliphate that accompanied the introduction of the Hellenic corpus posed many of the same challenges for Judaism that it did for Islam. Many Jews, particularly in the new bourgeoisie, were troubled by the apparent contradictions between religious revelation and belief, on the one hand, and science and philosophy (which in effect were one and the same), on the other. For example, Judaism—like Islam and Christian—held the dogma that the world had been created *ex nihilo*, whereas in the Aristotelian system it had been formed from eternal matter. Judaism held that the highest truths were those revealed by God, whereas a fundamental tenet of Hellenic philosophy was that all truths could be ascertained by the powers of reason. The competing claims to truth made by the numerous schools were openly debated in the cosmopolitan atmosphere of this period and served to increase many people's spiritual uncertainty. A chagrined Andalusian Muslim describes an intellectual forum in tenth century Baghdad at which:

> There were present not only people of various (Islamic) sects, but also unbelievers, Magians, materialists, atheists, Jews and Christians. . . . One of the unbelievers rose and said to the assembly: we are meeting here for a discussion. Its conditions are known to all. You, Muslims, are not allowed to argue from your books and prophetic traditions since we deny both. Everybody, therefore, has to limit himself to rational arguments. The whole assembly applauded these words.[24]

Jewish freethinkers, like their Muslim counterparts, make their appearance at this time.

One such Jewish dissident was the heretic Hiwi al-Balkhi. Like so many sectarians, he too was from the Persian part of the empire, and he was active in the eastern province of Khorasan during the mid-ninth century. As Ibn al-Rawandi and Abu Bakr al-Razi (also Persians) did with Islam, Hiwi denied the very foundation of Judaism as a revealed religion. He composed a book in which he raised two hundred questions attacking the Bible on rational grounds. He criticized the injustice of the biblical deity, denied miracles on the basis of experiential knowledge, and scoffed at the crude anthropomorphism. As noted above, the issues of anthropomorphism and divine justice were major concerns of the rationalist Muslim Mutazilite theologians and had been taken up by the Karaites as well. Although Hiwi's book is no longer extant, it enjoyed wide circulation at the time.

The Rabbinic response to sectarianism, philosophy, and freethinking: The challenges raised by sectarians like the Karaites, by freethinkers like Hiwi, and by Muslim polemicists, who eagerly seized upon the critiques of those Jewish dissidents, appeared all the more threatening because they touched upon genuine Jewish theological concerns that were also current in the general intellectual climate of the age. As they did with Karaism, to combat these challenges, mainstream Rabbanite Jews used contemporary philosophical methods and, of course, addressed the same burning issues as their critics.

The battle was taken up most effectively by one of the outstanding figures of medieval Judaism, Saadiah Gaon (882-942), the Egyptian-born head of the venerable Sura Academy. He met these challenges by offering a rational exposition of Judaism through philosophy. In order too dispel the spiritual doubt (Ar., *shubha*, a term also employed by the rationalist Mutazilite theologian and Saadiah's younger contemporary, Qâî Abd al-Jabbâr) that plagued his contemporaries, Saadiah composed the first systematic theology of medieval Rabbinic Judaism, his Book of Doctrines and Beliefs. He wrote the book in Arabic to make it more accessible to the educated layman, who was more likely to be perplexed by the conflicting views of the different religions, sects, and philosophical schools. Saadiah coopted many of the ideas and critiques—not to mention dialectic techniques—current among freethinking rationalists, Karaites, and the Mutazilite theologians of Islam. He argued that whatever appeared to conflict with reason in Scripture had to be interpreted allegorically. He offered what became the standard rational proofs for the doctrine of *creatio ex nihilo*, and he maintained the strongest possible stance against anthropomorphism, which henceforth remained the normative view of Rabbinic Judaism.

Saadiah laid the foundations upon which medieval Jewish scholastic theology and philosophy were built. His approach was very much along the lines of the Kalam theologians in Islam, particularly the Mutazilite school, and kalamic influence remained strong in mainstream Judaism within the Muslim world for the next two and a half centuries. Saadiah's successors at Sura, Samuel b. Hofni (d. 1013) and Dosa b. Saadiah (d. 1017), followed in his rationalist tradition. Samuel b. Hofni was particularly prolific and produced books in Arabic on kalamic topics, such as *Kitâb al-Asmâ' wa 'l-ifât* ("Book on Divine Names and Attributes"), *Kitâb al-Hidâya* ("Book of Guidance"), *Kitâb Uûl al-Dîn wa-Furû'uhu* ("Book on the Roots of Religion and its Branches"), and treatises like his *Ashar Masâ'il* ("Ten Questions"). Not only at Sura but also at its sister institution, the Pumbeditha Academy, was Saadiah's kalamic theological approach adopted. Hai b. Sherirah Gaon (939-1038), for example, although essentially a halakhist who criticized other geonim for "frequently reading the works of Gentiles" and who opposed the teaching of philosophy to children in Jewish schools, nevertheless took up in his responsa such major theological questions of the day as whether there is an inexorable, preordained term of life (Ar., *ajal*) for each individual.[25]

Throughout the major Jewish intellectual centers of the Dar al-Islam, from Spain to Persia, the study of philosophy came to be viewed as an integral part of the study of Torah. Indeed in some quarters, philosophy was accorded primacy.[26] However, even in Saadiah's own lifetime other philosophical trends made their appearance in Rabbanite Jewish circles. Neoplatonism, for example, came into vogue in the populous Jewish center of Qayrawan in Tunisia and shortly thereafter throughout Spain. For the Neoplatonists, such as Isaac b. Solomon Israeli (d. 950) and his disciple Dunash b. Tamim (d. after 956) in Qayrawan, or Solomon b. Gabirol (d. 1056) in Saragossa and Granada and Bahya b. Paquda (second half of the eleventh century) in Saragossa, God was conceived as the first cause from which emanates a hierarchical universe of hypostases. Unlike Saadiah, these Neoplatonic Jewish thinkers were not primarily concerned with proving the existence of God or justifying the doctrines of Judaism per se, but rather with understanding the relation of God to this world. They did, however, try to link their philosophical ideas with Jewish beliefs, just as the non-theologian Muslim philosophers—such as al-Kindi, al-Farabi and Ibn Sina—tried to do in their tradition.

During the middle of the twelfth century, Aristotelianism came to replace Neoplatonism as the dominant trend in Jewish religious philosophy. Although there had been some Jewish Aristotelians in tenth-century Iraq, in Spain this school came to the fore, beginning with Abraham b. Daud (d. 1180). The new trend exhibited a strict rationalism, in marked contrast to the mysticism of the Neoplatonists, as well as a more sophisticated awareness of the boundaries separating religious faith and philosophical reason than is found in kalamic theologians like Saadiah and Samuel b. Hofni.

Jewish Aristotelianism in the Islamic world reached its acme with Moses Maimonides (d. 1204). The greatest Jewish thinker of the entire Middle Ages, Maimonides was also a consummate halakhist and a man of science. He was keenly aware of the dilemma of the believing Jewish intellectual who had studied philosophy, was troubled by the contradictions of faith and reason, and found Saadiah's kalamic arguments, which were aimed at the educated layman, to be unsatisfying. For the sake of this type of elite intellectual, who was thoroughly grounded in both Jewish learning and philosophy, Maimonides composed his philosophic masterpiece *The Guide of the Perplexed*. This was essentially a work of philosophical exegesis, in which Maimonides undertook to explain in a thorough and systematic manner the anthropomorphic and anthropopathic terms in the Bible as well as obscure biblical parables. In order to limit his readership to a small elite, Maimonides deliberately cast his book in an esoteric and often contradictory style. Still, he did convey many of his philosophical ideas in a popular form in other works, as for example, in the opening and closing books of his great law code, the *Mishneh Torah*.

The Guide had a profound impact upon all subsequent medieval Jewish philosophers. Among the Jews of Christendom, in its Hebrew translation (*Moreh Nevukhim*), *The Guide* ignited a controversy that raged for centuries between rationalists and antirationalists. In the Islamic world, oddly enough, even among Maimonides' immediate descendants, *The Guide* came to be reinterpreted in a mystic light, and strict Aristotelianism gave way to a Neoplatonic harmonizing of diverse and incompatible of philosophical schools.

It was not only through philosophy that the majoritarian Jewish community of the medieval Islamic world met the challenges of sectarianism and of the powerful Arabo-Islamic general culture. The centrality of Scripture and of sacred language in Islamic civilization had provided the stimulus for the cultivation of the sciences of Arabic grammar, lexicography, and koranic exegesis. As with philosophy, the methodologies of the Islamic scholars had in turn been adopted by the Karaites, for whom the study of the Bible was of utmost religious importance. Again, Saadiah appears to have been in the vanguard of the Rabbanite response, once again coopting the very methods of the opposition. He provided some of the basic tools for Rabbanite scholars to counter Karaite interpretations of the Bible. He did this by composing pioneering studies in Hebrew grammar, the first Hebrew dictionary, *Sefer ha-Egron* (ed. Nehemiah Allony, Jerusalem, 1969), and a rational, philologically sound commentary, *Tawil*, to complement his Arabic translation, *Shar*, of the Bible.[27]

Saadiah's pioneering linguistic work was taken up and thoroughly developed by Rabbanite Jewish scholars in the western half of the Islamic world, again first in North Africa and shortly thereafter in Spain. Even before Saadiah, Judah b. Quraysh (second half of the ninth or perhaps early tenth century) in Tahert, Algeria, composed a treatise (*Risala*) on the Hebrew language in comparison with Aramaic and Arabic (ed. Dan Becker, Tel Aviv, 1984). Together with the grammatical treatises and dictionaries of Andalusian Jewish scholars such as Judah Hayyuj (945-1000), Jonah b. Janah (990-1050), and Moses b. Jiqatilla (eleventh century), Saadiah's and Ibn Quraysh's works became the standard references for biblical exegetes and Hebrew poets.

The aesthetic element in medieval Islamicate Judaism: The high, indeed lofty, status accorded to Arabic poetry and rhetoric in medieval Islamic civilization profoundly influenced the acculturated Jews of that world. This veneration of language was so ingrained in Islamic society that even a Jew like Moses ibn Ezra (d. after 1135) of Granada could make the astounding statement that, "Because the Arabs tribes excelled in their eloquence and rhetoric, they were able to extend their dominion over many languages and to overcome many nations, forcing them to accept their suzerainty."[28]

Nowhere were the aesthetic values of Islamic civilization more assimilated by Jews than in Muslim Spain. Thus, in al-Andalus during the tenth century, a new kind of Hebrew poetry arose, consciously modeled on the Arabic art form, with its rhyme and quantitative meters, classical language, and even its hedonist secular themes celebrating wine, the beauties of nature, and love (both hetero- and homosexual). However, unlike Arabic poetry, which was primarily, though not exclusively, secular in content, Andalusian Jewry also created a rich spiritual poetry employing the new, innovative style. This new Hebrew poetry was introduced into the synagogue service to be sung by the cantor—who was himself frequently a poet—between the prose texts of the prayers, supplanting much of the earlier, often opaque and highly didactic liturgical poetry (Heb., *piyyut*) that had developed in Palestine starting in the sixth century. The Hebrew liturgical poetry of Islamic Spain had all the intimacy and elegance of Arabic amatory poetry, only now the love being celebrated was between God and Israel or God and the individual soul. The earliest of the new *paytanim* (liturgical poets), Solomon ibn Gabirol (d. ca. 1057) for example, has God, the lover, implore his people: "Come to me at dawn, love/Carry me away/For in my heart I'm thirsting/To see my folk today."[29] Judah Halevi (d. 1141), the laureate of medieval Hebrew poets, apostrophizes God as the very seat of love itself: "From time's beginning, You were love's abode/My love encamped wherever it was you tented."[30] The very same poets who produced these sublime liturgical verses also wrote exquisite secular poetry, and it is this dichotomous tension between their Jewish spirituality and deep acculturation within the general, non-religious aspects of Islamic civilization that was so characteristic of many Jews in the medieval Muslim world and most particularly in al-Andalus.

The new style of liturgical poetry spread out of Spain and became a standard element in synagogue services throughout the provinces of the Islamic world. A good cantor was expected to be able to compose his own *piyyutim* and at the very least to be able to draw upon the compositions of the great poets. A young would-be cantor writes in a late twelfth- early thirteenth-century Geniza letter:

> I have left Damascus and intend to devote myself to the calling of a cantor. For this purpose, I have borrowed the diwans of Solomon the Little (the famous Ibn Gabirol) and of Judah ha-Levi—may their memory be blessed—and made excepts from them for my use.[31]

Poetry was so important among the Jews of the Islamic world that prosody became a required subject in the traditional curriculum of the Oriental and Sephardi yeshiva down to modern times, in marked contrast to the course of study in the European Ashkenazi academy.

Music was closely associated with poetry

in Islamic society, and the love of music that has always bordered on a passion in the Arabic-speaking lands was shared by Jews. Jews had been associated with music in the Muslim world from the days of the Islamic Renaissance. The Jew Abu 'l-Manur was court musician to the Umayyad emir of Spain, al-akam I in the early ninth century, and even the great theologian and polymath Saadiah Gaon had written about musical theory in his philosophical writing.[32] The Oriental synagogue was and remains a singing synagogue, in which almost all of the liturgy in sung out loud according Arabic musical modes and frequently to Arab popular melodies. This, in spite of the objections of no less a figure than Maimonides himself, who in a responsum to the Jewish community of Aleppo, states unequivocally that listening to Arab songs at any time, even without the words, is forbidden.[33] In the medieval Islamic world, it was not unusual for several cantors to officiate simultaneously at a Sabbath or holiday service or for individual members of the congregation to sing a particular prayer solo. Cantorial virtuosi traveled frequently for guest appearances in different communities. Some cantors even bore titles such as *ha-mumheh* (the expert), *ha-gadol* (the great), *nezer ha-hazzanim* (diadem of the cantors) or *pe'er ha-hazzanim* (glory of the cantors).[34]

Because of the high premium placed upon a cantor's poetic and musical talents, not every precentor's moral character was screened as carefully as it should have been prior to his appointment. In another responsum, Maimonides says that a cantor who comes to services intoxicated should not be allowed to officiate in any way (*Teshuvot ha-Rambam*, no. 165, pp. 314-315). A responsum probably written by Joseph b. Abitur (second half of the eleventh-first third of the twelfth century) notes the case of a cantor in Spain who is removed from office for immoral relations with a Gentile prostitute and an adolescent boy (*Teshuvot Geoney Mizrah u-Maarab*, ed. Joel Müller, Berlin, 1888, no. 171, p. 41). These examples probably reflect occasional but not entirely rare incidents. The ideal was summed up in the recommendation for a cantor preserved in

the Geniza documents, which emphasizes the man's "love of God, his religiosity, piety, and virtuousness, his pleasant manners, his eagerness to seek knowledge and excellence, and . . . his unblemished conduct."[35] The norm, though probably falling short of this ideal, was far closer to it than to the notorious exceptions.

Mysticism, pietism, and popular religiosity: Quotidian Judaism in the medieval Islamic world as reflected in the documents of the Cairo Geniza has been described by S.D. Goitein.[36] This was:

> a stern, straightforward, Talmudic type of piety, concerned with the strict fulfillment of the commandments and with the pursuit of the study required for their knowledge. The somewhat jejune character of their [i.e., the Geniza people's] religiosity was enhanced by the rigorous rationalism embraced by Jewish orthodoxy in the wake of centuries of secular and theological controversies, set into motion by the contact with Greek thought (of course, in Arabic garb).

The religion characterized by Goitein was the official establishmentarian faith, or "Great Way," of the bourgeoisie. There existed in addition others forms of religiosity, a "Lesser Way," both in popular strata of Jewish society and even among members of the elite. As noted above, some mystic and pietistic urges had already found expression in sectarian movements like the Isawiyya, the Yudghaniyya, and, to a certain extent, in Karaism. Jewish mystical pietists (Heb., *hasidim*) in eighth century Basra, may, as Goitein himself has suggested,[37] have had a significant formative influence on early Sufism (Islamic mysticism). Leading figures of the mainstream rationalist elite had devoted part of their wide-ranging attention to elite, Rabbinic mysticism. Both Saadiah Gaon and Isaac Israeli, for example, wrote commentaries on the *Sefer Yetzira*, a highly regard mystical text from late antiquity. Bahya b. Paquda, a *dayyan* (halakhic judge) in late-eleventh-century Saragossa combined Saadiah's rationalism with a pietism permeated with mystical overtones. His devotional handbook, The Guide to the Duties of the Heart,[38] dealt with the inner person and the soul's quest for spiritual perfection and union with the Divine Light. The book became a popular manual for pietists and mystics, and in its Hebrew translation (*Hobot ha-Lebabot*), came to enjoy great popularity among the Jewish masses in Christian Europe as well because of its homely warmth and sincerity. Bahya's mystic pietism shows affinities with the synthesis of Sufism and orthodoxy of his contemporary in the East, the great Muslim theologian al-Ghazali.

Even as Iraqi *hasidim* had influenced early Sufis in the eighth century, so did fully developed Sufism of the thirteenth century influence a Jewish hasidic movement in Ayyubid Egypt and Palestine. This movement was founded by Abraham b. Moses Maimonides (d. 1237), the son of the great philosopher, halakhist and physician, who succeeded his father as *ra'îs al-yahud/nagid* in Egypt and as a member of the royal medical staff. Abraham Maimonides openly admired Sufism, even going so far as to declare that some Muslim mystics were worthier disciples of the biblical prophets than many of his own contemporary coreligionists. He employed Sufi vocabulary, for example, referring to *unio mystica* as *wuûl* (lit., "arrival") and to asceticism as *zuhd*. He tried to revive ancient practices that had been abandoned in Jewish worship since Second Temple times, such as prostration during prayer, raising the hands when making supplications, and washing the feet before worship.

Like Bahya, he too produced a manual for pietists entitled *Kifâyat al-câbidîn* ("Complete Guide for Worshippers"), which bears a striking resemblance to the title of a work by his Muslim contemporary in Egypt, Abd al-Aîm al-Mundhirî (*Kifâyat al-mutacabbid*). However, his book did not enjoy the same renown as did Bahya's, nor was it translated into Hebrew. His innovations and the excessive, almost heretical-sounding expressions of mystical ecstasy by some of his followers aroused considerable opposition among other Jews, and the movement remained restricted to a very small circle of individuals, mainly among Abraham Maimonides' direct descendants. One of his son's, Obadiah, wrote a mystical work that is very much in the Sufi tradition, *al-Maqâla al-awiyya* ("The Treatise of the Pool") (complete Eng. trans. by Paul Fenton, London, 1981), and a grandson, David b. Joshua, wrote a manual for ascetics, *al-Murshid ila l-tafarrud wa 'l-murfid ila 'l-tajarrud* ("The Guide to Detachment and Aid to Isolation") (Ar. text and Hebrew trans. by Paul Fenton, Jerusalem, 1987). During the later Middle Ages, Jewish devotees of mysticism in Syria and Iran sometimes became more or less loosely associated with Sufi orders, and Jewish mystics in Yemen studied and cited the poetry of the great Muslim Sufis of the past.

In addition to pietism and mysticism, the Jews of the medieval Islamic world engaged in other forms of non-orthodox religiosity. Pilgrimage to holy shrines associated with miraculous past events or the tombs of prophets and saintly individuals were common. These popular pilgrimages were of a totally different character than the traditional Jewish "going up" (Heb., *aliyah*) to Jerusalem. The Karaite polemicist, Sahl b. Masliah, writing in the second half of the tenth century decries popular Rabbanite pilgrimages to the graves of holy men:

> How can I keep silent when some Jews follow the customs of idolaters? They sit among graves of saintly persons and spend nights among tombstones, while they seek favors from dead mean, saying, "O Jose the Galilean, grant me a cure!" or "Vouchsafe me a child!" They light lamps at the graves of saints and burn incense upon the brick altars before them and tie bowknots to the palm trees bearing the name of the saint as a charm for all kinds of diseases. They perform pilgrimage rites over the graves of these dead saints and make vows to them and appeal and pray to them to grant their requests.[39]

Jews from as far away as Spain and Morocco visited the putative tombs of the Prophet Ezekiel and Ezra the Scribe in Iraq. The twelfth-century traveler Benjamin of Tudela describes the "great gathering like a fair" that took place at Ezekiel's tomb during the High Holy Days. According to him, the camp of the Jewish pilgrims extended for two miles, and Arab merchants set up stalls to provide goods and services.[40] A scene such as this can still be observed to this day at annual Jewish pilgrimages in Morocco, Tunisia, and Egypt.

One important medieval Jewish shrine not associated with a tomb was the synagogue in Dammuh (site of ancient Memphis), just south of Old Cairo, where according to tradition Moses had prayed and performed miracles. The Muslim writer al-Maqrizi describes Dammuh as "the largest Jewish place of worship in the land of Egypt."[41] Pilgrims would make camp there in tents during the Pentecost festival. An eleventh-century Geniza document issued by the rabbinical court in Fustat banning instrumental music, dancing, games, entertainment (e.g., shadow puppet shows), unchaperoned females (except for very old women), brewing beer, men and boys sleeping under the same blanket, and social mixing of men and women, gives the distinct impression that such practices were in fact the norm at great pilgrimage gatherings.[42]

Not all shrines drew pilgrims from the far ends of the Dar al-Islam. Some were of a purely local nature, as for example the synagogue of Tatay in Lower Egypt, which possessed a highly venerated ancient Torah scroll. There is no evidence, however, for anything resembling a cult of local Jewish saints' tombs anywhere in the medieval Islamic world as there was throughout much of North Africa in early modern and modern times. The writers of Geniza letters never invoke angels. As Goitein has observed, "even the names of archangels appear only exceptionally as personal names, and that of Gabriel seems to be completely absent."[43] This may be due to the fact that most of the writers belonged to the educated, rationalist bourgeoisie. Geniza magic texts mention Metatron, the throne angel. The eleventh-century Andalusian Muslim polemicist Ibn Azm makes the sweeping categorical statement that Rabbanite Jews invoke Metatron on the night of Yom Kippur.[44] Ibn Azm, however, never hesitated to tell half truths and outright falsehoods for polemical purposes.

Although decried by rationalists such as Maimonides, magic, astrology, and use of amulets were widespread in all strata of Jewish society in the Middle Ages. An undated Geniza letter requests passages from the Song of Songs to cure dry skin and boils.[45] Other Geniza documents mention esoteric practices such as summoning up the *jinn* (supernatural spirits, genies), performing incantations, and fumigations.[46] But only with the general socioeconomic and intellectual decline of the Jews of the Islamic world at the end of the Middle Ages, together with their non-Jewish neighbors, did magical practices become ubiquitous among all levels of Jewish society.

Bibliography

Goitein, S.D., *A Mediterranean Society: The Jewish Communities of the Arab World as Portrayed in the Documents of the Cairo Geniza* (Berkeley and Los Angeles, 1971-1988).

Goitein, S.D., *Jews and Arabs: Their Contacts through the Ages* (3rd ed., New York, 1974).

Nemoy, Leon, ed. and trans., *Karaite Anthology* (New Haven and London, 1952).

Scheindlin, Raymond P., *The Gazelle: Medieval Hebrew Poems on God, Israel, and the Soul* (Philadelphia, 1991).

Stillman, Norman A., *The Jews of Arab Lands: A History and Source Book* (Philadelphia, 1979).

Wasserstrom, Steven M., *Between Muslim and Jew: The Problem of Symbiosis under Early Islam* (Princeton, 1995).

Wolfson, Harry A. Wolfson, *Repercussions of the Kalam in Jewish Philosophy* (Cambridge, Mass., 1979).

Notes

[1] See H.Z. Hirschberg, *Der Dîwân des as-Samaùal ibn 'Adijâ'* (Krakow, 1931).

[2] See H.Z. Hirschberg, *Yisra'el ba-'Arab* (Tel Aviv, 1946), pp. 112-116, and Ilsa Lichtenstadter, "Some References to Jews in Pre-Islamic Arabic Literature," in *PAAJR* 10, 1940, pp. 185-194.

[3] On the problems of identifying sources, see Julian Obermann, "Islamic Origins: A Study in Background and Foundation," in Nabih Faris, ed., *The Arab Heritage* (Princeton, 1944), pp. 58-120.

[4] Judah Even Shemuel, *Midreshey Ge'ullah: Pirqey ha-Apoqalipsah ha-Yehudit* (2nd ed., Jerusalem and Tel Aviv, 1953), p. 188.

[5] Norman A. Stillman, *The Jews of Arab Lands: A History and Source Book* (Philadelphia, 1979), p. 181. For other such texts, see ibid., pp. 178-179, 182, and 269-270.

[6] Ibid., pp. 171-175, and Marcus Nathan Adler, ed. and trans., *The Itinerary of Benjamin of Tudela* (New York, 1964).

[7] See Moshe Gil, "The Exilarchate," in Daniel Frank, ed., *The Jews of Medieval Islam: Community, Society, and Identity* (Leiden, 1995), pp. 33-65.

[8] See Menahem Ben-Sasson, *The Emergence of the Local Jewish Community in the Muslim World: Qayrawan, 800-1057* (Jerusalem, 1996);

and Norman A. Stillman, "Quelques renseignements biographiques sur Yôsêf Ibn ʿAwkal, médiateur entre les communautés juives du Maghreb et les Académies d'Irak," in REJ 132 (October-December 1973), pp. 529-542.

[9] Gideon Libson, p. 98, n. 105.

[10] For the major points of difference, see M. Margaliot, ha-Hilluqim she-beyn Anshe Mizrah u-Beney Eretz Yisra'el (Jerusalem, 1938), and B.M. Lewin, Otzar Hillup Minhagim beyn Beney Eretz Yisra'el u-beyn Beney Babel (Jerusalem, 1942).

[11] Ed., Daniel S. Goldschmit (Jerusalem, 1971); also, in 2 vols., ed. and trans. by David Hedegård (Lund, Sweden, 1951-1974).

[12] "The Comprehensive Book of Prayers and Praises," 2nd edition, ed. I. Davidson, S. Assaf, and B.I. Joel (Jerusalem, 1963).

[13] For a review of the scholarly debate, see Steven M. Wasserstrom, "The ʿIsawiyya Revisited," in Studia Islamica 75 (1992), pp. 37-41.

[14] Summarized in Ben Zion Dinur, Yisra'el ba-Golah (Tel Aviv, 1961), vol. 1, pt. 2, pp. 228-231.

[15] S.D. Goitein, Jews and Arabs: Their Contacts through the Ages, 3rd ed. (New York, 1974), pp. 168-170; Wasserstrom, op. cit., pp. 57-80, and Steven Wasserstrom, Between Muslim and Jew: The Problem of Symbiosis under Early Islam (Princeton, 1995), pp. 71-81.

[16] For the sources on Yudghan and Mushkan and their movements, see Dinur, op. cit., vol. 1, pt. 2, pp. 232-234, and Yaʿqûb al-Qirqisani, Kitâb al-Anwâr wa 'l-Marâqib: Code of Karaite Law, 4 vols., Leon Nemoy, ed. (New York, 1942), pp. 145 and 134-135.

[17] See Qirqisani, ibid., pp. 144-145.

[18] Called into doubt by Leon Nemoy, "Anan ben David: A Re-appraisal of the Historical Data," in Semitic Studies in Memory of Immanuel Löw (Budapest, 1947), pp. 239-248, but vigorously defended by Salo W. Baron, A Social and Religious History of the Jews (2nd ed., New York, 1957), vol. 5, pp. 388-389, n. 1.

[19] For a succinct summary of the arguments for such a link, see Bernard Dupuy, "Les karaite sont-ils les descendents des esseniens?" in Istina 29 (1984), pp. 139-151.

[20] See Michael Cook, "ʿAnan and Islam: The Origins of Karaite Scripturalism," in Jerusalem Studies in Arabic and Islam 9 (1987), pp. 161-182.

[21] Excerpts appear in Leon Nemoy, ed. and trans., Karaite Anthology (New Haven and London, 1952), pp. 23-29.

[22] Ibid., p. 52.

[23] Die Renaissance des Islams (Heidelberg, 1922).

[24] Al-umaydî, quoted by Alexander Altmann, ed. and trans., Saadya Gaon: Book of Doctrines and Beliefs (Oxford, 1946), p. 13.

[25] See Harry A. Wolfson, Repercussions of the Kalam in Jewish Philosophy (Cambridge, Mass., 1979), pp. 222-227.

[26] See Herbert A. Davidson, "The Study of

Philosophy as a Religious Obligation," in Goitein, op. cit., pp. 53-68.

[27] Joseph Derenbourg, et al., eds, Oeuvres complètes de R. Saadia Ben Iosef al-Fayyoûmî, 3 vols. in 2 (Paris, 1893-1899; repr. Hildesheim, 1979); also Moses Zucker, Rav Saadya Gaon's Translation of the Torah (New York, 1959 [Hebrew]).

[28] Moses ibn Ezra, Sefer Shirat Yisrael (Kitab al-Muâara wa 'l-Mudhâkara), Heb., trans. B. Halper (repr., Jerusalem, 1966), p. 62.

[29] Raymond P. Scheindlin, The Gazelle: Medieval Hebrew Poems on God, Israel, and the Soul (Philadelphia, 1991), p. 97.

[30] Ibid., p. 77.

[31] S.D. Goitein, A Mediterranean Society: The Jewish Communities of the Arab World as Portrayed in the Documents of the Cairo Geniza (Berkeley and Los Angeles, 1971-1988), vol. 2, p. 221.

[32] See Henry George Farmer, Sacadyah Gaon on the Influence of Music (London, 1943).

[33] Moses Maimonides, Teshuvot ha-Rambam, ed. Joshua Blau (Jerusalem, 1957), no. 224, pp. 398-400.

[34] Jacob Mann, The Jews in Egypt and in Palestine under the Fâtimid Caliphs (2nd ed., New York, 1970), p. 269; Goitein, op. cit., p. 223.

[35] Goitein, op. cit., p. 222.

[36] S.D. Goitein, ed., Religion in a Religious Age (Cambridge, 1974), p. 8.

[37] S.D. Goitein, Jews and Arabs: Their Contacts through the Ages, 3rd ed. (New York, 1974), pp. 149-151.

[38] Menahem Mansoor, The Book of Direction to the Duties of the Heart (London, 1973).

[39] "Epistle to Jacob b. Samuel," in Nemoy, Karaite Anthology, pp. 115-116.

[40] The Itinerary of Benjamin of Tudela, p. 44.

[41] al-Maqrîzî, al-Mawâʿi wa 'l-Iʿtibâr fî dhikr al-khia wa 'l-âthâr II, Bulaq, 1270 A.H., p. 464.

[42] TS 20.117v in Simha Assaf, Meqorot u-mehqarim betoldot Yisra'el (Jerusalem, 1946), pp. 160-162.

[43] Goitein, A Mediterranean Society, vol. 5, pp. 336-337.

[44] Quoted by Ignaz Goldziher, "Proben muhammedänischer Polemik gegen den Talmud," in Jeschurun 8, 1872, pp. 102-104.

[45] Richard Gottheil and William H. Worrell, eds., Fragments from the Cairo Genizah in the Freer Collection (New York, 1927), no. III, pp. 22-23.

[46] For a brief survey of the evidence, see Steven Wasserstrom, "The Magical Texts in the Cairo Genizah," in Joshua Blau and Stefan C. Reif, eds., Genizah Research after Ninety Years: The Case of Judaeo-Arabic (Cambridge, 1992), pp. 160-166.

NORMAN A. STILLMAN

JUDAISM, HISTORY OF. PART V.A. JUDAISM IN MODERN TIMES IN EUROPE: For the history of Judaism in Europe, "modern times" begin when, from the late eighteenth century, political change removed from Christianity its power to define culture. The militant secularism of the French Revolution sought to replace Christianity with a religion of reason. When Christianity no longer governed as the sole arbiter of the social order and political life. Rabbinic Judaism as set forth in Talmudic and related writings met competition within Jewry. The Rabbinic Judaism that had taken shape in the fifth century C.E. in response to triumphant Christianity and that had so long and so successfully sustained the life of the Jewish people now confronted skeptical questioning among people standing essentially outside of its system of truths. The received Judaism no longer answered the urgent questions critical to communities of Jews, and, as a result, new Judaisms took shape, dealing with other agenda of urgent questions and answering those questions in ways self-evidently right for those who believed. Each of these Judaisms claimed to continue in linear succession the Judaism that had flourished for so long, to develop in an incremental succession and so to connect, through the long past, to Sinai. But, in fact, each one responded to contemporary issues deemed urgent among one or another group of Jews.

The Rabbinic Judaism that had flourished addressed the agenda of Christianity and gave answers that, for holy Israel, proved self-evidently valid. Christianity in the West, like Islam in North Africa and the Near and Middle East, defined the world to which that Judaism responded, the world that made Judaism relevant for holy Israel. Therefore, when Christianity's agenda began to compete with secular ones, other Judaisms took shape as well, so that, just as Christianity faced competition from secularism, Communism, Nazism, nationalism, and hedonism (among others), so those same competing views of the world provoked the formation of new kinds of Judaism. This was the legacy of the political changes referred to as "Emancipation," which marked, in the case of Judaism in the West, the period that begins with the American Constitution and the French Revolution. In the nineteenth and twentieth centuries, these changes meant that, for the first time, the dominant Rabbinic Judaism would confront alternative visions of Judaism, one, as we shall see, framed around theological ideas, a second, around secular ideological ones.

Modern and contemporary Judaisms in the context of Rabbinic Judaism: What distinguishes the Judaic system of the dual Torah from its continuators and competition in the nineteenth and twentieth century is a simple trait. The Judaism of the dual Torah encompassed the whole of the existence of the Jews who found its truth self-evident, its definition of life ineluctable. In the way of life of that system, a Jew was not simply always a Jew, he or she was *only* a Jew. The newly emergent Judaisms acknowledged the former. Jews never stopped being Jews. The world would not let them, even if they wanted to. But the Judaism of the dual Torah made slight provision for Jews to be anything but Jews: the holy people had no other vocation, no alternative, to its holiness. Its history as a people different in kind from other peoples, its destiny at the end of time—these matched its distinctive holy way of life in the here and now. So Israel was always Israel and only Israel. But in modern times, Israel became one of several things that Jews would be: also Americans, also workers, also Israelis, among the twentieth-century Judaisms, but never only Israel, God's people. And that theory of Israel matches in social terms the conception of the individual person as well. For in the received Torah, the Jew lived out life in the rhythm of sanctification, realizing in concrete deeds the Torah's words, once more, not only always but *only* as a Jew. It was not a romance, it was a marriage.

The conception of the people Israel presents the key to interpreting this system. From antiquity forward, the Judaism of the dual Torah saw the people of Israel as solely that. But from the eighteenth century onward, Judaic systems took shape that saw Israel as that and more. They differed on the question, What more? They took issue, further, on the range of permissible differences, on issues of segregation versus integration. But all concurred that, in some ways, Jews would integrate. That concurrence by itself distinguished all modern Judaic systems from the received system of the dual Torah. In the systems of continuation of the nineteenth century, for instance, the Jew was a citizen as well as a Jew. That meant that being a Jew required reframing: a new theory of Israel, demanding also a fresh conception of the way of life of that Israel, and, it would follow, also a new world view to explain that way of life and situate it among the received texts. The mythic Judaisms of the twentieth century for their part accepted as given the multiple dimensions that took the measure of the Jew: individual, member of diverse groups, among them, a Jewish one. So the Jewish Socialist was a Socialist too, and between Zionism and Jews' other worlds, or between American Judaism and Jewish Americans' other concerns, competition for commitment could scarcely come to resolution. For in modern and contemporary times, the Jews concerned themselves with many things, even though, from the viewpoint of the world, a Jew might be only that. How did these new concerns arise?

Emancipation: Part of a larger movement of emancipation of serfs, women, slaves, Catholics (in Protestant countries, for instance, England and Ireland), "emancipation" encompassed the Jews as well. Benzion Dinur defines the process as follows:

> Jewish emancipation denotes the abolition of disabilities and inequities applied specially to Jews, the recognition of Jews as equal to other citizens, and the formal granting of the rights and duties of citizenship. Essentially the legal act of emancipation should have been simply the expression of the diminution of social hostility and psychological aversion toward Jews in the host nation . . . but the antipathy was not obliterated and constantly hampered the realization of equality even after it had been proclaimed by the state and included in the law.[1]

The political changes that fall into the process of the Jews' emancipation began in the eighteenth century, and, in fifty years, affected the long-term stability that, from Constantine onward, had characterized the Jews' social and political life. These political changes raised questions not previously found urgent, and, it follows, also precipi-

tated reflection on problems formerly neglected. The answers to the questions flowed logically and necessarily from the character of the questions themselves.

Dinur traces three periods in the history of the Jews' emancipation, from 1740-1789, ending with the French revolution, then from 1789-1878, the French revolution to the Congress of Berlin, and from 1878 to 1933, the Congress of Berlin to the Nazis' rise to power in Germany. The adoption of the American Constitution in 1787 confirmed the U.S. position on the matter. Jewish males enjoyed the rights of citizens along with all other whites. The first period marked the point at which the emancipation of the Jews first came under discussion, the second marked the period in which Western and Central European states accorded to the Jews the rights of citizens, and the third brought to the fore a period of new racism that, in the end, annihilated the Jews of Europe (fig. 71).

In the first period advocates of the Jews' emancipation maintained that religious intolerance accounted for the low caste-status assigned to the Jews. Liberating the Jews would mark another stage in overcoming religious intolerance. During this first period, the original ideas of Reform Judaism came to expression, although the important changes in religious doctrine and practice were realized only in the earlier part of the nineteenth century. In the second period, the French revolution brought Jews political rights in France, Belgium, Netherlands, Italy, Germany, and the Austro-Hungarian Empire. As Germany and Italy attained unification and Hungary independence, the Jews were accorded the rights and duties of citizenship. Dinur explains:

> It was stressed that keeping the Jews in a politically limited and socially inferior status was incompatible with the principle of civic equality . . . "it is the objective of every political organization to protect the natural rights of man," hence, "all citizens have the right to all the liberties and advantages of citizens, without exception."

Jews at that time entered the political and cultural life of the Western nations, including their overseas empires (hence Algerian Jews received French citizenship). During this second period, Reform Judaism reached its first stage of development, beginning in Germany. It made it possible for Jews to hold together the two things they deemed inseparable, their desire to remain Jewish and their wish also to be one with their "fellow citizens." By the middle of the nineteenth century, Reform had reached full expression and had won the support of a sizable part of German Jewry. In reaction against Reform, Orthodoxy came into existence. Orthodoxy no less than Reform asked how "Judaism" could co-exist with "German-ness," meaning citizenship in an undifferentiated republic of citizens. A centrist position, mediating between Reform and Orthodoxy, was worked out by theologians in what was then called the Historical School and what, in twentieth-century America, took the name of Conservative Judaism. The period from the French Revolution to the Congress of Berlin therefore saw the full efflorescence of all of the Judaisms of political modernization. All of these Judaisms characterized the Jews of Western Europe, and, later on, America. But in America, Reform, Orthodoxy, and the Historical School or Conservative Judaism radically changed in character, responding to the urgent issues of a different circumstance, producing self-evidently valid answers of a character not compatible with the nineteenth century statements of those same systems.

In the third period, anti-Semitism as a political and social movement attained power. Jews began to realize that, in Dinur's words, "the state's legal recognition of Jewish civic and political equality does not automatically bring social recognition of this equality." The Jews continued to form a separate group; they were racially "inferior." The impact of the new racism would be felt in the twentieth century. Judaisms of the twentieth century raised the questions of political repression and economic dislocation, as these faced the Jews of Eastern Europe and America.

Clearly, in the nineteenth century, particularly in Western countries, a new order revised the political settlement covering the Jews, in place for nearly the entire history of the West. From the time of Constantine forward, the Jews' essentially autonomous life as a protected minority had raised political questions that found answers of an essentially supernatural and theological character. But now the emancipation redefined those questions, asking about Jews not as a distinct group but about Jews as part of some other polity altogether than the Jewish one. Those Jews who simply passed over retain no interest for us; Karl Marx, converted to Christianity at an early age, produced no ideas important in the study of Judaism(s). But vast numbers of Jews in the West determined to remain Jewish and also to become something else. Their urgent question addressed the issue of how to be both Jewish and something else: a citizen of Germany or France or Britain. Still, that issue would not confront the Jews of the Russian Empire until World War I, and, together with the Jews the Austro-Hungarian Empire, Rumania, and other Eastern European areas, these formed the vast majority of the whole.

The nineteenth century Judaisms and the political question: Changes in the political circumstances in which Jews made their lives as well as in the economic conditions in which they made their living intensified issues that formerly had drawn slight attention and rendered inconsequential claims that had for so long demanded response. The Jews had formerly constituted a distinct group. Now in the West they formed part of an undifferentiated mass of citizens, all of them equal before the law, all of them subject to the same law. The Judaism of the dual Torah rested on the political premise that the Jews were governed by God's law and formed God's people. The two political premises—the one of the nation-state, the other of the Torah—scarcely permitted reconciliation. The consequent Judaic systems, Reform Judaism, Orthodox Judaism, positive Historical Judaism (in the U.S.A.: Conservative Judaism), each of them addressing issues regarded as acute and not merely chronic, in the nineteenth century alleged that they formed the natural next step in the unfolding of "the tradition," meaning the Judaic system of the dual Torah.

From the time of Constantine to the

nineteenth century, Jewry in Christendom sustained itself as a recognized, and ordinarily-tolerated minority. The contradictory doctrines of Christianity—the Jews as Christ-killers to be punished, the Jews as witnesses to be kept alive and ultimately converted at the second coming of Christ—held in an uneasy balance. The pluralistic character of some societies, for instance, that in Spain, the welcome accorded entrepreneurs in opening territories, for instance, Norman England, Hungary, Poland and Russia, White Russia and the Ukraine, in the early centuries of development—these account still more than doctrine for the long-term survival of Jews in Christian Europe. The Jews, like many others, formed not only a tolerated religious minority but something akin to a guild, specializing in certain occupations, e.g., crafts and commerce in the East. True, the centuries of essentially ordinary existence in the West ended with the Crusades, which forced Jewry to migrate to the eastern frontier of Europe. But, until the twentieth century, the Jews formed one of the peoples permanently settled in Europe, first in the West, later in the East. But it was only in modern times that the Jews as a whole found, or even aspired to, a position equivalent to that of the majority population in European societies.

Prior to that time the Jews found themselves subjected to legal restrictions as to where they might live and how they might earn a living. They enjoyed political and social rights of a most limited character. In the East, where most Jews lived in circumstances of segregation, they governed their own communities through their own administration and law. They spoke their own language, Yiddish, wore distinctive clothing, ate only their own food, controlled their own sector of the larger economy and ventured outside of it only seldom, and, in all, formed a distinct and distinctive group. Commonly, the villages in which they lived found Jews and Christians living side by side, but, in many of those villages, Jews formed the majority of the population. These facts made for long-term stability and autonomy. In the West, the Jews formed only a tiny proportion of the population, but, until modern times, lived equally segregated from the rest of the country, behind the barriers of language, custom, and economic calling. So the Jews for a long time formed a caste, a distinct and clearly defined group—but within the hierarchy ordered by the castes of the society at hand.

In that setting, Reform, Orthodoxy, and Conservative Judaism each make explicit a claim to stand in a linear, unitary, harmonious relationship with the dual Torah of Sinai, to form the necessary development of the Torah. Each of these three Judaisms negotiated issues of secularity, on the one side, and social and cultural and political change, on the other. None affirmed an essentially secular view, nor did any one of them formulate its systemic statement outside the framework of the dual Torah. These three main Judaisms born between 1800 and 1850, in the aftermath of the advent of modern politics, have now to be described.

First in time is Reform Judaism, coming to expression in the early part of the nineteenth century and making changes in Jewish liturgy, then in doctrine and in way of life. Reform Judaism recognized the legitimacy of making changes and regarded change as reform, yielding institutional Reform. Second was the reaction to Reform Judaism, called Orthodox Judaism, which in many ways was continuous with the Judaism of the dual Torah, but in some ways was as selective of elements of that Judaism as was Reform Judaism. Orthodox Judaism reached its first systematic expression in the middle of the nineteenth century. It held that Judaism lies beyond history, is the work of God, and constitutes a set of facts of the same order as the facts of nature. Hence, in its view, change is not reform, and Reform Judaism is not Judaism. Third in line and somewhat after Orthodox Judaism was positive Historical Judaism, known in the U.S.A. as Conservative Judaism, which occupied the center between the two others. This Judaism maintained that change could become reform, but only in accord with the principles by which legitimate change may be separated from illegitimate change. Conservative Judaism would discover those principles through historical study. In an age in which historical facts were taken to represent theological truths, the historicism of Conservative Judaism bore compelling weight.

The Jews of the West (extending, to be sure, to California in the farthest west of all), preoccupied with change in their political position, formed only a small minority of the Jews of the world. But their confrontation with political change proved paradigmatic. They invented the Judaisms of the nineteenth century. Each of these Judaic systems exhibited three characteristic traits. First, it asked how one could be both Jewish and something else, that is, also a citizen, a member of a nation. Second, it defined "Judaism" (that is, its system) as a religion, so leaving ample space for that something else, namely, nationality, whether German ("*Deutschtum und Judentum*," German-ness and Jewish-ness), or British, or French, or American. Third, it appealed to history to prove the continuity between its system and the received Judaism of the dual Torah. The resort to historical fact, the claim that the system at hand formed the linear development of the past, the natural increment of the entire "history" of Israel, the Jewish people, from the beginning to the new day—that essentially factual claim masked a profound conviction concerning self-evidence. The urgent question at hand—the political one—produced a self-evidently correct answer out of the history of politics constituted by historical narrative.

That appeal to history, particularly historical fact, characterizes all three Judaisms. The Reformers stated explicitly that theirs would be a Judaism built on fact. The facts of history, in particular, would guide Jews to the definition of what was essential and what could be dropped. History then formed the court of appeal—but also the necessary link, the critical point of continuity. The Historical School took the same position, but reached different conclusions. History would show how change could be effected, and the principles of historical change would then govern. Orthodoxy met the issue in a different way, maintaining that "Judaism" was above history, not a historical fact at all. But the Orthodox position would also appeal most forcefully to the past in its claim that Orthodoxy constituted the natural and complete continuation of "Judaism" in its true form. The importance of history in the theological thought of the nineteenth century Judaisms derives from the intellectual heritage of the age, with its stress on the nation-state as the definitive unit of society and on history as the mode of defining the culture and character of the nation-state. History as an instrument of reform, further, had served the Protestant Reformation, with its appeal to Scripture as against (mere) tradition, its claim that it would restore Christianity to its (historical) purity. Finally and most important, the supernaturalism of the inherited Judaism of the dual Torah, its emphasis upon God's active intervention in history, on miracles, on a perpetual concern for the natural implications of the supernatural will and covenant—that supernaturalism contradicted the rationalism of the age. The one thing the Jewish thinkers wished to accomplish was to show the rationalism, the reason—the normality—of the Judaisms they constructed. Appealing to (mere) facts of history, as against the unbelievable claims of a Scripture placed upon a positive and this-worldly foundation that religious view of the world that, in the received system of the dual Torah, rested upon a completely supernatural view of reality.

The three Judaisms of the age, which we see as continuous in important ways, thus took as their task the demonstration of how they formed out of the received and unwanted old Judaism something new, different, and acceptable. The Judaisms of the nineteenth century were born in the matrix of the received system of the dual Torah, among people who themselves grew up in a world in which *that* Judaism defined what people meant by Judaism. That is why the framers of the Judaisms of continuation could not evade the issue of continuity. They wished both to continue and also to innovate—and to justify innovation. And that desire affected Orthodoxy as much as Reform. In making changes, they appealed to the past for justification. But they pointed to those changes also as proof that they had overcome an unwanted past. The delicate balance between tradition and change attained by each of the Judaisms of continuation marks the genius of its inventors. All worked out the same equation: change but not too much, whatever the proportion a group found excessive.

Just as the questions before all three important Judaisms of the nineteenth century were the same, the answers of the three systems were remarkably congruent to one another. The three Judaisms of continuity exhibit striking traits in common. All looked backward at the received system of the dual Torah. All sought justification in precedent out of a holy and paradigmatic past. All viewed the documents of that system as canonical, differing, of course, on the relative merit of the several components. They concurred that proofs of their new propositions should derive from those canonical writings (or from some of them). All took for granted the enduring, God-given authority of those writings. None doubted that God had revealed the (written) Torah at Sinai. All looked for validating precedent in the received canon. Differing on issues important to both world view and way of life, all three Judaisms concurred on the importance of literacy in the received writings, on the lasting relevance of the symbolic system at hand, on the pertinence of the way of life (in some, if not in every, detail), on the power of the received Judaism of the dual Torah to stand in judgment on whatever, later, would serve to continue that Judaism.

True, the differences among the three Judaisms impressed their framers and with good reason. The Reformers rejected important components of the Judaism of the dual Torah and said so. Written Torah, yes; Oral Torah, no. The Orthodox explicitly denied the validity of changing anything, insisting on the facticity, the givenness, of the whole. The Conservatives, in appealing to historical precedent, shifted the premise of justification entirely. Written Torah, yes; Oral Torah, maybe. They sought what the Orthodox thought pointless and the Reform inconsequential, namely, justification for making some few changes in the present in continuation of the processes they held had effected development in the past. None of these points of important difference proved trivial.

But all of them, all together, should not obscure the powerful points of similarity that mark all three Judaisms as continuators of the Judaism of the dual Torah. The points at which each Judaism took its leave from the received system do not match. In the case of Reform, the break proved explicit: change carried out by articulate, conscious decision, so that change as a matter of policy enjoyed full legitimacy. And as for the positive Historical School and its continuators in Conservative Judaism, the gulf between faith and fact took the measure of the difference between the received system of the dual Torah and the statement of mere historical facts that, for the Historical School, served to document the faith. In saying that "things have changed in the past, and we can change them too," Reform established its primary position. It pointed to precedent and implicitly conceded the power of the received system to stand in judgment. All the more so did the Orthodox and Conservative theologians affirm that same power and place themselves under the judgment of the Judaism of the dual Torah. All three established a firm position within the continuation of that Judaism. Each claimed to take priority as the next step in the linear and incremental history of Judaism.

The twentieth century and its mythic ideologies: Three Judaisms were born in the twentieth century, two in 1897, one in 1967. The first was Jewish Socialism and Yiddishism, the second, Zionism, and the third, three generations later, the American Judaic system of Holocaust and Redemption. Jewish Socialism took shape in the Bund, a Jewish union organized in Poland in 1897. Zionism was founded in the World Zionist Organization, created in Basel 1897. American Judaism in the formulation under discussion came to powerful expression in the aftermath of the 1967 War in the Middle East. All three Judaic systems answered profoundly political questions. Their agenda attended to the status of the Jews as a group (Zionism, American Judaism), the definition of the Jews in the context of larger political and social change (Jewish Socialism, Zionism). It follows that the urgent questions addressed by the twentieth century Judaisms differed in kind from those found acute in the nineteenth century. In the twentieth century powerful forces for social and economic change took political form, in movements meant to shape government to the interests of particular classes or groups, the working classes or racial or ethnic entities, for instance. The Judaic systems of the century responded in kind.

To speak of "Judaic systems" in the context of the three exemplary twentieth-century systems broadens the sense of "Judaism" beyond its conventional limits to Judaic religious systems. For in the twentieth century, the three new and powerful modes of organizing a way of life, a world view, and a theory of who and what is "Israel" (a definition of "being Jewish"), Jewish Socialism wed to Yiddishism, Zionism, and the American Judaism of Holocaust and Redemption, all three mass movements, in no way conform to conventional definitions of religion, let alone of Judaisms. But no account of European Judaism in modern times can omit reference to the secular competition to the religious Judaisms of the day, for these defined the context in which Judaisms in the twentieth century carried on their programs. These are best called "Jewish" meaning, ethnic, but not "Judaic" meaning, religious, systems.

Jewish Socialism presented a Jewish-ethnic system congruent to the political task of economic reform through state action. The Jews would form unions and engage in mass activity of an economic and, ultimately, therefore of a political character. In that same century, the definition of citizenship, encompassing ethnic and genealogical traits, presented the Jews with the problem of how they were to find a place in a nation-state that understood itself in an exclusionary and exclusive, racist way—whether Nazi Germany or nationalist Poland, Hungary, Rumania, or revanchist and irredentist France. Zionism declared the Jews "a people, one people," and proposed as its purpose the creation of the Jewish State. Later on, shifting currents in American politics, a renewed ethnicism and emphasis on intrinsic traits of birth, rather than extrinsic ones of ability, called into question Jews' identification with the democratic system of America as that system defined permissible difference. A Jewish ethnicism, counterpart to the search for roots among diverse ethnic groups, responded with a tale of Jewish "uniqueness"—unique suffering—and unique Jewish ethnic salvation, redemption in the Jewish State—far away, to be sure. So three powerful and attractive movements, Jewish Socialism and Zionism and American Judaism—presented answers to critical issues confronting groups of Jews. All of these movements addressed political questions and responded with essentially political programs. Zionism wanted to create a Jewish state, American Judaism wanted the Jews to form an active political community on their own, and Jewish Socialism in its day framed the Jews into political, as much as economic, organizations, seeing the two as one, a single and inseparable mode of defining economic activity and public policy.

When we turn to Socialism, Zionism, and American Judaism as Jewish-ethnic systems, we need not ask whether they are old or new. All of them are new, without clear precedent and with slight pretense to the contrary. It follows that none of them proposed to legitimate its system by invoking precedents, proof-texts, or points of continuity in doctrine or deed. The two traits common to the twentieth century Judaisms contradict one another. First is the power to persuade by a logic deemed self-evident, and, second, the incapacity to last for very long. The half-life of a Judaism in this century appears to encompass not much more than a generation. True, institutions, long in dying, preserve the detritus of self-evident truth of long-ago, confusing us as to the vitality of what is, in fact, a corpse. Does this mean that the problems that precipitate rethinking the world and the way to live reach solution? Some do, "the Jewish problem" in its political definition, for example (though not solved as anyone in darkest nightmare anticipated); some do not, the issue of Jewish difference in America's open society remaining open, for instance: Jewish Americans still sort out the conflicting claims of segregation and integration.

The cultural issues addressed, and solved,

by Jewish Socialism and Yiddish—the Jews form a distinctive sector of the international working class, and Yiddish marks the point of acceptable difference—passed in a cataclysm of migration and mass murder. Millions of the Yiddish-speaking workers left for America and the West; millions of others were murdered; and within the Communist world, still other millions were swallowed up and lost all but the most attenuated connection to their Jewish origins: a name on an internal passport, yielding a life condemned to degradation for a distinction that, outside of the context of pathological hatred of Jews, makes no material difference. So when we observe that Judaisms prove transient, the reason is not always the same.

A single factor accounts for the impermanence of the Judaic systems of the twentieth century. The ideological Judaisms addressed transient moments and treated as particular and unique what are structural, permanent problems. As a result, none of the Judaisms that began in the twentieth century exhibits stability, all of them presently appearing to serve, for a generation or two, as the explanation in cosmic terms of rather humble circumstances. For not more than three generations Zionism thrived as an ideal for life and a solution to urgent problems. It essentially solved the meager "Jewish problem" left by World War II and, with the creation of the State of Israel, passed on into institutional continuations bereft of all ideological interest. Socialism and Yiddishism turn out to have expressed the ideals of exactly that sector of Jewry to which they spoke, the Yiddish-speaking workers. When the vast Yiddish-speaking populations were murdered, between 1941 and 1945, Yiddishism lost its natural constituency. Jewish Socialism in the U.S.A. thrived for that one generation, the immigrant one, that worked in factories; the Jewish unions then folded into the larger amalgam of unionism and lost their distinctive ethnic character; the Jewish voters, originally socialist or radical, found a comfortable home in New Deal Democracy in America. The Jewish Communists of Poland and the USSR in Stalin's time only with difficulty survived their revolution's success.

Disqualified by perfect faith in what they were doing, most of them lost out to the bureaucrats that made the new order permanent. So, in all, the Judaic systems of the morning of the century, eager in the light of day to exhibit their promise of a renewed Judaic world view and way of life, to bring a rebirth to "all humanity, not just the Jews," turned in the harsh light of afternoon desiccated faces and tottering gait. Not without reason do Israeli teenagers say, "When we get old, we'll talk in Yiddish."

Let us dwell on the odd contradiction between the self-evidence of the ideology and the transience of its appeal and heuristic power. Of American Judaism, we may scarcely speak; it is the birth of a single generation. Its power to mediate between a generation out of touch with its roots and a society willing to affirm ethnic difference— on carefully defined and limited bases to be sure—remains to be tested. Socialism, Yiddishism, and Zionism for their part share in common a transient character. Each came into existence for a generation that found itself in the middle, unable to continue what it had inherited, unable to hand on what it created. The way of life defined by Judaic systems of the twentieth century differed in yet a second way from the way of life of the Judaic systems of the nineteenth century. A devotee of a Judaism of the nineteenth century would do deeds that differed in quality and character from a devotee of another system altogether, e.g., either a Christian or a Socialist one. The way of life differed from any other; the categories were distinctive to the system. The ways of life of the twentieth century movements—whether essentially political, as in Zionism, or fundamentally economic, as in the Jewish labor unions of Jewish Socialism, or in category basically ethnic and cultural, as in American Judaism—all produced a culture of organizations, each such culture fitting comfortably into the category that encompassed all of them.

What the one who joined any of them did was pretty much what he or she would have done in any other organization: the flags had different colors, but the flag poles all were made of the same wood. We shall find difficult the identification of *systemically-distinctive* ways of life that differ among the Judaic systems at hand. All of them call for actions of a single kind: the building of organizations, institutions, bureaucracies, institutions of collective action. The contribution of the individual is to the support of the bureaucracy.

Every way of life requires action of the same order as every other way of life, and each system treats the devotee as a specialist in the doing of some few deeds. None any longer is a generalist, doing everything on his or her own. The labor of the individual in one system therefore hardly differs from the role of the individual in another Ordinarily what is asked for by all systems is the same thing: money, attendance at meetings, repeating of the viewpoint of the system. Yet that description misses the point, because it treats as trivial what to the participants meant life. In attending meetings, in giving money, people gave what, in the circumstances, they had to give. They went to meetings because they believed their presence mattered, to others and to themselves, as much as in attending services in worship of God pious people considered their presence important—holy. Paying dues marked identification with not the organization but the ideal and goal of the organization. So the way of life bore that same weight of profound commitment that the holy way of life had earlier sustained.

Besides evanescence and a certain uniformity of activity definitive of the way of life, all three Judaisms share a third trait as well. They each take up a position on the matter of historicism, appealing to facts of history in the formation and defense of the faith. Zionism, Reform, and, later, Conservative Judaism all constructed their positions on the foundation of that same conception of the facticity of history and its power, furthermore, to dictate, out of facts, the values and truths of not one time but all time.

Comparing the nineteenth and the twentieth century Judaisms: These Jewish ethnic systems radically differ from the Judaic ones that came to formation in the nineteenth century. That is for two reasons. First of all, on the surface the three Judaic systems of the twentieth century took up political, social,

economic, but not theological questions. That is self-evident. Second, while the nineteenth century Judaisms addressed issues particular to Jews, the matters of public policy of the twentieth century Judaic systems concerned everyone, not only Jews. So none of the Judaisms of the twentieth century proves congruent in each detail of structure to the continuator-Judaisms of the nineteenth. All of the new Judaisms intersected with comparable systems—like in character, unlike in content—among other Europeans and Americans. Socialism then is the genus, Jewish Socialism the species, American ethnic assertion the genus, American Judaism the species.

Accordingly, the twentieth century marked the move from a set of Judaisms that form species of a single genus—the Judaism of the dual Torah—to a set of Judaisms that bear less in common among themselves than they do between themselves and systems wholly autonomous of Judaic world-views and ways of life. The reason is clear. The issues addressed by the Judaisms of the twentieth century, the crises that made those issues urgent, did not affect Jews alone or mainly. The crises in common derived from economic dislocation, which generated socialism, and also Jewish Socialism; the reorganization of political entities, which formed the foundation of nationalism, and also Zionism; and the reconsideration of the theory of American society, which produced, alongside the total homogenization of American life, renewed interest in ethnic origins, and also American Judaism. So as is clear, the point of origin of the nineteenth century Judaisms locates perspective from the dual Torah. Jews in the twentieth century had other things on their minds.

The nineteenth century Judaisms made constant reference to the received system of the dual Torah, its writings, its values, its requirements, its viewpoints, its way of life. The twentieth century Judaisms did not. True, each Judaism born in the nineteenth century faced the task of validating change that all of the borning Judaisms in one way or another affirmed. But all of the new Judaisms articulated a principle of change guiding relationships with the received system, which continued to define the agenda of law and theology alike, and to which, in diverse ways to be sure, all the Judaisms recognized themselves as answerable. We cannot point to a similar relationship between the new Judaisms of the twentieth century and the received Judaism of the dual Torah. For none of them made much use of the intellectual resources of that system, found important issues deemed urgent within that system, or even regarded itself as answerable to the Judaism of the dual Torah.

For the twentieth century systems birth came about within another matrix altogether, the larger world of socialism and linguistic nationalism, for Jewish Socialism and Yiddishism, the realm of the nationalisms of the smaller peoples of Europe, rejecting the government of the international empires of Central and Eastern Europe, for Zionism, the reframing, in American culture, of the policy governing social and ethnic difference, for American Judaism. None of these Judaic systems of believing and behaving drew extensively on the received Judaic system of the dual Torah, and all of them for a time vastly overshadowed, in acceptance among the Jewish group, the Judaisms that did. So the passage of time, from the eighteenth to the twentieth century, produced a progressively radical attenuation of the bonds that joined the Jews to the Judaism of the dual Torah.

The Judaisms of the nineteenth century, first, retained certain close and nurturing ties to the Judaism of the dual Torah. All three of these nascent Judaisms confronted its issues, drew heavily on its symbolic system, cited its texts as proof-texts, eagerly referred to its sources in justification for the new formations. All of them looked backward and assumed responsibility toward that long past of the Judaism of the dual Torah, acknowledging its authority, accepting its program of thought, acceding to its way of life—if only by way of explicit rejection. But the Judaisms of the twentieth century in common treated with entire disinterest the same received Judaism of the dual Torah. They looked forward, and they drew heavily upon contemporary systems of belief and behavior. So they turned to the received system of the dual Torah only adventitiously, merely opportunistically, and—if truth be told—cynically. For that received Judaism provided not reasons but excuses. Appealing to its proof texts provided not simply authority for what people wanted to do anyhow, but mere entry to the mind and imagination of Jews themselves not far separated from the world that took for granted the truth of Scripture and the wisdom of the Oral Torah. So the shift from the Judaisms that responded to the received system and those that essentially ignored it except (at most) after the fact marked the true beginning of the modern age, that is, the point at which the old system held to be a set of self-evident truths gave way to a new set of systems, all of them equally self-evident to their adherents. What intervened was a span of self-consciousness, in which people saw choices and made decisions about what had formerly appeared obvious and beyond argument. At what cost did the shift come from a reading of the received texts to an ignoring of them? And what price did people pay when what served as a source of proof-texts for nineteenth century turned into a treasury of pretexts for twentieth century ideologists?

The Judaisms of the nineteenth century attained a high measure of self-consciousness because they had before their eyes the image of the innocent faith of their predecessors—and many in their own time as well. The Judaisms of the twentieth century, abandoning all pretense at a connection to the received Judaism, lost also the awareness that change took place, that people made choices, and, in all, that a dimension of decision-making took the measure of their Judaisms. So they entered a new phase of self-evidence, appealing now for vindication not to received texts but the obvious facts of the everyday world. History now proved propositions for the new Judaisms, and the text of those Judaisms was the world out there. Proof texts derived from headlines in newspapers. The continuators of the Judaism of the dual Torah developed systems of belief and behavior that invariably fell into the category of religions, in our setting, Judaisms. Whether or not the twentieth century successor-systems constitute religions, Judaisms, presents a

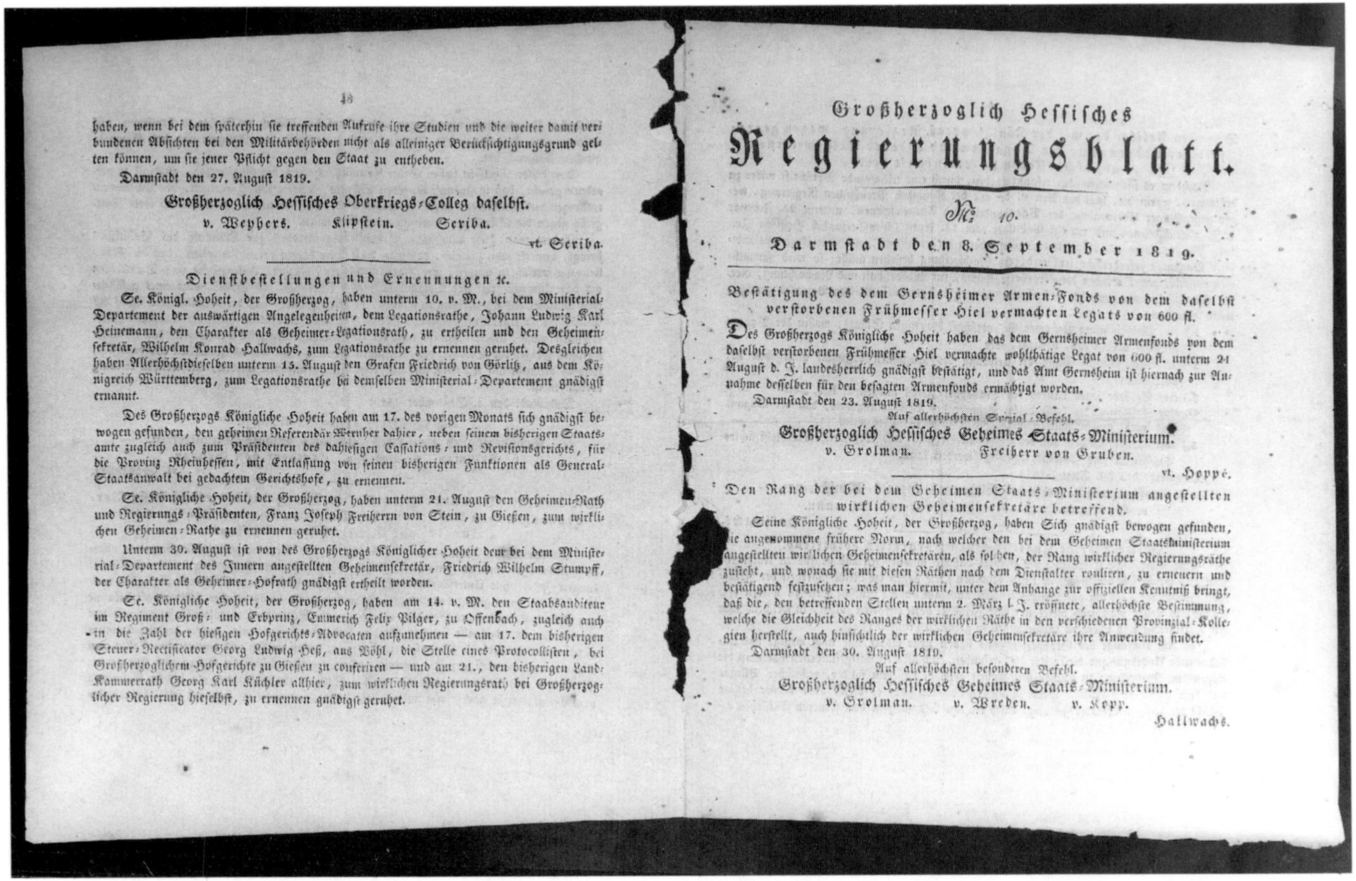

48

haben, wenn bei dem späterhin sie treffenden Aufrufe ihre Studien und die weiter damit verbundenen Absichten bei den Militärbehörden nicht als alleiniger Berücksichtigungsgrund gelten können, um sie jener Pflicht gegen den Staat zu entheben.

Darmstadt den 27. August 1819.

Großherzoglich Hessisches Oberkriegs-Colleg daselbst.

v. Weyhers. Klipstein. Scriba.

vt. Scriba.

Dienstbestellungen und Ernennungen ꝛc.

Se. Königl. Hoheit, der Großherzog, haben unterm 10. v. M., bei dem Ministerial-Departement der auswärtigen Angelegenheiten, dem Legationsrathe, Johann Ludwig Karl Heinemann, den Charakter als Geheimer-Legationsrath, zu ertheilen und den Geheimensekretär, Wilhelm Konrad Hallwachs, zum Legationsrathe zu ernennen geruhet. Desgleichen haben Allerhöchstdieselben unterm 15. August den Grafen Friedrich von Görlitz, aus dem Königreich Württemberg, zum Legationsrathe bei demselben Ministerial-Departement gnädigst ernannt.

Des Großherzogs Königliche Hoheit haben am 17. des vorigen Monats sich gnädigst bewogen gefunden, den geheimen Referendär Wernher dahier, neben seinem bisherigen Staatsamte zugleich auch zum Präsidenten des dahiesigen Cassations- und Revisionsgerichts, für die Provinz Rheinhessen, mit Entlassung von seinen bisherigen Funktionen als General-Staatsanwalt bei gedachtem Gerichtshofe, zu ernennen.

Se. Königliche Hoheit, der Großherzog, haben unterm 21. August den Geheimen-Rath und Regierungs-Präsidenten, Franz Joseph Freiherrn von Stein, zu Gießen, zum wirklichen Geheimen-Rathe zu ernennen geruhet.

Unterm 30. August ist von des Großherzogs Königlicher Hoheit dem bei dem Ministerial-Departement des Innern angestellten Geheimensekretär, Friedrich Wilhelm Stumpff, der Charakter als Geheimer-Hofrath gnädigst ertheilt worden.

Se. Königliche Hoheit, der Großherzog, haben am 14. v. M. den Staabsauditeur im Regiment Groß- und Erbprinz, Emmerich Felix Pilger, zu Offenbach, zugleich auch in die Zahl der hiesigen Hofgerichts-Advocaten aufzunehmen — am 17. dem bisherigen Steuer-Rectificator Georg Ludwig Heß, aus Wöhl, die Stelle eines Protocollisten, bei Großherzoglichem Hofgerichte zu Gießen zu conferiren — und am 21., den bisherigen Land-Kammerrath Georg Karl Küchler allhier, zum wirklichen Regierungsrath bei Großherzoglicher Regierung hieselbst, zu ernennen gnädigst geruhet.

Großherzoglich Hessisches

Regierungsblatt.

№ 10.

Darmstadt den 8. September 1819.

Bestätigung des dem Gernsheimer Armen-Fonds von dem daselbst verstorbenen Frühmesser Hiel vermachten Legats von 600 fl.

Des Großherzogs Königliche Hoheit haben das dem Gernsheimer Armenfonds von dem daselbst verstorbenen Frühmesser Hiel vermachte wohlthätige Legat von 600 fl. unterm 21 August d. J. landesherrlich gnädigst bestätigt, und das Amt Gernsheim ist hiernach zur Annahme desselben für den besagten Armenfonds ermächtigt worden.

Darmstadt den 23. August 1819.

Auf allerhöchsten Spezial-Befehl.

Großherzoglich Hessisches Geheimes Staats-Ministerium.

v. Grolman. Freiherr von Gruben.

vt. Hoppé.

Den Rang der bei dem Geheimen Staats-Ministerium angestellten wirklichen Geheimensekretäre betreffend.

Seine Königliche Hoheit, der Großherzog, haben Sich gnädigst bewogen gefunden, die angenommene frühere Norm, nach welcher den bei dem Geheimen Staatsministerium angestellten wirklichen Geheimensekretären, als solchen, der Rang wirklicher Regierungsräthe zusteht, und wonach sie mit diesen Räthen nach dem Dienstalter rouliren, zu erneuern und bestätigend festzusetzen; was man hiermit, unter dem Anhange zur offiziellen Kenntniß bringt, daß die, den betreffenden Stellen unterm 2. März l. J. eröffnete, allerhöchste Bestimmung, welche die Gleichheit des Ranges der wirklichen Räthe in den verschiedenen Provinzial-Kollegien herstellt, auch hinsichtlich der wirklichen Geheimensekretäre ihre Anwendung findet.

Darmstadt den 30. August 1819.

Auf allerhöchsten besonderen Befehl.

Großherzoglich Hessisches Geheimes Staats-Ministerium.

v. Grolman. v. Wreden. v. Kopp.

Hallwachs.

Figure 71. Proclamation by the Grand Duke of Hesse requiring more humane treatment of the Jews, Darmstadt, Germany, September 8, 1819.

Figure 72. Great Talmud Torah of Salonika, Greece, before the fire of 1917.

Figure 73. Religious leaders dine together to celebrate the donation of a Torah by Bela Weiss (right) to the Kazinczy synagogue, Budapest, Hungary, 1935.

Figure 74. View of Borneplatz synagogue decorated for the festival of Shavuot, Frankfurt, Germany, c. 1937-1938.

Figure 75. View of synagogue inside the Gergenstrasse Hospital, Frankfurt, Germany, c. 1938.

Figure 76. Interior of a synagogue in Vilna, Lithuanian Soviet Socialist Republic, 1985.
Photograph by Barbara Pfeffer.

Figure 77. Rabbi Leo Baeck with Mr. and Mrs. Martin Buber, undated.

question bearing only slight consequence. Clearly, Jewish Socialism and Zionism provided the deep meaning for the lives of millions of Jews, so, defining ways of life and world views and the nature of the people of Israel subject to both, they functioned entirely as did the religions, the Judaisms, of the nineteenth century and of the twentieth as well. But Socialism-Yiddishism and Zionism differ from the continuator-Judaisms, because neither invoked a supernatural God, revelation of God's will in the Torah, belief in Providence, or any other indicator of the presence of the family of closely-related religions, the Judaisms; and, moreover, their framers and founders did not claim otherwise. Had the framers alleged that theirs was a continuator-Judaism, we should have to introduce that fact into our analysis and interpretation, but none did. The Socialists took a position actively hostile to religion in all forms, and the Zionists compromised with the religious Judaisms of the day but in no way conceded that theirs was a competing Judaism. As to American Judaism, that forms a separate set of problems; but it suffices to observe that, in its contemporary form, in its appeal the salvific myth of Holocaust and Redemption, it crosses the border between a genuinely religious and an entirely secular system addressed to Jews, falling on both sides of the not-unmarked boundary between the one and the other.

Judaisms and facts, nineteenth and twentieth centuries: We may further place into perspective the Judaisms subject to analysis here by asking how each identified facts. Two sources of facts served, the past, for Zionism, and everyday, acutely contemporary experience, for Jewish Socialism and Yiddishism, as well as American Judaism. Zionism found for itself links to a remote past, leaping over distasteful (and contradictory) facts near at hand. History would supply the two things the Judaism required, first, acceptable models for a Jewish politics, second, a powerful link to the chosen land. The selective reconstruction of history, parallel to the selective piety of Orthodoxy, produced a well-composed ideology indeed, one based on the obvious, the factual, the self-evident.

But how different a claim on self-evidence and immediate credence did the other approaches present for themselves? For in place of the facts of history, they appealed to the facts of everyday life, of the streets and factories (for Jewish Socialism and Yiddishism), of the exclusion, actual and perceived, from the imagined society of undifferentiated America, joined with the (contradictory) quest for a distinct, if not wholly distinctive, place (for American Judaism). So the mode of thought—appeal to felt facts of life—proved uniform for the three ideologies.

And the basis for the power of these facts to make a difference is clear. The several Judaisms in common share enormously emotional appeals to the (self-evidently probative) experiences of history, meaning, what is happening today. Each framed a grievance for itself, a doctrine of resentment. For Zionism, statelessness; for Jewish Socialism and Yiddishism, economic deprivation; for American Judaism, a sense of alienation expressed that grievance, bringing to words the underlying feeling of resentment. The ideologies of the twentieth century Judaisms came after the fact of experience and emotion and explained the fact, rather than transforming feeling into sensibility and sentiment into an intellectual explanation of the world. The systems in common appeal to a self-evidence deriving from a visceral response to intolerable experience, near at hand. Unemployment and starvation made entirely credible the world-view and explanation of Jewish Socialism, made compelling the program of activity, the way of life, demanded thereby. Zionism formed into a single whole the experiences of remarkably diverse people living in widely separated places, showing that all those experiences formed a single fact, the experience of a single sort—exclusion, victimization, anti-Semitism—which Zionism could confront. American Judaism linked to an inchoate past the aspirations of a third and fourth generation of Jews who wanted desperately to be Jewish but in their own expe-rience and intellectual resources could find slight access to something to be called "Jewish."

Emotion—the emotion of resentment in

particular—for all formed the road within: strong feeling about suffering and redemption, for American Judaism; powerful appeal to concrete deed in the here and now by people who thought themselves helpless, for Zionism; outlet for the rage of the dispossessed, for the suffering workers of Czarist Russia and turn of the century America alike. So the power and appeal of the three ideological systems, all of them enjoying self-evidence for those for whom they answered basic questions, proved not only uniform, but also apt. For the problems taken up for solution—political, cultural, social, economic—raised for deep reflection the everyday and the factitious. What, after all, preoccupied the Jews in the twentieth century? Politics, economics, the crumbling of connection to a thousand-year-old culture, the Yiddish one, and a fifteen-hundred year old way of life and world view, the Judaism of the dual Torah. These were, as a matter of fact, things the most sanguine person could not ignore, experiences of the hour, education in the streets.

The end of Judaic "Systemopoeia" (system-formation): The twentieth century in fact has produced no new Judaic systems, only ethnic-Jewish ones, and, of those, the only mass movement still extant is the Judaism of Holocaust and Redemption. Except for that construction, all of the systems we have surveyed derive from the nineteenth century. From after the beginning of Reform Judaism at the start of the nineteenth century to the later twentieth century we identify three periods of enormous system-building, or, to invent a word, *systemopoeia*. At each of these, the manufacture of Judaic systems came into sharp focus: 1850-1860 for the systems of Orthodoxy and the positive Historical School, 1890-1900 for Jewish Socialism and Zionism, and 1967-1973 for the systems of American Judaism and American and Israeli reversionism encompassed within the Judaism of Holocaust and Redemption.

For a different calculation, beginning at the start of the nineteenth century in fact places all of the Judaic systems but one in the hundred years from 1800 to 1900: Reform, then, some decades later, in the middle of the century, Orthodoxy and the Historical School,

then, again some decades later, at the end of the century, Zionism and Jewish Socialism. It follows that nearly all of the Judaic systems of the nineteenth and twentieth centuries took shape within a span of not much more than a hundred years, from somewhat before 1800 to somewhat after 1900. During that period, all but one of the Judaisms we have surveyed had reached articulated statement, each with a clear picture of its required deeds and doctrines and definition of the Israel it wished to address. So, in all, the century at hand encompassed, in sequence, Reform, Orthodoxy, Conservative Judaism, Jewish Socialism and Yiddishism, as well as Zionism. We therefore wonder how it is possible that one period produced a range, only some of which we have surveyed, of Judaic systems of depth and enormous breadth that attracted mass support and persuaded many of the meaning of their lives, while the next three quarters of a century did not. What requires explanation is the end, not the beginning and fruition, of Judaic systemopoeia.

We may eliminate answers deriving from the mere accidents of political change; given the important shifts in the political circumstances of Israel, the Jewish people, we should have anticipated exercises in symbolic redefinition to accommodate the social change at hand. That is to say, the stimulus for system-building surely should have come from the creation of the Jewish state, an enormous event. The rise of the State of Israel fulfilled a system, the Zionist one, but replaced it with nothing pertinent to Jewry at large. But American Jewry presents the same picture. Wars and dislocations, migration and relocation—these in the past stimulated those large-scale reconsiderations that generated and sustained system-building in Jews' societies. The political changes affecting Jews in America, who became Jewish Americans in ways in which Jews did not become Jewish Germans or Jewish Frenchmen or Englishmen or women, yielded no encompassing system. The Judaic system of Holocaust and Redemption leaves unaffected the larger dimensions of human existence of Jewish Americans—and that is part of its power. When we consider the strength in the Judaisms of America, of Reform, Orthodoxy, and Historical or Conservative Judaism, we see the reality. The Judaic systems of the nineteenth century have endured in America, none of them facing significant competition of scale. That means millions of people moved from one world to another, changed in language, occupation, and virtually every other significant social and cultural indicator—and produced nothing more than a set of recapitulations of systems serviceable under utterly different circumstances. The failure of Israeli Jewry to generate system-building finds its match in the still more startling unproductivity of American Jewry. Nothing much has happened in either of the two massive communities of Israel in the twentieth century.

Political change should have precipitated fresh thought and experiment, and Judaic systems should have come forth. So change of an unprecedented order yielded a rehearsal of ideas familiar only from other contexts. Israeli nationalism as a Jewish version of third-world nationalism, American Judaism as a Jewish version of a national cultural malaise on account of a lost war—these set forth a set of stale notions altogether. Let me now recapitulate the question, before proceeding to my answer: why in the seventy-five years or so beyond World War I has Judaic system building (with the possible exception of the system of Judaic reversion) come to an end?

Three pertinent factors explain why no Judaic systems equivalent to Reform, Orthodoxy, Zionism, and the rest have come forth since the end of the nineteenth century: the Holocaust, the demise of intellect, and the triumph of large-scale organization.

The Holocaust: First of all comes the demographic factor. It is in two parts. First, the most productive sector of world Jewry perished. Second, the conditions that put forth the great systemic creations vanished with the six million who died. Stated as naked truth, not only too many (one is too many!), but the wrong Jews died. Judaic systems in all their variety emerged in Europe, not in America or in what was then Palestine and is now the State of Israel, and, within Europe, they came from Central and Eastern European Jewry. We may account

for the systemopoeia of Central and Eastern European Jews in two ways. First, the Jews in the East, in particular, formed a vast population with enormous learning and diverse interests. Second, the systems of the nineteenth and twentieth centuries arose out of a vast population lived in self-aware circumstances, not scattered and individual but composed and bonded. The Jews who perished formed enormous and self-conscious communities of vast intellectual riches.

To them, being Jewish constituted a collective enterprise, not an individual predilection. In the West, the prevailing attitude of mind identifies religion with belief, to the near-exclusion of behavior, and religion tends to identify itself with faith, so religion is understood as a personal state of mind or an individual's personal and private attitude. So the Judaic systems that took shape beyond 1900 exhibit that same Western bias not for society but self, not culture and community but conscience and character. Under such circumstances systemopoeia hardly flourishes, for systems speak of communities and create worlds of meaning, answer pressing public questions and produce broadly self-evident answers. The contrast makes the point, between the circumstance of reversionary systems of Judaisms, involving, as it does, individuals' "coming home" one by one, with the context of the ideological Judaic systems, all of them, in fact, mass movements and Jewish idiomatic statements of still larger mass movements. The demographic fact then speaks for itself. The reversionary systems of "return to tradition" demand a demographic base of one person, but Zionist and Socialist systems, millions. Yet everyone who has traced the history of Judaic systems in modern and contemporary times has found in the mass populations of Central and Eastern Europe the point of origin of nearly all systems. That fact then highlights our original observation, that the period of the preparation for, then the mass murder of, European Jewry, from the later 1930s to the mid-1940s, marked the end of Judaic systemopoeia. We cannot, then, underestimate the impact of the destruction of European Jewry. One of the as-yet untallied costs of the murder of six million Jews in Europe therefore encompasses the matter of system-building. The destruction of European Jewry in Eastern and Central Europe brought to an end for a very long time the great age of Judaic system-construction and explains the paralysis of imagination and will that has left the Jews to forage in the detritus of an earlier age: rehearsing other peoples' answers to other peoples' questions.

The demise of intellect: The second explanation for the end of systemopoeia is the as-yet unappreciated factor of sheer ignorance, the profound pathos of Jews' illiteracy in all books but the book of the streets and marketplaces of the day. That second factor, the utter loss of access to that permanent treasury of the human experience of Jewry preserved and handed on in the canonical Torah, has already impressed us: the extant raw materials of system-building now prove barren and leached. The Judaisms that survive provide ready access to emotional or political encounters, readily available to all—by definition. But they offer none to that confrontation of taste and judgment, intellect and reflection, that takes place in traditional cultures and with tradition: worlds in which words matter. People presently resort mainly to the immediately accessible experiences of emotions and of politics. We recall that the systems of the nineteenth and twentieth centuries made constant reference to the Judaism of the dual Torah, at first intimate, later on merely by way of allusion and rejection. The nineteenth century systems drew depth and breadth of vision from the received Judaism of the dual Torah, out of which they produced—by their own word—variations and continuations. So the received system and its continuators realized not only the world of perceived experience at hand. They also made accessible the alien but interesting human potentialities of other ages, other encounters altogether with the potentialities of life in society. The repertoire of human experience in the Judaism of the dual Torah presents as human options the opposite of the banal, the one-dimensional, the immediate. Jews received and used the heritage of human experience captured, as in amber, in the words of the dual Torah. So they did not have to make things up fresh every morning or rely only on that small sector of the range of human experience immediately accessible and near at hand. By contrast Israeli nationalism and American Judaism—the two most influential systems that move Jews to action in the world today—scarcely concern themselves with that Judaism. They find themselves left only with what is near at hand. They work with the raw materials made available by contemporary experience—emotions on the one side, politics on the other. Access to realms beyond requires learning in literature, the only resource for human experience beyond the immediate. But the Judaic systems of the twentieth century, except for the reversionary Judaisms, do not resort to the reading of books as a principal act of their way of life in the way in which the Judaism of the dual Torah and its continuators did and do. The consequence is a strikingly abbreviated agenda of issues, a remarkably one-dimensional program of urgent questions.

The triumph of large-scale organization: Third and distinct from the other two is the bureaucratization of Jewry in consequence of the tasks it rightly has identified as urgent. To meet the problems Jews find urgent, they have had to adopt a way of life of building and maintaining and working through very large organizations and institutions. The contemporary class structure of Jewry therefore places in positions of influence Jews who place slight value on matters of intellect and learning and that same system accords no sustained hearing to Jews who strive to reflect. The tasks are other, and they call forth other gifts than those of heart and mind. The exemplary experiences of those who exercise influence derives from politics, through law, from economic activity, through business, from institutional careers, through government, industry and the like. As the gifts of establishing routine take precedence over the endowments of charisma of an intellectual order, the experiences people know and understand—politics, emotions of ready access—serve, also, for the raw materials of Judaic system-building. Experiences that, in a Judaic context, people scarcely know, do not. This is yet another consequence of the ineluctable tasks of the twentieth century: to build large-scale organizations to solve large-scale problems. Organizations, in the nature of things, require specialization. The difference between the classes that produce systemic change today and those who created systems in the nineteenth and earlier twentieth centuries then proves striking. What brought it about, if not the great war conducted against the Jews, beginning not in 1933 but with the organization of political anti-Semitism joined to economic exclusion, from the 1880s onward. So in a profound sense, the type of structure now characteristic of Jewry represents another of the uncounted costs of the Holocaust.

Intellectuals create systems. Administrators do not, so when they need ideas, they call for propaganda and hire publicists and journalists. When we remember that all of the Judaic systems of the nineteenth and early twentieth centuries derive from intellectuals, we realize what has changed. Herzl was a journalist, for instance, and those who organized Jewish Socialism and brought Yiddishism all wrote books. The founders of the system of Reform Judaism were mainly scholars, rabbis, writers, dreamers, and other intellectuals. It is not because they were lawyers that the framers of the positive Historical School produced the historicistic system that they made. The emphases of Hirsch and other creators of Orthodoxy lay on doctrine, and all of them wrote important books and articles of a reflective and even philosophical character. So much for Reform, Orthodox, Conservative, Socialist-Yiddishist, and Zionist systems: the work of intellectuals, one and all.

These three factors, demographic, cultural, institutional, and bureaucratic, scarcely exhaust the potential explanation for the long span of time in which, it would appear, Jews have brought forth few Judaic systems, relying instead on those formed in a prior and different age and circumstance. They point directly or indirectly to the extraordinary price yet to be exacted from Jewry on account of the murder of six million Jews in Europe. The demographic loss requires no comment, and the passage of time from the

age in which the Judaism of the dual Torah predominated has already impressed us. Those causes are direct and immediate. But one has also to justify the correlation between mass murder and an exemplary leadership of lawyers and businessmen and politicians and generals. The answer is simple. Because of the crisis presented by the German nation's war against the Jews, the Jews had to do what they could to constitute themselves into a political entity, capable of mass action. So the leadership of the sort that came to the fore in the twentieth century responded to the requirement of that century, and thus the correlation between Holocaust and bureaucracy: that was what was needed. Administrators, not intellectuals, bureaucrats, not charismatic thinkers formed the cadre of the hour. In an age in which, to survive at all, Jews had to address the issues of politics and economics, build a state (in the State of Israel) and a massive and effective set of organizations capable of collective political action (in the U.S.A.), not sages but *politicians* in the deepest sense of the word, namely, those able to do the work of the polity, alone could do what had to be done. And they did come forward. They did their task, as well as one might have hoped. The time therefore demanded gifts other than those prized by intellectuals. And the correlation between mass murder and a culture of organizations proves exact: the war against the Jews called forth, from the Jews, people capable of building institutions to protect the collectivity of Israel, so far as anyone could be saved. Consequently much was saved. But much was lost.

Celebrating the victory of survival ought not obscure the cost. The end of the remarkable age of Judaic systemopoeia may prove a more serious charge against the future, a more calamitous cost of the destruction of European Jewry, than anyone has yet realized. More suffocated than Jews in gas chambers, but spirit too. The banality of survival forms a counterpoint to the banality of evil represented by the factories built to manufacture dead Jews in an age of the common and routine. So if people draw upon only their experience of emotions, inside, and politics without, then assign themselves the central position in the paradigm of humanity, seeing what they are as all they can become, we need not find that surprising. Who does otherwise, except for those with eyes upon a long past, a distant future: a vision? The system-builders, the intellectuals, book-readers, book-writers, truth-tellers—these are the ones who appeal to experience of the ages as precedent for the hour. That characterized all the Judaic systems born in the death-throes (as people thought at that time) of the received one: whether Reform theologians invoked the precedent of change or Orthodox ones of Sinai. Today Judaisms yield few system-builders, so we can scarcely ask for the rich perspectives, the striking initiatives, that yield compelling systems of life and thought, such as those characteristic of modern times in Europe.

Notes

[1] Benzion Dinur, "Emancipation," in *Encyclopaedia Judaica*, vol. 6, cols. 696-718. Quotation: col. 696.

JACOB NEUSNER

JUDAISM, HISTORY OF. PART. V.B. MODERN TIMES. THE MUSLIM WORLD: The expulsion of the Jews from Christian Spain in 1492 in a very real sense marked the beginning of modern times for the Jews of the Muslim world. Many of the exiles sought refuge in the Islamic kingdoms of the Maghreb, in Mamluk Egypt and the Levant, and in the expanding Ottoman Empire, which within a generation would take over all of the Middle East and North Africa between the borders of Persia and Morocco. These Sephardic refugees infused new vitality—demographically, culturally, and spiritually—into Islamicate Jewry, which had been in a state of overall decline since the middle of the thirteenth century. The ranks of the Sephardic Jews—Sephardim—in the Islamic lands continued to swell over the next seventy-five years as Conversos fleeing the terror of the Inquisition and seeking to return openly to Judaism also made their way into the Balkans, the Near East, and North Africa.

The tremendous influx of Iberian Jews into the Muslim world resulted in a structural dichotomy in the Jewish communities in all of the major coastal towns and cities, as well as many inland trading centers, where the newcomers settled. Henceforth, the Jewish community was divided into *megorashim* (exiles) and *toshavim* (indigenous Jews), each with separate synagogues and institutions, such as schools, law courts, and cemeteries. In some places (e.g., in Salonika), the *megorashim* were further divided into Castilians, Aragonese, and Portuguese, and even subdivided into congregations by city or region of origin. Thus, there were in communities with large concentrations of Sephardim separate congregations for Toledo, Cordoba, Lisbon, Majorca, Aragon, and Andalucía. These individual Sephardic congregations sometimes united in an umbrella communal organization (Heb., *qehillah*).

In Syria, where large numbers of Sicilian Jews settled after they were expelled from their homeland in 1497, they formed a distinct congregation alongside the Sephardic *megorashim* and the *toshavim*, who were called *mustacribin* (i.e., Arabized Jews). In Tunisia, the *toshavim/megorashim* dichotomy was represented by the *twansa/grana* (Tunisians/Livornese) split, because eventually most of the Sephardic newcomers came via the Italian port of Livorno, where they had become Italianized in speech and dress and continued to speak Italian, rather than Judeo-Spanish, after coming to Tunisia. In some regions, the *megorashim* so overwhelmed the *toshavim* numerically and culturally that the latter shrank to near extinction, as in the case of the Greek-speaking Romaniot Jews of Anatolia and the Balkans. The Romaniots, or *griegos* as the Sephardim called them, survived only in small numbers, mainly in the Greek interior. In other places, such as the North African interior and Syria, the numbers of Sephardic settlers were not sufficient to maintain a Spanish-speaking community, and the descendants of these *megorashim*, while maintaining a distinct identity, eventually went over to speaking the local Judeo-Arabic vernacular into which they introduced a greater or lesser number of Ladino terms.[1]

Although the influx of exiles from Iberia

during the late fifteenth and throughout the sixteenth century infused new blood into the Jewish communities of the Islamic world and provided a new scholarly Rabbinic elite that remained predominant through much of North Africa and the Middle East until the dissolution of these communities in the mid-twentieth century, there were tensions—more serious at first, but diminishing over time—between the older indigenous Jews and the newcomers. Some of these tensions were social and cultural, since the Sephardim frequently looked down upon the indigenous Jews. In Morocco, the *megorashim* disparagingly referred to the locals as *berberiscos* (Berbers/barbarians) and *forasteros* (outsiders). In the Levant, they referred to the local Arabic-speaking Jews as *moriscos* (Moors). There were also religious tensions resulting from differences of custom and Halakhic interpretation. In 1526, for example, a dispute erupted in Fez over the greater leniency of some Sephardim in the matter of inspecting the lungs of slaughtered animals to determine their kashrut. The controversy, which is described in detail by Hayyim Gagin, a leader of the Fasi *toshavim* at the time, split the community into two camps, both of which resorted to violence in the streets of the Jewish quarter and to lobbying with the Muslim rulers to intervene. The controversy over kashrut standards in Fez spilled over into other parts of the Maghreb, including Tlemcen and Oran in Algeria.[2] In Damascus, also during the sixteenth century, a number of religious controversies erupted between the *megorashim* and the *musta'ribin*, one of which involved the proper depth of a ritual pool (*mikveh*) in the Jewish bath house.[3]

In most Jewish communities of the Islamic world, the religious tensions between the *megorashim* and the *toshavim* eventually abated or disappeared altogether. Still, the social distance between members of the Sephardic elite and the indigenous Jewish population remained very real until well into the nineteenth, and, in some places, even into the twentieth century. But only in Tunisia did the division between the two groups actually worsen in later times. There, beginning in 1710, a schism developed between the in-digenous *twansa* and the Sephardic *grana* over the perennial issue of ritual slaughtering, resulting in a full-fledged break in relations between the two groups in 1741. Mutual ostracism between the branches of Tunisian Jewry continued into the first decades of the twentieth century.[4]

The Sephardic religious impact: Despite the social distance and the occasional controversies between the *megorashim* and the *toshavim*, the impact of the Sephardic newcomers upon the religious life of Middle Eastern and North African Jewry was tremendous. Sephardic rabbis comprised the majority of the religious elite in almost every country of the Muslim world with a Jewish population (excluding Yemen, Iraq, and Iran, where negligible or non-existent numbers of Sephardim settled). The Sephardic scholars who came to the Islamic world continued in their traditional role as legal authorities and decisors. The great law codes of Joseph Karo (1488-1575)—the *Beit Yosef* and the *Shulhan Aruk*—were both produced in this early Islamicate Sephardic milieu. Other great legal authorities of this foundational era included David b. Abi Zimra (1479-1573), known by the acronym Radbaz, in Cairo, Joseph b. Lev (1505-1580), known as the Rival, in Constantinople, Moses Trani (1500-1580), known as Mabit, who lived in Turkey and Syria, but eventually headed the Jewish in Safed, and Samuel de Medina (1506-1589), known as Maharashdam, in Salonika.[5] Sephardic Rabbinic families, such as the Ibn Danans, Serreros, and Tzarfatis in Morocco, the Boccaras in Tunisia, and the Abulafias, Hazzans, and Pallaches in the Levant, established dynasties of scholars that continued down to the nineteenth and twentieth centuries. Within two hundred years after the Spanish Expulsion, one could with justification refer as a whole to the Jews of the Middle East and North Africa (now commonly called in contemporary Hebrew *ha-separadim ve-edot ha-mizrah*—"the Sephardim and the communities of the Orient") as an organic—although by no means monolithic—entity sharing similar liturgical, legal, and customary traditions.

In addition to their Halakhic scholarship,

the Sephardic newcomers brought to the indigenous Jewish communities of the Islamic world strong messianic and mystical currents that had a lasting imprint upon Eastern Jewry. Iberia had been the center of the Kabbalah. The persecutions of the fifteenth century and the Expulsion, coupled with other momentous events of the time, such as the fall of Byzantium, the Ottoman conquest of the Middle East and much of North Africa, the discovery of the New World, and the Reformation, all heightened messianic and mystic enthusiasm. Rabbis like Abraham b. Eliezer ha-Levi (d. after 1528) and Jacob Berab (ca. 1474-1546) disseminated teachings that the messianic age was approaching. But it was the new kabbalistic system of Isaac Luria (1534-1572) that spread everywhere throughout the Islamic world through the popularity of the Lurianic prayerbook—known as *siddur ha-Ari*—that was popularized by Luria's disciple Hayyim Vital (1542-1620) in his *Shaar ha-Kavvanot* and by Shalom Sharabi (1720-1777) in his *Nehar Shalom*. Mystical prayerbooks of the Lurianic type became standard from Iran to Morocco. These prayerbooks were laced with *kavvanot*, mystical declarations of intent meant at heightening the worshipper's devotional concentration, and with *yihudim*, supererogatory prayers for the unification of God, the male monarch figure, with his female aspect, the Shekhina, which in kabbalistic mythology was personified as a divine consort.

The rapid spread of the Lurianic prayerbook, of kabbalistic mysticism, and of an entire Sephardic legal and religious tradition was due in no small measure to the introduction of printing presses into the Islamic world by the *megorashim*. Hebrew presses were established already in 1493 in Constantinople, 1513 in Salonika, and 1516 in Fez. More presses were established in Cairo and Safed in 1557 and in Damascus in 1605. These presses, the first of any kind in the Muslim world (there was no Turkish printing until the end of the eighteenth century and no Arabic printing until the nineteenth), spurred the widespread and relatively inexpensive dissemination of texts, making the Sephardic intellectual and spiritual impact all

the more powerful. Printed Hebrew books reached Jewish communities in isolated areas of the Islamic world, such as Yemen, where they were then copied by hand.[6]

During the sixteenth century, Safed in the Galilee became a great center for mystical and messianic activity, and, pushed by messianic expectation, the Jewish population in the Holy Land swelled by mid-century to approximately 10,000 souls. Messianic enthusiasm was not limited to mystic and pietist circles. Sephardic courtiers in Constantinople also tried to hasten the apocalypse with bold projects for the land of Israel. Doña Gracia Mendes and her nephew Don Joseph Nasi, for example, undertook the rebuilding as a Jewish city of Tiberias, which had fallen into ruin. They were no doubt spurred in part by the ancient tradition that the messiah would make his first appearance there.[7]

The intense ardor of Oriental Jewish messianism was finally dampened, but by no means extinguished, by the mass hysteria and subsequent disappoint created by the appearance of the false messiah Shabbetai Zevi in Gaza in 1665 and his subsequent apostasy in Edirne in 1666. Kabbalistic mysticism, on the other hand, remained a defining element in Oriental Jewish religious life. From the time of the Sephardic influx until the dissolution of Islamicate Jewry in the mid-twentieth century, societies dedicated to the study of mystical texts such as the Zohar became a common feature of Jewish life in the Islamic diaspora.

The popularity of such mystical societies was perhaps fostered in some measure as a Jewish parallel to the ubiquitous Sufi brotherhoods in the surrounding Muslim culture. Although in a few places—most notably, Persia—some Jews were attracted to peripheral association with the Sufi brotherhoods, for the most part, the mainstream Jewish *habarot* in the Islamic world continued to emphasize study and contemplation in the kabbalistic tradition, as it evolved in Iberia, generally eschewing the ecstatic practices (e.g., wild dancing in groups and induced trances) of the Muslim mystics. In the domain of popular religion, on the other hand, there was much more considerable commensality with the surrounding Islamic religiosity.

Popular religiosity, saint veneration, and pilgrimage: Although Jewish pilgrimages to holy sites were a common feature of popular piety in the Middle Ages, these had been primarily to places associated with antiquity, particularly, the biblical period, but also, albeit to a lesser extent, the talmudic age. During the sixteenth century, however, many more graves of Mishnaic and Talmudic rabbis were miraculously identified in Palestine and became loci of individual and organized pilgrimage. With the spread of the Lurianic Kabbalah and of collections of the miraculous deeds of Luria himself, entitled *Shivhey ha-Ari* ("The Praises of the Ari"), local pilgrimage sites begin to appear among many Jewish communities throughout the entire Muslim world, especially in North Africa. There, Berber popular religion, with its veneration of shrines associated with graves of holy men, sacred trees, groves, brooks, pools, rocks, and grottos, had been thoroughly syncretized with local Islam.

From the seventeenth to the twentieth century, shrines to venerated Jewish holy men, such as the tomb of Mori Shalom Shabazi (fl. seventeenth century) in Taiz, Yemen, the cairn of Amram b. Diwan (d. early eighteenth century) in Wazzan, Morocco, or the grave and synagogue of Hayy Tayyib (d. 1837) in Tunis, sprang up all over the Islamic world. The anniversaries of these individuals' deaths were designated their *hillula*, the Aramaic word for "wedding celebration," because at death the saint is wedded to the divine. This was a time of pilgrimage, and special commemorations took place to honor the *tzaddiq*, the pious departed: a *seudah* (religious collation), study session, or the singing of special hymns. By the twentieth century, in Morocco alone there were no fewer than 652 shrines to Jewish saints.[8] Lag B'Omer, which is associated in Jewish tradition with Simeon b. Yohai, one of the few wonder-working rabbis in the Talmudic literature and an important figure in Jewish mysticism, became the *hillula* par excellence for Jews throughout the Muslim world, a sort of Jewish All Saints' Day, characterized by visits to the graves of local holy men, special collations, and the singing of *piyyutim* about Bar Yohai and other saints.

Collections of these *piyyutim*—liturgical poems—were standard supplements to the regular prayerbooks. Some of these collections represented the work of single poet, such as the Yemenite master Shalom Shabazi or the Tunisian laureate Fraji Shawwat. The following Tunisian Judeo-Arabic *piyyut* is typical of the genre:[9]

> I envision you with pure intention.
> Without any ruse in my heart,
> I shall spend hundreds, even thousands
> Without counting, without measure.
> Your place is exalted and full of sweetness
>   for me.
> It is always in my thoughts, a joy for me.
> I shall expend my wealth for you
> For the constant good with which you reward
>   and favor me,
> O dear master, R. Simeon b. Yohai.

Collections circulated widely throughout the Jewish communities of the Islamic world. Thus, a manuscript of the anthology entitled *Rinat Yosef* by Joseph b. Yaish Abughanim, written in 1899, could end up in a collection of Yemenite manuscripts. Many of the Hebrew *piyyutim* of the Islamicate Jewish world, with their strong amatory, even erotic flavor, were influenced by the Syrian Sephardic *paytan*, Israel b. Moses Najarah (ca. 1555-ca. 1625), whose innovational poetry drew upon both Lurianic Kabbalah and the great prosodic tradition of Iberian Jewry.[10]

Over time, an extensive corpus of hagiographic literature connected with saint veneration, modeled on the *Shivhey ha-Ari*, also developed. *Maaseh nissim* (miraculous deeds), a sort of *legenda d'ora*, comprised another model, and yet a third genre was the biographical dictionary, a parallel to the encyclopedic collections in the surrounding Islamic society of the biographies of Sufi masters, known as *tarâjim*. A latter-day example of such a dictionary is Joseph b. Naim's *Malkhey Rabbanan* (Jerusalem, 1931).

In addition to the cult of dead saints, North African Jews widely venerated living holy men, who played a role clearly parallel to that of thaumaturgic Hasidic rebbes in Eastern Europe: of intercessor with the divine, dispenser of blessings, miraculous healer, and clairvoyant. Like the rebbes, some of these *tzaddiqim*, such as the Abuhatzeras and the Pintos, even established dynasties that continued after them for generations in North Africa and later in Israel. Such parallels are certainly due to the common influence of the Lurianic Kabbalah in both its intellectual and popular manifestations. Still, within the Sephardic and Oriental world, denominational movements, with distinctive theologies, separate communal organizations, and unique daily rituals, comparable to those of the Hasidic sects, never developed, and hence there never arose any major opposition comparable to the anti-Hasidic Lithuanian *mitnaggedim*. Even those Middle Eastern and North African rabbis who objected to the more exuberant and syncretistic practices of popular saint veneration tended to take a generally permissive attitude, due in part to saint veneration's ubiquity and in part to a desire to keep pilgrimages and other practices associated with such veneration as much as possible within Halakhic bounds. Thus, for example, while the great Iraqi legal decisor Yosef Hayyim (1833 or 1835-1909) ruled that the Jews of Arbil in Iraqi Kurdistan ought to abandon their custom of sacrificing cattle on the graves of *tzaddiqim* in times of drought, he did not forbid prayer at these places.[11] This tolerant attitude continues throughout much of the Sephardic world and in the state of Israel today, where saint veneration has undergone a major revival and is stronger than ever before (see below).

Religious responses to modernity: During the nineteenth and twentieth centuries, the Jews of the Middle East and North Africa, like their coreligionists in Europe and America, were subject to the transformational forces of modernity. However, the modernizing process was overall more gradual and less traumatic for Sephardic and Oriental Jews than it was for their Ashkenazic brethren. For the latter, modern times marked not only emancipation but the almost complete breakdown of traditional communal organization and authority, as well as an irrevocable and irreconcilable split into various religious movements (neo-traditionalist, quasi-traditionalist, and anti-traditionalist),

on the one hand, and secularist movements (Yiddish culturalism, Jewish socialism, and, most important of all, Zionism), on the other. Sephardic Jewry produced no Reform Judaism, no Historical-Positivism, no neo-Orthodoxy, and no ultra-Orthodoxy (although, as we shall see, the forms of the last two have evolved in Israel in recent years). Neither did it produce any anti-religious movements. Right up to the mass exodus of the Jewish population of the Muslim world in the mid-twentieth century, the Sephardic religious responses to the challenges of a world of unprecedented change came primarily from within the tradition itself, thus preserving both the viability and integrity of Sephardic Judaism. Even secularizing tendencies among the laity, on the whole, were manifest only in a lessening of personal ritual observance, even as those involved acknowledged the continuing validity of traditional religion and religious authority.

As a rule, the rabbis of the Middle East and North Africa, most of whom belonged to the elite *megorashim*, were far less confrontational in their attitude towards social, economic, and technological changes than were their traditionalist counterparts in Europe. Not that the rabbis in the Islamic world were happy with some of the results of modernity, such as a decline in the strictness of observance of mitzvot and in Jewish learning as well as laxer moral and social behavior among the laity. The Sephardic Rabbinic literature of the late nineteenth and early twentieth century is full of complaints about the erosion of communal discipline.[12] Yet, while disturbed by what they considered the negative consequences of Western cultural influences, these rabbis were not against modern civilization per se and believed that much that was positive might be learned from Europe. "If in each generation we were to forbid everything that has newly appeared among the uncircumcised and the gentiles, then we would be forbidding even some permissible things," writes the *Hakham Bashi* (Chief Rabbi) of Alexandria, Elijah Hazzan (1847/48-1908), a leading Sephardic legal decisor of the late nineteenth and early twentieth centuries.[13]

This typical Sephardic stance was the very opposite of the uncompromising reaction of such Ashkenazic traditionalists as Moses Sofer of Pressburg (known as the *Hatam Sofer*), whose rallying cry was, "Whatever is new is forbidden by the Torah in every instance." It also was contrary to the attitudes of many Muslim religious leaders at that time, who regarded everything connected with the penetration of modern Western civilization as a threat to traditional faith and its way of life. Indeed, in marked contrast to the resistance of both *mitnaggedim* and Hasidic rabbinical authorities in Eastern and Central Europe, Sephardic and Oriental rabbis generally exhibited a positive attitude towards the western, secular education that, beginning in the mid-nineteenth century, was becoming available to Middle Eastern and North African Jewry. Israel Moses Hazzan (d. 1863) in Egypt, Isaac Bengualíd (1789-1870) in Morocco, and Abdallah Somekh (1813-1889) in Iraq, for instance, all exhibited an open attitude towards the study of foreign languages and the introduction of secular subjects into the Jewish school curriculum.

Throughout the nineteenth and into the early twentieth century, there were, however, few indigenous attempts to establish modern Jewish religious schools in the Muslim countries. Two notable exceptions were Hakham Zaki Cohen's Tiferet Yisrael boarding school in Beirut, which operated from the 1870s until 1904, and Mori Yihyeh Qafih's Dar Da' (Heb., *dor de'a*—"generation of knowledge") school in Sana, Yemen, which was open only from 1909-1913. The principal disseminator of modern, western-style education among the Jews of the Islamic world was the Paris-based Alliance Israélite Universelle, founded in 1860. By the turn of the century, the Alliance had established a hundred schools in most of the major towns and cities with a Jewish community from Morocco to Persia. Although the Alliance's instructional program was primarily secularist, it did include a not insignificant religious component, which in the early days was taught by local rabbis and teachers, and many Jewish children supplemented their religious education with after-school classes at a traditional *talmud torah*.[14]

The only example of all-out, implacable religious opposition to the Alliance, and indeed to all modern schooling, came from the rabbis of the zealous island community of Jerba, Tunisia. Under the leadership of Moses Khalfon ha-Kohen (1874-1950), whose collection of *taqqanot* (regulations) and *minhagim* (customs), entitled *Berit Kehuna* ("The Covenant of the Priesthood"), became the authoritative code for local practice, Jerban Jewry developed a distinctive style of religiosity based upon intensive traditional education for all boys, followed by lifelong individual and group study. financial support for educating the children of poor families and subsidizing needy Torah scholars was undertaken by a public body known as *Vaad Or ha-Torah* ("Committee for the Light of the Torah"). This important focal point of Jerban communal life not only placed students into appropriate professions upon the completion of their formal schooling but also made sure that males regularly attended study groups thereafter.

As part of Jerban Jewry's distinctive ritualization of literacy, laymen were encouraged to set down in print their glosses and novellae to religious texts. This resulted in an enormous body of publications printed on Jerba's Hebrew press. Though mostly consisting of small pamphlets and specialized prayerbooks, these were considered a mark of Jerba's general scholarship and piety and contributed to the community's sense of elitism and being set apart from the rest of Tunisian Jewry. In addition to this factor and the Jerban Jews' geographical insularity, isolationism may have been influenced by the surrounding Ibadi Kharijite milieu, which cultivated a strict ideal of separation from the Sunni Muslims of the rest of Tunisia.[15]

The Jerban reaction to ever-encroaching modernity was exceptional. Most of the Sephardic religious leadership viewed the challenges of modern times as requiring neither rejection nor passive acceptance but rather active and creative engagement. Already in 1874, in his philosophical dialogue *Zikron Yerushalayim* ("Remembrance of Jerusalem"), Elijah Hazzan imagines a international Jewish assembly held in Tunis at which all the diverse currents of contemporary Jewry discuss the issues facing Judaism and the Jewish people.[16]

Because it was not faced with an all-out rebellion from within or a delegitimation of its authority from without, much of the Sephardic rabbinate viewed as one of its principal tasks the preservation of Jewish communal unity and the spiritual guidance of its members in the new age. Rather than trying to cut off or to restrain those who strayed from the paths of observance, and rather than trying to ordain ever-new strictures for their congregations, they tried to bring them into some degree of harmony with tradition. The *Hakham Bashi* of Cairo throughout the last decade of the nineteenth century and the first two decades of the twentieth, Raphael Aaron b. Simeon (1847/48-1928), summed up the widespread sentiment of most Oriental rabbis thus:[17]

> It is incumbent upon the man concerned with his religion and faith, who loves the people of his nation with a pure heart, to exert himself for their welfare and to seek to preserve their purity in whatever way he can find without pulling the cord of strictness to its limit.

A similar example of Oriental rabbis' generally tolerant and nuanced approach to increasingly secular tendencies among Middle Eastern and North African Jews may be seen in the reaction of Joseph Hayyim of Baghdad to Jews' frequenting of gentile coffeehouses on the Sabbath. While noting that it is preferable on the day of rest not to spend time in such idle pursuits, he merely cautions those who do go "to consume only what was prepared prior to their coming"[18] and so not to eat what what cooked specifically for them on the Sabbath.

In general, the Sephardic and Oriental rabbis also approached in a sober fashion, without any noticeable alarm, the Halakhic questions that arose from new technologies. For example, in 1877, Abdallah Somekh—regarded as the supreme Halakhic authority by the far-flung Iraqi Jewish colonies of merchants extending from India to China—ruled that it is permissible on Sabbaths and holi-

days to ride the railway within a city's limits, although not between cities, which would violate the Sabbath boundary. In his responsum, Somekh makes clear that he was familiar with the European Rabbinic literature on the subject, including the contrary opinions of scholars such as the Hatam Sofer, whom he mentions by name.[19] Somekh saw modern technology as raising technical problems, but he did not perceive it as part of a wider threat per se.

On the other hand, many Middle Eastern rabbis realized that the new technology indeed raised unprecedented questions for religious Jews and that Jewish tradition did not necessarily provide clear-cut answers to these questions. As Raphael Aaron b. Simeon observed:[20]

> New inventions . . . have proliferated in our generation which have increased and expanded man's wisdom with regard to the production of sophisticated articles of manufacture by means of knowledge and research into the basic foundations of creation. . . . Each day new inventions appear, of which our ancestors and forefathers never thought. The task of the teacher to respond to those who question him about these discoveries has become heavier. . . . For it is difficult to find parallels to them in our holy Talmud from which practical results may be obtained for teaching whether to forbid or to permit.

Perhaps because he lived in the modern metropolis of Cairo rather than provincial Baghdad, Ben Simeon felt acutely the daunting task of rendering Halakhic rulings concerning the new technology. But he was not overwhelmed by the challenge, nor did he shrink from it. Rather, he soberly states that religious authorities must exert themselves "with a clear and undisturbed mind and at leisure" as they traverse "the deep sea of the Talmud" in search of answers.

As a general rule, Middle Eastern and North African rabbis were less likely than their hard-line traditionalist counterparts in Central and Eastern Europe to oppose new practices simply because they conformed to gentile custom (*huqqat ha-goy*). Like the rabbis of the Talmudic era, they understood this principle to apply only to non-Jewish religious rituals and acts of immorality, not to practices that are morally or religiously neutral. "For if we were to forbid everything that had arisen first among the Christians and Muslims," writes Elijah Bekhor Hazzan, "we would be forbidding some permitted things as well."[21] This greater restraint in applying the principle of "gentile custom" to practices and modes adopted from the West was probably due to the Sephardic rabbinate's centuries-old openness to general culture and its greater willingness to look beyond the letter of the law. Indeed, sometimes Sephardic rabbis were willing to adopt new and innovative religious practices even though these had immediate roots outside of Judaism. During the 1920s and 1930s, for example, religious leaders such as David Prato in Alexandria and Jacob Boccara in Tunis introduced bat mitzvah/confirmation ceremonies for girls, who wore bride-like white dresses and veils similar to those used in churches for first communion.[22] Such experiments were exceptional, but they are indicative of a wider openness to Western modernizing influences.

Many leading rabbis in the Islamic world appear to have grasped that modernity was not a temporary phenomenon merely to be waited out. They also understood that it brought with it an unprecedented measure of individual freedom. Again, Raphael Aaron b. Simeon expresses this perception most eloquently:

> It was unheard of in any previous time that the governing authorities would loosen restraints so that an individual would be free in his religion and belief to the point that no one can say to him, "What does thou?" No on has the authority to chastise a person who commits a religious transgression, even if it is committed in public. This is the result of the freedom and liberty prevailing in the land.[23]

Ben Simeon understood that "freedom and liberty" might have positive as well as negative consequences. For example, Jews in British-controlled Egypt could hold public ceremonies, forbidden under traditional Muslim rule, "now—thank God—that freedom and liberty prevail in the land."[24] His colleague, Elijah Bekhor Hazzan, also refers to "freedom and liberty."[25] This grasp of the centrality of individual freedom accords precisely with sociologist Peter Berger's definition of modernization as "a shift from giveness to choice on the level of meaning."[26] Here again, the Sephardic rabbis stand in marked contrast to most Muslim religious leaders of the period, for whom words like "liberty" often denoted "libertinism."

Because of the Sephardic religious leadership's less confrontational nature and because of the overall conservatism of the surrounding Islamic society, the rabbis of the Middle East and North Africa maintained a considerable degree of their traditional communal authority and prestige. While many Sephardic rabbis were painfully aware of their own limitations, they were convinced that they could—and indeed did—effectively provide religious guidance to all sectors of the Jewish community, including the secularizing elements.

Religious nationalism: Modern Jewish nationalism—Zionism—was born and developed within Ashkenazic Jewry in Europe, and although it was rooted in two millennia of messianic hope for redemption and had religious branches, it was essentially a secularist movement. Before modern times, some of the most articulate voices of the traditional Jewish longing for Zion had emanated from the Sephardic and Oriental Jewish world. Judah Halevi, the poet laureate of medieval Andalusian Jewry, had given classic expression to this yearning in his sublime cycle of Hebrew verses known to later generations as the "Songs of Zion" (*Shirey Tzion*) and in his philosophical Judeo-Arabic dialogue, *The Kuzari*. As noted above, thousands of Sephardim settled in Ottoman Palestine in the sixteenth century, inspired in part by messianic expectations. In the centuries that followed, Sephardic and Oriental Jews maintained very strong, direct ties with the land of Israel to a much greater extent than did their brethren in Europe. This was due to the closer proximity of most of North African and Levantine Jewry to the Holy Land as well as to the fact that, until the colonial era, the vast majority of Oriental Jews lived in the Ottoman Empire, of which Palestine was just another province. Indeed, even those Oriental

Jews who lived outside Ottoman territory in Morocco to the West, or in Persia and Central Asia to the East, still felt that their ancestral homeland was within the same Islamic cultural world in which they lived. Emissaries from religious institutions in the four holy cities of Jerusalem, Hebron, Safed, and Tiberias made their rounds more frequently among the communities of the Middle East and North Africa than they did in more distant Europe, and they were an important medium of communication between the Yishuv—the Palestinian Jewish community—and the rest of Oriental Jewry.

Among Jews of the Islamic world, particularly among North African Jews, there was an established tradition of *aliyah* ("immigration;" literally, "ascent,") to the land of Israel going back to the Middle Ages. Until the nineteenth century, this was a matter of individual piety and not a group phenomenon. Numerous examples in Maghrebi responsa literature deal with the mitzvah—the religious obligation—of settling the Holy Land, with a considerable number of cases referring to wives who do not wish to accompany their husbands because of what they consider to be dangerous travel conditions. Rabbinic judges in the seventeenth and early eighteenth centuries tended to accept the wife's argument and required the husband to pay her the divorce settlement stipulated in her marriage contract before he set out. However, in the latter part of the eighteenth century, some Rabbinic authorities began to reject the wife's claim concerning the danger and permitted the husband to divorce her without payment. There are also cases of wives who wish to make *aliyah* whose husbands object. Because of the great mitzvah involved, the answer is invariably in the wife's favor. Questions in such instances only concern whether the woman may take her children with her, and, if so, whether this right is affected by the children's ages.

During the nineteenth century, *aliyah* to the land of Israel by Jews from the far ends of the Islamic world began to take on dramatic new proportions, impelled in part by messianic expectations and in part by difficult local conditions in the diaspora. Jews began emigrating from Kurdistan to Palestine in 1812, including several entire villages. Jews from Bukhara started coming to Israel in considerable numbers in 1868, with the specific goal of making Jerusalem a spiritual center for their community. In 1881, Yemenite Jews began pouring into Palestine in a wave that by the outbreak of World War I totaled some 3,000 individuals, between five and ten percent of Yemen's total Jewish population. Throughout the century, North African Jews arrived in a steady stream, and the Maghrebi community came to constitute large distinguishable units of the Jewish population in Jerusalem, Haifa, and Jaffa. Indeed, the revival of these towns in modern times was due in no small measure to the influx of these North African Jewish settlers. Though impelled primarily by religious sentiments, most of the North African and other Oriental Jewish immigrants to Palestine were not engaged exclusively in prayer and study; neither did they live off the *haluqqa* (the dole funded by the charity of coreligionists in the diaspora). Rather, in stark contrast to the majority of traditional Ashkenazic immigrants in the years prior to modern Zionist pioneering, they earned livelihoods through commerce, handicraft, and manual labor.

Although Zionism in both its political and cultural form evolved in Europe under the influence of European nationalist thinking, some Sephardic rabbis and lay intellectuals were independent forerunners of the Zionist movement. The earliest of these was Judah Bibas (1780-1852), the scion of a distinguished Moroccan Rabbinic family, born in Gibraltar where, for a while, he headed the yeshiva. He had received a secular education in Italy, and, in 1832, took a Rabbinic position on the island of Corfu. Inspired by the Italian Risorgimento and the Greek war of independence, Bibas broke with the traditional quietistic stance of waiting for messianic redemption. Instead, he advocated that Jews return to the land of Israel and wrest it by force if need be from the Turks. The most original notion in his theology was his reinterpretation of the spiritual concept of *teshuvah* (repentance) to its literal meaning, "return." Thus, he interpreted the Talmudic dictum "the matter [of redemption] depends only upon *teshuvah*" (B. San. 97b) to mean that redemption is not dependent solely upon repentance ("return to God") but upon physical return to the land of Israel.

Bibas did not commit his ideas to writing but preached them in Corfu and in the course of his travels in 1839 in the Ottoman and Austro-Hungarian Empires. During that year, he met Judah Alkalai (1798-1878), the *hakham* of Zemun in Croatia. Bibas had a profound impact upon Alkalai, who, because of his extensive publications and tireless efforts to spread his ideas throughout Europe, the Balkans, and the Levant, became the best known Sephardic harbinger of Zionism. At first, Alkalai's call for the Jews' return to their land seems to have been prompted by his own kabbalistic speculation and messianic calculations, as much as by Bibas's more nationalistic thinking. But even as he remained within his traditional categories of thought, he increasingly responded to specifically modern phenomena. His treatise *Minhat Yehudah* ("Judah's Offering"), written in 1840, viewed the Damascus Blood Libel of earlier that year as a sign of "the end of days" and a "birth pang of the messianic age." The treatise also, however, reflects how impressed he was by the mission of Sir Moses Montefiore and Adolphe Crémieux to the Levant on behalf of Damascene Jewry. The political power, influence, and energy of these two European Jewish leaders convinced him that they could turn to the rulers of the great powers and get them to grant freedom to Jews to return to their ancestral land, just as Nehemiah had prompted Cyrus the Great to do more than two millennia earlier. He also called for the convening of an international congress of Jewish leaders with full powers to make administrative decisions and raise funds for the resettlement of the Holy Land.[27]

Alkalai's religio-political thought evolved with time. His Zionism remained essentially a religious Zionism, but it became increasingly imbued with contemporary nationalistic sentiments. It was also permeated by a sense that the age was a new era in human history, as he eloquently proclaimed in his essay *Nehamat ha-Aretz* ("Consolation for the Land"), published in 1866:[28]

> The spirit of the times does not ask of the individual that he follow the arbitrariness of his heart, but rather that he seek the good of the collective. The spirit of the times has nothing to do with the Torah and divine service, for what the times require is without distinction of religion or people.... The spirit of the times demands freedom and liberty for the success of the nation. And thus it demands of us to proclaim liberty to those in captivity.... The spirit of the times requires all of the countries to establish their land and to raise up their language. Likewise, it requires of us to establish our living home and to raise up our sacred language and revive it.

Rabbi Alkalai clearly had come to identify the Jewish national revival not with an eschatological "end of days" but with a universal phenomenon that is the right, and indeed the duty, of all peoples everywhere. Such ideas were an integral part of modern European nationalist thought. So too is the belief expressed here that political revival is inextricably bound up with cultural revival. In fact, Alkalai's first book, *Darke Noam* ("Ways of Pleasantness"), published in 1839, was a Ladino grammar of Hebrew, although it was only some years later that, in his pamphlet *Meoded Anavim* ("Encouraging the Humble"), he actually called for a Hebrew language revival among Jews.[29]

Other Sephardic rabbis in the Near East and North Africa during the nineteenth century also expressed the need for a Hebrew language revival, or, at the very least, increased Hebrew language education. Israel Moses Hazzan published several appeals for Hebrew language study. In one of these, he points admiringly to the cultivation of classical Greek and Latin among Christians.[30] In Ottoman Turkey, Menahem Farhi wrote a Hebrew grammar in Ladino, entitled *Rav Pe'alim* (Constantinople, 1880), justifying his endeavor with the observation that other living languages are progressing. And Saul ha-Kohen in Tunis introduced his Hebrew grammar, *Lehem ha-Biqqurim* ("The Bread of the first Fruit Offering;" Livorno, 1870), with the justification that other nations are greatly interested in the study of their own language. In fact, throughout North Africa, rabbis frequently were found among the small circles of *maskilim* (members of the *Haskala*, the Jewish Enlightenment). Advocates of Hebrew linguistic revival, they subscribed—and even contributed articles—to Hebrew journals and read Hebrew books published in Europe and Palestine. In Essouira (Mogador), Morocco, David Elqayim wrote poems in praise of Hebrew. In one of these, he apostrophizes the mother tongue and calls upon it to arise and rejuvenate itself.[31] A few rabbis, such as Joseph Brami (1888-1924) in Tunis, even were active in modern Hebrew education.

Although Judah Alkalai's holistic, programmatic Zionism was unique, many other rabbis in the Islamic world shared his sentiments. Indeed, when Theodore Herzl and the World Zionist Organization came on the scene in 1897, there was no phenomenon in the Middle East and North Africa comparable to the *Protestrabbiner* in Germany. Most of the early Zionist societies in the Oriental Jewish communities included their spiritual leaders, who were frequently officers of the associations. Rabbis such as Jacob Boccara, the leader of the Grana community in Tunis, even attended early Zionist congresses in Europe as delegates. In Morocco, Tunisia, and Libya in particular, the rabbis perceived Zionism as a thoroughly natural expression of Judaism.

Zionism touched deep-seated spiritual chords within many sectors of Oriental Jewry. These chords were not exclusively religious in the modern Western sense, since in the Muslim world, and in Sephardic Judaism generally, the confessional community traditionally was understood in a corporate, national sense. In the late nineteenth and early twentieth centuries, the Zionist movement made modest, but not insignificant, inroads into most of the major urban Ladino- and Judaeo-Arabic-speaking communities of the Islamic world. It aroused widespread enthusiasm in the wake of the Balfour Declaration, the Allied victory, and the San Remo Conference. Crowds of thousands turned out for Zionist rallies in Cairo, Alexandria, and Tunis in 1917 and 1918. In the immediate post-

war years, several hundred families from Morocco made *aliyah* in a burst of semi-messianic fervor. There was also a smaller wave of immigrants numbering slightly over one thousand individuals, with similar numbers coming from Syria and Libya.

Religious opposition to Zionism remained virtually nonexistent among the Jews of the Middle East and North Africa. The only principal source of anti-Zionism was from the circles of the secularist Alliance Israélite Universelle, which had been overtly cool and covertly hostile to Zionism since its inception. Many members of the small, wealthy Jewish upper class were also tepid to Jewish nationalism. But the only strongly outspoken Rabbinic opponent to the movement was Sassoon Khadduri, who served as *Hakham Bashi* of Baghdad from 1927-1929 and was president of the community council from 1932-1949. At first a supporter of Zionism, in the late 1920s he became its implacable foe. His anti-Zionism was, however, purely political, not theological. Alarmed by the rise of the militant Arab nationalism in Iraq that identified itself with the Palestinian Arab cause, Khadduri believed that only a complete rejecting of Zionism would provide hope of protecting Iraqi Jewry from persecution or even destruction. He stayed behind in Baghdad after the Jews' mass exodus from Iraq in 1951, remaining the leading Jewish spokesman against Zionism in the Islamic world until his death in 1971.[32]

The only other significant spiritual leader among Oriental Jewry to voice any real opposition to Zionism was Hayyim Nahum, the French-educated, politically active Chief Rabbi of Egypt from 1925-1960. Though never a Zionist himself, Nahum had in fact acted as an intermediary between the Zionists and the Turkish authorities when he was *Hakham Bashi* of the Ottoman Empire (1909-1920). Like Khadduri, his rejection of Zionism was consistently political, never theological, and he studiously avoided scathing denunciations of the sort made by the Iraqi Chief Rabbi, even when under considerable pressure to do so.[33]

Both Sassoon Khadduri and Hayyim Nahum were exceptional figures, untypical of the Sephardic and Oriental Jewish rabbinate in many respects—and very different from one another. Neither of them may be considered in any way representative of the religious community's generally sympathetic attitude toward Zionism. Still, the widespread sympathy that so many Jews in the Middle East and North Africa felt for Zionism was rarely translated into active participation in the movement. This was for a number of reasons, including the disapproval of colonial authorities, the opposition of nationalist governments, and, from the late 1920s onward, mounting pan-Arab and pan-Islamic hostility. Oriental Jewry had no real tradition of political involvement or activism, so that, with the exception of Tunisia, membership in Zionist associations—even where legal—was always extremely limited.

Similarly, Zionist associations in the Middle Eastern and North African countries rarely sent delegates to the early World Zionist Congresses as they were entitled to do. This was due in part to their inexperience with parliamentary representation and in part due to the psychological and physical distance separating them from Western and Central Europe, where, before World War I, the congresses were held. But perhaps the most important reason for the lack of participation was that many Oriental and Sephardic Jews looked upon the World Zionist Organization with the utmost reverence and considered its leaders to be engaged in a divinely ordained enterprise that required only their unquestioning loyalty. This passivity would be abandoned only by a very small modernist and secularist minority during the course of the twentieth century. It remained the hallmark of the more traditional majority to the time of their mass *aliyah* and for sometime thereafter in their reestablished homeland.

Oriental and Sephardic Judaism in the late twentieth century: During the two decades following the establishment of the state of Israel, in the wake of mass emigration, most of the Jewish communities of the Islamic world shrank to near non-existence. With the exception of Morocco, Turkey, and Iran, only a small, vestigial, and for the most part moribund Jewish community remained behind.[34]

The great majority of Middle Eastern and North African Jews settled in Israel, where they and their descendants came to constitute more than half the Israeli Jewish population. A large number of North African Jews, including most of Algeria's Jews, also settled in France, where they too now comprise a majority of the Jews, not merely making an imprint upon French Jewry but totally transforming it. The most recent two chief rabbis of France, René Samuel Sirat (1981-1987) and Joseph Sitrouk (1987-present), were both North African born and are the first Sephardim to hold that office. There are also smaller, but sizable, émigré Jewish communities from the Islamic world in other European countries—for example, Libyan Jews in Italy, and Moroccan Jews in Spain and Belgium—as well as in Canada, the United States, Mexico, and South America. But for all intents and purposes, the vibrant centers of Islamicate Sephardic Jewry are now in Israel and to a certain extent France.

For their first two decades in their reestablished homeland, most of the Sephardic newcomers were religiously as well as politically invisible. In addition to the hardships they shared with all new immigrants, the Sephardic Jews experienced other problems. The Promised Land in which they had arrived had been founded by Ashkenazic pioneers from Eastern and Central Europe. The culture of the nascent state and its institutions were already in place and were stamped with a specifically European secularist, socialist, and utopian character. The official establishment Judaism was primarily Ashkenazic. Even though the Ottoman office of *Rishon le-Tzion* (*Hakham Bashi* of the Holy Land) continued to exist, it did so alongside the more influential Ashkenazic Chief Rabbinate, created under the British Mandate. As with so much in the early days of Israel, even in matters of religion the new Sephardic immigrants were dependent upon the established state institutions. The Ministry of Religious Affairs provided religiously-oriented public schools, houses of worship, prayerbooks, and an official government-salaried rabbinate, so that some of the traditional spiritual leaders who came to Israel with their communities experienced a loss of their authority.

Young Sephardim who entered the religious youth movements or went on to higher religious education usually found themselves in an Ashkenazic environment, and, since most of the Rabbinic colleges were also European-founded, new Sephardic rabbis were often trained in the Ashkenazic orthodox fashion, with its different world outlook, its distinct approach to piety, and even its own distinctive dress code. The powerful antireligious secularism of the Zionist political and cultural elite that dominated Israeli life also contributed to the weakening of traditional Sephardic authority, not only the authority of the old-time spiritual leadership but of the entire older generation of immigrants.

Although religious observance among members of the younger generation of Sephardim in Israel declined, this did not translate into the kind of wholesale disaffection from religion that characterized much of Ashkenazic secularity. A survey of Sephardic high school students in the late sixties showed that only about twenty percent defined themselves as non-religious, as compared to over half their Ashkenazic peers. Fully one third of Sephardic pupils, as compared to only a fifth of Ashkenazim, defined themselves as religious, while nearly half identified themselves as "traditional" (*masorti*), which in the Israeli context means observance of some Jewish practices, ranging, for example, from partial to consistent synagogue attendance or from observance of kashrut only at home to its careful observance outside as well.[35]

It is not uncommon to find *masorti* Sephardim who attend worship services on Shabbat morning and go to a football match or the beach that same afternoon. The Sephardic religious sector treats these compromises for the most part with the traditional tolerance, so that, despite a decline in synagogue attendance among young adults, synagogues have maintained their centrality in most Sephardic and Oriental communities. Indeed, one important manifestation of Sephardic and Ori-

ental religiosity that has reasserted itself in Israel with considerable vitality is the very one the Ashkenazic religious establishment tried to discourage, namely, non-universal Jewish rites that were part of local traditions in the diaspora, including the celebration of non-canonical holidays, such as the North African Mimouna, the Kurdish Sahrani, and more widespread practice of saint veneration, with its attendant *hillulot* and pilgrimages. The festivities of these non-canonical holidays and pilgrimages draw enormous numbers of people of all ages and all levels of religiosity, education, and socioeconomic status.[36]

The Mimouna and Sahrani are as much statements of ethnic pride and identity as religious occasions, somewhat parallel to Saint Patrick's Day in the United States. The required appearance at these celebrations of Israeli politicians of all stripes, as well as the participation of non-Sephardic merrymakers, who become honorary North Africans or Kurds for the day, are indicative of the perception of many Ashkenazic Israelis that these are ethnic rather than religious occasions. However, the main religious observances take place outside of public view at home and in the synagogue. The traditional Mimouna observances, for example, complete with blessings and ritual foods, are reserved for the home on the evening Passover ends, as an *isru hag*—a sort of minor holiday that occurs at the conclusion of each of the three major festivals.

Relatively little public manifestations of saint veneration occurred in Israel during the first decade following the mass *aliyah* from the Islamic world. This was due in part to the initial shock and passivity of the Sephardic immigrants as they adjusted to their new surroundings, as well as to the hard times and still primitive conditions prevailing in the young state, which made large scale pilgrimages to distant parts of the country unfeasible. At first, the observance of *hillulot* was confined to commemorative collations, chanting of liturgical poetry, and the recitation of mystical texts such as the Zohar at home. In the 1960s, synagogues named after *tzaddiqim* began to proliferate, and some became the sites of major annual *hillulot*. Around the same time, pilgrimages to the graves of holy men buried in Israel began to attract increasing numbers of people. These pilgrimages, which had been designated *ziyâra* ("visit") in the Arabic-, Persian-, and Eastern Ladino-speaking diaspora, came to be called *aliyah le-regel*, an evocative biblical phrase meaning "going up on foot" that was used for the three annual festival pilgrimages of ancient Temple times. The *hillula* of Simeon b. Yohai on Lag B'Omer at Meron in the Galilee has become the most important pilgrimage among Sephardim in Israel, attracting over 100,000 people each year.

A great many new pilgrimage sites have emerged in Israel in recent decades, and newly recognized individuals are continually being added to the pantheon of *tzaddiqim*. Among the more notable are the *hillulot* around the graves of the Tunisian Hayyim Huri, who died in Beer Sheba in 1957, and of the Moroccan thaumaturge, Israel Abu-hatzera, known as the Baba Sali, who died in the Negev town of Netivot in 1884 and whose portrait adorns the walls of countless kiosks and Middle Eastern style restaurants throughout Israel. Both of these pilgrimages now attract tens of thousands of participants of all ages as well as a steady stream of devotees throughout the year. The shrine built around Baba Sali's grave has become a popular place for Bar Mitzvah celebrations, and approximately fifty families a week pay a considerable amount of money to take out and read the Torah scroll from the shrine's ark.[37]

The proliferation of saints' shrines in Israel's so-called development towns (ironically, often the most underdeveloped communities in the country) may be in part a subconscious religious response to physical, economic, and social isolation and at the same time a means of establishing a deep spiritual intimacy with the new surroundings.[38] The vigorous reemergence of hagiolatry in Israel may also be viewed as a psychological response to the strains of military service and frequent wars. One Israeli ethnographer has noted an increase in reported miracles by *tzaddiqim* during military conflicts.[39] Notably, not only among the Sephardim in Israel

has saint veneration experienced a resurgence, but in the diaspora as well. Charter flights bring large groups to North Africa and Israel for *hillulot* and pilgrimages to tombs in Israel, Morocco, Tunisia, Egypt, and even Algeria. Recognizing the economic value of such tourism and also due to genuinely shared religious values, the Moroccan government has contributed to the upgrading and maintenance of Jewish saints' shrines and facilities for pilgrims adjacent to them.

The recent growth of Sephardic religious schools, youth movements, and political parties represents the adoption of some of the modes and norms, and, no less significantly, mentalities of Ashkenazic religiosity. The leaders of these new institutions are rabbis who studied in Ashkenazic yeshivot. These academies, whether of the neo-Orthodox or ultra-Orthodox variety, teach according to the Ashkenazic curriculum, which differs significantly in both content and style from the traditional Sephardic Rabbinic education. Whereas the Ashkenazic academy devotes most of its teaching to the Talmud and later commentaries through the discipline of theoretical casuistics (Heb.: *pilpul*), emphasizing almost exclusively the authority of texts, the traditional Sephardic academies of the diaspora had always offered a more broadly based education that included Bible and Hebrew prosody as well as a core of Talmudic studies. The Talmud was taught not so much through casuistry as through analytical study, and, in addition to textual authority, the Sephardic yeshivah placed considerable store in living tradition, emphasizing the practical application of Halakhah needed for communal service. Yet rabbis formed in the Ashkenazic mold now can be found serving Sephardic communities in France, Canada, and Morocco, as well as Israel.

The young Sephardic rabbis who came out of the Ashkenazic institutions were assimilated into the Eastern European yeshivah subculture. Out of this milieu emerged organizations like Reuben Elbaz's *Or ha-Hayyim* ("The Light of Life") outreach movement, which works to bring young penitents (Heb., *baalei teshuvah*) back to strict religious observance. *Or ha-Hayyim* is modeled on many similar Ashkenazic organizations. By the late 1980s, it boasted having more than 150 schools and clubs throughout Israel.[40]

In 1983, also out of the Ashkenazic yeshivah milieu, emerged the Shas Party (a Hebrew acronym for Sephardic Torah Guardians). By 1997, with ten seats in the Knesset, Shas had become the largest single religious party. Deeply dissatisfied with the blatant discrimination toward Sephardim in Ashkenazic yeshivah circles, the founders of Shas aimed at forming a separate Sephardic ultra-orthodox community, with its own schools and communal institutions. The Shas rabbis also wished to develop the kind of devoted following associated with great Ashkenazic leaders, such as the Lithuanian yeshivah heads and the Hasidic rebbes. Although a considerable cultural and spiritual gulf divides this new Ashkenazified Sephardic religious elite of Shas from the Sephardic masses, the party has enjoyed considerable support from the grass roots, in part as a protest against the Ashkenazic dominated parties and in part due to the great veneration that many traditionalist Sephardim still show their rabbis.

Indeed, some Ashkenazification has occurred among the Sephardic masses as well, the result, oddly enough, of Hasidism. Ever since the early 1950s, the Lubavitcher Habad movement has been actively proselytizing among Sephardim in North Africa, France, Israel, and North America. The Lubavitchers reach large numbers of Sephardim by their friendly and non-contemptuous manner and by making accommodations to Sephardic ritual and custom, which in any case have certain important elements in common with Hasidic practice. These commonalities include similar liturgies (the so-called *nusah sefard* or *nusah ha-ari*), veneration of holy men, and Lurianic Kabbalah. In the homes of North African Jews everywhere, it is not uncommon to find portraits of various Maghrebi *tzaddiqim* alongside that of the Lubavitcher Rebbe. Not only have the Lubavitchers conducted their outreach programs primarily on a popular level, but, in sharp contrast to the anti-Hasidic *mitnaggedim*, they have welcomed into the highest echelons

of their movement Sephardim who have attended their yeshivot and joined their ranks. However, despite their accommodating style, the Lubavitchers have grafted their own very specific brand of religiosity onto their Sephardic protégés, and those that actually join Habad are required to take on its distinctive customs and practices.

Whether acculturated by the yeshivah world of the Lithuanian *mitnaggedim* or the proselytizing enthusiasm of the Lubavitcher Hasidim, the Sephardim who have been affected have assimilated one common trait shared by both Ashkenazic groups: a degree of zealousness and an uncompromising spirit that is not only anti-secularist but anti-every form of religiosity that does not conform to their standards, that is closed to general culture, and that refuses to look outside the proverbial "four cubits of the law," understood in the most restrictive fashion. This growing Ashkenazified outlook is a far cry from that of most of traditional Sephardic Judaism. Most Sephardic and Oriental Jews have not been Ashkenazified, and many communities retain a religiosity that is without tension. However, the effects of Ashkenazic fundamentalist influence in the realm of religious world-view are increasing.

Bibliography

Dobrinsky, Herbert C., *A Treasury of Sephardic Laws and Customs* (New York and Hoboken, 1986).

Elazar, Daniel J., *The Other Jews: The Sephardim Today* (New York, 1989).

Shmuelevitz, Aryeh, *The Jews of the Ottoman Empire in the Late Fifteenth and the Sixteenth Centuries* (Leiden, 1984).

Stillman, Norman A., *The Jews of Arab Lands in Modern Times* (Philadelphia, 1991).

Stillman, Norman A., *The Language and Customs of the Jews of Sefrou, Morocco: An Ethnolinguistic Study* (Manchester, 1988).

Stillman, Norman A., *Sephardi Religious Responses to Modernity* (United Kingdom, 1995).

Notes

[1] For numerous examples, see Louis Brunot and Elie Malka, *Textes judéo-arabes de Fès* (Rabat, 1939), and idem, *Glossaire judéo-arabe de Fès* (Rabat, 1940).

[2] See Hayyim Gagin, *Etz Hayyim*, ed. Moshe Amar (Ramat Gan, 1987), pp. 67-173, and Abraham b. Tawah, *Seper Nopek*, Ohel David (Sassoon Collection) Ms. 714, JNUL Microfilm no. 1 S 9285.

[3] Aryeh Shmuelevitz, *The Jews of the Ottoman Empire in the Late Fifteenth and the Sixteenth Centuries* (Leiden, 1984), pp. 13-14.

[4] See Itzhaq Abrahami, *La Communauté Portugaise de Tunis et son Mémorial*, doc. diss., Bar-Ilan University (Ramat Gan, 1982), pp. 137-168 [Heb.].

[5] For detailed accounts of the lives and works or these and other outstanding figures of the first few generations of Sephardic decisors in the Islamic world, see Israel M. Goldman, *The Life and Times of Rabbi David Ibn Abi Zimra* (New York, 1970); Samuel Morell, *Precedent and Judicial Discretion: The Case of Joseph ibn Lev* (Atlanta, 1991); M. S. Goodblatt, *Jewish Life in Turkey in the XVIth Century as Reflected in the Legal Writings of Samuel de Medina* (New York, 1952).

[6] See A. Ya'ari, *ha-Depus ha-ivri ba-artzot ha-mizrah* (Jerusalem, 1936-1940) and Norman Golb, *Spertus College of Judaic Yemenite Manuscripts: An Illustrated Catalogue* (Chicago, 1972), p. 8, B1.

[7] See Cecil Roth *The House of Nasi: The Duke of Naxos* (Philadelphia, 1948), pp. 97-135.

[8] See Issachar Ben-Ami, *Culte des saints et pèlerinages judéo-musulmans au Maroc* (Paris, 1990), and Louis Voinot, *Pèlerinages judéo-musulmans du Maroc* (Paris, 1948).

[9] David Cohen, *Le parler arabe des Juifs de Tunis: Textes et documents linguistiques et ethnographiques* (Paris and the Hague, 1964), p. 94.

[10] See Joseph Yahalom, "R. Israel Najarah and the Revival of Hebrew Poetry in the East after the Expulsion from Spain," in *Pe'amim* 13, 1982, pp. 96-124 [Heb.].

[11] Joseph Hayyim, *Rav Pe'alim* 2, Jerusalem, 1979, pp. 61a-b, Resp. 31.

[12] Norman A. Stillman, *Sephardi Religious Responses to Modernity* (United Kingdom, 1995), p. 14.

[13] Elijah Bekhor Hazzan, *Ta'alumot Leb* 3 (Alexandria, 1902/3), p. 59a, Resp. 57.

[14] See Stillman, op. cit., pp. 15-19, and Norman A. Stillman, *The Jews of Arab Lands in Modern Times* (Philadelphia, 1991), pp. 23-25 and 29-34.

[15] Cf., Stillman, *The Jews of Arab Lands in Modern Times*, p. 18; and Abraham L. Udovitch and Lucette Valensi, *The Last Arab Jews: The Communities of Jerba, Tunisia* (New York, 1984), pp. 87-88.

[16] Elijah Hazzan, *Zikron Yerushalayim* (Livorno, 1874), pp. 48-117.

[17] Raphael Aaron b. Simeon, *Umi-Tzur Devash* (Jerusalem, 1914/15), p. 111a.

[18] Joseph Hayyim, *Ben Ish Hayy* 2 (Jerusalem, 1977), p. 48.

[19] Abdallah Somekh, *Zivhe Tzedeq*, pt. 2 (Jerusalem, 1986/87), Sec. *Shu't Orah Hayyim*, no. 23, pp. 25-26.

[20] *Umi-Tzur Devash*, p. 23a.

[21] *Ta'alumot Leb*, 3, p. 59a.

[22] For photographs of such attire, see Stillman, *The Jews of Arab Lands in Modern Times*, illus. between pp. 420 and 421.

[23] *Umi-Tzur Devash*, p. 111b.

[24] Raphael Aaron b. Simeon, *Nehar Mitzrayim*, Alexandria, 1907/08, p. 118b.

[25] *Ta'alumot Leb*, 4, p. 45a.

[26] Peter Berger, *Pyramids of Sacrifice* (New York, 1976), p. 186.

[27] Judah Alkalai, *Kitbe ha-Rab Yehudah Alqalai*, 2 vols., ed. Isaac Werfel (Jerusalem, 1944), vol. 1, pp. 179-182 and 195-196.

[28] Ibid., vol. 2, p. 529.

[29] Ibid., vol. 2, p. 487.

[30] Israel Moses Hazzan, *Words of Peace and Truth* (London, 1845), pp. 13-14.

[31] Joseph Chetrit, "New Consciousness of Anomaly and Language: The Beginnings of a Movement of Hebrew Enlightenment in Morocco at the End of the Nineteenth Century," in *Miqqedem Umiyyam*, vol. 3, ed. Joseph Chetrit and Zvi Yehuda (Haifa, 1986), pp. 129-168 [Heb.]; Elqayim's poem is on p. 145.

[32] For examples of Khadduri's pronouncements on Zionism, see Stillman, *The Jews of Arab Lands in Modern Times*, pp. 102 and 386-389.

[33] Concerning R. Nahum's ambivalent relationship to Zionism, see Esther Benbassa, *Haim Nahum: A Sephardic Chief Rabbi in Politics, 1892-1923* (Tuscaloosa and London, 1995), pp. 14-27, 36-38, and passim; and Gudrun Krämer, *The Jews in Modern Egypt, 1914-1952* (Seattle, 1989), pp. 97, 163-164, 192, and 195.

[34] For a survey of these remnant communities, see Norman A. Stillman, "Fading Shadows of the Past: Jews in the Islamic World," in William Frankel, ed., *Survey of Jewish Affairs 1989* (Oxford, 1989), pp. 157-170.

[35] See Simon N. Herman, *Israelis and Jews: The Continuity of an Identity* (New York, 1970), p. 130, table 97.

[36] Concerning the Mimouna and the Sahrani, see Harvey E. Goldberg, "The Mimuna and the Minority Status of Moroccan Jews," in *Ethnology* 17:1 (1978), pp. 75-87, and J. Halper and H. Abramovitz, "The Saharanei Celebration in Kurdistan and Israel," in Shlomo Deshen and Moshe Shokeid, eds., *Jews of the Middle East: Anthropological Perspectives Past and Present* (Tel Aviv, 1984) [Heb.].

[37] Tom Sawicki, "Inside the World of Mystic Healers," in *The Jerusalem Report*, January 27, 1994, p. 14.

[38] See E. Ben-Ari and Y. Bilu, "Saints' Sanctuaries in Israeli Development Towns: On a Mechanism of Urban Transformation," in *Urban Anthropology* 16:2, 1987, pp. 243-272.

[39] Issachar Ben-Ami, "Le-Heqer Folklor ha-Milhama: Motiv ha-Qedoshim," in S. Werses, N. Rotenstreich, and C. Shmeruk, eds., *Sefer Dob Sadan* (Jerusalem, 1977), pp. 87-104.

[40] Pinhas Landau, "The Sephardi Revolution," in *The Jerusalem Post International Edition*, June 27, 1987, p. 11.

NORMAN A. STILLMAN

JUDAISM, HISTORY OF, PART VI: THE PRACTICE OF JUDAISM IN 21ST CENTURY U.S.A.: How does one write about the coming century when the future insists on writing itself, in its own good time, more often than not, taking us by surprise and confounding all our certitudes? And how does one write about "Judaism" in the coming century when there has never been just one form of Judaism or Jewish practice in the past, and when the potential for manifold varieties in the future is almost beyond comprehension? Beyond the usual problems associated with prophecy—or even educated prognosis—this proliferation of Judaisms makes it almost impossible to predict the future. Indeed, we know too little about the religious practices of most American Jews today to extrapolate with any certainty about what they will be doing in another generation. And beyond this, having recently experienced such wholly unexpected events as the collapse of the Soviet Union, the dismantling of the Berlin Wall, the AIDS epidemic, and even the American stock market's soaring averages, we know that our imaginations are not up to the task of making pronouncements about what might happen next year, never mind in the next century.

Yet even if taking twentieth century history as prophetic is risky, Jews ignore the recent past at their peril. And so, by first identifying the trends that have brought us to the end of the twentieth century, we can perhaps begin to imagine what, if we do nothing at all, will continue in the future. But identifying these trends is only a first step; the harder work is to distinguish among them: Which trends must be accommodated because they are already too entrenched or advanced to be stopped? Which are still within our power to reverse or change? Even if we have the potential to stop or reverse certain trends, do the Jews, as a people, have the collective will and the communal strength to change the course of their own history?

American Jews at the end of the twentieth century: In the 1990 National Jewish Population Survey (NJPS), 8.2 million people reported living in "Jewish households." However, only slightly more than two-thirds of these Americans (5.5 million) are part of the "core Jewish population," that is, Jews by birth and/or current identification. Of the 5.5 million, 4.2 million adults and children were born Jewish and currently identify themselves as Jews; 1.1 million people were born Jewish but do not currently identify with any religion; and 185,000 are converts to Judaism. The remaining 2.7 million includes 210,000 Jews who have converted to other religions, 415,000 people who had a Jewish parent but were raised in another faith, 700,000 children under eighteen with a Jewish parent but being raised in another religion, and 1.35 million adult gentiles.

In looking towards the next century, the first consequential statistic from the NJPS is that, in 1990, there were 270,000 children under the age of five born to intermarried parents and being raised as Jews. These children represented more than half (56%) of all Jewish children in that age group. Barry Kosmin, director of research for Council of Jewish Federations, projects that if there is a rise of 5% in the intermarriage rate in the 1990s (modest compared to the 1970s and 1980s), by the year 2000, fully two-thirds of all Jewish children under five will derive from mixed-marriages.

The second consequential statistic is that, as a result of intermarriage, more than two million gentiles—1.35 million adults and 700,000 children under eighteen who are not being raised as Jews—now live in "Jewish households." Half a million of the 3.1 million "Jewish households" in the 1990 survey did not include any person who was a core Jew. And only 25% of children in households with a parent who currently identifies as Jewish and a non-Jewish parent were being raised as Jews; 45% were being raised in another religion (or in both religions), and 30% were being raised without any religion.[1]

These numbers take on added significance when we realize that, between 1970 and 1990, the total number of core Jews increased by only 1.8%, while the total population in Jewish households increased by 40.2%. As a result, by 1990, the number of "traditional" Jewish families was quite small: only 14%

of Jewish families contained a married Jewish father and mother with children. And, with a 52% intermarriage rate among those marrying since 1985 (62% among Reform Jews), the number of mixed-married families and the percentage of Jewish children born to these marriages is certain to increase.

Denominational affiliation: The 1990 NJPS reported that Reform Judaism had, for the first time, replaced Conservative Judaism as the largest single denomination in the United States. In 1970, 42% of Jews identified as Conservative; 33% as Reform; and 11% as Orthodox. In 1990, 42% identified as Reform; 38% as Conservative; and 7% as Orthodox. In addition, about 30,000 Jews identified with the Reconstructionist movement; an annual growth rate of 8-10% perhaps makes Reconstructionism Judaism's fastest growing denomination. Alongside this change in proportions away from Conservative Judaism, it is important to note that the character of Conservativism has also changed. In recent decades, while the Orthodox became more religiously right wing, the non-Orthodox movements are increasingly religiously liberal.[2]

Jewish-American generations: As we enter the 21st century, demographers generally break the American population into four generations: (1) *The Builder Generation*, born before 1945; (2) *The Baby Boom Generation*, born between 1946 and 1964; (3) *The Baby Bust Generation*, born between 1965 and 1983; and (4) *The Baby Boomlet Generation*, born after 1983.[3] Each of these generations has singular and common characteristics with ramifications for the future of American Jewish life. But over the next three decades, the most influential by far will continue to be the Baby Boom generation, the largest age cohort in American history. From the rapid expansion of the public schools to accommodate them in the 1950s, to the Vietnam War protests in the 1960s and 1970s, to the Baby "Boomlet" of their own children in the 1980s and 1990s, this generation has affected virtually every aspect of American life. At the turn of the century, the Baby Boomers will be at the height of their power; in their forties and fifties, they will comprise nearly one-third of the population.

While the American Jewish population falls into the same generational categories as the general population, Lawrence Hoffman, co-director of the Synagogue 2000 project, has broken down the American Jewish experience from the mid-1800s through the present into a slightly different set of generations. The first two American Jewish generations—*The Founders* (primarily Sephardic immigrants from Germany) and *The Preservers of Peoplehood* (primarily Ashkenazic immigrants from Eastern Europe)—were the parents (in some cases the grandparents) of the *Post-War Suburban Generation*. Dedicated to two primary Jewish goals—remembering the Holocaust and providing their children with a Jewish education—the post-War generation built, but rarely attended, innumerable synagogues in the suburbs. With Sunday schools that were often larger than sanctuaries, these congregations so shifted the emphasis of Jewish life away from adult learning and worship that, according to Hoffman, a new type of "pediatric Judaism" was born: The parents themselves expressed their Jewishness largely through educating their children and involvement in Jewish communal life and charitable activities, not through religion.

The vast majority of the children of the post-War generation—the Baby Boomers—accordingly attended religious school for some period of time. But many were permanently "turned off" by the poor education they received there. Even so, this first American Jewish generation, shaped as much by secular and non-family events and influences as by ethnic, religious and familial influences, has, in its fourth and fifth decades, become a generation of *Spirituality Seekers*. Now parents themselves, these Jews seek a different religious purpose in Judaism. With denominational loyalty at an all-time low, the pressure to respond to the needs of these seekers (many of whom are intermarried) will continue to drive Judaism in the beginning of the next century. Projects like Synagogue 2000 accordingly attempt to meet this generation's demands for a more personal religion, for greater spirituality and meaning, for deeper connection to a community by rethinking and reshaping institutional Judaism along with Jewish prayers and services, social action, and, especially, through ongoing learning.

By the second decade of the twenty-first century, however, much of the weight of power will pass to the fifth Jewish-American generation—the *"Baby Bust" Generation*. Born in the wake of the Baby Boom, between 1965 and 1983, their influence will be felt well into the middle of the century. For several reasons, many believe that these Jews will pose even greater challenges to traditional religion than either their parents or their older siblings. Unlike the Baby Boomers, many of these Jews are being raised outside of organized Judaism; many did not attend religious school, go to Jewish summer camps, or celebrate becoming Bar or Bat Mitzvah.

As a group, the Baby Busters have largely been neglected, not only by the mass media and societal planners but often by their own families. More than half of their parents' marriages (many of them intermarriages) ended in divorce, causing large numbers to be brought up in single-parent (mostly female-headed) households or the "blended" families created by their parents' remarriages, which have the greatest likelihood of being intermarriages. The majority of these young people lived in households in which both parents worked or, in the case of single-headed households, the resident parent worked.

One consequence of this upbringing is that this generation tends to look largely to media (television, movies, music, computers) and peers for direction, value judgments, and comfort. In the main, they distrust authority figures, whether parents, teachers, elected officials, or members of the clergy. They do not, for the most part, read newspapers or books; almost unanimously, they report getting their information from television or friends. If their grandparents were the radio generation and their parents the TV generation, the "Baby Bust" is the multimedia-and-technology generation, the first generation to grow up entirely in the television era; the first generation to mature with VCR technology; the first generation to experience the multi-

channel capacity of cable and satellite television; and, now, the first generation to grow up with the Internet and the World Wide Web. Constant exposure to these technologies has had a huge impact, creating limited (advertising-affected) attention spans, fragmenting audiences, and blurring the lines between content and advertising. And, with the proliferation of options, this generation is the first to have the power to almost completely control the programming they receive, unlike their parents' generation, which had only three commercial network stations and, later, one public television station, to choose among.

One result is that this generation shares fewer common visual images than immediately preceding ones. In addition, the television-generated "myths" this generation shares are less about how families should live (e.g., *Ozzie and Harriet, Father Knows Best, Donna Reed*), and more about how young people do live (e.g., *Friends, Melrose Place*, music videos). Needless to say, with greater openness in society, the images they encounter are more graphic in terms of sex and violence than at any time in the recent past. Other factors also have had major effects. The combination of a volatile, often stagnant economy and the enormous cohort of Baby Boomers right ahead of them has made it difficult for the Baby Busters to break into the workplace and nearly impossible for them to advance once they do. Many therefore are forced to live at home for much longer periods of adulthood than recent generations. The generation's economic situation, along with a general distrust of marriage, is also leading to ever-later marriages and will, most likely, lead to the birth of even fewer children than their parents had.

All of these things will have an impact on religious practice in the next century. At least one clergyman says that to attract the Baby Bust generation, religious groups will have to be able to provide them with "parafamily" settings (e.g., small classes, *havurot*), personal attention, local causes in which they can become involved, significantly shorter, fully participatory services with contemporary music, short, entertaining dramas (rather than sermons or lectures), and, over all, greater choice. This suggests the emergence of larger institutions that can offer such a range of programs. He goes on to offer specific directions and advice for clergy interested in building "Buster-friendly churches," advising them play down titles and use first names, to replace "churchy sounding words," like *foyer, vestibule*, and *sanctuary*, with common terms like *lobby* and *auditorium*, to provide child-care facilities, to dress casually, to use music similar to what they listen to in their cars and homes, and to install equipment Busters expect, such as air-conditioning and computers.[4]

Religious practices: It is difficult to say with any degree of accuracy what current religious practices really are, because the most commonly used measures—types and frequency of ritual observance—do not give a complete picture of American Jewish life. Nonetheless, because they are easy to identify, relatively clear in their meaning, and enable researchers to compare practices over time, these measures continue to be used most frequently.

According to these measures, over the past two decades ritual observance among American Jews has simultaneously decreased and increased: the number of Jews observing kashrut and Shabbat has declined, but the number attending a Passover seder, lighting Chanukah candles, and fasting on Yom Kippur appears to be rising. And, while attendance at weekly synagogue services (never high to begin with) continues to decline, significant numbers of Baby Boomers—like the generations before them, even if not yet in the same numbers—have begun to join synagogues in order to obtain a Jewish education for their children.

It had been no secret that between the 1960s and 1980s, the majority of American Jews had become far more assimilated. Nonetheless, the 1990 National Jewish Population Study—which revealed an intermarriage rate of 52% and unprecedentedly low levels of Jewish observance and affiliation—caused shock waves throughout the Jewish community. Since the report's release, the community has responded to this "continuity crisis" with major new efforts to keep the

children of intermarried Jews Jewish, to keep young people involved in Judaism, to more deeply engage Jews of all ages and all denominations in a more vibrant Judaism, and to "reinvent" synagogues and other central Jewish institutions. But despite these efforts, a great deal of trepidation about the future remains.

Ironically, at the same time that most Jews have been moving away from any practice of Judaism, a new wave of interest in more intensive religious practice has emerged in every part of the denominational spectrum. Samuel Heilman attributes to these "actively Jewish Jews," among other things, the intensification of Jewish education, particularly with regard to day schools, vigorous advocacy on behalf of Israel and Soviet Jewry, unlocking Jewish opportunities for women, and new forms of worship, like *havurot* and healing services. Looking only at this group, Heilman says, one finds a tremendous recent growth in all aspects of Jewish activity, showing that "for some there is commitment *and* content in American Jewish identity."[5] The problem, of course, is in the numbers, since secular Jews and ethnically-connected Jews outnumber actively Jewish Jews by about three-to-one. The question for the future thus concerns "whether these few [actively Jewish Jews] can continue to exert such influence and define the character of American Judaism, and whether they can continue to be actively Jewish while the majority drifts away toward a peripheral involvement with Judaism."[6]

Organized Judaism seems to be reacting to the "continuity crisis" in several different, often seemingly contradictory, ways. While leaders of all denominations declare themselves greatly troubled by high rates of intermarriage, they also take heart in the religious resurgence. For example, a recent study of the Conservative movement in America found that a "vibrant, living and continuity-minded Judaism" is "alive and kicking" throughout the United States—at least within Conservative synagogues. That study—the largest ever undertaken of a Jewish religious group in North America—reported that Conservative synagogues are "attracting a narrower but more intensely involved population of Jews who have far less ambivalence about Conservative Judaism than earlier members." The identification of a population of young Conservative Jews that is better educated and more actively involved than ever before—even if a high percentage of them does not consider kashrut or marrying a Jew important—gives the study's author reason for "sober optimism."[7]

The other three Jewish denominations—Reform, Orthodox, and Reconstructionist—as well as the Jewish Renewal movement have all recently issued equally optimistic statements about the future of their own movements and institutions, perhaps to counter the community-wide crisis mentality evoked by the recent statistics, perhaps also to reassure themselves. For example, Arthur Waskow, a leading figure in the Jewish Renewal movement, who was ordained a rabbi in 1995 by a committee made up of rabbis from the Hasidic, Reform, and Conservative movements and a feminist theologian, recently posted on the Internet a letter stating that the Renewal movement has "liberated new creativities in the Jewish people." He wrote:

> There are literally tens of thousands of people now living the kinds of Jewish life-practice that only a few dozen people were living just 25 years ago (Jewish meditation, new prayer language, dance as prayer, Rosh Hodesh, baby-girl covenantings, gay marriages, self-directed Pesach seders, adult bar/bat mitzvah, locally created prayerbooks, drushodrama (bibliodrama) for Torah study, new songs in new musical modes, an explosion of graphic arts, tallitot in color, etc. etc.).

In a speech to the Jewish Press Association (June, 1995), Eric Yoffie, the new president of Reform's Union of American Hebrew Congregations (UAHC), similarly suggested that, "The story of the American Jewish community is a story not of failure but of triumph," marked by grassroots interest in religious experience, study, and worship, to which the Reform movement, "the most optimistic of the religious movements, responds with hope and faith in the future."

In light of the recent shifts in the Jewish community, commentators have suggested

the need for more valid and meaningful yardsticks to measure the extent and depth of Jewish religious life. Such rethinking, however, poses problems. A significant issue is that most Jews continue to judge their *own* degree of connection to Judaism by using traditional measures of religious practice, especially going to worship services and observing kashrut. Indeed, it is increasingly the case that American Jews are so poorly educated about Judaism that they do not even know that there are Jewish practices other than these two. When considering taking religious practice more seriously in defining who is a Jew, some leaders fear that a more accurate definition might count out of the community many who now identify with but do not practice Judaism. On the other side, some worry that new definitions that reflect actual current practices would ratify those practices as "officially Jewish" and would so dilute the meaning of being a Jew that survey results would be even less useful than they are now.

Yet most keep coming back to the idea of new measures because they recognize that what is *not* now being measured may be more important and illuminating than what is. Social anthropologist Riv-Ellen Prell has noted, for example, that while social structuralists have discerned a difference in behavior among Jews over the past decades, because of the limitations of their methods, they have been unable to explain the significance of that behavior. In her words, "We do not know how Judaism is created in religious settings as opposed to nonreligious settings, such as secular philanthropic groups. In short, until recently, social scientists concerned with American Judaism have not asked how Jews are made Jews and why Jews remain Jews."[8]

What would we discover, she and others wonder, if we began to ask what attending a seder means to American Jews (is it just a family dinner or is it Jewishly meaningful?); what denominational identification means to them and how they choose it; how intermarried Jews—and their spouses—see themselves in relation to the Jewish community; what factors determine how intermarried raise their children; how the children of intermarried couples see themselves in relation to the Jewish community; how many American Jews are or would like to be engaged in the regular study of Torah, Talmud, or other Jewish texts; how many American Jews are engaged in social action and volunteer activity that they believe expresses their Jewishness; how many American Jews have incorporated practices learned from other faiths (e.g., meditation) into their own worship; how many have had a transformative religious experience, as a Jew or otherwise.

Significant trends in American society: The answers to questions such as these, so important in defining the future of Judaism in the U.S.A., are shaped by trends and societal shifts already underway and having profound effects on American Jews. The following reports on such central trends.

With the exception of some Orthodox Jews who have chosen to live apart, Jews have become more assimilated into American life over the past three decades than at any time in history. One reason is Jews' growing distance from the immigrant experience: nine out of ten American Jews were born in the U.S.A., and more than half have no foreign-born grandparents. Another reason is the Jewish community's greater social and geographic mobility as social and professional barriers have fallen and younger generations have moved away from their own families and out of Jewish neighborhoods.

Greater tolerance and access in American society have been enormously positive for American Jews, opening up a range of new educational, social, and vocational opportunities. Yet many also note these developments' negative impact on American Judaism. The most hotly-discussed consequence of greater openness is a much higher rate of intermarriage over the past decades. This is ironic: The higher rate of intermarriage is due, in large measure, to American Jews' being accepted, as Jews, in an increasingly open society. Greater interaction between Jews and non-Jews—in schools and neighborhoods, in social and business settings—has led to closer relationships of all kinds, with more Jews and gentiles than ever before seeing members of the other group as desirable marriage partners.

A second, not unmixed, result of greater tolerance is that levels of denominational loyalty have plummeted for all Americans, Christians as well as Jews. Most Americans now tell pollsters that they believe "all religions are good" and that "none is better than any other." In an era in which the two fastest growing political parties are "independent" and "absent from the polls," it should come as no surprise that religious affiliation too is no longer a given, no longer determined solely by the religion of one's parents. Yet many believe that the pendulum has swung too far when younger people overwhelmingly believe that everyone is free to choose a religion and equally free to choose again should something more attractive come along.

Finally, the tolerance and openness of the past three decades have led to an extraordinary proliferation of different family forms and an unprecedented acceptance of those following openly "alternative lifestyles"— gays and lesbians, single mothers, divorced parents. Yet even in an era in which the typical family of the 1950s—father in the workplace, mother at home, two children—is obsolete and the vast majority of Americans support individuals' right to live as they choose, polls consistently show that most do not see this as an entirely positive trend. While some religions have welcomed new family structures and others have not, *all* religions are forced by these profound changes to reexamine traditional doctrines on such issues as divorce, sexual orientation, and abortion.

Higher levels of education; adult education: The Baby Boomers are the most educated generation in American history. Twice as many went to college as their parents, three times as many as their grandparents, and their own children are following their lead.

Higher education has always been a broadening experience. But colleges and universities of the 1960s and 1970s exposed this generation to an unprecedented variety of ideas, people, and influences. Because of their huge numbers, just living and interacting with others on campus had an impact, opening students' eyes to diverse ways of living and believing and often showing them that "religious truth is itself something that is deeply personal and deemed by many as more relative than absolute." Along with opening the Baby Boomers up to new sexual and lifestyle choices, higher education was a context in which "[t]he so-called 'new religions'—Zen Buddhism, Meher Baba, Transcendental Meditation, and many others—also flourished, introducing students to Eastern spirituality."[9]

College was especially important in shaping Jewish Baby Boomers' futures: higher rates of university attendance, often at schools far away from home, and far greater social acceptability in those collegiate settings, inexorably led Jews to much closer relationships with non-Jews than their parents had. For the first time, intermarriage seemed possible to many young American Jews. Too, a new level of access to graduate and professional schools, and later to the professions and the corporate world, offered them a wide range of community identities. They simply did not have the same need their parents had to join Jewish, as opposed to secular, communal organizations.

The women of the Baby Boom generation were the first women to be educated at the same high levels as their brothers. Armed with degrees (often advanced degrees), they entered the work world in record numbers. The development of the first reliable and widely available birth control products also made them the first women in history able easily to control the timing of their families. These women have stayed in the labor force in record numbers, even after having children. One highly significant effect of this has been the disappearance of the backbone of communal life: the corps of women volunteers on which so many organizations, including religious ones, have depended for generations.

These trends' overall impact on religion should be clear. In every generation, education has been the best single predictor for a range of attitudes and values, such as racial tolerance, antisemitism, egalitarian roles, al-

ternative lifestyles, tolerance of nonconformity of all kinds, and adherence to traditional religious beliefs and practices. The same has held true for Baby Boomers, with the one exception of religious beliefs and practices. During the 1960s and 1970s, levels of religious belief, of worship attendance, and of participation in organized religion declined dramatically among all Baby Boomers, but the better educated dropped out of religion in much higher numbers than those with less education.[10]

Wade Clark Roof attributes this shift primarily to the emergence of new and more secular meaning systems. Generated by scholars and absorbed by Baby Boomers in colleges across the country, these alternative ways of looking at the world competed with theistic interpretations of the nature of reality. For instance, social scientific modes of explanation, which emphasize the role of social forces in shaping people's lives, gained ascendancy, somewhat replacing theories of God. "American-style individualism" also emerged as an alternative system of meaning, a system that holds an individual, rather than God or social forces, responsible for his or her own destiny. For many Baby Boomers, willpower and determination thus became the critical factors shaping a person's life and success.

Many have thus seen in the Baby Boomers a "generation of seekers," who ask questions "about the meaning of their lives, about what they want for themselves and their children" rather than simply adopting "the meanings and values handed down by our parents' religion, our ethnic heritage, our nationality."[11] In a similar vein, a recent article in *Publishers Weekly* described "the vigor of religion book sales," up 26.6% in the first three quarters of 1996 compared with a decrease of 7.7% in adult hardcovers overall. The author explains this as resulting from the decreased acceptance of the traditional religions of church and synagogue and the increased desire "to be affiliated on our own terms—accepting some teachings, rejecting others and frequently making our own decisions about ethical issues and spiritual practices."[12] This same spiritual quest is clearly followed by Jews of the Baby Boom generation.[13]

The rise of the religious right: Until quite recently, the rise of the religious right and the reversion to fundamentalism in the United States were entirely Christian phenomena. If Judaism and Jews were involved at all, it was as the enemy, since the vast majority of Jews were steadfast in their support for the continued separation of church and state and other key issues on the religious right's agenda. Over the past few years, however, right-wing Christians and right-wing Jews have found common cause, regularly joining together politically on a host of positions, from prohibiting abortion to ending church-state separation. To the degree these alliances continue, to the degree that religions continue to be split by political divisions, both liberals and conservatives will find that "the people with whom [they] share their values are not the people who are necessarily Jewish; while the ethnic or religious community that they have inherited is not the group with whom they count on sharing their deepest commitments."[14]

It bears noting, however, that this trend may not actually have much relevance to American Jewish life in the twenty-first century. Political activism coupled with very visible and aggressive outreach by the Orthodox to younger Jews has led many to believe that Orthodoxy has grown over the past generation and will continue to grow in the next. In fact, statistics show that Orthodoxy has not grown, but declined, in the U.S. Despite a somewhat higher Orthodox birthrate, the NJPS reports some shrinkage over the past two decades, from 11% of the American Jewish population to 7%. Similarly, while the younger generation of the Orthodox seems to maintain a higher allegiance to Orthodoxy than previous American generations, nearly all of those who have become Orthodox in recent years have done so because they married someone who is Orthodox.

The search for meaning and community: Prior generations resolved the need for community by becoming part of an ongoing religious group. As Baby Boomers continue this search, they confront their deep and abiding distrust of institutions, particularly ma-

jor, traditional ones, such as government and organized religion. This trait has and will continue to stand in the way of this generation's actually finding "community," just as it will affect the development of Jewish institutions in the twenty-first century.

The role of women: At the end of the twentieth century, women are reaching higher levels of education than ever before, entering and advancing in the labor force in record numbers, controlling the timing of childbearing, and deciding elections with their votes. In Jewish American life, women's roles have also changed dramatically. For example, over the past twenty-five years, the Reform, Conservative, and Reconstructionist movements all have begun to ordain women rabbis, and, in 1997, fully half of all Rabbinic students were women.

Not only the new roles women are assuming but also the ones they are leaving behind will have a major impact on Jewish life. For instance, as women—traditionally the moving force in bring families to services and determining which holidays they celebrate— have gone to work outside the home, they may be paying less attention to religious practice and attending synagogue less frequently. In addition, as noted above, the availability of women to volunteer has declined.

At the same time, a tremendous growth has resulted from the push for equality, bringing women to study groups and classes, to adult Bat Mitzvah, to the celebration of such women's life-cycle events as the once unknown ceremonies of *Shalom Bat* (welcoming a new-born daughter) and *Rosh Hodesh* (the festival of the New Moon), and to the creation of a growing body of scholarly, liturgical, and ritual works by and for Jewish women.

New economic realities: New economic realities have created much greater differentials of wealth than at any time in history, and many more families require two incomes. This means there is generally less family time, less leisure time, less time for volunteer activities, less time for religious study and worship. Even the upcoming intergenerational transference of unprecedented wealth may not help the Jewish community as a community. The $8 trillion expected to pass to the Baby Boomers over the next few decades will place in their hands the means for supporting the infrastructure of Jewish life: schools, organizations, and synagogues. But their greater assimilation and looser con-nections to organized religious life mean that funding for many of the institutions that underpin Judaism may well be reduced.

Social and geographic mobility: At the turn of the century, most extended Jewish families either lived together or within walking distance of one another. Once people settled in a place, they rarely left, often staying for generations. But in the postwar period, these patterns have changed dramatically. Extended families rarely live together now, and while Jews are still heavily concentrated in the Northeast (43.6%), they have begun to mirror mainstream America's shift to the Sunbelt regions, with nearly half of American Jews (45.1%) now living in the South and the West.

Because Jews in the Northeast have traditionally clustered in and outside of major cities, substantial Jewish communities still exist in this part of the country. In the south and West, however, Jews tend to be far more dispersed, with only a few major urban population centers. As a result, although there are more Jews living in these regions, Jewish life has not developed in the same way as in the Northeast: there are fewer synagogues, fewer communal organizations, fewer cultural and educational opportunities, and fewer potential marriage partners, which has led to higher rates of intermarriage than in more settled and populous Jewish communities.

The Jewish Baby Boomers, with their high levels of education and professional occupations, coupled with the growing freedom of choice about where to live, have increasingly moved away from their parents and out of areas of Jewish concentration. Working for others (rather than the more traditional Jewish self-employment) has meant transfers, weakening ties to Jewish communities and increasing opportunities for interaction with non-Jews in the workplace.

Growth in media and technology: Over the past two generations, Americans have changed their primary means of acquiring and sharing information at least three times: from books and newspapers to radio, from radio to television, and, finally, from television to computers. These new and pervasive media have had incalculable effects on society, ranging from the introduction of the notion of a shared, visual idiom—and the perception of common experience it engenders—to the plethora of information now available virtually instantaneously in one's home.

The Baby Boomers in particular watched history unfold in their living rooms. While the news—the assassination of President John F. Kennedy, the Vietnam War—simultaneously raised and dashed their hopes and expectations for the future, advertising taught them how to consume, and entertainment programming showed them how to live. Instancy and immediacy, the distinguishing features of television, became the way that Baby Boomers experience the world. For them, seeing, not reading, became the basis for believing, with all the implications this has for traditional religion and its intergenerational transmission.

American Jews tend to own more television sets, more VCRs, and more personal computers, on average, than the general population, reflecting both their affluence and their higher levels of education. And just as hundreds, perhaps thousands, of feature films, documentaries, and television programs with Jewish content have been created over the past decades, today efforts are underway to create Jewish-specific material for both old and new technologies, ranging from computer data bases to the Jewish Television Network, which weekly provides television stations around the country with blocks of programming on Jewish subjects, to more than five thousand Jewish Web sites, news groups, and Internet services, providing entertainment, information, and education to millions of people around the world. These new technologies certainly will lead to important changes in how people learn about, and make choices concerning, religious practice.

The future of American Jews and Judaism: Based on the information presented so far, a number of prognoses can be drawn regarding Judaism in the U.S.A. in the twenty-first century.

- In the next century, as a result of continued societal tolerance for difference and full access to all aspects of society, American Jews will become ever more assimilated.
- Already high rates of intermarriage will increase to as much as 70% in the 21st century.[15]
- Few of the grandchildren of those who intermarried in the last four decades of this century will be Jewish, since nine out of ten children of intermarriage marry gentiles, and only 5-10% of them raise their own children as Jews.
- While the Jewish population will decline, a growing number of Americans will have some familial connection to Judaism or will themselves be "partly Jewish." Even a generation later, over a third of the children of intermarriage celebrate Passover, and nearly a quarter celebrate Rosh Hashanah.
- American Jews will continue to view religious affiliation as optional, a matter not of birth or inheritance but of individual choice.
- Despite many efforts by organized Judaism, commitment to religious Judaism and affiliation with synagogues and Jewish organizations will not increase substantially, at least in the first part of the next century. Although some Baby Boomers will come late to organized religion, their participation will be balanced by the Boomers who cease to be members of synagogues when their children leave home.[16]
- The Baby Boom generation will continue its lifelong search for authenticity, celebration, and spiritual growth, but mostly outside of organized religion. A great many claim to be seeking a religion that provides structure and meaning to their lives, enables them to pass on values to their children, and takes significant action in the world. But most will continue looking to religion for "peak experiences," moments of transcendence or epiphany, and will not find this in Judaism or any other organized religion.
- Even when Boomers "return" to organized religion, they will continue in record numbers to switch into and out of religious denominations and to move across religions, showing low levels of loyalty to traditions, institutions, and brand names of all kinds. Choice in matters of faith and practice will continue to be taken for granted.
- The trend towards the "privatization of faith" will continue. Even those who belong to and participate in congregations will continue to "make religion personal," picking and choosing among not only Jewish practices and teachings but identifying and using other religions' traditions and practices to enhance their religious experiences.
- Unless major efforts are made to rethink and revitalize Jewish education, American Jews are likely to know even less than today about Judaism. Results similar to those of Steven Cohen's 1989 survey of American Jews, in which two-thirds of respondents thought that the most essential element of being "a good Jew" was "to lead an ethical and moral life," will continue to be seen.
- As their parents' generation dies out, there may be a concomitant drop in even the minimal levels of ritual observance now practiced by many in the younger generations. Without the older generation, many will find that they do not, on their own, have enough knowledge to lead a Passover seder, enough will to secure tickets to High Holiday services, or enough interest to light Chanukah candles.
- Despite all of this, the number of people identifying themselves as "Jewish" may not decline during the first part of the twenty-first century, since "identifying" is no longer correlated with "practicing" or even simply "affiliating" with Judaism as a religion. Like today, most Jews in America will define Jews as a "cultural group" (70%) or "ethnic group" (57%), rather than a purely religious group (49%). Almost all (96% today) will claim to be "proud to be a Jew," and nearly as many (90%) will believe a Jew can be "religious" even if he or she is not very observant.
- Affiliation with traditional religions, including Judaism, may begin to increase at the end of the second decade of the twenty-first century, as significant numbers of Baby Boomers reach older age. Up until now, they have not returned to traditional religion in the expected numbers, despite the expected "return factors"—getting married, settling into a community, and, most important, having children.[17] History, however, suggests one more moment when the Boomers may turn to religion, when they begin to confront their own mortality. It is also possible that more Baby Busters—who have fewer anti-institutional biases than their parents and older siblings—will join synagogues as they have children.

American Jewish religious institutions in the 21st century: At least partially in recognition of the ambivalent prognoses for American *Jews*, a revitalization already is underway in American Jewish religious *institutions*. The synagogue is already in the process of "reinventing" itself, Jewish education is being reconceptualized and strengthened, and nearly all religious institutions are adding special programs to meet the distinctive needs of the Baby Boom generation: *havurot*, women's study groups, family education courses, Jewish film festivals, social action workshops, and weekend-retreats on spirituality. Such developments are important, as studies already show that Jews choose synagogues on the basis of the following criteria. After denominational affiliation (58%), the most important factors are "a warm and friendly atmosphere" (46%), "the rabbi's personality/style/knowledge" (45%), "the quality of children's Jewish education" (43%), and "types of prayer services" (36%).[18] This points to several likely institutional developments in the twenty-first century:

- Education—for all age groups—will be taken seriously and become the primary focus for Jewish institutional activity. Even today, families say that the main reason they join synagogues is to educate their children Jewishly, and surveys show that $1 billion is spent annually on Jewish education in the United States. At the same time, however, for many, attendance is short-lived and sporadic. While the number of children enrolled in Jewish day schools has been increasing, the number in supplementary school programs has been decreasing, and only about 40% of Jewish children are currently enrolled in any Jewish school. In response, synagogues and other Jewish organizations have not only instituted a wide range of new curricular improvement and teacher training programs but have begun to return their attention to those who have always been Judaism's primary audience—adults.
- As part of this shift to education for adults, intensive family education programs will be put in place, both to provide remedial education to parents and to begin to move the center of gravity of Jewish learning and practice from the synagogue back to the home.
- There will be a new and stronger focus

on teachers. More than forty years ago, Abraham Joshua Heschel wrote: "What we need more than anything else is not textbooks but textpeople." In the twenty-first century, one of the primary focuses for Jewish institutions will be teachers: teacher training, teacher recruitment, higher salaries and better conditions, enhancement of Jewish teaching as a profession.
- In the next century, with the emphasis on a return to learning, there will be major efforts throughout the community to develop and implement new and expanded educational programs, focusing on life-long learning in all sectors of the community, including the home, and not only in formal school settings.[19]
- Educational programming for young people, both elementary school students and those who are post-Bar and Bat Mitzvah, will expand. The disaffection with Sunday schools and Hebrew schools experienced by many Baby Boomers has etched itself on the psyche of the American Jewish community, explaining the steady decline in numbers of students in after-school programs since the 1960s. Over the next decades, the now-familiar after-school and Sunday morning programs will gradually be displaced by new types of programming, including first-rate courses in Hebrew (both Biblical and modern), performing arts, community service, participation in mixed-age learning circles, and family education programs. Youth programs, summer camps, and Israel trips will all be expanded.
- The number of day schools that are competitive with the best secular schools will increase. Over the past quarter-century, the number of students attending full-time Jewish day schools has tripled. Of the approximately one million American Jewish children between the ages of two and eighteen, just under one-fifth, about 182,000 students, are enrolled in 636 schools. While more than three out of four of these students are in Orthodox institutions, the number of students in Conservative, Reform, and transdenominational schools has been growing rapidly.
- Despite the seemingly widespread enthusiasm for day schools, non-Orthodox day schools will continue to be clustered in major population centers, as the high costs of opening such schools, maintaining them over time, and paying tuition ($7,000-10,000 a year, on average), will continue to make them prohibitive for most communities and many families across the country.[20]

- Jewish pre-schools will continue to be extremely popular. Over the past decade, Jewish pre-schools have become the growth industry in Jewish education. The challenge for the next century will be to maintain parents' and children's involvement in the Jewish community after children move on to elementary school by providing families with a wide range of meaningful options for ongoing participation in Jewish learning and communal life.

- New technologies will be one key to Jewish education's success, just as they already have caught the imagination of the youngest generations. Technologies that allow a rich involvement with Judaism without leaving home have begun to be used by Jews in remote areas of the country, by Jews with limited time to study, and by Jews interested in finding out about Judaism but not ready to take the step of enrolling in a class at a local synagogue. In the twenty-first century, as the content begins to match the sophistication of the hardware, most of America—including most of the Jewish community—will be caught up in the technology revolution.

- In the next century, computer, satellite, and digital technologies will open up the possibilities for an entirely new relationship between American Jews and Jews in other parts of the world, especially in Israel. Not only will Jews from all over the world be able to access the same materials, they will be able to "speak" to one another across the Internet—by typing now but eventually by voice. This computer connection with Israel will be particularly important as the financial connection between American Jews and Israel changes and the community's leaders look for alternative ways to maintain, even strengthen, the overall relationship. finding new connections is not easy: In 1990, only a quarter (26.2%) of American Jews said they had visited Israel, and many of them had not been in decades. And because Americans now get most of their information from television, what they know of Israel comes mainly from disturbing reports on the nightly news. As a result, growing numbers are pinning their hopes on the Internet.

- To date, the most controversial uses of the Internet have been for prayer and religious ceremonies, and the debate will continue. For example, several well-attended "cyberseders" have been hosted on-line, primarily for college students away from home. But the questions abound: Does the "virtual community" of cyberspace bear any relationship to the kinds of "community" that have been the basis of Jewish life for thousands of years? Assuming that, for important reasons, Jewish law mandates a minyan, should Judaism approve of a minyan by computer?

- Despite the new technology, to the degree that any institution will be central to Jewish life, it will remain the synagogue. If a widespread revitalization of Jewish life depends on a return to Torah and a new emphasis on education, most believe that the only Jewish institution capable of sustaining such serious programs is the synagogue. Still, to survive, much about the synagogue will change. In addition to changes in Jewish education, synagogues are revising liturgy, broadening the uses of synagogue space, rethinking the role of rabbis and other professionals, and adding new kinds of music to services. Most synagogues have already begun to offer adult and family education programs and smaller, more participatory "alternative" services. Alongside traditional programs, synagogues are enhancing social action programs, focusing more on "spirituality," adding healing services, meditation sessions, women's prayer and study groups, addiction and recovery programs, and interfaith discussions.

- As the trends intensify towards personalized religion and full participation by congregation members in services and other activities, synagogues may become umbrella organizations, primarily offering shelter to numerous and varied smaller groups, in which the younger generations generally will seek and find community. In the next century, most affiliated Jews will become part of small groups within large congregations, with a person's "community" changing over time as his or her interests change.

- Larger synagogues will necessarily become the norm, since only large congregations will be able to offer a wide enough range of programming to families and adults. The downside of this trend is that it may mean that virtually every congregation, or even every member of every congregation, will have a slightly different "take" on Judaism. This would make it difficult for synagogues to act as the voice of Jewish authority in their own members' lives and virtually impossible to organize and run meaningful community-wide programs, trends possibly devastating to Judaism over time.

- A major question, particularly for Reform and transdenominational institutions, will be how to keep institutions Jewish when their members increasingly are not. One emerging solution is to create congregations specifically for intermarried couples, as a group of Reform Jews has done in Nashville. As one congregation member said, "The real goal is to raise our grandchildren as Jews. But if you exclude one partner in a marriage, you exclude them both, and their children."[21]

- Synagogues and institutions hoping to attract the younger generations must be fully committed to the full participation of women in every aspect of Jewish life and must be able to demonstrate that commitment through actions.[22] Significantly, as Lawrence Hoffman notes, the inclusion of women in Jewish life has created "a wave of internal immigration" and "more than doubled the ranks of the pool from which to select the leaders who will determine the destiny of the Jewish People."[23]

- Heightened attention to education cannot replace Judaism's focus on and commitment to social action. As Leonard Fein writes, "the pursuit of social justice has been understood as very near the heart of the matter. Study after study finds that Jews regard their commitment to social justice as even more essential an aspect of their Jewish expression than prayer, mastery of Hebrew, or regular synagogue attendance."[24]

- Nonetheless, two things must change in how American Judaism approaches social action. First, social action must be an integral element in the life of the whole community. Otherwise, young people will soon conclude that these activities bear little or no relevance to the real world of adults. Second, while the Hebrew phrase *tiqqun olam*—"correcting the world"—has become ubiquitous, most Jews today have almost no understanding of the texts and teachings from which the activities in which they are engaged arise. These connections must be consciously made through study, or the next generations will have even less of an idea of what is uniquely Jewish in these activities. Without those connections, these activities will probably have no significance for Jewish identity and continuity.

The American Jewish community in the 21st century: Overall, the interplay of two contrary trends will shape the Jewish community of the twenty-first century: 1) the resurgence of interest in a religious and spiritual connection will pull Jews (and others) toward Judaism, even as 2) rising rates of intermarriage may push them away. Although many wish for a decline in intermarriage, no one writing about American Jews today actually expects this to occur. The best case scenario suggests a plateauing of intermarriage at current levels (about 50%); the worst case posits an intermarriage rate that in the year 2000 hits 70% and keeps rising. Importantly, while intermarriage has increased substantially over the past decades, the percentage of marriage partners converting to Judaism has declined. In the 1950s and 1960s, about 40% of gentiles who married Jews converted before marriage. Today, only about 10% do so, although some convert after marriage, and others live as Jews without converting.[25]

At the same time, the resurgent interest in spirituality shows no sign of abating. For some families, these needs will readily be met by traditional forms of Judaism. For others—among them, those living in mixed-marriage households, those who seek transcendence through meditation and other Eastern practices, feminists, gays and lesbians, and others who still feel left out of many aspects of traditional religion—Judaism as it is today will not suffice. In the twenty-first century, either Judaism will change to meet the needs of new generations of spiritual seekers, or these people will look elsewhere.

Depending on how these issues are resolved, the Jewish community of the twenty-first century may look very different from today. On the one side, Judaism may become even more inclusive, with a spectrum of practices that runs from Orthodox to entirely new forms that incorporate the practices of other faiths and organizations (such as meditation and 12-step programs). Should this happen, many Jews will, of course, maintain that these new forms of practice are not Judaism at all. Alternatively, Judaism could become a much smaller but more religiously Jewish, more observant community. A third possibility is that significant change won't come in the first part of the next century at all but will take several generations to develop. Given how slow real change is, this is surely the likeliest possibility of the three.

Some, though, see a much greater coming upheaval, with American Judaism fragmenting, perhaps into a new form of Reform and

Reconstructionist Judaism that would become the home of the intermarried; perhaps in a merger of Conservative and Orthodox Judaism, with Conservative Judaism becoming the liberal wing of traditional Judaism; perhaps with all four denominations seeking to become independent of one another.

How might this happen? Today, Reform and Reconstructionist congregations are the only ones actively welcoming intermarried families, allowing the entire family, including the non-Jewish spouse, to become synagogue members.[26] In many Reform and Reconstructionist congregations, gentiles thus are allowed to, and increasingly do, sit on decision-making boards. Over time, many are certain, the high ratio of gentiles to Jews will inevitably and dramatically change these movements in particular and Judaism in general, with "the boundary between what is strictly or legitimately Jewish and what is not" becoming fuzzy or being lost entirely and the creation of families that easily move "between Christmas dinner at one set of grandparents and Passover seder at the other."[27]

While, as many have noted, there has never been just one Judaism, especially in the modern era, and while there is unlikely to be a fragmenting of Judaism in the short-term, in light of current trends, it is certainly conceivable that a major denominational split could occur during the next century. As the memberships of Reform and Reconstructionist congregations come to be made up more and more of interfaith families, the balance could shift: there might be as many gentiles as Jews in many congregations, with many of the Jews, themselves the progeny of intermarried couples, poorly educated (if educated at all) in Jewish traditions and teachings. At that point, it is not impossible that the religious content of synagogues—the liturgy, the teachings—could begin to change. Should that happen, these forms of "Judaism" will cease to be recognizable to more traditional Jews as Judaism, and a split would surely occur. Most important, as rates of intermarriage continue to increase, controversies—both within and between denominations—will arise about who is a Jew and whether limited resources should be used to support the actively Jewish minority or to reach out to the unaffiliated and intermarried majority.

For most Americans, intermarriage is a given. So long as America is an open society, no religious group will be safe from rising intermarriage. Indeed, not even the groups that have chosen largely to remove themselves from the temptations of American secular life have escaped unscathed. Already one study has shown that even the preponderantly, although not exclusively, Orthodox Jews who received a day school education in the 1970s and 1980s had an intermarriage rate of 43% for males and 22% for females.[28] And it is clear that for most American Jews, the discussion is over, despite the anguished outpourings about "Jewish continuity," despite the declarations that intermarriage is a "mortal threat" and a "spiritual Holocaust," despite the continuing task forces, studies, and conferences. For while most American Jews indicate that they are against intermarriage, this is true only in the abstract. When the intermarriage in question involves their own child, they tend to be much more accepting.

Even the communities' leaders seem to differentiate between what's right for "the community" and what's acceptable for their own children. A 1990 survey conducted by the Jewish Outreach Institute, which promotes Jewish continuity among interfaith families, asked 2,100 rabbis, Jewish federation heads, and other community professionals whether they would welcome a gentile son- or daughter-in-law into their homes to celebrate Jewish holidays. Well over 90% of all Reform and Conservative leaders, including rabbis, said yes, as did a majority of Orthodox lay leaders and a third of the Orthodox rabbis surveyed. This attitude is not surprising considering that 71% of respondents preferred that their children intermarry rather than not marry at all.[29]

Still, segments of the Jewish community are far from accepting intermarriage's inevitable consequences. The intra-denominational controversy over "Who is a Jew?"—with regard to both conversions by non-Orthodox rabbis and the Reform and Reconstructionist movements' controversial decision to recognize patrilineal as well as matrilineal descent—has been particularly bitter. More than a decade ago, Rabbi Irving Greenberg warned that by the turn of the century, there will be perhaps as many as half a million children accepted as Jewish by Reform and Reconstructionist congregations but not by the Conservative and Orthodox movements.[30] Picking up on this, Jack Wertheimer notes that "within a generation, there will be rabbis of patrilineal descent who will not be recognized *as Jewish* by Orthodox and Conservative rabbis." While it is still too early, Wertheimer continues, to tell whether this issue will "lead to further polarization or redouble efforts toward greater religious unity," the divisions over Jewish identity are not going to disappear.[31]

A second conflict, resulting from the growing political divisions in American life in general, will likely exacerbate the issue of who, or what, is a Jew. In the twenty-first century, within nearly every American religious group, ever-widening divisions between liberals and conservatives will emerge, with the Jews as no exception. Importantly, over the past decades, Americans have come to see themselves not primarily as Lutherans, Catholics, or Jews, but as liberals or conservatives. Alliances are now forged with like-minded people *across* religious lines, and "[o]n the left and on the right, Jews have thus reached the point where the people with whom they share their values are not the people who are necessarily Jewish; while the ethnic or religious community that they have inherited is not the group with whom they count on sharing their deepest commitments."[32] So the challenge of uniting American Judaism's socially and religiously diverse community will be exacerbated by the significant political diversity inside the Jewish community.

Possibilities for the American Jewish future: Earlier in this century, Rabbi Abraham Joshua Heschel wrote: "We are either the last, the dying Jews or else we are those who will give new life to our tradition. Rarely in our history has so much been dependent on one generation." Perhaps each generation believes it stands at the critical moment in Jewish history. But it is certainly true that today, on the threshold of the twenty-first century, American Jews once again see themselves as in crisis. And different this time is that nobody seems able to agree on which are the threats and which the opportunities.

To some, everything seems threatening. Even long-sought, finally-attained aspirations—such as unlimited access to and complete acceptance by the greater society—appear now to undermine Jewish continuity. For example, Rabbi Arthur Hertzberg, one of America's eminent social historians, is of the view that without dramatic changes in Judaism, acculturation and intermarriage will continue apace, and "American Jewish history will soon end, and become a part of American memory as a whole." Many others agree.[33]

On the other hand, some members of the community view everything—even higher rates of intermarriage and lower rates of observance, which throughout Jewish history have been seen as threats—as opportunities, for, these "transformationists" say, they force Jews and Judaism to "reimagine" the future and "reinvent" themselves, to find new and better ways to both reach out to and educate the younger, post-modern generations—whether they were born Jews or not. In the end, they say, Judaism will not only survive, it will emerge a stronger and far more vibrant faith.[34]

Is there any way now to tell who's right? Probably not. There are so many different, often competing, trends at work in the lives of American Jews today that one can spin out any number of equally plausible scenarios.

At the same time, nearly everybody seems to agree that, like the false reports of Mark Twain's death, the reports of Judaism's imminent demise are greatly exaggerated. Although there continues to be considerable alarm throughout the American community, it is hard to find anybody who believes that Judaism will actually disappear during the twenty-first century. Instead, the key question has now become: What will Judaism in America look like by the beginning of the twenty-second century?

Many forms of Judaism in the 21st century: Given the importance of choice in

American society, most Jews believe that, in the coming years, the number of options within Judaism will increase, not decrease. Jacob Neusner, for example, thinks we are "on the threshold of another great age of system-building." Such signs as "the formation of a distinctively Judaic politics" on both the Left and Right, "the *havura movement*, the renewal of Reconstructionism . . ., the development of an accessible Judaic mysticism . . ., and the development and framing of . . . a feminist Judaism," Neusner believes, show great promise.[35] Others point to new ways to express spirituality and worship, ranging from Bibliodrama and the arts to a more intensive focus on music and the introduction of new language and prayers.

In light of such developments, when Jewish leaders ask whether there will still be "one Judaism," what many are really asking concerns whether the increasing polarization between the Orthodox and the non-Orthodox will cause a complete break between traditional and liberal Jews. Will progressive and intermarried Jews and their families come to practice a form of religion so different from traditional Judaism that some Jews will not deem it Judaism at all?

While this is not a new issue, it has become far more pressing in recent years. In a 1985 paper that was widely discussed and debated, Irving Greenberg, an Orthodox rabbi and founder of the multi-denominational National Jewish Center for Learning and Leadership (CLAL), warned that both religious extremism and unreconcilable denominational positions on divisive issues (most particularly, the 1983 decision by the Reform movement to recognize patrilineal descent) had the potential for polarizing the Jewish people into two different religions by the year 2000.[36] Today, Greenberg believes the situation has deteriorated even farther, conceding only that his warning may have been off by a generation or two.[37]

Ironically, Orthodox Judaism and the more liberal denominations are moving further apart precisely at a time when the Reform movement is becoming more traditional. Eric Yoffie, the new head of the Reform Union of American Hebrew Congregations, recently critiqued American Jewry: "What is missing is a straightforward call for religious commitment; what is missing is the language of Torah and mitzvot." Not the usual Reform statement, as many have pointed out, and, in view of this shift, at least one observer predicts that over the next decade or two, the distinctions between the Reform, Reconstructionist and Conservative movements will narrow, leading the three to consider mergers of various kinds, including mergers of their seminaries.

Interestingly, such a development might occur alongside a parallel split in the community, between "traditional" Jews of all denominations and a new form or forms of Judaism—prompted by rising rates of intermarriage and disaffiliation with organized Judaism—that more traditional Jews do not believe are Judaism at all. Judaisms of individual "spirituality seekers" may be viewed as simply the latest in a series of varied incarnations of Judaism in America, as natural successors to Ethnic Judaism, Zionist Judaism, Suburban (or Pediatric) Judaism, and other forms of nineteenth and twentieth century American Judaism. Others, however, may view these as not "real" Judaism at all, yielding, they would say, too many core beliefs about covenant and community to American individualism and Christian notions of a "personal" God.

Notably, for all the problems caused by such assimilatory developments, with the exception of the ultra-Orthodox, Jews in this country will not willingly separate themselves from American society, even if they were convinced that this is what Jewish survival demands. American Jews are worried about Jewish continuity. But the vast majority believe that this worry is a more than reasonable price to pay for American acceptance and openness towards Jews. American Jews will continue to believe they can be American *and* Jewish, living fully in modern society *and* preserving Judaism.

Nonetheless, the majority of American Jews are beginning to recognize that Judaism and "Americanism" are not identical. While they share some fundamental values, most notably a commitment to justice and human dignity, the basic difference and biggest tension between the two is that America's primary teaching is seen by many to be commitment to self and individualism, while Judaism's primary teaching has always been commitment to community and people. Yet over the past few decades, as American Jews have become increasingly assimilated, the vast majority of them has absorbed more and more of the American attitude about self and individualism, in the process losing, or at least moving away from, Jewish commitments. Many believe this must change if Judaism is to survive, that "the Jewish community may have to adopt a view of Jewish identity as being at least partly in tension with the values of liberal, universalist modernity, and that any effort to strengthen 'the fabric of Jewish life' may necessarily entail challenging if not rejecting aspects of that very ethos, an ethos with which both secular Jewish leaders and many religious ones as well have been prominently allied."[38]

At the same time, many Jews and non-Jews are calling for *all* of American society to reject or at least to modify certain of these traditional American values. Recent works by Robert Bellah, Robert Putnam, Amitai Etzioni,[39] and others, have suggested that the health and strength of American society in the next century will depend on whether and how we can temper America's "first language" of individual self-fulfillment, achievement, and self-reliance with some of its "second language" of community, responsibility, and self-transcendence. Jonathan Woocher and others in the Jewish community have noted that while not unique to Jews, this is of particular importance to Jews, because the fundamental truths of Judaism are based so firmly in the "second language."

In sum, then, Jews must and will continue to struggle with the centuries-old dilemma of how to reconcile and live with both Torah and modernity, several centuries into an "uneasy encounter" with America still hoping to find ways to be fully American *and* fully Jewish. Most American Jews feel that being Jewish does not make them any different from other Americans. But, when looked at more closely, what this means is that for many, Judaism has become their way of being American.[40]

For there to be a hope of continuity in the face of ever-greater assimilation we will, then, have to identify ways for people fully to be both American and Jewish. This is a new problem, born of modernity, for in every previous age the overwhelming majority of Jews were allowed, and therefore had, only one identity. For centuries, Jewish continuity was achieved through Torah, through generation after generation of Jews' living out the religious core of their identity in their homes, in their individual study and observance of the Jewish way of life.

For twentieth-century America, however, study and observance have not been the primary vehicles for Jewish identity or community. Identity and community, rather, have been sustained by *non*-religious aspects of being Jewish, by "fighting for acceptance in the United States; creating our own social, recreational, and medical institutions; fighting anti-Semitism worldwide; saving Jews after the Holocaust; documenting the Holocaust; supporting a struggling emergent nation of Israel in its trials and tribulations, and adorning it with great quality institutions."[41] All critical, these issues worked to sustain what appeared to be a strong American Jewish community. The trouble, we have learned in recent years, is that these ways of being Jewish cannot transmit Judaism to the next generations. As new generations of Jews grow up, marry, and start their own families, many are finding that having inherited only the non-religious parts of Judaism, they have little or no idea of how they might build and sustain their own Jewish lives. More serious, they have little or no idea of *why* they should build and sustain Jewish lives.

In the end, the only way to keep twenty-first century Jews Jewish will be to make Judaism "so vibrant and so fulfilling that increasing number of people will be drawn to it—whether they were born Jews or not." Although few members of the Jewish community would argue with this statement by the UAHC's Eric Yoffie, there is not yet any widespread agreement about how Jews get from here to there. So far, actions have focused mainly on rethinking basic structures and institutions—the communal structure, synagogues, education, social action, the role of spirituality—and instituting new programs to meet emerging needs—family education, adult education, post-Bar and Bat Mitzvah programs, programs for college students and young adults. But most members of the community know that this is not enough: although Jewish education and Jewish institutions must be reconceived to meet the spiritual, educational, social, and communal needs of American Jews in the twenty-first century, educational systems and institutions are, ultimately, only tools in the service of Judaism. The question really is: What is the purpose of the Judaism for which we are educating and bringing people together? Is there a vibrant, new Judaism that will provide a coherent world view, a way of life, a social world, in which Jews can and will desire to live?

While there is not and may never be complete consensus, people from every part of the denominational spectrum are increasingly talking about a "vibrant and fulfilling" Judaism that uses the newest of Jewish ideas—new programs, structures, technologies—to support and advance the oldest of Jewish ideas—that being Jewish necessitates a commitment to the study and living of Torah as part of a distinct Jewish community. This, most are saying, must be the primary goal of American Judaism in the twenty-first century.

This has led to calls for a return to a Judaism "of laws, obligations and norms," to "a distinctive Jewish world view," including "institutions which emphasize Jewish particularism and foster strong identification with the group."[42] Along these lines, at his inauguration as head of the UAHC last year, Eric Yoffie called for a community-wide investment in education, to promote "the transmission of Torah across the generations." Similarly, even those well outside the leadership circles and traditional Judaism are calling for a return to a more distinctive form of Judaism. In a recent article in *Tikkun*, for instance, Nancy Kalikow Maxwell, a reference librarian from Florida, reflected on the current absence of a difference between Jews and non-Jews and wrote that the way to attract intermarried Jews was not to dilute Judaism but to return to "a vital, tradition-based Judaism. . . . Either we must accept that there is inherently no difference between Jews and non-Jews and allow Judaism to dissolve into the existing culture or we must reconstruct a Judaism that means more than just having a Jewish mother or liking bagels."[43]

Reflecting on the problem of creating such a Judaism, in the conclusion of one of his recent books, Professor Jacob Neusner asks:

> What can draw people together and persuade them in public, not only in private, to do one thing and not another and move them and shape their hearts—and also their minds?

The answer, he says, lies in "enchantment," recognizing that in the traditions of Judaism:[44]

> The words convey propositions, and rites stand for truths that we can express. But Judaic existence is not in the words, the emotions, and the attitudes alone. Judaism takes place through the arts, in enchantment that transforms, changing something into something else, somewhere into anywhere, some time into all time. And therefore we cannot say that Judaism *is*, rather, Judaism *takes place* at that moment at which in our imagination, expressed through media of heart and intellect beyond all speech, we enter into the circle of the sacred and, through words of enchantment, transform the world, if only for a moment. That is where God takes place.

And this, of course, will be true in the twenty-first century just as it has been in every other century of Jewish history.

Bibliography

Cohen, Naomi, *Jews in Christian America: The Pursuit of Religious Equality* (Oxford, 1993).

Heilman, Samuel C., *Portrait of American Jews: The Last Half of the 20th Century* (Seattle and London, 1995).

Lipset, Seymour Martin, and Raab, Earl, *Jews and the New American Scene* (Cambridge, 1995).

McClain, Ellen Jaffe, *Embracing the Stranger: Intermarriage and the Future of the American Jewish Community* (New York, 1995).

Notes

[1] Sidney Goldstein, "Profile of American Jewry," in *American Jewish Year Book 1992* (New York, 1992), p. 127.

[2] Samuel Heilman, *Portrait of American Jews. The Last Half of the 20th Century* (Seattle and London, 1995), p. 71.

[3] See, e.g., Paul Light, *Baby Boomers* (New York, 1988), and Gary L. McIntosh, *Three Generations: Riding the Waves of Change in Your Church* (Grand Rapids, 1995).

[4] McIntosh, ibid., pp. 144-157.

[5] Heilman, op. cit., p. 109.

[6] Ibid., pp. 110-111.

[7] Jack Wertheimer, "Conservative Synagogues and Their Members: The North American Survey of 1995-96" (Ratner Center for the Study of Conservative Judaism, The Jewish Theological Seminary, 1996).

[8] Riv-Ellen Prell, *Prayer & Community: The Havurah in American Judaism* (Detroit, 1989), p. 21.

[9] Wade Clark Roof, *A Generation of Seekers: The Spiritual Journeys of the Baby Boom Generation* (New York and San Francisco, 1993), pp. 51-52.

[10] See, e.g., Robert Wuthnow, *The Restructuring of American Religion: Society and Faith since World War II* (Princeton, 1988), pp. 153- 172, and Roof, op. cit., p. 52.

[11] Roof, op. cit., 1993, pp. 4-5.

[12] "New Road Maps for Searching Readers," *Publishers Weekly*, February 10, 1997, p. 29.

[13] Lawrence Hoffman, "Four Generations," *Synagogue 2000 Project Library*, Sections 3 and 4.

[14] Ibid., Section 4, p. 2.

[15] Barbara Skolnick Hoenig, *Jewish Environment Scan: Toward the Year 2000* (New York, 1992), p. 2.

[16] On the basis of the 1990 NJPS, researchers estimate that today 24% of Jews are actively engaged in Judaism, 20% are moderately engaged, and 56% are loosely engaged or disengaged (Jack Wertheimer, Charles S. Liebman, and Steven M. Cohen, "How to Save American Jews," in *Commentary*, January, 1996). Moving Jews into the actively or moderately engaged category is critical for the Jewish future since, at present, only 4% of the actively engaged and 10% of the moderately engaged intermarry, compared with 19% of the loosely engaged and 49% of the disengaged.

[17] Roof, op. cit., p. 164.

[18] Joel Streicker and Gary Tobin, "An Assessment of Synagogue Inreach and Outreach," in *The Koret Synagogue Initiative Executive Summary 1996*, p. 21, fig. 7.

[19] See Michael Zeldin, "Rethinking Jewish Education," in *Reform Judaism*, Spring, 1996.

[20] See Rachel Blustain, "Why More Parents are Choosing Jewish Day Schools," in *Moment*, February, 1997.

[21] Vince Beiser, "Intermarried with Children," in *The Jerusalem Report*, September 5, 1996.

[22] On this topic, see Sylvia Barack Fishman, "The Impact of Feminism," *American Jewish Yearbook 1989* (New York, 1989), pp. 3, 14-15.

[23] Hoffman, op. cit., Section 3, p. 4.

[24] Leonard Fein, "Without Social Justice, There Is No Torah," *Reform Judaism*, Fall, 1996.

[25] In the earlier period, the women almost always converted—either to or from Judaism. Now, the numbers of men and women converting is much more balanced. On this topic, see Goldstein, op. cit., pp. 124-28.

[26] Most Conservative congregations do not allow non-Jewish spouses formally to join the synagogues, though they are welcome to attend services and other synagogue events.

[27] Heilman, op. cit., p. 131.

[28] Sergio Della Pergola, "New Data on Demography and Identification among Jews in the U.S.: Trends, Inconsistencies, and Disagreements," in *Contemporary Jewry* (1991), p. 12.

[29] Vince Beiser, "Intermarried with Children," in *The Jerusalem Report*, September 5, 1996.

[30] Steven M. Cohen and Irving Greenberg, "The One in 2000 Controversy," in *Moment*, March, 1987, pp. 11-22.

[31] Jack Wertheimer, "Recent Trends in American Judaism," in *American Jewish Year Book 1989* (New York, 1989), p. 149.

[32] Hoffman, op. cit., Section 4.

[33] Arthur Hertzberg, *The Jews in America* (New York, 1989), p. 388. See Heilman, op. cit., pp. 161-62; Charles Liebman, quoted in Hertzberg, op. cit., pp. 383-84; and Charles Liebman, "A Grim Outlook," in *The Quality of American Jewish Life: Two Views* (New York, 1987), pp. 40-41.

[34] See, e.g., Hoffman, op. cit., section 4.

[35] Jacob Neusner, "Can Judaism Survive the 20th Century?" in *Tikkun*, July/August, 1989.

[36] Irving Greenberg, "Will There Be One Jewish People by the Year 2000?" in *Perspectives*, National Jewish Center for Learning and Leadership, June, 1985.

[37] On this and the following, see Yosef Abromowitz, "From Fantasy to Reality," in *Jewish Bulletin of Northern California*, 1995.

[38] Wertheimer, Liebman, and Cohen, op. cit.

[39] See Robert Bellah et al., *Habits of the Heart, A Good Society* (New York, 1991), Robert Putnam, "Bowling Alone", in *Journal of Democracy*, 6:1, Jan., 1995, pp. 65-78, and Amitai Etzioni, *The Spirit of Community* (New York, 1993).

[40] Steven M. Cohen, *Content or Continuity? The 1989 National Survey of American Jews* (New York, 1991), p. 57.

[41] Herbert Bronstein, *Chicago Jewish News*, 1996.

[42] Wertheimer, Liebman, and Cohen, op. cit.

[43] Nancy Kalikow Maxwell, "If You're So Smart, Why Are You Intermarried?," in *Tikkun*, vol. 12, no. 1 (January/February 1997), p. 43.

[44] Jacob Neusner, *Introduction to American Judaism: What the Books Say, What the People Do* (Minneapolis, 1994), pp. 161, 165.

LISA GOLDBERG AND JOEL ZAIMAN

JUDAISM, PHILOSOPHY AND THEOLOGY OF, MEDIEVAL: To some scholars and religious Jews philosophy is an import, which, like Solomon's harlot in Proverbs, lies in wait ready and willing to seduce unwitting Jews by means of her wiles and charms. To others, mainly the Jewish philosophers and historians of Jewish philosophy, philosophy is God's gift to humankind and is the road to ultimate happiness. It is thus not surprising that throughout its history Jewish philosophy manifests a certain ambivalence about its role and status within the Jewish religious experience. There is no doubt that the Bible is for the most part not a philosophical book, although it is not too hard to find philosophy in some of its components, such as Ecclesiastes and the Book of Job. Indeed, several scholars have claimed that some biblical books do evince the influence of Greek philosophical thought. Be that as it may, it is clear that the explicit and persistent impact of Hellenic speculative thought upon Judaism does not surface until the first century before the common era, when in Ptolemaic Egypt, specifically Alexandria, we discover Jews who wrote philosophical treatises and philosophical commentaries upon the Bible. The most famous example of this "birth of Jewish philosophy" was Philo of Alexandria (Philo Judaeus, c. 40 C.E.). Deeply influenced by Platonic philosophy Philo attempted to present to his Hellenized Jewish audience a Judaism that was both compatible with the best of Greek thought and consistent with the fundamental beliefs of the Bible as he understood them. Nevertheless, it must be admitted that Philo's project had little impact upon Jews and Judaism, in contrast to his significance for Christianity. Indeed, only in the sixteenth century was he retrieved for Judaism by several Italian Jewish scholars, whose latinity enabled them to read Latin translations of Philo. Accordingly, the history of the Jewish "naturalization" of philosophy began much later than Philo, with Saadia Gaon (882-942), whose importance for Jewish thought has been tremendous.

Saadia Gaon: Born and educated in Muslim Egypt, Saadia eventually settled in Iraq, then the cultural and political center of Islam. By that time some of the Greek philosophical and scientific legacy had been Arabicized and incorporated into Muslim theological literature, known as Kalam. One of the main purposes of Kalam, which had both Christian and Jewish representatives, was to defend the faith against pagan philosophical ideas that were hostile toward revealed religion and to refute the opposing claims of rival religions. In this sense Saadia's major speculative work, *The Book of Beliefs and Opinions*, is an excellent specimen of Jewish Kalam.

In the Introduction to this treatise Saadia clearly states his motives for writing the book and his methodology. He saw his generation as "perplexed," "drowning in an ocean of doubt," caused by a proliferation of philosophical doctrines and theological controversies. As the intellectual leader of his community, Saadia assumed the responsibility of acting as the "skilled swimmer" who would rescue his drowning co-religionists from the ocean of confusion. In addition to this bit of intellectual life-saving, Saadia wanted to offer the Jews of his day, and perhaps of the future as well, a Judaism fortified by philosophy, so that Jews would not just be believers but "purified" and mature followers of a religion that was philosophically respectable.

To this end Saadia set down the sources of truth that were going to be the parameters of his rational religion: 1) sense-perception; 2) self-evident principles; 3) rational inference; 4) reliable tradition. Saadia was no skeptic either with respect to (1) or (3); moreover, he believed that reason was in the possession of certain *a priori* principles that were "common notions," to use the Stoic phrase, such as the truth of the fundamental laws of logic and morality. Saadia affirmed the radical idea that tradition has to be consistent with the other three sources of truth: we are not entitled to believe what we "will to believe;" there are certain rational constraints set by sense experience and reason. This is a general theme in Saadia's writings, repeated in his biblical commentaries as well as his more speculative works. This principle also affected his Arabic translation of the Bible. For example, in Gen. 3:20 we read that Eve was the mother of all life. Since, obviously, this is false, the literal reading of the passage has to be rejected. Saadia therefore translates it, "Eve was the mother of all humans." In many respects Saadia was a religious rationalist or optimist who saw no real incompatibility between Judaism and reason.

Creation of the universe: One of the more controversial issues in medieval philosophical theology was the truth status of the opening verse of the Bible, which was also incorporated into the Quran. The creation of the world was a belief that had become authoritative for Jews, Christians, and Muslims; yet it was rejected by the leading Greek philosopher at this time, Aristotle, who claimed that the universe is eternal. Moreover, the creation of the universe was believed to have occurred *ex nihilo*, and this idea was not only rejected by Aristotle but by Plato as well, who believed that God did create the world, but out of some formless eternal matter. So Saadia had his hands full. His procedure is to prove first that the universe was created by God, second to show that God created the world *ex nihilo*, and finally to demonstrate that all rival theories of the world's generation are false.

Saadia offers four arguments in proof of the createdness of the universe, of which the first is especially interesting, since it uses Aristotle's physics to show that the universe is not eternal but created. The argument goes like this:

1. All bodies are finite in size and energy.
2. Having finite energy the body will eventually disintegrate, or pass away.
3. Whatever passes away has a beginning.

Hence, the world as a collection of finite bodies had a beginning.

To prove that the world was created *ex nihilo* Saadia presents several arguments, two of which are significant because of their subsequent influence upon later Jewish thinkers. first, Saadia claims that the biblical term *bara* used in Genesis 1.1 means "create *ex nihilo*." Unlike other biblical "making" verbs, such as *asah* or *yatzar*, the verb *bara*, has a special meaning that is reserved for God, who alone can create something from nothing. Second, if there were some eternal matter from which God fashioned the world, as Plato suggested, this matter, by virtue of its eternity, has a certain autonomy, or inde-

pendence. What or who can guarantee that it would be amenable to being shaped by God? Indeed, since it too is eternal, why should we think that God is the fashioner, not it?

In his discussion of the rival theories of creation, Saadia's considers the view that in creating the world God employed instruments or intermediary spiritual entities. Such a theme is found in Philo and in the Church Fathers, some of whom identify this instrument with Jesus. Saadia vigorously argues against this idea. He is especially concerned to defeat the claim that this idea appears explicitly in Prov. 8.22, which suggests that *wisdom* is premundane and served as God's instrument in creating the world. According to Saadia, all that Prov. 8.22 says is that God created the universe wisely, subject to order and design, nothing more.

The Torah: Living among Muslims and Christians Saadia had to deal with the claims that the Torah was no longer valid, having been superseded by the Gospels and having been abrogated by the Quran. Moreover, philosophically educated skeptics or deviationists had challenged the rationality of many of the commandments of the Torah. These opponents too had to be answered.

Responding to the Christian argument of supercession, Saadia shows that the Torah, which the Christian does accept, testifies to its own immutability (see Mal. 4:4-5 [Hebrew: 3:22-23]). Indeed, in the very chapter in Jeremiah where the Christian claims that a new testament will be forthcoming (Jer. 31:31-33), it is clearly stated that the laws of the Torah are as everlasting as the heavenly bodies (Jer. 31:33-35). To the Muslim argument of abrogation Saadia replies that if both the Torah and the Gospels have been annulled by the Quran, then it is possible that in the future the Quran itself will be abrogated by another revelation; indeed, the series of revealed but annullable laws could go on infinitely. But this is absurd. So, he argues, let us stay with the first and indeed only divinely revealed law, the Torah.

The question of the Torah's "rationality" is an old one. Philo and several of his Greek-Jewish colleagues undertook to show the reasonableness of the commandments in the face of Greek and Roman skeptics and scoffers, as well as Jews who were losing their faith. The rabbis formulated the compromise position, that the commandments are divided into two groups, those that have some rational purpose (*mishpatim*) and those that do not but must be followed simply because they have been revealed (*huqqim*). This distinction appears in Muslim Kalam, where the laws of Islam are classified as rational commandments or as revelational commandments. Saadia adopts this Kalam distinction in his effort to show the inherent reasonableness of the Torah. Although not going as far as Philo, who maintained that every commandment of the Torah has a reason, Saadia believes that even many of the so-called revelational laws (*huqqim*) have some utility. Consider, for example, impurity laws that prohibit entry into a holy place. Such commandments instill in the believer respect for the sanctity of certain specified locales. Or incest prohibitions: since contacts with the immediate members of the family of the opposite gender are frequent, if sexual intimacy were allowed promiscuity would ensue. Saadia is quite confident that God would not have given us laws that had no point whatsoever. This would be inconsistent with God's wisdom and goodness.

Saadia's analysis of the rational commandments is interesting for its Kantian flavor. Some of these commandments are the basic rules of morality that earlier Saadia had classified as self-evident, such as the prohibition against lying. For Saadia lying is irrational: a liar is someone who believes a certain proposition to be false yet at the same time affirms it. This violates the law of contradiction. A similar argument is given by Kant.

Human freedom: Another hotly contested issue in Muslim Kalam was the problem of human free-will. One challenge to its existence was the venerable dilemma between divine omniscience and human choice. If God knows everything, including the future, do people really have choice? Aristotle and some of his followers, such as Alexander of Aphrodisias, rejected the knowability of fu-

ture contingencies. But this was a price that believers in the Bible or the Quran could not afford. So some sort of reconciliation between the horns of the dilemma had to be found.

On this issue Saadia takes a very strong stand. Like Kant, Saadia claims that *ought* implies *can*: if we have duties we must have the power to fulfill them. Not only is this a principle of reason; it is clearly stated in the Torah (see Deut. 30:15-19). So human freedom is not limited either by divine power, as many Muslim theologians had maintained, nor by divine omniscience, as the Aristotelians had argued. With respect to the first position, Saadia claims that we alone are the agents of our actions. Unlike some of the Kalam, Saadia denies that God either gives man the capacity to act at the time of the action or that God is a co-agent. We have the power to make choices in so far as we are rational beings; we do not need anyone's help in making these choices. Otherwise, we would not be responsible for our actions; indeed, if another agent were involved, this agent would have to bear at least some of the responsibility for our actions, and what we do would not even be *our* actions!

But what about God's omniscience? Does the Bible not say that God knows our innermost thoughts and our future actions? Yes, it does, admits Saadia; but this does not imply that our actions are not free. One has to distinguish between knowing that some event will take place tomorrow and causing this event to come about tomorrow. If the latter were true, then the event in question would not be contingent, and we would not be free. But God's knowing this event does not cause the event. For example, if I shall choose to give some charity tomorrow, God knows that I shall make this choice; but God does not cause me to make this choice. I am the sole agent of my choices, even though God knows every such choice I shall make. (A similar resolution of the dilemma was given by Augustine.)

The soul and its immortality: The second half of Saadia's treatise is mainly devoted to a cluster of problems having to do with the general issue of reward and punishment, both individual and collective. In Judaism these are not neat issues. Moreover, they are complicated by doctrines that have either a distinctly political nature—the Messianic era—or some kind of apocalyptic character—resurrection of the dead. The Bible itself is not very clear on these topics. In a few passages it speaks about a day of judgment; in other places, again not too many, it refers to the soul, or spirit, returning to God. Only in the Book of Daniel, the latest book in the Bible, does a clear reference to the doctrine of the resurrection of the dead appear. It is not surprising that in Rabbinic literature one finds diverse and unsystematic discussions of these concepts.

Saadia may have been the first to attempt to formulate a theory of the "end of days," an account that integrates the various biblical and Rabbinic ideas on these subjects. First he discusses the nature of the soul. Although Saadia works with some kind of soul-body dualism, he does not exhibit the invidious distinctions and biases that Platonic or Cartesian dualisms do. The soul is made from a substance superior to that of which our body is made; indeed, this soul-substance is superior to that of the heavenly bodies. Accordingly, the soul mainly bears the responsibility for our actions; it makes the choices that our bodies carry out. In fact, the body is not, as the Platonists had maintained, intrinsically impure. It becomes impure if the soul chooses unwisely. The soul and its body are created together. Here Saadia departs again from Platonism, which had affirmed the pre-existence of the soul. By rejecting pre-existence Saadia is also able to deny transmigration, or metempsychosis. This does not mean, however, that the soul dies with the death of its body. When the latter dies, the soul survives in a "neutral waiting-room," the biblical "bundle of life," where it awaits the next stage in its career.

The second chapter in this story is the period Saadia refers to both as Resurrection of the Dead in This World and as the Time of Redemption. At this point matters get complicated, mainly because Saadia believes that there will be two resurrections. The first takes place in this world and is confined to the righteous of Israel and those Israelites who repent. Their souls return to their original bodies to enjoy a renewed life, a reward for all the sufferings Israel has endured. This period is also the time of the Messianic era, when a Davidic king will restore the kingdom of Israel and the exiles will be ingathered. Universal peace will reign and all the nations will worship God.

The final stage is what the rabbis called "The World-To-Come." At this time all souls return to their bodies and the complete individual is judged according to his or her merits. The sufferings of the innocent are recompensed and the hitherto unpunished prosperity of the sinners is replaced with appropriate calamities. This second resurrection is permanent: the righteous will enjoy their reward forever, just as the sinners will suffer their punishments forever. Since Rabbinic dicta stated that there would be no eating, drinking, or other mundane pursuits in the "world-to-come," Saadia characterizes this state literally as the "new heaven and earth" spoken of in Is. 65:17. Just as God created this world *ex nihilo*, God will destroy this world and make a new one having different natural properties, such as the absence of night and day. All the inhabitants of this new universe will worship God and enjoy everlasting divine illumination.

Jewish philosophy in Muslim Spain: Despite his important and pioneering intellectual achievements, Saadia was a bit behind the times. In his generation a new theoretical framework for both philosophy and religion had emerged, first in Islam and later in Judaism, that was to provide a radically different vocabulary and thought structure for the formulation of religious philosophy. Saadia's younger contemporary Muslim thinker in Iraq, Al-Farabi, was developing a systematic synthesis of the philosophies of Plato and Aristotle in such a way as to accommodate the main ideas of Islam. Actually, permeating his understanding of his two great Greek predecessors was the thought of another Greek philosophical genius, Plotinus, whose name was forgotten throughout the Middle Ages but whose ideas, often attributed to Aristotle, had a great impact upon medieval philosophy. Although Saadia's religious philosophy does not reflect this new wave of Neo-Platonic Aristotelianism, the next significant phase of Jewish philosophy does, albeit in a new locale: Jewish philosophy moved westward to Spain. Muslim Spain, Andalusia, now becomes a major cultural center for both Islam and Judaism; it is the breeding ground of important poets, philosophers, and scientists in both religions. Nor were religious studies neglected: biblical exegesis and Talmudic studies flourished. The two most important religious thinkers in Judaism in this period were the great poets Solomon ibn Gabirol and Judah Halevi, both of whom were philosophically adept and attuned to the newer philosophy, although each reacted to it in very different ways.

Solomon ibn Gabirol (1026-1050 or 1070): Gabirol had two very different careers until the middle of the nineteenth century. To Jews he was Shlomo the Hebrew poet who wrote some of the most moving religious poetry in the Hebrew language. Indeed, some of this poetry entered the liturgy of Sefardic Jewry. To Christian theologians, however, such as Albert the Great and Thomas Aquinas, he was Avicebrol or Avicebron, a Muslim or Christian Arab who had written an influential philosophical treatise, *The Source of Life*, originally in Arabic but surviving only in Latin translation. Only in the nineteenth century, when Solomon Munk identified the poet with the philosopher, did Gabirol return to Judaism intact.

The Source of Life, or as it was better known *Fons Vitae*, was never translated into Hebrew, although there is a medieval Hebrew epitome of it composed by Shem Tov Falaquera (d. 1290). A purely philosophical work written in dialogue form and containing no reference to the Bible, it is no wonder that Jews found it to be of no great interest or relevance. It was otherwise with his long philosophical poem *The Royal Crown*, which has been incorporated into Day of Atonement liturgy. Like *Fons Vitae* this poem expresses and formulates the dominant Plotinian-Aristotelian ideas of the period. But unlike the philosophical book the poem concretizes

these ideas in powerful verses that are redolent of the Bible and Rabbinic literature. Indeed, one can use the poem to get an appreciation of the extent to which medieval Platonism had become Judaized.

The paramount motif in Plotinian philosophy is the hierarchical structure of reality whose first element is the One, from which emanate Intellect, Soul, and then Nature. Since the latter is the domain of matter and duration, which for Platonic philosophers is inherently deficient, only the One, Intellect, and Soul really count. Indeed, not only do human souls originate from "on high," but our goal is to "revert" to the supernal realm, especially to the One, the source of everything. Gabirol's poem begins with the One, now called by his biblical names, and proceeds to develop a theology of the One that Jews can recognize and understand. But he is not content merely to translate into religious verse these Plotinian themes. Gabirol introduces an idea that is really foreign to Plotinus' necessatarian emanation scheme, divine will. Whereas for the philosophical Plotinian the lower forms and levels "flow" necessarily from the One, Gabirol's One, or better God, creates the universe voluntarily. Indeed, both here as well as in the *Fons Vitae*, divine will has an importance that almost undermines the original Plotinian metaphysics. Specialists have raised questions whether for Gabirol the will is a feature of the divine essence or a distinct hypostasis, or entity, that accounts for the creation of the universe *ex nihilo*. In either case, it is clear that Gabirol did not slavishly accept Plotinian necessatarianism, as did his Muslim counterparts, Al-Farabi and Ibn Sina.

Another interesting theme in the poem is the nature of the human soul. Like the Plotinian philosophers Gabirol asserts the supernal origin of the soul; after all, this is what Solomon the King had said in Ecclesiastes. And, again, like Plotinus, Gabirol speaks of the return of the soul to its origin, "the source of life." But unlike most Platonic philosophers Gabirol does not speak of the soul as imprisoned in the body or as descending from the supernal realm as the result of its sinful or imperfect nature. Rather, God creates the soul out of the superior substance of Intellect and then gives the soul to the body as its guide and governor. Yet, since the soul's origin is supernal, it too shares the inherent eternity of Intellect. Indeed, immortality is achieved through the life of intellectual and moral perfection, the true imitation of God.

Judah Halevi: The second great poet-philosopher of Jewish Andalusia was Judah Halevi (1085-1141). But unlike Gabirol, Halevi was born in Toledo when this important city was conquered by the Christians. This fact will be of some significance in Halevi's religious thought, as we shall see. Virtually all the standard histories of medieval Jewish philosophy include Halevi; but in an important sense he does not belong in such books, for he is more a critic of philosophy than a philosopher or philosophical theologian. Although well-versed in the medieval Muslim philosophical literature and possessed of an intellect capable of acute philosophical insight, Halevi undertook a defense of Judaism not only against its rival religions—Christianity and Islam—but philosophy as well. This "defense of a despised religion" is written in the form of a dialogue between a Jewish scholar and the King of the Khazars, a Turkish people that had settled in southern Russia in the eighth century and converted to Judaism. Halevi's treatise *The Kuzari* is an attempt to provide the rationale for the king's conversion and at the same time a response to the criticisms leveled against Judaism and the Jews by Christianity and Islam. Like Saadia and Gabirol, Halevi's philosophical language was Arabic, although he wrote all his poetry in Hebrew.

The *Kuzari* begins with the king's dream, in which an angel appears and tells him that, although his intentions are good, his religious practices are deficient. To correct this problem the king calls a philosopher to ask his advice. This opening scene is quite significant for two reasons. first, the dialogue begins with the king's having a religious experience that is akin in certain respects to prophecy; indeed a dream can be a form of prophecy. Second, unlike the historical sources that describe the king's conversion as having oc-

curred after his summoning representatives from the three scriptural religions, Halevi has a philosopher too appear—indeed makes him appear first. Even though the philosopher will soon leave, never to return in person, the presence of philosophy is apparent throughout the treatise. Halevi seems to be suggesting that perhaps the greatest threat to Judaism is philosophy. At any rate, the king proceeds to ask the philosopher what he believes. The philosopher responds by giving the king a summary of the Al-Farabi-Ibn Sina metaphysics, one that could have been subscribed to by Gabirol also. Throughout this philosophical presentation two themes are prominent: 1) the complete transcendence of God, to the point of God's not knowing individual things here on earth; and 2) human immortality consists in conjunction with the Agent Intellect, one of the supernal subordinate entities in the medieval synthesis of Aristotle and Plotinus. One consequence of this latter theme is that prophecy can result from this conjunction. The philosopher makes it clear that organized religion, especially its rituals, is not particularly important. Intellectual perfection is.

The king will have none of this. He has had an experience that no philosophical argument can dislodge. Moreover, in this dream he, a particular human being, was told that his deeds, especially his religious rituals, were not acceptable to God. Philosophical metaphysics is not adequate, especially the one he was given; the king wants something more. He wants to know how to act, and he needs to know this because the God who has spoken to him is concerned about him. Personal experience counts more than logic. The king dismisses the philosopher and calls a Christian and then a Muslim, for both believe in a deity who is concerned about humanity and who reveals its will to particular humans.

Although the Christian and Muslim differ in their theologies, they agree in two important respects: 1) they are theologians and begin their speeches with a creed specifying the fundamental beliefs of their religions; and 2) they both rest their theologies and their claims to prophetic authenticity upon Judaism. After all, both religions are based upon the Mosaic revelation. The king realizes that his initial disregard for Judaism, which was a "despised religion," was erroneous, and he now summons a Jewish scholar.

But the opening speech of the Jew disappoints the king. Instead of beginning with a creed containing a set of theological dogmas, the Jewish scholar recites a list of historical episodes in ancient Jewish history, to which the king angrily responds by accusing the Jews of particularity, a charge that has plagued Judaism for many centuries. The Jewish scholar is not bothered at all; indeed, he relishes in this particularity. After all, all historical facts are particular; moreover, the more particular they are the more unique they are. And this uniqueness proves the chosenness of Israel, a fact that the Christian and the Muslim both admit. So the fundamental fact of Judaism is its special status as the original and most authoritative revealed religion. So why not go with the original and forget the copies? The king does, converting to Judaism and importing Jews to teach his people his newly acquired religion.

So ends Book 1 of *The Kuzari*. How then does Halevi fill up the remaining four books? Remember that the king was initially told that deeds are very important to God; so much of Books 2 and 3 are devoted to detailed discussions of specific points of Jewish practice and law. But in Books 4 and 5 Halevi shifts gears and reverts to a discussion of philosophy, both as a general way of approaching God and as regards the specific doctrines of Kalam and the medieval Aristotelians. In Book 4 Halevi makes a sharp distinction between the way the philosophers come to know God and the way the prophets do. Whereas the former formulate theories wherein they attempt to give a description of the divine attributes in much the same way as the astronomer describes the heavenly constellations, the prophet acquires information about God via a personal experience of the divine. In Halevi's biblical language, the prophet sees, hears, indeed "tastes" God. Here Halevi's religious empiricism is most evident: not only is history preferred to logical inference but direct experience as well. According to Halevi the prophet is endowed with a "sixth sense" that enables him or her to experience things that are not perceived by others. This experience is irrefutable and sufficient. The proof of its truth is seen in the fact that prophets and their followers are prepared to die for their faith, an act for which philosophers for the most part are not famous.

The concluding book of the Kuzari is somewhat puzzling. The first half consists of a detailed exposition of philosophical solutions to some standard medieval philosophical problems, such as the issue of divine omniscience and the creation of the universe. Given Halevi's conclusion that the answers to these questions, to the extent that we need such answers, are given in the Torah and the oral tradition based upon it, it is surprising that at the end of his book Halevi would bother with these concerns. It is as if the philosopher of Book 1 has reappeared and is given another opportunity to present his case. But after this presentation another sudden shift occurs. The Jewish scholar decides to leave the king and to migrate to the Land of Israel, the place of prophecy and the only place the Jews are capable of a full and perfect practice of their religion. The king tries to dissuade him from going by reporting the various dangers that await him if he makes this journey, perhaps alluding to the wars between the Christians and Muslims for the Holy Land. But no use. The scholar affirms the centuries old Jewish commitment to the Land by actually going there himself. The liturgy of the prayer book has now become a reality.

Moses Maimonides: Although Maimonides (1135-1204) was no poet, in many respects he represents the high point of the Golden Age of Jewish Spain. Born in Cordoba, the birthplace and residence of another great medieval philosopher, Averroes (ibn Rushd, 1126-1198), Maimonides received his deep Rabbinic education in Spain, primarily from his father, and his secular learning from a variety of teachers, some of whom were Muslim. He and his family left Spain while he was in his early twenties because of the intolerant policies of the new Muslim rulers of Andalusia and eventually settled in Egypt;

yet, he always considered himself to be an Andalusian. In Egypt Maimonides became the chief physician to the Sultan and served several times as the official leader of the Jewish community, a position he merited by his enormous command of Rabbinic literature. His major contributions to Jewish legal studies were his *Commentary on the Mishnah* (written in Arabic) and his code of law *The Mishneh Torah* (written in Hebrew). Both works, however, contain something that previous and later legal books lacked: theology. In the earlier *Commentary* Maimonides often digresses to address theological issues; moreover, he formulates a creed consisting of thirteen basic beliefs. This list of dogmas is noteworthy not only for being one of the earliest attempts to propound a creed in Judaism but also for the use of philosophical terms and ideas in the formulation of these principles. For example, in explaining prophecy Maimonides introduces the reader to the theory of the Agent Intellect as the proximate cause or transmitter of the prophetic emanation (Sixth Principle). The same philosophical orientation is even more evident in the *Mishneh Toreh*, whose first book is devoted to a systematic presentation of the most important philosophical and theological ideas that are the foundations of the Jewish legal system. And again, Maimonides does not hesitate to acquaint his readers with the standard vocabulary of the philosophy and science of his day, which at this time was that of Aristotle, an Aristotle who had become less Plotinian but not entirely so.

But for Jewish philosophy his last major work, *The Guide of the Perplexed*, is of capital importance. Written in Arabic it was translated into Hebrew in Maimonides' own lifetime by Samuel ibn Tibbon, the son of Judah ibn Tibbon, who had translated Saadia's and Halevi's theological works. Almost immediately the *Guide* became the canonical text for the study of Jewish philosophical theology, a position it has retained even to this day; indeed, it was for many Yeshivah students their first exposure to philosophy, sometimes clandestine because of its controversial reputation. The *Guide* was also translated into Latin fairly early, and it had a

significant influence upon Christian medieval thought, especially upon Thomas Aquinas, who refers to Maimonides as "Rabbi Moses." The great German philosopher and mathematician Leibniz also read the *Guide* in Latin and made notes on it. It was probably the first philosophical book read by Spinoza, who in his *Theological-Political Treatise* criticizes it severely.

In several respects the *Guide* is a puzzling book. It attempts to resolve perplexities, but in many cases, because of the *Guide's* difficult nature, the reader is left in a more bewildered state than before. Maimonides explicitly states that this is not a philosophical book; nor is it a treatise in Kalam, as Saadia's *Book of Beliefs and Opinions* is. Ostensibly it is work of biblical exegesis. Most of Part 1 is devoted to an explanation of certain words and verses of the Torah that are particularly vexing primarily because of their anthropomorphic character. Maimonides assumes four principles about the Torah: 1) the language of the Bible is frequently equivocal and parabolic; 2) the Torah itself contains philosophical teachings, often hidden by its non-literal language; 3) these teachings are to be divulged only to those who are intellectually and morally prepared to receive them; and 4) these philosophical ideas are identical with what the Rabbis termed *maaseh bereshit* ("the works of creation") and *maaseh merkavah* ("the works of the divine chariot of Ezekiel"), the mystical teachings whose dissemination the rabbis reserved for the elite. Compounding the already complicated goals of the book, Maimonides concludes his Introduction by telling his reader that this work contains intentional contradictions, inserted in order to hide certain ideas from the unprepared. This latter point has occasioned considerable controversy, both in the medieval and modern periods, as to what Maimonides really believed. At any rate, the *Guide* has dominated all late medieval and early modern Jewish thought.

God: Maimonides' theology begins with two fundamental theorems: 1) God is absolutely one; and 2) God is utterly incorporeal. Although all Jews would certainly agree with the first, Maimonides' understanding of divine unicity is importantly different from the common view. To him God's oneness signifies primarily God's simplicity: the absence in God of any kind of plurality or compositeness. This notion of unicity will lead him to develop a radical conception of the divine attributes, as we shall see. God's incorporeality too had been a dogma for many Jewish thinkers before Maimonides; certainly Saadia and Halevi were insistent upon this theme. But in Maimonides this dogma is so important that he has no tolerance for anyone who denies or compromises it in any way. Indeed, the masses must be taught this doctrine, even though they may not understand why it is true. To believe that God has any corporeal characteristics is tantamount to idolatry, and this is punishable by death.

These two theorems lead Maimonides to a major reinterpretation of Scripture's language pertaining to God. Chapter after chapter of Part 1 of the Guide are devoted to showing that certain terms or phrases predicated of God in the Torah are not to be understood as implying any kind of corporeality. Thus, in the notoriously difficult verse wherein Moses is told that he will only be able to see God's "back" (Ex. 33:20-23), Maimonides reads this term as meaning that which is posterior to God, i.e., that which God has created. In other words, Moses is granted cognition of the natural world, not of the essence of God. Of greater significance and novelty is Maimonides' doctrine of divine attributes, a theme in medieval philosophy that had been developed for centuries. Maimonides claims that no attributes can be positively affirmed of God except attributes of action. Essential attributes cannot be affirmed, since they are definitional, and God cannot be defined; for to define something is to "split" it up into several properties, such that the defined thing is located in a classification scheme. But God cannot be confined to a taxonomical system of human contrivance. Nor can we ascribe to God either accidental or relational properties: not accidental attributes, because such attributes are such that they can be acquired or lost, and this would introduce change in God; nor relational properties, since they imply some sort of similarity between the related entities, but God is totally dissimilar to any thing created. So the only type of attribute we can positively affirm of God are actions, which are really not properties, i.e., adjectival, but doings, i.e., verbal. The latter do not imply any internal compositeness, change or comparison with God. Thus, when we say that God created the universe, we are just saying that the universe was brought into existence by something that itself has no cause for its existence. No subsistent property is being assigned to God as part of His essence along with other such properties, like goodness and justice.

But perhaps the most original feature of his theory is Maimonides' doctrine of negative attributes. Although earlier thinkers had recognized this type of description of God, they had also allowed other attributes to be asserted. Not so Maimonides. Indeed, for him negative attributes are the only philosophically legitimate kind of language we have to speak about God. The language of actions seems to be for him a concession to the masses. The true worshipper of God describes God in terms of what God is not. This is the best way to preserve divine simplicity. So, for example, when we want to say that God is one, we really should say "God is not many." In formulating the original proposition in negative form what we signify is that God is not the kind of entity that can be many, which property is applicable to everything other than God. Similarly, when we say of God that God is good, we really mean that God is not the kind of being that could be evil. In this sense, the doctrine of negative attributes is a version of the theory of category mistakes. The ascription of a positive attribute (other than an action) to God is not just a false assertion; it is non-sensical. It is like describing a number as red.

Creation of the universe: Part 2 of the Guide is devoted to two major themes in both the Torah and medieval philosophy: creation of the world and prophecy. By Maimonides' time both issues had become more complicated with the assimilation of Aristotelian philosophy, which denies creation and questions the legitimacy of prophecy. The sophisticated metaphysical cosmologies of

Al-Farabi and ibn Sina had reformulated or reinterpreted the traditional understanding of creation and prophecy, and for Maimonides these were fundamental principles of the Torah. So despite his great respect for Aristotle and Al-Farabi, Maimonides undertakes to defend the traditional idea of creation and to show that prophecy can be understood within a philosophical framework.

Maimonides begins by specifying the three theories of creation he considers worthy of consideration. first, he states the view of the Torah: creation *ex nihilo*. Like Saadia, Maimonides lays down the principle that God created the entire universe from no pre-existing matter. Time itself was created along with the creation of the world. Moreover, this creative act was voluntary and manifests purpose and design, since God is a free agent. The second theory Maimonides attributes to several thinkers, but he mentions only one by name, Plato. According to this theory, God creates the universe out of some eternal formless matter at the beginning of time. In a sense this view is a hybrid. Although it asserts the absolute beginning of the cosmos, it posits the eternity of matter. Finally, we have Aristotle's doctrine of the eternity of the universe: no creation at all, only the continuous, infinite duration of nature, both in the past as well as in the future.

There is one particular feature of Maimonides' representation of Aristotle's theory that is crucial to understanding why he believes this theory not only to be false but also to be clearly rejected as inimical to Judaism; it will also be a factor that Maimonides will use in his criticism of Aristotle's cosmology. According to Maimonides, Aristotle's world is governed by strict laws, allowing for no exceptions; it is also a universe in which there is no inherent design. Although for Aristotle there is one ultimate first Cause, God, who is in some way causally connected to nature, this God is not the maker of nature. Such a conception of both God and nature are unacceptable to and subversive of the Torah. This is so not because the first verse of the Bible says that God created the world, but because the deterministic naturalism of Aristotle undermines the belief in miracles, which idea expresses both the notions of the free activity of God and of his providence.

In general, we hold that the "gates of interpretation are not closed," meaning that we may interpret a biblical verse to satisfy a philosophical or scientific demand if we need to, i.e., if this philosophical teaching were proved. But in the case of creation, the gates of interpretation are closed, since the very existence of the Torah is subverted if the laws of the universe rule out miracles and divine providence. So it is not without justification that Maimonides considers creation to be the second most important principle in Judaism after the unity of God.

To defend the Torah doctrine of creation *ex nihilo* Maimonides adopts the following strategy. First he shows that the arguments for the eternity of the universe are invalid. Second, he argues that although neither the creation theory nor the eternity theory is provable, the former is a more plausible account of nature. Finally, he claims that two creation theories that rival the idea of creation *ex nihilo* are in the one case incoherent and in the other unproved. So there is no good reason to reject creation *ex nihilo*. Neither the compromise theory of the Muslim philosophers, that the universe is both eternal and created, nor the doctrine of Plato and others, that the world has been created out of eternal matter, commends itself against the idea of creation *ex nihilo*.

In invalidating the eternity arguments Maimonides first divides these arguments into two groups: the scientific arguments and the metaphysical arguments. He then constructs one clever counter argument that undermines all the scientific arguments and one counter argument to take care of the metaphysical difficulties. All of the scientific arguments assert that creation is absurd because the hypothesis of a first moment of time at which the world begins to exist is incompatible with the laws of physics. Maimonides exposes the invalidity of theses arguments by showing that they all assume that these laws are uniformly and universally retrodictable to every moment in the past. But this is to beg the question. The hypothesis of creation asserts that the first moment of the world's duration is unique: since it is first it is not bound to any prior moment by any law. It is in this sense a "free" event. Once created the universe does exhibit lawfulness; but this is a fact posterior to creation, not governing it. The metaphysical arguments for eternity are dismissed by the application of the doctrine of negative attributes. These arguments are variations on the theme that to create is to make something *absolutely* and as such it is an act that is motivated by some particular need or desire, thus entailing some change in the maker; otherwise, why would the maker make what he or she makes? Maimonides shows that such an argument presupposes a principle that is simply false, that God's will is like human volition. But we have already learned in Part One of the *Guide* that there is no analogy at all between the divine will and our will! With these refutations Maimonides feels free to conclude that the theory of creation has not been shown to be false; it is indeed a live option.

To show that creation is more plausible than the eternity hypothesis, Maimonides borrows an argument from the Kalam, a body of doctrines that he is usually reluctant to praise or to cite on his own behalf. This argument was known as the "Particularization Argument:" if two contrary or contradictory states of affairs are equally possible, then if one of them is the case, there needs to be a good reason why this particular state of affairs is true and its opposite is false. Now let us recall Maimonides' point that Aristotle's world is a deterministic one: accordingly, each and every event is governed by strict laws such that there are no exceptions or anomalies. Aristotle, as Maimonides interprets him, is committed to the principle of maximal rationality: everything in nature is explicable. The trouble is, claims the Particularization Argument, several anomalies occur in nature, especially in the celestial domain, where there should not be any, since for Aristotle this is where perfection reigns. Consider, for example, the variation in the colors of the illumination reflected by the planets. Venus' light is bluish, but that of Mars is reddish. Now according to Aristotle all the heavenly

bodies consist of the same perfect element, the aether, or quintessence. Thus these color variations cannot be explained internally. Nor can they be explained by their respective distances or motions, Maimonides claims. So they are "surds," natural phenomena that are not just rare, but anomalous. But they cease to be anomalous on the creation hypothesis. These various particularities are the results of divine will. God chooses to make Venus in such a way that it reflects a bluish color and Mars a reddish color. The creation theory then has greater explanatory power. It covers facts that the eternity theory cannot but, as a deterministic theory, should be able to explain. Maimonides makes it clear that this argument does not prove demonstratively that creation is true; but it does make creation a more credible hypothesis.

Finally, Maimonides eliminates the two other versions of creation: eternal creation and Platonic creation. The first is simply incoherent. It attempts to marry the notion that the universe is eternal to the idea that it has nevertheless been created by God with design. But how, Maimonides asks, can these two theses be combined? If the universe is a necessary emanation out of the first Cause, as it is for Al-Farabi and ibn Sina, how can it exhibit design and purpose, which are signs of creation? Indeed, there would be in such a world no contingency at all, and so miracles would be impossible. To the Platonic theory Maimonides shows more respect and tolerance. Unlike Aristotle or the Muslim philosophers Plato maintained that God willingly created the world at the beginning of time. This view allows for miracles. But since it has not been proved, Maimonides claims, there is no need to accept it. If it were proved, we would reinterpret Scripture accordingly; but since there is no such proof, we are free to follow tradition and accept creation *ex nihilo*.

Prophecy: With prophecy Maimonides' agenda was different. Aristotle had not denied prophecy altogether, and the Muslim philosophers had given it a place in their philosophical systems. It seems that here Maimonides' main opponent was the common understanding of prophecy. Although he will depart from the philosophers' account of prophecy in one important respect, his view is closer to that of Al-Farabi than it is to the doctrine of some fellow Jews, many of whom hold that God can at whim give prophecy to virtually anyone. After all, Amos was just a shepherd! Maimonides scornfully rejects this view and favors the idea of Al-Farabi that prophecy is a natural perfection that humans are capable of attaining so long as they satisfy certain conditions. A prophet must be morally sound, intellectually perfect, and have a strong imagination. But Maimonides disagrees with Al-Farabi in one important fact: according to the former, God can withhold prophecy from someone who is fit to receive it. As in all miracles divine will is operative, and in this sense prophecy, or better its absence, is a miracle. As in his theory of creation Maimonides thus preserves some element of contingency in the universe and freedom in God's will.

How does prophecy come about? Following Al-Farabi, Maimonides maintains that prophecy is one of several sorts of emanations, or influences, deriving from God via the mediation of the Agent Intellect, the lowest of the supernal intellects posited by the medieval Aristotelians, which the ordinary religious person calls an angel. The prophetic emanation first reaches the perfected intellect of the recipient and then the perfected imagination. If the emanation fails to reach or affect the imagination for some reason, then the individual is only able to engage in intellectual pursuits, such as philosophy or physics; if the emanation only affects the imagination, the person then is a politician or poet at best, a magician or diviner at worse. But if the emanation influences both faculties, we have a prophet, unless God intervenes. Perfection of these faculties is necessary since the prophet can and does receive philosophical or scientific truths, some of which he transmits to the masses. The prophet needs a good imagination in order to transmit these truths to the masses, since they can only understand them in a form that is accessible to the imaginative faculty, such as stories. This is one reason why the Torah uses poetic and parabolic language.

There is one important exception to this general account of prophecy. Already in his early Mishnah commentary Maimonides had listed as one of the basic principles of Judaism the uniqueness of Moses' prophecy. Indeed, Moses had attained the status of an angel, whereby he was no longer bound by bodily needs and lived the life of pure intellect; thus, he no longer needed the imagination in order to receive his prophecies. This point is repeated in the *Guide* and is used to argue that the term "prophet" applies to Moses and to the other prophets only in an equivocal sense. Moses' prophecy is then utterly intellectual.

Maimonides' exaltation of Moses represents an exegesis of several passages in the Torah where it is explicitly stated that Moses' prophecies were unique (Num. 12:8; Deut. 34:10). Unlike the other prophets Moses did not prophesize by means of a dream or vision: God spoke to God "face to face." This means to Maimonides that Moses received the prophetic emanation without the use of the imagination. Since for Maimonides, following Aristotle, God is intellect, the most intimate relation between God and man is intellectual (*Guide* 1:1). Moses had attained the highest level of proximity to God; hence his relationship with God was purely intellectual in the literal sense. It is for this reason, that no other prophet before or since Moses has ever arisen.

Providence: Part 3 of the *Guide* is diverse, discussing a variety of doctrines. But one of the most important of these themes is the question of divine providence, especially as it relates to the issue of evil and the suffering of the righteous. This latter point leads Maimonides to devote two chapters to an explanation of the Book of Job. However, his discussion of providence is enmeshed with another issue that was, as we have seen, of paramount importance, divine omniscience. Indeed, according to Maimonides, philosophers' denial of God's cognition of future contingent events, especially as they pertain to human affairs, follows from their denial of particular providence, the doctrine that God attends to the specific details in the lives of individual persons. Philosophers reject individual providence on empirical grounds: just look and see—the innocent suffer and the wicked prosper. If God had knowledge of particulars, he would not allow such an unjust distribution of goods and evils.

In the course of his analysis of omniscience Maimonides also addresses the issue of the compatibility of God's knowledge of the future with the contingency of future events. But his solution to this alleged dilemma differs from that of Saadia's. There is no real dilemma between divine omniscience and human freedom; there seems to be a problem only because we make the error of construing God's cognitive procedures on the model of own. But we have learned from Part 1 of the *Guide* that there is no analogy at all between God and us. So why do we persist in inferring from what is true of our cognitive experience to God's cognition? This venerable dilemma is simply a case of the fallacy of equivocation. Once we realize that God does not acquire knowledge as we do, we should then understand why God's knowledge of the future, especially of future contingencies, is not subject to the difficulties that our knowledge of them entails. God's cognitive logic is radically different from ours. God knows eternally; there literally is "nothing new under the sun" for God. Humans, on the other hand, derive their information as events take place. Our knowledge is always accumulating; God's knowledge is constant and immutable.

Once the question of omniscience has been resolved, Maimonides turns to the issue of providence. He first states the views of Epicurus, Aristotle, the Kalam, and the Torah. The Epicurean denial of providence is summarily dismissed, having been refuted by Aristotle. The Aristotelian theory is carefully represented, since it will turn out to be the doctrine that Maimonides considers to be the most significant rival to his own theory. Maimonides distinguishes between the two schools of Kalam, the Ashariyya and the Mutazaliyya, and rejects them both, although for different reasons. The Ashariyya doctrine is deficient because it denies human free will in favor of an extremely strong notion of divine power that annuls power in any crea-

ture: everything is the result of divine decree. The Mutazaliyya theory is a bit better since it accepts free will, albeit in a modified form; but it falters in its doctrines of complete divine providence, which it holds even extends to individual animals other than people.

Maimonides' account of the Torah's view of providence is complex. He distinguishes three different versions of the Torah's doctrine: 1) the doctrine of the masses, according to whom God extends his providence to all human beings individually and justly; 2) the view of some later Rabbinic sages, that God sometimes afflicts the righteous with suffering precisely because he loves them and wants them to earn a greater reward for bearing these afflictions with patience and faith; and 3) his own position, which explicitly denies this latter doctrine of "afflictions of love" as non-biblical. Maimonides proceeds to develop a modified Torah theory of providence, the chief novelty of which is his thesis that individual providence is a function of intellectual perfection. He makes it quite clear that Aristotle was almost right when he denied individual providence; he just failed to realize that there is individual providence in the human species. In the plant and animal world there is only general, or natural, providence: the provision of the means for the survival of the species. Individuals within those species are subject to chance. Individual humans, however, are able to become objects of divine concern if they live the life of the intellect, the ultimate goal of which is the love of God through knowledge. Since that which makes humans in the image of God is their intellect, it is only by means of intellect that we can merit individual providence. Thus, so long as the we devote ourselves to God by contemplating and knowing Him, we are "under God's wings;" as soon as this link is severed we are subject to the "arrows of fortune" just as the squirrels are.

The Torah: Since he was one of the great legal scholars in the history of Judaism, it is not surprising that even in his philosophical book the "Law" is a subject of concern. Like Saadia, Maimonides fully believes in the immutability of the Torah; he also believes in its essential rationality. Indeed, he maintains the latter thesis in a very strong form: virtually all of the commandments in the Torah have some purpose or rationale. His discussion of this topic is based upon the explicit rejection of the view, held by the masses and some legal scholars, that the divine commandments need not have reason at all. Such a view, Maimonides argues, is an insult to God. In working out the details of his philosophy of Jewish law, Maimonides borrows from his great legal code, the Mishneh Torah; in particular he uses the classification scheme of the earlier work to divide the whole corpus of the commandments into fourteen categories. He then discusses each category, assigning some general rationale for each one and providing in many cases specific reasons for the particular commandments that fall under each category. So, for example, the dietary prohibitions are not arbitrary decrees but rational means for the preservation of our health. Here Maimonides uses his medical expertise to good advantage. Certain animal meat is not good for us since it is fatty or unclean. God, the perfect lawgiver, thus has a good reason for commanding us not to eat pork. Other prohibitions are more symbolic; circumcision is commanded in order to teach us to curtail our sexual impulses.

Maimonides' *Guide* has had an enormous impact upon Jewish religious thought, just as his legal works have had. In spite of occasional opposition to the former book in both the medieval and modern periods, it is still studied by all Jews interested in a more sophisticated theological understanding of the Torah. Even though its Aristotelian framework is for the most part obsolete, it remains enlightening. In so far as the *Guide* is essentially a guide on how to read the Bible, it appeals to all those who still see the Torah as canonical yet do not subscribe to any particular reading of the Torah as canonical. As the "master of the *Guide*" has taught, "the gates of interpretation are not closed."

Jewish Averroism: The first translator of the *Guide*, Samuel ibn Tibbon, and its earliest commentators were not only disciples of Maimonides; they had another mentor, the great Cordoban commentator on Aristotle,

Averroes (ibn Rushd, 1126-1198). This "dual loyalty" resulted in 1) a particular interpretation of the *Guide* and 2) the development of a certain philosophical orientation that was more radical than what seemed to be its explicit teachings. Averroes' influence in the late middle ages was enormous. His commentaries on Aristotle became authoritative and his philosophical treatises were also important. This was not only true for Jewish philosophy but for Christian philosophy as well, so much so that in 1277 the Bishop of Paris had to issue a decree declaring the errors of Averroes and other thinkers, including Maimonides. But Averroes was the main target of his ire. And not without reason.

Jewish and Christian followers of Averroes were especially attracted to two particular doctrines in Averroes that did not sit well with the orthodox. First, Averroes had developed a version of the eternal creation theory that seemed to avoid some of the defects of the earlier formulations of this doctrine. In his view the language of emanation is minimized, if not eliminated all together, and the notion of God's eternal and infinite activity is preserved, from which he deduced the eternity of God's product, the world. The eternal cause produces an eternal effect. Second, in studying ideas on the soul and its immortality found in the late Greek commentators on Aristotle, as well as in his Muslim philosophical predecessors, Averroes concluded that human immortality consists in the conjunction and unification of the human mind with the Agent Intellect, such that no personal immortality resulted. All human intellects are one in the one Agent Intellect.

At this juncture in the history of medieval Jewish philosophy, southern France and Italy became the centers of philosophical study, especially of Averroes. Thinkers such as Isaac Albalag (c. end of the thirteenth century), Joseph ibn Caspi (1279-c. 1340) and Moses Narboni (c. 1300-c. 1362) were deeply influenced by Averroes and imported his understanding of Aristotle's philosophy into their own understanding of Maimonides' *Guide*, which had already become the canonical text for all medieval Jewish philosophers. These philosophers developed the doctrine of the esoteric teachings of the *Guide*, which in effect amounted to an Averroist reading of the book. Thus, for example, Maimonides' explicit defense of creation *ex nihilo* is disregarded as just an exoteric doctrine designed to appease and deceive the masses; in truth, Maimonides believed in eternal creation. Since Maimonides said relatively little, especially in the *Guide*, about immortality, the Jewish Averroists felt free to adopt Averroes' theory of conjunction with the Agent Intellect as their position on immortality. It is no wonder then that a sharp reaction to these philosophical "excesses" erupted in Spain and Southern France in the beginning of the fourteenth century, ultimately culminating in a ban against the study of philosophy. To no avail, however, since philosophical studies continued, especially under the guidance of Averroes, whose commentaries on Aristotle were avidly translated into Hebrew and later into Latin. Jewish Averroism persisted, at least until the early Renaissance: Elijah del Medigo (c. 1460-1493) wrote commentaries on Averroes and defended his general philosophical position.

Levi ben Gershom: The most significant response to Maimonides and Averroes that was both appreciative and critical came from the Provencal philosopher Levi ben Gershom (Gersonides, 1288-1344). Perhaps the most diverse and erudite of all medieval Jewish thinkers, Gersonides was particularly creative in the mathematical sciences, including astronomy, and biblical exegesis as well as philosophy. Although he did not write a major work in Jewish law, he was an excellent Talmudist, to whom several legal questions were addressed; moreover, his *Commentary on the Torah* is replete with detailed and subtle legal discussions. Beginning his philosophical career with super-commentaries on Averroes' commentaries on Aristotle, Levi eventually wrote an independent philosophical treatise entitled *"The Wars of the Lord"* (*Milhamot Hashem*). Originally designed as an essay on the question of creation, the scope of the treatise was expanded when Gersonides realized that this issue could not be divorced from several other crucial problems. The final version comprises six books,

some consisting of several parts. Each book is devoted to one main theme that had become a "disputed question." In actual fact, the work turned out to be the most comprehensive, detailed, and sophisticated philosophical book produced by a medieval Jew; virtually every topic in medieval metaphysics, natural philosophy, and psychology is treated, along with plentiful doses of astronomy and biology thrown in for good measure.

Although quite respectful of his philosophical mentors, Aristotle, Averroes, and Maimonides, Gersonides did not hesitate to criticize his teachers. Even his super-commentaries on Averroes exhibit a independent mind that is not reluctant to point out the defects in either Aristotle or Averroes. This is more evident in *The Wars of the Lord*. Indeed, each of its books can be considered a critique of a major thesis of one of his predecessors. Book 1: the rejection of Averroes' interpretation of Aristotle's psychology and the doctrine of immortality as conjunction with the Agent Intellect. Book 2: a defense of the validity and utility of extrasensory phenomena such as divination, dreams, and prophecy against the skepticism of Aristotle and others. Book 3: a solution of the problem of divine omniscience that departs significantly from that of Maimonides. Book 4: a defense of divine providence for individual humans, against Aristotle. Book 5: a general theory of cosmology, with particular emphasis upon the celestial domain, deviating from some basic ideas of Averroes. Book 6: a proof that the universe is created, not eternal, and that it was not created *ex nihilo* but from eternal formless matter.

Gersonides' boldness is best seen in Books 3 and 6, where he reaches conclusions that are "non-standard." In Book 3 he takes up the issue of God's knowledge: what can God know? For Gersonides this question involves the general problem of the domain of God's knowledge, in particular the issue whether God knows individual things; it also includes the venerable dilemma concerning the knowledge of future contingencies. In his discussion of this problem he subjects Maimonides' solution to severe criticism, especially his doctrine of negative attributes. If all the divine attributes, especially knowledge, are completely equivocal, as Maimonides claims, then we would never be in a position even to make negative statements about God; for in a negative proposition the attribute negated has to have the same meaning as it has in an affirmative proposition. Otherwise, we have committed the fallacy of equivocation. So the negative attribute solution to the problem of divine omniscience gets us nowhere. According to Levi, attributes are predicated of God in a manner that is intermediate between absolute equivocation and strict univocity. An attribute, such as knowledge, is said of God in a primary sense, whereas of Abraham it said secondarily; i.e., God knows things perfectly, whereas Abraham doesn't.

With Maimonides out of the way, Gersonides proceeds to develop his own theory of divine cognition. It is clear from his detailed discussion of the arguments of the philosophers against strong omniscience (the thesis that God knows absolutely everything) that Levi accepts their basic line of reasoning. Since individual things and events here on earth are spatial-temporal, knowledge of such phenomena must be obtained via sensory perception. But God does not have a sensory apparatus, since he is incorporeal. Indeed, God transcends space-time; so he cannot have knowledge of space-time individuals. Moreover, if anyone had knowledge of future contingent individual events, such events would lose their contingency. Gersonides clearly accepts the Aristotelian doctrine that foreknowledge is incompatible with contingency. A firm defender of human freedom he claims that God does not know what humans freely do. After all, if God really knew what Abraham would do to Isaac, why would He have tested him? A test implies some indeterminacy in outcomes. All God knew was that most people would refuse to sacrifice their only child; but he also knew that it is possible for at least one person to make this choice. Abraham was that person. So Gersonides' position is one of "weak omniscience:" God knows all that which is knowable; but future contingencies are not knowable. This is no imperfection in God,

no more than it is an imperfection in God that he cannot undo the past or commit suicide. Just as an omnipotent being is able to do everything that is doable, an omniscient being is able to know everything that is knowable. The content, then, of God's knowledge consists of the general laws of the universe, and this, according to Aristotle, is what knowledge really is.

The longest book in the treatise, Book 6 is devoted to the question of creation of the universe. Gersonides was not satisfied with Maimonides' treatment of the problem, and for two reasons. first, Maimonides had claimed that no proof for creation is possible or available, thus suggesting that certainty on this issue depends on faith. Gersonides was in no rush to run to the asylum of ignorance. He believed that reason was competent to solve all or most of the significant problems in metaphysics and natural philosophy. Second, he believed that the traditional doctrine of creation ex nihilo, to which Maimonides had at least given lip-service, was absurd. Accordingly, the question of creation had to be re-examined. Gersonides' strategy is as follows. First he proves that the universe was created at the very beginning of time; i.e., the past duration of the universe is finite. Second, he shows that creation ex nihilo is untenable and that a modified version of the Platonic theory of creation out of matter is the correct doctrine. Third, he presents detailed criticisms of the Aristotelian arguments for the eternity of the universe. finally, he turns to the Bible and demonstrates how his cosmogony is compatible with the account in Genesis 1.

Like Maimonides, Levi considers Aristotle to be his main adversary. To refute the eternity theory Gersonides takes two basic ideas of Aristotelian natural philosophy and uses them against Aristotle. First, Aristotle's concept of nature is teleological: natural phenomena exhibit ends, or goals. Within Aristotle's theory of explanation the telic, or final, cause plays an important role: the end of an acorn is to become an oak tree; the goal of a caterpillar is to be a butterfly. Moreover, living organisms display an internal structure that is teleological. The various organs and limbs of the animal or plant are so arranged and composed that the survival of the organism, at least for some time, is assured so long as nothing external interferes. Now Gersonides uses this teleological orientation to argue that telic phenomena imply a maker, indeed, a creator, unless they come about by chance. But chance phenomena are by definition rare; moreover, in the heavenly domain, which is Aristotle's favorite arena, there is no chance. So if we can find some telic features in the heavenly domain, we shall have proved that the celestial bodies have been created. And this is exactly what Levi does: he looks upwards and discovers that the heavenly bodies do exhibit telic properties. After all, the sun is responsible, Aristotle insists, for the cycle of generation and reproduction of living things on earth. This shows that these bodies are the "product of an agent," or creator. This argument is a version of the argument known later as "the argument from design;" or, as the Psalmist puts it, "The heavens declare the glory of God; the sky proclaims His handiwork" (Ps. 19:2).

Second, Aristotle's physics is finitistic; it especially avoids any notion of an actual infinite magnitude, such as an infinitely large body. Nevertheless, he does allow potential infinites. Time and motion, for example, are successively infinite in the sense that each moment of their duration succeeds the other without end, both in the past and in the future. Gersonides finds this theory to be incoherent. If time is truly infinite in the past, as the eternity theory claims, then it is really an actual, not potential, infinite. For past time is significantly different from future time in that every possible state of affairs in the past is either true or false: for example, that the Atlanta Braves won the World Series in 1995 is true. Moreover, every such fact literally "fills up" the past, such that there are no truth-value indeterminacies in the past. Past time then is real, or actual, since it is a closed system of facts, many of which have important consequences. Accordingly, the past is still with us. Now if the past is infinite, as Aristotle claims, it would be an actual infinite, which his physics denies. So here, as be-

fore, it turns out that Aristotle's philosophy is really committed to the creation, not eternity, of the world.

Having demonstrated the createdness of the world, Gersonides now has to show how it was created. Was it created *ex nihilo*? Despite his respect for tradition and especially for Maimonides, on this issue we must follow the truth, and the truth is that creation *ex nihilo*, as tradition understands it, is false. Here Gersonides leans heavily upon certain principles of Aristotle's physics, especially the impossibility of a vacuum in nature. Gersonides claims that the notion of making something out of absolute nothing implies the pre-mundane and post-mundane existence of a vacuum. Think of creation *ex nihilo* as the act of making a ball out of nothing and placing it in an empty box. Now before it was made and placed in that box, the box was empty but potentially fillable; in this sense the box was "vacuous" at one point. Moreover, after the ball has been made and placed in the box, there is still space in the box which can be filled up by other balls or different objects. Now this is the situation in the creation *ex nihilo* scenario: before creation there was empty space; after creation there is still space surrounding the world that can be filled up by other worlds or left unoccupied as a void. But for both Aristotle and Gersonides this is just absurd, since "nature abhors a vacuum." Accordingly, for Gersonides, God created the world out of some eternal formless body, as Plato suggested. This cosmogony is compatible with the belief in miracles, as Maimonides admitted, and can be actually found in the Torah. After all, we are not told that God ever created the waters! These primordial waters are the formless matter out of which God made the physical universe. Gersonides identifies this matter with Gen. 1:2's notion of the *bohu*, often translated *formlessness*.

Gersonides' impact upon posterity has been double edged. His philosophical ideas, especially those on omniscience and creation, were generally rejected and sharply criticized by later Jewish thinkers; nevertheless, they were taken seriously. Most of the important late medieval theologians devote considerable attention to Gersonides' arguments on these issues. On the other hand, Gersonides' scientific and exegetical works were appreciated and studied, the former often translated into Latin, the latter included in the printed editions of the Rabbinic Bible (*Miqraot Gedolot*). It is both ironic and amusing that one and the same student of the "Ralbag" (Rabbi Levi ben Gershom) will revere his biblical commentaries but vigorously reject some of the more radical theories of the *Wars of the Lord* or even deny that this work actually was written by the Ralbag!

The swan-song of Spanish-Jewish philosophy, Hasdai Crescas: From 1391-1492 the Jews of Spain suffered all kinds of tribulations and agonies, ultimately culminating in the Expulsion of 1492. Yet despite these calamities Jewish intellectual activity did not cease. Indeed, several of the more notable thinkers responded to these events in their literary works. For example, Hasdai Crescas (d. 1410) wrote a refutation of Christian dogmas at exactly the time when Spanish Jewry was exposed to a concerted and violent conversion campaign. His pupil Joseph Albo similarly wrote his *Iqqarim* (*Principles*) to meet the onslaught of Christian preachers, who forced the Jews to listen to their conversionary sermons in the synagogues. But Crescas' more important book is his treatise *Or Adonai* (*Light of the Lord*). This work too has a definite polemical character; but its target is not the Christians so much as it is those Jews—most notably Maimonides and Gersonides—who have adopted Aristotelian philosophy in order to understand and formulate the basic beliefs of Judaism. The *Light of the Lord* is ostensibly an alternative to Maimonides' great legal code the *Mishneh Torah*, which Crescas finds defective for several reasons, of which one is its inadequate presentation of Jewish theology. Since Maimonides prefaced his code with a discussion of the fundamental theological dogmas of Judaism, Crescas too begins his new code with a treatment of the Jewish creed; the second part of the work, which was to be devoted to law, was either never written or has not survived.

Crescas believed that Maimonides' attempt to formulate an authoritative creed had failed for two reasons: 1) it did not distinguish beliefs according to different levels of importance, for all it did was to provide a list of dogmas, without showing or explaining why these and not other beliefs were fundamental; 2) it presented these beliefs within an Aristotelian framework, which Crescas believed to be erroneous. So a new creed was necessary, one that would exhibit the logical and theological weight of each dogma and that would not be dependent upon faulty or unproved Aristotelian ideas. The immediate result of this undertaking is a creed that is arranged according to four levels of importance: 1) beliefs that are basic to any religion; 2) beliefs that are fundamental to any revealed religion; 3) teachings that are essential to Judaism; and 4) diverse and sometimes opposing ideas that one finds taught by Jewish sages but have no authoritative status. Thus, whereas the Jew must believe in all the ideas in categories 1-3, he is free to believe or not believe in any of those in the fourth group. For example, it is required for all to believe in God (category 1), since this belief defines what it is to be religious; it is incumbent upon anyone who accepts a revealed religion to believe in prophecy (category 2), since prophecy is the vehicle of revelation; for a Jew it is obligatory to accept the authority and immutability of the Torah (category 3); but a Jew need not believe either that the universe will be destroyed or will be everlasting (category 4). For Crescas then the content of Jewish belief manifests a clear logical structure that indicates why a particular dogma is a dogma and shows its relationship to other ideas in Jewish theology.

But the *Light of the Lord* is more significant for what it says about these various beliefs. For in Crescas' explanations of these ideas, his acuity and originality are evident. First, in his analysis of the dogmas in group 1, he exposes the basic errors in the Aristotelian physics and metaphysics that had provided the framework for Maimonides' philosophical theology of Judaism. Many of the axioms of Aristotle's physics are rejected. For example, Aristotle's denial of the actual infinite is sharply criticized: according to

Crescas an infinite body, an infinite number of individuals, or an infinite vacuum outside our world, indeed the possibility of plural universes—all of these hypotheses are genuine possibilities. Although Crescas' critique of Aristotle's physics was not intended to lay the groundwork for a new physics, but to show its irrelevance for Jewish theology, his arguments against Aristotle did open the way for more novel and fruitful ideas in natural philosophy.

Among the ideas included in the category 2 are the beliefs in divine omniscience and human choice: any revealed religion presupposes that God knows human beings and that we have the freedom to respond to God's commands. Crescas' discussions of these two topics are quite striking, perhaps radical. On the question of divine omniscience he holds the traditional strong view, defended by Saadia and Maimonides, that God knows everything, including future contingent affairs. But his defense of this position is original, at least in Jewish philosophy. He subscribes to the solution that had been suggested by several neo-Platonic thinkers, such as Proclus and Boethius, and that had been adopted by Thomas Aquinas: God has timeless knowledge of temporal facts, including contingent facts of the future. Since God is eternal in the sense of transcending time, God knows all facts in the "present;" i.e., he knows all facts simultaneously, even though in time these events happen successively. On the other hand, each contingent event remains contingent even though God's knowledge of it fixes its truth value. It is, as Crescas puts it, contingent in itself but necessary by virtue of its cause, which in this case is God's knowing it. Thus, although God eternally knows that Abraham would offer up Isaac as a sacrifice, this deed is not a necessary truth in the sense that $2 + 2 = 4$ is. It is conceivable that Abraham would refuse to kill Isaac; but, of course, if he had, God would have known it.

Crescas' analysis of choice is truly original, perhaps even radical, since he unabashedly and unambiguously affirms a deterministic account of human behavior. All human actions have causes from which they necessarily follow, just as all natural events are determined by causes. In this respect Crescas is a good Stoic determinist. Yet, he also believes that we have choice. How can the latter be reconciled with his adherence to determinism? No problem, or so he thinks. Our choices do have causes, like everything else; but choices and the resulting actions are necessary only in relation to these causes. In and of themselves our choices are logically contingent, just as they are even when God knows what they are. We would be bereft of choice if it were impossible for us to do other than what we in fact did. But this is usually not the case. Only when we are completely compelled by some external cause to do something, such that there is just no way we could have avoided what we were forced to do, do we have no choice. In this situation the agent feels the compulsion; the ensuing act is really not the agent's doing. Here Crescas' theory is similar to more modern philosophers, such as Hobbes, Spinoza, Hume, and J.S. Mill.

Crescas' most interesting discussion of an idea in the third group is his account of creation. first, unlike Maimonides or Gersonides he does not consider this principle to be a necessary presupposition of the Torah. True, it is taught in the Torah, but one could have a revealed religion whose authoritative text could have begun with, "God created an eternal universe." In short, the Torah does not stand or fall with the doctrine that the universe had a beginning. This means that for Crescas the doctrine of eternal creation, which for Maimonides was absurd, is at least logically plausible, and perhaps even the correct teaching of the Torah. In reaching this conclusion Crescas redefines the notion of creation *ex nihilo* in such a way that it becomes a temporally neutral idea. God creates *ex nihilo* in the sense that he is the first cause of the universe such that the world is dependent upon him and that God needs no matter to create the universe. Time does not enter in this definition at all. What counts is the rejection of Gersonides' doctrine of creation from matter: most of Crescas' attention is devoted to a refutation of Gersonides' theory, especially its reliance upon Aristotle's denial of the vacuum. Since for Crescas a vacuum is possible, he deems invalid arguments Gersonides proposed against creation *ex nihilo* that make use of Aristotle's physics.

Crescas' cosmology emphasizes divine omnipotence, understood as infinite power. Just as the neo-Platonist Proclus argued from an eternal cause to an eternal product, so Crescas argues from an infinitely powerful agent to an infinitely enduring world. Unlike Maimonides he has no difficulty with the idea that an eternal world can exhibit purpose or design; neither did Aquinas before him nor Leibniz after him. In this respect Crescas falls in line with a group of thinkers with whom he did not ordinarily have much sympathy, the Averroists, who believed in some form of eternal creation. On the other hand, he was well aware that Jewish tradition taught that the world did have a temporal beginning. So in order to reconcile his stress upon divine infinite power with this latter doctrine, he falls back upon a midrashic teaching, which Maimonides explicitly rejected, according to which God creates a series of worlds, perhaps *ad infinitum*. Whether this universe is eternal or is just one of an infinite series of created worlds does not matter so much; what matters is that in either case God's power is infinite. Here too we can see Crescas' willingness to depart from Aristotle's physics with respect to the doctrine of the infinite duration of the universe. It is logically possible for Crescas that the universe be destroyed and succeeded by another, a possibility that Gersonides had denied.

Although Crescas undertook a defense of Judaism not only against Christianity but against Jewish Aristotelianism as well, it turned out that some of his own interpretations of traditional Jewish doctrines were either too novel or radical. His disciple Joseph Albo was critical of his concept of choice, as were several other late medieval Spanish-Jewish thinkers, including traditionalists such as Isaac Arama. Nor was his sympathy for eternal creation unanimously appreciated. A number of scholars have argued, however, that some of these ideas are echoed in Spinoza, who mentions Crescas in one of his letters (Spinoza, Letter 12).

Isaac Abravanel: Don Isaac Abravanel can be regarded either as the last of the great medieval Jewish thinkers or as one of the first Renaissance Jewish philosophers. Like Crescas he too lived through the demise of Spanish Jewry. Even though he was a faithful financial consultant for the Spanish royal family, he was unable to persuade them not to issue the decree of Expulsion in 1492, and choosing not to convert he went into exile to Italy, where he died in 1509. Despite a long career in finance and diplomacy, he managed to find both time and energy to compose a variety of theological, philosophical and exegetical treatises. His two main concerns were the Bible and Maimonides. He wrote complete commentaries upon the Pentateuch, all the prophetic books, and Daniel; he did not complete his commentary on Maimonides' *Guide*, but did leave an extensive treatment of several of its parts, especially Maimonides' discussions of creation and prophecy. These latter topics were the two dominant theological interests of Abravanel. On creation he wrote his longest non-exegetical work *The Deeds of God*; on prophecy he wrote several books, none of which survived the tribulations of his years of exile. Yet his discussions on prophecy are plentiful in his biblical commentaries.

His most philosophical work, the late *Deeds of God* is devoted to a defense of the traditional doctrine of creation *ex nihilo*. Although comprehensive and thorough it is not a very original book, since it relies heavily upon the results of his predecessors, not only Jewish philosophers but also Christian and Muslim thinkers as well. Yet, it is an important work precisely because of its encyclopedic character; it is virtually a complete study of the whole problem of creation. Abravanel understands the doctrine of creation *ex nihilo* as did Saadia and Maimonides: God created the world at the first instant of time from no antecedent matter. But unlike Maimonides he believes 1) that this doctrine can be given a "virtual" proof, and 2) that the Platonic-Gersonidean theory of creation from matter is absolutely false and can be shown to be false. In the latter case, Abravanel relies primarily upon Crescas' refutations of Gersonides' vacuum arguments against creation *ex nihilo*. Moreover, he stresses the difference between logical impossibility and natural, or empirical, impossibility, and suggests that Gersonides and others failed to make clear which kind of impossibility is involved in the alleged absurdity of creation *ex nihilo*. If it is claimed that creation *ex nihilo* is impossible because it is incompatible with the laws of nature, this is conceded by the defender of this doctrine. But the defender maintains that although incompatible with the laws of physics, creation *ex nihilo* is logically possible. No law of logic is violated when it is alleged that God created the world from no antecedent matter. Indeed, it is precisely the defining feature of the divine agent that such an agent can do whatever is logically possible, although it may be naturally impossible to be done by a natural cause (e.g., the sun) or human agent. After all, God is infinitely powerful.

Unlike Maimonides, Abravanel has a more favorable attitude toward the Kalam arguments for creation. He likes in particular the argument constructed by John Philoponus and subsequently used by Saadia: the universe is essentially destructible; hence by virtue of Aristotle's own theorem—whatever is destructible is generable and, conversely, the universe is generated. Here another departure from Maimonides and Gersonides is evident. Abravanel believes that the world is destructible, and indeed will be destroyed and replaced with another one. He thus is closer to the second of Crescas' permissible cosmologies. On the other hand, he clearly rejects Crescas' first cosmological hypothesis, eternal creation, which he sees as an unacceptable compromise position that is hardly different from Aristotle's pure eternity theory.

Abravanel's prophetology is quite interesting and in some respects original, at least in the sense of deviating from the mainstream of Jewish medieval philosophers who, like Maimonides and Gersonides stressed its natural character. Not only in his commentary on Maimonides' *Guide* but throughout his biblical commentaries, Abravanel emphasizes the supra-natural character of prophecy. In particular he rejects the Maimonidean-Gersonidean doctrine that intellectual perfection, especially in philosophy, is a necessary condition for receiving the prophetic emanation. God can give prophecy to whomever he chooses. Abravanel thus defends the view that Maimonides labels as the doctrine of the fools. Moreover, Abravanel's severing of prophecy from the intellect allows him to recognize a type of prophetic inspiration that was not admitted by Maimonides, perceptual prophecy. Here only the perceptual faculties of the recipient are needed to be able to receive the prophetic emanation. This type of prophecy was experienced by the entire people of Israel at Mt. Sinai, when even the women and children heard the words of God. Surely they had not studied Aristotle's physics and metaphysics! Unlike ordinary perception, perceptual prophecy is caused by God, not some natural object; but like ordinary perception it is a direct form of cognition that is veridical. It is not to be confused with hallucinations or other types of illusion. Finally, Abravanel is skeptical of the theory of the Agent Intellect as the agent of prophecy. God can disclose his will without using an intermediary agent, just as he performs miracles directly. After all, prophecy is a kind of miracle in the first place.

Abravanel's immediate influence was through his biblical commentaries, which were studied and used by a number of later exegetes, such as Menasseh ben Israel (seventeenth century) and Malbim (nineteenth century). These commentaries still enjoy considerable popularity among traditional Jews. They are especially noteworthy for their insightful introductions and historical perspectives, in which some of the political affairs of his times are mentioned and discussed. Abravanel's philosophical, or perhaps his anti-philosophical, orientation was still medieval. Although he was somewhat familiar with the newer current of Platonic thought, it did not have a significant impact on his thinking. This was not the case with his son Judah, whose philosophical framework reflects the new Plato of the Italian Renaissance.

Jewish philosophy in the Italian Renaissance: Renaissance philosophy can be delineated by three novelties: 1) the revival of Plato and Plotinus; 2) the development of a purer, more secular Aristotle; and 3) the resurfacing of skepticism. It is primarily with respect to the first of these developments that Jewish philosophers in the Renaissance period made any significant contributions. In the last decade of the fifteenth century Marsilio Ficino translated into Latin the complete Greek texts of Plato and Plotinus, thus making available to Greek-less readers the main sources of ancient Platonism. Although Aristotle's authority and influence were still felt in the universities, interest in Platonism grew, especially in literary circles. Several Jewish thinkers participated in this Platonic revival, most notably Yohanan Alemanno, a teacher of Pico della Mirandola, and Judah Abravanel, the oldest son of Isaac. Unlike his father, Judah was not a financier and statesman, but a physician, who went into exile with his father but lived and practiced his profession mainly in Naples, not Venice, where Isaac eventually settled. But like his father Judah was a scholar and man of letters with a strong interest in philosophy; indeed, he was more a philosopher than his father, having no doubts about the value and importance of philosophy and its compatibility with Judaism.

One philosophical treatise by Judah (known in Italian as Leone Ebreo), *The Dialogues of Love*, has come down to us. Although it is not certain in which language he wrote it, its Italian and Spanish versions were very popular throughout the sixteenth and seventeenth centuries; Latin, French, and Hebrew translations were also available. *The Dialogues of Love* is notable for several reasons: 1) it was written or published first in a European language, not Hebrew; 2) one of its two characters is a woman; 3) it makes frequent references to Greek and Roman mythological themes, quite unusual in Jewish literature of this time; and 4) it has as its main theme love, or Eros, in all its forms. In this latter respect it is a "Jewish version" of Plato's *Symposium*, the most popular dialogue of Plato at this time, one that was not part of the medieval corpus of Plato's works.

Although Judah devotes considerable attention to love in its secular forms, he is primarily interested, as were his medieval predecessors, in love as a link between man and God. Like Maimonides he understands this link in terms of an intellectual bond that has become so filled with the passion to know God that it is indistinguishable from love. It is this intellectual love of God that enables us to attain ultimate felicity in this life as well as immortality, which like many medievals he sees as a form of conjunction. But whereas most of the medievals claimed that this conjunction obtains between the human intellect and the Agent Intellect, Judah identifies the latter with God. The immediate and personal relationship with God, characteristic of traditional Judaism, is thus retained, although given an interpretation in terms of the philosophical framework of Alexander of Aphrodesias, one of the chief ancient commentators on Aristotle.

Judah's Platonism is most evident in his cosmology, to which most of the third and final dialogue is devoted. Here he makes an explicit reference to Plotinus, as well as to Plato, and after discussing various theories of creation Judah suggests a doctrine that is very close to Plotinus' original emanation theory. On this view everything, including matter, emanates from God. The first emanated entity is Intellect (Plotinus), or First Intellect (Judah); the second emanated thing is the World-Soul; finally the physical world, or nature, emanates. Judah is non-committal as to whether this emanation process is temporal. In fact his language can be construed in such a way as to allow for an eternal creation theory. Judah reads this doctrine into the Bible by appealing to an old theme from Prov. 8:22-32, where wisdom is depicted as in some way God's "tool" or plan in the creation of the universe. Whereas the rabbis identified this wisdom with the Torah, Judah, like the Hellenic-Jewish philosophers Philo and the author of *The Wisdom of Solomon*, understands this "blueprint" as the place of the Platonic Forms, or in Plotinian terms, the Intellect.

The scientific revolution and Jewish thought. Joseph Solomon del Medigo: Although the main players in the scientific advances of the sixteenth and seventeenth centuries were not Jews, these new ideas did not pass unnoticed in Jewish intellectual circles, especially, but not only, in Italy, where Jews had been permitted to study in the universities for several centuries and were active in medicine. Of particular importance is the question of how these Jewish thinkers reacted to some of the more radical developments in the "new science" of Copernicus and Galileo. Perhaps the most interesting example of this phenomenon is the multifaceted Jewish physician, mathematician, and philosopher, Joseph Solomon del Medigo ("the Physician").

Joseph Solomon (1591-1655), although born in Crete, received most of his secular education in Italy, where he studied with Galileo in Padua. Like Judah Abravanel he practiced medicine, evidently not too successfully since he was always on the move; but his main interests were in mathematics and metaphysics. He may have been the first Jewish thinker to have accepted the new astronomy and physics of Galileo, whom he refers to as "my rabbi." In addition to his mathematical writings, he also wrote a number of philosophical treatises and works on kabbalah, in which he expresses an ambivalent attitude toward the mystical tradition, respectful but critical as well.

In two important respects Joseph Solomon continues the anti-Aristotelian critique of Crescas, whom he admired greatly: 1) he rejected much of the Aristotelian physics and metaphysics; and 2) he was sympathetic to the doctrine of eternal creation, which he interpreted in a Neo-Platonic-Kabbalistic fashion. Yet, unlike Crescas he was definitely in love with philosophy and attempted to forge a philosophical framework within which modern science, traditional Judaism, and a philosophically purified Kabbalah could be made to dwell together in harmony. Most significant in this attempt is his explicit rejection of the Aristotelian-Ptolemaic cosmology, especially the doctrine of the celestial spheres and their angelic, or intellectual, movers. There is, after all, no basis for these ideas in the Torah, nor in the new astronomy of Galileo and Kepler. Joseph Solomon was also open to the possibilities of plural worlds and life on these worlds. Like Galileo he was inclined towards an atomistic conception of matter, which he tried to read into the Kabbalah. It is not uninteresting to note that he spent several years in Amsterdam, where he had some of his works published by Menasseh ben Israel, who was one of Spinoza's teachers. Spinoza himself had one of Joseph Solomon's books in his library, just as he had a Spanish translation of Judah Abravanel's *Dialogues of Love*.

The end of a tradition. Spinoza (1632-1677): Baruch Spinoza's place within the history of Jewish philosophy is a disputed question. According to Julius Guttmann he really belongs to "the development of European thought" (Julius Guttmann, *Philosophies of Judaism*, N.Y., 1973, p. 301) and stands outside Jewish philosophy since he rejected Judaism and was rejected by the Jewish community of Amsterdam. Other scholars, most notably, Harry Wolfson, have claimed that Spinoza is part of Jewish philosophy, at least in so far as he was deeply influenced by several medieval Jewish thinkers, such as Maimonides and Crescas, even if he ultimately rejected or modified their views (Harry Wolfson, *The Philosophy of Spinoza*, N.Y., 1969). More recently, some scholars have situated Spinoza within a heterodox Marrano environment, where a critical stance toward traditional Judaism had appeared (Y. Yovel, *Spinoza and Other Heretics*, Princeton, 1989, vol. 1). Whatever Spinoza's attitude was toward his past, and by and large it was negative, it is clear that he saw himself as a "modern." His world was the world of Cartesian physics, which he interpreted in a strict deterministic and anti-teleological manner. This commitment to the "new science" was unqualified, and he participated in its development by engaging in research and experimentation in optics. But his main interest was in philosophy, and his comprehensive treatise *The Ethics* is a classic of modern European thought.

Spinoza's philosophy can be regarded as an internal critique of certain ideas in both medieval and Cartesian philosophy, ideas that Spinoza believed had some truth to them but did not go far enough. Consider Crescas' determinism: it correctly emphasized the causal networks operative in nature, especially in human behavior, but still admitted the notions of choice and purpose, both of which Spinoza rejected. If nature operates according to strict laws, which it does, then there is no room for miracles or contingency. Free will is an illusion. Everything that occurs had to take place just in the way that it has taken place. Moreover, nature is devoid of any purposes or goals; these are just fictions that humans foist upon nature. Nor do the medieval and Cartesian metaphysical and psychological dualisms fare any better. If, as Descartes had maintained, there is, strictly speaking, only one substance—God, a being that is self-caused and absolutely infinite, totally independent of anything else for its own existence—then why allow finite minds and bodies to be substances, albeit created ones? For Spinoza the latter are just finite modes, or effects, of God, i.e., entities that are not self-caused but are totally dependent upon something else. Moreover, if the medievals and Descartes want to maintain that God is the efficient cause of everything, including bodies, or extended things, then God must have the attribute of extension as well as the attribute of thought. Indeed, God has all the attributes since God is absolutely infinite. Thus Spinoza rejects any dualism between God and physical or extended nature. In fact, God is identical with nature, understood as an infinite, active, and autonomous system.

Most striking and perhaps most modern is Spinoza's criticism of psychological dualism, the doctrine that mind, or soul, and body are two radically different substances, or things, that are somehow united and interact with each other. Like many of his contemporaries, Spinoza believed that Descartes' attempt to explain mind-body union and interaction had failed. But unlike either Hobbes, who adopted a monistic materialistic psychology, or Leibniz, who favored a kind of mentalistic monism, Spinoza developed a "neutral monism," according to which everything, both God and modes, can be described under any attribute, including extension. For example, the idea or wish to do something, e.g., to go the movies instead of studying philosophy, can be described as some sort of bodily state (e.g., a certain electrical impulse in the brain) that causes the person to go out of the house and to the movies. However, we must not mix up our systems of description: if we want to describe and explain behavior in the language of thought, then we must tell the story in that language only; and the same is true for every other attribute. It should, however, be noted that in the *Ethics* there is a tendency to give greater weight to the attribute of extension; e.g., Spinoza tells us that if we want to know the mind's capacities, we should observe our bodies' capacities (*Ethics* 2.13, Scholium). Here Spinoza is close to current developments in cognitive science and neuroscience.

In his second major work, *The Theological-Political Treatise*, Spinoza's naturalization of the divine was applied to the specific problems of his day. Spinoza claimed here that the Bible is not a book of philosophical or scientific instruction, that it must be read in the context of the historical circumstances of its origins according to the methods of scientific inquiry. It is indeed, Spinoza admits, a book of moral education and guidance, but no more. This new "biblical science" became the challenge to almost all modern Jewish thinkers from Moses Mendelssohn in the eighteenth century to Emanuel Levinas in our own day. The question that Spinoza had put to himself and answered negatively— Can Judaism be maintained in the modern world?—has been the central issue for Jews who have adopted modern science and the historical-critical approach to the Bible but who want to answer Spinoza's question affirmatively. Although many Jewish thinkers have rejected Spinoza's bold naturalism and his dismissal of biblical revelation, many modern Jews have attempted to formulate a version of Judaism that is in some cases not too different from some of Spinoza's ideas (e.g., Mordechai Kaplan's Reconstructionism). Over fifty years ago the Jewish historian Joseph Klausner ascended Mt. Scopus in Jerusalem and announced that he, at least, was willing to annul the writ of excommunication and welcome Baruch back into the Jewish community. *De facto* this has happened. Almost all of Spinoza's writings have been translated into Hebrew; a Spinoza institute exists in Jerusalem; and Spinoza's doctrine of the separation of state and religion has become a cardinal axiom among Jews, at least among the non-orthodox. This "Judaization" of Spinoza may be an instance, perhaps ironic, of Maimonides' dictum, "the gates of interpretation are not closed."

Conclusion: Although philosophy entered the Jewish tradition as an outsider, it eventually became an integrated part of medieval Jewish literature. Even when it was attacked precisely as a foreign import, it was still studied, sometimes secretly. Frequently it was the avenue on which traditionally educated Jews traveled to the world of modern European culture. Many of the early modern Jewish philosophers, such as Moses Mendelssohn and Nachman Krochmal, were reared on Maimonides and other medieval Jewish thinkers. Although the philosophical-scientific frameworks of the medievals have now become antiquated or need revision, the works of a Saadia, Maimonides, or Gersonides can and have served as models of the application of reason to religion. If our philosophy and science are different, as they must be, it is still the case that many of our questions are the same as those of our medieval predecessors. Their answers to these questions are illustrative of the extent to which philosophy and science can live with Judaism in the same house. This will always be a central issue for those Jews who have accepted the opportunities and challenges of life in the secular world.

Bibliography

Guttmann, Julius, *The Philosophies of Judaism*, trans. D.W. Silverman (New York, 1964).

Isaac Abravanel, *The Principles of Faith*, trans. M. Kellner (London, 1982).

Levi ben Gershom (Gersonides), *The Wars of the Lord*, trans. S. Feldman, 3 vols. (Philadelphia, 1984-).

Moses Maimonides, *The Guide of the Perplexed*, trans. S. Pines (Chicago, 1963).

Saadia Gaon, *The Book of Beliefs and Opinions*, trans. S. Rosenblatt (New Haven, 1948).

SEYMOUR FELDMAN

JUDAISM, PHILOSOPHY AND THEOLOGY OF, IN MODERN TIMES IN EUROPE: Jewish religious thought since the eighteenth century is characterized by a grand paradox. Whereas the Jews' entry into the modern world has witnessed their increasing secularization, they have at the same time been preoccupied with theological questions. Indeed the pre-eminent task assumed by modern Jewish religious thought has been to re-articulate and even radically re-evaluate the theological presuppositions of Judaism in the light of the modern, secular experience.

Beginning with the proud, defiant humanism of the Renaissance and gaining dramatic momentum with the "new" science and cosmology heralded by Copernicus, Galileo, and Newton, the modalities of thought we now consider "modern" began to crystallize. The emergence of this bent of mind marked a radical shift in the regnant assumptions of western civilization regarding the nature of reality and the sources of authentic knowledge. The biblical teachings of creation, revelation, and miracles were virtually excluded from this picture of the world. The modern mind and sensibility are thus founded on a fundamentally new "image of knowledge," that is, the assumptions regarding what constitutes true knowledge—its sources, purpose, and principles of verification. Asserting the epistemological preeminence of reason and autonomous judgment and the dignity of a this-worldly happiness, the modern image of knowledge is said to be inherently antagonistic to the biblical image of knowledge, grounded as it is in the concepts of revealed truth, sacred scriptures, and an eschatological vision of human destiny.[1]

Heir to the biblical image of knowledge, modern Jewish thought seeks to come to terms with modern conceptions of truth and meaning. In this respect, of course, it is basically similar to modern religious thought in general. There are, however, specifics of the Jewish experience in modern Europe that determine the agenda and peculiar inflections of modern Jewish thought. It should, therefore, be recalled that Jews first encountered the modern world during the protracted struggle in eighteenth and nineteenth century Europe to attain political emancipation. This struggle was not merely a legal process but engaged Europe in an intense and wide-ranging debate assessing Judaism's eligibility to participate in the modern world. In the course of this two century-long debate Jews became, to say the least, exceedingly sensitive to the prevailing conceptions of Judaism in European culture. Not surprisingly, then, modern Jewish thought was often guided by an apologetic motive. Judaism's defensive posture was also prompted by the rise of modern, political and racial antisemitism that, to the dismay of many, was not confined to the mob but gained vocal support from more than a few intellectuals.

The integration of the Jews in the modern nation state and culture that was achieved despite persistent opposition led to a profound restructuring of Jewish life, both organizationally and culturally. The Jews were no longer under the obligatory rule of the rabbis and the Torah as they were in medieval times. In acquiring the political identity and culture of the "non-Jewish," secular society in which they lived, the Jews tended to lose much of their own distinctive culture, e.g., knowledge of Hebrew and the sacred texts of the tradition. Moreover, for many, the nation of Israel's covenantal relationship to God as a Chosen People—presently in exile but piously awaiting God's messiah and restoration to the Promised Land—was no longer self-evident and unambiguous.

Modern Jewish thought in Europe was thus charged with the task not only of explaining Judaism to non-Jews and to Jews estranged from the sources of their tradition, but also with re-thinking some of the fundamental concepts of the tradition that bear on the nature of the Jews as a people: covenant, election, exile (diaspora), the messiah, and the promise of national redemption—in general, the meaning of Jewish community, history, and destiny. These questions gained a unique urgency in the mid-twentieth century with the Holocaust and the establishment of the State of Israel. Whereas medieval Jewish philosophy was primarily concerned with the relatively circumscribed issues of reconciling faith and reason, modern Jewish thought accordingly has a broader and by necessity more protean purview, addressing the multiple dilemmas of the Jew in the modern world.

Baruch Spinoza: Paradoxically, modern Jewish thought may be said to have begun with Baruch Spinoza (1632-1673), or, rather, in response to this renegade sage. Incorrigibly heterodox, Spinoza was excommunicated by the Jewish community of his native Amsterdam. Not only did he remain an unrepentant heretic but also utterly indifferent to Judaism as a living faith. As a philosopher, he neither addressed Jewish issues nor expressed a commitment to Jewish continuity. Moreover, on the one occasion on which he did discuss Judaism, in his *Tractatus theologico-politicus* (1670), he limned a harsh and even denigrating picture of the religion of his ancestors. To be sure, he drew much from the medieval Jewish philosophers, whom he assiduously studied in his youth; but these ideas, borrowed from Maimonides, Crescas, and others, appertain to general philosophical issues and do not bear on specifically Jewish matters. Nonetheless, Spinoza has retained a salience in the modern Jewish consciousness.

This paradox is most often explained by the fact that Spinoza left Judaism without having converted to another historical religion—an act virtually impossible until the advent of the modern era. For this reason, he may be considered the first modern, secular Jew. Indeed, Spinoza has been refracted in the Jewish imagination as a symbol of the modern Jew, a richly inflected symbol that has evoked contrasting responses. To traditional Jews, who view modernity as a profound threat to Jewish life, Spinoza symbolized an unambiguously negative development. But secularized and acculturated Jews—proudly appreciative of the honored position Spinoza enjoys in the intellectual pantheon of modern culture—find in him a symbol authenticating their participation in the modern secular order. Still others, eager to be integrated into modern Europe, repeatedly emphasized that Spinoza was one of the earliest harbingers of liberal and democratic ideals. The Jews' claim to membership in the European polity thus was pristine and unimpeachable.[2]

Jewish thinkers of disparate ideologies, such as Reform Judaism and Socialist Zionism, have acclaimed Spinoza, especially pointing to the fact that despite his rejection of Judaism as a religion, he obdurately refused to become a Christian—a refusal that, as the first prime minister of the State of Israel, David Ben-Gurion opined, exemplified Jewish pride and honor. Although it might be erroneous to interpret Spinoza's integrity as abiding Jewishness, his decision to remain a "non-Christian" has a special resonance for modern Jews seeking to validate their secularity in Jewish terms.

Though an outcast, anathematized by the rabbis, Spinoza has thus played a surprisingly resilient role in the modern Jewish imagination. Still, his most enduring significance for Jewry remains philosophical. Spinoza was the first to articulate modernity's distinctive challenge to Judaism as a faith and way of life: Can Jews beholden to the modern "image of knowledge"—its conception of truth and procedures to attain such truth—still maintain a fidelity to Judaism as a divinely revealed religion?

This challenge was elaborated in his *Tractatus theologico-politicus*, in which the former rabbinical student concludes that Judaism is, in a word, an inauthentic religion. Analyzing its biblical origins, Spinoza argues that Judaism, including its ritual and ceremonial precepts, is basically only a legal construct designed to ensure the political stability of the Israelite state in which it first took shape. As a form of civic discipline, the religion of Israel is bereft of genuine spirituality and, worse, devoid of a discernible inclination to promote universal morality. Furthermore, Spinoza held, severed from the political commonwealth it was to serve, Judaism in the post-biblical period is an anachronism, indeed, a spiritually and intellectually vacuous phenomenon. Since the obligatory power of Judaism in its original setting is grounded in the coercive power of the state, the proud adherence of the Jews of the diaspora to their ancestral religion, with its burdensome ceremonial laws, is to be explained psychologically as an expression of an obstinate, atavistic patriotism. Spinoza also implied that the continued allegiance of the Jews to the Torah, to the laws of the Israelite state, is incompatible with citizenship in any other state.

In contrast to the intrinsically theocratic nature of Judaism, Spinoza observed, Christianity—embodied in the person of Jesus, who, unlike Moses, was not a political legislator but a moral teacher—is primarily interested in the promotion of charity and universal solidarity. Because this was his paramount concern, Spinoza emphasizes, Jesus was prepared to relinquish power to the temporal authorities. The original teachings of Jesus favor the separation of church and state, that is, they conform to Spinoza's political ideal. This approbation of Christianity, however, was not a religious affirmation; Spinoza merely wished to point out that Christianity, in its pristine expression at least, is compatible with the temperament and requirements of the modern age. In fact, in consonance with his critique of revelation (namely, that it is informed by the epistemologically imperfect category of "imagination" as opposed to reason), Spinoza had, as Hermann Cohen (1842-1918) noted, in effect, "placed religion altogether [that is, all theistic religions and not merely Judaism] outside the sphere of truth."

Indeed, arguing that truth can be achieved independently of religion, Spinoza was the first thinker since Philo of Alexandria in the Judeo-Christian world to construct a worldview involving no principles or axioms based on revelation. In this respect, Spinoza challenged Christian and Jewish thinkers alike. Moreover, while affirming the existence of God, he abjured the Judeo-Christian God—a transcendent, personal God who possesses an autonomous will and purpose—as a sad delusion. Similarly, he was the first to pursue biblical criticism in a systematic fashion and in general to employ an historical, "relativizing" perspective when dealing with religious questions. Thus this sixteenth century iconoclast adumbrated the philosophical issues that, in the modern world, would plague the person of faith and the Jew in particular. As Leo Strauss (1899-1973), one of the twentieth century's most sensitive students of Spinoza and a deeply thoughtful Jew observed, traditional Jewish faith and practice could be affirmed with intellectual integrity "only if Spinoza was wrong in every respect."

Moses Mendelssohn: The first Jew to take up the challenge posed by Spinoza was Moses Mendelssohn (1729-1786). Like many who would succeed him, he encountered the challenge both directly and as it was filtered through the culture of the Enlightenment, which had absorbed and even amplified Spinoza's critique of revealed religion in general and Judaism in particular. Affirming Judaism in the face of this critique, Mendelssohn's significance for modern Jewry is as much symbolic as philosophic. In contrast to Spinoza, he represents the possibility that the Jew's creative participation in modern secular culture need not negate a commitment to Judaism as a religious faith. Hailed by the Enlightenment as "the German Socrates," he remained a pious and proud Jew. Indeed, with the very beginning of his philosophical career, he was cast as a symbol. Not insignificantly, Mendelssohn's debut as a philosopher was occasioned by a debate among theater critics.

In 1754, Gotthold Ephraim Lessing (1729-1780), then a young playwright, published a play with a rather provocative title, "The Jews." This didactic play follows the heroic deeds of an amiable and handsome individual whose identity is revealed only at the end of the play. To the utter amazement of everyone he is a Jew! By portraying the Jew as humane and gracious, Lessing sought to combat the prevailing prejudice of his day, which held that a moral disposition—or, in Christian parlance, virtue—was attained only through the sanctifying grace of Jesus Christ. Like other advocates of the Enlightenment, Lessing maintained that reason was the true source of virtue, of human goodness. It followed that even those who denied Jesus Christ—even a Jew!—were capable of virtue!

The reception of Lessing's play was generally favorable, but it was faulted by some for lacking credibility. As one critic put it, the improbability of a "virtuous Jew" interfered with the enjoyment of an otherwise well crafted play. Lessing replied by publishing an anonymous letter from a manifestly cultured and high-minded Jew who protested the prejudices of the play's critics. "Let them further expose us to scorn and derision of all the world," he wrote, "only virtue, the one

solace of distressed souls, the one refuge of the forsaken, let them not seek wholly to deny us." To this protest, Lessing added, "He is really a Jew. A man of twenty and some years who without any guidance has achieved a great strength in languages, mathematics, in philosophy, in poetry. I regard him as a future honor of his people. . . .." The reference was to Moses Mendelssohn, whom Lessing befriended after having written the play and upon whom Lessing soon prevailed to publish his philosophical reflections, thereby to show the world that Jews could participate in the universal culture sponsored by reason, so as, according to the tenets of the Enlightenment, to attain virtue.

Thus the retiring Talmudic student, Moses, the son of the Torah scribe Mendel, began to write essays and monographs on a wide range of philosophical subjects: aesthetics, logic, psychology, and metaphysics. In these writings he associated himself with the school of philosophical rationalism developed by G.W. Leibniz and Christian Wolff. This school held that reason was the universal and self-sufficient source of knowledge, including the metaphysical truths of religion, that is, knowledge of God. Truth and virtue thus were equally available to all rational minds, unaided by any supernatural agency. Accordingly, the essence of religion did not lie in dogma or revealed truths but was contained in the rational verities of natural religion and the universal moral law rooted in them. Revelation was thus unnecessary for metaphysical knowledge, virtue, and eternal felicity.

More than the originality of his thought, Mendelssohn's contribution to philosophy was the force and lucidity with which he developed the principles of philosophical rationalism. His reputation as a philosopher was sealed with the publication in 1767 of *Phaedon,* one of the most widely translated and read books of its day. Following the form of Plato's classical dialogue, Mendelssohn sought to prove that the principle of morality required the concept of immortality of the soul. Significantly, he based his argument on reason and logic alone, and, although he made use of the metaphysical presupposition of natural religion, his interest was strictly philosophical. This *secular* focus was common to all of his writings on metaphysics, aesthetics, psychology, and epistemology. As such, Mendelssohn was not a *Jewish* philosopher. In fact, implicit in his writings was the assumption that his Judaism was irrelevant to his philosophical endeavors.

Accordingly, the Jewish savant was deeply shocked when in 1769 Johann Caspar Lavater, a Protestant minister who supported the Enlightenment, publicly challenged him to defend his fidelity to Judaism. Lavater's challenge was put forward in a preface to a German translation of the French philosopher Charles Bonnet's treatise offering a rational proof of the truth of Christian doctrine. Lavater requested the Mendelssohn read Bonnet's book and either refute his arguments or yield to them and convert to Christianity. In his reply, Mendelssohn reminded Lavater of the legally precarious position of the Jew in the gentile world—it was at the time still forbidden for him as a Jew even to visit Lavater in his native Geneva. It would thus be imprudent for him to engage in religious polemics. Pleading for tolerance, Mendelssohn concluded: "The contemptuous opinions one holds of a Jew I wish to refute through virtue and not through polemics."

Mendelssohn did not succeed in silencing Lavater or others who questioned the consistency of his simultaneous loyalty to the Enlightenment and Judaism. A series of pamphlets and books were published in quick succession that were overwhelmingly critical of Mendelssohn's position. He was chagrined to learn that while most of the authors of these works were able to reconcile their attachment to Christianity with their commitment to the principles of the Enlightenment, they could not accept—or rather refused to acknowledge—the possibility of Jews' adopting a similar position. The controversy opened a second period in Mendelssohn's public activity. He no longer could regard his Judaism as merely a private matter.

The boundaries between gentile and Jew were greater and far more intractable than Mendelssohn had assumed. He now became the leading spokesperson for the Jews in their struggle for tolerance and civil equality. At the same time, he endeavored to encourage his fellow Jews to seek integration into enlightened German and western culture. His translations of the Pentateuch into German (in the Hebrew alphabet, for few Jews then could read Latin letters) inaugurated a new era; it aroused the Jews' interest not only in the German language but also in the values of the Enlightenment (which in its Jewish expression was known as the *haskalah*). Indeed, he joined with other Jewish intellectuals in promoting *haskalah* among the Jewish masses, chiefly through educational reform.

In the political sphere, Mendelssohn's crowning achievement was to induce his friend Christian Wilhelm von Dohm to write a monumental monograph, "On the Civil Amelioration of the Jews" (*Über die bürgerliche Verbesserung der Juden*). Published in 1781, this was the first work to discuss in a systematic and enlightened manner the question of Jewish civil rights, later to be called emancipation. Its publication coincided with the Jewish reforms of Emperor Joseph II of Austria and helped focus the ensuing debate throughout Europe on the desirability of granting Jews civil rights. Mendelssohn, however, objected to Dohm's endorsement of the popular view of alleged Jewish commercial and moral corruption, which, Dohm contended, could be eliminated were the Jews integrated into the social and political fabric of the state.

Not only did this line of argument perpetuate a prejudice, it ultimately vitiated the enlightened premises of the appeal to grant Jews civil rights. This appeal, Mendelssohn pointed out, was based on a matter of pure principle, not on utilitarian considerations. Similarly he objected to Dohm's recommendation that the Jews retain their communal self-government, with the rabbis continuing to exercise their prerogative to excommunicate dissidents (and those who do not accept the moral codes required of them by the state). The Rabbinic right of excommunication, Mendelssohn contended, was incompatible with the spirit of tolerance and contradicted the principle of the separation of church and state.

As was to be anticipated, Mendelssohn's

call for the dissolution of Jewish legal autonomy and the revocation of the ecclesiastical power of the rabbis aroused the anger of the rabbinate. Unexpected, however, was the interpretation of his position by some non-Jews as implicitly conceding that Judaism was as Spinoza had argued, an anachronistic, essentially political religion. For, it was contended, the cancellation of Jewish legal autonomy and the coercive powers of the rabbis that Mendelssohn sought struck at the very heart of Judaism as a "system of law." Mendelssohn felt that now he had no alternative but to reply, and he wrote his first and only philosophical treatise in German on Judaism. Published in 1783, three years before his death, this statement was entitled *Jerusalem, or Religious Power and Judaism.* The title was apparently chosen in "proud defiance" of the assertion that, with Christianity, true worship of God had been removed from Jerusalem.[3]

The challenge that prompted the writing of *Jerusalem* implicitly confronted Mendelssohn with the demand to consider the question raised by Spinoza regarding the political and legal character of Judaism. He, of course, did not deny that the Torah allowed religion a role in the political life of biblical Israel. But his abiding fidelity to the faith of Israel obliged him to affirm, in contrast to Spinoza, that this role was consonant with genuine religious faith. On the other hand, his adherence to the principle of the separation of church and state required him to demonstrate that this role did not, again in contrast to Spinoza, exhaust the meaning and essence of Judaism. Mendelssohn would devote the first part of *Jerusalem* to a philosophical clarification of the relation between religion and state, making virtually no reference to Judaism *per se*. Speaking of religion in general, he insisted that the disavowal of ecclesiastical power does not mean that religion should have no relation to the state whatsoever.

Mendelssohn accordingly rejected the view propounded by John Locke, which was then popular among German liberals, that the temporal and eternal should be radically separate spheres. Such a view, Mendelssohn felt, encouraged people to neglect their mun-

dane moral duties in favor of the goals of spiritual life. The spiritual sphere, Mendelssohn held, must be brought to bear upon the public realm, for it lies uniquely in the power of the spiritual, that is, religion, to inculcate the right attitudes and sentiments (*Gesinnungen*) animating the ethical conduct in all facets of interpersonal life. In this respect, religion, indeed, has an important moral and educational role.

This emphasis on the public responsibilities of men and women of faith remains a salient motif of modern Jewish thought until this very day (see, in particular, Buber and Levinas). In Mendelssohn's view this role is to be confined to suasion and the cultivation of conscience. In contradistinction, the state, charged with regulating social relations, has the legitimate right to employ force to maintain the correctness and amiability of these relations—but only in the external sense of conformity to the law. The state and its coercive institutions cannot effect—and should not seek to influence—the inner life of the spirit and conscience. Neither the state nor the church (that is, religion in its formal, institutional embodiment) should seek to force one to subscribe to certain views or beliefs. Freedom of conscience and belief, Mendelssohn concluded, is thus absolute and indeed must be extended to all, Christians, Jews, Muslims, heretics, and dissidents.

Having clarified what he regarded as the proper theoretical perspective, in the second part of *Jerusalem*, Mendelssohn addressed the specific questions raised by his interlocutors with respect to Judaism. To be sure, he concedes, in the biblical state of Israel, ecclesiastical and civil law were identical. Nonetheless, he avers, it would be erroneous to regard that state as a theocracy. Although transgression of God's law was tantamount to a political offense, punishable under the law of the land, the state did not punish such wayward acts as heresies and unbelief, but simply as misdeeds. The Mosaic state did not seek to legislate or regulate opinion and belief, for, it was implicitly acknowledged, the inner life of the individual's relationship to God and truth cannot be dictated by law. Since the latter is the essential concern of the Torah, Israel's covenant with God was, in its deepest sense, not effected by the fall of the Temple and the eclipse of Jewish political sovereignty. Hence, continued adherence to the Torah and its laws is not at all an anachronism, nor does it, in the age of Enlightenment, militate against the Jew's commitment to the rule of reason and a liberal political ethic.

Mendelssohn now took the opportunity to address a particularly vexatious question posed by his fellow enlighteners, namely, whether his philosophical rationalism did not in effect mean that he was neither a Jew nor a Christian but a "naturalist." It seemed to more than one of Mendelssohn's contemporaries that his teaching that the eternal metaphysical truths of religion were universally available to all votaries of reason was inconsistent with his abiding attachment to Judaism, which, after all, purports to enjoy a privileged access to the revealed word of God. In his reply, Mendelssohn—the believing Jew—upheld his rejection of revelation as disclosure of divine truths, for this conception of revelation, he held, is an offense against reason. But, he continued, philosophical rationalism poses no special problem for Judaism, since Judaism is, he declared in his now famous dictum, "not a revealed religion but a revealed law." In contrast to Christianity, Judaism is not founded upon "doctrines, saving truths, or universally valid propositions of reason," but rather upon "laws, commandments . . ., instructions in the will of God." Mendelssohn suggested that the purpose of these commandments, as symbolic inscriptions of the eternal truths of reason, is to render the Jews ever alert to those truths, thus preventing them from succumbing to the idolatry of false ideas. Herein lies the meaning of Israel's election:

> The Jew were chosen by Providence to be a nation of priests, that is, a nation which through its laws and conduct . . . was to call wholesome and unadulterated ideas of God and His attributes continuously to the attention of the rest of mankind. It was a nation which, through its mere existence, as it were, would unceasingly teach, proclaim, preach, and strive to preserve these ideas among the nations.

Mendelssohn had thus paradoxically reduced Judaism to a body of ceremonial laws while at the same time expanding it into a universal religion of reason.

Mendelssohn's effort in this respect would characterize much of modern Jewish thought: unlike medieval Jewish philosophers, their modern descendants would no longer seek to reconcile revelation with reason, as two distinct but homologous bodies of truth, but would rather endeavor to demonstrate the significance of Judaism within the general framework of human reason and culture. Mendelssohn also anticipated another characteristic thrust of modern Jewish thought by his conception of Israel's "mission" to the nations—a notion that provided, as it were, a universalistic justification of Judaism's continued particularity.

Mendelssohn's definition of Judaism was not unproblematic, however. His delineation of the distinctive essence of Judaism as "revealed law" exposed Judaism to the charge—first developed by Mendelssohn's contemporary, Immanuel Kant—that Judaism is an inherently "heteronomous" religion of law that finds expression chiefly in religious ritual and ceremonies. As Kant regarded genuine religion to be the cultivation of moral autonomy, he deemed ritual and ceremony to be "false service to God" and accordingly depicted Judaism as a "pseudo-religion." Kant's indictment of Judaism—based largely on his reading of Mendelssohn (and Spinoza)—was repeated by many modern thinkers, especially those who shared the great philosopher's conception of enlightened culture and religion. At the same time, Mendelssohn's definition of Judaism satisfied few Jews. Traditionalists felt he ignored the unique creedal core of Judaism, and liberal Jews were unhappy (and not only because of Kant's critique) because of his emphasis on the ceremonial laws. Nonetheless, Mendelssohn's *Jerusalem* still stands as a monument to a Jew who sought to secure the integrity of his Judaism while actively pursuing modern culture.

Jewish opposition to modernity: More than Spinoza, the author of this defiant but dignified defense of Judaism's right to be part of the modern world became the exemplar of Jewish modernity. Eager to accommodate Judaism to the modern spirit, diverse Jews of varying theological tendencies claimed Mendelssohn as their spiritual progenitor. Even for Jewish opponents of the modern world Mendelssohn became a symbol of the new order—however, a symbol of betrayal.

The *spiritus rector* of Jewish orthodoxy as a self-conscious movement to guard the integrity of classical Judaism in the face of the putatively corrosive effects of the modern world, Rabbi Moses Sofer (1762-1839), popularly known as Hatam Sofer, regarded Mendelssohn as the insidious source of the contemporary Jew's self-destructive infatuation with "alien culture." In his last will and testament, he cautioned all God-fearing Jews "not to turn to evil and never engage in corruptible partnership with those fond of innovations, who, as a penalty for our sins, have strayed from the Almighty and His law! Do not touch the books of Rabbi Moses [Mendelssohn] of Dessau, and your foot will never slip! . . ." This document, written in 1837, that is, some fifty years after Mendelssohn's death, has been reprinted numerous times and still enjoys immense popularity among what are now called "ultra-Orthodox" Jewish circles (as opposed to Orthodox groups that seek some accommodation with the modern world).

The militant anti-modernism of these ultra-Orthodox circles, which dominated much of the traditional Jewish community in Eastern Europe, is distinguished by a deliberate self-enclosure. Although not totally ignorant of the modern world, they refused to acknowledge its most significant epistemological presuppositions and social and political values. It would be erroneous, however, to assume that ultra-Orthodoxy was moribund and spiritually stagnant; on the contrary, in its own terms, the movement was (and is) dynamic and creative. The nineteenth century actually witnessed a renaissance of Rabbinic learning, with the establishment of new talmudic academies sponsoring new methods and approaches to the study of the sacred texts and expressions of piety. Mention should be made of the yeshivot of Hatam Sofer in Pressburg, Hungary, and of Rabbi Hayyim

ben Isaac (1749-1821) of Volozhin, Lithuania; also notable is the pietistic movement founded by the Lithuanian rabbi, Israel Lipkin Salanter (1810-1883), known as Musar (literally, moral instruction), and it should be recalled that Hasidism, the movement of popular mystical piety, flourished in the nineteenth century.

The opposition of ultra-Orthodoxy to modernity is not as much epistemological as it is axiological. They view the modern world, given its social and political values, with profound suspicion, for it leads, in their judgment, to religious laxity and even defection. Even Hatam Sofer did not oppose certain secular studies *per se*, so long as they did not undermine the preeminence of Torah and Jewish tradition. Hence, whereas critical historical scholarship with its relativizing gaze was viewed as a threat, Orthodoxy was by and large indifferent to, and simply ignored, the epistemological and ontological issues raised by modern science, assuming a strictly instrumental attitude towards science and technology. Their sole objective was to protect the sanctity of the tradition and Torah.

But neither was modern science and its presuppositions a salient issue for Jewish modernists, who were principally exercised by the need to find a place for the Jews and Judaism in the modern world. Philosophically and theologically, as noted, this objective necessitated a delineation of Judaism's relevance to the development of a universal culture. Within the orbit of nineteenth century discourse, the principal vectors of this effort were provided by Kant, Schelling (1775-1854), and Hegel (1770-1831).

Because it viewed spiritual truths as developing and maturing in and through history, the philosophical idealism of Schelling and Hegel provided Jewish modernists, primarily associated with the Liberal or Reform Judaism that first crystallized in nineteenth century Germany, with the conceptual principles justifying the desired ritual and doctrinal change. To be true to the spiritual truths with which it had been entrusted, advocates of reform held, Judaism must be attuned to the dynamic thrust of history. Schelling's and Hegel's presupposition that the historical unfolding of the truths of reason and the spirit ineluctably lead to the progressive unification of human culture and sensibility also lent support to the Reformers' call for Jewish integration in general culture. But their affirmation of universal culture, in turn, posed a serious challenge to the enduring identity, and thus the continued particularity, of Judaism, in which all Liberal and Reform leaders continued to uphold.

Solomon Formstecher: The rabbi of the Liberal congregation of Offenbach, Germany, from 1842 until his death, Solomon Formstecher (1808-1889) used the teaching of Schelling to advance a theological exposition of Reform Judaism. His principal work, *Die Religion des Geistes* (*The Religion of Spirit*, 1841), was significantly subtitled, "A Scientific Description of Judaism according to its Character, Development and Mission to Humanity."

Following Schelling, Formstecher speaks of the divine as manifest in the realms of both spirit and nature. In contrast to Schelling, however, he does not regard these manifestations—spirit and nature—as co-equal aspects of the divine. Only as spirit—the realm of intellect, its self-consciousness and freedom—is the divine true to its very essence, that is, it is transcendent and thus above the laws and limits of nature.

Corresponding to these distinct manifestations of the divine are two ontologically distinct types of religion. The first, the "religion of nature," identifies the divine as "the soul of the world." This characteristically "pagan" conception, Formstecher contends, ineluctably prompts human beings to see a relationship with the divine by becoming one with the "soul of the world." In this regard, he notes, perhaps with reference to Spinoza, pantheism and speculative metaphysics, no matter how sophisticated, are at root pagan. The second type of religion, "the religion of spirit," regards God as transcendent, as a pure moral being utterly beyond nature and the grasp of reason. God, accordingly, is known only through self-revelation, and a human being's relationship to God can thus be established only through *imago dei*, the identification with God's *revealed* moral attributes

and the effort to realize those attributes in one's conduct. Judaism, Formstecher maintains, is the pristine, paradigmatic representative of the religion of spirit.

In the classical world, Judaism and paganism were diametrically opposed forces, hence Judaism's isolation. With the rise of Christianity and Islam, which propagated the *idea* of Judaism among the pagans, this isolation continued primarily because, by virtue of their mission to the gentiles, these two daughter religions had absorbed pagan elements. The perduring paganism of Christianity, according to Formstecher, was significantly modified by Protestantism, with its emphasis on the individual's spiritual self-transcendence. This development pointed to the eventual triumph of the *idea* of Judaism, that is, the religion of spirit.

The Enlightenment and the democratic state marked yet another decisive step in the universalization of the idea of Judaism. Acknowledging the individual's rational and moral autonomy, these two great decisive moments in the shaping of the modern ethos significantly empowered the individual and hence the possibility of his or her spiritual self-transcendence. The consequent overcoming of the pagan elements of culture signified by these developments, Formstecher argues, dialectically justifies the removal of all barriers between Jew and non-Jew. The emancipation of the Jews is thus not fortuitous but historically necessary. Yet until the pagan elements are fully eliminated from human sensibility and expression, the Jews are to persist as a distinct entity so as to safeguard the idea of the religion of spirit.

Nonetheless, concomitant to the progressive universalization of its founding "idea," Judaism should also undergo progressive change towards its ultimate union with the rest of humanity. Accordingly, Formstecher implores that "Rabbinic theocracy" and ritualism, which had hitherto secured the integrity and necessary isolation of Judaism during the long dark years of the diaspora, be gradually dismantled. As it joyfully enters the modern world, Judaism must appropriately discard its particularistic elements and streamline its "segregative" ceremonial life.

Religious reform is a dialectical imperative.

Samuel Hirsch: In contrast to Formstecher, Rabbi Samuel Hirsch (1815-1889), who emigrated to the U.S.A. in 1866 and became one the leading figures of the Reform movement there, did not regard the modern period as auguring the eventual amalgamation of Jewry into a new humanity, marking the end of its existence as a distinct religious community. The political and cultural integration of the Jews in the modern world, he held, was actually the occasion for Judaism truly to assert its distinctive spiritual reality and thus further its contribution to humanity. Correspondingly, he conceived of religious reform not as a means to facilitate the assimilation of the Jews but rather as the refinement of the spiritual content of Judaism, so as to facilitate its "mission" to the rest of the world. Hence, Hirsch insists, Reform Judaism is not to be viewed as easing the religious life of the Jews but rather as deepening their individual and collective responsibilities. Judaism, according to Hirsch, thus has a vital role to fulfill not simply, as Formstecher contends, in paving the road *to* but also *within* the modern world.

The specific task of Judaism in the modern period envisioned by Hirsch is to secure the "religious principle" threatened by the secular ethos dominating the period. By insisting that religion still has a role to play in the age in which reason had obtained a reigning position, Hirsch was challenging one of the cardinal propositions of Hegel. In contrast to his master, Hirsch did not regard religion as epistemologically inferior to reason. Religion need not yield its position to philosophy, for, in consonance with its authentic principle, religion, like the most refined expressions of philosophy, teaches that rational, moral freedom is the ground of human dignity and truth. But whereas philosophy suffices with abstract wisdom, according to Hirsch, religion encourages human beings to realize that the meaning of human existence lies in the concrete reality of autonomous moral decision and responsibility. Moreover, the religious principle brings one to the awareness that a transcendent God is the ultimate source of freedom and of one's ability

to transcend nature and its deterministic web of laws. In Judaism, the "classical" custodian of the religious principle, Hirsch explains, this function of religion had been exemplified by the notion of halakhah, the comprehensive religious law of the rabbis that sought to subordinate all aspects of natural life to the free act of devotion to God.

In the modern period, despite its allegiance to reason and the abstract principle of freedom, Hirsch argues, the actualization of genuine freedom is threatened by the determinism increasingly characteristic of the intellectual perceptions of the period. By consistently inducing a devotion to the concrete reality of freedom as a human-God reality, religion has a decisive advantage over the abstract teachings of reason. Philosophical reason thus has not, as Hegel thought, displaced religion. They are rather complementary modes of achieving human self-consciousness, with philosophy serving to give religious truths a conceptual clarity and religion guiding humans to a concrete actualization of freedom.

Hirsch developed this thesis in his *Die Religionsphilosophie der Juden* (*The Religious Philosophy of the Jews*, 1842). Consonant with this thesis, he teaches that the philosophy of Judaism is not found in abstract formulations but is discerned in its classical religious texts, which reflect the concrete life of the Jews. Aside from elucidating these texts and their theological presuppositions, he seeks to demonstrate that Judaism is not a historically moribund and thus anachronistic religion, totally irrelevant to the modern world, as Hegel and others held. The dialectic of Jewish history, he reasons, is fundamentally different from that governing pagan cultures, even from that of Christianity. In wedding itself to the pagan world, Christianity must perforce march through history in order to free itself of its pagan accretions. In contrast, Judaism does not require the purgatory of history and stands apart from both the pagan world and Christianity.

In the modern era, Judaism finds itself principally opposed to the regnant secular "neo-pagan" culture. Yet having inscribed freedom on its banner, the modern era presents Judaism with a unique opportunity to fulfill its pristine vocation to be "a light unto the nations." So that its universal message be as clarion as possible, Hirsch recommends that Judaism adjust its rite and public countenance in the direction proposed by Reform. But Judaism, Hirsch underscores, must endure. For in contrast to the past when God was revealed through miracles and prophecy, in the modern period God is manifest through the continued existence of the Jewish people and their faith. With Hirsch and Formstecher, we encounter a characteristic tension of modern Jewish thought. Judaism, they argued, is both within and beyond history. On the one hand, by celebrating the dynamic, historical character of Judaism, they could endorse the changes in the religious life of the Jews deemed necessary for their integration in the modern world. On the other, they placed Judaism or at least its spiritual core beyond history.

Samuel David Luzzatto: But it was not only Reform thinkers who mounted, as it were, a tightrope, seeking to balance Judaism between the pull of history and metahistory. The Italian religious philosopher Samuel David Luzzatto (1800-1865), a strict adherent of traditional Judaism, was also a pioneer of modern Jewish studies and a proponent of critical historical scholarship as a mode of reflecting upon the religious teachings of Israel. Frowning upon his colleagues who "study ancient Israel the way other scholars study ancient Egypt, Assyria, Babylon and Persia," he held that the antiquarianism and historical relativism attendant to the critical study of the sacred sources of the Jewish past could be avoided only if that study were "grounded in faith"—an existential commitment "to understand the Torah and the prophets as the Word of God, [and] to comprehend how, throughout our history, the spirit of God, our nation's inheritance, warred with the human spirit."

Nachman Krochmal: Luzzatto's older contemporary, Rabbi Nachman Krochmal (popularly known by his acronym, Ranak; 1785-1840) deemed the challenge posed by historical scholarship to tradition to require a far more elaborate defense. Krochmal,

who lived in the politically and socially conservative province of Galicia, where emancipation and religious reform were remote prospects, penned what he thought was an appropriate defense. His monumental Hebrew treatise, published posthumously in 1851, was entitled *Moreh Nevukhei ha-Zman* (*Guide for the Perplexed of the Time*). The title alludes to Maimonides' famous *Guide to the Perplexed* of 1190, and, similar to the great Spanish rabbi in his day, Krochmal sought to offer guidance to the perplexed of his generation.

Krochmal begins with the observation that Jewish youth are genuinely perplexed by the results of critical scholarship, which has cast doubt on the traditional view of Jewish history and in particular on the divine status of the foundational texts of Judaism, their composition and authority. An observant Jew, Krochmal notes that the faith of these youths will surely not be fortified by an obscurantist response; the enjoining of dogma in the face of the fruits of historical scholarship would only exacerbate their estrangement. Faith, as Maimonides argued, must be allied with reason; in our time, Krochmal contends, faith must be supported by a proper philosophical understanding of history. Krochmal's *Guide* sought to provide this, and hence its subtitle, *Gates to a Purified Faith*, referring to a faith purified through the crucible of philosophical reason.

Krochmal counseled the unequivocal acceptance of critical scholarship—the "scientific" evaluation of sources, the discovery of unknown and forgotten sources, and the appreciation of the historical conditioning of knowledge. Such scholarship need not, he held, undermine one's affirmation of the Torah as the word of God. To secure the authority of Judaism and its sources while acknowledging the validity of the insights and judgments of the historian, Krochmal developed an elaborate metaphysical conception of Jewish and world history. An autodidact in philosophy and modern European letters, who borrowed selectively from Hegel and Vico (as well as apparently Schelling and Fichte), he understood history as a dialectical process that proceeds through various cultural stages, each stage under the aegis of the "national spirit" of a particular people. Each of these peoples has its own life "cycle"— birth, development, maturity, decline, and dissolution. The "national spirit" of each is essentially particular and thus ephemeral.

In striking similarity to the philosophers of Reform Judaism—and there is no evidence of mutual influence—Krochmal contends that the Jewish people is an exception to this rule, for in essence it is "eternal," that is, a metahistorical people. To be sure, the Jewish people also knows the cycles of birth, growth, and decline, but, in its case, the cycle is continuously renewed. The eternality of the Jews is explained by the fact that, by virtue of the Torah, their "national spirit" is grounded in "the Absolute Spirit," a central Hegelian category that Krochmal identifies with the God of Israel. Indeed, the Jews are the agents of the Absolute Spirit as it unfolds in time, endowing world history with inner unity. In their sojourns in the diaspora, the Jews march through history, subject to all its forces. But, meeting all the "historical cultures" at their peak, they assimilate the truths of each. The Torah, which instructs and disciplines Israel to behold the One God as the principle of universal unity, allows the Jews to serve as the bearers of the comprehensive, "unified" knowledge of the evolving truth of history. Hence, although passing through—and clearly touched by—history, the Jews are in Krochmal's judgment ultimately a metahistorical, or better, a trans-historical, eternal people.

Implicit in Krochmal's exposition is that pious Jews who, as he put it, "love the Torah," need not fear "alien wisdom." He was of course aware that openness to the wisdom of the non-Jewish world not only exposed Jews to ways of thinking that challenged their beliefs but also confronted them with possible critiques of Judaism. Yet faith must be "purified" by a forthright consideration of these negative views, especially when voiced by thoughtful proponents of the modern sensibility. Hence, it is not surprising that Krochmal, as virtually all other Jewish religious thinkers in the nineteenth century, felt obliged to respond to Kant's conception of ethical piety as the ultimate form of true serv-

ice to God and to his attendant dismissal of Judaism as a misconceived expression of worship.

Even among thinkers whose primary concern was to develop *a la* Hegel and Schelling a philosophy of Jewish history, one discerns an attempt to come to terms with Kant's critique of Judaism as heteronomous pseudo-religion that deflects the heart from true, that is, ethical, service to God. Thinkers associated with every tendency in modern Judaism from Reform to neo-Orthodoxy shared the conviction that the faith of Israel properly understood actually promotes ethical piety. Even Luzzatto, a staunch traditionalist who expressly rejected the very premises of Kant's ethical rationalism, argued that Judaism is fundamentally a moral sentiment. Samson Raphael Hirsch (1808-1888), the founder of neo-Orthodoxy, which sought to accommodate "Torah-true" Judaism to the modern world, developed an elaborate exegesis of the mitzvot or the so-called laws of the Torah, indicating how each, even those of a seemingly pure ritualistic nature, in its distinctive manner, fosters the development of "moral consciousness."

Moritz Lazarus: Surely the most ambitious and systematic attempt to demonstrate Judaism's compatibility with Kant' conception of a religion of morality was a two volume work by Moritz Lazarus (1824-1903). A professor of philosophy at the University of Berlin and a prominent lay leader of Liberal Judaism in Germany, Lazarus duly entitled his work *Ethik des Judentums* (1898-1911; trans. from the German manuscript as *Ethics of Judaism*, 2 vols., 1900-1901). In developing his thesis, Lazarus drew upon the principles he had formulated in founding the discipline of *Völkerpsychologie*, the comparative psychological study of peoples, or what we would today call ethnic groups.

Elaborating Kant's metaphysical skepticism, Lazarus held that truth must be sought not in *a priori* abstractions but in an empirical psychological investigation, not of individual consciousness alone but of various societies and peoples as distinct entities. The philosopher as psychologist, accordingly, must study humankind from the historical and comparative cultural perspective, delineating the constitutive elements of its culture, conventions and developmental tendencies. With respect to the "psychological" study of Judaism, Lazarus proposed that the empirically apposite approach would be to examine the literary sources of classical Judaism as they most faithfully record the "will, intent and way of life" of the Jews. By insisting that only on the basis of such a study could Judaism be properly characterized, he abjured the speculative approach of Formstecher and Samuel Hirsch. He claimed to introduce Kantian categories not as speculative presuppositions but rather as heuristic principles that to his mind best organize and elucidate the "immanent" structure of Judaism, helping illuminate the objective unity of its "ethical cosmos."

Lazarus maintained that a study such as is presented in his *Ethics of Judaism* shows that Judaism is in effect a system of autonomous ethics; specifically, the rites and articles of faith of Judaism manifestly encourage the development of what Kant celebrated as the autonomous moral consciousness. As a religious system, however, Judaism is distinguished from purely rational ethics in that it enjoins one to regard oneself as subject to God as the author of moral precepts. This credal affirmation of God as the source of morality, however, contradicts the moral autonomy Lazarus identified as the ultimate meaning of Judaism—an apparent antinomy Lazarus solved by postulating that the moral law is an independent, objective truth to which even God is subordinate.

Crucial for Lazarus is the grounding of ethics in a belief that God endows moral action with a compelling sense of duty and obligation, which he felt the philosophical ethics of Kant failed to provide. Further, he observed, the ethical piety engendered by Judaism may be best characterized as "holiness," a quality of life that bespeaks neither a numinous nor transcendent reality but rather the indomitable conviction that a moral life is the ultimate meaning and purpose of existence.

Hermann Cohen: To Lazarus' profound disappointment, his *Ethics of Judaism* was severely criticized by the generation's most eminent Kantian philosopher, Hermann Cohen (1842-1918), the founder of the Marburg school of neo-Kantianism. Cohen faulted Lazarus for locating the source of Judaism's ethical teachings in the Jewish "folk-soul." To Cohen such a (questionable) concept, anchored as it is in psychology and history, undermines the reliability and certitude required in a genuine ethical system. Ethics must, he insists, derive its validity from rational, universal concepts. Jewish ethics is philosophically interesting and, indeed, compelling, he contends, because of its distinctive dependence on the concept of a universal, unique God, not just a phantasm of the Jewish folk-soul but a rationally defensible concept.

Cohen's critique was especially stinging for Lazarus not only because of the former's scholarly preeminence. Rather, like Lazarus, Cohen, who was also affiliated with Liberal Judaism, particularly in his later years, shared a conviction regarding the essential affinity between Judaism and Kant's ethical idealism. Interpreting the master's teachings in a somewhat novel fashion, Cohen understood ethics as not only addressing the individual but also in its fullest sense as summoning society to the "task" (*Aufgabe*) of molding the "future" according to the principle of a rationally determined, *a priori* moral "Ought." In his earlier writings, coinciding with his so-called Marburg period (1873-1912), he conceived of this task as a regulative principle that, when approximated, recedes into the future, such that the task is forever defined anew. The consequent eternity (or "asymptotic" nature) of the task, Cohen observes, required that the physical world—the *mise en scène* of the moral life—be conceived as also eternal, a presupposition that the natural sciences cannot confirm.

At this juncture, Cohen postulated the concept of God—the eternal, unique God of which the Hebrew Bible speaks—as the "guarantor" of the everlasting, eternally perduring existence of the world, thus assuring the realizability and rationally compelling quality of morality, albeit conceived as an eternal, unending task. Cohen held that this conception of ethics was anticipated by biblical monotheism, especially as refracted through the vision of the prophets of a messianic future that would witness the manifestation of God's oneness in the moral unity of humankind, as a divine promise and human, moral responsibility. For Cohen of the Marburg period, God was thus an idea, a postulate of ethical idealism, and, as such, religion, and Judaism in particular, gain their dignity and meaning by enriching ethics.

As the ideational prop supporting the ethical task, God for Cohen was thus not a personal God who enjoys an independent existence and relation to human beings. Hence, Cohen likewise did not regard religion as an autonomous spiritual reality but rather merely as the historical presupposition of ethics. His conception of God and religion, however, would undergo a far-reaching re-evaluation during the second period of his intellectual development, marked by his retirement in 1912 from his professorial chair in Marburg and departure for Berlin. Devoting himself there to Jewish life, Cohen seems to have subjected his thought to a fundamental revaluation. He now notes that ethics addresses the individual but as a representative of rational humanity and not existentially as an often tormented creature who stands alone. In contrast to ethics, Cohen of Berlin points outs, religion does address the individual existentially, especially through the notion of "sin," which Cohen understands as the individual's anguished realization of his or her own moral failings.

Sin and the concomitant feeling of guilt, Cohen observes, potentially leads the sinful individual to despair of his or her own moral worth and to abandon all subsequent moral effort. This self-estrangement attendant to sin requires, in Cohen's judgment, the concept of a forbearing God, who, by the act of forgiveness, rededicates the individual to the moral task. Religion is thus preeminently a series of acts of atonement , rites and prayers expressing remorse and repentance, focused on the belief in a merciful, forgiving God. The reconciliation between God and the human individual thus achieved requires in turn that God be conceived not as an idea but as a *being* who relates to the finite ever changing world of *becoming*, of which the individual is a part. Despite the fundamental ontological distinction separating them, being and becoming are interrelated through what Cohen called "correlation." God and the individual human being are "correlated" when the individual, cognizant of God's mercy, love, and concern, dedicates him or herself anew to emulating these divine qualities. Cohen spoke of correlation as a shared holiness, in which God and the individual are "co-workers" in the work of creation.

Cohen set forth these views in *Der Begriff der Religion im System der Philosophie* (*The Concept of Religion in the System of Philosophy*, 1915) and most forcefully in his *Religion of Reason from the Sources of Judaism* (*Religion der Vernunft aus dem Quellen der Judentums*, 1919). In this, his most enduring work, Cohen expounded his new conception of religion through a selective exegesis of the sources of classical Judaism in the Bible, Midrash, liturgy, and medieval Jewish philosophy. These traditional expressions of Jewish piety, Cohen argues, exemplify the most refined conception of religion.

The emerging portrait of Judaism as a faith of deep personal significance has suggested to many commentators that Cohen anticipated the existentialism characteristic of twentieth century Jewish theology, with its emphasis on the dialogical relationship between the individual and a living, personal God. Cohen, however, continued to speak of the "religion of reason," and his conception of God remained that of a God of ethics. And although he accorded prayer and ritual a dignity denied by Kant, Cohen still did not deem religious worship to be an independent reality enjoying a unique ontological and epistemological status. While not utterly absorbed into ethics, the "religion of reason" remained for Cohen ultimately ancillary to ethics. Religion, and Judaism in particular, is conceived as an instrument for enhancing moral consciousness (that is, moral reason) and, concomitantly, it facilitates acceptance of the responsibility of laboring to realize "the kingdom of God."

Despite Cohen's adumbration of some of

the salient features of twentieth century religious existentialism, his overarching moral theology renders him more a son of the previous century. Moral reason remained for Cohen the heart of religion, and thus it is not surprising that we read in *Religion of Reason* that "revelation is the creation of reason." This identification of reason and revelation, of course, was typical of nineteenth century philosophical idealism. For twentieth century religious existentialists, on the other hand, the point of departure was revelation understood as a meta-rational category pointing to God's free self-disclosure to human beings in their finite existence. In this respect, the transitional figure from nineteenth to twentieth century Jewish thought is not Cohen but an iconoclastic lay scholar, Solomon Ludwig Steinheim.

Solomon Ludwig Steinheim: A physician by profession, not affiliated with any denominational camp within the Jewish community in his native Germany or in Rome, where he spent the last twenty years of his life isolated from the organized Jewish community, Solomon Steinheim (1789-1866) has been called "the first [truly] Jewish theologian of the modern age. . . . He was [however] twenty years too late, and one hundred years too early" (Hans Joachim Schoeps). If one views Jewish thought from Mendelssohn to Cohen as a sustained effort to interpret Judaism as a religion of reason *par excellence*, then Steinheim stands alone in the nineteenth century.

In his monumental study *Offenbarung nach dem Lehrbegriff der Synagoge* (*Revelation according to the Doctrine of the Synagogue*, 4 vols., 1835-65), Steinheim sought to remove religion from the tutelage of reason, maintaining that religious truths are the "gift" of supernatural revelation. Recalling Kierkegaard's critique of Hegel, he held that the truths disclosed by revelation are incompatible and irreducible to reason. Further, he noted that the concept of supernatural revelation posits God as the creator who, unbounded by necessity, created the world freely and out of nothing, that is, *ex nihlio*. As such, revelation confirms the irrefragable human experience of freedom that reason burdened by the principle of universal neces-

sity perforce denies. Accordingly, Steinheim contends, reason must acknowledge the primacy of revelation.

In that God is the logical presupposition of revelation, Steinheim observes, the affirmation of the possibility of revelation perforce reestablishes the dignity and authority of God: "Our task is to present revelation [such that] we are constrained . . . to accept God. Therefore, it is for us to make a declaration, the exact opposite of Mendelssohn's and to prove the Old Testament was given not to reveal law but the living God" (*Offenbarung*, II, pp. 37-38). Revelation is thus not an object of faith but a definite cognitive phenomenon, and its content corresponds to the postulates of Kant's moral reason: God, freedom, and immortality. It also follows for Steinheim that not only these postulates are granted in revelation, but that the categorical imperatives of morality derive their authority from God and revelation. Judaism, he held, represents the ideal religion of revelation, its ritual laws being secondary to its moral code. Steinheim's conclusions regarding Judaism are hence unlike other nineteenth century Jewish thinkers, the crucial difference being that for him Judaism is a result of supernatural revelation.

Franz Rosenzweig: Steinheim affirmed revelation and the living God of Israel as postulates of reason, as logical deductions that emerge from reason's recognition of its own limitation. Revelation thus is not affirmed out of faith, nor is it attested on the basis of religious experience. This approach is strikingly similar to the path to religious faith taken by the twentieth century's most "God intoxicated" Jewish theologian, Franz Rosenzweig (1886-1929). Although he was apparently ignorant of Steinheim's writings, after concluding that reason is inherently incapable of answering some fundamental questions of existence, he too adopted what he called *Offenbarungsglaube*—a belief in revelation as a historical and existential possibility.

A highly assimilated Jew, Rosenzweig's adoption of religious faith initially took him to the threshold of the baptismal fount. His dramatic reversal of his decision to convert to

Christianity was accompanied by a resolve to explore Judaism, more precisely, traditional Jewish religious practice, as a framework in which to realize his faith in revelation. Such a faith, he held, must be the fulcrum of any genuine theology. Otherwise, he observed in his first essay on religious matters, one attains the strange anthropocentric, "godless" brew concocted by the nineteenth century, which, in placing religion within the realm of human sensibility alone, be it called "spiritual experience," "moral consciousness," or "folk soul," is in effect but an "atheistic theology." Theology, Rosenzweig asserts, must rather proceed from the divinely initiated event of revelation, of God's addressing human beings.

Rosenzweig developed his understanding of revelation as a divine address on the basis of a radical critique of philosophical idealism, with its quest for universal and thus timeless, abstract truths. In contrast to the ratiocination of the philosophers, revelation is in time, an occurrence whereby God establishes a relationship with time-bound individuals. Phenomenologically, this relationship is celebrated in the biblical traditions as love; the divine sounding of *Thou* to the temporally contingent *I* of the individual. God addresses individuals in their finite existence, calling them by their "first and last names," which distinguish them existentially from all others. In revelation, the contingent existence of individuals, encapsulated by the names they receive at birth, is thus confirmed in divine love and blessed with the kiss of eternity.

Occurring in time—within the contingent matrix of the lived life—revelation is inaccessible to a reason that only considers timeless essences. Yet, Rosenzweig emphasizes that this conception of revelation does not contradict reason; it merely delimits its sphere of validity. Properly understood, philosophical reason and faith are complementary. This affirmation of revelation allowed Rosenzweig to discern what many of his generation of assimilated German Jews had denied, that Judaism is a theocentric faith of enduring existential significance. He elaborated his conception of faith and of Judaism in *The Star*

of Redemption (*Stern der Erlösung*), a book he penned in the trenches of the First World War and published shortly thereafter.

A dense but clearly inspired volume, along with a systematic critique of the predominant philosophical traditions of the West, Rosenzweig's *Star* presents a phenomenological reconstruction of the inner life of the devout Jew, whose spiritual life is structured by the experienced realities of creation, revelation, and redemption. These interrelated spiritual realities—which begin experientially with revelation—are archetypically actualized in the liturgical calendar of the Jew: the daily prayer service, the Sabbath, the holidays, and festivals. Jewish liturgy, Rosenzweig avers, bears the soul of the Jew. As a preeminently liturgical community, the Jews follow a pattern of time that is not only sacred but also cyclical: the calendar of prayer that guides the Jews' passion and spiritual fantasy is set in a given yearly cycle.

Jewish calendrical time, thus, does not "grow" as secular time does from year to year but spins upon itself in a recurring pattern of liturgical celebration. Hence, the linear, ever unfolding time of the mundane world hardly affects the spiritual reality of the Jew. Accepting the nomenclature of the Church Fathers, Rosenzweig suggests that the Jewish people therefore is best depicted as a Synagogue, a community of prayer apart from history. But although it sequesters itself from history, unlike what is often charged by Christian critics and some philosophers, such as Hegel, the Synagogue is not irrelevant to ultimate human destiny. Standing apart from history, the Synagogue anticipates the spiritual reality of redemption. Thus, as an existential embodiment of the eschatological promise, the Synagogue inspires and prods the Church (which because of its divinely appointed mission to the gentiles must perforce march *through* history) to lead history to the goal of a world beyond history, that is, a world that has overcome division, strife, and war. For Rosenzweig, the Synagogue and the Church are hence complementary covenants, the former being the sustaining "fire," the latter the luminous "flame" of God's saving light.

In his later writings, after having completed the *Star*, Rosenzweig sought to incorporate more and more extra-liturgical aspects of traditional Judaism, from the commandment of keeping a kosher kitchen to that of Torah study. His approach to the ritual and ceremonial commandments, however, was distinctive. Unlike Orthodox Jews, he could not accept them on the basis of Rabbinic authority, for, as he remarked, "faith based on authority is not faith." His approach to "the Law," as he explained in a now famous openletter, entitled "The Builders," to Martin Buber, was rather to encourage each individual Jew to explore the sacramental and existential possibilities of the mitzvot, to determine which of these divinely ordained practices he or she personally feels called upon to fulfill. As he further elaborates his position to Buber with reference to a Rabbinic commentary on Is. 54:13, Jews are not only to regard themselves as God's obedient "children" (*banayikh*), but also as God's "builders" (*bonayikh*): every generation has the opportunity, indeed, the task, of recreating the law for itself. This non-dogmatic brand of traditionalism continues to guide many modern Jews who seek to reappropriate in undogmatic fashion traditional forms of Jewish piety and to reaffirm Judaism as a relationship with a living God. Indeed, Rosenzweig signally inspired the serious, non-apologetic theological reflection characteristic of much of Jewish religious thought in the twentieth century.

Martin Buber: Rosenzweig's legacy is frequently associated with that of the equally original religious thinker Martin Buber (1878-1965). Although they shared many theological presuppositions and cultural concerns, the two friends differed on some basic positions. Both conceived of revelation as essentially a divine-human dialogue, and both regarded the revalorization of the notion of revelation to be the urgent task for Jewish religious renewal. But whereas Rosenzweig envisioned that renewal to be bound to the life of prayer and ritual, Buber promoted a radical form of religious anarchism that exhibited little patience for the life of the synagogue and the mitzvot. Furthermore, Buber was a Zionist and thus emphatically rejected Rosenzweig's meta-historical view of Israel's vocation.

Buber's emergence as a genuine religious thinker was inaugurated with the publication of *I and Thou* (*Ich und Du*) in December, 1922, shortly before his forty-fifth birthday. His previous writings on spiritual matters, Jewish and otherwise, belonged to a genre of Romantic mysticism that Rosenzweig had expressly in mind when he wrote his essay on "atheistic theology." These writings were virtually devoid of any reference to the God of revelation. Only with his treatise on I-Thou, or dialogical, relationships, did Buber affirm faith as grounded in God's revealed word.

To be sure, Buber's conception of what the divine word entailed differed fundamentally from traditional teaching about the content of revelation. For Buber, revelation is homologous with what he calls dialogue. God, the Eternal Thou, addresses one through varied and fluid life-experiences—from the seemingly ephemeral and trivial to the grand and momentous—that demand a dialogical response. In this response one confirms the Thou, the unique presence of the other who stands before one awaiting that response. In uttering Thou (an actual speech-act is superfluous), the self, or I, in turn, finds its own presence confirmed. In its fullness, the life of dialogue is marked by mutuality. As a response to the continuously renewing presence of the other, dialogue must be born ever anew. The I-Thou response, Buber emphasizes, thus requires spontaneity and cannot be determined by fixed expressions, gestures, and prescribed deeds. It follows that the God revealed through the addressing presence of the immanent Thou that stands before one likewise requires spontaneity. Buber thus contends that the only authentic service to God is found in spontaneous responses to the Eternal God who turns to human beings through the protean flux of life. Although not utterly dismissing prayer and ritual as bearing the possibility of a spontaneous and hence authentic relation to God, Buber certainly did not regard them as paradigmatic forms of *devotio*.

Clearly such a conception of divine revelation conflicts fundamentally with the classical Jewish doctrine of revelation, which recognizes the Sinaitic presentation to Israel of the Torah as an historical event that, paradoxically, enjoys eternal authority. Further, his distance, bordering on antagonism, towards liturgical prayer and the mitzvot as the proper forms of divine service conflicts not only with traditional but with all expressions of institutional Jewish religious life. It was precisely Buber's anarchism that so irked Rosenzweig and led to his aforementioned open-letter, in which he challenged Buber to adopt a more constructive view of the mitzvot and institutional piety.

Acknowledging his anomalous position within Jewish religious thought, Buber insisted that he was not in a formal sense a theologian. He claimed to seek neither to justify revealed propositions about God nor to defend revealed scriptures and doctrine. He simply pointed to dialogue as the existential ground of one's relationship to God and as a meta-ethical principle that should determine the responses of an individual to the divine address as it is sounded through the web of everyday life. He held that this principle was at the heart of all great spiritual traditions, but particularly Judaism. The concept of dialogue can thus be employed as a hermeneutic lens to read the Hebrew Bible and other formative Jewish religious texts, such as those of Hasidism.

As a particular community of faith, Judaism is for Buber distinguished by its millennial and pristine witness to the dialogical principle both in its collective memory (enshrined in its central myths and sacred texts) and, ideally, in its current institutions. In fact, as a Zionist, he held that Jewish religious life in the diaspora had been falsely restricted to the synagogue and the home, thus losing hold of the primal thrust of the dialogical principle as a comprehensive ethic of service to God. By restoring the Jews to the sociological conditions of a full communal life, Zionism allows the Jews' public life, guided once again by the principle of dialogue, to be the essential realm of their relationship to God. The reappropriation of the public sphere as the dialogical responsibility of the community of faith, according to Buber, is in consonance

with the supreme injunction of the prophets to realize a just society. It thus constitutes the renewal of what he called Hebrew or biblical humanism.

Buber's religious anarchism and radical politics (to which his biblical humanism often led him) alienated many Jews committed to traditional forms of ritual and liturgical worship. On the other hand, his philosophy of dialogue has manifestly inspired others, especially those eager for extra-synagogal expressions of Jewish spirituality and commitment. Further, his conception of dialogue as a way to read sacred texts—which allows one to recognize the divine voice in those texts without necessarily accepting them uncritically—has had a seminal impact on contemporary Jewish studies and hermeneutical attitudes.

Together with Rosenzweig, Buber set the tone of Jewish religious thought in the twentieth century. Defying the denominational labels and apologetic predilections of the previous century, Jewish thought was now marked by an existential earnestness and a commitment to reappropriate for moderns traditional forms of Jewish piety and spirituality. These were deemed urgently relevant especially to lives buffeted by the many ambiguities of modernity. This reemergence of Judaism as an intellectually and spiritually compelling religious culture allowed the Jews of Germany in the 1930s to stand proud in the face of Nazi tyranny and to launch a "spiritual resistance" to the diabolical scheme to deprive them not only their civil rights but of their self-esteem.

Leo Baeck: The spiritual and human dignity of German Jewry in its "last and finest hours" was embodied in the person of Rabbi Leo Baeck (1874-1956; fig. 77). Although initially beholden to the apologetic, self-consciously rationalistic posture of nineteenth century Liberal Judaism, Baeck developed a theological position that was destined to serve as a courageous witness to Jewish faith. The religion of Israel, he held, is constituted by a dialectic of "commandment and mystery"—the abiding ethical affirmations of the Jews are perforce accompanied by a numinous experience of a living, just God.

This experience sustains the Jews and nurtures their trust in the world and in the ultimate triumph of the good. Baeck's was no naive faith, however. He was painfully cognizant of the evil spawned by a crazed humanity. But evil could, he taught, be overcome only if we resist despair by affirming human decency and the prophetic vision of a compassionate, just world.

In the dark days of the Shoah this vision became a hope-against-hope. The decimation of European Jewry, of course, also brought an abrupt halt to its vibrant and multifarious intellectual traditions. Those traditions were in part transplanted to the soil of North America and Israel. Surviving representatives of these traditions found particularly in the U.S.A. a supportive environment to continue their labors. The most seminal of these thinkers were two East European born thinkers, classmates at the University of Berlin in the late and early 1930, Abraham Joshua Heschel and Joseph Dov Soloveitchik.

Abraham Joshua Heschel: Emigrating to the U.S.A. in 1940, the Polish-born Heschel (1907-1972), scion of great Hasidic masters, developed a lyrical theology that drew its major conceptual apparatus from the philosopher Max Scheler (1874-1928), whose inspired efforts to rescue the cognitive dignity of subjective emotions exercised a tremendous attraction on his generation. Following Scheler, Heschel presented a phenomenological explication of his own subjective experience of faith as a believing Jew bound to the tradition of "halakhic holiness" and "prophetic consciousness."

Blending Hasidic spirituality—which, like Buber, with whom he worked closely while still in Germany, he held resonated the innermost truths of Jewish faith—with nuanced Western learning, Heschel sought to elaborate a conception of piety relevant to the contemporary Jew. Noting that western humanity's aptitude for faith has been dulled by technological, bourgeois civilization, he endeavored to reawaken the *sensus numinus*, the *a priori* sense of wonder and awe evoked by the mystery of life, which, like the Christian theologian and historian of religions Rudolf Otto (1869-1937), he regarded as the font of faith. To do this, he introduced his readers to the Hasidic-kabbalistic teaching that all of reality refracts the divine presence. He taught that the abiding mystery of existence, which even the most technological, pragmatic civilization can never truly eliminate, and which all individuals, often despite themselves, behold, is an intimation of the ineffable yet manifestly wondrous reality of God. Acknowledging God as the providential source of existence leads one beyond the absurd, "to the certainty of meaning." The apprehension of holiness "conquers absurdity." Indeed, "without holiness we would sink back into absurdity."

The inflections of Heschel's discourse bear the influence of existentialism, especially that of Kierkegaard. The nineteenth century Danish religious philosopher seems to have also provided Heschel with the language to help him conceptualize the existential logic of halakhah as creating an inner, "holy" reality that heightens one's sense of the divine presence. As a system of concrete, even mundane deeds, the halakhah ritualizes the prophetic teaching that faith is ultimately a "leap of action" (cf., Kierkegaard's concept of a "leap of faith"). We respond, that is, to God's presence by making God's work our own. Indeed, the covenantal relationship between God and Israel posits the possibility of an intimate partnership between human beings and God: our sins anger and sadden God, and, fearing and loving God, we resolve to bring God joy by sharing the divine's work to crown creation with justice and compassion (a theme already sounded by Leo Baeck and other representatives of European Liberal Judaism).

Despite his conviction that the "prophetic consciousness" captured the heart of traditional Judaism, Heschel's thought found its primary resonance not so much among the votaries of halakhah as among Jews in need of an interpretation of Judaism that would authenticate their participation as Jews in the humane causes of their day. Heschel's message of prophetic concern and responsibility thus spoke to a generation of American Jews in the 1960s and 1970s who felt themselves called upon to bear prophetic witness and join the struggle on behalf of civil rights for black Americans and to oppose what was regarded as an unjust war in Vietnam.

Joseph Dov Soloveitchik: A descendent of renowned Lithuanian Talmudic scholars, Rabbi Soloveitchik (1903-1993) emigrated to the U.S.A. in 1932, shortly after earning a Ph.D. with a dissertation on Hermann Cohen. Whereas Heschel structured his thought with a conceptual apparatus adapted from Scheler's phenomenology of emotions and existentialism, Soloveitchik wove his teachings from a synthetic skein of neo-Kantian and existentialist teachings. Hence, in contrast to Heschel, he developed a more dialectical view of the relation between technological civilization (which, to use Kantian parlance, unfolds in the phenomenal world) and the life of the mind and spirit (which dwells in the realm of noumenon). Halakhah allows the Jew to honor both spheres. A life wedded to halakhah, Soloveitchik taught, thus is not inherently antagonistic to the moral and cognitive concerns of technological civilization.

Indeed, by enhancing the quality of life, the halakhah augments the glory of God as the creator; accordingly, by participating—responsibly and creatively—in the efforts to advance scientific knowledge and its practical application, one furthers the work of creation. Moreover, by binding the individual to the community, halakhah implicitly encourages the cultivation of the social and gregarious personality required by technological civilization. At the same time, the halakhah accepts the individual's existential aloneness, overcoming the attendant isolation and anxiety through a "redemptive" love of God and Torah; the congregation of Jews forged by the Torah is a "covenantal community" that respects the solitary, existential reality of each of its members, joined in a common covenantal relationship, sacrally objectified by the halakhah, to God and each other. Like Heschel, Soloveitchik found a receptive audience in the U.S.A., where he primarily addressed American educated Orthodox Jews who, while embracing modernity, were perplexed by the increasingly ambiguous position of a person of faith and religious commitment in a pragmatic world with a pronounced secular bias. Rather than counseling the usual Orthodox posture of self-enclosure, Soloveitchik boldly accepted the pragmatic premises of modern civilization, even as he defended within the context of that civilization the integrity of "the halakhic man" conceived as *homo religiosus.*

Emmanuel Levinas: The slow but impressive reconstruction of European Jewry in the wake of the Shoah has given rise to a renewal of Jewish religious thought, most notably in France, where the Lithuanian born Emmanuel Levinas (1905-1995) is of singular importance. One of the most esteemed philosophers of post-World War II France, Levinas illuminates the religious meaning of Judaism through the metaphysical phenomenology he developed as a critique of Husserl's and Heidegger's concept of the other. The term "religious" requires some modification in the context of Levinas' thought, however. For him, Judaism is foremost a culture characterized by a distinctive ethical sensibility. Hence, "'Judaism' comes to signify a culture that is either the result or the foundation of the religion." This perspective allows Jews of decidedly secular as well as religious orientation to regard Levinas as a guide to reengage the spiritual heritage of Israel in a critical, reflective manner.

Levinas' point of departure is strikingly similar to that assumed by Rosenzweig in *The Star of Redemption,* an affinity of method and concern that Levinas readily acknowledged. The Greek philosophical tradition, to which the West is beholden, he observes, is fixated on an essentialist conception of being, insisting that all that is contingent yield to its imperious notion of necessary, lawful truths. Despite their appreciation of temporality, Levinas critically comments, even Heidegger and Husserl failed to break the hold of the "totalistic" and therefore totalizing Greek ontology. This break can be achieved only when one encounters the subjective reality of the other, which is beyond thought and thus by definition transcendent. The irreducible otherness—"alterity" is the term Levinas prefers—of the other whom one encounters compels one to reach out to the other by assuming a moral responsibility towards him or her. This moral experience of the other, Levinas points out in rebuke of Greek philosophical prejudices, is the only "knowledge" we have of the other.

This insight, Levinas argues, implicitly informs the Western humanist tradition. Alas, this tradition has been severely undermined by the anti-humanistic tendencies of contemporary western culture that masquerades as liberty, or rather a perverse concept of liberty that is unabashedly self-serving and egotistical. Levinas contrasts a liberty bereft of responsibility for the other with the Jewish-biblical concept of "a difficult liberty," which is the title of one of his most important collections of essays on Judaism. The Jew obtains transcendence and thus liberty by paradoxically living under God's law that requires ethical and social responsibility for the other. The biblical individual, Levinas observes, "discovers" his or her fellow human being before "discovering landscapes." As the custodian of biblical humanism, Levinas avers, Judaism defiantly proclaims to the contemporary world that liberty entails responsibility and obligation to others.

In elaborating this proposition, Levinas reads the Jewish sources, such as the Talmud, in the light of his dialogical ethics. He characterizes his reading as "aggadic," that is, he consciously reads the sources not with strict exegetical rigor or with halakhic, "normative" concern, but rather with the intention to cull insights and uncover the basic ethical impulses informing the texts. In a similar fashion, he re-reads the traditional categories of biblical faith; for instance, he presents revelation not as an historical event bearing a specific content but as the epiphany of the other inscribed in his or her face, the inimitable signature of absolute otherness. And "holiness" he understands as that moment when the material needs of others become one's spiritual needs.

Axiomatic to Levinas' dialogical ethics is a conception of the self that decisively challenges the prevailing understanding of the self in western culture, particularly in its bourgeois mold. The self is not enhanced by asserting its individuality but rather through its ethically responsible relationship to the other. Analogously, Judaism must be more than an identity, the defiant assertion of one' identity as a Jew in the face of assimilation and the horror of the Shoah. Judaism is rather a way of life, governed by the grammar of a specific religious-ethical discourse, that bears witness to the Other.

The discourse defining the Jewish way of life is open, and dialogically pursued. Indeed, Judaism as Levinas understands is a "religion for adults," meaning it is subject to constant debate, discussion, critical review, interpretation, commentary, in which divergent views are respected and encouraged. This conception of Judaism as a dynamic, plurality of voices that harmonize only in their commitment to making sense of the spiritual vocation of Israel in the modern world well summarizes the legacy of modern religious Jewish thought as it meets the next millennium.

Notes

[1] See Mendes-Flohr, "Images of Knowledge in Modern Jewish Thought," 1997.

[2] This argument is to be understood in the larger context of the Jewish struggle for emancipation and the concomitant need to counter objections that Jews were alien to European culture. The founders of modern Jewish studies—or *Wissenschaft des Judentums* as it was called in the nineteenth century—for instance, were guided by this apologetic motive. Through scholarly treatises on various aspects of Judaism, they would demonstrate that Jews made a lively and decisive contribution to the spiritual and intellectual history that ultimately nurtured the spirit of modern European.

[3] Cf., Altmann, *Moses Mendelssohn*, p. 514.

PAUL MENDES-FLOHR

JUDAISM, PHILOSOPHY AND THEOLOGY OF, IN THE STATE OF ISRAEL: The restoration of the Jews to their ancient patrimony in the land of Israel under Zionism raises a host of perhaps intractable theological questions. The foremost concerns the status and significance of a process initiated and carried out by humans that, throughout the ages, the custodians of Jewish faith taught would be realized only through the grace and direct action of God. In Jewish prayer and doctrine, the return of Israel's exiles to Zion was conceived to be a messianic event, providentially determined by the will of God, at God's appointed hour. Is not the Zionist project rather a usurpation of God's work, a mark of heretical impatience, not to speak of sinful hubris? Or, despite its secular passion and profane achievements, is Zionism to be ultimately regarded as the longed for redemption?

And with Jewish sovereignty reestablished, another salient question concerns the theological significance of the adjective "Jewish" when applied to a state's affairs conducted according to secular principles and considerations. Does the holiness of the land remove it from mundane geopolitical considerations? Does not the commandment to honor the land as the locus of the divine promise to the people of Israel supersede all pragmatic, even ethical, approaches to solving the conflict with the Arab residents of the land, who have their own competing national claims to the country? Can sovereignty over the land be shared with non-Jews?

Yehuda Alkalai and Zvi Hirsch Kalischer: Such questions were in part broached by two visionary Orthodox rabbis even before the Zionist movement was formally founded at the end of the nineteenth century. Yehuda Alkalai (1798-1878) and Zvi Hirsch Kalischer (1795-1894) both learned from the movements of national liberation that they witnessed in the respective countries of their residence—Alkalai served as a rabbi in Serbia; Kalischer in Posen, a Polish region that just before his birth had been annexed to Prussia. Inspired by the repeated rebellions of the Poles in the regions of their country that fell under Russian rule, the renowned Talmudic scholar Kalischer held that the Jews should take heart from the example of the Poles. "The beginning of the Redemption," he explained, "will come through natural causes by human effort . . . to gather the scattered of Israel into the Holy Land."[1] Kalischer called upon his fellow Jews to "cast aside the conventional view that the Messiah will suddenly sound a blast on the great trumpet and cause all the inhabitants of the earth to tremble."[2] Rabbi Alkalai concurred that the "ingathering of the exiles" will occur not by way of a "sudden miracle"[3] but "with the effort of the Jews themselves; they

must organize and unite, choose leaders, and leave the lands of exile."[4]

Isaac Jacob Reines: The envisioned political organization that would restore Jewish sovereignty was initiated by decidedly secular individuals, even—as in the case of Theodor Herzl (1860-1904), the founder of the World Zionist Organization (WZO)—by assimilated Jews. But Orthodox Jews were quick to organize themselves as a separate movement within the WZO. They were led by Isaac Jacob Reines (1837-1915), who had devoted his life to strengthening traditional Jewish society in eastern Europe, principally by promoting educational reform. The manifesto issued in 1902 at the founding of their movement, called Mizrahi, reads:

> In the lands of the Diaspora the soul of our people—our Holy Torah—can no longer be preserved in its full strength, nor can the commandments, which compromise the spiritual life of the people, be kept in their original purity, because the times are besieging us with difficult demands. It is difficult to respond to those demands without ignoring the holy treasure entrusted to us at Sinai. . . . Against his will each [of us] loses his Jewish self in the [non-Jewish] majority, for only in their midst can he fulfill all those secular requirements which the times demand of him. The people has found one remedy for this affliction—to direct their hearts to that one place which has always been the focus of our prayers . . .: Zion and Jerusalem. . . .
>
> It has therefore been agreed by all those who love the spirit of the people and are faithful to their God's Torah, that the reawakening of the hope of return to Zion will provide a solid foundation as well as quality to our people. It will serve as a focus for the ingathering of our spiritual forces and as a secure fortress for our Torah and its sanctity.[5]

What is significant in this statement is that it is a practical, not theological, endorsement of Zionism. It is clearly prompted by an emphatically practical concern, namely, how to stem the tide of secularization and assimilation. Under the conditions prevailing in the diaspora at this juncture in Jewish history, when the Jews of Europe are seeking integration into the new social and political order, the corresponding pull of secular culture has a deeply corrosive effect on Jewry's attachment to Torah. The hope of returning to

Zion awakened by Herzl's political program, the Mizrahi manifesto proclaims, will provide new cohesion and unity of purpose for the Jewish masses, enabling them to remain true to the Torah and to resist modern temptations. Significantly, the unabashed pragmatism that inspired this endorsement of Zionism led Mizrahi to support the so-called Uganda Program, a proposal that Herzl placed before the 1903 congress of the WZO, calling upon the movement to accept an offer of Great Britain to allow the establishment of a Jewish colony in His Majesty's East African Territory of Uganda. The proposed colony, Herzl argued, would allow for an immediate solution to the distress of millions of Jews. To Herzl's utter chagrin, the proposal was resolutely rejected by the majority of east European secular Zionists, especially those of a socialist, politically progressive orientation. They deemed the Uganda Program, irrespective of its practical merits, to be a betrayal of the dream of returning to Zion. Ironically, Herzl had to take solace in the enthusiastic support lent by the religious Zionists to his quest for a feasible solution to the Jewish Question.

Abraham Isaac Kook: Once Zionist settlement in the land of Israel gained momentum, religious Zionists took a dramatic turn from a pragmatic posture to a decidedly theological, even mystical, conception of the movement's objectives. This occurred principally under the tutelage of Rabbi Abraham Isaac Kook (1865-1935), who, in 1904, upon declining a prestigious Rabbinic post in Lithuania, emigrated to Palestine, where seventeen years later the British Mandatory government would appoint him the country's first Ashkenazic chief rabbi. Dedicated to a spiritual renaissance of Orthodox Jewry, Kook understood the religious significance of Zionism much in the manner that Alkalai and Kalischer did, namely as providence's use of secular forces to advance the redemption of Israel. Kook would give this view a profoundly mystical twist.

While still serving as a communal rabbi in his native Latvia, Kook was enthralled by the efforts of the "pioneers" (*halutzim*) of Zionism, the select band of idealistic youth who, since the 1890s, came to Palestine to "prepare" the land for the "ingathering of the exiles." Despite their often demonstrative irreligiosity, Kook regarded these *halutzim* as instruments of God's *Heilsplan*. Judging history from the perspective of the kabbalistic teaching that external events are but symbols of a deeper, hidden reality, he interpreted the "godless" actions of the *halutzim* on behalf of the Jewish people's restoration to Zion as symbolically reflecting a divinely appointed cosmic process of restoring a fragmented world to its primal harmony. He thus likened the *halutzim* to the workers who constructed the Temple. Although only the High Priest was entitled to enter the Holy of Holies, the sacred sanctuary of the Temple, and then only once a year, on the Day of Atonement, and only after a most complex procedure of ritual purification, during its construction the workers, sullied with the smut of their labors, were permitted to enter the Holy of Holies at will. The *halutzim* are the builders of the new Temple.[6]

In general Kook saw the increased secular activity characteristic of the modern age of social and scientific progress as part of a providential design to quicken the eschatological conclusion of history. The return of the Jews to their ancient domicile was but the most glorious symbol of the coming eschaton. Kook's messianic conviction was also sustained by his nigh-pantheistic appreciation of the holiness of the land of Israel. The land is suffused by the nurturing Presence of God. Accordingly, he wrote in apparently oblique criticism of Rabbi Reines that to "regard the land of Israel as merely a tool for establishing our national unity—or even for sustaining our religion in the Diaspora by preserving its proper character and its faith, piety, and observances—is a sterile notion; it is unworthy of the holiness of the land of Israel."[7]

The holiness of the land, Kook fervently proclaimed, transforms pious Jew and secularist alike. Focused in the Holy Land, "our entire spiritual heritage is presently being reabsorbed within its source and is reappearing in a new guise, much reduced in material extent but qualitatively very rich and luxuriant and full of vital force."[8] Dedicated to the rebuilding of Zion, secular and religious Jews alike "are called to a new world suffused with the highest light, to an epoch the glory of which will surpass that of all the great ages which have preceded."[9] With ecstatic, indeed, dythrambic tones, Kook adds, "all our people believes that we are in the first stage of the final Redemption. This deep faith is the very secret of its existence; it is the divine mystery implicit in its historical experience."[10]

With the vigorous, muscular energy of the *halutzim* in mind, Kook also counseled religious Jews to discard their contempt for physical labor and the cultivation of healthy, strong bodies:

> We have greatly occupied ourselves with the soul and have forsaken the holiness of the body. We have neglected health and physical progress, forgetting that our flesh is as sacred as our spirit. . . . Our return will succeed only if it will be marked, along with its spiritual glory, by a physical return which will create healthy flesh and blood, strong and well-formed bodies, and a fiery spirit encased in powerful muscles.[11]

The neglect of the physical has enfeebled the soul. With the renewal of the body through physical labor, the previously "weak soul will shine forth from the strong and holy flesh, as a symbol of the physical resurrection of the dead."[12]

Aaron David Gordon: But the glorification of labor and healthy bodies as religious values had already been articulated by a "secular"—at least in the formal sense of being non-observant—Zionist thinker, Aaron David Gordon (1856-1922). Similarly to Kook, Gordon discerned in the ethos of the *halutzim* extensive religious significance. At the age of fifty, he made the personal decision to relinquish the comforts of affluence and bourgeois eminence in Czarist Russia and to join the youthful *halutzim* in the labor of draining the swamps and tilling the soil of the land of Israel. Working tirelessly by day, he would write at night, exploring what he deemed the cosmic dimensions of the pioneering endeavor.

With a weave of kabbalistic-Hasidic doctrine and Russian populist ideas, especially drawn from the writings of Tolstoi, about the pristine dignity of the peasantry and a life rooted in nature, Gordon developed a mystical pantheism in which he celebrated agricultural labor as a supreme act of personal, national, and cosmic redemption. Toil on the land, he taught, integrates one into the "organic rhythms" of nature and the universe. The resulting experience of "the unity and purpose of the cosmos" is the core religious experience—an experience largely denied the Jews of the diaspora. This "intuitive experience," Gordon held, ultimately leads one to God (or rather to participate in the unity of the Godhead), regardless of one's faith and cognitive postures. For Gordon, an authentic relation to God had nothing to do with formal religious beliefs and ritual practice. In noting that God, or the hidden mystery of the cosmos, is approached through physical labor, he was quick to point out that biblical Hebrew employs the same word—*avodah*—to indicate both work and divine worship.

Asher Ginzberg: Zionism as a form of laicized spirituality was also the message of Ahad Ha'am, the *nom de plume* of Asher Ginzberg (1856-1929). Ahad Ha'am—meaning, in Hebrew, "one-of-the-people"—envisioned Zionism as effecting the reconstruction of Judaism as a secular but spiritually engaging national culture. Having abandoned in his twenties the religious faith of his Hasidic upbringing in Russia, Ahad Ha'am was acutely aware of the "spiritual crisis" afflicting his generation of Jews, for whom Judaism as a religious faith had ceased to command fidelity. In ever increasing numbers, young Jews were drawn to the secular-humanistic culture of the west, a culture, in Ahad Ha'am's judgment, of undeniable intellectual, ethical, and aesthetic power.

Ahad Ha'am further observed that the secular humanism of the contemporary world was expressed in non-Jewish languages and was supported by distinct national communities. This meant that the Jews' adoption of this new culture by definition entailed a weakening of their ties to their own people and to the Jewish religious culture. To stem the tide of acculturation and assimilation, Ahad Ha'am taught, Judaism must be similarly reformulated as a secular culture, grounded, in its case, in the indigenous humanistic values of Judaism, specifically, the ethical teachings of the Bible and the prophets. In this system, Hebrew would be reborn as the "national" language of the Jewish people. In Zion, a culturally autonomous Hebrew-speaking Jewish community would arise that, Ahad Ha'am affirmed, would by force of the example of its spiritually vital and creative culture inspire the Jews of the diaspora, where the vast majority of Jewry would by *force majeure* continue to dwell. Thus Judaism would adjust to the new secular reality even as a Jewish national consciousness was maintained.

Martin Buber: Dubbed the "agnostic rabbi," Ahad Ha'am held that the secularity inherent in modern culture entailed the irrevocable eclipse of religious faith. But other cultural Zionists held that secularism, although a necessary historical stage or condition, did not preclude Judaism's renewal as a meaningful religious faith. Martin Buber (1878-1965), who settled in the land of Israel in 1938, taught that the return to Zion and the labor of the *halutzim*—particularly as organized in the *kibbutzim* (agricultural communes), with their singular focus on egalitarian values and interpersonal solidarity—would allow for the emergence of new spiritual and religious expressions. Appealing to the Hasidic image of worshipping God in the "marketplace," that is, in the quotidian spheres of everyday life, Buber spoke of an extra-synagogal religiosity, meaning forms of religious conduct not mediated by ritual and liturgy. Indeed, he hoped that Zionism would free Jewish religiosity from the confines of the synagogue and allow it be translated into the matrix of "profane" interpersonal and intercommunal life. Identifying the "primal" religiosity of Judaism with what he called the ethic of dialogue, Buber taught that the centering of our spiritual life in the secular realm is consonant with the core intentions of the Bible. But because there are no clear, fast prescriptions for how to serve God in the "marketplace," Buber referred to his doctrine as "religious anarchism."

Gershom Scholem: Buber's friend Gershom Scholem (1897-1982), who settled in Jerusalem in 1923, also regarded himself as a religious anarchist, but insisted in contrast to Buber that his anarchism was only provisional. He longed for the renewal of the halakhah, Jewish law, for a disclosure of mitzvot—divine commandments—addressed to him as a post-traditional Jew. At the root of the crisis of Jewish religious faith and practice in the modern world, he contended, was the spiritually ossified and intellectually jejune Rabbinic conception of Judaism. His distinctive path to correcting these problems and revitalizing Judaism was through scholarship. The dean of Jewish studies in the twentieth century, Scholem employed the tools of a critical scholar to uncover dimensions and expressions of Jewish spirituality and imagination he held were suppressed by Orthodoxy and, later in the nineteenth century, by apologetic theologies and histories that defended specific conceptions of "normative" Judaism. Precisely because of its objective, non-prescriptive mode of inquiry, academic scholarship is capable of displaying the full canvas of Jewish spiritual options Unfettered by the defensive posture Jews are often led to assume in the diaspora, it—especially as pursued in an autonomous Jewish community—directly inspires religious renewal. Scholem additionally suggested that by identifying the varied well-springs of Jewish religious creativity, scholarship allows their nurturing waters to flow again. To this end he devoted his prodigious scholarly talents, researching the surprisingly ramified and hitherto little known or misperceived Jewish mystical tradition.

The impact of the establishment of the State: The establishment of the State of Israel in 1948 generated special theological problems for Orthodox supporters of Zionism, primarily concerning the messianic significance of the restoration of Jewish sovereignty in the land of Israel. Many regard this event as a miracle, a sign of divine providence pointing to the imminent advent of the messiah and divine redemption. In the flush of messianic euphoria, the chief rabbis of the nascent state took the rare step of introducing a new prayer into the time-bound traditional liturgy, recognizing God's causing "the beginning of our redemption to flower." On the other side, a significant minority of Orthodox opinion did, and continues to, oppose Zionism. This is precisely because of what it deems to be the movement's messianic pretensions, regarded as a sinful attempt to preempt God's judgment and redemptive deeds.

Yet even Orthodox Jews who support Zionism but are unwilling to view its political achievements in eschatological terms face a problem. They are obliged to reckon with the absence of traditional theological categories through which to comprehend the anomalous situation posed by the reestablishment of a Jewish commonwealth in the holy land and the concomitant nullification of the diaspora, in traditional Jewish terms, exile (*galut*), understood as the divinely decreed deprivation of Jewry's political independence in Zion. How is one to comprehend the theological status of the State if one denies it has eschatological significance and still regards the spiritual condition of the Jews (and existence at large) to be that of *galut*?

Yeshayahu Leibowitz: Since the early 1940s these issues have acquired sharp focus and popular attention through the sustained and invariably controversial efforts of Yeshayahu Leibowitz (1903-1994). Emigrating to the land of Israel in 1935 from his native Latvia (via Germany), Leibowitz joined the faculty of the Hebrew University, where he lectured in biological chemistry even as he assumed an active role in the public discourse of the country. Identifying with the religious rationalism of Maimonides, he was a proponent of a rigorously rational approach to religious and political questions, eschewing all that he regarded as platitudes and sentimental pieties. For Leibowitz, Zionism and the State of Israel have no messianic import whatsoever; indeed, he regards messianism as fundamentally a folkloristic accretion to Judaism that is best ignored by God-fearing Jews. He is particularly fond of citing Maimonides' admonition that one ought not preoccupy oneself with messianic speculations, for "they lead neither to fear [of God] nor to the love [of him]" (*Mishneh Torah*, Kings and Laws, 12:2).

Furthermore, Leibowitz argues, those who ascribe religious or any other intrinsic value to the Jewish state are committing the cardinal sin of idolatry, the worship of false gods. Still worse, the ascription of an intrinsic value to the state is the seed of fascism. This is because the Jewish state *per se*, like any other state, he insists, can at the most have but instrumental legitimacy, namely, to fulfill certain, specified functions on behalf of its citizenry. Accordingly, he sternly rebukes the "modern Sabbatians" (that is, followers of the seventeenth century pseudo-messiah Shabbetai Zevi) for their implicit fascism, seen in the fact that, for them, "the nation has become God, and the homeland Torah."[13]

Leibowitz thus refuses to regard Zionism as a religious phenomenon. He views it rather simply and solely as a movement for the *political* liberation of the Jewish people. Implicitly endorsing the founding principles of the religious party within Zionism, Mizrahi, of which he was a member, he calls upon religious Jews to rejoice in this fact and to greet the Zionist state as providing the framework for a fuller expression of halakhah and Israel's religious vocation. He conceives of this vocation in strictly theocentric terms. By accepting "the yoke of the kingdom of God," the Jews are preeminently God's servants, and not *vice versa*. Service to God—which he stipulates is the true meaning of religion—must be for its own sake, without any regard for one's spiritual, moral, and certainly not material well-being. Any conception of religion that emphasizes the enhancement of the individual's or community's fortunes, spiritual or material, is in effect anthropocentric, and, thus, according to Leibowitz's understanding, not true religion. Hence, he emphasizes, Judaism is not meant to render the Jews happier, spiritually edified, or more prosperous. Even the perfection of society and history, he contends, are essentially alien to Judaism. Politics, like morality and economics, lie outside the purview of religion *qua* service to God.

While Leibowitz does not object to humanistic and progressive political endeavors—in fact he was very much to the left in the Israeli political spectrum, especially after the Six Day War—he insists that these are in the realm of humans and their fallible judgment and as such are not to be theologically sanctified. Needless to say, Leibowitz's severe, almost priestly view of Judaism has evoked considerable, albeit seminal, discussion within both religious and secular circles of contemporary Israel.

David Hartman: One of Leibowitz's most sympathetic yet toughest critics within the Orthodox community of the State of Israel is an American-born and educated rabbi, David Hartman (1931-). Settling in Jerusalem in 1971, where he joined the faculty of the Hebrew University to teach Jewish philosophy, Hartman shares a similar intellectual background with Leibowitz. Both are heirs to the Lithuanian Rabbinic tradition, with its emphasis on a rational approach to reading sacred texts and to religious understanding, an orientation that for both was reinforced by their systematic study of Maimonides.

A student of Rabbi Joseph Soloveitchik (1903-1993), with whom he earned his Rabbinic ordination, Hartman's Zionist commitments were awakened by the Six Day War. Previously, under the sway of his mentor's religious, or better, halakhic existentialism, his principal concerns were outside of history—namely, the inner problems of the individual of faith. Then, in the weeks just prior to the Israeli-Arab war of June, 1967, when it seemed that the pending conflict with the Arab world might bring another Holocaust upon the Jews, he was confronted with the frightful reality of history. The euphoria engendered by the swift, unexpected victory of Israel's armed forces compelled him to give up a Rabbinic pulpit in Montreal and to join his fellow Jews who had "returned" to history under the aegis of Zionism and the State of Israel.

Hartman's decision to immigrate to Israel entailed a radical reevaluation of his biblical understanding of "halakhic spirituality," which hitherto he had understood as transposing the experience of God's presence from history to the mitzvot and their performance. To the degree that God was in history, the divine was experienced in symbolic time, reenacted and relived in the sacred narratives inscribed in the liturgy and religious calendar. Now, under the impact of the Six Day War, as Hartman explains in an autobiographical statement, "I returned to history as a Rabbinic Jew open to suggestions of God's presence in the events involving the fate of the living community of Israel."[14]

Hartman understands God's presence in the historical fortunes of the State of Israel, however, not as an eschatological drama. Boldly resisting the messianic enthusiasm that increasingly has gripped religious Zionism, Hartman insists that God does *not* act in history providentially, God does not intervene in human affairs, "mysteriously" directing historical events as vehicles of the divine will. The protagonists of history remain human beings, them alone. God enters history by virtue of human beings' conducting their political and social affairs in the light of the divine presence, that is, with a sense of responsibility before God. Religious meaning, Hartman underscores, inheres in actions of human beings but is not extrinsic to those actions; as such, those actions remain human and subject to critical, rational review. Hartman's God is, accordingly, a covenantal God. The Jew's relationship to God is mediated by Sinai. By taking the Jews back into history, Zionism offers them the opportunity to revitalize that relationship as a disciplined service to God in all possible spheres of human conduct.

In taking this position, Hartman is allied with Leibowitz in opposing the political and religious party *Gush 'Emunim*, "The Block of the Faithful"—faithful to the concept of "Greater Israel." This movement of religious Zionists, founded in 1974, views the Six Day War and the resulting "liberation" from the Arabs of the old city of Jerusalem and the "biblical" regions of Samaria and Judea as providential signs of the imminent denouement of history and the dawn of redemption. Israeli rule over these areas is, accordingly, by divine decree, and, hence, any political accommodation that grants Palestinian Arabs political sovereignty in these areas is a cardinal sin against the divine will. Against *Gush 'Emunim*, which, incidentally, draws much of its eschatological historiosophy from

Rav Kook, Hartman avers that God's will is known only in and through halakhah, and absolutely not otherwise.

Hartman gratefully acknowledges that it was Leibowitz who reminded him "how the love of Jews and the love of the land [of Israel] can become a source of modern Jewish idolatry."[15] Nonetheless, he holds that the State of Israel has immeasurable religious significance for the Jew. Although this significance is not of a metaphysical order, it is spiritual, at least in the sense that the Zionist experience may engender, notwithstanding the manifest dangers to which Leibowitz alerts us, religious sensibilities that render the individual "receptive to the living word of God."[16] This is what he means, he explains in a debate with Leibowitz, when he proclaims, "in making contact with the Land of Israel, one is led to make contact with the God of Israel."[17]

At the root of their difference stands a disagreement regarding religious anthropology. Leibowitz's paradigm of faith is the *aqeda*, Abraham's binding of Jacob at God's behest: faith, on this model, is a selfless obedience to God. For Hartman, by contrast, the model of faith is love, matrimonial love, in which the partners are bound to one another by a sense of mutual responsibility that accompanies them throughout the varied trials and tribulations of a life lived together. Love, he pointedly notes, "is rarely expressed in blind obedience."[18] Rather it entails passions, joy, even anger, and feelings of community—emotions that flower in an abiding commitment of responsibility. The life of halakhah, Hartman affirms, is traditional Judaism's normative grammar allowing for a disciplined expression of this love.

Enjoining the concept of a responsible love, Hartman extends the scope of his concerns to develop a meta-halakhic critique of religion in Israel. Objecting to the politicization of Judaism in the country, he openly expresses his abhorrence of the legally sanctioned monopoly of Orthodoxy and the consequent delegitimation of other conceptions of Jewish faith and practice. Similarly, he calls for the social and religious equality of women within Judaism. Further, in striking

contrast to his teacher, Rabbi Soloveitchik, he vigorously promotes theological dialogue with Christians and Muslims. The radical nature of these positions, certainly within the context of contemporary Israel, is anchored in Hartman's Zionism. Political sovereignty, he argues, provides the Jews of the State of Israel with the sociological and psychological conditions to assume an intellectual probity, free of all apologetic positions born of the insecurity of life in the diaspora—*galut*.

From the secure ground of a sovereign Jewish existence, Israeli Orthodoxy, Hartman contends, should courageously acknowledge the challenge of modernity, specifically as informed by the axiological and ethical sensibilities inspiring life in an open, pluralistic, democratic order. Hartman's assumption of the ethical and intellectual autonomy presupposed by these sensibilities in effect constitutes the meta-halakhic perspective with which he unflinchingly and critically examines the halakhic tradition in the light of those sensibilities. Yet it is crucial to note what renders Hartman's endorsement of the ethic of autonomous judgment meta-halakhic and not anti- or simply non-halakhic. This is the fact that for him autonomous judgment exists in dialectical tension with his overarching love for the halakhah and tradition, viewed as the matrix of Jewish faith and community. His radical critique of halakhah is from *within* the tradition. His message has gained increasing resonance within Israeli Orthodox circles by dint of his forceful, passionate presence as a teacher and by virtue of the Shalom Hartman Institute for Advanced Judaic Studies, which he founded in 1976 and at which he has gathered some of Israel's most thoughtful Orthodox Jewish men and women to engage in the type of study he recommends, in dialogue with secular Jews and believing Christians and Muslims.

Hartman and his colleagues would surely endorse Rabbi Kook's injunction that Zionism should not be an end itself. "It is proper," Kook wrote in his commentary to the prayerbook, "to nurture national honor and to seek to enhance it." Yet, he cautions, we should be ever vigilant, for humans are weak. "Preoccupied with the means—the increase of Israel's honor and status—[they] may easily forget the end—the glorification of the God of Israel and the world."[19]

Notes

[1] Letter to Amschel Meyer Rothschild, 1836, cited in Arthur Hertzberg, ed., *The Zionist Idea. A Historical Analysis and Reader* (Philadelphia, 1959), pp. 109-110.
[2] Kalischer, *Dreishat Tzion* [1862], 2nd ed. (Thorn, 1866), p. 178.
[3] Ibid.
[4] Cited in Hertzberg, op. cit., p. 106.
[5] The Mizrahi "Manifesto (1902)," in P. Mendes-Flohr and J. Reinharz, *The Jew in the Modern World. A Documentary History*, 2nd, rev. ed. (New York, 1995), p. 546.
[6] See Samuel Hugo Bergman, *Faith and Reason. Modern Jewish Thought* (New York, 1961), p. 135.
[7] Kook, "The Land of Israel," cited in Herzberg, op. cit., p. 419.
[8] Kook, "Lights of Rebirth," cited in Hertzberg, op. cit., p. 430.
[9] Ibid.
[10] Ibid.
[11] Ibid., p. 431.
[12] Ibid.
[13] *Judaism. The Jewish People and the State of Israel* (Hebrew: Tel Aviv, 1975), p. 271.
[14] *Joy and Responsibility* (Jerusalem, 1978), p. 7.
[15] *Conflicting Visions* (New York, 1990), p. 101.
[16] Ibid.
[17] *Joy and Responsibility*, p. 286.
[18] *Conflicting Visions*, p. 100.
[19] Cited in Bergman, op. cit., p. 137.

PAUL MENDES-FLOHR

JUDAISM, PHILOSOPHY AND THEOLOGY OF, IN MODERN TIMES, IN THE USA: American Jewish philosophy and theology focus on a range of disparate themes. Some of these reflect classical theological problems—for instance, the nature of God, the meaning of revelation, or hopes for salvation—or momentous historical events—the Nazi Holocaust and the establishment of the State of Israel, chief among them. Other themes respond to challenges facing American Jewry in particular, for instance, the meaning of Jewish rituals in a secular age, ways to balance adaptation to American life with retention of Jewish identity, and strategies for Jewish education in a pluralistic religious setting. Similarly the specifically America themes of American civil religion, interfaith coopera-

tion, and social problems dominate much of Jewish reflection.

In a recent work Harold Schulweis, a leading rabbi and thinker in America's Conservative Movement, examined this assortment of concerns.[1] His guiding image serves well as a metaphor for the totality of Jewish thinking in America. According to Schulweis, an idea of God serves as a mirror reflecting the several faces of American Jews (pp. xiii-xv). To be a Jewish thinker, accordingly, means to offer images of Judaism to American Jews, so they can discover whom they imagine themselves to be.

This function of Jewish thought appears as early as the life and writings of Gershom Mendes Sexias (1746-1816), who may well represent the earliest American Jewish thinking.[2] Sexias exemplifies Jewish thought in the United States of America in four ways. first, his position as religious leader discloses the close ties between the institutional standing of a thinker and the impetus to articulate a Jewish ideology. Although not an ordained rabbi, Sexias nevertheless served in a ministerial position in both New York and Philadelphia. Sexias celebrated the American spirit, and he supported the American revolutionary war as a patriot. He embraced the voluntary nature of religious affiliation in America, using it to his advantage in his life as a Jewish professional. Sexias adapted to differences among Jews in New York or in Philadelphia. This aspect of his career shows how as early as the eighteenth and nineteenth centuries, American Jewish thinkers had embraced the civil order and its emphasis on voluntarism.

Sexias was concerned that Judaism conform to what might be called "civil religion." Some sociologists perceive an American civil religion that lurks behind the particularity of Christianity in America.[3] The various institutions of religion in the United States—Roman Catholicism, Protestantism, and Judaism—contribute to this greater, shared, religiousness. The images by which Americans understand their history—its founding, its civil war, its involvement in European wars—draw upon biblical motifs and Jewish or Christian myth and literature. Sexias understood Judaism within this complex of American civil religiousness, and later Jewish thinkers agree with him. Some celebrate that religiousness, while others criticize it from the perspective of classical faith. Nevertheless, Sexias' sermons show that even the earliest Jewish writings in America confronted the reality of American civil religion.

Second, the particular ideology through which Sexias worked to situate Judaism within American society resonated with traditional Jewish symbols and images. His sermons made use of the theological vocabulary of classical Judaism. Whether addressing the needs of Jews or celebrating the reality of the United States, Sexias used biblical and Rabbinic language to describe the divinity, the idea of revelation (the Torah), and the mission for which the Jewish people has been chosen.

The use of such classical language, however, hardly disguises the untraditional nature of Sexias' ideas. American religion during this time seemed torn between two opposite poles. Thomas Paine's *The Age of Reason* (1794) represents one strand of thought. It opposes organized religion and demands that reason replace superstition. Paine's views were extreme, but other Americans such as Thomas Jefferson, Benjamin Franklin, and John Adams adapted his rationalism in a religiousness that has been called Deism. This religiousness emphasized a universal rational religion, of which Christianity was only one representative. It encouraged an acceptance of non-Christian religion that Sidney E. Mead describes as a "cosmopolitan, inclusive, universal theology."[4] These Deists held that Christianity preserves in its essence a rational and eternal core that is common to all true religion. They judge to be the most authentic that religion which resembles the rational faith in which all can believe.

In contrast to the Deists, revivalist preachers from the time of Jonathan Edwards (1703-1758) through his grandson Timothy Dwight (1752-1817), president of Yale from 1795-1817, emphasized the unworthiness of human reason, the sickness of the human soul, and the need for absolute reliance on the grace of the divinity. Harrowing portraits of damnation and Hell add urgency to the message of these preachers who seek to awaken their audience from the slumbers into which rationalism has lulled them. These preachers opposed both rationalism and Deism as false religions. Belief in such faiths would lead, they concluded, to damnation and suffering, not to salvation.

Between the Deists and the revivalist preachers stretches a gap that appears unbridgeable. Sexias, however, found both themes appropriate for his sermons. He preached rationalism and fear of divine retribution alike. His sermons reflect an eclectic Judaic thought that mixes Protestant imagery and Jewish symbolism. This ability to draw from various sources in the religious environment represents a third element in which Sexias anticipates later Jewish thinking. Jewish thinkers of the nineteenth and twentieth centuries, that is, follow Sexias in an integration of the diverse strands in American religious life.

Sexias legitimated Judaism on the basis of the canons of rationalism present in his day, without abandoning the equally powerful appeal of revivalist preaching. So too later Jewish theologians and philosophers examine Jewish religion using the philosophical criteria popular in their time. This final element in Sexias' Jewish thought introduces "philosophical" themes into American Jewish thinking. Sexias carefully balanced the theological rhetoric he gleaned from American revivalists with the rationalism derived from American philosophers. These two traditions, sometimes called those of "Jerusalem" and "Athens," continue to dominate American religious thinking.

Theology, based on Jerusalem's Hebrew Bible, and philosophy, drawn from Athens' Socratic tradition, contend with one another through the entire history of American religious thought. Some Jewish thinkers celebrate rationality and seek to show how Judaism conforms to it. Others deplore how rationalism limits belief to "natural" phenomena. They claim that true religion transcends both logic and science.

Perhaps John E. Smith, in his discussion

of American religious philosophy, offers the most accurate perspective on this issue. He remarks that the second half of the twentieth century provided a new stimulus for thinking about religion philosophically. Religious thinkers now, he claims, have come to "sense that neither a purely technical philosophy nor a purely fideistic theology will suffice." He traces the peculiar nature of contemporary theology to that double dissatisfaction.[5] Whatever their evaluation of the perceived contradiction between "Athens" and "Jerusalem," American Jewish thinkers address a philosophical concern by confronting rationalism and the Jewish tradition.

Sexias has already anticipated such a combination of faith and reason in his eighteenth century sermons. He offered his synthesis of Judaic, civil, and theological ideas unapologetically as authentic Judaism. More recent Jewish thinkers have faced a more daunting task of justifying and legitimating their presentation of Judaism in the eyes of other Jews and for the general community. These thinkers use one of three strategies. The first approach constructs a positive Judaism that affirms both Jewish tradition and the American context. This approach emphasizes the shared heritage that Jews hold in common with all other Americans. A second approach takes a more critical stance. Being Jewish, on this account, implies rejecting aspects of the general American culture, the pluralism of American religious life, or the trends of Western philosophy. This critical thought imagines the Jew as a maverick or gadfly in American society.

A final stance corresponds to a view now labeled as "postmodern," although some who exemplify it wrote well before the popularization of that term. As used here, postmodern refers to an imaginative approach to texts and reality that emphasizes the role of the reader in creating meaning. Texts interact with one another and with those who read them. This interaction creates the possibility that older texts will continually gain new meanings. Any single text may have multiple meanings depending on the other texts associated with it and on the background of the person reading it. The postmodern thus seeks to generate alternatives, to be suggestive rather than definitive, to cultivate dynamic change rather than static perfection. Judaism, on this reading, provides one set of resources by which postmoderns can advance this project.

Constructive approaches to American Jewish thought: Marc Lee Raphael describes the perilous situation of American Judaism in the nineteenth century. He notes that several challenges faced traditional belief—the scientific spirit, Ethical Culture, Spiritualism, and a general "indifference to all things Jewish." He comments that "religious leaders respond in such times with doctrinal or creedal statements of their faith."[6] American Reform Judaism articulated its credal platform as a constructive answer to the crisis it perceived. It defended its own institutional form as the most effective response to the dangers Judaism faced at the time. This impulse underlies several constructive movements in American Judaism. Again and again Jewish thinkers sought to meet the external challenge of the American environment by constructing an image of Judaism that justified and legitimated their way of being Jewish in America. Nineteenth century Reform thinkers like Isaac Meyer Wise, David Einhorn, and Kaufmann Kohler endeavored to produce a peculiarly American style of Judaism, that is, a "Minhag America." Early twentieth century thinkers like Samuel S. Cohon, Jacob Zvi Lauterbach, and David Neumark continued in that tradition. Thinkers like Eugene Borowitz and Alvin J. Reines represent more contemporary variations on that theme.

Conservative Jewish thinkers also exemplify a constructive imaging of American Judaism in their own likeness. Solomon Schechter, the guiding hand directing the growth of Conservative Judaism in America, saw in his idea of "Catholic Israel," a type of Jewish consciousness appropriate for the American setting. Other early Conservative leaders like Cyrus Adler and Israel Friedlander shaped the philosophy and theology of the movement while preserving diversity and pluralism. Still others such as Jacob Agus, Robert Gordis, and Simon Greenberg strengthened commitment to a pluralistic approach to theology. Recent thinkers such as Elliot Dorff, Yochanan Muffs, and Seymour Siegel have introduced into Conservative Jewish theological constructions current trends in modern thought.[7]

Orthodox Judaism in America represents itself as the Torah-true embodiment Judaic tradition. Yet pluralism also makes inroads into it. Orthodoxy has had two types of thinkers: resisters and accommodators. In the latter category, Samuel Belkin, Norman Lamm, Joseph Lookstein, Emmanuel Rackman Joseph Baer Soloveitchik, and Walter S. Wurzburger struggle to make sense of being an Orthodox Jew in the American context.[8] J. David Bleich, by contrast, presents halakhic thinking within a moral framework that confronts contemporary issues of medical ethics, business morality, political practice, and other questions facing Jews today. He combines a critical rejection of liberal compromises mixed with a willingness to engage himself with modern American problems. Even while opposing many contemporary trends, Bleich insists that the Judaism he presents benefits all Americans and not just Jews. Orthodox Judaism in America, no less than Reform or Conservative, includes thinkers who construct a theology that contributes positively to the general religious culture.

Another constructive approach in American Jewish thinking has focused on the nature of God and on this nature's implications for Jewish belief and practice. One tension arising here has been between supernaturalists, like Arthur A. Cohen, and naturalists, like Mordecai M. Kaplan. This distinction is similar to that between the Deists and the revivalist preachers. Supernaturalists, like the revivalists, accuse rationalism of undermining true belief. Too great a concern with the evidence of reason and nature, they hold, leads to skepticism and a shallow faith. Naturalists, however, claim that faith has credibility and persuasive power only if built on the firm foundation of fact and logic. They argue that supernaturalism ignores the real life situations in which human beings operate, holding that an emphasis on transcend-ence necessarily suggests a lack of concern with daily affairs.

We should be clear, however, that this sharp dichotomy drawn by each side in the debate tends to misrepresent the nuances of the conflicting positions. Mordecai Kaplan, for example, has far greater regard for theological precision than a simple "naturalistic" approach might suggest, while Cohen demonstrates a concern for the historical Jewish people and its practical needs that a simple "supernaturalism" might find surprising.[9] With that caveat in mind, however, the distinction between naturalist and supernaturalist still helps place various thinkers into proper perspective. Milton Steinberg and Jakob J. Petuchowski differ on many issues, but their common use of the supernaturalist mode unites them. Levi Olan and Henry Slonimsky exemplify very different intellectual traditions, yet the naturalistic approach they share underlies each one's theological system.

Naturalists and supernaturalists alike, no matter how they differ, agree in emphasizing the theological idea of covenant. Covenant implies a reciprocal agreement between the divine and the human in which God and Jews share in responsibility for improving the world. Covenantal stipulations obligate Jews to further the divine plan in the world. Jews, according to this view, must play an active role in actualizing God's design for humanity. This notion provides the basis on which American Jewish thinkers reinterpret the traditional idea of Jewish chosenness. The Bible asserts that the Jews are God's chosen people. Traditional Jewish theology maintains the same claim. At least superficially, this special status contradicts the American value of democracy and equality. Can a "chosen people" see itself as "equal" with all other religions in America? While "covenant" remains the key theological term, the problem it poses for American Jewish thinkers is that of "chosenness," of singling out one group from among others. Jewish thinkers address this issue in various ways.[10] Mordecai Kaplan rejects the idea of chosenness entirely. Others reinterpret it to apply to a specialized "vocation." Every religious group, according to that view, has its own divinely ordained task to perform, and Jews are "equal" to others not because they share the same tasks, but because all tasks are equally important.

Overall, Jewish theologians construct theories of Judaism for the several reasons we have enumerated: to support their institutional choices, to discover an appropriate balance between naturalism and supernaturalism, and to cope with the meaning of "covenant" and "chosenness." Jewish academics, no less than theologians, feel the impulse to construct an idea of Judaism. While historians of Jewish philosophy seem to devote themselves to objective scholarship alone, both the selectivity of their research and the impulses behind it show that they in fact share the same Judaic concerns and American orientation as the theologians. Jewish academics often explicitly intertwine scholarship and a commitment to creating a Judaism for the modern age.[11] Some of these use the Kantian approach to philosophy as a basis on which to argue for Judaism's compatibility with rationality. They thus offer constructive visions of Judaism that meet the philosophical challenges of contemporary American thinking. Existentialism, Postmodernism, or process thought provide some Jews with the basis for a new construction of Judaism.

Critical and postmodern approaches to American Jewish thought: Some American Jewish thinkers approach Judaism against the grain, as it were, opposing rather than conforming to the trends of history. They resist the tide of current thinking and claim that just as brushing against the grain makes bristles stand out more clearly, so, too, acting against popular ideas makes the truth more clear. Arthur Waskow writes of "Godwrestling," and the image is apt.[12] Judaism, understood from this perspective, stands in contrast to American culture and struggles to shape it. Religion, on this reading, wrestles for its life against secular values. Will Herberg and Eliezer Berkovits take up a similar stance, although they interpret authentic Judaism differently. Another critical approach, exemplified by Emil Fackenheim, learns from the Nazi Holocaust the necessity of distrusting

political bodies and elevates religious truth above social utility.

Other American Jewish philosophers also couch the encounter between Jerusalem and Athens as a contest rather than as a collaboration. Both Leo Strauss and David Novak argue that religious commitment goes beyond rational proof. The theologian begins with faith and will not concede primacy to philosophy and its methods. Novak, in particular, combines the two types of critical opposition. Contrasting the clarity of Jewish law, halakha, with the ineffectiveness of secular morality, he finds philosophy insufficient to supply Jews with a basis for Judaic living.[13]

Some recent thinkers suggest the model of Postmodernism. They legitimize a pluralistic reading of Judaism that encourages diversity and champions the under represented, such as Jewish women.[14] To accomplish this, they focus on the diverse ways in which the textual sources of Judaism generate several distinct images of Jewish meaning. Earlier American Jewish scholars such as Max Kadushin and Simon Rawidowicz provide direct antecedents for this approach. The emphasis on the dynamic meanings of Judaism that characterized the work of these thinkers molded the postmodern approach of Jewish thinkers today.

Other influences as well helped shape contemporary Jewish thinking. Richard L. Rubenstein's reflections on the Nazi Holocaust led him to a theology in which God represents the Holy Nothing from which all comes and to which it returns. This mystical insight underlies much of his later psychological and sociological writings that, finally, propose an inclusive, postmodern view of religion. The mystical element surfaces in several other modern Jewish thinkers, such as Zalman Schacter-Shalomi and Arthur Green, who draw on the mystical tradition to authorize and legitimate their pluralistic reading of Judaism.

The mystical turn in contemporary Jewish thought represents only one element contributing to a postmodern outlook. Another impressive use of a postmodern inclusiveness as the basis for a vision of Judaism occurs in the writings of Jewish feminists. While Judith

Plaskow offers a complete contemporary Jewish theology based on feminist images, others such as Judith Baskin, Lynn Davidman, Tamar Frankiel, Blu Greenberg, Riv-Ellen Prell, and Ellen Umansky have developed feminist Jewish visions of their own. These feminists offer a sometimes critical analysis of the Jewish past and a postmodern call for diversity in contemporary Judaism. Attention to suppressed voices leads to a responsive American Judaism built out of dialogue with others.

The nineteenth and twentieth century thinkers discussed in the following reflect the diversity of American Judaic thought. They are listed alphabetically rather than chronologically, since the major themes and concerns already adumbrated are consistent through both centuries. The key elements found in Gershom Sexias—an approach to civil religion, a reinterpretation of traditional Judaic beliefs and images, and a confrontation between Athens and Jerusalem—appear in the works of all of these thinkers. They struggle with the central questions of naturalism and supernaturalism, covenant and chosenness, reason and revelation, and the significance of historical events (in particular the Nazi Holocaust and the rebirth of a Jewish state). To gain a clear understanding of their positions requires that we also identify the type of thought or thinking they represent: Are they offering a construction of an American Judaism from an institutional standpoint, from the perspective of naturalism or supernaturalism, from a confrontation with the question of chosenness, or from an academic position? Are they critical or postmodern analysts of American Judaism? Do they describe Jewish religion as a corrective to secular society? Do they seek to inspire a greater diversity of Judaisms in America? These questions and issues shape the biographical descriptions which follow.

Jacob Bernard Agus (1911-): Agus has both studied the history of Jewish thought and philosophy and contributed to its modern manifestation. His approach celebrates the American philosophy that he thinks offers an insightful union of pragmatism and faith. His key idea is the essential polarity of all thought and experience. He sees this polarity in every aspect of Jewish religion, so that Judaism in his view creates a dialectic of faith and reason, of the God of experience and the God of rational thought, of the particularism of traditions and the universalism of the religious methods. His approach to Torah, the Jewish people, and to interfaith cooperation reflects this dialogic position.

The mission of Israel, according to Agus, must be to transform ethnicity into a universalistic dedication to ideals and values. Jews must "transmute" their nationalism into a "rededication" to the goals of "the Jewish spirit." Agus thus affirms the God of Athens and the God of Jerusalem equally, embracing a dialogue with America's religions and rejecting a Jewish parochialism. He contends that Judaism affirms both poles of religiousness—particularism and universalism—and thereby contributes to American civil religion.

Agus' major writings are *Guideposts in Modern Judaism: An Analysis of Current Trends in Jewish Thought* (New York, 1954); *The Meaning of Jewish History* (New York, 1963); *Dialogue and Tradition: The Challenges of Contemporary Judeo-Christian Thought* (New York, 1971); *The Jewish Quest: Essays on Basic Concepts of Jewish Theology* (New York, 1983).

Eliezer Berkovits (1908-): An articulate advocate for traditional Jewish thought in the United States, Berkovits might well deny that there is a specifically American aspect to his thinking. Still, he is keenly aware of his environment, presenting Judaism as a treasure house of biblical thinking and arguing that moderns need such a resource as they copes with a world devoid of spiritual guidance. As he perceives modernity, humanity faces a crisis of meaning and ethics. Historical events such as the Nazi Holocaust demonstrate the human potential for evil. Secular society creates an absence of values and a religious void. Human beings lack direction and significance in their lives. Berkovits offers Judaism as a solution to these problems, claiming that Judaism supplies valuable instruction not just for Jews but for all who seek meaning in an age marked by dilemmas of faith.

Berkovits shows a civil awareness that

expands beyond the Orthodox Jewish audience he specifically addresses. He has participated in general discussions in such forums as the journal *Sh'ma*, in which Reform, Conservative, Orthodox, and secular Jews enter into dialogue. His willingness to engage the entire range of Jewish opinion in America and to address non-Jews as well allows him to join in the civil religious context of the United States.

Berkovits affirms traditional Jewish practice and faith. He offers a critical appraisal of liberal Judaism by reasserting the supernaturalism of the divine, the divine source of revelation, and the transcendent purpose of the Jewish people. While he continues the philosophical tradition that reconciles Athens and Jerusalem in a single theory, his synthesis is critical. His approach to theodicy illustrates this stance. Berkovits, even in his earliest books, seriously considers the implication of real evil for theology. He refuses to develop a "solution" to theodicy, since that defies the limits of human ability. Nevertheless, he does suggest that by overcoming challenges people learn important lessons. That humanity must struggle with a world not yet perfected permits that freedom of choice necessary for moral responsibility. He sees the Holocaust as just another catastrophe in Jewish history. It, no less than the other challenges Jews have faced in the past, offers opportunities for sanctifying God and proclaiming the holiness of the divine even in the midst of darkest suffering. Suffering is a critical challenge for human beings. Berkovits interprets moral, theological, and philosophical issues in this critical fashion.

Berkovits' major philosophical writings are *God, Man and History: A Jewish Interpretation* (Second Edition. Middle Village, 1965); *Major Themes in Modern Philosophies of Judaism* (New York: 1974); and *Faith After the Holocaust* (New York: 1973).

Eugene B. Borowitz (1924-): A faculty member at the Hebrew Union College's New York campus, Borowitz is an active theological leader in Reform Jewish thinking, who has developed his major ideas within the framework of the concept of covenant. As he sees it, covenant entails partnership: between the divine and the human, among competing cultural systems, and among human communities. On the basis of this idea of shared responsibility, Borowitz advocates moderating the tension between modernity and tradition, between Jews and other nations, between political involvement and personal development. He writes on ethical questions, theological issues, and the history of Jewish thought. He participates widely in the intellectual activities of contemporary Jewish life. He created and is now co-senior editor of a popular journal, *Sh'ma*, that brings together Jewish thinkers from across the spectrum of Judaic theology and philosophy to discuss central issues of the day. He has engaged in dialogue with Christians and Buddhists as an expression of his view that "covenant" includes dialogue with thought from many traditions. One of his first works concerned not merely Jewish religious thought but religious existentialism generally.

Borowitz develops his understanding of Jewish thought by struggling to reconcile the needs of modernity with an inherited tradition. He admits, without apology, that Jews today understand themselves and their traditions in terms and categories borrowed from the gentile world. Balancing traditions and influences from several sources illustrates what Borowitz calls "covenant." By that phrase he implies a context for interaction and sharing, both between the divine and human and among human beings. This theological agenda animates every aspect of Borowitz's work. He sees himself as balancing the imperatives of the past against the commandments issuing from the present. He argues that the divine covenant with the Jews implies a struggle to balance the new and the old, the modern and the traditional, the parochial and the universal, and the individual and the social.

Borowitz recognizes the distinctive elements of the American environment and uses them to argue for dialogue, pluralism, and a responsive Judaism. He views that environment critically, noting a crisis of values, a conflict between concerns that in an earlier period had been seen as compatible. American Jews, he thinks, no longer know exactly who they are or what ideals they should uphold. Their dilemma, curiously, helps them in their search for a covenantal balance between inherited tradition and the immediate realities they meet in everyday life. Lacking absolute certainty, Jews today move haltingly between several alternatives. Jews, he thinks, have lost faith in Americanism as such, and he argues that this lack of faith may bring an unexpected return to Jewish roots. Jews also approach Judaic tradition with a fresh, challenging attitude, demanding to know the tradition that they affirm. Borowitz intimates a postmodern perspective by defining God as "the ground of our values." That definition sees divinity as a point of departure, a stimulus to thought and imagination, not an entity to be categorized or defined. Like many postmoderns, as well, Borowitz generates ethical norms and practices by an interplay of texts, contexts, and traditions. Taken together, his various efforts create a coordinated program of constructing a faith-filled Judaism appropriate for Jews today. Thus Borowitz affirms Israel as the chosen people without abandoning the universalism of the age of reason and the Enlightenment.

The most important of his works are *Choices in Modern Jewish Thought: A Partisan Guide* (2nd ed., West Orange, 1995); *Renewing the Covenant: A Theology for the Postmodern Jew* (Philadelphia, 1991); *Exploring Jewish Ethics: Papers on Covenant Responsibility* (Detroit, 1990); *The Masks Jews Wear: The Self-Deceptions of American Jewry* (Port Washington, 1980); and *A Layman's Introduction to Religious Existentialism* (Philadelphia, 1965).

Arthur A. Cohen (1928-1986): A publisher, novelist, and theologian, Cohen often stood in opposition to the theological consensus of American Jews. His thought challenges the naturalistic theologies that modern thinkers claimed must succeed the supernaturalism of traditional Jewish thinking. In his books, he criticized the optimistic syncretism of American religiosity manifest in the conception of a "Judeo-Christian tradition," arguing that an honest appraisal uncovers significant theological differences between Jews and Christians. Nevertheless, he recognized the relevance of Jewish religion for others, for instance confronting the theological challenge of the Nazi Holocaust in a slim but intense volume. He believed that the book offers "a theological language out of the calamity of Jewish historical existence which is not only relevant to Jews but to any other monotheist."[15]

This latter concern demonstrates that even Cohen recognizes the civil dimension of Judaism in the United States when it mobilizes moral and religious fervor to improve the quality of American spirituality. He calls upon Jews to renew their contact with the supernatural element in their tradition, because without it they lose sight of their mission and vocation. He argues that to believe in God means to believe that the world must be better than nature has made it. Jews must cultivate creative dissatisfaction in themselves and in others by pointing to a transcendent eschatological standard. The present, he argues, must be judged by how well it approximates the divine ideal.

Fully in tune with the pragmatic moralism of American thought, Cohen claims that God's failure to intervene intends to maintain human responsibility. God's agenda sets the human task, establishes the goals and purposes that surpass the natural givens of everyday life. God addresses each person intensely and individually. From that personal interaction not only the individual but the people of Israel as well learn the responsibilities and duties that God has established. Cohen's realistic assessment of contemporary America suggests that Jews and non-Jews alike have failed to live up to these duties. Depravity pervades the natural reality all believers confront. Cohen describes the task of both Jew and non-Jew today as struggling against that inherent evil surrounding everyone. Jews have experienced that evil directly in the Holocaust, but its poison pollutes all reality. In a post-Holocaust world, Cohen discerns a new meaning to Torah as prescriptive of the Jewish task and as a model for the non-Jew who shares the duty of preventing another outbreak of such radical evil.

His most extensive philosophical writings are *The Tremendum: A Theological Interpre-*

tation of the Holocaust (New York, 1981); *The Natural and Supernatural Jew: An Historical and Theological Introduction* (2nd revised ed., New York, 1979); and *The Myth of the Judeo-Christian Tradition* (New York, 1970).

Emil Fackenheim (1916-): Born in Halle, Germany, Fackenheim fled the Nazi's, eventually to become a Reform rabbi in Canada. After completing high school in 1935, he had left Halle to study in Berlin, thinking he could find a solution to the question of history and philosophy that bothered him. When in 1983 he left North America to settle in Israel, he found in that migration a culmination and completion of his search. His essays and philosophical works reflect his experiences and chart his religious quest. The earliest ones exhibit a philosophical intent and form. They do not mention Judaism explicitly even though they focus on such theological issues as the problem of faith and reason, of history and experience in contrast to thought and idealism. His subsequent books, more self-consciously Judaic in content and purpose, investigate the intersection of Athens and Jerusalem. Fackenheim affirms both, being unwilling to settle for either alone. This philosophical emphasis also shapes what has been Fackenheim's most influential reflections, on the significance of the Nazi Holocaust.

Fackenheim confronts Judaism with the major philosophical options in modern thought. The biblical stories of Elijah respond to the positivist critique of religion. Hegel's historical consciousness would seem to leave Judaism as a relic of a now transcended stage. Fackenheim seeks to preserve the best of Hegel without undermining the heritage of Moses, by showing philosophical alternatives beyond those Hegel imagined. Both Kant and Kierkegaard, he explains in several places, misunderstood the biblical story of Abraham, depicting an erroneous dichotomy between self-legislation and religious legislation and thereby mistaking the possibility of a morally responsible self-sacrifice. Fackenheim adds, however, that in a post-Holocaust world the self-sacrifice of a martyr becomes a moral abomination. He believes that the kingdom of God in the post-Holocaust world must be built by a humanity sensitive to social and political realities. He envisions that humanity tutored by a Jewish people ready to shoulder its cosmic burden, and by a true universalism. Fackenheim notes that it is from Jerusalem, not Athens, that humanity learns the need to transcend the parochial. The lessons of the Nazi Holocaust are meant not just for Jews but for all people. As Judaism has taught humanity to cherish the universal values, so it now teaches them to secure those ideas by political power.

Fackenheim's many works span several genre. Not only did he produce theological books and philosophical studies but also introductory texts meant for both adult and adolescent audiences. Among these are *Metaphysics and Historicity* (Milwaukee, 1961); *Encounters Between Judaism and Modern Philosophy: A Preface to Future Jewish Thought* (New York, 1980); *God's Presence in History: Jewish Affirmations and Philosophical Reflections* (New York, 1972); *The Jewish Return into History: Reflections in the Age of Auschwitz and a New Jerusalem* (New York, 1978); *To Mend The World: Foundations of Future Jewish Thought* (New York, 1982); *Quest For Past and Future: Essays in Jewish Theology* (Bloomington, 1968); *What is Judaism? An Interpretation for the Present Day* (New York, 1987). His many writings have been anthologized in Michael L. Morgan, ed., *The Jewish Thought of Emil Fackenheim: A Reader* (Detroit, 1987), and have occasioned scholarly discussion in Leonard Greenspan and G. Nicholson, eds., *Fackenheim: German Idealism and Jewish Thought* (Toronto, 1992).

Will Herberg (1906-1977): While his writings move from a radical Marxism to an equally radical conservatism, Will Herberg's thought exhibits several themes that remain constant throughout. Herberg shows a continual suspicion of the American way of life. He acknowledges it as the best possible secular ideology but also regards it as a danger to true faith. He maintains an insistence on the particularity and uniqueness of Jewish identity united with a demand for a universally valid moral code. Herberg places both Judaism and Christianity together as "biblical religions" in opposition to the civil religiousness of American democracy. He charges that the latter attempts to co-opt the former for idolatrous purposes. American religion, in his analysis, seeks to legitimate "all religion"—by which it means Judaism, Roman Catholicism, and Protestantism—as extensions of the economic and political concerns of the United States. Herberg considers this encroachment by civil religion on the particular religions dangerous. Religion, he claims, is ambiguous by nature. It provides comfort and spiritual sustenance, but it also challenges and criticizes its adherents. What Herberg calls "The American Way of Life" cannot do this, he believes, because it is too limited and narrow in scope. He opposes reducing Judaism or Christianity to a limited function subservient to American requirements of civility.

Not only is civil religion too narrow in focus, it also lacks the moral force of biblical religion. Herberg's approach to the conflict between Jerusalem and Athens focuses on the difference between the Abrahamic God of history and the Hellenic divine force. The personal God of Abraham, Herberg argues, works through holy history to create peoples obligated to fulfill the divine will. This divinity requires a decision for a faith that comes from beyond abstract reason as used by Greek philosophy and science, because it insists on this free responsibility. The Judaic approach, which he contrasts with "Greco-Oriental" spirituality, focuses on the divine will and the human obligations that flow from it. The contrast between Athens and Jerusalem becomes for Herberg the conflict between a salvation based on private, individual concerns and a redemption that emphasizes the reality of a corporate historical existence.

Herberg recognizes that American civil religion affirms the type of saving history that biblical tradition espouses. In itself he does not see American civil belief, "the American Way of Life," as necessarily idolatrous or evil. Herberg identifies an Americanized vision of Judaism and Christianity that blunts spirituality and converts the divine itself into an idol. From this perspective Herberg celebrates Judaic faith and practice

as a religious corrective to secularity.

Herberg expresses his philosophical and theological commitments in the following works: Bernhard Anderson, ed., *Faith Enacted as History: Essays in Biblical Theology* (Philadelphia, 1976); *Judaism and Modern Man: An Interpretation of Jewish Religion* (New York, 1951); *Protestant, Catholic, Jew: An Essay in American Religious Sociology* (Garden City, 1960). His work receives detailed analysis in Harry J. Ausmus, *Will Herberg: From Right to Right* (Chapel Hill, 1987).

Abraham Joshua Heschel (1907-1972): Recognized for his genius as a "translator of the Spirit," who transmutes traditional Jewish ideas into an American idiom, Heschel has been described as quintessentially American.[16] His work emerges from his feeling that Judaism is the "most misunderstood" of all religious traditions. Viewing Judaism as a dead religion, a relic of the past, Christians, on the one hand, both do Judaism an injustice and rob themselves of the benefit of its teachings. But Jews, on the other hand, equally misunderstand their tradition, focusing only on its parochial nature, on its ethnic component, so as to miss the universal relevance of its teachings. To rectify these misunderstandings, Heschel emphasizes a politics of piety and nostalgia that look to the Jewish past— to the Bible and to Polish Hasidism—to provide answers to American civil and religious problems. He creates a religious poetics of language in order to evoke the realities of God, Torah, and the Jewish people for a generation estranged from its roots.

Understanding Judaism correctly, Heschel insists, entails recognizing the difference between the Hellenic approach to reality and the Hebraic, the distinction between Athens and Jerusalem. Whereas the Greeks studied the world in order to understand it and moderns investigate reality in order to exploit it, biblical thinkers appreciated the world to enhance the reverence they felt toward it. By placing an awareness of the divine at the frontiers of the mind, Heschel seeks to recapture that experience of wonder and reverence. Religion, he thinks, arises at the point at which reason loses its ability to function. It suggests that reality spills over the boundaries of rationality. His language evokes the divine that stands beyond the mystery, that awaits every person on the other side of utilitarian and pragmatic thinking.

Heschel champions Hebraic thought generally and Jewish thought in particular as the contribution of Judaism to humanity as a whole. This universalistic perspective transforms the traditional Jewish self-understanding of "the chosen people." For Heschel, being chosen means having a mission to teach others the basic values of religious life. For him, these values spring from the generally human experience of the divine that lies on the other side of rationality, beyond the purview of Greek rationalism. Jews, Heschel thinks, must help all Americans regain a sensitivity to the Hebraic insights about the divine and help free them from the stultifying Greek rationalism.

Heschel presents this theology as applicable to every sensitive person. Although his books draw heavily on Jewish sources, he refuses to call his writing Jewish theology. Instead, he calls it "depth-theology." "Theology," he argues, focuses on the surface of religion—the external signs and practices that set one faith apart from another. It describes differences between traditions and addresses insiders within a specific religious group. "Depth-theology," by contrast, evokes the common experience shared by all human beings. It raises the existential questions that every person asks of life. Heschel's depth theology certainly exhibits the distinctive qualities of a Jewish theology. It uses the resources of the Torah and other Judaic texts, but Heschel contends that these become vehicles for guiding all people to general religious insight. From Torah he seeks to glean more than an explication of Judaism; he desires instruction that will comfort all people living in the tormented society of modernity.

To achieve this goal, Heschel moves beyond the narrow scope of philosophical questions. He applies Jewish teaching to the central civil issues of his day. In one of his most striking moves, he designates the "Negro crisis" as "God's gift to America." By this phrase, he means that America has been blessed by an obvious symptom of its racism.

The very explosiveness of the crisis makes it easier to confront. On the basis of Jewish experience, Judaic texts, and the teachings of Jewish leaders, Heschel redefines a social "emergency" as an opportunity, as a moment in which spiritual values can "emerge." This transformation of a social problem into a chance to develop positive responses characterizes Heschel's approach to civil questions. He analyzes the problems American society has coping with its elderly, the political questions arising from America's involvement in Southeast Asia, the dilemmas of conscience associated with Jewish concerns about religious freedom in the Soviet Union and with the survival of the modern State of Israel.

Heschel's major works are *A Passion For Truth* (New York, 1973); *God In Search of Man: A Philosophy of Judaism* (New York, 1966); *Israel: An Echo of Eternity* (New York, 1967); *Man is Not Alone: A Philosophy of Religion* (New York, 1951); *Man's Quest for God: Studies in Prayer and Symbolism* (New York, 1954); *The Insecurity of Freedom: Essays on Human Existence* (New York, 1967); *The Prophets* (Philadelphia, 1962). His writings have been anthologized in Fritz A. Rothschild, ed., *Between God and Man: An Interpretation of Judaism* (New York, 1959; revised, 1976); and in Jacob Neusner and Noam Neusner, eds., *To Grow In Wisdom* (Lanham, 1990).

Max Kadushin (1895-1980): Kadushin's approach to Rabbinic Judaism and the theology he derived from that approach influenced a generation of Conservative Jewish rabbis and scholars. Not widely known during his lifetime, his work has become more popular in a postmodern age. He has pointed to a way in which exegesis and interpretation can be used to understand theology and religious ideas. He finds in these methods an organic Judaic system that rivals the philosophic approaches of the Greek thinkers. This judgment relies on Kadushin's familiarity with classical philosophy. As someone trained in Greek thought, he felt that the Hellenic legacy in medieval Judaic thinking intruded as a foreign element and therefore condemned those medieval philosophers for departing from the inherent characteristics of Jewish religion.

Kadushin thought that the difference between organic Jewish thought and Hellenic philosophy lay in the approach each took to written texts. He identified this difference as one between the scientific method of dissection and self-distancing, on the one hand, and that of synthesis and engagement on the other. Athens and Jerusalem denote two ways of looking at texts, and Kadushin not only chose Jerusalem but devoted his writings to expounding the correct method for understanding the Judaic approach.

For postmoderns, Kadushin's locating of God's presence in Jewish worship has become extremely persuasive. Worship is more than just a collection of words. The words recited and the actions performed, Kadushin teaches, create moments in which the divine and human meet. He characterizes the basic element in Jewish prayer, the berakha, as a creative use of language. Through prayer, the worshiper comes into immediate relationship with the divine and feels God's presence experientially. Kadushin extended this insight about Jewish prayer into his understanding of the Torah as a whole. His hermeneutic reads texts as clusters of "value-concepts." Taken together the prayers convey ethical teachings about the importance of thankfulness, the value of the created world, and the significance of other people. Kadushin followed a procedure that today might be called "intertextual," analyzing clusters of words and concepts independently of the specific contexts in which they occurred. In this way, he evoked the organic structure behind Rabbinic writings as whole. This approach enabled him to show how aspects of Jewish thought that might appear chauvinistic or parochial were actually part of a universalist orientation. In particular, he elevated the idea of the "righteous gentile" to a position of prominence in Rabbinic thought. This openness to non-Jews makes Kadushin's view of Jewish chosenness acceptable within the egalitarian context of life in the United States. Israel's task in the world then, as defined by Kadushin, is fully compatible with the American democratic ideal.

Kadushin's major works are *Organic Thinking: A Study in Rabbinic Thought* (New York, 1938); *The Rabbinic Mind* (New York, 1951; second edition, 1965); and *Worship and Ethics: A Study in Rabbinic Judaism* (Evanston, 1964). A useful collection of studies on his work and its influence is Peter Ochs, ed., *Understanding the Rabbinic Mind: Essays on the Hermeneutic of Max Kadushin* (Atlanta, 1990).

Mordecai M. Kaplan (1881-1984): Kaplan's complete and impressive rethinking of Judaism continues to show new facets of meaning even in the contemporary Jewish context. By translating the Judaic tradition into pragmatic language, so that the elements of God, Torah, and Israel have significance in the modern context, he aimed not so much at creating an American Judaism as at providing American Jews with a persuasive rationale for remaining Jewish. He did this by making Jewish theological symbols vehicles for transmitting current philosophical meaning.

The idea of God, for Kaplan, represents a function, not a content. The idea of divinity, that is, refers to the common experience of discovering in the natural world unexpected support for human ideals and values. Expressing belief in God, on this reading, means affirming the surprise people feel when their highest concerns seem validated by "impersonal" nature. The word God thus signifies a response people have to the world, not an entity within the world. This view clearly rejects a supernaturalism, in which God is a super-human being who intervenes in the human sphere, just as a parent intervenes in a child's world. Kaplan's God is not a separate being who acts analogously to human beings, only in a more miraculous way, more powerfully and more perfectly than natural creatures can. Yet, while rejecting supernaturalism, Kaplan also refuses to call himself a naturalist. This is because his theology uses natural experience only as data pointing to something that transcends any single datum. He refers to his view instead as "transnaturalism," for it suggests that natural experience encounters a process that supports human development in a manner in which naturalistic analysis alone cannot allow.

Just as God refers to an experience associated with the process of self-development, so Torah refers to an experience associated with the process of assigning meaning to texts. Here again, Kaplan in the 1930s and 1940s anticipated the postmodern philosophies of the 1980s and 1990s. He sees Torah as texts awaiting meaning and understands "revelation" to comprise the effect of these texts on a community. When a community finds in certain written works the possibility of affirming and transcending its specific cultural context, then those works are to be recognized as "revealed." When Kaplan encourages loyalty to Torah, he refers to the process of using Jewish particularity as expressed in classical texts to address universal issues and general human concerns.

This understanding of Torah influences Kaplan's rather controversial view of Jewish identity. Although an avid Zionist, Kaplan rejected the theological concept of Jewish chosenness (this rejection may have led to his growing estrangement from Max Kadushin, who affirmed the idea). Kaplan hoped that the Jewish people would construct a transnational community that would model the democratic vision of participatory government. He looked to this potential as the major contribution that Jews could make to a confused modern society. This democracy in action was not a "justification" for Jewish survival—Jews he felt had the same right to survive as all other human communities. Instead he argued that the Jewish idea of covenant could offer a typology of communal democracy that would affirm individual freedom while encouraging group loyalty.

Kaplan's most influential work is *Judaism as a Civilization: Toward a Reconstruction of American-Jewish Life* (New York, 1967). Other important writings among his numerous publications are *A New Zionism* (second enlarged edition, New York, 1959); *Judaism Without Supernaturalism: The Only Alternative to Orthodoxy and Secularism* (New York, 1958); *Questions Jews Ask: Reconstructionist Answers* (New York, 1956); *The Future of the American Jew* (New York, 1967); and *The Meaning of God in Modern Jewish Religion* (New York, 1962). A useful study of his thought is S. Daniel Breslauer, *Mordecai Kaplan's Thought in a Postmodern Age* (Atlanta, 1994).

Kaufmann Kohler (1843-1926): While serving as rabbi of Temple Beth El in New York City, Kohler crafted the seminal statement of Reform Judaism referred to as the Pittsburgh Platform of 1885. As revealed in his platform, Kohler's thinking represented what has come to be referred to as classical Reform theology, emphasizing rationalism and ethics, both of which were prominent in American philosophy. Judaism, in Kohler's view, exemplified the ideal ethical monotheism. Its beliefs, practices, and above all ability to evolve and change marked it in his eyes as perfectly suited to the modern temperament. To maintain this position, he interpreted the various classical texts of the Jewish tradition as a philosophical rationalism. This required him to transform the historical and ritual aspects of Jewish experience into intellectual categories. In doing this, he neglected—and rejected—both the mystical elements in Judaism and the sociological sense of peoplehood advocated by European Jewish thinkers of his time. As later twentieth-century Jewish theologians increasingly turned to both mysticism and peoplehood as dominant, if alternative, ways of understanding Judaism, Kohler's formulation became marginalized.

In its nineteenth-century context, Kohler's Judaism had a great relevance and importance. His construction of Jewish religion was suited to the American Protestantism of his day, resembling the interpretation of Christianity offered by advocates of the Social Gospel, for instance, Walter Rauschenbusch (1861-1918), who proclaimed an ethical Christianity. Yet while many Christian theologians advocated an ethical philosophy, Kohler ignored their views and, in his defense of Judaism, branded all Christianity as a fundamentalistic irrationalism. This misrepresentation of Christian thought suggests the problem that Kohler faced. He wished to legitimize Judaism by pointing out a unique Judaic message that contributed an indispensable legacy to all humanity. He identified that message with rational ethics and so argued that, if Christian theologians had learned this lesson at all, they did so from Judaic, not Christian, sources.

Kohler interpreted the Jewish view of God in ethical terms. God's unity provided the basis on which humanity could develop a self-consciousness of its unity with all creation. Declaring the unity of God, for Kohler, affirms more than an abstract theory; instead, it gives expression to an experience of the interconnection of all things.

Rather than rejecting biblical miracles as supernaturalistic and irrational, Kohler insists that they function pedagogically. The miracles reported in the Bible, he argues, are merely external symbols of the one great miracle—the cosmic order. They draw attention to the rational purpose that animates creation. That recognition of order, he claims, is indispensable for ethics, for without the assurance of predictability and order, it would be impossible to practice the right and avoid immorality. Stories about miracles thus contribute to morality by reminding people of the ordered pattern which permeates reality.

The Torah, in Kohler's view, also serves a moral purpose by providing detailed instruction on how to live an ethical and moral life. Combining law and doctrine, the teachings of priest and prophet alike, its stimulates the highest virtues in every person. Kohler charts an evolution in the Bible from primitive symbols that perform this function to more elevated one. At one time, he thinks, the practice of circumcision taught people the self-discipline they needed to live morally. Later, he explains, the Sabbath with its regulations fulfills the same purpose, but on a higher level. Torah links human beings with the infinite divinity; it ennobles individuals so they can elevate the world as a whole. Judaism, as expressed in the Torah as Kohler reads it, thus is a programmatic battle against injustice and falsehood, aiming to "hallow every pursuit and endeavor."

That interpretation of Torah expresses Kohler's view of the purpose of the Jews as a chosen people. Jews are selected, Kohler thinks, to teach humanity the ethical truths essential for an ideal society. Kohler focuses on the "messianic age" that Jews are to es-

tablish rather than on a "messiah" who will inaugurate that age. He does this because he sees the Jewish task as one of active social amelioration. To be a Jew, he thinks, is "to be the messenger and champion of religious truth." The Jewish mission is not to bring a messiah, but rather to teach humanity how to institute a moral system of loving teachings. Kohler thinks that Jews today must conduct this mission in a more pluralistic fashion. While Judaism has indeed progressed from nationalism to universalism, he thinks it needs to take one further step. Jews should now recognize the validity of all ethical religions. While Kohler explicitly criticizes Christianity as a flawed faith, he applauds Christians when they include ethical monotheism within that faith. Jews, he thinks, should accept the fact that different groups call their ethical teachings by different names. When Jews discover that American Christians actually practice a type of Judaism, they can accept American pluralism as part of their own religious mission. This final step in the evolution of Judaism reflects Kohler's acceptance of the modern temperament, of the Jew's place in American society, and of the importance of pluralism in a democratic society.

Kohler's major theological work has been reprinted recently with an excellent introduction by Joseph C. Blau, in *Kohler, Kaufmann, Jewish Theology: Systematically and Historically Considered* (New York, 1968, reprint of 1918 edition).

Judith Plaskow (1947-): An ordained Conservative rabbi who has written pioneering books and articles, Plaskow offers what has been called "the first major attempt to provide a coherent vision of Judaism that incorporates women's experiences."[17] Indeed, Plaskow makes sensitivity to the spirituality of women the cornerstone of her thinking, perceiving all elements of Jewish theology through that prism.

A view of the divine, for Plaskow, shapes society; it offers the models used in judging human behavior and in evaluating the world in which people live. Jewish sources have provided some useful images that people today can reappropriate: the Shekinah (God's female aspect) and Lilith (an often maligned spirit who figures in medieval Jewish writings as a demon who refuses to accept the male power establishment).

These images, she thinks, enable contemporary Jews to use theology effectively. She argues for this because she thinks theology provides metaphors by which human beings understand themselves. With this is mind, she demands that a view of God must enable all human beings to discover their individual identity, and, therefore, she judges theology by the inclusiveness of its images. Traditional views of divinity silenced many members of the believing community, of which the silencing of women is only one example. A more suitable divine image must give voice to the formerly silenced ones.

Just as she views God as an expressive category rather than as an active, intervening being, so Plaskow defines Torah as a vehicle of memory, shaping the past in the perspective of the present. She recognizes that the texts that traditionally provided the vehicle for reshaping memory are embedded in male presuppositions. One cannot indulge in traditional exegesis, since the texts privilege the male reader. Despite this problem, Plaskow discovers ways of envisioning biblical ideas that transcend their male bias. She suggests a revolutionary alternative: transform texts from history, midrash, or liturgy into "living memories." The text dissolves into a pretext for an act of present being. It presents an occasion on which remembering transcends reading, on which response transcends obedience.

The biblical idea of Jews as the "chosen people," for example seems imbedded in a hierarchical system. God apparently selects one group among many for special favor. Plaskow rejects this idea as a negative influence on human life. Traditional views of the chosen people, she declares, have created hostile dichotomies—Israelis against Palestinians; Eastern European Jews against Oriental Jews; and, perhaps most crucial of all, male Jews against female Jews. She argues, however, that Jews today can see themselves as part of a group called together in egalitarian unity. Chosenness need not mean being

selected to be better than others but being open to sharing a community with others. Chosenness as the idea of inclusion, as an impulse to join with others, has a more positive meaning. Jews are "chosen" in the sense that they illustrate the basic human need for companionship, for social cohesion, and for equality. In this way a biblical concept rooted in divisiveness becomes the basis for a more universalistic and inclusive paradigm.

Plaskow complains that traditional Judaism places too great an emphasis on submission to authority. When Jewish women seek spirituality, they are told, she charges, to obey more rules, to learn more legal precepts. Jewish women may, in this way, repair the broken modern world in the process of repairing a traditional Judaism crippled under this burden of Jewish law. By articulating their Jewishness against the grain of tradition, Jewish women fulfill an important general mission—they testify to the need for revolution and change. Sexuality, redeemed in feminist Judaism, becomes less an obstacle requiring legal redress and more a source of personal power and expression. Jewish feminists show how human beings share the divine power of creation, how they actualize their partnership in creativity.

Plaskow's major work is *Standing Again at Sinai: Judaism From a Feminist Perspective* (San Francisco, 1990).

Simon Rawidowicz (1896-1957): Rawidowicz spent only nine of his 61 years in the United States, and many of his publications still are accessible only in Hebrew. Nevertheless as one of the architects of Brandeis University, he has exercised considerable influence on American Jewish thinking. Rawidowicz's contribution was to examine Jewish thinking as an act of "interpretation." It provides the means by which "thought" becomes established among the Jews and thus is a key to the survival of the Jewish people. Jewish thought provides a synthesis of Athens and Jerusalem, which Rawidowicz traces from Rabbinic times through the present day.

God, in this perspective, represents the ideal model of learning and interpretation. The divine is a dynamic principle which Rawidowicz, like Maimonides, as Rawidowicz interprets him, locates in the human being. This view anticipates postmodern intuitions of reality. There is no fixed order, no escape from contingent accidents of being. The divine finds its "permanence," as it were, in the very transient incarnation of human beings.

Rawidowicz reads Jewish texts to discover the same impulse to growth, change, and development that God models. "Interpretation" means more for him than just the eternal and essential aspect of Judaism. It is also the key to its texts. Rawidowicz rejects the static compilation of Torah that even as exalted a poet as Hayim Nahman Bialik created in his *Sefer Ha-Aggadah*.[18] Bialik reinterpreted traditional material in radical ways. His poetry evoked new meanings from biblical, talmudic, and medieval Jewish sources. Yet as an anthologist, Bialik pared down the tradition to meet narrow specifications, inventing set categories under which to organize the vast material he found. Rawidowicz considered such an approach antithetical to the Jewish spirit, limiting rather than expanding the potential meanings of the texts. Therefore he calls Bialik's desire for such an anthology and his exaltation of Jewish lore a "protest against poetry." Poetry requires anxiety, readiness for change, movement. Removing poetry from Torah, Rawidowicz contends, sacrifices the dynamic spirit of Judaism for the fixed content that spirit manifested during only one historical period. He advocated the "poetic" approach of continually changing the content of Judaism through radical interpretations. Such readiness to develop Jewish religion might alter its "meaning" but, he thought, would remain faithful to its spirit.

The same impulse to look to the spirit and not to a fixed content led Rawidowicz to reject the thinking of Zionists who divided Jews into diverse camps. There is but one "Israel," he contended, not a "diaspora" Judaism on the periphery and a "Zionist" Judaism at the center. The task of the modern Jew is to create a community in which scholars and community members work together to revive a dynamic Judaism. The legacy of the Nazi Holocaust is for Rawidowicz a call for a reborn Jewish learning. Jewish scholars, whose isolation, he insists, is thrust upon them and not freely chosen, require a cooperative community in which creative thinking can take place. Here Rawidowicz synthesizes Athens and Jerusalem into a universal academy for human learning. Not coincidentally, Brandeis University became, at least in his eyes as chair of the Graduate Department of Judaic Studies from its inauguration in 1953, just such a common ground of study.

His writings have been collected in Simon Rawidowicz, *Studies in Jewish Thought* (Philadelphia, 1974), which includes a foreword by Abram L. Sachar, a Biographical Introduction by Benjamin C.I. Ravid, and an editorial postscript by Nahum Glatzer; and in Benjamin C.I. Ravid, ed., *Israel, The Ever-Dying People, and Other Essays* (Rutherford, 1986).

Richard Lowell Rubenstein (1924-): Rubenstein has created an impressive corpus ranging from theological investigations to sociological studies. While his thought has developed and taken unexpected turns, it remains consistent in its theological elements. Indeed, after thirty years, he was able to produce a second edition of his *After Auschwitz* with only minor alterations.

Rubenstein translates Mordecai Kaplan's naturalism into a postmodern idiom. His view of the divine parallels that of the ancient Jewish mystics—God is the wholly Other from whom all things come and into which they are eventually reabsorbed. This divinity, like Kaplan's, does not intervene in human life, but rather provides the dynamic model for that life. Unlike Kaplan, however, Rubenstein, conditioned by the experience of the Nazi Holocaust in a way Kaplan was not, proposes a more pessimistic model. God symbolizes the varied possibilities of life, life's inevitable cycle of eternal return, but not an advance or progress toward ever higher human values. God stands for those limitations that, if confronted by a naive humanity, lead to despair. Recognizing the divine as a metaphor for inevitable human failure helps prepare modern Jews for the test of a world in which morality depends only on power.

This theology also underlies Rubenstein's idea of Torah. The ancient rabbis, he holds, practiced a type of disguised psychotherapy. Their tales and interpretations of Torah exposed Jews to their darkest inclinations and provided them with "self-perspective if not self-knowledge." Thus, even in grotesqueness, they provided a path to mental health. Rubenstein finds in the Jewish heritage anticipations of modern predicaments and measures, that in their time enabled Jews to cope with those challenges. Modern Jews, for the most part, he contends, can no longer accept the premises of the ancient texts. The naive assumptions no longer command respect and so the palliatives they offered no longer fulfill their original function. The Torah testifies to a truth that still endures, but it responds to that truth in ways that fail to achieve their purposes.

Rubenstein admits that some Jews today can still generate the mythic power of Torah and use it to fulfill their needs. The lessons of the Nazi Holocaust and its contemporary successors in this "age of triage," however, have taught most Jews to view the world more darkly and realistically. Rubenstein offers interpretations of the barbarity of modernity. He sees the event of Auschwitz, the sociology of modern mass destruction, and the psychology of religion as keys to understanding modern life. This idea underlies his defense of the modern State of Israel's military self-reliance and his view of the necessity for Jewish survival of the "tribalism" explicit in the idea of the "chosen people." Rubenstein not only naturalizes Jewish theology, but he makes that naturalization a model for all nations. From Auschwitz he derives a more realistic appraisal of how religion and politics intersect and reinforce one another. He regards this lesson as a harbinger of a future which will transcend traditional Judaic religiousness.

Rubenstein's presentation of these ideas makes his philosophy the touchstone against which other philosophies measure themselves.[19] His most important works are *After Auschwitz: History, Theology, and Contemporary Judaism* (Baltimore, 1992 [2nd ed.; first edition 1966]); *The Age of Triage: Fear and Hope in an Over-Crowded World* (Boston, 1983); *The Cunning of History: The Holocaust and the American Future* (New York, 1978); *Morality and Eros* (New York, 1970); and *The Religious Imagination: A Study in Psychoanalysis and Jewish Theology* (Indianapolis, 1968).

Joseph Baer Soloveitchik (1903-1993): For over forty years Rabbi Soloveitchik (sometimes called "the Rav," that is, the teacher, *par excellence*) lectured to American audiences speaking in Hebrew and Yiddish. He articulated a theology of Judaism based on the halakhic resources of the tradition but responding to the existential predicament of the modern Orthodox Jew. His thought developed philosophical ideas derived from Emmanuel Kant or neo-Kantians such as Hermann Cohen and from existentialists such as Soren Kierkegaard. He integrated this philosophical material with the Jewish legal corpus, using it as both an inspiration and as illustrative content for his writings. Despite his clear recognition of human irrationality, his rigorous thinking and intellectual proclivities identify him with the rationalist opponents of mysticism.

Soloveitchik generates several "ideal types" or typologies of religious experience. These imply that different temperaments or stages of development shape ways in which human beings interact with the divine. Drawing on the double account of the creation of human beings found in Genesis 1-4, Soloveitchik claims that the Bible presents two models of human personality, which he designates as "Adam I" and "Adam II." The first experiences partnership with the divinity through shared creativity. God sets humanity to work on perfecting the world, on mastering it and improving it. The second type of human recognizes the lonely isolation arising from the cosmic task. This "lonely man of faith" seeks redemption through God, through submission to the divine master. This type of religious person discovers a covenantal relationship with God that reassures the anxious self of its importance and worth.

Soloveitchik insists that both Adam I and Adam II are essential aspects of any religious life. Each person should combine elements from both types. Another of his dichotomous ideal types presents the same dilemma differently by speaking of halakhic and existential piety. These contrasting forms of religiousness can be identified too easily and imprecisely with the rational approach of Jewish legalism and the mystical approach of movements such as Polish Hasidism. Seen that way, Soloveitchik's thought may appear as an attempt to reconcile the divergent elements in his own personal biographical journey. A different approach sees these as models by which those engaged in traditional Jewish learning, who also confront a confusing modern predicament, learn to see themselves. Soloveitchik, on this reading, provides an existential hermeneutic by which to place oneself in the process of halakhic decision-making, in the on-going study of traditional Torah.

Soloveitchik offers these models to Jews caught between a commitment to Orthodox Jewish tradition and the modern American situation, addressing himself to the perplexed within his American audience. This audience helps explain why his typology is general rather than specific and why despite the universalism of his theory he still takes pains to distinguish between a Judaic and a Christian type of religiousness. The question facing him is how modern Orthodox Jews discover their humanity through Judaism and how their Judaism expresses their human situation. Soloveitchik does not need to justify Judaism as a mode of human living. He merely needs to show those for whom Judaism is the only alternative how it serves to illuminate their humanity.

Among his important writings are *Be-Sod Ha-Yahid veha-Yahad* (Jerusalem, 1978); *Halakhic Man* (Philadelphia, 1983); *The Halakhic Mind: An Essay on Jewish Tradition and Modern Thought* (New York, 1986). A useful study of his thought is given by Aaron Lichtenstein, "Joseph Soloveitchik," in Simon Noveck, ed., *Great Jewish Thinkers of the Twentieth Century* (Washington, 1963), pp. 281-297.

Leo Strauss (1899-1973): Strauss influenced a generation of scholars in political philosophy, constructing out of the legacy of the ancient thinkers—Plato, Judah Halevi, Moses Maimonides, a philosophy of Judaism

for a post Holocaust generation. His own intellectual journey took him from the existentialist philosopher Franz Rosenzweig, in whose Frankfurt Lehrhaus he studied, back through early modern thinkers such as Baruch Spinoza, Nicolo Machiavelli, and Thomas Hobbes, to the ancients, Plato, Maimonides, and Halevi. His experience of anti-semitism and Nazi murder of Jews played a crucial role in this intellectual development. He abandoned the modernist enterprise after discovering the catastrophes to which it led.

In the United States, he addressed a varied audience including students at the Hillel Foundation at the University of Chicago, Jewish intellectuals, and philosophers. Although couching his call differently to each group, Strauss' choice to return to the medievals and the Judaism of Moses Maimonides remains a focal point. He continually reiterates the superiority of the ancients to the moderns, in general, and to modern liberalism in particular. This attack on liberalism stimulates continuing controversy. Yet many who may disagree with Strauss' apparent conclusions often agree with his insight that careful writing requires careful reading.

His decision to reject existentialism derives from his belief that it "solves" the conflict between faith and reason too easily. It avoids confronting the issue rather than forcing a clear choice between the two alternatives. Strauss claims that no reconciliation can unite the biblical God of Judaism to the divinity discovered by the natural theology of the philosophers. The philosophers seek to know God's nature. Yet God's omnipotence means that no one can know the divine essence. That Spinoza sought to reveal that essence shows, for Strauss, that he stands with Athens and not Jerusalem. Medievals like Maimonides, he claims, were too perceptive to believe that the categories of being Jewish and being a philosopher were anything other than mutually exclusive. Announcing this axiom, Strauss urges a decision on modern Jews. They must either relinquish an imperialistic philosophy that tries to know all things or else be caught outside of Jerusalem.

Those inside Jerusalem have abandoned the task of choosing. They have affirmed unquestionably that which the authority of the past provides. Strauss emphasizes the irrational nature of Torah as a guide and teacher. To follow Torah means to forego the process of testing Torah truths against some putatively higher standard. It means recognizing that revelation provides "authoritative disclosure" in itself. Strauss recalls how the thought and person of Franz Rosenzweig attracted him to an existential commitment to a renewed Jewish life. Strauss, however, follows this thinking more radically than his mentor. It leads him first to a Zionist affirmation of the Jewish people and then to an acknowledgment that Zionism, correctly understood, should reinforce a completely Orthodox way of living. If Zionism tests the Jew's attachment to the Jewish people and its faith, then the test of Zionism itself lies in the authenticity of its adherence to Orthodox tradition.

At the heart of this argument lies Strauss' recognition that religion plays a political role in the creation of human communities. The idea of God, with its idea of an omnipotent power, enables a community to justify its politics, art, science, and laws. Divine dispensation, through religion, transforms these aspects of the civil order from arbitrary devices for social control into expressions of a natural pattern inherent in the world. Medieval Jewish philosophers, and one might guess Strauss himself, portray Jews as ideal citizens. They so describe them to tame the potentially dangerous impulses of individuals for the social good. By privatizing philosophy, by naturalizing civil law, and by socializing art, human beings express their most antisocial instincts in socially responsible ways. The purpose of the Jew as civil being would seem to reside in this exemplary function.

Strauss expresses his views about Jewish philosophy most clearly in Hilail Gildin, ed., *An Introduction to Political Philosophy: Ten Essays by Leo Strauss* (Detroit, 1989); *Persecution and the Art of Writing* (Glencoe, 1952); and *Philosophy and Law: Essays Toward the Understanding of Maimonides and His Predecessors* (Philadelphia, 1987). The controversy surrounding his thinking becomes clear by comparing two works devoted to his thought: Shadia B. Drury, *The Political Ideas of Leo Strauss* (New York, 1988) and Kenneth Hart Green, *Jew and Philosopher: The Return to Maimonides in the Jewish Thought of Leo Strauss* (Albany, 1993).

Harry Austryn Wolfson (1887-1974): Wolfson may not seem at first glance an original Judaic thinker, for his reputation is built on scholarly analysis of medieval Jewish thought. Nevertheless in several essays Wolfson demonstrates that he exemplifies creative American Judaic thought. When un-derstood through the prism of Wolfson's life, these more popular essays offer insight on Wolfson's academic approach. Both types of work reveal an effort to resolve the issues of God, Torah, and Israel in the context of American life.

Wolfson's view of the divine was ironically classical and unbending. He embraced the classical view of God that he discovered in religious philosophy from Philo through Spinoza as the only legitimate theological option. He scorned modernist thinkers who reinterpreted the meaning of "divinity" so that it lost all connection with traditional thought. Wolfson allowed faith a place in the world by admitting that scholarship only deals with "appearance" and that reality might point to a truth that academic science could not apprehend. He also held that academic science could establish just what that apprehension entailed. Any attempt to alter or dilute the traditional belief would render its force as a distinctive religious belief less powerful. Honesty, he claimed, demanded that Americans choose between the consequences of belief and the consequences of unbelief.

Wolfson's honesty prevented him from legitimating American Jewish denominationalism in its usual form. All types of institutional Judaism in America—whether Orthodox or liberal—seemed to be part of a conspiracy of deceit. At the same time, his scholarly agenda advanced a different sort of denominationalism. He read medieval philosophy as a single system, even when thinkers came to radically different conclusions, as occurred in Jewish, Muslim, and Christian religious thought. The system of Maimonides looks different from that of Halevi. The different schools of the Kalaam took divergent positions concerning the relationship between the Quran as Muslims read it and the heavenly Quran that God possesses. Yet they all begin from the identical point of departure, seeking to reconcile Greek philosophy and biblical religion. Wolfson's scholarship legitimates denominationalism, at least in the middle ages. Whether Judaic, Muslim, or Christian, all medieval religious philosophy, he declares, shared the common experience of mediating between two literary and intellectual traditions. It was this shared hermeneutics that allowed Wolfson to predict the time when Jews would "reclaim Jesus." From the perspective of the pluralism inherent in religious philosophy, he contends, Jesus appears as just another Rabbinic interpreter who sought to revise Judaic ways of reading the Bible.[20] While, for Wolfson, the only defensible theology is a classical one, the only acceptable practice is accommodation to pluralism as an adaptation to the American way of life.

Wolfson's scholarly studies include *The Philosophy of Spinoza: Unfolding the Latent Processes of His Reasoning* (Cambridge, 1935); *Philo: Foundations of Religious Philosophy in Judaism, Christianity and Islam* (Cambridge, 1947); Isadore Twersky, George H. Williams, eds., *Studies in the History of Philosophy and Religion* (Cambridge, 1973, 1977). Essays of equal scholarship but more popular in appeal appear in his *Religious Philosophy: A Group of Essays* (Cambridge, 1961).

Notes

[1] Harold M. Schulweis, *In God's Mirror: Reflections and Essays* (Hoboken, 1990).

[2] Jacob Raider Marcus, "The Handsome Young Priest in the Black Gown: The Personal World of Gershom Sexias," in *HUCA* 70-71, 1969-1970, pp. 409-467.

[3] Robert N. Bellah, "Civil Religion in America," in his *Beyond Belief: Essays on Religion in a Post-Traditional World* (New York, 1970), pp. 168-189.

[4] Sidney E. Mead, *The Nation With the Soul of a Church* (New York, 1975), p. 59.

[5] John E. Smith, *Themes in American Philosophy: Purpose Experience and Community* (New York, 1970), p. 242.

[6] Marc Lee Raphael, *Profiles in American Judaism: The Reform, Conservative, Orthodox, and Reconstructionist Traditions in Historical Perspective* (San Francisco, 1984), p. 16.

[7] See Seymour Siegel and Elliot Gertel, eds., *God in the Teachings of Conservative Judaism* (New York, 1985).

[8] See Jeffrey S. Gurock, "Resisters and Accommodators: Varieties of Orthodox Rabbis in America, 1886-1983," in Jacob Rader Marcus and Abraham J. Peck, eds., *The American Rabbinate: A Century of Continuity and Change, 1883-1983* (Hoboken, 1985), pp. 10-97.

[9] See Arthur A. Cohen and Mordecai M. Kaplan, *If Not Now, When? Conversations Between Mordecai Kaplan and Arthur A. Cohen* (New York, 1973).

[10] See Arnold M. Eisen, *The Chosen People in America: A Study of Jewish Religious Ideology* (Bloomington, 1983).

[11] See Steven S. Schwarzschild, *The Pursuit of the Ideal: Jewish Writings of Steven Schwarzschild*, Menachem Kellner, ed. (Albany, 1990), and Kenneth Seeskin, *Jewish Philosophy in a Secular Age* (Albany, 1990).

[12] See his *Godwrestling* (New York, 1978).

[13] See David Novak, *Halakhah in a Theological Dimension* (Chico, 1985).

[14] See Laurence J. Silberstein and Robert L. Cohn, eds., *The Other in Jewish Thought and History: Constructions of Jewish Culture and Identity* (New York, 1994).

[15] *The Tremendum: A Theological Interpretation of the Holocaust* (New York, 1981), p. xvi.

[16] Edward K. Kaplan, *Holiness in Words: Abraham Joshua Heschel's Poetics of Piety* (Albany, 1996), p. 12.

[17] Ellen M. Umansky, in Eugene Borowitz, *Choices in Modern Jewish Thought*, p. 317; see her entire discussion of Plaskow, pp. 317-325.

[18] Now translated by William G. Braude as *The Book of Legends: Sefer Ha-Aggadah, Legends from the Talmud and Midrash*; Hayim Nahman Bialik and Yehoshua Hana Ravnitzky, eds. (New York, 1992).

[19] See for example, Stephen K. Katz, *Post-Holocaust Dialogues: Critical Studies in Modern Jewish Thought* (New York, 1983), pp. 174-204.

[20] "How the Jews will Reclaim Jesus." Introductory Essay in Joseph Jacobs, ed., *Jesus as Others Saw Him* (New York, 1925).

S. DANIEL BRESLAUER

L

LANGUAGE(S) IN JUDAISM: Language, especially Hebrew, has a theological significance in Judaism not commonly associated with language in any other religion. Three reasons account for this: (1) the Hebrew Scripture's depiction of the world's being called into being through divine utterance, suggesting that Hebrew is the very language of creation, (2) the presence in Scripture of verbatim quotations of God, again in Hebrew, and (3) the many acts of piety prescribed in Scripture and Rabbinic documents that require writing out and/or reciting a text, again, usually in Hebrew, sometimes in Aramaic. Thus, while part of the legacy Judaism inherited from its ancient Near Eastern and Hellenistic antecedents is multilingualism, Hebrew, as the language of creation and revelation, has remained central. This centrality of language continued even as, over a period of centuries, Hebrew ceased to be a spoken language and was supplanted in daily Jewish life by other languages specific to Jews, the most famous and widely spoken of which were Yiddish and Ladino. Like Hebrew, these languages became part and parcel of Jewish religious identity, employed in the study of Torah and in private, and even some public, prayers.

The fact that Judaism is a religion of sacred languages is underscored by the realization that, in the modern period, the abandonment of these languages in favor of the languages of the Jews' host cultures was symptomatic of secularization over all. This was the case even in the State of Israel, where traditional Jewish languages were abandoned in favor of a new secular language, modern Hebrew. And yet, as the second millennium C.E. draws to a close, the Hebrew of modern Israel has come to provide for probably the greatest number of Jews in history a direct access to the spiritual treasures of the Hebrew Scripture and Rabbinic literature as well as a feeling of association with the entire history of the Jews, their religion, and culture. The revival of

Hebrew thus is perceived by many as part and parcel of the unfolding drama of God's messianic redemption, and Hebrew has retained its place not only as a language Jews speak but as a Jewish language, significant in the theology and, most important, eschatology, of Judaism.

To understand the significance of language in Judaism, we must begin with Scripture and, in particular, the creation narrative. Nine of the acts of creation described in Gen. 1:1-2:4a are introduced by the words, "and God said." Turning the very first word of the Bible, *Bereshit* ("in the beginning"), into a divine utterance, M. Ab. 5:1 determined that the cosmos came into being as a result of ten divine utterances. The later exegetical tradition found in this assertion of M. Ab. a restatement of Ps. 33:6, "By the word of the Lord the heavens were made," or of Ps. 33:9, "He said [a word], and it was [so]."

In Prov. 8:22, personified Wisdom declares that she was created at the very beginning of God's dominion, even before the watery abyss whose preexistence is taken for granted in Gen. 1:2. Moreover, personified Wisdom declares (Prov. 8:22-31) that, at the time of the creation of the cosmos, she accompanied God as a confidant. Already in Ps. 119 this personified Wisdom of Proverbs is identified with Torah, the same Torah that, in Ps. 119, as already in Deut. 17 and Neh. 9, comprises a God-given book of instructions concerning human behavior.

Simple logic suggests that if Wisdom is Torah and Wisdom is God's companion at Creation, then it was the Torah that accompanied God at Creation. It is a short step from this logical inference to the idea, first attested in the writings of the first century C.E. Alexandrian Jewish philosopher Philo, later in Gen. Rabbah 1:1, and still later among medieval Kabbalists, that the Torah was the blueprint used by God in creating the cosmos. It is, further, only a small step from this notion to the conclusion that the language of the Hebrew Scripture—and with it, the language of the Mishnah, the liturgy, most of the midrashic literature, and the language in which the rabbis of the two Talmuds express their definitive statements—is also the language of Creation. This means, ultimately, that the twenty-two letters of Hebrew's alphabet are the alphabet of Creation.

In keeping with this idea, B. Ber. 55a informs us that Judah had a tradition from Rab (late third century C.E.) that Bezalel, who was called upon to the fashion the vessels of the Tabernacle (Exod. 31:1-11) and implicitly, therefore, to build the Tabernacle itself, was able to do so because he knew how to combine the letters by which the world was created. Under Kabbalistic influence, this same theory of the power of the Hebrew alphabet comes to suggest even to some adherents of late twentieth century popular Judaism, especially in the State of Israel, that faulty-worded prayers and faulty-written *mezuzot* and *tefillin* can and do directly and adversely affect the health and well-being of persons and the cosmos.

Y. Meg. 1:9 notes that Eleazar and Yohanan—both late third century C.E. Palestinian Amoraim—disagreed regarding the meaning of Gen. 11:1: "The whole world was of one language and few words." One of these two rabbis (the Talmud seems neither to remember nor to care which) held that "and few words" means that from the beginning people spoke different languages but understood each other. The other rabbi holds that it means that prior to the confusion of tongues (Gen. 11:7-9) all people spoke God's language, that is, Hebrew.

An alternative understanding of Gen. 11:1, proposed by Hebrew University Assyriologist Aaron Shaffer and published by William W. Hallo,[1] translates Gen. 11:1, "All the earth was of one speech and corresponding words." This reading sees in this verse a reference to the bilingualism of ancient Near Eastern civilizations beginning in the third millennium B.C.E. It intimates that the bilingualism of Judaism is part of Judaism's legacy from the ancient Near East. Regardless of their real connection to Gen. 11:1, both the idea of Hebrew as God's language and the phenomena of bilingualism and multilingualism are

part and parcel of Jewish religious life from biblical times.

It was inferred from God's speaking Hebrew throughout Scripture that Hebrew is, in fact, God's holy tongue (see M. Sot. 7:1). This inference, combined with the availability of Hebrew as a spoken language in post-70 C.E. Palestine—albeit rivaled by both Aramaic and Greek—and coupled with the perspicacity of the Tannaim, especially Judah the Patriarch, tipped the scales in favor of Hebrew in general , though not in any particular dialect. Hebrew thus was designated and remained Judaism's unrivaled "holy tongue" for at least two millennia.

Interestingly enough, the only biblical text that explicitly associates Hebrew with the *religion* of Israel is Is. 19:19, which says that at some better time yet to be, "there shall be five [a round number meaning "many"?] towns in the land of Egypt speaking Canaanite [i.e., Hebrew] and swearing by the Lord of Hosts." The latter verse is part of a speech in which Isaiah (eighth century B.C.E.) declares in the name of God that Israel, Egypt, and Assyria will all be peoples of the one God. The passage suggests that the adoption of Hebrew will be a sign of Egypt's acceptance of the sovereignty of the Lord. Moreover, the use of Hebrew as an act of religious devotion is placed on a par with swearing by the Lord. Is. 19:19 is, therefore, the clearest Scriptural adumbration of the M. Sot. 7:1's conception of Hebrew as "holy tongue."

Note that in the Hebrew Scriptures, Aramaic appears either as the speech of outsiders (Gen. 31:47; Dan. 2:4) or as the language of Persian archives and diplomatic correspondence (Ezra 4:8-6:18; 7:12-26).

Hebrew and Greek as sacred languages among the Jews of Alexandria: The Letter of Aristeas attests to the belief that the Greek version of the Pentateuch, the Septuagint, no less than the Hebrew Pentateuch, was given by God in the presence of representatives of the twelve tribes of Israel. One consequence of this belief was the willingness of Philo Judaeus of Alexandria (first century C.E.) to derive lessons from Greek etymologies based upon the Septuagint just as he derives lessons from Hebrew etymologies based upon the Hebrew version. Rabbis of the Amoraic period and medieval Kabbalists continue to derive lessons from Greek etymologies of words in biblical Hebrew!

Thus, when the Mishnah appeared in its final form, c. 220 C.E., referring to Hebrew as "the holy language," it reckoned with a belief going back at least 400 years, that Greek no less than Hebrew is a sacred language in which both Scripture and liturgy may be sung in the synagogue. This legacy is reflected in 1) the abundant Greek inscriptions in synagogues and Jewish tombs in both Palestine and the diaspora; 2) the presence of both Greek and Hebrew versions of biblical books at Qumran alongside books of law (i.e., *serek*, a functional equivalent of Rabbinic *mishnah, halakhah*) in Hebrew and of biblical eisegesis in Hebrew and Aramaic but not in Greek (!); 3) the discussion in M. Meg. 1:8 of the permissibility of writing biblical books in Greek.

Language(s) in the Dead Sea Scrolls: E. Qimron, *The Hebrew of the Dead Sea Scrolls* (Atlanta, 1986, p. 116) explains that the Hebrew of the non-biblical scrolls recovered from Qumran is not an imitation of Biblical Hebrew but a continuation of Late Biblical Hebrew, a dialect attested in the biblical books of Eccl., 1-2 Chr., and perhaps Jonah and Cant. Moreover, Qimron shows that the Hebrew typical of Qumran shares with Mishnaic Hebrew, first attested as a living language in the Bar Kokhba letters from Wadi Murabbat (132-135 C.E.), not only such features of interest to linguists as the shift from *s* to *sh*, the non-assimilation of *nun* before another consonant, and the weakening of the guttural letters, but also 175 words either unattested in Biblical Hebrew or attested in wholly different meanings. Among these terms are *ger* in the sense "proselyte;" *minhag* meaning "custom;" *hummash* meaning "Pentateuch;" *abot* meaning "[the three] patriarchs"; *ben berit*, lit., "covenant member," meaning "Jew;" *seder* meaning "order;" and *talmud* meaning "learning."

It was argued by Rabin (*Qumran Scrolls*, Oxford, 1957, p. 67) that the persons who produced the Mishnah deliberately abandoned the use of Biblical Hebrew, the medium of the Dead Sea Scrolls, in favor of Mishnaic Hebrew in order to distinguish their teaching from that of the sectarians. In fact, too little is known either of the various Judaisms that antedate the Mishnah or of the various forms of Hebrew and Aramaic spoken in Palestine before and after the Mishnah to make it worthwhile to speculate on this issue. However, the Dead Sea Scrolls do reveal that, contrary to Max Kadushin in *The Rabbinic Mind* (New York, 1972, pp. 291-95), some of the most important valuational vocabulary and the underlying ideology that set apart the Judaism of the Mishnah from religious conceptions found in Hebrew Scripture derive from the legacy of some or even many of the Judaisms that existed in Second Temple times.

A special case is the Hebrew of the Qumran text called MMT or *Miqsat Ma'aseh ha-Torah* and dated to 159-152 B.C.E. Precisely because it bears the literary character of a public letter, its language, like that of the bodies (as against formulaic introductions and conclusions) of letters throughout the history of Semitic writing, closely resembles the spoken language of the author(s).[2] Most important for the role of language in post-70 Judaism is Qimron's statement: "Its [i.e., the language of MMT's] similarity [primarily in vocabulary] to MH [= Mishnaic Hebrew] results from the fact that both MMT and MH reflect spoken forms of Hebrew current in the Second Temple period."[3]

According to M. Meg. 1:8, phylacteries and *mezuzot* must be written in the square Hebrew characters that, according to Y. Meg. 1:9 and B. San. 21b, were brought to the land of Israel by Ezra the Scribe. Similarly, M. Meg. 2:2 stresses that the Scroll of Esther must be read on the Festival of Purim from a scroll written in the square Hebrew characters. As we know from the coins of the Hasmoneans in the second century B.C.E. as well as from the coins of Bar Kokhba (132-135 C.E.), Jews in the Second Temple period and later attempted to employ the paleo-Hebrew script for official purposes and preferred it to the square alphabet, which eventually prevailed. Among the biblical manuscripts from Qumran are fragments, or more, of copies of each of the books of the Hexateuch in paleo-Hebrew. Moreover, it was common scribal practice at Qumran to write the four letter proper name of God in paleo-Hebrew script even within the majority of biblical scrolls that employed the square characters for the remainder of the sacred text.

The latter usage of this script suggests that for the scribes of Qumran and for the ideologues in whose service they worked, the paleo-Hebrew script had a greater measure of sanctity and was to be employed if not in the transcription of biblical books at least in the transcription of the ineffable name. When, therefore, the Mishnah insists that certain sacred texts must be transcribed in square script (Heb., *Ashurit*), it is taking a very firm stand in what must have been a controversy during the Second Temple era, namely, whether or not Scriptures transcribed wholly or even partly in the relatively new square script should be employed. It is not beyond the realm of possibility that the insistence on a particular script to accompany the holy tongue was part of the program of state-building (or was it building a religion out of what had been a minor sect?), which made possible the creation of a religion based upon a law-code under the authority of the patriarch, who derived his authority from Roman law.

It is well known from early antiquity through the modern era that just as ethnic groups are associated with particular languages or dialects, so are particular political entities/religions associated with particular scripts. Five examples suffice: 1) the adoption of the Latin alphabet by modern Turkey to symbolize Turkey's westernization and turning away from the Middle East; 2) the distinction between Hindi and Urdu, which is essentially the writing of the same language in two different scripts, the former by Hindus using the Sanskrit alphabet and the latter by Muslims using Arabic script; 3) the oft-repeated pair of phrases in the biblical Book of Esther: "to each ethnic group according to its dialect; to each [of the 127] province[s] according to its [national] script;" 4) the na-

tional/religious lines drawn in Eastern Europe by the respective use of the Latin and Cyrillic alphabets; 5) the Soviet Communist regime's forcing of the Jews of the Kuba region of Azerbaijan to use first the Latin alphabet and later the Cyrillic alphabet in writing their ancestral Judeo-Tat language, thus severing a major tie of these Jews to their ancestral religion.

The employment in Hebrew biblical texts at Qumran of two different forms of the Hebrew alphabet, sometimes in combination, points to the Hasmonean and later attempt to revive the paleo-Hebrew script and treat it as holier than the square characters. Similarly, the Qumran texts reflect the tri-lingualism of Palestinian Jewry at the end of the Second Temple period. The fact that books of law found among the Dead Sea Scroll were written primarily in a form of Late Biblical Hebrew, which incorporated numerous elements that belong to a spoken dialect and whose continuation is Mishnaic Hebrew, suggests that it was no great innovation for Judah the Patriarch to compose his definitive law code in a form of that same dialect. Of course, he could have chosen Aramaic, as did the author of the Scroll of Fasts (Megillat Taanit), and the entire history of Judaism would have been different. Moreover, the bulk of the literature from Qumran, which expounds and expands upon the Bible, is also written in Late Biblical Hebrew. The one obvious exception is the Genesis Apocryphon, composed in Aramaic. Perhaps the fact that Rabbinic literature chose primarily to speak in Hebrew especially about biblical themes is part of the legacy of Second Temple Judaism, concerning which the Dead Sea Scrolls have permitted us a glimpse as through a glass darkly.

Some of the biblical manuscripts found at Qumran are written in Greek. The copying of biblical texts in Greek reflects the fact that from the third century B.C.E., Jews in both Palestine and elsewhere had been reading Scripture both publicly and privately in Greek as well as in Hebrew. Interestingly, but not surprisingly in light of the comparison to nation building elsewhere in human history, the Mishnah, which insists on square script for biblical texts written in the Hebrew language, does not attack or seem threatened by biblical texts written in Greek (M. Meg. 1:8). Unquestionably, it was the choice of Mishnaic Hebrew as against Aramaic or Greek, both of which were available and viable choices in 220 C.E. Palestine, first for the Mishnah and ultimately for the bulk of Rabbinic literature, that made it obvious to subsequent generations that Hebrew is "the holy tongue" and hence the proper and eternal language of the Jewish religion. What becomes equally obvious once one reckons with the historical fact that Hebrew, specifically Mishnaic Hebrew, was a living language in late Second Temple Palestine is that "holy tongue" in the context of M. Sot. is not analogous to nineteenth century B.C.E. Hittite as "language of the gods," that is, a dead language used *only* for liturgical purposes. Rather this is a value-laden statement designed to encourage the use of a language that is perceived as virtually the same language as that/those of the bulk of Hebrew Scripture.

It has long been noted that, in the same context in which Y. Meg. 1:9 refers to Aquila's version of the Pentateuch as the Tannaim's officially recognized Greek version of the Pentateuch, B. Meg. 3a refers to Targum Onkelos and Targum Jonathan respectively as the Babylonian Talmud's (and ultimately Judaism's) official Aramaic translations of the Pentateuch and Prophets. Obviously, the Babylonian Talmud, addressed initially to the Aramaic-speaking Jews of the Sassanian Empire, chose and prescribed Aramaic versions, which, whenever they depart ever so slightly from a literal rendering of the Hebrew, reflect and support that Talmud's version of Judaism. No less important is the Jerusalem Talmud's subtle insinuation that the Greek version *par excellence* is the in-house version produced by a disciple of Aqiba rather than the classic Septuagint.

Equally interesting is M. Meg. 1:8's strategy in fighting and winning the war over which language will be recognized as the one and only holy tongue. An anonymous suggestion that scriptural scrolls may be written in any language is followed by Gamaliel

II's assertion that sages had permitted such scrolls—employed for public reading in the synagogue—to be written only in [Hebrew and] Greek. Of course! The only ancient Jewish versions of Scripture that were ever considered divinely inspired and fit to be read as part of divine worship were the Hebrew and the Septuagint. The important point made by M. Meg. 1:8, however, is that phylacteries and *mezuzot*, unlike synagogue scrolls, may be written only in square script Hebrew. One very subtle message is that the texts contained in phylacteries and *mezuzot*, which are sealed up and read only by God, are written in God's language, that is, Hebrew and not Greek. Another subtle message is that the Mishnah fought its language battle by going directly into every Jewish home and dictating the rules for phylacteries and *mezuzot*. It wasted no energy on the boards of directors of Greek-singing synagogues.

Mishnaic Hebrew and Aramaic in the Rabbinic corpora: As we have seen, one of the spoken languages of the Jews of Palestine in the last two centuries B.C.E. and the first centuries C.E. was the Hebrew reflected later in the Mishnah, completed c. 220 C.E. Segal[4] prefers the term Mishnaic for the dialect, which nineteenth century Christian scholars called "New Hebrew." These scholars held that this language was simply a corrupt form of Biblical Hebrew, written by persons who were incapable of writing Hebrew properly. This view is consonant with the Christian theological belief that the religion expounded in the Mishnah is a corruption of the religion of ancient Israel.

Neusner (passim in his published works on the Rabbinic corpus), like Kutscher, uses the neutral term Middle Hebrew, reflecting the fact that Mishnaic Hebrew as a living language falls chronologically between Biblical Hebrew and Modern Hebrew. The Hebrew term *leshon mishnah* is employed by Rashi (1040-1105 C.E.) and his disciples to refer especially to the earlier phase of Rabbinic Hebrew reflected in the Mishnah, Tosefta, and other Tannaitic sources. While Yohanan b. Napha (fl. 275 C.E.) distinguishes between Biblical Hebrew, which he calls "Torah language," and Rabbinic Hebrew, which he calls "sages' language" (B. Hul. 137b; B. A.Z. 58b), M. Sot. 7:1 includes under the heading of "the holy tongue," both Biblical and Rabbinic Hebrew.

It is clear from M. Sot. 7:1, the exegesis thereof in the Tosefta and two Talmuds, and from the parallel passages in M. Ber. and M. Meg., that canonical liturgical texts existed in both forms of "the holy tongue." Whenever the rabbis believed that Scripture, oral tradition, or common sense required the recitation of a fixed canonical text, the recitation was to take place in "the holy tongue;" no sacred texts existed in any other language except for canonical versions of the Scripture in Greek (see M. Meg. 1:8 and Talmuds and commentaries ad loc.). When, however, Scripture, oral tradition, or common sense indicated that the primary concern was that a given liturgy be *understood* by ordinary people, the Mishnah and its ancient interpreters held that such a liturgy may be recited in any language, provided that the language is understood by the specific person. The ancient interpreters of the Mishnah also declared that, in most cases, even people ignorant of Hebrew could consider themselves to have fulfilled their religious duty if they read or listened to Scripture or other liturgy in that language (M. Meg. 2:1). Thus the Mishnah and its ancient exegetes expressed the conviction that Hebrew, without distinction as to dialect, is "the holy tongue."

In the very same way that the Mishnah inherited and did not seek to obliterate the tradition associated especially with Alexandria according to which Scripture could be written and read in Greek (M. Meg. 1:8), so did subsequent Rabbinic Judaism inherit and enhance the idea expressed at M. Sot. 7:1ff., namely, that both Biblical and Rabbinic Hebrew are "the holy tongue." Consequently, Mishnaic Hebrew is employed in the Babylonian Talmud for the transmission of authoritative statements attributed to Tannaim or Amoraim, formulations of prescribed behavior (*halakhah*), parables, expositions of Scripture, parables, and most traditions and anecdotes about the Tannaim and about past ages in general.[5]

It should, however, not be altogether surprising that both Talmuds employ Aramaic—Galilean Aramaic in the Jerusalem Talmud and Babylonian Aramaic in the Babylonian Talmud—in their respective discussions about the statements of Tannaim and Amoraim recorded in Mishnaic Hebrew as well as in anecdotes, which record ordinary conversations among Amoraim. One obvious fact is that, from the third century B.C.E. until the Arab conquest of the seventh century C.E., these Aramaic dialects were the standard speech of the Jews of Palestine and Babylonia respectively. But two other reasons may also explain the rather consistent use in both Talmuds of a form of Hebrew in framing authoritative statements and the use of Aramaic for the framework in which such statements are discussed.

First, as we noted above, bilingualism was an ingrained feature of the civilizations of the Near East from the third millennium B.C.E. Second, it is reasonable to suggest that the situation in life in which Aramaic was first perceived as the language used for exposition of a text recited in the holy tongue is the pre-Mishnaic Palestinian synagogue, in which the reading of the Pentateuch and the Prophets in the holy tongue was accompanied by an exposition in Aramaic. It is clear from M. Meg. 4:4ff. that with respect to the proper manner of reading Scripture and translating it into Aramaic, the Mishnah attempts to impose rules upon an entrenched practice, which presupposed the use of two distinct languages—Hebrew and Aramaic—in the studying of Torah, each with its own function.

If the elite group that produced, transmitted, and preserved the two Talmuds was equally at home in both Hebrew and Aramaic, why were the midrashic compositions composed in late Rabbinic Hebrew and not in Galilean Aramaic? One possible answer is that, just as Hebrew and Aramaic have distinct functions within the "Oral Law" represented by the two Talmuds—Hebrew for authoritative statements; Aramaic for discussion thereof—so in the exposition of Scripture do Rabbinic Hebrew and Aramaic have precise roles. These happen to be mirror images of their respective roles in the context of the Talmuds, for Aramaic is the medium of the translations of the Pentateuch and the Prophets, which the Babylonian Talmud itself designates as canonical (Onkelos for the Pentateuch, B. Meg. 3a; B. Qid. 49a; and Jonathan for the Early and Later Prophets, B. Meg. 3a). Both of these translations are for the most part, like the Septuagint and most classic translations of Scripture, word-for-word representations in another language of what Scripture states in "the holy tongue." If the literal representation of Scripture takes place in Aramaic, late Rabbinic Hebrew is assigned the task in both the Talmuds and the independent midrashic compositions of exposition and eisegesis of Scripture.

Another explanation of why the midrash compilations emanating from the land of Israel prior to the Arab conquest are composed primarily in late Rabbinic Hebrew rather than in Aramaic may, however, be suggested. Jacob Neusner, *Are the Talmuds Interchangeable?* (Atlanta, 1995, pp. 1-42), demonstrates that while the Jerusalem Talmud shares with the Babylonian Talmud the use of Aramaic in fixed phrases and technical words, the Jerusalem Talmud, unlike the Babylonian Talmud, does not employ Aramaic "as a medium of discourse sustained or abbreviated." In fact, Neusner demonstrates, "Hebrew predominates throughout [the Jerusalem Talmud] except in stories" (p. 4). It would appear, therefore, that 1) it was common practice in the Rabbinic subcultures that produced all of Rabbinic literature to produce eisegetical literature on the Bible in Rabbinic Hebrew rather than in Aramaic; and 2) the Rabbinic subculture of the land of Israel in general preferred Rabbinic Hebrew to Aramaic as a medium for setting forth Judaism, probably because, at least from the time of the Mishnah, Rabbinic Hebrew had been perceived as part of the holy tongue. It is conceivable, therefore, that this ingrained preference for Hebrew over Aramaic alongside the cultivation of Rabbinic Hebrew in the land of Israel paved the way in the geonic period for Babylonian Jewry's translating of Talmudic texts from Aramaic into Arabic, even as Palestinian Jews were translating those same texts from Aramaic into Rabbinic Hebrew.

No discussion of Mishnaic Hebrew and its function in the particular religious tradition(s) generated by the Mishnah is complete without taking note of Neusner's observations concerning the limited repertoire of literary forms that the Mishnah employs to convey its message(s) within the manifold possibilities available to it within the confines of the syntax, vocabulary, and grammar of Mishnaic Hebrew. The literary forms utilized are: 1) the simple declarative sentence, declaring that one who does so-and-so is such-and-such; 2) the duplicated sentence, in which it is asserted that as for one who does so-and-so, behold, that one is such-and-such; 3) mild apocopation, in which the subject of the sentence is cut off from the verb as follows: one who does so-and-so, it [what he has done] is such-and-such; 4) "Extreme apocopation, in which a series of clauses is presented, none of them tightly joined to what precedes or follows and all of them cut off from the predicate of the sentence;" and 5) "contrastive complex predicate:" one who does . . . is unclean, and one who does not . . . is clean."[6]

Chaim Rabin distinguishes within the Hebrew of the Rabbinic literature a language he holds to have been a rival of Late Biblical Hebrew during the latter half of the second century B.C.E. He refers to a literary dialect whose grammar and syntax are those of Mishnaic Hebrew but whose vocabulary is an admixture of Biblical Hebrew and Rabbinic Hebrew. This language, which he finds embedded in M. Yeb. 16:7, B. Qid. 66a, and in Sifra Num. 22, is the Hebrew dialect found also in the standard prayers of the Rabbinic Liturgy. Its characteristics are 1) Mishnaic sentence construction; 2) biblical accretions in syntax and inflection; and 3) the open vocabulary of natural poetry.

Further investigation reveals more idiosyncratic styles within the corpora commonly understood to have been written and preserved in early and late Rabbinic or Mishnaic Hebrew. Common to the use of all these dialects by the Jewish men and women who, from the promulgation of the Mishnah until now, as an act of piety, read the documents of Judaism in these dialects is the conviction enshrined in and propagated by M. Meg. and M. Sot., that collectively these dialects belong to "the holy tongue." Many acts of piety, listed in M. Sot. 7:1, can be performed in any language; but if Hebrew indeed is the holy tongue, why avail oneself of this option at all?

Aramaic, Hebrew, and Arabic in the religion of the geonic period: Blau[7] explains that the phase of the Arabic language called Middle Arabic originated among the lower strata of the native urban population in the Middle East soon after and as a consequence of the great Arab conquest of the seventh century C.E. He holds that under Arab rule urban Jews and Christians began speaking Middle Arabic as early as the seventh century C.E. However, no Jewish literary works in this language have been preserved prior to the ninth century C.E.

When, in the geonic period, Middle Arabic replaced Aramaic as the common speech throughout the Middle East, Palestinian *yeshivot* began to study both geonic books of *halakah*, such as *Halakhot Pesuqot*, and Talmudic texts in translations in Rabbinic Hebrew. In Babylonia, however, the Aramaic of the Babylonian Talmud continued to be the language of Rabbinic scholarship as late as the time of Hai Gaon (939-1038). Hence the Babylonian geonim usually wrote their responsa in Aramaic, often with the use of some Arabic terms. Blau holds that the adoption of Middle Arabic in place of Aramaic for prose writings on religious subjects was facilitated by the fact that Aramaic had never set apart the Jews of Babylonia from their gentile neighbors. If, prior to the Muslim conquest, Aramaic was a language shared by Jews and non-Jews (Mann, pp. 446-47; 554), by the ninth century, Middle Arabic had replaced Aramaic as the shared language of Jew and gentile throughout the Middle East and as far West as Spain.

Blau points out that in the medieval period Jews wrote Arabic in a number of styles. In medical texts and in letters from persons in high places, where the assumed readership was not specifically Jewish, Classical Arabic, the official literary language of the Muslim majority, based upon the language of the Quran, was employed with some elements of the spoken language, Middle Arabic. Maimonides (1135-1204) employed this style also in his Commentary on the Mishnah and in his *Guide to the Perplexed.* A semi-classical Middle Arabic employed for religious texts and private correspondence is reflected in Maimonides' responsa. Blau points out that the general use by the Jews of the Hebrew script in writing Arabic clearly shows the barrier that separated the bulk of Jewry from Arabic and Islamic culture.

With some very minor exceptions,[8] from the ninth century on, Jews in the Islamic world composed poetry in Biblical Hebrew. Blau identifies two reasons for this: 1) no tradition of religious poetry in Arabic existed and 2) poetry, by its nature, would have been written not in colloquial Middle Arabic but in Classical Arabic, which was no more accessible than Hebrew. Moreover, Saadiah (882-942) encouraged the composition of liturgical poems in Hebrew, and he established rules for writing such poetry. Another reason for the composition of liturgical poetry in Hebrew is that the Mishnah, followed by both Talmuds, had treated Hebrew as the holy language of the liturgy. Consequently, both the elaborate liturgical poems of pre-Islamic Hebrew *payyetanim*, such as Yannai and Kallir, which never fully achieved the status of normative, and the anonymous geonic poems, which to this day almost universally introduce the middle blessing of the *amidah* in each of the four Sabbath services, were composed in varieties of Hebrew.

Rabbinic Hebrew in the writings of medieval Ashkenazic Jewry, Ibn Ezra, and Maimonides: In the High Middle Ages in Central and Western Europe both Jews and Christians conversed in a variety of Romance and Germanic dialects. A shared convention of both Jews and Christians was that most important writing, such as law and Bible commentary, was done only in the languages of civilization—Hebrew for Jews and Latin for Christians—and not in the vulgar tongues of day-to-day discourse. Banitt[9] argues convincingly that Rashi's main purpose when, some 4382 times in his biblical commentaries, he renders Biblical Hebrew and Aramaic words in Northern Old French and, occasionally, in other languages, such as German, Italian, and Provençal, is to correct mistaken exegeses perpetuated in the commonly accepted oral translation of the Scriptures into the spoken languages of European Jewry.

Banitt's assumption[10] that Rashi's commentary was compiled from notes taken by his students from lectures Rashi gave in French is contradicted by the assertion of Rashi's grandson, Samuel b. Meir, in his Pentateuch Commentary at Num. 34:2, that his grandfather had written a commentary replete with line drawings! This is corroborated by surviving manuscripts of Rashi's Bible commentaries from 1233 C.E. onward. Since Rashi did compose commentaries on both the Bible and the Babylonian Talmud in Rabbinic Hebrew, which is very close to the Hebrew of the halakhic and aggadic midrashim, the question of the religious significance of Rashi's linguistic usage, which differs markedly from the Hebrew of other medieval Hebrew commentators, arises. As noted by Banitt,[11] Christians early on saw in Rashi's Bible commentary a counterpart to their own *glossa ordinaria*, which was a Latin summary of the commentaries of the Church Fathers, written in the margins of the biblical text. By composing a commentary, which not only summarized halakhah and aggadah but also contained Rashi's own observations concerning grammar, lexicography, syntax, history, and refutations of Christian exegesis, all couched in the linguistic idiom of *midrash*, Rashi's commentary succeeded at one and the same time in conveying two messages: 1) his commentary was the Jewish counterpart to the *glossa ordinaria*, using philological science to refute the Christian commentary; 2) his commentary spoke in the name of Rabbinic Judaism, not in the name of an individual commentator of the high middle ages.

So long as he lived in his native Spain, part and parcel of the Islamic world, Abraham ibn Ezra wrote prose in Middle Arabic and poetry in Biblical Hebrew. He thus adhered to the use of the two languages possibly established by Saadiah. When, however, Ibn

Ezra began his travels in the Christian lands of Italy and France, he, like Ashkenazic Jews before and after Rashi, composed biblical commentaries in Rabbinic Hebrew. Moses Nahmanides' later employment of Rabbinic Hebrew in Bible commentaries written in Christian Spain could not help but convey the notion that what was expressed therein was no less normative than the normative statements about God, the world, and behavior originally expressed in that dialect in the post-70 C.E. era.

Meanwhile, Moses Maimonides, who normally wrote in Middle Arabic, had the audacity to produce the Mishneh Torah, a compendium of Jewish belief and practice, beginning with what one was to believe about God. He used a linguistic medium that, no less than the one chosen by Rashi, Ibn Ezra, and, later, Nahmanides for their biblical commentaries, said as much if not more than his book's contents. While these other authors adopted a language drawn primarily from post-Mishnaic eisegetical literature, Maimonides went back to the peculiar idiom of the Mishnah, Tosefta, and the normative statements attributed to Amoraim in the two Talmuds. Rashi and his disciples call this "Mishnah language." Maimonides thus conveyed the idea that his compendium was normative, like the Mishnah itself. He succeeded, for, whenever they agreed with him, the subsequent codes of halakah, such as the Tur and Shulhan Aruk, copied him verbatim.

The languages of the Zohar: The collection of four distinct compositions commonly published and referred to as the Zohar exhibits three distinct dialects. First is the Hebrew found in the Hebrew parts of the *Midrash ha-Ne'elam*. This Hebrew, like the Hebrew of medieval Ashkenazic exegetical literature discussed above, imitates the Hebrew of the Rabbinic midrashic literature of late antiquity. In fact, it is a typically thirteenth century philosophical Hebrew of Spanish provenance.

The second, principal, language of the Zohar is the Aramaic of portions of the *Midrash ha-Ne'elam* and of the Zohar's main body. Its vocabulary combines the full gamut of the Aramaic dialects of the Rabbinic canon, from the Aramaic of Daniel and Ezra through the Galilean Aramaic of the Jerusalem Talmud and the Babylonian Aramaic of the Babylonian Talmud. However, the vocabulary and forms of the Babylonian Talmud and of the Aramaic translations of Scripture, which the Babylonian Talmud had declared canonical, predominate, for these were the Aramaic compositions that were the basis of Judaism in thirteenth century Spain. In the very same way that Rashi's Hebrew exhibits numerous expressions translated from French, so does the Zohar, like Nahmanides, exhibit numerous expressions derived from Spanish.

The third language of the Zohar is the Aramaic of the *Ra'aya Mehemna* and *Tiqqunim*, the two latest parts of this literature. The Aramaic of the body of the Zohar already existed as a model for the author(s) of these compositions. These compositions' Aramaic is however distinguished from that of the main body of the Zohar by the increased use of words borrowed from Spanish philosophical Hebrew and from Spanish itself.

In the same way that nineteenth century Christian Hebraists disparaged Mishnaic Hebrew as a corrupt form of Biblical Hebrew, so do rationalistic Judaic scholars of the nineteenth and twentieth centuries continue to justify their disparagement of medieval and modern Jewish mysticism by arguing that, based on poor knowledge of Semitic linguistics, the author(s) of the Zohar wrote bad Hebrew and worse Aramaic. Menahem Zevi Kaddari, *The Grammar of the Aramaic of the "Zohar"* (Jerusalem, 1971), points out that the author(s) of the Zohar "thought his thoughts in Hebrew and translated them—with a varying measure of success—into his peculiar, literary Aramaic."

This view, however, misses the genius of the Zohar's language. Among the interesting linguistic features of this created dialect are 1) the expression of the passive by the Hebrew *pu'al* and *nitpa'el;* 2) the expression of the passive of the intensive and causative forms of the verb by the *etpe'el,* which in ancient Babylonian Aramaic is used only as the passive of the *qal* (*pe'al*); and 3) the

adoption from Biblical Aramaic of the internal passive conjugation *pe'il.* Indeed, contrary to views such at that of Kaddari, we might argue that the creation of the Zohar's artificial Aramaic dialect out of diverse sources is a mark of extreme sophistication, no less remarkable than the artificial dialect created by Canaanite scribes in the fourteenth century B.C.E. or Maimonides' use of the dialect of the Mishnah to compose a comprehensive presentation of the beliefs and obligations of Judaism.

What was the religious significance and purpose of the Zohar's language? Had the primary purpose been to create the impression that the work was from the pen of Simeon b. Yohai, the author could have followed Maimonides' lead and used the language of the Mishnah. Alternatively, he could have followed the lead of Ashkenazic exegetes, whom he knows well and whose views he incorporates, and written entirely in midrashic Hebrew. Had he wanted to be esoteric and historically authentic, he might have chosen to write in pure Galilean Aramaic. Indeed, lest it be supposed that the Zohar was written in Aramaic to make it esoteric, it should be noted that it successfully prescribed the addition of several Aramaic prayers to the common Jewish liturgy.

The Zohar's linguistic sophistication and literary erudition leave no doubt that its author was capable of following these paths. He chose instead to compose a work that shared with the Babylonian Talmud the use of an Aramaic dress or framework for Hebrew ideas. The message was that the Zohar speaks with an authority equal to or even greater than that of the foundational book of Judaism, the Babylonian Talmud. Indeed, the Zohar was so successful in commanding this authority that the Shulhan Aruk, for example, frequently establishes the law as according with the Zohar against the Talmud, a remarkable feat.

Yiddish and Judeo-Arabic: While disagreeing regarding the precise time and place at which Yiddish became the common spoken language of Ashkenazic Jewry, historians agree that it is already attested by the middle of the thirteenth century C.E. At the onset of

World War II an estimated eleven million persons regarded Yiddish as their native tongue. That figure accounts for slightly less than two thirds of the world Jewish population at the time.

Most of the remaining seven million Jews were represented by the Jews of Muslim countries, who continued to use Judeo-Arabic for both the study of Torah and mundane purposes, with Hebrew serving only as the language of the liturgy. Yemen represents an unusual Jewish culture, in which most males achieved fluency in reading, writing, and speaking Hebrew alongside Judeo-Arabic. Goitein[12] notes that the men composed and sang songs on religious themes in Hebrew, while the women composed and sang songs on secular themes in colloquial Arabic.

Aside from those who spoke and read Arabic, Yiddish, and Ladino, at the onset of World War II, there were Jews, mostly but not exclusively descendants of Jews whose native language was Yiddish or Spanish, who employed in the study of Torah Dutch, English, German, Hungarian, Russian, and other languages, including a variety of specifically Jewish Iranian dialects.

Late in the post-World War II era, the disparaging of Yiddish by both Jews and non-Jews finally was understood often to represent a disguised attack upon Judaism, the majority of whose adherents, annihilated by the Nazi death machine, had spoken Yiddish. This negative attitude towards Yiddish ignored the fact that Yiddish shares with English the essential characteristic—obvious to native speaker and stranger alike—that its primary vocabulary is made up of two distinct languages. These are Hebrew and Middle High German in the case of Yiddish, and Norman French and Anglo-Saxon in the case of English. Even so, until after World War II, when disparagement of things Jewish ceased to be considered polite, even many Yiddish speakers thought of Yiddish simply as a jargon composed of incorrect German with an admixture of Hebrew.

We have already seen that the charge that a particular written and spoken language is a jargon or a mistake has been leveled at other Jewish languages—Mishnaic Hebrew

and Zoharic Aramaic—primarily for ideological reasons. In all fairness, this way of thinking has not been applied to Jewish languages alone. Until epigraphic archaeology revealed that New Testament Greek was simply the dialect spoken in the Middle East at the beginning of the Christian era, this Greek had long been perceived as a corrupt form of Attic Greek.

Other reasons also explain modern Jews' continuing belief that Yiddish is not really a language but only a jargon. Besides the close resemblance of most of Yiddish's non-Hebraic elements to standard German, the medieval notion survives that certain languages, principally Latin and Hebrew, are legitimate vehicles for the written communication of serious ideas, especially about religious subjects, while other languages are corrupt tongues employed by the unlettered. Early in modern times French, German, and English were admitted to the exclusive club of languages of high culture; Yiddish and many other languages of Central and Eastern Europe were admitted to this club only much later. Interestingly, as a result of such thinking, even when the Jews of liberal religious tendencies in Hungary abandoned Yiddish, they initially wrote about Jewish religious subjects in German, not wishing to exchange the uncultured Yiddish for uncultured Hungarian. Not surprisingly, both Yiddish and Modern Hebrew emerge as literary languages for *belles lettres* as well as for the writing of treatises about Jewish religious subjects precisely in conjunction with the emergence of national literatures as an expression of national consciousness in the other minority languages of Central and Eastern Europe, such as Czech, Slovak, Serbian, Romanian (figs. 78-79).

However, long before the post-World War II era, when scholars writing about Jews and Judaism could not yet bring themselves to say "Yiddish" rather than Judeo-German, and long before learned treatises on Jewish religious subjects were composed in Yiddish, Jews throughout Central Europe to the borders of the Russian Empire (which did not admit Jews until the partitions of Poland in the eighteenth century) utilized Yiddish to transmit an oral translation of the Bible and as the language of the cultic act of Torah study at all levels. Consequently, Yiddish remained until the last three decades of the twentieth century the primary language of Torah study throughout the Jewish world.

Indeed, the study of Torah in other languages, such as English and Modern Hebrew, was long regarded as unsound both pedagogically and religiously. One unhealthy result of this use of Yiddish in advanced instruction in Orthodox institutions was the tendency of most American and Israeli Jews to identify the study of Torah with the negative stereotypes of Eastern Europe and the old *Yishuv*, with poverty and the failure to adopt the manners and norms of Western civilization. Even so, interestingly enough, part of the legacy of Yiddish as the main language of instruction in *yeshivot* for as many as 700 years is the fact that, while both Christians who earn doctorates in Judaic subjects in American universities and Israeli graduates of Orthodox high schools pronounce Biblical Hebrew with ultimate accent, as befits any proper Semitic language, including Modern Hebrew, they pronounce Rabbinic Hebrew with penultimate accent. This tradition derives from Yiddish, the sacred language of instruction in the pre-World War II *yeshivot* of Poland and Lithuania.

Among Yiddish-speaking Jewry it was customary for women in particular to recite non-liturgical prayers in Yiddish. Men, however, were expected by and large to satisfy their religious obligations by reciting the Hebrew liturgy, even though, for the majority of Yiddish-speaking Jewry, this was largely incomprehensible. It is indeed ironic how the disparagement of both Yiddish and women created for Yiddish-speaking women spiritual opportunities that the men denied themselves.

Ladino: In Christian Spain the term Ladino, a derivative of the terms *Latinus* and *latino*, which originally designated classical Latin, referred to Romance languages in general, as opposed to Arabic. Secondarily, the term Ladino referred to the refined form of Spanish employed for the translation of Scripture and liturgy. In the context of a Jew-ish language, spoken and written by Jews of the Ottoman Empire, Ladino designates a petrified fifteenth century Spanish written in Hebrew script and containing a significant component of Hebrew and Aramaic derived from Judaism's sacred canonical literature. Considering that, in 1492, the Jews of Spain were given the choice of converting to Christianity and remaining in Spain or stubbornly adhering to Judaism and leaving, Ladino came into being by virtue of a difficult and conscious decision in the realm of faith. The continued use of this language was a function of the self-definition of its speakers as a religious community.

The most popular work composed in Ladino was *Me'am Lo'ez*, a commentary on the Bible that interprets the Hebrew Scriptures in light of the entire corpus of Rabbinic and Kabbalistic literature. Begun by Jacob Culi (d. 1732), it was continued by other writers including the late nineteenth century Raphael Hiyya Pontremoli. Reading of this work individually or in groups was regarded as an act of piety. A Hebrew translation became very popular in modern Israel.

Judeo-Persian: Just as medieval Muslims in Arabic-speaking lands did not write Middle Arabic, so did Iranian Muslims not write their local dialects but rather a standard literary Persian. Consequently, so-called Judeo-Persian represents, in fact, the writing down in Hebrew script of a variety of local dialects shared by Jews and non-Jews. Significant to the history of Judaism is the writing down in such dialects from the fourteenth century C.E. onward of 1) translations of Hebrew Scripture; 2) treatises on biblical lexicography, which attest to familiarity with the whole gamut of Rabbinic literature as well as the writings of Saadiah, Hai Gaon, Rashi, Abraham Ibn Ezra, and David Kimchi; 3) Jewish poetry on biblical themes. Outstanding authors of such poetry were fourteenth century Mawlana Shahin of Shiraz and sixteenth century Imrani of Shiraz.

Authors who wrote on aspects of Judaism in Tajiki, the Iranian dialect of Bukharan Jewry, included the eighteenth century Yusuf al-Yahudi and the nineteenth century Simon Hakham, who produced a monumental translation of the Bible. Another important Iranian Jewish dialect, which has yet to be adequately studied, is Judeo-Tat.[13]

The Case of Ethiopian Jewry: Just as for Rabbanite and Karaite Jews Hebrew was the holy language of Scripture and liturgy while a variety of languages—some of them specific to Jews—were employed both for the study of Torah and for mundane purposes, so did both the Jews of Ethiopia (prior to their arrival in the State of Israel) and the Christians of Ethiopia employ Ge'ez as the holy language of Scripture and liturgy while employing other languages, principally Amharic, the official modern language of Ethiopia, in both the expounding of Scripture and daily life. For a minority of Ethiopian Jews the spoken language was not Amharic but Tigriniya.

Since, however, the liturgy of the Beta Israel, or Jews of Ethiopia, includes passages in Agau, which, unlike South Semitic Ge'ez, Amharic, and Tigriniya, is an Hamitic language, it has been surmised that Agau, the spoken language of Beta Israel residing in Quara and Semyen, may have preceded Ge'ez as the liturgical or sacred language of Ethiopian Jewry.

The traditional Sabbath worship of the Beta Israel includes the reading of the Pentateuch in Ge'ez followed by its explanation in Amharic. Obviously, this practice corresponds to the reading of the Torah in Hebrew followed verse by verse by translation into Aramaic or Greek, attested in M. Meg. 1:8.

Other Jewish languages: In addition to Hebrew, Aramaic, Arabic, Yiddish, and Ladino, the Jews created numerous other languages characterized by Hebrew and Aramaic elements and the use of Hebrew script. Among these were Judeo-Provençal and Judeo-Catalan. An interesting case is the Neo-Aramaic dialect of the Jews of Kurdistan, who call their vernacular "Targum." This name recognizes this tongue as a form of the language of the Babylonian Talmud's official Aramaic translations of Scripture, called in Aramaic "Targum," meaning "translation." Judeo-Greek writings included translations of Hebrew Scripture and liturgical poetry, while Judeo-Italian writings included dictionaries,

translations of the Bible, the prayer book, Maimonides' *Guide of the Perplexed*, a thirteenth century Lamentation for the Ninth of Av and a Hymn in Honor of Queen Sabbath by the sixteenth century Kabbalist, Mordecai b. Judah Dato. A special instance of a Jewish dialect that, because it was never committed to writing by its native speakers, did not utilize the Hebrew alphabet is Judeo-Berber, spoken in the Atlas Mountains of Morocco. Like other Jewish languages, it was used to interpret the sacred texts of Judaism for the masses of Jews for whom Hebrew was largely incomprehensible.

Reform Judaism and the State of Israel: For the first time in many centuries, emancipation, or the promise of it, enabled Jews throughout Europe to participate in what many Jews and most Christians perceived as a higher culture. In Protestant countries where church services were conducted in the vernacular, traditional Jewish religious services conducted in Hebrew with some Aramaic elements seemed to typify Judaism's belonging to a bygone era. Protestantism's liturgy, said and sung in the vernacular, seemed to form a spiritual ladder to heaven; the liturgy of the synagogue, in both script and language increasingly foreign to emancipated Jews, seemed a veritable barrier to spirituality. While the introduction of vernacular sermons and choral and instrumental music characterized many synagogues throughout nineteenth century Europe, the singing of liturgy and Scripture in the traditional Hebrew and Aramaic did not appear problematic in those countries in which the Roman Catholic or Eastern Orthodox majority shared with the Jews the singing of liturgies and the reading of Scripture in dead languages, such as Church Latin and Church Slavonic, which most people did not understand.

Understandably, then, Reform Judaism's commitment from its inception to public worship partly or largely in the vernacular was especially appealing in those places in which the vernacular was employed in churches of the host culture and in which Jewish children and adults had little or no knowledge of either the Hebrew alphabet or language. Not surprisingly, Reform Judaism spread most rapidly in areas such as the American mid-West, South, and far-West, far removed from major aggregates of Jews able to establish schools for the teaching of Hebrew. Early on, Reformers found justification for reciting the liturgy in the vernacular in M. Sot. 7:1, which sanctions recitation of the basic synagogue prayers, the *Shema* and *Tefillah*, "in any language." By contrast, Zechariah Frankel, the putative founder of Conservative Judaism, argued that the public recitation of the liturgy in a language other than Hebrew effectively cut off synagogue attendees from the original language(s) of the canonical literature of Judaism.

By the middle of the twentieth century the typical American Jewish community outside of major population centers had two synagogues, an Orthodox one attended primarily by members of the immigrant generation, who retained some rudimentary knowledge of Hebrew script, enabling them to follow the services without very much comprehension, and a Reform synagogue in which the services were conducted largely in English with a few Hebrew prayers read by the rabbi, who was often the only one present who could decipher Hebrew script. Any reasonable visitor might have found it utterly hopeless that the younger generation in either of these synagogues would ever learn enough to understand even the minimal amount of Hebrew read in the Reform setting.

Three things changed this: 1) The new State of Israel transformed Hebrew from a dead language to the living language of a modern country whose emergence and survival were perceived as miraculous. Overnight the study of Hebrew was seen as only slightly more astonishing than the study of French or Spanish. 2) The Conservative movement in American Judaism, followed later by other Jewish movements, organized summer camps at which children and teenagers learned to sing the traditional liturgy in Hebrew, study Rabbinic literature in Hebrew and Aramaic, and speak modern Hebrew as a living language. Back home these children helped for a time to transform Conservative Judaism into the most dynamic

movement in American Jewry, some of them becoming rabbis and Judaic scholars in America and Israel. 3) Modern Orthodoxy, eventually followed by the other movements, created a network of private schools that combined teaching and practice of Judaism, the study of the classic texts of Judaism in Hebrew and Aramaic, the standard curriculum of the public schools, and modern Hebrew as a language of instruction taught by native speakers.

In due course even the right wing Orthodox began to understand that the use of Hebrew as the native speech of Israelis made both the synagogue and the study of the classic religious documents of Judaism universally accessible to the inhabitants of the State of Israel. One consequence of these developments in American and Israeli Judaism is that at the close of the millennium, American and Israeli Jews of every political and religious bent cross seas and continents to teach the Hebrew alphabet (the Mishnah's "Assyrian script"), the Hebrew language, and the sacred texts of Judaism to Jews who had no inkling of the existence of these things but a few years before. Notwithstanding the precarious existence of the State of Israel and a 50% rate of intermarriage in the diaspora, many Jews at the end of the twentieth century see in the rebirth of Hebrew as the official language of a Jewish state whose capital is Jerusalem a clear replication of Judaism's paradigm of Exile and Redemption. This provides a great impetus to learn and teach the Rabbinic canon. After almost two thousand years, M. Sot. and M. Meg. seem to have succeeded in their long term investment in "the holy tongue."

Conclusion: Epigraphic archaeology indicates that when Rabbinic Judaism came into being in the first century C.E., the Jews of Palestine employed in everyday life both Greek and Aramaic and to a much lesser extant a Hebrew dialect now designated Middle Hebrew. It was widely believed by Jews in the Hellenistic and Roman world that Greek, no less than Hebrew, was a language of divine revelation, because, according to a widely propagated legend, the Old Greek translation of the Pentateuch was no less

God-given than was the Hebrew version said to have been dictated by God to Moses. Nevertheless, the seminal document of Rabbinic Judaism dared to declare Hebrew—i.e., the disparate Hebrew dialects of Hebrew Scripture, of the liturgy inherited from the Second Temple and elaborated upon by the rabbis, and the Middle Hebrew in which Bar Kokhba had corresponded and in which Judah the Patriarch composed the Mishnah—to be collectively "the holy tongue."

Judah and his disciples succeeded in making Hebrew the language of all authoritative statements about Judaism for almost two millennia. Their success rested, no doubt, on the good fortune that, in Palestine, a substantial group of Jews already spoke Middle Hebrew. Additionally, the claim that Hebrew was *the* holy tongue derived its credibility from the fact that, in this language, God had created the universe and talked to Moses and the prophets.

Hebrew survived as a sacred language of prayer and the reading of sacred texts at least in part because, for almost two millennia, most Jews lived in environments in which their gentile neighbors also prayed and read Scriptures in holy languages (Latin, Church Slavonic, Classical Arabic) that were not spoken in everyday life. What Jews did mirrored in some ways what everyone did.

However almost miraculously, the shift that occurred in other cultures did not take place in Judaism. For in about the middle of the twentieth century, when most Jews found themselves in a world in which other peoples prayed and read Scriptures in modern spoken languages, Hebrew itself was reemployed as the language of a modern state. Suddenly, the study of Hebrew seemed to be more analogous to the study of French, German, or Spanish than to the study of Latin and Greek. In fact, this outward secularity masked Hebrew's continuing theological significance. The State of Israel was perceived by Jews and many gentiles as an aspect of God's long-awaited redemption. Consequently, the revival of Hebrew as the official language of the state was viewed as part and parcel of the return of the Jews to the Holy Land, as a harbinger of the messianic age.

At the end of the second millennium, Jews the world over see study and teaching of Hebrew as an aspect of finding their roots and achieving a level of spirituality. So Hebrew continues to have the value the Talmudic rabbis achieved for it, a value it would not have had they taken the easier paths of adopting Greek or Aramaic as the language of liturgy, Scripture, and religious discourse.

Bibliography
Kutscher, Eduard Yechezkel, *A History of the Hebrew Language* (Jerusalem, 1982).
Paper, Herbert, ed., *Jewish Languages, Theme and Variations* (Cambridge, 1978).
Spiegel, Shalom. *Hebrew Reborn* (Cleveland, 1962).
Weinreich, Max, *History of the Yiddish Language* (Chicago, 1980).

Notes
[1] "Bilingualism and the Beginnings of Translation," in Michael Fox, et al., eds., *Texts, Temples and Traditions* (Winona Lake, 1996), pp. 345-357.
[2] Elisha Qimron and John Strugnell, *Miqsat Ma'ase Ha-Torah* (Oxford, 1994), p. 108.
[3] Ibid.
[4] M.H. Segal, *A Grammar of Mishnaic Hebrew* (Oxford, 1927).
[5] Ibid., p. 4; Jacob Neusner, *The Discourse of the Bavli* (Atlanta, 1991), p. 12.
[6] Jacob Neusner, *Judaism as Philosophy* (New York, 1991), p. 282.
[7] Joshua Blau, *The Emergence and Linguistic Background of Judeo-Arabic: A Study of the Origins of Middle Arabic* (Jerusalem, 1981).
[8] See M. Steinschneider, "Introduction to the Arabic Literature of the Jews," *JQR* (old series), 12 [1900], pp. 312-313.
[9] Menahem Banitt, "Une langue fantome: le judéo-français," in *Revue de linguistiqueromane* 27 (1963), pp. 245-294.
[10] Op. cit., p. 10, n. 18; cf. p. 4, n. 14.
[11] Op. cit., p. 131.
[12] S.D. Goitein, "Women as Creators of Biblical Genres," in *Prooftexts* 8 (1988), pp. 1-8.
[13] Herbert Paper, ed., *Jewish Languages, Theme and Variations* (Cambridge, 1978).

MAYER GRUBER

LIFE CYCLE IN JUDAISM: Judaism defines a divinely ordained system of required behaviors, referred to as *mitzvot*, fulfillment of which expresses acquiescence to the divine will. Among these behaviors, life cycle ceremonies enhance worship of God by elevating otherwise ordinary moments into opportunities to fulfill God's demands. Even as life under foreign rule and over a period of thousands of years has created many distinctive Jewish cultures, through life cycle rituals, the Jewish people have maintained and been united by a not-quite-national, not-merely-religious, something-other-than-cultural, and more-than-just-ethnic identity. Life cycle ceremonies bind together Jews everywhere, enriching their lives both in the immediate physical and temporal present and in an imagined eternal and timeless realm. Through these celebrations, Jews sanctify crucial moments in individual and communal life, connecting each Jew to his or her family, each family to the community, and each community to the entire Jewish people and the entirety of Jewish history.

Birth: Creating new life by bringing children into the world is one of the most sacred and cherished duties under Jewish law, and the life cycle rituals surrounding birth reflect this special importance (fig. 80). In the ceremonies of baby naming, circumcision, and redemption of the first born, the newborn is brought into the fold and given a place among the Jewish people.

Brit milah, literally, "covenant of circumcision," often referred to in the Ashkenazic pronunciation, *bris milah*, or, simply, *bris*, is the religious rite of removal of the foreskin (prepuce) on the eighth day after the birth of a male child (figs. 43-44). Circumcision is a physical sign of the covenant between God and Israel, established with Abraham, reaffirmed at Sinai, and passed on through every generation. The significance of this biblical injunction, as understood by Jews today, is exemplified by the unique status of circumcision in Jewish law. Fulfillment of the commandment on the eighth day is so important that it takes precedence over the Sabbath; additionally, to be considered a Jew, even adult converts must undergo circumcision. Circumcision thus marks a boundary issue for Jews, defining who is a Jew; it is of such importance that even those who are the most marginal to the modern community continue to circumcise their sons.

The traditional ceremony, maintained especially by Orthodox and Conservative Jews, comprises four basic elements in which the mohel ("circumciser") performs the three necessary elements of circumcision: *milah*—the cutting off of the foreskin; *periah*—the tearing off and folding back of the mucous membrane to expose the glans; and *metzitzah*—the sucking of the blood from the wound. The other principal religious actors consist of the baby's father, the sandek (holder of the baby), and, in some communities, guests the family wishes to honor with participation. Literary evidence suggests that the liturgy for the circumcision ceremony was fixed during the medieval period, when a liturgical foundation from the Talmudic period was elaborated upon.[1]

Redemption of the first born (*pidyon haben*): Scripture assigns a special status to firstborns of humans, animals, and even fruit trees. A first born son, like all first "fruits," is to be dedicated to the service of God (Exod. 13:2, Num. 8:17, 8:6, 3:13); a rite of redemption is used as a symbolic release from this requirement of cultic service.

Following Scripture's explicit designation for God of one who "opens the womb," only a male child born vaginally is subject to the obligation of the first born and, hence, must be redeemed (B. Bek. 46a); those born of Cesarean section are exempt (Exod. 13:2, B. Bek 19a, 47b). Also, those born into the tribe of Levi, which includes members of the priestly caste, are exempt, as is the first born of the daughter of a priest (Exod. 13:2, B. Bek 13a). Following the explicit statement of Num. 3:40, redemption takes place when the child is a minimum of thirty days old (B. Bek. 49a, B. Men. 37a). Usually, the ceremony is performed on the thirty-first day (B. Bek. 49a), unless that day is a Sabbath or festival, when it occurs on the day following instead. The obligation to redeem the child falls on the father, but it may be fulfilled by the mother, grandparent, or court, if the father is unwilling or unable. A first born who was not redeemed as an infant can later redeem himself.

The redemption ceremony takes place at a *seudat mitzvah*, a celebratory meal such as accompanies many life cycle ceremonies. After ritual hand washing and breaking of bread, the child is brought in, often on a decorative tray. The father declares, "This

Figure 78. Wedding in the Forest (Chatunah Vaya'ar), by Ya'akov David Kamson, illustrated by Else Wentz-Vitar, Berlin, Germany, c. 1925. Secular books in Hebrew were a nineteenth century innovation. Previously, Hebrew was used only for prayer and the study of holy texts.

Figure 79. Three girls study Hebrew books at a synagogue in Tashkent, Uzbekistan, 1993.
Photograph by Zion Ozeri.

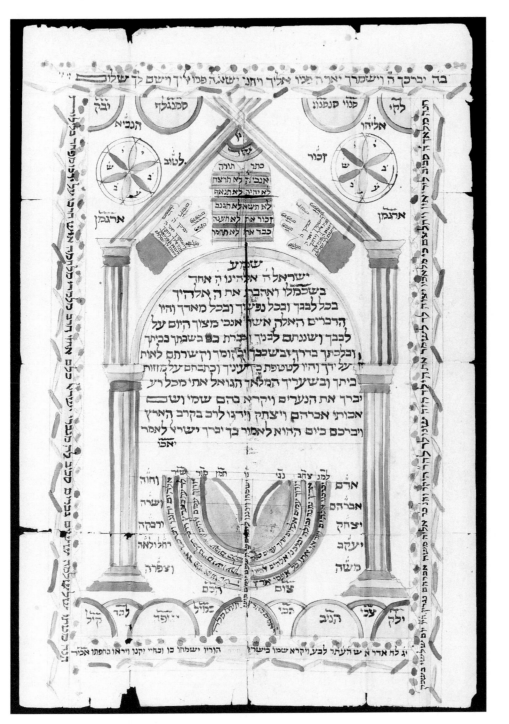

Figure 80. Aleph, an illuminated amulet created for the birth of Chaim (Herman) Negrin, dated according to the Hebrew calendar, 5670. Ioannina, Greece, 1910.

Figure 81. *Bar Mitzvah* boy of the Aronson family, New York, early 1900s.

Figure 82. *Bar Mitzvah* boy Hirsh Boyarsky with his parents, Rose and Louis, Brooklyn, June 12, 1960. Hirsh was born in Germany to Holocaust survivor parents. The family immigrated to the United States in 1948.

Figure 83. Brooklyn Hebrew Orphan Asylum girls at the time of their confirmation, Brooklyn, New York, 1920s.

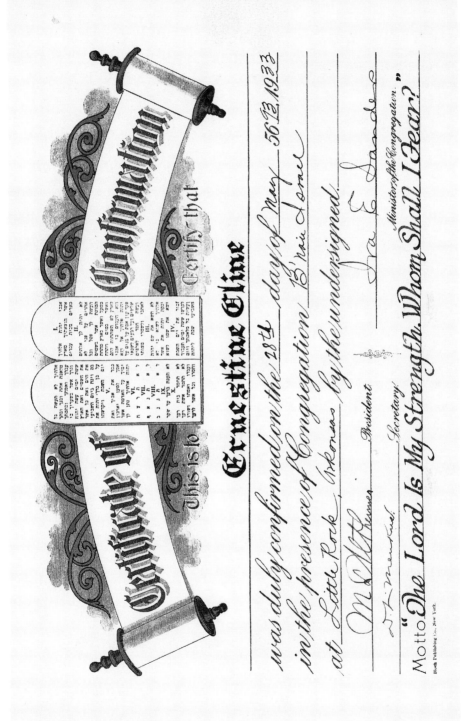

Figure 84. Confirmation certificate given to fifteen-year-old Ernestine Cline by Temple B'nai Israel, Little Rock, Arkansas, May 28, 1933.

Figure 85. Confirmation class on the steps of Congregation B'nai Israel, Little Rock, Arkansas, May 28, 1933.

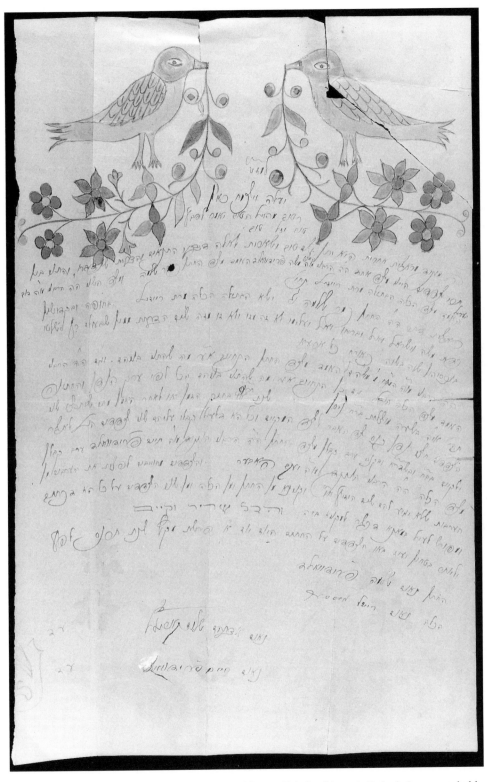

Figure 86. Engagement contract uniting Shlomo Friedwald and Raizel Isser, probably United States, late nineteenth century. This contract *(tna'im)* anticipates a wedding in the Hebrew month of Nisan.

Figure 87. Handwritten engagement *(tna'im)* and marriage contract *(ketubbah)* of Hayim Eliezer, son of Abraham Israel and D'vorah, daughter of David Mordechai, Teheran, Iran, 1898. The conditions of the *tna'im* are written in Judeo-Persian on the sides of the document.

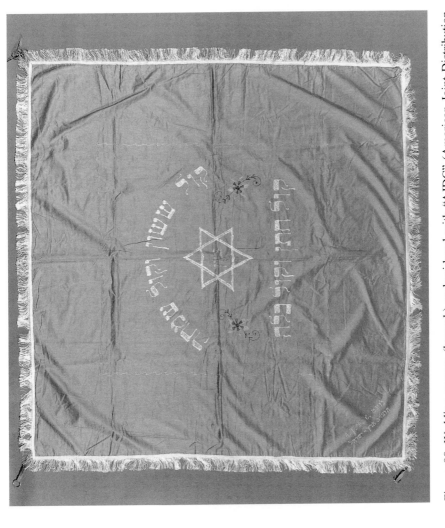

Figure 88. Wedding canopy (huppah) embroidered with "AJDC" (American Joint Distribution Committee), Palestine, c. 1945. Wedding canopies were made in Palestine for the JDC, to be used by Holocaust survivors who married in Displaced Persons camp.

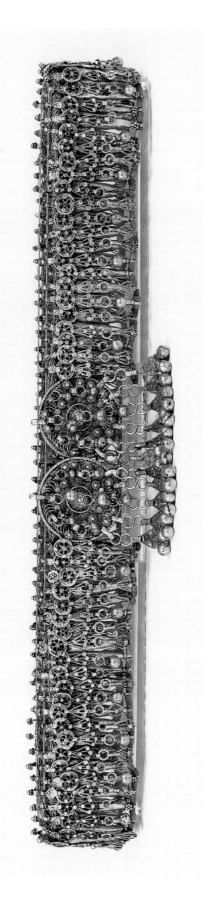

Figure 89. Wedding belt made of silver filigree with coral beads, Sana'a, Yemen, c. 1890. The Jewish silversmiths of Yemen were renowned for their fine craftsmanship.

Figure 90. Else Buxbaum and Seligmann Baer Bamberger celebrate their wedding, Würzburg, Germany, May 26, 1921.

Figure 91. Libus Seidenfeld and Max Rooz record their wedding day with a family portrait in the garden of the Seidenfeld home, Munkacs, Czechoslovakia, c. 1928-1929.

Figure 92. Jewish funeral in Allendorf, Germany, 1927.

Figure 93. Irwin, Yetta, and Sarah Maurer and Mani Steiller visit the grave of Shlomo Zalman ben Peretz ha-Levi and Yaakov ben-Zvi, Tarnow, Poland, 1922.

child is the first-born of his mother, and the holy one, blessed be he, has commanded that he be redeemed," followed by passages from Num. 18:16 and Exod. 13:2. The Kohen—a member of the priestly caste, who receives the redemption money in place of the child—then asks in Aramaic, "Which do you prefer: to give away your firstborn son, who is the first issue of his mother's womb, or to redeem him for five shekels, as you are required to do by the Torah?" The father indicates the latter and recites the blessing that pertains to the commandment of redemption, followed by the *shehekhianu*-blessing, which thanks God for allowing those present to have reached this milestone event. The priest accepts the money—five silver dollars are often used in the United States today—and, while swinging it in a circular fashion over the baby's head, says:

> This instead of that; this in exchange for that; this is pardoned because of that. May this son enter into life, into Torah, and into fear of heaven. May it be your will that just as he has entered into this redemption, so shall he enter into Torah, the marriage canopy, and good deeds. Amen.

The priest then blesses the baby, hands him back to the father, and blesses the wine. The meal follows the ceremony and is concluded with a special recitation of the Grace after Meals.

Baby naming: While Jews cherish the birth of a girl equally to that of a boy, no commandments comparable to circumcision or redemption apply. As a result, until recently, elaborate ceremonies have not accompanied a female birth. Traditionally, the baby has only been formally named, usually on the first Sabbath after birth, though this may be done on any day that the Torah is read during synagogue worship. In the traditional ceremony, the baby need not even be present. Rather, during the Torah reading, the father is called to the Torah (*aliyah*), and, after his participation in the reading, a blessing is recited for the mother and newborn. First, the mother is blessed "with her daughter who has been born to her in good fortune and for which her husband has come up to the Torah." After she is wished a complete re-

covery, the new baby is blessed and named with the formula: "let her name in Israel be _____ daughter of _____ (the father's Hebrew name)." As in the naming of a boy at the end of the circumcision ceremony, it then is urged that her parents are able to raise her to "Torah, the marital canopy, and good deeds."

Rites of passage: While the concept of a legal age of majority has always been fundamental to Jewish law and practice, the idea of celebrating the attainment of that age is comparatively new. The Torah does not explicitly mention an age necessary for religious majority, specifying only twenty as the minimum age at which one becomes required to bear arms (Num. 1). Nevertheless, the centuries old bar mitzvah ceremony and the fairly recent confirmation ceremony have become powerful rites of passage for adolescent Jews, their families, and the community at large.

Bar/Bat Mitzvah: This term, designating one who has become subject to the commandments, applies to a boy who has completed his thirteenth year or a girl who has completed her twelfth. These children now are considered adults and may serve as full participants in religious matters. They are responsible for fulfillment of all commandments appropriate to their gender and are liable to punishment or sanction for failure to fulfill religious obligations. Although one becomes bar/bat mitzvah—subject to the commandments as an adult—regardless of whether a formal acknowledgment has been made, the practice of the bar mitzvah ceremony—for boys—has been standard since at least the fourteenth century. The bat mitzvah ritual for girls is of much more recent origin.

The designation "bar mitzvah" appears first in the Talmud, where it refers to every grown member of the Jewish people (B. B.M. 96a). Thus it is synonymous with the Rabbinic terms *gadol*, meaning "adult," and *bar onshin*, literally, "subject to punishment." It also is used to refer to the time an individual reaches physical maturity (B. Kid. 16b). Soferim 18:7 speaks of taking the new bar mitzvah to the priests in the Temple in Jerusalem to receive a blessing. In the midrash, the age of thirteen is emphasized. According to Pirke d'Rabbi Eliezer 26, Abraham rejected his father's idols at this age. Gen. Rabbah 63:10, on Gen. 35:27, explains that Jacob and Esau parted ways at thirteen, with Jacob going to study Torah and Esau to worship idols. At thirteen a child becomes responsible for his own sins; until that point he relies on the merit of his father, who is responsible for him (Yalk. Ruth 600).

The first reference to a bar mitzvah ceremony comparable to the one still used today appears in the writings of Mordechai ben Hillel, cited by Jacob Halevi and Moses Isserles (Darkhe Moshe, Orah Hayyim 225:1). This ceremony consists of three basic parts: 1) a blessing recited by the father who, after being called to the Torah for an aliyah, thanks God for removing his responsibility for the sins of his son (*barukh shepetarani*) and the son's first time being called to participate in the reading of the Torah; 2) the *derashah*, in which the young adult delivers a Talmudic discourse; and 3) the *seudah*, a festive meal and communal celebration in honor of the bar mitzvah. This ceremony may occur on any day that the Torah is read, although most frequently it takes place on Sabbath morning. The regular worship service is performed but in a more festive atmosphere, often with the bar mitzvah leading all or part of the prayers. During the Torah service, the bar mitzvah generally reads the prophetic portion (haftarah), and often reads part or all of the Torah lection as well. The *derashah* traditionally is a Talmudic discourse and remains so in the Orthodox community; in many settings, however, it has become an opportunity for thanking parents and teachers and giving a more general speech (figs. 81-82).

In traditional Judaism, women do not lead congregational worship, so that, until recently, the bar mitzvah ceremony was used for boys alone. The bat mitzvah ceremony, which celebrates a young woman's maturation, was introduced in the United States by Mordechai Kaplan, the founder of Reconstructionist Judaism, in 1922, to mark his daughter's religious coming of age (fig. 117). It became widespread in the United States in the decades following World War II. In egalitarian synagogues, especially of the Reform, Reconstructionist, and Conservative movements, the bat mitzvah celebration is indistinguishable from the bar mitzvah of a boy, with the girl reciting the Torah, haftarah, and other prayers in the synagogue. In traditional settings, by contrast, the bat mitzvah often is marked at home or in school, not in the setting of public worship, in which women do not participate. In some orthodox settings, the father and brothers of the bat mitzvah are called to the Torah, followed by a special sermon given by or about the young woman.

Confirmation: Emphasizing that bar mitzvah age children are to immature to appreciate the seriousness of their coming of age, in the beginning of the nineteenth century in Germany, the Reform movement introduced to Judaism the confirmation rite. Borrowed from Protestant Christianity, confirmation originally was intended to replace the bar mitzvah celebration. Only later did it become an additional ceremony, usually marked together by an entire class of religious school students around age sixteen and during the holiday of Pentecost, which marks God's covenant with Israel (figs. 83-85). Since there is no traditional formula for this celebration, each class and each community develops its own ceremony, often combining declarations of faith, inspirational speeches, and music. Confirmation is not practiced in the Orthodox community, where it is generally derided as having no roots in Judaism.

Marriage: With the family unit at the center of Jewish life, the creation of a new family represents the continuity of the Jewish people and is awarded a very special place in Jewish tradition. As in other life cycle events, through the marriage ceremony, an otherwise personal event—a man and woman's consummating of their love—becomes an opportunity for the involvement of family, friends, and community and an occasion on which the individual's personal history is viewed on the backdrop of the past history and future salvation of the Jewish people as a whole.

The idea of the union of a man and woman in marriage goes back to the earliest biblical narratives and is dealt with extensively in the Rabbinic literature, which emphasizes marriage's primacy in Jewish Life. The Talmud states, "He who has no wife is not a proper man" (B. Yeb. 63). Similarly, the Shulkhan Arukh, definitive source of Jewish law, equates one who denies his instincts and fails to produce children with one who "shed blood, diminished the image of God, and made the Shekhinah depart from Israel." Conversely, "If one loves his wife as himself and honors her more than himself. . . .— of such a one, Scripture says, 'And you shall know that your tabernacle shall be in peace and you shall visit your habitation and you shall not sin' (Job 5:24)" (B. Yeb. 62b).

Historically, arranged marriages were common, and the matchmaker played an important role in Jewish life. Still, romance also has been known throughout history, and, in modern times, obviously, it is most common for individuals to choose for themselves who they marry. This idea is known as early as the Mishnah, which holds that, on the Day of Atonement and the fifteenth of Ab, unmarried girls dressed in white headed to the fields where men waited to choose brides.

In the Talmudic and medieval periods, the engagement of a man and woman was formalized in a ceremony called *shidukhin*, at which the financial conditions of the marriage (*tenaim*) were set (figs. 86-87). Today, some communities practice what is known as a *wort* (Yiddish for "word"), at which the couple informally announces the engagement, while the *tenaim* ceremony takes place immediately prior to the wedding. Generally, on the Sabbath prior to the wedding, the groom—in egalitarian communities, bride and groom—is honored with an aliyah and sometimes is showered with rice, nuts, or candy, in a tradition known in Yiddish as *aufruf*. According to the Jewish laws of family purity, the woman must immerse herself in a ritual bath (*mikveh*) before having sexual relations, so this too must take place before the wedding. Various other customs, not related to the actual wedding, are known. In some communities, the bride and groom do not see each other for a specified period of time; there is a distinctly Ashkenazic custom

of cemetery visitation at the graves of deceased parents; and we find the Oriental *hinnah* ceremony, in which the hands of the bride are painted red. Because marriage is viewed as a new beginning, it also is customary before the ceremony for both bride and groom to fast and to recite the confession of sins normally said during the afternoon service of the Day of Atonement.

Weddings may take place on any day other than a Sabbath, festival, day of public mourning, or during the period between Passover and Pentecost. The reason is that one may neither mix the holiness of a wedding with the holiness of a holiday, nor lesson the joy of the wedding with the sadness of mourning or other unhappiness (B. Bes. 36b-37a; B. M.K. 8b; Sh. Ar. OH 546, 339:4, 551:2, 493:1). Likewise, weddings are generally postponed in the event that a relative of the bride or groom dies, such that he or she becomes a mourner (B. Ket. 3b-4a). According to the Mishnah, virgins were wed on Wednesday, widows Thursday (M. Ket. 1:1), although this custom is not generally followed today.

Usually, the wedding takes place in the synagogue, but it may be performed anywhere. Some groups, including Hasidim, perform the ceremony outdoors. In all cases, the ceremony takes place under a wedding canopy (*huppah*), which may be elaborate or as simple as a prayer shawl supported on four sides (fig. 88). The canopy symbolizes the marital union and the couple's building a new home together. Although Jewish law does not require that a rabbi perform the ceremony, this has become customary. Preferably, the wedding ceremony should take place in the presence of quorum (*minyan*). Prior to the ceremony, the marriage contract (*ketubah*) is completed, signed by two witnesses, and acquired symbolically by the groom. Other pre-wedding customs found in some communities have no direct relationship to the wedding. These include a scholarly discourse offered by the groom, ashes placed on the forehead of the groom in memorial of the Temple in Jerusalem, and a ceremony known in Yiddish as *bedeken di kale*, in which the groom lowers the veil over the face of the bride and blesses her. Then candles are lit and the bride and groom are led in a procession to the *huppah*, where the actual ceremony takes place.

While Scripture makes no specific reference to a marriage ceremony, the rabbis interpret "taking a wife" (Deut. 24:1) to refer to a legal transaction in which the groom acquires the bride as property. The Talmudic literature knows three methods by which this acquisition may be effected: the acceptance by the bride of an object of monetary value, such as a ring or coin; a betrothal/consecration ceremony (referred to as *erusin* or *kiddushin*) that includes a written contract (*ketubah*); or through intercourse. Today, all three elements are combined in the wedding ceremony. Indeed, by the medieval period, Rabbinic legal decisors rejected the idea that a marriage could be completed through intercourse or monetary exchange alone, without a public consecration ceremony.

Today the *erusin* consists of two components: a sanctification ceremony with blessings and, at the heart of the legal transaction, the exchange of the ring. After the groom is escorted to the *huppah* in a procession that typically includes parents, the officiating rabbi says: "Blessed is the one who has come; may the one who is powerful . . . blessed . . . great . . . supreme above all bless the bride and groom." The bride approaches the groom and, in traditional ceremonies, circles him three or seven times, depending on custom. The rabbi then says: "Blessed is the one who has come; may the one who understands the speech of the rose among the thorns, the love of a bride, who is the joy of the beloved ones, bless the groom and the bride." The bride now stands to the right of the groom, facing the spot where the Temple in Jerusalem once stood. The rabbi recites a blessing over the wine, then one thanking God for detailing forbidden unions, followed by the bride and groom's drinking from the wine cup. At this point the groom, holding an unadorned gold ring (some communities use a coin) proclaims, "Behold, you are consecrated to me with this ring according to the law of Moses and Israel," after which he places the ring on the bride's index finger.

Now the *ketubah*, the marriage contract, is publicly read.

The ketubah enumerates the husband's ten obligations to his wife and his four rights to her property. He must provide her with sustenance and maintenance, and he is obligated to cohabit with her. Other obligations include alimony upon dissolution of the marriage, payment of medical expenses, a commitment to ransom her from captivity, to pay burial and related expenses, to support her and minor daughters through his estate upon his death, and to bequeath his property to the sons of the marriage. The husband's rights concern her property, for he is in essence acquiring her, and that entitles him to her property as well. Thus he has a right in her handiwork, property she discovers by chance, property she already owns, and he is the sole benefactor of her estate.

After the reading of the *ketubah*, the *nissuin*, sometimes referred to as *huppah*, follows. In ancient times the *huppah* likely was a tent in which the marriage was consummated. Today the marriage bond is created through the pronouncement by the officiating rabbi or anyone else of seven blessings (*shevah berakhot*).[2] The first blessing is pronounced over wine; the second refers to God's creating everything for his honor; the third recognizes God for fashioning the human being; the fourth expands upon the third, mentioning that human beings were fashioned in God's image; the fifth asks that God bring intense joy and exultation to the barren one—Zion—through the ingathering of her children; the sixth asks God to gladden the beloved companions as he gladdened Adam and Eve in Eden; the final blessing captures the messianic significance of the creation of each new family unit:

> Blessed are you, Lord our God, ruler over the universe, who created joy and gladness, groom and bride, mirth, glad song, pleasure, delight, love, fellowship, harmony, and companionship. Lord our God, let there soon be heard in the cities of Judah and the streets of Jerusalem the sound of joy and the sound of gladness, the voice of the groom and the voice of the bride, the sound of the groom's jubilance from their canopies and the youths from their feasts of song. Blessed are you,

Lord, who gladdens the groom with the bride.

Now groom and bride drink the wine, and, in the second stage of the *nissuin*, the groom steps on and breaks a glass, a memorial, it generally is believed, of the destruction of the Jerusalem Temple. The marriage celebration now is completed with *yihud*, a brief period of time that the bride and groom spend secluded together, representing symbolic consummation of the marriage. Thus, even if the validity of the present-day *huppah* ceremony were to be challenged, the couple would be deemed married under the Talmudic standard of cohabitation (Mishneh Torah, Ishut 10:1; Shulkhan Arukh EH 55:1).

Following the ceremony, the wedding is celebrated at a reception and then by seven days of festive meals and a full year of private rejoicing (figs. 90-91). This follows biblical precedent, since Genesis refers to Laban's gathering all the people for the wedding feast of Jacob and Leah (Gen. 29:22). At Gen. 29:27, he asks Jacob to "complete the week of this one"—understood to refer to a protracted wedding celebration—before continuing to work towards acquiring Rachel as a bride. The bridal week also appears at Judg. 14:12, where Samson allows the guests the seven days of the wedding feast to solve his riddle. At the initial wedding meal and the festive meals on each of the subsequent nights, the Grace after Meals includes a special introduction and a repetition of the seven blessing initially recited under the wedding canopy. To take part in this communal celebration, traditionally, couples remained at home for at least the first week following marriage. During this entire week, the groom is required to stay with the bride (B. Ket. 3a), ensuring that he devotes all his energies to her. The couple remains in a state of private celebration for the next full year, exempting the groom from certain ritual obligations and, in ancient times, from military service.

Forbidden marriages, divorce, Levirate marriage: A marriage is dissolved by the death of one partner, through the completion of a divorce procedure, or, in the case of a prohibited union, by a court. The seriousness of the rules governing these circumstances demonstrates the primacy of marriage in Jewish life.

While all efforts are made to encourage a husband and wife to remain together, Jewish law enumerates specific grounds for divorce, which normally entails the husband's giving the wife a *get*, that is, a writ of divorce. He may initiate the divorce on the grounds of her adultery, apostasy, immoral behavior, refusal of conjugal rights, inability to bear children, incurable disease, mental illness, refusal to cohabit, or in light of defects/diseases present before marriage but unknown to him. While a wife may not herself prepare a *get* so as to divorce her husband, where she alone desires divorce, she may petition a religious court (*bet din*), which has the power to compel the husband to divorce her. Grounds for such an action include his immoral behavior, habitual cruelty, incurable disease, engagement in an occupation that makes him revolting and prohibits cohabitation, sterility, refusal of conjugal rights, apostasy, refusal to support her, or if he has fled the country because of criminal behavior.

While such considerations are largely theoretical and hardly applied in the modern world, two sorts of conditions exist in which a court may initiate divorce without the petition of either party. In the first type of case, the marriage, though forbidden, is considered valid, so that a *get* is required. Such circumstances include marriage between incestuous relatives not of a close degree, marriage of a priest to a divorcee, marriage between a childless widow who has not been released from her obligation to marry her deceased husband's brother (Levirate marriage), a marriage in which the wife has engaged in adultery and the husband neglects himself to initiate divorce, and cases in which health considerations prevent intercourse. A second sort of circumstance does not require a *get*, for the marriage was never recognized to begin with. Such instances include an incestuous marriage between close relatives, marriage to a previously married woman who has not obtained a *get*, and cases in which a wife leaves her husband.

Ordinarily, death poses no problem for the dissolution of marriage. Still, various restrictions may apply, primarily controlling the widow's remarriage. She must wait a minimum of three months before remarrying, so that there is no question of correctly identifying the father of any child she subsequently carries. A nursing mother may not remarry until the child is weaned. Finally, a woman whose husband disappears but is not known to be dead may not remarry until adequate evidence of his death is manifest.

Levirate marriage takes place between a widow who's husband died childless and his brother (known as the levir). Halizah ("removal") is a ceremony that releases the woman from the obligation of Levirate marriage, allowing her to marry someone else. Although Levirate marriage itself no longer is practiced, traditional Jews still require halizah, formally releasing the widow from the biblically required union with her brother-in-law. The ceremony takes place before a court of five men, at least three of whom must be rabbis. In an initial meeting, the widow and levir are questioned regarding their desire not to marry, and instructions are given regarding the declarations that each must pronounce in Hebrew; the woman also is instructed to fast until the ceremony. In the ceremony, which takes place on the following day, a special shoe is removed from the levir's foot. The woman approaches him and proclaims in Hebrew, "My husband's brother refuses to raise up unto his brother a name in Israel; he will not perform the duty of a husband's brother unto me," to which he replies, "I do not want to take her." The widow then removes the shoe from his foot, tosses it away, and spits on the floor in front of him, saying, "So shall it be done unto the man that does not build up his brother's house, and his name shall be called in Israel, the house of him that had his shoe loosened." All present respond three times in unison, "he that had his shoe loosened." Concluding prayers are read by the judges, and often a certificate that the widow is free to remarry is drawn up.

Conversion: A *ger* (proselyte; literally, "stranger;" "client") is an individual born of a faith other than Judaism who undergoes the requirements of ritual immersion, circumcision (for males), and the instruction necessary to be counted as a member of the Jewish people.[3] Upon completion of these requirements, the proselyte is considered to achieve a new identity and is regarded as a Jew in every respect. B. Yeb. 47a elucidates the conversion procedure:

> If at the present time a man desires to become a proselyte, he is to be addressed as follows: "What reason do you have for becoming a proselyte? Do you not know that Israel at the present time is persecuted and oppressed, despised, harassed, and overcome by afflictions?" If he replies, "I know and yet am unworthy," he is accepted forthwith and given instructions in some of the minor and major commandments . . . he is also told of the punishment for the transgressions of the commandments . . . and the reward granted for their fulfillment.

During First and Second Temple times, a proselyte brought a sacrifice as well as undergoing circumcision and immersion, although, when a sacrifice was not possible, only circumcision and immersion were required (B. Ker. 9a). Conversion takes place before a religious court of three members (B. Yeb. 46b-47a). A proselyte is considered to undergo a spiritual rebirth and so is like a newborn child with no relation to his prior family (B. Yeb. 22a). Questions in the Mishnah regarding a proselyte's right to refer to the "God of our fathers" were settled by Maimonides in his letter to Obadiah, where he deemed proselytes to be children of Abraham through a spiritual connection.

For adults, the conversion procedure begins when, in the presence of two witnesses, the prospective proselyte is questioned regarding his or her knowledge of Judaism and intention to uphold the commandments. The ceremony then has two main components, circumcision (for men) and ritual immersion in a mikveh. The circumcision operation takes place in the presence of a religious court and resembles the ceremony for circumcising a newborn child. If the man already is circumcised, a very small amount of blood is drawn, a ritual act for the purpose of membership in the Jewish people. For women and men, the ceremony concludes with immersion followed by the recitation of the blessing for the immersion and the *shehekhianu*, used on all joyous occasions. While, generally, blessings are recited before performing a ritual act, in this case, the individual becomes a Jew only through the immersion; the blessings may be recited only once this transformation has taken place. Now the new convert also is welcomed to the Jewish people and given a Jewish name, the formula of which indicates that his or her father is the patriarch Abraham. Often, a male proselyte will don prayer shawl and phylacteries, and both men and women fulfill the commandment of saying the Shema-prayer for the first time.

The same basic formula is followed for children, with the exceptions that their parents are questioned regarding their intent to raise the child in the traditions of Judaism. Very small children are immersed by a member of the bet din, and if the child is too small to recite the blessing over the immersion, it is omitted. Additionally, the prayer welcoming the child and assigning a Jewish name is taken from the circumcision liturgy.

From its inception, the Reform movement rejected the two main components of conversion, circumcision and immersion, favoring instead only education and a declaration of faith. This has caused much controversy both in the United States and Canada and in Israel, where opinions differ over who may be considered a Jew according to religious law. Founders of the Reform movement were warm towards converts, and many actually were in favor of Jewish proselytizing. This led to much heated debate among Rabbinic authorities, and many of these repercussions are still felt today. Traditional Jews do not recognize the validity of non-Orthodox conversions, stressing that alongside circumcision and immersion, a convert must accept the responsibility to fulfill all the commandments. The issue is complicated Reform's acceptance of patrilineal descent as a criteria for Jewishness and its recognition as Jews of children born before a non-Jew converts. The movement thus does not see a need for conversion in cases in which the Orthodox would require one. The present status quo in Israel is not to recognize Jewish pluralism, effectively invalidating liberal religious procedures. Conversion to Judaism and its related issues have caused a growing rift between the traditional and liberal communities, a rift that it does not appear will be reconciled in the near future.

Death and mourning: Just as life begins with ceremonies shared by family, friends, and the larger community, so does it end. Because Judaism stresses the importance of life in this world, the rituals surrounding death focus primarily on the survivors, though proper preparation of the body and burial remain of the utmost importance.[4]

All efforts are made to comfort the sick and pray for them, in the hope that they will recover. One even is permitted to violate the Sabbath in order to comfort a dying person (B. Git. 28a). The dying person generally is not left alone, and it is considered both important and honorable to be present at the point of death (*yetziat neshamah*; "exit of the soul"). This transition to death is to be made as comfortable as possible, though when it seems that the final moments are near, the dying person is encouraged to recite the formal death-bed confession of sins. This is done as gently as possible with the words, "Confess your sins. Many confessed their sins and did not die, and many who did not confess died. In reward for having confessed, may you live; but everyone who confesses has a share in the world to come" (Yoreh Deah 338:1). A minimum confession is recorded at M. San. 6:2: "May my death be an atonement for all of my transgressions." A more complete confession reads (Yoreh Deah 337:2):

> I acknowledge before you, Lord, my God, and the God of my fathers, that my recovery and death are in your hand. May it be your will that you heal me with total recovery, but, if I die, may my death be an atonement for all the errors, iniquities, and willful sins that I have erred, sinned and transgressed before you. May you grant my share in the Garden of Eden and privilege me for the world to come that is concealed for the righteous.

The confession usually ends with the recitation of the Shema: "Hear, O Israel, the Lord is our God, the Lord is One."

Tradition recognized death to have occurred once breathing, heartbeat, pulse, and corneal reflexes cease. The body was not touched for eight minutes while a feather was laid over the lips to check for any sign of respiration. Once death is established, the eyes and mouth are closed and the limbs settled next to the body. The body is placed on the floor with the feet facing the door and covered with a sheet. Custom dictates that a candle should be lit and placed near the head, all mirrors covered, and stored water poured out. In modern situations, in which death often occurs in a hospital, these customs are not generally practiced. Still, in all settings, as a sign of respect for the dead, utmost care is taken to behave in a dignified manner before the body.

The burial society (*hevrah kadishah*) is comprised of religious Jews trained and committed to preparing the body for burial through the ritual process known as *taharah*. Through *taharah* ("purification"), the body is both physically cleaned and cleansed in a spiritual sense. Considered of great importance, this procedure is conducted with the utmost sobriety and solemnity. The *taharah* procedures are performed by individuals of the same sex as the deceased. The entire body, including the head, is washed with warm water. The fingers and toes are thoroughly cleansed, and the hair of the dead is combed. During the procedure, the body should not be placed face down, a degrading posture, but should be inclined, first on one side and then on the other. After the body has been thoroughly cleansed, it is washed with nine *kavin*, about twenty-four quarts, of water. This is done with the corpse placed in a standing position on the ground or upon straw, and the water poured over the head to run down over the entire body.

After this process is completed, the head is washed with a mixture of egg and wine. If a person died in a manner that blood continued flowing after death (including women who died in childbirth), the priority to bury all the remains of the person—including the blood—takes precedence over *taharah*, and the body is simply wrapped and buried in a sheet called a *sovev*. All Jews, regardless of gender, age, social, or economic status, are buried in the same white shrouds, known as *tachrichim*, stressing the equality found in death. These shrouds are made of linen, with-

out binding, seams, knots, or pockets and consist of a head dress (men), trousers, chemise, kittel, belt, and *sovev*. Men are wrapped in the prayer shawl they wore throughout their lifetime, with one fringe cut of, symbolizing the inability to continue fulfilling mitzvot. There are traditions to place some soil from the land of Israel and some shards of pottery in the casket, as well as to bend the fingers on the hand in a specific manner and to include some sort of utensil to aid the deceased in burrowing a tunnel to Israel at the time of the resurrection, though these two customs are derided in the Kitzur Shulkhan Arukh 197:5. The *taharah* and dressing are completed shortly before the funeral, and, immediately following, the deceased is laid to rest.

Members of the *hevrah kadishah* stay with the body constantly during the period between death and interment, reciting continuously from the Psalms. Gen. 3:19's reference to the human's return to the dust is understood to mean that the entire body should be buried as it was during life. Any blood that was lost after death, including blood stained clothing or even blood stained earth, must be collected and buried with the body. Because of this principle, Judaism expressly forbids cremation and embalming (unless considered necessary for health reasons) and frowns upon autopsies and organ transplant, unless they will save another's life. The dead are buried with anything that was worn as a part of the body (e.g., wigs, artificial teeth) but not jewelry or any other ornamentation.

Mourning: Mourning—*avelut*—is traditionally understood to encompass the expressions of grief and the religious observances followed by those who have lost a parent, child, sibling, or spouse, or which apply in the case of a treasured leader or after a national tragedy. Such practices have their foundation in Scripture, which, for instance, speaks of Abraham's purchasing a tomb and burying Sarah, and Reuben and Jacob's tearing of their clothes in mourning for Joseph. After Jacob's death, "Egypt bewailed him for seventy days" (Gen. 50:3), and the statement that "Joseph fell on his father's face" (Gen. 50:1) is interpreted as a fulfillment of God's promise to Jacob (Gen. 46:3), that "Joseph shall place his hands your eyes," that is, close them after death. The Torah also delineates which mourning practices are acceptable, ruling out pagan rites such as mutilation of the flesh (Lev. 21:5; Deut 14:1). The hagiographa and prophetic books contain many additional references to death and mourning practices.

Most of the mourning practices followed by Jews today thus have biblical precedent, and the Rabbinic literature, accordingly, records mourning rituals that have remained virtually unchanged to the present time. The Talmud holds that the mourning practices observed on the day of death derive from earliest biblical times, and it ascribes the establishment of the central seven day mourning period—shivah—to Moses (B. M.K. 34b, B. Ket. 25a). Concerned with maintaining the dignity of the deceased as well as of the living (B. San. 46b-47a), the rabbis of the Talmud record that three days are for weeping and seven are for lamenting (B. M.K. 27b). The number seven is derived from Amos 8:10, who says, "I will turn your feasts into mourning"—just as the feasts of Passover and Tabernacles are observed for seven days, so is mourning (B. M.K. 20). The Talmud even reports the observance of mourning for non-relatives: Ammi mourned thirty days for Yohanan (B. M.K. 25b), and it is said that one bares an arm and shoulder on the right side when mourning a brilliant scholar (hakham), the left side for the head of a bet din, and both sides for a prince (B. M.K. 22b). But indulging in excessive grief is forbidden, as it may cause a second tragedy; the Talmud recounts how one woman lost seven sons as a result of excessive mourning (B. M.K. 27b).

Judaism defines five distinct stages of mourning, allowing the individual systematically to cope with grief and gradually to reintegrate into the community. The first stage, aninut, is the period between death and burial. Shivah ("seven") is the following seven days, counted from the burial, during which period the mourners remain at home in the company of family and friends. Following shivah, a period ending thirty days after the funeral (shloshim) marks the gradual transition to normal life, and a final stage, observed only for parents, comprises the remainder of the twelve month period after death. In this period, the mourner reestablishes regular patterns of life and work but continues internally to mourn. This year is deemed sufficient time to recover from the loss, and tradition, in fact, prohibits mourning beyond the twelve months. Mourning for a leader or after a national catastrophe, as well as on public fast days, follows many of the same strictures observed in personal mourning.

During the period of aninut, between death and interment, the mourner is called an onen. In this most intense period of grief, the individual's inward feeling of isolation is expressed through various outward observances and abstentions from life's pleasures. The onen abstains from the consumption of meat, wine, and liquor, does not attend any festive meal or party, and often eats alone. The onen refrains from self-adornment—wearing new clothes, shaving, cutting the hair, wearing jewelry, donning phylacteries—as well as from bathing for pleasure and engaging in sexual relations. The individual ceases to do business and to study Torah, which is considered enjoyment, and is released from the obligations of prayer as well as many other commandments, including reciting the blessing over bread and Grace after Meals. In this period, accordingly, the onen may not be counted as a member of a prayer-quorum. While, even in this period, outward mourning is not permitted on the Sabbath and festivals, which are days of peace and holiness, personal restrictions like bathing for pleasure, sexual relations, and Torah study remain in effect.

Keriah, "rending the garments," was traditionally practiced during this period. This is an outward sign of mourning as well as a psychological tool used to express grief. Rending normally takes place at any of three times: upon hearing of the death, before the funeral service, or at the cemetery; if this procedure is somehow neglected or forgotten, however, it is performed upon recognition of the omission. It is customary to rend the outer clothing that is worn indoors: vest, jacket, sweater, or tie for men; dress, blouse, or sweater for women. Clothes may be changed before the rending takes place, and it not considered appropriate to wear new clothes during mourning. The initial cut is typically made with a knife or scissors and then torn approximately three inches. For parents, one rends the left side over the heart, and for other relatives in a less conspicuous place on the right side. With the rending, the blessing that recognizes God as the true judge (*dayan ha-'emet*) is pronounced, emphasizing the justness of the divine decree.

Children are exempt from rending, as are those too physically or mentally ill to perform it correctly or to appreciate its significance. It is forbidden for a bride or groom to infringe on the joy felt during their first week of marriage by performing rending. Though typically performed only for one's immediate relatives or spouse, rending is sometimes performed for one's in-laws or by a divorcee. For parents, the rend is worn through *shivah* and may be worn during *shloshim*; other relatives are permitted to change from the rent clothing during *shivah*. Many liberal communities have adopted the practice of rending a ribbon that is then pinned onto the outer clothing in place of rending a garment.

Jewish tradition does not sanction any effort to comfort the bereaved during the funeral service (*leviat hamet*) and burial (*kavurah*), which are performed as soon after death as possible. Emphasis is placed instead on honoring the deceased through proper prayer, eulogy, and burial. Jewish funeral services are typically brief and may take place at a funeral parlor, home, synagogue, or cemetery. The service consists of a selection of Psalms, a eulogy, and the chanting of the memorial prayer (*malei rachamim*). Commonly included in the service is Ps. 23, which, because it speaks of the intimate relationship between humans and God, is considered appropriate. Additionally, lines such as "Though I walk through the valley of the shadow of death, I fear no harm for you are with me" inspire hope in the bereaved. Also common is recitation of the collection of verses from various Psalms known as "What

is man" and other Psalms or readings appropriate to the individual's life. Often, for a woman, a selection from Proverbs known as "woman of valor" (*aishet hayil*) is recited.

In the eulogy, members of the family, close friends, or the officiating rabbi may address the community. The eulogy typically includes two elements: *hesped* (praising the deceased) and *bechi* (an expression of grief and loss). After the eulogy, the memorial prayer concludes the ceremony:

> O God full of compassion, you dwell on high! Grant perfect rest beneath the sheltering wings of your presence, among the holy and pure who shine as the brightness on the heavens, unto the soul of _____ who has gone unto eternity, and in whose memory charity is offered. May his repose be in paradise. May the Lord of mercy bring him under the cover of his wings forever, and may his soul be bound up in the bond of eternal life. May the Lord be his possession and may he rest in peace. Amen.

After the funeral service, the deceased is taken to the cemetery (fig. 92). Pallbearers are chosen from among the family and close friends, an important tribute to the dead. The somber funeral procession is considered an important last rite. Pallbearers typically escort the casket from the chapel to the hearse and, at the cemetery, from the hearse to the final resting place. During the procession, the bereaved walk behind the casket. Ps. 91 is recited and a number of pauses are made, symbolizing an unwillingness to end this final display of honor for the deceased. The passage *tziduk ha-din* ("justification of the divine decree") is said immediately before or just after interment, expressing acceptance of death. Family members, close friends, and honored members of the community usually begin the initial covering of the casket with dirt. Then a special burial kaddish—a doxology used often in Jewish liturgy—is recited, significantly different from other forms of this prayer in that it refers directly to resurrection of the dead.

Completion of the graveside service marks the transition from the period of *aninut* to *avelut*, in which the mourner begins to receive condolences. Traditionally, all present form two parallel lines through which the mourners pass. Those present greet the mourners with words of consolation: "May the Lord comfort you among the other mourners of Zion and Jerusalem." Upon exiting a graveyard, traditional Jews wash their hands in the ritual manner, having come into contact with the dead or, perhaps, as a way of saying that their hands are clean, that they have fulfilled all obligations attendant upon burial of the dead.

After burial, the mourners return home to a meal of condolence and begin the *shivah* observances, often referred to as "sitting *shivah*" because of the low stools, or "*shivah* benches," on which mourners traditionally sit. In general, relatives mourning together designate one location in which the mourning practices are observed, refereed to as a "*shivah* house." The *shivah* observance is obligatory for anyone mourning a parent, child, sibling, or spouse. It often takes place in the house of the deceased or in the home of one of the mourners. Because the observance holds that one must remain at home, surrounded by family and friends for an entire week, it remains a powerful ritual.

On the day of the funeral, the mourner typically fasts from dawn until after the burial, breaking the fast with a bland meal of bread, hard boiled eggs, cooked vegetables, and coffee or tea prepared by friends of the family. This meal, known as the meal of condolence, is an important time for the mourner to be with others, and it is not considered acceptable for one to prepare his or her own meal. Although, after interment, the most intense period of grief is considered to have passed, the meal is conducted in a solemn atmosphere. During this meal, as well as throughout the entire *shivah* week, it is customary for visitors not to speak until addressed by the mourner. It is considered inappropriate to ask a mourner how he or she feels, and the topic of conversation is generally confined to the virtues of the recently deceased. Candles are kindled and kept lit through the entire week to honor the memory of the dead. It customary to cover all mirrors in a house of mourning, for this is a time of isolation when the vanity of standing before a mirror is out of place.

At home for the entire week, the mourner is visited by members of the community. Comforting mourners is an obligation referred to as *gemilut hasadim*, an expression of true kindness. Typically, the community or extended family also makes arrangements to provide meals for the mourner's family. Guests come to the house for daily services, and it is very important that enough people are present to constitute a prayer quorum, so that the mourner may recite the mourner's kaddish. It is customary for the family and close friends to be present the first two days of *shivah* and for others to visit on the following days.

After *shivah*, the mourner begins the transition to normal life. *Shloshim*, which ends the mourning observances for relatives other than parents, begins at the conclusion of *shivah* and continues until the thirtieth day after burial. One may return to daily routines, though it is customary to continue abstaining from wearing new clothes, cutting the hair, and bathing for pleasure until one begins to receive comments regarding his or her disheveled appearance. Depending on the level of observance and knowledge of the community, this period may vary significantly from place to place. While a mourner may return to work and other obligations, in this period he or she does not attend social functions.

After *shloshim*, one continues mourning a parent until the anniversary of the death, called the yahrzeit. In this period of mourning, the individual often sits in a different place in the synagogue, makes an extra effort to study Torah, to act meritoriously, give charity, and to lead worship services in honor of the dead. But the most notable observance of this period of mourning, as during the initial days, is the recitation of the mourner's kaddish. A dramatic prayer in Aramaic, the mourner's kaddish is recited at every service, even on the Sabbath and festivals, when other mourning rituals are not carried out. This kaddish may only be recited in the presence of a minyan; the mourner therefore must surround him or herself with others in order to fulfill this obligation to a deceased parent. While the obligation is considered to last for a full year, it is customary to cease saying kaddish after eleven months. Traditionally, the obligation to say kaddish falls upon the son, though liberal movements have encouraged women to recite the kaddish as well.

At the conclusion of the year of mourning, it is customary to unveil the tombstone of the deceased, though this may occur earlier. The monument honors the deceased, marking a place for visitation, and clearly indicating a place descendants of the priestly caste, who are not to come into contact with the dead, must avoid. Alongside the removal of a cloth from the tombstone, symbolizing its erection, the unveiling ceremony includes a recitation of Psalms, the *malei rachamim* memorial prayer, and the mourner's kaddish. While Judaism does not condone excessive grave visitation, it is customary to visit the dead on the concluding day of *shivah* or *shloshim*, as well as on the anniversary of the death, fast days, before the high holidays, the eve of the months of Nisan and Elul, and, in the case of the graves of parents, before marriage (fig. 93). Upon visiting a grave for the first time in thirty days, one recites the memorial prayer and Psalms and often dedicates time to study of the Mishnah. Many Jews place a pebble on the tombstone as tangible evidence of the visit. This custom possibly derives from the period when graves were marked by piles of rocks.

The anniversary of death, or yahrzeit, is observed annually. The memorial prayer is recited on the Sabbath before the yahrzeit, and, on the anniversary itself, a candle is lit in the home, extra prayer, reflection, and Torah study take place, and charity is given. Some Jews also fast on this day. A memorial service for all the dead, called Yizkor, is a fixed part of the liturgy on the Day of Atonement, Passover, Pentecost, and Tabernacles. Traditionally, these memorial prayers are recited only by those who have lost a parent, with all others leaving the sanctuary during this dramatic liturgical rite. Many Jews also light candles in their homes on the holidays on which Yizkor is said, just as on the anniversary of the death.

Besides personal mourning observances, Judaism has six fast days that are public days of mourning, universally observed in traditional communities. Only the Day of Atonement is of biblical origin, with the other five commemorating historical tragedies that befell the Jewish people. On the Day of Atonement and Ninth of Ab (*tishah b'av*) one must abstain from eating, bathing, wearing cosmetics, wearing leather shoes, and engaging in marital relations from sundown until sundown the following day. The other days entail fasts that begin at sunrise; on these days, the other restrictions do not apply. The Fast of Esther commemorates the three day fast referred to at Esth. 4:16. The remaining four fast days commemorate the fall of Jerusalem. The seventeenth of Tammuz, first, marks the beginning of the fall of Jerusalem at the hands of the Romans. It also recalls the day Moses broke the tablets of the ten commandments, the burning of a Torah scroll and the erection of an idol in the Temple by the Greeks, and the Romans' forced cessation of the sacrificial cult. From this date and until the Ninth of Ab, three weeks of mourning are observed in commemoration of the fall of Jerusalem during the Roman siege. The Ninth of Ab itself then commemorates the destruction of the Jerusalem Temple; it is considered the saddest day of the Jewish year, especially as many other monumentally tragic events are associated with this day: the destruction of both Temples, King Edward's expulsion of the Jews from England in 1290, the Spanish Inquisition of 1492, and the outbreak of World War I. Finally, the fast of Gedaliah, commemorates the murder of a governor of Judah, and fast of the Tenth of Tevet commemorates the beginning of Nebuchadnezzar's siege of Jerusalem, which led to the destruction of the First Temple.

Throughout history, especially during the middle ages, various other public fasts were established and observed in varying locales, and although most are not observed today, personal fasts are observed on certain occasions, including in conjunction with an individual crisis or act of repentance. Two modern days of mourning also are observed by the world Jewish community: Holocaust Remembrance Day (*Yom haShoah*, 27 Nissan) commemorate the six million Jews murdered in Holocaust, and the Israeli Day of Remembrance (*Yom haZikkaron*, 4 Iyyar) commemorates the Israeli soldiers killed during Israel's War for Independence and subsequent battles for its existence.

Notes

[1] For a complete discussion of this ritual, including the text of the ceremony, see CIRCUMCISION.

[2] For a complete discussion of the wedding liturgy, see LITURGY OF JUDAISM, CONTENT AND THEOLOGY.

[3] On this topic, see also CONVERSION.

[4] On this topic, see as well DEATH AND AFTERLIFE, JUDAIC DOCTRINES OF.

WILLIAM SCOTT GREEN and J. MISHKIN

LITURGY OF JUDAISM, CONTENT AND THEOLOGY: Life under the law means praying—morning, noon, night, and at meals—both routinely and when something unusual happens. As a Jew in the classical tradition, one lives life constantly aware of the presence of God and always ready to praise and bless God. The way of Torah is the way of perpetual devotion to God. Here we look into the substance of that devotion: for what do pious Jews ask when they pray? For what do they thank God?

We find that Judaism's liturgy of home and synagogue expresses the theology of classical Judaism. In every synagogue that addresses God in the words of the classical prayerbook and that privileges the Pentateuch and aspires to live by its law, the theology of the Oral Torah imparts shape and structure to holy Israel's address to God. There, in the practiced piety of worship, the Written Torah is mediated through the Oral, the act and attitude of prayer given theological substance by the sages' account of God and the world. The sages teach Israel how to pray and what to say.

In the first six centuries C.E., the sages in the Oral Torah worked to delimit the liturgy. The halakhah delineates the order of common worship, defining its principal parts. The aggadah contains compositions of prayers in the names of various sages, and some of these are incorporated into the Siddur and Mahzor, the prayerbooks for daily worship, Sabbaths, and festivals, on the one side, and for the Days of Awe, on the other. But despite this Talmudic foundation, the detailed wording of both the Siddur and the Mahzor is first attested only centuries after the close of the Talmud of Babylonia. How, then, do we know that the liturgy of the Siddur and Mahzor, including rites of passage, in fact remains animated by the modes of thought characteristic of the sages of classical Judaism, who flourished some centuries before the liturgy reached the now-familiar wording?

The answer to this question will demonstrate that the liturgy indeed responds to the theology of the Oral Torah set forth by the sages of the Mishnah, Talmud, and Midrash. On the one hand, the intellectual traits of particular liturgies match modes of thought uniquely characteristic of the Oral Torah. On the other, liturgical motifs and themes join together in conformity to patterns established by the Oral Torah. These two traits demonstrate that the Oral Torah exercised a particular and highly distinctive—and therefore formative—influence upon the encounter between Israel and God in prayer.

The distinctive modes of thought characteristic of the sages but not of Scripture are evident in the remarkable power of the sages to recast history as paradigm. The sages reframed Scripture's history into laws governing the social order, turning events from singular, sequential, one-time and unique happenings into exemplary patterns. These encompass the past within the present and join future, present, and past onto a single plane of eternity. This mode of thought brings about the formation of liturgies in which all ages meet in one place, the great themes of existence coming together to reshape a very particular moment. That same mode of thought, moreover, insists on the union of the public and the private, the communal and the individual, all things subject to the same principle, explained in the same way.

The wedding liturgy: Two private liturgies realize the paradigmatic, as against the historical, mode of thought. First, this particularly Rabbinic mode of thought characterizes the prayer at the Jewish wedding, joining in one statement the motifs of creation, Adam, Eve, and Eden, the fall of Israel from the land of Israel, and the hoped-for restoration of humanity to Eden and Israel to Jerusalem and the Holy Land. The whole takes place out of time, in that "dream-time" that the Oral Torah creates. At a single moment all intersect. Here we find fully exposed the matter of life in that timeless world of an ever-present past. So too, the private and the public meet as well when a new family begins. Even as individual lover and beloved celebrate the uniqueness, the privacy of their love, they turn out to stand for Adam and Eve and to represent the very public hope for the restoration of Israel to the perfection of Eden in the Land. That imposes upon their love a heavy burden for the young, infatuated couple.

Here is where the liturgy utilizes theological modes of thought and casts them into moments of realization and reprise. What is striking is how the theme of Eden and alienation, land of Israel and exile, so typical of the theology of the Oral Torah, is reworked into a new pattern: from the loneliness and exile of the single life to the Eden and Jerusalem of the wedding canopy. The theme of exile and return is recapitulated, but now with the message that the joy of the bride and groom—standing, after all, for Israel and God—is a foretaste of what is last, that final reprise of creation, now in eternal perfection. The personal and the public join, the individuals before us embody and reenact the entirety of Israel's holy life, past to future:

> Praised are You, O Lord our God, King of the universe, Creator of the fruit of the vine.
> Praised are You, O Lord our God, King of the universe, who created all things for Your glory.
> Praised are You, O Lord our God, King of the universe, Creator of Adam.
> Praised are You, O Lord our God, King of the universe, who created man and woman in his image, fashioning woman from man as his mate, that together they might perpetuate life. Praised are You, O Lord, Creator of man.
> May Zion rejoice as her children are restored to her in joy. Praised are You, O Lord, who causes Zion to rejoice at her children's return.
> Grant perfect joy to these loving companions, as You did to the first man and woman in the Garden of Eden. Praised are You, O

> Lord, who grants the joy of bride and groom.
> Praised are You, O Lord our God, King of the universe, who created joy and gladness, bride and groom, mirth, song, delight and rejoicing, love and harmony, peace and companionship. O Lord our God, may there ever be heard in the cities of Judah and in the streets of Jerusalem voices of joy and gladness, voices of bridge and groom, the jubilant voices of those joined in marriage under the bridal canopy, the voices of young people feasting and signing. Praised are You, O Lord, who causes the groom to rejoice with his bride.[1]

The blessings speak of archetypical Israel, represented here and now by the bride and groom. They cover the great themes of the theology of the Oral Torah, excluding only one. We find creation, Adam, man and woman in God's image, after God's likeness; then comes the restoration of Israel to Zion; then the joy of Zion in her children and the loving companions in one another; then the evocation of the joy of the restoration—past, present, future, all in the here and now. The sole critical component of the theology of the Oral Torah omitted here concerns justice, on the one side, sin, repentance, and atonement, on the other, an omission that attests to sages' fine sense of what fits and what does not.

The theme of ancient paradise is introduced by the simple choice of the word *Adam*, just as we should expect. The myth of humanity's creation is rehearsed: man and woman are in God's image, together complete and whole, creators of life, "like God." Woman was fashioned from man together with him to perpetuate life. But this Adam and this Eve also are Israel, children of Zion the mother, as expressed in the fifth blessing. Israel is in exile, Zion lies in ruins. It is at that appropriate point that the restorationist motif enters: "Grant perfect joy to the loving companions," for they are creators of a new line in humankind—the new Adam, the new Eve; and their home—May it be the garden of Eden! And if joy is there, then "praised are you for the joy of bride and groom."

The concluding blessing returns to the theme of Jerusalem. Given the focus of the system as a whole, that hardly surprises. For the union of bridegroom and bride provides a foretaste of the new Eden that is coming. But that is only at the right moment, in the right setting, when Israel will have repented, atoned, and attained resurrection and therefore restoration to Eden, standing for the world to come. How is all this invoked? The liturgy conveys these motifs when it calls up the tragic hour of Jerusalem's first destruction. When everyone had given up hope, supposing with the end of Jerusalem had come the end of time, exile, the anti-Eden, only Jeremiah counseled renewed hope. With the enemy at the gate, he sang of coming gladness (Jer. 33:10-11):

> Thus says the Lord: In this place of which you say, "It is a waste, without man or beast," in the cities of Judah and the streets of Jerusalem that are desolate, without man or inhabitant or beast, there shall be heard again the voice of mirth and the voice of gladness, the voice of the bridegroom and the voice of the bride, the voice of those who sing as they bring thank-offerings to the house of the Lord. . . . For I shall restore the fortunes of the land as at first, says the Lord.

The intersection of characteristic motifs creates a timeless tableau. Just as here and now there stand Adam and Eve, so here and now in this wedding, the olden sorrow having been rehearsed, we listen to the voice of gladness that is coming. The joy of this new creation prefigures the joy of the messiah's coming, inaugurating the resurrection and judgment and the final restoration. The joy then will echo the joy of bride and groom before us. So the small space covered by the marriage-canopy is crowded indeed with persons and events. People who think historically and not paradigmatically can commemorate and celebrate. But they cannot embody or exemplify eternity in the here and now, the presence and past and future all at once. In this context, only the sages of the Oral Torah have formed a mode of thought that is capable of imagining such a convocation of persons and concatenation of events.

The Brit Milah: The same mode of thought marks other liturgies that celebrate events of the life-cycle. The entry of the male-child into the covenant of Abraham through the rite of circumcision, intensely personal (to the infant) and massively pub-

lic (to all Israel), forms another moment of timeless eternity. Specifically, in the case of a boy, a minor surgical rite becomes the mark of the renewal of the agreement between God and Israel, the covenant carved into the flesh of the penis of every Jewish male. The beginning of a new life renews the rule that governs Israel's relationship to God. So the private joy is reworked through words of enchantment—once more, sanctification—and so transformed into renewal of the community of Israel and God. Those present find themselves in another time, another place. Specific moments out of the past are recapitulated and specific personalities called to attendance. In the present instant, eternity is invoked at the moment of cutting off the foreskin of the penis. Calling the rite *brit milah*, the covenant of, or effected through, circumcision, invites Abraham to attend. *Brit milah* seals with the blood of an infant the contract between Israel and God, generation by generation, son by son.

The spoken words of this rite evoke within the intimacy of private life that which all share together: Israel, its covenant with God, its origin in Abraham, Isaac, Jacob. In the rite, God sees the family beyond time, joined by blood not of pedigree but circumcision, genealogy framed by fifty generations of loyalty to the covenant in blood and birth from the union of the womb of an Israelite woman with semen from the circumcised penis of her Israelite husband: this is the holy fruit of the womb. Four aspects turn the operation into a rite. When the ceremony begins, the assembly and the circumcisor—the mohel—together recite Num. 25:10-12:

> The Lord spoke to Moses saying, Phineas, son of Eleazar, son of Aaron, the priest, has turned my wrath from the Israelites by displaying among them his passion for me, so that I did not wipe out the Israelite people in my passion. Say therefore I grant him my covenant of peace.

Commenting on this passage, Lifsa Schachter states, "Phineas is identified with zealously opposing the . . . sins of sexual licentiousness and idolatry. He is best known for an event which occurred when the Israelites, whoring with Moabite women in the desert, were drawn to the worship of Baal-Peor. . . . Phineas leaped into the fray and through an act of double murder . . . quieted God's terrible wrath."[2]

Now the so-called "chair of Elijah" is set, so that the rite is conceived to take place in the presence of the prophet. The newborn son is set on that chair, and the congregation says, "This is the chair of Elijah, of blessed memory." To understand the invocation of Elijah, we first recall the pertinent biblical passage, in which Elijah complained to God that the people of Israel had forsaken the covenant (1 Kgs. 19:10-14). This passage stands behind a story in a medieval document, Pirke deRabbi Eliezer, that Elijah attends the rite of circumcision of every Jewish boy:[3]

> The Israelites were wont to circumcise until they were divided into two kingdoms. The kingdom of Ephraim cast off from themselves the covenant of circumcision. Elijah, may he be remembered for good, arose and was zealous with a mighty passion, and he adjured the heavens to send down neither dew nor rain upon the earth. Jezebel heard about it and sought to slay him.
>
> Elijah arose and prayed before the Holy One, blessed be he. The Holy One, blessed be he, said to him, " 'Are you better than your fathers' (1 Kgs. 19:4)? Esau sought to slay Jacob, but he fled before him, as it is said, 'And Jacob fled into the field of Aram' (Hos. 12:12).
>
> Elijah, may he be remembered for good, arose and fled from the land of Israel, and he betook himself to Mount Horeb, as it is said, "and he arose and ate and drank" (1 Kings 19:8).
>
> Then the Holy One, blessed be he, was revealed to him and said to him, "What are you doing here, Elijah"?
>
> He answered him saying, "I have been very zealous."
>
> The Holy One, blessed be he, said to him, "You are always zealous. You were zealous in Shittim on account of the immorality. For it is said, 'Phineas, the son of Eleazar, the son of Aaron the priest, turned my wrath away from the children of Israel, in that he was zealous with my zeal among them' (Num. 25:11).
>
> "Here you are also zealous. By your life! They shall not observe the covenant of circumcision until you see it done with your own eyes."
>
> Hence the sages have instituted the custom that people should have a seat of honor for the messenger of the covenant; for Elijah, may he be remembered for good, is called the messenger of the covenant, as it is said, 'And the messenger of the covenant, whom you delight in, behold he comes' (Mal. 3:1).

Thus the prophet Elijah is present whenever a Jewish son enters the covenant of Abraham, which is circumcision, witnessing the loyalty of the Jews to the covenant. Elijah further serves as the guardian for the newborn, just as he raised the child of the widow from the dead (1 Kgs. 17:17-24). Celebrating with the family of the newborn are not "all Israel" in general but a very specific personage. The gesture of setting the chair sets the stage for an event in the life of the family not of the child alone but of all Israel. The chair of Elijah, filled by the one who holds the child, sets the newborn baby into Elijah's lap. The enchantment thus extends through the furnishing of the room.

In the actual surgical act, we move from gesture to formula, with the mohel reciting a blessing regarding the obligation of circumcision immediately before the rite and the father reciting a blessing concerning the covenant just afterward:

> Praised are you . . . who sanctified us with your commandments and commanded us to bring the son into the covenant of Abraham our father.

The explicit invocation of Abraham's covenant turns a concrete action in the here and now into a simile of the paradigm and archetype. To this, those present respond: "Just as he has entered the covenant, so may he be introduced to Torah, the *huppah* [marriage canopy] and good deeds." Schachter interprets these words as follows:

> Torah—as against idolatry; in the presence of Phineas. . . . huppah, as against sexual licentiousness; in the presence of Abraham . . . to good deeds: For I have singled him out that he may instruct his children and his posterity to keep the way of the Lord by doing what is just and right (Gen. 18:18).[4]

In the transformation of the now of the birth of the son into the then of Abraham's covenant with God, people make a public event of a private joy. As historical personages join the occasion—Elijah complaining to God, Abraham obediently circumcising his sons, Phineas, calming God's wrath by an act of violence, with whom a covenant of peace then is made—so the private becomes a continuation of the shared history and destiny of a people.

The operation completed, the blessing for wine is recited, introducing yet a further occasion of enchantment:

> Praised are you, Lord our God, who sanctified the beloved from the womb and set a statute into his very flesh, and his parts sealed with the sign of the holy covenant. On this account, living God, our portion and rock, save the beloved of our flesh from destruction, for the sake of his covenant placed in our flesh. Blessed are you . . . who makes the covenant.

In the rite of circumcision, the covenant thus is transformed from a generality to something specific, concrete, fleshly. It is, moreover, understood to accomplish a very specific goal—as all religion means to attain concrete purposes—to secure a place for the child, a blessing for the child. By virtue of the rite, the child enters the covenant, meaning that he joins that unseen "Israel" that through blood enters an agreement with God. As a result, the blessing of the covenant is owing to the child. For covenants or contracts cut both ways.

The Grace after Meals: So much for the way in which sages' mode of thought shapes the liturgy, imposing the pattern of an ever-present past upon the present and turning present-tense time into a paradigm of what will be. What of those distinctive clusters of themes that the theology of the Oral Torah brings together?[5] A glance at the wedding liturgy defines what we should expect: Adam, creation, Israel, Zion; or joy, Jerusalem; or image of God, image of humankind. Other such clusters encompass Israel, gentile; this age, world to come; Eden, world to come; and so on. In fact, the Oral Torah yields a limited number of archetypal clusters, allowing for a nearly unlimited number of recombinations. But within the Oral Torah's theology, a certain few clusters suffice to animate the liturgy and supply its reference-points.

The theology of the Oral Torah combines many such components into a single narrative statement. Creation, revelation, redemption form one such paramount cluster; land, liberation, covenant, Torah, another; people of Israel, land of Israel, Jerusalem, restoration, a third. Above all, we must wonder, how do the several salvific symbols fit together in the larger mythic structure of creation, revelation, and redemption? In the Grace after Meals, recited whenever pious Jews eat bread, we see their interplay. To understand the setting, we must recall that in classical Judaism the table at which meals were eaten was regarded as the equivalent of the sacred altar in the Temple. Judaism taught that each Jew before eating had to attain the same state of ritual purity as the priest in the sacred act of making a sacrifice. So in the classic tradition, the Grace after Meals is recited in a sacerdotal circumstance. That is why the entire theology of the Oral Torah comes to realization in this simple liturgy:

> [1] Blessed art Thou, Lord our God, King of the Universe, who nourishes all the world by His goodness, in grace, in mercy, and in compassion: He gives bread to all flesh, for His mercy is everlasting. And because of His great goodness we have never lacked, and so may we never lack, sustenance—for the sake of His great Name. For He nourishes and feeds everyone, is good to all, and provides food for each one of the creatures He created.
>
> Blessed art Thou, O Lord, who feeds everyone.
>
> [2] We thank Thee, Lord our God, for having given our fathers as a heritage a pleasant, a good and spacious land; for having taken us out of the land of Egypt, for having redeemed us from the house of bondage; for Thy covenant, which Thou hast set as a seal in our flesh, for Thy Torah which Thou has taught us, for Thy statutes which Thou hast made known to us, for the life of grace and mercy Thou hast graciously bestowed upon us, and for the nourishment with which Thou dost nourish us and feed us always, every day, in every season, and every hour.
>
> For all these things, Lord our God, we thank and praise Thee; may Thy praises continually be in the mouth of every living thing, as it is written, And thou shalt eat and

be satisfied, and bless the Lord thy God for the good land which He hath given thee.

Blessed art Thou, O Lord, for the land and its food.

[3] O Lord our God, have pity on Thy people Israel, on Thy city Jerusalem, on Zion the place of Thy glory, on the royal house of David Thy Messiah, and on the great and holy house which is called by Thy Name. Our God, our Father, feed us and speed us, nourish us and make us flourish, unstintingly, O Lord our God, speedily free us from all distress.

And let us not, O Lord our God, find ourselves in need of gifts from flesh and blood, or of a loan from anyone save from Thy full, generous, abundant, wide-open hand; so we may never be humiliated, or put to shame.

O rebuild Jerusalem, the holy city, speedily in our day. Blessed art Thou, Lord, who in mercy will rebuild Jerusalem. Amen.

[4] Blessed art Thou, Lord our God, King of the Universe, Thou God, who art our Father, our powerful king, our creator and redeemer, who made us, our holy one, the holy one of Jacob, our sherpherd, shepherd of Israel, the good king, who visits His goodness upon all; for every single day He has brought good, He does bring good, He will bring good upon us; He has rewarded us, does regard, and will always reward us, with grace, mercy and compassion, amplitude, deliverance and prosperity, blessing and salvation, comfort, and a living, sustenance, pity and peace, and all good—let us not want any manner of good whatever.[6]

The context of grace is enjoyment of creation, the arena for creation is the land. The land lay at the end of redemption from Egyptian bondage. Holding it, enjoying it is a sign that the covenant is intact and in force and that the people is loyal to its part of the contract and God to his. The land, the Exodus, the covenant—these all depend upon the Torah, statutes, and a life of grace and mercy, here embodied in and evoked by the nourishment of the meal. Thanksgiving wells up, and the paragraph ends with praises for the land and its food.

This cluster on its own does not demand identification with the Oral Torah. The restorationist dynamic—Israel is to the Land as Adam is to Eden—is what signifies the hand of the sages. It is not merely a messianic prayer for the end of days, but a specific framing of the end in terms of the beginning, the

restoration of the people Israel to the land of Israel, that the liturgy bespeaks. The restorationist theme recurs throughout, redemption and hope for return, and then future prosperity in the land: "May God pity the people, the city, Zion, the royal house of the Messiah, the Holy Temple." The nourishment of this meal is but a foretaste of the nourishment of the messianic time, just as the joy of the wedding is a foretaste of the messianic rejoicing. Creation and recreation, exile and return—these are the particular clusters that point to the substrate of the sages' theology.

The Shema: The primary claim of the Oral Torah concerns God's creation of a world order over chaos, and, specifically, a world ordered by justice, a world ruled by God himself, and a world that would recover its original perfection. Here, in the Shema, we find the Judaic creed exactly as sages will have defined it. That is to say, the themes that converge here and the way in which they are articulated respond to the distinctive theological structure and system put forth by the sages. In maintaining that the Oral Torah imparted its imprint upon all that came afterward, and that this is a matter not of historical influence based on political sponsorship but inner logic, I point to formations such as the one before us here, the creed contained in the twice-daily recitation of the Shema.

Evening and morning, the pious Jew proclaims the unity and uniqueness of God. The proclamation is preceded and followed by blessings: two at the beginning, then the recitation of the *Shema* itself, then one at the end, creating a sequence that adduces creation, revelation, proclamation of God's unity and dominion, then redemption. The recitation of the Shema is introduced by a celebration of God as creator of the world. God daily creates an orderly world, a world ordered in goodness. That is what is important about creation. While the recitation of the Shema varies slightly morning and night, as appropriate to the time of day, the message, the creation of world order, does not. In the morning, one says,

Praised are You, O Lord our God, King of the universe.

You fix the cycles of light and darkness;
You ordain the order of all creation
You cause light to shine over the earth;
Your radiant mercy is upon its inhabitants.
In Your goodness the work of creation
Is continually renewed day by day. . . .
O cause a new light to shine on Zion;
May we all soon be worthy to behold its radiance.
Praised are You, O Lord, Creator of the heavenly bodies.[7]

The blessing in the morning celebrates light, ending with the new light when creation is renewed. The corresponding prayer in the evening refers to the setting of the sun. The natural order of the world thus elicits thanks and praise of God, who created the world and who actively guides the daily events of nature. Whatever happens in nature gives testimony to the sovereignty of the creator. And that testimony takes place in the most ordinary events: the orderly regularity of sunrise and sunset.

Through the Torah, Israel knows God not merely as creator but purposeful creator. There Israel encounters God as just, world order as a formulation of the benevolent, beneficent laws of life. Torah is the mark not merely of divine sovereignty and justice, but of divine grace and love. So goes the second blessing:

Deep is Your love for us, O Lord our God;
Bounteous is Your compassion and tenderness.

Now comes the pronouncement of the character of the world order: reliable, guided by compassion, to be learned through God's self-manifestation in the Torah:

You taught our fathers the laws of life,
And they trusted in You, Father and king,
For their sake be gracious to us, and teach us,
That we may learn Your laws and trust in You.
Father, merciful Father, have compassion upon us:
Endow us with discernment and understanding.
Grant us the will to study Your Torah,
To heed its words and to teach its precepts. . . .
Enlighten our eyes in Your Torah,
Open our hearts to Your commandments. . . .
Unite our thoughts with singleness of purpose
To hold You in reverence and in love. . . .
You have drawn us close to You;
We praise You and thank You in truth.
With love do we thankfully proclaim Your unity.
And praise You who chose Your people Israel in love.[8]

God, the creator, revealed his will for creation through the Torah, given to Israel his people. That Torah contains the "laws of life."

In the Shema, Torah—instruction through revelation—leads to the chief teaching of revelation, the premise of world order, the dominion of the one and only God. In proclaiming the following words, Israel accepts the rule of God and the yoke of the dominion of heaven: "Hear, O Israel, the Lord Our God, the Lord is One." This proclamation is followed by three Scriptural passages. The first is Deut. 6:5-9:

You shall love the Lord your God with all your heart, with all your soul, with all your might. And further, one must diligently teach one's children these words and talk of them everywhere and always, and place them on one's forehead, doorposts, and gates.

The second is Deut. 11:13-21, which emphasizes that if Jews keep the commandments, they will enjoy worldly blessings; but that, if they do not, they will be punished and disappear from the good land God gives them. The third is Num. 15:37-41, the commandment to wear fringes on the corners of one's garments.

Then comes the address to God, not as creator or revealer, but as redeemer. This prayer, predictably within the sages' framework, treats as comparable the redemption from Egypt and the redemption at the end of time, the one as the embodiment of the other:

You are our King and our father's King,
Our redeemer and our father's redeemer.
You are our creator. . . .
You have ever been our redeemer and deliverer
There can be no God but You. . . .

Now we turn to the initial formation of the paradigm of redemption, the liberation from Egypt, through the passage through the sea:

You, O Lord our God, rescued us from Egypt;

> You redeemed us from the house of bond-
> age. . . .
> You split apart the waters of the Red Sea,
> The faithful you rescued, the wicked
> drowned. . . .

As soon as redemption makes its appearance, the theme of arrogance and humility appears alongside, since, for sages, arrogance is the cause of sin and exile, humility elicits God's favor and brings about restoration:

> He humbles the proud and raises the lowly;
> He helps the needy and answers His people's
> call. . . .
> Rock of Israel, arise to Israel's defense!
> Fulfill Your promise to deliver Judah and
> Israel.
> Our redeemer is the Holy One of Israel,
> The Lord of hosts is His name.
> Praised are You, O Lord, redeemer of Israel.[9]

That God not only creates but also redeems is embodied in the redemption from Egyptian bondage. The congregation repeats the exultant song of Moses and the people at the Red Sea as participants in the salvation of old and of time to come. The stories of creation, the Exodus from Egypt, and the revelation of Torah at Sinai are repeated, not merely to recount what once happened but to recreate out of the reworked materials of everyday life the "true being"—life as it was, always is, and will be forever.

The Eighteen Benedictions—Hear our prayer, grant us peace: The Eighteen Benedictions—the Shemonah Esreh; also called the Amidah, "the standing prayer"—are recited in the morning, noon, and evening prayers. Some of these eighteen, in particular those at the beginning and the end, recur in Sabbath and festival prayers as well. The Eighteen Benedictions initially are said by each worshipper silently. Each individual prays by and for himself or herself, but together with other silent, praying individuals. These benedictions then are repeated aloud by the prayer leader, for prayer is both private and public, individual and collective. To contemplate the meaning of these prayers one should imagine a room full of people, all standing by themselves yet in close proximity, some swaying this way and that, all addressing themselves directly and intimately to God in a whisper or in a low tone. They

do not move their feet, for they are now standing before the king of kings, and it is not meet to shift and shuffle. If spoken to, they will not answer. Their attention is fixed upon the words of supplication, praise, and gratitude. When they begin, they bend their knees—so too toward the end—and at the conclusion they step back and withdraw from the divine presence. These, on ordinary days, are the words they say in the middle benedictions, which are specific to regular weekdays. The italicized words indicate the title of each subsequent benediction.

> *Wisdom-Repentance*
> You graciously endow man with intelli-
> gence;
> You teach him knowledge and understand-
> ing.
> Grant us knowledge, discernment, and wis-
> dom.
> Praised are You, O Lord, for the gift of
> knowledge.
> *Our Father, bring us back to Your Torah*
> Our King, draw us near to Your service;
> Lead us back to you truly repentant.
> Praised are You, O Lord, who welcomes
> repentance.
> *Forgiveness-Redemption*
> Our Father, forgive us, for we have sinned;
> Our King, pardon us, for we have trans-
> gressed;
> You forgive sin and pardon transgression.
> Praised are You, gracious and forgiving
> Lord.
> *Behold our affliction and deliver us.*
> Redeem us soon for the sake of Your name,
> For You are the mighty Redeemer.
> Praised are You, O Lord, Redeemer of Israel.
> *Heal Us—Bless Our Years*
> Heal us, O Lord, and we shall be healed;
> Help us and save us, for You are our glory.
> Grant perfect healing for all our afflictions,
> O faithful and merciful God of healing.
> Praised are You, O Lord, Healer of His
> people.
> O Lord our God! Make this a blessed year;
> May its varied produce bring us happiness.
> Bring blessing upon the whole earth.
> Bless the year with Your abounding good-
> ness.
> Praised are You, O Lord, who blesses our
> years.
> *Gather Our Exiles—Reign Over Us*
> South the great shofar to herald [our] free-
> dom;
> Raise high the banner to gather all exiles;
> Gather the dispersed from the corners of the
> earth.

Praised are You, O Lord, who gathers our exiles.

Restore our judges as in days of old;
Restore our counselors as in former times;
Remove from us sorrow and anguish.
Reign over us alone with loving kindness;
With justice and mercy sustain our cause.
Praised are You, O Lord, King who loves justice.

Humble the Arrogant-Sustain the Righteous
Frustrate the hopes of those who malign us;
Let all evil very soon disappear;
Let all Your enemies be speedily destroyed.
May You quickly uproot and crush the arrogant;
May You subdue and humble them in our time.
Praised are You, O Lord, who humbles the arrogant.

Let Your tender mercies, O Lord God, be stirred
For the righteous, the pious, the leaders of Israel,
Toward devoted scholars and faithful proselytes.
Be merciful to us of the house of Israel;
Reward all who trust in You;
Cast our lot with those who are faithful to You.
May we never come to despair, for our trust is in You.
Praised are You, O Lord, who sustains the righteous.

Favor Your City and Your People
Have mercy, O Lord, and return to Jerusalem, Your city;
May Your Presence dwell there as You promised.
Rebuild it now, in our days and for all time;
Re-establish there the majesty of David, Your servant.
Praised are You, O Lord, who rebuilds Jerusalem.

Bring to flower the shoot of Your servant David.
Hasten the advent of the Messianic redemption;
Each and every day we hope for Your deliverance.
Praised are You, O Lord, who assures our deliverance.

O Lord, our God, hear our cry!
Have compassion upon us and pity us;
Accept our prayer with loving favor.
You, O God, listen to entreaty and prayer.
O King, do not turn us away unanswered,
For You mercifully heed Your people's supplication.
Praised are You, O Lord, who is attentive to prayer.

O Lord, Our God, favor Your people Israel;

Accept with love Israel's offering of prayer;
May our worship be ever acceptable to You.
May our eyes witness Your return in mercy to Zion.
Praised are You, O Lord, whose Presence returns to Zion.

Our Thankfulness
We thank You, O Lord our God and God of our fathers,
Defender of our lives, Shield of our safety;
Through all generations we thank You and praise You.
Our lives are in Your hands, our souls in Your charge.
We thank You for the miracles which daily attend us,
For Your wonders and favor morning, noon, and night.
You are beneficent with boundless mercy and love.
From of old we have always placed our hope in You.
For all these blessings, O our King,
We shall ever praise and exalt You.
Every living creature thanks You, and praises You in truth.
O God, You are our deliverance and our help. Selah!
Praised are You, O Lord, for Your Goodness and Your glory.

Peace and Well-Being
Grant peace and well-being to the whole house of Israel;
Give us of Your grace, Your love, and Your mercy.
Bless us all, O our Father, with the light of Your Presence.
It is Your light that revealed to us Your life-giving Torah,
And taught us love and tenderness, justice, mercy, and peace.
May it please You to bless Your people in every season,
To bless them at all times with Your light of peace.
Praised are You, O Lord, who blesses Israel with peace.[10]

The first two petitions pertain to intelligence. Jews thank God for mind: knowledge, wisdom, discernment. But knowledge is for a purpose, and the purpose here is knowledge of Torah. Such discernment leads to the service of God and produces a spirit of repentance. We cannot pray without setting ourselves right with God, and that means repenting for what has separated us from God. Torah is the way to repentance and to return. So knowledge leads to Torah, Torah to repentance, and repentance to God. The logical next stop is the prayer for forgiveness. That is the sign of return. God forgives sin; God is gracious and forgiving. Once we discern what we have done wrong, through the guidance of Torah we seek to be forgiven. For sin leads to affliction, and affliction stands at the beginning of the way to God; once we have taken that way, we ask for our suffering to end; we beg redemption. This is then specified as we ask for healing, salvation, a blessed year. Healing without prosperity means we may suffer in good health or starve in a robust body. So along with the prayer for healing goes the supplication for worldly comfort.

The individual's task is done. But what of the community? Health and comfort are not enough. The world is unredeemed. Jews are enslaved, in exile, and alien. At the end of days a great shofar, or ram's horn, will sound to herald the messiah's coming. This is now besought. The Jewish people at prayer ask first for the proclamation of freedom, then for the ingathering of the exiles to the Promised Land. Establishing the messianic-kingdom, God needs also to restore a wise and benevolent government, good judges, good counselors, and loving justice.

Meanwhile Israel, the Jewish people, finds itself maligned. As the prayer sees things, the arrogant, hating Israel, hate God as well. They should be humbled. And the pious and righteous—the scholars, the faithful proselytes, the whole house of Israel that trusts in God—should be rewarded and sustained. Above all, God is asked to remember Jerusalem, to rebuild the city and again dwell there, setting up Jerusalem's messianic king, David, and making him prosper.

These are the themes of the daily prayer: personal atonement, good health, and good fortune; collective redemption, freedom, the end of alienation, good government, and true justice; the final and complete salvation of the Land and of Jerusalem by the messiah. At the end comes a prayer that prayer may be heard and found acceptable; then an expression of thanksgiving, not for what may come, but for the miracles and mercies already enjoyed morning, noon, and night. And at the end is the prayer for peace—a peace that consists of wholeness for the sacred community.

People who say such prayers do not wholly devote themselves to this world. True, they ask for peace, health, and prosperity. But these are transient. At the same moment they ask, in so many different ways, for eternity. They arise in the morning and speak of Jerusalem. At noon they make mention of the messiah. In the evening they end the day with talk of the shofar to herald freedom and the ingathering of the exiles. Living here in the profane, alien world, they constantly talk of going there—to the Holy Land and its perfect society. They address themselves to the end of days and the messiah's time. The praying community above all seeks the fulfillment and end of its—and humanity's—travail.

New Year and the Day of Atonement: Another most important liturgical exercise in reworking sages' theology brings us to the main principle of world order, God's just rule over creation. No more eloquent and powerful statement of that principle occurs than in the liturgy of the New Year—Rosh Hashanah—and the Day of Atonement— Yom Kippur—which together mark the Days of Awe, of solemn penitence, at the start of the autumn festival season. These occasions work out in concrete terms how the world order of justice extends to the here and now of patterned, orderly, everyday life. For on the first of these occasions, the New Year, each person is inscribed for life or death in the heavenly books for the coming year, and on the Day of Atonement the books are sealed. The synagogues on that day are filled with penitents. The New Year is called the birthday of the world: "This day the world was born." It is likewise a day of remembrance on which the deeds of all creatures are reviewed. On it God asserts his sovereignty:

> Our God and God of our Fathers, Rule over the whole world in Your honor . . . and appear in Your glorious might to all those who dwell in the civilization of Your world, so that everything made will know that You made it, and every creature discern that You

have created him, so that all in whose nostrils is breath may say, "The Lord, the God of Israel is king, and His kingdom extends over all."[11]

The themes of the liturgy are divine sovereignty, divine memory, and divine disclosure. These correspond to creation, revelation, and redemption. Sovereignty is established by creation of the world. Judgment depends upon law: "From the beginning You made this, Your purpose known. . . ." And therefore, since people have been told what God requires of them, they are judged:

> On this day sentence is passed upon countries, which to the sword and which to peace, which to famine and which to plenty, and each creature is judged today for life or death. Who is not judged on this day? For the remembrance of every creature comes before You, each man's deeds and destiny, words and way. . . .

The theme of revelation is further combined with redemption; the shofar, sounded in the synagogue during daily worship for a month before Rosh Hashanah, serves to unite the two:

> You did reveal yourself in a cloud of glory. . . . Out of heaven you made them [Israel] hear Your voice. . . . Amid thunder and lightning You revealed yourself to them, and while the shofar sounded You shined forth upon them. . . . Our God and God of our fathers, sound the great ram's horn for our freedom. Lift up the ensign to gather our exiles. . . . Lead us happily to Zion Your city, Jerusalem the place of Your sanctuary.

The complex themes of the New Year, the most "theological" of Jewish holy occasions, thus recapitulate a familiar cluster of motifs.

The most personal, solemn, and moving of the Days of Awe is the Day of Atonement, the Sabbath of Sabbaths, marked by fasting and continuous prayer. On it, the Jew makes confession:

> Our God and God of our fathers, may our prayer come before You. Do not hide yourself from our supplication, for we are not so arrogant or stiff-necked as to say before You. . . . We are righteous and have not sinned. But we have sinned.
> We are guilt laden, we have been faithless, we have robbed. . . .

We have committed iniquity, caused unrighteousness, have been presumptuous. We have counseled evil, scoffed, revolted, blasphemed. . . .[12]

The confession is built upon an alphabetical acrostic following the letters of the Hebrew alphabet, as if by making certain every letter is represented, God, who knows human secrets, will combine them into appropriate words. The very alphabet bears witness against us before God. Then:

> What shall we say before You who dwell on high? What shall we tell You who live in heaven? Do You not know all things, both the hidden and the revealed? You know the secrets of eternity, the most hidden mysteries of life. You search the innermost recesses, testing men's feelings and heart. Nothing is concealed from You or hidden from Your eyes. May it therefore be Your will to forgive us our sins, to pardon us for our iniquities, to grant remission for our transgressions.[13]

A further list of sins follows, again built on alphabetical lines. Prayers to be spoken by the congregation are all in the plural: "For the sin which we have sinned against You with the utterance of the lips. . . . For the sin which we have sinned before You openly and secretly. . . ." The community takes upon itself responsibility for all that is done in it. All Israel is part of one community, one body, and all are responsible for the acts of each. The sins confessed are mostly against society, against one's fellow; few pertain to ritual laws. At the end comes a final word:

> O my God, before I was formed, I was nothing. Not that I have been formed, it is as though I had not been formed, for I am dust in my life, more so after death. Behold I am before You like a vessel filled with shame and confusion. May it be Your will. . . . that I may no more sin, and forgive the sins I have already committed in Your abundant compassion.[14]

Israelites, within all Israel, see themselves before the just and merciful God: possessing no merits, yet hopeful of God's love and compassion.

Alenu: Every synagogue service concludes with a prayer prior to going forth, called *Alenu* from its first word in Hebrew. Like the

Exodus, the moment of the congregation's departure becomes a celebration of Israel's God, a self-conscious, articulated rehearsal of Israel's peoplehood. But now it is the end, rather than the beginning, of time that is important. When Jews go forth, they look forward:

> Let us praise Him, Lord over all the world;
> Let us acclaim Him, Author of all creation.
> He made our lot unlike that of other peoples;
> He assigned to us a unique destiny.
> We bend the knee, worship, and acknowledge
> The King of kings, the Holy One, praised is He.
> He unrolled the heavens and established the earth;
> His throne of glory is in the heavens above;
> His majestic Presence is in the loftiest heights.
> He and no other is God and faithful King,
> Even as we are told in His Torah:
> Remember now and always, that the Lord is God;
> Remember, no other is Lord of heaven and earth.
> We, therefore, hope in You, O Lord our God,
> That we shall soon see the triumph of Your might,
> That idolatry shall be removed from the earth,
> And false gods shall be utterly destroyed.
> Then will the world be a true kingdom of God,
> When all mankind will invoke Your name,
> And all the earth's wicked will return to You.
> Then all the inhabitants of the world will surely know
> That to You every knee must bend,
> Every tongue must pledge loyalty.
> Before You, O Lord, let them bow in worship,
> Let them give honor to Your glory.
> May they all accept the rule of Your kingdom.
> May You reign over them soon through all time.
> Sovereignty is Yours in glory, now and forever.
> So it is written in Your Torah:
> The Lord shall reign for ever and ever.[15]

In secular terms, Jews know that in some ways they form a separate, distinct group. In mythical reality they thank God they enjoy a unique destiny. They do not conclude with thanks for their particular being, but sing of

hope merely that the God who made their lot unlike that of all others will soon rule as sovereign over all. The secular difference, the unique destiny, is temporary. When the destiny is fulfilled, there will be no further difference. The natural eye beholds a social group with some particular cultural characteristics defining that group. The myth of peoplehood transforms *difference* into *destiny*.

Conclusion: A single, seamless statement, the Siddur and Mahzor, the Oral Torah and the Written Torah, severally and jointly say the same few things. That is why the worship of home and synagogue, with its enchanted and timeless world of ever-present eternity, is beyond all comprehending except within the framework of the Oral part of the Torah. But so too, sages will have insisted, the Oral part of the Torah for its part restates precisely the message, in exact balance and proportion, of the Written part. It too makes sense only within the framework of the Written part of the Torah. So, in sequence, the sages read from the Written Torah to the Oral one. And, reflecting on that reading, the theologians of the liturgy composed prayer to reframe in the second-person "you" of prayer personally addressed to the person of God precisely the result of that same reading: what the Torah teaches about God, Israel brings in prayer to God.

Bibliography

Jacob Neusner, *The Theology of the Oral Torah. Revealing the Justice of God* (Kingston and Montreal, 1998).

Notes

[1] Jules Harlow, ed., *A Rabbi's Manual* (New York, 1965), p. 45. The "seven blessings" said at a wedding are printed in traditional Jewish prayer books.

[2] Lifsa Schachter, "Reflections on the Brit Mila Ceremony," in *Conservative Judaism* 1986, 38, pp. 38-41.

[3] *Pirke deRabbi Eliezer*, trans. Gerald Friedlander (London, 1916), pp. 212-214.

[4] Op. cit., p. 41.

[5] In *The Theological Grammar of the Oral Torah* (Binghamton, 1997), II. *Syntax: Connections and Constructions*, I have catalogued one hundred fifty of them.

[6] Judah Goldin, trans., *The Grace After Meals* (New York, 1955), pp. 9, 15ff.

[7] *Weekday Prayer Book*, ed. by the Rabbinical Assembly of American Prayerbook Committee,

Rabbi Jules Harlow, Secretary (New York, 1962), p. 42.

[8] Ibid., pp. 45-56.

[9] Ibid., pp. 50ff.

[10] *Weekday Prayer Book*, ed. by the Rabbinical Assembly of America Prayerbook Committee, Rabbi Jules Harlow, Secretary (New York: Rabbinical Assembly, 1962).

[11] Traditional prayer; author's translation from the Hebrew.

[12] Jules Harlow, trans., *Mahzor* (New York, rep. 1995).

[13] Ibid.

[14] Ibid.

[15] Ibid., pp. 97-98.

JACOB NEUSNER

LITURGY OF JUDAISM: HISTORY AND FORM: The general term Jewish worship refers more specifically to Rabbinic worship, that is, the system of worship codified by the generations of authorities known loosely as "the rabbis." While Rabbinic myths date some liturgical customs as far back as Moses and even the patriarchs, it is in fact difficult to establish the existence of even elementary Rabbinic worship prior to the second century B.C.E. Only in the first century C.E. does the character of Rabbinic worship come clearly into focus. In particular we find that the Tannaim (c. 70-200 C.E.) are responsible for the structure of Rabbinic worship, while the much later Geonim (c. 757-1038) are responsible for canonizing a particular set of prayers that remains the liturgy of preference for later generations.

Scholars once believed that Jewish liturgy emerged from methodical Tannaitic consultations, arranged by authoritative Jewish central bodies, and representing a monolithic Rabbinic will. Philologists thus sought out putative "original texts" of prayer from which current variations had grown, and they attempted to determine the exact dates and circumstances that gave rise each incremental development. We now know that the Tannaim were a diverse group with often ineffective centralized authority; that despite general agreement on certain principles, variation of interpretation was the rule; and that, consequently, there are no single authoritative "original" prayers to be found. Instead, Tannaitic (and even Amoraic) worship is characterized by relatively freewheeling expressions of specific worship themes. There apparently was an abundance of equally old prayer texts, most of which have been lost to history.

Three institutions especially contributed to the earliest Rabbinic worship: the Temple, the *chavurah* and the synagogue. The Temple's destruction in 70 C.E. coincided with the earliest Tannaim who therefore knew its worship forms, and respected them as scripturally ordained. Succeeding Rabbinic generations accepted the Temple's sacrificial system as paradigmatic for ideal worship and looked forward to a rebuilt Temple with a restored cult at the end of time. Until then, they consciously modeled their own worship after real or imaginary cultic blueprints, characterizing prayer itself, for example, as "an offering of the lips," and announcing that the primary Rabbinic prayer, the *Tefillah*, had replaced the defunct *Tamid* or daily sacrifice.

Nonetheless, two alternative loci for worship, the *chavurah* and the synagogue, both of which had predated the Temple's fall, now rose to prominence. The *chavurah* (pl. *chavurot*) appears in our records by Pharisaic times. *Chavurot* are table-fellowship groups emphasizing worship around meals and featuring purity rules that liken average Israelites to priests and the table at which a meal is eaten to the Temple alter. They were either *ad hoc* gatherings or ongoing associations to celebrate such things as feast days and the birth of children. Out of this milieu grew the Passover *seder*, benedictions over food, and the grace after meals (*birkat hamazon*).

The synagogue too predates the Temple's fall, but not by the many centuries often imagined. Evident in the Gospels, and known both to Paul and to Josephus, the synagogue must have been well established by the first century C.E. But neither written nor archeological data indicate origins much prior to that, certainly not before the second century B.C.E. Sources prior to the Hasmonean revolt (167 B.C.E.)—including Daniel, written on its very eve—are alike in knowing nothing of synagogues, which, therefore can certainly *not* be dated to the Babylonian exile, as is often claimed.

Texts reflecting conditions in the second

and first centuries B.C.E. portray public worship also in village squares under the institutional aegis of a *ma'amad*. The *ma'amad* is described as an extension of the cult, that is, a local gathering at the time that the sacrifices were being offered in Jerusalem; but we hear also of a liturgy there, including the recitation of a *Tefillah* (the Rabbinic prayer *par excellence*) intended to achieve relief from drought. Earlier theory sometimes saw the synagogue as arising out of the *ma'amad*, though it now appears more likely that the synagogue was originally an unrelated, more general communal gathering place to which only eventually Rabbinic worship became attached.

We know little about the relationship of the rabbis to the early synagogue, but they seem at first to have preferred other institutions, especially the study milieu, for their prayers. The *ma'amad* ritual had been led by Elders (*zekenim*), and early synagogue worship was conducted by a new functionary, the *chazzan* (pl. *chazzanim*), a term used today for the synagogue cantor. But synagogue ritual was increasingly dominated by rabbis, to the point where today it is assumed (falsely) to have been the rabbis' place of prayer from the outset.

The synagogue and the *chavurah* (one's home) thus became twin liturgical foci following the Temple's fall. Though Jews can and do pray elsewhere, worship is normally enacted at set times in either or both of these locales, three times daily (see below) and even more extensively on holy days (figs. 94-96).

The liturgical text, the primacy of the blessing: Rabbinic prayers hark back to biblical prototypes, but they are unique in that they feature a standardized prose style known as a *berakhah*, that is, a blessing or benediction. Stylistic rules for framing benedictions evolved through the centuries, but were largely in place by the third century C.E. Blessings are either short or long. Short blessings are one-line formulas, beginning, "Blessed art Thou, Lord our God, Ruler of the Universe, who. . . ." Long blessings may or may not feature the introduction ("Blessed art Thou. . . ."), but they always conclude

with a *chatimah* (lit.: "seal") that sums up the blessing's theme; they are "long" in that the body of the blessing develops its theme, becoming, in essence, a small essay on some aspect of Rabbinic thought. Worship services comprise a variety of verbal material, but feature clusters of blessings strung one after the other. Of these, the following two stand out: the blessings that surround the *Shema* and the *Tefillah*, which are discussed below.

These "blessing-essays" are not the product of single authors; they are composite works reflecting centuries of oral transmission and editorial redaction. They thus betray the fact that the Rabbinic tradition is far from monolithic. One major strand, for example, is Jewish gnosticism (known generally as the praxis of *Yordei Merkavah*, the "Chariot" or "Throne" mystics) which from as early as the second or third centuries C.E. emphasized mantra-like formulas, word strings of synonyms that produced rhythmic regularity without any necessary cognitive enrichment; sometimes accompanied by fasting and body movement, this worship was trance-inducing, the goal being to join the heavenly angels seen by Isaiah (chap. 6), and to praise God with them.

At the same time, other Rabbinic strands stressed the cognitive pole of meaning, by mandating regular worship organized according to set themes. Indeed, for centuries, it was this unvarying thematic progression that identified worship as properly Rabbinic despite its many verbal manifestations in different synagogues. Generally speaking, each theme was allotted its own blessing, the style of which allowed for great variation, in that even after the basic rules for beginning and ending the blessing were in place, there still remained the blessing's body where the theme could be elaborated freely. Thus, expression of themes varied widely from place to place and even from time to time in the same place, as prayer leaders exercised considerable imagination in their renditions. Regardless of the vast differences in wording that resulted, however, the same *order* of blessings and, thus, the same progression of themes was the rule, so that even a highly unusual version of a worship service would be recognizable as just one more interesting delivery of the appropriate thematic elements.

From unfixed text to prayer book: Somewhere between the third and the eighth centuries the various strands of prayer coalesced into fixed liturgies. Lengthy poetic renditions known as *piyyutim* that originally, perhaps, were every-day alternatives used to express the benedictory themes, were eventually reserved for fast or feast days. The mystical mantra-like strata were combined with information-rich theological expressions of the themes. These developments produced final formulations of composite texts betraying both the affective and the cognitive poles of worship. Several such amalgams persisted for centuries, with two recognizable clusters of them taking shape: the Palestinian rite in Palestine and Egypt, and the Babylonian rite in the Tigris-Euphrates basin. The former remained particularly rich in poetry, preferring to continue the age-old tradition of encouraging novel expressions of the mandated blessings at the expense of a single "canonized" prayer text. The latter, however, chose fixity as its goal. It limited poetry to a bare minimum and established set texts to be recited from beginning to end of the standard worship services.

In the middle of the ninth century, Amram, the titular religious leader of Babylonian Jewry, announced his own particular set of texts as incumbent on all Jews. His decree, our first known comprehensive prayer book, is known as *Seder Rav Amram* ("The *Seder* [or order of prayers according to] Rav Amram"). It was accepted as normative by the young Jewish communities and in western Europe especially it eventually became the basis for all subsequent rites. Its power emerged in particular in the wake of Palestinian Jewry's destruction at the hands of the Crusaders and in light of the parallel success of the Babylonian legal tradition, which established Babylonia's cultural hegemony over its Palestinian parallel.

While *Seder Rav Amram* contained all Babylonian-required prayer texts for home and synagogue devotion, along with their legal (*halakhic*) regulations, it consciously omitted the Palestinian alternatives. Jewish worship was henceforth associated with the act of reading one's way through relevant paragraphs of a book, following the requisite guidelines regarding such things as bodily position, congregation/prayer-leader antiphony, and musical rendition. In the centuries that followed, the book was expanded with new poetry expressive of this or that community's identity. But before turning to these expansions, we should look briefly at the contents of *Seder Rav Amram*'s basic service, since it was to remain the essential outline of Jewish worship in all forms of Judaism to this day.

Outline of services, structure and theology: As an apt continuator of Rabbinic tradition, *Seder Rav Amram* does *not* feature texts of the Bible among its prayers. True, biblical citations abound: three of them (Deut. 6:4-9; 11:13-21; Num. 15:37-41) constitute the well-known *Shema Yisrael*, which is recited morning and evening; and psalms too appear here and there in their totality, especially in the psalm collections known as *Hallel*. But biblical snippets are generally embedded transcontextually in Rabbinic blessings, which redefine them according to Rabbinic interpretations. Even the *Shema* has been recast as only a centerpiece bracketed by introductory and concluding blessings; and psalmody is decidedly insignificant here, relative to the blessing structure that predominates. The theology of Rabbinic worship thus reflects the Rabbinic doctrine that the written Bible requires interpretation according to the insights of the oral tradition.

The most important worship units are (1) the *Shema* and its benedictions and (2) the *Tefillah*, "The Prayer [*par excellence*]," which singly or together have constituted the bulk of every synagogue service since the first century C.E., at least.

The *Shema* resembles a Jewish creed in which the assertion of God's unity is elaborated through the accompanying blessings that acknowledge God as (1) *Creator* of light and darkness, (2) *Revealer* of Torah (i.e., *Covenant-maker* with Israel), and (3) *Redeemer* of Israel from Egyptian bondage. God is thus the sole deity, responsible for creation, revelation, and redemption. Historical recollection is linked to eschatology, in that God's redeeming act at the Red Sea is the archetype for Israel's final deliverance at the end of created time when the covenant's promise comes ultimately to its fruition.

Eschatological hope figures even more prominently in the *Tefillah*, a series of nineteen (originally eighteen) benedictions, largely petitionary, organized at the end of the first century. God is asked to grant the necessary insight that leads to repentance and thus to divine pardon and salvation. The blessings that follow define the paradigmatic Rabbinic doctrine of salvation: God will heal the sick, restore fertility to the Land of Israel, return the exiles to their Land, reestablish the Jewish justice system, punish heretics, reward the righteous, rebuild Jerusalem, and bring the messiah son of David to rule in perfect peace.

Along with the *Shema* and the *Tefillah*, early worship featured the reading of the Torah (the first five books of the Bible), on Mondays, Thursdays, and Sabbaths. More than one lectionary seems to have been in effect: Palestinians favored the so-called triennial cycle (actually, a three and a half to four year cycle, despite its title), while Babylonian Jewry developed an annual cycle, which prevails today as a consequence of the Babylonian cultural victory typified by *Seder Rav Amram*. Sabbath mornings saw an additional reading (called *Haftarah*) drawn from the prophets (and the narrative books, like 1 and 2 Sam. or 1 and 2 Kgs., known also as "prophets" in Jewish tradition), and linked in some way to the primary Torah text. The reading of scripture was customarily followed by an interpretive sermon which ended with a *nechemta* (a word of hope), and then, with the *Kaddish*, a prayer calling for the coming of the reign of God. By the eighth century, the *Kaddish* was associated with mourning and assumed to benefit the dead, but its earliest appearance is as a concluding prayer to the study of Torah.

The rabbis favored private spirituality as well, and thus introduced benedictions (usually the short ones) as a means of injecting religious significance into everyday events, as disparate as eating an apple, seeing a rainbow, and going to the bathroom (at which time one was to marvel at and thank God for the system of ducts and tubes that constitute the human body). Similarly, benedictions preceded the performance of commandments (or *mitzvot*, sing.: *mitzvah*), affirming that the act about to be performed—kindling Chanukah lights, perhaps, or performing a circumcision—was of covenantal magnitude. Perhaps the most significant *mitzvah* was the study of Torah, understood generically as the ongoing revelation of God's word, and including both written scripture and oral tradition. Rabbinic spirituality favored such study every morning upon awakening, especially with texts describing the defunct Temple cult, as if reading about sacrifice was the next best thing to doing it. In his *Seder*, Amram included a particular collection of all such texts—the Bible and the rabbis on sacrifice, blessings over the *mitzvah* of Torah study, and benedictions related to the daily miracle of waking up to the world. But he appended these to the beginning of his synagogue liturgy, thus transforming home devotion into preliminary synagogue meditation and study. There it remains to this day, as does a second sort of introductory material Amram included: songs of praise highlighted by a *Hallel* (Pss. 145-150), and intended as preparatory "warm-up" for the statutory *Shema* and *Tefillah*, which remain the most significant rubrics of the daily service.

We saw above the petition for salvation, as defined in the *Tefillah* and as represented in the metaphor of the ultimate reign of God (from the *Kaddish*). But the arrival of God's promised realm presupposes the prior forgiveness of sin. The Amoraim, or rabbis of the Talmud (c. 200-550), thus suggested a daily confession following the *Tefillah*. Amram went further, including not only the opportunity for private devotion there, but also an official Supplication rubric (the *Tachanun*), composed of a collection of prayers acknowledging the lowliness of the human condition. These supplications later grew in importance among western European *Chasidei Ashkenaz* (see below), but were already present in Amram's *Seder*, as an apt continuation of the Amoraic religious anthropology that he inherited.

Thus, with but one exception, the *Alenu*, the major prayers of the daily morning service were in place by Amram's day. Beginning with (1) morning blessings and the study of texts about sacrifice, the worshipper then recited (2) a warm-up *Hallel* (psalms and songs of praise). These introduced the centrally significant (3) *Shema* and its blessings, and (4) *Tefillah*. The *Tefillah*, technically a replacement for the Temple *Tamid* sacrifice, conjured up the cult's penitential function, and led to (5) private prayer, especially the supplicatory *Tachanun*. On appropriate days, (6) scripture and (7) a sermon followed, but in any case (8) a concluding *Kaddish*, calling for God's promised reign on earth, was normative. The only important addition over the years has been the *Alenu*, composed originally as an introduction to Rosh Hashanah's blowing of the *Shofar*, but by the fourteenth century added to the concluding prayers. It too calls for God's ultimate reign on earth.

With slight alteration, the above outline of daily morning prayer (*shacharit*) characterizes every other synagogue service. Mandated afternoon (*minchah*) and evening (*'arvit* or *ma'ariv*) services featuring similar liturgies have by now coalesced into back-to-back services held at sunset. These daily occasions are suitably altered for Sabbaths, fasts, and festivals, when, in addition, the home as worship-setting usually looms larger than the daily norm. Thus, for example, Passover calls for additional synagogue poetry on the theme of the Exodus; but it also features the home *seder* ritual with family and friends. Home liturgy for Sabbaths and holy days include, above all, (1) the kindling of lights, along with a prayer called *Kiddush*, an announcement of the onset of sacred time; and (2) a *Havdalah* (or "separation") ceremony marking a "separation" between sacred and secular time, as the Sabbath or festival ends.

Medieval developments in Europe, structure and theology: *Seder Rav Amram* was followed by a second comprehensive prayer book, *Siddur Saadiah*, a compendium by the renowned tenth century philosopher, exegete, poet and polemicist: Saadiah Gaon.

Yet a third such book, no longer extant, is attributed to the last Gaon of our period, Hai (d. 1038). But Amram, especially, made an impact on all Europeans, who patterned their worship after his instructions and text. A broad division of rites into "Sefardic" as opposed to "Ashkenazic" differentiates later developments in the Iberian peninsula (*Sefarad*) from those in Northern Europe (France and Germany, known together as *Ashkenaz*). In both places, however, the texts grew in bulk as Spanish, French, German, and other Jews composed poetic additions, especially for holy days. In fourteenth century Ashkenaz, the expanding *siddur* (or "order" of prayer) was considered too bulky to be practical, and was split into: (1) a *siddur* for daily and Sabbath use; (2) a *Haggadah* for the Passover *seder*; and (3) a *machzor* for holy day prayers, often including a separate volume for each of the three pilgrim festivals (*Pesach* = Passover; *Shavuot* = Pentecost; and *Sukkot* = Tabernacles) and for the High Holy Days (*Rosh Hashanah* = New Year, and *Yom Kippur* = Day of Atonement). This prayer book taxonomy is common today.

The most important later medieval developments occurred in the mystical tradition that was in part continued, in part revived, and in part newly enriched, both in twelfth century Germany and in thirteenth and fourteenth century Spain—the latter tradition reaching its liturgical zenith in the sixteenth century Ottoman empire, especially in Galilee. Under the influence of medieval piety, particularly that of the mendicant monastic orders of the time, the former movement, known as *Chasidei Ashkenaz* ("The pietists of northern Europe") favored a severely penitential, even ascetic, attitude to prayer; and their influence was substantial in northern and eastern Europe, for centuries. The Spanish school, the Kabbalah—really a philosophy rooted in Provencal neo-Platonism, and transferred south over the Pyrenees—spread throughout the Mediterranean, especially to the Land of Israel, with the expulsion of Jews from Spain in 1492.

In terms of creativity and daring, only the founding Pharisees and Tannaim even approach these sixteenth century kabbalists, who not only composed an entirely novel service to introduce the Sabbath (*Kabbalat Shabbat*, which precedes regular worship on Friday evening), but also redefined the very goal of worship, introducing ecstatic practices reminiscent of the trance-inducing customs of earlier times. These included rote recitation of divine names and the use of music for self-hypnotic purposes. Implicit in their worship was a bold theology whereby (1) God and the universe are declared coterminous; (2) the human existential state is thus equivalent to God's; (3) as the dominant metaphor for the fractured state of being on earth (and in God!) we find the sexual image of an androgynous deity, whose male and female elements are divorced from each other and in anxious search for reunification. Worship is nothing less than the most important means to restore God's male and female parts to wholeness. Thus the normative Rabbinic theology contained in the manifest content of the benedictions was suppressed in favor of a hidden mystical meaning assumed to underlie the prayers. Worshippers were instructed to pray with only the secret meaning in mind. To facilitate that end, introductory meditations called *kavvanot* (sing.: *kavvanah*) were composed, sometimes with a prayer's hidden purpose expressly stated, and sometimes with it only alluded to. In the seventeenth century—and especially in the eighteenth, under the influence of Polish/Russian Chasidism, a theological outgrowth of Kabbalah—Kabbalistic thought spawned new prayer books replete with mystical *kavvanot*, as well as other more exotic innovations, such as diagrams pointing toward the divorced state of God, or to revived gnostic traditions regarding a dual world of light and darkness. These prayers reflected a new anthropology as well, featuring human beings as a reflection of a divided God and a divided world but yearning in prayer for the unity we call *shalom*—"peace" and "wholeness."

The theology implicit in the Jewish mode of worship: The message of worship comes from more than its words. The way of worship prescribed by the rabbis has theological and ecclesiological presuppositions. The primary expression of traditional wor-

ship is corporate. The Jew may pray privately any time, any place, and with any words, gestures, or songs. But the Jew *must* pray with the community three time daily. The congregation must include a quorum (or *minyan*) of at least ten men, the minimum necessary to represent the People Israel. (Traditional Judaism does not recognize women here. On modern-day attitudes to women in worship, see below.) The text is almost invariably first-person plural, "We," indicative of the corporate covenant being celebrated. The prayer leader is included with the people, for the leader functions technically only as a *sheliach tzibbur*, an "agent of the congregation," presenting the public's praise and petition to God. An implicit social contract underlies the relationship, as if, concerned that they may not achieve the proper spiritual dimension, the people give up their right to pray as they wish, and entrust this "public agent" with the power to represent them on high. If the agent proves inept or unfit in character, a new one is selected.

Thus the most important single person in traditional Jewish worship became the *chazzan*, who grew from humble origins as a general caretaker and prayer leader of the ancient synagogue to be the modern cantor, entrusted with the proper recitation of the liturgy. Without a monastic tradition, Jews did not develop unison singing as Christianity did, but it did specialize in the solo song, as the prayer leader chanted blessing after blessing, from the beginning to the end of the service. Ideally, the *chazzan* was held accountable for the highest musical, vocal, and textual competence, no small matter, given the growth of worship traditions over the years. Textual enrichment had gone hand in hand with increased musical sophistication. The Torah, unmarked as to vowels and musical signs, had to be read without error, according to the proper cantillation mode; and even the prayer texts required specific knowledge of *nusach*—the name given to the musical systems—that varied with the season of the year and the service of the day.

It became customary for *chazzan* and congregation to sing the service antiphonally, a custom still to be found in Conservative and

Reconstructionist congregations, but especially among the Orthodox. The congregation reads quickly through a prayer, each worshipper at a somewhat different speed, and often, out loud as well, a custom called *davvening*. The *chazzan*, who faces the same way as the congregation of which he is an integral part, listens for the noise to die down, indicating to him that everyone has finished the blessing in question. Then the *chazzan* repeats it, all or in part, but with the correct *nusach*, and, especially in recent Ashkenazic tradition, occasionally in extended melismatic form also, something akin to a jazz musician's improvisation around the melodies and harmonies of traditional tunes. This "dialogic" model, however, is ancient, going back to the very origin of Rabbinic worship, the implicit theological model being the angelic "dialogue" in Isaiah's vision, whereby two groups of angels face each other, alternately praising God. The *Sefardic* tradition, which moved from Spain and Portugal, mostly to Mediterranean countries where it was influenced by Muslim expressions of piety, largely retained the older congregational antiphony, by eschewing an elaborate cantorial solo tradition.

The dominant stance of the Jew before God is as giver of praise. Jews may be thankful—indeed, they must be—but they stand in covenantal partnership with God, such that the stance of receiving everything as a gift of pure grace, for which one can respond with nothing but intense gratitude alone, is somewhat alien to Jewish tradition. True, the famous prayer *Avinu Malkenu*, associated originally (second century) with fasts occasioned by a drought but now a staple for the high holy day period, pleads, "Have mercy on us . . . for we have no works." But a theology of *mitzvah* (covenantal commandment) could hardly hold that extreme notion; commandments (*mitzvot*) were nothing if not works. So despite human sin, God owes Israel something under covenantal terms. And Israel turns to God in a characteristically affirmative stance, praising the One from whom blessings flow and acknowledging God as their origin and source.

Turning even to private prayer, we see Judaism's communal focus, as well as another aspect of the Jewish world view, its appreciation of the cosmos as something valuable in its own right, an object to be enjoyed. Private prayer, it will be recalled, was established primarily around the memorization of set "short-form" blessings appropriate to acts of enjoyment or as introductions to performing commandments. In the latter category, we find once again the dominant image of the Jew as a member of a covenanted people, intent on performing covenantal acts with intentional awareness that they are precisely that, *mitzvot*, divine commands that one is fortunate enough to do. In the former case, we cannot miss the positive stance toward the world, which persists despite even the heightened penitential consciousness of the Chasidei Ashkenaz, who may have insisted on the sinfulness of humanity but never imputed such negativity to God's cosmos. Thus men and women are to enjoy the world, its fruit and its rainbows, its sages and its scholars, all of which, among other things, are to be greeted with pertinent blessings. Not only the sense of sight, but hearing too and even smell, are positively codified in blessing forms that celebrate their functions, for there are blessings on hearing good news (or bad news), on smelling fragrant flowers or herbs, and so on. The theology of Jewish worship insists that it is a sin to evade the world which God has prepared us to experience.

Modern developments, Europe: By the nineteenth century, post-Napoleonic Jewry in northern Europe found itself increasingly released from medieval ghettoes. Especially in large commercial and cultural capitals, enlightened Jewish communities faced the fact that their liturgy seemed still to be reflective of pre-modern consciousness. Beyond even the outmoded tenets of its troubling content, it was the manner of traditional prayer that Jews found disturbing. Services were long, entirely in Hebrew, lacking a sermon in the vernacular, and often conducted by cantors whose medieval style was deemed outmoded and not even in keeping with what tradition ideally demanded. The average service featured a noisy congregation of individualistic worshippers rocking back and forth and shouting prayers not at all in unison. This *davvening* hardly accorded with the dominant aesthetic of nineteenth century Europe, where worship was assumed to call for quietude, reverence, and decorum. Beginning in Alsace, but quickly spreading to Berlin, Hamburg, Vienna, and elsewhere, Jews initiated rapid and sometimes thorough worship reform.

Musically, the old modes and sounds were notated according to modern standards and recast so that "folk" music came out sounding like western classics. The *chazzan* was removed in favor of a singer and choir, who would render the tunes without the traditional cantorial embellishment. Rabbis learned to preach in German and to direct truncated worship services out of translated prayer books, stripped down to a basic liturgy; German translations or paraphrases omitted difficult-to-hold doctrines like the belief in bodily resurrection or an ultimate return from "exile" and emphasized the universalist strains of Jewish thought at the expense of particularistic ones. Of the two loci for Jewish worship, the home receded in importance, as Judaism shifted to the synagogue, which modern Jews saw as their "church."

European reform was not as far-reaching as it would become on American shores. Men generally still wore the traditional garb of prayer, a headcovering and a prayer shawl (*tallit*); and though women were granted theoretical equality as early as 1845 and admitted therefore into the praying community, they still sat in a separate section reserved for them. But the Reform Movement had been born.

Three Rabbinic conferences in mid-century featured deliberations of this religious "reformation" of Judaism, including such matters as the use of Hebrew in prayer. One rabbi—later claimed as the progenitor of the Conservative Movement—walked out of the proceedings when his liberal colleagues refused sufficiently to privilege Hebrew as a sacred tongue. In 1819 and again in 1841, a Hamburg congregation published a liberal prayer book, with resulting charges and counter-charges, condemnations and ex-

communications between traditionalists and modernists. But nineteenth century European politics was increasingly reactionary, so that the fight for change moved to America.

United States: American Jewish liturgy has gone through three stages. The first is the period known as Classical Reform, which reached its zenith in 1894/95, with the publication of a *Union Prayer Book* for Reform congregations. Reforms begun in Europe were carried through here, generally in a sweeping fashion undreamed of across the ocean. Worship featured short services almost entirely in English; it was dominated by western music sung by a hidden choir, and a sermon similar to what one would hear in an Episcopalian or Congregationalist church. Folk traditions like specialized worship garb and old-world customs like carrying the Torah through the congregation were erased. The mood was one of awe, and the worshippers were almost completely passive, expected to rise and sit in unison, sometimes to read some responses together, rarely ever to sing, and, by and large, to recognize the presence of God as a transcendent being suggested by the staid architectural and cultural magnificence which enfolded them.

The second stage developed in 1881 to 1924 with the migration to the United States of eastern European Jews, for whom classical Reform seemed cold and devoid of Jewish substance or feeling. The new immigrants crystallized into the Conservative Movement, which orchestrated worship styles similar to those they had known in eastern Europe but modernized in North American format and codified liturgically in 1946. By then, eastern Europeans had joined Reform Temples too, bringing with them a yearning for traditional melodies and the warmth of the folk culture that classical Reform had jettisoned. The depression and World War II then delayed rapid evolution for two decades, and the shock of the Holocaust as well as the need to build and then to support the State of Israel readjusted Jewish concern away from local spirituality and toward world politics. But the movement of Jews to the suburbs brought a recognizably different form of Jewish worship, especially for Reform Jews, whose classical style had been dependent on huge sanctuaries and pipe organs that no one in suburbia could afford, or, for that matter, even wanted any more. Of the greatest moment was a certain child-centeredness of the 1950s and '60s, which occasioned children's services and children's prayer books (especially among Conservative Jews), and froze adult liturgies in old forms that fewer and fewer adults attended, until the cultural revolution in the late '60s and '70s.

By then, the third stage, unleashed in part by the ambiance of a Vietnam generation, flower children, and a search for new forms of spirituality, had begun. Unhappiness with suburban worship and the need to express theologically the loss of the six million in the Holocaust, and the miracle of a modern Jewish state led to the publication of new adult prayer books. In 1972, the Reform Movement began ordaining women as rabbis and investing them as cantors, reforms that eventually were replicated by Conservative and Reconstructionist Jews as well, the result being a sudden burst of gender consciousness. (Reconstructionism, American Judaism's fourth movement, had broken away from Conservative Judaism, following the philosophy of Mordecai Kaplan, who retained traditional liturgy, but devoid of certain traditional Jewish beliefs, including a personal deity and chosen peoplehood.)

The liturgical renewal since the 1960s parallels a similar trend in North America at large, and even worldwide, wherever western religions and their liturgies have spread. Akin to a Third Great Awakening in American history or even a Second Reformation in the west generally, and abetted by technological innovations in the art of inexpensive mass printing, a virtual plethora of new liturgies are now available. An outstanding example is the *Artscroll* series, an Orthodox set of volumes that has virtually replaced earlier traditional prayer books in North American circles, and in England, even threatened to unseat the venerable *Singer Prayer Book* that has dominated British worship since 1890. It combines theological ultra-conservatism with traditional scholarship, even restoring old liturgical lines once removed by Jewish censors who had either frowned upon certain extreme statements of Jewish faith or feared hostile Gentile reaction to them.

In all three North American liberal movements too, new liturgies have multiplied as never before. They feature (1) modern English translation or altogether new creations alongside Hebrew originals; (2) the recapturing of poetry from the gamut of Jewish tradition, especially by Hebrew poets who exemplify a new Jewish cultural consciousness occasioned by Israel's rebirth; (3) creative ritual for the new Jewish holy days of *Yom Hashoah* (Holocaust Day) and *Yom Ha'atsma'ut* (Israel Independence Day); and (4) affirmation of gender egalitarianism through gender-inclusive language. Musically, Reform congregations have restored the cantor (now man or woman) in place of distant choirs and classical singers, and everywhere, traditional melodies vie with a new "American sound" created by a growing cadre of synagogue composers. Above all, we find an accent again on spirituality, not only in the synagogue, but in the home too, which, even in Reform ranks, is reemerging as a locus for the Jew's stance before God.

The newest trend as of the 1990s is an abundance of special services like New Moon (*Rosh Chodesh*) liturgies used by women's groups to exemplify women's spirituality and consciousness, and "healing services," usually *ad hoc* rituals that do not follow the normal times and structure for prayer, but which attract small groups to sing and pray for wholeness, peace of mind, and healing of body and soul. Of long-term interest is an apparent trend toward the abandonment of official movement liturgies, a development facilitated by computer technology and by social mores that have weakened the esteem accorded to centralized authority in general. More and more North American congregations use independently created liturgies, often created on their own or borrowed from each other, but not authorized by their movements. The proclivity of Judaism toward a centralized official text of prayer since Rav Amram in the ninth century may be coming to an end.

Bibliography

Elbogen, Ismar, *Jewish Liturgy: A Comprehensive History* (Philadelphia, 1993).

Hoffman, Lawrence A., and Nancy Wiener, "The Liturgical State of the World Union for Progressive Judaism," in *European Judaism* 24:1 (1991): 10-21.

Hoffman, Lawrence A., *Beyond the Text: a Holistic Approach to Liturgy* (Bloomington, 1987).

Hoffman, Lawrence A., *The Canonization of the Synagogue Service* (Notre Dame and London, 1979).

Langer, Ruth, To Worship God Properly (Cincinnati, 1998).

Reif, Stefan C., *Judaism and Hebrew Prayer* (Cambridge, 1993).

LAWRENCE A. HOFFMAN

M

MAGIC, MAGIC BOWLS, ASTROLOGY IN JUDAISM: Judaism, like most systems of religion, distinguishes between miracles—the extraordinary deeds of the true God or agents of the true God—and magic—the extraordinary deeds of false gods or their agents.[1] The former acts are judged good and acceptable, so that a person who is able to use the power of the divine for purposes the religion deems right and appropriate is thought of as a holy man, miracle worker, or sage. By contrast, a person—usually an outsider or practitioner of a different religion—who demonstrates similar abilities is derided as a witch, demon, or fiend.

This distinction between magic and miracle is crucial to our comprehension of the Hebrew Bible's most complete list of prohibited magical practices (Deut. 18:10-11):[2]

> There shall not be found among you any one who burns his son or his daughter as an offering, any one who practices divination, a soothsayer, or an augur, or a sorcerer, or a charmer, or a medium, or a wizard, or a necromancer.

This list of prohibited forms of divination and magical practices is echoed throughout the Bible, e.g., at Lev. 19:26, 19:31, and 20:1-6. Yet despite the directness of its condemnation of these practices, Scripture itself frequently speaks in neutral or positive language about a wide range of similar divinatory and magical acts. Interpreting dreams, using magic staffs, reciting blessings and curses, referring to oracles—these are but a few of the "magical" procedures that elsewhere figure prominently as suitable behaviors of the progenitors and heroes of the Israelite nation.

In making sense of these contradictions, we must be clear that the distinction between permitted and prohibited, miracle and magic, has less to do with what deed is attempted—with or without success—than with the systemic context in which the deed is carried out. At the heart of Israelite thinking is the certainty that what *we* accomplish involves a miracle and is good, while what *you* do is magic and evil. This distinction is prominent and important, for instance, in the story of Moses's confrontation with the magicians of Pharaoh (Exod. 7:11, 7:22, etc.).[3] Moses and Aaron, on the one side, and the Egyptians, on the other, perform the same actions and thus seem to have similar knowledge and powers (with the exception that Moses and Aaron's "magic" appears to be more powerful than the Egyptians'; see Exod. 7:12, where the serpent formed of Aaron's staff eats the serpents formed from the Egyptian magicians' staffs). But while they act in manners similar to the Egyptians, Moses and Aaron are not referred to by the negative title "magician" at all. The determining factor is neither their capacity to perform wonders nor the specific nature of the trick they perform. Those who do what we would call magic are characterized, rather, on the basis of the source of their knowledge and power: God vs. sorcery. Thus a distinction is made between what *we* Israelites know and can do with the help of our God, and what *you* non-Israelites know and can do through other, venal forces. In light of this distinction, as we already have seen, the Israelites' actions are in the category of miracle; those of the outsider are (mere) magic.

Magic in Rabbinic Judaism: Taking up the fundamental distinction introduced already by the Hebrew Scriptures, in the first centuries C.E. Rabbinic Judaism presented what to modern readers appears at first sight to be contradictory views of "magic." On the one hand, the rabbis condemn magic as one of the "ways of the Amorites" (M. Shab. 6:10), and they sanction its practitioners to death by stoning (M. San. 7:7). One who so much as whispers over a wound the words of Exod. 15:26 ("I will put none of the diseases upon you that I have put on the Egyptians, for I am the Lord who heals you") is said to lose his place in the world to come (M. San. 10:1). Indeed, it is reported that, to quell magical practices, Simeon b. Shetah hung eighty witches on a single day (M. San. 6:4). And yet, on the other hand, these same sources frequently describe without condemnation or concern miraculous or magical acts performed by both rabbis and common people. As our examination of the biblical legacy leads us to anticipate, these superficially contradictory attitudes do not emerge from a distinction the rabbis perceive in the character of what is done or attempted, but, rather, from their analysis of the particular qualities and purposes of the individual who carries out the act. In the Rabbinic view, an unusual events is "magic"—and culpable—or "miracle"—and laudable—depending upon who does it, in what context, and for what purpose. Exactly what is accomplished is rarely at issue at all.

For the rabbis, miracles are distinguished from magic primarily by the fact that the former are performed by a sage whose power derives from the merit earned through knowledge of Torah and a life of piety. In their academies, sages participated in the processes of revelation that yielded Torah. In doing this, they became more than simply partners with God, who himself had revealed Torah. Rather, insofar as what rabbis said and thought was understood to embody the precise thought and words of God,[4] Rabbinic texts equate sages themselves with scrolls of the Torah. This is explicit at Y. M.Q. 3:7:[5]

A. He who sees a disciple of a sage who has died is as if he sees a scroll of the Torah that has been burned.

B. R. Jacob bar Abayye in the name of R. Aha: "An elder who forgot his learning because of some accident that happened to him—they treat him with the sanctity owed to an ark [of the Torah]."

The Torah, God's revelation, is incarnate in the sage, who as a result can use the power of God to perform wonders. Like Moses, whose wonders were achieved through special capacities granted him by God, so the sage can carry out astounding acts that are deemed legitimate and appropriate. Indeed, a particular sage's prestige would be substantially enhanced should it become clear that his knowledge of Torah in conjunction with other characteristic Rabbinic virtues had given him supernatural powers (Y. Ta. 3:11.1V):

C. There was a house that was about to collapse over there [in Babylonia], and Rab set one of his disciples in the house, until they had cleared out everything from the house. When the disciple left the house, the house collapsed.

D. And there are those who say that it was R. Adda bar Ahwah.

E. Sages sent and said to him, "What sort of good deeds are to your credit [that you have that much merit]?"

F. He said to them, "In my whole life no man ever got to the synagogue in the morning before I did. I never left anybody there when I went out. I never walked four cubits without speaking words of Torah. Nor did I ever mention teachings of Torah in an inappropriate setting. I never laid out a bed and slept for a regular period of time. I never took great strides among the associates. I never called my fellow by a nickname. I never rejoiced in the embarrassment of my fellow. I never cursed my fellow when I was lying by myself in bed. I never walked over in the marketplace to someone who owed me money.

G. "In my entire life I never lost my temper in my household."

H. This was meant to carry out that which is stated as follows: "I will give heed to the way that is blameless. Oh when wilt thou come to me? I will walk with integrity of heart within my house" (Ps. 101:2).

The correlation of learning and virtuous behavior with the ability to work wonders is here explicit. The following passages, which appear at B. San. 67b-68a, ultimately make clear the way in which such laudable use of Rabbinical power is distinguished from the magical deeds performed by non-rabbis. The magic tricks of non-rabbis, but not those of a rabbi, render the lay magician culpable for death:

    A. There was a woman who tried to take dirt from under the feet of R. Hanina [for use against him in sorcery].

    B. He said to her, "If it works out for you, go do it, [for at Deut. 4:25] 'There is no one else besides him' is written."

    C. Can this be so [that Hanina permitted the woman to attempt a magical act]?

    D. [This seems impossible, since, at Deut. 4:25] "There is no one else besides him" is written.

    E. And [suggesting that sorcerers attempt to avail themselves of some different power] did not R. Yohanan say, "Why are they called sorcerers? Because they deny the power of the family above"?

    F. R. Hanina was in a special category, because he had a great deal of merit.

At issue in determining whether or not an act is forbidden as sorcery is the perceived source of the magical power. As D-E makes clear, what the sorcerer wishes to do is forbidden not because of the nature of the act but because it calls upon a power in heaven other than God. Hanina's different view is explained, F, as resulting from his own special character as a sage. He permits the woman's attempt against him because he holds her in fact to be powerless against God, who will protect him. The notion that sorcery, unlike the rabbis' own (permitted) acts, derives from outside powers, is developed in the continuation of the passage:

    A. Said R. Aibu bar Nigri said R. Hiyya bar Abba, "'With their sorcery' (Exod. 7:22) refers to magic through the agency of demons, 'with their enchantments' (Exod. 7:11) refers to sorcery without outside help.

    B. "This is as is said, 'And the flame of the sword that turns of itself' (Gen. 3:24) [that is, without outside aid]."

    C. Said Abayye, "If [the sorcerer] uses exact methods, it is through a demon.

    D. "If the sorcery does not work through exact methods, it is through enchantment."

Again, what distinguishes sorcery and enchantments from the rabbis' own permitted acts of wonders is that the former do not derive from the power of Torah. Sorcery, rather, uses demons or the magician's own personal powers. This notion, that magical deeds can be accomplished without the aid of an outside power at all, leads to a further distinction, described in the following, which also appears at B. San. 67b-68a:

    A. Said Abayye, "The laws of sorcery are like the laws of the Sabbath.

    B. "There are some actions that are punished by execution through stoning, some for which there is no penalty but which are forbidden, and some that are permitted to begin with.

    C. "He who does a deed is punishable by stoning, but he who merely creates an illusion does what is forbidden but is exempt from punishment [M. San. 7:11D].

    D. "And as to what is permitted to begin with, it accords with the matter involving R. Hanina and R. Oshaia.

    E. "Every Friday afternoon they would study the laws of creation and make for themselves a third-grown calf, and they would eat it."

The performance of illusions is not culpable. These are parlor tricks and, while they should not be performed, are distinguished from real acts of magic, which are punished by execution through stoning.[6] But the more important distinction here is between all such acts of magic, C, and the wonders accomplished by rabbis, E. The miracle performed by Hanina and Oshaia is permitted because it uses the power of God, which the rabbis attain through study of the laws of creation. While it is magic, it is "our" magic, accomplished through knowledge of Torah, and so permitted.

The rabbis thus distinguish the use of the power of Torah from deeds that are sorcery or "black" magic. In making this distinction, they in no way deny the existence and power of magical acts. Their point, rather, is simply to distinguish the miracles that knowledge of Torah allowed rabbis to do, which they deemed proper and acceptable, from what sorcerers do, which they view always as wrong. An important aspect of this distinction was the rabbis' certainty that, based upon the power of God and Torah, their power—like that of Moses—was greater than the power of (mere) magicians (B. San. 67b):

    A. Yannai came to an inn. He said to them, "Give me some water to drink." They brought him a flour-and-water drink.

    B. He saw that the woman's lips were moving. He poured out a little of the drink, and it turned into scorpions. He said to them, "I drank something of yours, now you take a drink of mine."

    C. He gave her something to drink, and she turned into an ass. He mounted her and went out to the market place.

    D. Her girl-friend came and nullified the charm, so he was seen riding around on a woman in the market place.

When Yannai is given a drink that, when spilled out, turns into scorpions, he repays the innkeeper with a potion that turned her into an ass. While the innkeeper's girlfriend is able to break the spell, the clear point here is that the rabbi, by using his powers, retained the upper hand. Not only did he escape the danger presented by sorcerers, but he was able to use his own power again such magicians, at least temporarily turning one of them into an ass. Strikingly, although the passage highlights the greater power of the rabbi, it also makes the point that, overall, there is no intrinsic difference between his magic and that of the non-rabbi. What he can do is pretty much what they are able to do, including their ability to undo the spell he has cast. So as we have seen all along, the distinction between miracles and magic is purely one of perspective: what distinguishes the two is the ultimate source of the power that makes the deed possible.[7]

In similar passages, the Talmud reports that Ashi knew of a person who could produce ribbons of silk from his nostrils; Hiyya speaks of an Arab who chopped up a camel and, by ringing a bell, caused it to come together again; Eliezer states that he taught Aqiba how to cause an entire field of cucumbers to grow and then to be harvested simply by saying a few words. These reports of magic performed by rabbis, common Jews, and non-Jews suggest that despite biblical and Rabbinic prohibitions against sorcery, the use of magic within the general culture of the Talmudic period had a significant impact upon Jewish society. Such practices were largely accepted as real and, when performed by sages who used the power of Torah, were deemed appropriate methods of protecting people from harm or of accomplishing other legitimate purposes.

Magic bowls: The Talmud portrays Jews in late antiquity as accepting and participating in the culture of magic/miracles of their age. The use of magical powers was seen as normal, and it was sanctioned so long as the person involved stood within the Rabbinic community and used magic for purposes accepted within Rabbinic religion. This implication of the literary sources is strengthened by archaeological evidence that reveals the extent to which the Jews of the Talmudic period, like the non-Jews of the cultures in which they lived, accepting and indeed depended upon the efficacy of magical spells for personal protection from demons and other ills.

This dependence is shown by a form of magical talisman found frequently in homes of the Talmudic period. The term "magic bowl" refers to a pottery bowl on which was written a magical formula used to drive away evil spirits or to invoke a deity's help in preserving and protecting individuals or a family. During the Talmudic period, in roughly 300-600 C.E., such bowls were in common use in Babylonia by Christians, Mazdeans, Mandeans, and Jews. While bowls in use in Jewish homes often were prepared by Jews who were not involved with or representative of the Rabbinical academies, certain Rabbinical figures also were deemed potent agents the citation of whose names could drive away particular demons. The names of these rabbis accordingly appear frequently on magic bowls and are invoked in spells written to protect an individual or property from demons. In this way, the Talmud's own image of the rabbi as a wonder-working holy man entered into and was utilized within the popular culture of the day.

The formulas used on magic bowls and the deities invoked are common across religious traditions. The bowls apparently were prepared by professionals, for instance, by Jews for both Jewish and non-Jewish use. A particular practitioner would be hired to produce a bowl not because of his religious or cultural origins but because of his reputation for success. This means that only certain references found on the extant bowls, but not features of design or the overall formulas used, signify the religious context in which the bowl was prepared. Mention of the rabbi Joshua b. Perahia, for instance, suggests a Jewish origin, while reference to Jesus the Messiah clearly suggests a Christian context. For the most part, however, even references to specific holy-men or the use of particular incantations are uniform across the religions. Identification of the bowls as Jewish, Christian, or Mandean accordingly usually depends primarily upon the script in which the incantation was prepared: Aramaic letters are Jewish; Syriac script indicates a Christian source; and Mandean lettering suggests a Mandean origin.

The majority of extant magic bowls were found during excavations in Nippur in 1888-1889. They were found upside down in the ruins of houses, with one or more bowl found in almost every house as well as in cemeteries, where they apparently served to lay ghosts at rest. The bowls were used by individuals and families seeking protection for houses and property, e.g., cattle, often with a particular concern for domestic sexual life and unborn babies. Frequent targets of the bowls are Lilis and Liliths, which personify sexual abnormality, prey upon women and children, and were understood to produce offspring with human beings.

The chief element of the bowls is an incantation composed of repeating phrases, words, or syllables believed to have the power to bind favorable powers, on the one side, or demons, on the other, to some designated action. Angels, in Jewish bowls, and deities, on pagan ones, frequently are adduced, and there appears to have been an attempt to use as many names as possible, to harness, as it were, as many forces as were available against as many demons as might be active. The spell's main power, however, derived from terminology declaring that the demon has been rendered unable to exercise its control, for instance, that it is "bound, sealed, countersealed, exorcised, hobbled, and silenced." The separation of a Lilith from her victim often is expressed in terms of a writ of divorce.

The incantations generally begin with an invocation, followed by the name of the client or clients, the categories of demons to be purged, the names of the angels or deities in which the spells are pronounced, and a conclusion. Jewish texts frequently refer to the angels Michael, Gabriel, and Raphael. The name Yahweh also occurs, often broken down into individual, repeated, letters or syllables.

The evidence of these magic bowls suggests the extent to which Jews, like other people of late antiquity, took for granted the existence of special powers in the universe. Deriving from deities or demons, from gods or from *the* God, these powers could be controlled and used to the benefit of those with special knowledge and/or piety. The Rabbinic literature, of course, distinguished the actions of Jews—rabbis and lay people alike—from those of non-Jews. What the former did, performed in the name of God, was accepted as right and good. It stood in contradistinction to the same acts performed by non-Jews, whose "sorcery" was seen as vile and dangerous. In the magic bowls we see the way in which, in the common culture of the people, even these distinctions were blurred. The Jewish community shared in the broader attitude of its day, accepting the existence of demons and depending upon people's ability, through incantations and spells, to protect themselves and their property.

Sefer HaRazim: An early work of Jewish mysticism, the "Book of Mysteries" sheds further light on the extent to which the mystical and magical doctrines of the Hellenistic world were familiar to and accepted by the Jews of the Talmudic period. The work details prayers and sacrifices to be offered to pagan and Jewish deities in magical ceremonies and includes an invocation of Helios in Greek, transliterated into Hebrew script. Sefer HaRazim contains deliberations on the angels, discussions of the seven heavens, and about thirty sets of instructions for those seeking to know the future, influence people in power, bring their enemies to ruin, be healed, speak with the moon and stars, and accomplish other similar desires. Authored by a Jew, the book is written in Mishnaic Hebrew and has a close philological relationship to the language of the magic bowls of its same period. Based upon content and style, the work probably belongs to the Talmudic period, although it possibly contains Greco-European magical texts from as late as the eighth century.

Sefer HaRazim originally was known from references scattered throughout the Sefer Raziel. It was reconstructed, apparently in its entirety, by Mordecai Margalioth on the basis of fragments from the Cairo genizah and Hebrew, Latin, and Arabic manuscripts. The relatively short book now contains about eight hundred lines divided into seven chapters. While composed in Hebrew, it is replete with transliterated Greek, representing the technical terms of Greek magic. The book includes the names of about seven hundred angels and, following its chapters on the lower six heavens, contains a chapter on the seventh heaven, dealing with God's throne and the throne of great light.

Astrology: The magic bowls, Sefer Ha-Razim, and the Talmudic theory of magic in general portray the existence in the universe of powers that can be exploited by those who know Torah. The idea that such powers can be employed in the service of humans is further developed in Talmudic discussions of astrology, which conceive the stars and planets to have a direct influence upon the direction of collective and individual human history.

This notion of a correspondence between what happens in the heavens and on earth is largely absent from the Hebrew Bible, which, in texts predating the Babylonian Exile, displays no astrological conceptions at all. First under Babylonian and then Hellenistic influence, such conceptions emerged only episodically in the biblical period. They appear in such texts as Is. 47:13, which reveals a negative attitude towards astrology: "You are wearied with your many counsels; let them stand forth and save you, those who divide the heavens, who gaze at the stars, who at the new moons predict what shall befall you." Dan. 2:27-30 similarly rejects the notion that astrologers can predict the future, even as it suggests that the future can be foretold insofar as the Israelite deity has made it explicitly known, for instance, in the king's dream:

> Daniel answered the king, "No wise men, enchanters, magicians, or astrologers can show to the king the mystery which the king has asked, but there is a God in heaven who reveals mysteries, and he has made known to King Nebuchadnez'zar what will be in the latter days. Your dream and the visions of your head as you lay in bed are these: To you, O king, as you lay in bed came thoughts of what would be hereafter, and he who reveals mysteries made known to you what is to be. But as for me, not because of any wisdom that I have more than all the living has this mystery been revealed to me, but in order that the interpretation may be made known to the king, and that you may know the thoughts of your mind."

Daniel strikingly denies the abilities of magicians and astrologers even as he asserts that the knowledge they *claim* to be able to provide is in fact available through himself. Utilizing the distinction with which we already have become familiar, Daniel asserts that the knowledge he is able to impart has nothing to do with magic or enchantments: Daniel knows what he knows because it is the will of the God of Israel that it be known. Thus we deal not with magic but with miracle, not with astrology but with revelation.

Knowledge of and interest in the science of astrology accordingly entered Talmudic Judaism not through the Hebrew Bible— which rejects this science—but through Greco-Roman culture. This is clear from the fact that the common Talmudic term for an astrologer uses not the designations found at Is. 47:13 ("those who divide the heavens," "those who gaze at the stars") or in the book of Daniel ("predictors") but terms originating in the Greco-Roman world itself: *astralog* ("astrologer") in the land of Israel, and *Caldei* ("Chaldeans") in Babylonia. These individuals are practitioners of a science referred to as *astralogia*, that is, the Greek term "astrology."

As in the case of the magic that the rabbis conceded non-Jews are in fact able to perform, so Rabbinic texts are clear that a direct correlation does exist between what occurs on earth and in heaven. Even so, the Talmudic rabbis overwhelmingly disapproved of the art of astrology. They held, on the one hand, that, under the direct protection of God, the Israelite nation is not subject to the stars. And they argued, on the other, that, even though astrologers can accurately predict the future, since they do not comprehend the manifold ways in which their predictions might be fulfilled, the knowledge is as likely to get their clients into trouble as it is to save them.

The basic notion of the correlation between heavenly and earthly events, along with the claim that Israel is not subject to that correlation, is made in the following passage at T. Suk. 2:5-6:

> A. On account of four sorts of deeds are the lights [of the heaven] eclipsed:
> B. because of counterfeiters, perjurers, people who raise small cattle, and people who cut down good trees.
> C. And because of four sorts of deeds are Israelite householders handed over to the government:
> D. because of holding on to writs of indebtedness that have already been paid, because of lending on interest, because of pledging funds to charity but not paying up, and because of having the power to protest and not protesting [wrong doing].

Actions on earth, A-B, have consequences in heaven. This is viewed, C-D, as parallel to the more common Israelite theodicy, which holds that Israelites' sinfulness is punished through the increased power of the gentile nations among whom the people of Israel dwell. The continuation of the passage, T. Suk. 2:6, makes a correlative point to A-B, explaining why astrology can work:

> A. When the lights [of the heaven] are in eclipse, it is a bad omen for the whole world.
> B. It is to be compared to a mortal king who built a palace and finished it and arranged a banquet, and then brought in the guests. He got mad at them and said to the servant, "Take away the light from them," so all of them turned out to be sitting in the dark.

> C. R. Meir would say, "When the lights of heaven are in eclipse, it is a bad omen for Israel, for they are used to blows.
> D. "It is to be compared to a teacher who came into the school house and said, 'Bring me the strap.' Now who gets worried? The one who is used to being strapped!"
> E. When the sun is in eclipse, it is a bad omen for the nations of the world.
> F. [When] the moon is in eclipse, it is a bad omen for Israel,
> G. since the gentiles reckon their calendar by the sun, and Israel by the moon.
> H. When it is in eclipse in the east, it is a bad omen for those who live in the east.
> I. When it is in eclipse in the west, it is a bad omen for those who live in the west.
> J. When it is in eclipse in-between, it is a bad omen for the whole world.
> K. When it turns red, it is a sign that punishment by the sword is coming into the world.
> L. When it is like sack-cloth, it is a sign that punishment by pestilence and famine are coming into the world.
> M. If [the lights of the heaven] are in eclipse at their entry [into sunset], the punishment will tarry. [When they are in eclipse] when they rise, the punishment is coming fast.
> N. And some say matters are reversed.
> O. You have no nation in the whole world that is smitten,[8] the god of which is not smitten right along with it,
> P. as it is said, "And against all the gods of Egypt I will execute judgments" (Exod. 12:12).
> Q. When Israel is occupied with Torah, they do not have to worry about all these omens,
> R. as it is said, "Thus says the Lord, 'Do not learn the way of the gentiles, nor be dismayed at the signs of the heavens, for the nations are dismayed at them'" (Jer. 10:2).

The long introduction at A-P sets up the main point, which is at Q-R. The science of astrology is in fact effective in predicting the future, except as regards the people of Israel when they are true to their covenant obligations. Then they can be certain that they are under the direct protection of God, so that they need have no concern for heavenly signs.

While denying that what is forecast in the stars applies to the people of Israel when the nation follows the covenant by occupying itself with Torah, the rabbis still are clear that they accept the basic premise of astrology. For they maintain that one's character and destiny are determined by the time of one's birth, either by the day of the week on which one is born or by the star that is ascendant at the exact time of the birth. The former view, which says that the day counts, is based on the notion of the power of God's acts of creation; the character of each day, in this view, is determined by the things that, in the beginning, God created on that day. But the other view accepts without hesitance the perspective of Greco-Roman culture, that the heavenly luminaries are gods that govern the earth. This point is explicit at B. Shab. 156a-b:

A. It was written in R. Joshua b. Levi's notebook, "One who is born on Sunday will be a man without 'one thing' in him."
B. What is the meaning of a man without "one thing" in him?
C. Should I say, without one good quality? But did not R. Ashi say, "I was born on Sunday"? So it must be, "A man without one thing to his disgrace."
D. But did not R. Ashi say, "I and Dimi bar Qaquzeta were born on Sunday: I am a king, and he is a *capo di capi*"?
E. Rather, it means, either wholly good or wholly bad. How come? Because light and darkness were created on that day.
F. [Reverting to the notebook:] "One who is born on Monday will be contentious. How come? Because the waters were divided that day. One who was born on a Tuesday will be wealthy and promiscuous. How come? Because herbs were created that day [and they multiply rapidly and commingle with other herbs]. One who was born on Wednesday will be wise and have a great memory. How come? Because that is the day on which the heavenly luminaries were hung up. One who was born on Thursday will do deeds of generosity. How come? Because fish and birds were created that day [and they are fed through God's generosity]. One who was born on Friday will be someone who makes the rounds [in his search for learning]."
G. Said R. Nahman bar Isaac, "One who makes the rounds to do religious deeds."
H. [Reverting to the notes:] "One who is born on the Sabbath will die on the Sabbath, because the preeminent Sabbath day was desecrated on his account."

I. Said Raba bar R. Shila, "And he will be called a great saint."

The continuation of this passage endorses the general principle of the validity of astrology but rejects the specific way in which Joshua b. Levi applies that principle. Hanina argues that the day on which a person is born is not specific enough to allow determination of his character. We must, rather, examine the state of the heavens at the exact time of birth.

J. R. Hanina said to [his disciples], "Go and tell Bar Levi [that is, R. Joshua], 'It is not the star that rules over the day in general on which one was born that governs, but the star that controlled that very hour that governs. He who was born under the sun will be an outstanding person; he will eat and drink of his own property, and his secrets will be uncovered; if he is a thief, he will not succeed. He who is born under Venus will be wealthy and promiscuous. How come? Because fire was created under that star. He who was born under Mercury will have a wonderful memory and be smart. How come? Because Mercury is the scribe of the sun. He who is born under the moon will be a man to suffer evil, building and destroying, destroying and building, eating and drinking what is not his, and his secrets will remain hidden. If he is a thief, he will be successful. He who is born under Saturn will be a man who never accomplishes what he sets out to do.'"
K. Others say, "All plans against him will be frustrated."
L. "He who is born under Jupiter [called 'righteous'] will be a person who habitually does righteousness."
M. R. Nahman bar Isaac said, "Doing righteousness in good deeds."
N. "He who is born under Mars will shed blood."
O. R. Ashi said, "That means he'll be a surgeon, thief, slaughterer, or circumciser."
P. Rabbah said, "I was born under Mars."
Q. Said Abbayye, "Yes, and you inflict punishment and kill [with words]."

As we already saw above, the Talmudic rabbis' acceptance of the accuracy of astrology belies their own sense that the knowledge it presents may not correctly predict what will happen to Israelites at all. For the people of Israel are directly subject to God, who, since he created the heavens, can change them around at will, rendering previous predictions worthless. This point is made in the continuation of the passage we have been reviewing at B. Shab. 156a-b:

A. It has been stated:
B. R. Hanina says, "One's star is what makes one smart, one's star is what gives wealth, and Israel is subject to the stars."
C. R. Yohanan said, "Israel is not subject to the stars."
D. And R. Yohanan is consistent with views expressed elsewhere, for said R. Yohanan, "How on the basis of Scripture do we know that Israel is not subject to the stars? As it is said, 'Thus says the Lord, Do not learn the way of the gentiles, nor be dismayed at the signs of the heavens, for the nations are dismayed at them' (Jer. 10:2). They are dismayed, but the Israelites are not dismayed."
E. And also Rab takes the view that Israel is not subject to the stars, for said R. Judah said Rab, "How on the basis of Scripture do we know that Israel is not subject to the stars? As it is said, 'And he brought him forth outside" (Gen. 15:5). Said Abraham before the Holy One, blessed be he, 'Lord of the world, "Someone born in my household is my heir" (Gen. 15:3).' He said to him, 'Not at all. "But he who will come forth out of your own loins" (Gen. 1:4).' He said before him, 'Lord of the world, I have closely examined my star, and I have seen that I am destined to have no children.' He said to him, 'Abandon this astrology of yours—Israel is not subject to astrology. Now what's your calculation? [156b] Is it that Jupiter stands in the west [and that is your constellation]? I'll turn it back and set it up in the East.' And so it is written, 'Who has raised up Jupiter from the east? He has summoned it for his sake' (Is. 41:2)."

When applied to Israelites, astrology is inaccurate, since God can change the order of the heavens. The authorities in the following add that such changes are not in the hands of God alone. Rather, the people of Israel's own actions—their adherence to Torah through the performance of acts of righteousness—have an equal power to change the future from that which astrology predicts:

A. It is also the position of Samuel that Israel is not subject to the stars.
B. For Samuel and Ablat [a gentile sage]

were in session, and some people were going along to a lake. Said Ablat to Samuel, "That man is going but won't come back; a snake will bite him and he'll die."
C. Said to him Samuel, "Indeed? Well, if he's an Israelite, he will go and come back."
D. While they were in session, he went and came back. Ablat got up and took off the man's knapsack and found in it a snake cut up and lying in two pieces.
E. Said Samuel to the man, "What did you do [today in particular]?"
F. He said to him, "Every day we tossed our bread into one pot and ate, but today one of us had no bread, and he was ashamed. I said to him, 'I will go and collect the bread.' When I came to him, I made as if I collected the bread, so he shouldn't be ashamed."
G. [Samuel] said to him, "You have carried out a religious duty."
H. Samuel went forth and expounded, "'But charity delivers from death' (Prov. 10:2)—not from a grotesque death, but from death itself."

The point is not that the gentile's prediction was objectively wrong, but that the specific actions of the Israelite had protected him from his expected fate.[9] Samuel, for his part, was able to anticipate this because of his own knowledge of Torah and its power. The relationship between Jewish sage and gentile seer thus is shown to be similar to the relationship between sage and magician. The rabbis take for granted the power of the magician and astrologer. At the same time, they comprehend these non-Jewish sciences to have very limited affect upon the Jewish community. Study of Torah and adherence to the covenant provide rabbis and Israelite lay-people with powers that far exceed those of gentile magic.

In line with this thinking, other Rabbinic texts adjure Israelites to stay away from astrology and to realize that their power lies in adherence to Torah. This point is explicit at Gen. Rab. XLIV:XII:

1.A. "And [God] brought him [that is, Abraham] outside [and said, 'Look toward heaven and number the stars, if you are able to number them']" (Gen. 15:5):
B. R. Joshua in the name of R. Levi,

"Now did he bring him outside of the world, that the text should say, 'And he brought him outside'? But the sense is that he showed him the open spaces of heaven, in line with this verse: 'While as yet he had not made the earth nor the open spaces' (Prov. 8:26)."

C. R. Judah b. R. Simon in the name of R. Yohanan: "He brought him above the vault of heaven. That is in line with the statement, 'Look toward heaven and number the stars,' and the meaning of the word 'look' is only 'from above to below.'"

D. Rabbis say, "[God told him], 'You are a prophet, not an astrologer, as it is said, "Now, therefore, restore the man's wife, for he is a prophet" (Gen. 20:7).'"

The anti-astrological polemic, invited by the reference of Gen. 15:5 to looking at the stars, is clear. God's purpose in having Abraham look at the stars was not to validate the claims of astrology, so far as these claims might be held to pertain to Israel. This is because, as is made explicit in the continuation of the passage, God, not the stars, governs the fate of the people of Israel:

2.A. In the time of Jeremiah the Israelites wanted to take up this principle [of astrology], but the Holy One, blessed be he, did not allow them to do so, in line with this verse: "Thus says the Lord, 'Do not learn the way of the nations, and do not be dismayed at the signs of heaven'" (Jer. 10:2).

B. Abraham, your forefather, wanted to take up this principle, but [God] did not allow him to do so.

3.A. Said R. Levi, "While the sandal is on your foot, step on the thorn. Someone who is placed below them should fear them, but you are placed above them, so should trample them down."

Israelites are above the nations of the world so that their fate is not ultimately determined by the heavenly bodies. It is, rather, controlled by God, in response to the Israelites' adherence to the covenant. This point, regarding the way in which the Israelites' can control their own fate, is elaborated in the following:

4.A. R. Yudan in the name of R. Eleazar: "Three things annul an evil decree [that is foreseen by astrology], and these are they: prayer, acts of charity, and repent-

ance. And all three of them may be located in a single verse of Scripture:

B. "'If my people, upon whom my name is called, shall humble themselves and pray [and seek my face, and turn from their evil ways, then I will forgive their sin]' (2 Chr. 7:14).

C. "'If my people, upon whom my name is called, shall humble themselves and pray' refers to prayer.

D. "'. . . and seek my face' refers to acts of charity, in line with this verse: 'I shall behold your face in acts of charity' (Ps. 17:15).

E. "'. . . and turn from their evil ways' refers to repentance.

F. "Then: 'I will forgive their sin.'"

G. R. Huna in the name of R. Joseph: "Also changing one's name and the doing of a good deed will have the same effect. We know that changing a name makes a difference from the case of Abraham and Sarah [see Gen. 17].

H. "We know that doing a good deed makes a difference from the case of the men of Nineveh, as it is said, 'And God saw their works, that they turned from their evil ways' (Jonah 3:10)."

I. Some say, "Also changing one's place of domicile, as it is said, 'And the Lord said to Abram, "Get you out of your country"' (Gen. 12:1)."

J. R. Mana said, "Also fasting [has the same effect], as it is said, 'The Lord answer you in the day of distress [interpreted here to mean the day of fasting]' (Ps. 20:20))."

K. Raba bar Mehasia and R. Hama bar Guria in the name of Rab: "Fasting is as good for a dream as fire for stubble."

L. Said R. Joseph, "That is so if it is done on the same day [as the dream], even if that is the Sabbath [on which it is ordinarily forbidden to fast]."

The fate of the people of Israel is determined not by the stars but directly by God, who responds to the Israelites' actions on earth. This means that the correspondence between heaven and earth is, for the Israelite people, the opposite of what the astrologers claim. Astrology claims that what happens in the heavens determines, or at least announces, the outcome of events on earth. Within the theology of Judaism, by contrast, people's actions on earth determine the response of God in heaven. This means that, within the Talmudic sources, God appropriately may be described as an astrologer (Gen. Rab. 1.IV):

2.A. R. Huna, R. Jeremiah in the name of R. Samuel b. R. Isaac: "Intention concerning the creation of Israel came before all else.

B. "The matter may be compared to the case of a king who married a noble lady but had no son with her. One time the king turned up in the market place, saying, 'Buy this ink, inkwell, and pen on account of my son.'

C. "People said, 'He has no son. Why does he need ink, inkwell, and pen?'

D. "But then people went and said, 'The king is an astrologer, so he sees into the future and he therefore is expecting to produce a son!'

E. "Along these same lines, if the Holy One, blessed be he, had not foreseen that, after twenty-six generations, the Israelites would be destined to accept the Torah, he would never have written in it, 'Command the children of Israel.'"

A similar point is made at Lev. Rab. 36.IV:

2.A. R. Berekhiah and R. Levi in the name of Samuel bar Nahman: "Abraham was saved from the furnace of fire only because of the merit of Jacob.

B. "The matter may be compared. To what is it like? It is like the case of someone who was judged before the ruler, and the judgment came forth from the ruler that he was to be put to death through burning.

C. "The ruler perceived through his astrological science that [the condemned man] was going to beget a daughter, who was going to be married to a king. He said, 'This one is worthy to be saved through the merit of the daughter that he is going to beget, who is going to be married to a king.'

D. "So in the case of Abraham, judgment against him came forth from Nimrod that he was to be put to death through burning. But the Holy One, blessed be he, foresaw that Jacob was going to come forth from him. So he said, 'That one is worthy of being saved on account of the merit of Jacob.'

E. "That is in line with the following verse of Scripture: 'Thus said the Lord to the House of Jacob, who redeemed Abraham' (Is. 29:22)."

God foresees what will happen on earth and acts accordingly. This means that the people are protected from the fate that the heavenly bodies dictate for the other nations. Astrol-ogy, according to the rabbis, had its place and purpose, and there were even individual sages who engaged in it (see, e.g., Deut. Rab. 8.VI). But like gentile magic in general, the rabbis saw neither a reason for Jews to participate in astrology nor any real threat from predictions made on the basis of astrology. The fate of the people of Israel, rather, was determined directly by God, who responded to the Israelites' engagement with Torah.

Astrology in the ancient synagogue: The rabbis' ambivalence towards astrology—their knowledge of and participation in it even as they denied its relevance—belies the place of astrological figures as a central motif of the synagogue of the Talmudic period. The prevalence of the zodiac in synagogue art is described by Bernard Goldman in his discussion of the fifth or sixth century C.E. mosaic zodiac preserved in the Beth Alpha synagogue:[10]

> The badly preserved mosaic floor of the synagogue at Yafia contains an animal circle, similar to that of Beth Alpha, but it is not clear whether it represents the zodiac or the Twelve Tribes. The synagogue of 'Ain Doug (Na'arah) contains an elaborately decorated mosaic floor with the wheel of the zodiac holding the center of the tripartite panel, much as at Beth Alpha; but, at 'Ain Doug an interlocking pattern containing animal and floral vignettes replaces the Akedah. In 1930, another historiated synagogue mosaic containing the zodiac was uncovered on Mt. Carmel at the village of 'Isfiya ('Esfia). Also, some of the relief decoration from the synagogue at Beth She'arim may have composed a zodiac design. The most recently discovered zodiac floor mosaic is one near Tiberias that also repeats the Beth Alpha format but, in style, is far closer to its Classical art sources. . . . There are several other probable references to the zodiac in synagogue architectural decorations; for example it is found on a fragmentary carved screen from er-Rafid. There is no question but that future excavations will bring to light additional examples.

The recurrence of the zodiac in synagogue after synagogue suggests its importance as more than a decorative or ornamental device. Rather, as the Talmudic sources make clear and as the continued appearance of the zodiac in later European Jewish art shows, the use of the zodiac in the synagogue of the Rabbinic period was consonant with its symbolic importance, an importance that extended from non-Jewish into Jewish metaphysics.

In classical sources, the zodiac symbolized the heavens. Through the image of the zodiac, "The artist transformed the starry path into a canopy, dome, arch, and frame to express the cosmic dimensions of the icon and ritual it enclosed" (Goldman, p. 61). Expressing this meaning, the zodiac had a natural place as a focal point of Jewish worship and ritual, as a "symbol of the heavens and constellations under whose aegis the destinies of nations and of men were ordered" (p. 64). Prayers for divine protection, for God's mercy and forgiveness from sin, for the coming of salvation appropriately were recited in a setting that depicted the divine and heavenly forces that could answer those prayers. Astrological symbols thus functioned in ancient synagogue not as mere ornamentation but as vivid representations of the Hellenized Jews' perception of the cosmic order.

At the center of the representation of the zodiac at Beth Alpha, as in the fourth century floor at Hamat Tiberias, and elsewhere, stood the sun-god Helios and his chariot. Despite the firm biblical, post-biblical, and Rabbinic literary traditions against the creation of images of what is on earth, let alone of foreign deities or of the invisible God of the Israelites, it seems almost certain that those who worshipped in these synagogues knew exactly what this portrayal of Helios symbolized. As E.R. Goodenough states, in their eyes this was "the divine charioteer of Hellenized Judaism, God himself,"[11] the God at whom all prayer and supplication was aimed. The medium of astrology and the symbols of the zodiac thus portrayed for the common Jew of the Talmudic period the cosmic order and the deity who had created that order and, with it, the entire world. This was the true God who responded to human prayer, controlling and shaping in the manner that astrology describes all that happens on earth.

Astrology in medieval Judaism: In the middle ages, especially in the orbit of Islam, Jews increasingly practiced astrology. A thorough knowledge of this art is evidenced in the Zohar and Sefer Raziel, and astrology is referred to frequently in medieval liturgical poetry, including the works of poets such as Kalir and Ibn Gabirol.[12] Well known Jewish astrologers of the ninth century were Jacob ibn Turik, whom Ibn Ezra says brought the astrological tables of the Hindus to Baghdad. Of the same period, some astrological works remain extant of Sahl b. Bishr al-Israeli, also known as Rabban al-Tabari ("the rabbi of Tabaristan").

In this period, the works of Islamic astrologers were translated by Jews into Hebrew. Ibn Ezra himself was an avid follower of astrology, which he referred to as a sublime science. He even translated into Hebrew the astrological work of Mashallah, the court astrologer of Almansur and Mamun, and he authored important works on the constellations and planets. Referring to astrology in his biblical commentaries, Ibn Ezra understood the heavens to represent the "book of life" in which people's fate is written. Still, in accordance with the inherited Talmudic perspective, he believed that this fate could be overruled by God, to whom humans accordingly have recourse in their quest to reshape their own destiny.

A similar approach appears in the commentary to Maimonides' Mishneh Torah of Abraham b. David of Posquieries (*Rabad*). While asserting the influence of the stars upon human destiny, he also avers that faith in God can overcome this influence. Maimonides, by contrast, alone among the major Rabbinic authorities of this period, opposed astrology and declared it explicitly forbidden by Lev. 19:26 ("You shall not practice augury or witchcraft"). Maimonides viewed astrology as a dangerous superstition, bordering on idolatry, that was "a disease on a science."

The last important Jewish astrologer was David Gans (in Germany, 1541-1613) Alongside his work on Jewish and general history (*Zemah David*), he wrote a work on cosmography (*Gebulat ha-Erez*), an astronomical treatise (*Magen David*), and a number of mathematical works. His *Nehmad ve-Naim*, which deals with astronomy and mathematical geography, contains a historical survey of the development of these subjects around the world.

The modern world and the emergence of science has largely brought an end to astronomy and the other magical practices known in Talmudic times.[13] One minor throw-back to that period is the contemporary use of the Hebrew phrase "Mazal Tov," literally "A good constellation," to mean "Good luck!" Similarly, following the approach of the Shulhan Aruch (*Yoreh Deah* 179, 2), some Jews continue to reject certain days of the week or month for weddings or other ventures.

Notes

[1] Jacob Neusner, "Science and Magic, Miracle and Magic in Formative Judaism: The System and the Difference," in Jacob Neusner, ed., *Religion, Science, and Magic in Concert and in Conflict* (New York, 1989), p. 61.

[2] On the following see Joanne Kuemmerlin-McClean, "Magic: Old Testament," in *ABD*, vol. 4, pp. 468-470.

[3] See too Elijah's confrontation with the prophets of Baal at 1 Kings 18:17-39.

[4] I paraphrase Jacob Neusner, "God: How, in Judaism, Do We Know God," in Jacob Neusner, ed., *Formative Judaism* (Seventh Series, Atlanta, 1993), p. 209.

[5] On this point, see Neusner, "Science and Magic," p. 69.

[6] The continuation of the passage explains how one can distinguish an illusion from an actual act of magic: Said Rav to R. Hiyya, "I myself saw a Tai-Arab take a sword and chop up a camel, then he rang a bell and the camel arose." [Hiyya] said to him, "After this was there blood or dung? [If not], it was merely an illusion."

[7] On these passages, see Neusner, "Science and Magic," pp. 71-75.

[8] In Hebrew, this is the same word elsewhere translated as "in eclipse."

[9] The same point is made in the subsequent paragraphs of B. Shab. 156b.

[10] *The Sacred Portal. A Primary Symbol in Ancient Judaic Art* (Detroit, 1966), p. 60.

[11] E.R. Goodenough, *Jewish Symbols in the Greco-Roman Period* (Princeton, 1953-1968), vol. VIII.2, pp. 214ff., cited in Goldman, p. 64.

[12] On the following, see Kaufmann Kohler, "Astrology, in Medieval Times," in Isadore Singer, ed., *Jewish Encyclopedia*, vol. 2, pp. 243-245.

[13] But, on the medieval Christian perception of the Jew as "full of sorcery," see Joshua Trachtenberg, *The Devil and the Jews. The Medieval Conception of the Jew and Its Relation to Modern Anti-Semitism* (Philadelphia and Jerusalem, 1983), pp. 57-75.

ALAN J. AVERY-PECK

MASCULINE AND FEMININE IN JUDAISM: Judaism in its classical documents joins traits explicitly marked as male to those explicitly classified as female and insists upon both in the formation of models of virtue. It therefore may be classified as androgynous, exhibiting the traits of both sexes as the religion itself defines those gender-qualities. In this world holy Israel is to emulate women's virtue as the condition of the coming of the Messiah. Women's capacity for devotion, selfless faith, and loyalty defines the model of what is required of Israel for its virtue.

Gender roles and the Judaic system: The sages of the normative writings, Mishnah, Talmud, Midrash, thought in terms of the holy community, not isolated individuals. Gender roles formed part of the larger statement that sages proposed to craft concerning the coherent life of the community overall. Sages' doctrine of feminine virtue, therefore, makes sense only within its larger systemic context. The dual Torah, beginning to end, taught that the Israelite was to exhibit the moral virtues of subservience, patience, endurance, and hope. These would translate into the emotional traits of humility and forbearance. And they would yield the social virtues of passivity and conciliation. The hero was one who overcame impulses; the truly virtuous person was the one who reconciled others by giving way before their opinions. All of these acts of self-abnegation and self-denial, accommodation rather than rebellion, required to begin with the right attitudes, sentiments, emotions, and impulses, and the single most dominant motif of the Rabbinic writings, start to finish, is their stress on the right attitude's leading to the right action, the correct intentionality's producing the besought decision. This required, above all, accommodating in one's heart to what could not be changed by one's action, specifically, the world as it was. Sages prepared Israel for the long centuries of subordination and alienation by inculcating attitudes that best suited people who could govern little more than how they felt about things. As we shall now see, sages themselves classified the besought virtues as feminine, and they proposed to feminize Israel, the holy people.

Feminine and masculine in Judaism:
When we speak of virtues as feminine and masculine, it is not to perpetuate contemporary stereotypes, but to pay close attention to sages' own judgment of matters. How do we know how the framers of the dual Torah, who bear the title "our sages of blessed memory," classify virtues, whether as masculine or as feminine? In the classical writings we have several systematic exegeses that focus on women and therefore permit us to characterize sages' conception of women's virtues, and it will follow, the virtues they classify as feminine. Sages' reading of the Scriptural books of Ruth and Esther and their treatment of Miriam the prophetess and other scriptural prophetesses provide access to their thinking on what characterizes the virtuous woman.

Among the expositions pertinent to that matter, however, none more reliably records sages' conception of the feminine and of the feminine in relationship to the masculine than their reading of the Song of Songs in the exegetical compilation Song of Songs Rabbah, a writing contemporary with the Talmud of Babylonia, ca. 600. There, in reading the Song of Songs as a statement of the relationship of God and Israel, Israel is identified as the female-beloved, God as the male-lover. We need not speculate, therefore, on correct traits for women; in the document at hand, they are those explicitly assigned to feminine Israel. So we now turn to a brief survey of what is said in so many words. Because of the critical place of Song of Songs Rabbah in the representation of androgynous Judaism and, in particular, the definition of the feminine component of the androgyneity, I cite representative passages at considerable length.

God and Israel in the metaphor of husband and wife: The first point is the most telling. The relationship of Israel to God is the same as the relationship of a wife to the husband, and this is explicit in Song of Songs Rabbah to Song 7:10:

    A. "I am my beloved's, and his desire is for me" (Song 7:10):
    B. There are three yearnings:
    C. The yearning of Israel is only for their

        Father who is in heaven, as it is said, "I am my beloved's, and his desire is for me."
    D. The yearning of a woman is only for her husband: "And your desire shall be for your husband" (Gen. 3:16).
    E. The yearning of the Evil Impulse is only for Cain and his ilk: "To you is its desire" (Gen. 4:7).

Here gender-relationships are explicitly characterized, and, with them, the traits associated with the genders as well.

The sages turn to everyday experience—the love of husband and wife—for a metaphor for God's love for Israel and Israel's love for God. And Israel is assigned the feminine role and the feminine virtues. It is difficult to identify a more extravagant form of praise for women's virtue, her capacity to love generously and in an act of unearned grace. When Solomon's song says, "O that you would kiss me with the kisses of your mouth! For your love is better than wine," (Song 1:2), sages of blessed memory think of how God kissed Israel. Reading the Song of Songs as a metaphor, the Judaic sages state in a systematic and orderly way their entire structure and system, and, along the way, permit us to identify the traits they associate with feminine Israel and masculine God, respectively. What is important here, however, is not the document's doctrinal message, but its implicit and tacit affirmations. The document does not set forth a great many explicit doctrines, but delivers its message through the description of attitudes and emotions. And our particular interest lies in the identification of the system's designative as feminine and masculine of clearly-defined attitudes and emotions. The writers mean to paint word-pictures, evoke feelings, speak empathetically, rather than only sympathetically. Song of Songs Rabbah tells how to think and feel, so as to form a heart at one with God.

Masculine virtue: No account of feminine virtue can accomplish its goals without cataloguing masculine virtue as well. Our survey of the feminine and the masculine in Song of Songs Rabbah begins with the clear characterization of God as masculine, Israel as feminine (6:2):

A. "My beloved has gone down to his garden, to the beds of spices, [to pasture his flock in the gardens, and to gather lilies]" (Song 6:2):

B. Said R. Yose b. R. Hanina, "As to this verse, the beginning of it is not the same as the end, and the end not the same as the beginning.

C. "The verse had only to say, 'My beloved has gone down to pasture in his garden,' but you say, 'in the gardens'!

D. "But 'my beloved' is the Holy One, blessed be he;

E. "'to his garden' refers to the world.

F. "'to the beds of spices' refers to Israel.

G. "'to pasture his flock in the gardens' refers to synagogues and school-houses.

H. "'and to gather lilies' speaks of picking [taking away in death] the righteous that are in Israel."

"My beloved" is God; the choice part of the garden, which is the world, is Israel, its synagogues and houses of study. Israel is now the faithful beloved, waiting patiently for her lover, always trusting in His faithfulness (Song of Songs Rabbah to Song 8:6).

A. "Set me as a seal upon your heart, as a seal upon your arm; for love is strong as death, jealousy is cruel as the grave. Its flashes are flashes of fire, a most vehement flame" (Song 8:6):

B. "for love is strong as death:"

C. As strong as death is the love with which the Holy One, blessed be he, loves Israel: "I have loved you says the Lord" (Mal. 1:2).

D. "jealousy is cruel as the grave:"

E. That is when they make him jealous with their idolatry: "They roused him to jealousy with strange gods" (Deut. 32:16). . . .

F. Another explanation of "for love is strong as death:"

G. As strong as death is the love with which a man loves his wife: "Enjoy life with the wife whom you love" (Prov. 9:9).

H. "jealousy is cruel as the grave:"

I. the jealousy that she causes in him and leads him to say to her, "Do not speak with such-and-so."

J. If she goes and speaks with that man, forthwith: "The spirit of jealousy comes upon him and he is jealous on account of his wife" (Num. 5:14).

Israel's feminine character is now well-established, and the ways in which the exegesis of the Song is worked out in response to that fact are clear. Then we have to ask ourselves,

precisely what kind of relationship does feminine Israel have with the masculine God? The answer is, the relationship of a wife to a husband.

Feminine Israel: Israel's status as God's beloved yields two important results. First, the metaphor is treated as neuter, in that, even though Israel is feminine, that fact bears no material consequence for the representation of Israel. The repertoire of word-symbols that convey the principal components of the structure of faith is set forth in terms of what is simply a useful metaphor. But the metaphor is not realized, e.g., in the formulation of traits set forth as unique to women and unique to feminine Israel by reason of its femininity. Representative of many pasages, the following, at Song of Songs Rabbah to Song 2:1, suffices to show how, despite the femininity of Israel, the framers are able to run through, without reference to gender, the principal elements of Israel's sacred history—Egypt, the Sea, Sinai, the subjugation to the kingdoms and the coming redemption by reason of Israel's faithfulness to the covenant:

A. "I am a rose of Sharon, [a lily of the valleys]" (Song 2:1):

B. Said the Community of Israel, "I am the one, and I am beloved.

C. "I am the one whom the Holy One, blessed be he, loved more than the seventy nations.

D. "I am a rose of Sharon:"

E. "For I made for him a shade through Bezalel [the words for shade and Bezalel use the same consonants as the word for rose]: 'And Bezalel made the ark' (Exod. 38:1)."

F. "of Sharon:"

G. "For I said before him a song [which word uses the same consonants as the word for Sharon] through Moses:

H. "'Then sang Moses and the children of Israel' (Exod. 15:1)."

I. Another explanation of the phrase, "I am a rose of Sharon:"

J. Said the Community of Israel, "I am the one, and I am beloved.

K. "I am the one who was hidden in the shadow of Egypt, but in a brief moment the Holy One, blessed be he, brought me together to Raamses, and I blossomed forth in good deeds like a rose, and I said before him this song: 'You shall have a song as in the night when a feast is sanctified' (Is. 30:29)."

L. Another explanation of the phrase, "I am a rose of Sharon:"

M. Said the Community of Israel, "I am the one, and I am beloved.

N. "I am the one who was hidden in the shadow of the sea, but in a brief moment I blossomed forth in good deeds like a rose, and I pointed to him with the finger (opposite to me): 'This is my God and I will glorify him' (Exod. 15:2)."

O. Another explanation of the phrase, "I am a rose of Sharon:"

P. Said the Community of Israel, "I am the one, and I am beloved.

Q. "I am the one who was hidden in the shadow of Mount Sinai, but in a brief moment I blossomed forth in good deeds like a lily in hand and in heart, and I said before him, 'All that the Lord has said we will do and obey' (Exod. 24:7)."

R. Another explanation of the phrase, "I am a rose of Sharon:"

S. Said the Community of Israel, "I am the one, and I am beloved.

T. "I am the one who was hidden and downtrodden in the shadow of the kingdoms. But tomorrow, when the Holy One, blessed be he, redeems me from the shadow of the kingdoms, I shall blossom forth like a lily and say before him a new song: 'Sing to the Lord a new song, for he has done marvelous things, his right hand and his holy arm have wrought salvation for him' (Ps. 98:1)."

To make the point that its author wishes to register, the foregoing passage does not require that Israel be represented as feminine. Nor do traits identified with femininity emerge. What we have is simply a review of standard high points in sages' theology of Israel's history: Egypt, the Sea, Sinai, then the whole of the intervening history homogenized into the single, dreadful time of subjugation to the kingdoms, and, finally, redemption, to which we shall return at the end.

The virtues of wives, portrayed as feminine, once more are those of loyalty and submission. This metaphor is exploited through the invocation of the wife's trust in the husband, the mark of the perfect wife. Israel follows wherever Moses, in behalf of God, leads; Israel trusts in God the way a woman who has accepted marriage trusts her husband (Song of Songs Rabbah to Song 4:12):

A. Berekhiah in the name of R. Judah b. R. Ilai: "It is written, 'And Moses led Israel onward from the Red Sea' (Exod. 15:22):

B. "He led them on from the sin committed at the sea.

C. "They said to him, 'Moses, our lord, where are you leading us?'

D. "He said to them, 'To Elim, from Elim to Alush, from Alush to Marah, from Marah to Rephidim, from Rephidim to Sinai.'

E. "They said to him, 'Indeed, wherever you go and lead us, we are with you.'

F. "The matter is comparable to the case of one who went and married a woman from a village. He said to her, 'Arise and come with me.'

G. "She said to him, 'From here to where?'

H. "He said to her, 'From here to Tiberias, from Tiberias to the Tannery, from the Tannery to the Upper Market, from the Upper Market to the Lower Market.'

I. "She said to him, 'Wherever you go and take me, I shall go with you.'

J. "So said the Israelites, 'My soul cleaves to you' (Ps. 63:9)."

Israel's feminine virtue must exceed even the wife's trust in the husband's protection. Israel also must care only for God, the way a wife's entire desire is solely for her husband. The point is unmistakable and critical. Israel is subject to an oath to wait patiently for God's redemption, not to rebel against the nations on its own; that is the concrete social politics meant to derive from the analogy of Israel's relationship to God to the wife's relationship to the husband: perfect submission, and also perfect trust. Rebellion against the nations stands for arrogance on Israel's part, an act of lack of trust and therefore lack of faithfulness. Implicit in this representation of the right relationship, of course, is the promise that feminine Israel will evoke from the masculine God the response of commitment and intervention: God will intervene to save Israel when Israel makes herself into the perfect wife of God.

The upshot is, Israel must fulfill the vocation of a woman, turn itself into a woman, serve God as a wife serves a husband. The question then follows: is it possible that the Judaism that has treated the present document as canonical asks men to turn themselves into women? And the answer is, that demand is stated in so many words. Here we find a full statement of the feminization of the masculine. The two brothers, Moses and Aaron, are compared to Israel's breasts, a reversal of gender-classifications that can hardly be more extreme or dramatic (Song of Songs Rabbah to Song 4:5):

A. "Your two breasts are like two fawns, twins of a gazelle, that feed among the lilies" (Song 4:5):
B. "Your two breasts are like two fawns:"
C. this refers to Moses and Aaron.
D. Just as a woman's breasts are her glory and her ornament,
E. so Moses and Aaron are the glory and the ornament of Israel.
F. Just as a woman's breasts are her charm, so Moses and Aaron are the charm of Israel.
G. Just as a woman's breasts are her honor and her praise, so Moses and Aaron are the honor and praise of Israel.
H. Just as a woman's breasts are full of milk, so Moses and Aaron are full of Torah.
I. Just as whatever a woman eats the infant eats and sucks, so all the Torah that our lord, Moses, learned he taught to Aaron: "And Moses told Aaron all the words of the Lord" (Exod. 4:28).
J. And rabbis say, "He actually revealed the Ineffable Name of God to him."
K. Just as one breast is not larger than the other, so Moses and Aaron were the same: "These are Moses and Aaron" (Exod. 6:27), "These are Aaron and Moses" (Exod. 6:26), so that in knowledge of the Torah Moses was not greater than Aaron, and Aaron was not greater than Moses.
L. Happy are these two brothers, who were created only for the glory of Israel.
M. That is what Samuel said, "It is the Lord that made Moses and Aaron and brought your fathers up" (1 Sam. 12:6).
N. Thus "Your two breasts are like two fawns:"
O. this refers to Moses and Aaron.

Not only are Moses and Aaron represented through feminine metaphors, so too are Abraham, Isaac, and Jacob, as well as the tribal progenitors, Jacob's sons.

In the following, feminine Israel is ornamented by all of the jewelry contained in the treasure of the Torah: all of the acts of faith are paraded as marks of the beauty of Israel in the explicit setting of Israel's feminine relationship to the masculine God (Song of Songs Rabbah to Song 1:15):

A. "Behold, you are beautiful, my love; behold, you are beautiful; [your eyes are doves]" (Song 1:15):
B. "Behold you are beautiful" in religious deeds,
C. "Behold you are beautiful" in acts of grace,
D. "Behold you are beautiful" in carrying out religious obligations of commission,
E. "Behold you are beautiful" in carrying out religious obligations of omission,
F. "Behold you are beautiful" in carrying out the religious duties of the home, in separating priestly ration and tithes,
G. "Behold you are beautiful" in carrying out the religious duties of the field, gleanings, forgotten sheaves, the corner of the field, poor person's tithe, and declaring the field ownerless.
H. "Behold you are beautiful" in observing the taboo against mixed species.
I. "Behold you are beautiful" in providing a linen cloak with woolen show-fringes.
J. "Behold you are beautiful" in [keeping the rules governing] planting,
K. "Behold you are beautiful" in keeping the taboo on uncircumcised produce,
L. "Behold you are beautiful" in keeping the laws on produce in the fourth year after the planting of an orchard,
M. "Behold you are beautiful" in circumcision,
N. "Behold you are beautiful" in trimming the wound,
O. "Behold you are beautiful" in reciting the Prayer,
P. "Behold you are beautiful" in reciting the Shema,
Q. "Behold you are beautiful" in putting a mezuzah on the doorpost of your house,
R. "Behold you are beautiful" in wearing phylacteries,
S. "Behold you are beautiful" in building the tabernacle for the Festival of Tabernacles,
T. "Behold you are beautiful" in taking the palm branch and etrog on the Festival of Tabernacles,
U. "Behold you are beautiful" in repentance,
V. "Behold you are beautiful" in good deeds,
W. "Behold you are beautiful" in this world,
X. "Behold you are beautiful" in the world to come.

Israel, then, is to exhibit the virtues explicitly assigned to women. God responds in a masculine manner. The feminine and masculine virtues complement one another, and neither is complete without the other. The process comes to fulfillment in the representation as feminine of all of the virtues, all of the saints and heroes, all of the acts of sanctification that God has commanded and that submissive Israel carries out. Once Israel is feminized, so too is everything else. Then the feminine virtues—submission, trust, perfect loyalty—are adopted by Israel. But that is only for now.

Sexuality and theology: How does the sexual imagery convey deep theological meaning? The message of Song of Songs Rabbah is that, if Israel is feminine now, she will resume her masculinity in the world to come. That is a much more subtle and profound statement, a judgment on the androgyneity of Israel that makes the union of traits, feminine and masculine, something other than a static portrait of a world at rest. In fact, the metaphor of the feminine Israel and the masculine God is subsumed within the more profound message of redemption and carries a critical element in that message: Israel must be patient, submissive, and deeply trusting in God now, so that, in the world to come, Israel may resume its fulfilled masculinity. In this age, Israel to God is as a wife to a husband. But in the age to come, Israel assumes masculine identity. It follows that Israel is represented as androgyne, feminine, then masculine (Song of Songs Rabbah to Song 5:3):

A. Berekhiah in the name of R. Samuel b. R. Nahman said, "The Israelites are compared to a woman.
B. "Just as an unmarried women receives a tenth part of the property of her father and takes her leave [for her husband's house when she gets married], so the Israelites inherited the land of the seven peoples, who form a tenth part of the seventy nations of the world.
C. "And because the Israelites inherited in the status of a woman, they said a song in the feminine form of that word, as in the following: 'Then sang Moses and the children of Israel this song [given in the feminine form] unto the Lord' (Exod. 15:1).
D. "But in the age to come they are destined to inherit like a man, who inherits all of the property of his father.
E. "That is in line with this verse of Scripture: 'From the east side to the west side:

Judah, one portion . . . Dan one, Asher one . . .' (Ez. 48:7), and so throughout.
F. "Then they will say a song in the masculine form of that word, as in the following: 'Sing to the Lord a new song' (Ps. 96:1).
G. "The word 'song' is given not in its feminine form but in its masculine form."
H. Berekiah and R. Joshua b. Levi: "Why are the Israelites compared to a woman?
I. "Just as a woman takes up a burden and puts it down [that is, becomes pregnant and gives birth], takes up a burden and puts it down, then takes up a burden and puts it down and then takes up no further burden,
J. "so the Israelites are subjugated and then redeemed, subjugated and then redeemed, but in the end are redeemed and will never again be subjugated.
K. "In this world, since their anguish is like the anguish of a woman in childbirth, they say the song before him using the feminine form of the word for song,
L. "but in the age to come, because their anguish will no longer be the anguish of a woman in childbirth, they will say their song using the masculine form of the word for song:
M. "'In that day this song [in the masculine form of the word] will be sung' (Is. 26:1)."

So the real message lies in the femininity of Israel in this world in contrast to its masculinity in the world to come. Not only so, but there is another qualification of considerable urgency. It is that feminine Israel is masculine in its aggressive relationship to the nations, and here, once more, we find what we may call temporal—or serial—androgyneity: feminine now, masculine in the age to come. It hardly needs repetition that the system is the work of men and states a masculine viewpoint, which makes the systemic androgyneity all the more remarkable. Israel is one thing to God, another to the nations; feminine and submissive to God, masculine and aggressive to the nations of the world. That point is now fundamental in our characterization of the whole. Israel is feminized only for a time; Israel is fully masculine in the end of time.

Serial androgeneity: Israel is serially androgynous: now feminine, later on, masculine. The following makes this point in respect to God as well, who responds to

Israel's character (Song of Songs Rabbah to Song 5:10):

A. ["What is your beloved more than another beloved, O fairest among women! What is your beloved more than another beloved, that you thus adjure us?;" Song 5:9]

B. "My beloved is all radiant and ruddy, distinguished among ten thousand" [Song 5:10).

C. The Israelites answer them, "'My beloved is all radiant and ruddy."

D. "radiant:" to me in the land of Egypt,

E. "and ruddy:" to the Egyptians.

F. "radiant:" in the land of Egypt, "For I will go through the land of Egypt" (Exod. 12:13).

G. "and ruddy:" "And the Lord overthrew the Egyptians" (Exod. 14:27).

H. "radiant:" at the Sea: "The children of Israel walked upon dry land in the midst of the sea" (Exod. 14:29).

I. "and ruddy:" to the Egyptians at the Sea: "And the Lord overthrew the Egyptians in the midst of the sea" (Exod. 14:27).

J. "radiant:" in the world to come.

K. "and ruddy:" in this world.

L. Levi b. R. Hayyata made three statements concerning the matter:

M. "'radiant:' on the Sabbath.

N. "'and ruddy:' on the other days of the week.

O. "radiant:" on the New Year.

P. "and ruddy:" on the other days of the year.

Q. "'radiant:' in this world.

R. "'and ruddy:' in the world to come.

S. "distinguished among ten thousand:"

T. Said R. Abba b. R. Kahana, "A mortal king is known by his ceremonial garments, but here, he is fire and his ministers are fire: 'And he came from the myriads holy' (Deut. 33:2).

U. "He is marked in the midst of 'the myriads holy.'"

Israel now is governed by others and so is deemed passive and, therefore, is classified by the patriarchal document as feminine. Israel is whole with God, but God and Israel cannot make peace with the nations of the world except on God's terms. In a subsequent passage, on Song 6:13, the invocation of the metaphor of dance, with God as the leader, Israel as the partner, underscores the wholly feminine representation of Israel once more: "like women—like the dance of the righteous." Then feminine Israel plays the role of the wife who stands as mediator between her husband and the world at large; the mother who holds the family together, now the family of the nations and the master, who is God.

Feminine and masculine emotions: The emotions encouraged by Judaism in its formative age, such as humility, forbearance, accommodation, a spirit of conciliation, exactly correspond to the political and social requirements of the Jews' condition in that time. The reason that the same repertoire of emotions persisted with no material change through the unfolding of the writings of the sages of that formative age was the constancy of the Jews' political and social condition. Emotions lay down judgments. They derive from rational cognition. What Judaism teaches the private person to feel links her or his heart to what Judaism states about the condition of Israel in history and of God in the cosmos. All form one reality, in supernatural world and nature, in time and in eternity wholly consubstantial (so to speak). In the innermost chambers of deepest feelings, the Israelite therefore lives out the public history and destiny of the people, Israel. The genius of Judaism, reason for its resilience and endurance, lies in its power to teach Jews in private to feel what in public they also must think about the condition of both self and nation. The world within, the world without, are so bonded, that one is never alone. The individual's life always is lived with the people. And, we now realize, the virtuous man, as much as the virtuous woman, will exhibit women's virtues of attitude and emotion.

An epitome of the sages' treatment of emotions yields a simple result. Early, middle, and late, a single doctrine and program dictated what people had to say on how Israel should tame its heart. Israel's virtues were to be those of the woman-Israel of Song of Songs Rabbah. And it is not difficult to see why. In this world, Israel was a vanquished nation, possessed of a broken spirit. Sages' Judaism for a defeated people prepared the nation for a long future. The vanquished people, the broken-hearted nation that had lost its city and its temple, had, moreover, produced another nation from its midst to take over its Scripture and much else. That defeated people, in its intellectuals, as represented in the Rabbinic sources, found refuge in a mode of thought that trained vision to see other things otherwise than as the eyes perceived them. And that general way of seeing things accounts also for the specific matter of the feminization of Israel: Israel now was to endure as a woman, so that, in the age to come, it would resume its masculine position among the nations: dominant and determinative. Among the diverse ways by which the weak and subordinated accommodate to their circumstance, the one of iron-willed pretense in life is most likely to yield the mode of thought at hand: things never are, because they cannot be, what they seem. The uniform tradition on emotions persisted intact because the social realities of Israel's life proved permanent, until, in our own time, they changed. The upshot was that Rabbinic Judaism's Israel was instructed on how to tame its heart and govern its wild emotions, to accept with resignation, to endure with patience, above all, to value the attitudes and emotions that made acceptance and reconciliation into matters of honor and dignity, and, therefore, also made endurance plausible: imitate the feminine virtues.

Deviations from the gender-ideal: How does the system treat deviation? In narrow terms, we refer to matters that Judaism in its classical statement does not contemplate. Reading the story of the creation of man and woman to state the norm, not only the normal, sages insisted that celibacy and monasticism contradict the way God formed nature: "It is not good for man to be alone; I will make a fitting helper for him" (Gen. 2:18); "Hence a man leaves his father and mother and clings to his wife, so that they become one flesh" (Gen. 2:24). These statements are taken explicitly to require marriage and the making of a family. The law of Judaism, set forth in the Mishnah and amplified in the two Talmuds, does not contemplate spinsterhood. The natural condition of woman, as we shall see, is marriage, and the correct location, a household—an extended family that also formed a unit of economic production. If a woman was widowed or divorced without children, she returned to her father's household, until she remarried. It was generally assumed that she would remarry within a year. Childlessness was never by intent. A single model prevailed: the woman married and in charge of her household—exactly as Proverbs 9:9, cited above, indicates.

And yet, were we to complete our account with the preceding paragraph, we should miss the critical, indeed the central concept of the classical statement of Judaism, one that feminizes the system at its very heart. It is the point at which the system does address deviancy in two of its critical aspects, first, the deviancy represented by ignorance of the Torah, and, second, the deviancy represented by sexuality in the form of prostitution. Here we come across what the Judaic system abhors: failure to master the Torah and therefore to know God as God is self-manifest; and, second, failure to take a position within the social order of holy Israel, God's community. The unlettered man, the society of whores—these represent the outer limits of the Israelite world. And here, we shall see in the following section, we come to the systemic center: the reversal of all rules, the transformation of all values. How so? In the texts we shall now discuss, the ignorant man embodies the highest virtue. The woman ready to sell her body realizes the deepest ideal. And, not only so, but, when all is said and done, it is the virtue represented by the deviant that is set forth as the center and soul of Judaism.

Zekhut—the heritage of virtue and its consequent entitlements: While people suppose that the Torah forms the symbolic center of Rabbinic Judaism, and study of the Torah the critical action, so that women, excluded from academies, find no place in Rabbinic Judaism at all, in fact when we reach the systemic center, we find that "the study of Torah" does not outweigh all else, not at all. Even the stories contained in the Talmud of the Land of Israel in which the priority and sanctity of the sage's knowledge of the Torah form the focus of discourse treat study of the Torah as contingent and merely instrumental. Time and again, knowledge of the Torah forms a way-station on a path to a more distant, more central goal: attaining *zekhut*, here translated as "the heritage of virtue and its consequent entitlements." Zekhut embodies the sages' own definition of feminine virtue. Torah-study is one means of attaining access to that heritage, of gaining *zekhut*. There are other equally suitable means, and, not only so, but the merit gained by Torah-study is no different from the merit gained by any and all other types of acts of supererogatory grace. And still more astonishing, a single remarkable action may produce *zekhut* of the same order as a lifetime of devotion to Torah-study, and a simple ass-driver through a noteworthy act of selfless behavior may attain the same level of *zekhut* as a learned sage.

Zekhut is gained for a person by an act of renunciation and self-abnegation, such that Heaven responds with an act of grace. Works of supererogation, which Heaven cannot compel but highly prizes, *zekhut* defines the very opposite of coercion. It is an act that no one could anticipate or demand, but an act of such remarkable selflessness that Heaven finds itself constrained to respond. That is why the systemic center is formed by an act, on Heaven's part, of responsive grace, meaning, grace one by definition cannot demand or compel, but only provoke. When we make ourselves less, Heaven makes us more; but we cannot force our will upon Heaven. When we ask about the feminization of Judaism, our attention rests upon this fact: the right relationship between Israel and God is the relationship that is not coerced, not manipulated, not imposed by a dominant party upon a subordinated one. It is a relationship of mutuality, negotiation, response to what is freely given through what cannot be demanded but only volunteered. The relationship, in other words, is a feminine, not a masculine, one, when measured by the prevailing, conventional stereotypes.

It is where Heaven cannot force its will upon us that *zekhut* intervenes. It is that exquisite balance between our will and Heaven's will that, in the end, brings to its perfect balance and entire fulfillment the exploration of the conflict of God's will and

our will that began with Adam and Eve at their last hour in Eden, and our first hour on earth. And, in context, the fact that we may inherit a treasury of *zekhut* from our ancestors logically follows: just as we inherit the human condition of the freedom to practice rebellion against God's word, so we inherit, from former generations, the results of another dimension of the human condition: our power to give willingly what none, even God, can by right or rule compel.

That is why the structure of Israel's political economy rested upon divine response to acts of will consisting of submission, on one's own, to the will of Heaven; these acts endowed Israel with a lien and entitlement upon Heaven. What we cannot by our own will impose, we can by the act of renunciation of our own will evoke. What we cannot accomplish through coercion, we can achieve through submission. God will do for us what we cannot do for ourselves, when we do for God what God cannot make us do. And that means, in a wholly concrete and tangible sense, love God with all the heart, the soul, the might, we have. God then stands above the rules of the created world, because God will respond not to what we do in conformity to the rules alone, but also to what we do beyond the requirement of the rules. God is above the rules, and we can gain a response from God when, on some one, unique occasion, we too do more than obey—but love, spontaneously and all at once, with the whole of our being. That is the conception of God that *zekhut*, as a conception of power in Heaven and power in humanity, contains. In the relationship between God and humanity expressed in the conception of *Zekhut*, we reach the understanding of what the Torah means when it tells us that we are in God's image and after God's likeness: we are then, "in our image," the very mirror-image of God. God's will forms the mirror-image of ours: when we are humble, God responds; when we demand, God withdraws.

When we come to the way in which *zekhut* is set forth, we find ourselves in a set of narratives of a rather special order. What is special about them is that women play a critical role, appear as heroines, win the attention and respect of the reader or listener. It is difficult to locate in Rabbinic literature before the Talmud of the Land of Israel—in the Mishnah, the Tosefta, or Sifra, for instance—stories in which women figure at all. So to take up a whole series of stories in which women are key-players comes as a surprise. But there is more. The story-teller on the surface makes the man the hero; he is the center of the narrative. And yet a second glance at what is coming shows us that the woman precipitates the tale, and her action, not the man's, represents the gift that cannot be compelled but only given; she is the one who freely sacrifices, and she also is represented as the source of wisdom. So our systemic reversal—something above the Torah and the study of the Torah takes priority—is matched by a still-less-predictable shift in narrative quality, with women portrayed as principal actors.

The three following texts define what the individual must do to gain *zekhut*. The point is that the deeds of the heroes of the story make them worthy of having their prayers answered, which is a mark of the working of *zekhut*. It is supererogatory, uncoerced deeds, those well beyond the strict requirements of the Torah, and even the limits of the law altogether, that transform the hero into a holy man, whose holiness served just like that of a sage marked as such by knowledge of the Torah The story that conveys the concept tells about the *zekhut* attained by a humble, poor, ignorant man. It is narrated to underline what he has done. But what provokes the event is an act of self-abnegation far greater than that willingly performed by the male hero, which is, the woman's readiness to sell herself into prostitution to save her husband. That is not a focus of the story but the given. But nothing has compelled the woman to surrender her body to save her husband; to the contrary, the marital obligations of a woman concern only conventional deeds, which indeed the Mishnah's law maintains may be coerced; failure to do these deeds may result in financial penalties inflicted on the woman in the settlement of her marriage-contract. So the story of the uncoerced act of selflessness is told about a man, but occasioned by a woman, and both actors in the story exhibit one and the same virtue.

Women at the center of the system of *Zekhut*: We note that, at the systemic center, women find entire equality with men; with no role whatever in the study of the Torah and no possibility of attaining political sagacity, women find a critical place in the sequence of actions that elicit from Heaven the admiring response that *zekhut* embodies. Indeed, a second reading of the stories shows that the hero is second to the heroine; it is the woman who, in each case, precipitates the occasion for the man's attainment of *zekhut*, and she, not he, exemplifies the highest pinnacle of selfless virtue. It follows, once more, that those reversals that signal the systemic center culminate in the (for so male a system as this one) ultimate reversal: woman at the height. Just as Torah-learning is subordinated, so man is subordinated; *zekhut*, the gift that can be given but not compelled, like love, in an unerring sense must be called the female virtue that sets atop a male system and structure.

It goes without saying that none of these stories refers explicitly to *zekhut*; all of them tell us about what it means to enjoy not an entitlement by inheritance alone, but a lien accomplished by one's own supererogatory acts of restraint. *Zekhut* integrates what has been differentiated. Holding together learning, virtue, and supernatural standing, by explaining how Torah-study transforms the learning man, *zekhut* further makes implausible those points of distinction between economics and politics that bore the systemic message of the Rabbis' initial philosophy, expressed in particular in the Mishnah. Hierarchical classification, with its demonstration of the upward-reaching unity of all being, gives way in the evolution of Rabbinic Judaism to a different and more compelling proposition: the unity of all being within the heritage of *zekhut*, to be attained equally and without differentiation in all the principal parts of the social order. The definition of *zekhut* therefore carries us to the heart of the integrating and integrated religious system of Judaism. And, we now see, at the center of matters is the virtue that sages themselves classify as feminine and can set forth only in the persons of women.

JACOB NEUSNER

MEDICAL ETHICS OF JUDAISM:[1] Recent advances in biomedical technology and therapeutic procedures have generated a moral crisis in modern medicine. The vast strides made in medical science and technology have created options that only a few decades earlier would have been relegated to the realm of science fiction. To a significant degree, humans now have the ability to exercise control over not only the ravages of disease but even over the very process of life and death. With the unfolding of new discoveries and techniques, the scientific and intellectual communities have developed a keen awareness of the ethical issues that arise out of our enhanced ability to control our destiny. In response to the concern for questions of this nature, the rapidly developing field of biomedical ethics has emerged.

Jews, to whom questions of medical ethics are quests not only for applicable humanitarian principles but also for divine guidance, must, of necessity, seek answers in the teachings of the Torah. "The Torah of God is perfect" (Ps. 19:8), and the discerning student will find its teachings eternally valid even in responding to newly-formulated queries. As physicians and patients turn to Rabbinic authorities for answers, Jewish scholars seek to elucidate and expound the teachings of the Torah in these areas of profound concern.

Judaism is guided by the concepts of the supreme sanctity of human life and of the dignity of humankind created in the image of God. The preservation of human life in Judaism is a divine commandment. Jewish law requires physicians to do everything in their power to prolong life but prohibits the use of measures that prolong the act of dying. The value attached to human life in Judaism is far greater than that in Christian tradition or in Anglo-Saxon common law. In order to save a life, all Jewish religious laws are automatically suspended; the only exceptions are those prohibiting idolatry, murder, and forbidden sexual relations such as incest.

In Jewish law and moral teaching, the value of human life is infinite and beyond measure, so that any part of life—even if only an hour or a second—is of precisely the same worth as seventy years of it.

In Judaism, the practice of medicine by a physician does not constitute an interference with the deliberate designs of divine providence. A physician does not play God by practicing medicine. In fact, a human physician not only has divine license to heal but is, in fact, obligated to heal. A physician in Judaism is prohibited from withholding healing skills and is not allowed to refuse to heal unless doing so would seriously endanger his or her own life.

Judaism is a "right-to-life" religion. This obligation to save lives is not only individual but also communal. A physician, who has knowledge and expertise far greater than that of a lay-person, is obligated to use medical skills to heal the sick and thereby prolong and preserve life. It is erroneous to suppose that having recourse to medicine shows lack of trust and confidence in God, the Healer. The Bible takes for granted the use of medical therapy and actually demands it. Although it is permissible but not mandatory in Jewish law to study medicine, a person who becomes a physician is obligated to use his skills and knowledge to heal the sick.

In Judaism, not only is a physician obligated to heal, but a patient is obligated to seek healing from human physicians and not rely only on faith healing. The Talmud states that no wise person should reside in a city that does not have a physician. The twelfth century Jewish scholar and physician Moses Maimonides rules that it is obligatory upon man to accustom himself to a regimen which preserves the body's health, and heals and fortifies it when it is ailing.

The extreme concern in Judaism about the preservation of health and the prolongation of life require that a woman's pregnancy be terminated if her life is in danger because of the pregnancy, that a woman use contraception if her life would be threatened by pregnancy, that an organ transplant be performed if it can save or prolong the life of a patient dying of organ failure, and that a postmortem examination be performed if the results of the autopsy may provide immediate lifesaving information to rescue another dying patient. Judaism also allows patients to accept experimental medical or surgical treatments provided no standard therapy is available and provided that the experimental therapy is administered by the most experienced physicians whose intent is to help the patient and not to just satisfy their academic curiosity. While Judaism prohibits cruelty to animals, it sanctions experimentation on animals to find cures for human illnesses, as long as the animal experiences little or no pain and suffering.

In Judaism, the infinite value of human life prohibits euthanasia or mercy killing in any form. Handicapped newborns, mentally retarded persons, psychotic persons, and patients dying of any illness or cause have the same right to life as anyone else, and nothing may be done to hasten their death. On the other hand, Judaism recognizes times when specific medical or surgical therapy is no longer indicated nor appropriate or desirable for a patient who is irreversibly, terminally ill. Under no circumstances, however, can general supportive care, including food and water, be withheld or withdrawn to hasten a patient's death.

In summary, Judaism considers each human being to be of supreme and infinite value. It is the obligation of individuals and society in general to preserve, hallow, and dignify human life and to care for the total needs of all persons to enable them to be healthy and productive members of society. This fundamental principle of the sanctity of life and the dignity of humankind as a creation of God is the underlying axiom upon which all medical ethical decision-making is based.

Sexuality and procreation, contraception: The importance of the biblical commandment to *be fruitful and multiply*, decreed first to Adam and Eve (Gen. 1:28), later to Noah and his sons (Gen. 9:1 and 9:7), and then to Jacob (Gen. 35:11), is discussed at B. Yeb. 63b as follows:

> Rabbi Eliezer stated: "He who does not engage in propagation of the race is as though

he sheds blood, for it is said, 'Whoever sheds the blood of man, by man shall his blood be shed' (Gen. 9:6). And this is immediately followed by the text, 'And you, be fruitful and multiply' (Gen. 9:7)." Rabbi Jacob said: "As though he has diminished the Divine Image, since it is said, 'For God made man in his own image' (Gen. 9:6), and this is immediately followed by 'And you, be fruitful and multiply.'" Ben Azzai said: "As though he sheds blood *and* diminishes the Divine Image."

Although one technically fulfills the commandment of procreation when one sires two children, there is another biblical precept of propagating the race. Therefore, contraception without specific medical or psychiatric indication is not condoned in Judaism even after one already has two children.

In a Jewish marriage, over and above the question of procreation, exist the conjugal rights of the wife, technically termed *onah*. Thus, nonprocreative intercourse—such as occurs when the wife is too young to bear children, when the wife is barren, pregnant, or postmenopausal, or following a hysterectomy—is not only allowed but required. The prohibition against improper emission of seed (*hashchatat zera*) is not involved or is canceled out so long as the intercourse is in the manner of procreation. Not only are such sexual activities permitted, but they are required by biblical law (see Ex. 21:10). "Marriage and marital relations are both independent of procreation, achieving the many desiderata spoken of in talmudic, *responsa* and mystic literatures."[2] Such goals include fulfilling the wife's desire, allowing physical release of the husband's sexual pressures, and maintaining marital harmony and domestic peace.

Several methods of contraception are described in the Bible and Talmud. *Coitus interruptus*, perhaps the sin or Er and Onen (Gen. 38:7-10) is unequivocally condemned as stated by Maimonides (Mishneh Torah, *Hilchot Issurei Biyah* 21:18):

> It is forbidden to expend semen to no purpose. Consequently, a man should not thresh within and ejaculate without. . . . As for masturbators, not only do they commit a strictly forbidden act, but they are also excommunicated. Concerning them it is written, "Your

hands are full of blood" (Is. 1:15), and it is regarded as equivalent to killing a human being.

A similar prohibition is found in all other codes of Jewish law. The Talmud discusses four methods and techniques employed by women to prevent conception: using the safe period, making twisting movements following intercourse, using an oral contraceptive, and using an absorbent material during intercourse. There seems to be no impropriety in the use of the safe period when birth control is required, such as in situations of hazard to the mother. By its use, however, the commandment of procreation and the wife's conjugal rights (*onah*) are both frustrated. Furthermore, the unreliability of this method makes it unacceptable in cases of danger to life.

An ancient method of contraception involves the woman's making violent and twisting movements following intercourse in order to spill her husband's seed. This method is described in the Talmud by Rabbi Jose, who is of the opinion that "a woman who plays harlot turns over in order to prevent conception" (B. Ket. 37a). The Talmud further entitles a woman to receive her marriage settlement (*ketubah*) if the husband imposes a vow obligating her to produce violent movements immediately after intercourse to avoid conception (ibid.).

At least two talmudic discussions speak of a "cup of roots" or sterility potion (B. Yeb. 65b and B. Shab. 109b-110a). The ingredients of this oral contraceptive potion are enumerated at B. Shab. 110a and include Alexandrian gum, liquid alum, and garden crocus, pulverized and mixed with beer or wine. The oral contraceptive Pill of today seems equivalent under the law to this cup of roots. It allows intercourse to proceed in a natural and unimpeded manner, thus allowing fulfillment of the wife's conjugal rights. Furthermore, whereas the effect of the cup of roots is permanent, the effect of the Pill is temporary. No improper emission of seed is involved in the use of the Pill.[3] It appears, however, that without medical indication oral contraceptives should not be used before the commandment of procreation (that is, the

birth of at least two children) is fulfilled. Furthermore, the question of the safety of the Pill is of both medical and Jewish legal concern. Certainly, women for whom medical contraindications make the use of oral contraceptives dangerous would be prohibited by Jewish law from taking them. Other deleterious side effects must also be taken into consideration. At the moment, however, the Pill seems to be the least objectionable method of birth control in Jewish law.

An enormous body of Rabbinic *responsa* deals with contraception. The most permissive view is that of sixteenth-century Rabbi Shlomo Luria, who allows the wife to apply a tampon before intercourse if a conception and pregnancy would prove dangerous. Many subsequent writers have supported this view. On the other hand, a school of nonpermissivists does not allow any impediment to natural intercourse.

When pregnancy would be hazardous, the pessary or diaphragm is allowed by numerous authorities because it does not interfere with the normal coital act. This is not the case with the condom, which constitutes an improper interference and is strictly prohibited. Chemical spermicides and douches are other contraceptive methods that leave the sex act alone and are thus permitted by many *responsa* writers, although only in the case of danger to the mother from pregnancy. Whether spermicides or diaphragms are preferable under Jewish law is a matter of debate. As for intrauterine contraceptive devices, recent medical evidence indicates that these prevent conception by inhibiting proper implantation of the fertilized ovum in the wall of the uterus. If this is so, then their abortifacient action would prohibit their use, as their action is akin to abortion.

In summary, Jewish authorities prohibit contraception by any method when no medical or psychiatric threat to the mother or child exists. The duty of procreation, which is primarily a commandment to men, coupled with the conjugal rights of the wife in Jewish law, militates against the use of the condom, *coitus interruptus*, or abstinence under any circumstances. When pregnancy would be hazardous, and when the use of birth control is given Rabbinic sanction, a hierarchy of acceptability emerges from the talmudic and later Rabbinic sources. Most acceptable are contraceptive means that least interfere with the natural sexual act and that permit the full mobility of the sperm along its natural course. According to Feldman, "Oral contraception by pill enjoys preferred status as the least objectionable method of birth control."[4]

Artificial insemination: The possibility of pregnancy without the sexual union of man and woman was recognized by the sages of the Talmud (B. Hag. 14b), who believed a pregnant virgin when she denied having coitus. She may have accidentally conceived in a bathhouse where a man had previously discharged semen, reasoned the rabbis. Other Jewish sources support the possibility of pregnancy *sine concubito*. Legal and ethical questions relating to a physician's intentionally inseminating a woman without her having coitus with the sperm donor are as follow.[5]

Artificial insemination using the semen of a donor (AID) other than the husband is considered by most Rabbinic opinion to be an abomination and strictly prohibited for a variety of reasons. Some authorities regard AID as adultery, which would require the husband to divorce his wife and the wife to forfeit the *ketubah* (marriage settlement or contract). These authorities further regard the physician and the donor as guilty for involvement in this act akin to adultery. Most Rabbinic opinion, however, states that when a sexual act is not involved, the woman is not guilty of adultery and is not prohibited from continued cohabitation with her husband.

Rabbinic opinion is divided on the status of the resulting child. Most rabbis consider the offspring to be legitimate, but a small minority consider the child to be illegitimate. According to the opinion of a considerable number of rabbis, the child, whether legitimate or illegitimate, is the offspring of the donor in all respects (that is, inheritance, support, custody, incest, levirate marriage, and the like). Some rabbis state that, although the child is considered to be the donor's offspring in all respects, the donor has not fulfilled the commandment of procreation. A minority of Rabbinic authorities assert that the child is not considered the donor's offspring at all.

Rabbinic opinion is nearly unanimous that the husband's semen may be inserted artificially if there is no other way for the wife to become pregnant. However, certain qualifications exist. The couple must wait a reasonable period of time after their marriage until there is medical proof of the absolute necessity for artificial insemination by husband (AIH). According to many authorities, the insemination may not be performed during the wife's monthly period of ritual impurity. It is permitted to obtain sperm from the husband both for analysis or insemination, but there is a difference of opinion about how to procure it. Masturbation should be avoided if at all possible; *coitus interruptus* or the use of a condom seem to be the preferred methods.

Note that many important legal and moral considerations that cannot be enunciated in the presentation of general principles may weigh heavily upon the verdict in any given situation. Therefore, it is advisable to submit each individual case to Rabbinic judgment, which, in turn, will be based upon expert medical advice and other prevailing circumstances.

New reproductive technologies: In 1978, Louise Brown, the world's first "test tube" baby was born as a result of in vitro fertilization (IVF), the process of mixing an egg with sperm in a laboratory dish to achieve fertilization, then transferring the early embryo to a woman's uterus with the hope that it will successfully implant and lead to the birth of a healthy child. In the case of Louise Brown, the sperm and egg used were from Mr. and Mrs. Brown. Often the embryo is implanted into the uterus of a woman other than the egg donor; the sperm may also be obtained from a man other than the husband. This technique is characterized by some as science at its best and by others as immoral meddling.

Surrogate parenting is not a technology but a social arrangement that uses reproductive technology (either artificial insemination or in vitro fertilization) to enable a woman to produce a child for another couple, who usually are unable to have a natural child by natural means. Surrogate parenting is characterized by the intention to separate the genetic and/or gestational aspects of childbearing from parental rights and responsibilities through an agreement to transfer the infant and all maternal rights at birth.[6]

One underlying theme in considering the legal issues and moral dilemmas posed by these new techniques is the motivation behind the actions of the concerned parties. At one extreme are the sperm donors and surrogate mothers who are often motivated by a desire for money. On the other end of the spectrum are the couples who have been trying unsuccessfully for years to have a child and who finally resort to one of these methods. Their motivation is pure and represents their burning desire to have a child. Many ethical and moral conflicts arise because the motivation of one party (the sperm donor or surrogate mother) is different from the motivation of the other (the husband and wife). Few ethical concerns are posed by the case of the husband and wife who resort to in vitro fertilization using their own egg and sperm, or that of the young woman with Hodgkin disease or other cancer who cryopreserves her eggs to be able to have children with her own spouse later. Such cases pose very few moral dilemmas other than those of the propriety or religious permissibility of artificial insemination and in vitro fertilization.

In Britain, a blue-ribbon committee headed by Dame Mary Warnock issued a report stating that sperm and egg donations and in vitro fertilization are acceptable techniques for treating infertility.[7] The committee took a pragmatic view of surrogate motherhood, based heavily on the fear of commercial exploitation, or "womb leasing." In response to both the Warnock committee report and the hostile mood of the British public towards commercial surrogacy, the British government passed the Surrogate Arrangements Act of 1985, which makes it a criminal offense to benefit from commercial surrogacy. Voluntary surrogacy, however, is still within the law.

In the United States, several state legislatures are considering laws to ban commercial surrogacy without making voluntary arrangements illegal. The American Medical Association, the American College of Obstetricians and Gynecologists, and the American Fertility Society, among others, have all issued guidelines about the proper use of these new reproductive technologies.[8]

From the Jewish viewpoint, is it tampering with life itself to perform in vitro fertilization? Is it interfering with the divine plan for humanity? If God's will is for a man and/or a woman to be infertile, who are we to undertake test-tube fertilization and embryo reimplantation into the natural or genetic mother, or into a host or surrogate mother, to overcome the infertility problem? Judaism teaches that nature was created by God for humans to use to their advantage and benefit. Hence, animal experimentation is certainly permissible, provided one minimizes the pain or discomfort to the animal. The production of hormones (such as insulin) from bacteria, in tissue cultures, or in animals by recombinant DNA technology for people's benefit also seems permissible. Gene therapy, such as in the replacement of the missing or defective gene in Tay-Sachs disease or in hemophilia, if and when it becomes medically possible, may also be sanctioned in Jewish law. But are we permitted to alter humanity by such measures as in vitro fertilization, transfer of the embryo from a woman inseminated with her husband's (or a donor's) sperm into another woman's womb, artificial gestation in a test tube or glass womb, sex organ or gene transplants, or genetic screening and counseling?

The Committee on Medical Ethics of the Federation of Jewish Philanthropies of New York concluded that a fertilized egg not in the womb, but in an environment in which it can never attain viability (a test tube) does not have humanhood and may be discarded or used for the advancement of scientific knowledge.[9] It should be stressed that, even in the absence of Jewish legal or moral objections to in vitro fertilization using the husband's sperm, no woman is required to submit to this procedure. The obligations of women, whether by reason of the scriptural exhortation to populate the universe or by virtue of the marital contract, are limited to bearing children by means of natural intercourse.[10]

In summary, artificial insemination, in vitro fertilization, surrogate motherhood, and cryopreservation of sperm, eggs, or fertilized zygotes for later use are strongly opposed by some rabbis on moral and ethical grounds and just as strongly justified by others. On the one hand, human procreation should not be converted into the "manufacture" of progeny. The intimate love joining husband and wife together should not be broken by the "biologization" of family life. On the other hand, in Judaism infertility is considered to be an illness—physiological, emotional or both—and the physician's duty and mandate is to heal illness and to overcome, if possible, somatic and emotional strains related to the illness. To help a couple to have their own child through the modern technologies of artificial insemination or in vitro fertilization seems to be within the physician's purview and might even strengthen the bonds of the marriage and the family structure. The use of host or surrogate mothers for the convenience of couples able to conceive by normal coitus cannot be condoned. However, an infertile Jewish couple may have recourse to the new reproductive technologies, including the use of a surrogate mother in the absence of alternatives, in order to effect pregnancy and by so doing preserve their marriage and bring themselves happiness.

Abortion: The Jewish legal and moral attitude toward abortion based on biblical, talmudic and Rabbinic sources including the *responsa* literature has been described in detail in English by Feldman,[11] Bleich,[12] Jakobovits,[13] and Rosner.[14] In Jewish law, an unborn fetus is not considered to be a person (Hebrew: *nefesh*, literally: soul) until it is born. The fetus is regarded as part of its mother's body and not a separate being until it begins to egress from the womb during parturition. Until forty days after conception, the fertilized egg is considered "mere fluid." Intentional abortion is not mentioned directly in the Bible, but a case of accidental abortion is discussed in Ex. 21:22-23, which states:

> When men fight and one of them pushes a pregnant woman and a miscarriage results,

but no other misfortune ensues, the one responsible shall be fined as the woman's husband may exact from him, the payment to be based on judges' reckoning. But if other misfortune ensues, the penalty shall be life for life.

Most biblical commentators interpret "no other misfortune" to mean no fatal injury to the woman following her miscarriage. In that case, the attacker pays only financial compensation for having unintentionally caused the miscarriage, no differently than if he had accidentally injured the woman elsewhere on her body. Thus, when the mother is otherwise unharmed following trauma to her abdomen that causes the fetus to be lost, the only concern is to have the one responsible pay damages to the woman and her husband for the loss of the fetus.

The major talmudic source for abortion rulings in Judaism discusses a case of danger to the mother (M. Oh. 7:6):

> If a woman is having difficulty in giving birth [and her life is in danger], one cuts up the fetus within her womb and extracts it limb by limb, because her life takes precedence over that of the fetus. But if the greater part was already born, one may not touch it, for one may not set aside one person's life [*nefesh*] for that of another.

The commentators explain that the fetus is not considered to be a *nefesh*, or person, until it has left the womb and entered the air of the world; one is, therefore, permitted to destroy it to save the mother's life. Once the head or greater part of the body of the infant comes out, the infant may not be harmed, because it is considered as fully born and, in Judaism, one may not sacrifice one life to save another.

There are many other talmudic sources which support the non-person status of the unborn fetus. In fact, during the first forty days of conception, the Talmud (B. Yeb. 69b, B. Nid. 30b, and M. Ker. 1:3) considers the fertilized zygote to be nothing more than "mere fluid." However, after forty days have elapsed, the fetus is deemed to have been fashioned or formed. Laws of ritual uncleanness must be observed for abortuses older than forty days, implying that the unborn fetus, although not considered to be a living person, still has considerable status. In fact, Jewish law allows one to desecrate the Sabbath to save the life or preserve the health of an unborn fetus so that "the child may observe many Sabbaths later."

The permissibility to kill the unborn fetus to save the mother's life rests upon the fact that such an embryo is not considered a person (*nefesh*) until it is born. Maimonides and Karo present another reason for allowing abortion or embryotomy prior to birth where the mother's life is endangered—the argument of "pursuit," which understands the fetus to be "pursuing" the mother. Maimonides (Mishneh Torah, *Hilchot Rotzeach* 1:9) states:

> if a pregnant woman is having difficulty in giving birth, the child inside her may be excised, either by drugs or manually [i.e., surgery], because it is regarded as pursuing her in order to kill her. But if its head has been born, it must not be touched, for one may not set aside one human life for that of another, and this happening is the course of nature [i.e., an act of God: the mother is pursued by heaven, not the fetus].

An identical statement is found in Karo's Code (Shulchan Aruch, *Choshen Mishpat* 425:2). Many Rabbinic authorities ask, How can the argument of pursuit be invoked here? Since the child does not intend to kill the mother, it appears to be a case of heavenly pursuit.

One answer is offered by Feinstein[15] and others who state that it is unclear whether the fetus is "pursuing" the mother or vice versa since it is an "act of God." Therefore, because the mother is a person and the fetus is not, it is permissible to sacrifice the fetus to save the mother's life. Once the baby is born, both mother and child are persons, and one may not touch the newborn because one may not sacrifice one life to save another.

If an unborn child is not considered a person or *nefesh*, why should its destruction not be allowed under all circumstances? Why is only a threat to the mother's life or health an acceptable reason for therapeutic abortion? Many reasons are offered. First, interference with pregnancy would constitute expulsion of semen for naught, an act akin to *coitus interruptus* and strictly prohibited in Jewish law. Second, the unborn fetus, although not a person, would have sufficient status, if it were aborted after forty days of conception, to require its mother to undergo the same ritual purification process required if she had given birth to a live child. The same process is also prescribed for a woman who has a spontaneous miscarriage. Thus, the fetus can be considered to be a "partial person."

Third, one is not permitted to wound oneself. A woman undergoing abortion by manipulative means is considered to be intentionally wounding herself. Fourth, abortion entails some danger, and Jewish law prohibits intentionally placing oneself in danger. Fifth, many rabbis prohibit abortion when there is no threat to the mother, because they deem such termination of pregnancy an appurtenance of murder and so morally forbidden. The unborn fetus is a potential person that, without interference, will be born and achieve the status of a person. The final and perhaps most important consideration in prohibiting abortion on demand in Jewish law is the fact that the Talmud permits abortion only when the mother's life is endangered. The implication is that when the mother's life is not at stake, it is prohibited to destroy the unborn fetus.

In summary, most Rabbinic authorities would prohibit therapeutic abortion in cases such as the mother's exposure to German measles or to thalidomide early in pregnancy, because there are no fetal indications for abortion in Judaism (for more extensive discussion, see below). By contrast, most rabbis permit and even mandate abortion when the health or life of the mother is threatened. Some authorities are stringent and require the mother's life to be in mortal danger, however remote that danger, whereas others permit abortion for a less serious threat to the mother's health. Such dangers to maternal health may include deafness, cancer, pain, or psychiatric illness. The psychiatric indication for abortion must be certified by competent medical opinion or by previous experiences of mental illness in the mother, such as a postpartum nervous breakdown. Additionally, if the mother becomes pregnant while nursing a child and the pregnancy changes her milk, thereby endangering the suckling's life, abortion is permitted.

A new moral and legal issue relates to a woman pregnant with multiple fetuses either naturally or as a result of hormonal treatment or following in vitro fertilization and implantation of multiple embryos. The mother of multiple fetuses is subject to a very high rate of complications in pregnancy, and there is also a high rate of fetal morbidity and mortality. One option is to selectively abort one or more fetuses so that the others remaining have a better chance of surviving.

In Judaism, abortion of one or more fetuses is never allowed for the sake of the fetus. Abortion is permissible and even mandated only where the pregnancy, simple or multiple, poses a serious danger to the mother's physical or mental health or constitutes a threat to her life. Because multiple pregnancies are associated with a high rate of serious maternal complications, such as preeclampsia, eclampsia, bleeding, uterine atony, and urinary tract infections, it might be permissible to destroy one or more fetuses in a multiple gestation situation to reduce or eliminate these serious risks to the mother.

Tay-Sachs screening and abortion: Debate continues about screening large numbers of Jewish people for the carrier state of Tay-Sachs disease and performing amniocentesis for the prenatal detection of the fatal disease. With rare exceptions, the authors of articles, pamphlets, and booklets relating to Tay-Sachs disease recommend abortion if the amniocentesis reveals an affected child. To eliminate Tay-Sachs disease by selectively terminating affected pregnancies may not be acceptable in Judaism, although some rabbis do sanction such procedures. Although local support for Tay-Sachs screening programs may be active, such support is usually limited to detecting the carrier state and does not include performing amniocentesis with the sole intention of aborting the fetus if it is found to have Tay-Sachs disease.

There are reasons to think twice before undertaking mass screening programs. What are the psychological problems created by discovering that one is a carrier for a fatal genetic disease? Should a known carrier refuse to marry a mate who has not been tested? Should partners break up an engagement or a marriage when they learn through a screening program that they are both carriers? Should a young person inquire about the Tay-Sachs status of a member of the opposite sex prior to meeting that individual socially? When should a person who knows that he or she is a carrier inform an intended spouse? Should we sacrifice primary prevention of Tay-Sachs disease through mate selection to avoid the psycho-social consequences? Is this method of disease prevention an attractive aspect of genetic screening for carriers?

One must remember that twenty-nine of thirty Jews tested for the carrier state are found to be free of the Tay-Sachs gene. It is certainly desirable for these twenty-nine to have peace of mind. However, is the anxiety of the thirtieth person on learning that he or she is a carrier sufficiently great to warrant not testing at all? Obviously not! But one cannot minimize the possible psycho-social trauma to such an individual.

The social stigma of being a carrier of the Tay-Sachs gene is not fully appreciated. Misinformed or uninformed people may look at carriers in the same way that, half a century ago, people looked at patients with epilepsy and leprosy: as individuals afflicted with a "taboo" disease who should be shunned and ostracized from normal social contact. Discrimination against carriers of Tay-Sachs disease may also occur in a variety of areas, if the experience of sickle-cell screening is repeated. Individuals found to have sickle-cell trait were dismissed from their jobs. Several life insurance companies charged higher premiums for individuals with sickle-cell trait or refused to insure them at all. Is this fate also to be suffered by people who, on screening, are found to be carriers of the Tay-Sachs gene? Total confidentiality in screening might avoid such problems and should be an essential part of all such programs.

If Tay-Sachs screening intends to assure that those who need it will receive genetic counseling about reproductive and mating options, few will argue against screening. If the purpose, however, is to suggest to couples at risk the benefits of prenatal diagnosis by amniocentesis, a procedure that may be contrary to the religious dictates of the client, then screening should not be performed. There is little doubt that screening for hypertension, diabetes, and other common conditions that, although not curable, can be controlled by medical therapy, is highly desirable and should be done. There is less certainty that the benefits of Tay-Sachs screening outweigh the disadvantages, although we can give a qualified affirmative answer to this question. But it is clear that those who plan or conduct any screening program must consider the religious teachings of the Jewish people if they want to have the cooperation of the rabbinate and compliance from the clients.

If amniocentesis reveals a fetus affected with Tay-Sachs disease, is abortion permissible in Jewish law? Rabbi Moshe Feinstein condemns abortion for Tay-Sachs disease because abortion is not allowed for the sake of the fetus.[16] On the other hand, Rabbi Eliezer Yehudah Waldenberg allows termination of pregnancy for Tay-Sachs disease because "the defect, the anguish, the shame, the physical and mental pain and suffering of the parents are inestimable."[17] Hence, abortion would be sanctioned by most rabbis to preserve the mother's sanity. Moreover, if a woman who suffered a nervous breakdown following the birth (or death) of a child with Tay-Sachs disease becomes pregnant again, and is so distraught with the knowledge that she may be carrying another child with the fatal disease that she threatens suicide, Jewish law would allow am-niocentesis. If this procedure reveals an unaffected fetus, the pregnancy will continue to term. If the am-niocentesis indicates a homozygous fetus with Tay-Sachs disease, the couple should consult a rabbi about whether or not an abortion should be performed.

Death and dying: Because of advances in medical technology, some people who in an earlier era would have died are today alive and well. Others who would have died are now alive but in a coma or a chronic vegetative state. Medical technology has created as many problems as it has solved. The new technology denies the physician a simple physiological end point for life. The result is a series of difficult questions to be faced by the patient, physician, and family:

> When is a person dead so that his organs can be removed for organ transplantation? Dare we remove kidneys from a donor whose heart is still beating? Is it cruel in the presence of a fatal disease, in the agonal hours, to prolong life (or dying) by the use of life-support machines? What should be done and what should not be done for a terminally ill patient? Should an eighty-year-old man with terminal prostatic cancer be treated differently from a child with leukemia? Who is to weigh the value of a few more days of life? Who is to decide—the physician? the patient? the family?—when the end should come? Should the patient have the option to choose a peaceful death without exposure to the seemingly relentless application of medical technology? Should the physician discuss this option with the patient? To what extent does any individual own his own death? Does a person have the right to select how and when to die? Is such a decision by the patient akin to suicide? What is an individual's responsibility to personal life and health?

Judaism's response to questions such as these emerges from its understanding that life is a gift of God to be held in trust. One is duty bound to care for one's life and health. Only God gives life and, hence, only God can take it away. This individual responsibility for the preservation of life and health is apart from the duty of one person (including a physician) toward another's life and health, and society's responsibility concerning the life and health of its citizens. Specific responses of Judaism to central areas of concern follow.

Euthanasia: Jewish teaching on mercy killing is based on the principle of the infinite value of human life. Since even a second of life has value, one is obligated to provide all necessary care even to patients who have only a few moments of life left. One is prohibited from doing anything that hastens death.

The Talmud clearly enunciates Judaism's objection to euthanasia when it states that a dying patient (Hebrew: *gosses*) is regarded as a living person in all respects (Semachot 1:1ff and B. Shab. 151b). All acts performed on the dead to delay putrefaction of the body and to prepare it for burial—such as binding the jaws, stopping up the openings, rubbing, washing or placing sand or salt on the body—are prohibited on a moribund patient, "lest they hasten the death of the patient by even a few moments." This rule is codified by Maimonides (Mishneh Torah, *Hilchot Avel* 4:5), Karo (Shulchan Aruch, *Yoreh Deah* #339) and others. He who unnecessarily touches the eyes of a dying patient when the soul is about to depart is shedding blood. The situation is compared to a flickering flame which is extinguished as soon as one touches it. On the other hand, Rabbi Moshe Isserles, known as *Ramah*, states (gloss Shulchan Aruch, *Yoreh Deah* #339:1):

> If there is anything that causes a hindrance to the departure of the soul such as the presence near the patient's house of a knocking noise such as wood chopping or if there is salt on the patient's tongue; and these hinder the soul's departure, then it is permissible to remove them from there because there is no act involved in this at all but only the removal of the impediment.

From these and other sources, Jakobovits[18] and other rabbis conclude that any form of active euthanasia is strictly prohibited and condemned as plain murder. Anyone who kills a dying person is liable to the death penalty as a common murderer. At the same time, Jewish law sanctions the withdrawal of any factor—whether extraneous to the patient or not—that may artificially delay the patient's demise in the final phase. Jakobovits is quick to point out, however, that all the Jewish sources refer to a *gosses* in whom death is expected to be imminent—three days or less in Rabbinic references. Thus, passive euthanasia for a patient who may yet live for weeks or months may not necessarily be condoned. Furthermore, in the case of an incurably ill person in severe pain, agony, or distress, the removal of an impediment that hinders the soul's departure, although permitted in Jewish law, may not be analogous to withholding the medical therapy that is perhaps sustaining the patient's life, albeit unnaturally. The impediments spoken of in Jewish law, whether far removed from the patient (as exemplified by the noise of wood chopping) or in physical contact with him (such as salt on the patient's tongue), do not constitute any part of the therapeutic methods and equipment employed in the medical management of this patient. For this reason, these impediments may be removed. However, it may be permissible to discontinue the use of instruments and machinery specifically designed and used in the treatment of incurably ill patients when one is certain that in doing so one is shortening the act of dying and not interrupting life.

Treatment of the terminally ill: The most extensive discussion in the recent literature of the treatment of the terminally ill is that by Rabbi Moshe Feinstein, who states that physicians are not obligated to administer special medical therapy to prolong a life of pain and suffering of a patient who cannot be cured and cannot live much longer; nature may be allowed to take its course.[19] While it is prohibited to administer any medication or do any act to hasten the patient's death by even a moment, pain-relief medications should be administered even if the patient is not yet considered a *gosses* in whom death is imminent, even at the risk of depressing the patient's respiratory center and hastening his death. This is provided that the medications are prescribed solely for pain relief and not to hasten death. Rabbi Eliezer Waldenberg also supports this view and reiterates that physicians are obligated to do everything possible to save the life of a dying patient, even if the patient will live only for a brief period, and even if the patient is suffering.[20] Any action that results in hastening the death of a dying patient is forbidden and considered an act of murder.

Feinstein also asserts that a seriously ill patient with respiratory difficulties should be given oxygen even if he cannot be cured, because oxygen relieves discomfort. There are times, continues Feinstein, when it is appropriate to pray for the death of a suffering, dying patient. Still, one must in no way hasten the patient's death, such that, for instance, care must even be exercised not to touch a dying patient unnecessarily. When a patient is suffering from advanced cancer and cannot be cured, and medications can only prolong the painful suffering, the patient should be so informed and asked if he or she wishes to receive such medications. They do not need to be administered to a person who refuses them, because life would be prolonged only for suffering. One is not obligated or even permitted to initiate artificial life support or other resuscitative efforts if it is obvious that the patient is terminally, irreversibly ill with no chance of recovery. This position is clearly supported by Isserles, who permits and even requires the withdrawal of any impediment to the departure of the soul. On the other hand, if the treatment has a reasonable chance of producing a remission of the illness and prolonging the patient's life, the patient is obligated to accept such treatment.

Feinstein also rules that if a patient with an incurable illness, such as metastatic cancer, develops an intercurrent illness that is treatable and often completely reversible, such as pneumonia or a urinary tract infection, it is obligatory to treat the intercurrent illness.[21] If the underlying incurable illness is very painful and the patient refuses additional palliative therapy, however, it is not obligatory to administer medications that will only prolong a life of suffering without any hope of cure. Even if the patient is unable to voice an opinion in this matter, one can consult with immediate family members about what the patient would have desired had he or she been able to express a preference. Such decisions should be made in consultation with a competent rabbi and the most expert physicians.

Specifically addressing the giving of food and fluids by nasogastric tube or intravenous route, Feinstein states:

> . . . it is clear that an incurably ill patient who cannot eat normally must be fed intravenously since such feeding strengthens the patient somewhat even if the patient does not feel anything [i.e., is comatose]. Food is not at all comparable to medication since food is a natural substance which all living creatures require to maintain life.

Many other modern Rabbinic authorities support the view that a dying patient must be given food, fluids, oxygen, antibiotics, and pain relief drugs. Every moment of life is precious, and all measures must be taken to preserve even a few moments of life. When a patient's situation is deemed by physicians to be hopeless, however, one is not obligated to institute life-prolonging or resuscitative treatments.

In summary, Jewish law requires the physician to do everything in his power to prolong life but prohibits the use of measures that prolong the act of dying. Euthanasia accordingly is opposed without qualification in Jewish law, which condemns as sheer murder any active or deliberate hastening of death, done with or without the patient's consent. Some Rabbinic views do not allow any relaxation of efforts, however artificial and ultimately hopeless they are, to prolong life. Others, however, do not require the physician to resort to "heroic" methods, but sanction the omission of machines and artificial life-support systems that only serve to draw out the dying patient's agony, provided, however, that basic care (such as food and good nursing) is provided.

Jewish teaching proclaims the sanctity of human life. The physician is given divine license to heal but not to hasten death. When a physician has nothing further to offer a patient medically or surgically, the physician's license to heal ends and he or she becomes no different from a lay person, morally obligated to help another human in distress. A dying patient is no exception to this obligation. The physician, family, friends, nurses, social workers, and other individuals close to the dying patient are all obligated to provide supportive—including psycho-social and emotional—care until the very end. Fluids and nutrition are part and parcel of that supportive care, no different from washing, turning, talking to, singing with, reading to, or just listening to the dying patient. There are times when specific medical and/or surgical therapy are no longer indicated, appropriate or desirable for an irreversibly ill, dying patient. However, under no circumstances can general supportive measures be abandoned, to hasten the patient's demise.

Because the decisions about withholding specific therapy for a terminally ill patient;

discontinuing life-support systems; employing resuscitative measures in a given situation; and withholding or withdrawing fluids, nutrition, and oxygen are complex and not free of the personal and emotional involvement and biases of family members and physicians, it is advisable to consult with a competent rabbi on a case-by-case basis.

The living will: The living will is a legal document that recognizes the right of an adult to instruct a physician to withhold life-sustaining procedures in the event of the person's inability to do so while in a terminal condition. The living will is designed to promote the patient's autonomy while removing the obligation of the physician and the patient's family to make onerous decisions. Experience with the living will indicates that it can either help or hinder clinical decision making. Jewish law, for its part, is opposed to the concept of the living will because it holds that the patient does not have the right to die. A person, rather, has an obligation to live. Only God gives and takes life. Humans do not have full title over their life or body. They are charged with preserving, dignifying, and hallowing that life.

A central problem with the living will emerges from the fact that it is extremely difficult to make accurate predictions for critically ill patients and to determine whether a patient is irreversibly ill and whether death is imminent. The provisions of the living will sometimes can be activated prematurely. Alternatively, the existence of a living will may deprive the patient of the full efforts of the medical team, who might not use the usual vigor and aggressive approach dictated by the patient's condition.

Other problems also occur. If a patient changes his or her mind while a living will is in effect but fails to formally rescind the declaration, it may be activated without proper "informed consent." Additionally, patients often write living wills to avoid having to live with intractable pain; however, should the time arrive that a patient is in intractable pain, medical science may have developed methods to deal with his pain. A patient who signs a living will thus thinks that he is opting for a painless, conscious, dignified,

decent, comfortable, peaceful, and natural death. In fact, what the patient perceives as the "right to die" may backfire. The living will only protects the right to refuse treatment; it does not guarantee a peaceful, easy death.

Definition of death: The classic definition of death in Jewish law is the irreversible absence of spontaneous respiration.[22] Some rabbis also require complete cessation of cardiac activity. One must use all available medical means to ascertain with certainty that respiratory and cardiac functions have indeed irreversibly ceased.

Rabbi Moshe Tendler introduced the concept of physiologic decapitation or whole brain including brain stem death in Judaism as an acceptable definition of death even if cardiac function has not ceased.[23] Thus, if it can be definitely demonstrated that all of a patient's brain functions, including brain stem function, have ceased, the patient is legally dead in Jewish law, because he is equated with a decapitated individual whose heart may still be beating. Brain stem function can be accurately evaluated by a variety of neurological tests, including the "apnea test" and other simple, safe, highly specific and highly reliable indicators of absence of blood flow to the entire brain to confirm total irreversible brain death. According to Tendler, Rabbi Moshe Feinstein,[24] whose *responsum* on heart transplantation begins with a discussion of decapitation, supports the aforementioned position that complete and permanent absence of any brain-related vital bodily function is recognized as death in Jewish law.

In a more recent *responsum*, Rabbi Feinstein further supports the acceptability of total irreversible whole brain death as an absolute definition of death.[25] Feinstein again reiterates the classic definition of death as the total irreversible cessation of respiration. He then states that, if by injecting a substance into the vein of a patient, physicians can ascertain that there is no circulation to the brain—meaning no connection between the brain and the rest of the body—the patient is legally dead in Judaism because he is equivalent to a decapitated person. Where the test is available, continues Feinstein, it should be used.

The classic respiratory and circulatory death is in reality brain death. Irreversible respiratory arrest is indicative of brain death. A brain dead person is like a physiologically decapitated individual. The requirement of Maimonides to "wait awhile" to confirm that the patient is dead is that amount of time it takes after the heart and lungs stop until the brain dies, that is to say, a few minutes.

In summary, all rabbis agree that the classic definition of death in Judaism is the irreversible absence of spontaneous respiration and heartbeat in a patient with no bodily motion. According to this definition, death may be pronounced following a brief waiting period after breathing has ceased. In the present era, when it is recognized that hypothermia or drug overdose can result in depression of the respiratory center with absence of spontaneous respiration and even heartbeat, this classic definition of death is insufficient. Hence, wherever resuscitation is deemed possible, no matter how remote the chance, it must be attempted. Some Rabbinic scholars do not accept total brain death as a criterion for establishing death, other than to confirm death in a patient who already has irreversible absence of spontaneous respiration and no heartbeat. The only exception may be the situation of decapitation, in which immediate death is assumed, even if the heart may still be briefly beating. Whether or not irreversible whole brain including brain stem death, as evidenced by sophisticated medical testing, is the Jewish legal equivalent of decapitation, is presently a matter of intense debate in Rabbinic circles.

Autopsy: Since Judaism teaches that man is created in the image of God, every dignity must be extended to the human body in death as in life. For this reason the body must be regarded as inviolate and, except in certain limited circumstances, Jewish law does not sanction the performance of autopsies. The consensus of Rabbinic opinion, however, holds that postmortem examinations may and sometimes must be performed for the purpose of gaining specific information of immediate benefit in the treatment of other patients already afflicted by a life-threatening disease. A case in point would be a person with cancer who died after receiving an experimental drug or drug combination. Postmortem examination to ascertain possible toxicity in order to prevent potential harm to other patients on the same course of treatment, or to obtain information concerning the therapeutic efficacy of the drug or drug combination, would be warranted according to Jewish law when such information is deemed to be essential in the treatment of other patients already suffering from the same illness.

Another situation in which autopsy is not only allowed but probably mandated involves life-threatening infectious disease such as Legionnaires' disease. At a convention in Philadelphia in 1976, several hundred Legionnaires were afflicted with a pneumonia-like illness, and many died. Jewish law would probably dictate autopsy on those who died in order to discover the offending organism (now known) and treatment (now available) so as to save the lives of the other patients afflicted, many of whom were dying of the same illness.

The dominant consideration in permitting an autopsy is the immediacy of the constructive application of the findings. This "here and now" principle, once limited to the medical needs of a local community, can now be extended through the excellence of communication and scientific reporting to the whole medical world. Results of autopsies in New York can be available in London in a matter of minutes. Routine autopsies cannot be sanctioned, however, although great benefit may accrue at some distant future time.

Another area where autopsy is permissible in Jewish law is genetic disease. A postmortem examination may be performed on a child who dies of a fatal genetic disease in order to obtain information that might save the lives of future children in that family who may be afflicted with the same disease. Although the baby whose life is to be saved has not yet been born or even conceived, the "here and now" principle is rabbinically satisfied in the case of lethal genetic diseases.

When an autopsy is sanctioned in Jewish law, certain considerations must be observed.

The autopsy should be done as a surgical procedure with the deceased given the same dignity, respect, and consideration that would be accorded a living patient undergoing an operation. It should be performed in dignified surroundings. The deceased should be draped and only the area of incision exposed. Proper decorum should be observed, and the behavior of the surgical-pathological staff should be appropriate to the situation. In a typical autopsy, an incision is made along the entire length of the abdominal and thoracic cavities, and internal organs, including the brain, are examined. Such a complete autopsy is not countenanced when—as is often the case—all pertinent potentially life-saving information may be acquired by means of a much more limited incision and examination of only those organs or areas crucial for obtaining this information. For example, in Legionnaires' disease, a postmortem examination limited to the chest would have provided the necessary information about the cause and cure of this disease for the purpose of immediately saving the lives of afflicted patients. Finally, organs may not be removed if they can be examined *in situ*. All organs and body fluids must be returned for burial.

A special autopsy consent form has been prepared by the Federation of Jewish Philanthropies of New York in consultation with a number of physicians and legal scholars. It is designed to provide for detailed specification of the nature and scope of the postmortem examination for which permission is sought. This consent form requires the physician to state in precise clinical terms the information sought and to specify the area to be incised and the organs to be examined to obtain such information. The authorization signed by the next of kin limits the extent of the postmortem procedure to that which is absolutely necessary in order to secure pertinent, potentially life-saving information of immediate applicability. Use of the consent form morally and legally obligates the pathologist to respect the directives of the next of kin. It specifies the limitations placed upon the autopsy procedure and ensures that all organs, tissues, and fluids will be returned for burial as required by Jewish law.[26]

Embalming and cremation: The Medical Ethics Committee of the Federation of Jewish Philanthropies of New York, in its *Compendium on Medical Ethics*, summarizes the Jewish view of procedures after death:

> The inviolate right of a person to life, which differentiates mankind from all other animal species, extends an aura of holiness over the body even after the Divine soul leaves it. The body, like the soul, is the property of the One who created it. It is therefore not permitted to injure or mutilate the body except when overriding consideration for the preservation of life and health make such action necessary. . . . Reverent treatment of the body and speedy interment are biblically-ordained precepts. Cremation, freeze-storage of the body, and above-ground burial crypts, are all in violation of Jewish law and practice. The duty to bury in the ground applies to all parts of the body and is the obligation of the next of kin. Even where testamentary direction to be cremated has been given, Jewish law requires that it be ignored as an unwarranted desecration of the body.[27]

For a more detailed discussion of embalming and cremation in the classic Jewish sources and recent Rabbinic writings, the reader is referred elsewhere.[28]

Suicide: Judaism regards suicide as a criminal act and strictly forbidden by Jewish law. The cases of suicide in the Bible as well as those in the Apocrypha, Talmud, and Midrash took placed under unusual and extenuating conditions.

In general a suicide is not accorded full burial honors. The Talmud and codes of Jewish law decree that rending one's garments, delivering memorial addresses, and other rites of mourning that are an honor for the dead are not to be performed for a suicide. The strict definition of a suicide for which these laws apply is only one who had previously announced the intention and then killed himself immediately thereafter by the announced method. Children are never regarded as deliberate suicides and are afforded all burial rites. Similarly, those who commit suicide under extreme physical or mental strain, or while not in full possession of their faculties, or in order to atone for past sins are not considered as willful suicides, and none of the burial and mourning rites are withheld.

These considerations may condone the numerous acts of suicide and martyrdom committed by Jews throughout the centuries, from the priests who leaped into the flames of the burning Jerusalem-Temple to the martyred Jews in the time of the Crusades, from the Jewish suicides during the medieval persecutions to the martyred Jews in more recent pogroms. Only for the sanctification of the name of the Lord would a Jew intentionally take his or her own life or allow it to be taken as a symbol of extreme faith in God. Otherwise intentional suicide would be strictly forbidden, because it constitutes a denial of the Divine creation of man, of the immortality of the soul, and of the atonement of death.[29]

Other medical ethical issues—Organ transplantation: The Jewish and legal moral issues concerning the transplantation of a human organ can be conveniently subdivided into those which pertain to the recipient, those that involve the physician or medical team, and those that primarily affect the donor.

In regard to the recipient, does the transplanted organ become a permanent part of the recipient, or must it be returned to the donor upon the eventual death of the recipient? The donor may long since have been buried, and his identity and/or burial site may not be known. Furthermore, where a diseased organ such as a heart, liver, or lung is removed before implantation of a new organ, what does one do with the "old" or diseased organ? Can one just discard it? Must it be buried? Can one incinerate it or place it in formalin for preservation? Must it be treated with respect as part of a human being who was created in the image of God? This problem is not unique to organ transplantation but applies to any organ or part removed from a living human being. Thus, the rabbis discuss whether or not a gallbladder, stomach, uterus, appendix, foot, leg, or other diseased organ or limb removed at surgery or traumatically avulsed requires burial. An entire chapter in Rabbi Joseph Karo's *Code of Jewish Law* is devoted to this question (*Yoreh Deah* 374).

Another question concerns whether or not the recipient is allowed to subject himself to the danger of the operative procedure. In Judaism, it is not proper intentionally to wound oneself for no valid medical reason.[30] Does this rule apply to surgery in general and to an organ transplant in particular? Furthermore, does the recipient transgress the biblical commandments "Only take heed, and keep your soul diligently" and "Therefore take good heed to yourselves" (Deut. 4:9 and 4:15), which both the Talmud and Maimonides interpret to mean the removal (i.e., avoidance) of all danger to one's physical well-being (B. Ber. 32b; Mishneh Torah, *Hilchot Rotzeach* 11:4)?

Another Jewish legal issue concerns a recipient who is a priest (Kohen), who is commanded not to become ritually defiled by corpse contact (Lev. 21:1-3). Does this question of ritual defilement[31] apply to an organ from a dead donor, which is now to be implanted into a priest? Finally, what are the Jewish priorities, if any, for choosing a recipient in view of the shortage of organ donors? Such priorities are enumerated in the Talmud (B. Hor. 13a, 13b, and 14a). Do they apply to organ transplant recipients, or should medical criteria be used exclusively in the selection of recipients?

In regard to the physician or medical team performing the organ transplant there are two major issues. Does an organ transplant constitute standard medical therapy or human experimentation but with therapeutic intent? Corneal and kidney transplants can be considered to be standard medical therapy, whereas lung and liver transplants should still be viewed as experimental. Physicians are obliged to heal the sick using all standard therapies available. Human experimentation is permissible in Jewish law under specific restricted conditions.[32] The more difficult issue is the establishment of criteria for determining whether a prospective donor is dead, for if the donor is still alive when the physician performing an organ transplantation removed one or more of his organs, the physician would be guilty of murder. The definition of death in Jewish law is discussed above. In relation to heart transplantation, the question of "killing" the recipient is also raised by several rabbis. When the recipient's diseased heart is removed prior to the implantation of a new heart, the patient is without a heart. Is the patient equivalent to a corpse (*nevelah*) or a non-viable person (*terefah*)? If so, are the physicians guilty of murder? Obviously not!

There are numerous Jewish legal questions concerning the organ donor: First is the establishment of the death of the donor before any organ is removed for transplantation. Second, there is the biblical prohibition of desecrating or mutilating the dead (B. Ar. 7a, B. Hul. 11b, and B. B.B. 154b). How can one remove an organ for transplantation without desecrating the body? There is also a biblical prohibition against deriving benefit from the dead.[33] The recipient of an organ from a deceased person certainly derives benefit from the dead! Furthermore, there is a biblical prohibition against delaying the burial of the dead[34] as well as the positive commandment of burying the dead.[35] Another halakhic consideration is that of ritual defilement for priests in the same room with either the donor or only the donor's organ or organs.[36] Do such organs transmit ritual defilement? Finally, in Jewish law is permission necessary either from the deceased prior to his demise or from the next of kin? Is one "robbing the dead" if one fails to obtain consent? Does the deceased have total rights over his or her body, or does it belong to God, who gave it on loan for the duration of life?

The answer to all these questions is based on the fact that a person dying of organ failure is classified as dangerously ill, and saving such a person (*pikuach nefesh*) takes precedence over all biblical and Rabbinic commandments except murder, idolatry, and forbidden sexual relations. Even restoring sight to a blind person is classified as *pikuach nefesh*, since the blind individual may fall down a flight of stairs or be hit by a bus when crossing the street.[37] Thus, all organ transplants are permissible and even mandatory, provided the donor is deceased when donor organs are removed for transplantation. Live donors can be used for kidney and bone marrow transplantation because the risk to the donor is very small. In this regard Ezekiel's prophecy of God's promise is poignant: "And a new heart will I give you, and a new spirit will I put within you, and I will take away the stone heart out of your flesh, and I will give you a heart of flesh" (Ez. 11:19 and 36:26). Although this scriptural reference is obviously meant in a figurative and spiritual sense, it seems vividly to depict the epoch of cardiac and other organ transplantation.

Animal experimentation: Jewish law not only forbids cruelty to animals but requires that we be kind to them, have compassion for them, and treat them humanely. Thus, if one sees an animal collapsing under a heavy burden, one must unload it. One may not muzzle an animal to deprive it of food while it is working. In fact, one may not partake of any food until one has first assured the provision of food for one's animals. That animals may not work on the Sabbath is a rule enunciated among the Ten Commandments, indicating that care of and kindness to animals are of profound importance for the humanizing of man.

These and other biblical and Rabbinic moral and legal rules concerning the treatment of animals are based on the principle that animals are part of God's creation for which man bears responsibility. Maimonides offers an insight into these rules in stating that the prohibition of causing suffering to animals was set down with a view to perfecting humans so that we do not acquire moral habits of cruelty. We should not inflict pain gratuitously without any utility but should be kind and merciful even with a chance or stray animal. We are forbidden to eat a limb cut off from a living animal because this act would make us acquire the habit of cruelty. The same reason is given for the rule forbidding the slaughtering of an animal and its young on the same day and the commandment to release the mother bird before taking the young.[38]

There are many additional rules the rabbis enacted to guard animals against hunger, overwork, disease, distress, and suffering. Wanton hunting and killing of animals for sport is prohibited. It is forbidden to inflict a blemish on an animal. Numerous Sabbath laws relating to forbidden acts are waived when such acts are intended to relieve pain of an animal. People are not permitted to buy animals unless they can properly care and provide for them.

On the other hand, Judaism also espouses the concept that everything God created in this world was created to serve mankind. Animals may thus be used as beasts of burden and for food, providing they are humanely slaughtered. Scientific experiments upon laboratory animals during the course of medical research designed to yield information that might lead to cure of disease are sanctioned by Jewish law as legitimate utilization of animals for the benefit of mankind. However, wherever possible, pain or discomfort should be eliminated or minimized by analgesia, anesthesia, or other means. The pain does not serve to satisfy a legitimate human need and its infliction is prohibited. In addition, animal experimentation is only permissible by Jewish law if its purpose is to obtain practical benefits to mankind and not simply the satisfaction of intellectual curiosity. Furthermore, if alternative means of obtaining the same information are available, such as tissue culture studies, animal experimentation might be considered to fall under the category of unnecessary cruelty to animals and be prohibited.

Alternative therapies: More and more patients are seeking alternative therapies or more natural forms of therapy such as naturopathy, acupuncture, chiropractic, herbal remedies, and vitamin and mineral therapies. Contrary to stereotypes, patients who seek unproven methods tend to be well-educated, upper middle class, and not necessarily terminal or even beyond hope of cure or remission by conventional treatments. Many practitioners of unorthodox cancer care are licensed physicians who specialize in homeopathic or naturopathic medicine.

Why do people seek out alternative therapies? They may be discouraged and despair about the realities of conventional cancer treatment. Fear, side-effects, previous negative experiences, and a desire by the patient for more supportive care are other reasons. People are unhappy with the disease oriented technologic, authoritarian health care system. They may reject conventional care, because they are attracted to the ideology

which includes an emphasis on self-care.

Since Judaism considers a human life to have infinite value, physicians and other health-care givers are obligated to heal the sick and prolong life. Physicians are not only given divine license to practice medicine, but are also mandated to use their skills to heal the sick. Failure or refusal to do so, with resultant negative impact on the patient, constitutes a transgression on the part of the physician. Physicians must be well-trained in traditional medicine and licensed by the authorities. Patients similarly are duty bound to seek healing from a physician when they are ill and not to rely solely on divine intervention or faith healing. Patients are charged with preserving their health and restoring it when ailing in order to be able to serve the Lord in a state of good health. Quackery is not condoned in Judaism whether or not it is practiced by physicians. Those who deceive patients into accepting quack remedies "are destined for Gehenna" (B. Qid. 4:14).

On the other hand, Judaism seems to sanction certain alternative therapies, such as prayers, faith healing, amulets, incantations, and the like, when used as a supplement to traditional medical therapy. Only the substitution of prayer for rational healing is condemned. Quackery, superstition, sorcery, and witchcraft are abhorrent practices in Judaism, but confidence in the healing powers of God through prayer and contrition is encouraged and has its place of honor alongside traditional scientific medicine.[39]

Rationing and priorities in Judaism: Health care reform is being driven in part to control costs. Organ transplantation, hemodialysis, sophisticated cardiac and other surgery, in vitro fertilization and other reproductive technologies, magnetic resonance imaging and other advanced diagnostic tools are all very costly. The care of small premature babies, patients with AIDS, and the elderly with chronic physical or mental disabilities is extremely expensive. We can no longer afford to pay for everything for everybody. Despite the varied and extensive health technology available nowadays, including a multitude of diagnostic and therapeutic modalities, not all needs can be met.

The classic talmudic source which discusses priorities (i.e., rationing) teaches that a man takes precedence over a woman in matters concerning the saving of life because he has more commandments to fulfill (M. Hor. 3:7). A woman takes precedence over a man in respect of clothing, because her shame is greater if she must wear shabby clothing. A woman also takes precedence over a man in ransoming them from captivity, because she may be raped by her captors. If a man and his father and his teacher were kidnapped, his ransom takes precedence over his teacher, and his teacher takes precedence over his father, while his mother takes precedence over all of them. A scholar takes precedence over a king of Israel, for if a scholar dies there is none to replace him, while all Israel are eligible for kingship. A king takes precedence over a High Priest, and a High Priest takes precedence over a prophet (B. Hor. 13a).

It seems from this talmudic discussion that Judaism considers religious status, personal dignity, social worth, and even inherited station in life as factors that determine priorities and precedences in the allocation of ransom money or other scarce resources. Yet such an approach is in direct contrast to the cardinal Jewish principle that one may not sacrifice one human life to save another (B. San. 72b; M. Oh. 7:6, etc.). The reason, as cited in the Talmud, is because one person's blood is no redder than the blood of another (B. Pes. 25b), indicating that all lives are of equal value. The infinite value of human life, that is, disallows the sacrificing of one life to save another since all lives are of equal value. This rule implies that no qualitative distinctions should be made between people. Yet, the Talmud cited above lists orders of precedence based on social worth, religious status and personal dignity!

How, then, does Judaism approach the problem of scarce medical resources? If only one dialysis machine is available but several patients dying of kidney failure urgently need dialysis, how does one decide who gets dialyzed and who is left to die for lack of additional dialysis machines? If two patients need a life saving medication but only enough medicine is available for one patient, whose life is saved and whose is not? Should the precedences relating to religious status, social worth and personal dignity be considered as enumerated in the Talmud? How can such an approach be reconciled with the fact that no person's blood is redder than any other person's blood and that qualitative distinctions in the saving of life, according to Jewish law, should not be made?

A classic example of "lifeboat ethics" is described at B. B.M. 62a, which speaks of two people traveling in the desert far from civilization, and only one has a canteen of water. If both drink the water, they will both die, but if only one drinks, he can reach civilization but the other will die. Ben Petura rules that it is better that both should drink and die rather than one behold his companion's death. But Rabbi Aqiba rules that only the one who owns the canteen drinks, because the biblical verse "that your brother may live beside you" (Lev. 25:36) means that "your life takes precedence over his life." Rabbi Aqiba's reasoning seems to be self-evident. A person is obligated to save another's life if the latter is drowning or mauled by beasts or attacked by robbers (B. San. 73a; Mishneh Torah, *Hilchot Rotzeach* 1:14). If one fails to do so, one violates the biblical precept "you shall not stand forth against the life of your neighbor" (Lev. 19:16). This injunction is not applicable when one's own life would be endangered in the attempt to save the other. The other's life is secondary to one's own when both are at stake because "his blood is no redder than yours." The final legal ruling in the case of the single canteen of water is in accordance with the opinion of Rabbi Aqiba.

How are these classic biblical and talmudic sources applied to modern medical situations involving triage, the allocation of scarce medical resources and rationing? Are the criteria used by society to ration services and to determine the allocation of scarce resources different from those used by individuals in the conduct of their private lives? Are the ethical standards different for society and for individuals. Rabbi Moshe Tendler states that "societal ethics are more than individual ethics. Whereas individual ethics must be taken into account in societal decisions, there is more to society than the individuals in it."[40] Support for this position can be found in several classic Jewish sources. The Talmud states that, to prevent abuses, captives should not be ransomed for more than their value (M. Git. 2:6). The kidnappers must not be encouraged to seize more people and make excessive ransom demands that will impoverish the community. If society had to pay large sums of money to ransom kidnap victims, that money could not be allocated to other pressing societal needs. B. Git. 45a continues:

> Come and hear: Levi ben Darga ransomed his daughter for 13,000 dinari of gold [showing that an individual is allowed to pay exorbitant fees if he wishes, and the reason why society may not spend large sums of money to redeem captives is to protect the community].

It is thus clear that a man is allowed and perhaps obligated to ransom his wife or daughter for a very large amount of money. The underlying point of the Talmud is that societal ethical standards differ from those to be used by individuals in the allocation of scarce financial, medical or other resources. Society may not expend an inordinate amount of its limited resources to redeem captives, although the rich may pay their entire fortune to ransom a close relative. Clearly, a distinction is made in Judaism between societal ethics and individual ethics.

An individual physician must treat all patients equally, usually on a first come, first served basis. The physician must do whatever is necessary to care for the patient irrespective of cost. The physician should not be involved in rationing at the bedside. The physician's only concern should be the here and now of the patient. Society, however, must be concerned about long range planning and future generations and can, therefore, make decisions based on considerations of cost or social status (Judaism gives priority to orphans and widows). Hence, governmental spending caps are consistent with Judaic teaching.

AIDS—A Jewish view: The acquired immunodeficiency syndrome (AIDS) has been described as this century's greatest health peril. Many thousands of patients have already died from the disease and there is no cure yet available. The emotional toll on patients with AIDS, their families, and their caregivers is enormous. Most patients with AIDS are intravenous drug users or homosexuals.

Judaism condemns homosexuality as an immoral act characterized in the Torah as an abomination. We are nevertheless duty bound to defend the basic rights to which homosexuals are entitled. The Torah teaches that even one who is tried, convicted, and executed for a capital crime is still entitled to the respect due to any human being created in the image of God. Thus, the corpse may not go unburied overnight (Deut. 21:23). The plight of Jewish AIDS victims doomed to almost certain death should arouse our compassion.

In Judaism, the value of human life is infinite. Whether a person is a homosexual or not, we are obligated to give him proper care if he is sick, charity if he is needy, food if he is hungry, and a burial after death. If he breaks a law of the Torah, he will be punished according to the transgression. Even if AIDS were a punishment by God for the sin of homosexuality, Jewish tradition teaches us that such a divine affliction may serve as an atonement for that sin, or the patient may repent while ill, making the AIDS victim even more deserving of our mercy and lovingkindness as a fellow Jew.

The compassion of Jewish law in requiring treatment for AIDS patients, however, should not be confused with acquiescence to the behavior of homosexuals who develop AIDS. Under no circumstances does Judaism condone homosexuality, which Judaism characterizes as an abomination. Nevertheless, the patient with AIDS should be treated and his life saved. To stand idly by and see the homosexual die without trying to help is prohibited (Lev. 19:16). Evil should be banned, but the evildoers should be helped to repent (Ps. 104:35).

Other issues: This essay presents the Jewish attitude toward five major topics relating to sexuality and procreation (that is, the beginning of life), seven major topics relating to death and dying (that is, the end of life), and five other medical ethical topics. There are obviously many other medical ethical questions that are beyond the scope of this chapter. Such questions include truth telling and professional secrecy, sterilization, transsexual surgery, sex-preselection, genetic engineering, hazardous medical and/or surgical therapy, human experimentation, among many others.

For example, how does Judaism view a physician's treating close members of his or her own family? May a male physician care for his own mother? May a female physician minister to her own brother? Does Jewish law prohibit cigarette smoking based on the danger to life it represents? Are people not charged with preserving, dignifying and sustaining their God given life? Smoking would seem to be in direct conflict with this charge, since lung and other cancers, cardiac and chronic lung ailments, and other maladies are common consequences of smoking. Are Jewish physicians obligated to inform their patients of these considerations?

Does Judaism recognize the concept of risk-benefit ratio? Does Judaic law consider the statistical probability of prolonging life versus the mortality rate or the odds of shortening life? May a dying patient be exposed to a hazardous therapeutic procedure that offers a slim chance of a cure, even though the chances of survival are much less than even? How does one define "slim"? If a physician cannot recommend a specific experimental treatment or procedure on the basis of sound scientific principles, may he or she offer it as a "one chance in a million?" Would Judaism prefer an approach in which a patient's health is left to chance?

One area in medical ethics that is just beginning to receive the attention of Rabbinic scholars is mental illness and psychiatry. What does Judaism have to say about transsexual surgery, transvestitism, alcoholism, drug addiction, psychotherapy, psychotropic drug therapy, and a host of related issues?

Conclusion: In the Jewish tradition, a physician is given specific divine license to practice medicine. According to Maimonides and other codifiers of Jewish law, it is in fact an obligation upon the physician to use medical skills to heal the sick. Not only is the physician permitted and even obligated to minister to the sick, but also the patient is obligated to care for his or her own health and life. People do not have title over their life or body. They are charged with preserving, dignifying and hallowing that life. They must eat and drink to sustain themselves and must seek healing when ill.

Another cardinal principle in Judaism is that human life is of infinite value. The preservation of human life takes precedence over all but three biblical commandments: the prohibitions against idolatry, murder, and forbidden sexual relations such as incest. Life's value is absolute and supreme. Thus, an old man or woman, a mentally retarded person, a deformed baby, or a dying cancer patient have the same right to life as healthy people in their prime of life. In order to preserve a human life, the Sabbath and even the Day of Atonement may be desecrated and all other rules and laws (save the above three) are suspended for the overriding consideration of saving a human life. The corollary of this principle is that one is prohibited from doing anything that might shorten a life even for a very short time, since every moment of human life is of infinite value.

These and other principles of Judaism guide the Jewish physician in the practice of medicine. As more physicians become familiar with the Judaic principles relating to the practice of medicine, and as more rabbis become aware of the daily ethical judgments required of the physician, the answers to ethical queries such as those reviewed above become more readily available. Such answers need to be consonant with the physician's ability to practice medicine, using the most up-to-date advances in medical science and biomedical technology. However, such answers must also remain true to traditional Judaic teachings as transmitted by God to Moses and the children of Israel.

Notes
[1] An earlier version of this entry was published as "Jewish Medical Ethics," in *The Journal of*

Clinical Ethics 6, num. 3 (1995). It is used here with permission.

2 David Feldman, *Birth Control in Jewish Law* (New York, 1968), p. 60.

3 Moshe Feinstein, *Iggrot Moshe*, vol. 1, *Even Haezer* #65.

4 Feldman, op. cit, p. 248.

5 See Fred Rosner, *Modern Medicine and Jewish Ethics* (New York, 1986), pp. 91-105.

6 The New York State Task Force on Life and the Law, *Surrogate Parenting. Analysis and Recommendations for Public Policy* (New York, May, 1988).

7 *Report of the Committee of Inquiry into Human Fertilization and Embryology*, Cond 9314 (London, HM Stationary Office, 1984).

8 Fred Rosner, et al., "Ethical Considerations of Reproductive Technologies," in *New York State Journal of Medicine*, 1987, vol. 87, pp. 398-401.

9 David Feldman and Fred Rosner, eds., *Compendium on Medical Ethics. Jewish Moral, Ethical and Religious Principles in Medical Practice* (Sixth edition, N.Y.: Federation of Jewish Philanthropies, 1984), pp. 51-52.

10 J. David Bleich, *Judaism and Healing. Halakhic Perspectives* (New York, 1981), p. 88.

11 David Feldman, *Marital Relations, Birth Control and Abortion in Jewish Law* (New York, 1975), pp. 152-294.

12 J. David Bleich, *Contemporary Halakhik Problems* (New York, 1977), pp. 325-371.

13 I. Jakobovits, "Jewish Views on Abortion," in Rosner and Bleich, *Jewish Bioethics* (N.Y., 1979), pp. 118-133.

14 Fred Rosner, "Abortion," in Rosner and Bleich, op. cit., pp. 139-160.

15 *Iggrot Moshe, Choshen Mishpat*, part 2, #71.

16 *Halachah Urefuah* (Jerusalem, 1980), vol. 1, pp. 304-306.

17 *Tzitz Eliezer*, vol. 13, #102, and in *Assia*, vol. 13, 1976, pp. 8-10.

18 *Jewish Medical Ethics* (N.Y., 1975), pp. 119-125

19 *Iggrot Moshe, Choshen Mishpat*, part 2, #73-75.

20 *Tzitz Eliezer*, vol. 5, #28:5; vol. 9, #46; vol. 10, #25; vol. 13, #87 and #89; vol. 14, #80-81; vol. 15, #37.

21 Fred Rosner, "Rabbi Moshe Feinstein on the Treatment of the Terminally Ill," in *Judaism*, 1988, vol. 37, pp. 188-198.

22 Fred Rosner, "Definition of Death in Jewish Law," in *New York State Journal of Medicine*, 1983, vol. 83, pp. 973-978.

23 F. Veith, J. Fein, M. Tendler, et al., "Brain Death 1. A Status Report of Medical and Ethical Considerations," in *Journal of the American Medical Association*, 1977, vol. 238, pp. 1651-1655.

24 *Iggrot Moshe, Yoreh Deah*, part 2, #174.

25 Ibid., part 3, #132.

26 Fred Rosner, *Modern Medicine and Jewish Ethics*, pp. 313-333.

27 Feldman and Rosner, *A Compendium on Medical Ethics . . .*, p. 109.

28 Fred Rosner, *Modern Medicine and Jewish Ethics*, pp. 335-350.

29 Fred Rosner, *Modern Medicine and Jewish Ethics*, pp. 247-261.

30 Mishneh Torah, *Hilchot Shevuot* 5:17 and *Hilchot Chovel Umazik* 5:1, based on B. B.Q. 91b.

31 Shulchan Aruch, *Yoreh Deah* 369:1 and 374:2.

32 Fred Rosner and J. David Bleich, *Jewish Bioethics* (New York, 1971), pp. 377-397.

33 Shulchan Aruch, *Yoreh Deah* 349:1-2 and Mishneh Torah, *Hilchot Avel* 14:21, based on B. A.Z. 29b.

34 Shulchan Aruch, *Yoreh Deah* 357:1 based on "his body shall not remain all night upon the tree" (Deut. 21:23). See also B. San. 46b.

35 Mishneh Torah, *Hilchot Avel* 12:1, based on "but thou shalt surely bury him on that day" (Deut. 21:23). See also B. San. 46b and Y. Naz. 7:1.

36 Mishneh Torah, *Hilchot Tumat Met* 3:1, and Shulchan Aruch, *Yoreh Deah* 369:1.

37 I.Y. Unterman, *Shevet Miyehudah* (Jerusalem, 1955), pp. 313-322.

38 *Guide for the Perplexed* 3:17 and 3:48.

39 Fred Rosner, *Modern Medicine and Jewish Ethics*, pp. 419-432.

40 M. Tendler, "Rabbinic Comment on Triage of Resources," in *The Mount Sinai Journal of Medicine,* 1984, vol. 51, pp. 106-109.

FRED ROSNER

MESSIAH: Probably no religious idea seems more fundamental to Judaism or more essentially Jewish than that of the messiah, Israel's eschatological redeemer. It is widely supposed that Judaism is a messianic religion and that hope for the messiah's appearance is the major focus of, and driving force behind, Jewish religious belief and behavior. Indeed, two commonplaces of western history are that, in first century Palestine, enhanced Jewish anticipation of the messiah's arrival was the backdrop for the emergence of Christianity and that conflicting opinions about the messiah's appearance, identity, activity, and implications caused the division between Judaism and Christianity. The idea of the messiah thus appears fundamental to the structure and character of Judaism and therefore to the emergence of Christianity.

But recent research suggests that these assumptions need qualification. Judaism's scripture, the Hebrew Bible, contains no doctrine of an eschatological redeemer and does not use the term "messiah" to refer to one. Postbiblical Jewish texts—the Apocrypha, Pseudepigrapha, Dead Sea Scrolls, the writings of Philo and Josephus—use the term "messiah" infrequently and inconsistently. On their basis, there is no reason to think that the Jews of first century Palestine were anticipating a messiah. The idea of the messiah is barely present in the Mishnah, the foundational document of Rabbinic Judaism. A key reason for the unclarity about the messiah in these texts is that the Temple-centered religion practiced in Jerusalem and described in Scripture, which dominated ancient Judaism and is the basis of all other forms of Judaism, provides no religious role for a savior. God alone is Israel's—and therefore humanity's—redeemer. In this religion, living according to God's design—ethically and ritually—maintains Israel's relationship with God, including the forgiveness of sin. "Levitical religion," as we might call it, offers no religious function for a messiah that is not already covered in some other way.

Of all the Jewish writings of the Second Temple and immediate post-destruction periods, only the New Testament—which became Christianity's scripture—offers the rudiments of a coherent doctrine of the messiah. Early Christian teaching about Jesus (though perhaps not Jesus' own teaching about himself) ultimately shifted the focus of redemption from God to the messiah. This shift, which made the messiah the medium of humanity's salvation, altered Judaism's structure and produced a new religion.

Ancient and medieval Rabbinic writings as well as the synagogue liturgy contain the category of "messiah." But, as in earlier writings, the pictures in these varied literatures are not consistent. In the Talmuds, "the messiah" is a secondary category, subordinate to the generative and more central components of the Rabbinic religious system. In Jacob Neusner's words, in Rabbinic literature, the messiah

> does not define a categorical imperative in the way that Israel and the gentiles, . . . sin and atonement, resurrection and the world to come, all do. . . . The Messiah-theme forms a subset of several categories and by itself does not take up an autonomous presence in the theology of the Oral Torah. The Messiah-theme fits into the primary categories but is itself divisible among them.

In this sense, for most forms of Judaism in ancient and medieval times, the messiah is present in, but not essential to, the workings of the Jewish religion.

There is one important exception and one significant qualification to this generalization. The career of Shabbetai Sevi (1626-1676), Judaism's most famous false messiah (and the movements that flowed from his messianic claims) is the exception. In 1666, Shabbetai Sevi, a charismatic figure born in Smyrna, was regarded as the messiah by substantial portions of the Jewish world. In an unprecedented act, he converted to Islam. Shabbetai Sevi's principal spokesman and interpreter, Nathan of Gaza, employed the doctrines of Lurianic Kabbalah to explain this conversion as a redemptive act that brought the world closer to salvation. Sabbateanism shifts the focus of Israel's redemption from God to the messiah and thereby alters Judaism's fundamental morphology.

The significant qualification concerns the matter of exile. For most of its history, Judaism has existed without a native center. Its scripture, theology, liturgy, practices, and most of its writings assume that Judaism's adherents are living as aliens, away from their native territory. The figure of the messiah emerges from the loss of the Davidic dynasty and of Israel's political autonomy. The messiah-theme, therefore, is inextricably bound up with the notion of exile, and the Jews' recovery of the land they regard as theirs inevitably has messianic overtones. By realizing the ancient promise of restoration, the contemporary establishment of a Jewish polity in the land of Israel raises unprecedented questions about the religious meaning of return from exile in terms of classic Jewish ideas of the messiah.

The following describes the main contours of the idea of the messiah in Judaism, with particular attention to the ancient period and to the interactions between the traditional Jewish messianism and Zionism. Its focus is on the place of the messiah-theme in the structure of Jewish religion rather than on messianism as the broad ideology of Jewish redemption. The so-called "messianic" movements that appeared in nearly every century sought—but failed—to ameliorate the position of the Jews, and they did not foster major changes in the workings of Judaism itself.

Israelite antecedents: The term "messiah" means "anointed" or "anointed one." In ancient Israel, as in other Near Eastern cultures, the smearing or pouring of oil conferred leadership status on an individual, usually a priest, prophet, or king. The shift from the conception of the "messiah" as simply a current leader—a duly anointed king or judge, for instance—to the idea of a future redeemer for Israel is a function of both the nature of the Davidic monarchy and its dissolution after the destruction of the first Temple in 586/587 B.C.E. The conception of kingship represented by the divine promise that David's house will rule Israel in perpetuity—for example, in 2 Sam. 7—lays a foundation for the Israelite belief in an ideal future king, whose appearance fulfills that promise. Such a figure is the object of both hope and speculation in the writings of Israel's exilic and post-exilic prophets. The loss of the monarchy, political sovereignty, and the land of Israel itself constituted a cultural trauma that was written deep into Israel's national literature. The transformation of that literature into Judaism's scripture and the land of Israel's continued subjugation to foreign powers (save for a century of Hasmonean rule) institutionalized the trauma and made an ideal Davidic monarch and the exiles' return to the land conventional components of Jewish views of redemption. These hopes persist to varying degrees and forms throughout the history and literature of Judaism.

Jewish texts from biblical through the post-70 periods illustrate a progressive idealization of the future "anointed" king. Their speculations about the future king's rule range from restorative—an idealized but this-worldly Davidic kingdom—to utopian—an almost magical age of idyllic perfection. This development seems to be the basis of the idea of a divinely ordained figure who will redeem Israel at the end of time or the end of the age. As we shall see below, such figures, most of whom are not called "messiah," appear in Jewish literature from the Second Temple period. The wish for a new or ideal Davidic king retained its currency in several Jewish circles during the Second Temple period.

Jewish expectation of a restored Davidic monarchy intensified with the exiles' return from the Babylonian exile and ultimate rebuilding of the Temple during the Persian period, 540-330 B.C.E. However, the colonial context generated an important modification in ideas about Israel's redeemer. Persian rule allowed the Jews autonomy in "ritual and sacred institutions," which valorized the priesthood at the expense of the Davidic monarchy. Zechariah's claim (Zech. 3) that post-exilic Israel would be ruled by a diarchy—a king and a priest—responds to colonial policy by diminishing Israelite political claims in the face of non-Jewish rule.[1]

Continued foreign domination of the Jews in the land of Israel generated a *de facto* distinction between religion and politics that effectively removed the king from the realm of religion. For example, in the Bible, the Israelite king has no role in divine worship and is not responsible for the fall of rain. Moreover the cult is developed in the desert, not in a state. This literary strategy keeps the cult far from royalty and separates the issue of holiness from the question of Israel's sovereignty. A people rather than a polity, the Bible's Israel is bound together by its relationship to the cult, not to the throne. This clearly is an effort by the priestly authorities to focus Israel's relation to God around the cult rather than the state. Nothing in the cultic structure or narrative encourages the development of either monarchy or sovereignty.

Though the king was central in the period of the First Temple, in the Second Temple period, the priests were the dominant cultural and religious figures. Their vision of the nature and maintenance of Israel's relationship to God is spelled out in their editing of the Pentateuch. The religion they advocated—"levitical religion"—constitutes the background against which most of the relevant early Jewish texts about the messiah were written and shapes the contours of the messiah in later Judaism.

Levitical religion and the messiah: Judaism in the ancient Mediterranean was highly diverse, but its varieties were neither equally distributed nor uniformly influential and important. Between the Persian period and 70 C.E., the dominant form of Judaism was the Jerusalem Temple and its cult. The religion represented by the Temple and its priestly personnel conceived of the life of Israel as a comprehensive and integrated system of disciplined engagement with God. That engagement largely took the form of prescribed and repeated behaviors, directed by a caste of priests, that revolved around and focused on a sacred center, a stable reference point—the Holy of Holies—where access to God was certain to occur. Before the Holy of Holies stood the altar, on which the priests offered animal and other sacrifices daily to maintain Israel's relationship with God and to secure God's forgiveness of sin, both individual and collective.

A religion of cult and sacrifice, as levitical religion was, is extremely powerful and difficult to abandon because it guarantees that one is in the presence of God. The Temple is the *Domus Dei*, the house of the god, and the priestly rituals maintain God's presence there. The life and death drama of the sacrifices graphically illustrates what is at stake in being right with God, and the rising smoke is tangible evidence that the relationship with God remains solid. Levitical religion is appealing and effective because it is immediate and concrete. Its interests and traits explain why it provides little place for a future messianic redeemer.

Levitical religion is a religion of distinctions. It maps out a system of categories—usually binary opposites such as clean/unclean, fit/unfit, holy/profane—in which everything that matters has its place. A major distinction is the absolute distinction between the living and the dead. The two states must not be confused or conjoined. The priests have no funerary responsibilities and are forbidden to come in contact with dead human bodies, which are regarded as a source of uncleanness. But, in levitical religion human death is religiously insignificant. It is a fact, and there is no effort to transcend it or triumph over it.

Levitical religion emphasizes the integration of mind and body. It maintains order

through acts of conscious labor: proper moral actions and attitudes; correct offering of sacrifices; observance of food and sexual taboos; tithing of produce; celebration of Sabbaths and festivals; and so forth. In levitical religion, there is no categorical difference between what we now call ethics and ritual. Telling the truth, honoring one's parents, observing the Sabbath, and eating permitted food are all important and equally obligatory. Levitical religion is a religion of sanctification. Through conscious action Israel becomes a holy people and repairs any ruptures in its relationship with God.

Because it is centered around the Temple, levitical religion conceives of time cyclically. Every year as a repetition of every other year. The priestly writers thought paradigmatically rather than diachronically. Their ultimate interest is in nurturing and maintaining the already established relationship between God and Israel. Their preferred literary form was the list—for instance, the genealogies and series of rules of the Pentateuch's P document—rather than narrative.

The goal of levitical religion is not to escape the world but to preserve the present. There is no attempt to do away with the current social structure. Rather, everything in levitical religion reinforces the priestly vision of the cosmic order. For example, the festivals described in Leviticus—Passover, Booths, Pentecost, the New Year—are all intimately tied in to the cycle of the seasons. The Sabbath, which seems unique in the ancient near east, illustrates how levitical religion celebrates the received order of creation. The Sabbath commemorates the creation of the world. Israel rests as God rested at the end of the seventh day. This powerfully reinforces the idea that the order of creation is good, to be celebrated, and to be preserved.

In its ritual and its writing, levitical religion promulgated a synchronic vision of a centered, structured, hierarchical, and orderly reality. Its practitioners celebrated precision, lineage, precedent, and concreteness and had an exceedingly low tolerance for uncertainty, confusion, and ambiguity.

A religion of having what you want and

keeping it, levitical religion in principle has no religious need for a redeemer, savior, or messiah. The consistent message of the priestly editing of Scripture is that so long as the altar is effective, Israel's relationship with God is secure. In levitical religion, there is nothing religious a messiah can do that the altar cannot do. A redeemer is religiously unnecessary.

Rabbinic Judaism is the primary heir and continuator of the levitical religion represented in Scripture. Emerging from the destruction of the Second Temple in 70 C.E., its aim, in the absence of the altar, was to preserve Scripture's priestly ideals largely undisturbed. Rabbinic Judaism substituted piety, good deeds, and study of Torah for the altar, and it replaced the Holy of Holies with the sacred Torah scroll. Halakhah, Rabbinic religious praxis, derives from, and shares the values of, the levitical religion outlined in Scripture. Living rabbinically is comprised of a host of behaviors—ethical acts, good deeds, charity; food, purity, and kinship taboos, observance of Sabbaths, holy days, festivals, and prayer—that depend on and promulgate levitical categories. Hence, in Rabbinic Judaism and the forms of Judaism that follow it, the messiah will play an ancillary role and have little impact on religious practice.

Although the levitical worldview dominated and shaped the development of the messiah-theme in Judaism, it did not and could not extinguish the vision of redemption associated with a future or ideal Davidic king. So long as the Jews regard themselves as in exile, the wish for an heir of David who would lead the people back to its land remains a persistent leitmotif. In this sense, despite the levitical effort to limit redemption to the realm of religion, the messiah-theme always had the potential to be political.

The messiah in Second Temple literature: Any notion of a messianic belief or idea in ancient Judaism necessarily presupposes that "messiah" was a focal and evocative native category for ancient Jews. But a review of Israelite and early Judaic literature, the textual record produced and initially preserved by Jews, makes such a conclusion dubious at best. The noun *mashiah* ("anointed"

or "anointed one") occurs thirty-eight times in the Hebrew Bible, where it applies twice to the patriarchs, six times to the high priest, once to Cyrus, and twenty-nine times to the Israelite king, primarily Saul and secondarily David or an unnamed Davidic monarch. In these contexts the term denotes one invested, usually by God, with power and leadership, but never an eschatological figure. Ironically, in the apocalyptic book of Daniel (9:25f.), where an eschatological messiah would be appropriate, the term refers to a murdered high priest.

The term "messiah" has scant and inconsistent use in early Jewish texts. Most of the Dead Sea Scrolls and the Pseudepigrapha, and the entire Apocrypha, contain no reference to "the messiah." Moreover, a messiah is neither essential to the apocalyptic genre nor a prominent feature of ancient apocalyptic writings. A rapid survey of the most pertinent materials helps to justify these generalizations.

The Maccabean documents, which disdain the revival of the Davidic dynasty, ignore the term. There is no messiah in Jubilees, nor in Enoch 1-36 and 91-104, nor in the Assumption of Moses, nor in 2 Enoch, nor in the Sibylline Oracles. The messiah is absent from Josephus' description of Judaism in both *Antiquities* and *Against Apion*, and also from the writings of Philo.

In Ben Sira, which has no interest in a future redeemer, the "anointed one" or "messiah" is the Israelite king—a this-worldly, political leader. The Qumran scrolls report two messiahs, one Davidic and one priestly, who are not necessarily eschatological figures. The scrolls also apply the term to the prophets. In Psalms of Solomon 17, which is neither apocalyptic nor eschatological, the messiah is an idealized, future Davidic king who also exhibits traits of sage and teacher. The term appears only twice in the Similitudes of Enoch (1 Enoch 37-71), where it denotes not a king but a transcendent, heavenly figure. In any case, its use in Enoch is dwarfed by other titles, such as "the Chosen One" and "the Son of Man." The half-dozen references in the first century text 4 Ezra offer conflicting pictures of the messiah. In 7:28ff.

the messiah dies an unredeeming death before the eschaton, but later chapters portray him as announcing and executing the final judgment. In 2 Baruch, which contains five references, the term applies primarily to a warrior, the slayer of Israel's enemies. In the Mishnah's legal contexts, messiah refers to an anointed priest, and the messiah as redeemer is negligible.

These texts offer little evidence of sustained thought or evolving Judaic reflection about the messiah. Thus, in early Jewish literature, the term "messiah" is notable primarily for its indeterminacy.

The messiah and early Christian writing: In light of its insignificance in these texts, it is legitimate to ask why the category "the messiah" came to be seen as a fundamental and generative component of Israelite religion and early Judaism and why it persists as a major religious category in the west. It is fair to ask how so much has come to be written about an allegedly Jewish conception in which so many ancient Jewish texts manifest such little interest.

The hegemony of Christianity in the western world answers this question. The primacy of "the messiah" as a religious category and subject of academic study derives directly from early Christian word choice, theology, and apologetics. In contrast to the relatively infrequent references to the term "messiah" in Jewish literature cited above, the New Testament uses the term three hundred and fifty times, two hundred and seventy of them in Paul's epistles. In particular, two aspects of New Testament writing were determinative for the western conception of the messiah.

First, early Christian writers attached the word *christos*, the Greek for *mashiah*, to Jesus' name, either as a title or a surname. This usage valorizes *christos* and thereby makes "messiah" seem a revealing and important category and thus a subject to be studied. To be persuaded that this use of the word *christos* itself was pivotal in shaping later understanding, one need simply imagine the consequences for western history, religion, and theology had, for example, "lord," "son of man," or "rabbi" prevailed instead as Jesus' cognomen.

Second, New Testament authors, particularly of the gospels of Matthew and Luke, made the Hebrew scriptures into a harbinger of Jesus' career, suffering, and death. The "promise-fulfillment" motif, which casts Jesus as a foreseen figure, is perhaps the major achievement of New Testament apologetics. Apparently a later development of early Christian writing, the motif is a major focus of neither Paul's letters, the Q source, nor the Gospel of Mark.

It is richly articulated and elaborated in the Gospel of Matthew, particularly in Matthew's distinctive use of fulfillment formulas ("All this happened in order to fulfill what the Lord declared through the prophet . . .") to make various prophetic statements into predictions of Jesus' birth and career. Nearly half of those statements are not predictions about the future but the prophets' comments about Israel's past or their own present. This suggests that the fulfillment formulas and their attached verses are the results of *post facto* choice rather than remnants of an exegetical heritage. As in the *pesher* commentaries in the Dead Sea Scrolls, early Christians sought to ground their current experience in scripture and so read the present into the text.

The ideology for the motif is explicit at Luke 24:13-27. On the road to Emmaeus, two disciples unknowingly encounter the risen Jesus and express their disbelief at his death, which seems to disconfirm their early supposition about him ("But we had been hoping that he was the man to liberate Israel"). Jesus rebukes their lack of perception and claims that his death was predicted in the Hebrew scriptures ("Then he began with Moses and all the prophets and explained to them the passages which referred to himself in every part of the scriptures"). The Hebrew scriptures are thus classified as anterior literature, the messiah's textual antecedent.

The "promise-fulfillment" motif, along with the (conflicting) genealogies devised by Matthew and Luke (Mat. 1:1-17; Luke 3:23-38) embed Jesus in the Hebrew scriptures and forge an indelible continuity between him (and thus the early Christians) and Israel. By naming Jesus *christos*, giving him an Israelite pedigree, and depicting him and his death as foretold and predetermined, early Christian writers gave the figure of the messiah a diachronic dimension. They situated the messiah's origin not in the present but in Israelite antiquity and thus established the Hebrew scriptures as a sequence of auguries. Reading Scripture became, and to a large extent has remained, an exercise in deciphering and tracing a linear progression of portents. It was not simply, as Paul claimed, that the messiah exhibited a typological similarity to important biblical characters such as Adam. Rather, the messiah was rooted in Israel's past and his appearance could be tracked and plotted, perhaps even calculated, through time. On the model provided by Matthew and Luke, the messiah emerges not as an abrupt response to a contemporary crisis, but as the ultimate fulfillment of centuries of accumulated hope and intensifying expectation, the culmination and completion of an ancient Israelite tradition.

This strategy of representation established an enduring convention of western discourse about the messiah. The model limned by an apologetic use of Scripture was accepted by later scholarship as a literary fact and a historical reality, not only of Scripture itself but also of Israelite and Jewish religion.

The messiah in Rabbinic Judaism: In contrast to the New Testament, Rabbinic literature did not develop a consistent doctrine of the messiah or his role. The Rabbinic picture of the messiah and his activity varies according to document, time, and Rabbinic authority. In general, Rabbinic literature depicts the messiah as secondary to the major and generative categories of the Rabbinic system.

According to Jacob Neusner, the Mishnah develops a religion of sanctification that has a "teleology without eschatology." Consequently, it lacks a doctrine of "the Messiah."

> In the system of the Mishnah—vast and encompassing as it is—we look in vain for a doctrine of the Messiah. There "messiah" serves as a taxonomic indicator, e.g., distinguishing one type of priest or general from some other. There is no doctrine of the Messiah, coming at the end of time; in the Mishnah's system, matters focus on other issues

entirely. Although the figure of a Messiah does appear, when the framers of the Mishnah spoke of "the Messiah," they meant a high priest designated and consecrated to office in a certain way, and not in some other way. The reference to "days of the Messiah" constitutes a conventional division of history at the end time but before the ultimate end. But that category of time plays no consequential role in the teleological framework established within the Mishnah. Accordingly, the Mishnah's framers constructed a system of Judaism in which the entire teleological dimension reached full exposure while hardly invoking the person or functions of a messianic figure of any kind. . . . For the purpose of our inquiry, the main thing is a simple fact, namely, that salvation comes through sanctification. The salvific figure, then becomes an instrument of consecration and so fits into an ahistorical system quite different from the one built around the Messiah.[2]

As the primary heir of levitical religion, the Mishnah offers neither a picture of "the Messiah" nor an articulated religious role for one. Its ahistorical vision does not conceive of a dramatic redemption at the end of time. Rather, through the life of piety and the performance of commandments, Israel restores and enacts the ideal conditions of creation and the Garden of Eden. Since Israel's destiny is to be a "holy people," she fulfills her teleology through sanctification. In the Mishnah, therefore, the performance of commandments does not—and cannot—produce the messiah or cause the messiah to come. The commandments are effective in their own terms and not because of some additional consequence that they generate. The Mishnah's worldview makes the messiah virtually irrelevant to the practice of Judaism, and any notion of the messiah as redeemer must stand essentially outside of the Mishnaic system.

The logic of any religious system disciplines the thought and imagination that take place within it. But it cannot restrain thinking that goes on outside it. Since the Mishnah contains no doctrine or description of the messiah, it could neither shape nor block messianic speculation in later Rabbinic Judaism. Hence, post-Mishnaic Rabbinic texts exhibit a wide range of thinking about the messiah. At one end of the spectrum of opinion is the view that severs the messiah completely from the exercise of religion. It holds that the messiah will come unexpectedly, when God, not Israel, determines it. Nothing Israel can do will make the messiah appear. A related view is the Rabbinic posture of messianic quietism, which explicitly warns Israel against trying to "force" God's hand in bringing redemption. The following text illustrates (Song of Songs Rabbah 2:7; Neusner, trans.):[3]

> R. Helbo says, ". . . He imposed an oath on Israel not to rebel against the kingdoms and not to force the end, not to reveal its mysteries to the nations of the world, and not to go up from the exile by force."

This passage suggests that God actually imposed on Israel four "oaths" concerning the end, each one requiring Israel to be patient and passive, to await God's decision. It reflects both the desire for redemption and as the concern that something fundamental will be violated if Israel tries to generate it herself. Both of these positions seem to accord with the Mishnah's worldview.

By contrast, a virtual connection between piety and redemption occurs for the first time at Y. Taanit 1:1.

> A. "The oracle concerning Dumah. One is calling to me from Seir, 'Watchman, what of the night? Watchman, what of the night?'" (Is. 21:11).
> B. The Israelites said to Isaiah, "O our Rabbi, Isaiah, what will come for us out of this night?"
> C. He said to them, "Wait for me, until I can present the question."
> D. Once he had asked the question, he came back to them.
> E. They said to him, "Watchman, what of the night? What did the Guardian of the ages tell you?"
> F. He said to them, "The watchman says, 'Morning comes; and also the night. If you will inquire, inquire; come back again' (Is. 21:12)."
> G. They said to him, "Also the night?"
> H. He said to them, "It is not what you are thinking. But there will be morning for the righteous, and night for the wicked, morning for Israel, and night for idolaters."
> I. They said to him, "When?"
> J. He said to them, "Whenever you want, he too wants [it to be]—if you want it, he wants it."
> K. They said to him, "What is standing in the way?"
> L. He said to them, "Repentance: 'Come back again' (Is. 21:12)."
> M. R. Aha in the name of R. Tanhum b. R. Hiyya, "If Israel repents for one day, forthwith the son of David will come."
> N. "What is the Scriptural basis? 'O that today you would hearken to his voice!' (Ps. 95:7)."
> O. Said R. Levi, "If Israel would keep a single Sabbath in the proper way, forthwith the son of David will come."
> P. "What is the Scriptural basis for this view? 'Moses said, Eat it today, for today is a Sabbath to the Lord; today you will not find it in the field' (Exod. 16:25)."
> Q. "And it says, 'For thus said the Lord God, the Holy One of Israel, "In returning and rest you shall be saved; in quietness and in trust shall be your strength." And you would not' (Is. 30:15)."

As Neusner observes:

> First, the system of religious observance, including study of Torah, is explicitly invoked as having salvific power. Second, the persistent hope of the people for the coming of the Messiah is linked to the system of Rabbinic observance and belief. In this way, the austere program of the Mishnah, with no trace of a promise that the Messiah will come if and when the system is fully realized, finds a new development. A teleology lacking all eschatological dimension here gives way to an explicitly messianic statement that the purpose of the law is to attain Israel's salvation: "If you want it, God wants it too." The one thing Israel commands is its own heart; the power it yet exercises is the power to repent. These suffice. The entire history of humanity will respond to Israel's will, to what happens in Israel's heart and soul. And, with Temple in ruins, repentance can take place only within the heart and mind.[4]

But even this view, which marks a shift from the Mishnah's position, does not give the messiah a role in religious practice. In all Rabbinic texts, the messiah remains subordinate to Torah. He leads Israel to redemption and so is a precursor, but not the redeemer himself. The messiah gathers Israel from exile and leads Israel to judgment, but the judgment itself is performed by God. The subordination of the messiah to God is evident in the varied roles the Talmuds assign to the messiah and the sometimes conflicting description of his tasks. Again, Neusner's research makes the point:

> Like Elijah, the Messiah is forerunner and precursor, but he is hardly an enduring player in the eschatological drama. Only God is. Time and again we shall see that the Messiah refers back to God for instructions on what he is to do. A mark of categorical subordination of the Messiah-theme is the diversity of Messiahs, each with his own story. One Messiah comes out of the line of Joseph, another out of the line of David. Both Messiahs (and others in that same classification, for example, the Messiah who is anointed to be high priest in charge of the army [Deut. 20:2-7, Mishnah-tractate Sotah Chapter Eight]), are mortal and subject to the human condition. One Messiah is murdered, replaced by another. The Messiah, moreover, is subject to the impulse to do evil, like any other man. The Messiah plays a transient role in the eschatological drama. People want the Messiah to come—that is the premise of the stories told in connection with repentance—but that is only because he will inaugurate the eschatological drama, not because, on his own, he will bring the drama to its conclusion. Only God will.[5]

The diversity in Rabbinic messianic thought underscores the persistence of the Mishnaic view: the messiah is not integral to the practice of Judaism.

The essential unrelatedness of the messiah to Judaic piety also is evident in ancient rabbis' inability to craft a consistent position on the messiah's impact on the performance of the halakhah. The following passage illustrates (B. Shab. 151a):

> A. R. Simeon b. Eleazar says, "'. . . and the years draw nigh when you shall say, I have no pleasure in them' (Ec. 12:1)—this refers to the days of the messiah, in which there is neither merit nor guilt."
> B. This differs from what Samuel said, for said Samuel, "The only difference between this world and the days of the messiah is Israel's servitude to the nations of the world. As it is said, 'For the poor will never cease out of the Land' (Deut. 15:11)."

The position ascribed to Simeon b. Eleazar can be understood to mean that in the time of the messiah, the commandments will no longer apply. By contrast, the view attributed

to Samuel suggests that religious life after the messiah's arrival will be identical to that before it. Other Rabbinic passages suggest that the days of the messiah will signal the performance of more religious acts, particularly those of the sacrificial cult, than are practiced in this world. The more prevalent view accords with Samuel, and it appears throughout the Judaic literature of antiquity. W.D. Davies' classic study shows that:

> . . . we found in the Old Testament, the Apocrypha and Pseudepigrapha and in the Rabbinical sources the profound conviction that obedience to the Torah would be a dominant mark of the Messianic age. . . . Generally, our sources revealed the expectation that the Torah in its existing form would persist into the Messianic age when its obscurities would be made plain, and when there would be certain natural adaptations and changes. . . .[6]

That the coming of the messiah does not automatically affect religious practice suggests that there is little systemic relationship between the two in the structure of Judaism.

The diversity in the messiah-theme persisted through the middle ages. Medieval Jewish thinkers held different views about Israel's redemption. Maimonides held a restorative view and envisioned a messiah who, without miracles or wonders, would signal the end of foreign domination of Israel. Nahmanides made the separation between Judaic piety and redemption explicit: "Our Law and Truth and Justice are not dependent upon a Messiah."[7] Alongside these views, however, a series of apocalyptic works appeared, such as *The Book of Zerubbabel*, which offered fantastic visions of the end, including a cosmic battle between a satanic figure named Armilus, who defeats the Messiah ben Joseph but is then defeated by the Messiah ben David. H.H. Ben Sasson observes that Jewish medieval apocalyptic literature is notable for the

> complete absence from it of any doctrinal religious or ideological elements. In these works the future is described as an inevitable end of the world as known and the beginning of a new one. In none of these works is there any explanation as to why anything is going to happen or what a Jew should do to help in the great task of bringing about redemption.[8]

The disconnect between religion and redemption described by Ben Sasson conforms to the basic position of levitical religion.

The messianic religion of Shabbetai Sevi: A definitive change from the position of levitical religion occurs in the case of Shabbetai Sevi. His career and the movements that follow him have been described in detail by G. Scholem and only a brief recapitulation is given here.

Shabbetai Sevi is the most famous false messiah in Judaism. Born in Smyrna, educated in Egypt and Jerusalem, he was both brilliant and delusional. His had a strange early career, replete with instances of violating various rules of halakhic behavior. In 1665, he connected with a figure named Nathan of Gaza, who proclaimed him to be the messiah. Nathan was to become the principal interpreter—the Paul—of Shabbateanism.

In the mid-17th century, Lurianic Kabbalah became a powerful ideology that deeply affected the worldview of Jews across Europe and the Mediterranean. It held that there had been a dislocation within the Godhead and that "sparks" of divinity had become lodged in the evil, material world. The performance of commandments released the dislocated sparks to their proper place and moved the cosmos closer to redemption. Unlike Levitical religion, Lurianism thus attributed redemptive power to discrete acts of halakhic conformity. It moreover taught that the process of cosmic restoration was nearly complete and that the final redemption was on the verge of occurring.

Nathan of Gaza shared the Lurianic position and, in May, 1665, declared that Shabbetai Sevi would soon inaugurate the final redemption. At that time, Shabbetai Sevi went to Smyrna and proclaimed himself to be messiah. The announcement created an enormous stir in the Jewish world, and in February, 1666, Shabbetai Sevi was arrested by the Turkish authorities. On September 16, he was brought to the Turkish Sultan, who was staying in Adrianople, and offered the choice of converting to Islam or being beheaded. Shabbetai Sevi chose to convert, for which he received a pension from the Turks.

Nathan of Gaza used Lurianic teaching to make this unprecedented move seem plausible. He claimed that by converting to Islam, Shabbetai Sevi had entered the realm of evil to release the last trapped sparks of divinity and to begin the redemption of the world. The conversion, he insisted, was a subterfuge. It looked like apostasy, but it was really redemption. Although most of the Jewish world rejected this teaching, some groups continued to believe in Shabbetai Sevi after his death in 1676. They developed practices in imitation of him, on the argument that the best way to fulfill the Torah was to violate it. In Europe, a figure named Jacob Frank (1726-1791) formed a Sabbatean group that converted to Roman Catholicism. Another group that converted to Islam.

Lurianic Kabbalah and the Sabbatean movement represent a break with the structure of levitical religion in the claim that the performance of commandments is redemptive and can move Israel closer to redemption. In effect, it shifts responsibility for Israel's redemption from God to Israel. Aspects of this ideology, as we shall see below, appear in modern Lubavitch Hasidism.

The messiah, "messianism," and Zionism: With the exception of the Sabbatean movement and some smaller messianic outbreaks, the Rabbinic prohibition against "forcing" the end dominated Jewish thinking about the messiah until the modern period. On this view, the Jewish people was to remain passively in exile and not agitate for redemption. The messiah's arrival was promised, and the Jews were not to doubt the divine plan by their own impatience. This idea of passivity did not preclude the necessity of individual repentance as a precondition to redemption, but it did prohibit the possibility that human political initiative could have a legitimate role in hastening redemption. Throughout the history of Judaism, the "oaths" against forcing the end cited above evoke the abyss between the human, historical and the divine, metaphysical spheres that can only be crossed with the messiah's appearance.

In premodern Judaism, the "oaths" were deemed nonbinding. In modern Hasidic and

Western Orthodox thought, however, they appear as a central motif. Aviezer Ravitzky argues that this can be explained by the emergence of Jewish nationalism and Zionism, which challenged Judaism's established posture of passivity in exile.[9]

As we have seen, Judaism is a quintessential religion of exile. Return to the land of Israel, therefore, signaled a systemic change, a decisive alteration in Israel's condition. That is why in the modern age the messianic question acquires a unique urgency in the history of Judaism. New trends in European thought and emerging historical realities—both of which influenced Judaism—exposed the ideological tensions inherent in the history of Jewish thinking about the messiah. The physical return to the Land of Israel may have been redemption for secular Jews, but it was a problem for many Jewish—particularly Orthodox—religious thinkers.

Modern European nationalism and the beginnings of Zionism: Influenced by nineteenth century European struggles for national sovereignty and "receptiveness to innovation," two Orthodox thinkers argued for a significant reassessment of classical Jewish passivity. Rabbi Judah Alkalai (Serbia, d. 1878) and Rabbi Zvi Hirsch Kalischer (Prussia, d. 1874), developed an activist and worldly idea of redemption. Known as the "Harbingers of Zionism," these rabbis and their followers imagined redemption to be a utopian process of gradual realization, rather than the sudden, complete realization of their contemporaries. Thus, they advocated gradual immigration and agricultural settlement of the land of Israel as a "necessary and organic step toward full redemption."

The Harbingers derived textual support from a distinctive reading of classical Jewish literature. They distinguished between the "messianic process" and the "messianic goal," the former to be made manifest in worldly, historical terms the latter to burst forth in the sudden, miraculous coming of the messiah. This imagery is based on classical sources in which the redemptive, metaphysical messiah—the Messiah ben David—is thought to follow the appearance of an historical messiah—the Messiah ben Joseph—

associated with the last great, apocalyptic battles. Thus the Harbingers focused on a classical tension between history and redemption using the figure of Messiah ben Joseph as proof that historical initiative has a legitimate role in collective redemption. The Harbingers were among the first representatives of a new activist conception of redemption in which human initiative and political, historical developments could have real implications for the coming of the messiah.

The Harbingers provoked criticism from contemporary Jewish thinkers for breaking with the traditional commitment to Jewish quietism. Many Orthodox thinkers found problematic the idea that the Jews' political and social activism could be ways of advancing what previously had been seen as a plan for the world in God's hands alone, and therefore religiously meaningful. Rabbi Isaac Jacob Reines (who laid down the ideological foundations of the Mizrachi [religious-Zionist] movement) developed the most articulate arguments against the ideology of the Harbingers. Reines objected to the Harbingers' distinction between "messianic process" and "messianic goal" on the grounds that redemption was to be achieved solely though supernatural means. He acknowledges the religious value of settling the land, because it seeks to improve the living circumstances of the Jewish community. But it must not be confused with actual metaphysical redemption, which he understood in its traditional utopian mold. Reines cautiously affirms the settlement of the land, but denies that such historical developments have anything to do with the Jewish people's redemption. Still, even his moderate stance in certain respects would have facilitated the emergence of a contemporary Zionist messianism, since it allows religious settlers to cooperate with secular pioneers. These religious traditionalists thus could participate in a utopian social and political movement without fear of violating the traditional prohibition against forcing the End.

The possibility of maintaining such a moderate ideology, however, was doomed to failure. The agent of this failure was the explosive confrontation between traditional understandings of Jewish messianism and the emergence of organized Zionism. Zionism sought to achieve partial salvation in the present through human, political initiative. Moreover, Zionist leaders aimed to reconstitute Jewish nationhood under a secular banner. Both Zionism and traditional messianism sought to end the exile from the land of Israel, cultivate the land, and achieve the social reform of the Jewish people. Transcending these commonalties were irreducible differences of opinion about the meaning of these goals. Ultimately, a moderate stance was too fragile to survive the volatile mix of ideological similarities and differences. Over time, extreme schools of Jewish religious thought developed in direct response to the Zionist challenge. Reines' moderate ideology was replaced by radical anti-Zionism and religious Zionism. Both movements employ a utopian model of redemption, but they interpret the meaning of the Zionist endeavor (and the Holocaust) in radically different ways.

The majority of Orthodox leaders condemned Zionism from its beginnings. At first, their critique focused mainly on the secular character of the movement and its leaders and on the unrealistic, impractical nature of the endeavor. But the challenge Zionism presented to traditional ideas about the nature of collective Jewish redemption became the central motif in anti-Zionist criticism. In 1899, the Lubavitcher Rebbe, Rabbi Shalom Dov Baer Schneersohn, laid the ideological ground of this ultra-Orthodox critique of Zionism. He argued that Zionism is essentially opposed to the classical Jewish messianism because it sought to bring about the redemption of the Jewish people through ordinary human political initiative rather than through the supernatural and miraculous arrival of the messiah. Instead of attempting to force the end of history through impatient and arrogant politics, the Jewish people ought to remain in exile, passively waiting for the eschaton to arrive by metaphysical means.

Schneersohn argued that redemption must be sudden and complete (the utopian model). But secularization is comprehensive and therefore blocks precondition of the messiah's arrival: the total realization of a repentant world. Jewish identity is intrinsically bound up with a traditional messianic commitment to passivity. To achieve a Jewish nation, the Zionists must erode Jewish identity. Thus Schneersohn conceives of Zionism as unavoidably opposed to authentic Jewish religion. Within this ideological context the passivity in exile is transformed from a persistent Rabbinic theme into a normative article of faith. Only in confrontation with Zionism—a modern ideology—does the fear of forcing the End achieve normative stature and centrality. After Schneersohn, this theological critique becomes the primary theme in the radical critique of Zionism.

Schneersohn may have been the first to articulate an anti-Zionist ideology, but Rabbi Moshe Teitelbaum, the Satmar Rebbe, produced a comprehensive theory of anti-Zionism. For Teitelbaum, Zionism is the anti-messianic work of Satan himself. Indeed the improbable success of Zionism is proof of its satanic assistance, for only with the aid of Satan could the antimessianic Zionists overcome the inherent holiness of the land of Israel. In this view, the state is *de facto* destructive. The very fact of its existence, and not its policies, is the problem. Not even the passage of religious laws ("Torah legislation") can ameliorate the secular nature of the state, such that any active participation or influence in Israeli government indirectly legitimates a corrupt, heretical entity. The only proper response to the fact of the state is criticism and protest from a distance.

But not all Orthodox thinkers cleaved to the theology of passivity. Some were able to completely rethink the inherited messianic ideal to create a sort of messianism that makes sense of their own experiences and desires, particularly in the settling of the land. This competing school of thought sees the Zionist project as a legitimate first step in the divine *process* of redemption. The ideological founder of religious Zionism, Rabbi Abraham Isaac Kook, interpreted Zionism not as a manifestation of human arrogance and impatience but as the latest symbol of God's concern for the Jewish people and the beginning of a new, post-exilic phase in Jewish history devoid of historical passivity. Religious Zionism attempts to close the gap set up between historical and messianic reality in traditional Jewish imagination. It positions the state of Israel within the ongoing march toward collective redemption and interprets the Zionist project in the traditional religious categories of sin, repentance, and redemption.

Religious Zionist ideology is essentially messianism in the temporal absence of a personal savior. It is "messianism without a messiah." It holds that human collective action begins the process of redemption, and the messiah will appear to conclude and mature this process. Thus redemption is a process, a series of steps leading to eventual redemption conceived in traditional utopian terms, but in which human action has a legitimate role to play.

The question of human initiative in the advent of the messianic age has classical origins. The Kabbalistic teachers "taught the messianic redemption was the collective responsibility of the fellowship or community as a whole." These mystics understood the messiah's arrival as the culmination of a process of collective repentance. Human spiritual purification was the precondition of the messiah's arrival. The religious Zionists added to this classical understanding by seeing religious meaning in political, historical developments. Thus, their ideology attempts to fuse the political and the theological; the image of the Jewish state is that of a fully integrated "theopolitical whole." As it reshapes classical Jewish thinking about the messiah, religious Zionism creates a modern Jewish messianism that works in categories foreign to the Christian ideologies that constitute the established western perception of what the messiah is about.

Due to their dialectical understanding of history and progress, Kook and his followers, are able to maintain their optimism even in the face of what may appear to be national disappointment. The religious Zionists—grounded in Kook's dialectic—interpret social, political, military, and cultural upheaval and revolution as integral elements of the determined march towards redemption. Kook's

son and ideological heir, Rabbi Zvi Yehudah Kook (1891-1981), voices this interpretative tendency in his treatment of the Holocaust. He sees the destruction of European Jewry as the necessary expurgation of a wretched, Jewish culture of exile. The Holocaust proves to be a "kind of shattering, the destruction of a rotten culture (that of exile) for the sake of national rebirth and the fulfillment of the vision of the revealed End."

The elder Kook interprets the actions of secular Zionist pioneers through his dialectic perspective. They represent an unconscious movement towards repentance, and the return to the land—even for apparently secular reasons—can be affirmed as the beginning of a process in which eventually all Jews in the land will realize their inner, religious nature and live according to the dictates of the Torah and the halakhah. Utopian redemption will ultimately arrive in the form of the messiah when the secularists consciously turn to a purification of their ways and affirm the relevance and authority of traditional Torah Judaism.[10] This interpretation allows Kook and his ideological brethren to assimilate seemingly objectionable elements of the state. What might be construed as apostasy becomes in the hands of the religious Zionists one more integral and necessary challenge on the inevitable road to messianic redemption.

It should be noted that messianic determinism—the belief that redemption is the inevitable end of human history—does not necessarily preclude human responsibility. Although the elder Kook finds religious and messianic significance in the objective historical development of the state, he nevertheless affirms that redemption is not possible until the Jewish people take full responsibility for their own spiritual repentance. Thus, Kook maintains a seemingly delicate position: The End is inevitably on hand, but ultimate redemption does not annul human responsibility, it requires it.[11]

Religious determinism in both the radical anti-Zionist and religious Zionist camps reveals that the fundamental conflict revolves around the "essence" of the Zionist enterprise. Neither school of thought believes in partial redemption. The redemption of the Jewish people will be utopian: sudden and complete. The legitimacy of Zionism does not depend on Israeli social and political reality. For the anti-Zionists and religious Zionists, the question of Zionism ultimately rests on their distinctive understandings of the relationship between human initiative and divine revelation.

The Lubavitch Hasidic movement—A contemporary case of acute messianism: The Hasidic sect known as Habad Lubavitch maintains an extraordinarily public image in the Jewish world. This is largely due to its ability to harness the cultural and technological elements of modernity for the propagation of its traditional religious message.[12] Apart from this extraordinary feature, the Habad movement also presents a cogent illustration of the effect the Zionist movement has had on traditional messianic ideologies.

Earlier generations of Habad leadership refrained from speaking on the possibility of collective messianic redemption and chose instead to focus on the nature of individual redemption.[13] Yet today, the Habad movement is characterized by extraordinarily explicit messianic discourse and fervor. The key historical factor in this transformation has been the emergence and relative success of Zionism.

That Zionism should have transformed the self-understanding of Habad so significantly is ironic if we recall that a Habad Rebbe, Shalom Dov Baer Schneersohn, was among the most virulent opponents of Zionism, rejecting outright its legitimacy and authority on traditional theological grounds. Yet the pending destruction of European Jewry prompted a later Habad Rebbe, Joseph Isaac Schneersohn, to publicly yearn for the coming of the messiah. His declaration that redemption was approaching was derived from the collective experience of his followers, the suffering brought on by the systematic destruction of the Holocaust. Rabbi Joseph Isaac, amid the reality of the Holocaust, did not interpret it as punishment for Zionist agitation or as the divine removal of an accursed exile culture. He drew on classical Jewish sources and saw the Holocaust as the "birth pangs" of redemption, the advent of unendurable suffering thought to precede the messianic age.[14]

Under the leadership of the most recent Lubavitcher Rebbe, Menachem Mendel Schneersohn, this messianic fervor reached its most fevered pitch. Unlike Joseph Isaac, who called out for redemption in the wake of profound suffering, Menachem Mendel affirmed a "messianism of prosperity." He interpreted historical events such as the collapse of the Soviet Union and the end of the cold war as explicit indications that the world was moving closer to full observance of the Noachide laws and thus cosmic redemption was approaching.[15]

Yet this messianism of prosperity obviously requires constant stimuli to maintain its optimism, and the history of contemporary Habad shows that this is precisely what has occurred. At the end of Passover in April, 1991, Menachem Mendel confessed to his followers that he had expended all of his spiritual energy and that the arrival of the coming messiah rested on their individual repentance. On Shabbat Pinhas, July 6, 1991, the Rebbe aroused even greater emotional fervor when he discussed the coming messiah more explicitly than ever before. Lastly, to further elevate the emotional frenzy, Habad followers began to speak of their Rebbe in terms traditionally reserved for the messiah.[16] After the death of the Lubavitcher Rebbe in July, 1994, some of his followers began to assert that he is the messiah. In the fall, 1996, the Israeli Weekly *Sihat Ha-Geullah* revised the standard messianist slogan to read: "May our Master, Teacher, and Creator (instead of 'Rabbi'), the King Messiah live forever." A number of other Lubavitch publications suggested that the Rebbe should be the focus of prayers.

While the belief that the Rebbe is the messiah seems limited to particular circles within Lubavitch Hasidism and cannot be said to reflect the ideology of the entire movement, the messianism associated with Habad has been criticized as a new form of Zionist activism. Fixating on the messianic question and engaging in prayer and repentance with the explicit expectation of bringing about the messiah appeared to some in the Haredi community as an example of forcing the End.[17] The new and dramatic claim that the Rebbe is the Messiah also has generated charges of heresy, because the focus on the Rebbe as, for example, "our Creator" seems to alter the form and basis of Judaism. However, despite some controversy over this issue, Lubavitch Hasidism retains its legitimacy within the larger Judaic world. The radical messianic declarations of some of its members have not been seen to push Habad beyond the pale.

Conclusion: Judaism is grounded in the experience of exile. Ancient Jews, certain that they were God's people always, drew creatively on their Israelite culture and heritage to develop two major responses to the twin challenges of national dislocation and chronic political oppression. The first was the hope for an ideal national leader—often, but not always, from the royal Davidic dynasty—whose work could range from leading the people home to an ideal kingdom to the establishment of a new cosmic order. The idea of "the messiah," an individual savior or redeemer of Israel, derives from this conception. The second response was the establishment of levitical religion, a system of ethics and piety that both maintained and manifested the distinctive relationship between Israel and God. Although initially centered around the Temple and its cult, levitical religion—particularly as adapted and transformed by Rabbinic Judaism—could be performed anywhere.

These two responses are not mutually exclusive, but they are systemically independent of one another. Neither requires the other. Judaism is an extension of levitical religion. The idea of an individual messiah existed alongside, but was never fully integrated into, the levitical system of ethics and piety that constituted the core of Rabbinic Judaism. Structurally, Judaism does not require a messiah to justify fulfilling the commandments. Indeed, a persistent strain of Rabbinic teaching holds that the commandments will apply after the messiah appears. Despite references to the restored Jerusalem and future heir of David, the synagogue liturgy celebrates God, not the messiah, as Israel's redeemer and looks forward to the restoration of the Temple cult. Except for Sabbateanism and the forms of religion that emerge from it, there is no assumption that the commandments are performed to make the messiah arrive.

Because the category of the messiah is extrinsic to the system of Jewish religious practice, it is subject to speculation. In the varied forms Judaism has taken over time, there was and remains a wide range of opinions about what the messiah will be and do. These opinions in themselves do not constitute grounds for separation from Judaism. The figure of the messiah surely is present in Jewish religious imagination, but hope for the messiah's arrival is not the driving force of Jewish religious life. Modern and contemporary developments in Zionism and the State of Israel have posed fresh questions to the classical view. How these will be answered still remains to be seen.

Notes
[1] This analysis relies on Shemaryahu Talmon, "The Concepts of Masiah and Messianism in Early Judaism," in J.H. Charlesworth, ed., *The Messiah* (Minneapolis, 1992), pp. 79-115. The cited words are on p. 106.
[2] William Scott Green and Jacob Neusner, *The Messiah in Ancient Judaism* (Atlanta, 1999).
[3] Also see B. Ket. 111a.
[4] Ibid.
[5] Ibid.
[6] W.D. Davies, *Torah in the Messianic Age and/or the Age to Come* (Philadelphia, 1952), pp. 64-66, 84.
[7] H.H. Ben Sasson, "Messianic Movements," in *Encyclopedia Judaica*, vol. 11, col. 1263.
[8] Ibid., vol. 11, col. 1413.
[9] Aviezer Ravitzky, *Messianism, Zionism, and Jewish Religious Radicalism* (Chicago, 1996). This section is based on Ravitsky's research.
[10] Ibid., pp. 112-113.
[11] Ibid., p. 130.
[12] Ibid., p. 182.
[13] Ibid., pp. 193-194.
[14] Ibid., p. 195.
[15] Ibid., p. 197.
[16] Ibid., p. 197.
[17] Ibid., p. 201.

WILLIAM SCOTT GREEN
JED SILVERSTEIN

MIRACLES IN JUDAISM, THE CLASSICAL STATEMENT: Extraordinary events that have no possible human or natural cause are recognized in the Hebrew Bible and in later forms of Judaism as deriving from the direct intervention of God in the human sphere. In the Rabbinic literature, such occurrences are referred to simply by the term *nes*, signifying a "wondrous event" and roughly comparable to the English term "miracle."[1] In the Hebrew Bible, by contrast, events that violate the natural order much more commonly are designated as "signs" (*otot, mofetim*),[2] a term that points to the distinctive role miracles play in ancient Israelite theology. This is because, in the Hebrew Bible, God performs miracles—breaks directly into the physical world—for the explicit purpose of demonstrating his power and informing people of his specific desires and particular plans. In light of this purpose, events such as the ten plagues that God brought against the Egyptians are not adequately described through the simple concept of "miracle," that is, as extraordinary occurrences with no natural explanation. Rather, within the Hebrew Bible, these remarkable happenings have a specific theological function: they are signs of the absolute power of the Israelite deity and proof that Moses indeed speaks for that deity when he states what is expected of the Egyptians.

The characteristic function of miracles in the Hebrew Bible is clear from Scripture's recognition of a difference between a miracle and a mere magic trick. The Bible understands that magic can successfully be performed by magicians of all peoples (Exod. 7:22) and is not a source of knowledge about God or God's will.[3] Scripture sees miracles, by contrast, as unparalleled manifestations of God's will that function as saving acts on behalf of God's people. Miracles are at once signs of what God desires and proof of God's ability to accomplish his will.

The important point is that, in the biblical view, people come to know God, God's qualities, and God's demands on Israel and the world only insofar as God personally and directly takes the initiative to reveal these things. In the Hebrew Bible, knowledge of God and of what God desires of humankind does not result from theological or philosophical speculation. It is known, rather, from the wondrous deeds through which God reveals himself in the world. As in the case of the Exodus from Egypt, such signs occur in particular in the context of God's saving acts, *niflaot*, through which the deity expresses his sovereignty and brings salvation to his people. But such miracles pertain as well to individuals, as in the marvelous works of God described in the Psalms (see, e.g., Ps. 9:1-2). In all, miracles constitute the foundation for the Israelites' acceptance of God's sovereignty, as Is. 25:1-2 makes explicit:

> O Lord, thou art my God; I will exalt thee, I will praise thy name; for thou hast done wonderful things,[4] plans formed of old, faithful and sure. For thou hast made the city a heap, the fortified city a ruin; the palace of aliens is a city no more, it will never be rebuilt.

From the destruction of a fortified city to the placement of a rainbow in the heaven (Gen. 9:13), God's extraordinary acts instruct people of God's will and assure them of God's continued saving powers.

The historical context for changing perspectives on miracles: Before we examine the Rabbinic development of the biblical conception of miracles, let us reflect upon the biblical view's power in the periods of the Jewish commonwealths, in which it was shaped. While the First Temple stood, the people of Israel rightly perceived themselves as the great and mighty nation they understood God to have intended them to be. They recognized at the foundation of their success the power of a God who fought their battles and assured their victories. Even the decline of Israelite power in the sixth and fifth centuries B.C.E., represented in the destruction of the first Temple and the Babylonian exile, did little to supplant this view. The people understood that they were exiled because of their sins. The same God who wrought miracles on behalf of a faithful nation logically would break into history to bring punishment upon a sinful one. The almost immediate rebuilding of the Temple, the emergence of the Second Commonwealth, and the fact that for hundreds of years Jewish life went on largely as it always had meant that throughout biblical times the image of a God who exercised power directly in the human sphere was not significantly challenged.

Such a challenge, as we shall now see, occurred in the first centuries C.E., in the period that gave rise to Rabbinic Judaism. For this Judaism developed in a period of devastating events of history that forced Jews carefully to evaluate who they were, what they believed, and how they would face an increasingly inhospitable world. Conceived in the period following the war with Rome that, in the first century, led to the destruction of the second Jerusalem Temple, the Rabbinic program for Judaism was shaped in the immediate aftermath of the devastating Bar Kokhba Revolt of the second century, which left as many as half a million Jews dead and which resulted in Jerusalem's being turned into a Roman colony, with a temple of Jupiter Capitolinus erected on the Temple Mount. The Rabbinic program then achieved its classical formulation and gained control over the Jewish nation as a whole in the fourth-sixth centuries, the period of the firm establishment of Christianity as the official religion of the Roman world.

As a result of these historical events, both the political and theological contexts in which Jews previously had interpreted the events of history—viewing them as the result of the miraculous intervention of God into the human sphere—had been dramatically altered. If God could work miracles, why did he now not miraculously return the nation to its former glory? Rather than denying the power of God, on the one hand, or promising that miracles should be again expected, on the other, the sages who shaped Rabbinic Judaism addressed this question by entirely rethinking the inherited biblical perspective on what can and should be expected of God. The destruction of the Temple and the failed revolt under Bar Kokhba had made clear to these rabbis that the Jewish people were not well served by ambitious political leaders who insisted that God would immediately and miraculously fulfill the biblical promise of Jewish sovereignty over the holy land. In the Rabbinic view, rather, Jews were better off forgetting the notion of God's wondrous actions in history, accepting, instead, Roman political domination. Under this domination, rather than depending upon miracles, they would develop modes of piety independent of priestly and nationalistic aspirations, unconcerned with what was happening on the stage of history.

The result of this thinking was that, under Rabbinic leadership, Jews would continue to pray for the rebuilding of the Temple, the re-establishment of animal sacrifice, and renewed Israelite sovereignty, to be achieved, to be sure, through God's personal and miraculous intervention in history. But these things now were seen not as matters for this day but as signifiers of the advent of the messianic age. They would be events of the end of time, not aspects of this world, expected to come about today or tomorrow. The Rabbinic ideology thus refocused the people's concerns from the events of political history, which are, after all, far beyond the control of the individual, to events within the life and control of each person and family. What came to matter were the every-day details of life, the recurring actions that, day-in and day-out, define who we are and that demarcate what is truly important to us. How do we relate to family and community? By what ethic do we carry out our business dealings? How do we acknowledge our debt to God not for the events of history but for everyday things, for the food we eat and for the wonders of the universe evidenced in the daily rising and setting of the sun?

Certainly the rabbis understand the observance of a detailed system of ritual and communal law as directly affecting God, as leading God to act on the people's behalf. But, through the Rabbinic system, Israelites were made to recognize that they should expect no quick, spectacular response as had occurred, for instance, in the period of the Exodus from Egypt or, more recently, in the return, after one generation, from the Babylonian exile. A messiah would come, but only in some distant future. And, in light of the battles and bloodshed that were understood to come along with the messianic event, people should not even be too desirous of living in that coming time.

In this way, those who created Rabbinic Judaism responded to the critical theological problem of their day. God's presence and love of the people had always been represented in his mighty deeds on behalf of the people. Insofar as such deeds no longer could be expected, let alone depended upon, Rabbinic religion located a new proof for the existence of God and a new explanation for how the people could be assured of God's continued care and providential concern. The people, the rabbis said, must find God in their everyday lives rather than expect God to appear to them in miraculous acts of intervention into human history.

Miracles in Rabbinic Judaism: In line with their new thinking, even as the Talmudic rabbis acknowledged that miracles occur and are evidence of God's action in the world, they proposed that such miracles are neither an appropriate foundation for faith nor the expected method through which God should in their own day protect individuals or the Israelite people as a whole. One explanation for the cessation of divine miracles was that contemporary generations were not as pious and worthy of miraculous intervention as earlier ones had been (B. Ber. 4a):

  A. "Till your people pass over, O Lord, till your people pass over, that you have acquired" [Exod. 15:16].
  B. "Till your people pass over" refers to the [Israelites'] first entry into the Land [in Joshua's time].
  C. "Till your people pass over, that you have acquired" refers to the second entry into the Land [in the time of Ezra and Nehemiah. The point is that a miracle was promised not only for the first entry but also for the second. Why did no miracle occur the second time around?]
  D. On the basis of this statement, sages have said, "The Israelites were worthy of having a miracle performed for them in the time of Ezra also, just as it had been performed for them in the time of Joshua b. Nun, but sin caused [the miracle to be withheld]."

The rabbis understood later generations to have been more sinful than former ones, and this brought an end to miracles. To the extent that they understood miracles to have continued to occur past the biblical age at all

(and even up to their own day), the later rabbis saw even this possibility as having diminished over the period of a few generation (B. Ber. 20a):

  A. Said R. Papa to Abayye, "What makes the difference that the former authorities had miracles done for them, while miracles are not done for us?
  B. "If it is because of the issue of learning Tannaite traditions. In the time of R. Judah, all they learned to repeat was the matter of Damages, while, for our part, we repeat all six divisions [of the Mishnah and their associated Tannaite traditions].
  C. "And when R. Judah would come to the passage in tractate Uqsin [that begins], 'A woman who presses vegetables in a pot . . .' (M. Uqs. 2:1), or, some say, 'Olives pressed with their leaves are clean' (M. Uqs. 2:1), he would say [nothing more than], 'Here I see the issues raised by Rab and Samuel for reflection.' But when we repeat tractate Uqsin, we have thirteen sessions [to devote to the matter].
  D. "Yet when R. Judah would take off one sandal [in preparation for a fast for rain], it would rain right away, while we torture ourselves and cry out, and no one [in heaven] pays attention to us."
  E. [Abayye] said to [Papa], "The former authorities would give their lives for the sanctification of the Divine Name, while we do not give our lives for the sanctification of the Divine Name."

Torah study was widely regarded as the foundation of piety and a source of access to God's power. But rabbis of the Talmudic period saw even this power has having been closed off to themselves, the result of their lessened overall righteousness. The later generations, as a result, were no longer worthy of miracles (B. San. 94b):

  A. What is the meaning of this verse: "When aforetime the land of Zebulun and the land of Naphtali lightened its burden, but in later times it was made heavy by the way of the sea, beyond Jordan, in Galilee of the nations" (Is. 8:23)?
  B. It was not like the early generations, who made the yoke of the Torah light for themselves, but the later generations, who made the yoke of the Torah heavy for themselves.
  C. And these [early generations] were worthy that a miracle should be done for

them, just as was done for those who passed through the sea and trampled over the Jordan.

Overall these passages argue that miracles are done only for particularly deserving people. Later generations have failed to live up to God's expectations and therefore are unworthy of miracles. While in the context of the first centuries, this approach served well to explain the circumstance of the Israelite nation (as the liturgy puts it, "Because of our sins we have been exiled from our land. . . ."), it is actually quite different from the approach to miracles expressed, as we have seen, in the Hebrew Scriptures. For in the Bible, miracles are not simply or even primarily a reward for piety. As in the case of the Exodus from Egypt, referred to in this passage at C, miracles are, rather, a method by which God initially expresses his divine will, providing the Israelite nation with the evidence they need to accept his lordship, and leading them to accept the covenant and abide by its law.[5]

We thus see the extent to which the apparent cessation of miracles in the period of the rabbis has led them entirely to rethink the biblical attitude, which held it reasonable for a person to pray for or depend upon God's miraculous intervention. The rabbis, by contrast, insist that one should not endanger him or herself in anticipation of a saving miracle (B. Ta. 20b, B. Ket. 61b). Rather, they went so far as to consider the human expectation of or demand for the miraculous to be folly, even when that expectation pertained not to a personal desire but to the fulfillment of a goal clearly shared by God (M. A.Z. 4:7):

A. They asked sages in Rome, "If [God] is not in favor of idolatry, why does he not wipe it away?"

B. They said to them, "If people worshipped something of which the world had no need, he certainly would wipe it away.

C. "But, lo, people worship the sun, moon, stars, and planets.

D. "Now do you think he is going to wipe out his world because of idiots?"

E. They said to them, "If so, let him destroy something [associated with idolatry] of which the world has no need, and leave something that the world needs!"

F. They said to them, "Then we should strengthen the hands of those who wor-

ship things [which would not be destroyed], for then they would say, 'Now you know full well that they are gods, for, lo, they were not wiped out!'"

God, in this passage's view, cannot be expected to perform miracles even in order to accomplish a purpose in keeping with God's own plan and desires. In a point that is echoed throughout the Rabbinic discussion of miracles, the text argues that this is the case not because God does not desire to perform such miracles but because they would not work. God, in the example given here, does not wipe out idolatry since, in the nature of things, doing so would also destroy needed aspects of the world or, at least, would wind up strengthening the very beliefs God wishes in the first place to eradicate. The rabbis thus imagine God's power to be restricted by the logic that confines human reasoning and action. Miracles, even if they were still to occur, would have to conform to the logic and order of the world as humans perceive it. How different this is from the miraculous events of the Exodus, in which, for instance, God placed all of Egypt in darkness while the Israelites had light (Exod. 10:22-23). While crediting God with tremendous power, the rabbis, by contrast, do not conceive God to have the ability to violate the basic principles by which events normally unfold.

In line with this sense of the limitations faced even by God in working miracles, the rabbis understood the miracles described in the Bible to have been preordained, arranged by God at the time of creation, when, for instance, the manna consumed by the Israelites after the Exodus from Egypt and the mouth of Balaam's talking ass were created (M. Ab. 5:6; see Exod. Rab. 21:6). They even understood God to have been able to split the sea at the time of the Exodus only because, when he created the world, God had stipulated with the sea that, on this specific occasion, it would disrupt its normal flow (Exod. Rab. 21:6). Had it not been for this prior agreement, the rabbis argue, God could not have split the sea at all. Miracles thus were not seen as actually interrupting the natural order; they were rather a part of that order, only appearing to people as extraordinary.

Even while continuing in the Bible's comprehension that God reveals his will through miracles, the rabbis reject the notion that, in their own day, such a course of action on God's part is either appropriate or acceptable. The rabbis see in God's miraculous deeds, rather, an attempt inappropriately to coerce the people to accept God's rule. And, in apparent contrast to Scripture, they are adamant that such a coerced "faith" is not a legitimate faith at all. Thus the rabbis go so far as to reject God's redeeming of the people from Egypt as an appropriate foundation for the Israelites' accepting of the covenant (B. Shab. 88a):

A. "And they [that is, the people of Israel, after the Exodus, camped at Sinai] stood below the mount" (Exod. 19:17):
B. Actually underneath the mountain.
C. Said R. Abdimi bar Hama bar Hasa, "This teaches that the Holy One, blessed be he, held the mountain over Israel like a cask and said to them, 'If you accept the Torah, well and good, and if not, then there is where your grave will be.'"
D. Said R. Aha bar Jacob, "On this basis there is ground for a powerful protest against the Torah [since it was imposed by force]."
E. Said Raba, "Nonetheless, the generation of the time of Ahasuerus accepted it, as it is written, 'The Jews ordained and took it upon themselves'[6] (Est. 9:27)—they confirmed what the others [at the time of Sinai] had already accepted."

The passage argues that God's actions against the Egyptians did more than to help the Israelites to recognize God's power and sovereignty. Rather, God's miracles created a circumstance of compulsion, in which the people of Israel had no choice but to accept the Torah. The nation had just witnessed God's overwhelming power, including the deity's willingness to drown an entire army. The people now stood in the wilderness with no where to go, no means of defending themselves, and insufficient provisions. The rabbis imagine this circumstance as being comparable to standing "beneath" Sinai, for the people's refusal to accept God's covenant would certainly have meant their being left to die in the wilderness. Rejection of the covenant would lead to death as surely as if

the mountain literally were dropped on them.

In the rabbis' reading, then, the miracle of the Exodus and the wondrous events at Sinai were too coercive properly to form the foundation of a meaningful faith.[7] God's actions bordered on the inappropriate. People cannot legitimately be compelled to accept the obligations of faith (or of any other contract), and therefore the Israelites had grounds for a protest against the Torah, acceptance of which appears to have been coerced.

Alongside this reading of the events of Sinai, the rabbis propose that Scripture contains a different, appropriate model of faith. This is exemplified by what happened in the period of Esther and Mordechai, described in the above passage at E. In the story of the book of Esther, as in the account of the Exodus, the Jews faced a very real enemy. But in the story of Esther, they appear, at least on the surface, to fight this enemy through their own strength and determination. God is never mentioned in the book of Esther, and the Jews' victory, while depicted as miraculous, involves no violation of the natural order, no wondrous deeds attributed directly to the God of Israel. The rabbis recognize that, in this setting, it was up to the people themselves to discern in their own human victory evidence of God's presence. In light of their personal, theological interpretation of what had happened, the people of the time of Esther chose on their own volition to confirm the covenant. In this the rabbis find the appropriate foundation for the people of Israel's continuing commitment to the covenant.

In all, the rabbis reject miracles as an appropriate means through which God may assure the people's acceptance of the covenant and promote adherence to the divine will. Rather, in the Rabbinic view, the people of Israel must themselves be the primary actors in the emergence of their own national history and in the development of their faith. Within such thinking, God's wondrous actions in the human sphere are things of the past not only because God has ceased to perform such deeds or because the people no longer are worthy of them. To an equal extent, wonders no longer occur because they are too coercive to be useful in the evolution of the people's faith and in the expansion of the nation's relationship with God.

This view of the impact of God's wondrous deeds does not mean that the rabbis held miracles entirely to have ceased. Rather, the sages rethought the nature and purpose of God's saving acts. As in the Rabbinic reading of the story of Esther, they increasingly viewed as miraculous the results of human endeavor. Additionally, they focused upon the day-to-day wonders of the world around them, seeing miracles in even the smallest aspects of everyday life. Such things as a person's recovery from an illness now proved God's continued presence and never ending concern for the people of Israel (B. Ned. 41a):

> A. R. Alexandri also said in the name of R. Hiyya bar Abba, "Greater is the miracle that is done for a sick person than the miracle that was done for Hananiah, Mishael, and Azariah [Dan. 3]. That of Hananiah, Mishael, and Azariah was fire made by man, which anybody can put out, but that of a sick person is fire made by Heaven, and who can put that out?"

Similarly, the earth's provision to people of sufficient food could be viewed as a miracle greater than the final redemption of the entire people (B. Pes. 118a):

> A. Said R. Yohanan, "Providing food for a person is more difficult than redemption, for with respect to redemption, it is written, 'The angel who has redeemed me from all evil' (Gen. 48:16), suggesting that an everyday angel was enough [to provide redemption]; [but] with respect to food [it says]: 'the God who has fed me' [Gen. 48:15, suggesting that God himself must do this]."

In this approach to interpreting events in the world around them, people are led not to expect a miraculous redemption or any kind of divine interventions into the cosmic order. Such things, in the Rabbinic view, are unnecessary as proof of the existence of God or of God's concern for the people of Israel. Rather, just as the people are to serve God through observance of the covenant and

through righteousness in everyday activities, so the everyday events of nature prove God's continuing providential concern. The flow of day and night, the rhythm of the seasons, the earth's providing of food were now to be recognized as greater miracles than those reported in Scripture, in which God's intervention in the physical world gave birth to extraordinary events that changed history. In the Rabbinic reading, miracles were no longer to be viewed primarily as events in which God loudly proclaimed his presence and will. Miracles, rather, occurred quietly, every day, and it was the responsibility of the people to identify them and to learn from them.

In a period in which God no longer seemed to act in history to save the people, the rabbis thus recognized a new imperative. In the first centuries, the people were in a new position *vis-à-vis* God. Now they needed themselves to buttress their faith by identifying God's presence and power in the operation of the natural order and by locating a divine element within their own conduct and in the exercise of their own strength. The Hebrew Bible had taken it as axiomatic that God's qualities and demands on Israel would be known through God's miraculous revelation, exactly as had occurred in the theophany on Sinai. Now the people themselves would be responsible for finding and interpreting God's will, without the help of God's direct intervention into the human sphere.

This point is particularly clear in the rabbis' complete rejection of the notion that, in their day, as at Sinai, God had the right to make his will known to people by miraculously breaking into the human order so as to inform them of the content of covenantal law. In the Rabbinic, unlike the biblical, perspective, such knowledge of the divine is left up to people alone to discover. This they do through their active intellectual engagement with the already revealed law. The possibility of God's miraculous intervention into the legal debates through which the rabbis discern the law was contemplated. But this interference was neither welcome nor effective,[8] as the often cited story of the Oven of Akhnai makes clear (B. B.M. 59b):

A. On that day, R. Eliezer brought forward all of the arguments in the world, but they [that is, the other rabbis] did not accept them from him.

B. Said he to them, "If the law agrees with me, let this carob-tree prove it!" The carob-tree was torn a hundred cubits out of its place.

C. They said to him, "No proof can be brought from a carob-tree."

D. He said to them, "If the law agrees with me, let the stream of water prove it!" The stream of water flowed backward.

E. Again they said to him, "No proof can be brought from a stream of water."

F. Again he said to them, "If the law agrees with me, let the walls of this house of study prove it!" The walls tilted, about to fall.

G. R. Joshua rebuked the walls, saying, "When disciples of sages are engaged in a legal dispute, what role do you walls play?"

H. Hence, they did not fall, in honor of R. Joshua; but nor did they resume the upright, in honor of R. Eliezer.

I. Again [Eliezer] said to them, "If the law agrees with me let it be proved from heaven!" An echo came forth [from heaven] and said, "Why do you dispute with R. Eliezer? For in all matters, the law agrees with him!"

J. But R. Joshua arose and exclaimed [citing Deut. 30:12], "It [the law] is not in heaven!"

K. [Later] R. Nathan met Elijah [the prophet] and asked him, "What did the holy one, blessed be he, do at that time?"

L. [Elijah] replied, "He laughed, saying, 'My sons have defeated me! My sons have defeated me!"

The passage strikingly rejects the idea that God's miraculous intervention into the human sphere, in this case, into the activities of the study house, is acceptable. The story asserts rather that the law is defined by a vote of the majority of sages, who determine proper conduct based upon their wisdom and knowledge, and who give no heed to supernatural interference. What is the nature of the "defeat," about which God laughs? God chuckles over the unexpected result of his own success as a parent. God has created and nurtured children, imbued them with such a sense of responsibility and intellectual cunning that they insist on living in a world of their own making. They no longer desire or will accept God's interference—even God's miraculous intervention—into what they see as their affairs.

In their original setting in the book of Deuteronomy, God's words, "*It is not in heaven*," mean only that people cannot deny that they know the law and are able to follow it. Now these words come back to haunt God. If the Torah is on earth and not in heaven, if it is in the people's mouth and heart, then God may no longer interfere in its interpretation. The law is among the sages. They are empowered to engage in reasoned debate and then to vote. They thereby take over the role of God in revealing Torah.

But there is an even more significant way in which God's children have defeated him. This is in the fact that God, as much as the people, is bound by the rules of Torah. God, just like the people, must accept and follow the logically decided view of the sages on earth. That which they deem holy and right becomes, in a cosmic sense, even in God's mind, holy and right. The human mind and intellect come to determine the content of God's mind and intellect. They—and not miraculous deeds of God—define the ultimate reality in the world.

The Rabbinic passages we have reviewed suggest the extent to which the Rabbinic conception of miracles reflects a significant shift from the biblical to the Rabbinic understanding of God. The biblical system had cherished God's brilliant acts in history, the signs and miracles that showed the people God's power and that comforted them, even when they were punished, by assuring them of the absolute logic and justice in the world. But living in a period in which such logic was elusive and in which the punishments received by the Jewish people fit no known crime, the rabbis rejected the old approach. The problem was not simply that the biblical conception was flawed and did not reflect the reality that the rabbis knew. Rather, they saw the biblical dependence upon miracles as an inappropriate path to piety. For the rabbis as for the Bible's authorship, God was present, to be worshipped and trusted to fulfill the terms of the covenant made at Sinai. But for the rabbis unlike the Bible's authors, the source and foundation of the people's faith, their desire to worship God, and their acceptance of the terms of the covenant needed to derive from their own independent recognition of the truth of God's presence and power. The determination of the people to love and worship God needed to be independent of any expectation of God's present-day miraculous intervention into human history.

The rabbis thus rejected the notion that it is appropriate for God to control people or force them into obedience through voices from heaven, miracles, divine messengers, or even by descending to earth personally to fight their battles. Instead, in the Rabbinic view, it is up to individual Jews to find the otherwise hidden God. This they are to do by acting responsibly in pursuing justice, promoting what is good, observing the law and even, when times demand it, by fighting their own battles to save themselves, as happened in the time of Esther and Mordechai. In everyday acts of goodness and self-protection—whether they seem to change the world or not—the people are to appreciate the presence of God and to find strength in the knowledge that they are following God's path.

The rabbis in this way reject the coercion implicit in a system in which God forces belief and conformity to his will through displays of power. Central to Rabbinic faith, instead, is the individual's coming to find God through contact with the compelling divine word—that is, Torah. In this system, the individual is brought into the world of faith and worship by his or her own initiative. This is not in response to God's spectacular miracles but as an aspect of a spiritual and national awakening in which the people come to recognize the presence of God in their own human abilities and intellect.

In an odd way, exactly by placing the power to define Torah in human hands, the rabbis make the powerful point that, despite the way the events of history made things seem, God still exists, still rules over the people and land of Israel, and still can be depended upon to bring redemption. It is only

for these reasons that Torah still matters at all, still must be explicated, still must be followed. But, in the Rabbinic system, the God who had been understood to make and destroy nations, to show his will through splendid and miraculous deeds, is pictured as moving rather in response to the intentions and perceptions of everyday Jews who engage in the study of, and therefore the creation of, revelation; who lead their daily lives in accordance with divine precepts; who eat their food as though their home-tables are the Temple altar; and who live their lives as though they are a kingdom of priests.

At the heart of this Rabbinic approach is the notion that knowledge of God results not primarily from God's self-revelation in history. It depends rather upon humanity's proper grasp of the Torah, requiring the Jews' active engagement with the details of revelation, through sagacity, erudition, and human intelligence. According to Rabbinic Judaism, it is through thinking about Torah, not by witnessing and interpreting divine miracles, that the Jew asks the deeper question of what can be known about God. Thinking about Torah, the rabbis hold, reveals God's thought in God's own words.[9] Through this human participation in revelation comes the possibility of returning the world to the way God meant it to be when, on the seventh day of creation, God saw that what he had created was good.

The rabbis responded to the devastating events of their day by rejecting the simplistic biblical view that all history attests to God's will. But they did not therefore withdraw from that history into a world of ritual or cultic action. Rather, Jews came increasingly to insist that the individual has the power and the obligation to use his or her intellect to define and then to work to create a new and better world, a world of holiness and sanctification, a world as we know it should be, wish it to be, and, if we only imagine intently enough and work hard enough, will assure that it someday will be. In confrontation with the real world in which people lived, the biblical image of God's power to act through miracles yielded the belief that *people themselves have and must use their power to transform the world.* It is here, rather than in God's intervention in the human realm, that the rabbis saw the real miracle of God's power.[10]

Notes

[1] Thus M. Ab. 5:4 states, "Ten wonders were done for our fathers in Egypt, and ten at the Sea." The point is that the process through which the Israelites were redeemed from Egyptian bondage was miraculous. But this statement in itself makes no particular theological point.

[2] In Scripture, the term *nes* occurs in the sense of miracle only once, Num. 26:10. Otherwise, it refers to a long pole on which an object or banner can be placed for display (Num. 21:8-9, Is. 30:17 and 33:23). On the general conception of miracles in biblical and later Rabbinic thinking, see Jacob Licht, "Miracle," *EJ*, vol. 12, col. 73, and Yair Zakovitch, "Miracle (OT)," *ABD*, vol. 4, pp. 845-846.

[3] On this point, see MAGIC.

[4] *Fele*, from the same root as the term *niflaot*.

[5] This is exactly what occurs at 1 Kings 18:21-39. At Elijah's behest, God miraculously sends a fire from heaven to ignite offerings laid out for him. This leads the people, who had been tending towards the worship of Baal, to declare, "The Lord, he is God." As in Egypt, the miracle thus precedes the people's affirmation of Yahweh as their God.

[6] The verse continues: "and their descendants and all who joined them, that without fail they would keep these two days according to what was written and at the time appointed every year."

[7] On this reading of the passage, see Irving Greenberg, *The Jewish Way. Living the Holidays* (New York, 1993), pp. 249-252.

[8] Note by contrast Exod. 18:14-26's story about Moses's establishing a system of judges. While these judges were to help settle disputes among the people, their commission did not in any way impinge upon God's absolute authority. Thus they were to handle only the clear-cut matters, in which the law already was known. But any hard case, in which there was a question of law, was to be brought to Moses, who would continue as before to "represent the people before God and bring their cases to God" (Exod. 18:19).

[9] I paraphrase Jacob Neusner, "God: How, in Judaism, Do We Know God," in Jacob Neusner, ed., *Formative Judaism* (Seventh Series, Atlanta, 1993), p. 209.

[10] On medieval Jewish philosophers' understanding of miracles, see JUDAISM, PHILOSOPHY AND THEOLOGY OF, IN MEDIEVAL TIMES.

ALAN J. AVERY-PECK

MONOTHEISM: In Judaism, monotheism refers to the belief in one God, who is all-powerful and just. In Judaism's view, the will of the one, unique God, made manifest through the Torah, governs, and, further, God's will for both private life and public activity is rational. That is to say, within man's understanding of reason, God's will is just. And by "just," sages understood the commonsense meaning: fair, equitable, proportionate, commensurate. In place of fate or impersonal destiny, chance, or simply irrational, inexplicable chaos, God's plan and purpose everywhere come to realization. So the Torah identifies God's will as the active and causative force in the lives of individuals and nations.

Only through appeal to that fundamental principle of one God's imposing a just order can we make sense of the specific convictions of Judaism on any particular subject. Whatever ideas sages propose to account for the situation of Israel in public or the individual in private, whether the resolution of the historical crisis in the coming of the messiah and the nations' standing in judgment by the criterion of the Torah or the advent of the world to come—all of these massive presences in sages' thinking about the here and now, the past and the future, rested on the same conviction: an exact, prevailing justice explained the meaning of all things. It was a reciprocal process because the same reasonable justice ruled small and great transactions without distinction. Not only so, but, for sages, that conviction required an act not of faith but of rational inquiry into the record of reality that Judaism finds in Scripture.

Monotheism is not a matter of arithmetic—one God against many gods. It is a completely different way of explaining the world. Monotheism posits one God, wholly other than humanity, transcendent over nature, in charge of all things, responsible for all reality. And monotheism as set forth by Judaism (and its offspring Christianity and Islam) insists that the one, all powerful God is good, merciful, and just. While a religion of numerous gods finds many solutions to one problem, a religion of only one God presents one to many. Life is seldom fair. Rules rarely work. To explain the reason why, polytheisms adduce multiple causes of chaos, a god per anomaly. Diverse gods do various things, so, it stands to reason, ordinarily outcomes conflict. Monotheism by nature explains many things in a single way. One God rules. Life is meant to be fair, and just rules are supposed to describe what is ordinary, all in the name of that one and only God. So in monotheism a simple logic governs to limit ways of making sense of things. But that logic contains its own dialectics. If one true God has done everything, then, since this God is all-powerful and omniscient, all things are credited to, and blamed on, him. In that case, God can be either good or bad, just or unjust—but not both.

Responding to the generative dialectics of monotheism, Judaism systematically reveals the justice of the one and only God of all creation. God is not only God but also good. Appealing to the facts of Scripture, the Written part of the Torah, in the documents of the Oral part of the Torah, the sages in the first six centuries C.E. constructed a coherent theology, a cogent structure and logical system, to expose the justice of God.

On what basis do the sages of Judaism insist upon the justice of God? To answer the question of the source of probative evidence for the principle that the world is reliable and orderly by reason of justice, we turn to the concrete evidence that they held demonstrated their point. When sages opened Scripture to find out how, in the detail of concrete cases, the judge of all the world is bound by the rules of justice and systematically does justice, like philosophers in natural history, they looked not for the occasional but the enduring: not for the singular moment but the routine pattern. One-shot proof-texts mattered less than governing paradigms. Sages were theologians before they were exegetes, and they were exegetes because they were theologians. So, while proof from specific texts they showed to emerge from details, they used hermeneutics to hold details together in a single coherent whole. That is why they composed their account of the workings of the principle of measure for measure—whether for divine punishment or for divine reward—out of cases in which God does not intervene, but in which the very nature of things, the ordinary course of events, showed the workings of the principle.

What would suffice, then, to make a point that—we must assume—people in general deem counter-intuitive? For who from Job onward assumed that the ordinary course of everyday events proves the justice (and the goodness) of God? More lost the faith because the here and now violated the rule of justice than gained the faith because it did. So, to begin with, sages framed for themselves what we might call a null-hypothesis, that is to say, a hypothesis that they would test to prove the opposite of what they sought to show. They asked themselves this question: if justice did not govern, how should we know it? The answer is, we should find not a correlation but a disproportion between sin and consequent result, or penalty, between crime and punishment.

The null-hypothesis framed the question of order through justice in its most palpable, material form. It is not enough to show that sin or crime provoke divine response, that God penalizes them. Justice in the here and now counts. The penalty must fit the crime, measure must match measure, and the more exact the result to the cause, the more compelling the proof of immediate and concrete justice as the building block of world order that sages would put forth out of Scripture. That is the point at which justice is transformed from a vague generality—a mere sentiment—to a precise and measurable dimension of the actual social order of morality: how things hold together when subject to tension, at the pressure-points of structure, not merely how they are arrayed in general. Here, in fact, is how God made the world, what is good about the creation that God pronounced good.

That is why, when sages examined the facts of Scripture to establish that principle of rationality and order in conformity to the requirements of justice and equity, what impressed them was not the inevitability but the precision of justice. Scripture portrays the world order as fundamentally just and reasonable, and it does so in countless ways. But Scripture encompasses the complaint of Job and the reflection of Ecclesiastes. Sages for their part identified those cases that transcended generalities and established the facticity of proportionate justice, treating them as not only exemplary but probative. They set forth their proposition and amassed evidence in support of it.

When God judges and sentences, not only is the judgment fair but the penalty fits the crime with frightening precision. But so too, when God judges and awards a decision of merit, the reward proves equally exact. These two together, the match of sin and penalty, meritorious deed and reward, then are shown to explain the point and purpose of one detail after another, and, all together, they add up to the portrait of a world order that is fundamentally and essentially just—the starting point and foundation of all else.

Here is sages' account of God's justice, which is always commensurate, both for reward and punishment, in consequence of which the present permits us to peer into the future with certainty of what is going to happen. What we note is sages' identification of the precision of justice, the exact match of action and reaction, each step in the sin, each step in the response, and, above all, the immediacy of God's presence in the entire transaction. They draw general conclusions from the specifics of the law that Scripture sets forth, and that is where systematic thinking about takes over from exegetical learning about cases (M. Sot. 1:7):

> A. By that same measure by which a person metes out [to others], do they mete out to him:
> B. She primped herself for sin, the Omnipresent made her repulsive.
> C. She exposed herself for sin, the Omnipresent exposed her.
> D. With the thigh she began to sin, and afterward with the belly, therefore the thigh suffers the curse first, and afterward the belly.
> E. But the rest of the body does not escape [punishment].

The course of response of the woman accused of adultery to her drinking of the bitter water that is supposed to produce one result for the guilty, another for the innocent, is described in Scripture in this language: "If no man has lain with you . . . be free from this water of bitterness that brings the curse. But if you have gone astray . . . then the Lord make you an execration . . . when the Lord makes your thigh fall away and your body swell; may this water . . . pass into your bowels and make your body swell and your thigh fall away" (Num. 5:20-22). This is amplified and expanded, extended to the entire rite, where the woman is disheveled; then the order, thigh, belly, shows the perfect precision of the penalty. What Scripture treats as a case, sages transform into a generalization, so making Scripture yield governing rules. And the main point, that God governs justly, derived from those rules based on the facts of Scripture.

The same passage proceeds to further cases that prove the same point: where the sin begins, there the punishment also commences; but also, where an act of virtue takes its point, there divine reward focuses as well. Merely listing the following names, without spelling out details, for the cognoscenti of Scripture will have made that point: Samson, Absalom, Miriam, Joseph, and Moses. Knowing how Samson and Absalom match, also Miriam, Joseph, and Moses, would then suffice to establish the paired and matched general principles (M. Sot. 1:8):

> A. Samson followed his eyes [where they led him], therefore the Philistines put out his eyes, since it is said, "And the Philistines laid hold on him and put out his eyes" (Judg. 16:21).
> B. Absalom was proud of his hair, therefore he was hung by his hair [2 Sam. 14:25-26].
> C. And since he had sexual relations with ten concubines of his father, therefore they thrust ten spear heads into his body, since it is said, "And ten young men that carried Jacob's armor surrounded and smote Absalom and killed him" (2 Sam. 18:15).
> D. And since he stole three hearts—his father's, the court's, and the Israelite's—since it is said, "And Absalom stole the heart of the men of Israel" (2 Sam. 15:6)—therefore three darts were thrust into him, since it is said, "And he took three darts in his hand and thrust them through the heart of Absalom" (2 Sam. 18:14).

Justice requires not only punishment of the sinner or the guilty but reward of the righteous and the good, and so sages find ample, systematic evidence in Scripture for both sides of the equation of justice (M. Sot. 1:9-10):

> 1:9A. And so is it on the good side:
>   B. Miriam waited a while for Moses, since it is said, "And his sister stood afar off" (Exod. 2:4), therefore, Israel waited on her seven days in the wilderness, since it is said, "And the people did not travel on until Miriam was brought in again" (Num. 12:15).
> 1:10A. Joseph had the merit of burying his father, and none of his brothers was greater than he, since it is said, "And Joseph went up to bury his father . . . and there went up with him both chariots and horsemen" (Gen. 50:7, 9).
>   B. We have none so great as Joseph, for only Moses took care of his [bones].
>   C. Moses had the merit of burying the bones of Joseph, and none in Israel was greater than he, since it is said, "And Moses took the bones of Joseph with him" (Exod. 13:19).
>   D. We have none so great as Moses, for only the Holy One blessed be he took care of his [bones], since it is said, "And he buried him in the valley" (Deut. 34:6).
>   E. And not of Moses alone have they stated [this rule], but of all righteous people, since it is said, "And your righteousness shall go before you. The glory of the Lord shall gather you [in death]" (Is. 58:8).

Scripture provides the main probative evidence for the anticipation that God will match the act of merit with an appropriate reward and the sin with an appropriate punishment. The proposition begins, however, with general observations as to how things are, M. 1:7, and not with specific allusions to proof-texts; the character of the law set forth in Scripture is reflected upon. The accumulated cases yield the generalization.

It follows that Judaism conveys the picture of world order based on God's justice and equity. The categorical structure of the Oral Torah encompasses the components, God and humanity; the Torah; Israel and the nations. The working-system of the Torah finds its dynamic in the struggle between God's plan for creation—to create a perfect world of justice—and human will. That dialectic embodies in a single paradigm the events contained in the sequences, rebellion, sin, punishment, repentance, and atonement; exile and return; or the disruption of world order and the restoration of world order. None of these categories and propositions is new; anyone familiar with the principal components of the faith and piety of Judaism, the Written Torah, the Oral Torah, and the liturgy of home and synagogue, will find them paramount.

The Torah's formulation of monotheism takes the form of a story. That simple story tells about a world governed by the moral order imposed by God's ultimate reason and justice, set forth in the Torah of Sinai, in oral and written media, and realized by God in Israel. Therein is found the governing, integrating theology of the Torah. The generative doctrine of God's perfect justice in the divine creation and governance of the world is what imparts integrity to the details and proportion to the whole. That story portraying the requirements of justification encompasses the entire tale of humanity in general and its counterpart, Israel in particular. The tale provides a dense record of the reasonable rules that account for what happens in public and, by way of complement and match, at home, to the people and to individuals. The four principles of the Torah's monotheist theology of a just God are these:

1. God formed creation in accord with a plan, which the Torah reveals. World order can be shown by the facts of nature and society set forth in that plan to conform to a pattern of reason based upon justice. Those who possess the Torah—Israel—know God and those who do not—the gentiles—reject God in favor of idols. What happens to each of the two sectors of humanity, respectively, responds to their relationship with God. Israel in the present age is subordinate to the nations, because God has designated the gentiles as the medium for penalizing Israel's rebellion, intending through Israel's subordination and exile to provoke Israel to repent. Private life as much as the public order conforms to the principle that God rules justly in a creation of perfection and stasis.

2. The perfection of creation, realized in

the rule of exact justice, is signified by the timelessness of the world of human affairs, their conformity to a few enduring paradigms that transcend change (theology of history). No present, past, or future marks time, but only the recapitulation of those patterns. Perfection is further embodied in the unchanging relationships of the social commonwealth (theology of political economy), which assure that scarce resources, once allocated, remain in stasis. A further indication of perfection lies in the complementarity of the components of creation, on the one side, and, finally, the correspondence between God and humans, in God's image (theological anthropology), on the other.

3. Israel's condition, public and personal, marks flaws in creation. What disrupts perfection is the sole power capable of standing on its own against God's power, and that is human will. What people control and God cannot coerce is the human capacity to form intention and therefore to choose either arrogantly to defy, or humbly to love, God. People defy God, and the sin that results from this rebellion flaws creation and disrupts world order (theological theodicy). The paradigm of the rebellion of Adam in Eden governs, the act of arrogant rebellion leading to exile from Eden thus accounting for the condition of humanity. But, as in the original transaction of alienation and consequent exile, God retains the power to encourage repentance through punishing human arrogance. In mercy, moreover, God exercises the power to respond to repentance with forgiveness, that is, a change of attitude evoking a counterpart change. Since, commanding their own will, people also have the power to initiate the process of reconciliation with God, through repentance, an act of humility, they may restore the perfection of that order that through arrogance they have marred.

4. God ultimately will restore that perfection that embodied the divine plan for creation. In the work of restoration, death that comes about by reason of sin will die, the dead will be raised and judged for their deeds in this life , and most of them, having been justified, will go on to eternal life in the world

to come. The paradigm of humanity restored to Eden is realized in Israel's return to the land of Israel. In that world or age to come, however, the sector of humanity that through the Torah knows God will encompass all of people. Idolaters will perish, and humanity that comprises Israel at the end will know the one true God and spend eternity in God's light.

If we translate into the narrative of Israel, from the beginning to the calamity of the destruction of the (first) Temple, what is set forth in both abstract and concrete ways in the formulation of monotheism that we find in the Oral Torah, we turn out to state a reprise of the theology of monotheism that we find in the Written Torah. This is, in particular, located in the Authorized History laid out in Genesis through Kings and amplified by the principal prophets. Furthermore, the liturgy of synagogue and home recapitulates characteristic modes of thought of the Oral Torah and reworks its distinctive constructions of exemplary figures, events, and conceptions.

So here, beginning with the integrating basics, encompassing the entire expanse of creation and humanity, from first to last things, are the ideas that impart structure and order and sustain the whole. Starting with the doctrine of world order that is just and concluding with eternal life, here is the simple logic that animates all the parts and makes them cohere. The generative categories prove not only imperative and irreducible but also logically sequential. Each of the four parts of the theology of monotheism—[1] the perfectly just character of world order, [2] indications of its perfection, [3] sources of its imperfection, [4] media for the restoration of world order and their results—belongs in its place; set in any other sequence, the four units become incomprehensible.

In spelling out in concrete terms the theology of monotheism, sages set forth the rational version of the stories of Scripture: creation and its flaws, Eden and the loss of Eden. But their logic, involving as it did the insistence on a perfect and unchanging world, created by the perfect and just God, sought out what complements and completes the account. Thus, they taught how Eden is to be recovered. Adam and his counterpart, Israel, in the cosmic drama acted out every day, here and now, in the humble details of Israel's ordinary life embodied the simple story of the world: unflawed creation, spoiled by man's act of will, restored by Israel's act of repentance. The rationality of an orderly and balanced world set forth in the Oral Torah comes to full realization in the match of Eden and the land of Israel, Adam and Israel, the paradise and paradise lost, with one difference. Adam had no Torah, Israel does. Adam could not regain Eden. But Israel can and will regain the land. Sages' teleology imposed itself on eschatology, so forming a theory of last things corresponding to first things, in a theology of restoration.

Private life conformed; it too revealed that same flawless character that the world does—when reason takes over, and exception is explained (away). Exchanges of goods—scarce resources—likewise aimed at a perfect balance. Time, for sages, stood still, history bore no meaning, all things could be shown to exemplify rules and embody regularities. Scripture then conveyed lessons of not history and its admonitions but logic—the logic of creation and its inner tension—and its inexorable result.

Sages in these proportionate, balanced and measured components revealed a world of rules and exposed a realm of justice and therefore rational explanation. It was the kingdom of heaven, so sages called it, meaning the kingdom of God. They accordingly conceived of a philosophical Eden out of Scripture's account—its authorized history of the world from Eden to the return to Zion. What the observed facts of nature taught philosophers, the revealed facts of Scripture taught Judaism's sages. Therein theology differs from philosophy—but, in the Oral Torah in particular, the difference is there and there alone and no where else.

A single statement of that view in general suffices to call attention to the regularities and order, the correspondences, that sages found linked nature and humankind in a perfect match. Stated very simply, to sages, humanity and nature correspond. God created the same matching traits in nature and in humans (Abot deR. Natan XXXI:III.1):

A. R. Yose the Galilean says, "Whatever the Holy One, blessed be he, created on earth, he created also in man. To what may the matter be compared? To someone who took a piece of wood and wanted to make many forms on it but had no room to make them, so he was distressed. But someone who draws forms on the earth can go on drawing and can spread them out as far as he likes.

B. "But the Holy One, blessed be he, may his great name be blessed for ever and ever, in his wisdom and understanding created the whole of the world, created the heaven and the earth, above and below, and created in man whatever he created in his world.

C. "In the world he created forests, and in man he created forests: the hairs on his head.

D. "In the world he created wild beasts and in man he created wild beasts: lice.

E. "In the world he created channels and in man he created channels: his ears.

F. "In the world he created wind and in man he created wind: his breath.

G. "In the world he created the sun and in man he created the sun: his forehead.

H. "Stagnant waters in the world, stagnant waters in man: his nose [namely, rheum].

I. "Salt water in the world, salt water in man: his urine.

J. "Streams in the world, streams in man: man's tears.

K. "Walls in the world, walls in man: his lips.

L. "Doors in the world, doors in man, his teeth.

M. "Firmaments in the world, firmaments in man, his tongue.

N. "Fresh water in the world, fresh water in man: his spit.

O. "Stars in the world, stars in the man: his cheeks.

P. "Towers in the world, towers in man: his neck.

Q. "Masts in the world, masts in man: his arms.

R. "Pins in the world, pins in man: his fingers.

S. "A king in the world [that is, God], a king in man: his head.

T. "Grape clusters in the world, grape clusters in man: his breasts.

U. "Counselors in the world, counselors in man: his kidneys.

V. "Millstones in the world, millstones

in man: his intestines [which grind up food].

W. "Mashing mills in the world, and mashing mills in man: the spleen.

X. "Pits in the world, a pit in man: the belly button.

Y. "Flowing streams in the world and a flowing stream in man: his blood.

Z. "Trees in the world and trees in man: his bones.

AA. "Hills in the world and hills in man: his buttocks.

BB. "pestle and mortar in the world and pestle and mortar in man: the joints.

CC. "Horses in the world and horses in man: the legs.

DD. "The angel of death in the world and the angel of death in man: his heels.

EE. "Mountains and valleys in the world and mountains and valleys in man: when he is standing, he is like a mountain, when he is lying down, he is like a valley.

FF. "Thus you have learned that whatever the Holy One, blessed be he, created on earth, he created also in man."

Shorn of theological and mythic language, the statement says no less than natural philosophy does in its insistence upon the teleology of nature, its hierarchical order. As philosophers follow a procedure of comparison and contrast, resting on the systematic sifting of the data of nature, so too do sages. But here, nature and Scripture (without differentiation as to source or effect of derivation from nature rather than from Scripture) yield correspondences that are deemed concrete and exact.

Intellectuals to their core, confident of the capacity to contemplate, to conceive in mind for speculative analysis a real world that corresponds to the world realized alone in mind, sages insist upon the primacy of reason. Logic ruled. It was logic that they had the capacity to discern. All things can be made to make sense. Proper analysis transforms the apparent chaos of nature's data into the compelling order of purposeful system and structure as the one God created the world: streams in the world, streams in mind, a world of complement and balance. A vast and ordered universe yields its secrets to those who discern regularity in close reading of actualities. Then, in place of mysteries come reliable knowledge, facts that yield

the laws of life. When they answered the question, Whence the knowledge of the rules of the ordered society, the world of balance and proportion in all things and of equitable exchange formed by the one God?, sages took their leave of philosophers. Instead of reading nature, they read the Torah. In place of searching for regularities of nature, they found patterns in the Torah. Instead of an abstract, natural teleology, to be defined through systematic work of hierarchical classification, comparison and contrast, they invoked the will of God. This will they showed to be dependable, regulated by rules humans can discern, wholly rational, entirely just. Then, instead of an inquiry into natural history, guided by considerations of hierarchy, order, and ultimate purpose, sages contemplated the condition of Israel, explaining how those same principles of intent and order governed, the same modes of rational explanation functioned, the same media of reasoned thought in the form of applied reason and practical logic guided thought. That is what distinguished sages from philosophers and turned them into theologians: the privileged source of truth that the Torah constituted.

Take, for example, the heart of the system of the Torah, the conviction of one God's rule of a world of order that is to be explained by appeal to the principles of justice. Then events serve as the source of moral truth. Destiny is dictated by God, and God's hegemony realizes a morality defined by justice. So justice, not chance, governs Israel, specifically, God's plan. For God has a purpose in what he does with Israel. This point is set forth by reference to exemplary actions, a narrative of what counts. God sent Israel down into Egypt to have occasion to perform miracles, so that the whole world would know that he is God and there is no other (Sifre Deut. CCCVI:XXX.2ff.):

2.A. "And how on the basis of Scripture do you say that our ancestors went down to Egypt only so that the Holy One, blessed be he, might do wonders and acts of might, and so that his great name might be sanctified in the world?

B. "As it is said, 'And it came to pass in the course of that long time that the king of Egypt died . . . and God heard their groaning, and God remembered his covenant' (Exod. 2:23-24).

C. "And it is said, 'For the name of the Lord I proclaim; give glory to our God.'

The purposeful character of God's actions now is spelled out in further cases:

3.A. "And how on the basis of Scripture do we know that the Omnipresent brought punishments and the ten plagues on Pharaoh and on the Egyptians only so that his great name might be sanctified in the world?

B. "For to begin with it is said, 'Who is the Lord, that I should listen to his voice?' (Exod. 5:2).

C. "But in the end: 'The Lord is righteous, and I and my people are wicked' (Exod. 9:27).

We move from the punishment of Egypt to the miracles done for Israel, also purposefully:

4.A. "And how on the basis of Scripture do we know that the Omnipresent did wonders and acts of might at the sea and at the Jordan and at the Arnon streams only so that his great name might be sanctified in the world?

B. "As it is said, 'And it came to pass, when all the kings of the Amorites that were beyond the Jordan westward, and all the kings of the Canaanites [that were by the sea, heard how the Lord has dried up the waters of the Jordan from before the children of Israel until they had passed over, their heart melted]' (Josh. 5:1).

C. "And so Rahab says to the messengers of Joshua, 'For we have heard how the Lord dried up the water of the Red Sea before you' (Josh. 2:10).

D. "Scripture says, 'For the name of the Lord I proclaim; give glory to our God.'

Not only miracles, but suffering and martyrdom serve God's purpose:

5.A. "And how on the basis of Scripture do we know that Daniel went down into the lions' den only so that the Holy One, blessed be he, might have occasion to do wonders and acts of might, and so that his great name might be sanctified in the world?

B. "As it is said, 'For the name of the Lord I proclaim; give glory to our God.'

C. "And Scripture says, 'I make a decree, that in all the dominions of my kingdom men tremble and fear before the God of Daniel . . .' (Dan. 6:27-28).

6.A. "And how on the basis of Scripture do you maintain that Hananiah, Mishael, and Azariah went into the fiery oven only so that the Holy One, blessed be he, might have occasion to do for them wonders and acts of might, and so that his great name might be sanctified in the world?

B. "As it is said, 'It seems good to me to declare the signs and wonders that God Most High has done for me . . . how great are his signs, and how mighty are his wonders, his kingdom is an everlasting kingdom' (Dan. 3:32-33)."

Important here are two traits of mind. First, theological truth is discovered in revealed Scripture. But then, second, the facts that are adduced are ordered into generalizations that are subject to the tests of verification or falsification: philosophical modes of thought applied to the data of theology: the search for the logic of God. What philosophers of Judaism accomplished in medieval times, joining Torah to reason, sages accomplished in the very process of formulating the Torah, oral and written, for the ages.

What is at stake in monotheism as set forth by the Torah? It is an explanation of Israel's present condition, and, still more urgent, identification of the operative reasons that will lead to viable hypotheses concerning Israel's future prospects. The present properly analyzed and explained contains within itself the entire past, the whole future, all together, all at once. We turn to Abram because we wish out of the past to know the future and because we take as fact that Israel's future recapitulates the past of Abram. God has laid out matters from beginning to end; Scripture not only records the past but provides the key, through patterns we can identify in the present, to the future. The premise of analysis then is, when we understand the facts in hand, we also can learn the rules. So in a world created in accord with the requirements of exact balance, proportion, correspondence, complementarity, and commensurability. There are no mysteries, only facts not yet noticed, analyses not yet undertaken, propositions not yet proved.

How to explain the present? The sages' explanation of the justice of God identifies the rational principle that is involved. Scripture's facts do not suffice, reason is demanded. Rationality thus is established by appeal not to the given of Scripture but to the conviction that the familiar traits of perfection characterize creation and the creator. Sages do not paraphrase or recapitulate Scripture and its narrative, they transform Scripture into facts to be analyzed and reconstructed. The results yield self-evidently valid doctrines. These prove to be few but paramount: the perfection of creation, the centrality of the Torah as a source of established facts, the subservience of God—therefore creation and history—to the same reason that animates the mind of humankind. All things are subject to the rules of logic and order that the human mind obeys, and explanation in the end must derive from the sources of nature and its laws and the Torah and its regularities, each recapitulating the mind and will of the loving and merciful and reasonable God, in whose image, after whose likeness, humankind is made.

What of the future? Sages compared themselves to prophets and insisted that their knowledge of the Torah provided a key to the future. Knowing why noteworthy things take place provided them with that key. For a model of anticipation will extrapolate from the results of analysis and explanation those governing rules of an orderly world that define a useful hypothesis concerning the future. Having identified regularities and defined descriptive laws, then accounted for those rules by spelling out the systemic reasons behind them, sages had every reason to peer over the beckoning horizon. For their basic conviction affirmed the order and regularity of creation, its perfection. If, therefore, they knew the rules and how they worked (including remissions of the rules), sages insisted they could predict how the future would take shape as well.

In its statement of monotheism, therefore, the Torah tells the story of how God created the world and sustains creation through the just moral order realized in the people to whom God made himself known, holy Israel. The theology narrates the unfolding tale of humanity from the creation of the world to the resurrection of the dead to eternal life with God. It sustains complex articulation and extension without losing coherence. That story is told in several distinct forms of discourse, mythic-narrative, exegetical, analytical and argumentative, in media of law and of lore, in statements of a general character and cases examined on their own or treated as exemplary. That sustaining story conveys a cogent logic, self-evident principles of reason and rationality. From a few governing principles or convictions, the entire story spins itself out into the finest details.

JACOB NEUSNER

MUSIC IN JUDAISM: While one typically expects a cultural group's music to be homogeneous and definable through melodic or rhythmic musical characteristics, due to the complex history of the Jewish people, Jewish music is neither homogeneous nor definable. Instead, reflecting the variety of the Jews' contacts with local cultures throughout time, Jewish music is largely to be characterized as an adaptation of music from local cultures within a Jewish context. But this fact—the absence of a universal feature that defines Jewish music—should not be construed to diminish its value or importance. It reflects, rather, the richness of Jewish musical culture, which must always be considered within its particular culture and historical place.

The history of Jewish music is known from a variety of sources. Written ones include the Bible, Midrash, Mishnah, Talmud, responsa literature, and certain historical accounts, including Philo, Josephus, the Qumran scrolls, and even the Christian Bible. These provide the primary basis for understanding the evolving role of music in Jewish life. Non-written materials, including physical evidence of musical instruments, are also important, as is iconography from frescoes, mosaics, pottery decorations, and images on coins that represent music's use. Additionally, notated musical sources provide the most concrete record, although, unfortunately, musical notation of Jewish music prior to 1700 is minimal and only a few manuscripts are extant.[1] Thus, an oral tradition provides the richest source of melodic materials. Several regional traditions, for instance, are represented in Abraham Zvi Idelsohn monumental collection, *Thesaurus of Hebrew-Oriental Melodies*, published in ten volumes between 1914 and 1932,[2] including Yemen, Iraq, Persia, Syria, the "Jerusalem-Sephardic" tradition,[3] Morocco, Eastern Europe, and Central Europe. Idelsohn's collection provided the basis for study throughout the twentieth century. Finally, present day recordings have added a vast dimension to what is available for examination.[4]

Despite this range of materials, the limited notated sources mean that broad assertions regarding universal features of Jewish music are hard to support. Attempts to uncover the sound of Jewish music from antiquity based on modern practices are especially problematic. For example, Rabbinic sources dating back two thousand years refer to the melodic recitation of the Bible, and some scholars imagine that Jews from Yemen have faithfully maintained that tradition, so as to present a living record of two thousand year old cantillation.[5] But such claims, based on conjecture, lack merit, for an ongoing question concerns the dating of contemporary oral traditions. To what extent do present Ashkenazic and Sephardic practices represent the continuation of an oral tradition rooted in the past? Each situation must be considered on its own merits, so that, today, ethnomusicologists generally stress the in-depth study of a single tradition rather than trying to postulate broad, and often unprovable, theories on the universal nature of music in various cultures or across time.

Music in ancient times: The Hebrew Bible contains approximately 350 references to instruments, song, and singing, the vast majority of them in the prophetic books and Hagiographa (while over 130 references to music appear in the Psalms, only twenty appear in the entire Pentateuch). The references concern three major contexts for music: historical events, prophecy, and lamentations. Historical events include miraculous moments, at which God's power is praised and

exalted, for instance, when the Egyptians were destroyed in the sea (Exod. 15:1-18, 15:21) and Hannah's "Song of Praise" after childbirth (1 Sam 2). Music marked other events as well: the blast of the ram's horn at the giving of the ten commandments (Exod. 19:13-19, 20:15), and its use to move groups of people (Num. 10:1-10), to call men to battle (Zech. 9:14-15), to welcome them victoriously from battle (1 Sam. 18:6-7), and to announce festivals and the Jubilee (Lev. 23:24, 25:9, Num. 29:1). Instruments also are associated with the transport of the ark to Jerusalem (2 Sam. 6:5, 1 Chr. 13:8), the establishment and reconstitution of the Temple service (2 Kgs. 12:14; 1 Chr. 15:16-28), and anointing of kings (1 Sam. 10:5; 1 Kgs. 1:34; 2 Kgs. 11:14).

Music's role in prophecy is deduced from David's playing of the harp, which cured Saul's depression (1 Sam. 16:14-23) by driving away an evil spirit. Other passages specifically indicate that prophets played music to bring out the divine presence of God (1 Sam. 10:5, 2 Kgs. 3:15). Finally, the use of music in lamentations is plentiful in the bible. This first instance is David's lament over Saul and Jonathan (2 Sam. 1:19-27). Biblical passages also mention mourning (1 Kgs. 13:30; Jer. 48:36), newly composed laments by men and women (2 Chr. 35:25), and the ceasing of music after the destruction of the Temple (Lam. 5:14).[6] Other contexts of music include entertainment for the rich and the kings' courts (2 Sam. 19:36; Amos 6:5; Eccl. 2:8), the inclusion of bells on the tunic of the high priest (Exod. 28:33-34, 39:25-26), and farewell ceremonies (Gen. 31:27). In all these cases, no detail is given of the type of music or the nature of the sound.

Music in the Jerusalem Temple: While the bible gives no indication of music's use in Temple worship or sacrifice, this is discussed in the Rabbinic literature, which knows of instrumental and vocal practices and the use of psalms (see, e.g., M. Ar. 2:3-6). The rabbis' depiction of the use of instruments refers to three categories: percussion, wind, and string.[7] One percussion instrument was used, the *tziltzelim*, a pair of cymbals. A drum was not used, perhaps due to its association with noisy celebrations or, perhaps, with women's activities (e.g., Exod. 15:21 and 1 Sam 18:6-7).[8] Wind instruments included the shofar and *hotzotzerah* (a trumpet) to signal events. The flute was also used, but restricted to the twelve festal days (M. Ar. 2:3). The reed pipe, mentioned at Gen. 4:21, was not used, perhaps due to the plethora of post-biblical references to its use for ritually unclean purposes. String instruments included the *kinnor* and *nevel*, lyre instruments with strings fastened to a frame, most likely originating in Asia Minor.

Levites aged thirty to fifty and young boys, who added "sweetness" (M. Ar. 2:6), sang. The literature discusses their training (M. Hul. 24a), vocal tricks (M. Yom. 3:11), and a responsorial singing style (M. Sot. 5:4, B. Sot. 30b; M. Suk. 3:11, B. Suk. 38b). A minimum and maximum number of instruments is given. The minimum of twelve for a regular weekday included two *nevel*, nine *kinnor*, and one cymbal. This intentionally balanced the minimum of twelve Levitical singers (Ar. 2:3-6). It is unclear if the Levites sang with the instruments or *a cappella*.

M. Tam. 5-7 illustrate music's use within the service. After opening benedictions from the priests, sacrifices were offered. The *magrepha* (a large rake used for clearing the ashes) was thrown forcefully on the ground to summon other priests and Levites into the Temple; ritually unclean members were sent to the eastern gate. Two priests stood by the altar and blew trumpets with the sounds of *teki'ah, teru'ah*, and *teki'ah*. Then the cymbal player sounded the cymbal, and the Levites sang a text from the Psalms. The trumpet blowing was repeated, participants prostrated themselves, and the Levites continued singing. M. Tam. 7:4 lists the daily psalm texts.

The use of psalms in the Temple service is intriguing, since specific psalms' introductory lines—*incipits*—offer clues to their specific use and may even provide evidence for the use of music. *Incipits* may signify a melodic description, direction, or place of use or performance. Melodic descriptions include a particular person or group, e.g., Korah (Ps. 87) and Asaph (Ps. 77); a style of performance in a melodic scale, e.g., "*al ha- she-*

minit" (Pss. 6, 12); or use of an instrument, such as "*nehilot*" (flute; Ps. 5), "*shiggayon*" (Ps. 7), "*gitit*" (Pss. 8 and 81), "*alamot*" (Ps. 46);[9] cue words of a known song, such as "*ayelet ha-shahar*" (the hind of the dawn; Ps. 22) or "*shoshanim*" (roses; Pss. 45, 80). The term "*selah*" appears in the middle of Pss. 46-50. Although this term is variously understood, it possibly indicates a point of pause at which the singing stopped and instruments were played. Three groups of psalms are known for their specific use in Temple worship: the Psalms of Ascent (Pss. 120-134), sung on the steps of the Temple during the festival of Tabernacles (M. Suk. 5:4, B. Suk. 51a-b);[10] the "*hallel*" (Pss. 113-118), recited on the celebration of the new month and the three pilgrimage festivals; and "*halleluyah*" (Pss. 146-150), the final five psalms, seen as the most exalted form of Godly praise, but whose exact use in the Temple service is unclear.

Music in the liturgy: Music's role in Jewish liturgy developed alongside the canonization of the liturgical worship, which, though begun in Second Temple times, occurred primarily after the destruction in 70 C.E., when liturgical recitation replaced sacrifice and the focus of Jewish ritual shifted to the synagogue. The earliest complete compilation of prayer, the *Seder Rav Amram*, dates to the ninth century and includes biblical (particularly psalmodic), Rabbinic, and poetic texts.

Unlike the relatively small amount of poetry, neither the biblical nor Rabbinic passages that comprise the core of Jewish liturgy—e.g., the Shema and the Eighteen Benedictions—make extensive use of meter or rhyme. But other well known portions of the prayer, developed in later centuries in various Jewish communities, have rich traditions of melodic settings. These texts include *Ein Ke'lohenu*, by an unknown author, present in prayer books as early as that of *Amram; Adon Olam*, also by an unknown author and in almost every liturgical rite since the fourteenth century; and *Yigdal*, based on Maimonides thirteen articles of faith, probably composed in the first half of the fourteenth century.

In general, Jewish liturgy is divided into two rites, Ashkenazic and Sephardic, distinguished by small differences in the order of the prayers and the inclusion or exclusion of some psalms and various liturgical poems. But the statutory prayers of the two rites are the same, with only slight differences in wording. The Sephardic rite, a development originally from Spain, influenced the local rites of those European and Middle Eastern communities that received an influx of Spanish Jews after the expulsion from Spain in the sixteenth century.

Prior to the circulation of settings of liturgical texts beginning in the seventh century, the non-statutory sections of the liturgy were improvised, as, presumably, was the melodic recitation. The *hazzan*—cantor—thus created texts spontaneously. Some thus speculate that the term *hazzan* comes from *harzan*—to versify.[11] Only in the geonic period, at the same time that the liturgical text was codified, did the *hazzan* became the religious officiant who led prayers. Thus, the musical expression of the liturgy grew out of liturgical need, function, and aesthetics.

Musical types in the reading of sacred texts: Forms of liturgical music during the first millennia are best viewed topically rather than historically, that is, by examining independently cantillation (the melodic recitation of biblical texts), psalmody (the recitation of psalms or groupings of psalms), and liturgical chant (a broad range of melodic styles for non-biblical portions of the liturgy). These musical contexts encompass the core concerns of liturgical music.

Cantillation: Biblical cantillation occurs whenever the bible is read publicly, on Monday, Thursday, and the Sabbath during morning worship as well as on Sabbath afternoons and holidays. While the melodic recitation of the bible is mentioned in the Talmud (B. Meg. 3a), the actual process of cantillation was first formalized into a system by Aaron b. Moses b. Asher during 900-930 C.E. He lived in Tiberias, and his system of cantillation symbols, *ta'amei ha'miqrah* in Hebrew, is referred to as the "Ben Asher" or "Tiberian" system. These signs, placed above and below the biblical text, provided grammat-

ical indications for proper syntax and sentence division (see Illustration 2). The shapes of the signs indicate grammatical or musical function, visual representation of melodic contour, or the shape of hand signs used to indicate the melody.[12] This later practice is mentioned at B. Ber. 62a, and Rashi comments that, even in his time, the eleventh century, the practice was still used. It remains today in some Yemenite communities.

Sephardic and Ashkenazic communities differ in their melodic interpretation of these signs (Illustration 1 compares a sampling of melodic recitations for Song 1:1-3). Avigdor Herzog defines five regional styles: Yemenite, Ashkenazic, Middle Eastern and North African, Jerusalem Sephardic, and North Mediterranean.[13] Some traditions supply the specific melodic unit for each sign; others use larger melodic units for a phrase. The transcriptions of Song 1:1-3 thus can be divided into two general styles. The first three renditions, from Babylonia, Egypt and Palestine, and Morocco, are narrow in melodic range, within a fifth, and move stepwise; the last two, Spanish and Portuguese and Ashkenazic-Lithuanian, are more expansive melodically, covering a larger range and containing more melodic leaps. The first three also are more regular rhythmically than the latter two, in all exemplifying how some communities applied melodic formulas to the text rather then to each sign.[14] Traditions that apply a melody to each sign, such as the Spanish and Portuguese and Lithuanian, follow the rhythm of the text and are freer metrically. Song 1:1-3 provides an interesting contrast, since Middle Eastern communities typically sing this text in its entirety to usher in the Sabbath. A regular rhythm keeps members of the congregation together during the recitation, facilitating group singing.

Particular circumstances also influence melodic renditions of the Bible. Used in different books, for instance, the same signs yield different melodies.[15] Further, since the signs do not indicate specific pitches, one must rely on their oral interpretations for each book, and specific passages within a book may have unique circumstances that determine melody. For instance, the ten commandments

Illustration 1. Cantillation of *Shir HaShirim* 1:1-3

Illustration 1. Cont.

d) Spanish and Portuguese

Shir — ha - shi - rim — a - sher - lish - lo - mo. — Yi - sha -
ke - ni mi - n' - shi - kot — pi - hu, ki to - vim do - de - ka mi -
ya - yin. L' - rei - ah sh'ma - nei - ka to - vim, she - men tu - rak sh' -
me - ka, al ken — a - la - mot — a - he - vu - - ka.

e) Ashkenazic–Lithuanian (A. W. Binder)

Shir ha - shi - rim — a - sher lish - lo - mo. — Yi - sha - ke - ni mi - n' - shi - kot
pi - hu, ki to - vim — do - de - ka mi - ya - yin. L' - rei - ah sh' - ma - nei - ka to -
vim, — she - men tu - rak — sh' - me - ka, al ken — a - la - mot a - he - vu - ka.

Illustration 2. Biblical Cantillation Signs for *Shir HaShirim* 1:1-3

שִׁיר הַשִּׁירִים אֲשֶׁר לִשְׁלֹמֹה: יִשָּׁקֵנִי מִנְּשִׁיקוֹת פִּיהוּ כִּי

טוֹבִים דֹּדֶיךָ מִיָּיִן: לְרֵיחַ שְׁמָנֶיךָ טוֹבִים שֶׁמֶן תּוּרַק שְׁמֶךָ עַל

כֵּן עֲלָמוֹת אֲהֵבוּךָ:

The Song of Songs, by Solomon. Oh, give me of the kisses of your mouth, for your love is more delightful than wine. Your ointments yield a sweet fragrance, Your name is like finest oil-- therefore do maidens love you.

Illustration 3. Jewish Prayer Modes Used in Shabbat Liturgy

a) HaShem Malak

L'- ku —— n'- ra - n'- na la- do- shem, na - ri - a l'- tsur yish - e - nu...

Ar- ba- im sha nah a- kut — b' - dor, va- o- mar —— am to- ei lei- vav hem, —— v' - hem ——

lo yad'- u d'- ra - kai. A- sher —— nishba- ti v'- a- pi, im y'- vo - un el m'- nu - ha - ti. ——

b) Magen Avot

Sho - ken ad ma- rom v'- ka- dosh sh'- mo. V' - ka - tuv: ra - n'- nu tsa- di- kim ba- do-

shem lay- sha- rim na- vah t' - hi - lah. B'- fi —— y'- sha - rim tit - hal- lal. Uv- di- vrei tsa- di-

kim tit- ba- rak. U- vil- shon ha- si- dim tit - ro- mam. Uv- ke - rev k'- do shim tit - kadash.

Illustration 3. Cont.

c) Ahavah Rabbah

Tsur Yis - ra - el ku - mah b' - ez - rat Yis - ra - el, uf - deh

kin - u - me - ka Y' - hu - dah v' - Yis - ra - el. Go - a - le - nu A - doshem ts' - va - ot sh' - mo,

k' - dosh Yis - ra - el. Ba - ruk a - tah, A - do - shem, ga - al Yis - ra - el.

d) Three Jewish Prayer Modes used in "K'dushah"

Magen Avot on 'E'   HaShem Malak on 'A'   Ahavah Rabbah on 'E'

Magen Avot on 'E'

N' - ka - desh et shim - ka ba - o - lam, k' - shem she - mak - di - shim

o - to bish - mei ma - rom, ka - ka - tuv al yad n' - vi - e - ka, v' - ka - ra

HaShem Malak on 4th scale degree ('A')

zeh el zeh v' - a - mar: Az b' - kol ra - ash ga - dol

a - dir v' - ha - zak mash - mi - im kol,

Ahavah Rabbah on 'E'

mit - nas' - im l' - u - mat s' - ra - fim, l' - u - ma - tam ba - ruk yo - me - ru:

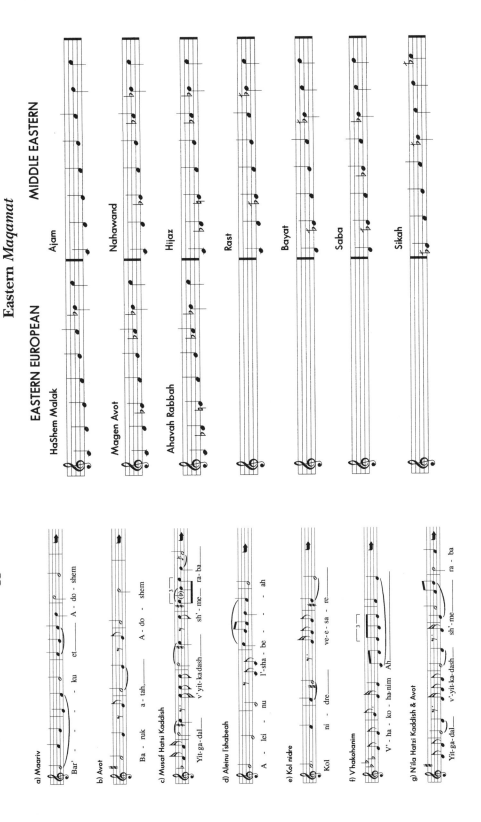

Illustration 5. Eastern European *Nusah* and Middle Eastern *Maqamat*

Illustration 4. *MiSinai Niggunim*

Illustration 6. Sephardic Liturgy *"Nishmat Kol Haï"*

Illustration 6. Cont.

Illustration 6. Cont.

have a special melody, and tragic portions of the book of Esther are highlighted with melodies from the intonation of Lamentations.

Psalmody: Unlike Torah reading, psalm chanting (except for the psalm of the day) is not a required ritual practice. As a result, the rendering of psalms is not always systematic within a community. Used mostly within the introductory part of the liturgy, they are known as "*pesuke dezimrah*" in Ashkenazic liturgy and "*zemirot*" in Sephardic liturgy. In some communities, psalms are recited by each individual, with the leader only indicating the conclusion of each; but other communities recite psalms publicly. In general, Sephardic practices are more systematic, using regular musical formulas, than Ashkenazic ones. Interestingly, the reverse is true with biblical cantillation.

For the psalms, a system of signs with melodic indications is a lost art. Typically, psalm chanting consists only of an introductory phrase, a medial recitation note, and a final phrase.[16] This process of intonation outlines the important structural notes of a mode. An example is the Moroccan recitation of Song 1:1-3 (Illustration 1c), which works similarly to psalm chanting. The ending phrase of each line of text uses the same formula (see the five-note pattern over the words "*lish-lo-mo*," line 1, and "*a-he-vu-ka*," line 3). The melodic contour of each of the three lines of text accommodates the text of each line; the major melodic activity can be seen as a descent from the note "g." The melodic line covering the first sentence (the first ten notes) then is expanded upon and varied in each of the two subsequent lines, just as Illustrations 1a and 1b, from other Middle Eastern communities, make use of a consistent ending formula with medial recitation on a specific note. The musical evolution based on formulaic beginnings and endings thus makes up the melodic process of psalmody.[17]

Liturgical chant: With the development of the liturgy, the *hazzan's* role became formalized, and so did the liturgical chant. During the last quarter of the first millennium, the *hazzan* became the congregational prayer leader, facilitating prayer through musical recitation. Musical developments thus kept

pace with textual innovations, although we know more about the later than the former. In addition, the development of the liturgical poem—*piyyut*—during this period saw a growth in the use of rhyme and meter and of music as a means to express a text.

Liturgical chant combines the musical features of biblical chant and psalmody. The solo chant of the prayer leader alternates between free recitation, based upon melodic cells similar to biblical cantillation, and the formulaic process of continuing melodic evolution, found in psalmody. In the Ashkenazic tradition, liturgical chant gave way to *nusah*, the Jewish prayer mode system, with melodies that mark the liturgical year. Similarly, the Sephardic tradition marks the liturgy with specific melodies, the Middle Eastern tradition, for instance, making use of Arabic modes, the *maqamat*. Within all traditions, solo chant became known as *hazzanut*, the specialized art of the *hazzan*, who intricately combined the careful recitation of the text with various melodic strategies so as to express prayer. This often led to melodic excess that rabbis, even as early as the geonic period, tried to ban. But congregants increasingly desired new aesthetic innovations through which they would experience prayer with a deeper spiritual connection. In later centuries and in various locales, the tension between rabbis and cantors thus grew in tandem with each officiant's desire to control congregants' religious needs and aesthetic desires.

Requirements in Jewish law: Jewish law, codified in the sixteenth century Shulhan Arukh, had much to say about the use of music in prayer, in many aspects continuing concerns known already from the first millennia. After the destruction of the Second Temple, playing musical instruments was forbidden on the Sabbath and festivals (*Orach Hayyim* 338:10; see B. Erub. 104a and B. Sot. 48a). On other days, rabbis only allowed music when connected to a joyous celebration—typically, the example of a wedding is cited—since music created a joyous mood that should be limited to a religious celebration (*Orach Hayyim* 560:3; see also B. Sot. 49a). Comments on melodies are infrequent, yet they do reveal important points: the community's High Holidays melodies should not be changed (*Orach Hayyim* 619:1); priests (*kohanim*) who bless the congregation should always sing the same melody, so that they do not get muddled (*Orach Hayyim* 128:21); extending prayers with a beautiful melody is appropriate to express the pleasantness of the Sabbath (Rema on *Orach Hayyim* 281:1); a prayer leader who uses foreign melodies should be removed (Rema on *Orach Hayyim* 53:25).

The community prayer leader was to be a man, since the voice of a woman could lead to sexually indecent behavior (*Orach Hayyim* 75:3; see also B. Ber. 24a and B. Qid. 70a-70b).[18] He should be modest, acceptable to the public (presumably in his personal demeanor), possess a pleasant voice, and be knowledgeable in reading the Bible (*Orach Hayyim* 53:4; see also B. Ta. 16a). The prayer leader preferably should be an older person who is wise, ethical, and known for doing good deeds (*Orach Hayyim* 53:5; see also Mishneh Torah, *Ahavah, Tefilah* 8:11). In all, the prayer leader's personal characteristics are more important than his voice. Music thus was to be a vehicle toward prayer but not an end in and of itself.

Musical developments (1000-1500): During the first quarter of the second millennium, the Jews' approach to music was more receptive than creative.[19] Evidence for this is the new theoretical understanding of music and developments in poetry. The cultural climate in Spain saw the resurgence of Greek philosophical components, and Jewish philosophers followed their Islamic contemporaries. Thus, the last chapter of Saadiah Gaon's *Book of Faith and Knowledge* deals with the eight rhythmical modes applied to music. Others followed the Greek philosophers' interpretations, focusing on music's place in understanding the cosmos. But even as these theoretical writings placed music on a philosophical level, during the thirteenth century, others stressed music's impact on the soul: "the soul can only be affected by pleasing melodies," wrote Maimonides (*Guide of the Perplexed* 3:45). Thus, music was esteemed as a vehicle to affect one's mood and

to foster a more intense, experiential relationship with God. But intention was emphasized: one should use music for spiritual purposes rather than entertainment. Later, this point was rearticulated and expanded by Kabbalists and Hasidim.

Since there is no extant notated music to divulge stylistic characteristics, texts must serve as evidence. The increased interest in poetry with regular meter and rhyme surely had an impact on music. Much of the influence for new poetry grew out of the rich cultural life in Spain during its Golden Age (1100-1300). Many indications suggest that Hebrew poetry was sung, and, as this poetry proliferated, so too did the music. In 1145, Abraham ibn Ezra wrote that sung poetry should be written in equal metrical units. Presumably the regularity of poetic meter was somehow followed through musical expression. But exactly how is not clear:[20]

> It is evident from examples that a "metrical" tune need not be syllabic: a series of short notes may appear on a long syllable. To judge from present practice, however, the absolute identity of poetic and musical rhythm is relatively rare. More often the tune is given its own rhythms, but even then it will be symmetrical or cyclic, like a metrical scheme.

Jewish communities throughout Europe grew in their use of regular metered tunes, which facilitated group singing and stability of melodies.

The adaptation of music from surrounding cultures began during this period has continued until the present, despite Rabbinic opinions typically prohibiting this borrowing, for fear that engagement with non-Jewish culture would weaken Jewish life. Still, wandering Jewish minstrels played for both Jews and gentiles, suggesting their familiarity with the variety of music of their European locations. Some Jews even desired to sing the love songs of troubadours. Sources indicate that they felt their musical artistry had been lost to the Christians, so that, by absorbing Christian music, Jewish artistry would be appropriately renewed. Others argued that sanctifying unholy melodies through Jewish religious use restores Godliness to the world.

Whichever the explanation, it is important that Jews engaged in musical adaptation to suit their aesthetic tastes, which changed over time and in various geographic locales.

Music in Ashkenazic liturgy (1500-1900): Jews migrated into European steadily during the fourteenth and fifteenth centuries. By the sixteenth century, two sub-groups within Ashkenazic Jewish practice were formed, the *Minhag Ashkenaz*, denoting Western Europe (sometimes known as *Minhag Rinus*, Rhineland) and *Minhag Polin*, in Eastern Europe, particularly denoting Poland. Both trends retained the same prayer chants and cantillation motives, and even as each grew slowly into its own, migrating cantors helped melodies travel between the two regions. Thus, congregations were exposed to an array of musical innovations and renderings of prayer.[21]

With enlightenment and the dawn of modernity, Ashkenazic musical practices began to be codified, and the oral tradition was documented in written form. But the tension between preservation and creation was ongoing. Cantors and community members wanted new tunes, while others, most notably rabbis, wished to preserve older ones. This would, presumably, slow the rate of influence of surrounding non-Jewish musical practices. Cantors were known by name for the musical personalities they brought to the recitation of prayers; in some communities composers too were identifiable. Thus, the diversity of musical practice increased even as musical traditions were firmly established and put into writing.

Musical types in Ashkenazic liturgy—Cantillation: The system of cantillation in the Ashkenazic tradition continued to receive a significant amount of attention by both practitioners and scholars. The exactitude of pronunciation and syntax was carefully maintained. Communities carefully followed the instruction of *Sefer Hasidim* (twelfth century, §302):

The various cantillation chants date back to antiquity. Therefore, you should not read the Torah using the chant intended for Prophets or Writings, or vice versa. Use the appropriate intonation for each section of the *Tanakh*,

because these chants are all laws handed down to Moses on Mt. Sinai, as it says, "God replied with a voice" (Exod. 19:19).

Six different melodic systems of reciting the Bible emerged, with the musical signs codified by Ben Asher interpreted according to the specific book and occasion of use. The six systems distinguish 1) the regular reading of the Pentateuch; 2) High Holiday reading of the Pentateuch; 3) the prophets; 4) the scroll of Esther; 5) the scrolls of Ruth, Song of Songs, and Ecclesiastes; 6) the scroll of Lamentations. The Eastern European tradition became dominant, perpetuated among Ashkenazic Jews in America,[22] while the Central European tradition became the standard practice in London.

Jewish prayer modes: The mainstay of Ashkenazic liturgy is prayer modes, or *nusah*.[23] Prayer modes operate like other musical modes defined by two parameters: scalar definition and a stock of melodies variously applied. The number of modes used in the Jewish tradition is debated,[24] though the generally accepted practice today, part of the pedagogy in American cantorial schools, is the use of three modes, named for the opening words of the liturgical passage in which they first appear in Sabbath liturgy: *HaShem Malak, Magen Avot*, and *Ahavah Rabbah*.[25] Hence, music and text are closely associated. Illustration 3 shows prayer modes and their usage.

The *HaShem Malak* mode is similar intervallically to the western major scale with a lowered seventh (the D-natural in Illustration 3c). In most instances, a prayer mode is defined by its four lowest notes (or tetrachord; note the differences in the lower tetrachords in Illustrations 3b and 3c). The melodic example of "*L'ku n'ran'na*" in Illustration 3a displays the typical pattern of the *HaShem Malak* mode. Like psalmody, the prayer modes consist of an opening, medial, and closing formula. The melodic ascent of the first, third, and fifth notes of the mode (E-G#-B) opens this prayer, and the ending is marked by the fourth, third, and first notes of the mode (A-G#-E; see the last three notes on the first line). The next two lines of Illustration 3a, starting with the text "*Arbaim* shanah," expand the melodic outline of the first line. As the *hazzan* continues the recitation, the *HaShem Malak* mode is developed. An additional feature here is its affective association: the *HaShem Malak* mode is equated with the grandeur of God's strength.

Illustration 3b provides an example of *Magen Avot*. Note the intervallic similarity to the Western minor scale. The textual portion provided in this example comes from the start of the cantor's prayers in the Sabbath morning service. The initial gesture of this mode is characterized by a leap up to the fifth note of the mode (B), followed by a descent emphasizing the three lowest notes (G-F#-E). The typical ending of this mode emphasizes the fourth and final notes of the mode (A and E; see the last two notes of the third line). Different notes are emphasized than in the *HaShem Malak* mode. *Magen Avot* is known as the didactic mode, since it is used for extended declamation of text and does not make use of extensive melodic elaboration.

Often called the most "Jewish" of the Jewish prayer modes, *Ahavah Rabbah* is displayed in Illustration 3c. Its essential feature is the augmented second interval between the second and third notes of the mode (F and G#). There is no western equivalent to this mode, though many have compared it to a similar scale found in Eastern European folk music, and much of the Hassidic musical repertoire makes use of it, as, curiously, does the Jewish standard "*Hava Nagila.*" The liturgical text "*Tsur Yisrael,*" the last portion sung by the cantor prior to the Amida, provides an effective example, Illustration 3c. Note the frequent movement between the second and third scale degree (F and G#), such that the unique augmented second interval is heard. *Ahavah Rabbah* means "great love" and aptly reflects the affective association of this mode, which musically expresses the "great love" for God through a unique musical sound.

Other sections of the cantor's recitation use all three modes, and the differing quality of each expresses the unique subtleties of the text. Illustration 3d, taken from the Sanctification (*K'dushah*), the climatic exaltation in the public repetition of the Amida, displays

this. This portion begins in *Magen Avot* on "E" and continues through the third line. The text states that "We will sanctify Your Name in the world just as they [the angles] sanctify it in the highest heavens;" the didactic mode of *Magen Avot* thus is appropriate. The text continues, "Then, with the sound of great rushing, mighty and strong, they make their voice heard," a fitting context for the *HaShem Malak* mode, which expresses the grandeur of God, conveyed through the might and strength of the heavenly voices. On the last line, the mode changes to *Ahavah Rabbah* on "E" to the words "*mitnas'im l'umat s'rafim,*" which means, "raising themselves up toward the Serafim [angles], those facing them say. . . ." The point at which one is elevated towards the angel, the intimate and expressive mode associated with the great love of God, *Ahavah Rabbah*, is used. This illustrates a typical progression in Ashkenazic liturgical music, demonstrating how the prayer modes aptly express the meaning of the text and provide a symbolic commentary. *Hazzanut* is filled with such intricate details of combined textual and musical meaning.

Liturgical melodies: Liturgical melodies in Ashkenazic practice can be divided into two categories: *MiSinai niggunim*—literally, melodies from Mt. Sinai—and metrical tunes. These two categories contain known melodies that are sung by the cantor, congregation, or both, and are associated with particular liturgical sections at specific times during the year. The *MiSinai niggunim* represent the oldest body of melodies in the Ashkenazic tradition and encompass the recurrent melodies of the High Holidays and pilgrimage festivals. Their name is not literally understood. Many note the similarity to the phrase "*halakhah l'Moshe MiSinai*"— "a law given to Moses at Sinai," which, in Talmudic discourse, denotes a law without a biblical source. Avenary attributes the musical application of the term to A.Z. Idelsohn,[26] who attributes it to a statement in *Sefer Hasidim* (§817). The Maharil (ca. 1365-1427) frequently commented on the preservation of local musical customs (leading to the designation of some melodies as *niggunei Maharil*). Idelsohn himself saw a dual origin to these melodies, oriental and medieval German.[27] No collection or tabulation of all of them exists. Illustration 4 gives the opening phrases of several *MiSinai niggunim* for the High Holidays. Note the distinctive character of each. *MiSinai niggunim* differ from prayer modes in that they comprise set tunes of greater length. But these musical types are similar in that they flexibly apply the melody or melodic fragment to the text. Since there is no exact correspondence between text and melody, interpretations vary.

In addition to the recurring melodic phrases of the *MiSinai niggunim*, the Ashkenazic tradition contains a vast array of metrical tunes, distinct in their use of regular rhythm, which facilitates congregational singing. The German tradition in particular made regular use of metrical tunes. Well known liturgical melodies in this category are: *Yigdal*, a liturgical poem sung at the end of Sabbath morning prayers; *Maoz tzur*, a poem sung on Hanukkah; *Eli tsiyon*, sung on Tisha B'av, which commemorates the destruction of both Jerusalem Temples, at the end of the reading of liturgical poems. All three melodies are in wide circulation and sung by modern day Ashkenazic Jews worldwide.

Performance practice: Ashkenazic liturgical performance practice consists of solo passages sung by the cantor and choral responses or refrains (fig. 97). The cantor's portions frequently comprise a few words or lines at the end of the liturgical text, known as a *hatima*, "seal." Illustration 3 demonstrates this. The congregational response may be a word, such as *Amen*, or a phrase of text, done freely and therefore not notated in musical manuscripts. One particular performance practice is worth noting. During the seventeenth and eighteenth centuries, the aesthetic beauty of music in the synagogue was enriched by having the cantor assisted by two others, the three together known as the *meshorerim*—"singers." One participant was a boy, referred to as the "singer;" the other was a man, known as the "bass." Many musical manuscripts of this period indicate a melodic line to be sung by one of the three participants. Evidence for this practice is also found in plates in prayer books, e.g., the *Leipzig Mahzor*, which show the *hazzan* and assistants.

Changing attitudes toward music: During various periods preceding the Jewish enlightenment of the nineteenth century, communities sought unique musical innovations. Most noteworthy are Italian Jewish composers of the early seventeenth century and Amsterdam composers of the early eighteenth century. Based on an image of music in the ancient Temple, Leon Modena, a rabbi in Ferrara, sought to reestablish artistic beauty in the synagogue. In 1605, he installed up to eight singers for polyphonic singing, a style contemporary for his time. Similar developments appeared thereafter in other cities. The best known composer was Salamone de Rossi (ca. 1570-ca. 1630), whose synagogue compositions *Ha-Shirim Asher li-Shelomo* (Venice, 1622-1623; reprinted: New York, 1953) display his fluency in the High Renaissance musical style. His interweaving of polyphonic musical lines with block chords is similar to that of Giovanni Gabrieli. Rossi was also a noted composer in the court of Mantua. Other Jewish composers of this time in Italy were Davit Civita and Alegre Porto. But not all composers of music for Jewish occasions in Amsterdam were Jewish, e.g., Lidarti and Casceres. Although the musical developments in these communities were short lived and not maintained as a musical tradition, they reflect the desire to engage in artistic music like that of the surroundings. Later generations drew from the outside as a basis for innovation, and the music reached new heights.

Ideological proponents of the Jewish enlightenment, *Haskalah*, sought to integrate the totality of Judaism—philosophy, culture, and religious practice—into the western sphere of knowledge. Opponents favored an inward approach, seeking to solidify traditional Jewish practices with greater intensity. Musical practices, likewise, reflected a desire for incorporating external influence while, at the same time, keeping elements of the tradition, such as the *MiSinai niggunim*. Synagogue compositions of this period thus added Baroque musical interludes to traditional melodies. These musical interludes were excesses and are elaborations of the *meshorerim* practice, with each of the three participants, but most often the singer and bass, given an opportunity for melodic embellishments. At the same time, internal musical manifestations appear in Hasidic communities, which sought spiritual beauty not through elite practices but through an ecstatic experience that elevated the soul. While Hasidic music also drew from the surroundings—from folk tunes and many other sources—artistry was not the goal. Singing in the synagogue, at home, and for other occasions intended to create a deeper commitment to Judaism.

Central European cantorial and synagogue music: The most significant development in Central European cantorial and synagogue music resulted from liturgical and aesthetic changes of the Reform movement. Although changes in various Central European cities began in the late 1700s and early 1800s, Reform did not take shape in an established fashion until the mid-nineteenth century. Israel Jacobson (1768-1829), a merchant by profession, initiated many changes, including elimination of the cantor, use of Protestant hymns with Hebrew words, sermons in German, confirmation for boys and girls, and the reading, not cantillation, of the Bible. With the exception of the elimination of the *hazzan*, most of his changes were incorporated into the Reform service later in the nineteenth century and thereafter. Congregations replaced traditional Jewish music with hymnal singing in the Protestant style and in some cases literally supplied known German Protestant hymns with Hebrew words. Jacobson introduced the first synagogue organ in Seesen in 1810. Short lived there, in 1818 the practice continued in Hamburg, which became an important city for the furtherance of Reform.

Moderate Reform was musically led by Salomon Sulzer (1804-1890), who trained many cantors and whose impact on synagogue music was unprecedented and long lasting. From 1926, he officiated at the New Synagogue in Vienna, elevating the office of cantor with his fine musicianship; his singing was admired by Schubert and Liszt. Sulzer's lasting contribution is his *Shir Zion*, published in two volumes (1840 and 1866; reprinted in three volumes: New York, 1953). The work collects his compositions and others he commissioned. His goal was to "purify" the traditional Jewish melodies, as he felt ornate Baroque musical elaborations inappropriate to the dignity of the service. Demonstrating the changes he made to synagogue music is Sulzer's rendition of the *Mi-Sinai niggun* "*Alenu*." He preferred a straight forward lyrical melodic setting of the text, as can be seen in the symmetrical phrases in the opening melodic line. In addition, he sought to harmonize this melody within the rules of musical art current in his time. This setting thus begins in the key of "D," and the tenor and basses end in that key with the words "*w'gorolenu k'chol hamonom*." It then follows with a choral and cantor section in the key of "Bb." The modulation from "D" to "Bb" exemplifies the third-relationship found in the music of nineteenth century Romantic composers such as Schubert, Liszt, and Mendelssohn. Sulzer wrote out the music for the cantor and choir, with no improvisation or congregational singing possible or desired.

Another significant figure in Central European synagogue music was Louis Lewandowski (1821-1894), who served as a choral director and composer in Berlin at the Old Synagogue in the Heidereutergasse, and, after 1866, at the New Synagogue. His musical compositions appear in two well known publications: *Kol Rinah U'T'fillah* (1871), for one and two voices (reprint: New York, 1953) and *Todah W'simrah* (1876-1882), for four voices and soli, optional organ accompaniment (reprint: New York, 1953). Lewandowski's musical compositions in *Kol Rinah U'T'fillah* contain simple choral responses designed for ease of use with congregations. The *Todah W'simrah* compositions often include organ accompaniment that were doublings of the choral or filled in the solo melodic line. When sung with the accompaniment, this adds a rich texture, but the optional indication displays Lewandowski's recognition that not all congregations would want or be able to afford an organist.

In Lewandowski's *Todah W'simrah* collection is his rendition of the *MiSinai niggun* "*Alenu.*" Like Sulzer, Lewandowski sets the known melody into a regular meter with symmetrical phrasing. In some respects, this setting is simpler rhythmically than Sulzer's. Note that Lewandowski engages the choir in a responsorial manner with the cantor (beginning with the word "*Wanachnu*"). His contributions to synagogue music can be seen as a refinement of Sulzer's efforts. Lewandowski provided settings of traditional melodies and also wrote unique compositions, some based on, some independent of *nusah*. His music had a major impact in both Reform and traditional synagogues throughout Europe and America from the nineteenth century and well into the twentieth.

Central European musical changes were in practice throughout the region: Sulzer in Vienna and Lewandowski in Berlin had the greatest impact. Another significant figure was Samuel Naumbourg (1815-1880), who trained in Munich and served at a congregation in Paris from 1843. While his pieces also are based on traditional material, he, too, incorporated the various musical styles of his surroundings, including Parisian grand opera.

Eastern European cantorial and synagogue music: The Eastern European cantorial style remained traditional in focus, as few Eastern European synagogues incorporated the reforms commonly found in Central Europe, for instance, the use of an organ. Adherence to traditional melodies and the prayer modes thus pervaded the region, even as some cantors came to Vienna to study with Sulzer and incorporated his musical innovations in a style appropriate for Eastern European. Nissan Blumenthal (1805-1903), for instance, was born in the Ukraine and introduced German style music at the Brody synagogue in Odessa. He founded a choir school in 1841 and developed choral singing in four voices, though few of his musical compositions are extant. During the second half of the nineteenth century choral compositions became more common.

Two examples of "*Alenu*" settings demonstrate the innovations of Eastern European synagogue music and its differences from the Central European style. Abraham Baer Birnbaum (1864-1922) was a cantor in Poland, and his setting of "*Alenu,*" in *Amanut Ha Chazanut* (1908, 1912 reprint: New York, 1953) makes more use of the choir throughout, whereas Sulzer and Lewandowski only used it at the end. Birnbaum's settings also do not use symmetrical phrases. Eliezer Gerovich (1844-1913), a student of Nissan Blumenthal, began as a *hazzan* at the Choral Synagogue in Berdichev. After 1887, he was chief cantor in Rostov-on-Don. His setting of "*Alenu,*" in *Shire T'filoh* (1897 reprint: New York, 1953), makes use of an extremely ornate cantorial opening prior to the choir's entrance. Like Birnbaum, he did not use symmetrical phrases; melodic freedom was desired.

The hallmark of the Eastern European style is the use of recurring melodic fragments to convey a deep emotional feeling, ornate musical embellishments that transport the listener into a spiritual realm. Word repetition was not uncommon. The nicely patterned phrases of Central Europe came to be known as *hazzanut ha-seder*, that is, orderly *hazzanut*, in contrast to the free and ornate Eastern European style, known as *hazzanut ha-regesh*, or emotional *hazzanut*. This latter style became the foundation for the Golden Age of the cantorate in America in the first decades of the twentieth century (see below). But these distinct styles were also intermingled in the compositions of cantors immersed in the Eastern European musical world who also studied with men such as Sulzer. Edward Birnbaum (1855-1920), who not only composed but was also an important Jewish musical scholar, is an apt example. Born and trained in Cracow, he later studied with Sulzer for three years. His compositions for his synagogue in Koenigsberg show a balanced style synthesizing Central and Eastern European musical elements.

Paraliturgical musical practices: Musical practices in non-liturgical settings reflect many of the same stylistic influences found in the synagogue. These settings include religious occasions, such as life cycle events (circumcision, bar mitzvah, weddings, and holidays) and meals, when the singing of songs with religious themes (*zemirot*), many of them based on poetic texts from the Golden Age of Spain, was common practice. Many of the *zemirot* in the Ashkenazic tradition use melodies similar to those found in the surrounding communities.

Hasidic communities found a variety of other occasions for singing songs both with and without words. The latter, called *niggunim*, are sung to a variety of syllables, e.g., "Ay, yai, yai," "Bum, bum, bum," and "Tra, la, la." Some even understood specific vocables to have significant meaning. Melodies appear in two or more repeated sections, with the second, or later section, on a higher melodic level than the first. This provides a feeling of ascending toward ecstasy. Melodies appear in the *Ahavah Rabbah* prayer mode or others (see Illustration 3). A *niggun* with a regular rhythm is known as a *stam niggun*, a regular tune, whereas a melody without a regular rhythmic pulse, in a free cantorial style, is called a *devequt niggun*, an ecstatic melody sung at a special occasions to reach a deep spiritual state.

Music in Sephardic liturgy: Due to the diversity of Sephardic liturgical music, its study presents significant difficulties. The problem is compounded when one considers that the Sephardic practices are still maintained orally, and only a limited amount of the repertoire has been notated and collected. In addition, Sephardic liturgical music has not received the same amount of study as Ashkenazic, and, hence, the research to draw upon is limited.

One other point deserves mention. The term "Sephardic" has been variously understood in Judaic studies. The word "*Sepharad*" appears at Obad. 1:20 and is thought to refer to the Iberian Peninsula. The term Sephardic refers to Spanish Jews and their descendants in various points of relocation. Use of the term becomes problematic when these Spanish descendants relocated to other existing communities. In some cases the Spanish Jewish traditions replaced existing practices as, over time, these immigrant Jews mixed with the local Jewish culture. Here we use "Sephardic" primarily to mean "non-Ashkenazic," recognizing that it is illegitimate to treat Sephardic Jewry as a single community that has remained unchanged over time.

Influences of Arabic music and poetry: In medieval Spain, Arabic culture richly influenced Judaism. Especially in the period known as the Golden Age of Spain (eleventh-thirteenth centuries), Jewish culture flourished in unprecedented ways, with every dimension of Jewish religious and cultural life drawing from a free interaction between Jew and non-Jew.

Most notably, in this period, theoretical writing on the nature of music permanently influenced the way music was viewed. Islamic scholars followed the ancient Greeks in examining musical phenomena through acoustics and other abstract principles. In *Emunot ve-De'ot* (933), Saadiah Gaon discussed the way in which eight types of musical rhythm affect the human temper and mood. Similar ideas appear in the works of Arabic writers on music, such as Al-Kindi (d. ca. 874). Other Jewish writers applied Saadiah's ideas to musical-moral phenomena and biblical events, such as David's harp playing for Saul. Hence, the Arabic discussion of music was fused with Jewish concepts.

The creation of liturgical poetry, *piyyutim*, significantly affected music. As Arabic poetry increased in prominence through new rhyme schemes and a consistent use of meter, so Hebrew poetry was influenced through the work of Dunsah Labrat (tenth century) and others. With the expulsion of 1492, descendants of this rich tradition took these poetic methods with them. One significant figure was Israel Najara (1550-1620), who created new Jewish songs by replacing Turkish, Arabic, Spanish, and Greek words with Hebrew ones. In this process, some of the sounds or assonance of the text were incorporated into his Hebrew poetry, and often the melody was adapted to fit this new text. Thus, Sephardic music, both past and present, is defined by adaptation.

Musical influences and major regional styles: Sephardic liturgical music falls under four major regional styles: Spanish and Portuguese, Moroccan, *Edot hamizrah* (Middle

Eastern or Arabic), and Yemenite.[28] The first two styles include the liturgy of Jews from Spain and Morocco, whose descendants traveled to Western Europe, England, and Amsterdam, as well as the Americas, both North and South, and developed a more westernized tradition. These descendants from Spain, like the others discussed below, took their tradition to these new locations and then adapted. Moroccan Jewry received a large number of Spanish Jewish refugees during the fifteenth and sixteenth centuries, and Jewish musical traditions from Morocco have been continually influenced by local Spanish traditions, such as Andalusian. The two other musical styles, *Edot hamizrah* and Yemenite, are influenced by Arabic music. Spanish elements within these traditions are faint or nonexistent. The *Edot hamizrah* include the Jews of the Levant (Syrian, Lebanon, Iraq, Iran, Egypt, and other neighboring locales). The Arabic modal system, known as *maqamat*, is deeply incorporated into their liturgical and paraliturgical practices. The Yemenite tradition also makes use of Arabic practices. Other traditions, such as Turkish, combine some of these styles. The geographical location between Morocco and the Middle East also affected Turkish Jewish music, which contains Spanish and Arabic elements. Other Jewish traditions, such as Bukharan and Ethiopian, are in their early stages of study.[29]

The three musical types already discussed for Ashkenazic liturgy likewise apply to Sephardic liturgy, with different factors generating the rendering within each community.

Cantillation: Sephardic communities differ in their use of cantillation. As discussed above, most *Edot hamizrah* and Yemenite renderings of sacred texts follow the formulaic features of psalmody, though this may differ for communities that adhere to a specific melody for each of the cantillation signs. *Edot hamizrah* renderings, found in Illustrations 1a-c, represent a more normative practice for texts other than the Torah. The books of the prophets and each of the various writings may have different melodic formulas. The main cantillation signs that receive emphasis are: "*pasek*" (end of biblical sentence); "*atnah*" (mid-sentence pause); and "*katon*"[30]

(end of a smaller grammatical clause). Therefore, the renderings found in Illustrations 1a-c for the Song of Songs illustrate a process used in other books. The Spanish and Portuguese tradition differs in using a specific melody for each cantillation sign (Illustration 1d).

Chanting of prayer: Sephardic traditions lack the equivalent of Ashkenazic prayer modes or *nusah*. Rather, prayers are chanted to known melodies or improvised. In the Spanish and Portuguese tradition, however, chanting patterns exist for the portions in which the *hazzan* prays individually. Interestingly, the chanting pattern for the Amida in the Spanish and Portuguese tradition is similar to the Moroccan. Many of the *Edot hamizrah* communities adhere to the Arabic modal system in some manner. Some of these modes include notes one-quarter in distance, which is unlike Western scales, in which one-half is the smallest interval (see Illustration 5 with quarter tones in the following maqamat: Rast, Bayat, Saba, Sikah).

The Syrian Aleppo tradition provides a useful example. In the eighteenth century, and most likely earlier, Aleppo cantors developed a system of associating the weekly biblical reading with a *maqam* (singular for Arabic mode). Sad events in the biblical reading, such as the death of Sara the matriarch or the building of the Golden Calf, were associated with a *maqam* with a sad affect. Other associations exist for happy readings. This *maqam* does not affect the biblical reading, which always follows the same *maqam*, but only the cantor's rendering of the first portion of the Sabbath morning prayer, which is made to evoke the feeling of the Torah reading for the day, e.g., happy or sad. Some liturgical pieces are sung with known melodies in the *maqam* of the day; others are improvised melodically. This practice is kept alive by Syrian cantors throughout the world,[31] and Jewish traditions deriving from the Ottoman Empire follow a similar practice. These include liturgical traditions in Turkey, Iraq, and other neighboring regions.

Liturgical melodies: Illustration 6 provides renditions of three Sephardic traditions. The text "*Nishmat Kol Hai*" ("The soul of every living thing . . .") begins the cantor's prayers on Sabbath morning. In this example, the Spanish and Portuguese rendition appears on the first line of each system throughout, the Turkish is on the second, and the Syrian on the third. The Spanish and Portuguese rendition and the Syrian are the most distinct. The former possesses a consistent rhythm and is not melodically ornate. The latter is freer rhythmically, indicated in the transcription with no meter, with more notes per word. The Turkish rendition falls stylistically between the other two, with a consistent rhythm and some slight embellishments throughout. All three renditions are similar in that they repeat musical phrases, but distinct when the musical material is repeated. The Spanish and Portuguese rendition begins with a repeated "Gb" followed by a descent; this same phrase begins with slight modifications over the words "*v'ruah.*" The Turkish rendition begins on a "G," descends stepwise quickly to "E," and then leaps up to a "B." This melody repeats with the word "*t'faer.*" The Syrian rendition begins on a "G" with a dotted quarter note. This melody repeats with the word "*Adoshem.*" Thus, each community renders this, or any, liturgical text differently, expressing distinct nuances of the text.

Sephardic liturgical music regularly focuses on congregational participation but differs in where in the liturgy this occurs. In Illustration 6, only the Spanish and Portuguese tradition has *Nishmat Kol Hai* sung congregationally. The Syrian and Turkish assign this text to the cantor alone. The Spanish and Portuguese rendition facilitated group singing through a regular rhythm and more simple stepwise musical line. In the Syrian and even the Moroccan tradition, the *hazzan* begins with a known melody and then improvises. While group singing appears in all traditions, different parts of the liturgy are emphasized. The *Qaddish* and *Qedusha* are emphasized by congregational singing, but the highlighting of liturgical passages between these phrases differs by community. Choral singing only appears in the Sephardic traditions influenced by Western music in European locales. This is evident in the Spanish and Portuguese tradition, which has a rich heritage of many nineteenth and twentieth century liturgical choral compositions.[32] Choral singing is not practiced in Moroccan, *Edot hamizrah*, and Yemenite traditions.

Liturgical performance: The practice of lively congregational singing describes Sephardic liturgy. While many portions are recited by the *hazzan*, as required by Jewish law, congregational participation is enthusiastic and joyful. Unlike the Ashkenazic practice, in which the cantor intones the last two to three lines of a liturgical text, Sephardic *hazzanim* recite the entire liturgical text out loud. Congregants may join in the recitation, which some do in an undertone. The uniqueness of the Sephardic tradition is not only displayed by the melodies used but also by the liturgical performance practice itself, which combines active and passive participation.

Music in paraliturgical contexts: Many liturgical melodies are adaptations of melodies used elsewhere within each tradition, most often adapted from *piyyutim*. The venerable tradition of Israel ben Moses Najara (1555-1625?), author of hundreds of poems and table hymns, thus is kept alive in Yemenite, Moroccan, Turkish, and Syrian communities up to the present. In many instances, following Najara's practice, liturgical melodies were taken from non-Jewish songs that became so popular that they appear in a variety of secular and religious contexts. Distinctions between sacred and secular thus are often arbitrary, as many melodies are used in both settings.[33]

The main context for singing *piyyutim* is the celebration of a holiday or life cycle event. Specific texts are associated with particular holidays and are sung in the synagogue or at home during meals, especially on paraliturgical occasions, events designated for religious enrichment but not mandated or required. One occasion is the *bakkashot*, or *nuba*, in the Moroccan tradition, practiced in some Syrian and Moroccan communities. Participants go to the synagogue at midnight or early in the morning before sunrise and sing supplications. This is intended to elevate the spirit prior to the formal morning prayers.

The *piyyutim*, like the liturgy, draw from

biblical, Rabbinic, and mystical texts, in many instances expressing or amplifying an idea from the midrash. This rich body of poetry follows the model of the Golden Age of Spain, when poets took rhyme schemes and meter from surrounding poetry. Often, a popular non-Jewish song provided inspiration.

Judeo-Spanish songs: A venerable tradition of Spanish Jews is Ladino culture. Its written and spoken dialect, Ladino, represents more than a language, illustrating the synthesis of Jewish and Spanish culture. The rich tradition of this cultural connection from the Golden Age has continued, with the amount preserved versus new influence varying among Sephardic Jews over the past five hundred years. Thus, for Jews in Morocco, Spanish influence has been ongoing, whereas Jews in Turkey and Greece have had more Middle Eastern influence. Some historians hold that the venerable musical forms of these Sephardic Jews, the *ballad* and *romancero*, are time honored traditions, faithfully transmitted and untouched by new cultural influence. Modern scholars, however, have been unable to validate this claim.[34] In all events, Ladino music has deep roots, and, as with other forms of Jewish music, a unique musical tradition is both perpetuated and revitalized by modern performers.

Judeo-Spanish music has long been conserved by women. Many of the texts of the *romancero* and *ballad* deal with women's experiences in life cycle events, are passionate or erotic poetry, or present epic tales or stories. Dirges related to the deaths of individuals in untimely and other circumstances are known as *endechas*. The *coplas*, short holiday songs, also complement the Judeo-Spanish musical repertoire. Marriage has been a particularly rich source of music for Sephardic women. The preparation of the bride for the ritual bath prior to the wedding, a bride's dowry, and her relationship with her mother-in-law are subjects of Judeo-Spanish wedding songs.

Musicologist Israel Katz, who has devoted his scholarly efforts to understanding present manifestations of Judeo-Spanish songs, distinguishes between two musical types of *ballad*. The Western Mediterranean, or Moroccan, Judeo-Spanish singing style includes regular phrases and rhythms with few embellishments. Many performers of Judeo-Spanish music within this style incorporate Spanish and Moorish musical styles. The Eastern Mediterranean, or Turkish and Balkan, Judeo-Spanish singing style, by contrast, includes more melodic embellishments in a freer and, often, less regular rhythm. Over time these two styles have merged. Katz postulates that a third grouping may exist if one includes the *ballad* style of Greece.[35]

Ashkenazic and Sephardic liturgical musical traditions: Although once the focus of musicological studies—like Idelsohn's major work *Jewish Music in Its Historical Development* (New York, 1929)—comparative analysis, which is fraught with difficulties, is no longer the goal of research. Rather, scholars seek to explore the details and complexities of a single tradition in order as fully as possible to understand its nuances. One problem with comparison is that, while similar practices appear across cultural settings—for example, both Syrian and Eastern European Jews sing the *Qaddish* during Sabbath morning prayers—significant independent cultural factors may govern the actual use of music in a particular portion of the liturgy.[36] The following discussion of the similarities of and differences between Ashkenazic and Sephardic liturgy thus intends only to help define each tradition, not to claim that both traditions originated from the same source.

An interesting similarity is the parallel between the Ashkenazic and Sephardic Western and Eastern traditions. The Central European Ashkenazic tradition involves the congregation through singing, making use of many liturgical melodies and presenting the service in a formal manner with limited melodic improvisation. The same is true of the Spanish and Portuguese tradition that represents the Western Sephardic practice. The Ashkenazic Eastern European tradition, in contrast, makes use of solo singing by the cantor, melodic improvisation during prayers, and less congregational singing and metrical melodies. So too the *Edot hamizrah* traditions make use of the same musical liturgical principles. In each of Ashkenazic and Sephardic corresponding traditions, Western or Eastern, while the principles are similar, the aesthetic vehicle differs. Hybrid traditions exist both in Ashkenazic and Sephardic practices. For example, some Eastern European cantors who lived close to Western European cities combined both Central and Eastern European practices. So too with Sephardic practices, such as the Moroccan tradition that combines both Spanish and Portuguese musical stylistic features and those of the *Edot hamizrah*.

An important feature of Ashkenazic and Sephardic practice is the use of modes. One way to illustrate the similarities is to compare the Eastern European *nusah* and the Middle Eastern use of *maqamat*, as in Illustration 5. The scalar content of the Eastern European *nusah* even has parallels with some of the Middle Eastern *maqamat*. For instance, the Eastern European *HaShem Malak* is similar to the Middle Eastern *maqam Ajam*; the only exception is that the seventh degree of the scale in the former is lowered, which is not the case in *Ajam*. Other similarities can be seen between *Magen Avot* and *Nahawand* as well as between *Ahavah Rabbah* and *Hijaz*. The remaining Middle Eastern *maqamat* shown in Illustration 5 have no European parallels, since these *maqamat* make use of quarter flats, a note between "Eb" and "E" for example, which do not exist in the Western scale.

While these similarities have been noted by many scholars[37] and are interesting, they ignore function, which is crucial, since different usages may alter the surface features of similar scalar construction. For example, in the Syrian liturgical tradition, the entire morning service (*shaharit*) uses the same *maqam* from "*Nishmat kol hai*" through the *Qaddish*, and *Amidah*. In the Eastern European tradition, by contrast, during the equivalent portion of the morning service, the cantor makes use of all three of the prayer modes. In this approach, the same mode is used from week to week for the same prayer; while the amount of improvisation varies, the mode remains the same. But in the Middle Eastern tradition, the mode changes from week to week, in line, as we have seen, with

the mood of the Torah reading. Overall, then, the mode in the Eastern European tradition matches the mood of the particular text. But in the Middle Eastern tradition, the mood of the *maqam* is imposed upon the text, so as to create a desired affect throughout the prayers, not just on each isolated liturgical section. Mode and *maqam*, even though they sometimes sound similar, thus function quite differently.

Similarities also exist in Ashkenazic and Sephardic paraliturgical usages. The Ashkenazic Hassidic *niggun* elevates participant's level of *devequt*, adhesion to God. Music, that is, lifts one's spirit. Likewise *bakkashot* among Moroccan and Syrian Jews function as ecstatic singing. While the same end is achieved in each context, cultural differences determine the specific format and content of the ritual.

Differences: Ashkenazic and Sephardic music grew out of distinctive cultural traditions that determined musical aesthetics as well as repertoire. An interesting way to illustrate differences between and within the traditions is to consider the role of the *hazzan* and the nature of the service. In the respective western traditions—Central European in the Ashkenazic, and Spanish and Portuguese in the Sephardic—metrical melodies, formality, and a concern for dignity motivate the cantor. Yet these Western traditions differ in that innovation of new melodies or new renditions based on traditional melodies was allowed only within the Central European Ashkenazic tradition. But the Spanish and Portuguese tradition limited change, preferring the same melodies and very little innovation of new melodies in the liturgical cycle.

Moreover, in contrast to both these Western practices stands the modal improvisation of the Eastern European and *Edot hamizrah* traditions. The elaborate manner in which modal music, either a Jewish prayer mode or a *maqam*, is intertwined with the reciting of the text provides for unique artistry. Melodic improvisation that follows rules within each tradition leads to a spontaneous experience of prayer. Even so, where an *Edot hamizrah* cantor encourages the congregation to participate with certain melodies throughout the service, Eastern European cantors limit the congregation to an accompanying role by humming chord tones at key phrase changes. In the late nineteenth and early twentieth century, choral writing is found in larger Eastern European synagogues. In general, Ashkenazic liturgical music focuses on the end product, based on style, taste, and quality of the music. Sephardic liturgical music differs through the encouragement of congregational participation and the end goal of singing to express prayer, so that experiencing the moment may override the need for "high" art music.

The portions of the liturgical text emphasized musically also differ. In morning worship in Eastern European tradition, the cantor begins at *Shokhen ad* and continues with three separate texts: *Befi yehsarim, Shechen hovat*, and *barukh atah . . . melekh gadol betishbahot*. In the *Edot hamizrah* tradition, by contrast, the *hazzan* begins with *Nishmat kol hai* and continues with *Shav'at aniyim* and *Kel hahodaot*. The traditions also differ in their conceptions of liturgical music. Central and Eastern European traditions, unlike the Sephardic, use the category of *MiSinai niggunim*. Still, Sephardic communities have melodies considered very old that do not change from year to year, in particular those used on the High Holidays.

Music in modern synagogue life: American synagogue music has undergone distinct changes in the last century, so as both to continue the European legacy and to react to influences from American culture. Although the seventeenth century settlers in America were Sephardic, their influence was overshadowed by European immigration in the nineteenth century. German Jews were the first to arrive after 1820, but the mass migration of Eastern European Jews beginning in 1880 ultimately dominated American Judaism. This immigrant period, 1880-1930, became known as the Golden Age of the Cantorate. The cantors associated with it, born and trained in Eastern Europe before coming to America, either had regular pulpits for the entire year or were engaged only for the High Holidays, often commanding large salaries.

Radio broadcasts, 78 rpm recordings, and concerts proliferated this musical artistry. The recordings provide a lasting record, freezing the sound of the Golden Age for future generations. Great cantors include Yossele Rosenblatt (1882-1933), Leib Glantz (1898-1964), Mordecai Hershman (1888-1940), Leibele Waldman (1907-1969), Pierre Pinchik (1900-1971), Moshe Koussevitzky (1899-1966), and his brother David (1891-1985). So admired were these cantors that people came from long distances to hear them sing at concerts and services. Pierre Pinchik's "*Elokai N'Shamah*," illustrates some of the characteristics of their music. Growing out of the Eastern European nineteenth century tradition, Pinchik's chanting of this portion of the morning liturgy uses a slowly unfolding melody that begins with a narrow range and expands. The word repetition, "*n'shamah, n'shamah shenatata bi*," helps elongate the musical phrase and maintain a plaintive feeling. The *Magen Avot* mode and *HaShem Malak* mode are used. The long musical phrases make use of ascending and descending ornamental figures indicative of artistic vocal embellishments. The Golden Age of the Cantorate thus briefly fused vocal artistry and impassioned prayer in a distinctive style that has become the definitive form of *hazzanut*.

The Reform movement that began in Central Europe quickly spread in America, with the music of Sulzer and Lewandowski soon making its way across the ocean. By the second quarter of the twentieth century, composers sought additionally to innovate the music of the synagogue to the musical style of the twentieth century. Men such as Abraham Binder (1895-1966), Isadore Freed (1900-1960), and Lazare Weiner (1897-1982) took traditional European tunes and reworked them in accordance with Jewish prayer modes, thus producing harmonies not typically found in Western music. Binder and Freed were motivated by the same desires as Sulzer and Lewandowski in the nineteenth century, to develop known melodies for cantor, choir, and organ in a dignified and tasteful manner according to the music of the surrounding culture.

Ernest Bloch (1880-1959), a well known American composer, premiered his *Avodath ha-Kodesh* (Sacred Service) in 1933 for cantor, choir, orchestra, and narrator. The great acclaim elevated this work of Jewish liturgy to the status of an oratorio. Towards the middle of the twentieth century, two composers, Max Helfman (1901-1963) and Max Janowski (1912-1991), wrote compositions that have become standards for the High Holidays, Helfman's "*Sh'ma Koleinu*" and Janwoski's "*Avinu Malkeinu*." During the second half of the twentieth century, musical tastes have preferred more accessible music. Composers such as Michael Isaacson draw from a variety of musical styles, both classical and contemporary, for synagogue compositions. He and others also use folk, popular, and Israeli songs. To provide interest and variety, cantors in Reform synagogues today sing diverse musical compositions from the past 150 years.

The denominations within American Judaism, Reform through Orthodox, deal with similar concerns with respect to music in the synagogue. One issue is the role of the cantor as prayer facilitator and the place of congregational involvement, an issue that is inherent in the combining in varying practices of American congregations of the rhythmically precise Central European and the rhythmically free Eastern European traditions. Indeed, where Reform synagogues were once the source of artistic innovations, this trend now has diminished in favor of participatory services. Thus, while trained cantors and many congregants still desire to utilize music that draws from the rich musical history of the Jewish tradition, others prefer more accessible music that facilitates their participation. Music thus may draw from the Jewish tradition, including Hasidic and Israeli melodies; but folk and popular styles predominate.

The use of music in Conservative synagogues is comparable to the Reform. Even as traditional melodies are more commonly heard in Conservative synagogues, the *ha-vurah* movement that began in the 1970s created a trend of empowering the laity to participate in and shape services. The end result has been an increase in congregational involvement and a cantor who often functions primarily as educator and facilitator of congregational participation. But, particularly on the High Holidays and at special events, the rich legacy of liturgical music is still heard, combining the artistry of cantorial recitatives taken from or inspired by the Golden Age of the Cantorate, compositions based on the traditional prayer modes, and liturgical chants, sometimes with volunteer or professional choirs.

Within Orthodox synagogues, music generally serves a more functional purpose. A professional cantor is rarer here than in Reform and Conservative congregations, and the role of prayer leader (*baal tefilah*) is just that, with vocal embellishments kept to a minimum and congregational involvement primary. As in the other movements, traditional melodies are more commonly heard on the High Holidays, the only time when, in many Orthodox synagogues, a cantor may be employed. Orthodox congregations differ in their use of *nusah*. Some prefer Israeli melodies or tunes from songs popular in the community. While some are critical of the lack of artistry seen in this popular influence on liturgical music,[38] others embrace it as a way to encourage synagogue attendance. In all events, we see here the continuation of the trend that has long been a part of Jewish synagogue music's history.

Prior to the contemporary formation of cantorial programs in rabbinical seminaries, individuals learned *hazzanut* through apprenticeship and life experience, including singing in synagogue choirs. But after World War II, several programs developed to train cantors. The first, in 1948, was the Reforms movement's School of Sacred Music at the Hebrew Union College—Jewish Institute of Religion in New York. The Conservative movement's Jewish Theological Seminary of America opened its Cantors Institute in 1952, and, in 1964, the Cantorial Training Institute at Yeshiva University began preparing cantors to serve Orthodox synagogues.

Music outside the synagogue: The proliferation of popular Jewish music is a recent phenomenon worth noting. It is estimated that close to four thousand recordings of Jewish music have been made over the last twenty-five years. This can be attributed both to the American born Jewish baby boom population, which wants its own form of Jewish music to express its Jewish cultural and religious roots and to the now low cost of recording technology and cheap and easy production and distribution of cassette recordings and CDs. Many see Shlomo Carelbach as the father of popular Jewish music. He combined simple folk and popular music with traditional Jewish elements, such as a Hassidic style of participation in songs with consistent and driving rhythms. Perhaps most influential were his concerts, in which he shared stories and life experiences to reinforce Jewish identity. Other performers serve different segments of the community. Mordechai Ben David and Avraham Fried perform for Orthodox audiences throughout the world; Debbie Friedman performs for Reform and Conservative audiences; and hundreds of other artists use music to deepen commitment to Judaism.

Popular Jewish music is a unique art form. Traditional Hebrew texts are used in addition to English. The English songs are particularly unique, in that their texts discuss religious issues, often presenting a message concerning the modern religious experience. The popularity of the involved artists is growing steadily and has produced a small industry of producers and distributors.[39]

Other contexts: Traditional European forms of Jewish music from contexts outside the synagogue have been perpetuated throughout the twentieth century and illustrate the endurance of certain musical genres. *Klezmer* is the instrumental tradition of Eastern European Jewry, often heard today on joyous occasions. This music reflects a musical process or context rather than a genre; there is no particular form or style of music known as *klezmer*. Certain genres, though, are illustrative of the syncretized, or adaptable, musical process, for example, the *doina*, which grows out of the Eastern European tra-

dition of solo instrumental music. Throughout the region, this is known under different names. The *doina* played by Jewish musicians is taken both from the Romanian *doina* and the musical sounds of a *hazzan*. A *doina* slowly unfolds, followed by rapid undulations. This is very similar to the musical components of *hazzanut* from the Golden Age of the Cantorate. Like other *klezmer* selections, the prayer modes link this repertoire with the music heard in the synagogue.

A remarkable feature of *klezmer* is its ability to absorb a variety of influences and remain viable as a unique entity. Both in Europe and America, *klezmorim* played at both Jewish and non-Jewish events, indicating that these Jewish musicians were well aware of, and participated in, the music of their surroundings. Once in America, jazz and other influences also were reflected in *klezmer*. Interest in *klezmer*, recorded on 78s and heard on radio broadcasts, waned in the 1940s, but the past two decades have seen a re-vitalization of this music in America and abroad.[40] A new generation of Jewish musicians has discovered the musical roots of its heritage and sought to perpetuate it in traditional and more innovative forms. Leading groups that draw from this tradition and innovate new compositions are Kapelye, The Andy Statmun Quartet, Klezmer Conservatory Band, Brave Old World, and the Klezmatics.

Yiddish and Ladino songs also are perpetuated in the present. Many popular Yiddish songs were composed for the Yiddish theater, founded by Abraham Goldfaden (1840-1908). Yiddish and Ladino songs also continue to be sung for entertainment and in casual contexts, such as lullabies. Interestingly, like *klezmer*, their musical language draws from similar phrases heard in the synagogue, the music is based on the Jewish Prayer modes.

Other examples include a wide variety of folk and art contexts. Religious and secular summer camps and programs throughout the year make use of a wide variety of music to educate children and teenagers in Jewish concepts and religious practices. For nearly sixty years, further, new music has been composed in Israel, including children's songs, popular music, and folk songs with Zionist themes. Folk singer Naomi Shemer's "*Al Kol Eleh*" (For All These Things) and "*Yerushalayim shel Zahav*" (Jerusalem of Gold) have heightened the feeling of solidarity in the country and captured the enduring importance of Israel as the home of the Jewish people. The synthesis of traditional Jewish musical styles and forms in both sacred and secular contexts, combined with a contemporary classical idiom, has been the goal of several noted composers in Israel. The most significant was Paul Ben-Haim (1897-1984), who drew from a wide variety of Jewish and non-Jewish musical styles.

Many have argued the nature of the "Jewish" elements in Israeli music, questioning whether Israeli music is a national form or a Jewish one. The same debate encompasses American composers of note, such as Leonard Bernstein (1918-1990), whose "Jeremiah" (1942) and "Kaddish" (1963) symphonies make use of Jewish themes but also seek acceptance in the broader world of Western music. Many art music composers and popular song writers thus continue in the historical tradition of Jewish musicians, composing music that draws from the Jewish past but that, attentive to current forms as well, inspires a present generation to perpetuate Judaism.

Bibliography

Gradenwitz, Peter, *The Music of Israel* (New York, 1949; rev., 1978).

Idelsohn, Abraham Z., *Jewish Music in its Historical Development* (New York, 1929).

Nulman, Macy, *Concise Encyclopedia of Jewish Music* (New York, 1975).

Shiloah, Amnon, *Jewish Musical Traditions* (Detroit, 1992).

Werner, Eric, *The Sacred Bridge: The Interdependence of Liturgy and Music in Synagogue and Church during the First Millennium* (New York, 1959-1984).

Sources for Musical Illustrations

1. Cantillation of *Shir HaShirim* 1:1-3
   a. Babylonia: Idelsohn HOM, vol. 2, p. 54.
   b. Egypt and Palestine: Idelsohn HOM, vol. 2, pp. 54-55.
   c. Morocco: Idelsohn HOM, vol. 5, p. 41.
   d. Spanish and Portuguese, Abraham Lopes

Cardozo, *Selected Sephardic Chants* (New York, 1991), pp. 18-19.
   e. Ashkenazic-Lithuanina (A.W. Binder): from A.W. Binder, *Biblical Chant* (New York, 1959).
2. Biblical Cantillation Signs.
3. Jewish Prayer Modes Used in Shabbat Liturgy: Idelsohn HOM, vol. 8, pp. 8, 16, 18, 19.
4. MiSinai Niggunim: Hanoch Avenary, "Music," in *Encyclopedia Judaica*, vol. 12, cols. 151-152.
5. Eastern European *Nusah* and Middle Eastern *Maqamat*
6. Sephardic Liturgy "*Nishmat Kol Hai*"
   a. Spanish and Portuguese: Transcription of recording, *Shearith Israel Choir: Music of Congregation Shearith Israel*, "Songs of the Sabbath," vol. 2, side A, band 8; transcription by Mark Kligman.
   b. Turkey: Cantor Isaac Behar, *Sephardic Sabbath Chants* (Cedarhurst, 1992), p. 72.
   c. Syria: Cantor Isaac Cabasso, Sephardic Archives, Brooklyn NY; transcription by Mark Kligman.

Notes

[1] The earliest are the notations of a twelfth-century cleric, Obadiah, found in the Cairo Genizah. See Israel Adler, "The Notated Synagogue Chants of the 12th Century of Obadiah, the Norman Proselyte," in Eric Werner, ed., *Contributions to a Historical Study of Jewish Music* (New York, 1976). These have been recorded as *Chants Mystiques: Hidden Treasures of a Living Tradition* (PolyGram Special Markets, 1995). Biblical cantillation was first notated melodically by Johannes Reuchlin, *De accentibus et orthographia linguae hebraicae* (Haguenau, 1518). See Hanoch Avenary, *The Ashkenazic Tradition of Biblical Chant Between 1500 and 1900* (Tel Aviv, 1978).

[2] For a useful guide to this collection, see Eliyahu Schleifer, "Idelsohn's Scholarly and Literary Publications: An Annotated Bibliography," in *Yuval* vol. 5, *The Abraham Zvi Idelsohn Memorial Volume* (1986), pp. 63-92.

[3] This refers to Sephardic Jews of the Levant who immigrated to Israel during the late nineteenth and early twentieth centuries. In Israel, they developed a unified and identifiable musical and liturgical tradition rather than differentiating themselves by country of origin.

[4] The National Sound Archives of the Jewish National University Library in Jerusalem claims as of 1996 to hold 6,500 reels, 1,000 cassettes, 400 discs, and 12,730 records and other forms of recordings.

[5] Abraham Z. Idelsohn, *Jewish Music in its Historical Development* (New York, 1929), pp. 35-71.

[6] Singing and instrument playing at funerals is discussed at M. Shab. 23:4, M. B.M. 6:1, M. Ket. 4:4, and M. M.Q. 3:8.

[7] See Bathja Bayer, "Music, History, Biblical

Period," in *Encyclopedia Judaica*, vol. 12, cols. 559-566, and Eric Werner, "Jewish Music," in *The New Grove Dictionary of Music and Musicians* (New York, 1980), pp. 618-620.

[8] Werner, ibid., p. 619.

[9] The words *"shiggayon," "gitit,"* and *"alamot"* are often left untranslated, since their exact meaning is uncertain.

[10] Alternatively, these psalms were composed on the return from Babylon to Jerusalem or on the pilgrimage up to Mt. Zion on the three festivals.

[11] Macy Nulman, *Concise Encyclopedia of Jewish Music* (New York, 1975), p. 102. But note that the term once referred to a teacher of children (M. Shab. 1:3), superintendent of prayer (M. Yom. 7:1, M. Sot. 7:8), or one who announced the order of the proceedings (Y. Ber. 4:7, 9d).

[12] Hanoch Avenary, *Studies in the Hebrew, Syrian and Greek Liturgical Recitative* (Jerusalem, 1963).

[13] "Masoretic Accents," in *Encyclopedia Judaica*, vol. 11, cols. 1098-1112.

[14] For a thorough study of Yemenite cantillation in a style similar to psalmody, see Uri Sharvit, "The Realization of Biblical Cantillation Symbols (*Te'amim*) in the Jewish Yemenite Tradition," in *YUVAL* 4 (1982), pp. 179-210.

[15] Twenty-one of the Bible's books—known as the *Khaf-Aleph* (that is, "twenty-one") books—utilize signs that function the same grammatically. The three other books, with a different use of signs, are know as *EMeT: Eiyov* (Job), *Mishlei* (Proverbs), and *Tehillim* (Psalms).

[16] Hanoch Avenary, "Music," in *Encyclopedia Judaica*, vol. 12, cols. 571-576.

[17] The Christian use of psalms led many scholars to believe that the early music of the church was based on Jewish models: Idelsohn, *Jewish Music in Its Historical Development*, pp. 62-64, and Eric Werner in his seminal *The Sacred Bridge* (New York, 1959-1984). Chant scholars see Werner's conclusions as speculative: Peter Jeffrey, "Werner's *The Sacred Bridge*, Volume 2: A Review Essay," in *Jewish Quarterly Review* 77 (1987), pp. 283-298.

[18] Treatment of the female voice in Jewish law is complicated. The Talmud prohibits a man's hearing a women's voice during recitation of the Shema. Is this the only context in which it is prohibited? Opinions vary. See Saul Berman, "Kol 'Isha," in Leo Landman, ed., *Rabbi Joseph H. Lookstein Memorial Volume* (New York, 1980), pp. 45-66.

[19] Avenary, "Music," col. 592.

[20] Ibid., col. 595.

[21] The difference between western and eastern traditions is documented in Abraham Baer, *Baal T'Fillah* (1865; reprint: New York, 1953).

[22] A useful resource that clearly documents the Eastern European practice is A.W. Binder, *Biblical Chant* (New York, 1959).

[23] The term *nusah* also refers to a liturgical tradition, either *"nusah Ashkenaz"* or *"nusah Sep-*

harad," corresponding to the Ashkenazic or Sephardic liturgical tradition. The Yiddish term is *"shtayger."*

[24] Hanoch Avenary, "The Concept of Mode in European Synagogue Chant," in *YUVAL*, vol. 2 (1971), pp. 11-12.

[25] This practice derives from Baruch Cohon, "Structure of the Synagogue Prayer Chant," in *Journal of the American Musicological Society* 3, 1950, pp. 17-32 (reprinted: *Journal of Synagogue Music* 11/1, 1981).

[26] Hanoch Avenary, "The Cantorial Fantasia of the Eighteenth and Nineteenth Centuries: A Late Manifestation of the Musical Trope," in *YUVAL*, vol. 1, 1968, pp. 68, note 6.

[27] A.Z. Idelsohn, "Der Missinai-Gesang der deutschen Synagoge," *Zeitschrift für Musikwissenschaft*, vol. 8, 1926, pp. 449-472; a revised version appears in English in his *Thesaurus of Hebrew-Oriental Melodies*, vol. 7, 1933, chap. 5. Werner took Idelsohn's ideas a step further and noted parallels between the *MiSinai niggun "Aleinu l'shabeah"* and a Gregorian chant, "Sanctus and Agnus Dei," of the ninth mass. See *A Voice Still Heard* (University Park and London, 1976), pp. 43-45.

[28] This discussion looks at twentieth century practices. Due to the lack of historical sources, we use a comparative approach, understanding these traditions through their similarities and differences. But similarities between two geographically distinct Jewish cultures do not necessarily indicate the existence of a single "original" practice.

[29] Mark Slobin, "Notes on Bukharan Music in Israel," in *YUVAL*, vol. 4 (1982), pp. 225-239; Kay Kaufman Shelemay, *Music, Ritual and Falasha History* (East Lansing, 1986).

[30] These cantillation signs are equivalent to the Ashkenazic *sof pasuk, etnahta,* and *zakef katon.*

[31] See Mark Kligman, "Modes of Prayer: Arabic *Maqamat* in the Sabbath Morning Liturgical Music of the Syrian Jews in Brooklyn," Ph.D. dissertation, New York University, 1997.

[32] Edwin Seroussi, *Spanish-Portuguese Synagogue Music in Nineteenth-Century Reform Sources from Hamburg: Ancient Tradition in the Dawn of Modernity* (Jerusalem, 1996).

[33] Kay Kaufman Shelemay, "The Study of Sacred Music: A Perspective from Ethnomusicology," in Paul Brainard, ed., *Reflections on the Sacred: The Musicological Perspective* (New Haven, 1994), pp. 26-33.

[34] On the former view, see Edith Gerson-Kiwi, "On the Musical Sources of the Judeo-Hispanic Romance," in *The Musical Quarterly* 50, 1964, pp. 31-43 (reprinted in *Migrations and Mutations of the Music in East and West— Selected Writings*, Tel Aviv, 1980). On the latter, see Israel J. Katz, "The 'Myth' of the Sephardic Musical Legacy from Spain," in *Proceedings of the Fifth World Congress of Jewish Studies* 4, 1973, pp. 237-43, and Kay Kaufman Shelemay "Mythologies and

Realities in the Study of Jewish Music," in *Journal of the International Institute for Traditional Music* 37/1, 1995, pp. 24-38.

[35] Israel J. Katz, "A Judeo-Spanish Romancero," in *Ethnomusicology* 12/1, 1968, pp. 72-85.

[36] Amnon Shiloah, *Jewish Musical Traditions* (Detroit, 1992), pp. 13-15.

[37] Idelsohn, *Jewish Music in Its Historical Development*, p. 88; Johanna Spector, "Chant and Cantillation," in *Musica Judaica* 9 (1986-1987), p. 12.

[38] Samuel Adler, "Sacred Music in a Secular Age," in Janet Walton and Lawrence Hoffman, eds., *Sacred Sound and Social Change* (Notre Dame and London, 1992), pp. 289-299.

[39] Mark Kligman, "On the Creators and Consumers of Orthodox Popular Music in Brooklyn," in *YIVO Annual*, vol. 23 (1996), pp. 259-293.

[40] Mark Slobin, "Klezmer Music: An American Ethnic Genre," in *Yearbook for Traditional Music* 16 (1984), pp. 34-41.

MARK KLIGMAN

MYSTICISM, JUDAISM AND: It is a commonplace in the history of religions to assume that most, if not all, religions have a tradition of mysticism associated with them. Generally speaking, the mystical element is linked to intense and often extreme forms of consciousness that relate one way or another to an encountering of ultimate reality, identified in theisitc religions as God. But can we really speak of a universalist phenomenon called "mysticism"? Or is it better to speak of mysticism relative to the specific context in which it appears? If the former, what are the defining qualities of this cross cultural phenomenon? If the latter, how can we continue to use the word "mysticism" to refer to diverse phenomena from different sociopolitical and ideological settings?

To date, there is no universal consensus among scholars regarding the precise meaning of the term "mysticism." Indeed, in recent years, a number of scholars have challenged the popular conception of mysticism as a perennial philosophy hardly altered by differences of clime or creed, according to the felicitous and memorable phrasing of William James. Thus, in contrast to earlier phases of the scholarly debate, it is now generally assumed that one must be careful to distinguish the mystical phenomenon as it appears in each religious or cultural context. In one form or another, this contextualist orientation

has had a major impact on the way scholars view mysticism in the history of religions. Being more attentive to context, however, does not necessarily preclude the possibility of positing a basis for comparative analysis. On the contrary, precisely such attentiveness to detail may allow one to speak most meaningfully of mysticism in a comparative perspective.

It therefore may still be viable to chart common characteristics of mysticism, even if we must then decipher clearly how each of these characteristics is manifest in the particular context. Some of the recurring characteristics that may be culled from the literary testimonies of mystics in various traditions are as follows:

(1) Standing in the immediate presence of the ultimate ground of being, the formless and nameless source in which the multiplicity of beings is unified in a non-differentiated manner (an orientation that is sometimes designated as pantheism or acosmism).

(2) Union with this ground of being, which is predicated on overcoming the ontological boundary separating it from the self (either in the sense of absorption or of deification).

(3) The intuitive experience of the preontological ground of being characterized by the transcendence of the correlation of opposites, which marks the formal logical structure that conditions the human account of everyday experience.

(4) Secret gnosis and poetic inspiration gained through the disclosure of this ground of being, which is the absence that makes possible the presencing of all beings.

(5) The inevitable need to express the ineffability of the ultimate experience, which is related to the recognition that language itself is the only adequate means through which thought leads to the unspoken.

(6) Special meditational techniques and contemplative practices that induce the ecstasy or enlightenment that ensues from the encounter with the nothingness of being.

(7) The adoption of an ascetic lifestyle, related principally to a negative assessment of the material body and the concomitant need to curtail, if not abrogate, physical pleasures, a lifestyle that in some traditions betokens liberation of consciousness and/or messianic redemption.

Many scholars still identify as quintessential the experience of the oneness of reality in the unity of consciousness. Mysticism is defined, therefore, as the immediate and direct encounter with the one true source of all being. Through the contemplative experience of this oneness, all things are unified. The splintering of consciousness into subject and object is thus overcome in the *unio mystica*. For that reason the contemplative state often is marked as that which cannot be expressed. The conventional dichotomies of linguistic expression yield the silence of mystical enlightenment.

A recurring aspect of the *via mystica*, indeed, according to many, the distinguishing feature of mysticism, is the quest for this underlying unity in reality. As Ludwig Wittgenstein put it in his *Tractus*, "The feeling of the world as a limited whole is the mystical feeling" (6.45). The nature of the unitive consciousness may vary from tradition to tradition. For Christian, Jew, and Muslim, the transcendent being of scriptural faith is the personal God (theism), and thus the mystical experience is often portrayed in these traditions as a particular way of life that facilitates encountering the divine presence. However, in these very traditions (especially as they evolved in the Middle Ages, in part due to the influence of Neoplatonic thought), the experience of the mystic may point beyond the morphic form to that which is absent in its presence. Alternatively, the mystical element in these religions may take the form of nature mysticism or pantheism, which in some measure approximates the expression of a mystical animus in Eastern traditions. For example, the Hindu mystic confronts the ground of being as the impersonal. Hence, the mysticism of Hinduism, reflected in Sankara and Vedanta, is sometimes referred to in Western modes of discourse as monistic. For the Chinese mystic, whether Buddhist or Taoist, the unitive source is the force of nature or the cosmic play that is expressed in the polarity of the way, the being that is nothing and the nothing that is being. In the different religious traditions, moreover, there is evidence for what William Stace calls the introvertive as opposed to the extrovertive

mysticism, that is, the discovery of the ultimate unity in the internal world of mind, heart, or soul. The one in which the many is unified is thus found at the bottom of one's self, which is absorbed or expanded into the grand self or spirit, the consciousness of being as such.

The texture of the mystical union likewise may vary from one religion to another. Some mystics describe a complete annihilation of self within the consciousness of spirit, whereas other mystics, theistic in nature, stress communion with the personal God. Communion, as distinct from union, preserves the sense of individuality of the mystic even as she or he is unified with the divine. In the latter case, moreover, the unitive experience is often related to erotic imagery, an especially apt field of symbolic discourse insofar as, in the experience of sexual union, boundaries of embodied self are traversed even as identities of personality are preserved. So the mystic stands in relation to the divine.

Esotericism and the role of secrecy in Jewish mysticism: The distinctive turn to mysticism in the Jewish tradition requires an esoteric dimension. The employment of the term "mysticism" is more than the cultivation of experiences that are in some sense replications of prophetic epiphanies. What makes these re/visions the subject matter of mysticism within the religious history of Judaism is the further presumption regarding the hidden significance these experiences are supposed to preserve. The symbolic language of poetic description represents not only the narrative recounting of an experience, which may in any case overflow the linguistic boundaries or normal modes of discourse (as Wittgenstein and others have argued); on the contrary, the poetic symbol for visionary and exegete alike is a marker on the way that brings the archaic meaning of the novel experience into the light of day. The act of mystical reading, therefore, facilitates a process of revisioning, and thus the gap separating text and experience, vision and interpretation, is effectively closed. However, as Norman O. Brown once pointed out, the nature of mystery as such, to be distinguished from the sense of wonder that is the source of philosophy, involves the secret, which must display itself in words that remain concealed. In this respect, the occult embraces the character of the poetic word, for poetry, too, is predicated on the paradox of saying that which cannot be said, uttering a truth that remains veiled in its revelation.[1]

The contextualization of the mystical within a framework of esotericism is characteristic of the hermeneutical strategy employed repeatedly in the sources that scholars have studied under the rubric of Jewish mysticism. Indeed, I would suggest that the more appropriate term to characterize this body of lore is esotericism, *hokhmat ha-nistar*, a set of doctrines and practices that are deemed secretive and must therefore be transmitted orally to a small circle of initiates. It is plausible that in *Sefer Yesirah*, one of the earliest documents of Jewish mystical and magical speculation, parts of which may derive from occult circles active in late antiquity, we have a reference to just such a practice. The text has been preserved as a composite made up of distinct units welded together in a complicated and for the most part inscrutable process of redaction. In one of the distinct tradition-complexes preserved in the first part of the text that deals with the enigmatic term *sefirot*, we read of an injunction to search out the nature of these ten *sefirot* in what appears to be a meditational practice of visualization. This is followed, however, by the suggestion that one must retreat from the contemplative gaze, for "upon this matter was the covenant made," *'al davar zeh nikhrat ha-berit.* Although this passage is not entirely transparent, it appears to allude to some practice whereby a fraternity of mystics were bound together by an oath of secrecy related to the visionary contemplation of the imaginal form of the divine anthropos.

In subsequent generations, we often find more explicit references to practices of such a nature. Medieval kabbalistic texts contain constant reminders that the esoteric doctrines and practices must be conveyed by oral transmission from master to disciple. Ostensibly, this would privilege orality as the main vehicle by which the mystical secrets were transmitted. Yet, the act of oral transmission

should not be construed simply as an intellectual exercise. On the contrary, the very process of transmitting and receiving secrets is a form of visionary gnosis. The speaking of the word by the master is not only the linguistic context within which the mystical experience takes shape, but it is itself a form of that experience. Moreover, inasmuch as later kabbalists presumed that the secrets were encoded in the biblical (and to some degree Rabbinic) texts, there is no rigid division of orality and literacy, spoken and written language. The oral exposition of the secret requires the exegesis of a canonical text. This I take to be the hermeneutical circle that informs us about the very core of the mystical phenomenon within Judaism.

Placing the notion of secrecy at the center of our focus facilitates as well the appreciation of a constant dialectic that has characterized the nature of the mystical experience articulated in the Jewish sources: the concomitant concealment and disclosure of secretive matters. This is expressed, for instance, by the Zoharic description of the divine as "hidden but revealed." Concealment and disclosure are not mutually exclusive antinomies separable by the power of logical reasoning into distinct categories; on the contrary, in the lived experience of mystical insight, the two overlap such that the concealment is a form of disclosure and the disclosure a form of concealment. Indeed, the insight for the kabbalists with respect to the nature of secrecy is that the process of unveiling is itself a form of concealment. This paradoxical experience is often expressed by kabbalists through the image of a garment applied to the light by which the divine is manifest: from one perspective the garment conceals, but from another it reveals. In the mystical gnosis, these are not logical antinomies. On the contrary, the garment reveals in the manner that it conceals that which it reveals, and it conceals in the manner that it reveals that which it conceals.

Vision of the glory and the ocularcentric nature of Jewish mysticism: The demarcation of the mystical phenomenon within the history of Judaism is a particularly difficult matter that has eluded the grasp of most scholars who labor in this field. There are many reasons for the difficulty in establishing a precise taxonomy for Jewish mysticism, not least of which is the impressive degree of factual/textual specificity that characterizes this multifaceted phenomenon—if we are even correct in referring to a "phenomenon" in the singular. How do we isolate a critical nerve that animates the mystical element in its multiple historical configurations? Perhaps it is not possible. Where does one even begin to chart the history of Jewish mysticism? Indeed, we must even ask, Is the term "Jewish mysticism" the most effective way to describe the many phenomena that scholars have come to classify under this rubric?

A scholar's decision regarding what can be considered part of the history of Jewish mysticism very much depends on a hermeneutical decision concerning the nature of mysticism more generally. For many years, the field has been determined by Gershom Scholem's decision to begin the history of Jewish mysticism in the postbiblical period. Thus, while acknowledging that intense religious moments were captured in the literary narrative of Scripture, Scholem was rather adamant on insisting that no personality mentioned in the biblical text could be considered properly a mystic and no experience recorded therein mystical. But is this the only or even the best response? Is there a way of construing mysticism such that it might encompass the extraordinary experiences of the divine, traces of which have been left behind in the biblical texts? Is it legitimate to characterize some of these experiences as moments of mystical illumination? In particular, can we look anew at descriptions of the glory (*kavod*) and of the name (*shem*) in different strata of ancient Israelite culture to discern the possible sources for two of the major foci of later mystical thinking? Can we, that is, hold Scripture up as a lens through which to re/vision ancient theosophic traditions about the divine glory and its holy name without being accused of uncritical traditionalism or anachronism?

If we identify the mystical phenomenon in the history of Judaism more precisely in terms of the criterion of standing in the presence of God, often experienced in the theophanic image of the divine anthropos, then it may indeed be plausible to speak of mysticism in a biblical context. As I have argued in several studies, the contemplation of the imaginal body of God, which entails the meditative construction of the form of the divine anthropos in the imagination, is a recurring theme in ancient and medieval Jewish mysticism and in the ethical and homiletical literature based thereon.[2] With respect to this seminal issue, it is necessary to contextualize the mystical phenomenon in a broader phenomenological framework: the history of Judaism has been marked by a perennial clash between the view that God is not susceptible to portrayal by images and the basic religious need to imagine the divine in figurative representation. Precisely some such need lies at the heart of the mystical vision within the aniconic traditions of Judaism. The problem of the visionary experience of God represents one of the major axes about which the wheel of Jewish mystical speculation in its various permutations turns. Indeed, literary evidence attests that the religious experience described in the different currents of Jewish mysticism is overwhelmingly visual. Ironically enough, the lack of fixed iconic representation in ancient Israelite religion and subsequently in the diverse forms of Judaism from the period of the Second Temple onwards provided the ongoing context for the imaginative visualization of divinity.

It is certainly the case that mystics in subsequent stages of Jewish history envisioned the biblical material in precisely these terms. What emerged as the central concern of the prophetic tradition of ancient Israel was the visionary capabilities of imaging God in fire, cloud, or human form. It is for this very reason that Ezekiel, the sixth-century prophet who dwelt both in the land of Israel and in Babylonia, emerged as the key figure in the mystical currents of postbiblical Judaism. The vision that Ezekiel recounted in the first and tenth chapters of his book became the prototype of mystical vision, which some rabbis in the Palestinian academies of the first and second centuries C.E. actually thought better not studied publicly or even read as a prophetic portion on the holiday of Pentecost, rabbinically the commemoration of the Sinaitic revelation of the Torah. Current liturgical practice reflects the alternative view that allowed for the use of the first chapter in the synagogue. And for good reason: there is an intrinsic connection between the theophany at Sinai and the epiphany of the glory upon the chariot/throne, a symbolic message that needs to be carried through ritual praxis. Heeding that message properly will go a long way in establishing the taxonomy of the term mysticism when applied to subsequent stages in Jewish history.

The culmination of Ezekiel's visionary encounter is the imaging of what the prophet refers to as the "appearance of the likeness of a human," *demut kemar'eh adam*, seated upon the "appearance of a throne," *demut kisse'*, which was "in the likeness of a sapphire stone," *kemar'eh even sappir* (Ezek. 1:26). The human form is further described in images of luminosity. Thus, above the loins, he is depicted by the neologism *hashmal*, which clearly has something to do with a radiant presence, and from the loins down he is characterized as the splendor surrounded by light, also described as the aura of the rainbow. Rather than viewing this elaborate vision as a circumlocution to avoid attributing an explicitly anthropomorphic image to the glory, it is necessary to recognize in the scriptural text a theophanic tradition regarding the anthropomorphic shape of the divine. In the variegated history of Jewish mysticism, the vision of Ezekiel served this very purpose. Beyond the attribution of an imaginal body to the glory, in and of itself an extremely important dimension of the biblical conception of the divine epiphany, the particular image of enthronement later served as a key symbolic depiction of the sacred union in the divine realm between the masculine glory and the feminine throne. This union was interpreted by mystics through the generations as alluding to the secret of *ma'aseh merkavah*, the esoteric account of the chariot.

The mythic image of the glory riding upon the chariot thus assumed supreme significance in Jewish mystical sources, for it conveyed symbolically the notion of the *hieros gamos*. Already in one of the compositions that is part of the ancient mystical speculation on the chariot, *Hekhalot Rabbati*, the throne is described as the bride who addresses the glorious king, or her bridegroom, and entreats him to glorify himself by sitting upon her.[3] The use of the enthronement motif to convey the erotic union of masculine and feminine potencies in the divine should not come as a surprise given the sense of power that is related to the image of enthronement, on the one hand, and the eroticized nature of power relations, on the other. Certainly, in later kabbalistic texts, the sexually charged implications of this image are fully exploited. Thus, to cite one illustration, a passage from the Zohar is recited liturgically by certain communities prior to the start of the Friday evening service, under the title *Raza' de-shabbat*, the mystery of Sabbath (Zohar 2:135a-b):

> The blessed holy one is one above, and he does not sit upon his throne of glory until she is unified in the secret of the one as he is, so that they will be one together with one. . . . The prayer of Sabbath evening: the holy throne of glory is unified in the secret of the one and she is prepared for the supernal holy king to rest upon her.

The mystical significance of the evening prayer, therefore, is related to the process of unifying the throne, which is the feminine principle, or the Shekhina, so that she is prepared to be unified with the holy king who sits upon her, clearly a euphemistic expression of the holy union between the male and female.

The philosophical principle underlying the mythical symbol is articulated succinctly by the sixteenth-century kabbalist Moses Cordovero:[4]

> Just as there is a sublime delight for the throne when the glory dwells and hovers upon her, for she receives the good from the supernal benefactor, so too the supernal benefactor delights, and the glory is elevated and rests inasmuch as it bestows goodness, dwells, and hovers upon his throne, for it is his way to benefit that which is other than him.

Without ignoring the important historical developments that have characterized the evolution of the mystical phenomenon in Judaism, I would advocate the acceptance of some unchanging structures of thought that have had an impact on both belief and practice. The symbolic image of the male glory sitting upon the female throne is an example of precisely such a structure. The enduring appeal of the mythic image of enthronement on the remarkably fluid and fertile imagination of the Jewish mystics attests to its ability to call forth a primordial symbol that dramatically conveys the sense of divine power and unity. Furthermore, the experience of visualizing the enthroned glory affords the mystic visionary the opportunity to participate in the most sacred moment in the divine realm, wherein the masculine and feminine potencies are united in erotic embrace. The witnessing of this experience eroticizes the texture of the mystic's own visionary encounter. The nexus of vision and eros adds yet another dimension to the centrality of the notion of secrecy to the Jewish mystical tradition. That is, the erotic nature of the visionary experience necessitates the concealment of that which is visualized; indeed, it is the hiddenness of the divine that is the ultimate object of the vision. The ultimate paradox that marks the way of the mystical vision in the Jewish sources can be formulated simply: the God that is seen is the invisible God.

Imagination and mystical intentionality: The epistemological foundation for the vision of God in Jewish mystical sources is located in the symbolic imagination, that is, the divine element of the soul that enables one to gain access to the realm of incorporeality by transferring or transmuting sensory data and/or rational concepts into symbols. The primary function of the imagination, therefore, may be viewed as poetical. Through the images within the heart, the locus of the imagination, the divine, whose pure essence is incompatible with all form, is nevertheless manifest in a form belonging to the imaginative presence. The paradox that the hidden God appears to human beings in multiple forms—including, most significantly, that of an anthropos—is the enduring legacy of the prophetic tradition that has informed and challenged Judaism throughout the ages. Moreover, the role of the imaginal as a symbolic intermediary allowing for the imaging of the imageless God is rooted in biblical and Rabbinic texts, although it is developed and articulated most fully in the medieval mystical literature.

Central to all the major schools of Jewish mysticism in the middle ages is the presumption regarding the representation of God as an anthropomorphic shape within the imagination of the mystic, primarily in the context of contemplative prayer. The recurring emphasis on the visualization of the divine anthropos in the texts of the German Pietists, the ecstatic and the theosophic kabbalists, indicates that in the Jewish mystical tradition the abstract object is rendered in concrete images in the contemplative vision. The visual encounter operative in the three trends of medieval Jewish mysticism attests to the convergence of anthropomorphism and theomorphism: God is imaged in human terms because the human is imaged in divine terms. In seeing God, one sees oneself, for in seeing oneself, one sees God. This, I assume, is the hermeneutical claim that lies at the phenomenological core of Jewish mysticism in all of its diverse manifestations.

Moreover, the experience of union, which, as noted, is so often designated the distinctive mark of mystical experience, is realized only to the extent that one cleaves to the form of God that one has visualized in one's imagination. From that vantage point, the imagination, which medieval mystical sources frequently locate in the heart, is the throne upon which the divine presence dwells. The critical aspect of intention in Jewish mystical literature, therefore, is not union with God *per se*, but the anthropomorphic representation and visual apprehension of God that ensues from the state of conjunction. To avoid potential misunderstanding, let me emphasize that I am not denying that unitive experiences were cultivated by medieval Jewish mystics, in some cases based on a Neoplatonic paradigm and in other cases betraying the influence of the Aristotelian model as it informed the mystical praxis of ecstatic kabbalah. My point is rather that these experiences of union served the ultimate goal of inducing mystical consciousness, which is the immediate and direct presence of God visually comprehended as an imaginal body. Unitive experience, therefore, must be contextualized in a broader phenomenological framework that concerns encountering the immediacy of the divine presence. One of the fundamental ways this is achieved in the Jewish mystical tradition is the visual contemplation of God's form in liturgical worship. Precisely this feature lies at the heart of the Rabbinic literature's conception of *kavvanah*— the intentionality required in prayer.[5]

Indeed, the praxis of *kavvanah* described in the various forms of kabbalistic speculation is predicated on the representation of the *sefirot*, understood either as the divine hypostases (in the theosophic kabbalah) or the luminous intellects that manifest the providential overflow of God (in the prophetic kabbalah), as an anthropomorphic shape within the imaginative faculty of the mystic. My understanding contrasts sharply with Scholem's characterization of meditation as it appears in kabbalistic literature from the middle of the thirteenth century as a contemplation by the intellect, whose objects are neither images nor visions, but non-sensual matters such as words, names, or thoughts.[6] No one could argue with the claim that the ultimate object of meditation in the main currents of the kabbalistic orientation consists of the *sefirot*, the spiritual entities that make up the divine pleroma. The important point, however, is that these entities, whatever their ontological status vis-à-vis the infinite Godhead, are phenomenally experienced only insofar as they are configured and instantiated in particular sentient forms within human consciousness. Contemplation of the linguistic structures mentioned by Scholem—words, names, and thoughts—is itself dependent on the imaginary visualization of these structures. One must, therefore, raise questions about Scholem's sweeping attempt to contrast the Christian and the kabbalistic doctrines of meditation on the grounds that in Christian mysticism there is centrally a pictorial and concrete subject, such as the suffer-

ing of Christ, that is given to the meditator, whereas in the kabbalah, the subject of contemplation is abstract and cannot be visualized, such as the tetragrammaton and its combinations.[7] The textual evidence from the major currents of the medieval Jewish mystical tradition indicates just the contrary: the divine names, and especially the tetragrammaton, serve as the object of contemplation only to the degree that they assume morphic (and, in many instances, anthropomorphic) shape in the mind of the mystic. The mindfulness achieved by meditative ascent affirmed in kabbalistic texts is not a state of abstract emptiness, a peeling away of all material form from consciousness to attain the illumination of formless absorption as one finds, for instance, in Buddhist meditation.[8] Quite the opposite: contemplation eventuates in the polishing of the mind so that reflected in the mirror of the imagination is the concrete image of the divine anthropos.

Many sources could be cited to support my contention, but in this context I make reference to two examples from the sixteenth-century. The first is from Joseph Karo, who thus comments in his mystical diary:[9]

> If your thoughts cleave to Me constantly, nothing shall be lacking, and you shall be of those who stand before Me perpetually, for you should always imagine (*tesayyer*) in your soul that you are standing before Me and doing My service. . . . Therefore, you should take care to stand before Me constantly without any interruption, and your body and your limbs should be purified in the manner of Enoch, whose flesh became torches of fire and balls of flame.

To stand before God constantly, presented here as the essential datum of *devequt* —the experience of mystical communion—implies that one mentally forms an image of the divine presence in the shape of an anthropos. But to stand vis-à-vis God, to re/present the glory visually, is predicated further on the ontological metamorphosis of the physical person into a spiritual being.[10] The paradigm of this transubstantiation is the figure of Enoch who, according to ancient Jewish tradition, was transformed from mortal flesh into the fiery essence of the angelic Metatron. Karo does not speak of the obliteration of the body but its purification. The image of fire as the means for the transfiguration of the carnal body into a psychic body recurs in Karo's writing, and it is often linked with the symbol of the sacrificial burnt-offering, such that the individual who undergoes this transformation is considered to be a sacrifice offered up to God.[11] The important point for our analysis is that the bodily vision of God's spirit is vouchsafed only to one whose own body has been spiritually transfigured.

The second illustration of my point is derived from Hayyim Vital, the preeminent disciple of Isaac Luria. The reappropriation of corporeal images as part of the mystical understanding of *kavvanah* is poignantly conveyed in a passage from the fourth part of Vital's *Sha'arei Qedushah*.[12] Vital characterizes the "secret of communion and the perfect intention" as a state in which one must constantly see oneself as "a soul without any body." One who attains this disembodiment, which is related by Vital to the spiritual exercise of *hitbodedut*, is able to draw upon himself the "holiness of the Holy Spirit" when he prays or recites psalms.[13] The pietistic path described by Vital actually involves five stages of attainment: the secret of conjunction (*hitdabbequt*), the secret of equanimity (*hishtavvut*), the secret of meditation (*hitbodedut*), the comprehension of the Holy Spirit (*ruah ha-qodesh*), and the experience of prophecy (*nevu'ah*).[14] One who has the requisite moral and religious virtues can embark upon this fivefold spiritual path that leads ultimately to prophecy, which is understood as the imaginative representation of the imageless God.

Consistent with other sixteenth-century kabbalists, who in turn based their views on older meditational tracts and manuals, Vital considers subjugation of the body (achieved through specific acts of asceticism) as the necessary precondition for the mystical experience of contemplation, described primarily as the visionary communion with the divine. To receive supernal illumination, the soul must be completely separated from the body, emptied of all material sensations and corporeal desires.[15] The point is stated explicitly in another passage:[16]

> The person must meditate in his thought (*yitboded be-mahshavto*) until the utmost limit, and he should separate his body from his soul as if he does not feel that he is garbed in matter at all, but he is entirely a soul. To the degree that he separates from matter his comprehension is augmented . . . if any corporeal thought comes to him, the thought of his soul ceases to be conjoined to the supernal entities and he does not comprehend anything, for the supernal holiness does not dwell on a person when he is attached to matter even [in the measure of] a hairsbreadth.

The ultimate secret of the prophetic experience is the imaginative representation of the divine as an anthropos. Only one who transforms the physical body into something spiritual—a process presented in the relevant texts as an angelification of the mystic—is capable of imaging the divine forms in bodily images.[17]

Annihilation of self, therefore, is a means for cleansing the imaginative faculty. Hence, immediately after Vital finishes the characterization of *hitbodedut* as the radical stripping away of all things corporeal, he cites a passage from the anonymous kabbalistic treatise, *Ma'arekhet ha-'Elohut*, which deals with the esoteric gnosis of the *Shi'ur Qomah*, a cluster of older texts that attribute explicit dimensions to the limbs of the creator, and the anthropomorphic nature implied by the scriptural account of prophetic visions.[18] The ultimate secret of the prophetic experience is the imaginative representation of the divine as an anthropos. The point is represented ideally in a remark of Judah Hayyat in his commentary to *Ma'arekhet ha-'Elohut*, which Vital himself cites in this context:[19]

> The lower anthropos is a throne for the supernal anthropos, for the physical limbs that are in him allude to the spiritual limbs above, which are the divine potencies, and not for naught does it say, "Let us make Adam in our image" (Gen. 1:26). Inasmuch as this image is the image of the spiritual, supernal anthropos, and the prophet is the physical man who, in the moment of prophecy, is almost transformed into a spiritual entity, and his external senses almost depart from him, thus he sees the image of an anthropos, just as he sees his image in a glass mirror.

The distinguishing feature of prophecy, according to Vital, is the conjunction of the soul to its ontological root in the realm of the *sefirot*, an experience predicated on the purification, rather than the nullification, of the body. Thus, Vital characterizes the "matter of prophecy" in the third part of *Sha'arei Qodesh* as follows:[20]

> When a person is in pure matter without any of the filth of the evil inclination and without any of the faculties of the elemental soul, and he has no sin that blemishes some root in the roots of his soul, and he prepares himself to be conjoined to his supernal root, then he can be conjoined to it. Even though he is worthy of this, he must remove his soul entirely and separate it from all corporeal matters, and then he can be conjoined to his spiritual root.

In another passage from this section of the text, Vital goes so far as to compare this separation to a simulated death: "He should close his eyes and separate his thought from all matters of this world as if his soul departed from him like one who has died who feels nothing at all."[21] This deathlike separation, however, does not entail the complete abrogation of corporeal images from prophetic vision, a wiping clean of the mirror of consciousness, as it were; on the contrary, as Vital goes on to describe at great length, a consequence of the soul's separation from the body is the imaginative ascent to the divine realm that culminates in the spiritual entities' assuming corporeal form within the imagination.[22]

The task that Vital here assigns to the prophet conforms to what he elsewhere defines as the more general task of the life of piety. The purpose of the conjunction of the soul and God, the rejoining of the part to the whole, is the spiritual vision of the divine accorded the soul.[23] This vision, once again, is depicted in terms of the ancient esoteric *Shi'ur Qomah*, i.e., the *sefirot* are configured as an anthropos in the human mind. The sinful soul is compared to a copper mirror so full of stains and rust that nothing can be seen in it; by contrast, the pure soul is like a clear and bright mirror in which the "supernal, holy things take shape."[24] That the visualization of the divine form is the ultimate goal of *devequt* and the true intent of *kavvanah*

may be deduced from Vital's admonition to the reader that:[25]

> he should place the name [of God] before his eyes, as it is written, "I am ever mindful of the Lord's presence" (Ps. 16:8), and he should intend to conjoin his thought to it, and he should not cease even for a moment; this is the secret of "to cleave to him" (Deut. 11:22), "and to him shall you cleave" (Deut. 10:20).

Kavvanah is predicated on a visual image of the letters of the tetragrammaton, in which are contained the ten *sefirot* that are configured in the shape of an anthropos. The experience of *devequt*, moreover, is realized only to the extent that one cleaves to the form of God that one has visualized in one's imagination. From that vantage point, the imagination—frequently designated, as we have said, as the heart—is the throne upon which the Shekhina dwells.[26]

The body of the text and the text of the body: Another assumption shared by the various trends of Jewish esotericism is that the luminous form of the glory visualized as the anthropomorphic shape upon the throne is simultaneously experienced in terms of the letters of the divine name (or names). The convergence of these two fields of symbolic discourse is attested in the *Shi'ur Qomah* fragments, which provide a detailed account of the stature of the body of the creator both in terms of extraordinary measurements and seemingly unintelligible names. It is plausible that these were originally two distinct strands of tradition that were blended together at a particular stage in the redactional process. The essential point, however, is that the text was received in such a way that it was presumed that the two strands belonged together, and hence what is most corporeal is the literal. The body is the name, and the name is the body.

The convergence of these two symbolic modes had a major impact on the medieval kabbalistic literature. In the theosophic tradition, the potencies of the Godhead, the ten *sefirot*, are visually configured in the shape of an anthropos, but the limbs of that body are composed ultimately of the letters of the divine names associated with each of those potencies, which are all derived from the one name, the tetragrammaton. Indeed, the position affirmed generally by kabbalists of a theosophic orientation is that the ultimate nature of corporeality is related to the linguistic structure that underlies the material substratum. The point is underscored in the following remark of the eighteenth-century Rabbinic figure Jonathan Eybeschuetz, who noted that the kabbalists "received from the prophets who saw the camp of God, and they saw that [the divine matters] are all letters, which are described as a very bright and resplendent light."[27]

Encapsulated in this succinct remark are the two main fields of symbolic discourse employed by kabbalists in the attempt to depict the nature of the divine reality, light and language. For many kabbalists, the two fields are related to the thirty-two paths of wisdom mentioned in *Sefer Yesirah*, which comprise the ten *sefirot* and the twenty-two letters of the Hebrew alphabet. But the word *sefirot* itself is sufficient to convey this dual sense, because that word apparently derives from the root *SFR*, which can be vocalized as *sefer*, book, but is also associated with the word *sappir*, a sapphire. Additionally, the root *SFR* can be vocalized as *safar*, to count. No single English word can adequately account for the richness of the range of semantic meaning linked to the term *sefirot*, which denotes concurrently the sense of luminosity (*sappir*), speech (*sefer*), and enumeration (*safar*). At the heart of the mystical experience that informs the world of the kabbalists is the convergence of these three fields of discourse: the potencies of the divine are experienced as the translucent letters that are enumerated within the book written by God.

The kabbalists' preponderant utilization of anthropomorphic imagery to depict the divine is predicated on the presumption that the Hebrew letters assigned to each of the relevant limbs constitute the reality of the body on both the human and the divine planes of being.[28] For the kabbalists, therefore, the use of human terms to speak about matters divine is not simply understood in the philosophical manner as an approximate way to speak of God, a concession to the inevitable limitations of embodied human beings who desire to speak of that which is disembodied. On the contrary, the examples of anthropomorphism in the canonical texts of Scripture indicate that the nature of human corporeality can only be understood in light of the divine corporeality, which is constituted ultimately by the letters of the name. The point is expressed succinctly by Joseph Gikatilla, a Spanish kabbalist who was active at the time of the composition of the Zohar in the late-thirteenth and early-fourteenth centuries: "The intention of the forms of the limbs that are in us is that they are made in the image of signs (*be-dimyon simmanim*), the hidden, supernal matters that the mind cannot know except in the manner of signification (*ke-dimyon zikkaron*)."[29]

In line with Maimonides, Gikatilla rejects the possibility of interpreting biblical anthropomorphisms in a literal sense, since God does not have a physical body. On the other hand, he differs from Maimonides to the degree that he does not deny that there is an ontological reality to the divine that can only be conveyed in anthropomorphic terms. What is unique to the kabbalistic perspective articulated by Gikatilla is that the limbs of the physical body signify the limbs of the spiritual body, for the reality of the former, much like that of the latter, is constituted by the letters that make up the corporeal matter. The kabbalists express this idea as well by their repeated claim that the Torah in its mystical essence is the name of God, which is identical with the body of the divine.[30] In contrast to the Christological doctrine of the incarnation of the word in the flesh of Jesus, the Jewish esoteric tradition is based on the notion of the body as text and the text as body rather than the identification of a particular historical figure as the embodiment of the divine teaching. In the final analysis, the image of the Torah as an anthropos is an imaginal symbol, for only in the eye of the imagination does the scroll of the Torah assume the shape of a human form, which is of course identified as the ideal Israel.

The convergence of bodily and linguistic symbolism is also a central component of the kabbalistic teaching of the ecstatic-prophetic school espoused particularly by the thirteenth-century mystic, Abraham Abulafia. For Abulafia, not only is the esoteric wisdom of the divine chariot brought about by knowledge of the various combinations and permutations of the names of God, but vision of the chariot itself consists of the very letters that are constitutive elements of the names.[31] The ecstatic vision of the letters is not simply the means to achieve union with God; it is, to an extent, the end of the process. The culminating stage in the *via mystica* is a vision of the letters of the divine names, especially the tetragrammaton, originating in the intellectual and imaginative powers. These letters are visualized simultaneously as an anthropos. Gazing upon the divine name, therefore, is akin to beholding the divine form as constituted within one's imagination. This vision results from the conjunction of the human intellect with the divine, but, like all prophecy, following the view of Maimonides and his Islamic predecessors, there must be an imaginative component. The latter is described either as the form of the letters or that of an anthropos. Both of these constitute a figurative depiction of the Active Intellect, personified as Metatron, who is also identified as the scroll of the Torah in its mystical essence.[32]

Conclusion: This presentation of some of the main elements that have shaped the contours of the mystical phenomenon in the religious history of Judaism can be broadly defined as morphological in nature, to be distinguished from the typological orientation that has been utilized by scholars since the nineteenth century. The typologies are helpful, but they ultimately fail to capture the complex relationship between the various trends that have been expressed in the thoughts and practices of the different mystics. Thus, for example, the distinction between magic and mysticism is very problematic, insofar as magical texts often embrace components of the mystical tradition, and the mystical texts, components of the magical tradition. In the abstract, one may certainly draw the line between mysticism and magic, but it is very difficult in concrete examples culled from the primary sources of either phenomenon to maintain a clear and well-defined distinction. The centrality of the power of the divine and angelic names in both mystical and magical sources illustrates the blurring of the line that separates these two pursuits.

Similarly, with respect to the typological distinction between ecstatic and theosophic kabbalah, the line separating the two is not always apparent.[33] Thus, the theosophic traditions expressed in medieval kabbalistic sources are often enough related to the cultivation of visionary and contemplative experiences that lead to ecstasy, whereas the ecstatic kabbalah embraces a meditational practice that is itself rooted in an ontology that presupposes a theosophic understanding of the divine nature. What is stated by theosophic and ecstatic kabbalists is the emphasis on the knowledge of the name, which is the defining feature of the occult wisdom of the kabbalah. Moreover, for both ecstatic and theosophic kabbalists, knowledge of the name occasions the experience of *devequt*, conjunction with the divine that may be experienced as communion or even union of the soul and God. According to the kabbalists, the ultimate purpose of the religious life is for one to attain this state of conjunction, which in the last analysis is an expression of self-realization. The deeper self that the kabbalist comes to be through knowledge of the divine is at the same time the true essence of the world. Although the Jewish mystics have tried to preserve the distinction between God, self, and world, it is not entirely clear that they have succeeded, for in the blaze of the mystical vision, all reality becomes one. To see God, therefore, is to see oneself reflected in the mirror of the text of the world.

Bibliography

Scholem, Gershom, *Major Trends in Jewish Mysticism* (New York, 1956).
Scholem, Gershom, *On the Kabbalah and Its Symbolism* (New York, 1969).
Werblowsky, R.J. Zwi, *Joseph Karo: Lawyer and Mystic* (Philadelphia, 1977).
Wolfson, Elliot R., *Through a Speculum that Shines: Vision and Imagination in Medieval Jewish Mysticism* (Princeton, 1994).

Notes

[1] N.O. Brown, *Apocalypse and/or Metamorphosis* (Berkeley, 1991), p. 3.

[2] See, in particular, E.R. Wolfson, *Through a Speculum that Shines: Vision and Imagination in Medieval Jewish Mysticism* (Princeton, 1994).

[3] Ibid., pp. 98-105.

[4] *Zohar 'im Perush 'Or Yaqar*, 17 (Jerusalem, 1989), p. 11.

[5] Elliot R. Wolfson, "Iconic Visualization and the Imaginal Body of God: The Role of Intention in the Rabbinic Conception of Prayer," in *Modern Theology* 12 (1996): 137-162.

[6] *Kabbalah* (Jerusalem, 1974), p. 369. See also Scholem's characterization in "The Concept of Kavvanah in the Early Kabbalah," in A. Jospe, ed., *Studies in Jewish Thought: An Anthology of German Jewish Scholarship* (Detroit, 1981), pp. 162-180; idem, *Origins of the Kabbalah*, R.J. Zwi Werblowsky, ed. (Princeton, 1987), pp. 195-196, 243-244, 414-419; idem, *The Messianic Idea in Judaism* (New York, 1971), pp. 217-218.

[7] *Kabbalah*, p. 371.

[8] See S.W. Laycock, *Mind as Mirror and the Mirroring of Mind: Buddhist Reflections on Western Phenomenology* (Albany, 1994), pp. 76-78. For an approach to Jewish mystical texts more congenial to the model I have rejected, see D. Matt, "Ayin: The Concept of Nothingness in Jewish Mysticism," in R.K.C. Forman, ed., *The Problem of Pure Consciousness: Mysticism and Philosophy* (New York, 1990), pp. 121-159, now reprinted with slight modifications in L. Fine, ed., *Essential Papers on Kabbalah* (New York, 1995), pp. 67-108. While apophatic statements appear in Jewish mystical literature, I would argue that the encounter with the divine nothing is an experience of God's presence as absence rather than an experience of the absence of God's presence. See my "Negative Theology and Positive Assertion in the Early Kabbalah," in *Da'at* 32-33 (1994), pp. v-xxii. A similar argument has been made by Bernard McGinn for the negative or apophatic mystics in the history of Western Christianity. See his *The Foundations of Mysticism: Origins to the Fifth Century* (New York, 1991), pp. xvii-xix and *The Growth of Mysticism: Gregory the Great Through the 12th Century* (New York, 1994), pp. x-xi.

[9] *Maggid Mesharim* (Petah Tiqvah, 1990), pp. 149-150. On the role of *kavvanah* and the experience of *devequt* in Karo's thought, see R.J. Zwi Werblowsky, *Joseph Karo: Lawyer and Mystic* (Philadelphia, 1977), pp. 162-163; M. Pachter, "The Concept of Devekut in the Homiletical Ethical Writings of 16th Century Safed," in I. Twersky, ed., *Studies in Medieval Jewish History and Literature*, vol. 2 (Cambridge, 1984), pp. 193-209.

[10] In *Maggid Mesharim*, p. 37, Karo relates the spiritualizing transformation through ascent to martyrdom, symbolized primarily in terms of sacrificial imagery. On the symbolic correlation of death and *devequt*, cf. *Maggid Mesharim*, p. 139. See Werblowsky, *Joseph Karo*, pp. 153-154; Pachter, "Concept of Devekut," pp. 199-202. The nexus of *kavvanah*, visual apprehension of the Shekhina, and the eradication of the bodily sense, is already implied in earlier kabbalistic sources, such as the passage from David ben Judah he-Hasid translated and discussed by Scholem, "Concept of Kavvanah," p. 169.

[11] See Pachter, "Concept of Devekut," pp. 200-201.

[12] For a description of this part of *Sha'arei Qedushah*, including a list of Vital's major sources, see L. Fine, "Recitation of Mishnah as a Vehicle for Mystical Inspiration: A Contemplative Technique Taught by Hayyim Vital," in *Revue des Études Juives* 141 (1982), pp. 188-189. The mystical techniques recommended by Vital to attain a contemplative state of communion, consisting mainly of unifications (*yihudim*), conjurations (*hashba'ot*), and adjurations by divine or angelic names (*hazkarot ha-shemot*), are discussed by Werblowsky, *Joseph Karo*, pp. 71-83. See also Pachter, "Concept of Devekut," pp. 225-229; L. Fine, "Maggidic Revelation in the Teachings of Isaac Luria," in J. Reinharz and D. Swetschinski, eds., *Mystics, Philosophers and Politicians* (Durham, 1982), pp. 141-157; idem, "The Contemplative Practice of Yihudim in Lurianic Kabbalah," in A. Green, ed., *Jewish Spirituality From the Sixteenth-Century Revival to the Present* (New York, 1987), pp. 64-98.

[13] *Sha'arei Qedushah*, IV.2, in *Ketavim Hadashim le-Rabbenu Hayyim Vital* (Jerusalem, 1988), p. 10.

[14] Ibid., p. 9.

[15] On the role of asceticism in kabbalistic pietism, especially in sixteenth-century texts, see Werblowsky, *Joseph Karo*, pp. 38-83, 113-118, 149-152, 161-165; Pachter, "Concept of Devekut," pp. 200-210; L. Fine, "Purifying the Body in the Name of the Soul: The Problem of the Body in Sixteenth-Century Kabbalah," in *People of the Body: Jews and Judaism from an Embodied Perspective*, pp. 117-142. For a discussion of the ascetic tendencies in earlier kabbalah, see B. Safran, "Rabbi Azriel and Nahmanides: Two Views of the Fall of Man," in I. Twersky, ed., *Rabbi Moses Nahmanides (Ramban): Explorations in His Religious and Literary Virtuosity* (Cambridge, 1983), pp. 75-106; E.R. Wolfson, "Eunuchs Who Keep the Sabbath: Becoming Male and the Ascetic Ideal in Thirteenth-Century Jewish Mysticism," in J.J. Cohen and B. Wheeler, eds., *Becoming Male in the Middle Ages* (New York, 1997), pp. 151-185.

[16] *Sha'arei Qedushah*, IV.2, in *Ketavim Hadashim le-Rabbenu Hayyim Vital*, p. 5.

[17] Consider the following passage in the anonymous kabbalistic treatise *Sullam ha-'Aliyyah*, ed. J.E. Parush (Jerusalem, 1989), p. 73: "All this is in order to separate the soul and to purify it from all the physical forms and entities. . . . And when it is in this condition, he will prepare his true thought to form in his heart and in his intellect as if he were sitting above in the heaven of heavens before the Holy One, blessed be he, and in the midst of the splendor, the effulgence, and the

majesty of his *Shekhinah*, and it is as if he were to see the Holy One, blessed be he, sitting like a high and exalted king."

[18] *Ma'arekhet ha-'Elohut* (Jerusalem, 1963), ch. 10, 142b-144b; for discussion of this passage, see Wolfson, *Through a Speculum that Shines*, p. 325.

[19] *Sha'arei Qedushah*, IV.2, in *Ketavim Hadashim le-Rabbenu Hayyim Vital*, p. 12, citing *Ma'arekhet ha-'Elohut*, 143a.

[20] *Sha'arei Qedushah*, III.5, p. 89.

[21] Ibid., III.8, p. 101.

[22] *Sha'arei Qedushah*, III.5, pp. 89-90; and see analysis of this passage in Wolfson, *Through a Speculum that Shines*, pp. 320-323. See also Werblowsky, *Joseph Karo*, pp. 65-71; E.R. Wolfson, "Weeping, Death, and Spiritual Ascent in Sixteenth-Century Jewish Mysticism," in *Death, Ecstasy, and Other Worldly Journeys*, pp. 209-247. On the description of *devequt* as an ecstatic separation of the soul from the body and its consequent restoration to the divine, cf. *Sha'arei Qedushah*, III.2., pp. 80 and 84.

[23] See, by contrast, the characterization of *kavvanah* in sixteenth-century Lurianic material given by Scholem, *Major Trends in Jewish Mysticism* (New York, 1956), pp. 276-278. Scholem emphasizes that, for the Lurianic kabbalists, *kavvanah*, which involves concentrating on the mystical meaning associated with each word, is the way that leads to *devequt*, the kabbalistic equivalent of *unio mystica*. True to fashion, however, he does not mention the visionary quality of the experience.

[24] *'Olat Tamid* (Jerusalem, 1907), 46a-b. This passage appears in some editions of *Sha'ar Ruah ha-Qodesh*, for example the version of this text published in *Kitvei Rabbenu ha-'Ari* (Jerusalem, 1963), 11:39. For discussion, see Wolfson, *Through a Speculum that Shines*, pp. 323-324, and Fine, "Purifying the Body," pp. 131-132. Cf., *Sha'arei Qedushah*, IV.2, in *Ketavim Hadashim le-Rabbenu Hayyim Vital*, p. 15.

[25] *Sha'arei Qedushah*, III.4, pp. 87-88.

[26] This aspect of *devequt* in the writings of Jewish mystics was duly noted by Werblowsky, *Joseph Karo*, pp. 58-59. Interestingly, Werblowsky suggests that the idea expressed by kabbalists that the mystic's heart is the true dwelling of God may betray the influence of Sufism. For a more recent study of this possibility, see P. Fenton, "La 'Hitbodedut' chez les premiers Qabbalists en Orient et chez les Soufis," in R. Goetschel, ed., *Prière, mystique et Judaïsme* (Paris, 1987), pp. 133-157, and idem, "The Influences of Sufism on the Kabbalah in Safed," *Mahanayyim* 6 (1993), pp. 170-179 (in Hebrew).

[27] *Shem 'Olam*, A. Jellinek, ed. (Vienna, 1891), p. 11.

[28] See E.R. Wolfson, "Anthropomorphic Imagery and Letter Symbolism in the Zohar," in *Jerusalem Studies in Jewish Thought* 8 (1989), pp. 147-181 (in Hebrew).

[29] *Sha'arei 'Orah*, J. Ben-Shlomo, ed. (Jerusalem, 1981), 1:49.

[30] See G. Scholem, *On the Kabbalah and Its Symbolism* (New York, 1969), pp. 32-86.

[31] See M. Idel, *The Mystical Experience in Abraham Abulafia* (Albany, 1988), pp. 95-100.

[32] See Scholem, *Major Trends*, p. 141; M. Idel, *Language, Torah, and Hermeneutics in Abraham Abulafia* (Albany, 1989), pp. 35-38, 77-79, and 163 n. 33.

[33] For fuller discussion of this issue, see E.R. Wolfson, "The Doctrine of Sefirot in the Prophetic Kabbalah of Abraham Abulafia," in *Jewish Studies Quarterly* 2 (1995), pp. 336-371 and 3 (1996), pp. 47-84; idem, "Mystical Rationalization of the Commandments in the Prophetic Kabbalah of Abraham Abulafia," in A. Ivry, A. Arkush, and E.R. Wolfson, eds., *Perspectives on Jewish Thought and Mysticism* (Reading, 1997), pp. 311-360.

ELLIOT R. WOLFSON

MYTHOLOGY, JUDAISM AND: The renowned historian of religion and student of religious myth, Mircea Eliade, commented that the term "myth" as used today has become "somewhat equivocal." In ordinary usage the term means a false idea, a story that lacks truth. By contrast, as used by "ethnologists, sociologists, and historians of religions" the term indicates a "sacred" story, a narrative that serves as an "exemplary model." The two definitions conflict. While the second emphasizes myth's positive characteristics, the first is pejorative, holding that myth lacks the rigor of science, reflects superstition and naive belief, and has no place in modern life. Eliade traces this conflict from ancient through the modern times,[1] himself defending myth and arguing for its supreme value within all human culture. According to Eliade, the function of myth is "to reveal models and, in so doing, to give a meaning to the World (sic) and to human life."[2] Such models, he says, are indispensable for all human existence.

Another view recently has become popular. Myth, as understood today, takes its meaning from its original Greek sense of "story." To call something a myth is to denote not its significance, truth, or accuracy, but its form, content, and purpose. Since, in this view, myth is a literary form, a type of narrative, linguistic analysis holds the key to its meaning, purpose, and value. Accordingly, structuralists like Claude Levi-Strauss[3] look to the form of a narrative to determine whether it is myth. They see myth as a type of language, a linguistic trop, in which mythic symbols work as a vocabulary. On the most obvious level, this means that, rather than speaking directly about sexuality and conflict, stories will use erotic symbols, such as serpents and apples. On a more complex level, motifs such as rescue from danger, ascent to heaven, and descent to the nether world develop particular meanings within the literary system.

This approach to myth holds that audiences learn to interpret mythic symbols, recognizing the significance of a tale concerning the "one forbidden thing," whether what is forbidden is opening a certain door, eating a certain food, or looking at a person's face. When more than one such motif occurs, there will be a "grammar" that determines their arrangement. Thus, whether an exile or a quest follows the breaking of the forbidden thing may have important significance beyond the specific details of the particular story.[4]

Even when viewed as a kind of language, myth can be interpreted positively or negatively. It may be seen as providing a structure and framework for meaning, so as to reinforce the status quo; or it can be used as the occasion for ever-new meanings, an opportunity to challenge accepted traditions. In evaluating this dichotomy, Umberto Eco contrasts the ancient and medieval understanding of myth with the modern view. He thinks that earlier approaches used myth as a way to *limit* the unfettered imagination. By drawing mythic pictures, authors established a framework for thinking. In this setting, myth did not encourage reckless speculation, because it provided a concrete image against which thinkers had to measure their words. Like philosophy, myth thus was a way of controlling the tendency for people to follow their most whimsical thoughts, what Eco calls "the exaggerated fecundity of symbols." By contrast to this approach, Eco opposes what he sees as the recent use of myth as a license to imagine whatever the thinker wishes. Myth, that is, has come to offer an excuse to generate ever more outrageous models of reality. Eco laments that a thinker today "no longer recognizes the discipline that myths impose on the symbols they involve."[5]

The following presentation of Jewish myth uses the model of language and avoids the temptation to evaluate myth as either a positive or negative force in human life. We take myth to be a certain formal genre—that of a story. But while every text discussed here shares this narrative characteristic, it must be understood that not all stories count as myths. A second characteristic that defines myth is function. In general, we understand narratives as mythic when they provide models for human behavior, human society, or human perception of reality. Scholars however debate the specifics. Some claim that myth conveys a view of the world, an image of the cosmos. Others discover in myth psychological paradigms that allow people to cope with their inner conflicts. A related approach interprets mythic function as sociological or political. Finally some identify an imaginative function of myth, evoking and provoking human creativity. A final characteristic of myth lies in its content, the message that the texts transmit. The language of myth not only functions in specific ways but uses a specific set of ideas to achieve its goals. That complex of concepts creates the content of a particular mythology.

History and myth: Since the nineteenth century, this variety of approaches to myth has influenced the way Jewish scholars investigate the relationship of mythology and Judaism. Indeed, Jews who study myth today debate its significance by offering the same array of positive and negative evaluations as are found among students of myth generally.[6] Most modern scholars of Judaism, for instance, deem the story of creation in Genesis 1:1-2:4 either to be a "myth" or to preserve mythic elements. By this they do not mean that it is a fiction or that its science is inaccurate. Even evolution, most students of religion aver, presents a mythic view of the universe. The creation story qualifies as myth because it tells a story designed to provide a model of reality, to point to the ordered and designed quality of the world in which we live.

Many Jewish scholars hail what they see as this mythic aspect of the story. It shows, they say, that Jews created a viable paradigm of reality that continues even today to influence the way people think. Other scholars disagree, seeing "myth" in general as a primitive way of regarding the world. These scholars privilege non-mythic models of reality and argue that the Genesis story itself is the first example of exactly such a non-mythic depiction. In this view, any mythic elements of the creation story have been transformed in the book of Genesis from narrative into objective descriptions of the observed world. The story therefore is not to be interpreted as "myth" at all. While members of each group agree that myth means something other than "fiction," or "inaccurate science," they disagree in their definitions of myth. Examining those who see Jewish myth negatively and those who see it positively reveals the variety of definitions held by scholars of Jewish mythology today.

The biblical scholar Yehezkel Kaufmann exemplifies the approach of those who deny that biblical accounts rightly are deemed mythological. He considers the central contribution of monotheism to human culture to be its depiction of a world unified by the grand design of its single maker. Whereas polytheism's mythic stories offered several competing models of reality, monotheism, Kaufmann argues, initiated a scientific mode of thinking. Polytheists required myth because they lacked the basis for a predictable, ordered exploration of the empirical world. They relied on suggestive mythic pictures because the multitude of divinities left them at the mercy of arbitrary and contradictory supernatural forces. Jewish monotheism, in contrast, leaves no room for mythic narratives, because it regards all reality as evidence for a single, understandable pattern. Observation, historical progress, and human development replace myth as a means for comprehending the world. While Kaufmann acknowledges that elements in the Hebrew Bible draw on stories from ancient polythe-

istic myth, he insists that the author of the biblical narratives transformed pagan motifs into a view of reality based on science and history. Myth, understood this way, opposes history and science; its exemplary models represent a now outmoded way of comprehending the cosmos.[7]

Another biblical scholar, Henri Frankfort, advances a similar critique of myth. Frankfort posits two spheres in which human beings create "reality:" that of history and that of ritual. The Bible, according to him, propels human beings to act in the world around them, to change reality, to progress to higher stages of existence. Myth, on the other hand, points backward to eternal time, to a world that exists beside and beyond our current existence. Myth invokes ritual as the sphere in which people make the most difference. By acting in ritual prayer, song, and drama, people recreate and thus recapture an ideal reality of which they have lost sight. Mythic thinking detracts from history not because it provides unscientific models of the world, but because it elevates cultic action over historical deeds. It yearns for a return to primal perfection rather than an advance to a future utopia.[8]

Both Kaufmann and Frankfort argue that myth substitutes for history. This theory meets opposition from many biblical scholars who deny that the Bible anticipates modern intellectual approaches. Some argue that the historical veneer in biblical narratives cannot disguise the basic mythic elements that are present.[9] The reliance on miracles and folk lore within the biblical narratives suggests to such readers that the Bible has hardly gone far beyond the pagan materials it incorporates. They claim therefore that the Bible more accurately is interpreted within the context of ancient pre-scientific and pre-historical thinking than as a proto-modern breakthrough. Other thinkers refuse to choose between myth and history, describing the Bible instead as encompassing both categories within a unique type of writing called "epic."[10] This strategy, however, only deflects the discussion slightly. The question remains what should one do with a content that seems equally historical and non-historical.

Martin Buber offers a positive interpretation of myth by suggesting that the category "history" itself be reconsidered. History, for Buber, provides the context within which the human meeting with others occurs. The external "historical" events, which people chronicle, merely offer a backdrop for the "I-thou" encounter, the face-to-face embrace of one "self" with another. This perspective enables Buber to defend myth within Judaism, and, indeed, he examined the entire range of Jewish mythology within his unique I-Thou perspective.[11] His writings on the Bible analyze its texts to discover their potential for stimulating I-Thou meeting. In this account, myth represents a type of language that requires recitation for vitalization. When the written word becomes an enacted sound, creating a "speech-act," language gains vitality. Buber believes that such recitation, such speaking, acts creatively. It evokes a special dimension of being that, while as palpably real as ordinary experience, nevertheless enables people to move beyond ordinary limitations. Myth, for Buber, acts like a special language, a set of words that, when spoken, change existence. To speak, in this sense, is to perform an action. Myth, therefore, consists of language used to accomplish a deed, of "speech-acts" that create a sense of intimacy and connection to God. For Kaufmann and Frankfort, myth serves a pseudo-historical function; for Buber, it prepares the way for the only authentic history possible.

An approach similar to Buber's not only sees myth as conveying the true historical message, but elevates it above so-called "modern" historical approaches. Myth, on this view, represents an alternative to logical reasoning and history, but not a rival to it. It amplifies the human relationship to the cosmos. Science, history, and logic help humanity make use of the world in which they live. Myth, in this claim, teaches people how to relate immediately to the world and its creator.[12] This type of relation seems to exemplify what Buber meant by the "I-Thou" encounter. It moves beyond objective history to the history of the living subject, of the person, in relationship to another self. Myth, on this reading, opens the way to an unmediated meeting with the other, a meeting more difficult to achieve through texts of either science or history. While Henri Frankfort criticized pre-biblical thought as mythic because it stimulates ritual action rather than historical deeds, John L. McKenzie celebrates the ability of myth to reveal a meaning that transcends the mundane events that make up historical experience.

Another approach regards myth as a type of non-historical narrative that contains within it evidence about the history of its makers. Jonathan Z. Smith, for example, identifies the function of myth as primarily historical. Through a functionalist approach, he uncovers the "history in myth." Myth functions, on his reading, as a reflection and repository of evidence concerning a group's past.[13] The question for Smith is not whether or not the Bible thought it was writing history. Historians do not often realize the mythic aspects of what they write, and myth makers do not often recognize the history within their myths. In both cases the "function" of historical or mythic writing is more a matter of the reader's perception than of the author's intent.

Some thinkers, like Mircea Eliade, go beyond identifying a positive historical function in myth. They claim that myth offers a unique contribution to human existence that no other human phenomenon, whether historical or psychological, can fulfill. Only through myth, they claim, do people discover the transcendent realm of the eternal that surpasses historical time (see Eliade, ibid.). Elie Wiesel similarly finds in myth a vehicle for conveying a moral orientation to the world that historical narrative lacks. Without myth, history lapses into a record of one event after another. With myth, history takes on moral significance; it becomes a series of choices that define the moral stature of human beings.[14] Here the function of myth cannot be replaced by history or philosophy, although the content of myth may use both of these as its building blocks.

Whether contending against myth, championing its cause, or arguing for its moral relevance, these thinkers analyze the truth claims that myth advances. Those who oppose myth think that its claims refer to the same data as those of science and history, with myth providing only imprecise and impressionistic images of that data. Whether due to the influence of polytheism or to a pre-scientific attitude toward nature, this mythic imprecision renders it a poor anticipation of true history. Another view, however, sees myth as a realm of being parallel to but not identical with that of empirical studies. Whether identified with Buber's "I-Thou" meeting or with some moral dimension, myth points to a reality that history cannot comprehend.

We shall see below that some Jewish myths do indeed seem to overlap with empirical history, while other mythic texts point beyond that sphere—some to morality and others to a different theological realm. Contemporary students of Jewish myth accordingly need not limit mythic texts to a single truth claim. Instead they may posit the various possible claims evoked by a particular story, and in so doing explore a variety of ways of construing the meaning of that text.

Social, political, and psychological functions of myth: Myth may function as an alternative to history, acting within the political or sociological sphere to provide a unifying ideology or social consensus, articulating a particular group's highest values and aspirations. In this function, political myth serves several purposes. It can stabilize a society by reinforcing existing views of leadership and civil order. It can also destabilize the social norms by introducing new paradigms and models of politics. Often one mythic image may perform both purposes, providing stability in a time of crisis precisely by challenging the accepted image of the world order. Many Jewish texts may be deemed mythic precisely because of their political function.[15]

Mythic texts also function psychologically. Some regard this function as dangerous and primitive, deriving from an immature period in the evolution of human thought, which must be replaced by more mature thinking. In this case, however, psychological maturity rather than science and history replace outmoded myth. Rene Girard argues this

case with persuasive passion,[16] seeing myth as fulfilling a psychological and sociological function of justifying violence. Though mythology, he argues, a society projects its violence outward onto a scapegoat. For instance, myths of the Greek god Zeus and of the Scandinavian Baldr exonerate their heroes from charges of mass murder.

Girard argues that through such myth a people learns to accept its own violence as necessary and even virtuous. The Bible, in contrast, recognizes the violence that its "heroes" perpetrate but *criticizes* it. Just as the Roman myth of the building of Rome depends upon the fratricide of its twin founders, so in the Bible civilization begins with Cain's fratricidal murder of Abel. Yet the Bible refuses to exonerate Cain and consistently reveals the perils of violence and its inevitable destruction of human society. For Girard this willingness to face up to violence and offer no excuses for it indicates an abandonment of myth. While for Girard both mythic and non-mythic stories offer exemplary models of human behavior, they differ on the basis of content. Myth disguises violence and hides it under good intentions; the Bible, by rejecting myth, takes an honest look at the violent human psyche. For Girard such honesty represents a mature approach, while myth is symptomatic of an immature unwillingness to face facts.

Psychologists, however, do not invariably take a negative view of myth and its functions. The psychological study of myth, begun by such pioneers as Freud and Jung, often reflects the tension already found in theorists of myth generally; some evaluate it positively and some negatively (see Segal, ibid., pp. 11-17). Erich Fromm exemplifies a positive approach to biblical and Jewish myth, claiming that while some myths reinforce immature psychological responses to reality, others aid mature development. He hails Jewish myth for serving the latter function.[17] Beyond simply defending myth, some scholars condemn cultures defined by "amythia," that is, the rejection of myth. They argue that such a rejection deprives people of the tools provided by the unconscious for self-discovery. On this reading, people living in a society cursed with amythia remain blind to their inner nature, unable to cope with the buried truths hidden in their psyches.[18] Judaism, or at least its myths, offers Jews an opportunity to gain insight into their dilemmas and problems. Jewish myth functions therapeutically as a useful tool as modern Jews seek to understand hidden personality traits.

We shall illustrate below that Jewish myth functions in diverse ways and cannot be limited to a single purpose, whether sociological, political, or psychological. These stories sometimes unite a society and sometimes fragment it. They sometimes enable people to confront the darker parts of their personality and at other times allow them to find a refuge from their deepest fears. A careful student of myth avoids branding one social consequence of myth "functional" and another "dysfunctional" or labeling one psychological result of myth "mature" and another "immature." The scholarly task must be to discover both the psychological and sociological repercussions of myth and to allow readers to draw their own conclusions. The variety of mythic types parallels the variety of human needs and should be understood within the context of human diversity.

Imagination and modern myth: Myth in the modern world seems distinctly different from traditional mythology. Contemporary life proliferates models of reality that could well bear the title "myth." As Roland Barthes, who defines myth as any language that refers to reality rather than seeking to create it, suggests, the ordinary perceptions ingrained into the social fabric provide the myths by which people live. Myth, he thus argues, reproduces reality without seeking to create something new. He offers as examples of myth the latest cinematic icon, popular styles in dress, and commercial advertising.[19]

Modern Jewish writing reflects exactly such an influence of myth. Movements like Reform Judaism, Zionism, and Yiddishism create mythic images to legitimate their new and distinctive constructions of Judaism. Indeed, myth seems particularly prominent in Jewish political ideology today. Yet some thinkers complain that seeing a use of myth in these political contexts has transformed what had always been defined as a religious phenomenon into an "ordinary" one. Calling Zionism a myth, that is, cheapens the term, insofar as, in service to an ideology, mythic narratives fails to perform the creative function of "true" myth. They hold, by contrast, that myth is always a positive force, *creating* a view of reality and initiating a believer into it. If modern myth reduces this power of creativity to political expediency, then it has forfeited its most important function.[20]

Political myth, however, is only one form of modern Jewish mythology. Jewish myth often acts as a catalyst for the imagination. Reading Jewish myth, contemporary Jews may glimpse new ways of conceiving of themselves and their tradition. Modern Jews, for instance, have explored the mystical tradition exposed by Gershom Scholem and have found in its depths resources for reinventing what it means to be a Jew. The sexual references, the plethora of symbols, and the mythic narratives appeal to them as an alternative to secular society. Other modern Jews, however, criticize this fascination with the fantastic and mythic. Both Walter Benjamin and Franz Rosenzweig emphasized the ethical rather than the mythic. Duty and task, understanding history and working to redeem it, became central to their vision of a renewed Judaism. Jewish renewal sometimes espouses the mythic as a source of strength and sometimes rejects it as a diversion from moral matters.[21]

The choice between renewal through myth or renewal through ethics may be too stark. Emmanuel Levinas, for example, agrees with Rosenzweig's emphasis on ethics. Nevertheless, he finds a use for Jewish myth. Myth offers an opportunity for reflection; it challenges Jews to "demythologize" its meaning—to interpret its symbolism. Levinas asserts that no single demythologization is ever final. Indeed, he says, Jewish creativity depends on demythologizing ancient texts. The problem, according to Levinas, comes only when myth takes itself too literally. He celebrates Jewish tradition as a "demythologizing of what was already demythologized, a quest for meaning to be renewed."[22] This view looks at myth as an irritant ready to be converted into a pearl. Levinas does not oppose myth as the point of departure for new and rational interpretations, for what he calls demythologization. But when Jews refuse to defuse myth, when they celebrate its imaginative function, then he thinks they have moved beyond the essential teachings of Judaism.[23] The correct use of myth breeds a greater sense of ethical responsibility and moral awareness, not a lessened one.

Levinas' approach intimates a way of reading Jewish myth that mediates between those who view it negatively and those who interpret it positively. Whether myth contributes positively to modern Judaism or whether it undermines it, mythic elements do indeed intrude in Judaic religion today. The survey that below devotes attention to modern Jewish myth-makers without suggesting an evaluation of their effect on Jewish religion. Clearly modern Jewish myths differ from previous Jewish mythology. The decision as to whether that novelty strengthens or weakens the tradition does not lie with students of mythology. Thus we sketch the variety of modern myths as testimony to the continuing power of myth-making within Jewish religious life.

Content of Jewish myth: Jewish myths, defined structurally as Jewish narratives and functionally as the use of these narratives to convey a world view, to accomplish social, political, and psychological goals, and to stimulate imagination, exhibit certain common characteristics. The content of Jewish mythology, that is, unites it through different centuries and transcends the uses to which it has been put. While each period yields specific myths formed out of the historical and literary material of that period, other myths remain constant throughout Judaism's historical development. All of these myths fall into three broad categories: the cosmological, the anthropological, and the political.

The cosmological myth describes the creation of the world and evokes a sense of the reality existing outside of human activity. It projects an image of the natural environment in which people find themselves. Sometimes it suggests a supportive, positive environment; sometimes it implies a broken cosmos

that presents obstacles for humanity to overcome. The usual content of cosmological myth is a "creation narrative," describing how this world came into being. Sometimes, however, cosmology lies embedded in a hymn of praise or a prophetic sermon. Creation as a general subject offers a key to this type of Jewish myth.

Anthropological myth concentrates on the human role in the world and the questions raised by that role. What purpose does humanity serve? What is the nature of human beings? What effect does humanity have on the non-human world? While Jewish mythic texts sometimes pose these questions very generally, most often they examine them from a more narrow focus. Jewish myth moves quickly from an evoking of humanity and its general task to a description of the duties of Jews in particular. Anthropological myths tend to focus on God's revelation to the Jews and how that revelation reveals human potentials and problems, actualizing the former and correcting the latter.

Political myth focuses on the nature of the Jewish people, its history and its destiny. Mythic narratives of this type illuminate the changing fortunes of a people whose national life often underwent dramatic alterations. Jews were exiled from their land; they experienced periods of power and times of political oppression; they evaluated military, political, and religious claims to leadership; they hoped for a "redemption" that would restore them to political independence. Not only national liberation and subjugation, but also shifting leadership groups influenced the political myths of Judaism. Often several competing political myths exist, each speaking for a specific power group within a single context. The two central images associated with this type of myth are exile and redemption, although related subjects such as the messiah often surface as well. Political myths suggest why exile occurred, explain how and when redemption will come about, and depict the nature of the messianic leader and the importance of that leader either as a sign of the redemption or as the agent bringing it about.

Scholars of Judaism debate the meaning, significance, function, and validity of each of these mythic types, offering linguistic, functionalist, and content oriented interpretations. Some investigators argue that each period of Jewish history creates its own mythic vocabulary. The symbolic language used by Jews in the period of the Bible, they suggest, reflects ancient Near Eastern influences. The mythic vocabulary of the Rabbinic period exhibits relationships to Hellenistic culture. Medieval Jewish philosophers draw on one mythic tradition, while medieval Jewish mystics express themselves using a distinctive mythology of their own. Using this paradigm, the modern period appears as a dramatic break with the past.

This model, which uses historical context to understand myth, has several flaws. The historicist approach appeals to our need for exact knowledge, for explanatory theories. But precisely because it offers what are apparently absolute answers and certain facts, chronology proves a false friend. First, as already noted, the major thematic content remains consistent across the different periods. Second, associating mythic texts with particular contexts of time and space confuses a literary reality with a historical one. The myths discussed here occur in writings, in textual expressions. The texts themselves cannot provide evidence as to whether these myths represent a "majority" or "minority" view. Relying on history to decode myths often obscures the way mythic alternatives compete with one another. No single group of myths represents a univocal, unambivalent function. Without recognizing this diversity, a scholar might impose a single meaning on a varied and conflicting body of data.

The approach used here maintains a traditional four-fold periodization of biblical, Rabbinic, medieval, and modern times[24] and refers specifically to the written documents that emerged in each period. The Bible, of course, is a single work (although it turns out to be an anthology). Rabbinic texts are often conflicting sets of writings representing a range of religious, social, and political views. By "medieval" is meant two sorts of mythic texts, those of Jewish philosophers written under the influence of Greek, Muslim, and Christian thought, and those of Jewish mys-

tics up through the nineteenth and twentieth centuries. Looking for myth in the modern period requires a broader definition of appropriate textual data. What constitutes the "modern" in this essay ranges from ideological writings by Zionists, feminists, and other political or religious activists to what has been called "belle lettres," that is, essays, poetry, novels, and short stories. To understand the mythic language of these texts, one must examine their literary form. Rather than begin with a historical sketch against which to decode myths in each section, the survey that follows looks to the literary structure in which the myths are imbedded. After establishing the framework within which the myths occur, each section summarizes and analyzes the central mythic content. In each case, the texts refer to creation, revelation, exile, and redemption.

Myth in the Hebrew Bible: The Hebrew Bible took shape as an anthology of religious literature. It contains several distinct genres of writing and often presents several competing descriptions of the same event, contradictory versions of similar laws, or opposing theological theories about reality. The mythical elements in this anthology share the diversity found in the other genres represented. Narratives containing myths, prophetic sermons alluding to them, or poetic evocations of mythic themes combine to make the Bible a rich resource for scholarship on myth.[25] Some myths take the shape of narratives concerning critical events in the human past— the creation of the world, a catastrophic flood, the founding of cities, the development of national identities. These myths show striking similarity to narratives found in texts associated with other ancient Near Eastern civilizations,[26] and one mode of understanding biblical myth, accordingly, is through comparison to these other stories.

Myth, however, appears in biblical writings other than narratives, and another approach to biblical myth takes these varied genres as its point of departure. Anthropologists, that is, have analyzed biblical narrative, law, and ritual to discover within them myth that functions psychologically or sociologically.[27] Laws, for instance, may evoke a mythic understanding of the world. The rule that fruitful trees, like Hebrew males, must be "circumcised" suggests a myth concerning productivity. A "cut" that judiciously prunes a living organism may, contrary to common expectations, increase, rather than decrease, fruitfulness. This intimates a vision of the world and may even serve a social or psychological function appropriate for myth. Sometimes even an apparently dull genealogy listing a king's forbears, for instance, may have surprising implications. The inclusion of a mother of doubtful purity or of an incestuous heritage may serve one of several mythic purposes. Even the story of a ritual sacrifice, the carving up of a carcass and the precise distribution of its parts, may reconcile people to a disjointed life or may confront them with the chaos inside themselves.

An alternative way of decoding biblical myth emphasizes the communal context in which these myths appear. A postcritical stance looks at biblical narratives as the possession of a community and discovers their significance in the collective consciousness of the group. This approach involves two related ideas. The first is that of intertextuality. Michael Fishbane teases out an intertextual code in which history becomes myth and myth history in a series of texts that refer back to each other.[28] The variety among the myths of creation, differences separating views of revelation, and the multi-polar visions of exile and redemption become, in this approach, equal participants in a vast community of meanings.

The second element is that of subjectivity. If there is a community of meaning within a text, then its final significance arises within a concrete community of others. The reading community as well as the communal library that is read provides a key to myth. This element entails a subjectivity by which a reader becomes engaged not only with texts but with a living community of other people. Myth takes on significance when the reader asks, "What does this mean for us?" By reading the myths with a postmodern openness that allows several meanings, this approach refuses to proclaim any single explanation of myth paramount. Instead it privileges and

deems most important an affective link with the community.[29]

In content, biblical myth evokes diverse models of creation, human nature, and the redemptive process. Images of creation occur throughout the Hebrew Bible from the famous creation stories in Genesis through references in the prophets and the Psalms. Three variant themes appear in these stories. One theme, found in its fullest expression in Gen. 1:1-2:4 but also intimated in Isaiah 40, emphasizes an organic development in which one creation emanates out of another through progressively fine differentiation. Light emerges when differentiated from darkness, land from the differentiation of sky and water, one type of animal arises from differentiation from another. This creative pattern parallels biological procreation in which new beings derive from previous ones.

A second pattern, illustrated in prophetic and Psalmic materials (see Is. 14, Ezek. 28; 51:9-13, Ps. 104:1-13), emphasizes conflict and drama. God struggles with the recalcitrant powers of chaos and darkness. The divinity vanquishes them by setting limits to the raging waters, subduing the sea monsters, and reducing an originally powerful but rebellious humanity—sometimes seen as a prince in a great garden—to more manageable proportions.

A third mythic strand, found in Gen. 2:4b-4:24, for example, mediates between these two. In it, compromise and negotiation replace either organic creation or a battle against chaos. God experiments with the world, using a more mechanistic model. In this model God creates in an analogous way to human construction; the world is God's because "he made it," just as artisans own the work of their hands.

What function might these stories serve? Some interpreters claim that they reveal repressed psychological tensions. Theodor Reik, for example, finds in Gen. 2-3 a reversal of the natural order by which women give birth to men. He understands this as a mythic way to confront men with their ambivalence toward women and childbirth.[30] Edmund Leach claims that each mythic narrative reiterates the same "persistent sequence of binary discriminations," and thus he discovers a unity underlying the narrative complexity. All three versions of creation are interacting possibilities referring to the range of human experience (see Leach, op. cit., pp. 7-23). Reik affirms the conflict among the myths, while Leach sees the diversity transcended by a deeper unity.

The myths of creation offer a complex set of diverse narratives that different scholars perceive as fulfilling sometimes opposite functions. The same variety characterizes the anthropological myths of the Bible. Basic to that variety is a single judgment concerning human nature: human beings need control and refinement. The Bible describes several continuing conflicts among people: between males and females, between shepherds, farmers, and urbanites, between generations, among siblings, and among the conflicting impulses within the human psyche. These stories set the stage for the laws and rituals of the Bible. In its central anthropological concern, biblical legislation presupposes the need for a mechanism, attuned to these basic realities of human nature, that can provide such refinement and control. While myth implies narrative and story, it thus may surface as the foundation of ethical and ritual imperatives.

Biblical rituals exemplify a type of law that implies a myth. Sometimes the myth attached to a ritual is clear: both Gen. 17 and Exod. 4 supply the ritual of circumcision with a narrative setting. At other times the mythic substratum of the ritual needs to be excavated. Upon examination, two general types of myth underlie biblical legislation. One set of rituals demands that people submit to a superior and supernatural power. Human nature is so degenerate and sinful that people cannot rescue themselves. Their natural inclinations overpower them despite themselves. They require divine assistance to ameliorate themselves. A divinely revealed ritual transforms and perfects their nature. To perform this ritual, priest are entrusted with special powers and precise directions to follow. By putting the procedure into effect, they can work a miraculous change on their people, for instance, sprinkling the blood of sacrificial animals so that the community becomes pure (see, e.g., Lev. 16).

The myth that generates this first type of ritual describes humanity as requiring supernatural assistance through priestly intermediaries. Another type of ritual presupposes a myth that conceives of every person as a potential priest and the people of Israel as a "nation of priests" (Exod. 19:6). According to this myth, all Israelites, not just priests, participate in the rituals that transform human nature. The rituals enable those who perform them to transcend their natural limitations and so assume a human nature that, through obedience to divine commandments, can develop positive and successful traits. Lev. 17-26 sets out moral, dietary, and sexual laws that every Israelite must observe to ensure the well-being of the community. Negative aspects of human nature come under the control of divine legislation. Lev. 11:1-46 establishes permitted and forbidden foods. No explanation of these ritual restrictions occurs in the biblical text, yet the implication of Lev. 26 seems to apply here as well: obedience to the rules brings prosperity and success, disobedience leads to chaos and disaster.

These diverse rituals with their different mythic presuppositions have occasioned scholarly debate concerning the meaning of biblical myth. In the nineteenth century, the anthropologist W. Robertson Smith offered a striking analysis of biblical ritual and myth. He understood the religious practices, the myth and ritual, described in the Bible within the context of ancient Semitic religion generally. Smith thus read biblical ritual as testifying to a social myth of a "blood bond" by which human beings absorb into themselves the spirit of that which is sacrificed. Through this absorption they create a spiritual link among all who have shared in the sacrifice.[31] The myth of a new reality created by the extraordinary activities of sacrificing and consuming a victim underlies and legitimates the ritual act.

The contemporary anthropologist Mary Douglas has focused attention on the dietary laws, examining the ordered and rational nature of their categorization of reality. Douglas sees the mythic world-view illuminated by dietary restrictions as emphasizing wholeness and completeness. While the world may not always look pure and perfect, the biblical structure offers a model of how it should manifest itself. The myth expresses itself as a story of creation: "God's work through the blessing is essentially to create order, through which men's affairs prosper."[32] In effect, however, the operative myth concerns human abilities. Not only does God create a perfect world, human beings as well can imitate the divine and exemplify that divine order in the way they control their own lives.

We see that, as with creation myths, so concerning the meaning of anthropological ones, analysts differ. Some emphasize the transformative power of ritual and the myths supporting it. Others emphasize how ritual, because of its underlying myths, empowers human action. These different understandings of anthropological myth may actually be complementary rather than contradictory, for, at times, the bible seems to advocate one understanding of human nature and at other times another. The different strands in the mythic material intertwine in strange ways.

The same complexity occurs in the Bible's political myths, as is illustrated especially well by the pivotal story of the Exodus from Egypt. According to this myth, Israel began as a nation when God appointed Moses to lead a group of slaves from bondage in Egypt to a land promised to their progenitors. The Bible tells this story in several different ways. Sometimes the story emphasizes a miraculous escape from slavery followed by inheritance of the promised land (Ps. 105:23-44). Elsewhere we find an intermediary stage during which the people refuse to obey God and demonstrate their rebellious character (Ps. 106:7-39). Other biblical texts locate a divine revelation on Mount Sinai during the intermediary period (Neh. 9:9-25). These variations reveal three different ways in which Israel understands itself. The people may derive its identity from the land it has inherited. The national homeland, the culture of place and language, appears as the identifying marks of an Israelite in the first myth. The second myth focuses on national char-

acter rather than national geography. The rebellious social response of the people typifies their political order. Israel in this paradigm appears as an unruly social unit needing strict rules and guidance. The third paradigm understands Israel as a people of revelation, with the central and defining moment of the Exodus being the receiving of Torah in the wilderness. To be a member of this people implies neither a national homeland nor an inherent nature. Instead it depends on accepting the teachings of revelation. To become part of this people means to follow Torah.

Frank Cross interprets the range of Exodus myths as reflecting changing views of reality (op. cit., pp. 88-174), to which he associates as well changing myths of creation. The motif of Israel's holy war in which a slave people conquers its land parallels the myth of God's creation as a conquest of chaos. The Exodus understood as an explanation for national dispersion and political failure resembles the myth that views creation as a story of compromise and people's continual disappointing of God. Finally, the Exodus as the occasion of Torah points to an eschatological future, to a new creation in which the promises of Torah find fulfillment. This orientation imputes a divine intention to Torah that will inevitably be realized. In all these cases, the myth affirms the status quo and, whether triumphant, defeatist, or optimistic, the myth gives a reason to accept present conditions.

The Exodus myth contrasts with a related political myth—often called "messianic"—that anticipates a future time of social change and revolution. The term "messiah" literally refers to an anointed political or religious leader. Messianic myth, however, describes the ideal characteristics of such a leader. The Bible often presents heroes of the past in an idealized way. Their genealogical pedigree, their youthful experience, and their heroic exploits provide a model for later generations. Sometimes a former leader articulates this idealized picture: the Bible records the words of both King David and King Solomon in such a mythic fashion. At other times a prophetic speech will enumerate the virtues expected of a true leader.

Yet other myths look to the end of time without explicit reference to a messianic hero. These eschatological myths often reverse the myths of creation and portray a return to chaos. They imagine a penultimate battle among supernal beings followed by a new creation that corrects the abuses of the contemporary world order. Biblical myth offers conflicting portraits of this final sequence of events as well as of the nature and function of a messianic leader.

These myths yield diverse interpretations. Both Gershom Scholem and Walter Benjamin recognized dangerous political implications in messianic change, which they viewed as disturbing, as disruptive of the status quo. Despite this agreement, they disagreed about the desirability of a messianic myth (Handelman, op. cit., pp. 35-46, 118, 161). Benjamin, for his part, often identified his own politics with the messianic, with his stressing of the need to end "history," to make a radical beginning. The messianic was not a goal toward which people strove but rather a break with all previous progress, a break Benjamin found essential for the renewal of human society. Unlike Benjamin, Scholem did not embrace this alteration but sought to avoid it. He was suspicious of the messianic because he held that it disrupted society. By contrast to both these scholars, Frank Cross sees biblical political myth, including that of the Exodus, as conservative, breeding acceptance of the status quo.

As with anthropological myth or creation mythology, one need not imagine biblical political myth as fulfilling only one single function. Biblical mythology, rather, shows diversity and hence inspires diverse responses among students of myth. It embraces creation myths of conflict, organic birth, and negotiated compromise. Some interpreters explain this in terms of the dynamic conflicts within the human psyche. Others see it as a manifestation of the basic binary structure of human consciousness.

Biblical anthropology sometimes despairs of human nature and trusts only to miraculously revealed rituals that change that nature. Other biblical myths envision human nature more positively and advance a ritualism that urges humanity to imitate the rationality of the deity. Again analysts divide over whether that myth creates a "blood bond" of initiated members or whether it merely draws attention to the rationality of the universe. Finally the political myth of the Exodus, understood in one of several ways, contrasts with the political myth of the messiah, in any of its manifestations. Some theorists of myth focus on the conservative nature of the Exodus myth, while others emphasize the radicality of the messianic myth. In every case, the Bible exemplifies variety and diversity both in the data it provides and in the way scholars have understood it.

Rabbinic mythology: What is "Rabbinic" mythology? Gary Porton introduces his *Understanding Rabbinic Midrash: Texts and Commentary* (New Jersey, 1985, pp. 1-5) with a useful contrast between the modern, everyday usage of the term "rabbi" and its technical meaning applied to texts produced in late antiquity. He notes that the term "Rabbinic refers to the way of life, the beliefs, the ideas, the ideals, and the behaviors of the rabbis of late antiquity" (ibid., p. 4). These traits as illustrated by one set of "Rabbinic" writings from antiquity need not be identical with those found in other sets of writings. While Porton traces some common presuppositions of the Rabbinic genre of midrash, he also painstakingly articulates the differences among the various collections he studies. Other scholars approach this material as an intertextual whole in which one set of writings supplements another. In order to discover the Rabbinic use of the parable, for example, David Stern brings illustrations from a varied range of sources. Daniel Boyarin looks to the "gapped and dialogical" nature of texts to find a single perspective.[33]

Despite their clear disagreements, both approaches to Rabbinic literature concur regarding the centrality of the "Torah myth," which holds that the surest guide to truth is the divine revelation as interpreted and taught by the rabbis of antiquity. The myth of Torah permeates Rabbinic texts: Torah is the key to redemption, it is the focal experience of revelation, and it is a mirror of God's own activities. This myth, created and sustained by rabbis, the scholarly experts in Torah, not only reinforced the power of these leaders but may indeed have shaped it. Creation myths confirmed the magical ability of these men; revelation myths legitimated their status; myths of redemption provided an alternative to a failed political program.[34]

Rabbinic creation myths, like biblical ones, present several conflicting cosmologies. Some myths depict God's creating the world out of himself. One text claims that he wrapped himself in a prayer shawl and irradiated creation from his luminous being (Gen. Rab. 3:4). Other texts portray God's acting as an artisan (ibid. 1:1), an architect who uses Torah as the blueprint for the cosmos. Still other depictions imagine God as a king who consults with angelic courtiers, like a father who acts out of mercy toward his children, or like a judge who invokes pure justice. These descriptions reveal a remarkable ambivalence. On the one hand, God appears as a wise and benevolent architect of the world. On the other hand, divine creative power often seems arbitrary, judgmental, or dangerously potent. God is both a creator who loves the creation and a supernatural being whose creative force can overwhelm the creation.

Of course these various views are all anthropomorphic; they consider divine creativity based on an analogy with human creativity. That creativity, strikingly, accords with the creative actions that rabbis themselves pursue. The Jew who looks to Torah, these texts assume, has the potential to imitate the divine, both in the positive sense of being creative and in the negative sense of possessing a potentially lethal force. Public worship offers the rabbis one sphere of power and control, for God obligingly creates the world by engaging in prayer. The rabbis sometimes serve as artisans, either literally or as architects of the social order. The rabbis may engage in political activities like courtiers, demand respect from their disciples as fathers expect from their children, or pronounce legal decisions like a judge. In every case the type of action that the rabbis actually carry out is imagined as a possible creative deed of the divine.

This analogy suggests that rabbis imitate divine creativity, which has clear, positive possibilities. Rabbis like God can control the natural world. In time of drought they bring rain; in time of scarcity they create living animals out of clay. Yet a negative misuse of this potential also may occur. Powers can be used to undermine society rather than help it. Some Rabbinic texts warn against speculating about divine creativity. Cautionary tales suggest the dangers involved as those who try to use creative power consume themselves or others in the attempt.

Stories of inter-Rabbinic conflict often focus on this question of creative power. One such story tells of the miracle worker Honi the Circle-Drawer (B. Ta. 23a). Several elements combine in the tale. First, Honi clearly imitates the divine power over nature. When a drought appears he first reprimands people for trusting him and not God, and when he pleads to God for rain he calls the people ignorant ones who "cannot tell the difference between their father in heaven and their father here on earth." Yet his power has its limits. God, the rabbis say, should punish him. In fact, the story tells how he finally must implore God to send him death as a release from a life impossible to maintain. This myth expresses the ambivalence of power, the problems of political authority. When compared with tales of other miracle workers, Honi appears as one possible model for imitating divine creativity measured against other models of strikingly different ways for rabbis to exemplify the divine creativity.[35]

The diversity in this appraisal of the divine creative forces appears as well in an understanding of human nature. Richard L. Rubenstein suggests the Rabbinic myths balance human freedom against the experience of human limitations. The aim, he states "is not to deny freedom to the creature, but to allow as much freedom as is consistent with the inherent limitations and structure of the created order."[36] Torah, for the rabbis, prescribes that domain of limited freedom. Myths depicting the revelation of Torah convey a sense of the ambivalent nature of human beings. The central scene of these myths of revelation is that of Moses' ascent to Sinai to receive the Torah. In some depictions God provides Torah as a gift to a ready and willing people; in others the nation must be coerced into accepting God's revealed law. Some narratives describe Moses' ascent and receiving of the gift without incident. Other tales picture him contending against the angels who would rather the Torah remain with them. Some versions of the event describe revelation as a once and forever act; other versions claim that an echo of the divine voice never ceases.

The diversity of descriptions applies as well to ways in which those who follow after the event of revelation can recapture it. Some stories claim that a modern Jew seeking knowledge of revelation must attain the same level of competence as Moses, must become an adept able to ascend to the angelic powers to gain access to the continuing flow of Torah. In other cases, being a disciple of a sage, learning at the feet of one who has inherited Torah from the past, suffices. Revelation after Moses occurs through the authorized channels of teaching.

The ambivalence toward human nature—its potential and its problems—not only prescribes a "limited freedom" as Rubenstein suggests. The same combination of attraction and wariness that the texts attribute to creation also occurs in the myths about Torah. Torah can cure, but it can also poison. Perhaps the most dramatic illustration of this ambivalence occurs in the stories told about one of the most perplexing Rabbinic figures, R. Aqiba.[37] Aqiba ben Joseph begins as an ignorant shepherd who falls in love with a rich man's daughter. This erotic connection motivates him to become a scholar. Scholarship transforms him, and he develops into a subtle interpreter of the Torah. His interpretations are said to perplex even Moses. Yet Aqiba also becomes a political activist. While at first acting as mediator for Rabbinic conflicts, he eventually leads a revolt against Rome. His activism leads him into imprisonment and finally execution by the Romans. The stories tell that when brought out to his death, Aqiba expounded the meaning of the Shema-prayer, which cites Deuteronomy 6:4. Dying with the words "The Lord is One" on his lips, Aqiba, according to the story, died by "the kiss of God."

Aqiba certainly finds a "cure" in the Torah for his ignorance and his erotic impulses. He channels these into the Rabbinic activity of study. Yet Aqiba also finds himself drawn to an activist path that leads to death. Not a successful revolt against the Romans but a beautiful death (euthanasia, in its literal meaning) awaits him. Scholars of this material debate the meaning of this story. Herbert Basser, for example, takes Daniel Boyarin to task for making Aqiba's martyrdom into an exaltation of a beautiful death.[38] The story itself, however, seems intentionally ambiguous, pointing to the diverse possibilities of the effect of Torah on a person's life.

The political myths of Rabbinic texts offer equally ambivalent treatments of earlier motifs.[39] Often, the idea of the messiah fades into the background, and political models of Jewish communal life take shape independently of a messianic hope. Two tales seem particularly remarkable. One again involves Aqiba, who, according to Rabbinic sources, supported the messianic uprising under Simeon bar Kokhba. Despite warnings from his colleagues, Aqiba engaged in a disastrous project that led to his death. In the Rabbinic sources, that death, however, transfigured him, and by means of his Torah knowledge, he gained entrance into the World to Come. Aqiba's claim to immortality thus is shown to lie not in his political activity but in his understanding of Torah piety. In another tale, Yohanan ben Zakkai reveals how piety replaces politics. During the siege of Jerusalem, he feigns death to escape the city and enter the camp of the besieger, Vespasian. Through a false death that gains him permission to begin a Rabbinic academy, he ensures the life of Judaism. Again and again in this literature, life thus emerges from Torah and not through worldly politics.

These two stories illustrate what Richard Rubenstein saw as an exaltation of powerlessness. He comments that powerlessness is often "praised as indispensable for maintaining the monotheistic and ethical purity of Judaism" (*The Religious Imagination*, p. 33). Yet the two stories have very different versions of the response to powerlessness. The story of Aqiba sees two alternatives: either political revolution or martyrdom. Aqiba's final transfiguration shows the glory of the latter. The story of Yohanan, however, sees another alternative, that of a creative avoidance of politics altogether. Jews need not resist the political order nor submit to it. They can withdraw to a spiritual piety that keeps them beyond the reach of the political.

This tension between the political alternatives suggested in the stories of Aqiba and Yohanan parallels the tensions in the cosmological and anthropological myths as well. The Rabbinic material raises alternative possibilities for the conception of the world, for understanding human nature, and for comprehending the political order. Theorists of myth who look at this material may choose to emphasize one or the other pole. Yet the ambivalence transcends any easy decision for one alternative over another.

Medieval myths: In medieval times, Jews living under Christian or Muslim domination produced legal works, poetic liturgy, philosophical treatises, and mystical writings. Deriving from the philosophers and mystics, the mythical texts of this period share many themes and motifs with biblical and Rabbinic myth. They place a special emphasis on techniques for discovering truth and develop systems within which truth must be evaluated. In this enterprise, Jewish legalists, philosophers, and mystics offered competing systems of reality that, though sometimes combined in an uneasy alliance, more often conflicted as each sought to dominate Jewish consciousness.[40] Even so, within these works, the common search for mythic expression overrides the differences between the philosophical and mystical systems. Gershom Scholem, therefore, is wrong when he contrasts the philosophers and rabbis on the one hand to the mystics on the other and associates myth only with the latter.[41] The difference between the two is not in the act of using myth but only in the images expressing it. Both philosophers and mystics use their favorite images to reinforce a systematic cosmology that includes creation, revelation, and redemption. At the heart of both philosophical and mystical myth lies the desire for a unified universe, a cosmos in which every element hangs together as part of a coherent whole.

Yehuda Liebes and Elliot Wolfson examine how mystical symbols and tropes generally use concrete, anthropomorphic images to communicate mythic conceptions of creation, revelation, and redemption. They demonstrate the complex interweaving of inherited themes and new perspectives on the world.[42] Remarkably, these myths often couch their narratives in gendered language, portraying the divine not merely as gendered, but multi-gendered. The divine potencies include both male and female properties. The dramatic schema tends to envision a remasculinization of the feminine, a reincorporation of the darker, more elusive side of the divinity within the luminosity of the male side. While this erotic theme has, understandably, attracted psychological analysis, a more recent trend understands these myths as imaginative constructions of language. Postmodern philosophy provides categories useful when decoding and deconstructing the meaning of this language.

The myths occurring in philosophical writing have received less attention. Their presence in preaching, however, gives evidence for their popularity among sophisticated thinkers.[43] Using rigorous argumentation, philosophical myths compile proofs of God's existence, rational interpretations of the revelational process, and sophisticated renderings of messianic prophecies. Upon examination, however, these outward forms disguise the inner purpose. The philosopher exposes a human side barely hidden by the appearance of detached rationalism. The true subject, as David Novak argues, is not the idea of God but the image of humanity and its social implications.[44] Philosophical myths function both anthropologically and politically to ground Jewish life and practice in human experience. Not only did philosophers seek to provide rational explanations of Jewish myths concerning creation, revelation, and redemption, but they also created myths in the style of Plato's allegories and illustrations to communicate the truths of rationalism. The concern to bridge the gap between the Bible and its historical paradigm and Greek science with its distinctive view of cosmic reality animated the medieval philosophical enterprise.[45]

Medieval Jewish philosophers asked three central questions: whether God created freely or of necessity, whether an eternal matter co-exists with God, and whether the world has been brought into existence for a purpose. These three questions are central in medieval philosophical discussions of creation, because they are crucial to a reconciliation of biblical theory and the philosophies of Plato, Aristotle, and the Stoics. From Philo of Alexandria and Isaac Israeli through Isaac Abrabanel and Hasdai Crescas, Jewish thinkers provided divergent answers to the question of whether the biblical view was compatible with the rationalistic one. While offering a distinctive harmonization, each thinker, maintained the rationality of the Torah and its principles. Some described creation as an act in which the divine authorized an intellectual principle to construct the universe. Others argued that creation out of an eternal pre-existent matter in no way impairs the divine uniqueness. Others claim that while human reason is fitted for explaining what occurs within the created world, it lacks the equipment necessary to comprehend creation itself. In each of these ways Jewish thinkers construed the universe as compatible with human reason and within the Judaic and the Greek frameworks of thought alike.

Jewish mystics faced a similar problem. Philosophers harmonize their experience of rational truth with the texts of Jewish tradition. Mystics harmonize their experience of transcendent truth with those same texts. Both groups create a mythology that corresponds to their confrontation with reality. Philosophers ask how texts correspond to the teaching they feel reveals the actual workings of the world. Mystics evoke from the same texts a reality that mirrors the sufferings and possibilities of their own lives.

The variety of creation stories that mystics tell mirrors Jewish experiences with reality. Some stories focus on conflict. They suggest that the creation event precipitates a crisis in which the skeleton of reality cracks, in which

sparks of holiness are trapped in an evil substance, or in which the ordered structure of the universe gets wrenched out of joint. Other stories portray a more tranquil sequence. In these stories one divine force flows out into another, generative powers exercise their natural potencies, or successive generations recapitulate the original divine order. These different images merge themes found in classical Rabbinic works, in Greek mystery religions, in Neo-Platonism, and in Gnostic speculation. Often the same mystical images reappear in very different creation myths. The variety involved serves a single purpose, to establish the basis on which coherence arises out of what is plainly and undeniably a fragmented world. Mystics use a unity of images to express a variety of cosmologies to give an encoded description of how Jews encounter reality. The multi-layered imaginative vocabulary offers continuity despite diversity. It thereby reassures Jews that even as different Jewish groups and individuals generate divisive experiences, a common set of symbols unites them.

This desire for unity within diversity receives a strange twist in the consideration of Torah and its implication for understanding human nature. Although admitting that revelation must be associated with Moses and Mount Sinai, both philosophers and mystics focus attention on decoding that revelation through prophetic insight. The original revelation, as it were, hides the golden apples of prophecy behind silver filigree, protecting but also disguising it. Special techniques enable an interpreter to gain access to the one true meaning of revelation despite the variety that apparently shines out from the various windows in the filigree. Mystics compared this process to that of divesting a woman of her garments and then, through unification with her, restoring her original power by re-incorporating her into the original cosmic pattern. Philosophers also recognized that gleaning truth occurs in a gradual process. They compared this process to glimpsing the world during a stormy night through flashes of lightning that provide sporadic vision. While the narrative images used by mystics and philosophers differ, the myth itself remains the same. In both cases, revelation, even if it occurred once in the past, requires a ladder of intellectual and spiritual ascension to be reappropriated in the present. The ability to receive the truths of revelation reveals the true nature of the adept who has attained this skill.

That ladder of ascension that provides access to revelation involves a progressive amelioration of human nature. Some myths portray this process as weaning the intellect from its bodily sheath. Ascetic training, intellectual rigor, and disassociation from immorality fashion a prophetic personality. One myth describes the soul as a mirror in which divine truth may reflect itself. Corruption and concern with material things darkens and obscures the mirror. The prophet has cleansed the surface of the mirror so that it shines and reflects the divinity clearly. Some myths see prophetic power as flowing necessarily from this act of self-cleansing. Others declare that God, in the last resort, must decide whether an adept receives that for which he has prepared. Nevertheless, even here, the preparation follows a necessary and logical path.

Other myths describe more dramatic and arbitrary divine actions. According to one myth, Jews have a special place in the divine plan. They possess a peculiar potential for prophecy. Which of them becomes a prophet is, to some extent, an arbitrary decision of God, for the divinity chooses the instrument who will receive the influx of holy spirit. Yet, even in this case, certain prerequisites appear necessary. Several writers maintain that prophetic inspiration occurs only in the land of Israel. Additionally, many traditional Judaic elements and practices become prerequisites for prophecy: Hebrew is the language of prophecy, performance of certain rites and rituals makes prophecy more likely, knowledge of Rabbinic law is a necessity for becoming a prophet. While God is seen as acting according to the divine will, and not of necessity, some actions more than others are understood to draw one closer to that divine will. Some myths, finally, suggest that only certain exalted souls can become prophets. An individual might be born with such a

soul, gain it by identification with an earlier hero or through a specially provided divine grace. In these myths a mystical or philosophical teacher guides adepts on their way, showing them how to think philosophically or how to potentiate the powers latent in themselves.

The myths of revelation given by both philosophers and mystics in the medieval period seem to serve a sociological function. They justify the claims of certain leadership groups to elite status. Against those leaders who argue that only mastery of the Judaic legal system provides authority, these myths legitimate others whose ability to perform miracles, intellectual prowess, or insight into the human spirit demonstrates their superiority. The use of gendered language suggests a psychological dimension in these myths. The incorporation of the feminine within the male offers a paradigmatic model for psychological wholeness, for the integration of the masculine and feminine aspects of the psyche, as Carl Jung would express it. Put differently, this means that a mystic must possess a well-balanced psyche. Taken together, the three elements in the Jewish anthropological myths of the medieval period draw a picture of an ideal leader. The true leader, these myths suggest, must possess an imagination capable of generating ever-new meanings from the inherited texts of Judaism, a sociological status of honor within the community, and psychological health.

The myth of Torah evinces strong ties to cosmological myths of creation. Several intertwined metaphors permeate stories of creation and myths of prophetic understanding of revelation alike. The metaphors of light, sparks of divinity, and flashes of illumination see darkness as an alien force invading and obscuring creation. The metaphors of erotic yearning, of desire for reunification with one's primal source, and the need to reintegrate the female within the male reflect an uneasiness and discomfort within experience, a sense that reality has lost its original wholeness and integrity. These metaphors surface in discussions of revelation as well. The true leader is the one who has grasped the true unity of creation and who recognizes the place of human beings in the scheme of creation and in repairing damage to the world. The prophetic reader of Torah penetrates the mysteries of eroticism in the supernatural and masters the potent forces hidden within both creation and revelation.

Medieval theories of salvation and redemption might appear to mirror these political considerations. They do tend to reflect the historical context of the elite leaders who formulated them. Their distinctive concern, however, seems more ideological and philosophical than political. Two types of speculation predominate; one focuses on the salvation of the worthy individual and the other on the triumphant success of the Jewish people. While related to the culturally different experiences of Ashkenazic and Sephardic Jewry, these two also reflect certain common features.[46] Both integrate a conception of the ideal universe, a diagnosis of the problems of present existence, and a systematic view of reality. A dramatic illustration of such an integrated myth of redemption is that of the Golem.[47] The myth describes how an exalted adept can construct a model human being from inert matter and, through the use of the magic inherent in Hebrew letters, vitalize that image. By doing this, the adept retraces the stages by which divine power flows into the world and imitates God's creative force. This myth provides a symbol of redemption. It evokes a time when the perfect order has been restored and matter has become reunited with its spiritual source. The prophetic seer initiates redemption by reversing the process of creation. This redemptive myth integrates a cosmology portraying the downward flow of divine forces with a prophetic myth of a mystic master and the eschatological vision of a material world elevated to spirituality.

Even the messianic myths of the period share this orientation. Although the philosophers Moses Maimonides and Judah Halevi have different criteria for the messianic fulfillment, both expect a political revival of the Jewish people. Both describe the rebirth of prophecy and the civil independence of the Jewish people. This expectation of a this-worldly messianic time corresponds to the philosophical system in which politics, imagination, and prophecy are intertwined. The logical and political cosmic reality that the philosophers sketch in their theories of truth finds fulfillment in the politics of redemption. Both Halevi and Maimonides posit certain enduring realities in the world of experience, and these realities in turn shape their messianic expectation.

Jewish mystics, like the philosophers, disagreed on the implication of messianic redemption but agreed that redemption must be understood in terms of both myths of creation and myths of prophecy. Mystics often describe the messiah as appearing as the result of restoring the world to its pristine state. This ideal assumes a crisis at creation that disrupted the order of reality. It envisions the mystic sage as a prophet who, through an esoteric study of Torah, has mastered a way to reverse the original crisis and repair the damage. The figure of the messiah, in this myth, symbolically represents the return to that ideal condition disrupted at creation and repaired by prophecy. A second myth, however, portrays the messianic world as entirely new, utterly unprecedented. The messiah that the mystic summons will alter cosmic reality. The mystic uses his skills to induce the coming of this agent of great change. This myth understands both creation and the purposes of prophecy differently from the first. In this view, redemption as transformation occurs because creation began as a challenge or an invitation to human creativity. The human being who knows the secrets of Torah can fulfill the original human task.

These two myths differ in their specific demands on the mystic and in their depiction of the cosmic alteration that the messianic time entails. Yet they can be coupled (the Zohar, for example, contains both myths side by side), since the main point is that redemption involves cosmic events. These myths serve less of a political function and act more to reinforce the general picture of reality that the thinker wishes to express.

Jewish philosophers and mystics offer a

varied set of cosmological, anthropological, and political myths. Yet this variety points to an even deeper diversity among medieval Jewish thinkers. Philosophers disagreed concerning the underlying structure of reality and the place of revelation and redemption within that structure. Mystics contested with one another to see which image of reality would prevail. Yehuda Liebes notes the consequence of this competition. He argues that myth occurs spontaneously in human culture. To this natural religious expression, the Kabbalah adds, he contends, "systematic formulation . . . rigid frameworks." The structuring of myth by rival thinkers creates rival frameworks. This in turn weakens the "personal, spontaneous vitality" of myth. Whether or not Liebes is right in seeing the Kabbalah as a diminution of myth, he demonstrates how medieval Jewish thinking expressed itself in competitive systems of myth.

Modern Jewish myths: Modern myth looks distinctively, almost essentially, different from pre-modern myth. When novels and newspapers, commercial advertisements and religious tracts, and cinematic art no less than philosophy provide mythology, the line between the mythic and the non-mythic blurs. Such blurred distinctions lead beyond modernity to postmodernity. Jacques Derrida locates this dichotomy between "mythus" and "logos" as far back as Plato's dialogues, and he criticizes any easy demarcation between "myth" and "truth," "poetry" and "philosophy" as misleading. Many Jewish thinkers today agree with this critique. Derrida's own sense of standing beyond Hellenism and Hebraism strikes a resonating chord among contemporary Jews who read Jewish texts, both modern and ancient, in deconstructionist fashion. Derrida, who stands beyond myth and logos, thus offers a hermeneutics that allows Jewish interpreters of myth to transform logos into myth and myth into logos.[48]

That process of blurring the lines between myth and philosophy began at the dawn of modernity, as Jewish theologians adapted the symbols and texts of Judaism to the major myths of the European Enlightenment. Religious ideologies replaced religious philosophies as the basic expression of Jewish belief.

Secular Jewish leaders communicated an ideological program through the use of Judaic symbols and practices. Yet these apparently "secular" and "realistic" approaches to Judaism actually contained much that is mythic.

This secular myth derives from poets, novelists, politicians, and scholars. Sometimes they provide what could be called a new type of midrash, a reworking of ancient themes to convey new perspectives on reality.[49] Martin Buber, Isaac Loeb Peretz, Micah Joseph Ben Gorion, Hayyim Nahman Bialik, and Saul Tchernikowsky offer mythic presentations of older material in a new guise. That old material does not disguise the novelty in the reality these writers present. The new myths reflect an experience of alienation, secularization, and discontent. They use the older mythic images to create a new story, to tell a new tale.

Some of these myths—like those of the Zionists, who construct diverse myths out of the Judaic past to legitimize their nationalistic interpretation of Judaism[50]—describe one kind of political reality. Other contemporary Jewish myths focus on a different political reality. For instance, groups of Jews often excluded from the community of Judaic culture—women, homosexuals, and other "strangers"—find that they too can tell their story by using the images of older Jewish mythology.[51] Women often complain that the Judaic mythic heritage preserves stereotyped views of women. Yet they use that heritage as a resource for creating new myths intended to liberate Jews today from gender-related constrictions.[52]

A set of Jewish myths centered on the twin events that marked the midpoint of the twentieth-century—the Nazi slaughter of six million Jews and the rebirth of an independent Jewish state—has influenced contemporary thinkers.[53] These historical occurrences become the basis for a new way of understanding reality, human nature, and Jewish political hope. Indeed, some modern theologians diagnose these events as symptoms of a failure of mythology. They hold that the Holocaust occurred because the modern nation state usurped control of myth. The

State of Israel, in turn, flounders because of its government's realistic politics devoid of mythic power. In this view, new myths—whether in political ideology, in literary forms, or in theological terms—must replace the old ones that have been abandoned.[54] Thinkers must reappropriate older motifs from the Judaic past to provide a new framework within which to understand the disasters and triumphs of modern Jewish history.

Transformed conceptions of the world impelled Jewish theologians, novelists, and poets from the nineteenth century onwards to refashion traditional Jewish myth. One prevalent myth proclaimed inevitable humanistic progress. History appeared as a dynamic advancement from one stage of civilization to an ever higher one. Scientific and social progress seemed built into the fabric of the universe. Thinkers proclaimed faith in humanity's irreversible triumph over the evils of war, inequity, and intolerance, over the challenges of a recalcitrant natural environment, and over the dark depths of the human spirit.

This myth sometimes expresses itself as an affirmation of universalism. It offers the optimistic picture of a united humanity, sharing a basic concern for the divine and sensitivity to transcendence independent of parochial religious traditions. It celebrates a common human interest in the welfare of others. Human beings care for one another, this myth claims, because they have compassion for one another. The myth takes this word literally, reading compassion as "com" "passion," a "feeling" of "withness." People, it is argued, possess the ability sympathetically to identify with the suffering of every other person. Liberal Jewish movements, whether religious in nature like classical Reform or political in orientation like Jewish socialism, seize upon this myth of a compassionate human nature.

The events of the mid-twentieth century challenged that optimistic myth of progress. The Nazi slaughter of six million Jews has emerged as a symbol of the irreducible and permanent residue of evil in human life. The death camps of Nazi Germany, of Auschwitz in particular, stand as poignant images of unredeemable evil. The world does not progress toward ever higher stages. Instead, it continually frustrates human efforts to improve the cosmos, human society, and human nature.

Taking its cue from this myth, Zionism sketches a humanity mired in self-interest, inevitably drawn into economic, social, and political conflict. Zionism responds to this human nature by proclaiming the need for Jewish self-defense, for Jewish self-affirmation and self-distinction. The Zionist offers the myth of the "new man," who awakens to a new day in the Jewish homeland (the male-exclusive term is used intentionally here; the Zionist vision focused on masculinity and Jewish strength). Living as a natural man, the Jew in Israel unabashedly celebrates his individuality and parochial identity. This "new man" has liberated himself from universality to embrace his own true nature.

Recognition of irredeemable evil and acceptance of parochialism lead to some unexpected mythology. Jewish women, so obviously excluded from the Zionist mythology, recreate a Judaism more congenial to their gender. They often create a myth parallel to that of the Zionists. Just as Zionists claim that Jew and non-Jew can never be reconciled, so women sometimes aver that the opposition between men and women cannot be reconciled. Just as Zionists call for a new homeland and a new man, so Jewish feminists seek a refuge of their own and an exclusive community made up of new "womyn" (a locution developed to avoid the offensive term "man"). They insist that only a society of women, often a specifically lesbian community, can protect them from male predation. The ancient Jewish myth of Lilith, a night demon whose femininity sometimes transmogrifies itself into masculine power, takes on a new shape. Lilith in the new myth seeks her own kind, other women, forges an alliance with the more compliant woman "Eve" and liberates herself from the bondage under which men have dominated her. Other Jewish women take a more optimistic view of human nature. They, like the universalists rather than the Zionists, foresee an inclusive community where male and female work together in unity and cooperation. They too reread biblical texts and later mythic works, finding in the Kabbalah's images of the female aspect of the deity sources of self-understanding that reinforce their hope for inclusion.

Both Zionists and Jewish feminists who embrace the pessimistic view of human nature anticipate a redemptive community composed of like-minded members. Political programs seeking to constitute such communities differ according to their myths concerning human impulses. Some advocate a violence in establishing independence; others seek a more pacifistic ideal. Yet each group imagines a new social order that will affirm its distinct identity and its right to maintain this distinctiveness. Universalists portray a strikingly contrary ideal. The new world order of harmony and inclusion that they imagine builds on their hopes for progress and the utilization of the best in human nature. They often describe a tolerant, progressive, and open society as the ultimate achievement of an enlightened humanity.

Many Jews, especially those in the United States of America, are caught between the two modern myths. The American civil myth ostensibly supports tolerance, diversity, and inclusion. It considers progress and the compassionate nature of humanity as building blocks in creating an open society. The myth of the Nazi Holocaust, however, and the celebratory myth of Zionism introduce a pessimistic note into American Jewry's self-understanding. Accepting these myths creates a tension with the civil religion that is difficult for modern Jews to resolve. The modern myths of universalism and particularism, of optimistic and pessimistic conceptions of human nature, and of exclusive versus inclusive communities compete for the allegiance of these Jews.

Many who feel this tension sense it only dimly; others externalize it as the result of political or psychological factors. Whatever the explanation, the tension itself has led to a mythic expression. Jewish writers beginning in the nineteenth century and continuing through the fiction and poetry produced by contemporary Jewish authors in Israel, the United States, and in Europe, portray Jews alienated from themselves. Jews who were "banished from their father's table" and have not found themselves at home in the non-Jewish world symbolize the chaos of modern experience.[55] The myth of the Jew as a displaced person, buffeted by the winds of sexual, social, and political confusion, reappears in the novels, poetry, theology, and even scholarship of modern Jewish writers.

This mythic complex parallels even as it replaces earlier mythic constructs of Judaism, and it, like its predecessors, points forward to new myths as yet uncharted by scholarship. While modern Jewish myth appears strikingly different from its predecessors, in fact it displays the same characteristics that they do, in particular the transformation of logos into myth and myth into logos made explicit in previous mythic writing. The biblical stories of creation, rituals associated with revelation, and the messianic epics cast a competition of ideas into mythic vocabulary, yet cannot disguise the ideological conflicts they embody. Rabbinic myths elicit varied interpretations because they make the psychological and political diversity of their times transparent. Medieval philosophers and mystics translated their rival systems of thought into myth, making the myth a champion of their philosophy. The modern use of Jewish myth, whether to defend excluded members of the Jewish community or to transform Jewish national consciousness, not only fits into the paradigms established by earlier expressions of Jewish mythology but makes those paradigms more explicit and self-conscious.

Notes

[1] Mircea Eliade, *Myth and Reality*, William R. Trask, ed. (New York: 1963), pp. 1-2, 139-193.

[2] Ibid., p. 145.

[3] "The Structural Study of Myth," in his *Structural Anthropology* (New York, 1963), pp. 204-231.

[4] See Albert Spaulding Cook, *Myth and Language* (Bloomington, 1980), and Philip Wheelwright, "The Semantic Approach to Myth," in Thomas A. Sebeok, ed., *Myth: A Symposium* (Bloomington, 1968), pp. 154-168.

[5] Umberto Eco, *The Limits of Interpretation* (Bloomington, 1990), p. 21.

[6] See Maurice Olender, *The Languages of Paradise: Race, Religion and Philology in the Nineteenth Century* (Cambridge, 1992), and Robert A. Segal, "In Defense of Mythology: The

History of Modern Theories of Myth," in *Annals of Scholarship* 1:1, 1980, pp. 3-49.

[7] See Yehezkel Kaufmann, *The Religion of Israel: From Its Beginnings to the Babylonian Exile* (Chicago, 1960), pp. 77, 244, 316.

[8] H.A. Frankfort, John A. Wilson, and Thordild Jacobsen, *Before Philosophy: The Intellectual Adventure of Ancient Man* (Baltimore, 1949), pp. 15-16.

[9] See Ignac Goldziher, *Mythology among the Hebrews and Its Historical Development* (New York, 1967).

[10] See Frank Moore Cross, *Canaanite Myth and Hebrew Epic: Essays in the History of the Religion of Israel* (Cambridge, 1973), and Theodor Hiebert, *Yahwist's Landscape: Nature and Religion in Early Israel* (New York, 1996), p. 80.

[11] See S. Daniel Breslauer, *Martin Buber on Myth: An Introduction* (New York, 1990).

[12] John L. McKenzie, "Myth and the Old Testament," in his *Myths and Realities: Studies in Biblical Theology* (London, 1963), pp. 182-200.

[13] See Jonathan Z. Smith, "The Unknown God: Myth in History," in his *Imagining Religion: From Babylon to Jonestown* (Chicago, 1982), pp. 66-89.

[14] Elie Wiesel, "Myth and History," in Alan M. Olson, ed., *Myth, Symbol, and Reality* (Notre Dame, 1980), pp. 20-30.

[15] See Gilbert Cuthbertson, *Political Myth and Epic* (East Lansing, 1975), and Christopher G. Flood, *Political Myth: A Theoretical Introduction* (New York, 1996).

[16] See the discussion in Richard J. Golsan, *Rene Girard and Myth: An Introduction* (New York, 1993); the analysis in James Williams, *The Bible, Violence and the Sacred: The Liberation from the Myth of Sanctioned Violence* (San Francisco, 1991); and the primary writings in Rene Girard, *Things Hidden since the Foundation of the World* (Stanford, 1987), and his *The Scapegoat* (Baltimore, 1986).

[17] See his *The Forgotten Language: An Introduction to the Understanding of Dreams, Fairy Tales and Myths* (New York, 1951); *The Dogma of Christ and Other Essays on Psychology, Religion, and Culture* (New York, 1963), and *You Shall Be As Gods: A Radical Interpretation of the Old Testament and its Tradition* (New York, 1966).

[18] Loyal D. Rue, *Amythia: Crisis in the Natural History of Western Culture* (Tuscaloosa, 1989).

[19] Roland Barthes, *Mythologies* (London, 1993).

[20] See Galit Hasan-Rokem, "Myth," in Arthur A. Cohen and Paul Mendes-Flohr, eds., *Contemporary Jewish Religious Thought: Original Essays on Critical Concepts, Movements, and Belief* (New York), pp. 657-661.

[21] See Susan A. Handelman, *Fragments of Redemption: Jewish Thought and Literary Theory in Benjamin, Scholem, and Levinas* (Bloomington, 1991).

[22] Emmanuel Levinas, *In the Time of the Nations* (Bloomington, 1994), p. 168.

[23] Emmanuel Levinas, *Nine Talmudic Readings* (Bloomington, 1994), p. 94.

[24] Even this terminology immediately raises questions. The first two terms describe texts: the Bible and so-called "Rabbinic literature." While more genuinely "chronological," the other terms represent a peculiarly Western European view of history.

[25] See Walter Beltz, *God and the Gods: Myths of the Bible* (New York, 1983); Theodor H. Gaster, *Myth, Legend and Custom in the Old Testament* (New York, 1975); and Benedikt Otzen, *Myths in the Old Testament* (London, 1980).

[26] See Dorothy Irvin, *Mytharion: The Comparison of Tales from the Old Testament with the Ancient Near East* (Neukirchen-Vluyn, 1978).

[27] See Edmund Leach, *Genesis as Myth and Other Essays* (London, 1969), and Howard Eilberg-Schwartz, *The Savage in Judaism: An Anthropology of Israelite Religion and Ancient Judaism* (Bloomington, 1990).

[28] Michael A. Fishbane, *Text and Texture: Close Readings of Selected Biblical Texts* (New York, 1979).

[29] See Peter Ochs, ed., *The Return to Scripture in Judaism and Christianity: Essays in Postcritical Scriptural Interpretation* (New York, 1993).

[30] See his *The Creation of Woman* (New York, 1960), especially his conclusions, pp. 141-148.

[31] W. Robertson Smith, *The Religion of the Semites: The Fundamental Institutions* (New York, 1972), pp. 312-387.

[32] Mary Douglas, "The Abominations of Leviticus," in her *Purity and Danger: An Analysis of Concepts of Pollution and Taboo* (Baltimore, 1966), pp. 54-72 and especially p. 63.

[33] See Daniel Boyarin, *Intertextuality and the Reading of Midrash* (Bloomington, 1990), and David Stern, *Parables in Midrash: Narrative and Exegesis in Rabbinic Literature* (Cambridge, 1991).

[34] See Jacob Neusner, *A History of the Jews in Babylonia* (Leiden, 1966-1970), and his *There We Sat Down: The Story of Classical Judaism in the Period in which It Was Taking Shape* (Nashville, 1972).

[35] See Kaufmann Kohler, "Abba Father: Title of Spiritual Leader and Saint," in *JQR* 13: 1901, pp. 567-580.

[36] *The Religious Imagination: A Study in Psychoanalysis and Jewish Theology* (Boston, 1968), p. 147.

[37] See Michael Fishbane, *The Kiss of God: Spiritual and Mystical Death in Judaism* (Seattle, 1994).

[38] See Herbert Basser, "Boyarin's Intertextuality and the Reading of Midrash," in *JQR* ns. 81:3-4, p. 432.

[39] See Jacob Neusner, William Scott Green, and Ernest S. Frerichs, eds., *Judaisms and Their Messiahs at the Turn of the Christian Century* (New York, 1987).

[40] See Meir Benayahu, "Kabbalah and Halakha: A Confrontation," [Heb] in *Daat: A Journal*

of Jewish Philosophy and Kabbalah 5.1980, pp. 61-115.

[41] See Gershom G. Scholem, *Major Trends in Jewish Mysticism* (New York, 1963), pp. 34-38, and his *On the Kabbalah and Its Symbolism* (New York, 1965), pp. 87-117.

[42] See Yehuda Liebes, *Studies in Jewish Myth and Jewish Messianism* (Albany, 1993), and his *Studies in the Zohar* (Albany, 1993); Elliot R. Wolfson, *Through A Speculum that Shines: Vision and Imagination in Medieval Jewish Mysticism* (Princeton, 1994); and his *Circle in the Square: Studies in the Use of Gender in Kabbalistic Symbolism* (New York, 1995).

[43] See Robert Bonfil, "Preaching as Mediation between Elite and Popular Cultures: The Case of Judah Del Bene," in David B. Ruderman, ed., *Preachers of the Italian Ghetto* (Berkeley, 1992), pp. 67-88.

[44] See David Novak, "Are Philosophical Proofs of the Existence of God Theologically Meaningful?," in Seymour Siegel and Elliot Gertel, eds., *God in the Teachings of Conservative Judaism* (New York, 1985), pp. 188-200.

[45] See the essays collected in David Novak and Norbert Samuelson, eds., *Creation and the End of Days: Judaism and Scientific Cosmology* (Lanham, 1986).

[46] See Gerson D. Cohen, "The Soteriology of R. Abraham Maimuni," and "Messianic Postures of Ashkenazim and Sephardim," in his *Studies in the Variety of Rabbinic Cultures* (Philadelphia, 1991), pp. 209-242 and 271-297.

[47] Moshe Idel, *Golem: Jewish Magical and Mystical Traditions on the Artificial Anthropoid* (Albany, 1990).

[48] See the intriguing essay by Geoffrey Bennington, "Mosaic Fragment: If Derrida were an Egyptian," in David Wood, ed., *Derrida: A Critical Reader* (Oxford, 1992), pp. 97-119.

[49] See David C. Jacobson, *Modern Midrash: The Retelling of Traditional Jewish Narratives by Twentieth Century Hebrew Writers* (Albany, 1987).

[50] See Menachem M. Kellner, "Messianic Postures in Israel Today," in *ModJud* 6. 1986, pp. 197-289.

[51] See Laurence J. Silberstein, "Others Within and Others Without: Rethinking Jewish Identity and Culture," in Laurence J. Silberstein and Robert L. Cohn, eds., *The Other in Jewish Thought and History: Constructions of Jewish Culture and Identity* (New York, 1994), pp. 1-34.

[52] See Howard Eilberg-Schwartz and Wendy Doniger, eds., *Off With Her Head! The Denial of Women's Identity in Myth, Religion, and Culture* (Berkeley, 1995).

[53] See Jacob Neusner, *Stranger at Home: Zionism, "The Holocaust," and American Judaism* (Chicago, 1981).

[54] See Peter J. Haas, *Morality after Auschwitz: The Radical Challenge of the Nazi Ethic* (Philadelphia, 1988).

[55] See Alan Mintz, *Banished from Their Father's Table: Loss of Faith and Hebrew Autobiography* (Bloomington, 1989).

S. Daniel Breslauer

N

Natural Science, Judaism and: The familiarity of names such as Freud, Einstein, and Feynman suggests that, since the latter half of the nineteenth century, Jews have been at the forefront of scientific advancement. Almost one hundred Jews have been awarded Nobel prizes in chemistry, physics, and medicine. This is 20% of these prizes, far out of proportion to the number of Jews in the world's population. Nobel prizes, however, mark only individual success, leaving us to inquire whether the extraordinary achievements of some Jews, most of whom had little knowledge of or attachment to Judaism, reflect anything of the value placed by Judaism on inquiry into the physical world. Is there, that is to say, any connection between Jewish thought and scientific discovery?

The Bible and natural science: In answering this question, we must be aware, first of all, that today's concept of "natural science" is a product of the modern era. Only relatively recently has science, an organized observational discipline, been separated from philosophy, on the one hand, and from magic, on the other. Indeed, some areas of investigation, such as psychology and the social sciences, are still struggling to extricate themselves from this pre-modern inheritance. To comprehend the roots of later attitudes to the natural world, we begin with the Bible. For, in contrast with later Jewish and Christian texts, the Hebrew Scriptures, other than in a few late passages, do not support a dualism of body and spirit and consequently do not disparage the material world as such. Even in the historically late opening chapter of Genesis, nature—that is, the material world—is affirmed as God's creation, therefore good. This attitude is fully borne out in hymns such as Ps. 104.

The Scottish theologian Thomas Torrance has argued that the Hebrew Scriptures' monistic world-view is more conducive to scientific progress than the "Greek" dualism of body and spirit that, he maintains, pervades Greek and Roman thought.[1] This may be so but cannot explain modern Jews' disproportionate contribution to scientific endeavor. This is because all pre-modern forms of Judaism exhibit the dualism of body and soul missing from Scripture; some of them—particularly the Kabbalistic forms—are almost Gnostic in contrasting the evil of the material world with the goodness of the world of spirit.

Most of the Bible—Ecclesiastes is unclear on the point—assumes that the world was designed and created by God and that it is run by God who every now and then intervenes directly to make sure that the divine purposes, for instance bringing the Israelites out of Egypt, are fulfilled. This concept of design, or purpose, harmonized well enough with Aristotelian science, which was teleological, but has been increasingly questioned by philosophers at least since Descartes and is no longer a useful scientific hypothesis. The concept of an intervening God ready to pull miracles out of a hat to save the chosen people runs counter not only to mechanistic science but scarcely less so to the probabilistic science of the twentieth century, and, for quite different reasons, it was undermined by reflection on the Holocaust.

The Bible's hostility to magic is noteworthy but does not necessarily denote denial of magic's reality and efficacy; this was to become a major point in the controversies of the Maimunists and anti-Maimunists in the Middle Ages. The omission from Gen. 1 of all reference to demons and other non-natural beings is perhaps the closest the Bible comes to outright denial of their existence.

Proto-science—The classification of phenomena: The biblical approach to the natural world is not restricted to an appreciation of its order and beauty or the power or wisdom of its creator. From time to time, there is in addition strong evidence of systematic thought, of attempts to classify phenomena and to evaluate their relationships. The creation scheme of Gen. 1, for instance, is well-ordered and hierarchical, reflecting and perpetuating structures of the society that produced it. Some modern commentators—we refer below to Rosenzweig—discover in it a dynamic quality, of movement from chaos to order, culminating in divine perfection on the seventh day. But it can just as well be read as a story of the already perfect God's creating a perfect, static universe, inhabited by distinct and immutable species in fixed hierarchical relationships with one another.

A carefully devised classification of the natural order also underlies the ordered lists of birds, beasts, and sundry creatures in Lev. 11 and Deut. 18. Mary Douglas has drawn attention to the sophistication of these lists and to the fact that the creatures forbidden for consumption are precisely those that appear anomalous in this classification, which she relates to that of Gen. 1. "Proper" animals are domesticated (cow, sheep, goat), and they chew the cud and have cloven hooves; but the camel and the pig are anomalous, for they lack these characteristics.[2] Similarly, Lev. 13 presents a systematic description of "leprosy" that can only be the result of careful and extended observation.

On the other hand, despite its numerous illuminating references to natural phenomena, Job rarely transcends the merely descriptive, as in chapter 28 on mining, and chapters 38-41, where God overwhelms Job with awesome descriptions of everything from the crocodile to the Pleiades but considers him incapable of appreciating a coherent taxonomy. The Bible thus not only repeatedly affirms the wonder and wisdom of the natural world but, from time to time, incorporates and in some ways transforms the available science. As we shall now see, these features persist in Rabbinic Judaism.

The Talmud—Science subordinated to religion: Since the late nineteenth century several studies have been made of natural science—especially medicine and mathematics—in the Talmud and Midrash. These studies must be regarded with caution, since they typically predate or ignore modern scholarship on the formation of Rabbinic texts, they impose modern notions of natural science on the rabbis, and they generalize on the basis of limited or ambiguous evidence. Beyond these methodological problems, it is clear that, even if some of the rabbis possessed scientific knowledge, the redactors of the Rabbinic works did not, and, consequently, scientific observations were likely to be omitted or at least mangled in transmission. Additionally, particularly outside Babylonia through most of the period under consideration, "Rabbinic" Jews were a minority among Jews. No one knows what most other Jews were doing, whether they were competent astronomers or physicians or what part they played in mediating such scientific knowledge as was possessed by the rabbis.

Despite these caveats, the Rabbinic literature does illuminate the rabbis' general perspective, in which the sciences, while not disparaged, were treated as ancillary to Jewish law. Thus M. Ab. 3:23 reads: "R. Eleazar Hisma said, 'The sacrifices of birds and the counting of days of purification for menstruants are major topics of law; [the calculation of] seasons and geometry [*gematriyot*] are [mere] byways of wisdom.'"

The rabbis believed that Scripture was both inerrant and comprehensive; it contained all knowledge and was the source of all truth. It thus worried them that some useful knowledge, such as that of astronomy and medicine, appeared to originate elsewhere. Further, having contrived an opposition between Greek (bad) and Jew (good), they resisted acknowledging any debt to Greek learning. So they insisted that all knowledge of created things was divinely revealed and that other nations had "borrowed" this knowledge from the Jews. The third century Palestinian Amora Yohanan accordingly interpreted Deut. 4:6—"For this is your wisdom and understanding in the eyes of the nations"—as referring to Jewish pre-eminence in astronomical calculation (B.

Shab. 75a). Similarly, the rabbis understood medical remedies to be recorded in a book of cures concealed by Hezekiah (see below) and hence to be of "Jewish" origin, and they frequently read "facts" of nature into biblical verses.

But the rabbis' observations on nature are rarely original and not always sound. By the Middle Ages, Jewish physicians therefore abandoned Rabbinic medicine in favor of Hippocrates and Galen. Later, in the early modern period, Rabbinic cosmology too proved embarrassing. Yet other Rabbinic observations were not known to be erroneous until more recently, for instance, that lice are not generated spontaneously from sweat or dirt[3] or that mushrooms are not nourished from the soil (B. Ber. 40b). Some aggadic statements on nature are presumably not meant to be taken literally, but where is the line to be drawn? Did the rabbis really think there was a river, Sambatyon, that hurled great stones throughout the week and rested on the Sabbath (Midrash Tanhuma Warsaw edition, *Ki Tissa* 33)?

Astronomy in the Talmud: The third century Babylonian Amora Samuel claimed extensive knowledge of medicine and astronomy. He had a reputation for eye salves (B. Shab. 108b) and asserted that he had remedies for all bad eating habits except three (B. B.M. 113b). He also declared: "The paths of heaven are as familiar to me as the streets of Nehardea" (B. Ber. 58b). Even so, as he left no pharmacopoeia, no star atlas, nor a map of Nehardea, it is impossible to assess any of these claims. Samuel calculated the *tekufa*—the average period between solstice and equinox, or precisely a quarter of the solar year—at 91 days and 7 1/2 hours (B. Erub. 56a). This coincides with the length of the Julian year, and, because it is inaccurate, the Jewish festivals now occur on average almost two weeks later in the year than they should. A more accurate figure of 91 days, 7 hours, 28 minutes, 51.34 seconds is attributed by Jewish scholars from about the tenth century to Samuel's contemporary Adda bar Ahava. This value is close to that given by Hipparchus in the second century

B.C.E., but it is not mentioned in the Talmud, and the link with Adda bar Ahava is spurious.[4] If Samuel's estimate of the *tekufa* were correct, it would recur at the same moment of the same day in the week once every twenty eight years. The recurrence of this "great cycle" is marked by the ceremony of *qiddush ha-hama* ("sanctification of the sun"), when, it was thought, the sun, moon, stars, and constellations were in the relative positions they occupied at creation (B. Ber. 59a, as explained by Rashi).

A "small cycle" of nineteen years, though not mentioned in the Talmud, is basic to the harmonization of the solar and lunar calendars. Outside Rabbinic literature, it is known as the Metonic cycle, after the fifth century B.C.E. Greek astronomer Meton, who noticed that nineteen solar years equal almost exactly 235 lunar months. Meton thus assumed the same length for the solar year as Samuel. It is probable that the *tekufa* attributed to Adda bar Ahava was arrived at by the simple expedient of dividing 235 lunations by nineteen to establish the length of the solar year and dividing that by four.

M. A.Z. 3:1 rules that a statue (in human form) with a ball in its hand must be assumed to be an idol. On this, Y. A.Z. 18b comments:

> "A ball," because the world is made like a ball. R. Jonah said, "When Alexander of Macedon wanted to ascend, he went up, and up, and up, until he saw the world like a ball and the sea like a dish; that is why they sculpted him with a ball in his hand." Then [why not] picture him with a dish in his hand? He ruled over the earth only, but the Holy One, blessed be he, rules also over the sea *and* the dry land.

This is frequently cited as evidence that the rabbis—at least, the Palestinians—knew that the earth was a sphere. It would not be surprising, in the aftermath of the Alexandrian astronomer Ptolemy (90-168) and several centuries after Aristotle had demonstrated the sphericity of the earth (*De caelo* 2.13), if they did. However, the image of a ball floating in a dish of water does not fit; if the rabbis had clearly understood the concept of a spheri-

cal earth they would have imagined a ball part water, part earth, not a dish; nor does the "dish" image fit the notion of the spherical earth floating in the "lower waters" of creation. The common treatment of this subject exemplifies a misreading of Rabbinic sources for apologetic reasons, in this case to demonstrate that the rabbis got their science right. Much less ambiguous are numerous aggadic statements implying that the earth is flat (for instance, B. Pes. 93b-94; B. Hag. 12b; B. Tam. 32a); but these are "explained away" or ignored by the apologists.

Comets are discussed in the Talmud, but even Samuel conceded he did not understand them (B. Ber. 58a). One that appeared every seventy years is mentioned and has inevitably been identified with Halley's, though it is unclear why it should mislead mariners, who presumably would not mistake it for a star. Possibly what is meant is a nova or supernova, not a comet at all; that would not appear at regular intervals, but somebody might have thought it did.

Medicine and biology in the Talmud: The Babylonian Talmud contains several collections of remedies introduced by the third century teacher Abayye with the words "my mother told me"—an attribution to be taken not at its face value but as editorial semantics for "popular tradition." Some of the remedies are common-sense, as, for instance, to turn the seam of a baby's swaddling cloth outwards so as not to cause injury (B. Shab. 134a) Others concern the formulae and repetition of spells (B. Shab. 66b), and many relate to diet (B. Ket. 10b) or the correct use of plants and herbs.

Alongside such folk medicines, demons, possession, and the evil eye—notably absent from the Hebrew scriptures—figure commonly in Rabbinic literature. In recent years, numerous Hebrew amulets and incantation bowls from the first to fifth centuries have been recovered, many of them written by non-Jews evidently hoping to capture the efficacy of "Jewish magic," held in high repute in late antiquity.[5] Still, a more scientific attitude to medicine and healing clearly always prevailed in some circles. Even with regard to amulets, the Talmud distinguishes between those regarded as tested and reliable and those not so regarded (B. Shab. 53a-b), a distinction that presupposes a modicum of experiment and observation.

Several scholars in modern times, following the pioneering work of Julius Preuss (1861-1913),[6] have discussed Talmudic anatomy and physiology. This is not an easy exercise, for no Talmudic treatise concerns either of these subjects. To assess Talmudic anatomy, therefore, one has to work with material such as a list of body parts compiled in connection with laws of ritual purity (M. Oh. 1:8) or lists of defects that render priests or sacrificial animals unacceptable for Temple service (M. Bek. 6 and 7) or that render an animal or bird impermissible for consumption (M. Hul. 3). Such knowledge of physiology as is preserved in the Talmud has to do with matters like childbirth and sexual relations that are regulated by the law or is implied in random comments on nature, divine providence, and the like. We know very little about the actual practice of medicine by Jews in the Talmudic era, and the Talmud is concerned not with the art of medicine *per se* but with the law. Thus it has preserved only those elements of medical science needed for correct interpretation and application of the Halakhah. As Edward A. Boyden has written, "although the Mishnaic portion of the Talmud, when redacted, was contemporary with Galen, and the commentaries of the Gemara were post-Galenic, the stage of development of Talmudic medicine is nearer that of the Hippocratic school. . . ."[7]

Just as today one might learn quite a lot about issues in medical ethics from studying the law reports, but little of the relevant basic science, we are able from the Talmud to assess the rabbis' ethical presuppositions but remain in the dark as to their finer understanding of anatomy and physiology.

The independent status of science in the Middle Ages: The subordination of science to Jewish law was challenged by a number of medieval philosophers, foremost among them Bahya ibn Pakuda (eleventh century Spain). Bahya picked up the biblical concept of nature as testifying to the greatness of God as creator and argued that the study of nature *per se* led to faith in its infinitely wise maker.[8]

Moses Maimonides (1135/8-1204) struggled to incorporate a duty to study natural science within his all-embracing legal system. He subsumed this work under the command to love God (Mishneh Torah, *Hilkhot Yesodei ha-Torah* 2:2):

> How does one love and fear him? When a person reflects on his works and his great and wonderful creations and perceives in them his infinite and boundless wisdom, he immediately loves, praises, glorifies and fervently desires to know this great name. . . .

Then, in a fine example of the popular scientific genre of the time, Maimonides proceeds to give the reader a summary of cosmology, consisting of an account of the heavenly spheres and of the theory of the four elements. This basic science is not needed for the implementation of any specific law, unlike the principles of medicine and the details of calendrical calculation that Maimonides includes respectively under the laws on self-preservation and the determination of the new moon. It is an end in itself, part of the contemplation on the divine mystery that to Maimonides is the ultimate human felicity and the ultimate objective of obedience to the commandments.[9]

In keeping with this attitude, Maimonides was clear that tradition alone did not impart credibility or authority to scientific claims. What could be scientifically tested should be. Thus he observed (*Guide* 3:14) that the astronomy of the rabbis was neither accurate nor authoritative, since mathematics was not fully developed in their time and their statements on these topics did not derive from prophetic revelation. He similarly was an outspoken critic of the astrology practiced by Jews in his own day, which he denounced in a letter to the rabbis of Marseilles as a pseudo-science, claiming he had carried out empirical tests on various astrological theories. In his Mishneh Torah (*Laws of Idolatry* 11:16), he formulated a general rejection of pseudo-sciences:

> And all these matters [astrology, necromancy, etc.] are falsehood and deceit, by means of which idolatrous priests in ancient

times misled the people of the nations to follow them. It is not fitting that [the people of] Israel, who are wise and learned, should be attracted by such nonsense or entertain the possibility that there is any benefit in it; as it is said, "Surely there is no divination in Jacob, and no augury in Israel" (Num. 23:23), and "Those nations whose place you are taking listen to soothsayers and augurs, but the Lord your God does not permit you to do this" (Deut. 18:14). Whoever believes in such things, or anything like them, and thinks that they are true, though the Torah forbade them, is a fool, an ignoramus, and in the category of women and children whose comprehension is imperfect.

Though Maimonides was preceded in his rejection of astrology by Bahya ibn Pakuda and, half-heartedly, by Judah Halevi, his enlightened view convinced few scholars in his time and had virtually no impact on popular belief. Even the Vilna Gaon sharply criticized him for denying the existence of demons.[10] Today some orthodox leaders still endorse such beliefs, as well as astrology, on the grounds that they were held by the rabbis of the Talmud.

Astronomy, astrology, mathematics, physics in the Middle Ages: The need to calculate the calendar forced Jews to engage in astronomy, and since, despite their pretentions, they really had no indigenous tradition, to accomplish this, they were obliged to work with Muslims and Christians. The result was that they not only acted as translators, assisting in the transmission of Indian and Arab astronomy to the West, but made original contributions, in the compilation of tables, in observation, and in the design of astronomical instruments.

By means of their Hebrew or Latin translations of the Arabic translations, commentaries, and compilations of Ptolemy's *Almagest*, Jews contributed to the transmission of Arabic-language science to scholastic Europe and hence to the renaissance. One of the first Hebrew translations of the Arabic version of the *Almagest* was made by Jacob Anatoli between the years 1231 and 1235. Ibn Aflah's *Kitab al-Hayd* ("The Book of Astronomy"), important for its critical appraisal of the Ptolemaic system, was translated into Hebrew by Moses ibn Tibbon in 1274.

Translation of ancient learning from Greek into Arabic (sometimes via Syriac), then into Hebrew and from Hebrew into Latin, was unlikely to preserve the original author's intentions. But while Europeans were busy rediscovering Greek, several Arabic essays were translated directly by Jews into European languages, especially Latin and Spanish. These constituted a major vehicle for the progress of astronomy. For instance, in 1256, Judah b. Moses ha-Kohen of Toledo translated into Spanish Abd al-Rahman al-Sufi's *Book of the Stars* under the title *Libro de las figuras* and Ibn Abu al-Rijal's astrological treatise *Kitab al-Barie* under the title *Libro complido*.

Similarly, the heretic Jew Sind ibn Ali (829-833) was a principal contributor to the astronomical tables of Caliph Maimun. Before 1136, Abraham bar Hiyya compiled a set of tables based on the calculations of the Arab Al-Battani (d. 929). Abraham ibn Ezra (1092-1167), Isaac Israeli (ninth to tenth century), and several other Hebrew authors compiled astronomical tables, and twelve Jewish astronomers, under the leadership of the Cordovan astronomer, Ibn Arzarkali (Azarchel), helped to compile the Toledo Tables in the twelfth century.

The famous "Alphonsine Tables" were prepared in Toledo for King Alfonso X of León and Castile under the direction of the Jewish astronomers Judah ben Moses ha-Cohen and Isaac ibn Sa'id. Completed in 1252, these tables were based on the geocentric Ptolemaic theory and enabled astronomers to calculate eclipses and the positions of the planets for any given moment. They were an important source of information for Copernicus, whose own work superseded theirs in the 1550s. Among many other sets of tables drawn up by Jewish astronomers were those by Levi ben Gershom (1288-1344) and by Abraham Zacuto (ca. 1452-1515), whose tables and *Almanach Perpetuum* in Latin and Spanish were used by Columbus on his voyages.

Observations and inventions in the Middle Ages: Astronomy was an important science that involved many Jewish scholars of the middle ages. The *B'raita diShmuel* or

Sod ha-ʿibbur, which deals with the principles of intercalating the calendar, is regarded by some as the first original Hebrew work on astronomy in the Middle Ages. Pseudonymously attributed to the Amora Samuel, it was compiled no earlier than the ninth century and applies Arab astronomy to Jewish calendrical problems. Another Jew, Mashaallah (ca. 800), whose Hebrew name was possibly Joab or Joel, served the caliphs in Baghdad. His essay on lunar eclipses, astral conjunctions, and seasons of the year is preserved in Hebrew. The ninth century Persian Jewish astronomer Andruzager b. Zadi Faruch may be identical with Eliezer b. Faruch, to whom the eleventh century Arab chronologist al-Biruni attributed the fixing of the Jewish calendar.

In Spain, Abraham bar Hiyya, in addition to his astronomical calendars and Latin translations of Arabic astrological works, wrote several original books. Those that were translated into Latin had a significant influence on the development of European science. Abraham ibn Ezra, though devoted to astrology, wrote several astronomical works, some of which describe types of astrolabes. The handwritten notes of Isaac ibn Saʾid (of Alphonsine table fame) on his observations of lunar eclipses are still extant.

In 1310, Isaac ben Joseph Israeli composed *Yesod Olam*, a study of astronomy and cosmography, incorporating an original method for calculating the parallax of the moon. He also wrote *Shaʾar ha-Shamayim* on periods and seasons and *Sefer Shaʾar ha-Milluʾim* on the movement of the planets, their order, and positions.

Gersonides (Levi ben Gershom, or Ralbag; 1288-1344) devoted the first section of the fifth book of his philosophical treatise *Milhamot Adonai* ("Wars of the Lord") to astronomy. He explains in detail his discovery, or improvement, of the cross-staff, a device for measuring angles and spherical distances, which became known in Europe as *baculus Jacobi* ("Jacob's staff"), and he describes his method of passing a light ray from a star through a small aperture in a darkened chamber on to a board—the first recorded use of the *camera obscura*. Among his achievements was the measurement of the relationship of the diameters of the sun and the moon to the lengths of their apparent orbits and the relationship between the parts of the surfaces covered during an eclipse and the size of the total area. This led him, in chapter 9, to reject some of the basic assumptions of the Ptolemaic system. Part of the book was translated into Latin in 1342.

Other Jewish inventors of astronomical instruments in the later Middle Ages include Jacob ben Machir, who invented an improved quadrant, for measuring angles; Isaac ben Solomon ben Zaddik al Hadib, who invented a new instrument that was a combination of astrolabe and quadrant; and Jacob (Bonet) de Lattes (fifteenth to sixteenth centuries), who designed a device in the shape of a ring for measuring the height of the sun and the stars. Zacuto improved the astrolabe.[11]

The Zohar on the earth's shape: Several scholars have repeated the erroneous claim that "some 250 years before Copernicus the Zohar stated that 'the whole earth spins in a circle like a ball; the one part is up when the other part is down; the one part is light when the other is dark, it is day in the one part and night in the other.'"[12] What the text actually says is (*Zohar Vayiqra* 10a):

> It is further explained in the book of Rav Hamnuna the Elder that the whole *yishuv* [the inhabited part of the earth] is round like a ball,[13] some below and some above, and all these creatures are of different appearance because [they live in] different climates. . . .

> So there is a place in the *yishuv*, that when it is light for these it is dark for those, when it is day for these it is night for those, and there is a place where it is all day and there is no night except for a brief moment.

So far as the effects of longitude are concerned, this statement of the Zohar does not go beyond the much earlier, well-known statements of Jewish authorities such as Judah Halevi (Kuzari 2:20) and Zerahia Halevi of Gerona.[14] However, the Zohar introduces a gratuitous error by inventing "a place where it is all day and there is no night except for a brief moment," overlooking the fact that in those latitudes in which daylight is constant for part of the year, darkness is constant at other times.

Hasdai Crescas (1340-1412) on physics: In his *Or Hashem* (1410), the Spanish Jewish philosopher Hasdai Crescas concedes the eternity of the world and sacrifices human free will to natural causality. At the same time, he rejects the *via negativa* in theology and "denies that man's true perfection and ultimately human immortality are to be gained by intellectual development, and makes goodness, rather than thought, the central attribute of the deity."[15]

Crescas attempts to undermine Aristotelian philosophy by disproving Aristotle's physics.[16] He

> answers Aristotle's proofs of the impossibility of an infinite magnitude, an infinite place, or a vacuum. He rejects Aristotle's definition of time: his definition of place: the theory that two elements, fire and air, are endowed with an absolute lightness that causes them to rise, and the theory that all four physical elements have their proper natural places . . . is the cause of their natural motion. The drift of Crescas' critique is toward a conception of infinite space, with the possibility of infinite worlds, and the uniformity of nature.[17]

But this summary by Davidson overlooks the most revolutionary aspect of Crescas' natural philosophy, his assertion that the heavens and earth are subject to the same system of natural law.[18]

Crescas was read by Pico della Miranda and directly influenced Spinoza. Some of his ideas are similar to those for which Giordano Bruno was burned at the stake; both of them may have been indebted to fourteenth century Parisian scholastics.[19]

Medicine and biology in the Middle Ages: A systematic scientific approach to medicine appears in Jewish sources only in the Middle Ages, when the influence of the Hippocratic School and Galen is prominent. The earliest known medical works written by a Jew are the Arabic treatises of Isaac Israeli (ca. 855-955). The *Book of Asaph* or *Book of Healing*, of which several versions exist, is the oldest Hebrew medical treatise, cited in some form perhaps as early as the tenth century.[20] Asaph the Physician, the supposed author, to whom a version of the Hippocratic

oath[21] subsequently in use by Jewish physicians is attributed, cannot be identified. The book—at least in one manuscript—contains "treatises on the Persian months, physiology, embryology, the four periods of man's life, the four winds [that is, humors], diseases of various organs, hygiene, medicinal plants, medical calendar, the practice of medicine, as well as an antidotarium, urinology, aphorisms, and the Hippocratic oath."[22] It is interesting that it draws not on the ample medical material in the Talmud but on "the books of the wise men of India" and a "book of the ancients." It ascribes the origin of medicine to Shem, son of Noah, who received it from angels. The contents clearly show dependence on Galen, Hippocrates, and Dioscorides, indicating that the practice of Jewish physicians was modeled not on Rabbinic sources but on "scientific" medicine.

Many Greek medical works were translated into Hebrew, generally from Arabic rather than the original language and often with the commentaries of leading medieval Muslim scholars. Opinions vary as to the originality of Jewish contributions to medicine, but there is no doubt that Jews played a significant role in the transfer of ancient Greek medical knowledge, together with later Islamic insights, to the west during the renaissance. Sadly, the great European universities formed at that time excluded Jews, so that although many individual Jews acquired medical knowledge and gained high reputations for their skills, only converted Jews such as Amatus Lusitanus[23] were able to play a full part in the development of the science before modern times.

But the systematic scientific approach created problems for traditionalists, since it rejected folk elements and superstitions included in the Talmud. Maimonides, in the short regimen of health he includes as a single chapter in his Mishneh Torah (*Hilkhot Deot* 4), casts aside tradition in favor of Galen and his own contemporaries. The remark of the commentator *Migdal Oz* that "everything in the chapter is based on principles derived from the sages and scattered through the Talmud" is wide of the mark. The truth is that Maimonides did not believe the sages had an adequate knowledge of medicine or that such knowledge could be obtained by the investigation of traditional texts. The Torah taught not the details of medical science but rather that one should seek the best advice obtainable from whatever source it might come.

The theological approach to healing: Jewish theology understands God to be all-powerful, merciful, and compassionate, God's providence extending to all creatures. Presumably, then, individuals who are sick and suffer do so not by accident but by God's design, whether on account of sin or in some way to refine them. This being the case, Jews pray to God to seek forgiveness and, if it is God's will, healing. This raises an important issue: if it is not God's will to heal, then, by utilizing the art of medicine to heal ourselves, do we not thwart God's will? If, for instance, God purposely "creates" an individual with a defective kidney, do we not circumvent God's will by replacing it with a healthy one or by offering dialysis? As a result of such thinking, some Karaites objected to the practice of medicine. Nahmanides (1194-1270) likewise held that God would protect from sickness any individual who served God in complete faith and that, ideally, the sick person should turn to repentance not to doctors, even though the Torah granted "permission for the doctor to heal" (commentary on Lev. 26:11).

The Talmud relates that Hezekiah, king of Judah, took six initiatives without consulting the sages; *post factum* they approved of three but not of the others (B. Ber. 10b and parallels). Among those they did approve was his initiative in hiding away the *sefer refuot* ("book of cures"). Most commentators assume that the book listed herbs God had created to cure each and every human malady. Hezekiah hid the book, explains Rashi, "because their heart was not humbled for the sick but they were healed immediately," that is, because the certainty of cure led people to ignore God. Maimonides, to whom it was inconceivable that the sages should approve of the deliberate suppression of beneficial medical information or resources, rejects this explanation. In his opinion, the book contained cures forbidden by the Torah, such

as astrological talismans. To leave it around would have been positively dangerous; moreover, the "cures" were worthless (commentary on M. Pes. 4, end).

The predominant Jewish view is indeed that endorsed by Maimonides, that the practice of medicine is not only permissible but virtuous. That the art of medicine is licit is inferred in the Talmud from the rules of compensation for injury: a malefactor must compensate the victim for pain, injury, shame, loss of earnings, and medical care, which indicates that doctors are allowed to practice (B. B.Q. 85a). Similarly, Joseph Karo (1488-1575), in his *Shulhan Arukh* (*Yore Deah* 236:1), states, ". . . [to heal] is a positive obligation, tantamount to the saving of life, and one who avoids doing it sheds blood, even though there is someone else available to [effect the cure], since the patient does not respond equally to every doctor;" one may practice medicine only if duly authorized by a Jewish religious court.

David ben Samuel haLevi (1586-1667) expressed theologically the relationship between "permission" to heal and the "obligation" to heal (Taz, on *Shulhan Arukh Yore Deah* 236:1):

> True healing is through prayer, for healing is from heaven, as it is written, "I have smitten, and I shall heal" (Deut. 32:39). But not everyone is worthy of this [special divine intervention]; hence it is necessary to achieve healing by natural means. He, blessed be He, agreed to this, and gave healing through natural cures; this is what is meant by "He gave permission to heal." Since human beings have got into this state [of having to rely on natural cures], doctors are obliged to effect cures [by natural means].

By being subsumed within the divine commandments, the practice of medicine becomes part of the spirituality of Judaism. Nevertheless, the specific remedies used by the physician are not determined by the religious tradition itself but by the science of medicine.

Natural science in the early modern period: Jonathan Israels has demonstrated that Jews, at least in western Europe, commenced reintegration with the host societies in the mid-sixteenth century and exerted a profound influence on subsequent European cultural and economic development.[24] André Néher[25] and others have shown the extent to which Jews such as David Gans were in direct contact with some of the leading scientific minds of the age. Ephraim Kupfer argued that there was a strong current of rationalist culture and philosophical activity among German Jews in the late fourteenth and early fifteenth centuries and that this stimulated similar interests among Polish Jews in the late sixteenth century.[26] Ruderman rightly observes, however, that the distinction between physics and metaphysics was a new feature of sixteenth century Jewish thought, reflecting an emergent consensus in Christian thought on the relationship between science and faith.

Moses Isserles (1520-72) in Cracow was "audacious"[27] in publishing a commentary on the Hebrew translation of Peurbach's *Theoricae Novae Planetorum* and was put on the defensive for his "Aristotelian" ideas by the more conservative Solomon Luria (ca. 1510-1574).[28] But often one becomes aware of the clash between observational science and Jewish tradition indirectly, through a defensive posture in the Halakhah. Luria himself, for instance, discusses a group of Talmudic statements in which advice is given on the avoidance of dangerous foods or eating habits, such as eating meat and fish together. Referring also to remedies and to protective measures against demons, he writes, "There is an ancient ban of excommunication on those who rely on the cures prescribed in the Talmud. [This is so that we should] not bring the sages into disrepute, for [people] do not know that there are differences in place and in time. . . ."[29] The question of "nature's having changed" had been mooted some centuries earlier by the Tosafists (at B. M.Q. 11a, s.v., *Kavra*), but with the new Age of Discovery had become far more acute.

The Copernican revolution: On May 24, 1543, on his death bed, Nicholas Copernicus received the first printed copy of his *De revolutionibus orbium coelestium*, completed thirteen years earlier, in which, though he was careful not to make the *substantive* claim that the earth orbited the sun, he demonstrated the mathematical elegance of calculating heav-

enly motions on the assumption that it did.

To what extent did Copernicus' revival of Aristarchus' heliocentric conception of the universe disturb traditional Jewish thought? Certainly, it was some time before the Copernican theory gained acceptance; as late as 1616, the Inquisition condemned Copernicus' book, and Galileo was tried in 1632. As knowledge of it spread, two problems presented themselves. The obvious one was that, in purely mathematical terms, it contradicted the Ptolemaic theory, which by this period had been incorporated into Jewish as well as Christian theology. However, what was in the long run far more serious was that it implied, as Crescas had suggested, that the stars and other "heavenly" bodies constituted a single physical system with the earth; the heavens thus were dethroned—in Max Weber's term, "disenchanted." The whole medieval fabric of a chain of being leading down from the One, through the heavenly spheres, to the earth and its lowly inhabitants, collapsed. No longer did it make sense to speak of a God who lived, literally, in the sky.

Maharal (Judah Loew ben Bezalel), responding to Azariah dei Rossi's skepticism with regard to Talmudic aggada, attempted, in his last published work (*Be'er ha-Gola*, section 6) to defend B. Pes. 94b:

> The rabbis taught: The sages of Israel say the sphere is fixed and the constellations rotate; the sages of the nations say the constellations are fixed and the sphere rotates. . . . Rabbi said, their words seem more correct than ours, since wells are cool in the day and hot at night.

Whether the passage has anything to do with the geocentric/heliocentric debate, as Maharal and others thought, is doubtful. Maharal, at any rate, remained faithful to the Rabbinic view of cosmogony, which he identifies with the Ptolemaic. For, he said—in a passage that contains the first, albeit oblique, reference to Copernicus in Hebrew—it was received by them from Moses at Sinai, who received it from God, who alone can possibly know the truth (*Netivot Olam, Netiv ha-Torah*).

In one respect, however, Maharal may have been influenced by Copernicus; he vehemently attacks Maimonides' contention that the spheres are intelligent beings (second preface to *Gevurot Hashem*), thus perhaps yielding to the pressure for "disenchantment" of the heavens. In the same passage he expounds his "double truth" theory, that the plane of spiritual reality, though generally synchronized with that of physical reality, occasionally departs from it, as in miracles such as the sun's standing still for Joshua; the "true" spiritual sun stopped, but the "mere" physical sun continued on its course.[30] This very convenient notion enables Maharal to have his cake and to eat it. Science (of the "nations") is perfectly valid and a legitimate activity but deals only with superficial appearance, whereas Torah truth (the unique possession of Israel) deals with essences, spirituality, ultimate reality. The two cannot contradict each other because they do not really meet, and the truth of Torah, like the people of Israel, is superior and eternal.

Maharal's disciple David Gans (1541-1613) was a colleague, or at least acquaintance, of both Tycho Brahe (1546-1601), self-styled last of the astronomers, and the latter's disciple Kepler (1571-1630), designated by Brahe to clear up the few remaining details. In *Nehmad ve-Na'im* (1613), Gans offered the first Hebrew exposition of the Copernican system; like Kepler himself, he rejected its substantive implications. Unlike Maharal, he thought that truth was one.

The Cretian polymath Joseph Solomon Delmedigo (1591-1655) was a pupil of Galileo and the first Hebrew writer to use logarithms. In his *Elim* he expounds the works of al-Battani and Copernicus, apparently endorsing the latter. Tobias ben Moses Cohen, known as Tuviyyah ha-Rofé (1652-1729), "the physician", in his *Ma'aseh Tuviyyah* (Venice, 1707-1708), reviews the heliocentric view but rejects it, principally on religious and traditional grounds, denouncing Copernicus as the "first-born of Satan."[31]

The early modern period—Conversos and natural science: Among the descendants of the *converso* Jews who remained in Spain after 1492 and Portugal after 1497 were many who achieved eminence in medicine. Among the most notable was Amatus Lusitanus (1511-1567), famous for dissect-

ing corpses, for his work on *materia medica*, and for attending Pope Julius III. Several times accused (as a Christian) of heresy, after two peaceful years in Ragusa (Dubrovnik), he moved in 1558 to Salonika, where he openly practiced Judaism and eventually died of the plague.

The *converso* émigrés who, from the end of the sixteenth century, were able to return to Judaism in the Netherlands and elsewhere in Europe formed new and intellectually restless Jewish communities. The medical professionals among them were held in high repute for their skills. But did they contribute significantly to the scientific revolution in the field of medicine? While Josef Kaplan thinks not, David Ruderman stresses the contribution they made to shaping a new Jewish cultural identity: "Several of them even contributed to discussions of the nature of religious belief and epistemological uncertainty, even applying their own rational and naturalistic susceptibilities to a radical rereading of the biblical text and the Jewish religious tradition."[32] Ruderman specifies three in particular: Francisco (1551-1623), whose *Quod nihil scitur* (Lyons, 1581) exhibits a constructive skepticism that, critical of Aristotle, emphasizes the need for experiment,[33] and Isaac La Peyrère (1596-1676) and Baruch (Benedict) Spinoza (1632-77), who exemplify the application of scientific techniques to biblical study. Richard Popkin has argued that this, even more than Copernican cosmology, undermined the theological foundations of Judaism and Christianity.[34]

Jewish medical studies at Padua: It is estimated that between 1520 and 1605, 29 Jews received medical diplomas from the University of Padua, then governed by Venice; between 1617 and 1816, at least 320 Jews graduated there.[35] Many must have attended university without matriculating, and some trained at the very small number of other universities that from time to time admitted Jews. In addition to their medical training, students at Padua studied logic, philosophy, and what might nowadays be known as a liberal arts curriculum.

Among the most famous graduates were Tobias Cohen, whom we met above, Joseph

Delmedigo, and Joseph Hamitz. Such men, all of whom had a thorough grounding in Jewish studies, and many of whom were rabbis, formed a distinct cultural and intellectual Jewish elite that not only bridged the gap between the Jewish and non-Jewish worlds but was uniquely placed to attempt to resolve the conflicts of science and religion.

Science and religion in the modern period: Since the seventeenth century, science has conflicted with religious tradition in the following ways:

(a) Innumerable instances have arisen of scientific results contradicting statements made by religious authority.
(b) The requirement that theory be supported by reproducible experimental evidence has not only cast doubt on earlier statements on nature by religious authorities but has undermined the traditional religious method of deriving information about the world out of traditional texts.
(c) The teleology that characterized the Aristotelian understanding of nature and conveniently supported the Argument from Design, which holds that creation has a purpose, has been abandoned.

The broad result of this has been a denominational split within Judaism. The Reformist branch, established as a separate movement in the early nineteenth century for sociopolitical as well as intellectual reasons, has accepted the scientific revolution in principle, to the extent that conflicts (a) and (b) are no longer perceived as threatening; however, its theologians have not satisfactorily dealt with (c). The Orthodox range from outright denial of scientific results to a variety of accommodations and reinterpretations designed to safeguard the integrity of the traditional doctrine of *Torah min ha-Shamayim*, that is, divine revelation.[36]

One ancient strategy to preserve the Torah's authority in the face of science is to demonstrate that all science is contained in the Torah itself. Thus Pinhas Eliyahu ben Meir of Vilna, in his *Sefer ha-Brit* (Petrkow, 1913; first published 1797), offers a remarkable review of almost every branch of science, ranging from physiology to mechanics and from astronomy to meteorology—all in terms of the theory of the four elements and

a geocentric Ptolemaic universe (1:7)! His stated objective is to assist people to attain the Holy Spirit; but, in that Enlightenment period, he undoubtedly intends both to demonstrate that "all is in the Torah" and that the great sages knew science before the gentiles "discovered" it. Pinhas Eliyahu may be responding to the work of the David Nieto[37] or the Jewish representatives of "physico-theology," such as the colorful Mordechai Gumpel Schnaber Levison.[38]

More recently, inevitably, the computer has been recruited in the attempt to demonstrate that everything is in the Torah. Michael Drosnin[39] reports the following method: The text of the Torah, consisting of just over 300,000 Hebrew letters, is fed into the computer, and regurgitated as a matrix of n lines, each consisting of a sequence of letters extracted from the text at intervals of n letters. Thus, 102 lines might be generated in which the first line contains the first letter, the 103rd letter and so on, and the bottom line the 102nd letter, the 204th letter, and so on. The computer then hunts for strings of letters occurring forwards or backwards, up or down, diagonally, in sequence or in intervals, anywhere in the matrix. So, for instance, when n was made equal to a certain number, a sequence comprising a possible Hebrew spelling of "Newton" occurred in one vertical line. Not far away, but in another direction, a Hebrew term for gravity was located. The researchers argue that, since no human being in the days of Moses could have known that over three thousand years later a man called Newton would discover gravity, the Torah could only have been composed by the all-knowing God, who concealed within it all knowledge and all future events, even people's names. It would be tedious to refute this nonsense. But the book has become popular and should be seen for what it is—a *reductio ad absurdum* of the whole enterprise of reading into holy texts what is patently not there, and thus missing the point of what *is* there.

Special problems—evolution, creation, and teleology: "How great are your works, O Lord; with wisdom have you made them all" (Ps. 104:24). The Jewish, Christian, and Muslim religions, whether in pious or philosophical mode, have consistently drawn attention to the manifestation of God's wisdom in creation. Thus, the main challenge to religion of Darwinian and post-Darwinian theory is that it undermines the traditional notion of creation by conscious design, of creation with a purpose. That is, it undermines the teleological science that had ruled since the days of Aristotle and was vital to the Argument from Design.

By contrast, Descartes (1596-1650) held that all change and movement in the physical world were to be explained in purely mechanical terms; Spinoza (1634-77) scathingly dismissed the idea of final causes in nature as a superstition, a figment of the human imagination (see *Ethics*, appendix to part I); and David Hume (1711-1776) reduced causation to mere "association of ideas."[40] Teleology, as a scientific hypothesis, was dead.

But it was not buried. This final rite was performed in 1859, when Charles Darwin at last released his *Origin of Species* like a bombshell upon the Victorian scene. Evolution poses three challenges to the traditional understanding of the biblical creation story:

(a) It claims, against the Bible, that people existed long before six thousand years ago, when Adam and Eve supposedly were created.
(b) It denies a special act of creation of humankind, asserting the continuity of life forms and the heredity of *homo sapiens* from more primitive species of animal.
(c) It posits a process—natural selection—by which human beings, as well as other creatures, could come to exist without having been specifically planned.

The last of these ideas was at the same time the most fundamental challenge to faith and the weakest part of the theory. For Darwin had no plausible explanation of how variation occurred or indeed of the reproductive process itself. Almost a century after the announcement of Darwin's hypothesis, Watson and Crick at Cambridge together with Rosalind Franklin in London unraveled the structure of DNA. At last a coherent model was available for a self-replicating molecule able to carry the information needed for the formation of a new individual organism. Minor, accidental variations in the code could be responsible for variation within a species and, cumulatively, for the evolution of distinct new species. Nowadays, with genetic modification at the molecular level an everyday technology and much of the human genome itself decoded, Dawkins' "selfish gene"[41] has come of age. The idea of human beings or any other creatures being "designed" has become superfluous.

In the nineteenth and early twentieth century some Orthodox thinkers felt they could accommodate evolution within a traditional Jewish scheme. Several, including Israel Lipschutz (1782-1860),[42] noted the parallel between the evolution of species and the statement attributed to Abbahu (Gen. Rabbah 9:2), that "The Holy One, blessed be he, repeatedly created worlds and destroyed them until he made this one." Rav Kook (1865-1935) observed that Kabbalah recognizes an ongoing process of redemption, a completion of creation, analogous to evolution.[43] J.H. Hertz appended to his commentary on Genesis a note in which he asserts:

> . . . there is, therefore, nothing inherently un-Jewish in the evolutionary conception of the origin and growth of forms of existence from the simple to the complex, and from the lowest to the highest. The Biblical account itself gives expression to the same general truth of gradual ascent from amorphous chaos to order . . . *insisting, however, that each stage is no product of chance, but is an act of Divine will*, realizing the Divine purpose, and receiving the seal of the Divine approval. . . .[44]

While these and others grasped the idea of evolution as progress, they failed to understand that "progress" of this kind does not require design. They addressed the minor question of how a progression of life, even one extended far beyond the few thousand years allowed by Scripture, can be reconciled with tradition, but not the major theological issue: Why is God needed, not simply as the "ground of being," but as author and guide of specific events?

Probability: Some argue that the state of things is statistically so improbable that it can only have come about through the direct will of an intelligent creator. For example, Edward H. Simon,[45] a molecular biologist, calculated "the average time it would take a random sequence of three hundred base pairs to evolve by chance mutation into a blue print for an enzyme, assuming a population of bacteria in steady state growth at a rate of one division (generation) per hour, with an average mutation rate of 10^{-8}/base pair/division." He concluded that 6×10^6 linear generations would be required for the new enzyme to arise by chance. If one applies the same sort of calculation to a higher animal, such as one of us, and bears in mind the large number of proteins coded in sequence in each of the large number of human genes, it is fairly obvious that we could not have evolved within the known time scale of the universe. Simon cautiously states, "These calculations do not PROVE anything." But he makes it pretty obvious that he wants us to think that organic evolution is impossible within the time-scale of our universe and hence that there must be a creator who has designed and created individual species. His identification as an "Orthodox Jewish Scientist" is a sign that he identifies this creator with the God of Jewish tradition and accepts the authenticity of the communications attributed to him by that tradition, though of course none of this follows from his argument. It is the characteristic leap from "architect" to "creator" that was resisted by Kant.

But are calculations of this type to be taken seriously, even when adopted by an atheist such as Fred Hoyle who draws from them the conclusion that life on earth must have been "seeded" from elsewhere ("Panspermia")?[46] I think not. The calculations are for the most part simply wrong, because they entirely ignore the dynamic nature of biological evolution.

The error is this. One can easily calculate the number of possible permutations of a sequence, *n* units long, of four amino acid radicals, which can occur in any order and any proportion of the four. The human genome consists of a sequence in the order of 10^{10} amino acids, and the number of possible permutations of a sequence that long is wildly beyond anything that could be conceived as actually being implemented within

our universe. But biological systems do not churn out permutations like supercomputers. They follow a very limited number of possible evolutionary paths. The dynamics of the system restrict the ways in which a particular system can be modified, and interaction with the environment places still more limitations on the paths actually followed. All this makes it far less improbable that some sort of complex system could arise within the available time-scale. Bearing in mind the constraints imposed by the dynamics of biological systems, it is not absurdly unlikely that a species of our degree of complexity could have arisen, without the special intervention of a creator, within the earth's time-scale.

Cosmology—the Big Bang: Medieval philosophers, we have seen, were bothered by the theory, attributed to Aristotle, than the universe was eternal, not created. Until the latter part of the twentieth century, scientific cosmology remained wedded to the assumption that the universe had no beginning or end, or at least none that could be subjected to any empirical test. By the 1960s, however, the Big Bang theory had become dominant and remains so. Observations are best explained on the basis that the universe is finite, bounded, and expanding; extrapolating backwards from the current rate of expansion yields a point of origin roughly fifteen billion years ago.

Theologians, Jewish as well as Christian, have welcomed this as confirmation of Genesis,[47] which, unlike medieval Aristotelianism, does acknowledge a point of origin, which it is but a small step to identify with divine creation. But theologians should not rejoice prematurely, since:

(a) Some theorists propose that the universe is simply undergoing one of an indefinite, possibly infinite, series of phases of expansion and contraction, so that it in fact has no beginning.
(b) Some have argued that the concept of a first moment of time is meaningless (this is very different from saying that time stretches back infinitely).
(c) Genesis states that the *earth* was created at the beginning—a view rejected by all astronomers.

(d) There is no evident correspondence between the six days of creation in Genesis and the fifteen billion years of modern cosmology or even the five billion years of earth history, with regard to either periods of time or order of events.

Even the modern view of cosmology thus seems hardly to support the traditional biblical view of a purposeful and well organized creation by a divine being.

Franz Rosenzweig on religion and science: Franz Rosenzweig (1886-1929), in the first part of his *Star of Redemption*, uses vector analysis and calculus as analogies to indicate that creation "moves" in a certain direction. But these are never more than loose analogies, any more than his A = A, A = B, and B = A are equations in a mathematical sense. Rosenzweig was dropping mathematical words into a conversation to impress his readers rather than actually doing philosophy of science.

"Creation," in Rosenzweig's view, expresses the relationship between God and the world, as "revelation" expresses the relationship between God and humanity, and "redemption" that between humanity and the world. God has no "end" but relates to humanity (revelation) and world (creation), in an atemporal, asymptotic process. Norbert Samuelson finds in common between Rosenzweig and the medieval Jewish philosophers the fact that "creation is seen as a single act set outside the bounds of time in which the universe is understood as a movement from God in the direction of a moral ideal."[48] Maybe. But most medieval Jewish philosophers held emphatically that the universe *did* have a beginning, out of nothing, five thousand plus years ago. They did *not* view the concept of beginning as an "asymptote."

Yeshayahu Leibowitz on religion and science: Yeshayahu Leibowitz (1903-1994) was a professor of organic and biochemistry and neurophysiology at the Hebrew University and a practicing Orthodox Jew. This double life is reflected in his simplistic philosophy, according to which science and religion do not conflict, since they occupy totally distinct domains.[49] Judaism, according to Leibowitz, is a religious and historical phenomenon characterized by a recognition of the duty to serve God according to Jewish religious law; there is no such thing as Jewish philosophy, theology, mysticism, or science, and, thus, there is no problem of the relationship between religion and science. Unfortunately for this solution, Judaism is not remotely as Leibowitz describes it, for it has repeatedly made claims to authority in domains we would now wish to reserve for science.

Joseph Dov (Baer) Soloveitchik on religion and science: J.D. Soloveitchik (1903-1993) likewise reduced Torah to Halakhah.[50] Torah narratives have as their purpose the determination of law; even the creation story is not cosmogony or metaphysics but Halakhah—the law that we should engage in the creative activity of Torah. But he does acknowledge that Torah addresses natural phenomena, so that Torah and nature do not occupy distinct domains; however, the Man of Religion, the Man of Science, and the Man of Halakhah each brings a different set of *a priori* concepts with which to confront the world. Each looks at the same tree or sunset. But where the Man of Religion responds with awe, and the Man of Science by measuring in accordance with his *a priori* laws, the Man of Halakhah confronts the tree or the sunset with the *a priori* laws of the Torah of Moses and decides what blessing to pronounce, whether the time has come for evening prayer, and so on.

Norbert Samuelson on religion and science: Norbert Samuelson (1936-) attempts to show the congruence, or at least compatibility, of modern cosmology with biblical and later Jewish accounts of creation. He indicates four aspects of the Jewish concept of creation that interface with contemporary scientific cosmology:[51] (1) the nature and origin of the universe in relation to time, (2) the role of space in the story of creation, (3) the relation of the actual physical universe to other possible universes, and (4) the relationship between the domains of science and ethics from a religious perspective. Genesis defines the first of these by stating, "In the beginning . . .;" the second, by the assertion of creation out of what was formless and void; the third, by its separation of heaven and earth; and the fourth, by the repeated declaration, "It was good." How does contemporary science handle these aspects of cosmogony?

The Big Bang theory posits a definite beginning for the cosmos, and one might have expected Samuelson, like more traditional "creationists," to seize on this as confirmation of Genesis. However, he cannot do this, since both his and Rosenzweig's "plain" readings of Genesis suggest an "atemporal" creation. Samuelson might perhaps have committed himself to Stephen Hawking's view that the concept of a first moment of time is meaningless; instead, he muddies the waters by referring to theories of parallel universes, inflationary universes, reversibility of time, and the like. Unfortunately, current mathematical descriptions of the history of the universe are so counter-intuitive that in attempting to put them into ordinary language, let alone the language of Genesis, one is drawn to paradox and confusion.

Much the same happens when Samuelson invokes quantum mechanics. Many people, including physicists such as Niels Bohr himself, have written as if quantum mechanics pointed to some sort of indefiniteness or undecidedness in the physical universe itself. But, as John L. Casti recently remarked, "the equation governing the wave function of a quantum phenomenon provides a causal explanation for every observation (completeness) and is well defined at each instant in time (consistency). The notorious 'paradoxes' of quantum mechanics arise because we insist on thinking of the quantum object as a classical one."[52]

Jewish thought and scientific discovery: Jacob Neusner has observed that "the ways of making connections and drawing conclusions, specifically the mixed logics of the dual Torah in its ultimate canonical statement, produced a different sort of learning from the philosophical, the scientific;"[53] therefore, he argues, there is "no science in the mind of Judaism." It is true that the logic that characterizes Talmudic argumentation differs from that of the experimental or theoretical scientist.[54] But the question we have addressed is

not whether there is "science in the mind of Judaism" but whether there is "science in the mind of Jews." As we have seen, there is.

Thus we answer the question posed at the beginning, "Is there any *organic* connection between Jewish thought and scientific discovery?," with a subdued affirmative. The Talmud itself demands, if in an ancillary role, answers to astronomical and biological questions and does not always obtain those answers by its usual "logic of fixed association." Moreover, "Jewish thought" is larger than the Talmud, ranging from biblical awe at God's creation, to the philosophies of the Middle Ages, to excitement at the new philosophies and scientific conceptions at the onset of modernity, to contemporary concern about conservation of the environment, all of which generate interest in the way the natural world works. The precise forms in which the normal human inquisitiveness of Jews has been channeled have been influenced by social and economic pressures as well as tradition, but we should not doubt that the love of learning and inquiry encouraged within Jewish tradition have stimulated scientific inquiry by Jews.

Notes

[1] See *The Christian Frame of Mind: Reason, Order, and Openness in Theology and Natural Science* (Colorado Springs, 1989).

[2] Mary Douglas, *Purity and Danger: An Analysis of Concepts of Pollution and Taboo* (London and Henley, 1966), chapter 3.

[3] B. Shab. 107b. Aristotle, in *De generatione animalium*, held that oysters, mussels, mosquitoes, flies and some plants were spontaneously generated. Pliny adds more species. The fourth century Christian Lactantius pointed to abiogenesis as nature's demonstration of the possibility of the virgin birth. Even Pasteur, in the nineteenth century, did not finally lay abiogenesis to rest.

[4] W.H. Feldman, *Rabbinic Mathematics and Astronomy* (London, 1931; reissued: New York, undated), pp. 74-76. Maimonides, Mishneh Torah *Qiddush ha-Hodesh* 9 and 10, explains both calculations of the *tekufah*. Feldman does not mention the so-called *B'raita d'Rav Adda bar Ahava*, in which Adda's *tekufah* is specified, but undoubtedly it is pseudepigraphic, like the *B'raita di-Shmuel*; possibly an attempt to claim a Jewish origin for Hipparchus' calculation.

[5] See, for instance, J. Naveh and S. Shaked, *Aramaic and Hebrew Incantations of Late Antiquity* (Jerusalem and Leiden, 1985) and J. Naveh S. and Shaked, *Amulets and Magic Bowls: Aramaic*

Incantations of Late Antiquity (Jerusalem, 1992).

⁶ Julius Preuss, *Biblical and Talmudic Medicine* (New York, 1978); E. Carmoly, *Histoire des médicins juifs anciens et modernes* (Brussels, 1944); H. Friedenwald, *The Jews and Medicine*, 2 vols. (Baltimore, 1944; reprint: New York, 1962), an others.

⁷ S.I. Levin and Edward A. Boyden, *The Kosher Code of the Orthodox Jew* (New York, 1969), p. vi.

⁸ Bahya ibn Pakuda, *Duties of the Heart*, tr. M. Hymanson, 2 vols. (Jerusalem, 1962), vol. 1, second treatise, chapters 1-6.

⁹ Hava Tirosh-Samuelson, in a forthcoming work based on her Jacobs Lectures, Oxford, 1997.

¹⁰ Regarding Bahya, see Y.T. Langermann, "Maimonides' Repudiation of Astrology," in *Maimonidean Studies* 2 (1991), 125/6, n. 9. For Halevi, see *Kuzari* 4:9, which rejects astrology as it does not yield certain results and is not a revealed science. For the position of the Vilna Gaon, see *Biur ha-Gra* note 13 on *Shulhan Arukh Yore Deah* 179.

¹¹ On the preceding, see Arthur Beer, "Astronomy," in *Encyclopaedia Judaica*. See also S. Gandz, *Studies in Hebrew Mathematics and Astronomy* (New York, 1970).

¹² Beer, op. cit. Like others who cite the Zohar, Beer fails to give a precise reference.

¹³ "*mitgalgala be-agula ke-kadur.*" To translate this "revolves like a ball," though linguistically possible, seems tendentious; one would require unambiguous evidence that the author of the Zohar meant "revolve" and this is not forthcoming.

¹⁴ *Baal ha-Maor* end of *Rosh Hashana* chapter 1 (p. 5 in the Vilna Alfasi).

¹⁵ Herbert A. Davidson, in *Dictionary of Scientific Biography* (New York, 1971), vol. 3, p. 470.

¹⁶ Harry Austryn Wolfson, *Crescas' Critique of Aristotle: Problems of Aristotle's Physics in Jewish and Arabic Philosophy* (Cambridge, 1929).

¹⁷ Davidson, op. cit.

¹⁸ Wolfson, op. cit., pp. 118-121.

¹⁹ Shlomo Pines, in his Hebrew work *Post-Thomistic Scholasticism and the Theories of Hasdai Crescas* (Jerusalem, 1966), suggests this link.

²⁰ Elinor Lieber, "Asaf's *Book of Medicines: A Hebrew Encyclopedia of Greek and Jewish Medicine, Possibly Compiled in Byzantium on an Indian Model*," in *Dumbarton Oaks Papers* 38 (1984), pp. 233-49.

²¹ Lieber, ibid., p. 244: "While this shows many affinities with the Hippocratic Oath, it is not taken from it directly.... From the literary point of view it constitutes a remarkable mosaic of Biblical phrases."

²² Richard Gottheil, "Asaph," in *The Jewish Encyclopedia*, vol. 2, p. 162.

²³ See H. Friedenwald, *The Jews and Medicine* (Baltimore, 1944), vol. 1, p. 333.

²⁴ J. Israels, *European Jewry in the Age of Mercantilism, 1550-1750* (Oxford, 1985).

²⁵ André Néher, *Jewish Thought and the Scientific Revolution of the Sixteenth Century: David Gans (1541-1613) and His Times* (Oxford, 1986).

²⁶ E. Kupfer, "Concerning the Cultural Image of Ashkenazic Jewry and Its Sages in the Fourteenth and Fifteenth Centuries," in *Tarbiz* 42 (1972/3), pp. 113-147. See also David B. Ruderman, *Jewish Thought and Scientific Discovery in Early Modern Europe* (New Haven and London, 1995), pp. 55ff.

²⁷ Ruderman, op. cit., p. 72.

²⁸ The correspondence between Isserles and Luria—in Isserles' *Responsa*, ed. Asher Ziff, (Jerusalem, 1971), nos. 5-8—superficially concerns a certain type of lesion; no. 7 is a little less veiled.

²⁹ Solomon Luria, *Yam shel Shlomo* on *Hullin* 8 #12.

³⁰ See Tamar Ross, "The Miracle as an Additional Dimension in the Thought of the Maharal of Prague" (Hebrew), in *Da'at* 17 (1986), pp. 81-96, and Ruderman, op. cit., pp. 78-79.

³¹ See André Néher, "Copernicus in the Hebraic Literature from the Sixteenth to the Eighteenth Century," in *Journal of History of Ideas* 38 (1977), pp. 219-21; H. Levine, "Paradise Not Surrendered: Jewish Reactions to Copernicus and the Growth of Modern Science," in R.S. Cohen and M.W. Wartofsky, eds., *Epistemology, Methodology, and the Social Sciences* (Boston, 1983), pp. 210-212.

³² Ruderman, op. cit., p. 276.

³³ See José Faur, *In the Shadow of History: Jews and Conversos at the Dawn of Modernity* (Albany, 1992), pp. 87-109.

³⁴ On La Peyrère, see R. Popkin, *Isaac La Peyrère: His Life, Work and Influence* (Leiden, 1987) and Y. Kaplan, H. Méchoulan, and R. Popkin, *Menasseh ben Israel and His World* (Leiden, 1989).

³⁵ Ruderman, op. cit., p. 105.

³⁶ Of the copious Orthodox writing on this theme in recent decades the following is a sample: *Proceedings of the Association of Orthodox Jewish Scientists* (New York: 1970 onwards); Norman Lamm, *Torah U-Madda: The Encounter of Religious Learning and Worldly Knowledge in the Jewish Tradition* (Northvale, 1990); E. Lederhendler, *Jewish Responses to Modernity* (New York and London, 1994); L. Levi, *Torah and Science: Their Interplay in the World Scheme* (Jerusalem, 1983); Moshe Schatz, *Sparks of the Hidden Light: Seeing the Unified Nature of Reality through Kabbalah* (Jerusalem, 1996).

³⁷ Ruderman, op. cit., chapter 11; J.J. Petuchowski, *The Theology of Haham David Nieto* (New York, 1970).

³⁸ Ruderman, op. cit., chapter 12.

³⁹ *The Torah Code* (London, 1997).

⁴⁰ David Hume, *An Enquiry Concerning Human Understanding* (first published in 1748), section III.

⁴¹ Richard Dawkins, *The Selfish Gene* (Oxford and New York, 1976) and *The Blind Watchmaker* (Longman, 1986).

[42] See #3 of his *D'rush Or ha-Hayyim*, appended to the Order Neziqin (first published 1845) in many editions of his commentary *Tiferet Israel* on the Mishnah. The sermon, on life after death, was delivered in Danzig on the intermediate Sabbath of Passover, 1842, and therefore antedates the full-blown Darwinian theory of evolution by natural selection.

[43] See for instance *Orot ha-Qodesh* (Jerusalem, 1938), ns. 559 and 565.

[44] J.H. Hertz, *Pentateuch and Haftorahs: Hebrew Text English Translation and Commentary* 2nd edition (London, 1965), p. 194. The work was first published in 1936. The emphasis is his.

[45] Edward H. Simon, "Gene Creation," in A. Carmell and C. Domb, eds., *Challenge: Torah Views on Science and Its Problems* (London and Jerusalem, 1976), pp. 208-215.

[46] Fred Hoyle and Chandra Wickramasinghe, *Our Place in the Cosmos* (London, 1993).

[47] See, e.g., Aron Barth, *The Creation in the Light of Modern Science* (Jerusalem, 1968).

[48] Norbert M. Samuelson: *Judaism and the Doctrine of Creation* (Cambridge, 1994), p. 98.

[49] Yeshayahu Leibowitz, *Judaism, Human Values and the Jewish State*, ed. Eliezer Goldman (Cambridge and London, 1992).

[50] See *Halachic Man* (Philadelphia, 1983) and *The Halachic Mind: An Essay on Jewish Tradition and Modern Thought* (New York, 1986). This account considers only the former work.

[51] Op. cit., p. 221.

[52] *Scientific American*, October, 1996, p. 79.

[53] Jacob Neusner, *The Making of the Mind of Judaism: The Formative Age* (Atlanta, 1987), p. 140.

[54] M. Fisch, op. cit., has contested this.

NORMAN SOLOMON

NORTH AMERICA, PRACTICE OF JUDAISM IN: The Jews in the U.S.A. and Canada form an ethnic group, meaning, a group that bears in common certain indicative traits of behavior and conduct, origin and outlook. Many of the members of the Jewish ethnic group also practice the religion, Judaism. Judaism is the religion of a single people, because, by its own theology, when a person adopts the faith of Judaism and its way of life and world view, that person also enters into the social entity, "Israel," meaning in Judaism, the holy people, God's first love, to whom the Torah is revealed. But that same term, "Israel," also signifies in common usage the Jews, or, more recently, the State of Israel in the Land of Israel. Consequently, we deal with ambiguity when we speak of the Jews and Judaism and the various senses and meanings of "Israel"

that circulate, quite properly, among them and in the world at large. But there is no Judaism without real people, practicing a living faith, and since the people who practice Judaism are not only Judaists—practitioners of the religion—but also, by definition, Jews who may not be Judaists at all, in trying to describe the lived and practiced religion, Judaism, in North America, we find ourselves at the boundary between religion and society.

Judaism in the U.S.A. finds definition in a variety of organized religious movements, with approximately half of all Jews who regard themselves as practitioners of Judaism identifying themselves with Reform Judaism, a third with Conservative Judaism, and perhaps ten per cent with Orthodox Judaism. In the U.S.A. Jews further form an ethnic group with a strong identification in politics—from 80 to 90% of them voting for the Democratic party in any given election. Within the ethnic group, it is estimated, of 6.5 million, approximately 4 to 4.5 million practice a form of Judaism.

The demography of U.S. and Canadian Jewry: Since the Jews form an ethnic group and encompass also practitioners of the religion, Judaism, in various forms, we are wise to approach the description of the practice of the religion by first taking account of the population within which the religion is practiced. In America, most Jews live in cities, indeed, in the largest metropolitan areas. We can get some idea of what this means by comparing the distribution of Jewish and non-Jewish populations in America. Consider this: 54 percent of American Jews live in the Northeast, whereas only a quarter of non-Jews live there. By contrast, about the same percentage of Jews and non-Jews live in the Western region of the United States (17 percent of each group), and Jews are significantly under represented in the South (17 percent of Jews compared to 34 percent of non-Jews) and in the North Central region (12 percent of Jews compared to 26 percent of non-Jews). Indeed, there are only 10 states where Jews have a population size of over 100,000, and together these account for 87 percent of all U.S. Jewry. Canadian Jewry is similarly concentrated in Toronto and Montreal (there is a sizable community in Winnipeg, too).

Current social studies of Judaism in America yield a consensus that all surveys have produced.[1] The U.S.A. contains a "Jewishly identified population" of some 6,840,000. Of these, 4.2 million identify themselves as born Jews with the religion, Judaism. They embody all the Judaisms that flourish in North America. Another 1.1 million call themselves born Jews with no religion. Adults of Jewish parentage with some other religion than Judaism are 415,000. Born of Jewish parents, raised as Jewish, and converted to some other religion are 210,000. Jews by choice ("converts") are 185,000. Children under 18 being raised in a religion other than Judaism are 700,000 (Kosmin, p. 4). It follows that the "core Jewish population" is 5.5 million, of which approximately 80%—4.4 million—are Jews by religion.

The Ethnic and the Religious in U.S. and Canadian Judaism: There are Jews who are atheists and Jews who are Orthodox, and many in-between (figs. 98-101). If a Jew who does not practice Judaism converts to some religion other than Judaism, he is generally thought to have dropped out of the ethnic group. But what the books say Judaism is and how Judaism is practiced in North American Jewry do not correspond in all details. If it is to keep dietary taboos, not to eat pork or lobster or mix dairy products with meat, then many Jews—perhaps 90% of them—are excluded. And if it is to "love your neighbor as yourself" (Lev. 19:18), then while everybody tries, few succeed. Indeed, while one person who practices Judaism thinks that religious practices are vital, another, who also practices Judaism, does not.

Why these uncertainties, these contradictions in defining Jews and Judaism? Behind them lie two fundamental problems in Judaism. The first comprises the complex and at times almost oppositional relationship between ethnic and religious definitions of Judaism. All branches of Judaism select Jews along ethnic lines according to their birth. For instance, Orthodox and Conservative Judaism (terms explained below) define the Jew as a person born of a Jewish mother, and Reform Judaism, as a person born of a Jewish mother or father. But Judaism speaks of "Israel," meaning the Jewish people as Christianity speaks of "the Church." That is, religious criteria operate too. The line between the supernatural social entity, called into being by God in God's service, and the this-worldly social group, formed by people of common background and culture, is a very fine one. In Judaism it is difficult to make out.

The second problem is a by-product of this conflict between religious and ethnic definitions of Judaism: North American Jews do not agree on what Judaism is. Indeed, since being Jewish also makes a person automatically part of "Israel," meaning God's holy people, the opinions of individual Jews are often considered authoritative and even representative of Judaism. That explains why we have so many forms of Judaism. In the U.S.A. and Canada, and overseas as well, there are at least four organized forms of Judaism or, as we shall term them, four Judaisms: Orthodox, Reform, Conservative, Reconstructionist. Orthodox Judaism believes in a literal way that God gave the Torah, both written (that is, the "Old" Testament, as Christianity knows it) and oral (that is, the traditions written down after 70 C.E. and the final destruction of the temple by the rabbis who evolved to replace the priests). It keeps the law as God-given. Reform Judaism emphasizes change. It considers the Torah a statement of eternal principles in historical language and terms, and consequently believes that it can be changed to respond to new conditions. Indeed, it abandons much of the original Torah as no longer relevant. Conservative Judaism, by contrast, affirms the God-given standing of the Torah but accommodates change. As for Reconstructionist Judaism, it sees the faith as the historical religious civilization of the Jews and identifies God in naturalist rather than supernatural terms. That is, the more recent Judaisms move further and further from the notion of Torah as their divinely inspired, authoritative text.

Moreover, although in the State of Israel only Orthodoxy is recognized by the State, Orthodox Jews in Israel and around the world, including in North America, are divided among themselves. So we have to take the classification "Orthodox Judaism" and subdivide that too. In its place stand Orthodox Judaisms, many, diverse, and fiercely competitive. All Orthodox Judaisms affirm the God-given authority of the Torah (and are therefore "Orthodox"), but they differ among themselves on how to interpret the Torah—and even on who should interpret and apply its law—as vigorously as they disagree with Reform Judaism.

The geography of Judaism: Jews exhibit traits that indicate their social continuity and corporate cohesion in the context of their various homelands. The sociologist and demographer Calvin Goldscheider, among others, has shown that the Jews form a distinctive social group and that the indicators of their difference are sharply etched and well framed. Goldscheider writes: "A detailed examination of family, marriage, childbearing, social class, residence, occupation and education among Jews and non-Jews leads to the unmistakable conclusion that Jews are different. Their distinctiveness as a community is further reinforced by religious and ethnic forms of cohesiveness."[2]

Goldscheider's point is that although difference is defined in different ways in different places, everywhere the sense of being different, of being "unique," characterizes Jews. Of course, since difference is defined differently in different places, what makes a Jew different in one place will not mark him and not be recognized as a difference somewhere else. For instance, in America people think that bagels are a Jewish bread, or that corned beef is a Jewish dish, but to outsiders, American Jews appear to be Jewish Americans—and more American than Jewish. Similarly, in Morocco and Algeria, some forms of wheat used to be prepared in a way that Moroccans and Algerians considered specific to Jews and therefore Jewish, but in America we recognize no specifically Jewish way to prepare wheat.

What kind of traits mark the group off from others in one context and another? Family, stratification of Jewish society, and diverse characteristics of ethnicity all identify the Jews as a group distinctive in their larger social setting. Goldscheider writes:

> The distinctive features of American Jewish life imply bonds and linkages among Jews which form the multiple bases of communal continuity. These ties are structural as well as cultural; they reflect deeply embedded forms of family, educational, job and residence patterns, reinforced by religious and ethnic-communal behavior, cemented by shared lifestyles and values.[3]

That is, Jewish difference is distributed across socio-economic patterns. It appears in the form of marriage, type of family, place of residence, degree of mobility a Jew enjoys in that society. That is, we see it in his occupation, education, economic status—his social class with its communal affiliation and identification and behavior. When we consider these phenomena, we see that Jews do exhibit qualities in common. For instance, they live together, forming Jewish neighborhoods; they work in a few specific types of occupations; they marry within the group. As a result, Americans think, for example, that psychiatry is a Jewish profession while professional football is not. By contrast, in the State of Israel, Jews are identified (as was the case in biblical times) as farmers and soldiers. None of these are inherently Jewish occupations, of course, any more than they are Norwegian. But in specific contexts they indeed indicate a person's Jewishness. And thus they justify describing the Jews as a socio-ethnic group, not merely as individuals who happen to believe the same things and so have the same religion.

The geographical demography of Judaism: Realizing that there are various Judaisms in the world, we ask what characterizes the practice of Judaism in various places where Jews form ethnic groups or communities. On this matter, Goldscheider observes, "The extent and variation of contemporary Judaism—the religiosity and religious commitments of Jews—defy simple definition and classification." For most Jews there is limited evidence on the degree of Jewish identification, religious practice, ritual observance, or other indicators of Judaism. This is true despite the highly organized character, e.g., congregational, institutional, of Jewish communities and synagogue and Rabbinical associations.

An examination of some rough indicators of Judaism reveals the following profile for the largest communities in the United States. National American data show that about 85 percent of the adult Jewish population in the United States identify themselves with one of the three major denominations—Orthodox, Conservative or Reform (which are generally ranked from higher to lower in intensity of religious observance). As noted above, overall, about 11 percent identify with the Orthodox, 42 percent with Conservative Judaism and 33 percent with Reform Judaism.[4]

Goldscheider points out, further, that variation in this identification and practice of Judaism is also reflected in ritual practices and synagogue attendance. Nationally, data from a 1970-71 survey showed that about 30 percent of the Jews observed the dietary rules, 13 percent attended synagogue frequently, 24 percent were members of two or more Jewish organizations. Data from New York (1981) show that about 90 percent of adult Jews attend a Passover Seder, 80 percent observe the December festival of Hanukkah, 70 percent have a *Mezuzah* (an amulet) on the doorpost of their houses as Scripture requires, 67 percent fast on Yom Kippur (the Day of Atonement), 36 percent buy only kosher meats, and 30 percent keep two sets of dishes, one for meat and the other for dairy, as the Talmud requires. Few Jews attend services weekly (14 percent of the men in New York); most attend a few times a year. About 30 percent of the men never attend. Again, Jews in other American communities, particularly in the west show lower levels of ritual observance and synagogue attendance. Canadian Jewry is much like American Jewry; Orthodoxy competes with strong Reform and Conservative Judaisms there too.

How Jews view Judaism and "Being Jewish:" The distinction between the ethnic and the religious—takes on weight when we examine popular opinion on whether the Jews are a religious group, an ethnic group, a cultural group, or a nationality. Kosmin's report states (p. 28):

Being Jewish as defined by cultural group membership is the clear preference of three of the four identity groups [Jews by birth, religion, Judaism; Jews by choice, converts; Jews by birth with no religion; born and raised Jewish, converted out; adults of Jewish parentage with another current religion]. Definition in terms of ethnic group was the second highest and was cited more frequently than the religious concept by every Jewish identity group.

Jews who thought of themselves as a religious group were 49% of those who said they were born Jews, religion Judaism; 35% of born Jews with no religion; 56% of born and raised Jews who converted out; and 40% of adults of Jewish parents with another current religion.

The further figure that affects our study—besides the 4.4 million, which defines its parameters—concerns intermarriage patterns. At this time, 68% of all currently married Jews by birth (1.7 million) are married to someone who was also born Jewish. But, in the language of Kosmin's report:

The choice of marriage partners has changed dramatically over the past few decades. In recent years just over half of born Jews who married, at any age, whether for the first time or not, chose a spouse who was born a Gentile and has remained so, while less than 5% of these marriages include a non-Jewish partner who became a Jew by choice. As a result, since 1985, twice as many mixed couples, that is, born Jew with gentile spouse, have been created as Jewish couples (Jewish with Jewish spouse). This picture . . . tends to underestimate the total frequency, because it does not include currently born-Jews divorced or separated from an intermarriage nor Jew-Gentile unmarried couple relationships and living arrangements.

Wertheimer too comments on the matter of intermarriage, in these terms: "Intermarriage has exploded on the American Jewish scene since the mid-1960s, rapidly rising in incident to the point where as many as two out of five Jews who wed marry a partner who was not born Jewish." In Reform Judaism he reports, 31% of the lay leaders of Reform temples reported having a child married to a non-Jewish spouse. So the first thing that captures our attention is that the single most important building block of Judaism, the family, the expression in the here and now of the sacred genealogy of Israel, wobbles.

Religious beliefs: Restricting our attention to the Judaists and the secular Jews (Kosmin's born Jews, religion Judaism, and his born Jews with no religion), what do we learn about religious beliefs?

[1] The Torah is the actual word of God: 13% concur (but 10% of born Jews with no religion do too, not a very impressive differential).

[2] The Torah is the inspired word of God, but not everything should be taken literally word for word: 38% of Judaists concur, and 19% of the secularists.

[3] The Torah is an ancient book of history and moral precepts recorded by man: 45% of the Judaists, 63% of the secularist Jews concur.

[4] And 4% of the Judaists and 8% of the secularists had no opinion.

By the criterion of belief in the basic proposition of the Judaism of the dual Torah, that the Torah is the word of God, 13% of the Judaists concur; another 38% agree that the Torah is the inspired word of God but not literally so; and another 45% value the Torah. If we were to posit that these numbers represent Orthodox, Conservative, and Reform Judaisms, we should not be far off the mark.

In fact, the denominational figures Kosmin's report gives are as follows (current Jewish denominational preferences of adult Jews by religion = our Judaists):

Of the Judaists, 80% are Reform or Conservative, approximately 7% Orthodox; and the high level of identification with Orthodoxy is strictly a phenomenon in the greater New York City area. Elsewhere, the percentage of Orthodox Jews in the community of Judaists is still lower (Wertheimer, p. 80). The denominational choice of the rest is scattered. A slightly earlier study by Kosmin (for 1987) divided the Jews in general as: 2% Reconstructionist, 9% Orthodox, 29 percent Reform, 34 percent Conservative, and 26 per-

cent "other" or "just Jewish." It is not clear whether the distinction between Jews and Judaists is reflected in these figures, but the upshot is not in doubt (cf. Wertheimer, pp. 80-81).

Kosmin further observes (p. 32) that there is "a general trend of movement away from traditional Judaism. While one quarter of the born Jewish religion Judaism group was raised in Orthodox households, only 7% report themselves as Orthodox now." Not only so, but "nearly 90% of those now Orthodox were raised as such, thus indicating any movement toward Orthodoxy is relatively small. In contrast to the Orthodox, the Conservative and Reform drew heavily from one or both of the major denominations; one third of the Conservatives were raised as Orthodox, and one-quarter of the Reform as Conservative, with an additional 12% having been raised Orthodox."

Wertheimer too observes that the trend is away from Orthodoxy and from Conservatism as well and toward Reform Judaism: "Nationally, the Conservative movement still commands the allegiance of a plurality of Jews, albeit a shrinking plurality. The main beneficiary of Orthodox and Conservative losses seems to be the Reform movement" (Wertheimer, p. 80). As to synagogue affiliation, Kosmin comments (p. 37): "Synagogue affiliation is the most widespread form of formal Jewish connection, but it characterized only 41% of the entirely Jewish households." He further notes that there is a discrepancy between calling oneself Reform and belonging to a Reform temple; "The distribution of the 860,000 households reporting synagogue membership across the denominations shows that the Reform plurality, which was evidenced in denominational preferences, does not translate directly into affiliation. By contrast, the Orthodox are more successful in affiliating their potential constituency."

	Proportion of those polled	Proportion of households
Orthodox	6.6%	16%
Conservative	37.8%	43%
Reform	42.4%	35%
Reconstructionist	1.4%	2%
Just Jewish	5.4%	

Religious practices among the faithful:
How about religious practice of the Judaists?
Here the figures cover only three matters:

fast on the Day of Atonement	61%
attend synagogue on high holidays	59%
attend synagogue weekly	11%

Every study for several decades has replicated these results: lots of people go to Passover seders, a great many also observe the so-called High Holy Days (in the Torah: "the days of awe," that is, Rosh Hashshanah, the New Year, and Yom Hakkippurim, the Day of Atonement). So we may ask, why do people who do not participate in public prayer weekly (or daily) come to synagogue worship for the New Year and the Day of Atonement, that is to say, why do approximately half of the Judaists who worship in community at all do so only three days a year? How do they know what is fit and proper: this day, not that?[5]

Religious practices in the home: As to rites at home and household practices, Kosmin shifts to entirely Jewish households, as against mixed Jewish and gentile households, that is, from the Judaist to the Jewish (and a sensible shift at that):

attend Passover seder	86%
never have Christmas tree	82%
light Hanukkah candles	77%
light Sabbath candles	44%
belong to a synagogue	41%
eat kosher meat all the time	17%

What makes Passover different from all other holidays? Clearly, that question must come up first of all. What makes Sabbath candles (all the more so, the weekly Sabbath as a holy day of rest) only half so important as Hanukkah candles (one week out of the year)?

Since the Torah devotes considerable attention to the foods that may sustain the life of holy Israel, and since the ethnic Jews too identify foods as particularly Jewish, we may ask about the matter of observance of dietary rules in Conservative Judaism, which affirms them and regards them as a key-indicator of piety. Charles S. Liebman and Saul Shapiro report[6] that among the Conservative Jews they surveyed, 5% of the men and 6.4% of the women state that they observe the dietary laws both at home and away (by the standards of Conservative Judaism, which are somewhat more lenient then those of Orthodoxy); 29.2% of the men and 28.8% of the women have kosher homes but do not keep the dietary taboos away from them. Approximately a third of the Conservative homes, then, appear to be conducted in accord with the laws of kosher food. Liebman and Shapiro comment that the home of the parents of those in this group also was kosher, and observance of the dietary laws correlates with Jewish education:

> Of the children receiving a day school education, 66% come from kosher homes; of all those who attended Camp Ramah [a Jewish educational summer camp run by the Conservative movement], 53% came from kosher homes; this despite the fact that only 34% of the parents report their homes are kosher. The differences are even more dramatic if one bears in mind that a disproportionate number of older Conservative synagogue members have kosher homes, which means that their children were educated at a time when day school education was much less widespread in the Jewish community.

Essential religious practices in North American Judaism: Along these same lines Steven M. Cohen introduces the metaphor of "an artichoke syndrome," where, he says, "the outer layers of the most traditional forms of Jewish expression are peeled away until only the most essential and minimal core of involvement remains, and then that also succumbs to the forces of assimilation . . . according to assimilationist expectations, ritual observance and other indicators of Jewish involvement decline successively from parents to children."[7] But current studies do not "support a theory predicting uniform decline in ritual practice from one generation to the next. Rather, it suggest intergenerational flux with a limited movement toward a low level of observance entailing Passover Seder attendance, Hanukkah candle lighting, and fasting on Yom Kippur."[8] In yet other studies, Steven M. Cohen speaks of "moderately affiliated Jews," who nearly-unanimously "celebrate High Holidays, Hanukkah and Passover, belong to synagogues when their children approach age 12 and 13, send their children

Figure 94. Synagogue services on the morning of Sukkot, Bukhara, Uzbek Soviet Socialist Republic, 1985. Photograph by Barbara Pfeffer.

Figure 95. Interior of a synagogue in Salonika, Greece, undated.

Figure 96. A service at the excavated ancient synagogue on Masada combines history and spirituality, Israel, 1992. Photograph by Richard T. Nowitz.

Figure 97. Male choir of Hinenstraat synagogue, Amsterdam, Holland, undated.

Figure 98. Days of Awe services at the farm of Moses Bloom, Norwood, New Jersey, 1919. This rural area had no rabbi, but people from various communities gathered to hold services together.

Figure 99. Jewish New Year's card, New York, September 1908.

Figure 100. Passover seder at the home of Fannie and Charles Rosenblat, New York, c. 1943-1945.

Figure 101. Hasidic Jews at a farbrengen (festive gathering) at the Lubavitch headquarters in Crown Heights, Brooklyn, New York, 1970s. Photograph by Barbara Pfeffer.

to afternoon school or Sunday school, and at least occasionally support the Federation ['UJA'] campaigns."[9]

Cohen speaks of "broad affection for Jewish family, food, and festivals." Here, Cohen's report provides especially valuable data. He explains "why Jews feel so affectionate toward their holidays:"

> One theme common to the six items [celebrated by from 70 to over 90% surveyed] is family. Holidays are meaningful because they connect Jews with their family-related memories, experiences, and aspirations. Respondents say that they want to be with their families on Jewish holidays, that they recall fond childhood memories at those times, and that they especially want to connect their own children with Jewish traditions at holiday time. Moreover, holidays evoke a certain transcendent significance; they have ethnic and religious import; they connect one with the history of the Jewish people, and they bear a meaningful religious message. Last, food . . . constitutes a major element in Jews' affection for the holidays.[10]

The holidays that are most widely celebrated in this report remain the same as in the others: Passover, Hanukkah, and the High Holy Days. By contrast, "relatively few respondents highly value three activities: observing the Sabbath, adult Jewish education, and keeping kosher." The question comes to the fore once again: why those rites and not others, why those rites in preference to others?

How about Israeli matters? Among the Judaists, 31% have visited the State of Israel, 35% have close family or friends living there; among the ethnic-Jews (not Judaists), the figures are 11% and 20%. Here is another question: what makes the State of Israel so important to the Judaists?

And, along the same lines come charity, including Israel-centered charity (UJA for instance) (once more speaking of entirely Jewish households:

contributed to a Jewish charity in 1989	62%
contributed to UJA/Federation campaign in 1989	45%
celebrated Israeli independence day	18%

And, for comparison:

contributed to a secular charity in 1989	67%
contributed to a political campaign in 1988-1990	36%

Commenting on the Kosmin report, Ari L. Goldman (New York Times, Friday, June 7, 1991), commented, "In a radical change from just a generation ago, American Jews today are as likely to marry non-Jews as Jews. But even as this assimilation accelerates, Jews are clinging to religious traditions."

The state of contemporary Jewish religious life: Covering a variety of issues, Jack Wertheimer proposes to "evaluate the state of contemporary Jewish religious life" (Wertheimer, p. 63), with special attention to changing patterns of religious observance, which concern this inquiry into the contrast between book-Judaism and practiced Judaism. Orthodoxy, conceded by all parties to be closest in popular observance to the Judaism described in the holy books, retains its young people, but at the same time loses its older population, a disproportionately large component of its numbers, to death, with from two to three times as many Orthodox Jews over age 65 as between 18 and 45; so the gap between the books as lived by everyday Jews and the conduct of the generality of Jews is growing wider. Synagogue attendance rates vary, but decline. In the early 1980s, Wertheimer says, approximately 44 percent of Americans claimed they attended services weekly, and 24 percent of American Jews did; but that figure is high. Wertheimer says, "In most communities between one third and one-half of all Jews attend religious services either never or only on the High Holy Days" (p. 85).

Dividing the country by communities, e.g., New York, Philadelphia, Baltimore Washington, St. Louis, Miami, and the like, yields various statistics on diverse religious practices. For the sake of simplifying the picture—for the variations are not formidable—we shall review Wertheimer's "practice of selected observances, by community" (pp. 88ff.):

These figures show a fair amount of variation, but, overall, confirm the impressions formed in the Kosmin study. Some religious practices are widespread, others not. Not only so, but if we distinguish, as Kosmin does, between those who say they are Jews by religion and those who say they are not, the probability is that the percentages of Judaists who practice the rites listed here is higher than indicated.

The available figures rarely tell us about other rites. For instance, what percentage of Jews who marry other Jews and who also identify as Judaists marry in a Judaic rite, and what percentage do not? So too, what percentage of Jews circumcise their sons, and, if they do so, do they do so eight days after birth, through the offices of a ritual circumciser (mohel), or do they use a doctor and pass on the religious rite altogether? Here we have some intriguing data. Cohen notes,[11] that:

what "a good Jew" wants. We shall return to that anomaly in due course.

What percentage of Jews are buried by a rabbi and buried in a Jewish cemetery, what percentage of Judaists have Judaic last rites, and so forth? Here we rely on guess work, but the naked eye strongly suggests that most Jews who marry other Jews have a religious rite for the wedding; most Judaists are buried with Judaic rites; the rite of circumcision tends, among Reform Jews, to be transformed into a (merely) surgical operation, but is exceedingly common among American Jews. These and other impressions do not have the same authority as the results of the surveys just now quoted. They suffice to suggest that Judaists practice rites of passage—circumcision or some other rite at the birth of a child (syna-

	New York	Philadelphia	St. Louis	Phoenix	Rochester
attends seder	89%	89%	71%	81%	80%
lights Hanukkah candles	76%	78%	80%	78%	78%
has mezuzah	70%	71%	76%	57%	NA
fasts on Yom Kippur	67%	67%	NA	NA	63%
lights Sabbath candles	37%	32%	28%	NA	33%
buys only kosher meat	36%	NA	19%	NA	NA
uses two sets of dishes, meat and dairy	30%	16%	15%	9%	23%
handles no money on the Sabbath	12%	NA	NA	4%	NA
refrains from transport on the Sabbath	NA	5%	5%	4%	NA
has Christmas tree (sometimes or frequently)	NA	NA	14%	NA	15%

a large proportion, 55%, of respondents say it is extremely important that their children have sons ritually circumcised; another 18% say it is very important. These proportions far exceed those on marrying another Jew—33% say marrying another Jew is extremely important for their children, as opposed to the 55% for circumcising their grandsons.

The upshot is somewhat curious: grandparents are more concerned that their grandsons be circumcised than that their sons marry Jewish women; since the child of a gentile woman is, in the law of Judaism, gentile, it turns out that these grandparents favor the circumcision of (specified) gentiles as part of

gogue service for naming sons and daughters, for instance); bar or bat mitzvah (for boys and girls respectively); marriage by a rabbi and a cantor under a Judaic marriage canopy; Jewish burial. Add to this very high levels of observance of Passover, Hanukkah, and some other home rites, and we form the impression of a religion that enjoys substantial everyday observance of rites that involve the family (rites of passage) and the home (Passover).

Alongside these rites of family and home, it would be a considerable error to ignore certain broadly practiced activities that characterize Jews in America and that form a major, public component of their community. Philanthropic and political activities, for instance, are carried out under a deeply Judaic aspect, frequently explained within the framework of Judaism. So there is a public and communal Judaism, as much as Judaism for home and family, which must be taken into account as we describe the practices of Jews in North America.

The moderately affiliated; the center in U.S. and Canadian Judaism: To describe the large center of American Jews, those who are both ethnically Jewish and religiously Judaic—estimated by Steven M. Cohen to number about half of the American Jews—we may use the terms Cohen has provided. He gives these generalizations that pertain to our problem:[12]

> The moderately affiliated are proud of their identity as Jews, of Jews generally, and of Judaism.
> They combine universalist and particularist impulses; they are ambivalent about giving public expression to their genuinely felt attachment to things Jewish.
> They are especially fond of the widely celebrated Jewish holidays as well as the family experiences and special foods that are associated with them.
> They celebrate High Holidays, Hanukkah and Passover as well as most major American civic holidays . . .
> They vest importance in those Jewish activities they perform; and they regard those activities they fail to undertake as of little import. Accordingly, they are happy with themselves as Jews; they believe they are "good Jews."
> Their primary Jewish goal for their children is for them to maintain Jewish family continuity . . .
> The Holocaust and anti-Semitism are among the most powerful Jewish symbols . . .
> The moderately affiliated believe God exists, but they have little faith in an active and personal God.
> They are voluntarists, they affirm a right to select those Jewish customs they regard as personally meaningful, and unlike many intensive Jews, most of the moderately affiliated reject the obligatory nature of halakhah [laws, norms].
> They endorse broad, abstract principles of Jewish life (such as knowing the fundamentals of Judaism) but fail to support narrower,

more concrete normative demands (such as regular text study or sending their children to Jewish day schools).
> The moderately affiliated prefer in-marriage but fail to oppose out-marriage with a great sense of urgency.
> They support [the State of] Israel, but only as a subordinate concern, one lacking any significant influence on the private sphere of Jewish practice.
> To the moderately affiliated, "good Jews" are those who affiliate with other Jews and Jewish institutions.

We have before us the description of a mass of Judaists, who in some ways conform, and in other ways do not conform, to book-Judaism. Their religion presents us with a problem of interpretation: how do these people know the difference between what matters and what doesn't, not only Passover as against Pentecost (Shabuot) fifty days later; but circumcision as against intermarriage; the Holocaust and anti-Semitism as against the State of Israel; the existence of God as against God's active caring? The key lies in Cohen's description: "they affirm a right to select."

American Judaism of Holocaust and Redemption: Another self-evidently valid Judaism, besides the Judaism that all "good Jews" agree defines the norm, flourishes in North America. It is different from the Judaists' Judaism, and we also know it is practiced, alongside the Judaists' Judaism, by nearly all Judaists, as well as by the generality of Jews not Judaists. The key figures come in the following form:

contributed to a Jewish charity in 1989	62%
contributed to UJA/Federation campaign in 1989	45%

Add to this list political action in behalf of the State of Israel, e.g., contributing to a lobby such as American-Israel Political Action Committee ("AIPAC"), writing letters to members of Congress, voting for candidates who favor the State of Israel and against those who oppose it, and you have a set of actions not primary to or not known in book-Judaism, but very important for Judaists as much as for Jews. And, since these activities not only define traits of "good Jews," and so enjoy such normative status as exists in

Judaism in North America, they have to be seen as practical actions that express deeply-held convictions and formative attitudes: rites of some kind. So we turn to the question of another Judaism, moving from the rites, rapidly considered, to the tale of transcendence that turns an action into a rite, and a story into a narrative bearing transcendent meaning.

"The Holocaust" of the Judaism of Holocaust and Redemption refers to the murder of six million Jewish children, women, and men in Europe in 1933 through 1945 by the Germans. "The Redemption" is the creation of the State of Israel. Both events constitute essentially political happenings; a government did the one, a state and government emerged from the other. And both events involved collectivities acting in the realm of public policy. "The Holocaust" then corresponds in the here and now to anti-Semitism, exclusion, alienation, which Jews experience solely by reason of being Jewish. And, while authentic anti-Semitism—hatred of Jews as the cause of all evil, loathing of Judaism as a wicked religion, pointing to Jews as the source of every disaster—flourishes only on the lunatic fringe of politics, on the one side, and in certain circles of racist ideologues, white and black, on the other, the experience of difference is a commonplace and routine experience for North American Jews—and that is by definition! The one shared, public, corporate, communal experience all Jews have is that they are different from gentiles. The Judaism of the dual Torah explains that difference as destiny and invokes the covenant to explain it, the category of sanctification to justify it. The Judaism of Holocaust and Redemption explains that difference differently. But while only some Jews find a correspondence between covenant and imagined status as God's holy people, all Jews see themselves on a continuum with the Holocaust: if I were there, I too would have been gassed and cremated.

So to state this Judaism in a few words: the world view of the Judaism of Holocaust and Redemption stresses the unique character of the murders of European Jews, the providential and redemptive meaning of the creation of the State of Israel. The Judaism

of Holocaust and Redemption accordingly requires active work in raising money and political support for the State of Israel. Different from Zionism, which held that Jews should live in a Jewish State, this system serves, in particular, to give Jews living in America a reason and an explanation for being Jewish. This Judaism therefore lays particular stress on the complementarity of the political experiences of mid-twentieth century Jewry: the mass murder in death factories of six million of the Jews of Europe, and the creation of the State of Israel three years after the end of the massacre. These events, together seen as providential, as we see, bear the names Holocaust, for the murders, and redemption, for the formation of the State of Israel in the aftermath. The system as a whole presents an encompassing transcendent message, linking one event to the other as an instructive pattern and moves Jews to follow a particular set of actions, rather than other sorts, as it tells them why they should be Jewish. In all, the civil religion of Jewry addresses issues of definition of the group and the policies it should follow to sustain its on-going life and protect its integrity.

So how do we know one Judaism from another, and, in this setting, how shall we tell one set of Judaists from another? We distinguish one Judaism from another by examining the myth, ritual, and symbolic structure of a Judaic system and comparing the results with the myth, ritual, and symbolic structure of another Judaic system. And we are not going to tell one set of Judaists from another, for we shall soon realize that each Judaism addresses a distinct range of social experience; the Judaism that emerges from the holy books predominates at home and in the family, reshaping life-cycle events; the other Judaism addresses the experience of people not at home or in private but in their lives together and in community. So the one Judaism, with its rituals and transcendent tale, explains one component of the social world, the other, a different component of that same social world, and the same Judaists who worship on the Day of Atonement *but* not on the Sabbath are the ones who support the

State of Israel *but* do not go to live there. In each case, "good Jews" know how to pick and choose. But each of the two Judaisms serves in its place, to make sense of its assigned realm of human experience, the private and the public, respectively.

The ritual of that other Judaism involves political action and enormous communal organization and activity. Its counterpart to the Day of Atonement is the fund raising dinner of the local Jewish Federation and Welfare Fund and United Jewish Appeal campaign for the State of Israel and other Jewish causes. Its counterpart to the bar or bat mitzvah is a summer vacation in the State of Israel. Its equivalent to the intense moments of marriage and death is the pilgrimage to Auschwitz followed by a flight to Jerusalem and procession to the Western wall in Jerusalem. Its places of worship comprise Holocaust Museums, and its moments of celebration, commemorations of the Holocaust on a day set aside for that purpose. Its "study of the Torah" involves visits to Holocaust Museums and courses on the German war against the Jews and the death factories of Europe. Its memorial of the destruction of the Temple finds expression in recitations of how the Germans massacred these Jews by firing squads, those by asphyxiation, and the others by driving them into a barn and setting it on fire, men, women, and children. These things really happened, of course, but long ago and far away, just as Sinai really happened, long ago too. But recovered by memory, they live and inform, just as much as Sinai is constantly remembered in the Torah, in the covenant.

The power of the Judaism of Holocaust and Redemption differs not at all in its appeal to facts reconstituted in vivid imagination, that is, the power of memory; but the memories are different. Memory is evoked by rite when social experience corresponds to the message of the rite, and the received tradition remains inert when nothing in our experience makes its message plausible. In the case of the Judaism of Holocaust and Redemption the experience to which it appeals for plausibility is immediate, and it accurately replicates, in the language of history, a felt social experience of Jews in North America: their sense that difference far from defining destiny shades over into disability and discrimination. Holocaust states in extreme form what gentiles are capable of doing and have done to Jews. And Redemption provides the remission of the horror of history.

But why is it that the Judaism of the books, that is, the Judaism of the dual Torah, finds a firm position in the shared imagination of Judaists in one part of the social order, the familiar and personal and private, while the Judaism of Holocaust and Redemption occupies the center of the social order that is public, corporate, and communal? Judaic public behavior extends to what is communal, public, and corporate: "contribute to Jewish charity," "give to UJA." And Judaists also are activists in Jewry when shared and public action of a political character is demanded of "all good Jews." The consensus of Judaists focuses upon corporate as much as private dimensions of the social order. It is not that Judaism has been privatized and individualized at all. Rather a distinct Judaism, one that answers another sort of questions altogether, has taken shape and has entered the center of public life and activity, taking the place of those elements of the program of public life and activity set forth by the received, book-Judaism.

So the appearance of indifference to the corporate dimensions of the holy life of book-Judaism should not deceive us. Not only do Jews form a corporate community and share a substantial range of social experience. That shared public life itself takes shape in response to a Judaism and forms a religious system—but it is not the same Judaism, the same religious system, that governs in private life. The reason is that this other Judaism answers the urgent questions that the community at large asks itself, and, it follows, its answers are found self-evidently true, therefore its rites predominate, and other rites for the community fall by the way.

That shared social experience in politics also takes form in transformations of the given into a gift, so that the *is* of the everyday polity shades into the *as if* of another time and place, as much as is the case in the transformation by the Judaism of the dual Torah of the passage of the individual through the cycle of life. We shall now see that American and Canadian Jews in politics as much as in private life see themselves in the model of an imagined paradigm, one in substance different from, but in structure the same as, the Passover Seder, that is, "as if they were liberated." Jews conduct public business with remarkable unanimity, as though they were somewhere else and someone else than where and what they are. Specifically, in politics, history, in society, even in economics, Jews in North America may not only point to shared traits and experience but also claim to exhibit a viewpoint in common that leads to readily discerned patterns of belief and behavior.

American and Canadian Jews do share a transforming perspective, which imparts to their public, as much as to their private, vision a different set of spectacles from those worn by everybody else in the sheltering society of America or Canada. There is not only a Jewish-ethnic, but a Judaic-religious corporate experience out there in public life, and, while it self-evidently does not lead to the synagogue, it does enchant vision and change perspective and persons. There are cosmic narratives and rites to which people respond, even though they are not those of the received Judaism. And the Judaic system that takes the place, in the life of the community at large, of the received Judaism indeed occupies its share of the place reserved for the unique, the self-evident truths beyond argument.

What is this other Judaism, the Judaism of Holocaust and Redemption? In politics, history, in society, Jews in North America respond to the Judaism of the Holocaust and Redemption in such a way as to imagine they are someone else, living somewhere else, at another time and circumstance. That vision transforms families into an Israel, a community. The somewhere else is Poland in 1944, on the one hand, and the earthly Jerusalem, on the other, and the vision turns them from reasonably secure citizens of America or Canada into insecure refugees finding hope

and life in the land, and State, of Israel. Public events commemorate, so that "we" were there in "Auschwitz," which stands for all of the centers for the murder of Jews, and "we" share, too, in the everyday life of that faraway place in which we do not live but should, the State of Israel. That transformation of time and of place, no less than the recasting accomplished by the Passover Seder or the rite of *berit milah*—circumcision—or *huppah*—marriage—turns people into something other than what they are in the here and now.

The issues of this public Judaism, the civil religion of North American Jewry are perceived to be political. That means, the questions to which this Judaism provides answers are raised by peoples' public and social experience, not the experience of home and family and the passage through life from birth to death. But the power of that Judaism to turn things into something other than what they seem, to teach lessons that change the everyday into the remarkable—that power works as does the power of the other Judaism to make me Adam or one of the people of Israel who crossed the Red Sea.

The lessons of the two Judaisms, of course, are not the same. The Judaism of the dual Torah teaches about the sanctification of the everyday in the road toward the salvation of the holy people. The Judaism of Holocaust and Redemption tells me that the everyday—the here and the now of home and family—ends not in a new Eden but in a cloud of gas; that salvation lies today, if I will it, but not here and not now. And it teaches me not only not to trouble to sanctify, but also not even to trust, the present circumstance.

The transcendent message of the Judaism of Holocaust and Redemption comes to expression in the words of the great theologian of the Judaism of Holocaust and Redemption, Emil Fackenheim, who maintains that "the Holocaust" has produced an eleventh commandment, "Not to hand Hitler any more victories." The commanding voice of Sinai gave Ten Commandments, the commanding voice of Auschwitz, that eleventh. The Ten call for us to become like God in the ways in which the image of God may be graven, which is, by keeping the Sabbath and honoring the other and having no other gods but God. The eleventh tells us what we must not do; it appeals not to love God but to spite a man. So does politics transform. The Judaism of Holocaust and Redemption supplies the words that make another world of this one. Those words moreover, change the assembly of like-minded individuals into occasions for the celebration of the group and the commemoration of its shared memories.

Not only so, but events defined, meetings called, moments identified as distinctive and holy, by that Judaism of Holocaust and Redemption mark the public calendar and draw people from home and family to collectivity and community—those events, and, except for specified reasons, not the occasions of the sacred calendar of the synagogue, that is, the life of Israel as defined by the Torah. Just as in the U.S.A. religions address the realm of individuals and families while a civil religion defines public discourse on matters of value and ultimate concern, so the Judaism of the dual Torah forms the counterpart to Christianity, and the Judaism of Holocaust and Redemption constitutes Jewry's civil religion.

That explains how the Judaism of Holocaust and Redemption affirms and explains in this-worldly terms the Jews' distinctiveness. When did this Judaism come to the fore? It forms, within Jewry, a chapter in a larger movement of ethnic assertion in America. Attaining popularity in the late 1960s, the Judaism of Holocaust and Redemption came to the surface at the same time that black assertion, Italo-American and Polish-American affirmation, feminism, and movements for self-esteem without regard to sexual preference attained prominence. That movement of rediscovery of difference responded to the completion of the work of assimilation to American civilization and its norms.

Once people spoke English without a foreign accent, the could think about learning Polish or Yiddish or Norwegian once more. It then became safe and charming. Just as when black students demanded what they deemed ethnically characteristic food, so Jewish students discovered they wanted kosher food too. In that context the Judaism of

Holocaust and Redemption came into sharp focus, with its answers to unavoidable questions deemed to relate to public policy: who are we? Why should we be Jewish? What does it mean to be Jewish? How do we relate to Jews in other times and places? What is "Israel" Meaning the State of Israel to us, and what are we to it? Who are we in American society? These and other questions form the agenda for the Judaism of Holocaust and Redemption.

The power of the Judaism of the Holocaust and Redemption to frame Jews' public policy—to the near-exclusion of the Judaism of the dual Torah—may be shown very simply. The Holocaust formed the question, redemption in the form of the creation of the State of Israel, the answer, for all universally-appealing Jewish public activity and discourse. Synagogues except for specified occasions appeal to a few, but activities that express the competing Judaism appeal to nearly everybody. That is to say, nearly all American Jews identify with the State of Israel and regard its welfare as more than a secular good, but a metaphysical necessity: the other chapter of the Holocaust. Nearly all American Jews are more than just supporters of the State of Israel. They also regard their own "being Jewish" as inextricably bound up with the meaning they impute to the Jewish state. In many ways every day of their lives these Jews relive the terror-filled years in which European Jews were wiped out— *and every day they do something about it.*

It is as if people spent their lives trying to live out a cosmic myth, and, through rites of expiation and regeneration, accomplished the goal of purification and renewal. Access to the life of feeling and experience, to the way of life that made one distinctive without leaving the person terribly different from everybody else—emerged in the Judaic system of Holocaust and Redemption. The Judaism of Holocaust and Redemption presents an immediately accessible message, cast in extreme emotions of terror and triumph, its round of endless activity demanding only spare time. That Judaism realizes in a poignant way the conflicting demands of Jewish Americans to be intensely Jewish, but only once in a while, providing a means of expressing difference in public and in politics while not exacting much of a cost in meaningful everyday difference from others.

At issue, therefore, is not whether Jews see and do things together. They do. At issue is whether or not they do *religious* things together, and still more concretely why they share or appeal and respond to some, but not other, religious things. For the realm of the sacred touches their passage through life and draws them into contact with others principally through home and family. What people do together and share also passes under the transforming power of imagination. What they do not share is not subject to that metamorphosis of vision that changes the *is* into the *what if?* Everything that, in the religious life of Judaism, works its wonder for the generality of Jews proves personal and familial, not communal—and that despite the remarkable facts of Jewish distinctiveness within the larger society of America and, all the more so, Canada. The social experience forms the premise of the religious life.

But the Jews' social experience of polity and community does not match the religious experience of home and family. Hence the religious side to things conforms to the boundaries of family, and the public experience of politics, economics, and society that Jews share comes to expression in quite different ways altogether. Two fundamental reasons explain the present state of affairs, which finds the religion, Judaism, intensely affective in the private life and remarkably irrelevant to the public. The one is the prevailing attitude toward religion and its correct realm, the other is the Jews' reading of their experience of the twentieth century, which has defined as the paramount mode of interpreting social experience a paradigm other than that deriving from the life of that Israel that is the holy people of mind and imagination, therefore also of sanctification and salvation.

If the received Judaism thrives in the private life of home and family, where, in general, religion in North America is understood to work its wonders, that other Judaism makes its way in the public arena, where, in general, politics and public policy, viewed as distinct from religion, function. That other Judaism, the one of Holocaust and Redemption rather than Eden, Sinai, and the World to Come, we recognize, is political in its themes and character, cosmic truth and rites. The world view of the Judaism of Holocaust and Redemption evokes political, historical events—the destruction of the Jews in Europe, the creation of the state of Israel, two events of a wholly political character. It treats these events as unique, just as the Judaism of the dual Torah treats Eden and Adam's fall, Sinai, and the coming redemption, as unique. It finds in these events the ultimate meaning of the life of the Jews together as Israel, and it therefore defines an Israel for itself—the State of Israel in particular—just as the Judaism of the dual Torah finds in Eden, Sinai, and the World to Come the meaning of the life of Israel and so defines for itself an Israel too: the holy Israel, the social entity different in its very essence from all other social entities. That other Judaism, the Judaism of Holocaust and Redemption, addresses the issues of politics and public policy that Jews take up in their collective social activity.

Why this, not that, in the practice of Judaism in North America: The catalogue of rites and myths North American Jews neglect or dismiss exceeds—and also in anomalous ways simply differs from—the list of beliefs and practices that, for Judaists, define "a good Jew." That single sentence could easily suffice to state the message of this chapter, if the conventional agenda sufficed. But at stake is not a list of this and that, but a principle of differentiation, and, for that purpose, we require both a generalization and an example thereof.

1) Judaists identify with the religious world of the Judaism of the dual Torah experiences of the individual that are plausibly transformed in rites of passage and events in the home and family into encounters with transcendence. That is why the social imagination of Jewry engages with Judaism in its narrative of the rites of the passage through life, on the one side, and of a social experi-

ence mediating between home and family and the sheltering world, on the other. Circumcision and the Passover banquet-Seder bear in common a single social referent: family, home, and experiences of essentially private life. The theological message of the rites corresponds to the social experience of the faithful that practice those rites.

2) Rites that focus on community and public affairs, by contrast, fail because they invoke in common another social referent: society beyond individual and family. So there is one set of social experiences that correspond to the myth and ritual of individual, home, and family; there is another set of social experiences that correspond to the transcendent tale and ritual of corporate Jewry, Israel all together. And they do not seem to match, intersecting in many people's lives to be sure, but hardly corresponding in the essentials of symbol, myth, and ritual.

In Protestant North America people commonly see religion as something personal and private; prayer, for example, therefore speaks for the individual. No wonder, then, that those enchanted words and gestures that, for their part, Jews adopt transform the inner life, recognize life's transitions and turn them into rites of passage. It is part of a larger prejudice that religion and rite speak to the heart of the particular person. What can be changed by rite then is first of all personal and private, not social, not an issue of culture, not affective in politics, not part of the public interest. What people do when they respond to religion, therefore, affects an interior world—a world with little bearing on the realities of public discourse: what—in general terms—should we do about nuclear weapons or in terms of Judaism how we should organize and imagine society? The transformations of religion do not involve the world, or even of the self as representative of other selves, but mainly the individual at the most unique and unrepresentative. If God speaks to me in particular, then the message, by definition, is mine, not someone else's. Religion, the totality of these private messages (within the present theory) therefore does not make itself available for communication in public

discourse, and that by definition too. Religion plays no public role. It is a matter not of public activity but of what people happen to believe or do in private, a matter mainly of the heart.

When religion addresses what actually happens to people living together, and when the message it conveys conforms to their sense of self-evidence (that is the same thing twice), then religion governs. What the books say will accurately describe what the people do. When religion pertains, but its message jars, what the books say people may do, but they may not to it in the way the books direct. And when the social order and the religious system do not correspond at all, then people will conclude "good Jews do this, not that." So religion lives in the perceived, social experience that people have; its ideas prove not right or wrong, not even persuasive or implausible, but self-evidently true because they are descriptive, or obviously irrelevant because they are not descriptive, of the world as lived out in the social world. Conscience is the creation of community, theological truth subject to the disposition of common sense, that is to say, a sense of what is fitting and just made common by being shared.

The rites that speak to the subjectivity and individuality of circumstance lay stress on private person, recognize and accord priority to the autonomous individual. What people find personally relevant they accept; for them, the words evoke meaning and make worlds. The rites that speak to the community out there beyond family, to the corporate existence of people who see themselves as part of a social entity beyond, scarcely resonate. The context therefore accounts for the difference and even for variations. Jews live one by one, family by family. Words that speak to that individuality work wonders. Jews do not form a corporate community but only families. Words that address the commonality of Israel not as the congregation of individual Jews but as a community bound by law to do some things together, fall unheard, mere magic, not wonder-working at all.

Jews respond to the holy occasions that speak of the individual including the family, while they have difficulty dealing with the ones that address the collectivity of public experience then pertains not to Jews alone but to life in the open society created by Protestant Christianity and shared by Protestants with all comers, on terms of rough equality. The enchantment wrought by life in the democratic West should not be missed: the "I" even before God remains always the "I," and the "we" is just that many "I"s formed into families—only that, not something more *and something else.* Israel before God is made up of Israelites, individual and family, counted solely one by one, family by family. For the sum of the whole is merely the same as the parts. But it is magic that makes the whole greater than the sum of the parts.

In North America Judaism as a religion encompasses what is personal and familial. But that definition of religion proves insufficient to cover Judaic religious systems that flourish. The Jews as a political entity put forth a separate system, one that concerns not religion, which is not supposed to intervene in political action, but public policy. Judaism in public policy produces political action in favor of the State of Israel, or Soviet Jewry, or other important matters of the corporate community. Judaism in private affects the individual and the family and is not supposed to play a role in politics at all. That pattern conforms to the Protestant model of religion, and the Jews have accomplished conformity to it by the formation of two Judaisms. A consideration of the Protestant pattern, which separates not the institutions of Church from the activities of the state, but the entire public polity from the inner life, will show us how to make sense of the choices that characterize the practice of Judaism in North America.

Religion is understood in Protestant North America as something private and interior, individual and subjective: how I feel all by myself, not what I do with other people. Religion is something you believe, all by yourself, not something you do with other people. The prevailing attitude of mind identifies religion with belief, to the near-exclusion of behavior. Religion is understood as a personal state of mind or an individual's personal and private attitude. When we study

religion, the present picture suggests, we ask about not society but self, not about culture and community but about conscience and character. Religion speaks of individuals and not groups: faith and its substance, and, beyond faith, the things that faith represents: faith reified, hence, religion. William Scott Green further comments in more general terms as follows:

> The basic attitude of mind characteristic of the study of religion holds that religion is certainly in your soul, likely in your heart, perhaps in your mind, but never in your body. That attitude encourages us to construe religion cerebrally and individually, to think in terms of beliefs and the believer, rather than in terms of behavior and community. The lens provided by this prejudice draws our attention to the intense and obsessive belief called "faith," so religion is understood as a state of mind, the object of intellectual or emotional commitment, the result of decisions to believe or to have faith. According to this model, people have religion but they do not do their religion. Thus we tend to devalue behavior and performance, to make it epiphenomenal and of course to emphasize thinking and reflecting, the practice of theology, as a primary activity of religious people. . . . The famous slogan that "ritual recapitulates myth" follows this model by assigning priority to the story and to peoples' believing the story, and makes behavior simply an imitation, an aping, a mere acting out.[13]

Now as we reflect on Green's observations, we of course recognize what is at stake. It is the definition of religion, or, rather, what matters in or about religion, emerging from Protestant theology and Protestant religious experience. For when we lay heavy emphasis on faith to the exclusion of works, on the individual to rather than on society, conscience instead of culture, when we treat behavior and performance by groups as less important and thinking, reflecting, theology and belief as more important, we simply adopt as normative for academic scholarship convictions critical to the Protestant Reformation. Judaisms in their historical expressions place emphasis at least equally on religion as a matter of works and not faith alone, behavior and community as well as belief and conscience. Religion is something that people do, and they do it together. Religion is not something people merely have, as individuals. But in the context in which religion is personal and subjective, not public and shared, the practice of Judaism in North America fits well.

Notes

[1] I consulted a variety of books and articles, but mainly rely upon Steven M. Cohen, *Content or Continuity? Alternative Bases for Commitment* (New York, 1991), Jack Wertheimer, "Recent Trends in American Judaism," *American Jewish Yearbook, 1989* (New York and Philadelphia, 1989) (from this point: Wertheimer); and Barry A. Kosmin, Sidney Goldstein, Joseph Waksberg, Nava Lerer, Ariella Keysar, and Jeffrey Scheckner, *Highlights of the CJF [Council of Jewish Federations]* 1990 National Jewish Population Survey (N.Y.: Council of Jewish Federations, 1991) (from this point: Kosmin). Michael Satlow provided, in addition, these items: M. Sklare and J. Greenbaum, *Jewish Identity on the Suburban Frontier: A Study of Group Survival in the Open Society* (New York, 1967), pp. 49-96; Charles Liebman and S. Shapiro, "A Survey of the Conservative Movement and Some of its Religious Attitudes" (unpublished; dated N.Y., 1979), pp. 17-24; Samuel Heilman and Steven M. Cohen, *Cosmopolitans and Parochials: Modern Orthodox Jews in America* (New York, 1987), pp. 39-111, 207-216, 222-227, 235-244; Samuel Heilman and Steven M. Cohen, "Ritual Variation among Modern Orthodox Jews in the United States," in *Studies in Contemporary Jewry* (Jerusalem, 1986) 2:164-187; and S. Cohen, *American Assimilation or Jewish Revival?* (Bloomington, 1988), pp. 71-81, 130. Professor Calvin Goldscheider provided the following: Calvin Goldscheider, "Jewish Individuals and Jewish Communities: Using Survey Data to Measure the Quality of American Jewish Life" (Unpublished MS, prepared for the Third Sydney Hollander Memorial Conference on Policy Implications of the 1990 National Jewish Population Survey, July, 1991); Calvin Goldscheider, "The Structural Context of American Jewish Continuity: Social Class, Ethnicity, and Religion" (unpublished paper, presented at the American Sociological Association, Cincinnati, 1991). Note also Gary A. Tobin, "From Alarms to Open Arms," in *Hadassah Magazine*, December, 1991, pp. 22ff.; Arthur J. Magida, "The Pull of Passover," in *Baltimore Jewish Times* April 17, 1992, pp. 58ff.; Samuel C. Heilman, *Jewish Unity and Diversity. A Survey of American Rabbis and Rabbinical Students* (New York, 1991).

[2] Calvin Goldscheider, *Jewish Continuity and Change. Emerging Patterns in America* (Bloomington, 1986), p. 170.

[3] Ibid., p. 171.

[4] There is, of course, variation in denominational identification within the United States. In 1981, for example, the distribution in New York, the largest Jewish community in the world, was 13 percent Orthodox, 35 percent Conservative and 29 percent Reform. About one-fourth of New York Jews define themselves denominationally as either "other" or "none." In St. Louis, there were fewer Conservative Jews but more Reform Jews. In the western states the proportion Reform and "other-none" tends to be higher.

[5] This question and the similar ones posed in the following sections are answered at the end of this chapter.

[6] In "A Survey of the Conservative Movement and Some of its Religious Attitudes," Unpublished MS dated September, 1979; Library of the Jewish Theological Seminary of America.

[7] Steven M. Cohen, *American Assimilation or Jewish Revival?*, p. 80.

[8] *American Assimilation or Jewish Revival?*, p. 81.

[9] Steven M. Cohen, *Content or Continuity? Alternative Bases for Commitment* (New York, 1991), p. 4. Cohen distinguishes between "the Jewish-identity patterns of the more involved and passionate elites from those of the more numerous, marginally affiliated Jews, those with roughly average levels of Jewish involvement and emotional investment.... One may be called 'commitment to content' and the other 'commitment to continuity.' alternatively ... 'commitment to ideology' versus 'commitment to identity.'"

[10] Pp. 14-15.

[11] *Content or Continuity*, p. 21.

[12] *Content or Continuity*, pp. 41-2.

[13] Personal letter, January 17, 1985.

JACOB NEUSNER

O

ORTHODOX JUDAISM: Many people reasonably identify all "traditional" or "observant" Judaism with Orthodoxy, and they furthermore take for granted that all traditional Judaisms are pretty much the same. But a wide variety of Judaisms affirm the Torah, oral and written, and abide by its laws, as interpreted by their particular masters, who differ from one another on many important points. Thus, rather than simply signifying "observant" Judaism in general, the designation "Orthodox" refers to a very particular Judaic religious system, one that affirms the divine revelation and eternal authority of the Torah, oral and written, but that favors the integration of the Jews ("holy Israel") into the national life of the countries of their birth. Other "observant" Judaisms affirm the Torah but favor the segregation of the holy Israel from other people in the countries where they live, including the state of Israel. Indicators such as clothing, language, and, above all, education differentiate integrationist from segregationist Judaisms. Orthodoxy identifies with the former, integrationist category, and a wide variety of other Judaisms fall into the latter, segregationist category.

When Jews who kept the law of the Torah, for example as it dictated food choices and use of leisure time (to speak of the Sabbath and festivals in secular terms), sent their children to secular schools, in addition to or instead of solely Jewish ones, or when, in Jewish schools, they included in the curriculum subjects outside of the sciences of the Torah, they crossed the boundary between the received and the new Judaism. For in the nineteenth century the notion that science or German or Latin or philosophy deserved serious study, while not alien to important exemplars of the received system of the dual Torah, struck as wrong those for whom the received system remained self-evidently right. Those Jews did not send their children to gentile schools, and in Jewish schools did not include in the curriculum other than Torah-study.

Integrationist, Orthodox Judaism come into being in Germany in the middle of the nineteenth century among Jews who rejected Reform and made a self-conscious decision to remain within the way of life and world view that they had known and cherished all their lives. They framed the issues in terms of change and history. The Reformers held that Judaism could change, and that Judaism was a product of history. The Orthodox opponents denied that Judaism could change and insisted that Judaism derived from God's will at Sinai and was eternal and supernatural, not historical and man-made. In these two convictions, of course, the Orthodox recapitulated the convictions of the received system. But in their appeal to the given, the traditional, they found more persuasive some components of that system than they did others, and in the picking and choosing, in the articulation of the view that Judaism formed a religion to be seen as distinct and autonomous of politics, society, "the rest of life," they entered that same world of self-conscious believing that the Reformers also explored.

Orthodox Judaism is that Judaic system that mediates between the received Judaism of the dual Torah and the requirements of living a life integrated in modern circumstances. It dealt with the same urgent questions as did Reform Judaism, questions raised by political emancipation, but it gave different answers to them. Orthodoxy maintains the world-view of the received dual Torah, constantly citing its sayings and adhering with only trivial variations to the bulk of its norms for the everyday life. At the same time Orthodoxy holds that Jews who adhere to the dual Torah may wear clothing that non-Jews wear and do not have to wear distinctively Jewish clothing; live within a common economy and not practice distinctively Jewish professions (however, in a given setting, these professions may be defined), and, in diverse ways, take up a life not readily distinguished in important characteristics from the life lived by people in general.

So for Orthodoxy a portion of Israel's life may prove secular, in that the Torah does not dictate and so sanctify all details under all circumstances. Since the Judaism of the dual Torah presupposed not only the supernatural entity, Israel, but also a way of life that in important ways distinguished that supernatural entity from the social world at large, the power of Orthodoxy to find an accommodation for Jews who valued the received way of life and world view and also planned to make their lives in an essentially integrated social world proves formidable. The difference between Orthodoxy and the system of the dual Torah therefore comes to expression in social policy: integration, however circumscribed, versus the total separation of the holy people.

Many see Orthodox Judaism as the same as "the tradition," what is natural and normal, holding that Orthodoxy now stands for how things always were, for all time. But the term Orthodoxy" takes on meaning only in the contrast to Reform, so in a simple sense, Orthodoxy owes its life to Reform Judaism. The term first surfaced in 1795,[1] and over all covers all Jews who believe that God revealed the dual Torah at Sinai and that Jews must carry out the requirements of Jewish law contained in the Torah as interpreted by the sages through time. Obviously, so long as that position struck as self-evident the generality of Jewry at large, Orthodoxy as a distinct and organized Judaism did not exist. It did not have to. What is interesting is the point at which two events took place: first, the recognition of the received system, "the tradition" as Orthodoxy, second, the specification of the received system as religion. The two of course go together. So long as the Judaism of the dual Torah enjoys recognition as a set of self-evident truths, those truths add up not to something so distinct as "religion" but to a general statement of how things are: all of life explained and harmonized in one whole account.

The view that the received system was "traditional" came first. That identification of truth as tradition came about when the received system met the challenge of competing Judaisms. Then, in behalf of the received way of life and world view addressed to supernatural Israel, people said that the Judaism of the dual Torah was established of old, the right, the only way of seeing and doing things, how things have been and should be naturally and normally: "Tradition." But that is a category that contains within itself an alternative, namely, change, as in "tradition and change."

Only when the system lost its power of self-evidence did it enter, among other apologetic categories, the classification, "the Tradition." And that came about when Orthodoxy met head on the challenge of change called Reform. We understand why the category of tradition, the received way of doing things, became critical to the framers of Orthodoxy when we examine the counter claim. That is

to say, just as the Reformers justified change, the Orthodox theologians denied that change was ever possible, so Walter Wurzburger: "Orthodoxy looks upon attempts to adjust Judaism to the 'spirit of the time' as utterly incompatible with the entire thrust of normative Judaism which holds that the revealed will of God rather than the values of any given age are the ultimate standard."[2]

The position outlined by the new, Orthodox theologians followed the agenda laid forth by the Reformers. If the Reform made minor changes in liturgy and its conduct, the Orthodox rejected even those that, under other circumstances, might have found acceptance. Saying prayers in the vernacular, for example, provoked strong opposition. But everyone knew that some of the prayers, said in Aramaic, in fact were in the vernacular of the earlier age. The Orthodox thought that these changes, not reforms at all, represented only the first step of a process leading Jews out of the Judaic world altogether, so, as Wurzburger says, "The slightest tampering with tradition was condemned."

If we ask where did the received system of the dual Torah prevail, and where, by contrast, did Orthodoxy come to full expression, we may follow the spreading out of railway lines, the growth of new industry, the shifts in political status accorded to, among other citizens, Jews, changes in the educational system, in all, the entire process of political change, economic and social, demographic and cultural shifts of a radical and fundamental nature. Where the changes came early in the nineteenth century, Reform Judaism met them in its way, and Orthodoxy in its way. Where change came later in the century, as in the case of Russian Poland, the eastern provinces of the Austro-Hungarian Empire, and Russia itself, there, in villages contentedly following the old ways, the received system endured. Again, in an age of mass migration from Eastern Europe to America and other western democracies, those who experienced the upheaval of leaving home and country met the challenge of change either by accepting new ways of seeing things or articulately and in full self-awareness reaffirming the familiar ones, once more, Reform or Orthodoxy. We may, therefore, characterize the received system as a way of life and world view wedded to an ancient people's homelands, the villages and small towns of central and eastern Europe, and Orthodoxy as the heir of that received system as it came to expression in the towns and cities of central and Western Europe and America. That rule of thumb, with certain exceptions, allows us to distinguish between the piety of a milieu and the theological conviction of a self-conscious community. Or we may accept the familiar distinction between tradition and articulate Orthodoxy, a distinction with its own freight of apologetics to be sure.

When, therefore, we explain by reference to political and economic change the beginnings of Reform Judaism, we also understand the point of origin of Orthodoxy as distinct and organized. Clearly, the beginnings of Orthodoxy took place in the areas where Reform made its way, hence in Germany and in Hungary. In Germany, where Reform attracted the majority of not a few Jewish communities, the Orthodox faced a challenge indeed. Critical to their conviction was the notion that "Israel," all of the Jews, bore responsibility to carry out the law of the Torah. But the community's institutions in the hands of the Reform did not obey the law of the Torah as the Orthodox understood it. So, in the end, Orthodoxy took that step that marked it as a self-conscious Judaism. Orthodoxy separated from the established community altogether. The Orthodox set up their own organization and seceded from the community at large. The next step prohibited Orthodox Jews from participating in non-Orthodox organizations altogether. Isaac Breuer, a leading theologian of Orthodoxy, would ultimately take the position that "refusal to espouse the cause of separation was interpreted as being equivalent to the rejection of the absolute sovereignty of God."[3]

The matter of accommodating to the world at large, of course, did not allow for so easy an answer as mere separation. The specific issue—integration or segregation—concerned preparation for life in the large politics and economic life of the country, and that meant secular education, involving not only language and science, but history and literature, matters of values. Orthodoxy proved diverse, with two wings to be distinguished, one rejecting secular learning as well as all dealing with non-Orthodox Jews, the other cooperating with non-Orthodox and secular Jews and accepting the value of secular education. That position in no way affected loyalty to the law of Judaism, e.g., belief in God's revelation of the one whole Torah at Sinai. The point at which the received system and Orthodox split requires specification. In concrete terms we know the one from the other by the evaluation of secular education. Proponents of the received system never accommodated themselves to secular education, while the Orthodox in Germany and Hungary persistently affirmed it. That represents a remarkable shift, since central to the received system of the dual Torah is study of Torah—Torah, not philosophy.

Explaining where we find the one and the other, Katzburg works with the distinction we have already made, between an unbroken system and one that has undergone a serious caesura with the familiar condition of the past. He states:

> In Eastern Europe until World War I, Orthodoxy preserved without a break its traditional ways of life and the time-honored educational framework. In general, the mainstream of Jewish life was identified with Orthodoxy, while Haskalah [Jewish Enlightenment, which applied to the Judaic setting the skeptical attitudes of the French Enlightenment] and secularization were regarded as deviations. Hence there was no ground wherein a Western type of Orthodoxy could take root. . . . European Orthodoxy in the 19th and the beginning of the 20th centuries was significantly influenced by the move from small settlements to urban centers . . . as well as by emigration. Within the small German communities there was a kind of popular Orthodoxy, deeply attached to tradition and to local customs, and when it moved to the large cities this element brought with it a vitality and rootedness to Jewish tradition. . . .[4]

Katzburg's observations provide important guidance. He authoritatively defines the difference between Orthodoxy and "tradition." So he tells us how to distinguish the received system accepted as self-evident, and an essentially selective, therefore by definition new system, called Orthodoxy. In particular he guides us in telling the one from the other and where to expect to find, in particular, the articulated, therefore, self-conscious affirmation of "tradition" that characterizes Orthodoxy but does not occur in the world of the dual Torah as it glided in its eternal orbit of the seasons and of unchanging time.

Old and new in Orthodoxy: Urban Orthodox Jews experienced change, daily encountered Jews unlike themselves, no longer lived in that stable Judaic society in which the received Torah formed the given of life. Pretense that Jews faced no choices scarcely represented a possibility. Nor did the generality of the Jews propose, in the West, to preserve a separate language or to renounce political rights. So Orthodoxy made its peace with change, no less than did Reform. The educational program that led Jews out of the received culture of the dual Torah, the use of the vernacular, the acceptance of political rights, the renunciation of Jewish garments, education for women, abolition of the power of the community to coerce the individual—these and many other originally Reform positions characterized the Orthodoxy that emerged, another new Judaism, in the nineteenth century.

If we ask, how new was the Orthodox system? we find ambiguous answers. In conviction, in way of life, in world view, we may hardly call it new at all. For the bulk of its substantive positions found ample precedent in the received dual Torah. From its affirmation of God's revelation of a dual Torah to its acceptance of the detailed authority of the law and customs, from its strict observance of the law to its unwillingness to change a detail of public worship, Orthodoxy rightly pointed to its strong links with the chain of tradition. But Orthodoxy still constituted a sect within the Jewish group. Its definition of the "Israel" to whom it wished to speak and the definition characteristic of the dual Torah hardly coincide. The Judaism of the dual Torah addressed all Jews, and Orthodoxy recognized that it could not do so. Orthodoxy acquiesced in a situation that lay

beyond the imagination of the framers of the Judaism of the dual Torah.

True, the Orthodox had no choice. Their seceding from the community and forming their own institutions ratified the simple fact that they could not work with the Reformers. But the upshot remains the same. That supernatural entity, Israel, gave up its place and a natural Israel, a this-worldly political fact, succeeded. Pained though Orthodoxy was by the fact, it nonetheless accommodated the new social reality—and affirmed it by reshaping the sense of Israel in the supernatural dimension. Their Judaism no less than the Judaism of the Reformers stood for something new, a birth not a renewal—a political response to a new politics. True enough, for Orthodoxy the politics was that of the Jewish community, divided as it was among diverse visions of the political standing of Israel, the Jewish people. For the Reform, by contrast, the new politics derived from the establishment of the category of neutral citizenship in an encompassing nation-state. But the political shifts flowed from the same large-scale changes in Israel's consciousness and character, and, it follows, Orthodoxy as much as Reform represented a set of self-evident answers to political questions that none could evade.

To claim that the Orthodox went in search of proof-texts for a system formed and defined in advance, of course, misrepresents the reality—but not by much. For once the system of a self-conscious and deliberate Orthodoxy took shape, much picking and choosing, assigning of priorities to some things and not others—these would follow naturally. And the upshot of it all remains the same: a new system, a way of life much like the received one, but readily differentiated; a world view congruent to the received one, but with its own points of interest and emphasis; and, above all, a social referent, an "Israel" quite beyond the limits of the one posited by the dual Torah. Orthodoxy represents the most interesting challenge to the hypothesis announced at the outset.

In general, no Judaism recapitulates any other. Each begins on its own, defining the questions it wished to answer and laying forth the responses it finds self-evidently true, only then going back to the canon of received documents in search of proof-texts. Every Judaism therefore commences in the definition (to believers: the discovery) of its canon. Orthodoxy surely forms an enormous exception to such a proposed rule. For its canon recognized the same books, accorded the same status and authority as in the antecedent system. Yet that is only part of the story. Orthodoxy also produced books to which the received system of the dual Torah could afford no counterpart—and vice versa. Orthodoxy addressed questions not pertinent to the received system or to the world that it constructed. Its answers of course violated important givens of the received system. The single most significant trait of Orthodoxy, we shall now see, is its power to see the "Torah" as "Judaism," the category-shift that changed everything else (or, that ratified all other changes).

Judaism enters the category, "religion:" The category "religion," with its counterpart, "secular," recognizes as distinct from "all of life" matters having to do with the church, the life of faith, the secular as against the sacred. Those distinctions were lost on the received system of the dual Torah, of course, which legislated for matters we should today regard as entirely secular or neutral, for example, the institutions of state (e.g., king, priest, army). We have already noted that in the received system as it took shape in Eastern and Central Europe, Jews wore garments regarded as distinctively Jewish, and some important traits of these garments indeed derived from the Torah. They pursued sciences that only Jews studied, for instance, the Talmud and its commentaries. In these and other ways, the Torah encompassed all of the life of Israel, the holy people. The recognition that Jews were like others, that the Torah fell into a category into which other and comparable matters fell—that recognition was long in coming.

For Christians it had become a commonplace in Germany and other Western countries to see "religion" as distinct from other components of the social and political system. While the Church in Russia identified

with the Tsarist state, or with the national aspirations of the Polish people, for example, in Germany two churches, Catholic and Protestant, competed. The terrible wars of the Reformation in the sixteenth and seventeenth centuries, which ruined Germany, had led to the uneasy compromise that the prince might choose the religion of his principality, and, from that self-aware choice, people understood that "the way of life and world view" in fact constituted a religion, and that one religion might be compared with some other. By the nineteenth century, moreover, the separation of church and state ratified the important distinction between religion, where difference would be tolerated, and the secular, where citizens were pretty much the same.

That fact of political consciousness in the West reached the Judaic world only in the late eighteenth century for some intellectuals, and in the nineteenth century for large numbers of others. It registered, then, as a fundamental shift in the understanding and interpretation of "the Torah," now seen, among Orthodox as much as among Reform, as "Judaism," an -ism alongside other -isms. A mark of the creative power of the Jews who formed the Orthodox Judaic system derives from their capacity to shift the fundamental category in which they framed their system. The basic shift in category is what made Orthodoxy a Judaism on its own, not simply a restatement, essentially in established classifications, of the received system of the dual Torah.

If we ask how Orthodox Judaism, so profoundly rooted in the canonical writings and received convictions of the Judaism of the dual Torah, at the same time made provision for the issues of political and cultural change at hand, we recognize the importance of the shift in category contributed by Orthodoxy. For Orthodoxy, within the sector of the received system, made provision for the difference between sacred and secular, so within Judaic systems identified as a religion, Judaism, what the received system had called the Torah, encompassing and symmetrical with the whole of the life of Judaic society. Specifically, Orthodox Judaism took the view that one could observe the rules of the Judaic system of the ages and at the same time keep the laws of the state. More important, Orthodox Judaism took full account of the duties of citizenship, so far as being a good citizen imposed the expectation of conformity in certain aspects of everyday life. So a category, "religion," could contain the Torah, and another category, "the secular," could allow Jews a place in the accepted civic life of the country. The importance of the category-shift therefore lies in its power to accommodate the political change so important, also, to Reform Judaism. The Jews' differences from others would fit into categories in which difference was (in Jews' minds at any rate) acceptable, and would not violate those lines to which all citizens had to adhere.

To review the fundamental shift represented by the distinction between secular and religious, we recall our original observation that Jews no longer wished to wear distinctively Jewish clothing, for example, or to speak a Jewish language, or to pursue only Jewish learning under Jewish auspices. Yet the received system, giving expression to the rules of sanctification of the holy people, did entail wearing Jewish clothing, speaking a Jewish language, learning only, or mainly, Jewish sciences. So clothing, language, and education now fell into the category of the secular, while other equally important aspects of everyday life remained in the category of the sacred. Orthodox Judaism, as it came into existence in Germany and other Western countries, therefore found it possible by recognizing the category of the secular to accept the language, clothing, and learning of those countries. And these matters serve only to exemplify a larger acceptance of gentile ways, not all but enough to lessen the differences between the Holy People and the nations. Political change of a profound order, which made Jews call into question some aspects of the received system—if not most or all of them, as would be the case for Reform Judaism—presented to Jews who gave expression to Orthodox Judaism the issues at hand: how separate, how integrated? And the answers required picking and choosing, different things to be sure, just as much as, in principle, the Reform Jews picked and

choose. Both Judaisms understood that somethings were sacred, others not, and that understanding marked these Judaisms off from the system of the dual Torah.

Once the category-shift had taken place, the difference was to be measured in degree, not kind. For Orthodox Jews maintained those distinctive beliefs of a political character in the future coming of the Messiah and the reconstitution of the Jewish nation in its own land that Reform Jews rejected. But, placing these convictions in the distant future, the Orthodox Jews nonetheless prepared for a protracted interim of life within the nation at hand, like the Reform different in religion, not in nationality as represented by citizenship. What follows for our inquiry is that Orthodoxy, as much as Reform, signals remarkable changes in the Jews' political situation and—more important—aspiration. They did want to be different, but not so different as the received system would have made them.

Still, Orthodoxy in its nineteenth century formulation laid claim to carry forward, in continuous and unbroken relationship, "the tradition." That claim assuredly demands a serious hearing, for the things that Orthodoxy taught, the way of life it required, the Israel to whom it spoke, the doctrines it deemed revealed by God to Moses at Sinai—all of these conformed more or less exactly to the system of the received Judaism of the dual Torah as people then knew it. So any consideration of the issue of a linear and incremental history of Judaism has to take at face value the character, and not merely the claim, of Orthodoxy. But we do not have without reflection to concede that claim. Each Judaism, after all, demands study not in categories defined by its own claims of continuity, but in those defined by its own distinctive and characteristic choices. For a system takes shape and then makes choices—in that order. But the issue facing us in Orthodoxy is whether or not Orthodoxy can be said to make choices at all. For is it not what it says it is, "just Judaism"? Indeed so, but the dual Torah of the received tradition hardly generated the base-category, "Judaism." And "Judaism," Orthodox or otherwise, is not "Torah."

That is the point at which making self-conscious choices enters discourse. For the Orthodoxy of the nineteenth century—that is, the Judaism that named itself "Orthodox"—exhibited certain traits of mind that marked its framers as distinctive, that is, as separate from the received Judaism of the dual Torah as the founders of Reform Judaism. To state the matter simply: by adopting for themselves the category, religion, and by recognizing a distinction between religion and the secular, the holy and other categories of existence, the founders of Orthodoxy performed an act of choice and selectivity. And that defines them as self-conscious and shows that the received system for them was not self-evident. It was no longer definitive of the very facts of being as it had been and remained for those for whom it was self-evident.

The Torah found itself transformed into an object, a thing out there, a matter of choice, deliberation, affirmation. In that sense Orthodoxy recognized a break in the line of the received "tradition" and proposed to repair the break: a self-conscious, modern decision. The issues addressed by Orthodoxy, the questions its framers found ineluctable—these take second place. The primary consideration in our assessment of the claim of Orthodoxy to carry forward, in a straight line, the incremental history of a single Judaism, carries us to the fundamental categories within which Orthodoxy pursued its thought, but the Judaism of the dual Torah did not. The Judaism of the dual Torah had no word for Judaism; Orthodoxy did (and does).

So let us dwell on this matter of the category, Judaism, a species of the genus, religion. The fact is that those Jews for whom the received Judaism retained the standing of self-evident truth in no way recognized the distinctions implicit in the category, religion. Those distinctions separated one dimension of existence from others, specifically, the matter of faith and religious action from all other matters, such as politics, economic life, incidental aspects of every day life such as clothing, vocation and avocation, and the like. As I have stressed, the Judaism of the dual Torah, for its part, encompasses every dimension of human existence, both personal and public, both private and political. The Jews constitute a supernatural people; their politics form the public dimension of their holiness, and their personal lives match the most visible and blatant rules of public policy. The whole forms a single fabric, an indivisible and totally coherent entity, at once social and cultural, economic and political—and, above all, religious. The recognition, therefore, that we may distinguish the religious from the political, or concede as distinct any dimension of a person's life or of the life of the community of Judaism, forms powerful evidence that a fresh system has come into existence.

For nineteenth century Reform and Orthodox theologians alike, the category "Judaism" defined what people said when they wished all together and all at once to describe what the Jews believe, or the Jewish religion, or similar matters covering religious ideas viewed as a system and as a whole. It therefore constituted a philosophical category, an -ism, instructing thinkers to seek the system and order and structure of ideas: the doctrine of this, the doctrine of that, in Juda-ism. The nineteenth century Judaic religious thinkers invoked the category, Judaism, when they proposed to speak of the whole of Judaic religious existence. Available to the Judaism of the dual Torah are other categories, other words, to tell how to select and organize and order data: all together, all at once to speak of the whole.

To the Jews who abided within the received Judaism of the dual Torah, the discovery of Orthodoxy therefore represented an innovation, a shift from the self-evident truths of the Torah. For their word for Judaism was Torah, and when they spoke of the whole all at once, they used the word Torah—and they also spoke of different things from the things encompassed by Judaism. For the received Judaism of the dual Torah did not use the word the nineteenth century theologians used when speaking of the things of which they spoke when they said, Juda-ism. The received system not only used a different word, but in fact referred to different things. The two categories—Judaism and Torah—which are supposed to refer to the same data in the same social world, in fact encompass different data from those taken in categorically, by Judaism. So we contrast the two distinct categories, Judaism and Torah.

Judaism falls into the classification of a philosophy or ideology or theology, a logos, a word, while *Torah* fell into the classification of a symbol, that is, a symbol that in itself encompassed the whole of the system that the category at hand was meant to describe. The species "-ism" falls into the classification of the genus, logos, while the species, Torah, while using words, transcends words. It falls into a different classification, a species of the genus symbol. How so? The "*-ism*" category does not invoke an encompassing symbol but a system of thought. Judaism is an it, an object, a classification, an action. Torah, for its part, is an everything in one thing, a symbol. I cannot imagine a more separate and unlike set of categories than Judaism and Torah, even though both encompassed the same way of life and world view and addressed the same social group. So Torah as a category serves as a symbol, everywhere present in detail and holding all the details together. Judaism as a category serves as a statement of the main points: the intellectual substrate of it all.

The conception of Judaism as an organized body of doctrine, as in the sentence, *Judaism teaches,* or *Judaism says,* derives from an age in which people further had determined that Judaism belonged to the category of religion, and, of still more definitive importance, a religion was something that *teaches* or *says.* That is to say, Judaism is a religion, and a religion to begin with is (whatever else it is) a composition of beliefs. That age is the one at hand, the nineteenth century, and the category of religion as a distinct entity emerges from Protestant theological thought. For in Protestant theological terms, one is saved by faith. But the very components of that sentence, one—individual, not the people or holy nation, saved—personally, not in history, and saved, not sanctified, faith—not mitzvot—in fact prove incomprehensible in the categories constructed by Torah. Constructions of Judaic dogmas, the specification of a right doctrine—an orthodoxy—and the insistence that

one can speak of religion apart from such adventitious matters as clothing and education (for the Orthodox of Germany who dressed like other Germans and studied in Universities, not only in yeshivas) or food (for the Reform) testify to the same fact: the end of self-evidence, the substitution of the distinction between religion and secularity, the creation of *Judaism* as the definitive category.

In fact in the idiomatic language of Torah-speech one cannot make such a statement in that way about, or in the name of, Judaism—not an operative category at all. In accord with the modes of thought and speech of the received Judaism of the dual Torah, one has to speak as subject of Israel, not one, to address not only individual life but all of historical time, so saved by itself does not suffice, further to invoke the verb, since the category of sanctification, not only salvation must find its place, and, finally, one native to the speech of the Torah will use the words of mitzvot, not of faith alone. So the sentence serves for Protestant Christianity but not for the Torah. Of course "Judaism," Orthodox or Reform, for its part will also teach things and lay down doctrines, even dogmas.

The counterpart, in the realm of self-evidence comprised by the received Judaism of the dual Torah, of the statement, *Judaism teaches,* can only be, *the Torah requires,* and the predicate of such a sentence would be not, . . . *that God is one,* but, . . . *that you say a blessing before eating bread.* The category, Judaism, encompasses, classifies and organizes, doctrines: the faith, which, by the way, an individual adopts and professes. The category, Torah, teaches what "we," God's holy people, are and what "we" must do. The counterpart to the statement of Judaism, "God is one," then is, ". . . who has sanctified us by his commandments and commanded us to. . . ." The one teaches, that is, speaks of intellectual matters and beliefs, the latter demands—social actions and deeds of us, matters of public consequence—including, by the way, affirming such doctrines as God's unity, the resurrection of the dead, the coming of the Messiah, the revelation of the Torah at Sinai, and on and on: "we" can rival the Protestants in heroic deeds of faith. So it is true, the faith demands deeds, and deeds presuppose faith. But, categorically, the emphasis is what it is: Torah, on God's revelation, the canon, on Israel and its social way of life; Judaism, on a system of belief. That is a significant difference between the two categories.

Equally true, one would (speaking systemically) also *study Torah*. But what one studied was not an intellectual system of theology or philosophy, rather a document of revealed Scripture and law. That is not to suggest that the theologians of Judaism, Orthodox or Reform, of the nineteenth century, did not believe that God is one, or that the philosophers who taught that "Judaism teaches ethical monotheism" did not concur that, on that account, one has to say a blessing before eating bread. But the categories are different, and, in consequence, so too the composites of knowledge. A book on Judaism explains the doctrines, the theology or philosophy, of Judaism. A book of the holy Torah expounds God's will as revealed in "the one whole Torah of Moses, our rabbi," as sages teach and embody God's will. I cannot imagine two more different books, and the reason is that they represent totally different categories of intelligible discourse and of knowledge. Proof, of course, is that the latter books are literally unreadable. They form part of a genuinely oral exercise, to be cited sentence by sentence and expounded in the setting of other sentences, from other books, the whole made cogent by the speaker. That process of homogenization is how Torah works as a generative category. It obscures other lines of structure and order.

True, the two distinct categories come to bear upon the same body of data, the same holy books. But the consequent compositions—selections of facts, ordering of facts, analyses of facts, statements of conclusion and interpretation and above all, modes of public discourse, meaning who says what to whom—bear no relationship to one another, none whatsoever. Indeed, the compositions more likely than not do not even adduce the same facts, or even refer to them.

How is it that the category I see as imposed, extrinsic, and deductive, namely, "Judaism," attained the status of self-evidence? Categories serve because they are self-evident to a large group of people. In the case at hand, therefore, Judaism serves because it enjoys self-evidence as part of a larger set of categories that are equally self-evident. In all of these categories, religion constitutes a statement of belief distinct from other aspects and dimensions of human existence, so religions form a body of well-composed "-isms." So whence the category, "Judaism"? The source of the categorical power of "Judaism" derives from the Protestant philosophical heritage that has defined scholarship, including category formation, from the time of Kant onward. "*Juda*" + "*ism*" do not constitute self-evident, let alone definitive, categories—except where they do. Judaism constitutes a category asymmetrical to the evidence adduced in its study. The category does not work because the principle of formation is philosophical and does not emerge from an unmediated encounter with the Torah. Orthodoxy can have come into existence only in Germany, and, indeed, only in that part of Germany in which the philosophical heritage of Kant and Hegel defined the categories of thought, also, for religion.

Samson Raphael Hirsch: The importance of Hirsch (1808-1888), first great intellect of Orthodoxy, derives from his philosophy of joining Torah with secular education, producing a synthesis of Torah and modern culture. He represents the strikingly new Judaism at hand, exhibiting both its strong tie to the received system but also its innovative and essentially new character. Sometimes called "neo-Orthodox,"[5] Hirsch's position, which laid stress on the possibility of living in the secular world and sustaining a fully Orthodox life, rallied the Jews of the counter-reformation. But Hirsch and his followers took over one principal position of Reform, the possibility of integrating Jews in modern society. What made Hirsch significant was that he took that view not only on utilitarian grounds, as Samet says, "but also through the acceptance of its scale of values, aiming at creating a symbiosis between traditional Orthodoxy and modern German-European culture; both in theory and in practice this meant abandonment of Torah study for its own sake and adopting instead an increased concentration on practical halakhah."[6] On that basis we rightly identify Orthodoxy as a distinct Judaism from the system of the dual Torah. Hirsch himself studied at the University of Bonn, specializing in classical languages, history, and philosophy.[7] So he did not think one had to spend all his time studying Torah, and in going to a university he implicitly affirmed that he could not define, within Torah-study, all modes of learning. Gentile professors knew things worth knowing. By contrast, of course, continuators of the Judaism of the dual Torah thought exactly the opposite: whatever is worth knowing is in the Torah.

In his rabbinical posts, Hirsch published a number of works to appeal to the younger generation. His ideal for them was the formation of a personality that would be both enlightened and observant, that is to say, educated in Western knowledge and observant of the Judaic way of life. This ideal took shape through an educational program that encompassed Hebrew language and holy literature, and also German, mathematics, sciences, and the like. In this way he proposed to respond to the Reformers' view that Judaism in its received form constituted a barrier between Jews and German society. The Reformers saw the received way of life as an obstacle to the sort of integration they thought wholesome and good. Hirsch concurred in the ideal and differed on detail. Distinctive Jewish clothing, in Hirsch's view, enjoyed a low priority. Quite to the contrary, he himself wore a ministerial gown at public worship, which did not win the approbation of the traditionalists, and when he preached, he encompassed not only the law of the Torah but other biblical matters, equally an innovation. Hirsch argued that Judaism and secular education could form a union. This would require the recognition of externals, which could be set aside, and the emphasis on the principles, which would not change. So Hirsch espoused what, in the ideas of those fully within the mentality of self-evidence, constituted selective piety, and, while the details differed, therefore fell within the classification of reform.

In his selections Hirsch included changes in the conduct of the liturgy, involving a choir, congregational singing, sermons in the vernacular—a generation earlier sure marks of Reform. But he required prayers to be said only in Hebrew and Jewish subjects to be taught in that language, and he opposed all changes in the Prayer Book itself. At the same time he sustained organizational relationships with the Reformers and tried to avoid schism. By mid-career, however, toward the middle of the century, Hirsch could not tolerate the Reformers' abrogation of the dietary laws and those affecting marital relationships, and he made his break, accusing the Reformers of disrupting Israel's unity. In the following decades he encouraged Orthodox Jews to leave the congregations dominated by Reform, even if that was the only accessible synagogue. Separationist synagogues thus formed in the larger community.

We come now to Hirsch's framing of issues of doctrine. He constructed an affirmative system, not a negative one. His principal argument stressed that the teachings of the Torah constitute facts beyond all doubt, as much as the facts of nature do not allow for doubt. This view of the essential facticity—the absolute givenness—of the Torah led to the further conviction that human beings may not deny the Torah's teachings even when they do not grasp the Torah's meaning. Wisdom is contained within the Torah, God's will is to be found there. Just as the physical laws of nature are not conditioned by human search, so the rules of God's wisdom are unaffected by human search. The Torah constitutes an objective reality, and, in Katz's words, its laws form "an objective disposition of an established order that is not dependent on the will of the individual or society, and hence not even on historical processes."[8] Humanity nonetheless may through time gain religious truth.

What makes Israel different is that they gain access to the truth not through experience but through direct revelation. Gentile truth is truth, but derives from observation and experience. What Israel knows through the Torah comes through a different medium.

That people then stands outside of history and does not have to learn religious truth through the passage of history and changes over time. Israel forms a supernatural entity, a view certainly in accord with the Judaism of the dual Torah. But when it came to explaining the way of life at hand, Hirsch went his own way. Hirsch pursued a theory of the practice of the religious life through concrete deeds—the commandments—in a highly speculative and philosophical way. He maintained that each of the deeds of the way of life represented something beyond itself, served as a symbol, not as an end in itself. So when a Jew carries out a holy deed, the deed serves to make concrete a revealed truth. This mode of thought transforms the way of life into an exercise in applied theology and practical, practiced belief. Specifically, in Katz's words:

> The performance of a commandment is not determined by simple devotion but by attachment to the religious thought represented in symbolic form by the commandment. Symbolic meanings must be attributed . . . particular to commandments which are described by the Torah itself as signs . . . and commandments which are established as pointing to historical events . . . and commandments whose entire content testifies to their symbolic character."[9]

The diverse commandments all together stand for three principles: justice, love, and "the education of ourselves and others."

Hirsch's theory of who is Israel stood at the opposite pole from that of Abraham Geiger and the Reformers. To them Israel fell into the classification of a religious community, that alone. To Hirsch Israel constituted a people, not a religious congregation, and Hirsch spoke of "national Jewish consciousness:" "The Jewish people, though it carries the Torah with it in all the lands of its dispersion, will never find its table and lamp except in the Holy Land." Israel performs a mission among the nations, to teach "that God is the source of blessing." Israel then falls between, forming its own category, because it has a state system, in the land, but also a life outside.[10] In outlining this position, Hirsch of course reaffirmed the theory of the supernatural Israel laid forth in the dual

Torah. The power of the national ideal for Hirsch lay in its polemical force against the assimilationists and Reformers, whom he treated as indistinguishable:

> The contempt with which the assimilationists treat David's [fallen] tabernacle and the prayer for the sacrificial service clearly reveals the extent of their rebellion against Torah and their complete disavowal of the entire realm of Judaism. They gather the ignorant about them to whom the Book of Books, the Divine national document of their Jewish past and future, is closed with seven seals. With a conceit engendered by stupidity and a perfidy born from hatred they point to God's Temple and the Divine Service in Zion as the unholy center of the 'bloody cult of sacrifices.' Consequently, they make certain to eliminate any reference to the restoration of the Temple service from our prayers. . . . The 'cultured, refined' sons and daughters of our time must turn away with utter disgust from their 'pre-historic, crude' ancestors who worship their god with bloody sacrifices. . . .

Hirsch reviews the long line of exalted leaders who affirmed sacrifice and who were not crude, e.g., Moses, Isaiah, Jeremiah, and on. Then he concludes:

> The Jewish sacrifice expresses the highest ideal of man's and the nation's moral challenge Blood and kidney, head and limbs symbolize our service of God with every drop of blood, every emotion, every particle of our being. By performing the act of sacrifice at the place chosen by God as the site of His Law, we proclaim our determination to fulfill our lofty moral and ethical tasks to enable God to bless the site of the national vow with the presence of this glory and with the fullness of this love and grace.[11]

Hirsch's spiritualization of the sacrifices, in an ample tradition of precedent to be sure, derives from the challenge of Reform. Demanding an acceptance at face value of the Torah as the revelation of God's wisdom, Hirsch nonetheless made the effort to appeal to more than the givenness of the Torah and its commandments.

On the contrary, he entered into argument in the same terms—spiritualization, lofty moral and ethical tasks—as did the Reformers. That marks his thought as new and responsive to a fresh set of issues. As to the Reformers, he met them on their ground, as he had to, and his principal points of insistence to begin with derived from the issues defined by others. That is why we may find for him a suitable place in the larger setting of discourse among the Judaisms of the nineteenth century, all of them products of the end of self-evidence and the beginning of a self-conscious explanation for what had formerly, and elsewhere in the age at hand, the authority of the absolutely given. We see that fact most clearly when we take up a single stunning instance of the possibility of locating the several Judaisms on a single continuum: the doctrine of the Torah, what it is, where it comes from.

The issue of revelation and the Dual Torah: The Judaism of the dual Torah by definition maintained that not only the Hebrew Scriptures ("Old Testament") but also the entire canon of Rabbinic writings constituted that one whole Torah that Moses received at Sinai. The three Judaisms of the nineteenth century met that issue head-on. Each of the possibilities—only Scripture, everything, some things but not others—found proponents. The consequent theory of revelation had to explain the origin and authority of each of the components of the received canon. And, further, that theory of revelation had to explain what, precisely, revelation meant. The position of Orthodoxy on this matter takes on significance only in the larger context of the debate with Reform. Reform through Geiger took the view that revelation was progressive. The Bible derived from "the religious genius of the Jewish people." Orthodoxy through Hirsch, for example, saw the Torah as wholly and completely God's word. A middle position, represented by Conservative Judaism, espoused both views. God revealed the written Torah, which was supplemented by "the ongoing revelation manifesting itself throughout history in the spirit of the Jewish people."[12]

Orthodoxy of course could not concur. The issue pertained to the historical identification of those responsible for the Rabbinic writings. The Conservatives, in the person of Zechariah Frankel, a contemporary of Hirsch, maintained that the whole of the Rabbinic corpus derived from scribes and their successors. These authorities adapted the system of Scripture by inventing the notion of the oral Torah. The Orthodox could not concede such a break. The positive historical school, in Wurzburger's description, held that "the religious consciousness of the Jewish people provided the supreme religious authority, [while] the Orthodox position rested upon the belief in the supernatural origin of the Torah which was addressed to a 'Chosen People.'" So the theory of who is Israel joined to the issue of revelation: how, what, when. The Orthodox position, as outlined by Hirsch, saw Israel as a supernatural people that has in hand a supernatural revelation. The entirety of the dual Torah and the writings flowing from it constitute that revelation. Quite how this notion of a long sequence of revealed documents differs from the conception of a progressive revelation is not entirely clear, but in context it made a considerable difference. For in his affirmation of the entirety of the Torah, written and oral, as the revealed will of God, Hirsch marked the limns of Orthodoxy and made them coincide with the precise boundaries of the received dual Torah. Whether those to whom the supernatural character of Israel and the entirety of Torah formed self-evident truths will have understood Hirsch's careful explanations of matters outside of the received modes of apologetics, however, must come under doubt. For the one thing the traditionalist grasped, the absolute givenness of the whole, Hirsch could not concede. How do we know it? Because he explained and explained and explained.

What is new in Orthodoxy: That Hirsch's Orthodoxy flows directly out of the received system no one doubts. But it also takes a position separate from that system in both doctrine and method. Hirsch spent much energy defending the practice of the religious duties called commandments, such as circumcision, the wearing of fringes on garments, the use, in morning worship, of *tefillin* (commonly translated phylacteries), and the sacrificial cult and Temple. These he treats not as mere data—givens of the holy life. Rather, he transforms them into symbols of a meaning beyond. And that exercise, in his context, testifies to the utter self-consciousness of the Judaism at hand, hence to the formation of a new Judaism out of received materials, no less than Reform Judaism constituted a new Judaism out of those same received materials. For the sole necessity for making up such symbolic explanations derived from decision: defend these, at all costs. Equivalent explanations and a counterpart process of articulated defense of the holy way of life hardly struck as equivalently urgent the contemporaries of Hirsch living in the villages of the East.

When, therefore, Hirsch invoked the parallel, to which we have already alluded, between the study of nature and the study of the Torah, he expressed the freshness, the inventiveness, of his own system, thereby testifying to the self-consciousness at hand. A sizable abstract provides a good view of Hirsch's excellent mode of thought and argument:

> One word here concerning the proper method of Torah investigation. Two revelations are open before us, that is, nature and the Torah. In nature all phenomena stand before us as indisputable facts, and we can only endeavor a posteriori to ascertain the law of each and the connection of all. Abstract demonstration of the truth, or rather, the probability of theoretical explanations of the acts of nature, is an unnatural proceeding. The right method is to verify our assumptions by the known facts, and the highest attainable degree of certainty is to be able to say: 'The facts agree with our assumption'—that is, all the phenomena observed can be explained according to our theory. A single contradictory phenomenon will make our theory untenable. We must, therefore, acquire all the knowledge possible concerning the object of our investigation and know it, if possible, in its totality. If, however, all efforts should fail in disclosing the inner law and connection of phenomena revealed to us as facts in nature, the facts remain, nevertheless, undeniable and cannot be reasoned away.
>
> The same principles must be applied to the investigation of the Torah. In the Torah, even as in nature, God is the ultimate cause. In the Torah, even as in nature, no fact may be denied, even though the reason and the connection may not be understood. What is true in nature is true also in the Torah: the traces of divine wisdom must ever be sought. Its ordinances must be accepted in their entirety as undeniable phenomena and must be studied in accordance with their connection to each other, and the subject to which they relate. Our conjectures must be tested by their precepts, and our highest certainty here also can only be that everything stands in harmony with our theory.
>
> In nature the phenomena are recognized as facts, though their cause and relationship to each other may not be understood and are independent of our investigation. So too the ordinances of the Torah must be law for us, even if we do not comprehend the reason and the purpose of a single one. Our fulfillment of the commandments must not depend on our investigations.[13]

Here we have the counterpart, in argument, to Hirsch's theory of Torah and worldly learning. Just as Hirsch maintained the union of the two, so in the deepest structure of his thought he worked out that same union. Natural science dictated rules of inquiry, specifically, the requirement that we explain phenomena through a theory that we can test. The phenomenon is the given. Then, for the Torah, the requirements of the Torah constitute the givens, which demand explanation, but which must be accepted as facts even when explanation fails. Clearly, Hirsch addressed an audience that had come to doubt the facticity of the facts of the Torah in a way in which none doubted the facticity of the facts of nature.

Once we compare the Torah to nature, the Torah no longer defines the world-view and the way of life at hand. Rather, the Torah takes its place as part of a larger world-view and way of life, one in which the Israelite-human being (in Hirsch's happy concept) has to accommodate both the received of the Torah and the given of nature. The insistence that the process of accommodation—"studied in accordance with their connection . . . and the subject to which they relate"—testifies to a world view essentially distinct from the one of the received system of the dual Torah. In this new world view the Torah demands explanation, its rules find themselves reduced to the lesser dimensions of an apologia of symbolism, so that they form not givens in an enduring and eternal way of life, but objects of analysis, defense, above all, reasoned decision. True, Hirsch insisted, "Our fulfillment of the commandments must not depend on our investigations." But the investigations must go forward, and that, in and of itself, tells us we deal with a new Judaism.

Orthodoxy never claimed to mark the natural next step in the history of Judaism. Orthodoxy saw itself as nothing other than Judaism. In its near-total symmetry with the received system, Orthodoxy surely made a powerful case for that claim. But the fact that the case had to be made, the context and conditions of contention—these form the indicators that another Judaism was coming into being. The asymmetrical points, moreover, demand attention, though, on their own, they should not decisively refute the position of Orthodoxy. What does is the existence of an Orthodoxy at all. The single most interesting instance of a Judaism of self-consciousness, Orthodoxy defends propositions that, in the received system, scarcely reached a level of articulate discourse, for instance, the absolute necessity to conform to the holy way of life of the Torah. The necessity for making such an argument testifies to the fact that people, within Orthodoxy, thought they confronted the need to choose and did choose.

True, the choices, from the viewpoint of Orthodoxy, fell in the right direction. But Orthodoxy formed an act of restoration and renewal, therefore an act of innovation. The modes of argument of Hirsch, representative as they are of the mentality of the Orthodoxy he defined, call into question the linear descent of Orthodoxy from what people called "tradition." An incremental progress, perhaps, but a lineal and unbroken journey, no. But even the incremental theory of the history of Judaism, which, in the case of Orthodoxy, identifies Hirsch's Orthodoxy with the system of the dual Torah, fails to take note of facts, and, as Hirsch himself argues, that failure suffices. The facts that people, Hirsch included, made clear-cut choices, identifying some things as essential, others not (clothing, for one important instance). If the piety of Reform proved selective, the selections that Hirsch made place him into the classification,

also, of one who sorted out change and made changes. Just as the Reformers of the nineteenth century laid emphasis on the points of continuity they located between themselves and the past, so, of course, did the Orthodox (and, from their perspective, with better reason). Just as the Orthodox of the nineteenth century specify what mattered more than something else, so of course, did the Reform (and, from their perspective, with greater relevance to the situation at hand).

The political changes that in the aggregate created an abyss between the Judaism of the dual Torah and the new, theological Judaisms of the nineteenth century affected both the Reform and the Orthodox of the age. They stood in a single line—one that broke off en route to (so to speak) Sinai, that is, to the Judaism of the dual Torah. So in Orthodoxy we find powerful indication of a system standing in an incremental relationship with the received system, but still more striking symptoms of a system formed afresh and anew.

Continuity or new creation? Both—but, therefore, by definition, new creation. Piety selected is by definition piety invented, and Hirsch emerges as one of the intellectually powerful creators of a Judaism. "Torah and secular learning" defined a new world view, dictated a new way of life, and addressed a different Israel, from the Judaism of the dual Torah. To those who received that dual Torah as self-evident what the Torah did not accommodate was secular learning. The Torah as they received it did not approve changes in the familiar way of life, and did not know an Israel other than the one at hand. So the perfect faith of Orthodoxy sustained a wonderfully selective piety. The human greatness of Hirsch and the large number of Jews who found self-evident the possibility of living the dual life of Jew and German or Jew and American? It lay in the power of the imagination to locate in a new circumstance a rationale for inventing tradition.

The human achievement of Orthodoxy demands more than routine notice. Living in a world that only grudgingly accommodated difference and did not like Jews' difference in particular, the Orthodox followed the rhythm of the week to the climax of the Sabbath, of the seasons to the climactic moments of the festivals. They adhered to their own pattern of daily life, with prayers morning, noon, and night. They married only within the holy people. They ate only food that had been prepared in accord with the rules of sanctification. They honored philosophy and culture, true, but these they measured by their own revealed truth as well. It was not easy for them to keep the faith when so many within Jewry, and so many more outside, wanted Jews to be pretty much the same as everyone else. The human costs cannot have proved trivial. To affirm when the world denies, to keep the faith against all evidence—that represents that faith that in other settings people honored. It was not easy for either the Orthodox of Germany or the immigrant Jews of America, who in an ocean voyage moved from the world of self-evident faith to the one of insistent denial of the faith.

Notes

[1] Nathaniel Katzburg and Walter S. Wurzburger, "Orthodoxy," *Encyclopaedia Judaica*, vol. 12, col. 1486-1493.

[2] Op. cit., col. 1487.

[3] Op. cit., col. 1488.

[4] Op. cit., col. 1490.

[5] Moshe Shraga Samet, "Neo-Orthodoxy," *Encylopaedia Judaica*, vol. 12, col. 956-958.

[6] Op. cit., col. 957.

[7] Simha Katz, "Samson (ben) Raphael Hirsch," *Encyclopaedia Judaica*, vol. 8, col. 508-515.

[8] Op. cit., col. 512-513.

[9] Op. cit., col. 513.

[10] Op. cit., col. 514.

[11] Samson Raphael Hirsch, *The Collected Writings* (New York and Jerusalem, 1984), vol. 1, pp. 388-389.

[12] Wurzburger, col. 1489.

[13] Hirsch, op. cit., vol. III, pp. xiii-xiv.

JACOB NEUSNER

OTHER RELIGIONS, JUDAIC DOCTRINES OF: Judaism is primarily an inward looking religion. Its theology defines Judaism's own goals, aspirations, and problems but seldom evidences any concern for, or interest in, those outside its faith community.[1] While traditional Jews believe that their deity daily (re-)creates the entire world,[2] controls all of the world's activities, and is the God of all humankind, still they focus on the fact that at Sinai God entered into a special relationship with the People Israel in particular. Judaism focuses almost without exception on that exclusive covenant and on its implications for the everyday life of Jews. Only at a secondary level are the present and future states of non-Jews of concern. God created all of humankind, and everyone has an obligation to do YHWH's will; however, in the Jewish view, God, not the people of Israel, is responsible for assuring non-Jews' compliance. For that reason the beliefs, actions, and status of non-Jews in the eyes of God receive relatively little attention in Jewish sources.

Rabbinic perspectives on non-Jews: The Rabbinic texts of the first centuries C.E. exhibit so little interest in non-Jews that they seldom even distinguish among the variety of non-Jewish religions and ethnic groups. While the rabbis define fine distinctions among different types of Jews, they lump together virtually all non-Israelites.[3] Humanity is divided between us and them, Israelites, *benai yisrael*, and "nations," *goyim*. Seldom do the Rabbinic documents clearly differentiate among Christians, non-Christians, worshippers of Zeus, followers of the Isis cult, or devotees of any other religious system other than Judaism. In the Talmud and midrashic texts, all non-Israelites are *goyim*, and, unless otherwise noted, gentiles are idolaters, "worshippers of the stars and planets," or those who practice "a strange ritual."[4]

The earliest Rabbinic texts, the Mishnah and the Tosefta, discuss non-Israelites primarily in order to sharpen and refine their definition of Israelites. One's identity is created by comparison to that of others, so that the first step in my determining who is like me is to delineate the traits of those who are not like me.[5] Because the sages of the Mishnah and Tosefta are not interested in gentiles *qua* gentiles, they offer us little specific or detailed information about them or their religions. The earliest Rabbinic documents, the Mishnah and Tosefta, deal with the non-Jew from the Jewish point of view and in terms of specifically Rabbinic legal categories and paradigms. References to non-Jews thus serve to illuminate the laws that apply to Jews without telling us much about the non-

Jews at all. In response to specific social, religious, and political situations that forced Jews to interact more immediately with non-Jews, later Jewish documents—the Talmuds and midrashic books—by contrast, do discuss other religious systems that were active in ancient Palestine and Babylonia. But these comments too are always from the Jewish point of view and tend to be schematic and generalized, reflecting the propagandistic needs of the talmudic authors rather than the reality of the non-Jewish religion and culture. For example, they spend much more time discussing *Ba'al Peor* and the *Asherot*, idols known from biblical times, than they do the Christianity or religion of the Magi contemporary in their own day.

Although YHWH is the God of the People Israel and the deity of all humankind, the Bible and the Rabbinic texts do not have the same religious expectations for non-Israelites as they do for Israelites. With the exception of Isaiah 45, the Hebrew Bible does not insist that the non-Israelite nations give up their idols and idolatrous rituals. Scripture condemns *Israelites* who worship idols because this violates the covenant between them and YHWH. But the Bible does not insist that in the present era the other nations give up their gods. The nations' idols may be useless and silly, but because the "nations" have not had the same religio-historical experiences as the Israelites, they do not have the same obligations as the People Israel. In light of the Sinai covenant, idolatry represents a danger to the Israelites and must not be tolerated in their midst. As a result, gentiles who wish to reside among Israelites must give up their idolatrous rituals. But other gentiles need not. As David Novak states, "For although idolatry is frequently ridiculed in Scripture as nonsense, it is nonsense for only the people of Israel who are to know better because of the covenant. Gentiles, therefore, cannot be faulted for their own idolatry as long as they do not infect the people of Israel with it" (Novak, p. 37). Gentiles "cannot be morally faulted for unfaithfulness to a covenant in which they themselves are not participants" (Novak, p. 38).

The opinion of the Rabbinic documents is slightly more complicated (Stern, pp. 27-29, 141-162, 187-197). Again, all Jewish practice of idolatry is condemned, and the major concern of *Avodah Zarah*, the talmudic tractate on idolatry, is to guarantee that Israelites have no opportunity to engage in, to appear to engage in, or to aid a gentile who engages in idolatry. At the same time, the inclusion of a prohibition against idolatry in the Noachide laws,[6] the seven obligations the rabbis understood to be incumbent even upon gentiles, indicates that at least some rabbis expected "righteous" gentiles also to give up their idolatrous ways. But this view is tempered by others that accept idolatry as a fact of gentile culture and that do not seem overly concerned with it (see, e.g., B. Hul. 13b). And while the rabbis generally hold that all idolatrous shrines must be eliminated from the Land of Israel, YHWH's Land, they do not apply this rule to other geographical regions. So, as in the Mishnah, later Rabbinic texts are not concerned with what non-Jews do within their own social or geographical areas. Non-Jews are of no major concern unless Israelites come into contact with them. Only at that point, in order to regulate the Israelites' actions, must the rabbis also imagine restrictions to be applicable to gentiles.

The Jewish perspective on early Christianity: For the most part, it should have been fairly easy to distinguish between Judaism and the other religions of the ancient world. Non-Jews' deities were different, their sacred books were uniquely theirs, their rituals were foreign, and their ethnic identity was distinctive. However, with the advent of Christianity the situation became ambiguous. Christians claimed to be monotheistic, appropriated the Hebrew Bible (albeit in Greek) as its own Scripture, and took the God of the Bible as their own deity. Originating in YHWH's Holy Land and among YHWH's covenanted people, the believers in Christ challenged Judaism at its very core. Christianity was not a "strange ritual" in the usual sense of the term; in fact, this religion must have appeared to the rabbis to be all *too* familiar. It clearly seemed recognizable and familiar to numerous Palestinian Jews, for they soon became followers of what started as a Jewish sect and quickly became a separate religion. Indeed, only in the middle of the third century C.E. were Romans able to distinguish between Jews and Christians at all.

In light of Christianity's clear challenge to Rabbinic Judaism, it is surprising that we do not find more overt discussions of this religion.[7] One reason may be that medieval Christian censors deleted or forced the Jews to alter overt references to Christians and Christianity. But even this being the case, it appears clear that Christianity was not a major focus within the Rabbinic corpus. The rabbis identify a few figures as Christians or even as Jesus himself, and s small number of Rabbinic discussions, especially in the *midrashim*, clearly refer to Christianity. Some midrashic and talmudic discussions even appear to be oblique answers to the Christian challenge. But not every Rabbinic text that discusses the unity of YHWH was a response to the Christian notion of the trinity, nor need every reference to humanity's inherent goodness have been a response to the doctrine of original sin.[8] In short, the Rabbinic documents provide little information concerning the rabbis' opinion of Christianity, other than the fact that it was treated like every other non-Jewish system. It was primarily ignored.[9]

The paucity of overt references to Christianity in the Rabbinic texts may be attributed to several factors. Early Christianity was viewed by the Jewish and Roman authorities as a Jewish sect. It is doubtful that the early rabbis saw Christianity as any more threatening than any other of the various messianic movements found within the Jewish population of the first century C.E. Many probably thought that it was best to ignore these people, assuming that eventually they would see the folly of their ways. This would have been the case especially after Jesus' ignoble death. While there is some evidence that early on Jews worked to persuade the Roman authorities that the Christians posed a threat to the social order and the Empire's well-being, by the fourth century, a thoroughly gentile Christianity was a formidable force within the Roman Empire and the religion of the Emperors. Eventually, disparag-

ing remarks about Christianity or even theological challenges were severely punished.

Throughout the New Testament there are indications that the Jews persecuted the early Christians. In Gal. 5:11 Paul claims that he is persecuted because he does not require gentiles to be circumcised before joining the Church. In 2 Cor. 11:24-25 Paul writes, "Five times I have received at the hands of the Jews the forty lashes less one. Three times I have been beaten with rods; once was I stoned." The flogging of thirty-nine lashes was a recognized Jewish method of punishment; a whole tractate of the Mishnah, *Makkot*, focuses on the lashes. Stoning was also an accepted form of punishment or execution for specific violations of Jewish law. However, it is impossible to determine if these acts were those of a community, a mob, or individuals.[10] The evidence in Acts is similarly ambiguous with regard to the organized nature of the persecutions (Seltzer, pp. 58-65). Claudia Seltzer notes that because the Jews depended on Roman largess for their peace and prosperity, they would have objected to Christian missionaries' disrupting the status quo. She writes, "The Jews may have worried that they would be guilty by association with Jewish Christian missionaries and incur Roman displeasure" (p. 23). This of course assumes that the Romans did not view the Christians of Paul's letters and the Book of Acts as distinct from Palestinian Jews. With regard to these Jewish attempts to suppress early Christianity, Jack T. Sanders writes: [11]

> The Temple leadership . . . sought periodically to destroy Christianity. . . . In and near Jerusalem . . . Paul first carried out and later received synagogue punishment directed against Christian missionaries. I have been able to unearth no good direct cause of this hostility towards the Jewish Christians other than the fact that some renegades among them, like Paul, admitted gentiles . . . without requiring those gentiles to become proselytes to Judaism [by being circumcised]. There is also the possibility of a continuing criticism of the Temple cultus on the part of self-righteous Christians resident in Jerusalem. . . . For the period between the wars . . . our evidence shifts to Galilee, where we find Jewish Christians being excluded from syna-

gogues and declared heretics. . . . [D]eveloping Rabbinic Judaism finds them guilty of the heresy of making Jesus equal to God and causing enmity and strife between God and his people.

Sanders also stresses that the Christians' opposition to the Temple, the Jewish "cultural symbol par excellence," would have put them outside of the main symbolic system of Judaism. He further maintains that their attacks on the Torah and the law must have appeared to be subversive to the leaders of the Jewish community (p. 99). But these same practices led to no similar persecutions of groups that remained within Judaism. The Babylonian Talmud attributes to first and second century sages a major disagreement concerning the necessity of circumcising converts.[12] Furthermore, those who lived at Qumran believed that the Temple in Jerusalem had been corrupted by its present leadership and that the "wicked priest" had killed the "Teacher of Righteousness." Yet, there is no evidence of Jewish persecutions of those who followed the practices of Qumran, just as the rabbis who would have accepted uncircumcised converts were accorded no approbation.

The Jewish documents suggest that between the revolts of 70 and 135 C.E., Christianity was lumped together with the other Jewish heresies under the category of *minut* (Sanders, p. 128), Jewish sectarianism; Christians were not viewed as a distinct religion. Seltzer, for instance, finds no evidence in the Synoptic Gospels that Jews viewed Christians as outsiders (pp. 42-43). She argues that in the early days of the movement, Jewish crowds in Jerusalem were "curious and amazed by the miracles and words of early Christian preachers" (p. 57). While Acts 19 points to Paul's preaching in Ephesus as the final point of the positive Jewish response to his message, Acts 23 describes some Pharisees in Jerusalem as arguing in support of Paul before the Sanhedrin (pp. 57-58). Surely Acts contains many references to Paul's sufferings at the hands of the Jews. But Seltzer concludes that these are literary and rhetorical devices and have little historical value (pp. 58-65).

The evidence from most of the early Chris-

tian and Jewish sources indicates that at first the Jews considered the Christians to be a Jewish group, even if, from the start, at least some Christians saw themselves as distinct from other Jews (Seltzer, pp. 185-188). While Nero appears able to differentiate between Jews and Christians, Domitian was either unable or unwilling to do so (Simon, p. 117). By the middle of the second century, the situation changed. The Martyrdom of Polycarp, the Gospel of Peter, and some early inscriptions indicate that the Jews now considered Christians to be outsiders, and that the former turned to the Roman authorities to suppress the followers of Jesus (Seltzer, pp. 114-125). Thus, after the Bar Kokhba war, "in the eyes of ancient Judaism, Christianity represented not merely an arbitrary break in the tradition but a revolutionary innovation" (Simon, p. 78).

Jews defined Christians as deviant because Christianity challenged their own Jewish identity. At stake, that is, were not mere theological differences. This meant that as Christianity became more and more influenced by its new gentile members, the Jewish community strove to separate itself from the new religion in order to establish firmly its own uniqueness. Sanders concludes (p. 141):

> The Jewish leadership punished early Christianity not primarily because the Christians were following deviant halakhah or because they called Jesus God, or because they proclaimed a crucified Messiah, or even because they criticized the temple cultus and questioned the validity of Torah, but because events were leading enforcers of Judaic identity to maintain the boundaries of Judaism while the Christians were breaking though those boundaries in one way or another.

Interestingly, it is likely that the codification of the Mishnah at about this same time stems from the same urge firmly to establish the parameters of Jewish identity.

Writings from this period reflect the extent to which the conflict between Judaism and Christianity was, as much as about theology, an argument about self-identity. Justin's *Dialogue with Trypho*, for instance, pays careful attention to demonstrating the validity of Christ and Christianity on the basis of the

Hebrew Bible. He attempts to demonstrate that the Hebrew Bible's references to the election of the Jews refer to the Christians. The *Dialogue* contains a substantial number of references to the Jewish mistreatment of Christians, including their attacks, ridicule, curses and slanders. Within this context, Justin often mentions the Jews' hatred of Christians (Seltzer, pp. 135-146; Sanders, p. 50).

In his *Contra Celsus*, Origin shows that the disputes between the Jews and Christians focused on Jesus' life, with the Jews claiming that Jesus' disciples invented the tales about his life, such as the virgin birth. In truth, according to Origin's Jews, Jesus was an illegitimate child, and the story of his resurrection was a pure fabrication by his disciples, a band of lowlifes and rabbles. In addition, the Jews do not understand how the Christians can claim to accept the Hebrew Bible when they ignore the commandments (Seltzer, pp. 149-154).

The early Church Fathers are consistent in their claims that the Jews debated the Christians concerning correct interpretations of the Hebrew Bible, Jesus' legitimacy, and the truth of his resurrection. Jerome, Cyril of Jerusalem, and Eusebius all maintain that the Jews initiated these conversations and debates (Simon, p. 177). While these assertions by Christian writers may be historically accurate, they may also be a way for the Church Fathers to underscore their position that Judaism now had to defend itself from Christianity's claims to be God's chosen people.

Once Christianity became the official religion of the Roman emperors and the Empire, the position of Judaism and Jews dramatically changed. From the time of Julius Caesar, Judaism had been a legitimate religion within the Empire, and the Jews enjoyed the right to practice their ancient traditions. They were freed from certain obligations incumbent upon other citizens, such as participating in official pagan rituals connected to the political process. In addition, they were permitted to send a regular assessment to Jerusalem to support the Temple.

With the failure of the two wars against Rome, many of these rights had been eliminated or curtailed. The Jews were not allowed to enter Jerusalem, and the Temple half-*sheqel* now went to the Emperor. But, the Jews still were held in fairly high regard by the Roman officials, as the Rabbinic stories about Judah the Patriarch and the Emperor indicate (Simon, pp. 126-132). The situation changed completely after Constantine's conversion, and by the beginning of the fifth century Christianity enjoyed the status of *religio*, while the term *superstitio* applied to Judaism.[13] Roman-Christian law now sought to confine the scope of Judaism and the power of Jews. The Theodotian and Justinian codes reduced the ability of Jews to interact socially, politically, and economically with Christians and other non-Jews. The Empire's law codes sought to isolate the Jews as much as possible. It became illegal for Jews to disparage Christians or to try to encourage Jewish converts to Christianity to return to their native faith.[14]

The Jewish view of Christians and Christianity in the medieval period: Pope Gregory I (590-604) set the tone for much of the Christian medieval legislation and mythology concerning the Jews. As long as the Jews acted in accordance with Church law, they would be permitted to worship in their synagogues freely and without interference. Similarly, they should not be subject to forced baptism. Gregory saw a theological importance to the continued presence of the Jews in Christian lands. He maintained that God has allowed the Jews to live among Christians, so that they might bear witness to the truth of Christian doctrine. As long as the Jews were scattered throughout Christendom and lived as second-class citizens under Christian domination, the truth of the Christian claim that they alone enjoy God's favor would be manifest to everyone (Cohen, pp. 36-38).

Christianity took a good deal of time to convert Europe and to put its plan with regard to the Jews into place. After Charlemagne converted on Christmas day, 800, he and his descendants treated the Jews extremely well. The Carolingian rulers understood and profited from the Jews' international economic contacts, and the relationships between Jews and non-Jews were quite positive. Jews had a virtual monopoly on the import and export of goods within the empire. Although Church leaders such as Agobard objected to the positive treatment of the Jews, their position remained stable throughout much of the tenth century.

The Crusades and the widespread desire to rid the world of non-Christians and heretics poisoned the European atmosphere in which Jews interacted with Christians. The Jewish communities of the Lorraine and near the Rhine were among the first to suffer at the hands of the Crusaders, beginning in January, 1096. The practice of *qiddush haShem*, of committing suicide rather than betraying Judaism and God, became common within some European Jewish communities at this time.[15] The thirteenth century witnessed the first examples of the papacy's interfering with the free practice of Judaism. Both Gregory IX and Innocent IV investigated the Talmud and had copies burned. Clement IV in 1267 extended the Inquisition's authority to Jews who were suspected of influencing Christians, thus promoted the heresy of Judaizing Christianity (Cohen, pp. 38-40).

Little Jewish literature has survived from the early Middle Ages, and before the twelfth century there are no Jewish works that discuss Christianity. In any case, before the twelfth century Christianity did not pose a real threat to Judaism. The advent of the Crusades was an overt indication of the changing European landscape, as more and more the Jews found themselves in a tenuous situation. Eventually, they came to live in a world politically, economically, and socially dominated by hostile Christians. Within this environment Jews enjoyed few inherent rights, and they faced a constant external threat to their integrity and stability as a people and as a religion. Christianity openly challenged the Jews to demonstrate that the Christians were not correct in their interpretations of the Jewish Bible, in their descriptions of the trinitarian deity of the Old and New Testaments, and in their claim to the rewards of the Jewish covenant.

The medieval Jewish biblical commentators sought to re-establish the absolute validity of the Rabbinic interpretations of the biblical texts. Within his authoritative biblical commentary, Solomon b. Isaac of Troyes (1040-1105), known as Rashi, emphasized the Jewish interpretations of those verses that were central to the Christian community (Cohen, p. 141). In late antiquity the Jews had rejected allegorical interpretations, a method widespread among Christian exegetes, in favor of the literal reading of biblical texts (Simon, p. 150). Rashi claimed that his commentary sought to expound only the *peshat*, the simple meaning of the verses. In addition, he drew freely and often upon the wealth of Rabbinic midrashic interpretations available to him. Rashi set the pattern for latter commentators, such as Samuel b. Meir, his grandson, and Joseph Qara, one of his first students. The Jews believed that by undercutting the Christian interpretations of the Bible they could underscore Christianity's implausibility.[16]

Joseph Kimhi's (ca. 1105-1170) *Book of the Covenant* is most probably the first European Jewish anti-Christian polemic. He argued that the conduct of the Jews demonstrates that they are God's people. The Jews, not the Christians, follow the Ten Commandments, live moral lives, teach their children to fear God, and regularly give to charity. Only the Christian ascetics, who are not representative of Christianity as a whole, live similar exemplary lives. Kimhi's work, like most of the rest of the medieval anti-Christian Jewish polemical literature, frequently revolved around the biblical text. As the thirteenth century *Old Book of Polemic*, an anonymous collection of Jewish anti-Christian arguments current among Franco-German Jews, demonstrates, to the Jews, Christianity was irrational and its interpretations of the Hebrew Bible unreasonable. Jews often initiated discussions with Christians over doctrinal questions under the assumption that Christianity's irrationality could be demonstrated easily. Although many of the Christological interpretations were rather far-fetched, others were taken seriously by Jewish writers. Often the Jewish commentator would point to the verse's context and argue that the passage referred to historical figures, not to the messiah. Another approach was to note that when read in its entirety, the Bible consistently maintained that the messiah would be a human being who would usher in a period of idyllic peace in the world. By pointing to the contemporary political situation, the Jews challenged the Christian claim that the world had changed with the advent of Jesus. By rejecting the Christian allegorical interpretations of the Hebrew Bible, the Jews maintained that the ritual law continued to be binding; the biblical verses that described it meant exactly what they said (Berger, pp. 7-15).

The Jews often challenged the rationality of Christian dogma. While some Jews conceded that it was theoretically possible for God to have caused a virgin to conceive and bear a child, many held that the Incarnation was impossible, even for an omnipotent deity. The Jewish views on human nature and God's justice would not allow them to accept the doctrine of original sin, the universal damnation of humankind, or the fact that unbaptized infants could not enter heaven. The Jewish writers were disdainful of Jesus' miracles, and they often expressed wonderment that those events impressed Jesus' followers (Berger, p. 15). The trinity also was a subject of much Jewish criticism. At the end of the twelfth century, David Kimhi argued that logically, a father must proceed a son; therefore, it is impossible for Jesus and God to be coexistent. This whole trend of Jewish argument was summarized by Nahmanides, who wrote that Christian doctrine is irrational and not accepted by nature.[17]

Thus, Jews challenged the logic of Christianity's doctrinal claims, the Christian interpretations of Scripture, and also the Christian reading of history. David Kimhi objected to the Christian claim that its validity was established by the fact that it had spread throughout the world, for Ishmael and Israel, among other nations, had not accepted it (Talmage, p. 75). In the sixteenth century, Isaac b. Abraham of Troki rejected the Christian argument that its age demonstrated the truth of its theological claims. He pointed out that Islam is a thousand years old (Talmage, p. 15), and Judaism is over three thousand years old. Nahmanides even noted that the Muslim em-

pire was much larger than that controlled by Rome and the Christians (Talmage, p. 86).

These polemical responses to Christianity did not represent an organized effort by the Jewish community to refute the Christian claims or arguments. Rather, they were *ad hoc* or *ad hominem*. Further, while this literature shows a direct interest in and desire to discredit Christianity, most of the Jewish literature and thought in this period simply continued the Rabbinic practice of ignoring the non-Jewish world and its religions. And, despite the clear anti-Christian polemic within the sphere of social legislation, Christianity by this period was held by Jews not to be a form of idolatry at all. This meant that, in most regards, Christians were considered to be appropriate business partners for Jews.

Indeed, the major issue facing Jews who had to interact socially and economically with Christians was the question of idolatry. Rabbinic law forbids Jews from supporting idolatry, even indirectly. M. A. Z. 1:1 forbids Jews from engaging in business dealings with idolaters for three days before their festivals, and in the following passage, Ishmael forbids business dealings three days after their festivals as well. If Christians are idolaters and Sunday constitutes a religious festival, business dealings between Jews and Christians would be virtually prohibited. Similarly, the Talmud forbids Jews from deriving benefit from wine with which an idolater has come into contact at any stage in its production, from the picking of the grapes to bottling. If Christians are idolaters, from whom do Jews purchase wine for their various ritual needs? Therefore, for the medieval Jew, the question of whether Christianity was a form of monotheism or just one more idolatrous religion had important practical consequences.

Maimonides, who lived under Muslim rule and had no direct knowledge of or experience with Christians, classified Christianity as idolatry and, on the basis of Ishmael's ruling in the Mishnah, forbade all business dealings with them. In light of the icons churches contained, he also declared these places idolatrous shrines and did not permit Jews to visit them or live in towns that contained them. Christianity had negated the authority of the Torah, rejected the commandments, and elevated Jesus above Moses, creating an erroneous messianism. It was a polytheistic faith, and for that reason it could not be a repository of divine revelation.[18]

Although Maimonides rejected Christianity's assertion that it was a monotheistic religion, he did find a positive role for it in the messianic scheme. Christianity can bring the world to the worship of the One God because it finds its roots within the Hebrew Bible. Maimonides writes (Novak, p. 64):

> It is permitted to teach the commandments to Christians and to draw them to our religion . . . [because] the uncircumcised ones believe that the version of the torah has not changed, only they interpret it with their faulty exegesis. . . . But when the Scriptural texts shall be interpreted with correct exegesis it is possible that they shall return to what is best. There is nothing that they shall find in their Scriptures that differs from ours.

At present, Christianity is idolatrous because it has misinterpreted the Hebrew Bible, and trinitarian doctrines have misled Christians to place icons within their churches. However, because they accept the Divine character of the Hebrew Scriptures, they can, in theory, be taught the correct interpretations, so that they will discard their erroneous beliefs and practices. But, until that time, they must be treated as idolaters, "and all Torah restrictions pertaining to idolaters pertain to them" (Novak, p. 57).

Maimonides lived in an Islamic environment, and he had the luxury of condemning a Christianity with which he had no direct contact. The sages living within Christian Europe had no such luxury, and so many of them expressed a different view. These authorities were careful to limit the application to Christians of Talmudic law. For instance, the Talmud explains that the Mishnah forbids Jews from engaging in business dealings with gentiles near the time of their festivals specifically out of fear that the gentiles would use the money they received to support idol worship. Jacob Tam, a twelfth century French sage, accordingly ruled that Jews could do business with Christians in any item

except those that were designed specifically for a religious purpose. But the simple exchange of money was no matter of concern. For even if one were to classify Christians as idolaters, one cannot distinguish the money they will use to support their religion from money they employ for non-religious purposes. Jews need not fear that the funds they pay the Christians will be improperly used.

More than this, Tam in fact did not consider Christians to be idolaters. This is clear in his treatment of the Talmudic rule that prohibits Jews from drinking or benefiting from the wine of non-Jews, which is based on the Talmudic belief that all gentiles 1) dedicate a small portion of any wine with which they came into contact to their idols (B. San. 60b, B. A.Z. 29b), that they 2) would be thinking of their idols when they purchased the wine, or 3) that trading in wine would lead to extended social interactions which would finally end up in intermarriage (B. A.Z. 36b). While not permitting Jews to drink wine with which Christians had come into contact, Tam, following his grandfather, Rashi, permitted Jews to derive other benefit from gentile wine, which meant they could buy and sell it for profit. Tam's position implies that he has placed the Christians somewhere between Jews and the Talmud's idolaters (Novak, pp. 45-46).

Tam faced another problem that forced him to express clearly his understanding of Christian worship. In the Talmud, Samuel's father prohibits Jews from entering into a partnership with non-Jews, because the gentile will "become obligated to swear an oath by his god" (B. San. 63b). While the rabbi's original intention may have been to permit the Jew to enter into a partnership as long as he did not require his gentile partner to take an oath by the latter's god, this eventually became an absolute prohibition against business partnerships between Jews and non-Jews. Tam, facing a very different environment from that of the talmudic sages, excludes Christians from the Talmud's restrictions. He argued that although the Christians are thinking about the true God, they swear by the names of their saints, "to whom they did not ascribe divinity. . . ." Even though they associate the name of God with something else, "we do not find that it is forbidden to indirectly cause others to perform such association" (Novak, pp. 46-47).

In his efforts to sanction interaction between Jews and Christians, Menahem b. Solomon, known as Ha-Meiri, a fourteenth century Provensal sage, focused on Christianity's moral code. He argued that Christians are righteous gentiles, because they accept the seven Noachide commandments as Scripturally ordained. This means they have rejected polytheism. While the Talmud presumed that gentiles were idolaters, Ha-Meiri presumes that Christians are not idolaters. The legal liabilities the Talmud placed upon gentiles therefore do not apply to medieval Christians (Novak, pp. 53-54), the exact opposite of Maimonides' view. Whenever the Torah mentions *your brother*, ha-Meiri wrote, it refers to *all* those who believe in God, including Christians.

Finally, along these same lines, Rabbi Moses Rivkes, a seventeenth-century Lithuanian Talmudist, wrote:

> The rabbis of the Talmud meant by the term "idolaters" the pagans who lived in their time, who worshipped the stars and the planets and did not believe in the Exodus from Egypt and in the creation of the world out of nothing. But the nations under whose benevolent shadow we, the Jewish nation, are exiled and are dispersed among them, they do believe in the creation of the world out of nothing and the Exodus from Egypt and in the essentials of the Faith, and their whole intention is toward the Maker of heaven and earth, as other authorities have said . . . the nations do believe all of this (Novak, p. 49).

So we see the extent to which, living under Christian domination and in close contact with Christianity, Jews came to see Christianity as a separate, but legitimate, religion, the followers of which were appropriate partners in business and other economic dealings.

The evidence from the medieval sources illustrates the complexity of attempting to delineate the Jewish view of Christianity. Within the polemical treatises, the debate literature, and the Rabbinic commentaries, we find many negative assessments of Christian biblical interpretation, doctrine, and practice.

On the other hand, in the responsa literature and the medieval talmudic commentaries we find texts that distinguish medieval Christians from idolaters. While the medieval rabbis agreed that the Christians had misinterpreted the Hebrew Bible, the mere fact that they had accepted it as divinely revealed distinguished them from the idol worshippers referred to in the Talmud. Depending on the context in which the rabbi wrote, this could or could not be an important datum to consider when talking about Christianity.

Jewish attitudes towards non-Jews in modern times: The Enlightenment forever changed the world in which the Jews lived. From the end of the eighteenth century to the end of the nineteenth century western European Jews moved inch by inch toward the centers of modern Western society. In theory, at least, the Jews could become fully participating citizens of enlightened countries. Political and social theorists put forth numerous arguments for granting the Jews citizenship and more or less equal access to the educational, political, economic, and social institutions of the day. The western European Jews, especially those in Germany, believed that they were on the verge of having the same rights and privileges as their Christian neighbors. Some liberal rabbis wrote as if they were living in the messianic age or at least close to its advent.

These changes in the social, political, and economic spheres went hand in hand with changes in intellectual paradigms. Experimentation replaced theology as the primary means of gaining secure knowledge about the world, its workings, and its inhabitants. Even as science was daily demonstrating the complexity of the world, people such as Newton and Galileo were ascertaining "laws" that explained natural phenomena. The eternal varities that the human mind and the divine mind had previously held in common no longer were the source of all knowledge nor an adequate explanation of the human situation and condition. Reason and analysis based on sense perception along with experimentation replaced religious truths and revelation as the source of knowledge and understanding. Pascal (1623-1662) had explained the human condition in terms of the fall of Adam and Eve. Rousseau (1844-1910) explained it through a theory of the social contract.

This new thought carried over into a new understanding of religion. No longer would religious doctrine be self-validating. Reason, not revelation, rather, would provide an adequate source of knowledge of the Deity and the nature of a valid religion. Only those religious claims that could be verified through rational inquiry were to be important. And because reason was universal to humankind, rational natural religion was the same for all peoples. Many Jewish and Christian theologians agreed on what should constitute a rational religion, so that some viewed Judaism, Christianity, and Islam as equally valid. Religious coercion has no justification, and a valid religion's feelings of superiority are self-contradictory. The only way that one can determine whether or not a particular religion is a true expression of the divine is by assessing the morality and rationality of its believers. A true religion must produce moral followers.[19]

While the particularities of the various religious systems cannot be rationally established, many believed that one could argue on the basis of rational analysis that certain religious propositions are true. A theory of natural religion was developed, which held that one could rationally demonstrate the God exits, that God is benevolent, and that human beings have immortal souls. A system that has these three elements and that produces moral followers thus would be deemed a valid religion and would deserve the respect of all humankind. For this reason, enlightened Jews came to view the religious claims of Judaism and Christianity as valid to the extent, and only to the extent, that those claims were rational and resulted in proper human action.

Educated in languages, math, philosophy, and poetry, Moses Mendelssohn (1729-1786) embodied the traits of the enlightenment and hence was viewed by gentiles with both respect and amazement. No Jew before him had achieved equal status as a philosopher and arbiter of cultural values. While Mendelssohn had no personal desire publicly to defend Ju-

daism or to evaluate Christianity, in 1769 the noted Swiss theologian Johann Caspar Lavater challenged him to refute the "obvious" truth of Christianity or to do what any rational person would do, convert to the religion whose truth he could not deny. Unable to ignore this public challenge Mendelssohn was forced to respond. In doing so, he judged Christianity on the same terms on which he judged Judaism: a "true" religion had to be rational and to lead its followers to live moral and ethical lives.

In carrying out his analysis Mendelssohn, argued that, to meet the standards of a "true" religion, Christianity needed to eliminate its irrational dogma, for instance, that Jesus rejected Mosaic law. If this were done, then, he argued, even Jews could accept Jesus as a "prophet and messenger of God," sent "to preach the holy doctrine of virtue and its rewards in another life to a depraved human race" (Meyer, 36). But this was not the Christianity that Mendelssohn knew. Rather, it held that Jesus abrogated the law, and it depended on stories of Jesus' miracles. While such stories, as well as a reliance on revelation, in fact occur in every religion, Mendelssohn argued that these things do not establish a religion's truth. Otherwise we would have only "testimonies against testimonies," and no reasonable or rational arguments could verify the contradictory claims. In the end, therefore, based upon an evaluation of Christianity's theology and beliefs, Mendelssohn judged it to be inferior to Judaism. Judaism—with the exception of the ritual law—was a purely rational and true religion, while Christianity rested on a dogma that could not withstand rational evaluation.

Although Mendelssohn believed that Judaism had a stronger claim to being a rational religion than did Christianity, he still argued that the latter religion was appropriate to its own followers. It was irrational, he felt, for any religion to claim that salvation was limited only to its own adherents, a small segment of humanity. Rather, each group—including Christians—would gain salvation through its own ethics and religion. Each rational religion was unique, but each one was an equally acceptable path by which its own followers could achieve salvation.[20]

Following Mendelssohn's lead, a range of new attitudes towards Christianity began to emerge among Jewish thinkers, most of them intent upon finding a point of rapprochement between the two previously antagonistic faiths. Thus, Jews began to emphasize Christianity's essential Jewishness. By identifying Christianity's Jewish roots, Jews could relate to some of its practices and beliefs, even as they rejected elements that challenged the legitimacy of Judaism. A leader of German Reform Judaism, Abraham Geiger (1810-184), for instance, subordinated Christianity to Judaism by placing both Jesus and Christianity within the context of classical Rabbinic Judaism. He argued that Jesus was a Pharisee with strong Galilean roots, a man of deep inner conviction and spirituality. Like many other Jews of his time, Jesus thought he was the Messiah, but his lack of originality prevented him from forming a new religion. Only Paul successfully developed Jesus' messianic claims so as to create a new faith. In this way, Geiger was able to acknowledge Jesus as an important religious figure within first century Judaism, while rejecting Christianity and its messianic claims about Jesus.

Geiger found Christianity's strength to be its struggle to overcome people's natural instincts and to unite humankind. Its shortcomings were its vision of a new world order that left no room for the old world, so that it had to reject everything that preceded it. Christianity strove to stand above humankind and demanded an exclusive loyalty from all of its followers. Because Christianity believes that the final page of human history was written almost two thousand years ago, no real progress in human life is possible without the messianic age. Because Christianity fails to recognize Judaism's self-sufficiency and the fact that Christianity itself grew from a particular form of Judaism, it has rejected all of Judaism instead of just the particular legalistic forms that were common in late antiquity and that Geiger himself abandoned (Jacob, pp. 40-47).

Focusing on the Gospel of Matthew, Samuel Hirsch, 1815-1889, another German Reform rabbi, described Jesus in the same terms that he would any nineteenth century Reform Jew. Matthew, in Hirsch's view, describes a Jesus who lived his life according to the best ideals of Judaism. All that Jesus taught was found in the Mosaic teachings and the words of the biblical prophets. John altered Matthew's accurate description and turned Jesus into an abstraction rather than a person. Paul's assessment of the law and Judaism was accurate for the Judaism that he encountered, but he did not fully understand the depth of breadth of Judaism. For Hirsch, Paul's mission was to prepare the gentile world for accepting Jesus' religion, the ethical and prophetic ideals of Judaism as exemplified in the Sermon on the Mount (Jacob, pp. 53-55). In this vein, Salomon Formstecher (1808-1889) even argued that Christianity's mission was to bring the world to Judaism. Christianity enclosed the truths of Judaism in pagan metaphysics, so that it was comprehensible to the pagans and could lead them to Judaism (Jacob, pp. 57-59). Like Geiger, these other Reform rabbis thus were able to separate Jesus' teachings and personality from later Christianity. They held that Jesus taught a form of Judaism not much different from that which they themselves taught. But Paul, the later Gospel writers, and the Church distorted Jesus' message and created a religion at odds with Judaism. What was true and valuable in Jesus' thought were those items he had found in his Jewish religion.

The American Reform rabbinate, which also stressed the rational and ethical side of Judaism, dealt with Christianity in ways similar to its German counterparts. These American rabbis faced a strong missionary movement in America, which had widespread support in many Christian communities. Like their German contemporaries, the American Reform rabbis placed Jesus within the context of Judaism, so as to argue that early Christianity had no unique doctrines. In this way, true Christianity was nothing but Judaism, and only those learned in classical Judaism could speak authoritatively about Christianity.

Isaac Meyer Wise (1818-1900), the founder of American Reform Judaism, rejected the notion that Jesus' martyrdom was necessary for humanity's salvation, claiming instead that the doctrine of vicarious atonement has no basis in the Gospels. Jesus, he held, accepted the title of messiah at Peter's urging, in order to increase popular support for a Jewish revolt against Rome. Then, when Jesus realized that the Romans were about to massacre the Jews gathered in Jerusalem, he voluntarily accepted execution in order to prevent the Roman slaughter of the Jews. The "novel myth" of Jesus' death was designed to impress the pagan mind. The Gospels' descriptions of Jesus' crucifixion are an unhistorical "conglomeration of contradictions and improbabilities."[21]

Wise argues that Christianity's universal religious and ethical elements are independent of Jesus or the Christian story. One thus could be a good Christian and still reject a belief in Jesus or in the truth of the Gospels. Christianity's triumph was its success in spreading its moral doctrine among the pagan nations of the ancient world and medieval Europe. Its Christological doctrines are so irrational that they cannot be accepted by the majority of humankind, nor can they be the basis of a meaningful religiosity (Jacob, pp. 71-81; Berlin, pp. 49-50). Wise, unlike many of his contemporaries, also argued that Paul was a loyal Jew who spread Jesus' doctrines to the gentile world. His universalistic ideas and ideals are to be admired (Berlin, pp. 62-63).

Kaufman Kohler (1843-1926) described Jesus as an Essene wonder worker, deeply embedded in the eschatological and apocalyptic Jewish doctrines of the first century. Because he believed that the end of the world was near, Jesus preached the value of poverty, chastity, asceticism, passivity in the face of evil, and opposition to the priesthood (Berlin, p. 50). Paul, a Hellenistic Jew, was influenced by gnosticism and the Hermes literature. His mission was to bring the gentiles to the higher ethical standards of Judaism. While he succeeded in doing this, he failed to achieve universal success, because he divided the world between Christians and Jews instead of between Jews and gentiles (Berlin, p. 61).

In all, we see that the leaders of nineteenth century German and American Reform Juda-ism interpreted early Christianity as a form of modern Reform Judaism. In this way they could acknowledge Jesus, and perhaps even Paul, to be important religious leaders and argue for a harmonious relationship between Jews and Christians. If modern Christians would divest themselves of the late antique and medieval distortions of the original message of Jesus in the same way that Reform Jews had rejected the talmudic and medieval distortions of the original biblical and prophetic teachings, the two religions, projecting similar messages, could dwell in harmony.

Franz Rosenzweig (1886-1929), one of the most original Jewish thinkers of the early part of the twentieth century, had a cousin and close friend who converted to Christianity; he himself was on the verge of conversion when he returned to Judaism after a *Kol Nidre* service, on the eve of the Day of Atonement. In the context of this personal experience, he came to see all religions as having some validity, but with Judaism and Christianity standing apart from the rest. Both of them, in his view, has a central place in God's plan for the world.

Rosenzweig altered the terms of the Jewish analysis of Christianity, arguing that philosophy and true religion are phenomenologically the same, both comprising dialogues. However, the content of these dialogues are different. Because of this, Rosenzweig maintains that both Christianity and Judaism are necessary in the world and that each has a role to play in bringing humanity closer to God. But despite their similar functions, Judaism and Christianity are essentially different. Unlike the thinkers discussed above, Rosenzweig does not try to amalgamate Judaism and Christianity. He insists instead that each maintains its distinctiveness, for only in that way can he find a reason for both of them to exist.

Rosenzweig believed that every person had the potential to confront the Divine, which for him meant to enter into a dialogue with God. While only the biblical faiths, Judaism and Christianity, expressed the truth of the relationship between God and humanity, valid revelatory experiences could also occur in non-biblical contexts, the result of a primordial connection between humanity and God. This primal relationship is apparent in God's question to Adam, Gen. 3:9, "Where are you?," to which human beings must render an answer. Any person can answer that question, and in that answer each one defines himself or herself as religious, atheistic, agnostic, or pantheistic.[22]

Insofar as the relationship between God and human beings was natural and primordial, Rosenzweig argued that it could be expressed in diverse modes, all of them authentic. This means that the content of revelation is as important as the experience. Authentic revelation, that is, does not end merely in ecstasy, enlightenment, knowledge, or dogma. The essence of true revelation is the awareness that God is near and that God commands. The proper human response to that revelation is to recognize God's presence and to fulfill God's commandment, a commandment to love. There must be a human response to what God has revealed, a response that creates a dialogue (Miller, p. 66). And this dialogue, according to Rosenzweig, is the same as that which comprises philosophy, in which the participants do not know ahead of time what the other or even themselves will say. Indeed, it is in the dialogue of revelation that Rosenzweig find the perfect example of his own new philosophy (Miller, pp. 58-59).

The dialogue-model explains how there can be more than one authentic expression of the revealed truth. If revelation contained only propositions, there could be only one system that contained the truth (Miller, p. 83). But if revelation is a dialogue that depends on both human and divine actions, there can be several authentic modes of expression.

Rosenzweig argued that Judaism and Christianity are both necessary for humankind, because neither contains the whole truth, which is only with God. Only at the end of time when Judaism and Christianity have each fulfilled its mission will they both become irrelevant. Rosenzweig constructs the image of the sun and its rays in order to show the relationship between Judaism and Christianity. Judaism is self-absorbed, like the burning core of the sun. Christianity goes out into the world, like the sun's rays. Primacy belongs to Judaism, but its message

cannot be disseminated without Christianity (Novak, pp. 100-101).

In order to explain why Christianity, but not Judaism, must seek converts, Rosenzweig compares Judaism to the infinity of a point that "only consists of that fact that it is never erased; thus it preserves itself in the eternal self-preservation of procreative blood." Judaism's essence makes it possible for it to sustain itself without bringing in people from the outside. A point is always the same; it does not need to be added to in order to maintain itself. Christianity, on the other hand, is similar to the infinity of a line that "consists of the very possibility of unrestricted extension." To reach infinity, Christianity must seek converts, just as a line can extend itself only by being added to. In this way, Rosenzweig justifies Christianity's attempt to convert non-Christians, even though this is an aspect of Christianity that most Jews find objectionable (Novak, p. 102).

A crucial difference between Judaism and Christianity is that Judaism's eternal nature and uniqueness lie in its direct relationship to God. Christianity is correct when it claims that no Christian can reach the Father except through the Son. This is not true for Jews, who do not need the Church or the Son because they have already reached God. The rest of humankind, however, does not have this direct contact with God and so require the mediating power of Christianity: "Any and every Jew feels in the depth of his soul that the Christian relation to God . . . is particularly and extremely poverty-stricken and ceremonious; namely, that as Christians one has to claim from someone else, whoever he may be, to call God 'our Father'" (Novak, p. 104). Miller (p. 95) summarizes Rosenzweig's view as follows:

> The Christocentric character of Christianity, which is essential to it, renders it incapable of being simultaneously theocentric. Thus, from the viewpoint of Judaism, it remains in some sense godless. On the other hand, the love of God manifested in Christ is so vibrantly incarnate for Christianity that Judaism seems by comparison loveless.

Judaism views God and God's kingdom as essentially and ultimately real. Christianity considers Christ and the interim kingdom, that break in the eternal course of history that occurred at Jesus' birth, as essentially real. Because Judaism does not accept a break in the eternal thread of history from creation to the end of time (Miller, p. 95), the two faiths are irreconcilably different. They have two completely different foci (Miller, p. 108). Despite this fact, the Jews' existence and their maintaining a direct connection to God prevents Christian expansion from degenerating into paganism. This is what would occur if that expansion were for its own sake and not for the sake of God. Without Judaism, the sun, Christianity, the rays of the sun, would not continue to shine.

In addition, Christianity faces three potential problems, and the continued existence of Judaism prevents these problems from becoming realities. Left unchecked 1) the Spirit could lead in any direction and not necessarily to God; 2) the Son of Man could become the Truth instead of God; 3) God would become All-in-All not the One above all (Novak, p. 105). Judaism and its direct, unmediated relationship to God thus puts the divine in its proper perspective for all humankind, including Christians.

Just as Judaism is necessary for Christianity, so the former needs the latter in order to fulfill its mission on earth. Christianity permits all of the nations to be included in the revealed relationship with God. If Judaism were in this way to focus its concern on the rest of the nations of the world, it would lose the unique intensity of its special relationship to God. Judaism must accept the importance of Christianity's universalistic mission, undertaken for the sake of final redemption of humanity (Novak, p. 109).

Rosenzweig argued that Judaism and Christianity were necessary and complementary religions. Each was distinct but each needed the other in order to be able to fulfill its mission. Rosenzweig's contemporary and collaborator Martin Buber (1878-1965) took a different stand. Like Rosenzweig, Buber recognized the differences between Christianity and Judaism. But unlike his colleague, Buber followed the tact of viewing true Christianity as a kind of authentic Judaism. The Jewishness Buber wanted to find in Jesus was the same Jewishness he sought to discover in Judaism. For Buber, Jesus was an authentic Jew who experienced and taught about the proper relationship to God (Novak, p. 81):

> From my youth onwards I have found in Jesus my great brother. That Christianity has regarded and does regard him as God and Savior has always appeared to me a fact of the highest importance which, for his sake and my own, I must endeavor to understand. I am more than certain that a great place belongs to him in Israel's history of faith and that this place cannot be described by any of the usual categories.

Buber believed that Jesus experienced God spontaneously and spiritually; he did not reach God through the legalism of either Paul or the rabbis. Buber finds the real Jesus in Matthew's Sermon on the Mount (Novak, p. 84). The Christian dogma of Christ is a later development constructed by Paul and the Church, and this forms as much of a barrier to an intimate relationship between humans and the divine as does the dogma of legalistic Judaism (Novak, p. 85).

Also like Rosenzweig, Buber believed in the possibility that each religion has an authentic revelation that is valid for those who believe in the system. Thus, he justifies his perspective that religions are matters of personal choice and that all peoples' beliefs are equally valid. The conflicts among religious persons result from the fact that only those within the faith community can appreciate a given religion and find its core. The Christianity of the Sermon on the Mount, for instance, is an authentic path to God. The Jews ability to acknowledge this path is, however, contravened by Christology's demands that Jews accept that a radical change occurred in the world with Jesus birth, life, and death. This Jews cannot accept (Jacob, pp. 173-174):

> We know that the history of the world has not yet been shattered to its very core, that the world is not yet redeemed. We feel the lack of redemption of the world. We do not perceive a caesura in the course of history. We acknowledge no mid-point in it, but only a goal. The goal of the way of God who does not pause upon his way.

Buber believed that Judaism and Christianity were each authentic and unique; however, "the mystery of the other one is internal . . . and cannot be perceived from without" (Jacob, p. 174). It is God's mystery that both faiths exist side by side: "We should acknowledge our fundamental difference and impart to each other with unreserved confidence our knowledge of the unity of this house, a unity which we hope will one day surround us without divisions. We will seve, until the day when we may be united in common service" (Jacob, p. 174).

Buber's view of Christianity was not as philosophically consistent as Rosenzweig's. Buber found a common ground between Judaism and Christianity in the spirituality he saw as shared by Jesus' message and that of prophetic Judaism. Unfortunately, he thought, that commonality was destroyed by Paul and the Church on one side and by Rabbinic legalism on the other. While each religion has its place in the present world, their distinctiveness has prevented Jews and Christians today from working together.

Jewish perceptions of Christianity after the Holocaust: The events of the twentieth century dramatically changed the relationship between Jews and Christians. The Holocaust forever altered the way in which Jews of the second half of this century would view non-Jews. While Christianity did not cause the Holocaust, many of its myths and images supported European anti-Judaism and justified the Nazis' murder of Europe's Jews. There were many Christians and Church leaders who endangered themselves in order to protect Jews. But many more supported and executed the Nazis' plans, and many did so in the name of Jesus and Christianity. While the Nazis also killed many Christians, many, even most, of the murderers of the Jews were baptized followers of Christ. Contemporary Christians struggle with this truth, as do current Jewish thinkers.

Two other events have proven important for Jews attempting to comprehend the relationship between Judaism and Christianity. The creation of the State of Israel in 1948 challenged medieval and modern Christian doctrine concerning the superiority of Christianity and the divine rejection of Jews and Judaism. From the Jewish point of view, the failure of the Vatican, the World Council of Churches, and other international Christian organizations to support Israel in the Six Day War was also significant. This disproved the previous Jewish assumption that, in the aftermath of the Holocaust, Christians would feel compelled to assist Jews who were again threatened with extinction.

The complexity of the post-Holocaust Jewish view of Christianity can be seen through a brief review of the ideas expressed by Eliezer Berkovits, an orthodox rabbi, Richard L. Rubenstein, a conservative rabbi who is a university professor and theologian, and Emil L. Fackenheim, a professor of philosophy and survivor of Sachsenhausen. As we shall see, while all three see a connection between Christianity and the Nazi ideology that created the Holocaust, they differ regarding the implications of that connection.

These thinkers' understanding of the relationship between the historical attitude of Christians towards Jews and the Holocaust is as follows. Berkovits[23] focuses on the previous centuries of Christian anti-Jewish teachings (pp. 18-26): "Without the contempt and hatred for the Jews planted by Christianity in the hearts of the multitude of its followers, Nazism's crime against the Jewish people could never have been conceived, much less executed" (p. 42). Rubenstein[24] holds that a Christian invention, the "mythological Jew," provided the images and the models for the Nazis. This was the Jew viewed not like other humans, but as either Jesus or Judas, as the divine or the paradigmatic betrayers. In this regard, medieval descriptions of the Jews as the devil's surrogates, God-killers, provided a fertile ground for Nazi propaganda (p. 21). Fackenheim,[25] finally, sees a close connection between Nazi anti-semitism and the religious and social doctrines of Christian (pp. 54-55).

Christianity's ancient and medieval images of the Jews thus are understood to have provided the Nazis with the raw material upon which to ground their war against the Jews. Further, the failure of the largely Christian West, let alone the Vatican, to respond to the Nazi onslaught becomes significant for the

Jewish view of modern Christianity. Focusing upon Christianity's failure to act, Berkovits argues that that religion has entirely lost its moral underpinning, that the Vatican and the other churches have "lost all claim to moral and spiritual leadership in the world" (p. 16). Fackenheim holds a similar view, noting in particular that the same anti-Semitism that permitted many Christians to accept the Nazi slaughter of the Jews still finds expression today in Christians' reading of the Holocaust as a universal evil not particular to the Jews at all. Fackenheim goes so far as to deem to be an aspect of anti-semitism what he views as Christians' failure to be even-handed in judging the competing claims of Israelis and Arabs (Fackenheim, p. 56):

> Why did the Christian press remain undisturbed by nineteen years of Jordanian control of the Christian holy places (and desecration of Jewish cemeteries and synagogues), but become greatly agitated by Israeli control? Why does it fill its pages with accounts of the plight of Arab refugees but rarely even mention the nearly as numerous Jewish refugees from Arab countries? Why are there moral equations between Israel's claims to the right to exist and Arab claims to the right to destroy her?

In the end, all three see little chance of a real Jewish-Christian dialogue unless Christianity rethinks its traditional images of the Jews. Berkovits maintains that the only reason Christianity is willing even to think about engaging in ecumenical discussions is its loss of worldly power. Rubenstein has written that "unless Israel is the vessel of God's revelation to humanity, it is difficult to proclaim Christ as the fulfillment and climax of that revelation. . . . I see no way believing Christians can demythologize Israel's special relation to God without radically altering the meaning of Christian faith" (p. 21). This means that Christianity cannot imagine the Jew as a normal human being (p. 56).

In the wake of the Holocaust, Jewish theologians have challenged Christian thinkers to rework Christianity's traditional pictures of the Jews, which played a role in the Nazi onslaught and which prevented and still prevent many Christians from responding positively to Jews in dire straits. Until this occurs, many contemporary Jewish thinkers believe it will be impossible for contemporary Jews and Christians to view one another as caring human beings and to respond to one another in appropriate ways.

Conclusions: At its core, Judaism is a self-contained religious system that has little concern for the non-Jew. Judaism's principle effort has been to define clearly the ways in which Jews can fulfill the terms of the covenant entered into between God and the Jewish People at Sinai. To the extent that Jews, in contact with large non-Jewish populations, have needed to make sense of the "other," their views have changed according to the specific needs defined by the intellectual, cultural, political, economic, and social environments of each age. As a result, it is largely impossible to speak of *the* Jewish attitude towards the non-Jew. Still, we can draw several general conclusions.

The most important point is that, through history, the Jewish definition of the non-Jew has been an aspect of Jewish self-definition and the legitimization of Judaism. Through their image of the "other," Jews, like other peoples, have defined what it means to be a member of their particular group. Second, Jewish attitudes towards non-Jews have changed from age to age depending upon the actual nature of the contact between Jew and gentile and in light of the particular social and economic needs of the time. Jewish thinking about the non-Jew thus has for the most part not been a primarily theological enterprise. It is, rather, the outcome of the real life experiences of Jews living as a minority within non-Jewish cultures and nations.

Because Christianity depends upon the Jewish scriptures, the Jewish deity, and the Jewish mythological view of itself, it has presented a major challenge to Jewish thinkers. While other religions of late antiquity were obviously different from Judaism, and so could largely be ignored, Christianity appeared to be and claimed to be *very* similar. Throughout history, the two religions thus have sought at both theoretical and practical levels clearly to distinguish between themselves. The result is that Jewish views of Christianity have been multi-faceted and complex, emerging from the particular historical contexts in which they served to make sense of Jewish experience. This being the case, projecting the future course of Jewish understanding of the non-Jew appears futile, as impossible as accurately foreseeing the course of human events in general.

Bibliography

Berlin, George L., *Defending the Faith: Nineteenth-Century American Jewish Writings on Christianity and Jesus* (Albany, 1989).

Cohen, Mark R., *Under Crescent and Cross: The Jews in the Middle Ages* (Princeton, 1994).

Porton, Gary G., *Goyim: Gentiles and Israelites in Mishnah-Tosefta* (Atlanta, 1988).

Porton, Gary G., *The Stranger Within Your Gates: Converts and Conversion in Rabbinic Literature* (Chicago, 1994).

Sanders, Jack T., *Schismatics, Sectarians, Dissidents, Deviants: The First One Hundred Years of Jewish-Christian Relations* (Valley Forge, 1993).

Seltzer, Claudia, *Jewish Responses to Early Christians: History and Polemics 30-150 C.E.* (Minneapolis, 1994).

Notes

[1] On this, see, for example, Gary G. Porton, *Goyim: Gentiles and Israelites in Mishnah-Tosefta* (Atlanta, 1988).

[2] The morning prayers state: "Blessed are you, YHWH, sovereign of the universe, former of light and creator of darkness, maker of peace and creator of all. Who, in his mercy, gives light to the earth and to those who dwell on it. And in his goodness, daily renews creation. . . ."

[3] William S. Green, "Otherness Within: Toward a Theory of Difference in Rabbinic Judaism," in Jacob Neusner and Ernest S. Frerichs, *"To See Ourselves as Others See Us:" Christians, Jews, "Others" in Late Antiquity* (Chico, 1985), pp. 49-70.

[4] See the discussions in Sacha Stern, *Jewish Identity in Early Rabbinic Writings* (Leiden, 1994).

[5] For a partial bibliography of ethnicity, see those items listed in Porton.

[6] David Novak, *The Image of the Non-Jew in Judaism* (New York, 1983).

[7] Jacob Neusner, *Judaism and Its Social Metaphors* (Cambridge, 1989), pp. 88-89.

[8] See the careful discussion of these issues in Neusner, pp. 97-106, 145-163. See also Marcel Simon, *Verus Israel: A Study of the Relations between Christians and Jews in the Roman Empire (135-425)* (London, 1986), pp. 187-193.

[9] While many have understood the Rabbinic discussions of the *minim*—a term designating Jewish sectarians—to be directed specifically towards Christians (Simon, pp. 197-199), this seems to be an oversimplification. While Christians, or at least the Jewish followers of Jesus, were probably in-

cluded in the designation *minim*, the category is much broader and includes many other Jewish dissidents and heretics. Recent scholarship has demonstrated that the rabbis' concern with the *minim* is no indication of their specific interest in Christianity. See Reuven Kimelman, "*Birkat Ha-Minim* and the Lack of Evidence for an Anti-Christian Jewish Prayer in Late Antiquity," in E.P. Sanders, A.I. Baumgartern, and Alan Mendelson, *Jewish and Christian Self-Definition: Volume Two. Aspects of Judaism in the Graeco-Roman Period* (Philadelphia, 1981), pp. 226-244.

[10] Claudia Seltzer, *Jewish Responses to Early Christians: History and Polemics 30-150 C.E.* (Minneapolis, 1994), pp. 21-22.

[11] Jack T. Sanders, *Schismatics, Sectarians, Dissidents, Deviants: The First One Hundred Years of Jewish-Christian Relations* (Valley Forge, 1993), p. 81.

[12] On the Rabbinic controversy concerning the circumcision of converts see Gary G. Porton, *The Stranger Within Your Gates: Converts and Conversion in Rabbinic Literature* (Chicago, 1994), pp. 139-148.

[13] Mark R. Cohen, *Under Crescent and Cross: The Jews in the Middle Ages* (Princeton, 1994), p. 34.

[14] M. Avi-Yonah, *The Jews of Palestine: A Political History from the Bar Kokhba War to the Arab Conquest* (New York, 1976), pp. 213-220, 246-251.

[15] H.H. Ben-Sasson, *A History of the Jewish People* (Cambridge, 1976), pp. 413-420.

[16] David Berger, *The Jewish-Christian Debate in the High Middle Ages* (Philadelphia, 1979), p. 8.

[17] F.E. Talmage, *Disputation and Dialogue: Readings in the Jewish Christian Encounter* (New York, 1975), pp. 86.

[18] David Novak, *Jewish-Christian Dialogue: A Jewish Justification* (New York and Oxford, 1989), pp. 57-61.

[19] Michael A. Meyer, *The Origins of the Modern Jew: Jewish Identity and European Culture in Germany, 1749-1824* (Detroit, 1967), pp. 11-56.

[20] Walter Jacob, *Christianity through Jewish Eyes: The Quest for Common Ground* (Cincinnati, 1974), pp. 18-22.

[21] George L. Berlin, *Defending the Faith: Nineteenth-Century American Jewish Writings on Christianity and Jesus* (Albany, 1989), p. 49.

[22] Ronald H. Miller, *Dialogue and Disagreement: Franz Rosenzweig's Relevance to Contemporary Jewish-Christian Understanding* (Lanham, New York, London, 1989), pp. 59-62.

[23] Eliezer Berkovits, *Faith After the Holocaust* (New York, 1973).

[24] Richard L. Rubenstein, *After Auschwitz: Radical Theology and Contemporary Judaism* (Indianapolis, New York, Kansas City, 1966).

[25] Emil L. Fackenheim, *The Jewish Return into History: Reflections in the Age of Auschwitz and a New Jerusalem* (New York, 1978).

GARY G. PORTON